Not For Tourists™ Guide to **LOS ANGELES**

2004

Not For Tourists Inc New York

Published and designed by:

Not For Tourists, Inc.

NFT™ NOT FOR TOURISTS™ Guide to **LOS ANGELES** 2004

www.notfortourists.com

Concept by
Jane Pirone

Information Design
Jane Pirone
Rob Tallia
Scot Covey
Diana Pizzari

Editor
Jane Pirone

Managing Editor
Diana Pizzari
Rob Tallia

City Editor
Beth Deitchman

Writing and Editing
Beth Deitchman
Diana Pizzari
Rob Tallia
Jane Pirone

Database Design
Scot Covey

Graphic Design / Production
Scot Covey
Ana Albu
James Martinez
Yun Zan

Contributors
Stan Chandler
David Gruenberg
Caroline Halili
Camille Jacks
Gregory Kuntz
Eric Loo
Angelica Martinez
Monique McIntyre
Kurt Mortensen
Donna Reyes
Christina Yu

Research / Data Entry
Diana Pizzari
Annie Holt
Shannon Browne
Aniela Srocynski
Sherry Wasserman
Anne-Cecile Bourget
Sharyn Jackson

Proofing
Jack Schieffer

Printed in China
ISBN# 0-9740131-1-0 $19.95

Every effort has been made to ensure that the information in this book is as up-to-date as possible at press time. However, many details are liable to change—as we have learned. The publishers can not accept responsibility for any consequences arising from use of this book.

Dear **NFT**™ User:

When Jane and Rob, my fearless leaders back in New York, asked me to write this letter they'd hoped it would reflect what's going on in my city "now." I had no easy answer and worried that I was missing some crucial part of the L.A. zeitgeist. But a warm, cozy feeling came over me as I realized that there's a sameness to life in L.A. and that can be pretty darned comforting.

We live in a city where it's possible to chart the change of seasons by the colors of the Juicy Couture tracksuits women wear to their yoga class, by whether we're watching *The Sopranos* or *Sex and the City* on HBO, and by looking at the marquee of the nearest multiplex—Halle Berry emerging from the sea in a bikini, making men feel good? Summer. Halle Berry locked in an embrace with Billy Bob Thornton, imploring him to make her "feel good?" Better grab a sweater as you leave the house.

That's not to say that L.A. never changes. This year, Downtown is experiencing a growth spurt. The Standard Hotel is all the rage, with a rooftop bar that some say has the best view in L.A. And we're eagerly awaiting the opening of the Frank Gehry-designed Disney Hall, which many believe will be L.A.'s answer to Sydney's Opera House. There's a burgeoning art scene in Chinatown and a brand new cathedral, Our Lady of Angels, which seems to have been built without the use of any right angles at all.

NFT has undergone subtle changes as well. We've updated and expanded our restaurant and nightlife sections, and we have also added a list of both major (The Rose Bowl) and not so major—but not to be missed—events (Tofu Festival, anyone?). And we at NFT looked at our fellow Angelenos and noticed that many of them are small… and loud… and adorably cute… Why, they're children! They're everywhere—heck, I've even got one myself. We're very excited about the addition of "not for grown-ups," a section designed to help parents navigate this fair city with a child and keep their sanity in the process.

As always, I'd like to thank Jane and Rob for giving me the opportunity to learn about my hometown and share this morass with the rest of you. Thanks also go to Diana (Go USA Netball!), Scot, Alli, Annie, and the rest of the folks back in NYC.

So enjoy the book and keep it close—in your passenger seat, perhaps, amidst the Coffee Bean empties and candy bar wrappers. The book improves with age and with your feedback—comments, questions, complaints, etc.—so log on to www.notfortourists.com and tell us what you think.

Here's hoping you find what you need.

Beth Deitchman
NFT-Los Angeles, City Editor

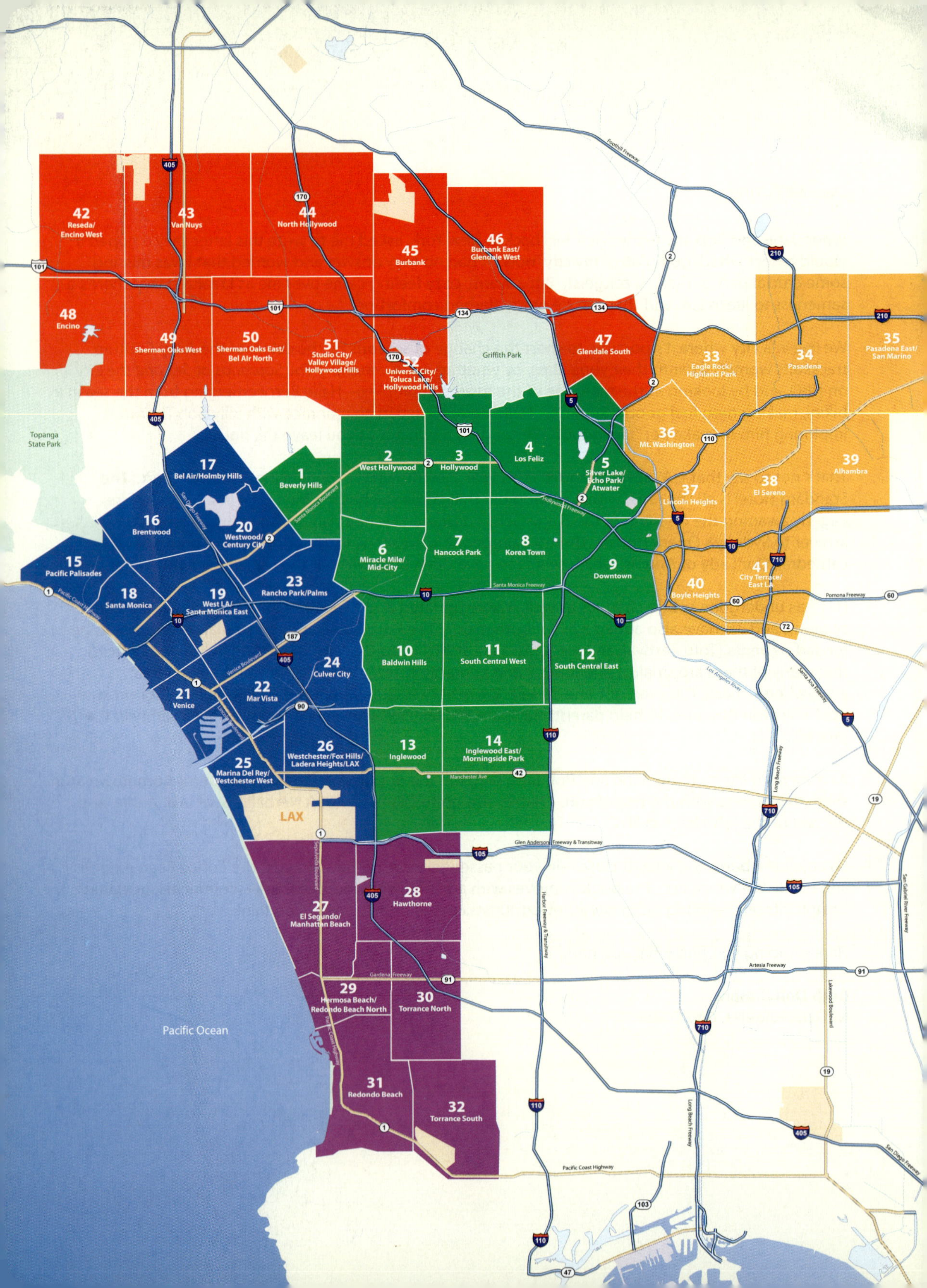

405
101
42 Reseda/Encino West
43 Van Nuys
170
44 North Hollywood
45 Burbank
46 Burbank East/Glendale West
Foothill Freeway
2
210
48 Encino
49 Sherman Oaks West
50 Sherman Oaks East/Bel Air North
51 Studio City/Valley Village/Hollywood Hills
101
134
134
52 Universal City/Toluca Lake/Hollywood Hills
170
Griffith Park
47 Glendale South
2
33 Eagle Rock/Highland Park
34 Pasadena
35 Pasadena East/San Marino
210
Topanga State Park
405
17 Bel Air/Holmby Hills
1 Beverly Hills
2 West Hollywood
2
101
3 Hollywood
4 Los Feliz
5 Silver Lake/Echo Park/Atwater
5
36 Mt. Washington
110
39 Alhambra
16 Brentwood
20 Westwood/Century City
2
Hollywood Freeway
2
37 Lincoln Heights
38 El Sereno
5
15 Pacific Palisades
18 Santa Monica
19 West LA/Santa Monica East
23 Rancho Park/Palms
6 Miracle Mile/Mid-City
7 Hancock Park
8 Korea Town
9 Downtown
Santa Monica Freeway
10
41 City Terrace/East LA
710
1
Pacific Coast Highway
10
187
40 Boyle Heights
60
Pomona Freeway
60
405
24 Culver City
10
10 Baldwin Hills
11 South Central West
12 South Central East
72
22 Mar Vista
90
21 Venice
Venice Boulevard
Los Angeles River
Santa Ana Freeway
26 Westchester/Fox Hills/Ladera Heights/LAX
13 Inglewood
14 Inglewood East/Morningside Park
110
5
25 Marina Del Rey/Westchester West
Manchester Ave
42
LAX
1
Long Beach Freeway
19
105
Glen Anderson Freeway & Transitway
105
710
28 Hawthorne
405
Harbor Freeway & Transitway
27 El Segundo/Manhattan Beach
Artesia Freeway
91
Gardena Freeway
91
Lakewood Boulevard
29 Hermosa Beach/Redondo Beach North
30 Torrance North
710
Pacific Ocean
19
31 Redondo Beach
1
32 Torrance South
110
405
San Diego Freeway
Pacific Coast Highway
103
110
47

Table of Contents

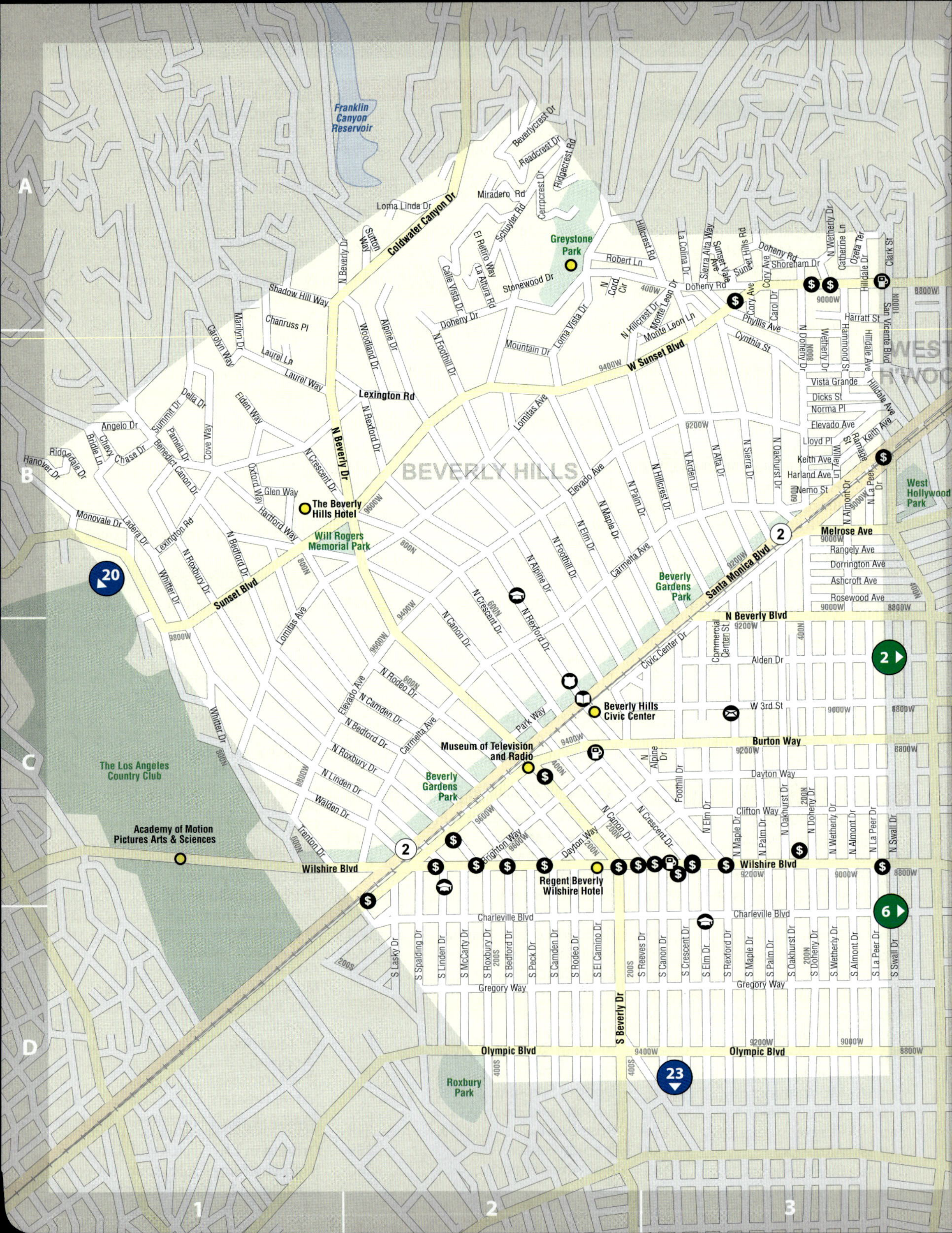

N
Franklin Canyon Reservoir
Greystone Park
Loma Linda Dr
Coldwater Canyon Dr
Miradero Rd
Beverlycrest Dr
Readcrest Dr
Ridgecrest Rd
Cerrocrest Dr
Schuyler Rd
El Retiro Way
La Altura Rd
Calle Vista Dr
Stonewood Dr
Robert Ln
N Cord Cir
400W
Hillcrest Rd
La Colina Dr
Sierra Alta Way
Sunset Vale Ave
Sunset Hills Rd
Doheny Rd
N Wetherly Dr
Catherine Ln
Ozeta Ter
Clark St
Sutton Way
N Beverly Dr
Shadow Hill Way
Doheny Dr
Mountain Dr
Loma Vista Dr
N Hillcrest Dr
Monte Leon Dr
Monte Leon Ln
Doheny Rd
Cory Ave
Carol Dr
Shoreham Dr
N Doheny Dr
Hildale Dr
San Vicente Blvd
WEST H'WOOD
8800W
9000W
10000
Marilyn Dr
Chanruss Pl
Carolyn Way
Alpine Dr
Woodland Dr
Laurel Ln
Laurel Way
Lexington Rd
N Rexford Dr
N Foothill Dr
W Sunset Blvd
9400W
Lomitas Ave
Phyllis Ave
Cynthia St
N Doheny Dr
Harratt St
Vista Grande
Dicks St
Norma Pl
Elevado Ave
Lloyd Pl
Hammond St
Hildale Ave
Ramage St
Keith Ave
Keith Ave
Harland Ave
Nemo St
9200W
Della Dr
Eiden Way
Summit Dr
Angelo Dr
Chevy Chase Dr
Pamela Dr
Benedict Canyon Dr
Loma Vista Dr
N Crescent Dr
Oxford Way
Glen Way
Hartford Way
The Beverly Hills Hotel
BEVERLY HILLS
Elevado Ave
N Maple Dr
N Palm Dr
N Hillcrest Dr
N Arden Dr
N Alta Dr
N Sierra Dr
N Oakhurst Dr
N La Peer Dr
N Almont Dr
N Almont Dr
West Hollywood Park
Ridgedale Dr
Hanover Dr
Bridle Ln
Ladera Dr
Monovale Dr
Lexington Rd
N Bedford Dr
N Roxbury Dr
Whittier Dr
Will Rogers Memorial Park
N Alpine Dr
N Crescent Dr
Elevado Ave
Carmelita Ave
N Elm Dr
Beverly Gardens Park
Santa Monica Blvd
2
Melrose Ave
9000W
Rangely Ave
Dorrington Ave
Ashcroft Ave
Rosewood Ave
9000W
8800W
20
Sunset Blvd
800N
9600W
9800W
800N
Lomitas Ave
N Canon Dr
N Rodeo Dr
N Camden Dr
N Bedford Dr
N Roxbury Dr
N Linden Dr
Walden Dr
Trenton Dr
Carmelita Ave
N Rexford Dr
N Foothill Dr
Park Way
Beverly Hills Civic Center
Civic Center Dr
Commercial Center St
N Beverly Blvd
Alden Dr
W 3rd St
Burton Way
9000W
9200W
400W
N Beverly Blvd
8800W
2
C
The Los Angeles Country Club
Academy of Motion Pictures Arts & Sciences
600N
9400W
Museum of Television and Radio
Beverly Gardens Park
9600W
Dayton Way
Brighton Way
200N
N Canon Dr
N Crescent Dr
Dayton Way
Clifton Way
Alpine Dr
Foothill Dr
N Elm Dr
N Maple Dr
N Palm Dr
N Oakhurst Dr
N Doheny Dr
N Wetherly Dr
N Almont Dr
N La Peer Dr
N Swall Dr
2
Wilshire Blvd
Regent Beverly Wilshire Hotel
Wilshire Blvd
9200W
9000W
8800W
6
Charleville Blvd
Charleville Blvd
S Lasky Dr
S Spalding Dr
S Linden Dr
S McCarty Dr
S Roxbury Dr
200S
S Bedford Dr
S Peck Dr
S Camden Dr
S Rodeo Dr
S El Camino Dr
S Beverly Dr
S Reeves Dr
S Canon Dr
S Crescent Dr
S Elm Dr
S Rexford Dr
S Maple Dr
S Palm Dr
S Oakhurst Dr
S Doheny Dr
S Wetherly Dr
S Almont Dr
S La Peer Dr
S Swall Dr
Gregory Way
Gregory Way
200S
Olympic Blvd
9400W
400S
Olympic Blvd
9200W
9000W
8800W
23
Roxbury Park
400S
A
B
C
D
1
2
3

The one-way streets and heavy foot traffic can make navigating Beverly Hills a challenge. Luckily, there are plenty of well-marked parking lots throughout the city, so your best bet is to rest your car for a few hours and tackle this area on foot.

$ Banks

- **Bank of America** · 460 N Beverly Dr
- **Bank of America** · 9461 Wilshire Blvd
- **Bank of the West** · 9401 Wilshire Blvd
- **California National Bank** · 9100 Wilshire Blvd
- **California National Bank** · 9916 Santa Monica Blvd
- **Citibank** · 9059 W Sunset Blvd
- **City National Bank** · 400 N Roxbury Dr
- **City National Bank** · 9229 W Sunset Blvd
- **Comercia Bank** · 9757 Wilshire Blvd
- **First Republic Bank** · 9593 Wilshire Blvd
- **Manufacturers Bank** · 9701 Wilshire Blvd
- **Union Bank** · 9460 Wilshire Blvd
- **United National Bank** · 450 N Roxbury Dr
- **US Bank** · 9595 Wilshire Blvd
- **Washington Mutual** · 9245 Wilshire Blvd
- **Wells Fargo Bank** · 9354 Wilshire Blvd
- **Western Financial Bank** · 9107 Wilshire Blvd

Gas Stations

- **76** · 427 N Crescent Dr
- **76** · 9460 W Olympic Blvd
- **Chevron** · 9378 Wilshire Blvd

Landmarks

- **Academy of Motion Picture Arts & Sciences** · 8949 Wilshire Blvd
- **Beverly Hills Civic Center** · Rexford Dr & Santa Monica Blvd
- **Beverly Hills Hotel** · 9641 Sunset Blvd
- **Greystone Park** · 905 Loma Vista Dr
- **Museum of Television and Radio** · 465 N Beverly Dr
- **Regent Beverly Wilshire Hotel** · 9500 Wilshire Blvd

Libraries

- **Beverly Hills Public Library** · 444 N Rexford Dr · 310-288-2220

24-Hour Pharmacies

- **Rite-Aid** · 300 N Canon Dr · 310-273-3561

Police

- **Beverly Hills Police** · 464 N Rexford Dr · 310-550-4951

Post Offices

- 312 S Beverly Dr
- 323 N Crescent Dr
- 325 N Maple Dr

Schools

- **Beverly Vista Elementary School** · 200 S Elm Dr
- **Good Shepherd Catholic** · 148 S Linden Dr
- **Hawthorne Elementary** · 624 N Rexford Dr

Supermarkets

- **Pavilions** · 9467 W Olympic Blvd
- **Whole Foods Market** · 239 N Crescent Dr

Map 1 • Beverly Hills

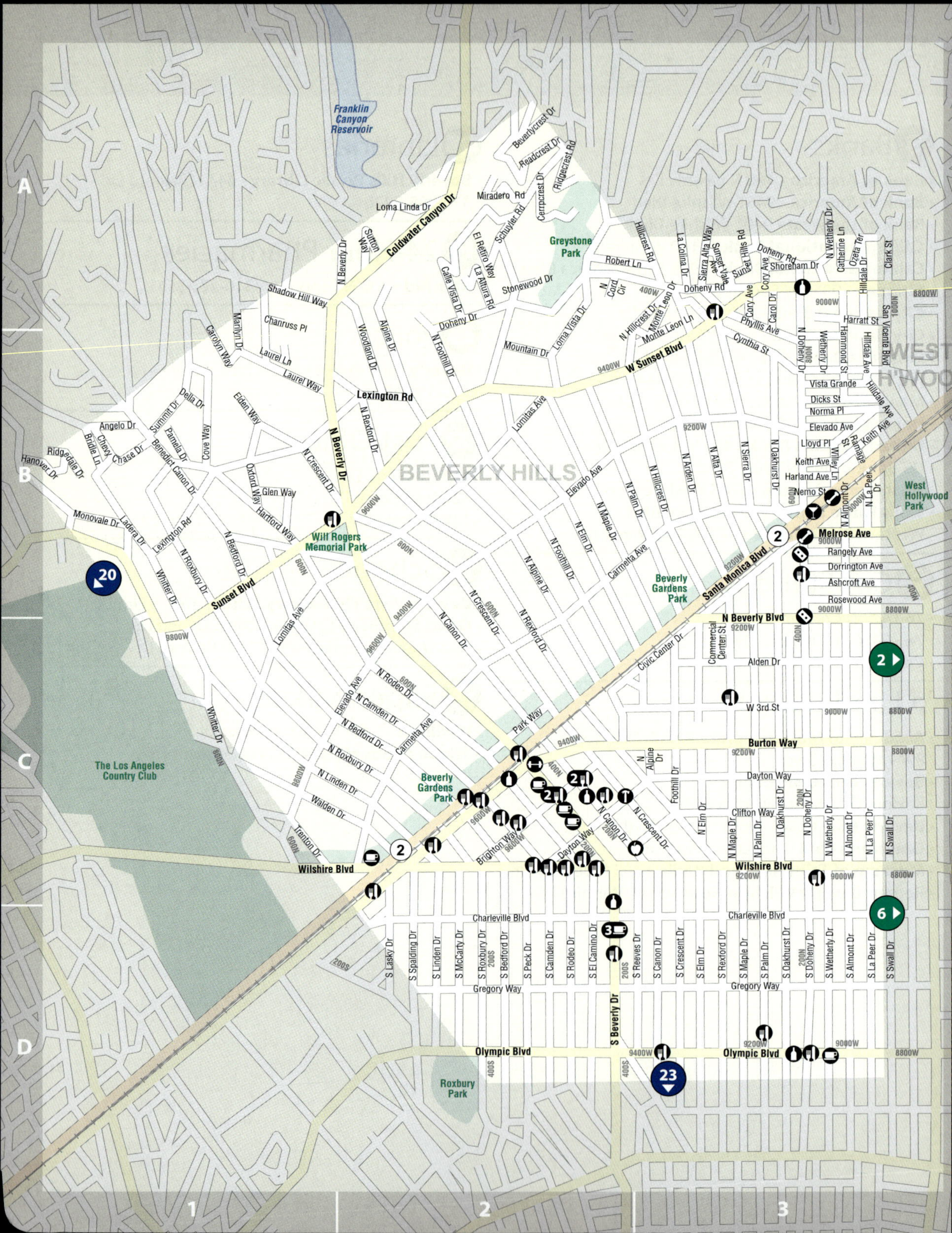

Beverly Hills: swimming pools, movie stars… This remains true long after the Beverly Hillbillies had their digs here. This high end, exclusive area of the city of angels offers small boutique shopping and fine dining. Plus, where else in the city can you cross a street diagonally?

Clubs

- **Avalon Hotel Bar** • 9400 W Olympic Blvd • 310-277-5221
- **Coconut Club** • 9876 Wilshire Blvd • 310-285-1358
- **Good Bar** • 9229 Sunset Blvd • 310-271-8355
- **Joya** • 242 N Beverly Dr • 310-888-8811
- **Peninsula Hotel** • 9882 Santa Monica Blvd • 310-551-2888
- **Regent Beverly Wilshire** • 9500 Wilshire Blvd • 310-275-5200
- **Trader Vic's** • 9876 Wilshire Blvd • 310-276-6345

Coffee

- **Coffee Bean & Tea Leaf** • 233 S Beverly Dr
- **Coffee Bean & Tea Leaf** • 445 N Beverly Dr
- **Graffeo Coffee Roasting** • 315 N Beverly Dr
- **Peet's Coffee & Tea** • 258 S Beverly Dr
- **Starbucks** • 202 S Beverly Dr
- **Starbucks** • 428 N Beverly Dr
- **Starbucks** • 9844 Wilshire Blvd

Farmer's Markets

- **Beverly Hills** • 200 N Canon Dr • Sun 9-1

Gyms

- **Studio C** • 435 N Beverly Dr • 310-273-2351

Hardware Stores

- **Pioneer & Lucerne Hardware** • 315 N Crescent Dr • 310-276-1167

Liquor Stores

- **Wine Merchant** • 9467 Santa Monica Blvd
- **Wine Shop** • 350 N Canon Dr

Pet Stores

- **Elite Animals** • 9040 Santa Monica Blvd • 310-888-0115

Restaurants

- **Baja Fresh** • 475 N Beverly Dr • 310-858-6690
- **Barney Greengrass** • 9570 Wilshire Blvd • 310-777-5877
- **Belvedere, The** • 9882 Little Santa Monica Blvd • 310-788-2306
- **Blue on Blue** • 9400 W Olympic Blvd • 310-277-5221
- **Brighton Coffee Shop** • 9600 Brighton Way • 310-276-7732
- **Cafe Talesai** • 9198 W Olympic Blvd • 310-271-9345
- **Crustacean** • 9646 Santa Monica Blvd • 310-205-8990
- **Da Pasquale** • 9749 Santa Monica Blvd • 310-859-3884
- **El Torito Grill** • 9595 Wilshire Blvd • 310-550-1599
- **Farm of Beverly Hills** • 439 N Beverly Dr • 310-273-5578
- **Ginza Sushi-Ko** • 218 N Rodeo Dr • 310-247-8939
- **Grill, The** • 9560 Dayton Way • 310-276-0615
- **Joss** • 9255 Sunset Blvd • 310-276-1886
- **Kate Mantilini** • 9101 Wilshire Blvd • 310-278-3699
- **La Scala** • 410 N Canon Dr • 310-275-0579
- **Le Pain Quotidien** • 9630 Little Santa Monica Blvd • 310-859-1100
- **Mandarin, The** • 430 N Camden Dr • 323-272-0267
- **Maple Drive** • 345 N Maple Dr • 310-274-9800
- **Mastro** • 246 N Canon Dr • 310-888-8782
- **Mulberry Street Pizzeria** • 240 S Beverly Dr • 310-247-8100
- **Mulberry Street Pizzeria** • 347 N Canon Dr • 310-247-8988
- **Nate 'n Al's** • 414 N Beverly Dr • 310-274-0101
- **Nic's** • 453 N Canon Dr • 310-550-5707
- **Polo Lounge** • 9641 Sunset Blvd • 310-276-2251
- **Regent Beverly Wilshire** • 9500 Wilshire Blvd • 310-275-5200
- **Trader Vic's** • 9876 Wilshire Blvd • 310-276-6345
- **Xi'an** • 362 N Canon Dr • 310-275-3345

Shopping

- **Caviarteria** • 158 S Beverly Dr • 310-285-9773
- **Cheese Store of Beverly Hills** • 419 N Beverly Dr • 310-278-2855
- **Fishland** • 9150 W Olympic Blvd • 310-271-2553
- **Mrs Beasley's/Miss Grace Lemon Cake Co** • 255 1/2 S Beverly Dr • 310-281-8096

Video Rental

- **Video Collection** • 470 N Doheny Dr • 310-273-7700

Map 2 • West Hollywood

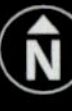

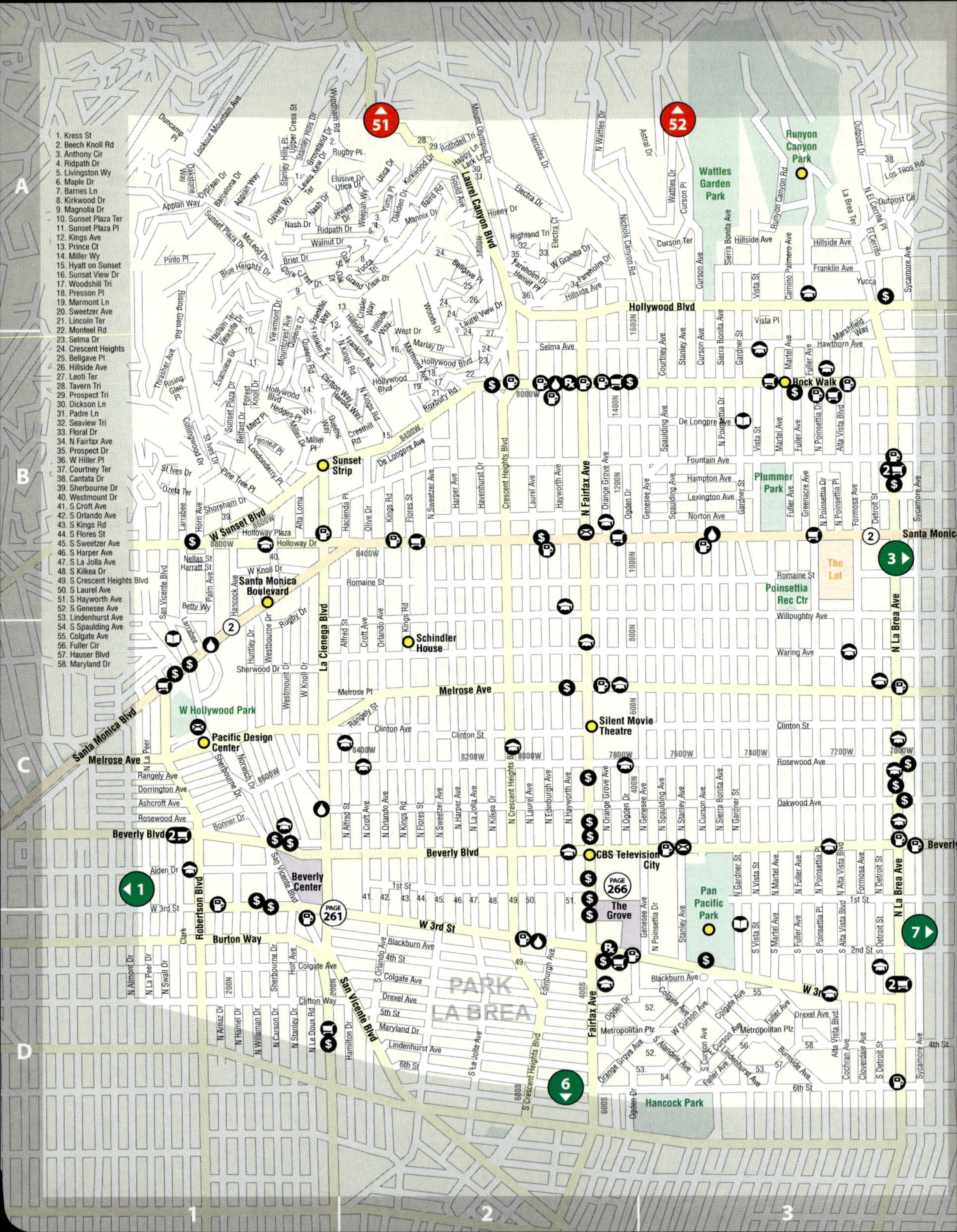
1. Kress St
2. Beech Knoll Rd
3. Anthony Cir
4. Ridpath Dr
5. Livingston Wy
6. Maple Dr
7. Barnes Ln
8. Kirkwood Dr
9. Magnolia Dr
10. Sunset Plaza Ter
11. Sunset Plaza Pl
12. Kings Ave
13. Prince Ct
14. Miller Wy
15. Hyatt on Sunset
16. Sunset View Dr
17. Woodshill Tri
18. Presson Pl
19. Marmont Ln
20. Sweetzer Ave
21. Lincoln Ter
22. Monteel Rd
23. Selma Dr
24. Crescent Heights
25. Bellgave Pl
26. Hillside Ave
27. Leoti Ter
28. Tavern Tri
29. Prospect Tri
30. Dickson Ln
31. Padre Ln
32. Seaview Tri
33. Floral Dr
34. N Fairfax Ave
35. Prospect Dr
36. W Hiller Pl
37. Courtney Ter
38. Cantata Dr
39. Sherbourne Dr
40. Westmount Dr
41. S Croft Ave
42. S Orlando Ave
43. S Kings Rd
44. S Flores St
45. S Sweetzer Ave
46. S Harper Ave
47. S La Jolla Ave
48. S Kilkea Dr
49. S Crescent Heights Blvd
50. S Laurel Ave
51. S Hayworth Ave
52. S Genesee Ave
53. Lindenhurst Ave
54. S Spaulding Ave
55. Colgate Ave
56. Fuller Cir
57. Hauser Blvd
58. Maryland Dr
51
52
Runyon Canyon Park
Wattles Garden Park
Hollywood Blvd
Laurel Canyon Blvd
Rock Walk
Sunset Strip
W Sunset Blvd
Plummer Park
Santa Monica
The Lot
Poinsettia Rec Ctr
Santa Monica Boulevard
Schindler House
La Cienega Blvd
N Fairfax Ave
Melrose Ave
W Hollywood Park
Pacific Design Center
Silent Movie Theatre
Santa Monica Blvd
N La Brea Ave
Beverly Blvd
CBS Television City
Beverly Center
PAGE 261
PAGE 266
The Grove
Pan Pacific Park
W 3rd St
Burton Way
Robertson Blvd
San Vicente Blvd
PARK LA BREA
Fairfax Ave
Hancock Park
A
B
C
D
1
2
3

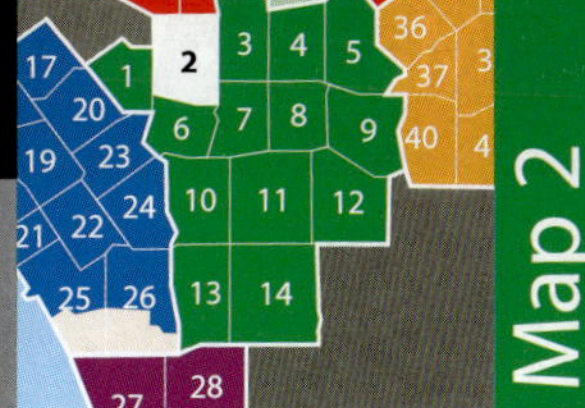

West Hollywood is one of the most diverse cities we know, boasting large factions of older Russian immigrants living side by side with WeHo's sizeable gay population, to name just two groups. This eclectic quality is most visible on Fairfax Avenue, where improv comedy theatres and thrift stores co-exist alongside kosher bakeries serving up freshly baked challah.

$ Banks

- **Bank of America** · 466 N La Brea Ave
- **Bank of America** · 7800 W Sunset Blvd
- **Bank of America** · 7900 Melrose Ave
- **Bank of America** · 8025 Santa Monica Blvd
- **Bank of America** · 8655 Beverly Blvd
- **Bank of America** · 8921 Santa Monica Blvd
- **Bank of America** · 9021 Sunset Blvd
- **California National Bank** · 145 S Fairfax Ave
- **Citibank** · 300 S Fairfax Ave
- **Citibank** · 7257 W Sunset Blvd
- **Citibank** · 8900 Santa Monica Blvd
- **First Federal Bank** · 400 N La Brea Ave
- **First Federal Bank** · 464 N Fairfax Ave
- **First Federal Bank** · 8653 Beverly Blvd
- **First Professional Bank** · 8600 W 3rd St
- **First Regional Bank** · 7083 Hollywood Blvd
- **Gilmore Bank** · 7929 W 3rd St
- **National Bank of California** · 145 S Fairfax Ave
- **US Bank** · 8901 Santa Monica Blvd
- **Washington Mutual** · 310 N Fairfax Ave
- **Washington Mutual** · 449 N La Brea Ave
- **Washington Mutual** · 6120 W 3rd St
- **Washington Mutual** · 8150 W Sunset Blvd
- **Wells Fargo Bank** · 100 N La Cienega Blvd
- **Wells Fargo Bank** · 1233 N La Brea Ave
- **Wells Fargo Bank** · 137 N Fairfax Ave
- **Wells Fargo Bank** · 8625 W 3rd St

Car Washes

- **Apollo Car Wash** · 7617 Santa Monica Blvd
- **Majestic Car Wash** · 8017 W 3rd St
- **Royal Car Wash** · 431 N La Cienega Blvd
- **Santa Palm Car Wash** · 8787 Santa Monica Blvd
- **Sunset Car Wash** · 7955 W Sunset Blvd

Gas Stations

- **76** · 5436 W 6th St
- **76** · 7751 Beverly Blvd
- **76** · 7979 W Sunset Blvd
- **76** · 8755 W 3rd St
- **Arco** · 7564 Santa Monica Blvd
- **Arco** · 7901 W Sunset Blvd
- **Chevron** · 1107 N La Cienega Blvd
- **Chevron** · 7020 Beverly Blvd
- **Chevron** · 7100 Melrose Ave
- **Chevron** · 7861 Melrose Ave
- **Chevron** · 7955 W Sunset Blvd
- **Chevron** · 8017 W 3rd St
- **Chevron** · 8101 W Sunset Blvd
- **Exxon** · 8020 Santa Monica Blvd
- **Mobil** · 307 N La Brea Ave
- **Mobil** · 7100 W Sunset Blvd
- **Mobil** · 7865 W Sunset Blvd
- **Mobil** · 8380 Santa Monica Blvd
- **Mobil** · 8489 Beverly Blvd
- **Shell** · 1309 N La Brea Ave

Hospitals

- **Cedars-Sinai Medical Ctr** · 8700 Beverly Blvd · 310-423-3277

Landmarks

- **CBS Television City** · Beverly Blvd & N Fairfax Ave
- **Pacific Design Center** · Melrose Ave & San Vicente Blvd
- **Pan Pacific Park** · 7600 Beverly Blvd
- **Rock Walk** · 7435 Sunset Blvd
- **Runyon Canyon Park** · Franklin Ave & Fuller Dr
- **Santa Monica Blvd** · Between La Cienega Blvd & Robertson Blvd
- **Schindler House** · 833 N Kings Rd
- **Silent Movie Theatre** · 611 N Fairfax Ave
- **Sunset Strip** · Sunset Blvd between N Doheny Dr & N Fairfax Ave

Libraries

- **Fairfax Branch Library** · 161 S Gardner St · 323-936-6191
- **Los Angeles Library** · 1403 N Gardner St · 323-876-2741
- **West Hollywood Public Library** · 715 N San Vicente Blvd · 310-652-5340

24-Hour Pharmacies

- **Rite Aid** · 7900 W Sunset Blvd · 323-876-4466
- **Sav-On** · 6360 W 3rd St · 323-937-3030

Post Offices

- 1125 N Fairfax Ave
- 7610 Beverly Blvd
- 820 N San Vicente Blvd

Schools

- **Aldonderry** · 8730 Alden Dr
- **Bais Tzivia Girls' School** · 7269 Beverly Blvd
- **Bais Yaakov School for Girls** · 461 N La Brea Ave
- **Center for Early Education** · 563 N Alfred St
- **Cheder Menachem** · 7215 Waring Ave
- **Cheder of Los Angeles** · 348 N La Brea Ave
- **Daniel Murphy Catholic High School** · 241 S Detroit St
- **Fairfax Senior High School** · 7850 Melrose Ave
- **Fountain Day School** · 1128 N Orange Grove Ave
- **Gardner Street Elementary** · 7450 Hawthorn Ave
- **Hancock Park Elementary** · 408 S Fairfax Ave
- **Just Like Mom's Preschool/Kindergarten** · 1535 N Poinsettia Pl
- **Laurel Elementary** · 925 N Hayworth Ave
- **Maimonides Academy** · 310 N Huntley
- **Melrose Ave Elementary** · 731 N Detroit St
- **Ofman Learning Center** · 812 N Fairfax Ave
- **Pacific Hills** · 8628 Holloway Dr
- **Perutz Jacob Hebrew Academy** · 7951 Beverly Blvd
- **Rosewood Ave Elementary** · 503 N Croft Ave
- **Temple Israel Day School** · 7300 Hollywood Blvd
- **West Coast Talmudical Seminary** · 7215 Waring Ave
- **Whitman Continuation** · 7795 Rosewood Ave
- **Yeshiva Gedolah of Los Angeles** · 5822 W 3rd St
- **Yeshiva Rav Isaacsohn** · 540 N La Brea Ave

Supermarkets

- **Bristol Farms** · 7880 W Sunset Blvd
- **Bristol Farms** · 9039 Beverly Blvd
- **Gelson's Markets** · 8330 Santa Monica Blvd
- **Jon's Marketplace** · 1234 N La Brea Ave
- **Pavilions** · 8969 Santa Monica Blvd
- **Ralph's** · 100 N La Cienega Blvd
- **Ralph's** · 1233 N La Brea Ave
- **Ralph's** · 260 S La Brea Ave
- **Ralph's** · 7257 Sunset Blvd
- **Ralph's** · 9040 Beverly Blvd
- **Trader Joe's** · 263 S La Brea Ave
- **Trader Joe's** · 7304 Santa Monica Blvd
- **Trader Joe's** · 8611 Santa Monica Blvd
- **Whole Foods Market** · 6350 W 3rd St
- **Whole Foods Market** · 7871 Santa Monica Blvd

Map 2 • West Hollywood

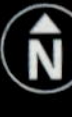

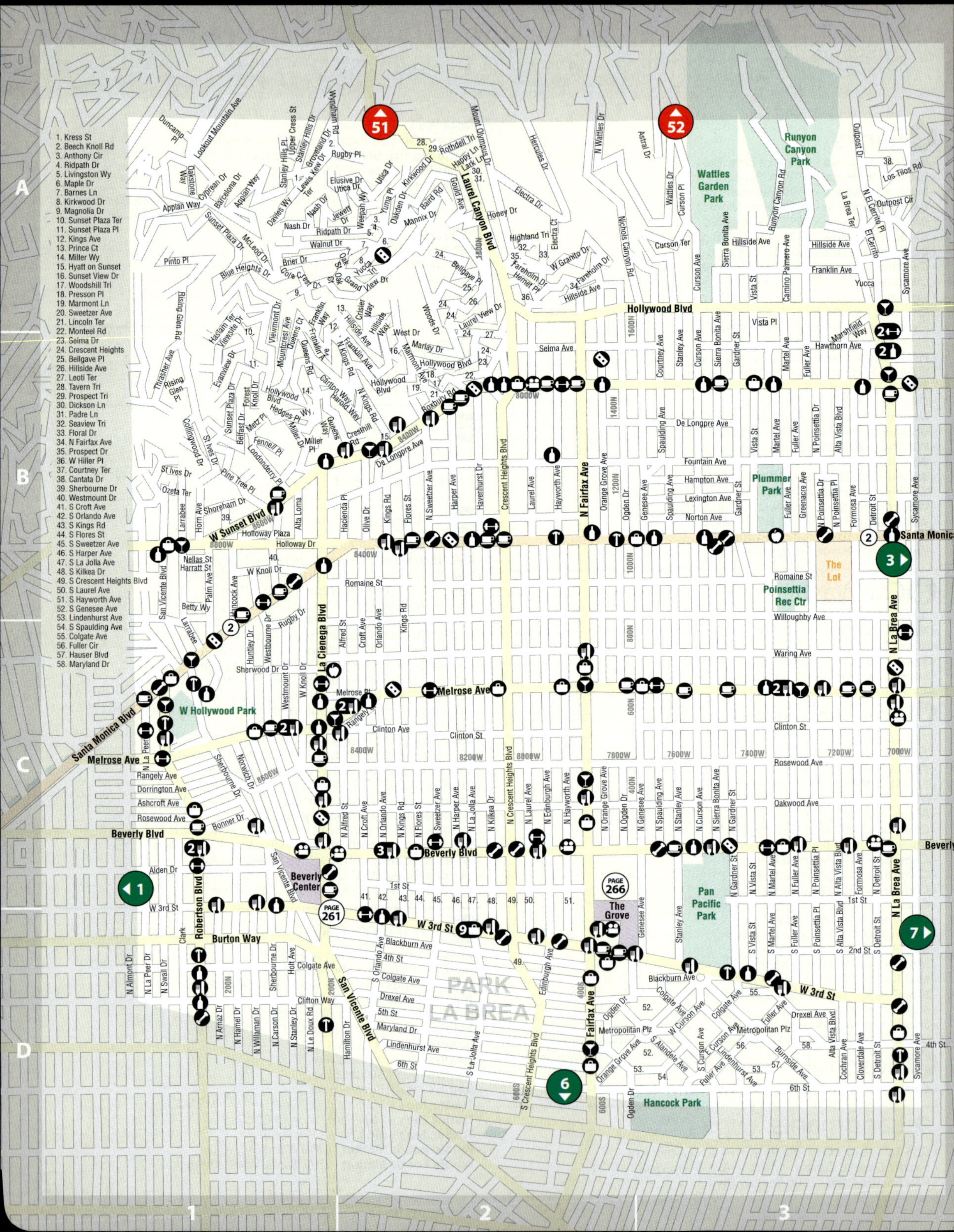
1. Kress St
2. Beech Knoll Rd
3. Anthony Cir
4. Ridpath Dr
5. Livingston Wy
6. Maple Dr
7. Barnes Ln
8. Kirkwood Dr
9. Magnolia Dr
10. Sunset Plaza Ter
11. Sunset Plaza Pl
12. Kings Ave
13. Prince Ct
14. Miller Wy
15. Hyatt on Sunset
16. Sunset View Dr
17. Woodshill Tri
18. Presson Pl
19. Marmont Ln
20. Sweetzer Ave
21. Lincoln Ter
22. Monteel Rd
23. Selma Dr
24. Crescent Heights
25. Bellgave Pl
26. Hillside Ave
27. Leoti Ter
28. Tavern Tri
29. Prospect Tri
30. Dickson Ln
31. Padre Ln
32. Seaview Tri
33. Floral Dr
34. N Fairfax Ave
35. Prospect Dr
36. W Hiller Pl
37. Courtney Ter
38. Cantata Dr
39. Sherbourne Dr
40. Westmount Dr
41. S Croft Ave
42. S Orlando Ave
43. S Kings Rd
44. S Flores St
45. S Sweetzer Ave
46. S Harper Ave
47. S La Jolla Ave
48. S Kilkea Dr
49. S Crescent Heights Blvd
50. S Laurel Ave
51. S Hayworth Ave
52. S Genesee Ave
53. Lindenhurst Ave
54. S Spaulding Ave
55. Colgate Ave
56. Fuller Cir
57. Hauser Blvd
58. Maryland Dr
N
A
B
C
D
1
2
3
51
52
Wattles Garden Park
Runyon Canyon Park
Laurel Canyon Blvd
Hollywood Blvd
W Sunset Blvd
Santa Monica Blvd
Melrose Ave
Beverly Blvd
W 3rd St
Burton Way
La Cienega Blvd
N Fairfax Ave
N La Brea Ave
Crescent Heights Blvd
Robertson Blvd
San Vicente Blvd
Plummer Park
The Lot
Poinsettia Rec Ctr
W Hollywood Park
Beverly Center
PAGE 261
PAGE 266
The Grove
Pan Pacific Park
PARK LA BREA
Hancock Park
Fountain Ave
De Longpre Ave
Romaine St
Willoughby Ave
Waring Ave
Clinton St
Rosewood Ave
Oakwood Ave
Selma Ave
Hawthorn Ave
Franklin Ave
Hillside Ave
Holloway Dr
Blackburn Ave
6th St
1
3
6
7

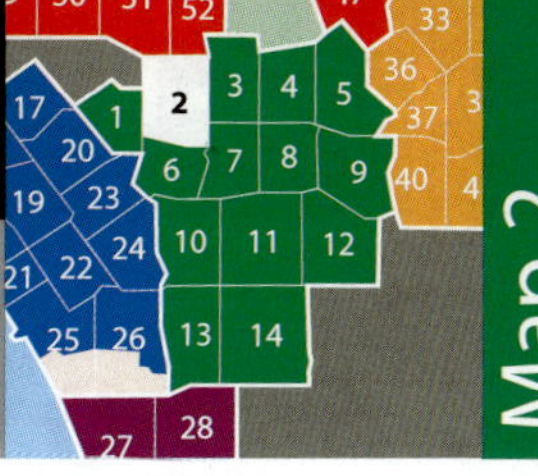

In West Hollywood, there is always something to do, somewhere to shop, and someone to watch. We think a great day would start with a hike at Runyon Canyon Park—which has killer views all the way to the ocean—followed by a day of shopping at the new Grove at the Farmer's Market and ending with dinner at Cynthia's restaurant, where you absolutely must order her famous berry cobbler for dessert.

Clubs
- **Bar Marmont** • 8221 W Sunset Blvd • 323-650-0575
- **Barfly** • 8730 Sunset Blvd • 310-360-9490
- **Barney's Beanery** • 8447 Santa Monica Blvd • 323-654-2287
- **Bel Age Hotel** • 1020 N San Vicente Blvd • 310-854-1111
- **Chateau Marmont** • 8221 Sunset Blvd • 323-656-1010
- **Dominick's** • 8715 Beverly Blvd • 310-652-7272
- **Dublins** • 8240 Sunset Blvd • 323-656-0100
- **El Carmen Tequila & Taco Bar** • 8138 W 3rd St • 323-852-1552
- **El Coyote** • 7312 Beverly Blvd • 323-939-2255
- **Farmer's Market Bars** • Corner 3rd St and Fairfax Ave • 323-933-9211
- **Fenix Lounge** • 8385 W Sunset Blvd • 323-654-7100
- **Formosa Café** • 7156 Santa Monica Blvd • 323-850-9050
- **Garden of Eden** • 7080 Hollywood Blvd • 323-465-3336
- **Genghis Cohen** • 740 N Fairfax Ave • 323-653-0640
- **House of Blues** • 8430 Sunset Blvd • 323-848-5100
- **Jones** • 7205 Santa Monica Blvd • 323-850-1727
- **Largo** • 432 N Fairfax Ave • 323-852-1073
- **Lava Lounge** • 1533 N La Brea Ave • 323-876-6612
- **Lola's** • 945 N Fairfax Ave • 213-736-5652
- **Louis XIV** • 606 N La Brea Ave • 323-394-5102
- **Max's** • 442 N Fairfax Ave • 323-651-4421
- **Molly Malone's** • 575 S Fairfax Ave • 323-935-1577
- **North** • 8029 W Sunset Blvd • 323-654-1313
- **Rage** • 8911 Santa Monica Blvd • 310-652-7055
- **Roxy** • 9009 Sunset Blvd • 310-276-2222
- **Saddle Ranch Chop House** • 8371 W Sunset Blvd • 323-656-2007
- **Snake Pit Ale House** • 7529 Melrose Ave • 323-852-9390
- **The Bar at the Four Season Hotel** • 300 S Doheny Dr • 310-273-2222
- **The Factory/Ultra Suede** • 661 N Robertson Blvd • 310-724-8181
- **The Gate** • 643 N La Cienega Blvd • 310-289-8808
- **The Lounge** • 9077 Hollywood Blvd • 323-228-4830
- **The Rainbow** • 9015 Sunset Blvd • 310-278-4232
- **The Ruby** • 7070 Hollywood Blvd • 323-467-7070
- **The Skybar** • 8440 W Sunset Blvd • 323-650-8999
- **The Standard Hotel Lobby** • 8300 W Sunset Blvd • 323-654-2800
- **The Troubadour** • 9081 Santa Monica Blvd • 310-276-6168
- **Viper Room** • 8852 Sunset Blvd • 310-358-1880
- **Whiskey Bar** • 1200 N Alta Loma Rd • 310-657-0612
- **Whisky A Go Go** • 8901 Sunset Blvd • 310-652-4202

Coffee
- **At Coffee Shop** • 7200 Melrose Ave
- **Basix Coffee** • 8329 Santa Monica Blvd
- **Bob's Coffee & Donuts** • 6333 W 3rd St
- **Buzz Coffee** • 7623 Beverly Blvd
- **Buzz Coffee** • 8000 Sunset Blvd
- **Buzz Coffee** • 8200 Santa Monica Blvd
- **Coffee Bean & Tea Leaf** • 6333 W 3rd St
- **Coffee Bean & Tea Leaf** • 7502 Melrose Ave
- **Coffee Bean & Tea Leaf** • 7915 W Sunset Blvd
- **Coffee Bean & Tea Leaf** • 8591 W Sunset Blvd
- **Coffee Bean & Tea Leaf** • 8735 Santa Monica Blvd
- **Coffee Bean & Tea Leaf** • 8793 Beverly Blvd
- **Coffee House** • 8226 W Sunset Blvd
- **Daily Grind** • 7801 Melrose Ave
- **Galaxy Gallery** • 7224 Melrose Ave
- **Royal Coffee & Tea** • 8151 Santa Monica Blvd
- **Starbucks** • 100 N La Cienega Blvd
- **Starbucks** • 6333 W 3rd St
- **Starbucks** • 7055 W Sunset Blvd
- **Starbucks** • 7122 Beverly Blvd
- **Starbucks** • 7624 Melrose Ave
- **Starbucks** • 8595 Santa Monica Blvd
- **Starbucks** • 8949 Santa Monica Blvd
- **Top Fuel Kawfee House** • 7554 W Sunset Blvd
- **Urth Caffe** • 8565 Melrose Ave

Farmer's Markets
- **Melrose Place** • Between La Cienega and Orlando
- **Plummer Park** • 7377 Santa Monica Blvd • Mon 9-2

Gyms
- **24-Hour Fitness** • 8612 Santa Monica Blvd • 310-652-7440
- **Angel City Gym** • 8816 Melrose Ave • 310-858-6812
- **Beverly Hills Health & Fitness** • 8301 Beverly Blvd • 323-658-6999
- **Body Sculpting LA** • 630 N La Cienega Blvd • 310-657-4140
- **Boulevard Health** • 120 N Robertson Blvd • 310-659-5002
- **Crunch** • 8000 W Sunset Blvd • 323-654-4550
- **Custom Fitness** • 7709 Melrose Ave • 323-653-8683
- **Easton Gym** • 8053 Beverly Blvd • 323-651-3636
- **Golding Fitness** • 8416 W 3rd St • 323-655-4602
- **Groove Fitness** • 1626 N La Brea Ave • 323-960-0660
- **Hollywood Gym** • 1551 N La Brea Ave • 323-845-1420
- **In Training** • 7416 Beverly Blvd • 323-937-3539
- **Ultra Body Fitness** • 828 N La Brea Ave • 323-464-5300
- **Winsor Fitness** • 8204 Melrose Ave
- **Workout Warehouse** • 650 N La Peer Dr • 310-358-1838

Hardware Stores
- **Anawalt Lumber** • 641 N Robertson Blvd • 310-652-6202
- **Carter Hardware** • 153 N Robertson Blvd • 310-657-1940
- **Design Hardware** • 6053 W 3rd St • 323-930-1330
- **Koontz Hardware** • 8914 Santa Monica Blvd • 310-652-0123
- **Laurel Hardware** • 7984 Santa Monica Blvd • 323-656-9605
- **Liz's Antique Hardware** • 453 S La Brea Ave • 323-939-4403
- **Restoration Hardware** • 131 N La Cienega Blvd • 310-360-9651
- **Tashman Screens & Hardware** • 7769 Santa Monica Blvd • 323-656-7028

Liquor Stores
- **Almor Liquors** • 7855 W Sunset Blvd
- **Bicentennial 13** • 7613 Beverly Blvd
- **Carmel Liquor** • 8200 Santa Monica Blvd
- **Consumers Liquor** • 7151 W Sunset Blvd
- **Crown Liquor Store** • 130 N Robertson Blvd
- **Du Vin Wine & Spirits** • 540 N San Vicente Blvd
- **Fountain Liquor & Mkt** • 7952 Fountain Ave
- **Gil Turner's Fine Wine & Sprts** • 9101 W Sunset Blvd
- **Golden Rule Liquor** • 7753 Santa Monica Blvd
- **Greenblatt's Delicatessen** • 8017 W Sunset Blvd
- **John & Pete's Liquor** • 621 N La Cienega Blvd
- **La Brea Discount Liquor** • 707 S La Brea Ave
- **Lee's Liquors** • 8572 W 3rd St
- **Limelite Liquors** • 1649 N La Brea Ave
- **Liquor Locker** • 8161 W Sunset Blvd
- **Liquor Time** • 7873 Santa Monica Blvd
- **Melrose Liquors** • 7435 Melrose Ave
- **Monaco Liquor** • 8513 Santa Monica Blvd
- **Mr S Liquor Mart** • 7580 W Sunset Blvd
- **Park Plaza Liquor & Wine Cllr** • 6015 W 3rd St
- **Pink Dot Market Deli/Grocery** • 8495 W Sunset Blvd
- **Robert Burns Liquor** • 157 N Robertson Blvd
- **Roman's Liquor** • 1529 N La Brea Ave
- **S & S Liquor** • 7600 Santa Monica Blvd
- **St Regis Liquors** • 8401 W 3rd St
- **Sun Bee Food & Liquor Mart** • 8860 W Sunset Blvd
- **Sunset Plaza Liquors** • 7365 W Sunset Blvd
- **Y M Liquor** • 7119 Santa Monica Blvd

Movie Theaters
- **AMC Beverly Connection** • 100 N La Cienega Blvd
- **Laemmle Fairfax** • 7907 Beverly Blvd
- **Laemmle Sunset 5 Theatres** • 8000 W Sunset Blvd
- **Loews Beverly Center 13** • 8522 Beverly Blvd
- **New Beverly Cinema** • 7165 Beverly Blvd
- **Pacific Theatres - The Grove Stadium 14** • 189 The Grove Dr
- **Regent Showcase Theatre** • 614 N La Brea Ave

Pet Stores
- **Amazon Rainforest Pet Shop** • 7505 Santa Monica Blvd • 323-969-8382
- **Animal Crackers** • 8023 Beverly Blvd • 310-659-1919
- **Animal Farm Pet Shop** • 8928 Santa Monica Blvd • 310-659-2498
- **Aquarium Stock** • 8070 Beverly Blvd • 323-653-8930
- **Centinela Feed & Pet Supplies** • 331 N Robertson Blvd • 310-246-0367
- **Chateau Marmutt** • 8128 W 3rd St • 323-653-2062
- **Collar & Leash Pet Food & Supl** • 8555 Santa Monica Blvd • 310-657-6638
- **Dog House** • 5959 W 3rd St • 323-549-9663
- **For Birds Only** • 8273 Santa Monica Blvd • 323-848-8361
- **For Pets Only** • 310 S La Brea Ave • 323-934-8303
- **Gays Pet Grooming** • 7547 Santa Monica Blvd • 323-874-1886
- **Oranda Aquarium** • 7318 1/2 Santa Monica Blvd • 323-876-5059
- **Pet Love** • 131 N La Cienega Blvd • 310-659-8490
- **Petco** • 200 S La Brea Ave • 323-934-8444
- **Petco** • 608 N Doheny Dr • 310-274-7862
- **Pets Spa** • 248 Santa Monica Blvd • 323-654-6758
- **Pour La Pooch** • 7617 Beverly Blvd • 323-934-0940

Restaurants
- **Ago** • 8478 Melrose Ave • 323-655-6333
- **Amici** • 469 N Doheny Dr • 310-858-0271
- **Angeli Caffe** • 7274 Melrose Ave • 323-936-9086
- **Angelini Osteria** • 7313 Beverly Blvd • 323-297-0070
- **Authentic Café** • 7605 Beverly Blvd • 323-939-4626
- **Balboa** • The Grafton Hotel, 8462 W Sunset Blvd • 323-650-8383
- **Barefoot Bar & Grill** • 8722 W 3rd St • 310-276-6223
- **Basix Cafe** • 8333 Santa Monica Blvd • 323-848-2460
- **Bistro 21** • 846 N La Cienega Blvd • 310-967-0021
- **Bossa Nova** • 685 N Robertson Blvd • 310-657-5070
- **Cadillac Café** • 359 N La Cienega Blvd • 310-657-6591
- **Café Angelino** • 8735 W 3rd St • 310-246-1177
- **Cafe Med** • 8615 Sunset Blvd • 310-652-0445
- **Café Pranzo** • 8514 W 3rd St • 310-652-7755

Restaurants (continued)
- **Campanile** • 624 S La Brea Ter • 323-938-1447
- **Canter's Deli** • 419 N Fairfax Ave • 323-651-2030
- **Chaya Brasserie** • 8741 Alden Dr • 310-859-8833
- **Chianti** • 7383 Melrose Ave • 323-653-8333
- **Chianti Cucina** • 7383 Melrose Ave • 323-653-8333
- **Cynthia's** • 8370 W 3rd St • 323-658-7851
- **Doughboys** • 8136 W 3rd St • 323-651-4202
- **East India Grill** • 345 N La Brea Ter • 323-936-8844
- **Ed's Coffee Shop** • 460 N Robertson Blvd • 310-659-8625
- **Farm of Beverly Hills** • 189 The Grove Dr • 323-525-1699
- **Fish Grill** • 7226 Beverly Blvd • 323-937-7162
- **Flora Kitchen** • 460 S La Brea Ave • 323-931-9900
- **Genghis Cohen** • 740 N Fairfax Ave • 323-653-0640
- **Gumbo Pot** • 6333 W 3rd St • 323-933-0358
- **Hirozen** • 8385 Beverly Blvd • 323-653-0470
- **House of Blues** • 8430 Sunset Blvd • 323-848-5100
- **Hugo's** • 8401 Santa Monica Blvd • 323-654-3993
- **Ivy, The** • 113 N Robertson Blvd • 310-274-8303
- **Jar** • 8225 Beverly Blvd • 323-655-6566
- **King's Road Cafe** • 8361 Beverly Blvd • 323-655-9044
- **Kokomo** • Inside Farmer's Market, at 3rd St & Fairfax Ave • 323-933-0773
- **Le Pain Quotidien** • 8607 Melrose Ave • 310-854-3700
- **Lucques** • 8474 Melrose Ave • 323-655-6277
- **Mandarette** • 8386 Beverly Blvd • 323-655-6115
- **Manhattan Won Ton Company** • 151 S Doheny Dr • 310-888-2804
- **Newsroom Café** • 120 N Robertson Blvd • 310-652-4444
- **Noura Café** • 8479 Melrose Ave • 323-651-4581
- **Pig, The** • 612 N La Brea Ave • 323-935-1116
- **Pink's Famous Chili Dogs** • 709 N La Brea Ave • 323-931-4223
- **Quality Food & Beverage** • 8030 W 3rd St • 323-658-5959
- **Real Food Daily** • 414 N La Cienega Blvd • 310-289-9910
- **Saddle Ranch Chop House** • 8371 Sunset Blvd • 323-656-2007
- **Sweet Lady Jane** • 8360 Melrose Ave • 323-653-7145
- **Swingers** • 8020 Beverly Blvd • 323-653-5858
- **Tail o' the Pup** • 329 N San Vicente Blvd • 323-652-4517
- **The Standard** • 8300 Sunset Blvd • 323-650-9090
- **Urth Caffé** • 8565 Melrose Ave • 310-659-0628
- **Yabu** • 521 N La Cienega Blvd • 310-854-0400

Shopping
- **Book Soup** • 8818 Sunset Blvd • 310-659-3110
- **Button Store** • 8344 W 3rd St • 323-658-5473
- **Centerfold Newsstand** • 716 N Fairfax Ave • 323-651-4822
- **Chado Tea Room** • 8422 1/2 W 3rd St • 323-655-2056
- **Chateau Marmutt** • 8128 W 3rd St • 323-653-2062
- **Denim Doctor** • 8044 W 3rd St • 323-852-0171
- **Fred Segal** • 8100 Melrose Ave • 323-651-4129
- **Golden Apple** • 7711 Melrose Ave • 323-658-6047
- **Guitar Center** • 7425 Sunset Blvd • 323-874-1060
- **I. Martin** • 8330 Beverly Blvd • 323-653-6900
- **Illume** • 8302 W 3rd St • 800-245-5863
- **Kbond** • 7257 Beverly Blvd • 323-939-8866
- **Malia Mills** • 7972 Melrose Ave • 323-655-4709
- **Mani's Bakery** • 519 S Fairfax Ave • 323-938-8800
- **Mr Marcel's** • 6333 W 3rd St (Farmers Market) • 323-935-9451
- **Plastica** • 8405 W 3rd St • 323-655-1051
- **Pleasure Chest** • 7733 Santa Monica Blvd • 323-650-1022
- **Pulp** • 456 S La Brea Ave • 323-937-3506
- **Sam Ash Music** • 8000 Sunset Blvd • 323-654-4922
- **Samy's Camera** • 431 S Fairfax Ave • 323-938-4400
- **Solomon's** • 447 N Fairfax Ave • 323-653-9045
- **Soolip** • 8646 Melrose Ave • 310-360-0545
- **Splash Bath & Body** • 8934 Santa Monica Blvd • 310-657-7627
- **Storyopolis** • 116 N Robertson Blvd • 310-358-2500
- **The Cook's Library** • 8373 W 3rd St • 310-665-3141
- **Trashy Lingerie** • 402 La Cienega Blvd • 310-652-4543
- **Traveler's Bookcase** • 8375 W 3rd St • 310-665-0575
- **Zipper** • 8316 W 3rd St • 323-662-9463

Video Rental
- **20-20 Video** • 8208 Santa Monica Blvd • 323-656-2300
- **20-20 Video** • 7515 Beverly Blvd • 323-935-2020
- **20-20 Video** • 7064 W Sunset Blvd • 323-957-2020
- **94 Video** • 8178 W Sunset Blvd • 323-654-7911
- **Blockbuster** • 1508 N Orange Grove Ave • 323-851-2688
- **Blockbuster** • 330 N La Cienega Blvd • 310-659-8366
- **Movies & More** • 8302 Melrose Ave • 323-658-5151
- **Rocket Video** • 726 N La Brea Ave • 323-965-1100
- **Top One Video** • 901 N Fairfax Ave • 323-654-0434
- **Video West** • 805 Larrabee St • 310-659-5762

1. Timmons Tri
2. Macal Pl
3. Bryn Mawr Ct
4. Fink Pl
5. San Marco Cir
6. Lorenzo Dr
7. Whitley Ter
8. Fairfield Ave
9. Watsonia Ct
10. High Tower Dr
11. Los Altos Pl
12. Yeager Pl
13. Rockledge Rd
14. Woodland Wy
15. Paramount Dr
16. Bella Vista Wy
17. Holly Hill
18. Wilcox Ave
19. Hollyridge Pl
20. W Allview Ter
21. E Allview Ter
22. Manola Wy
23. Argosy Wy
24. Tuxedo Ter
25. High Oak Dr

HOLLYWOOD

Hollywood Reservoir
Griffith Park
Runyon Canyon Park
Mulholland Dr
Hollywood Bowl
PAGE 318
Hollywood Freeway
Hollywood Wax Museum
Mann's Chinese Theatre
Pantages Theatre
Capitol Records Building
Hollywood Walk of Fame
Hollywood Blvd
Hollywood Forever Cemetery
Paramount Studios
Wilshire Country Club

W Sunset Blvd
Santa Monica Blvd
Melrose Ave
Beverly Blvd
Franklin Ave
N Cahuenga Blvd
N Beachwood Dr
N Gower St
Vine St
N Highland Ave
N Las Palmas Ave
N Cherokee Ave
Fountain Ave
Lexington Ave
Romaine St
Barton Ave
Willoughby Ave
Waring Ave
Clinton St
Rosewood Ave
Oakwood Ave

Hollywood is becoming trendy again. Young people are snatching up apartments in the neighborhood as quickly as developers can tear down the 1920s buildings and remodel them. Hollywood Blvd. still isn't the safest place to walk alone at night, but nothing beats living in the heart of it all.

$ Banks

- **Bank of America** · 6300 W Sunset Blvd
- **Washington Mutual** · 1500 Vine St
- **Wells Fargo Bank** · 5609 W Sunset Blvd
- **Wells Fargo Bank** · 6320 W Sunset Blvd

Car Washes

- **Ambassador Car Wash** · 6061 Santa Monica Blvd
- **Celebrity Car Wash** · 901 Vine St
- **Cook's Corner Smog** · 5925 Melrose Ave
- **Melrose Car Wash** · 5080 Melrose Ave
- **Paramount Car Wash** · 1411 N Highland Ave

Gas Stations

- **76** · 4700 Beverly Blvd
- **76** · 5890 Hollywood Blvd
- **76** · 6051 Franklin Ave
- **76** · 6537 Melrose Ave
- **76** · 6678 Santa Monica Blvd
- **Arco** · 5175 Melrose Ave
- **Arco** · 6100 Franklin Ave
- **Chevron** · 1787 N Highland Ave
- **Chevron** · 1934 N Cahuenga Blvd
- **Chevron** · 5700 Melrose Ave
- **Mobil** · 1051 N Highland Ave
- **Mobil** · 5700 Hollywood Blvd
- **Mobil** · 5857 W Sunset Blvd
- **Mobil** · 6228 Franklin Ave
- **Mobil** · 6301 Santa Monica Blvd
- **Mobil** · 6601 Melrose Ave
- **Shell** · 5657 W Sunset Blvd
- **Shell** · 6420 Franklin Ave
- **Texaco** · 859 N Highland Ave

Hospitals

- **Hollywood Community Hospital** · 6245 De Longpre Ave · 323-462-2271

Landmarks

- **Capitol Records Building** · 1750 N Vine St
- **Hollywood Bowl** · 2301 N Highland Ave
- **Hollywood Forever Cemetery** · 6000 Santa Monica Blvd
- **Hollywood Walk of Fame** · Hollywood Blvd from N Gower St to La Brea Ter
- **Hollywood Wax Museum** · 6767 Hollywood Blvd
- **Mann's Chinese Theatre** · 6925 Hollywood Blvd
- **Pantages Theatre** · 6233 Hollywood Blvd
- **Paramount Pictures** · 5555 Melrose Ave

Libraries

- **Frances Howard Goldwyn Library** · 1623 Ivar Ave · 323-856-8260
- **John C Fremont Library** · 6121 Melrose Ave · 323-962-3521

Police

- **Los Angeles County Park Police** · 2101 N Highland Ave · 323-845-0080
- **Los Angeles Police Dept** · 1358 Wilcox Ave · 213-485-4302

Post Offices

- 1425 N Cherokee Ave
- 1615 Wilcox Ave
- 6457 Santa Monica Blvd

Schools

- **ABC Educational Center** · 1129 Cole Ave
- **Bancroft Middle School** · 6750 Romaine St
- **Blessed Sacrament** · 6641 W Sunset Blvd
- **Booth High School** · 2670 Griffin Ave
- **Cheremoya Ave Elemenary** · 6017 Franklin Ave
- **Christ The King Elementary** · 617 N Arden Blvd
- **Grant Elementary** · 1530 N Wilton Pl
- **Hollywood Little Red School House** · 1248 N Highland Ave
- **Hollywood Senior High School** · 1521 N Highland Ave
- **Le Conte Middle School** · 1316 N Bronson Ave
- **Learning Connection** · 2528 Canyon Dr
- **Los Angeles Hankook Middle/High School** · 5120 Melrose Ave
- **Oaks School** · 6817 Franklin Ave
- **Page Private School** · 565 N Larchmont Blvd
- **Santa Monica Boulevard Elementary** · 1022 N Van Ness Ave
- **Selma Ave Elementary** · 6611 Selma Ave
- **Soledad Enrichment Action** · 1717 N Gramercy Pl
- **Tca Arshag Dickranian Armenian** · 1200 N Cahuenga Blvd
- **Van Ness Ave Elementary** · 501 N Van Ness Ave
- **Vine Street Elementary** · 955 Vine St

Supermarkets

- **Gelson's Markets** · 5877 Franklin Ave
- **Pavilions** · 727 Vine St
- **Stop N Shop** · 1123 Vine St
- **Von's** · 727 N Vine St

Map 3 · Hollywood

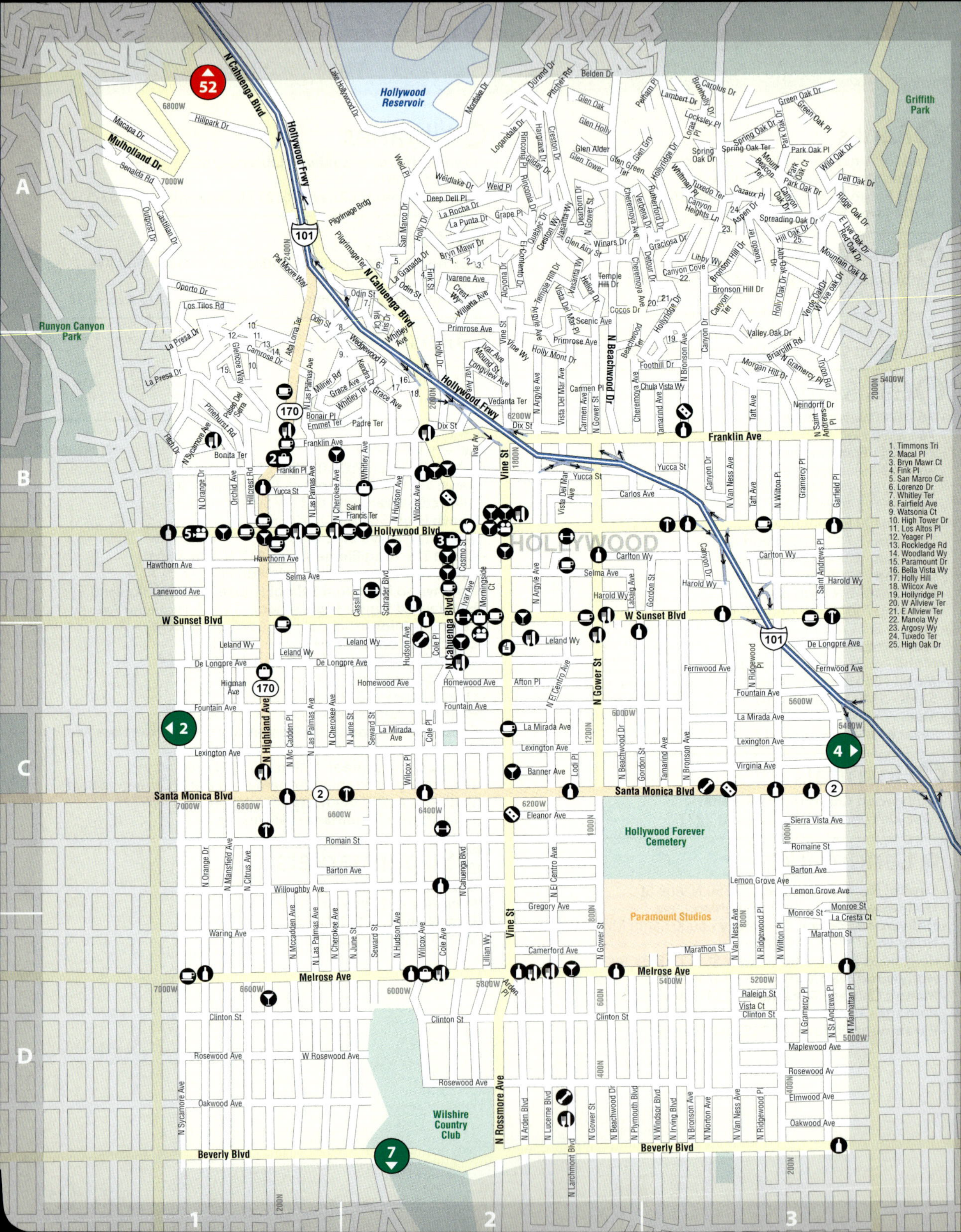

The rebirth of Hollywood is here! Well, sort of. Though Hollywood is working to flush out the kitschy souvenir stores that litter the Boulevard, for now it remains a tourist trap. The swanky new Hollywood & Highland shopping complex has become a focal point, but Hollywood is still all about the nightlife. Several not-to-be-missed bars have opened in the past year, and several larger nightclubs are planned along Cahuenga Blvd.

24-Hour Copy Centers

- **Kinko's** · 1440 Vine St · 323-871-1300

Clubs

- **AD** · 836 N Highland Ave · 323-467-3000
- **Beauty Bar** · 1638 N Cahuenga Blvd · 323-464-7676
- **Birds** · 5925 Franklin Ave · 323-465-0175
- **Blue** · 1642 Las Palmas Ave · 323-462-7442
- **Boardner's** · 1642 N Cherokee Ave · 323-462-9621
- **Burgundy Room** · 1621 1/2 Cahuenga Blvd · 323-465-7530
- **Cat & Fiddle** · 6530 W Sunset Blvd · 323-468-3800
- **Catalina Bar & Grill** · 1640 N Cahuenga Blvd · 323-466-2210
- **Cinespace** · 6356 Hollywood Blvd · 323-228-4830
- **Daddy's** · 1610 N Vine St · 323-463-7777
- **Deep** · 1707 N Vine St · 323-462-1144
- **El Floridita** · 1253 N Vine St · 323-871-8612
- **For Stars Shoes** · 6364 Hollywood Blvd · 323-462-6448
- **Frolic Room** · 6245 Hollywood Blvd · 323-462-5890
- **Goldfinger's** · 6423 Yucca St · 323-962-2913
- **Hollywood Athletic Club** · 6525 Sunset Blvd · 323-462-6262
- **Joseph's** · 1775 Ivar Ave · 323-462-8697
- **Knitting Factory** · 7021 Hollywood Blvd · 323-463-0204
- **La Palmas Supper Club** · 1714 N Las Palmas Ave · 323-464-0171
- **Musso & Frank Grill Bar** · 6667 Hollywood Blvd · 323-467-5123
- **Nacional** · 1645 N Wilcox Ave · 323-962-7712
- **Sunset Room** · 1430 N Cahuenga Blvd · 323-463-0004
- **The Baked Potato Hollywood** · 6266 Sunset Blvd · 323-461-6400
- **The Cinegrill** · 7000 Hollywood Blvd · 323-466-7000
- **The Highlands** · 6801 Hollywood Blvd · 323-461-9800
- **The Larchmont** · 5657 Melrose Ave ·
- **the room** · 1626 N Cahuenga Blvd · 323-462-7196
- **The Well** · 6255 W Sunset Blvd · 323-467-9355
- **Three of Clubs** · 1123 N Vine St · 323-462-6441
- **White Lotus** · 1743 N Cahuenga Ave · 323-463-0060

Coffee

- **Coffee Bean & Tea Leaf** · 6255 W Sunset Blvd
- **Expresso Mi Cultura Books & Coffee** · 5625 Hollywood Blvd
- **Goldberg's Famous Coffee Bar** · 6767 W Sunset Blvd
- **Green Room** · 6752 Hollywood Blvd
- **Space Booth** · 1233 Vine St
- **Starbucks** · 1900 N Highland Ave
- **Starbucks** · 5615 W Sunset Blvd
- **Starbucks** · 6102 W Sunset Blvd
- **Starbucks** · 6745 Hollywood Blvd
- **Starbucks** · 6801 Hollywood Blvd
- **Stir Crazy Coffee Shop** · 6917 Melrose Ave
- **The Hotel Café** · 1625 Cahuenga Blvd
- **Tully's Coffee** · 7000 Hollywood Blvd
- **Via Roma Cafe** · 1611 N El Centro Ave
- **Wise Shane** · 2034 1/2 N Highland Ave

Farmer's Markets

- **Hollywood** · Ivar St & Hollywood Blvd · Sun 8:30-1

Gyms

- **24-Hour Fitness** · 6360 Sunset Blvd ·
- **Bally Total Fitness** · 1628 N El Centro Ave · 323-461-0227
- **Gold's Gym** · 1016 Cole Ave · 323-462-7012
- **Hollywood YMCA** · 1553 N Schrader Blvd

Hardware Stores

- **Anawalt Lumber Company** · 1001 Highland Ave · 323-464-1600
- **Home Depot** · 5600 W Sunset Blvd · 323-461-3303
- **Rompage Hardware** · 5916 Hollywood Blvd · 323-467-2129
- **Terry Lumber** · 6641 Santa Monica Blvd · 323-469-1951

Liquor Stores

- **Al's Liquor Store** · 5550 Melrose Ave
- **Bogie's Liquor** · 5753 Melrose Ave
- **Carlton Liquor** · 1610 N Gower St
- **Gary's Liquor** · 5067 Melrose Ave
- **Highland Liquor** · 1770 N Highland Ave
- **Hollywood Liquors** · 7040 Hollywood Blvd
- **Howie's Liquor & Junior Market** · 5645 Santa Monica Blvd
- **Hudson Liquor & Delicatessen** · 6023 Melrose Ave
- **La Vida Liquors** · 6007 W Sunset Blvd
- **Liquor & Food Mart** · 4657 Beverly Blvd
- **Liquor To Go Go** · 5901 Hollywood Blvd
- **P & J Liquor** · 6170 Santa Monica Blvd
- **P & J Liquor-Deli** · 6480 Santa Monica Blvd
- **Pla-Boy Liquor** · 6435 Yucca St
- **Quaker State Liquor Store** · 6901 Melrose Ave
- **Spirit Shoppe & Deli** · 6443 W Sunset Blvd
- **St Andrews Liquor Store** · 5566 Hollywood Blvd
- **Studio Liquor** · 6759 Santa Monica Blvd
- **Sunset Market & Liquor** · 5825 W Sunset Blvd
- **Tony's Liquors** · 5707 Santa Monica Blvd
- **Victor's Liquor & Delicatessen** · 1915 N Bronson Ave
- **Wilcox Liquor Store** · 1515 1/2 Wilcox Ave

Movie Theaters

- **AMC Hollywood Galaxy Cinema** · 7021 Hollywood Blvd
- **Egyptian Theater** · 6712 Hollywood Blvd
- **El Capitan** · 6838 Hollywood Blvd
- **Grauman's Chinese Theatre** · 6925 Hollywood Blvd
- **Mann Chinese 6** · 6801 Hollywood Blvd
- **Vine Theatre** · 6321 Hollywood Blvd

Pet Stores

- **Animal Ark Pet Shop** · 1434 Wilcox Ave · 323-464-6965
- **Barking Lot** · 336 N Larchmont Blvd · 323-464-3031
- **Yo Aquarium** · 5846 Santa Monica Blvd · 323-871-2730

Restaurants

- **Ammo** · 1155 N Highland Ave · 323-871-2666
- **Cat N' Fiddle Pub & Restaurant** · 6530 W Sunset Blvd · 323-468-3800
- **Chan Dara** · 310 N Larchmont Blvd · 323-467-1052
- **Hola** · 1807 N Cahuenga Blvd · 323-466-0000
- **Hollywood & Vine Diner** · 6263 Hollywood Blvd · 323-461-2345
- **House, The** · 5750 Melrose Ave · 323-462-4687
- **Les Deux Cafes** · 1638 N Las Palmas Ave · 310-465-0509
- **Miceli's** · 1646 N Las Palmas Ave · 323-466-3438
- **Musso & Frank** · 6667 Hollywood Blvd · 301-467-7788
- **Off Vine** · 6263 Leland Way · 301-962-1900
- **Patina** · 5955 Melrose Ave · 310-467-1108
- **Roscoe's Chicken & Waffles** · 1514 N Gower St · 323-466-7453
- **Sunset Room** · 1430 N Cahuenga Blvd · 323-463-0004
- **The Pig & Whistle** · 6714 Hollywood Blvd · 323-463-0000
- **Yamakasa** · 1900 N Highland Ave · 323-882-6524
- **Yamashiro** · 1999 Sycamore Ave · 323-466-5125
- **Zumaya** · 5722 Melrose Ave · 323-464-0624

Shopping

- **Amoeba Music** · 6400 Sunset Blvd · 310-245-6400
- **Blest Boutique** · 1634 Cahuenga Blvd · 323-467-0180
- **Cahuenga World News** · 1652 N Cahuenga Blvd · 323-465-4357
- **Conservatory Florist** · 1900 N Highland Ave · 323-851-6290
- **Definitive Music** · 1628 N Cahuenga Blvd · 323-728-4345
- **Hollywood Hills Beauty Center and Spa** · 1915 N Highland Ave · 323-874-5159
- **Larry Edmunds Cinema and Theater Bookshop** · 6644 Hollywood Blvd · 323-463-3273
- **Ray the Retoucher** · 1330 N Highland Ave · 323-463-0555
- **Vine American Party Store** · 5969 Melrose Ave · 323-467-7124

Video Rental

- **Holly Hills Video** · 1931 N Bronson Ave · 323-463-1750
- **SKG Video Rental** · 1051 Vine St · 323-465-4005
- **Super Video** · 5810 Santa Monica Blvd · 323-465-0927
- **Yucca Video** · 1817 N Cahuenga Blvd · 323-465-2376

Map 4 • Los Feliz

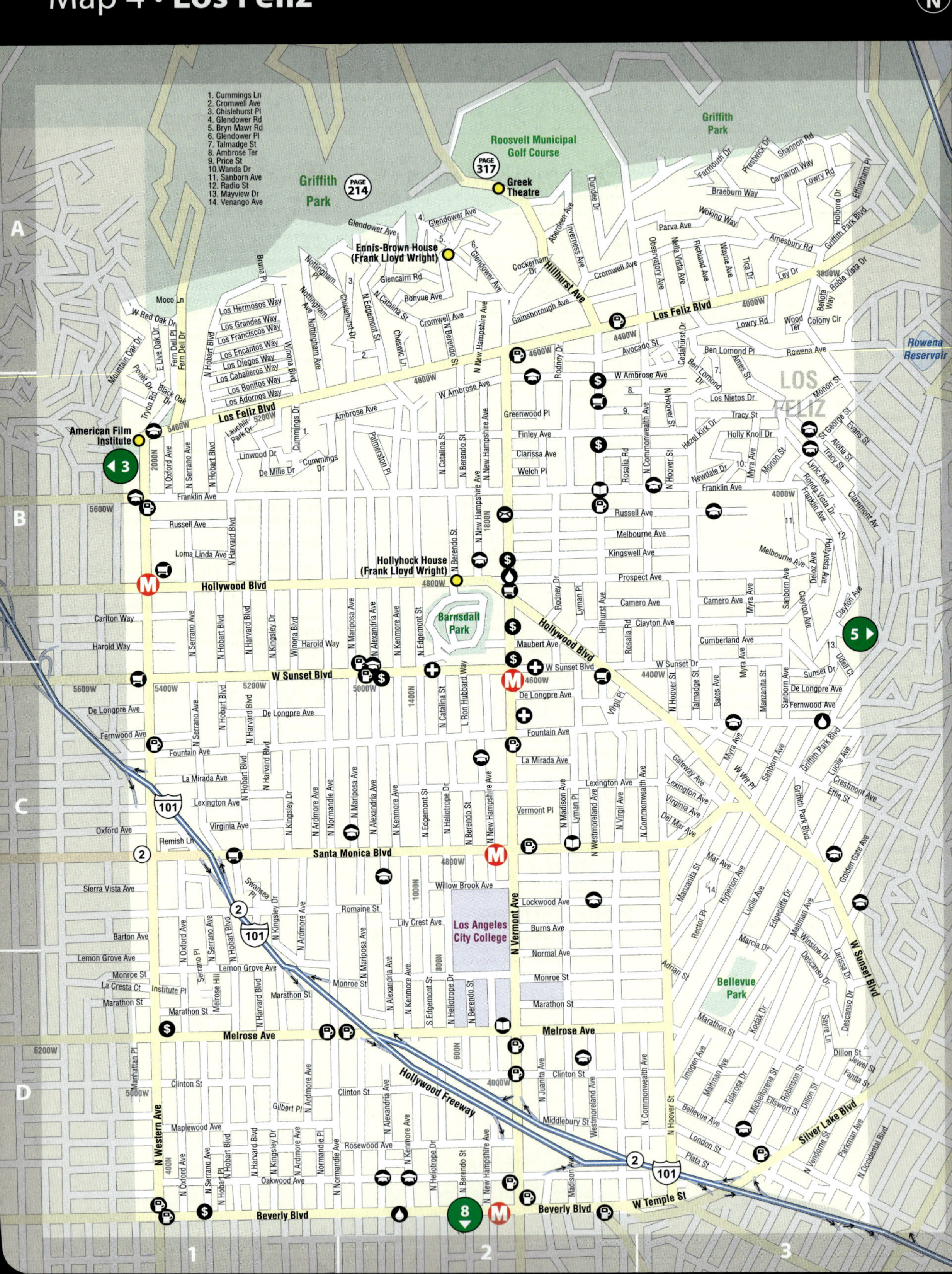

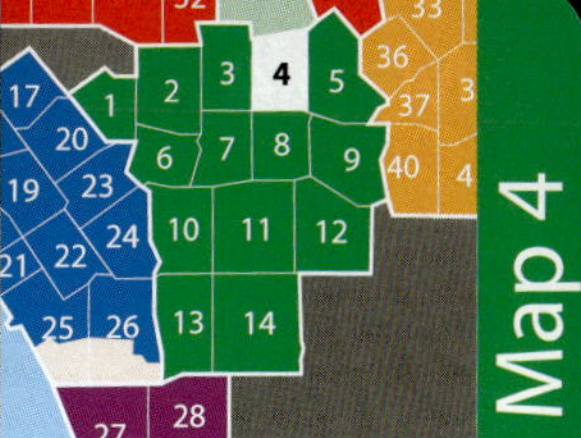

Not one but two houses designed by Frank Lloyd Wright can be found in Los Feliz. Tours are available and are an alternative to the Griffith Park Observatory, which has closed for three years of renovations. We hope they don't touch the James Dean statue, commemorating his role in "Rebel Without a Cause," which was partially shot at the Observatory.

$ Banks

- **Bank of America** • 1715 N Vermont Ave
- **Bank of America** • 2035 Hillhurst Ave
- **Bank of America** • 4975 Melrose Ave
- **California National Bank** • 4500 Beverly Blvd
- **Citibank** • 1965 Hillhurst Ave
- **Citibank** • 5000 Sunset Blvd
- **Washington Mutual** • 1600 N Vermont Ave
- **Wells Fargo Bank** • 1534 N Vermont Ave

Car Washes

- **American Elite Car Wash** • 1821 Hyperion Ave
- **Beverly Catalina Car Wash** • 4000 Beverly Blvd
- **Hollymont Car Wash & Detail** • 1666 N Vermont Ave

Gas Stations

- **76** • 1270 N Vermont Ave
- **76** • 1300 N Western Ave
- **76** • 304 N Vermont Ave
- **76** • 4600 Melrose Ave
- **76** • 591 N Vermont Ave
- **Arco** • 5025 W Sunset Blvd
- **Chevron** • 1276 N Western Ave
- **Chevron** • 1868 N Western Ave
- **Chevron** • 1869 Hillhurst Ave
- **Chevron** • 2134 N Vermont Ave
- **Chevron** • 4590 Melrose Ave
- **Chevron** • 4666 Santa Monica Blvd
- **Mobil** • 4605 Beverly Blvd
- **Mobil** • 515 Silver Lake Blvd
- **Mobil** • 655 N Western Ave
- **Mobil** • 657 N Vermont Ave
- **Shell** • 341 N Vermont Ave
- **Shell** • 5007 W Sunset Blvd
- **Texaco** • 4456 Los Feliz Blvd

Hospitals

- **Children's Hospital** • 4650 W Sunset Blvd • 323-660-2450
- **Kaiser Foundation Hospital** • 4867 W Sunset Blvd • 323-783-4011
- **Queen of Angels Hospital** • 1300 N Vermont Ave • 213-413-3000

Landmarks

- **American Film Institute** • 2021 N Western Ave
- **Ennis-Brown House (Frank Lloyd Wright)** • 2607 Glendower Ave
- **Greek Theatre** • 2700 N Vermont Ave
- **Hollyhock House (Frank Lloyd Wright)** • 4800 Hollywood Blvd

Libraries

- **Braille Institute Library** • 4205 Melrose Ave • 323-660-3880
- **Cahuenga Library** • 4591 Santa Monica Blvd • 323-664-6418
- **Los Feliz Branch Library** • 1874 Hillhurst Ave • 323-913-4710

Post Offices

- 1825 N Vermont Ave

Schools

- **Alexandria Avenue Elementary** • 4211 Oakwood Ave
- **American Film Institute** • 2021 N Western Ave
- **Bellevue Avenue Primary Center** • 610 N Micheltorena St
- **Crestmoore** • 1253 N New Hampshire Ave
- **Dayton Heights Elementary** • 607 N Westmoreland Ave
- **Franklin Ave Elementary** • 1910 N Commonwealth Ave
- **Funtime Nursery and Day Care** • 400 N Kenmore Ave
- **Immaculate Heart** • 5515 Franklin Ave
- **John Marshall High School** • 3939 Tracy St
- **King Junior High School** • 4201 Fountain Ave
- **Lockwood Ave Elementary** • 4345 Lockwood Ave
- **Los Angeles City College** • 855 N Vermont Ave
- **Los Feliz Elementary** • 1740 N New Hampshire Ave
- **Lycee International De Los Angeles** • 4155 Russell Ave
- **Marshall Senior High School** • 3939 Tracy St
- **Micheltorena Street Elementary** • 1511 Micheltorena St
- **Our Mother of Good Counsel** • 4622 Ambrose Ave
- **Ramona Elementary** • 1133 N Mariposa Ave
- **Rose Alex Pilibos Arm** • 1615 N Alexandria Ave
- **St Casimir** • 2714 St George St
- **St Francis of Assisi Parish** • 1550 Maltman Ave
- **Thomas S King Junior High School** • 4201 Fountain Ave

Supermarkets

- **Albertson's** • 2035 Hillhurst Ave
- **Food 4 Less** • 5420 W Sunset Blvd
- **Jon's Marketplace** • 1601 N Vermont Ave
- **Jon's Marketplace** • 5315 Santa Monica Blvd
- **Ralph's** • 5429 Hollywood Blvd
- **Von's** • 4520 W Sunset Blvd

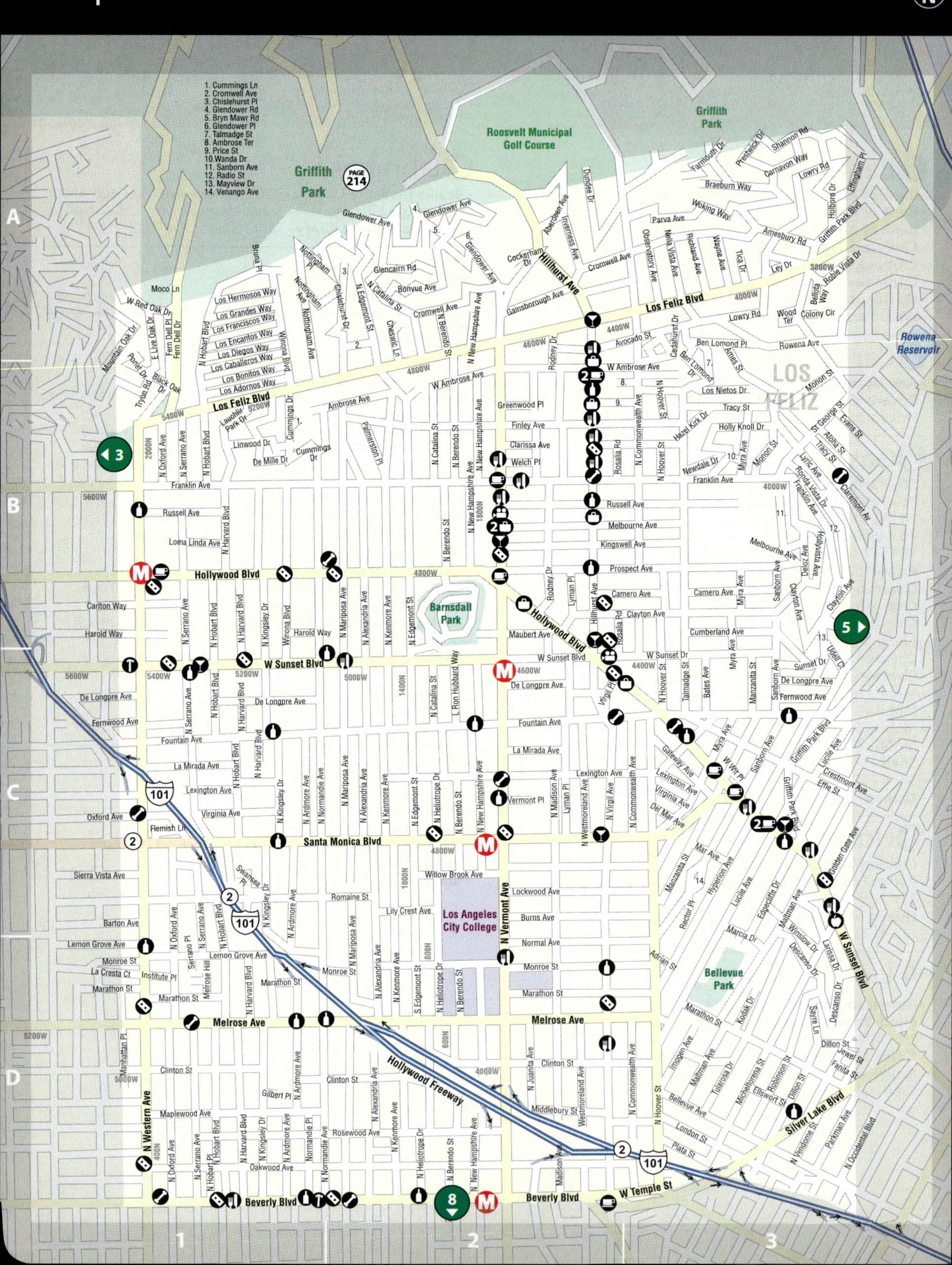
Map 4 · Los Feliz
N
1. Cummings Ln
2. Cromwell Ave
3. Chislehurst Pl
4. Glendower Rd
5. Bryn Mawr Rd
6. Glendower Pl
7. Talmadge St
8. Ambrose Ter
9. Price St
10. Wanda Dr
11. Sanborn Ave
12. Radio St
13. Mayview Dr
14. Venango Ave
PAGE 214
Griffith Park
Roosevelt Municipal Golf Course
Griffith Park
LOS FELIZ
Rowena Reservoir
Barnsdall Park
Los Angeles City College
Bellevue Park
Los Feliz Blvd
Hollywood Blvd
W Sunset Blvd
Santa Monica Blvd
Melrose Ave
Beverly Blvd
Hollywood Freeway
Silver Lake Blvd
W Sunset Blvd
W Temple St
101
2
A
B
C
D
1
2
3
3
5
8

Los Feliz is off the beaten path and there's no quick way to reach it, but once you do, you'll find a funky, artsy neighborhood with few chains. Instead, the neighborhood's establishments reflect the eclectic nature of its residents. Marty and Elayne, lounge singers at the Dresden Room, are an L.A. institution.

Clubs

- **Akbar** • 4356 W Sunset Blvd • 323-665-6810
- **Bar Vermont** • 1712 N Vermont ave • 323-661-6163
- **Tantra Bar** • 3705 W Sunset Blvd • 323-663-9090
- **The Derby** • 4500 Los Feliz Blvd • 323-663-8979
- **The Dresden Room** • 1760 N Vermont Ave • 323-665-4294
- **The Garage** • 4519 Santa Monica Blvd • 323-662-6166
- **The Good Luck Bar** • 1514 Hillhurst Ave • 323-666-3524
- **Tiki Ti** • 4427 W Sunset Blvd • 323-669-9381
- **Ye Rustic Inn** • 1831 Hillhurst Ave • 323-662-5757

Coffee

- **Café Los Feliz** • 2118 Hillhurst Ave
- **Cafe Stella** • 3932 W Sunset Blvd
- **Casbah Cafe** • 3900 W Sunset Blvd
- **Coffee Bean & Tea Leaf** • 2081 Hillhurst Ave
- **i2i-World Cafe** • 3823 W Sunset Blvd
- **Psychobabble** • 1866 N Vermont Ave
- **Starbucks** • 1700 N Vermont Ave
- **Starbucks** • 5453 Hollywood Blvd
- **Tsunami Coffee House** • 4019 W Sunset Blvd

Farmer's Markets

- **Sunset Junction** • 3700 W Sunset Blvd • Sat 8-1

Hardware Stores

- **B & M Hardware** • 4226 Beverly Blvd • 213-388-7655
- **Orchard Supply Hardware** • 5525 W Sunset Blvd • 323-871-1707

Liquor Stores

- **Beverly Mart Liquors** • 4003 Beverly Blvd
- **Big Mac's Liquor** • 3735 W Sunset Blvd
- **Bill's Liquor** • 5334 W Sunset Blvd
- **Cap N' Cork Junior Market** • 1700 Hillhurst Ave
- **Esquire Liquor Shop** • 5201 Santa Monica Blvd
- **Fountain Liquor** • 4711 Fountain Ave
- **Golden Fountain Liquor & Mkt** • 5203 Fountain Ave
- **Grand Liquor & Junior Market** • 4669 Melrose Ave
- **Hillhurst Liquor** • 2060 Hillhurst Ave
- **I & A Liquor Store** • 701 N Normandie Ave
- **Ink Cigarettes & Liquor** • 5063 W Sunset Blvd
- **J B Liquor** • 1185 N Vermont Ave
- **Lee's Liquor Mart** • 3907 Fountain Ave
- **Liquor Center** • 861 1/2 N Western Ave
- **Michael's Liquor** • 4323 W Sunset Blvd
- **Mikron Liquor** • 631 Silver Lake Blvd
- **Pacific Liquors** • 4228 Beverly Blvd
- **Pink Elephant Liquors** • 1836 N Western Ave
- **Robin's Liquor** • 5102 Hollywood Blvd
- **Village Liquor Mart** • 1859 Hillhurst Ave
- **Virgil Liquors** • 780 N Virgil Ave

Movie Theaters

- **Los Feliz 3 Theater** • 1822 N Vermont Ave
- **Vista Theatre** • 4473 Sunset Blvd

Pet Stores

- **Beverly & Normandie Pets** • 4152 Beverly Blvd • 213-382-9314
- **Bird Kingdom & Pet Shop** • 4562 Beverly Blvd • 323-461-5538
- **California Solutions** • 2332 Claremont Ave • 323-667-0693
- **Collar & Leash** • 4327 W Sunset Blvd • 323-665-2215
- **Damian's Tropical Fish** • 1144 N Western Ave • 323-466-7140
- **Fish on the Wall** • 4901 Melrose Ave • 323-468-0103
- **Fish Tale** • 4364 Fountain Ave • 323-665-0350
- **For Pets Only** • 1903 Hillhurst Ave • 323-664-4211
- **J's Dog & Cat Grooming** • 5065 Hollywood Blvd • 323-667-1255
- **Kim's Pets & Fish** • 1187 N Vermont Ave • 323-664-3338
- **Young's Tropical Fish** • 1953 Hillhurst Ave • 323-663-5665

Restaurants

- **Café Stella** • 3932 Sunset Blvd • 323-666-0265
- **Cha Cha Cha** • 656 N Virgil Ave • 323-664-7723
- **El Conquistador** • 3701 Sunset Blvd • 323-666-5136
- **Electric Lotus** • 4656 Franklin Ave • 323-953-0040
- **Fred 62** • 1850 N Vermont Ave • 323-667-0062
- **Mexico City** • 2121 Hillhurst Ave • 323-661-7227
- **Millie's** • 3524 Sunset Blvd • 323-664-0404
- **Palermo** • 1858 N Vermont Ave • 323-663-1178
- **Shin** • 1972 Hillhurst Ave • 323-664-1891
- **Trattoria Farfalla** • 1978 Hillhurst Ave • 323-661-7365
- **Vida** • 1930 Hillhurst Ave • 323-660-4446
- **Vito's Pizza** • 814 N Vermont Ave • 323-667-2723
- **Zankou Chicken** • 5065 W Sunset Blvd • 323-665-7845

Shopping

- **Eastside Records** • 1813 Hillhurst Ave • 323-913-7461
- **LS** • 2120 Hillhurst Ave •
- **Naturemart & Bulk Bin** • 2080 Hillhurst Ave • 323-667-1677
- **Squaresville** • 1800 N Vermont Ave • 323-669-8464
- **Uncle Jer's** • 4459 W Sunset Blvd • 323-662-6710
- **Wacko** • 4633 Hollywood Blvd • 323-663-0122

Video Rental

- **20-20 Video** • 5420 W Sunset Blvd • 323-467-2020
- **4 Star Video Group** • 5211 W Sunset Blvd • 323-663-6991
- **A-1 Video** • 1100 N Vermont Ave • 323-669-1230
- **Blockbuster** • 4470 Sunset Blvd • 323-661-0791
- **Blockbuster** • 5445 Hollywood Blvd • 323-467-0481
- **Express Video** • 365 S Western Ave • 213-381-2647
- **Five Stars Video (Thai)** • 5155 Hollywood Blvd • 323-665-9547
- **Hollynorm Video** • 5068 Hollywood Blvd • 323-662-5003
- **Hollywood Video** • 1075 N Western Ave • 323-464-0294
- **Jerry's Video Room** • 1904 Hillhurst Ave • 323-666-7471
- **LA Video** • 720 N Western Ave • 323-465-0705
- **LA Video & Music** • 711 N Virgil Ave • 323-663-0116
- **MJB Video** • 4459 Beverly Blvd • 323-666-5099
- **Mondo Video A-Go-Go** • 1718 N Vermont Ave • 323-953-8896
- **Video Hot** • 4207 Beverly Blvd • 323-668-1616
- **Video Market** • 3607 W Sunset Blvd • 323-663-6000
- **Winn Video** • 4855 Santa Monica Blvd • 323-953-9732

Map 5 • Silver Lake / Echo Park / Atwater

If you only know Silverlake and Echo Park from driving along Sunset Blvd. on your way to Dodger Stadium, you are only getting a fraction of the story. The heart of these neighborhoods is to be found north of Sunset on winding and steep streets that offer sweeping views of downtown. Atwater Village is one of the best-kept residential secrets in town, perfect for dog-walking, bike riding, and hedge-clipping.

$ Banks

- **Bank of America** · 1572 W Sunset Blvd
- **Bank of America** · 2420 Glendale Blvd
- **Citibank** · 1900 Sunset Blvd
- **Citibank** · 2450 Glendale Blvd
- **East West Bank** · 2496 Glendale Blvd
- **Jackson Federal Bank** · 3355 Glendale Blvd
- **Wells Fargo Bank** · 1342 N Alvarado St
- **Wells Fargo Bank** · 3250 Glendale Blvd

Car Washes

- **Best Way Hand Car Wash** · 1185 W Sunset Blvd
- **Coin-Op Car Wash** · 3128 W Sunset Blvd
- **Los Feliz Car Wash** · 3013 Los Feliz Blvd
- **R & S Car Wash** · 2473 Glendale Blvd
- **Sunset-East Car Wash** · 2040 W Sunset Blvd

Gas Stations

- **76** · 1000 Elysian Park Ave
- **76** · 1340 Glendale Blvd
- **76** · 2580 Glendale Blvd
- **76** · 3070 Glendale Blvd
- **Arco** · 1605 Glendale Blvd
- **Arco** · 2466 Riverside Dr
- **Arco** · 3073 Los Feliz Blvd
- **Chevron** · 2427 Fletcher Dr
- **Chevron** · 3050 Los Feliz Blvd
- **Diamond Shamrock** · 2918 Riverside Dr
- **Shell** · 3047 Glendale Blvd
- **Shell** · 3053 Los Feliz Blvd

○ Landmarks

- **Dodger Stadium** · 1000 Elysian Park Ave
- **Echo Park** · Glendale Blvd & Park Ave
- **Jengen's Recreation Center Building** · 1700 W Sunset Blvd
- **Police Academy** · 1880 Academy Dr
- **Richard Neutra houses** · 2200 Silver Lake Blvd
- **Rowena Reservoir** · Hyperion Ave & Rowena Ave
- **Silver Lake Reservoir** · Silverlake Blvd & Duane St

Libraries

- **Atwater Library** · 3379 Glendale Blvd · 323-664-1353

24-Hour Pharmacies

- **Sav-On** · 2530 Glendale Blvd · 323-666-6555

Post Offices

- 1525 N Alvarado St
- 3370 Glendale Blvd

Schools

- **Allesandro Elementary** · 2210 Riverside Dr
- **Atwater Avenue Elementary** · 3271 Silver Lake Blvd
- **Baxter Montessori** · 2101 Echo Park Ave
- **Carroll Rees Academy** · 3031 Angus St
- **Clifford Street Elementary** · 2150 Duane St
- **Elysian Heights Elementary** · 1562 Baxter St
- **Glenfeliz Blvd Elementary** · 3955 Glenfeliz Blvd
- **Golden West Christian School** · 1310 Liberty St
- **Holy Trinity** · 3716 Boyce Ave
- **Ivanhoe Elementary** · 2828 W Herkimer St
- **Kids' World** · 2442 Hyperion Ave
- **LA International Christian School** · 2301 Bellevue Ave
- **La Senda Antigua Charter School** · 2240 Clifford St
- **Learning Kingdom** · 2772 Rowena Ave
- **Logan Street Elementary** · 1711 Montana St
- **Mayberry Street Elementary** · 2414 Mayberry St
- **Solano Ave Elementary** · 615 Solano Ave
- **St Teresa of Avila** · 2223 Fargo St

Supermarkets

- **Gelson's Markets** · 2725 Hyperion Ave
- **Ralph's** · 2520 Glendale Blvd
- **Trader Joe's** · 2738 Hyperion Ave
- **Von's** · 1342 N Alvarado St

N

Griffith Park
Forest Lawn Memorial Park (Glendale)
Elysian Park
Echo Park
Echo Lake
Silver Lake Reservoir
Rowena Reservoir
Dodger Stadium
PAGE 256

Los Angeles River
Los Feliz Blvd
Glendale Blvd
San Fernando Rd
Glendale Freeway
Golden State Freeway
Riverside Dr
Fletcher Dr
Hyperion Ave
Silver Lake Blvd
W Silver Lake Dr
N Silver Lake Dr
Stadium Way
Academy Rd
Silver Lake Blvd
W Sunset Blvd
Sunset Blvd
N Alvarado St
N Rampart Blvd
Echo Park Ave
Hollywood Freeway
Pasadena Freeway
N San Fernando Rd

1. Los Feliz Pl
2. Princeton St
3. Hyperion Ave
4. Avenel Ter
5. Claremont Ave
6. Entrance Dr
7. Rokeby St
8. Hawick St
9. Redrock Ct
10. Silver Lea Ter
11. Childs Ct
12. Drury Ln
13. Meadow Valley Ter
14. Silverado Ter
15. Panorama Ter
16. Ivan Ct
17. Lakeview Ter W
18. Lakeview Ter E
19. Deane St
20. Ripple St
21. Roselin Pl
22. Audre Pl
23. Gleneden St
24. Crystal St
25. Peru St
26. Landa St
27. McCready Ave
28. Silver Ridge Wy
29. Earl Ct
30. Fair Oak View Ter
31. Oak Glen Pl
32. Moore St
33. Cove Wy
34. Allesandro Wy
35. Rockford Rd
36. Waterloo St
37. Cedar Lodge Ter
38. Edgecliff Dr
39. Maltman Ave
40. Fall Ave
41. San Jacinto St
42. Swan Pl
43. Webster Ave
44. Cicero Dr
45. Murray Cir
46. Fargo St
47. Champlain Ter
48. Loma Vista Pl
49. Lake Shore Ave
50. Niles Pl
51. Twin Oak St
52. Baxter Pl
53. Murray Cir
54. Berkeley Cir
55. Branden St
56. Duane St
57. Armitage St
58. Marsden St
59. Paul Ter
60. Galveston St
61. Macbeth St
62. Morton Wk
63. Aqua Pura Dr
64. Eilet Pl
65. N Bonnie Brae St
66. Everett Pl
67. Boylston St
68. Alpine St

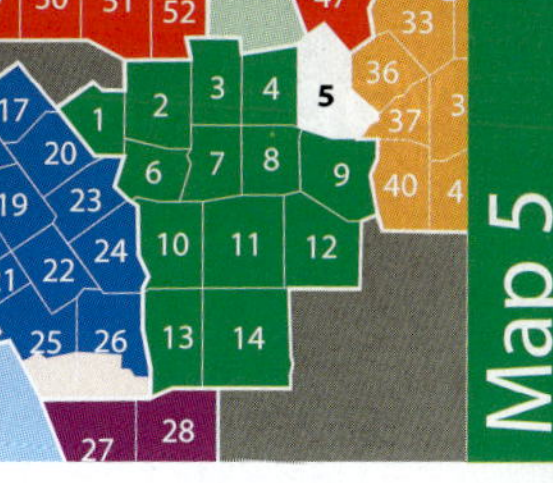

By day, the real entertainment is people-watching in the cafes and shops along Hyperion, Sunset, Rowena, Silverlake, and Glendale Blvd. By night, the action moves indoors to hotspots like Spaceland, the Silverlake Lounge, and the Short Stop (which, according to Rolling Stone, is the "Coolest Bar in America"). For late, late entertainment, we recommend the gender-bending after-hours parade in and around the Astro Family Restaurant.

 Clubs

- **Bigfoot Lounge** · 3172 Los Feliz Blvd · 323-662-9227
- **Silverlake Lounge** · 2906 Sunset Blvd · 323-663-9636
- **Spaceland** · 1717 Silver Lake Blvd · 323-661-4380
- **The Red Lion Tavern** · 2366 Glendale Blvd · 323-662-5337
- **The Roost** · 3100 Los Feliz Blvd · 323-664-7272
- **The Short Stop** · 1455 W Sunset Blvd · 213-250-5902
- **The Tam O'Shanter** · 2980 Los Feliz Blvd · 323-664-0228

 Coffee

- **Coffee Table** · 2930 Rowena Ave
- **Moca Max** · 1616 S Central Ave
- **Myrna's Espresso & Yogurt** · 2660 Griffith Park Blvd
- **Silverlake Coffee** · 2388 Glendale Blvd
- **Starbucks** · 2134 W Sunset Blvd
- **Starbucks** · 2560 Glendale Blvd
- **The Downbeat Cafe** · 1202 N Alvarado St

 Gyms

- **Body Builders Gym** · 2516 Hyperion Ave · 323-668-0802
- **MJ Fitness Club** · 1816 W Sunset Blvd · 213-484-9870

 Hardware Stores

- **Baller Hardware & Building** · 2505 Hyperion Ave · 323-665-4149

 Liquor Stores

- **Bill's Liquor Store** · 3150 Glendale Blvd
- **Bogie's Liquor** · 2560 Hyperion Ave
- **House of Spirits** · 1314 Echo Park Ave
- **King Liquors** · 2105 W Sunset Blvd
- **Kopper Keg Liquors** · 3237 Glendale Blvd
- **Liquor Royale** · 1508 W Sunset Blvd
- **Los Feliz Liquor** · 3006 Los Feliz Blvd
- **M & W Liquors** · 2801 Fletcher Dr
- **Plaza Liquors** · 2829 W Sunset Blvd
- **Ray's Liquor** · 2730 Fletcher Dr
- **Silver Glen Liquor** · 2474 Glendale Blvd
- **Silver Lake Liquor** · 1620 Silver Lake Blvd
- **Silversun Liquor** · 2901 W Sunset Blvd

Pet Stores

- **Catts & Dogs Pet Boutique** · 2833 Hyperion Ave · 323-953-8383
- **Jimmy's Pet Store** · 1540 Glendale Blvd · 213-413-8013
- **LA Tropical Fish Pet & Supplies** · 1373 W Sunset Blvd · 213-482-9131
- **Pampered Birds** · 3183 Glendale Blvd · 323-662-7807
- **Tiffany's Pet Food** · 2854 W Sunset Blvd · 323-662-7173

Restaurants

- **Astro Family Restaurant** · 2300 Fletcher Dr · 323-663-9241
- **Chameau** · 2520 Hyperion Ave · 323-953-1973
- **Les Freres Taix** · 1911 W Sunset Blvd · 213-484-1265
- **Osteria Nonni** · 3219 Glendale Blvd · 323-666-7133
- **Police Academy Café** · 1880 Academy Dr · 323-221-5222
- **Tam O'Shanter** · 2980 Los Feliz Blvd · 323-664-0228

Shopping

- **Rockaway Records** · 2395 Glendale Blvd · 323-664-3232

Video Rental

- **20-20 Video** · 2522 Glendale Blvd · 323-665-2020
- **50 50 Video** · 1717 W Sunset Blvd · 213-353-0406
- **Asian Star Video (Chinese & Thai)** · 1498 W Sunset Blvd · 213-481-2896
- **Blockbuster** · 2656 Griffith Park Blvd · 323-665-6764
- **Cookie Video Rental** · 2501 W Sunset Blvd · 213-484-2317
- **Go Video** · 2147 W Sunset Blvd · 213-413-0860
- **Silverlake Video** · 3206 Glendale Blvd · 323-666-5570
- **Video Channel** · 1501 W Sunset Blvd · 213-481-8218
- **Video Czar** · 3332 Glendale Blvd · 323-661-2978
- **Video House** · 1864 Glendale Blvd · 323-663-9175
- **Video Hut** · 2732 Hyperion Ave · 323-660-1166
- **Video Journeys** · 2730 Griffith Park Blvd · 323-663-5857
- **Videoactive** · 2522 Hyperion Ave · 323-669-8544

Map 6 · Miracle Mile / Mid-City
N
Wilshire Blvd
1
2
7
23
10
BEVERLY HILLS
La Cienega Park
LACMA West
LA County Museum of Art
La Brea Tar Pits
George C. Page Museum of La Brea Discoveries
Hancock Park
Peterson Auto Museum
Craft & Folk Art Museum
Lula Washington Dance Theatre
Ballona Creek
Santa Monica Freeway
N Robertson Blvd
S Clark Dr
S Arnaz Dr
S Hamel Dr
S Willaman Dr
S Carson Rd
S Stanley Dr
S Le Doux Rd
Charleville Blvd
Gregory Way
Chalmers Dr
N La Cienega Blvd
N Gale Dr
S La Cienega Blvd
S Gale Dr
Tower Dr
Gregory Way
S Hamilto Dr
Orange St
Capistrano Way
Commodore Sloat Dr
San Ysidro Way
Santa Ynez Way
Hayes Dr
Moore Dr
Sweetzer Dr
Foster Dr
Carrillo Dr
Carmel Way
San Diego Way
San Gabriel
Warner Dr
Del Valle Dr
Barrows Dr
Mc Carthy Vista
San Vicente Blvd
W Olympic Blvd
W Olympic Pl
W Olympic Pl
S Robertson Blvd
S Woodster St
S Shenandoah St
S Bedford St
S Sherbourne Dr
S Holt Ave
S Alfred St
S Orlando Ave
Alvira St
S La Jolla Ave
Crescent Heights Blvd
Stearns Dr
S Point View St
S Hayworth Ave
Edgewood Pl
Whitworth Dr
Whitworth Dr
Packard St
S Fairfax Ave
Roland Walk
S Genesee Ave
S Spaulding Ave
S Alandale Ave
S Stanley Ave
S Curson Ave
S Sierra Bonita Ave
S Masselin Ave
Hauser Blvd
S Ridgeley Ave
S Burnside Ave
S Dunsmuir Ave
S Cochran Ave
S Cloverdale Ave
S Detroit St
S Sycamore Ave
S La Brea Ave
Wilshire Blvd
W 8th St
W 9th St
W Olympic Blvd
Edgewood Pl
W 12th St
Edgewood Ave
Meadowbrook Ave
San Vicente Blvd
Packard St
S Redondo Blvd
S Sycamore Dr
S Orange Dr
Alcott St
Saturn St
Whitworth Dr
Alcott St
Saturn St
Homer St
Cashio St
Pickford St
Homer St
Key St
Preuss Rd
Livonia Ave
Guthrie Ave
David Ave
S Robertson Blvd
S Corning St
S Garth Ave
Charlton St
S Stanley Ave
S Curson Ave
Carmona Ave
Hauser Blvd
Dockweiler Pl
W Pico Blvd
W Pico Blvd
Saturn St
Pickford Pl
Airdrome St
Airdrome St
S Corning St
S Garth Ave
W 18th St
S La Cienega Blvd
S Fairfax Ave
Crescent Heights Blvd
Stearns Dr
S Point View St
Hi Point St
S Hayworth Ave
Sawyer St
W 18th St
Sawyer St
Venice Blvd
Venice Blvd
Guthrie Ave
Charlton St
Buchard Ave
David Ave
Glennie Ln
W Washington Blvd
S Orange Grove Ave
S Genesee Ave
S Spaulding Ave
S Stanley Ave
Thurman Ave
Clyde Ave
Cologne St
Bangor St
Clyde Ave
Carmona Ave
Hauser Blvd
S Ridgeley Dr
S Burnside Ave
S Dunsmuir Ave
S Cochran Ave
Cochran Pl
S Cloverdale Ave
S Redondo Blvd
S Sycamore Ave
S Orange Dr
S Mansfield Ave
W 20th St
W 21st St
W 23rd St
Bangor St
Alsace Ave
Pickford St
S La Brea Ave
Glennie Ln
Apple St
Venice Blvd
S Marvin Ave
S Curson Ave
S Marvin Ave
Elsmere Ave
S Sierra Bonita Ave
10
187
10
10
1
2
3
A
B
C
D

"Miracle Mile" refers to the stretch of Wilshire Blvd. that used to be home to glamorous shopping destinations like Bullocks, a now-defunct department store that currently serves as part of Southwestern Law School. But the Miracle Mile is still home to many of the city's major museums, including the somewhat underrated L.A. County Museum of Art and the equally overrated La Brea Tar Pits.

$ Banks

- **Bank Leumi USA** · 8383 Wilshire Blvd
- **Bank of America** · 5304 Wilshire Blvd
- **Bank of America** · 8381 Wilshire Blvd
- **Bank of America** · 8501 W Pico Blvd
- **Bank of America** · 8760 Wilshire Blvd
- **California Bank & Trust** · 6500 Wilshire Blvd
- **California National Bank** · 5900 Wilshire Blvd
- **Citibank** · 5660 Wilshire Blvd
- **Citibank** · 8485 Wilshire Blvd
- **City National Bank** · 6100 Wilshire Blvd
- **Washington Mutual** · 8484 Wilshire Blvd
- **Wells Fargo Bank** · 5601 Wilshire Blvd
- **Wells Fargo Bank** · 6245 Wilshire Blvd

Car Washes

- **Expert Car Wash** · 900 S La Brea Ave
- **La Cienega Car Wash** · 1907 S La Cienega Blvd

Gas Stations

- **76** · 1004 S La Cienega Blvd
- **76** · 1515 S La Brea Ave
- **Arco** · 5301 W Olympic Blvd
- **Arco** · 5420 Venice Blvd
- **Arco** · 8770 W Olympic Blvd
- **Chevron** · 1865 S La Brea Ave
- **Chevron** · 2065 S La Cienega Blvd
- **Chevron** · 391 S Robertson Blvd
- **Exxon** · 1460 S La Cienega Blvd
- **Mobil** · 2305 S La Cienega Blvd
- **Mobil** · 8567 Wilshire Blvd
- **Shell** · 1502 S Robertson Blvd
- **Shell** · 1606 S La Brea Ave
- **Shell** · 2339 S La Brea Ave
- **Shell** · 5164 W Washington Blvd
- **Shell** · 6107 W Olympic Blvd
- **Shell** · 8500 W Pico Blvd

Hospitals

- **Kaiser Foundation Hospital** · 6041 Cadillac Ave · 323-857-2201
- **Midway Hospital** · 5925 San Vicente Blvd · 323-938-3161

Landmarks

- **Craft & Folk Art Museum** · 5800 Wilshire Blvd
- **George C Page Museum of La Brea Discoveries** · 5801 Wilshire Blvd
- **LA Country Museum of Art** · 5905 Wilshire Blvd
- **La Brea Tar Pits** · Wilshire Blvd & S Curson Ave
- **LACMA West (former May Co Building)** · 6067 Wilshire Blvd
- **Lula Washington Dance Theatre** · 5041 W Pico Blvd
- **Petersen Automotive Museum** · 6060 Wilshire Blvd

Libraries

- **Art Research Library** · 5905 Wilshire Blvd · 323-857-6118
- **Goethe Institute-Los Angeles** · 5750 Wilshire Blvd · 323-525-3388
- **LACMA Visual Resource Center** · 5905 Wilshire Blvd · 323-857-6116
- **Robertson Library** · 1719 S Robertson Blvd · 310-840-2147

24-Hour Pharmacies

- **Walgreens** · 8770 W Pico Blvd · 310-275-1344

Police

- **Los Angeles Police Dept** · 4861 Venice Blvd · 213-485-4022

Post Offices

- 1270 S Alfred St
- 4960 W Washington Blvd
- 5350 Wilshire Blvd

Schools

- **Bais Chana** · 9041 W Pico Blvd
- **Bais Chaya Mushka** · 9017 W Pico Blvd
- **Carthay Center Elementary** · 6351 W Olympic Blvd
- **Cathedral Chapel** · 755 S Cochran Ave
- **Crescent Heights Boulevard Elementary** · 1661 S Crescent Heights Blvd
- **Donna Ro** · 4946 W 20th St
- **Frances Hatch** · 4930 Venice Blvd
- **Hillel Hebrew Academy** · 9120 W Olympic Blvd
- **Holy Spirit Elementary** · 1418 S Burnside Ave
- **Horace Mann Elementary** · 8701 Charleville Blvd
- **Joannes Taylor** · 1372 S Cochran Ave
- **Kabbalah Center** · 1062 S Robertson Blvd
- **Los Angeles Center for Enriched Studies** · 5931 W 18th St
- **Marvin Ave Children's Center** · 2341 S Curson Ave
- **Marvin Elementary** · 2341 S Curson Ave
- **Ohr Haemet Institute for Girls** · 1030 S Robertson Blvd
- **Page Private School** · 419 S Robertson Blvd
- **Rabbi Jacob Pressman Academy** · 1055 S La Cienega Blvd
- **Rejoice in Jesus Christian School** · 1304 S Cochran Ave
- **Saturn Street Elementary** · 5360 Saturn St
- **Savoy Junior Academy** · 5211 Venice Blvd
- **Shalhevet High School** · 910 S Fairfax Ave
- **Shenandoah Street Elementary** · 2450 S Shenandoah St
- **St Mary Magdalen Catholic** · 1223 S Corning St
- **Torat Hayim Hebrew Academy** · 1210 S La Cienega Blvd
- **Yeshiva University High of Los Angeles** · 1619 S Robertson Blvd

Supermarkets

- **Ralph's** · 5601 Wilshire Blvd
- **Von's** · 1430 S Fairfax Ave

Map 6 · Miracle Mile / Mid-City
N
A
B
C
D
1
2
3
Wilshire Blvd
N Robertson Blvd
S Clark Dr
S Arnaz Dr
S Hamel Dr
S Willaman Dr
S Carson Rd
S Stanley Dr
S Le Doux Rd
Charleville Blvd
Gregory Way
S La Cienega Blvd
N La Cienega Blvd
S Hamilto Dr
N Gale Dr
S Gale Dr
S Tower Dr
Gregory Way
La Cienega Park
Chalmers Dr
BEVERLY HILLS
Sweetzer Dr
Santa Ynez Way
6600W
Moore Dr
Hayes Dr
Foster Dr
Commodore Sloat Dr
San Gabriel Way
Capistrano Way
Orange St
Mc Carthy
Warner Dr
Costa
San Diego Way
Del Valle Dr
Barrows Dr
Carmel Way
Cazilio Dr
San Vicente Blvd
S Fairfax
Roland Walk
S Genesee Ave
S Spaulding Ave
Alandele Ave
S Stanley Ave
S Curson Ave
S Sierra Bonita Ave
S Masselin Ave
Hauser Blvd
S Ridgeley Dr
S Burnside Ave
S Dunsmuir Ave
S Cochran Ave
S Cloverdale Ave
S Detroit St
S Sycamore Ave
S La Brea Ave
Wilshire B
W 8th St
W 9th St
W Olympic Blvd
W Olympic Blvd
5600W
5400W
W Olympic Pl
S Alfred St
S Orlando Ave
S La Jolla Ave
Alvira St
Crescent Heights Blvd
Stearns Dr
S Point View St
HI Point St
S Hayworth Ave
Edgwood Pl
Whitworth Dr
Packard St
Edgewood Pl
Edgewood Pl
Meadowbrook Blvd
S Redondo Blvd
S Sycamore Ave
S Orange Dr
W 12th St
San Vicente Blvd
Packard St
S Robertson Blvd
S Woodstar St
S Shenandoah St
S Bedford St
S Sherbourne Dr
S Holt Ave
S Corning St
Whitworth Dr
8600W
Alcott St
Saturn St
8600W
Alcott St
Saturn St
Homer St
Pickford St
6000W
W Pico Blvd
S Stanley Ave
S Curson Ave
S Sierra Bonita Ave
Masselin Ave
Carmona Ave
Hauser Blvd
S Ridgeley Dr
Dockweiler Pl
S Burnside Ave
S Dunsmuir Ave
S Cochran Ave
Packard St
5400W
W Pico Blvd
Homer St
Key St
Alvira St
Stearns Dr
S Point View St
HI Point St
Saturn St
Pickford St
Preuss Rd
Airdrome St
S Corning St
S Garth Ave
6000W
Airdrome St
Pickford Pl
Pickford St
S Orange Grove Ave
S Ogden Dr
S Genesee Ave
S Spaulding Ave
S Stanley Ave
Elsmere Ave
S Curson Ave
S Sierra Bonita Ave
Carmona Ave
Venice Blvd
S Dunsmuir Ave
5200W
S Cochran Ave
S Orange Dr
S Mansfield Ave
S La Brea Ave
1600S
23
Livonia Ave
S Robertson Blvd
Guthrie Ave
David Ave
W 18th St
S La Cienega Blvd
Sawyer St
Chariton St
Crescent Heights Blvd
Stearns Dr
S Point View St
S Hayworth Ave
W 18th St
1800S
5800W
Sawyer St
Guthrie Ave
S Genesee Ave
S Spaulding Ave
Thurman Ave
Clyde Ave
S Curson Ave
S Marvin Ave
Carmona Ave
S Ridgeley Dr
S Burnside Ave
Cochran Pl
S Cochran Ave
S Cloverdale Ave
S Redondo Blvd
Alsace Ave
S Sycamore Ave
Pickford St
S Mansfield Ave
S La Brea Ave
W 20th St
W 21st St
7
2000S
S Shenandoah St
S Hahn Ave
S Holt Ave
Cadillac Ave
S Corning St
S Garth Ave
Chariton St
David Ave
Burchard Ave
Venice Blvd
Ballona Creek
2200S
Cologne St
Bangor St
Clyde Ave
W Washington Blvd
S Marvin Ave
Carmona Ave
Hauser Blvd
S Ridgeley Dr
S Burnside Ave
S Dunsmuir Ave
S Cochran Ave
S Cloverdale Ave
S Redondo Blvd
Alsace Ave
S Sycamore Ave
S Orange Dr
S Mansfield Ave
2000S
W 23rd St
Glennie Ln
Glennie Ln
Apple St
Bangor St
10
187
10
10
Santa Monica Freeway
Hancock Park

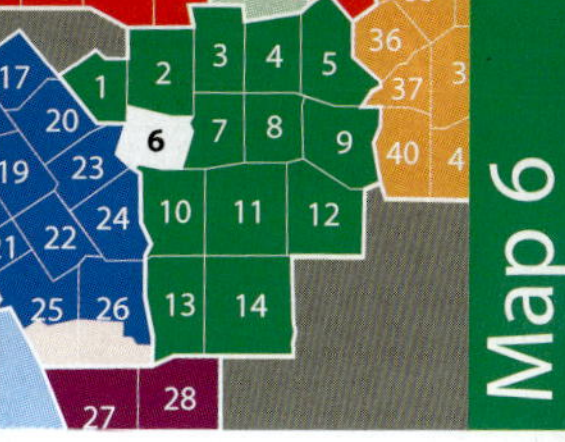

After a long economic slump, Mid-City and Miracle Mile are back with renovated museums, hot nightspots, and a booming Ethiopian community. Activities range from high-end art galleries to $1.00 burritos for a midnight snack.

24-Hour Copy Centers
- **Kinko's** • 5500 Wilshire Blvd • 323-937-0126
- **Kinko's** • 6157 W Pico Blvd • 323-653-4947

Clubs
- **Conga Room** • 5364 Wilshire Blvd • 323-938-1696
- **El Rey** • 5515 Wilshire Blvd • 323-936-4790
- **The Joint** • 8771 W Pico Blvd • 310-275-2619
- **The Mint** • 6010 Pico Blvd • 323-954-9630
- **Tom Bergin's Tavern** • 840 S Fairfax Ave • 323-936-7151

Coffee
- **Café Latte** • 6254 Wilshire Blvd
- **Coffee Break** • 1507 1/2 S Robertson Blvd
- **International Coffee & Tea** • 1945 S La Cienega Blvd
- **La Peer Coffee Shop** • 8120 Wilshire Blvd
- **Starbucks** • 1258 S La Brea Ave
- **Starbucks** • 6066 W Olympic Blvd
- **Starbucks** • 8783 W Pico Blvd
- **Starbucks** • 9049 W Olympic Blvd
- **Taistee Coffee Shop** • 6200 Wilshire Blvd

Farmer's Markets
- **Farmers' Market** • 1801 La Cienega Blvd • Thu 3-7

Gyms
- **Bolder Fitness** • 8810 W Pico Blvd • 310-276-5505
- **LA Fitness Sports Clubs** • 5950 Wilshire Blvd • 323-934-6150
- **LA Fitness Sports Club** • 1833 La Cienega Blvd • 310-202-6823
- **Meridian Sports Club** • 5750 Wilshire Blvd • 323-933-5875
- **Quick's Fitness Center** • 473 S Robertson Blvd • 310-271-7933

Liquor Stores
- **Beverly Hills Beverage** • 8328 Wilshire Blvd
- **L & E Liquors** • 1298 S La Brea Ave
- **La Brea Liquor** • 1617 S La Brea Ave
- **La Brea Liquor & Junior Market** • 718 S La Brea Ave
- **Le Chateau Wine & Spirits** • 6252 Wilshire Blvd
- **Liquorama Liquor Store** • 4979 W Washington Blvd
- **Midtown Junior Market & Liquor** • 5956 W Olympic Blvd
- **Mike's Liquor** • 5390 W Washington Blvd
- **Okay Liquor Store** • 5500 W Pico Blvd
- **PM Liquor** • 1976 S La Cienega Blvd
- **Redondo Liquor** • 5156 W Washington Blvd
- **Sunshine Liquor** • 5677 W Pico Blvd
- **Teddy's Liquor & Market** • 2112 S La Brea Ave
- **Thriftown Mkt & Liquor** • 2043 S La Cienega Blvd
- **Vendome Wine & Spirits** • 9153 W Olympic Blvd

Movie Theaters
- **Cecchi Gori Fine Arts Theatre** • 8556 Wilshire Blvd
- **Laemmle Music Hall Theatre** • 9036 Wilshire Blvd

Pet Stores
- **Angeles City Pet Hospital** • 5777 Pico Blvd • 323-933-8406
- **Pet Club** • 778 S La Brea Ave • 323-933-8811
- **Petco** • 1475 S Robertson Blvd • 310-282-8166
- **Tamid Enterprises** • 1633 Stauton Ave • 213-747-4547

Restaurants
- **Brasserie Des Artistes** • 8300 Wilshire Blvd • 323-655-6196
- **Caffé Latte** • 6254 Wilshire Blvd • 323-936-5213
- **Crazy Fish** • 9105 W Olympic Blvd • 310-550-8547
- **La Boca del Conga Room** • 5370 Wilshire Blvd • 323-938-1696
- **Lucy's** • 1371 S La Brea Ave • 323-938-4337
- **Mo Better Meatty Meat Burgers** • 5855 W Pico Blvd • 323-938-6558
- **Natalee Thai** • 998 S Robertson Blvd • 310-855-9380
- **Nyala** • 1076 S Fairfax Ave • 323-936-2486
- **Rosalind's** • 1044 S Fairfax Ave • 323-936-2486
- **Roscoe's Chicken & Waffles** • 5006 W Pico Blvd • 323-934-4405
- **Temple** • 14 N La Cienega Blvd • 310-360-9460
- **Versailles** • 1415 S La Cienega Blvd • 310-289-0392
- **Wi Jammin** • 5103 Pico Blvd • 323-965-9809

Shopping
- **Ace Gallery** • 5514 Wilshire Blvd • 323-935-4411
- **Albertson Wedding Chapel** • 5318 Wilshire Blvd • 323-937-4919
- **Bang a Drum** • 1255 S La Brea Ave • 800-495-1109
- **City Spa** • 5325 Pico Blvd • 323-933-5954
- **Feldmar Watch** • 9000 W Pico Blvd • 310-272-1196
- **Hansen's Cakes** • 1072 S Fairfax Ave • 323-936-4332
- **Kitson** • 115 S Robertson Blvd • 310-859-2652
- **Marinello Beauty School** • 6111 Wilshire Blvd • 323-938-2005
- **Miauhaus** • 1201 S La Brea Ave • 323-933-6150
- **Oh My Nappy Hair!** • 805 S La Brea Ave • 323-939-3999
- **Up Health Merchants** • 1017 S Fairfax Ave • 323-935-3020

Video Rental
- **20-20 Video** • 6161 W Pico Blvd • 310-551-2020
- **Blockbuster Video** • 270 S Robertson Blvd • 310-854-0991
- **Blockbuster Video** • 5353 Wilshire Blvd • 323-934-8367
- **Blockbuster Video** • 6340 Wilshire Blvd • 323-782-9733
- **Hollywood Video** • 3939 Crenshaw Blvd • 323-937-5647
- **Hollywood Video** • 5522 Wilshire Blvd • 323-937-5647
- **La Brea Video** • 752 S La Brea Ave • 323-936-1274
- **Top Video** • 4972 W Pico Blvd • 323-935-6960

N

Wilshire Country Club

HANCOCK PARK

COUNTRY CLUB PARK

MID-CITY

Los Angeles High Memorial Park

Harold A Henry Park

Queen Anne Rec Center

Getty House

Los Altos Apartments

Wilshire Ebell Theatre & Club

Wiltern Theatre

PAGE 321

Wilshire Blvd

Wilshire Blvd

W 1st St

W 2nd St

W 3rd St

W 3rd St

W 4th St

W 5th St

W 6th St

Carling Way

W 8th St

W 8th St

W 8th St

W 9th St

W 9th St

W 9th St

W 9th St

W 10th St

W 10th St

W 11th St

W 11th St

W 11th St

W 12th St

W 12th St

W 12th St

W Olympic Blvd

Edgewood Pl

Edgewood Pl

Le Claire Pl

Queen Anne Pl

Country Club Dr

Country Club Dr

San Vicente Blvd

W Pico Blvd

W Pico Blvd

Victoria Park Dr

Nadeau Dr

Victoria Park Pl

Lomita St

W 16th Pl

St Charles Pl

W 15th St

W 17th St

W 17th St

W 16th Pl

Saturn St

St Charles Pl

W 17th St

St Elmo Dr

St Elmo Dr

W 18th St

W 18th St

W 18th St

Pickford St

Mascot St

Pickford St

W Washington Blvd

W Washington Blvd

W 20th St

W 20th St

W 21st St

W 21st St

W 21st St

W 21st St

W 21st St

W 22nd Pl

W 22nd St

W 23rd St

W 23rd St

W 23rd St

W 23rd St

W 23rd St

Santa Monica Frwy

Ingraham St

Leeward Ave

Francis Ave

San Marion St

Dockweiler St

Venice Blvd

Westminster Ave

1. Abbey Pl
2. 11th Pl
3. W 11th St
4. W 12th St
5. S Ridgewood Pl

N Sycamore Ave
N Orange Dr
N Mansfield Ave
N Citrus Ave
N Highland Ave
N Mccadden Pl
N Las Palmas Ave
N June St
N Hudson Ave
N Hudson N
Hudson Pl

S Sycamore Ave
S Orange Dr
S Mansfield Ave
S Citrus Ave
S Highland Ave
S Mccadden Pl
S Las Palmas Ave
S June St
S Hudson Ave
S Rimpau Blvd
S Muirfield Rd

N Arden Blvd
N Lucerne Blvd
N Gower St
N Beachwood Dr
N Plymouth Blvd
N Windsor Blvd
N Irving Blvd
N Norton Ave
N Van Ness Ave
N Ridgewood Pl
N Wilton Pl
N Gramercy Pl

S Rossmore Ave
S Arden Blvd
S Lucerne Blvd
S Larchmont Blvd
S Plymouth Blvd
S Windsor Blvd
S Irving Blvd
S Norton Ave
S Van Ness Ave
S Wilton Pl
S Gramercy Pl

Wilton Dr
S Wilton Pl
S Wilton Pl
S Gramercy Pl
S St Andrews Ave
Council St

Lorraine Blvd
Crenshaw Blvd

S Bronson Ave
S Norton Ave
S Van Ness Ave

Westchester Pl
S Wilton Pl
S Gramercy Pl
S Gramercy Dr
S St Andrews Pl

3rd Ave
Westchester Pl
S Wilton Pl
Wilton Pl

S Highland Ave
S Longwood Ave
S Tremaine Ave
Keniston Ave
S Mullen Ave
S Muirfield Rd
Fremont Pl
Fremont Pl

S Citrus Ave
S Highland Ave
S Longwood Ave
S Tremaine Ave
Keniston Ave
S Hudson Ave
S Rimpau Blvd
S Mullen Ave
S Muirfield Rd
West Blvd
Queen Anne Pl
S Lucerne Blvd
S Plymouth Blvd
S Windsor Blvd
S Victoria Ave
S Bronson Ave
S Norton Ave
5th Ave
4th Ave
3rd Ave

Highland Av
Highland Dr
S Longwood Ave
S View St
S Rimpau Blvd
S Harcourt Ave
S Palm Grove Ave
S Claudina Av
Vineyard Av
Hillcrest Dr
West Blvd
Buckingham Rd
Virginia Rd
Wellington Rd
La Fayette Rd
S Victoria Ave

W Lucerne Ave

S Victoria Ave
10th Ave
9th Ave
8th Ave
7th Ave
6th Ave
5th Ave
4th Ave
3rd Ave
2nd Ave

S Van Ness Ave
S Wilton Pl
S Gramercy Pl
S St Andrews Pl

Arlington Ave
S Van Ness Ave
Cimarron St

2nd Ave
S Gramercy Pl

10

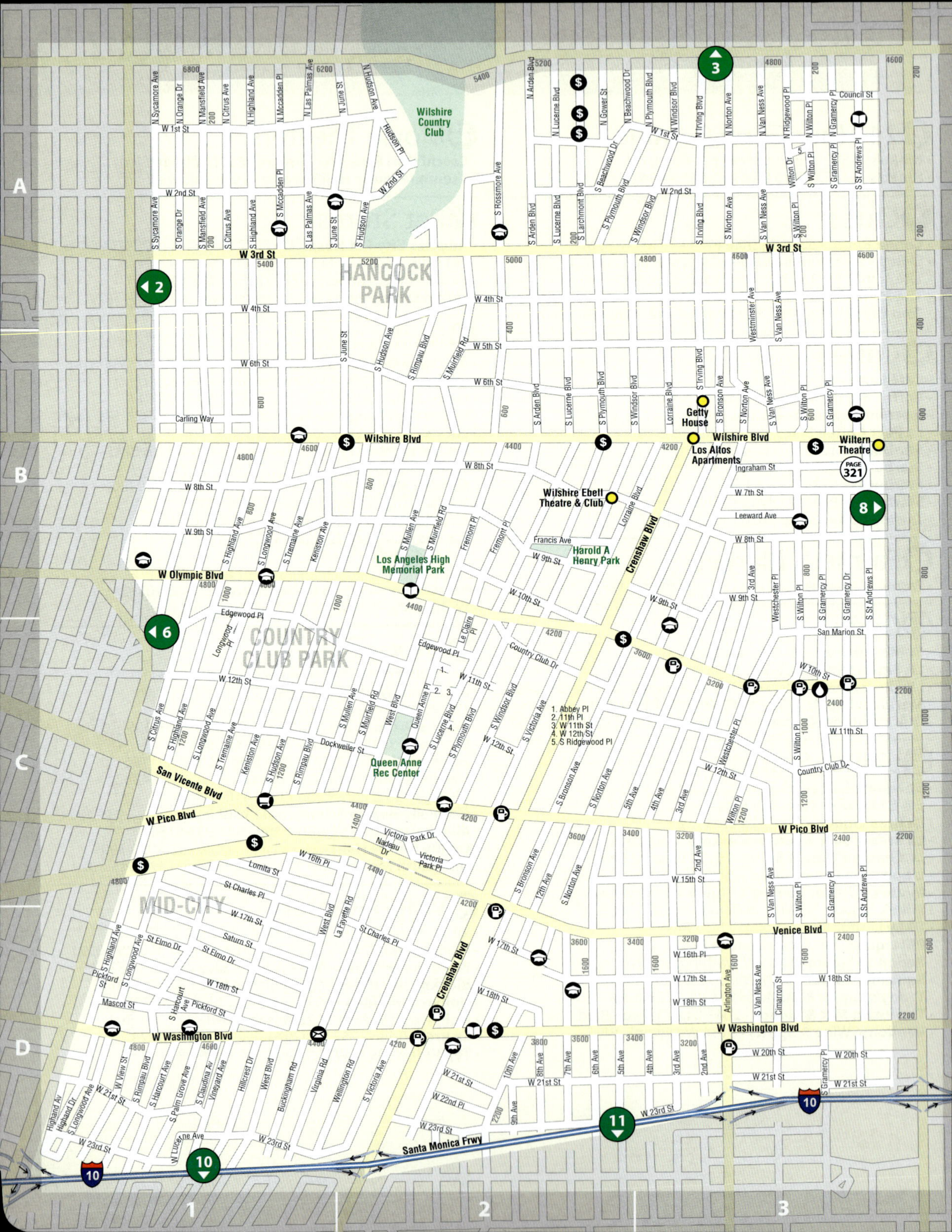

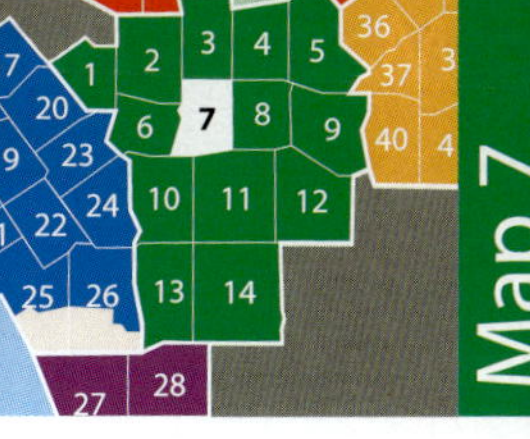

Though primarily a residential area, Hancock Park has a lot to offer, architecturally speaking. This is where the studio moguls from Hollywood's golden age used to live, and the mansions that lie on either side of 6th Street are worth a trip to see. Another "must" is the Wiltern Theatre, a medium-sized venue that is a great place to hear a concert.

Banks

- **Bank of America** · 100 N Larchmont Blvd
- **Bank of America** · 4077 W Washington Blvd
- **Bank of America** · 4649 Venice Blvd
- **Broadway Federal Bank** · 4800 Wilshire Blvd
- **Broadway Federal Bank** · 4835 Venice Blvd
- **Hanmi Bank** · 3737 W Olympic Blvd
- **Washington Mutual** · 101 N Larchmont Blvd
- **Washington Mutual** · 4333 Wilshire Blvd
- **Wells Fargo Bank** · 245 N Larchmont Blvd

Car Washes

- **Olympic Car Wash** · 3554 W Olympic Blvd

Gas Stations

- **76** · 3477 W Olympic Blvd
- **76** · 3481 W Olympic Blvd
- **76** · 3554 W Olympic Blvd
- **76** · 4176 Venice Blvd
- **Arco** · 4169 Pico Blvd
- **Chevron** · 1009 Crenshaw Blvd
- **Chevron** · 1907 Arlington Ave
- **Mobil** · 1925 Crenshaw Blvd
- **Mobil** · 3950 W Olympic Blvd

Landmarks

- **Getty House (Mayor's official residence)** · 605 S Irving Blvd
- **Los Altos Apartments** · 4121 Wilshire Blvd
- **Wilshire Ebell Theatre & Club** · 4401 W 8th St
- **Wiltern Theatre** · 3780 Wilshire Blvd

Libraries

- **Memorial Branch Library** · 4625 W Olympic Blvd · 323-938-2732
- **Washington Irving Branch Library** · 4117 W Washington Blvd · 323-734-6303
- **Wilshire Library** · 149 N St Andrews Pl · 323-957-4550

Post Offices

- 4040 W Washington Blvd

Schools

- **Alta Loma Elementary** · 1745 Vineyard Ave
- **Arlington Heights Elementary** · 1717 7th Ave
- **John Burroughs Middle School** · 600 S McCadden Pl
- **Los Angeles Senior High School** · 4650 W Olympic Blvd
- **Marlborough** · 250 S Rossmore Ave
- **Mount Vernon Middle School** · 4066 W 17th St
- **Pico Pre-School #2** · 4410 W Pico Blvd
- **Pio Pico Elementary** · 1512 S Arlington
- **Queen Anne Place Elementary** · 1212 Queen Anne Pl
- **Roennes** · 4701 W Washington Blvd
- **Simmons Institute** · 4865 W Washington Blvd
- **St Gregory Nazianzen** · 911 S Norton Ave
- **St James** · 625 S St Andrews Pl
- **St Paul Elementary** · 1908 S Bronson Ave
- **Third Street Elementary** · 201 S June St
- **Thompsons Learning Village** · 1932 10th Ave
- **Wilshire Crest Elementary** · 5241 W Olympic Blvd
- **Wilshire Elementary** · 4900 Wilshire Blvd
- **Wilton Place Elementary** · 745 S Wilton Pl
- **Yavneh Hebrew Academy** · 5353 W 3rd St

Supermarkets

- **Ralph's** · 4760 W Pico Blvd

N

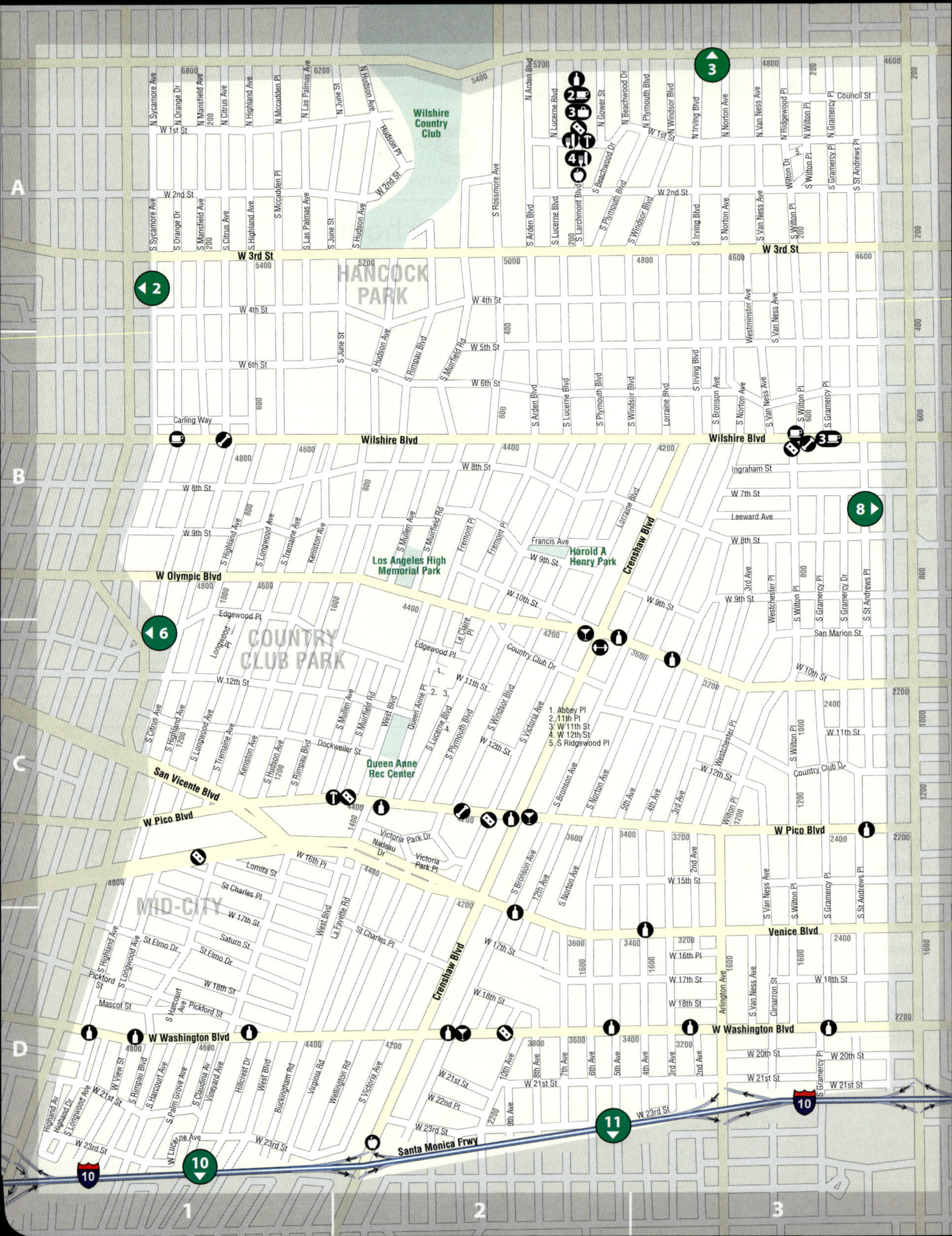

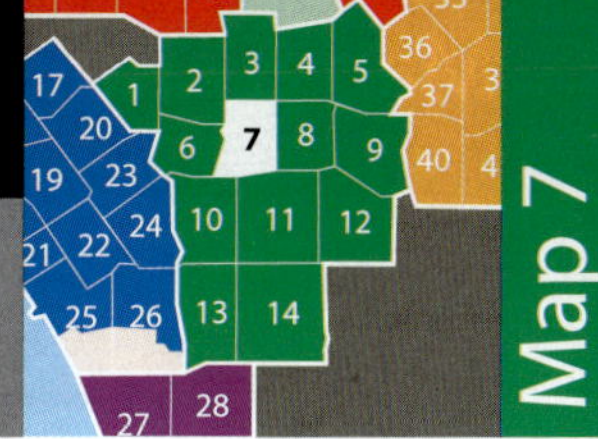

Larchmont Village has the feel of a small town's main street. Its high-end boutiques are unusual but fun. The Larchmont Beauty Center might be the best store of its kind in the city, and we think that the Larchmont Village Pizzeria is also at the top of its class. You'll often find aspiring actor Dennis Woodruff and his distinctive, graffitied car parked somewhere along the street. Don't say you weren't warned.

Clubs

- **Jewel's Catch One** • 4067 W Pico Blvd • 323-737-1159
- **Mixed Nuts Comedy Club** • 4000 W Washington Blvd • 323-735-6622
- **Voodoo** • 4120 W Olympic Blvd • 323-930-9600

Coffee

- **Cafe Americano** • 4001 Wilshire Blvd
- **Cafe Monet** • 3774 Wilshire Blvd
- **Coffee Bean & Tea Leaf** • 135 N Larchmont Blvd
- **Coffeecana** • 3959 Wilshire Blvd
- **Expresso Roma** • 124 N Larchmont Blvd
- **Hwa Sun Ji Tea & Coffee** • 3960 Wilshire Blvd
- **Starbucks** • 206 N Larchmont Blvd
- **Starbucks** • 5020 Wilshire Blvd

 Farmer's Markets

- **Larchmont Farmers Market** • Larchmont Blvd between Third & Beverly • Sun 10-2
- **Torrance** • 2200 Crenshaw Blvd • Tue 8-1

Hardware Stores

- **Larchmont Hardware** • 152 N Larchmont Blvd • 323-463-5783
- **Orchard Supply Hardware** • 4801 Venice Blvd • 323-930-6060

Liquor Stores

- **AWG Liquor** • 4161 W Washington Blvd
- **Grand Prize Liquor & Deli** • 4555 W Washington Blvd
- **Jack's Cigars** • 3720 W Olympic Blvd
- **LA Liquor** • 4816 W Washington Blvd
- **L & J Liquor** • 4111 Venice Blvd
- **Larchmont Village Wine & Spirits** • 223 N Larchmont Blvd
- **Midway Liquor** • 3186 W Pico Blvd
- **Olympic Mart Liquors** • 3533 W Olympic Blvd
- **Relay Liquor Store** • 3230 W Washington Blvd
- **Showplace Liquors** • 3401 Venice Blvd
- **Sixth Avenue Liquor Store** • 3526 W Washington Blvd
- **T & G Liquor Store** • 4879 W Washington Blvd
- **Three Jays Liquor** • 2333 W Washington Blvd
- **Tony's Liquor** • 4485 W Pico Blvd
- **Victoria Plaza Liquors** • 4226 W Pico Blvd

Pet Stores

- **Fumi's Tropical Fish** • 4211 W Pico Blvd • 323-939-5255
- **Kyoto Aquarium** • 3952 Wilshire Blvd • 213-487-7302
- **Pat McKay** • 5040 Wilshire Blvd • 323-456-0320

Restaurants

- **Kiku Sushi** • 246 N Larchmont Blvd • 323-464-1294
- **La Luna** • 113 N Larchmont Blvd • 323-962-2130
- **Larchmont Village Pizzeria** • 131 N Larchmont Blvd •
- **Le Petit Greek** • 127 N Larchmont Blvd • 323-464-5160
- **Prado** • 244 N Larchmont Blvd • 323-467-3871

Shopping

- **Landis Department Store** • 138 N Larchmont Blvd • 323-465-7998
- **Larchmont Beauty Center** • 208 N Larchmont Blvd • 323-466-6859
- **Larchmont News Stand** • 230 N Larchmont Blvd •

Video Rental

- **Blockbuster** • 147 N Larchmont Blvd • 323-461-3341
- **No 1 Video** • 4409 W Pico Blvd • 323-932-6299
- **Oscar Video (Korean)** • 4001 Wilshire Blvd • 213-384-7770
- **Pico Video** • 4236 W Pico Blvd • 323-939-1933
- **Planet Video** • 4737 Venice Blvd • 323-936-6343
- **Video 21** • 4020 W Washington Blvd • 323-730-8927

Council St
Beverly Blvd
W Temple St
Hollywood Freeway 101
5
2

A

N Oxford Ave
S Oxford Ave
W 1st St
N Serrano Ave
S Serrano Ave
N Hobart Blvd
S Hobart Blvd
N Harvard Blvd
S Harvard Blvd
N Kingsley Dr
S Kingsley Dr
N Ardmore Ave
S Ardmore Ave
N Normandie Ave
S Normandie Ave
N Mariposa Ave
S Mariposa Ave
N Alexandria Ave
S Alexandria Ave
N Edgemont St
S Edgemont St
N Kenmore Ave
S Kenmore Ave
N Catalina St
S Catalina St
N Berendo St
S Berendo St
N New Hampshire Ave
S New Hampshire Ave

Council St
Council St

W 1st St

W 2nd St

W 2nd St

Cosmopolitan St
N Commonwealth Ave
Council St

White House Pl
N Madison Ave

Bimini Pl
N Juanita Ave

Robinson St
N Dillon St
N Vendome St
S Vendome St
N Reno St
S Reno St
Parkman Ave
N Lafayette Park Pl
Dryden Pl

W Temple St
N Hoover St

Council St
Glassell St

Beverly Blvd
S Occidental Blvd

N Benton Way
N Rampart Blvd
N Coronado St
N Carondelet St

200

B

S Manhattan Pl
W 3rd St
4200
4000
3800
3600
3400
3200

W 4th St
WILSHIRE CENTER
Diana St
Geneva St
Shatto Rec Ctr
W 4th St

W 5th St

W 6th St

400

3800
600
3600
3400

2
Wilshire Blvd

WESTLAKE

S Commonwealth Ave

W 3rd St
3000
2800
2600

W 4th St
W 5th St
2400

S Hoover St
Ocean View Ave
2800
2600
W 6th St

Lafayette Park

2400

S Benton Way
S La Fayette Park Pl
S Occidental Blvd
S Dillon St
S Reno St
S Vendome St
S Commonwealth Ave

S Rampart Blvd
S Coronado St
S Carondelet St
W 2nd St
N Coronado St
N Carondelet St

W 4th St
W 5th St
S Park View St

400
800
S Park View St
S Grand View St
S Lake St

Shatto Pl
S Westmoreland Ave
Southwestern Law School
Wilshire Pl
Sunset Pl
Wilshire Blvd

MacArthur Park
MacArthur Lake

2600
2200

Leeward Ave
Magnolia Ave

W 7th St

W 8th St

800

Francis Ave

James M Wood Blvd
San Marino St

9

7

KOREATOWN
S Manhattan Pl
S Western Ave
Connecticut St

James M Wood Blvd

Ardmore Playground

S Ardmore Ave
Irolo St
S Normandie Ave
S Mariposa Ave
Fedora St
S Kenmore Ave
S Catalina St
S Berendo St
S New Hampshire Ave

Monette Pl
San Marino St

W Olympic Blvd
3000
2800

S Coronado St
S Carondelet St
S Park View St
S Grand View St
S Lake St

W 10th St

W Olympic Blvd
2200
2000

S Alvarado St
S Westlake Ave
S Bonnie Brae St
S Burlington Ave
Beacon Ave

C

W 11th St
Harrington Ave
S Serrano Ave
S Hobart Blvd
S Harvard Blvd
S Kingsley Dr
S Ardmore Ave
Irolo St
S Normandie Ave
S Mariposa Ave
Fedora St
S Kenmore Ave
Dewey Ave
S Catalina St
S Berendo St
S New Hampshire Ave
S Vermont Ave
S Westmoreland Ave
Elden Ave
Magnolia Ave
Arapahoe St

W 12th St
W 12th Pl
1200

W 12th St
2200
2000

W 11th St
1600

W Pico Blvd
3000
2800
2600
2400
Menlo Ave
2200

S Oxford Ave
S Westlake Ave
W Pico Blvd
1200

W 14th St
W 14th St
W 15th St
Cambridge St

1400
S Oxford Ave
S Hobart Blvd
S Harvard Blvd
S Kingsley Dr
S Ardmore Ave
Roosevelt Ave
S Normandie Ave
1400
Orchard Ave
W 14th St
W 15th St

Pomers Pl
Alvarado Ter
Courtland St
Malvern Ave
W 14th St

Venice Blvd
2000

Normandie Playground
1800

W 17th St
1600
W 17th Pl
Menlo Ave
1400

S Hoover St
Constance St
S Union Ave
Valencia St

Venice Blvd
1200

D

S Manhattan Pl
W 18th St
1800

S Oxford Ave
Westmoreland Blvd
S Hobart Blvd
S Harvard Blvd
S Kingsley Dr
S Ardmore Ave
Roosevelt Ave
S Normandie Ave

Rosedale Cemetery

Walton Ave
S Catalina St
S Berendo St
S New Hampshire Ave
1800
Menlo Ave
1600
S Westmoreland Ave
Orchard Ave
New England St
Magnolia Ave
Arapahoe St
Wilmot St

W 17th St
W 18th St

S Bonnie Brae St
S Burlington Ave
S Union Ave
Toberman St
Albany St
W 15th St
W 17th St
W 18th St
Oak St

W Washington Blvd
2200
1800
1600
1000

S Oxford Ave
S La Salle Ave
S Normandie Ave
Cordova St
S Mariposa Ave
Raymond Ave
S Budlong Ave
Cordova St
Orchard Ave
New England Pl
Arapahoe St

10
Santa Monica Freeway
W 20th St
W 20th St
11
Menlo Ave
W 21st St
10
12

1
2
3

"K-Town" was hit hard by the L.A. riots, but it has bounced back with a vengeance. There's lots to do at night, from classy supper clubs like the Atlas Bar & Grill to much more no-frills Korean BBQ restaurants from which you emerge smelling like you've been in the hibachi along with your dinner. The Mexican restaurant, El Cholo, is an L.A. institution, having been open in the same location for over 70 years.

$ Banks

- **Banco Popular** · 3360 W Olympic Blvd
- **Bank of America** · 1232 S Vermont Ave
- **Bank of America** · 3045 Wilshire Blvd
- **Bank of America** · 3320 W Olympic Blvd
- **Bank of America** · 3442 Wilshire Blvd
- **Bank of the West** · 3347 Wilshire Blvd
- **California Bank & Trust** · 3250 Wilshire Blvd
- **California Center Bank** · 2222 W Olympic Blvd
- **California Center Bank** · 3435 Wilshire Blvd
- **California Center Bank** · 3525 W 8th St
- **California Center Bank** · 4301 W 3rd St
- **California Korea Bank** · 3099 W Olympic Blvd
- **California Korea Bank** · 3530 Wilshire Blvd
- **Citibank** · 270 N Vermont Ave
- **Citibank** · 3530 Wilshire Blvd
- **City National Bank** · 1730 W Olympic Blvd
- **First Federal Bank** · 351 S Vermont Ave
- **Hanmi Bank** · 120 S Western Ave
- **Hanmi Bank** · 2610 W Olympic Blvd
- **Hanmi Bank** · 3660 Wilshire Blvd
- **Nara Bank** · 2727 W Olympic Blvd
- **Nara Bank** · 3680 Wilshire Blvd
- **Nara Bank** · 3701 Wilshire Blvd
- **Pacific Union Bank** · 3099 W Olympic Blvd
- **Pacific Union Bank** · 3245 Wilshire Blvd
- **Pacific Union Bank** · 928 S Western Ave
- **Pacific Union Bank** · 933 S Vermont Ave
- **Washington Mutual** · 3701 Wilshire Blvd
- **Washington Mutual** · 3731 Wilshire Blvd
- **Wells Fargo Bank** · 3550 Wilshire Blvd
- **Wells Fargo Bank** · 670 S Western Ave
- **Wilshire State Bank** · 3200 Wilshire Blvd
- **Wilshire State Bank** · 841 S Western Ave

◯ Car Washes

- **4th & Western Car Wash** · 401 S Western Ave
- **Auto Spa Hand Car Wash** · 128 S Western Ave
- **M & M Car Wash** · 2400 W Pico Blvd
- **Pico Car Wash** · 3131 W Pico Blvd
- **Silverlake Car Wash** · 3595 Beverly Blvd
- **Wilshire Car Wash** · 505 S Vermont Ave

ⓅGas Stations

- **76** · 1000 S Vermont Ave
- **76** · 3501 W 3rd St
- **76** · 4000 W 6th St
- **76** · 801 S Hoover St
- **76** · 801 S Western Ave
- **Arco** · 3325 W 6th St
- **Chevron** · 1570 S Western Ave
- **Chevron** · 2503 W Pico Blvd
- **Chevron** · 3625 Beverly Blvd
- **Chevron** · 3817 W 3rd St
- **Mobil** · 1904 W Washington Blvd
- **Mobil** · 1940 S Hoover St
- **Mobil** · 2608 W Temple St
- **Mobil** · 958 S Alvarado St
- **Shell** · 1303 S Western Ave
- **Shell** · 270 S Western Ave
- **Shell** · 700 S Vermont Ave
- **Texaco** · 3401 W 8th St

● Landmarks

- **MacArthur Park** · Wilshire Blvd & S Alvarado St
- **Southwestern Law School** · 3050 Wilshire Blvd

Libraries

- **Felipe De Neve Branch-LA Library** · 2820 W 6th St · 213-384-7676
- **Pio Pico Koreatown Library** · 694 S Oxford Ave · 213-368-7647

Rx 24-Hour Pharmacies

- **Rite-Aid** · 334 S Vermont Ave · 213-381-5257
- **Walgreens** · 3201 W 6th St · 213-251-0078

Police

- **Los Angeles Police Dept** · 2710 W Temple St · 213-485-4061

✉ Post Offices

- 2390 W Pico Blvd
- 265 S Western Ave
- 3751 W 6th St

Schools

- **Berendo Middle School** · 1157 S Berendo St
- **Berkeley Hall** · 16000 Mulholland Dr
- **Bishop Conaty-Our Lady of Love** · 2900 W Pico Blvd
- **Cahuenga Elementary** · 220 S Hobart Blvd
- **Cal Tech** · California Blvd & Hill Ave
- **Commonwealth Avenue Elementary** · 215 S Commonwealth Ave
- **First Lutheran School of LA** · 3119 W 6th St
- **Green Pastures Academy** · 600 S Lafayette Park Pl
- **Hobart Boulevard Elementary** · 980 S Hobart Blvd
- **Hoover Street Elementary** · 2726 Francis Ave
- **Linden Center West** · 2706 Wilshire Blvd
- **Los Angeles Christian** · 2001 S Vermont Ave
- **Los Angeles Elementary** · 1211 S Hobart Blvd
- **Loyola High School** · 1901 Venice Blvd
- **Magnolia Ave Elementary** · 1626 Orchard Ave
- **Mid-Wilshire Christian** · 221 S Juanita Ave
- **New Horizon School LA Campus** · 434 S Vermont Ave
- **Phillips Academy** · 3404 W 1st St
- **Pilgrim** · 540 S Commonwealth Ave
- **Politi Elementary** · 2481 W 11th St
- **Precious Blood** · 307 S Occidental Blvd
- **St Brendan's** · 238 S Manhattan Pl
- **St Thomas Apostle Elementary** · 2632 W 15th St
- **Virgil Middle School** · 152 N Vermont Ave
- **White House Primary Center** · 108 S Bimini Pl

Supermarkets

- **Food 4 Less** · 1091 S Hoover St
- **Food 4 Less** · 1717 S Western Ave
- **Jon's Supermarket** · 1500 W Pico Blvd
- **Jon's Supermarket** · 3334 W 8th St
- **Jon's Supermarket** · 3667 W 3rd St
- **Jon's Supermarket** · 840 S Alvarado St
- **Ralph's** · 3410 W 3rd St
- **Ralph's** · 670 S Western Ave
- **Von's** · 3461 W 3rd St

N

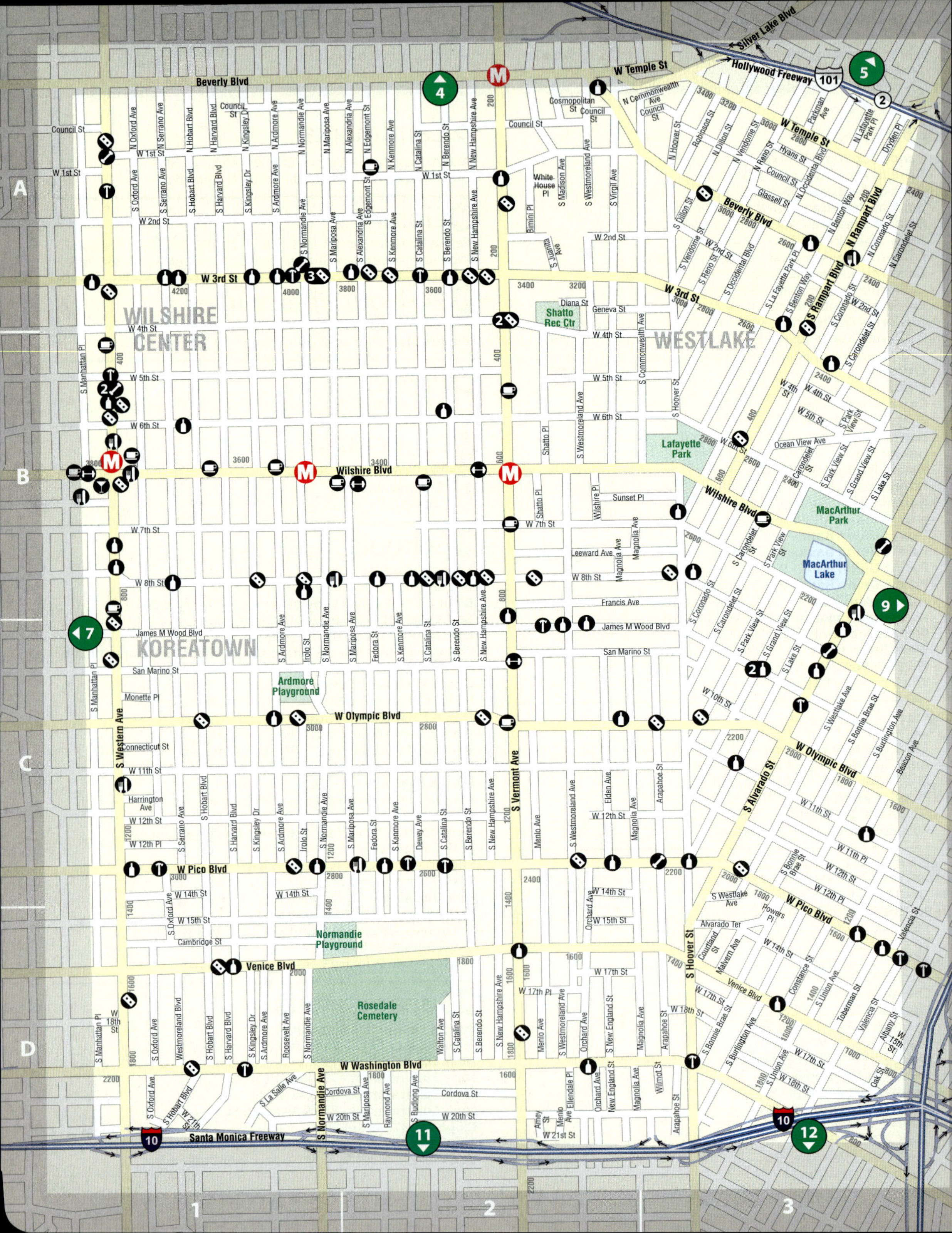

Council St
Beverly Blvd
W Temple St
Hollywood Freeway 101
Silver Lake Blvd
5
2
Cosmopolitan St
Council St
N Commonwealth Ave
Council St
W Temple St
3400 3200
3000
Robinson St
N Hoover St
N Dillon St
N Vendome St
N Reno St
Fackman Ave
N Benton Way
N Lafayette Park Pl
N Rampart Blvd
N Coronado St
N Carondelet St
Dryden Pl
2400
2200
N Oxford Ave
N Serrano Ave
N Hobart Blvd
N Harvard Blvd
Council St
N Kingsley Dr
N Ardmore Ave
N Normandie Ave
N Mariposa Ave
N Alexandria Ave
N Edgemont St
N Kenmore Ave
N Catalina St
N Berendo St
N New Hampshire Ave
Council St
W 1st St
White House Pl
S Madison Ave
S Westmoreland Ave
S Virgil Ave
Council St
Glassell St
Beverly Blvd
3000 2800
2600
S Vendome St
S Reno St
S La Fayette Park Pl
S Benton Way
S Coronado St
S Carondelet St
4
M
A
W 1st St
W 1st St
W 2nd St
W 3rd St
S Oxford Ave
S Serrano Ave
S Hobart Blvd
S Harvard Blvd
S Kingsley Dr
S Ardmore Ave
S Normandie Ave
S Mariposa Ave
S Alexandria Ave
S Edgemont St
S Kenmore Ave
S Catalina St
S Berendo St
S New Hampshire Ave
Bimini Pl
S Juanita Ave
W 2nd St
W 3rd St
200
3400 3200
Diana St
Geneva St
W 3rd St
S Occidental Blvd
S La Fayette Park Pl
W 2nd St
W 4th St
2600
S Coronado St
WILSHIRE CENTER
W 4th St
4200
4000
3800
3600
Shatto Rec Ctr
WESTLAKE
W 4th St
W 4th St
2400
W 4th St
W 5th St
S Park View St
W 5th St
400
2B
400
W 5th St
S Commonwealth Ave
S Hoover St
W 5th St
2600 2400
S Manhattan Pl
600
Shatto Pl
S Westmoreland Ave
Lafayette Park
2800 2600
Ocean View Ave
Carondelet St
S Park View St
S Grand View St
S Lake St
W 6th St
W 6th St
W 6th St
600
B
3800
3600
3400
Wilshire Blvd
600
Shatto Pl
Wilshire Pl
Sunset Pl
Wilshire Blvd
2600 2400
MacArthur Park
S Lake Pl
M
M
M
W 7th St
W 7th St
Leeward Ave
Magnolia Ave
Wilshire Blvd
MacArthur Lake
W 7th St
Francis Ave
2600
S Carondelet St
S Park View St
S Grand View St
2200
9
W 8th St
800
W 8th St
James M Wood Blvd
San Marino St
S Coronado St
S Carondelet St
S Park View St
S Grand View St
S Lake St
S Westlake Ave
S Bonnie Brae St
S Burlington Ave
7
KOREATOWN
San Marino St
Monette Pl
S Manhattan Pl
S Western Ave
Ardmore Playground
S Ardmore Ave
Irolo St
S Normandie Ave
S Mariposa Ave
Fedora St
S Kenmore Ave
S Catalina St
S Berendo St
S New Hampshire Ave
James M Wood Blvd
San Marino St
W 10th St
21
W Olympic Blvd
2000
S Bonnie Brae St
S Burlington Ave
Beacon Ave
Connecticut St
W Olympic Blvd
3000
2800
W Olympic Blvd
S Vermont Ave
2200
S Alvarado St
W Olympic Blvd
1800
C
W 11th St
Harrington Ave
W 11th St
1600
Elden Ave
Magnolia Ave
Arapahoe St
W 11th St
W 12th St
W 12th Pl
1200
S Hobart Blvd
S Harvard Blvd
S Kingsley Dr
S Ardmore Ave
Irolo St
S Normandie Ave
S Mariposa Ave
Fedora St
S Kenmore Ave
Dewey Ave
S Catalina St
S Berendo St
Menlo Ave
S Westmoreland Ave
W 12th St
1200
S Bonnie Brae St
S Westlake Ave
W 11th Pl
W 12th Pl
W Pico Blvd
S Serrano Ave
W Pico Blvd
3000
2800
1200
2600
1400
2400
W 14th St
W 15th St
2000
Powers Pl
1600
Valencia St
S Oxford Ave
W 14th St
W 14th St
Orchard Ave
Alvarado Ter
S Westlake Ave
W 12th Pl
W 15th St
Cambridge St
Normandie Playground
1400
W 15th St
1800
Courtland St
Malvern Ave
Constance St
S Union Ave
Tobesman St
Valencia St
Albany St
W 15th St
Venice Blvd
2000
1800
1600
W 17th St
S Hoover St
W 17th Pl
Powers Pl
Venice Blvd
W 14th St
Oak St
W 1600
S Manhattan Pl
W 18th St
Rosedale Cemetery
1800 1600
W 17th Pl
W 18th St
Venice Blvd
New England St
Orchard Ave
Magnolia Ave
Arapahoe St
S Bonnie Brae Ave
S Burlington Ave
S Union Ave
W 17th St
1200
Constance St
1400
D
S Manhattan Pl
S Oxford Ave
Westmoreland Blvd
S Hobart Blvd
S Harvard Blvd
S Kingsley Dr
S Ardmore Ave
Roosevelt Ave
S Normandie Ave
Walton Ave
S Catalina St
S Berendo St
Menlo Ave
S Westmoreland Ave
Orchard Ave
S New England St
Magnolia Ave
Arapahoe St
S Bonnie Brae Ave
S Burlington Ave
S Union Ave
W 17th St
1000
W Washington Blvd
2200
S Oxford Ave
W 21st St
S La Salle Ave
Cordova St
S Mariposa Ave
S Budlong Ave
Raymond Ave
Cordova St
1600
Arney
Menlo
New England Pl
Orchard Ave
New England St
Magnolia Ave
Wilmot St
Arapahoe St
W 18th St
1800
800
10
10
12
Santa Monica Freeway
11
S Normandie Ave
W 20th St
W 20th St
W 21st St
1
2
3

If we had only two more meals to enjoy, one might be a steak at Taylor's Prime Steaks. However, the other would most definitely be Korean Barbecue at Soot Bull Jeep. The experience is neither for vegetarians nor for the faint of heart, but the marinated pork and Spencer Steak are absolutely delicious.

Clubs
- **Atlas Bar & Grill** · 3760 Wilshire Blvd · 213-380-8400
- **La Fonda De Los Camperos** · 2501 Wilshire Blvd · 213-380-5055

Coffee
- **Baristar** · 698 S Vermont Ave
- **Cafe Aristo** · 664 S Catalina St
- **Coffee House Cona** · 425 S Western Ave
- **Coffee World** · 3500 Wilshire Blvd
- **Coffee Zone** · 3240 Wilshire Blvd
- **Coffeetime** · 851 1/2 S Western Ave
- **Espresso Plus** · 2500 Wilshire Blvd
- **Essence Coffee** · 3458 1/2 Wilshire Blvd
- **Smooth Moove** · 115 N Edgemont St
- **Starbucks** · 3680 Wilshire Blvd
- **Vienna Coffee** · 2716 W Olympic Blvd
- **Zen Cafe** · 3324 Wilshire Blvd

Gyms
- **24-Hour Fitness** · 3699 Wilshire Blvd · 213-388-2700
- **Natura Sports Health Club** · 3240 Wilshire Blvd · 213-637-9640
- **Wilshire Center Health Club** · 3440 Wilshire Blvd · 213-388-4111

Hardware Stores
- **A & B Hardware** · 513 S Western Ave · 213-389-6529
- **Alvarado Paint & Hardware** · 915 S Alvarado St · 213-382-1305
- **Callahan Hardware** · 139 S Western Ave · 213-387-3336
- **Catalina Hardware & Paint** · 3615 W 3rd St · 213-384-3059
- **D & D Hardware** · 2831 James M Wood Blvd · 213-386-6220
- **Hoover Hardware** · 1243 W Washington Blvd · 213-746-1775
- **J & C Hardware** · 1426 W Pico Blvd · 213-748-1530
- **LA Hardware** · 4027 W 3rd St · 213-388-4644
- **Orlando's Key Shop & Hardware** · 2024 W Washington Blvd · 323-737-5017
- **Pico Building Supply** · 2595 W Pico Blvd · 213-388-5102
- **Tool Max Hardware** · 2656 W Pico Blvd · 213-386-5284
- **Villanueva's Hardware** · 3030 W Pico Blvd · 323-737-1099

Liquor Stores
- **3rd Street Liquors Store** · 4023 W 3rd St
- **77 Liquor & Market** · 3200 W 8th St
- **8 O K Liquors** · 749 S Western Ave
- **A & A Liquor Market** · 111 S Vermont Ave
- **Albert Liquor Mart** · 3088 W Pico Blvd
- **Amigos Liquor 2** · 2601 W 7th St
- **Amigos Liquor & Market** · 3010 W 7th St
- **Ardmore Liquor** · 4056 W 3rd St
- **Ashibi Liquor** · 4376 W 3rd St
- **Bengal Liquor** · 3600 W 3rd St
- **Catalina Liquor** · 3130 W 8th St
- **Cheyenne Liquor Store** · 1611 S Vermont Ave
- **Crest Liquors** · 2543 W 3rd St
- **Dick's Beverage House** · 3315 W 6th St
- **El Serrano Liquor** · 3833 W 6th St
- **Garden Liquor Store** · 1479 W Washington Blvd
- **Gary's Liquors** · 2171 Venice Blvd
- **Gourmet Liquors** · 826 S Alvarado St
- **Hiro's Liquor & Groceries** · 2340 W Pico Blvd
- **Hobart Liquor** · 4212 W 3rd St
- **Hope Liquor Market** · 687 S Hoover St
- **Imperial Liquor** · 1602 W Pico Blvd
- **J & F Liquor Store** · 1512 W Pico Blvd
- **J & H Liquors** · 1154 Venice Blvd
- **Jeff's Liquor Store** · 1683 W 11th St
- **Kumano Liquor Mart** · 2801 W Pico Blvd
- **Lake Liquor Store** · 2202 W 11th St
- **Lawrence Liquor & Junior Market** · 2301 W James M Wood Blvd
- **Lee's Ladd Liquor** · 4217 W 3rd St
- **Midge's Liquor & Market** · 2201 W Pico Blvd
- **Nadee's Liquor Store** · 863 S Vermont Ave
- **Occidental Liquor** · 2755 Beverly Blvd
- **Ocean Liquor** · 760 S Alvarado St
- **Olympic Liquors** · 3060 W Olympic Blvd
- **Oxford Mini Mart** · 3502 W 8th St
- **Park Liquor Store** · 3554 Beverly Blvd
- **Service Liquor House** · 3803 W 3rd St
- **Silver Liquor & Delicatessen** · 2717 W 3rd St
- **Superior Liquor Store** · 2700 W Pico Blvd
- **Tighi Liquor** · 2701 W 8th St
- **Topper Liquor** · 3061 W 8th St
- **West Seven Liquor Store** · 707 S Western Ave
- **Western Liquor** · 553 S Western Ave
- **Westmoreland Market** · 2800 James M Wood Blvd

Pet Stores
- **Blanquis Pet & Supplies** · 2251 W Pico Blvd · 212-487-1290
- **Hobby Life Center** · 517 S Western Ave · 323-262-9999
- **Mike's Pet Shop** · 622 1/2 S Alvarado St · 213-483-5316
- **Normandie Pet & Supplies** · 4000 W 3rd St · 213-385-0431
- **Rancho Pet** · 804 S Alvarado St · 213-380-1220
- **Western Pet Center** · 533 S Western Ave · 213-381-3435
- **World Pet Shop & Bonsai** · 151 N Western Ave · 323-469-9977

Restaurants
- **Atlas Bar & Grill** · 3760 Wilshire Blvd · 213-380-8400
- **El Cholo** · 1121 S Western Ave · 323-734-2773
- **El Farolito** · 2737 W Pico Blvd · 323-731-4329
- **LA Farm** · 3000 W Olympic Blvd · 310-449-4000
- **Soot Bull Jeep** · 3136 W 8th St · 213-387-3865
- **Taylor's Prime Steaks** · 3361 W 8th St · 213-382-8449
- **Tommy's** · 2575 Beverly Blvd · 213-389-9060
- **Woo Lae Oak** · 623 S Western Ave · 213-384-2244

Video Rental
- **20-20 Video** · 142 S Vermont Ave · 213-380-0202
- **20-20 Video** · 1833 S Vermont Ave · 323-734-2020
- **3rd Street Video (Korean)** · 3559 W 3rd St · 213-739-5935
- **50 50 Video** · 2411 W Olympic Blvd · 213-384-4585
- **A & T Video Center** · 272 S Rampart Blvd · 213-387-6161
- **Blockbuster** · 2190 W Washington Blvd · 323-373-2082
- **Blockbuster** · 2377 W Pico Blvd · 213-383-2927
- **Blockbuster** · 4005 W 3rd St · 213-252-3133
- **Central Video (Korean)** · 3072 W 8th St · 213-389-2111
- **Chasis Video** · 2703 W 8th St · 213-385-7727
- **Cinema Story** · 401 S Vermont Ave · 213-383-6211
- **Club Video (Filipino)** · 4031 W 3rd St · 213-380-3575
- **Corner Video (Korean)** · 2528 W Olympic Blvd · 213-388-2255
- **East-West Video (Korean)** · 3328 W 8th St · 213-385-6181
- **El Chasis Video** · 2980 W 8th St · 213-385-4702
- **Excalibur Video** · 1724 S Western Ave · 323-731-1801
- **Han Nam Video (Korean)** · 2716 W Olympic Blvd · 213-487-1225
- **Hollywood Video** · 650 S Western Ave · 213-385-7233
- **J & J Video** · 3101 Beverly Blvd · 213-380-4169
- **Korea Town Video (Korean)** · 928 S Western Ave · 213-480-8080
- **Korean Video Store (Korean)** · 401 S Vermont Ave · 213-386-7116
- **LA Korean Video (Korean)** · 326 S Western Ave · 213-389-4989
- **Lucky Video (Korean)** · 124 N Western Ave · 323-460-4398
- **Mickey Video (Korean)** · 3134 W Olympic Blvd · 323-732-8399
- **Opaane Video Store** · 3967 W 6th St · 213-427-9855
- **P & J (Korean)** · 555 S Western Ave · 213-380-6699
- **Planet Video** · 2026 W Pico Blvd · 213-381-1884
- **Super Video (Korean)** · 3388 W 8th St · 213-380-0550
- **Video Target** · 3128 W 8th St · 213-487-6035
- **Video Tek** · 849 S Western Ave · 213-382-0714
- **Virgil Video** · 2161 Venice Blvd · 323-734-6007
- **Westside Video** · 2709 W 6th St · 213-384-4725

Echo Park
Echo Lake
Dodger Stadium

W Temple St
Beverly Blvd
W 3rd St
S Alvarado St
Glendale Blvd
Beverly Blvd
W 3rd St
Wilshire Blvd
W 6th St
W Olympic Blvd
W Pico Blvd

Elysian Park Ave
Stadium Way
Pasadena Frwy
W Sunset Blvd
Hollywood Frwy
W Temple St
W Cesar E Chavez Ave
Harbor Frwy & Transitway

N Broadway
N Spring St
N Main St
LA Co. Main Jail
Union Station
Olvera Street
Chinatown
El Pueblo De Los Angeles State Hist Park
Instituto Cultural Mexicano
E Cesar E Chavez Ave
Santa Ana Frwy
N Mission Rd

N Figueroa St
N Grand Ave
N Hope St
Music Center
MOCA
WTC
W Kosciuszko Way
Central Park
Angel's Flight
Pershing Square
City Hall
MOCA Geffen
Japanese American National Museum
E 1st St
E Temple St
E Commercial St
S Central Ave
S Alameda St
S San Pedro St
Los Angeles River

Grand Central Market
W 3rd St
W 7th St
W 8th St
Museum of Neon Art
S Grand Ave
S Flower St
S Olive St
S Hill St
S Broadway
S Main St
S Los Angeles St
S San Julian St

LA Convention Center
Staples Center
W Pico Blvd
W Olympic Blvd
PAGE 231
S Figueroa St
Venice Blvd
W Washington Blvd
W Adams Blvd
LA Trade/Technical College
S Figueroa St
S Broadway
S Main St
S San Pedro St
S Central Ave
Santa Monica Frwy
E Olympic Blvd
E Washington Blvd

E 4th St
E 5th St
E 6th St
E 7th St
E Olympic Blvd
S Santa Fe Ave
Produce St
Wholesale St
Industrial St
E 7th St
Bay St
Sacramento St
E 8th St

1. Onizuka St
2. Woodworth Ct
3. Azusa St
4. Japanese Pz
5. N Central Ave
6. Hewitt St
7. Avery St
8. Merrick St
9. W Gen Thaddeus Kosciuszko Way
10. Prudent St
11. Llewellyn St
12. Magdalena St
13. Cardinal St
14. Bamboo Ln
15. Gin Ling Way
16. Jing
17. Lei Min Way
18. Mei Ling Way
19. Sun Mun Way
20. Chung King Rd
21. Doyle Pl
22. Adobe St
23. Court St
24. S N Boylston St
25. Victor St
26. Mignonette St
27. S Boylston St
28. S Boylston St
29. S Bixel St
30. Lake Shore
31. Pizarro St
32. Rosenell Ter
33. S Edgeware Rd
34. Linwood Ave
35. W 12th Dr
36. Emerald Dr
37. Convention Center
38. Diamond St

L.A.'s downtown area is relatively small compared to that of most major cities, and it's possible to live in Los Angeles without ever setting foot there—though that would be a mistake. Grand Central Market, Union Station, and Olvera Street, where traditional Mexican goods are still sold, are all located in the downtown area and are some of the most "L.A." spots you'll find in the city.

$ Banks

- **Banco Popular** · 354 S Spring St
- **Bank of America** · 100 S Broadway
- **Bank of America** · 103 E Cesar E Chavez Ave
- **Bank of America** · 1127 S Hill St
- **Bank of America** · 1625 W Olympic Blvd
- **Bank of America** · 2101 W 6th St
- **Bank of America** · 300 S Grand Ave
- **Bank of America** · 355 S Grand Ave
- **Bank of America** · 525 S Flower St
- **Bank of America** · 550 S Hill St
- **Bank of America** · 555 S Flower St
- **Bank of America** · 590 S Central Ave
- **Bank of America** · 600 Wilshire Blvd
- **Bank of America** · 850 N Broadway
- **Bank of the West** · 300 S Grand Ave
- **Bank of the West** · 333 S Alameda St
- **Bank of the West** · 601 S Figueroa St
- **California Bank & Trust** · 101 S San Pedro St
- **California Bank & Trust** · 550 S Hope St
- **California Center Bank** · 1059 S San Pedro St
- **California Center Bank** · 1126 Santee St
- **California Center Bank** · 1205 S Broadway
- **California Korea Bank** · 401 E 11th St
- **California National Bank** · 221 S Figueroa St
- **Cathay Bank** · 777 N Broadway
- **Citibank** · 324 E 1st St
- **Citibank** · 787 W 5th St
- **City National Bank** · 606 S Olive St
- **City National Bank** · 633 W 5th St
- **Comerica Bank** · 201 N Figueroa St
- **East West Bank** · 624 S Grand Ave
- **East West Bank** · 942 N Broadway
- **Far East National Bank** · 350 S Grand Ave
- **Far East National Bank** · 977 N Broadway
- **First Bank & Trust** · 711 W College St
- **First Republic Bank** · 900 W 7th St
- **First Republic Bank** · 901 W 7th St
- **General Bank** · 800 W 6th St
- **Hanmi Bank** · 950 S Los Angeles St
- **International Bank of California** · 2323 Beverly Blvd
- **International Bank of California** · 888 S Figueroa St
- **Manufacturers Bank** · 135 E 9th St
- **Manufacturers Bank** · 200 S San Pedro St
- **Manufacturers Bank** · 515 S Figueroa St
- **Nara Bank** · 1122 Wall St
- **Pacific Commerce Bank** · 408 E 2nd St
- **Pacific Union Bank** · 401 E 11th St
- **Preferred Bank** · 601 S Figueroa St
- **Union Bank** · 120 S San Pedro St
- **Union Bank** · 445 S Figueroa St
- **Union Bank** · 900 S Main St
- **United California Bank** · 300 S Grand Ave
- **United California Bank** · 601 S Figueroa St
- **United Commercial Bank** · 767 N Hill St
- **Washington Mutual** · 400 S Hope St
- **Washington Mutual** · 855 S Hill St
- **Washington Mutual** · 888 W 7th St
- **Wells Fargo Bank** · 1200 Wilshire Blvd
- **Wells Fargo Bank** · 1244 E 8th St
- **Wells Fargo Bank** · 1831 W 3rd St
- **Wells Fargo Bank** · 333 S Grand Ave
- **Wells Fargo Bank** · 333 S Spring St
- **Wells Fargo Bank** · 707 Wilshire Blvd
- **Wells Fargo Bank** · 988 N Hill St
- **Wilshire State Bank** · 1122 Maple Ave

Car Washes

- **Daisy Shell** · 400 N Alvarado St
- **Downtown Car Wash** · 811 W Olympic Blvd
- **Joe's Car Wash** · 400 E 7th St
- **Mario's Hand Wash & Detailing** · 1000 Wilshire Blvd
- **Onik's Truck Service** · 647 Mateo St
- **Sunset Car Wash** · 811 W Olympic Blvd
- **Valet Car Wash** · 355 S Grand Ave
- **Valet Car Wash** · 725 S Figueroa St

Gas Stations

- **76** · 1031 W 2nd St
- **76** · 1307 W 6th St
- **76** · 1800 E Olympic Blvd
- **Arco** · 1045 Blaine St
- **Arco** · 2041 Beverly Blvd
- **Arco** · 2106 W Temple St
- **Arco** · 221 S Figueroa St
- **Arco** · 333 S Hope St
- **Arco** · 866 W Cesar E Chavez Ave
- **Beacon Oil** · 812 S Main St
- **Chevron** · 1516 S Main St
- **Chevron** · 1600 W Olympic Blvd
- **Chevron** · 501 Glendale Blvd
- **Chevron** · 811 W Olympic Blvd
- **Chevron** · 900 N Hill St
- **Chevron** · 901 N Alameda St
- **Mobil** · 520 N Alameda St
- **Shell** · 1520 Santa Fe Ave
- **Shell** · 1541 S Central Ave
- **Shell** · 1551 W 7th St
- **Texaco** · 500 S Alameda St
- **Texaco** · 504 W Olympic Blvd

Hospitals

- **California Hospital Medical** · 1338 S Hope St · 213-742-5555
- **California Hospital Medical** · 1401 S Grand Ave · 213-748-3855
- **City of Angels Medical Center** · 1711 W Temple St · 213-989-6100
- **Good Samaritan Hospital** · 1225 Wilshire Blvd · 213-977-2121
- **Pacific Alliance Medical Center** · 531 W College St · 213-624-8411

Landmarks

- **Angel's Flight** · W 4th St & Hill St
- **Chinatown** · 700-1000 N Broadway
- **City Hall** · 200 N Spring St
- **Grand Central Market** · 317 S Broadway
- **Instituto Cultural Mexicano** · 125 Paseo de la Plaza
- **Japanese American National Museum** · 369 E 1st St
- **LA Convention Center** · 1201 S Figueroa St
- **MOCA** · 250 S Grand Ave
- **MOCA at the Geffen Contemporary** · 152 N Central Ave
- **Museum of Neon Art** · 501 W Olympic Blvd
- **Music Center** · 135 N Grand Ave
- **Olvera Street** · Olvera St
- **Staples Center** · 1111 S Figueroa St
- **Union Station** · 800 N Alameda St
- **World Trade Center** · 350 S Figueroa St

Libraries

- **Chinatown Branch Library** · 639 N Hlll St · 213-620-0925
- **City Attorney's Library** · 200 N Main St · 213-485-5400
- **Echo Park Library** · 1410 W Temple St · 213-250-7808
- **Franklin D Murphy Library** · 244 S San Pedro St · 213-628-2725
- **LA County Law Library** · 301 W 1st St · 213-629-3531
- **Little Tokyo Library** · 244 S Alameda St · 213-612-0525
- **Los Angeles Central Library** · 630 W 5th St · 213-228-7000
- **MPA Library** · 1 Gateway Plz · 213-922-4859
- **Water & Power Library** · 111 N Hope St · 213-367-1995

Police

- **Los Angeles Police Dept** · 150 N Los Angeles St · 213-485-2121
- **Los Angeles Police Dept** · 251 E 6th St · 213-485-3294

Post Offices

- · 100 W Olympic Blvd
- · 1808 W 7th St
- · 300 N Los Angeles St
- · 350 S Grand Ave
- · 505 S Flower St
- · 508 S Spring St
- · 760 N Main St

Schools

- **10th Street Elementary** · 1000 Grattan St
- **9th Street Elementary** · 920 Towne Ave
- **Ann Street Elementary** · 126 E Bloom St
- **Belmont Senior High School** · 1575 W 2nd St
- **Camino Nuevo Charter Academy** · 697 S Burlington Ave
- **Castelar Elementary** · 840 Yale St
- **City of Angels** · 1320 W 3rd St
- **Downtown Business High** · 1081 W Temple St
- **Esperanza Elementary** · 680 Little St
- **Gratts Elementary** · 309 Lucas Ave
- **Immaculate Conception** · 830 Green Ave
- **LA Trade/Technical College** · 400 W Washington Blvd
- **Metropolitan Continuation** · 727 Wilson St
- **Newmark Continuation** · 135 Witmer St
- **Our Lady of Loretto** · 250 N Union Ave
- **Plasencia Elementary** · 1321 Cortez St
- **Rosemont Ave Elementary** · 421 Rosemont Ave
- **St Nicholas Child Care Primary** · 2300 W 3rd St
- **St Turibius Elementary** · 1524 Essex St
- **Union Avenue Elementary** · 150 S Burlington Ave

Supermarkets

- **Jon's Supermarket** · 1500 W 6th St
- **Ron's** · 805 S Main St
- **Trader Joe's** · 216 E Alameda St

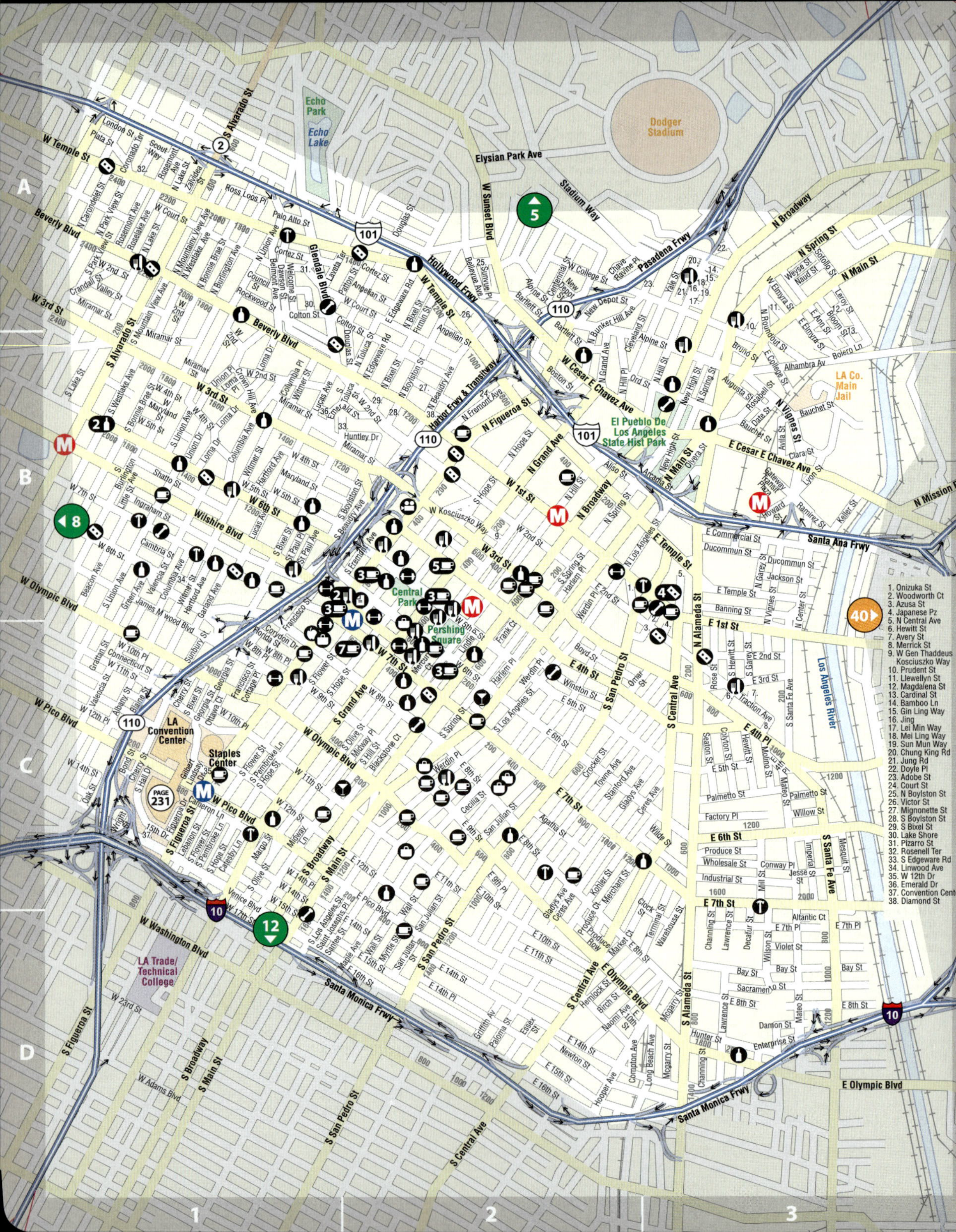

1. Onizuka St
2. Woodworth Ct
3. Azusa St
4. Japanese Pz
5. N Central Ave
6. Hewitt St
7. Avery St
8. Merrick St
9. W Gen Thaddeus Kosciuszko Way
10. Prudent St
11. Llewellyn St
12. Magdalena St
13. Cardinal St
14. Bamboo Ln
15. Gin Ling Way
16. Jing
17. Lei Min Way
18. Mei Ling Way
19. Sun Mun Way
20. Chung King Rd
21. Jung Rd
22. Doyle Pl
23. Adobe St
24. Court St
25. N Boylston St
26. Victor St
27. Mignonette St
28. S Boylston St
29. S Bixel St
30. Lake Shore
31. Pizarro St
32. Rosenell Ter
33. S Edgeware Rd
34. Linwood Ave
35. W 12th Dr
36. Emerald Dr
37. Convention Center
38. Diamond St

Philippe, the Original (located at 1001 N. Alameda Street) is the birthplace of the French dip sandwich. Legend has it that Philippe accidentally dropped a French roll into a pan of drippings while he was making a sandwich. The customer liked the concoction so much that he brought his friends back the following day, and a deli staple was born.

24-Hour Copy Centers
- **Kinko's** · 835 Wilshire Blvd · 213-892-1700

Clubs
- **Downtown LA Standard** · 550 S Flower St · 213-892-8080
- **Mayan** · 1038 S Hill St · 213-746-4287
- **Stock Exchange** · 618 S Spring St · 213-487-3877

Coffee
- **706 Coffee Shop** · 706 S Hill St
- **Bayo's** · 719 S Main St
- **Blue Diamond** · 633 S Hill St
- **Cafe Take 5** · 328 E 1st St
- **Caffe Bellagio** · 1149 S Hill St
- **Coffee Bean & Tea Leaf** · 210 E Olympic Blvd
- **Coffee Bean & Tea Leaf** · 801 W 7th St
- **Coffee Buzz** · 573 E Pico Blvd
- **Coffee Shop** · 911 Wilshire Blvd
- **Coffee Sin** · 1125 Wall St
- **Coffee Time** · 790 Gladys Ave
- **Corner Bakery Café** · 801 S Figueroa St
- **Essence Coffee** · 733 W 7th St
- **Gourmet Coffee & Nuts** · 505 S Flower St
- **Happy Time Snack** · 819 Santee St
- **Hill's Cafe** · 317 S Broadway
- **Jolt-Bar Cafe** · 1055 W 7th St
- **Jolt-Bar Cafe** · 317 S Broadway
- **Larry's Cookie** · 221 N Figueroa St
- **Moose's Juices** · 444 S Flower St
- **Park Central Coffee Shop** · 412 W 6th St
- **Pasqua Storeroom** · 355 S Grand Ave
- **Pasqual Coffee Bars** · 300 S Grand Ave
- **Pasquini Imports** · 1501 W Olympic Blvd
- **Primo's Expresso Americana** · 333 S Spring St
- **Starbucks** · 10925 Atlantic Ave
- **Starbucks** · 1201 S Figueroa St
- **Starbucks** · 138 S Central Ave
- **Starbucks** · 1601 Wilshire Blvd
- **Starbucks** · 217 N Hill St
- **Starbucks** · 300 E 9th St
- **Starbucks** · 330 S Hope St
- **Starbucks** · 333 S Hope St
- **Starbucks** · 350 S Grand Ave
- **Starbucks** · 400 S Hope St
- **Starbucks** · 444 S Flower St
- **Starbucks** · 445 S Figueroa St
- **Starbucks** · 505 S Flower St
- **Starbucks** · 555 W 5th St
- **Starbucks** · 601 W 5th St
- **Starbucks** · 633 W 5th St
- **Starbucks** · 695 S Figueroa St
- **Starbucks** · 735 S Figueroa St
- **Starbucks** · 800 W 6th St
- **Stop-In Coffee** · 926 S Los Angeles St
- **Trimana Restaurant** · 615 W 6th St
- **Wall Street Cafe** · 949 Wall St

Farmer's Markets
- **7 Fig** · 735 S Figueroa St · Thu 11-3, Sat 10-4

Gyms
- **24-Hour Fitness** · 505 S Flower St · 213-683-1400
- **Bally Total Fitness** · 700 S Flower St · 213-624-3933
- **Century Sports Club** · 420 W Olympic Blvd · 323-954-1020
- **Gold's Gym** · 735 S Figueroa St · 213-688-1441
- **Los Angeles Athletic Club** · 431 W 7th St ·
- **Millennium Biltmore Hotel Health** · 506 S Grand Ave · 213-612-1567
- **Sanwa Health Spa** · 120 S Los Angeles St · 213-687-4597

Hardware Stores
- **7th & Union Hardware** · 1622 W 7th St · 213-483-5138
- **Anzen Hardware & Supplies** · 309 E 1st St · 213-628-2068
- **Cooper Hardware & Paint** · 1645 W Temple St · 213-483-3353
- **Douglas Hardware** · 1811 E 7th St · 213-622-4666
- **DSW Hardware** · 1317 S Grand Ave · 213-747-1305
- **La Campana Hardware** · 1322 W 12 Pl · 213-483-6331
- **Terminal Hardware** · 824 E 8th St · 213-624-4078

Liquor Stores
- **Annex Liquors** · 1607 W 6th St
- **Bixel Liquor Store** · 467 S Bixel St
- **Duke's Liquor Store** · 818 S San Pedro St
- **Elf's Liquor** · 1324 W 7th St
- **Esquire Liquors & Deli** · 619 1/2 S Olive St
- **French Kitchen** · 404 S Figueroa St
- **Friendly Liquor Store** · 1553 W 8th St
- **George's Liquor Store** · 1300 W Temple St
- **George's Liquor Store** · 700 N Broadway
- **Gourmet Liquors** · 1476 W 3rd St
- **Gourmet Wine & Spirits** · 505 S Flower St
- **Grand Central Public Market** · 317 S Broadway
- **Hope's Market** · 1216 W 7th St
- **Jack's Market** · 520 E 5th St
- **Jo's Liquor** · 333 W Pico Blvd
- **K & K Liquor** · 1246 E 7th St
- **Lee's Liquor** · 1800 W 6th St
- **Macy Liquor Store** · 111 W Cesar E Chavez Ave
- **Mark's Liquor** · 1259 W 6th St
- **OT Liquor** · 1920 E Olympic Blvd
- **Pete's Liquor** · 1234 Maple Ave
- **Sam's Corner Liquor Store** · 2001 W 6th St
- **Sorrento Liquor Store** · 801 W Cesar E Chavez Ave
- **TD Beer & Wine** · 1948 E 7th St
- **Union Liquor Store** · 1703 Beverly Blvd

Movie Theaters
- **Laemmle's Grande** · 349 S Figueroa St

Pet Stores
- **Al's Pet Supplies** · 430 S Los Angeles St · 213-622-1215
- **Liberty Fish & Pet Shop** · 665 N Broadway · 213-628-9664
- **Magic Cat** · 123 Astronaut Onizuka St · 213-625-1786
- **Morales Pet Shop** · 222 Glendale Blvd · 213-482-9622
- **Trinity Animal Hospital** · 1504 S Main St · 530-623-5757

Restaurants
- **Brooklyn Bagel** · 2217 Beverly Blvd · 213-413-4114
- **California Roll & Sushi Fish** · 727 W 7th St · 213-489-0238
- **Checkers** · 535 S Grand Ave · 213-624-0000
- **Cicada** · 617 S Olive St · 213-488-9488
- **Ciudad** · 445 S Figueroa St · 213-486-5171
- **El Cholo** · 1025 Wilshire Blvd · 310-417-1910
- **Emerson's** · 606 S Olive St · 213-623-3006
- **Emerson's** · 862 S Los Angeles St · 213-623-8807
- **Empress Pavillion** · 988 N Hill St · 213-617-9898
- **Engine Co No 28** · 644 S Figueroa St · 213-624-6996
- **Mrs Beasley's** · 735 S Figueroa St · 213-228-0227
- **Nick & Stef's Steakhouse** · 330 S Hope St · 213-680-0330
- **NY Pizza** · 518 W 6th St · 213-614-1100
- **Original Pantry Cafe** · 877 S Figueroa St · 213-972-9279
- **Pacific Dining Car** · 1310 W 6th St · 213-483-6000
- **Philippe, the Original** · 1001 N Alameda St · 213-628-3781
- **Seoul Jung Korean** · 930 Wilshire Blvd · 213-888-7777
- **Soul Folks Café** · 714 Traction Ave · 213-613-0381
- **Yang Chow** · 819 N Broadway · 213-625-0811

Shopping
- **7 + Fig at Ernst & Young Plaza** · 735 S Figueroa St · 213-955-7150
- **California Market Center** · 110 E 9th St · 866-746-7262
- **LA Flower Market** · 766 Wall St · 213-622-1966
- **Moskatel's** · 738 S Wall St · 213-689-4590
- **Santee Alley** · Midway between Santee St and Maple Ave, from 12th St to Olympic Blvd ·
- **Thomas Bros Map Store** · 521 W 6th St · 213-627-4018

Video Rental
- **B & C Video Rental** · 1416 W 6th St · 213-484-5383
- **Blockbuster** · 1830 W 8th St · 213-250-1292
- **Echo Echo Video** · 220 Glendale Blvd · 213-250-9105
- **Gemini Video** · 2424 W Temple St · 213-389-2030
- **Global Video** · 123 S Figueroa St · 213-680-1779
- **Global Video** · 800 W 2nd St ·
- **J Wave** · 319 E 2nd St · 213-687-9920
- **Peter's Video Center** · 1226 W 7th St · 213-891-1927
- **Sevan Video (Turkish)** · 640 S Hill St · 213-622-5735
- **Sun Video** · 450 E 2nd St ·
- **Tokyo Market (Japanese)** · 339 E 1st St · 213-620-0033
- **Video Hot** · 2110 Beverly Blvd · 213-413-5433
- **Video Paradise (Japanese)** · 321 E 1st St · 213-625-2671
- **Video Z** · 1460 W Temple St · 213-481-0996

1. Smiley Dr
2. S Curson Ave
3. Carmona Ave
4. S Ridgeley Dr
5. S Burnside Ave
6. S Dunshuir Ave
7. Highlight Pl
8. S Ridgeley Dr
9. S Burnside Ave
10. Wrighcrest Dr
11. Stillwater Dr
12. Don Arturo Pl
13. Don Pablo Pl
14. Don Alegre Pl
15. Don Tapia Pl
16. Baldwin Villa Driveway
17. Don Alberto Pl
18. Don Porfirio Pl
19. Fairway Blvd
20. Addington Wy
21. Chasar Pl
22. Whelan Pl
23. Valdina Pl
24. Springhill Pl
25. Adale Pl
26. Springdale Dr

One of the strangest sights in L.A. is the oil wells located just off of La Cienega. There are over 1,000 that still produce oil and gas, as well as process oil drilled from other locations around L.A.

$ Banks

- **Bank of America** • 2907 Crenshaw Blvd
- **Bank of America** • 3615 S La Brea Ave
- **Bank of America** • 3945 Crenshaw Blvd
- **California Bank & Trust** • 3810 Crenshaw Blvd
- **US Bank** • 3605 S La Brea Ave
- **Wells Fargo Bank** • 3480 S La Brea Ave
- **Wells Fargo Bank** • 3649 Stocker St

Car Washes

- **Crenshaw Car Wash** • 4220 Crenshaw Blvd
- **Slauson Hand Car Wash** • 3615 W Slauson Ave

Gas Stations

- **76** • 5100 W Jefferson Blvd
- **Arco** • 3412 Crenshaw Blvd
- **Arco** • 4661 W Slauson Ave
- **Arco** • 5884 Washington Blvd
- **Chevron** • 2538 Crenshaw Blvd
- **Chevron** • 3063 Crenshaw Blvd
- **Chevron** • 3742 S La Brea Ave
- **Chevron** • 4081 Marlton Ave
- **Chevron** • 4701 W Slauson Ave
- **Mobil** • 4380 W Adams Blvd
- **Mobil** • 5776 Washington Blvd
- **Shell** • 2545 S Crenshaw Blvd
- **Shell** • 3300 S La Cienega Blvd
- **Shell** • 3645 Crenshaw Blvd
- **Shell** • 4044 W Martin Luther King Jr Blvd
- **Shell** • 4660 W Slauson Ave

Landmarks

- **Baldwin Hills Village Oil Wells** •
  East of La Cienega Blvd
- **Kenneth Hahn State Recreation Area** •
  4100 S La Cienega Blvd

Libraries

- **Baldwin Hills Library** • 2906 S La Brea Ave •
  323-733-1196
- **View Park Library** • 3854 W 54th St • 323-293-5371

Post Offices

- 3650 W Martin Luther King Jr Blvd
- 3894 Crenshaw Blvd

Schools

- **54th Street Elementary** • 5501 Eileen Ave
- **Alpha Elementary** • 5252 W Adams Blvd
- **Applied Learning Academy** • 3855 W Slauson Ave
- **Ascension Lutheran** • 5820 West Blvd
- **Baldwin Hills Elementary** • 5421 Rodeo Rd
- **Cienega Elementary** • 2611 S Orange Dr
- **Cleophas Oliver Learning Center** •
  4449 W Adams Blvd
- **Coliseum Street Elementary** • 4400 Coliseum St
- **Dorsey Senior High School** • 3537 Farmdale Ave
- **Ebony Learning Tree School** • 3906 W Slauson Ave
- **Foundation for the Junior Blind** •
  5300 Angeles Vista Blvd
- **Hillcrest Drive Elementary** • 4041 Hillcrest Dr
- **Mt Cavalry Christian School** • 3770 Santa Rosalia Dr
- **New Roads** • 5753 Rodeo Rd
- **Slausen Learning Center** • 4000 W Slauson Ave
- **Soledad Enrichment Action** • 4324 W Jefferson Blvd
- **St Bernadette Elementary** • 4196 Marlton Ave
- **St Paul's Presbyterian Preschool** • 5100 Coliseum St
- **View Park Continuation** • 4701 Rodeo Rd
- **View Park Preparatory Accelerated Charter School** •
  3751 W 54th St
- **Virginia Road Elementary** • 2925 Virginia Rd
- **West Angeles Christian Academy** •
  3010 S Crenshaw Blvd
- **Wilkerson Academy of Learning** • 3740 Don Felipe Dr
- **Windsor Hills Math and Science Elementary** •
  5215 Overdale Dr

Supermarkets

- **Albertson's** • 3480 S La Brea Ave
- **Albertson's** • 3901 Crenshaw Blvd
- **Ralph's** • 3670 Crenshaw Blvd
- **Ralph's** • 5080 Rodeo Rd
- **Ralph's** • 5212 W Adams Blvd

Map 10 • Baldwin Hills

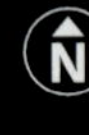

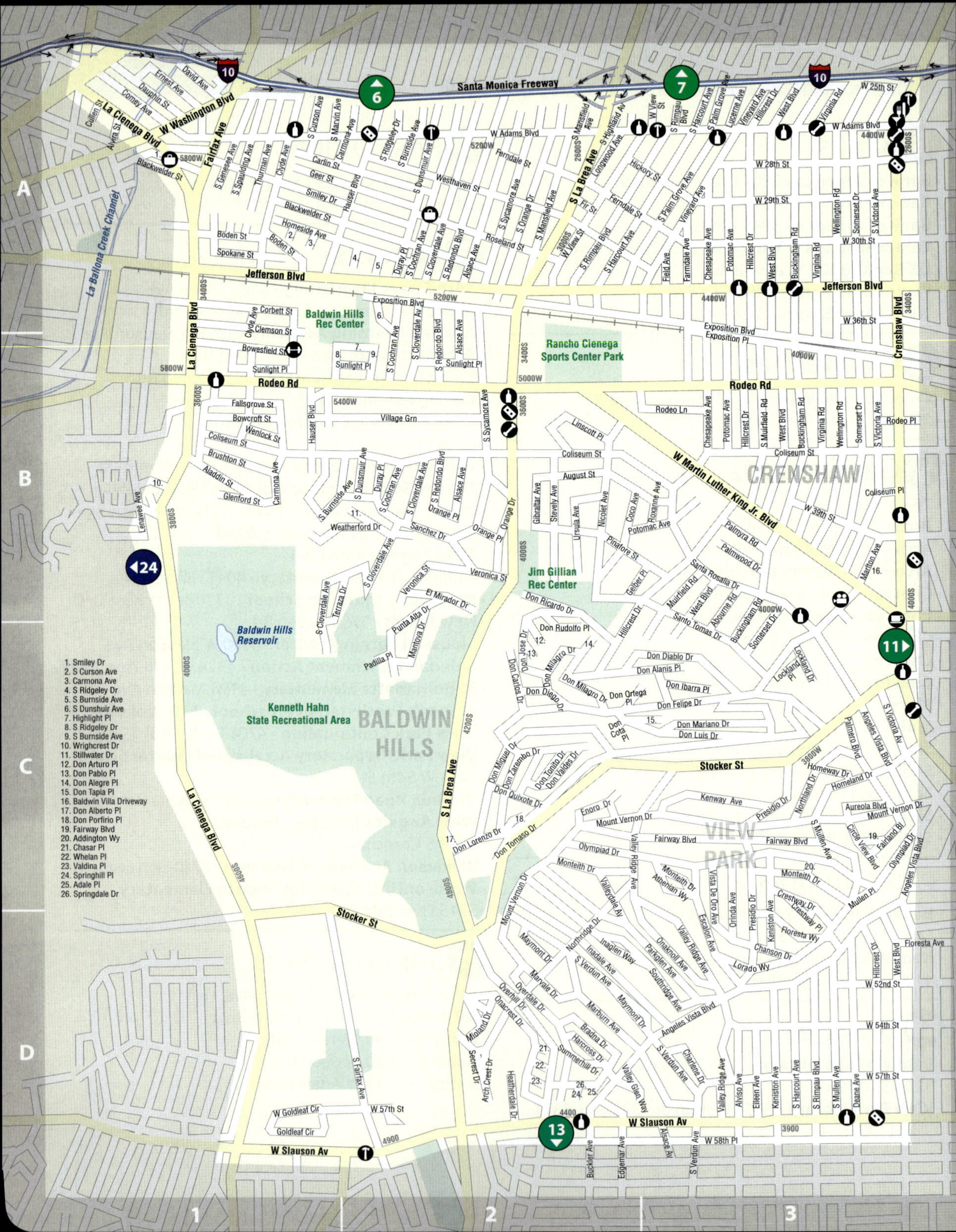

Santa Monica Freeway
10
6
7
11
13
24
W Washington Blvd
La Cienega Blvd
Fairfax Ave
Jefferson Blvd
Exposition Blvd
Rodeo Rd
W Adams Blvd
S La Brea Ave
W Martin Luther King Jr. Blvd
Crenshaw Blvd
Stocker St
W Slauson Av
Baldwin Hills Rec Center
Rancho Cienega Sports Center Park
Jim Gillian Rec Center
Baldwin Hills Reservoir
Kenneth Hahn State Recreational Area
BALDWIN HILLS
CRENSHAW
VIEW PARK
La Ballona Creek Channel
1. Smiley Dr
2. S Curson Ave
3. Carmona Ave
4. S Ridgeley Dr
5. S Burnside Ave
6. S Dunshuir Ave
7. Highlight Pl
8. S Ridgeley Dr
9. S Burnside Ave
10. Wrighcrest Dr
11. Stillwater Dr
12. Don Arturo Pl
13. Don Pablo Pl
14. Don Alegre Pl
15. Don Tapia Pl
16. Baldwin Villa Driveway
17. Don Alberto Pl
18. Don Porfirio Pl
19. Fairway Blvd
20. Addington Wy
21. Chasar Pl
22. Whelan Pl
23. Valdina Pl
24. Springhill Pl
25. Adale Pl
26. Springdale Dr
A
B
C
D
1
2
3

Sundries / Entertainment

Leblond's Normandie Pate, on Cochran, almost makes you think you've been spirited away from the auto repair shops and strip malls that surround the bakery, and dropped into a Parisian café for a petit dejeuner.

Clubs

- **Café Club Fais Do-Do** · 5257 W Adams Blvd · 323-954-8080
- **The Living Room** · 2636 Crenshaw Blvd · 323-735-8748

Coffee

- **Ethio Gourmet Cafe** · 3650 W Martin Luther King Jr Blvd

Hardware Stores

- **Homebase Home Improvement** · 4925 W Slauson Ave · 323-298-1155
- **Paintcraft Supply & Hardware** · 2620 Crenshaw Blvd · 323-733-9157
- **Slater Hardware** · 5365 W Adams Blvd · 323-932-1942
- **Sonora Hardware** · 4860 W Adams Blvd · 323-766-1396

Liquor Stores

- **Adams Liquor** · 4620 W Adams Blvd
- **Arcade Liquor Store** · 4431 1/2 W Slauson Ave
- **Baldwin Hills Liquor** · 3629 S La Brea Ave
- **Bell's Liquor** · 3869 Santa Rosalia Dr
- **Bottle Bar Liquor Store** · 2642 Crenshaw Blvd
- **Cabin Liquor Store** · 5633 W Adams Blvd
- **Gubby's Liquor Store** · 4800 W Adams Blvd
- **Holiday Liquor Market** · 4966 W Adams Blvd
- **Jan-Ett's Liquor** · 4028 W Jefferson Blvd
- **Liquor Bank & Deli** · 3600 Stocker St
- **PG's Liquor** · 4407 W Jefferson Blvd
- **T & D's Liquor Store** · 3860 W Slauson Ave
- **Tag's Liquor Store** · 3866 Crenshaw Blvd
- **Wine Cellar** · 5747 Rodeo Rd

Movie Theaters

- **Magic Johnson Theatre 15** · 4020 Marlton Ave

Pet Stores

- **James' Tropical Fish** · 4273 Crenshaw Blvd · 323-294-6490
- **Pet Center** · 4105 W Jefferson Blvd · 323-734-1445
- **Pets Planet** · 3651 S La Brea Ave · 323-293-1212
- **Tokyo Aquarium** · 4600 W Adams Blvd · 323-735-7553

Restaurants

- **Leo's BBQ** · 2619 Crenshaw Blvd · 323-733-1186

Shopping

- **Graphaids** · 3030 S La Cienega Blvd · 310-204-1212
- **Leblond's Normandie Pate** · 3022 S Cochran Ave · 323-939-5528

Video Rental

- **Home Video Club** · 2803 Crenshaw Blvd · 323-730-1322
- **King Video** · 5500 W Adams Blvd · 323-931-6028
- **LA Hit Video** · 3653 S La Brea Ave · 323-290-1655
- **Rick's Video** · 3608 W Slauson Ave · 323-299-2950
- **Video Club** · 4130 Crenshaw Blvd · 323-294-8997

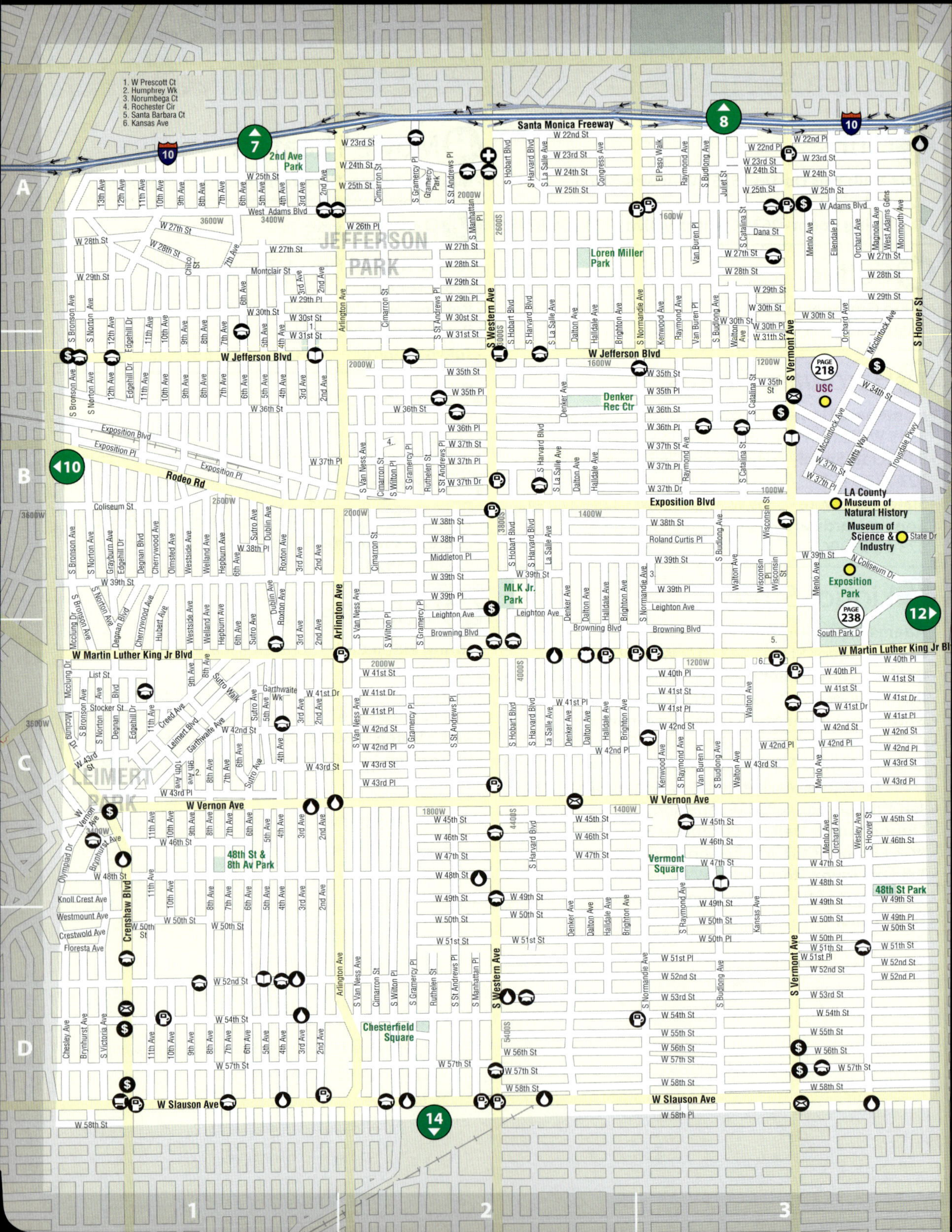

Map 11 · South Central West

N

1. W Prescott Ct
2. Humphrey Wk
3. Norumbega Ct
4. Rochester Cir
5. Santa Barbara Ct
6. Kansas Ave

Santa Monica Freeway

10

7

8

10

A

2nd Ave Park

W 23rd St
W 24th St
W 25th St
W 22nd Pl
W 23rd St
W 24th St
W 25th St

W 22nd Pl
W 23rd St
W 24th St
W 25th St
W 22nd Pl

West Adams Blvd
3600W
3400W

W 26th Pl
W 27th St
W 28th St
W 29th St

JEFFERSON PARK

Loren Miller Park

W Adams Blvd
W 27th St
W 28th St
W 29th St

Menlo Ave
Ellendale Pl
Orchard Ave
Magnolia Ave
West Adams Gdns
Monmouth Ave

S Hoover St

13th Ave
12th Ave
11th Ave
10th Ave
9th Ave
8th Ave
7th Ave
6th Ave
5th Ave
4th Ave
3rd Ave
2nd Ave

W 27th St
Montclair Ave
W 28th St
Chico St
W 29th St
3rd Ave
2nd Ave
W 29th Pl

Arlington Ave
Cimarron St

W 27th St
W 28th St
W 29th St
W 30th St
W 30st St
W 31st St

S St Andrews Pl

S Western Ave
S Hobart Blvd
S Harvard Blvd
S La Salle Ave

Dalton Ave
Halldale Ave
Brighton Ave

S Normandie Ave
Kenwood Ave
Raymond Ave
Van Buren Pl
S Budlong Ave
Walton Ave

S Vermont Ave

W 27th St
W 28th St
W 29th St
W 30th St
W 31st St

Orchard Ave
Mcclintock Ave

W 30th St
W 31st St

B

10

W Jefferson Blvd

W 30th St
W 31st St
4th Ave
5th Ave

W Jefferson Blvd

W 35th St
W 35th Pl
W 36th St
W 37th St
W 37th Pl
W 37th Dr

W Jefferson Blvd

1600W

W 35th St
W 35th Pl
W 36th St
W 36th Pl
W 37th St
W 37th Pl
W 37th Dr

PAGE 218
USC

1200W
W 34th St

S Bronson Ave
S Norton Ave
12th Ave
Edgehill Dr
11th Ave
10th Ave
9th Ave
8th Ave
7th Ave
6th Ave
5th Ave
4th Ave
3rd Ave
2nd Ave

Exposition Blvd
Exposition Pl
Exposition Pl

Rodeo Rd

S Van Ness Ave
Cimarron St
S Wilton St
Rutherlen St
S St Andrews Pl
S Gramercy Pl

Denker Ave

Denker Rec Ctr

S Harvard Blvd
S La Salle Ave
Dalton Ave
Halldale Ave

S Catalina St

McClintock Ave
Watts Way
Trousdale Pkwy

LA County Museum of Natural History

Museum of Science & Industry
State Dr

2500W
2000W

Exposition Blvd

1400W
1000W

W 38th St
W 38th Pl
Middleton Pl
W 39th St
W 39th Pl

MLK Jr. Park

Leighton Ave
Browning Blvd

N Coliseum Dr

Exposition Park

PAGE 238

12

Coliseum St
S Bronson Ave
S Norton Ave
Grayburn Ave
Edgehill Dr
Olmsted Ave
Cherrywood Ave
Westside Ave
Welland Ave
Hepburn Ave
6th Ave
Dublin Ave
Roxton Ave
3rd Ave
2nd Ave

Cimarron St

W 38th St
W 38th Pl
W 39th St
W 39th Pl

S Hobart Blvd
S Harvard Blvd
La Salle Ave

Roland Curtis Pl

W 38th St

W 39th St

Denker Ave
Dalton Ave
Halldale Ave
Brighton Ave

S Normandie Ave

Leighton Ave
Browning Blvd

Walton Ave
Wisconsin St
Wisconsin St

Menlo Ave

W 39th St

South Park Dr

C

W Martin Luther King Jr Blvd

Arlington Ave

Leighton Ave
Browning Blvd

W Martin Luther King Jr Blvd

W 40th Pl

W Martin Luther King Jr Bl
W 40th Pl

List St
S Bronson Ave
Ave
9th Ave
8th Ave
Sutro Walk
Mcclung Dr S
S Norton
Degnan
Edgehill Dr
11th Ave
Creed Ave
Leimert Blvd
Garthwaite Ave
8th Ave
7th Ave
Sutro Ave
6th Ave
5th Ave
4th Ave
Sutro Ave
10th Ave

Garthwaite Wk
Sutro Ave
5th Ave
3rd Ave
2nd Ave

W 41st St
W 41st Dr
W 41st Pl
W 42nd St
W 42nd Pl
W 43rd St
W 43rd Pl

S Van Ness Ave
W 40th Pl
2000W

S Wilton Pl
S Gramercy Pl
S St Andrews Pl

W 41st St
W 41st Dr
W 41st Pl
W 42nd St
W 42nd Pl
W 43rd St
W 43rd Pl

4000S

S Hobart Blvd
S Harvard Blvd
La Salle Ave
Denker Ave
Halldale Ave
Brighton Ave

Kenwood Ave
S Raymond Ave
Van Buren Pl
S Budlong Ave
Walton Ave

W 40th Pl
W 41st St
W 41st Dr
W 41st Pl
W 42nd St
W 42nd Pl
W 43rd St

Menlo Ave

W 40th Pl
W 41st St
W 41st Dr
W 41st Pl
W 42nd St
W 42nd Pl
W 43rd St

Mcclung Dr
S Bronson Ave
S Norton
Degnan
Edgehill Dr
11th Ave
Stocker St

LEIMERT PARK

W Vernon Ave

W Vernon Ave

W Vernon Ave

W 43rd Pl

Chesley Ave
Brynhurst Ave
S Victoria Ave
11th Ave
10th Ave
9th Ave
8th Ave
7th Ave
6th Ave
5th Ave
4th Ave
3rd Ave
2nd Ave

Crenshaw Blvd

Olympiad Dr
Brynhurst Ave

W Vernon Ave
W 46th St
48th St & 8th Av Park
W 48th St

Knoll Crest Ave
Westmount Ave
Crestwold Ave
Floresta Ave

W 50th St
W 50th St

W 45th St
W 46th St
W 47th St
W 48th St
W 49th St
W 50th St
W 51st St

1800W

S Harvard Blvd

W 45th St
W 46th St
W 47th St

W 48th St

W 49th St
W 50th St
W 51st St

4400S

Denker Ave
Dalton Ave
Halldale Ave
Brighton Ave

S Western Ave

1400W

Vermont Square

S Raymond Ave

W 45th St
W 46th St
W 47th St
W 48th St
W 49th St
W 50th St
W 50th Pl

S Normandie Ave
S Budlong Ave
Kansas Ave

Menlo Ave
Orchard Ave
Wesley Ave
S Hoover St

48th St Park

W 45th St
W 46th St

W 48th St
W 49th St
W 49th Pl
W 50th St
W 50th Pl
W 51st St
W 51st Pl
W 52nd St

W 52nd St
W 52nd St

D

Chesterfield Square

W 52nd St
W 54th St

Arlington Ave
S Van Ness Ave
Cimarron St
S Wilton Pl
S Gramercy Pl
Ruthelen St
S St Andrews Pl
S Manhattan Pl

S Western Ave

5400S

W 52nd St
W 53rd St
W 54th St
W 55th St
W 56th St
W 57th St
W 58th St

S Normandie Ave

W 52nd St
W 53rd St
W 54th St
W 55th St
W 56th St
W 57th St

W 57th St
W 57th St
W 58th St

W Slauson Ave

W Slauson Ave

14

W 58th St
W 58th Pl

Leimert Park Village (bordered by Vernon Ave., Crenshaw Blvd., 43rd St., and Leimert Blvd.) is a shopping and arts district with an emphasis on African-American culture. If you check the area out, you'll find awesome jazz clubs, sidewalk chess games, and terrific soul food.

$ Banks

- **Bank of America** • 4103 S Western Ave
- **Bank of America** • 5471 Crenshaw Blvd
- **Bank of America** • 5700 S Vermont Ave
- **Bank of America** • 985 W Jefferson Blvd
- **Citibank** • 3615 S Vermont Ave
- **Downey Savings & Loan** • 2600 S Vermont Ave
- **Union Bank** • 3501 W Jefferson Blvd
- **US Bank** • 5760 Crenshaw Blvd
- **Washington Mutual** • 4401 Crenshaw Blvd
- **Washington Mutual** • 5717 S Vermont Ave

Car Washes

- **100 Percent Car Wash** • 2500 W 54th St
- **A Moment's Notice Hand Carwash** • 4727 Crenshaw Blvd
- **Crystal Shine Hand Car Wash** • 2601 W Slauson Ave
- **Flores Hand Car Wash** • 2027 W Slauson Ave
- **Flores Hand Car Wash** • 5201 S Western Ave
- **Red Carpet Carwash** • 1620 W Martin Luther King Jr Blvd
- **Riley's Car Wash** • 2500 W Vernon Ave
- **Slauson Hand Car Wash** • 1680 W Slauson Ave
- **Squeaky Clean Detail** • 2315 W Vernon Ave
- **Touch of Class Hand Car Wash** • 1763 W 48th St
- **V & A Car Wash** • 5845 S Hoover St

Gas Stations

- **76** • 2330 W Slauson Ave
- **76** • 3774 S Western Ave
- **76** • 5816 S Western Ave
- **Arco** • 1355 W Martin Luther King Jr Blvd
- **Arco** • 1515 W Martin Luther King Jr Blvd
- **Arco** • 3227 W 54th St
- **Arco** • 5407 S Normandie Ave
- **Arco** • 5804 Crenshaw Blvd
- **Chevron** • 1691 W Adams Blvd
- **Chevron** • 2202 S Vermont Ave
- **Mobil** • 3770 S Western Ave
- **Shell** • 1010 W Martin Luther King Jr Blvd
- **Shell** • 1403 W Adams Blvd
- **Shell** • 1404 W Martin Luther King Jr Blvd
- **Shell** • 2215 W Martin Luther King Jr Blvd
- **Shell** • 2603 S Normandie Ave
- **Shell** • 4404 S Western Ave

Landmarks

- **Exposition Park** • Menlo Ave & S Park Dr
- **LA County Museum of Natural History** • 900 Exposition Blvd
- **Museum of Science & Industry** • 700 State Dr
- **University of Southern California** • Trousdale Pkwy

Libraries

- **Exposition Park Library** • 3665 S Vermont Ave • 323-732-0169
- **Jefferson Library** • 2211 W Jefferson Blvd • 323-734-8573
- **Los Angeles City Library** • 2700 W 52nd St • 323-292-4328
- **Vermont Square Branch Library** • 1201 W 48th St • 323-290-7405

Police

- **Los Angeles Police Dept** • 1546 W Martin Luther King Jr Blvd • 213-485-2582

Post Offices

- 1515 W Vernon Ave
- 3585 S Vermont Ave
- 5472 Crenshaw Blvd
- 5832 S Vermont Ave

Schools

- **24th Street Elementary** • 2055 W 24th St
- **36th St** • 1771 W 36th St
- **36th St Children's Center** • 3556 S St Andrews Pl
- **37th Street Children** • 1204 W 36th Pl
- **42nd Street Elementary** • 4231 4th Ave
- **52nd Street Elementary** • 816 W 51st St
- **Angeles Mesa Elementary** • 2611 W 52nd St
- **Audubon Middle School** • 4120 11th Ave
- **Bright Elementary** • 1771 W 36th St
- **Burton Green** • 3787 S Vermont Ave
- **Cecil L Murray Educational Center** • 2400 S Western Ave
- **Creative Learning Center** • 1729 W Martin Luther King Jr Blvd
- **Crenshaw Senior High School** • 5010 11th Ave
- **Dorothy Brown** • 3502 S Normandie Ave
- **Foshay Junior High School** • 3751 S Harvard Blvd
- **Golden Day** • 4476 Crenshaw Blvd
- **Holy Name of Jesus Elementary** • 1955 W Jefferson Blvd
- **King Elementary** • 3989 S Hobart Blvd
- **Leon Garr Learning Institute** • 5101 S Western Ave
- **Lewis Metropolitan Christian School** • 4900 S Western Ave
- **Little Citizens Westside Academy** • 4256 S Western Ave
- **Little Scholars** • 1712 W Jefferson Blvd
- **Manual Arts Senior High School** • 4131 S Vermont Ave
- **Marcus Garvey** • 2916 W Slauson Ave
- **Marie Fegan Schools** • 2069 W Slauson Ave
- **Menlo Ave Elementary** • 4156 Menlo Ave
- **Mid City Magnet School** • 3150 W Adams Blvd
- **Nativity** • 943 W 57th St
- **New Life Academy** • 3200 W Adams Blvd
- **Normandie Avenue Elementary** • 4505 S Raymond Ave
- **Quardobah** • 3420 W Jefferson Blvd
- **Sixth Ave Elementary** • 3109 6th Ave
- **St Agnes** • 1428 W Adams Blvd
- **St Cecilia Elementary** • 4224 S Normandie Ave
- **Testimonial Christian School** • 5701 S Western Ave
- **Transfiguration** • 4020 Roxton Ave
- **United World Christian Educational Center** • 5125 Crenshaw Blvd
- **University of Southern California** • Trousdale Pkwy
- **Vermont Ave Elementary** • 1435 W 27th St
- **Weemes Elementary** • 1260 W 36th Pl
- **Western Avenue Elementary** • 1724 W 53rd St
- **Westside Academy/Little Citizens** • 3411 12th Ave
- **Widney High School** • 2302 S Gramercy Pl
- **Young Continuation** • 3051 W 52nd St

Supermarkets

- **Food 4 Less** • 1748 S Jefferson Blvd
- **Food 4 Less** • 1820 W Slauson Ave
- **Ralph's** • 2600 S Vermont Ave
- **Ralph's** • 3300 W Slauson Ave
- **Ralph's** • 4030 S Western Ave

Santa Monica Freeway

1. W Prescott Ct
2. Humphrey Wk
3. Norumbega Ct
4. Rochester Cir
5. Santa Barbara Ct
6. Kansas Ave

JEFFERSON PARK

2nd Ave Park

Loren Miller Park

Denker Rec Ctr

MLK Jr. Park

Exposition Park

LEIMERT PARK

48th St & 8th Av Park

Vermont Square

48th St Park

Chesterfield Square

USC — PAGE 218

PAGE 238 — South Park Dr

West Adams Blvd · W Jefferson Blvd · Rodeo Rd · Exposition Blvd · W Martin Luther King Jr Blvd · W Vernon Ave · W Slauson Ave · Crenshaw Blvd · S Western Ave · S Normandie Ave · S Vermont Ave · S Hoover St · Arlington Ave · Leimert Blvd · Coliseum St · Exposition Pl

N Coliseum Dr · State Dr · South Park Dr · McClintock Ave · Watt Way · Trousdale Pkwy

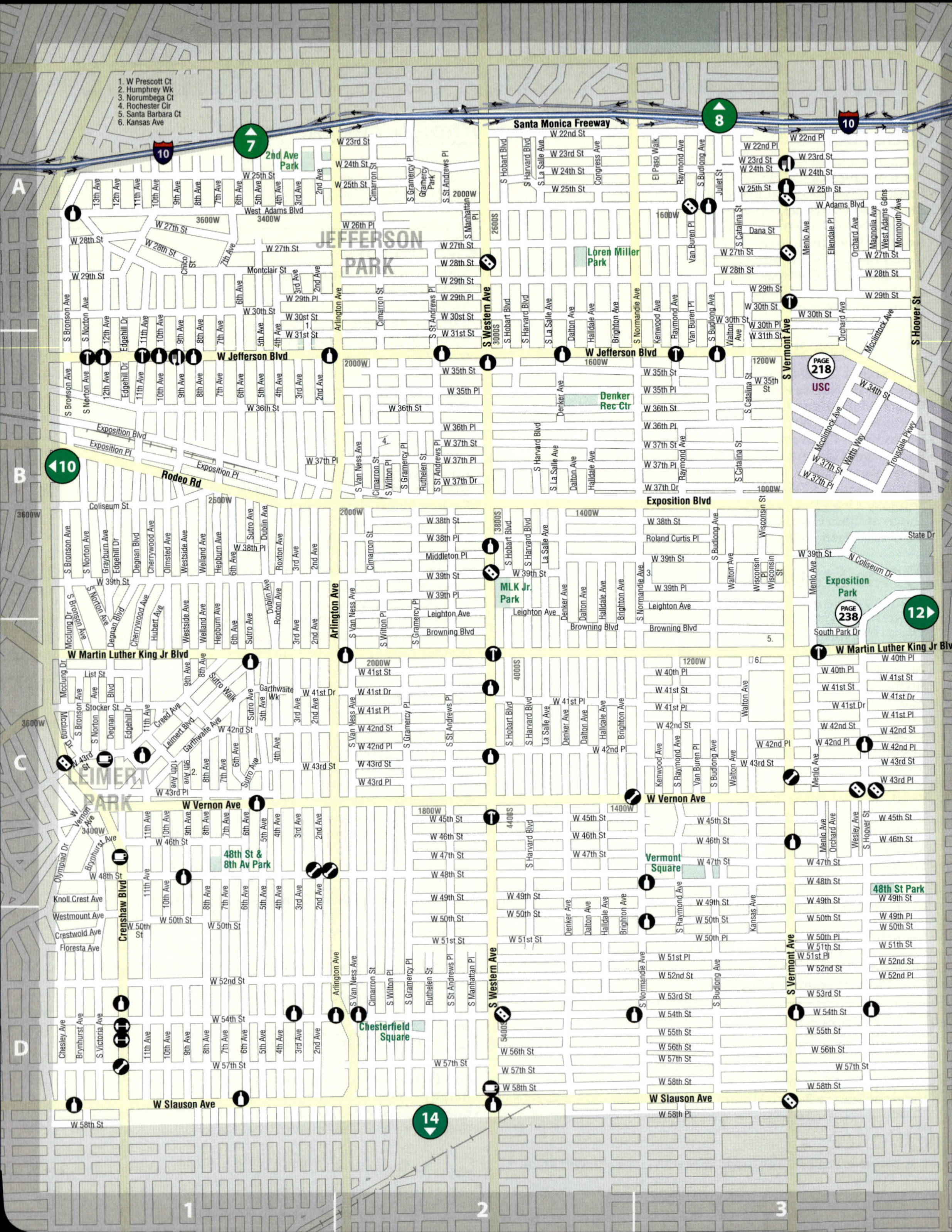

Harold & Belle's Restaurant may have the best Cajun and Creole cooking this side of the Mississippi. We recommend the gumbo!

 Clubs

- **Babe's Ricky Inn** • 4339 Leimert Blvd • 323-295-9112

Coffee

- **Lucy Florence Coffee House** • 4305 Degnan Blvd
- **Starbucks** • 1800 W Slauson Ave
- **Wrapture Coffee House** • 4711 Crenshaw Blvd

Farmer's Markets

- **Farmers' Market** • W Adams Blvd & S Vermont Ave • Wed 1-6

Gyms

- **Black Diamond Enterprises** • 5436 Crenshaw Blvd • 323-291-0294
- **One Stop Fitness Center** • 5426 Crenshaw Blvd • 323-292-2298

Hardware Stores

- **Bell Sales** • 910 W Martin Luther King Jr Blvd • 323-234-7883
- **Bravo's Hardware** • 1439 W Jefferson Blvd • 323-735-3777
- **J & J Hardware** • 1755 W Martin Luther King Jr Blvd • 323-290-0909
- **Kay Hardware & Garden Supplies** • 3318 W Jefferson Blvd • 323-732-6966
- **Peterson's Hardware** • 4831 S Western Ave • 323-292-5310
- **Tak's Hardware & Garden Supply** • 3007 W Jefferson Blvd • 323-737-7775
- **True Value Hardware** • 2929 S Vermont Ave • 323-734-4477

Liquor Stores

- **7 Kings Liquor** • 4051 Leimert Blvd
- **Abic Liquor** • 3115 S Western Ave
- **Adlong Liquor** • 1550 W Adams Blvd
- **B & O Liquor Store** • 1339 W Jefferson Blvd
- **Bloom Liquor** • 2718 W Vernon Ave
- **Century Liquor** • 2115 W Jefferson Blvd
- **Century Liquor** • 2301 W 54th St
- **Century Liquor** • 3894 S Western Ave
- **F & J Liquor** • 5360 Crenshaw Blvd
- **Fairway Liquor Market** • 5400 S Hoover St
- **Fifty-Fourth Van Ness** • 2201 W 54th St
- **Ford's Liquor & Delicatessen** • 4629 S Western Ave

- **G & I Liquor** • 3504 W Slauson Ave
- **Gee-Gee Liquors** • 5028 S Normandie Ave
- **Hubert's Liquor** • 4307 Leimert Blvd
- **Jerry's Market & Liquor** • 4279 S Vermont Ave
- **Jesse's Liquor** • 2527 W 54th St
- **John's Liquor** • 2428 S Vermont Ave
- **Kenny's Liquor** • 3104 W 48th St
- **LA Liquor** • 1403 W 54th St
- **Lucky Liquor Store** • 2109 W Martin Luther King Jr Blvd
- **Marvin's Liquor & Deli** • 1650 W Jefferson Blvd
- **Ninth Avenue Liquor Store** • 2833 W Jefferson Blvd
- **Saki Liquor Store** • 3300 W Jefferson Blvd
- **Slauson Liquor** • 2825 W Slauson Ave
- **St Andrews Place Liquors** • 1894 W Jefferson Blvd
- **T's Liquor Store** • 3019 W Jefferson Blvd
- **Two & One Liquor Store** • 4829 S Normandie Ave
- **West-Vern Liquor** • 4381 S Western Ave
- **Wine Barrel Liquors** • 4250 S Hoover St

Movie Theaters

- **California Science Center IMAX** • 700 State Dr

Pet Stores

- **Darell Pet Supply** • 2369 W 48th St • 323-295-3124
- **Dog Lovers of America** • 5702 Crenshaw Blvd • 323-298-8811
- **El Eden Pet Shop** • 4403 S Normandie Ave • 323-263-3138
- **M & R Pet Supplies** • 2367 W 48th St • 323-299-9536
- **Tong's Tropical Fish & Pets** • 4327 S Vermont Ave • 323-235-4370

Restaurants

- **Harold & Belle's** • 2920 W Jefferson Blvd • 323-735-9023
- **La Barca** • 2414 S Vermont Ave • 323-758-7433

Video Rental

- **Alpha Video** • 807 W Vernon Ave • 323-233-8930
- **Blockbuster** • 5323 S Western Ave • 323-290-7691
- **Blockbuster** • 728 W Vernon Ave • 323-238-0146
- **Blockbuster** • 4299 Crenshaw Blvd • 323-295-7233
- **Echo Video & Mini Mart** • 2701 S Western Ave • 323-735-7411
- **Johnny's Video** • 2709 S Vermont Ave • 323-733-0862
- **Omni Video** • 5862 S Vermont Ave • 323-759-7100
- **Video World** • 2600 S Vermont Ave • 323-733-1877

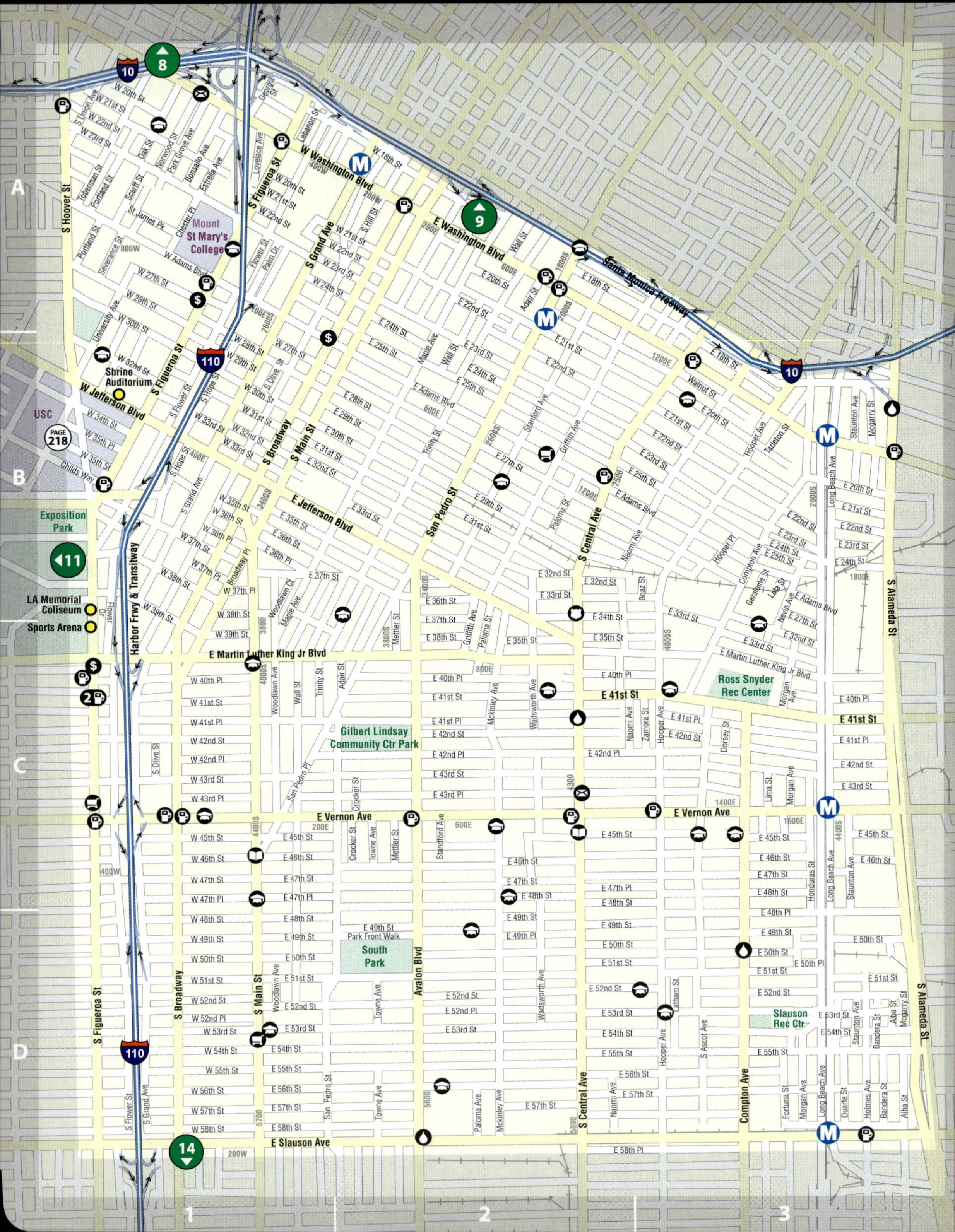

N

Grid references (left margin): A, B, C, D

Bottom columns: 1, 2, 3

Freeways: I-10, I-110

Connector tiles: 8, 9, 11, 14

Key places and labels:

Mount St Mary's College
Shrine Auditorium
W Jefferson Blvd
USC
PAGE 218
Exposition Park
LA Memorial Coliseum
Sports Arena
Childs Way
Gilbert Lindsay Community Ctr Park
South Park
Park Front Walk
Ross Snyder Rec Center
Slauson Rec Ctr
E Martin Luther King Jr Blvd

Streets and avenues:

S Hoover St
Toberman St
Portland St
Scarff St
St James Pk
Severance St
University Ave
Oak St
Norwood St
Park Grove Ave
Bonsallo Ave
Estrella Ave
Flower St
Palm Dr
Lovelace St
Lebanon St
Georgia St
S Figueroa St
S Grand Ave
Flower St
S Hope St
S Olive St
S Broadway
S Main St
Trinity St
San Pedro St
S Central Ave
Maple Ave
Wall St
Stanford Ave
Griffith Ave
Compton Ave
Paloma St
Naomi Ave
Hooper Ave
Ascot Ave
Staunton Ave
Long Beach Ave
S Alameda St
Mateo St
Tarleton St
Walnut St
Geraldine St
Zamora St
Boaz St
Morgan Ave
Dorsey St
Latham St
Honduras St
Fortuna St
Duarte St
Holmes Ave
Bandera St
Alba St
McGarry St
Luma St
Harbor Frwy & Transitway
S Flower St

Cross streets (numbered):

W 20th St, W 21st St, W 22nd St, W 23rd St, W 18th St
W Washington Blvd, E Washington Blvd
W 24th St, W 27th St, W 28th St, W 30th St, W 31st St, W 32nd St, W 33rd St, W 34th St, W 35th St, W 35th Pl
W Adams Blvd, E Adams Blvd
E 18th St, E 20th St, E 21st St, E 22nd St, E 23rd St, E 24th St, E 25th St, E 27th St, E 28th St, E 29th St, E 30th St, E 31st St, E 32nd St, E 33rd St, E 34th St, E 35th St, E 36th St, E 37th St, E 38th St
W 36th St, W 37th St, W 37th Pl, W 38th St, W 39th St
E Jefferson Blvd
E Martin Luther King Jr Blvd
W 40th Pl, W 41st St, W 42nd St, W 42nd Pl, W 43rd St, W 43rd Pl
E 40th Pl, E 41st St, E 41st Pl, E 42nd St, E 42nd Pl, E 43rd St
E Vernon Ave
W 45th St, W 46th St, W 47th St, W 47th Pl, W 48th St, W 49th St, W 50th St, W 51st St, W 52nd St, W 52nd Pl, W 53rd St, W 54th St, W 55th St, W 56th St, W 57th St, W 58th St
E 45th St, E 46th St, E 47th St, E 47th Pl, E 48th St, E 49th St, E 49th Pl, E 50th St, E 51st St, E 52nd St, E 52nd Pl, E 53rd St, E 54th St, E 55th St, E 56th St, E 57th St, E 58th St
E Slauson Ave
E 58th Pl
Avalon Blvd
Woodlawn Ave
Crocker St
Mettler St
Towne Ave
Standford Ave
McKinley Ave
Wadsworth Ave
Kevin Ave
Mevin Ave

Freeways/landmarks:

Santa Monica Freeway
Santa Monica Freeway

Grid coordinates labels: 200W, 400W, 800W, 200E, 400E, 600E, 800E, 1200E, 1400E, 1600E, 2000E, 2500E, 2600S, 3400S, 3800S, 4000S, 4400S, 5600, 5700, 5800

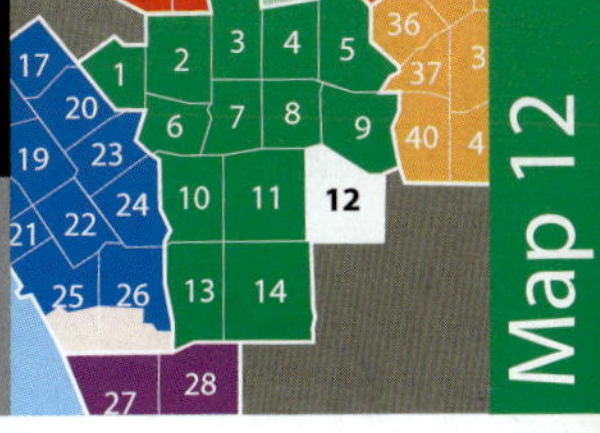

Most Westsiders are familiar with this area for one reason: the Shrine Auditorium, which frequently hosts the Oscars and Emmys, along with the occasional rock concert. It may surprise many to know that the Shrine Auditorium is used most often by the Shriners. The Shrine's vast size and unique appearance, which resembles an Arabian mosque, make it a great landmark when navigating the area or giving directions.

$ Banks

- **Bank of America** · 2703 S Figueroa St
- **Broadway Federal Bank** · 4001 S Figueroa St
- **Wells Fargo Bank** · 141 W Adams Blvd

Car Washes

- **Bull's Truck Wash** · 1625 S Alameda St
- **Manuel's Car Wash** · 5821 Avalon Blvd
- **Martinez Hand Car Wash** · 5000 Compton Ave
- **Westland Car Wash** · 4166 S Central Ave

Gas Stations

- **76** · 1900 S Broadway
- **76** · 505 W Vernon Ave
- **Arco** · 1800 E Slauson Ave
- **Arco** · 2211 S Hoover St
- **Arco** · 4424 S Central Ave
- **Arco** · 4442 S Avalon Blvd
- **Chevron** · 3584 S Figueroa St
- **Chevron** · 4000 S Figueroa St
- **Chevron** · 4088 S Figueroa St
- **Chevron** · 525 W Washington Blvd
- **Chevron** · 650 E Washington Blvd
- **Mobil** · 1690 S Alameda St
- **Mobil** · 2620 S Figueroa St
- **Mobil** · 315 W Vernon Ave
- **Shell** · 1285 E Vernon Ave
- **Shell** · 1317 E Washington Blvd
- **Shell** · 1900 S San Pedro St
- **Shell** · 2603 S Central Ave
- **Shell** · 4380 S Broadway
- **Shell** · 4403 S Figueroa St

Landmarks

- **LA Memorial Coliseum** · 3911 S Figueroa St
- **Shrine Auditorium** · 665 W Jefferson Blvd
- **Sports Arena** · 3939 S Figueroa St

Libraries

- **Los Angeles Library** · 4504 S Central Ave · 323-234-9106
- **Los Angeles Library** · 4607 S Main St · 323-234-1685

Police

- **Los Angeles Police Dept** · 3400 S Central Ave · 323-846-6547

Post Offices

- 4352 S Central Ave
- 819 W Washington Blvd

Schools

- **20th Street Elementary** · 1353 E 20th St
- **28th Street Elementary** · 2807 Stanford Ave
- **32nd Street USE Performing Arts** · 822 W 32nd St
- **49th Street Elementary** · 750 E 49th St
- **Accelerated School** · 116 E Martin Luther King Jr Blvd
- **Adams Middle School** · 151 W 30th St
- **Arco Iris Primary Center** · 4504 Ascot Ave
- **Ascot Ave Elementary** · 1447 E 45th St
- **Carver Middle School** · 4410 McKinley Ave
- **Holy Cross Middle School** · 104 W 47th Pl
- **Hooper Ave Elementary** · 1225 E 52nd St
- **Jefferson Community Adult School** · 1319 E 41st St
- **Jefferson New Middle School** · 644 E 56th St
- **Jefferson Senior High School** · 1319 E 41st St
- **John Adams Middle School** · 151 W 30th St
- **Los Angeles Academy Middle School** · 644 E 56th St
- **Main Street Elementary** · 129 E 53rd St
- **Mount St Mary's College** · 10 Chester Pl
- **Nevin Ave Elementary** · 1569 E 32nd St
- **Norwood Street Elementary** · 2020 Oak St
- **Page Multicultural Learning Academy** · 216 W Vernon Ave
- **San Pedro Street Elementary** · 1635 S San Pedro St
- **St Odilia** · 5300 Hooper Ave
- **St Vincent** · 2333 S Figueroa St
- **Temple Baptist Church Star Charter** · 2120 Estella Ave
- **Trinity Street Elementary** · 3736 Trinity St
- **University of Southern California** · Trousdale Pkwy
- **Victory Baptist Day Elementary** · 892 E 48th St
- **Wadsworth Ave Elementary** · 981 E 41st St
- **West Vernon Avenue Elementary** · 4312 S Grand Ave

Supermarkets

- **Food 4 Less** · 5318 S Main St
- **Jon's Supermarket** · 1011 E Adams Blvd
- **Ralph's** · 4360 S Figueroa St

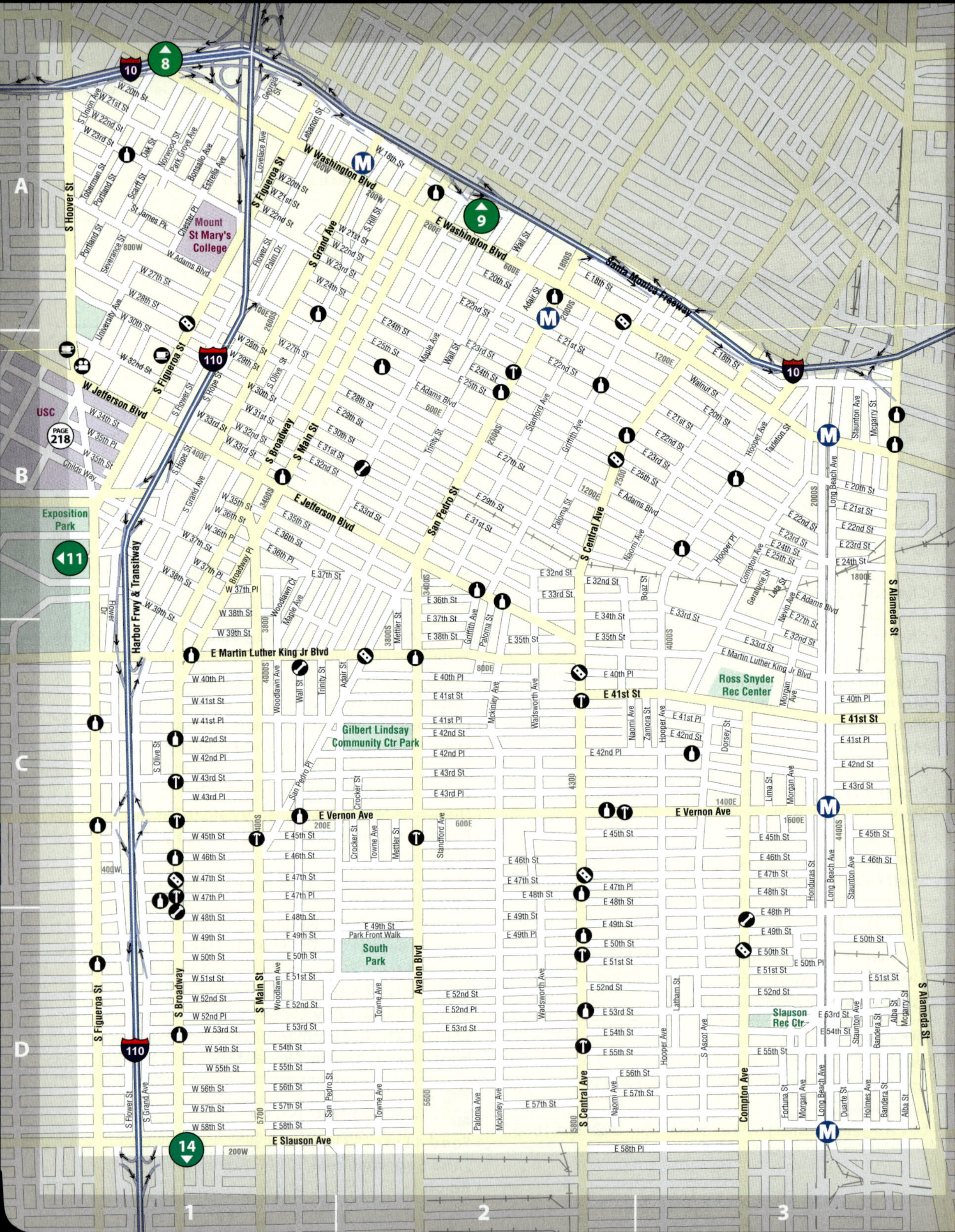

N
10
8
S Union Ave
W 20th St
W 21st St
W 22nd St
W 23rd St
Oak St
Norwood St
Park Grove Ave
Estrella Ave
Toberman St
Portland St
Scarff St
St James Pk
Georgia St
Lebanon St
Lovelace Ave
S Figueroa St
W Washington Blvd
W 18th St
400W
W Washington Blvd
E Washington Blvd
9
200E
Wall St
Adair St
Santa Monica Freeway
Mount St Mary's College
Flower St
Palm Dr
W Adams Blvd
Portland St
Severance St
800W
University Ave
W 27th St
W 28th St
W 30th St
W 32nd St
S Grand Ave
W 21st St
W 22nd St
W 23rd St
W 24th St
S Hill St
E 20th St
E 22nd St
E 23rd St
E 24th St
E 21st St
E 22nd St
E 18th St
2400S
1200E
M
M
Adair St
S Flower St
S Hope St
260E
W 28th St
W 27th St
W 29th St
400E
E 24th St
E 25th St
Maple Ave
Wall St
Trinity St
Stanford Ave
Griffith Ave
E Adams Blvd
600E
Walnut St
E 20th St
Hooper Ave
Talt St
E 18th St
10
M
Staunton Ave
Mcgarry St
110
W Jefferson Blvd
S Figueroa St
USC
PAGE 218
W 34th St
W 35th St Pl
W 35th St
Childs Way
S Flower St
S Hope St
400E
S Olive St
W 30th St
W 31st St
W 32nd St
W 33rd St
S Broadway
S Main St
W 27th St
W 28th St
W 29th St
W 30th St
E 31st St
E 32nd St
San Pedro St
E 27th St
E 29th St
E 31st St
2200S
Paloma St
Naomi Ave
S Central Ave
E Adams Blvd
1200E
2500
E 25th St
E 23rd St
E 22nd St
E 21st St
Hooper Ave
Compton Ave
Geraghty St
Lata St
Nevin Ave
E 27th St
E Adams Blvd
E 22nd St
E 23rd St
E 24th St
1800E
S Alameda St
Long Beach Ave
E 20th St
E 21st St
E 22nd St
E 23rd St
E 24th St
Exposition Park
11
S Grand Ave
Broadway Pl
Maple Ave
Woodlawn Ct
W 35th St
W 36th St
W 37th St
W 38th St
W 37th Pl
W 39th St
E Jefferson Blvd
E 33rd St
E 35th St
E 36th St
E 37th St
E 38th St
Griffith Ave
Paloma St
3400S
800E
E 32nd St
E 33rd St
E 34th St
E 35th St
4000S
Boaz St
E 33rd St
E 32nd St
E Martin Luther King Jr Blvd
Harbor Frwy & Transitway
Flower Dr
E Martin Luther King Jr Blvd
3800
3800S
Mettler St
Adair St
Trinity St
E 40th Pl
E 41st St
E 40th Pl
E 41st St
Morgan Ave
Ross Snyder Rec Center
E 40th Pl
E 41st St
W 40th Pl
W 41st St
W 41st Pl
Woodlawn Ave
Wall St
4400S
Mckinley Ave
Wadsworth Ave
Naomi Ave
Zamora Ave
Hooper Ave
Dorsey St
E 41st St
S Olive St
W 42nd St
W 42nd St
W 43rd St
W 43rd St
Gilbert Lindsay Community Ctr Park
E 42nd Pl
E 42nd Pl
E 43rd St
E 43rd Pl
4300
E 41st Pl
E 42nd Pl
Lima St
Morgan Ave
E 42nd Pl
E 43rd St
M
E 41st Pl
E 42nd St
E 43rd St
San Pedro St
Crocker St
Crocker St
Towne Ave
Standford Ave
Mettler St
E Vernon Ave
200E
600E
E Vernon Ave
1400E
E Vernon Ave
1600E
M
400W
W 45th St
W 46th St
W 47th St
W 47th Pl
W 48th St
E 45th St
E 46th St
E 47th St
E 47th Pl
E 48th St
E 46th St
E 47th St
E 48th St
E 49th St
Latham St
S Ascot Ave
Honduras St
Staunton Ave
E 45th St
E 46th St
E 47th St
E 48th St
E 45th St
E 46th St
E 47th Pl
E 48th Pl
S Broadway
S Main St
Woodlawn Ave
W 49th St
W 50th St
W 51st St
W 52nd St
W 52nd Pl
E 49th St
E 50th St
E 49th St
Park Front Walk
South Park
Avalon Blvd
E 49th Pl
E 50th St
E 51st St
E 49th St
E 50th St
E 51st St
E 48th Pl
E 49th St
E 50th St
M
E 51st St
W 53rd St
W 54th St
W 55th St
E 51st St
E 52nd St
E 52nd Pl
E 53rd St
E 53rd St
Towne Ave
E 52nd St
E 53rd St
E 54th St
E 55th St
Hooper Ave
Slauson Rec Ctr
Fortuna St
Morgan Ave
Bandera St
Staunton Ave
Mcgarry St
Alba St
E 51st St
E 52nd St
E 53rd St
E 54th St
E 55th St
110
W 56th St
W 57th St
W 58th St
S Figueroa St
S Grand Ave
S Flower St
E 54th St
E 55th St
E 56th St
E 57th St
E 58th St
San Pedro St
Paloma Ave
Mckinley Ave
5600
5700
5800
E 56th St
E 57th St
Naomi Ave
S Central Ave
Compton Ave
Long Beach Ave
Duarte St
Holmes Ave
Bandera St
Alba St
S Alameda St
14
200W
E Slauson Ave
E Slauson Ave
E 58th Pl
A
B
C
D
1
2
3

 Coffee

- **Coffee Factory** · 3014 S Figueroa St
- **Starbucks** · 3303 S Hoover St

Hardware Stores

- **Avalon Tools & Supplies** · 4514 Avalon Blvd · 323-232-6516
- **Banner Hardware** · 4412 S Broadway · 323-231-9012
- **Central Hardware** · 5010 S Central Ave · 323-231-5659
- **Garcia Hardware** · 2414 S San Pedro St · 213-749-0992
- **Jalisco Hardware** · 5423 S Central Ave · 323-231-3340
- **Los Perritos Tools** · 4725 S Broadway · 323-232-1602
- **Main Building Materials** · 4308 S Broadway · 323-235-6253
- **Marce's** · 4500 S Main St · 323-233-9320
- **Munoz Hardware** · 4121 S Central Ave · 323-234-3623
- **Villanuevas Hardware** · 1177 E Vernon Ave · 323-234-6340

Liquor Stores

- **A & D Mini-Mart** · 4006 Avalon Blvd
- **A & J Liquor** · 2527 S Hill St
- **A & J Liquor** · 200 E Vernon Ave
- **Ace Liquor** · 2525 Griffith Ave
- **Bestway Liquors** · 4157 S Figueroa St
- **C & C Liquor** · 4606 S Broadway
- **Central Liquor Mart** · 5000 S Central Ave
- **Davis Liquor & Deli** · 1367 E 42nd Pl
- **Empire Liquor & Market** · 1100 E 22nd St
- **Express Liquor Store** · 1601 S Alameda St
- **Gordon's Liquor & Wines** · 842 E Jefferson Blvd
- **Harry's Corner** · 2315 S Central Ave
- **JKO Liquor** · 255 E Adams Blvd
- **Johnny's Liquor** · 4000 Broadway Pl
- **Kimbo Liquor** · 1161 E Vernon Ave
- **Koko's Liquor** · 5029 S Figueroa St
- **Lee's Market & Liquor** · 936 W 23rd St
- **Louie's Liquor Market** · 908 E Jefferson Blvd
- **Main Street Market** · 3327 S Main St
- **Maple Liquor** · 2401 S San Pedro St
- **Reggie's Liquor & Junior Market** · 4426 S Figueroa St
- **Reggie's Liquor & Junior Market** · 2700 Hooper Ave
- **Sam's Liquor & Market** · 1813 S Main St
- **Steve's Liquor** · 1501 E 22nd St
- **Times Square Liquor** · 4200 S Broadway
- **Toni's Liquor & Deli** · 5955 West Blvd
- **Wally's Liquor Market** · 1955 S San Pedro St
- **Webb's Liquor Store & Sundries** · 4762 S Central Ave

 Movie Theaters

- **Flagship University Village 3** · 3323 S Hoover St

Pet Stores

- **Granero Santa Cruz** · 4876 Compton Ave · 323-235-4707
- **John's Pet Supplies** · 4031 Wall St · 323-231-1414
- **Maple Pets & Supplies** · 3121 Maple Ave · 323-232-8080
- **Maria's Pet Shop** · 4757 S Broadway · 323-234-7887

Video Rental

- **Compton Video** · 5035 Compton Ave · 323-233-2822
- **Danny Boy Video** · 2506 S Central Ave · 323-234-4412
- **Eve's Video** · 4068 S Central Ave · 323-234-0473
- **Hernandez Video** · 4754 S Central Ave · 323-231-0213
- **Perfect Video** · 4005 S San Pedro St · 323-846-8545
- **Roger's Video** · 830 E Washington Blvd · 213-747-2461
- **Video Hits** · 2813 S Figueroa St · 213-748-2928
- **Video Hut** · 4711 S Broadway · 323-232-1662

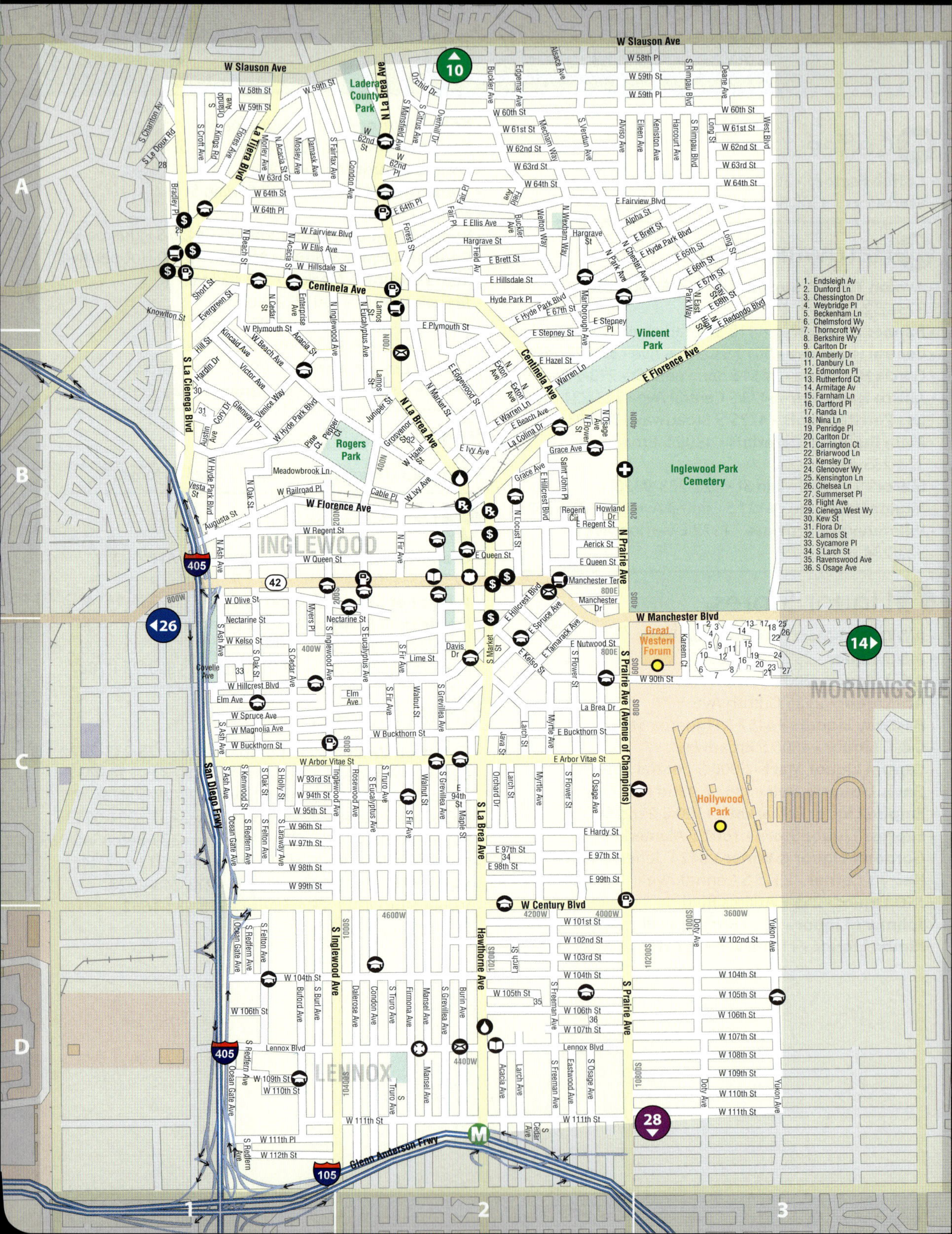

INGLEWOOD
LENNOX
MORNINGSIDE
Ladera County Park
Rogers Park
Vincent Park
Inglewood Park Cemetery
Great Western Forum
Hollywood Park
W Slauson Ave
W Manchester Blvd
W Century Blvd
W Florence Ave
E Florence Ave
Centinela Ave
N La Brea Ave
S La Brea Ave
S La Cienega Blvd
Hawthorne Ave
S Prairie Ave (Avenue of Champions)
N Prairie Ave
S Inglewood Ave
San Diego Frwy
Glenn Anderson Frwy
W Arbor Vitae St
E Arbor Vitae St
La Tijera Blvd
Lennox Blvd
1. Endsleigh Av
2. Dunford Ln
3. Chessington Dr
4. Weybridge Pl
5. Beckenham Ln
6. Chelmsford Wy
7. Thorncroft Wy
8. Berkshire Wy
9. Carlton Dr
10. Amberly Dr
11. Danbury Ln
12. Edmonton Pl
13. Rutherford Ct
14. Armitage Av
15. Farnham Ln
16. Dartford Pl
17. Randa Ln
18. Nina Ln
19. Penridge Pl
20. Carlton Dr
21. Carrington Ct
22. Briarwood Ln
23. Kensley Dr
24. Glenover Wy
25. Kensington Ln
26. Chelsea Ln
27. Summerset Pl
28. Flight Ave
29. Cienega West Wy
30. Kew St
31. Flora Dr
32. Lamos St
33. Sycamore Pl
34. S Larch St
35. Ravenswood Ave
36. S Osage Ave

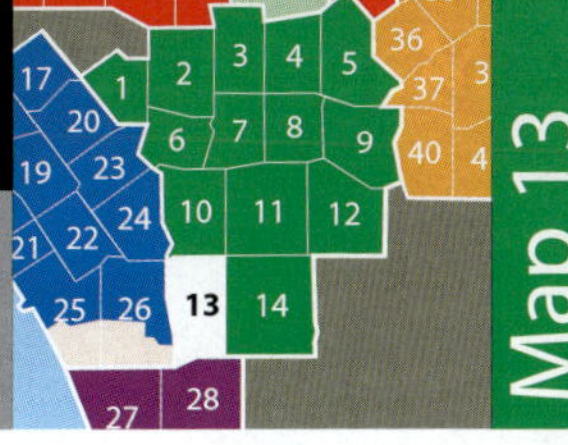

The Forum used to be home to the Lakers, Kings, and Sparks and was considered L.A.'s premier place to see a sporting event. But then Staples Center opened and lured virtually every L.A. team—and most major rock concerts—away. The Forum was recently purchased by the Faithful Central Bible Church, who still rent the arena for events like ice shows and the circus, but who now hold Sunday services on the very space where Magic Johnson once played.

$ Banks

- **Bank of America** · 330 E Manchester Blvd
- **Bank of America** · 6611 La Cienega Westway St
- **Broadway Federal Bank** · 170 N Market St
- **Union Bank** · 5245 W Centinela Ave
- **Union Bank** · 6719 La Tijera Blvd
- **Washington Mutual** · 355 E Manchester Blvd
- **Wells Fargo Bank** · 400 S Market St

Car Washes

- **Inglewood Car Wash** · 320 N La Brea Ave
- **Lennox Car Wash** · 10709 Hawthorne Blvd

Gas Stations

- **76** · 1430 N La Brea Ave
- **76** · 633 W Manchester Blvd
- **Alliance** · 145 E Manchester Blvd
- **Chevron** · 4015 W Century Blvd
- **Mobil** · 1007 N La Brea Ave
- **Mobil** · 5215 W Centinela Ave
- **Unified** · 1244 S Inglewood Ave

Hospitals

- **Centinela Hospital Medical Center** · 555 E Hardy St · 310-673-4660
- **Daniel Freeman Memorial Hospital** · 333 N Prairie Ave · 310-674-7050

Landmarks

- **Hollywood Park** · 1050 S Prairie Ave
- **Great Western Forum** · Manchester Ave & Prairie Ave

Libraries

- **Inglewood City Library** · 101 W Manchester Blvd · 310-412-5380
- **Lennox LA County Library** · 4359 Lennox Blvd · 310-674-0385

24-Hour Pharmacies

- **Sav-On** · 222 Market St · 310-671-0441
- **Walgreens** · 230 N La Brea Ave · 310-671-2049

Police

- **Inglewood Police Dept** · 1 W Manchester Blvd · 310-412-5210

Post Offices

- 300 E Hillcrest Blvd
- 4443 Lennox Blvd
- 811 N La Brea Ave

Schools

- **A F Williams Christian Academy** · 1437 W Centinela Ave
- **Academy for Early Learning** · 1020 N Park Ave
- **Basics Plus Learning Academy** · 4323 W Century Blvd
- **Buford Elementary** · 4919 W 109th St
- **Centinela Elementary** · 1123 Marlborough Ave
- **Communion Christian Academy** · 6201 S La Brea Ave
- **Coporate Preparatory Academy** · 101 N La Brea Ave
- **Crozier Junior High School** · 151 N Grevillea Ave
- **Felton Elementary** · 10417 Felton Ave
- **Good Shepherd Lutheran** · 901 Maple Ave
- **Highland Elementary** · 430 Venice Way
- **Hillcrest High School** · 441 W Hillcrest Blvd
- **Hudnall Elementary** · 331 Olive St
- **Inglewood Ave Kindergarten** · 215 S Inglewood Ave
- **Inglewood Christian School** · 215 E Hillcrest Blvd
- **Inglewood High School** · 231 S Grevillea Ave
- **Inglewood Middle School** · 151 N Grevillea Ave
- **Jefferson Elementary** · 10322 Condon Ave
- **Kelso Elementary** · 809 E Kelso St
- **La Tijera Elementary** · 1415 S La Tijera Blvd
- **Morningside High School** · 10500 Yukon Ave
- **Oak Street Elementary** · 633 S Oak St
- **Parent Elementary** · 5354 W 64th St
- **Payne Elementary** · 215 W 94th St
- **Playtime Preschool/Kindergarten** · 220 S Eucalyptus Ave
- **Saint Mary's Academy** · 701 Grace Ave
- **Saluson Learning Center** · 260 N Locust St
- **St John's Chrysostom Elementary** · 530 E Florence Ave
- **Tender Care Kindergarten** · 336 E Spruce Ave
- **University of Children** · 1518 Centinela Ave
- **Whelan Elementary** · 4125 W 105th St
- **Wiz** · 121 W Arbor Vitae
- **Worthington Elementary** · 11101 Yukon Ave

Supermarkets

- **Ralph's** · 5245 W Centinela Ave
- **Ralph's** · 950 N La Brea Ave
- **Von's** · 500 Manchester Ter

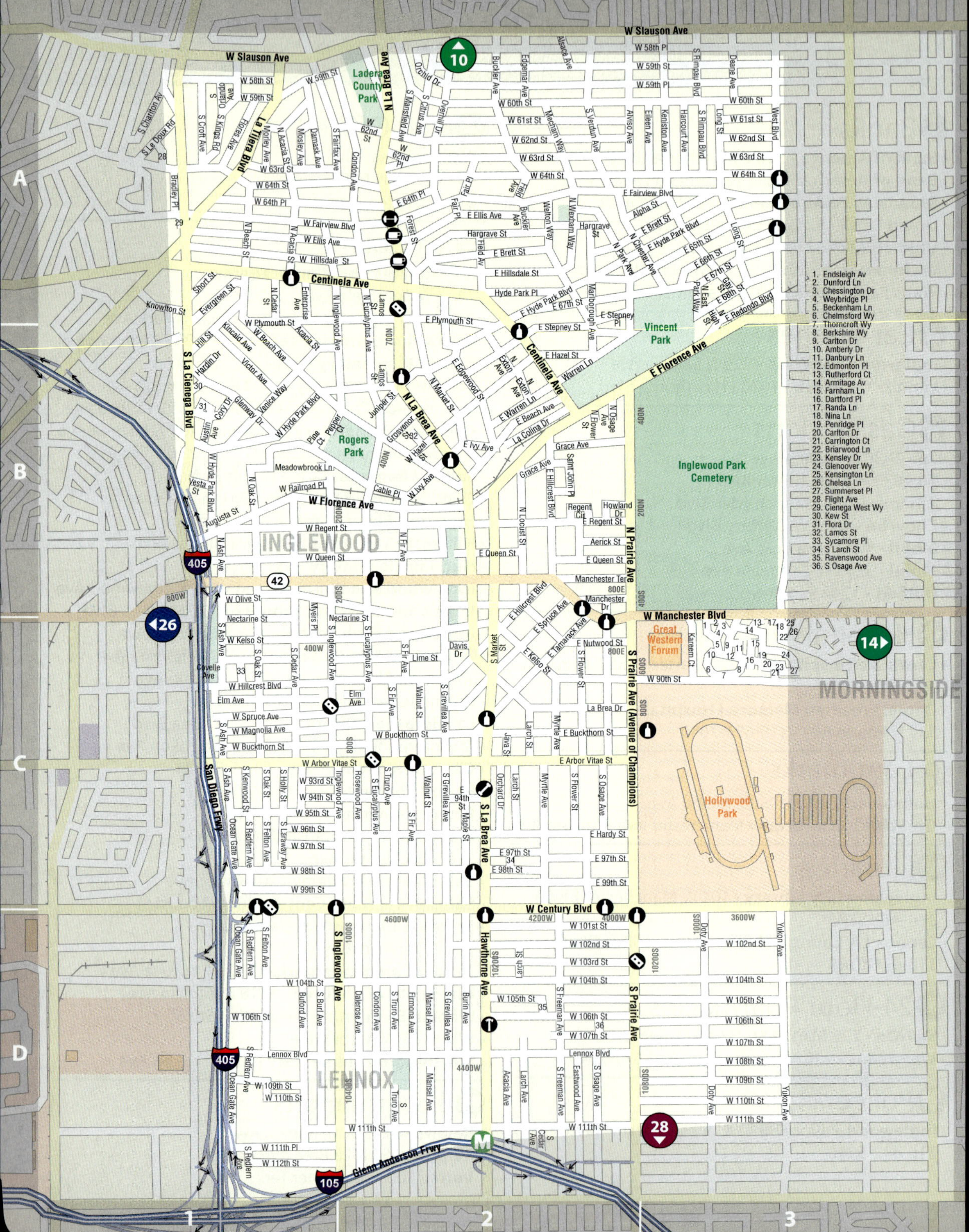

W Slauson Ave
W Slauson Ave
Ladera County Park
10
W 58th St
W 59th St
N La Brea Blvd
Orchid Dr
Overhill Dr
N Mansfield Ave
S Citrus Ave
N Citrus Ave
W 62nd
W 58th St
W 59th St
Flores Blvd
S L'e Doux Av
S Charlton Av
S Osapo Av
S Kings Rd
S Croft St
Mosley Ave
Damascus Ave
N Fairfax Ave
Condon Ave
W 60th St
W 61st St
W 62nd St
W 63rd St
W 64th St
S Verdun Ave
Meehan Way
Field Ave
Walton Ave
N Wheelam Way
Hargrave St
Alsace Ave
Edgemar Ave
Buckler Ave
Eileen Ave
Kenniston Ave
Harcourt Ave
S Rimpau Blvd
Deane Ave
West Blvd
W 58th Pl
W 59th St
W 59th St
W 60th St
W 61st St
W 62nd St
W 63rd St
W 64th St
La Tijera Blvd
N Beach St
N Acacia St
N Ellis Ave
Short St
Evergreen St
Enterprise
Knowlton St
Kincaid Ave
Hardin Dr
Hill St
N Cedar St
N Inglewood Ave
N Eucalyptus Ave
N La Brea Ave
Lamos St
Lamos St
Fir Ave
W 63rd St
W 64th St
W 64th Pl
W Fairview Blvd
N Acacia Ave
W Ellis Ave
W Hillsdale Ave
Centinela Ave
W Plymouth St
W Beach Ave
Acacia St
Victor Ave
Venice Way
Glenway Dr
Cory Dr
Unisky
Fairt
Field Ave
E Ellis Ave
E Brett St
E Hillsdale St
E Plymouth St
E Stepney St
E Hazel St
Forest
N Wheelam Way
Hargrave St
Alpha St
Marlborough Ave
N Hyde Park Blvd
N Chester Ave
E Fairview Blvd
E Brett St
E Hyde Park Blvd
E 65th St
E 66th St
E 67th St
Hyde Park Pl
E Hyde Park Blvd
E Stepney Pl
Vincent Park
Long St
N East High
N Redondo Blvd
E 68th St
E Florence Ave
E Florence Ave
Inglewood Park Cemetery
N Prairie Ave
Warren Ln
Grace Ave
Saint John Pl
Grace Ave
Regent
Howland
Aerick St
E Queen St
N Locust St
N 40th
N 40th
N Osage Ave
N Flower Ave
N 79th Ave
E Warren Ln
E Beach Ave
E Ivy Ave
E Market St
Exton Ave
E Edgewood Ave
Junpier St
Grosvenor St
N Market St
N Fisher St
E Ivy Ave
Cable Pl
W Ivy Ave
W Florence Ave
INGLEWOOD
Rogers Park
Meadowbrook Ln
W Railroad Pl
Vesta St
Augusta St
N Oak St
N Ash Ave
405
42
26
W Regent St
W Queen St
W Olive St
Nectarine St
S Inglewood Ave
S Ash St
S Kelso St
S Oak St
S Cedar Ave
Myers Pl
Nectarine St
S Eucalyptus Ave
E Queen St
E Spruce Ave
Manchester Ter
Manchester Dr
W Manchester Blvd
Great Western Forum
Kareem Ct
S Prairie Ave (Avenue of Champions)
S Prairie Ave
W 90th St
MORNINGSIDE
14
Hollywood Park
Lime St
Fir St
Elm Ave
Walnut St
Davis Dr
Java St
Larch St
Myrtle Ave
S Flower Ave
S Osage Ave
La Brea Dr
E Buckthorn St
E Arbor Vitae St
E Hardy St
E 97th St
E 98th St
E 99th St
W Century Blvd
W Hillcrest Blvd
Elm Ave
W Spruce Ave
W Magnolia Ave
W Buckthorn St
W Arbor Vitae St
W 93rd St
W 94th St
W 95th St
W 96th St
W 97th St
W 98th St
W 99th St
San Diego Frwy
S Ash Ave
S Kenwood St
S Oak St
S Holly St
Inglewood Ave
Rosewood Ave
S Eucalyptus Ave
S Truro Ave
S Grevillea Ave
Walnut St
S Fir St
Maple St
Orchid Dr
Larch St
S La Brea Ave
S Osage Ave
S Flower Ave
E Buckthorn St
S Larch St
S Redfern Ave
Ocean Gate Ave
S Felton Ave
S Larawey Ave
Covelle Ave
W 100th St
W 101st St
W 102nd St
W 103rd St
W 104th St
W 105th St
W 106th St
W 107th St
W 108th St
W 109th St
W 110th St
W 111th St
Doty Ave
Yukon Ave
S Prairie Ave
Eastwood Ave
S Osage Ave
28
405
105
Glenn Anderson Frwy
LENNOX
Lennox Blvd
W 109th St
W 110th St
W 111th St
W 111th Pl
W 112th St
S Redfern
S Cedar Ave
Hawthorne Ave
S Inglewood Ave
Buford Ave
Burl Ave
Dalerose Ave
Condon Ave
Truro Ave
Mansel Ave
Firmona Ave
S Grevillea Ave
Burin Ave
S Freeman Ave
S Freeman Ave
W 104th St
W 105th St
W 106th St
W 107th St
1. Endsleigh Av
2. Dunford Ln
3. Chessington Dr
4. Weybridge Pl
5. Beckenham Ln
6. Chelmsford Wy
7. Thorncroft Wy
8. Berkshire Wy
9. Carlton Dr
10. Amberly Dr
11. Danbury Ln
12. Edmonton Pl
13. Rutherford Ct
14. Armitage Av
15. Farnham Ln
16. Dartford Pl
17. Randa Ln
18. Nina Ln
19. Penridge Pl
20. Carlton Dr
21. Carrington Ct
22. Briarwood Ln
23. Kensley Dr
24. Glenoover Wy
25. Kensington Pl
26. Chelsea Ln
27. Summerset Pl
28. Flight Ave
29. Cienega West Wy
30. Kew St
31. Flora Dr
32. Lennos St
33. Sycamore Pl
34. S Larch St
35. Ravenswood Ave
36. S Osage Ave

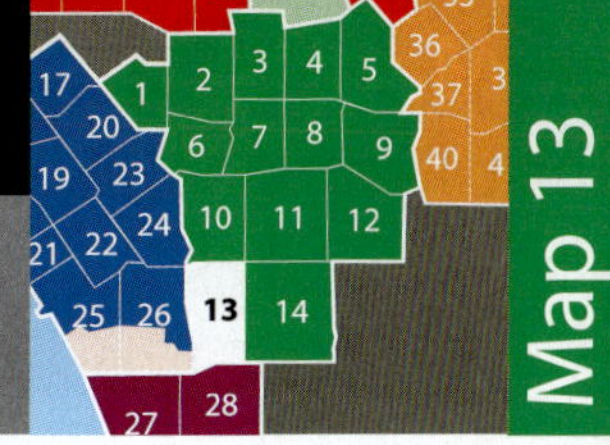

During its racing season, Hollywood Park makes a concerted effort to lure younger patrons with low prices and Friday night rock concerts. But since the Motels and Frankie Goes To Hollywood have been recent headliners, they might want to try a bit harder. If you're into betting on the ponies, Hollywood Park is the only place to go.

Coffee

- **Cafe Future & Gallery** · 1314 N La Brea Ave
- **East Ellis Coffee House** · 1139 N La Brea Ave

Gyms

- **Huff N Puff Gym** · 1321 N La Brea Ave · 310-672-5055

Hardware Stores

- **Inglewood Pipe & Supply** · 10600 Hawthorne Blvd · 323-678-6261

Liquor Stores

- **Airport Liquors & Groceries** · 420 N La Brea Ave
- **Andy's Liquor** · 440 W Manchester Blvd
- **Arena Liquor & Mini Market** · 816 E Manchester Blvd
- **B & B Liquor** · 4082 W Century Blvd
- **Banks of Scotland Liquor Store** · 5014 W Century Blvd
- **Forum Liquors** · 801 S Prairie Ave
- **Happy Time Liquors** · 730 N La Brea Ave
- **Hyde Park Jr Liquor** · 622 Centinela Ave
- **JR's Liquor** · 10025 S Inglewood Ave
- **Liquorette** · 1400 Centinela Ave
- **Martino's Liquor** · 706 E Manchester Blvd
- **Mr B's Liquor Marts** · 10025 S Prairie Ave
- **Nelson's Liquor Store** · 1435 N 64th St
- **Penny-Pincher Junior Market** · 6430 West Blvd
- **Speedy Spot Liquor** · 1190 S La Brea Ave
- **Tran's Liquor** · 10021 Hawthorne Blvd
- **Will's Liquor Jr Market & Mxcn** · 6513 West Blvd

Pet Stores

- **Distributors Feed Co** · 4435 Lennox Blvd · 310-677-0200
- **Inglewood Pet Shop** · 979 S La Brea Ave · 310-677-2225

Video Rental

- **Blockbuster** · 500 E Manchester Blvd · 310-680-9860
- **Carrousel Video** · 913 S Inglewood Ave · 310-677-1888
- **Hollywood Video** · 425 E Manchester Blvd · 310-677-6510
- **Starr Video** · 313 W Arbor Vitae St · 310-680-7325
- **Video Plus** · 933 N La Brea Ave · 310-412-3105
- **Video Vision** · 5006 W Century Blvd · 310-674-0004
- **Zacatecas Video** · 10302 S Prairie Ave · 310-419-7948

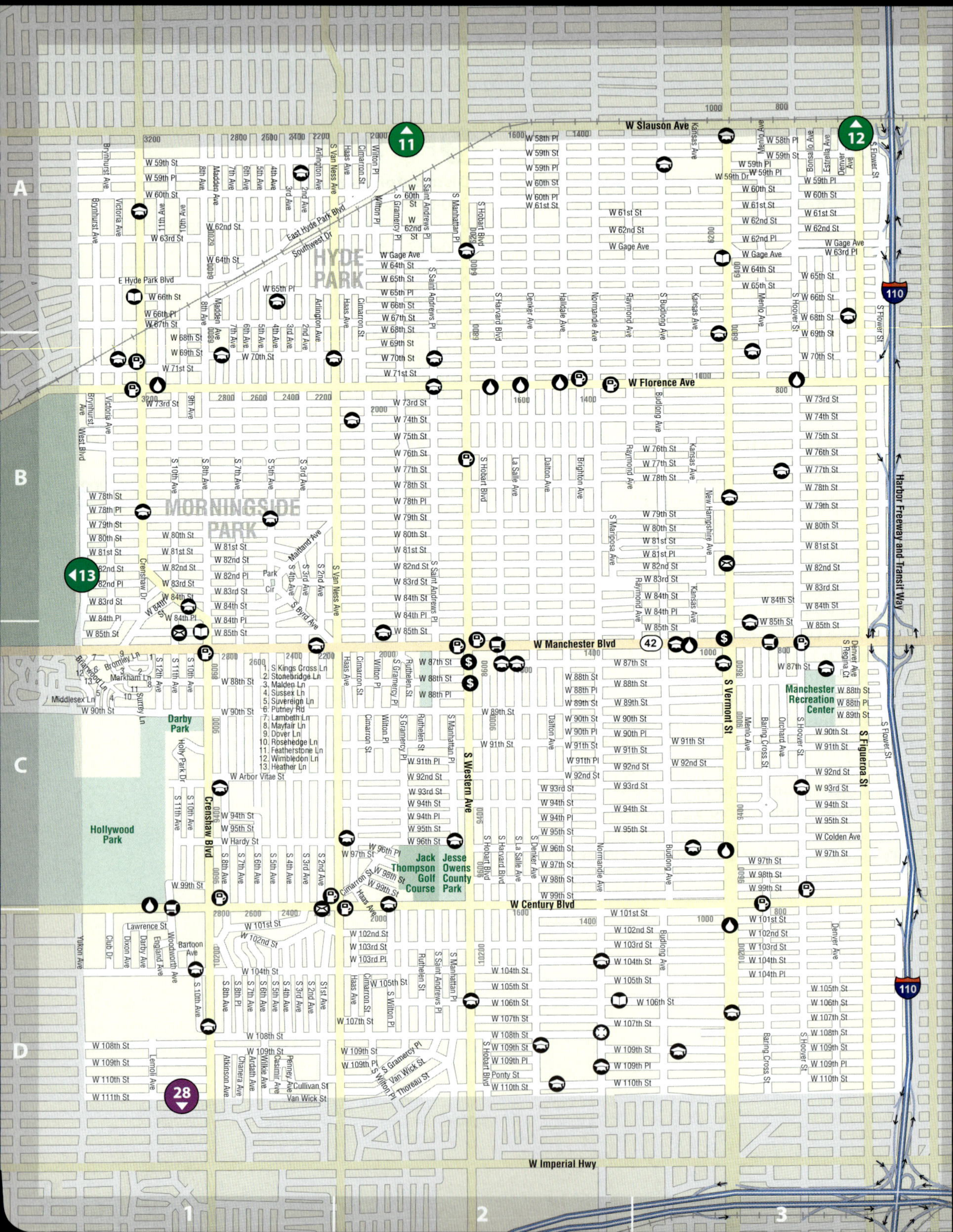
N
HYDE PARK
MORNINGSIDE PARK
W Slauson Ave
W Florence Ave
W Manchester Blvd
W Century Blvd
W Imperial Hwy
Crenshaw Blvd
S Western Ave
S Vermont St
S Figueroa St
Harbor Freeway and Transit Way
East Hyde Park Blvd
Southwest Dr
E Hyde Park Blvd
West Blvd
S Van Ness Ave
S Hobart Blvd
S Saint Andrews Pl
S Manhattan Pl
S Budlong Ave
Normandie Ave
Kansas Ave
S Hoover St
Menlo Ave
Darby Park
Hollywood Park
Manchester Recreation Center
Jack Thompson Golf Course
Jesse Owens County Park
1. S Kings Cross Ln
2. Stonebridge Ln
3. Malden Ln
4. Sussex Ln
5. Sovereign Ln
6. Putney Rd
7. Lambeth Ln
8. Mayfair Ln
9. Dover Ln
10. Rosehedge Ln
11. Featherstone Ln
12. Wimbledon Ln
13. Heather Ln
11
12
13
28
42
110
A
B
C
D
1
2
3

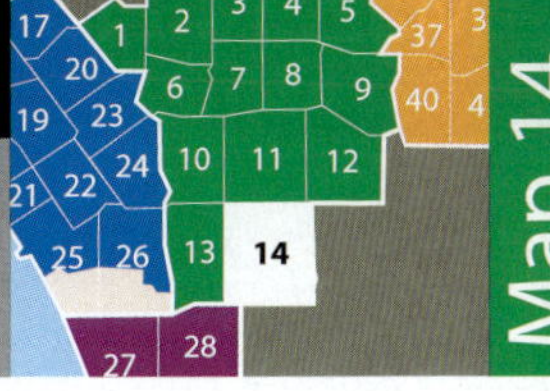

Back in the 1920s, Inglewood was briefly thought of as the "Chinchilla Capital of the World." But the community has largely outgrown its agricultural roots and is now a thriving city with highrises and a population of over 100,000.

$ Banks

- **Bank of America** · 8701 S Western Ave
- **Union Bank** · 8811 S Western Ave
- **Washington Mutual** · 1027 W Manchester Ave

Car Washes

- **Deryl with the Curl Hand Car Wash** · 1454 W Florence Ave
- **Hollypark Car Wash** · 3350 W Century Blvd
- **Manchester Car Wash** · 1111 W Manchester Ave
- **Mike's Hand Car Wash** · 10135 S Vermont Ave
- **Personal Touch Hand Car Wash** · 1624 W Florence Ave
- **Saycey Hand Car Wash** · 9719 S Vermont Ave
- **Spot Car Wash** · 801 W Florence Ave
- **Super Shine Hand Car Wash** · 1724 W Florence Ave
- **Supreme Car Wash** · 3312 W Florence Ave

Gas Stations

- **76** · 1350 W Florence Ave
- **Arco** · 1403 Century Blvd
- **Arco** · 3411 W Florence Ave
- **Arco** · 7600 S Western Ave
- **Mobil** · 1400 W Florence Ave
- **Mobil** · 1803 W Manchester Ave
- **Mobil** · 3016 W Century Blvd
- **Mobil** · 7130 Crenshaw Blvd
- **Mobil** · 850 W Century Blvd
- **Shell** · 2138 W Century Blvd
- **Shell** · 3107 W Manchester Blvd
- **Shell** · 8611 S Western Ave
- **Shell** · 9920 S Hoover St
- **Young's** · 800 W Manchester Ave

Libraries

- **Hyde Park Branch Library** · 6527 Crenshaw Blvd · 323-750-7241
- **John Muir Library** · 1005 W 64th St · 323-789-4800
- **Los Angeles Public Library** · 1340 W 106th St · 323-757-9373
- **Morningside Park Library** · 3202 W 85th St · 310-412-5400

Post Offices

- 2200 W Century Blvd
- 3212 W 85th St
- 8200 S Vermont Ave

Schools

- **59th Street Elementary** · 5939 2nd Ave
- **68th Street Elementary** · 612 W 68th St
- **74th St Elementary** · 2112 W 74th St
- **95th Street Preparatory School** · 1109 W 96th St
- **Ambassadors Christ Christian School** · 1400 104th St
- **Bret Harte Middle School** · 9301 S Hoover St
- **Budlong Ave Elementary** · 5940 S Budlong Ave
- **Cavalry Christian School** · 2400 W 85th St
- **Century Park Elementary** · 10935 Spinning Ave
- **Children's Enrichment Center** · 2309 W Manchester Blvd
- **Cleophas Oliver Learning Academy** · 1902 W Florence Ave
- **Ellington High School** · 1541 W 110th St
- **Faith Childrens Center** · 2057 W Century Blvd
- **Faith Lutheran Church** · 3320 W 85th St
- **First Church of God Christian School** · 2941 W 70th St
- **Frederick K C Price** · 7901 S Vermont Ave
- **Freeman Elementary** · 2602 W 79th St
- **Greers Child Care Center** · 6806 S Vermont Ave
- **Horace Mann Middle School** · 7001 S St Andrews Pl
- **Hyde Park Charter Elementary** · 3140 Hyde Park Blvd
- **John Muir Middle School** · 5929 S Vermont Ave
- **Kay Anthony's Elementary** · 8420 Crenshaw Blvd
- **Kay Anthony's Pre-School** · 8702 Crenshaw Blvd
- **La Salle Avenue Elementary** · 8715 La Salle Ave
- **Lane Elementary** · 9330 S 8th Ave
- **Little People Preschool** · 1713 W 108th St
- **Manchester Ave Elementary** · 661 W 87th St
- **Manhattan Place Elementary** · 1850 W 96th St
- **Miller Elementary** · 830 W 77th St
- **Monroe Magnet School** · 10711 S 10th Ave
- **Nelson S Western Ave** · 10531 S Western Ave
- **New West Technical Academy** · 10513 S Vermont Ave
- **Nikka Tiffany** · 7112 S Victoria Ave
- **Normandie Christian School** · 6306 S Normandie Ave
- **Raymond Ave Elementary** · 7511 Raymond Ave
- **San Pedro Academy** · 1145 W Manchester Ave
- **Shabach Christian Preparatory School** · 8711 S Harvard Bl
- **St Anselm's** · 7019 S Van Ness Ave
- **St Eugene's Catholic** · 9521 Haas Ave
- **St John the Evangelist** · 6102 Crenshaw Blvd
- **St Michael's Elementary** · 1027 W 87th St
- **St Raphael's Elementary** · 924 W 70th St
- **Washington High Preparatory School** · 10860 S Denker Ave
- **West Adams Academy** · 6625 4th Ave
- **Woodcrest Elementary** · 1151 W 109th St
- **Woodcrest Nazarene** · 10936 S Normandie Ave
- **Woodworth Elementary** · 3200 W 104th St
- **Youth Opportunities** · 943 W 85th St

Supermarkets

- **Food 4 Less** · 3200 W Century Blvd
- **Ralph's** · 1730 W Manchester Ave
- **Ralph's** · 8620 Orchard Ave

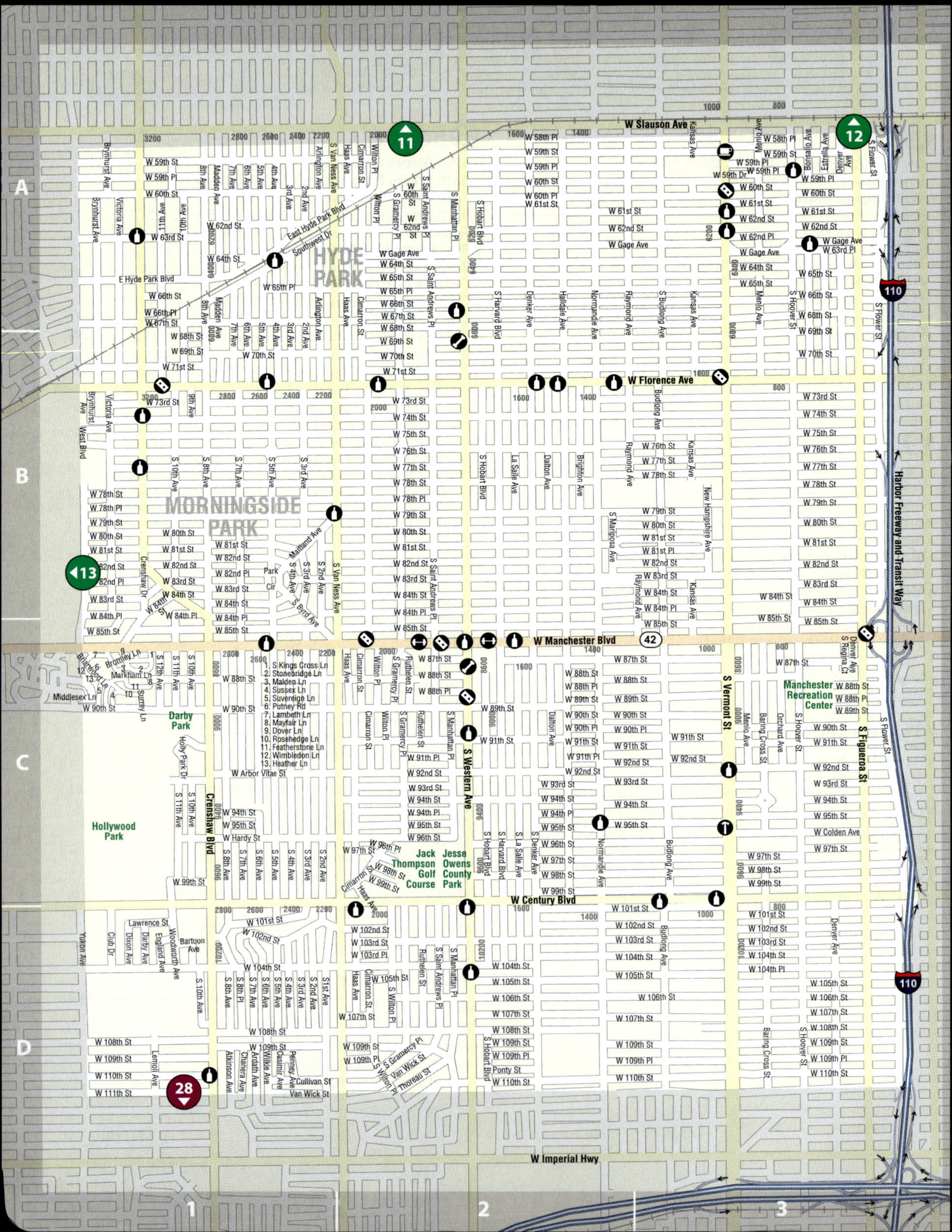

N
W Slauson Ave
W Florence Ave
W Manchester Blvd
42
W Century Blvd
W Imperial Hwy
HYDE PARK
MORNINGSIDE PARK
Darby Park
Hollywood Park
Jack Thompson Golf Course
Jesse Owens County Park
Manchester Recreation Center
Harbor Freeway and Transit Way
110
S Western Ave
S Vermont St
S Figueroa St
Crenshaw Blvd
Crenshaw Dr
S Van Ness Ave
S Hobart Blvd
S Normandie Ave
Budlong Ave
Kansas Ave
S Hoover St
S Flower St
East Hyde Park Blvd
Southwest Dr
E Hyde Park Blvd
West Blvd
Victoria Ave
Brynhurst Ave
Arlington Ave
S Manhattan Pl
S Saint Andrews Pl
S Gramercy Pl
Wilton Pl
Cimarron St
Haas Ave
1. S Kings Cross Ln
2. Stonebridge Ln
3. Malden Ln
4. Sussex Ln
5. Sovereign Ln
6. Putney Rd
7. Lambeth Ln
8. Mayfair Ln
9. Dover Ln
10. Rosehedge Ln
11. Featherstone Ln
12. Wimbledon Ln
13. Heather Ln
W Arbor Vitae St
Middlesex Ln
Bromley Ln
Markham Ln
W Gage Ave
W 58th Pl
W 59th St
W 61st St
W 62nd St
W 73rd St
W 84th St
W 85th St
W 87th St
W 88th St
W 90th St
W 91th St
W 95th St
W 101st St
W 104th St
W 108th St
W 110th St
W 111th St
Cullivan St
Van Wick St
Lawrence St
Bartoon Ave
Yukon Ave
Club Dr
Lemoli Ave
11
12
13
28
1
2
3
A
B
C
D

The Inglewood Chamber of Commerce co-sponsors an annual "Golf Classic." This tournament is not held in Inglewood, however, but behind the Orange Curtain, inexplicably, in Los Alamitos. Look for it every June.

Coffee

- **Good Donut** · 6001 S Vermont Ave

Gyms

- **Manchester Health Club** · 1943 W Manchester Ave · 323-971-9671
- **One On One** · 8726 S Western Ave · 323-751-3029

Hardware Stores

- **Abe Lecour Hardware** · 9609 S Vermont Ave · 323-777-4503

Liquor Stores

- **Bottoms Up Liquor** · 6424 S Vermont Ave
- **Bufkin Liquor** · 2063 W Florence Ave
- **Dave's Liquors** · 9317 S Vermont Ave
- **Frank's Liquor** · 8720 S Western Ave
- **Gin's Liquor Store** · 11001 Crenshaw Blvd
- **Holiday Liquor** · 9150 S Western Ave
- **J's Liquor** · 1005 W Century Blvd
- **M & J Liquor** · 7405 Crenshaw Blvd
- **Maple Liquors** · 10421 S Western Ave
- **Mr Spirits Liquor Store** · 6818 S Western Ave
- **Ralph's Drive-In Liquor** · 2130 W Century Blvd
- **Red Liquor Market** · 2600 Southwest Dr
- **Red's Liquor Store** · 1201 W Century Blvd
- **S M & B's Liquors** · 9467 S Normandie Ave
- **San's Liquor & Market** · 7911 S Van Ness Ave
- **Shyrea's Liquor** · 1753 W Century Blvd
- **Silver Dollar Liquor** · 1650 W Manchester Ave
- **Sunshine Liquor** · 2619 W Florence Ave
- **Susie's Liquor** · 5953 S Hoover St
- **Tom's Liquor Store II** · 1355 W Florence Ave
- **Vee's Liquor** · 7707 Crenshaw Blvd
- **Vermont Liquor Mkt** · 6107 S Vermont Ave

Pet Stores

- **R & T Pet & Feed Enterprise** · 6819 S Western Ave · 323-751-5136
- **RT Pet & Food General Warehouse** · 8902 S Western Ave · 323-778-1400

Video Rental

- **A & N Video** · 519 W Manchester Ave · 323-971-6249
- **Blockbuster** · 3330 W Florence Ave · 323-789-7991
- **Blockbuster** · 8811 S Western Ave · 323-750-2947
- **Jenny Video** · 6025 S Vermont Ave · 323-753-3288
- **Video Entertainment** · 2107 W Manchester Ave · 323-753-5609
- **Video Place** · 1013 W Florence Ave · 323-750-1084

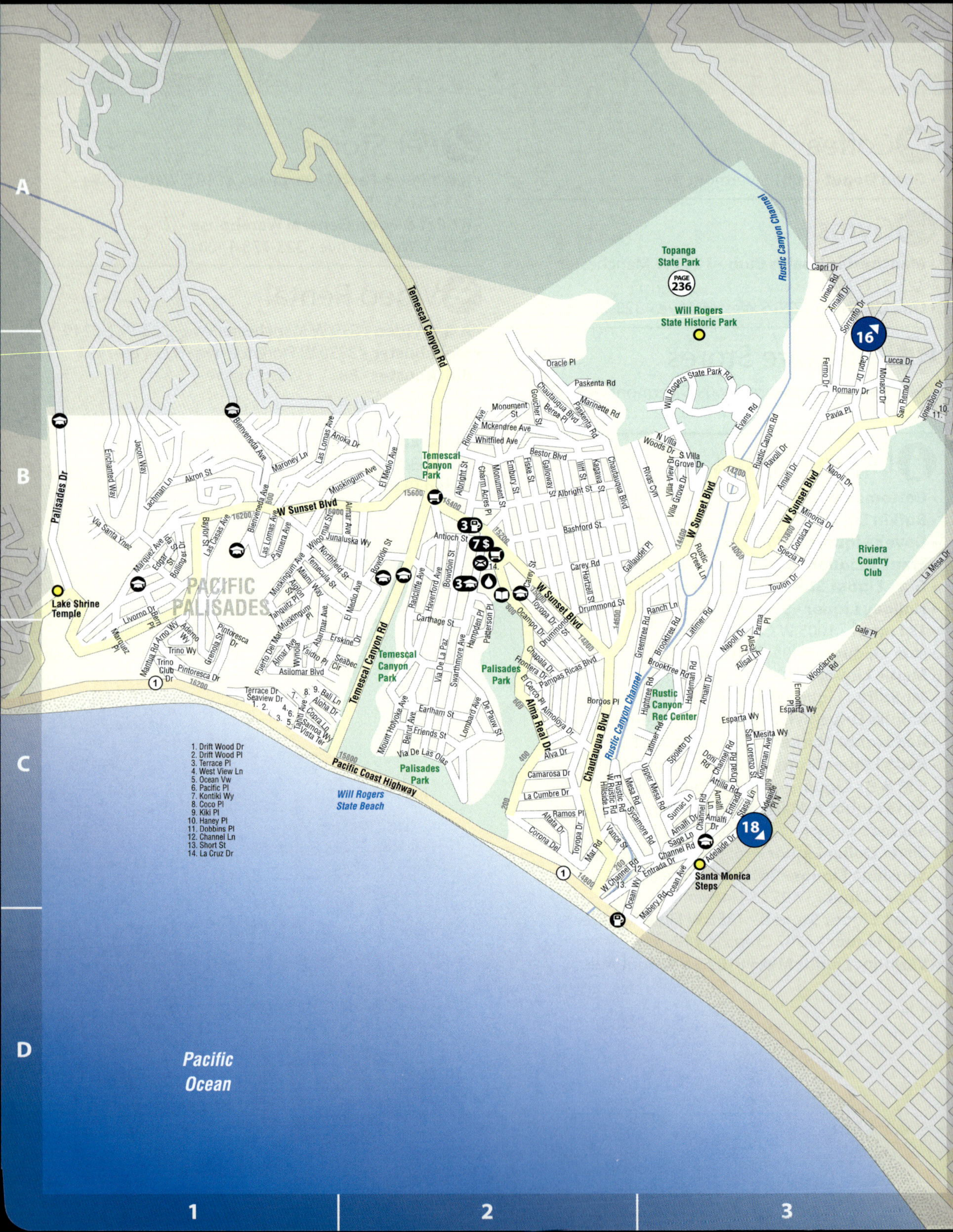

Map 15 • Pacific Palisades

The Palisades are one of L.A.'s most beautiful areas, and the area is home to many celebs and movie moguls—as the lavish homes might suggest. Though technically in Santa Monica, the 4th Street Steps are a popular place for people-watching, and an unusual workout. Whether you walk or run up the imposing stairway, you'll be sucking air by the time you reach the top.

$ Banks

- **Bank of America** · 15314 W Sunset Blvd
- **California National Bank** · 15305 W Sunset Blvd
- **Citibank** · 15215 Sunset Blvd
- **First Federal Bank** · 15135 W Sunset Blvd
- **US Bank** · 15245 W Sunset Blvd
- **Washington Mutual** · 15200 W Sunset Blvd
- **Wells Fargo Bank** · 1012 Swarthmore Ave

Car Washes

- **Palisades Car Wash** · 890 Alma Real Dr

Gas Stations

- **76** · 15400 W Sunset Blvd
- **Chevron** · 14791 Pacific Coast Hwy
- **Mobil** · 15281 W Sunset Blvd
- **Shell** · 15401 W Sunset Blvd

Landmarks

- **Santa Monica Steps** · 4th St & Adelaide Dr
- **Self Realization Fellowship Lake Shrine Temple** · Sunset Blvd near Palisades Dr
- **Will Rogers State Park** · Sunset Blvd

Libraries

- **Pacific Palisades Library** · 861 Alma Real Dr · 310-459-2754

Post Offices

- 15209 W Sunset Blvd
- 15243 La Cruz Dr

Schools

- **Archer School for Girls** · 15240 La Cruz Dr
- **Calvary Christian School** · 701 Palisades Dr
- **Canyon Elementary** · 421 Entrada Dr
- **Corpus Christi Catholic School** · 890 Toyopa Dr
- **Marquez Elementary** · 16821 Marquez Ave
- **Pacific Palisades Elementary** · 800 Via De La Paz
- **Palisades Charter High School** · 15777 Bowdoin St
- **Saint Matthews Episcopal** · 1031 Bienveneda Ave
- **Temescal Canyon High School** · 777 Temescal Canyon Rd
- **Village School** · 780 Swarthmore Ave

Supermarkets

- **Gelson's Markets** · 15424 W Sunset Blvd
- **Ralph's** · 15120 W Sunset Blvd

N

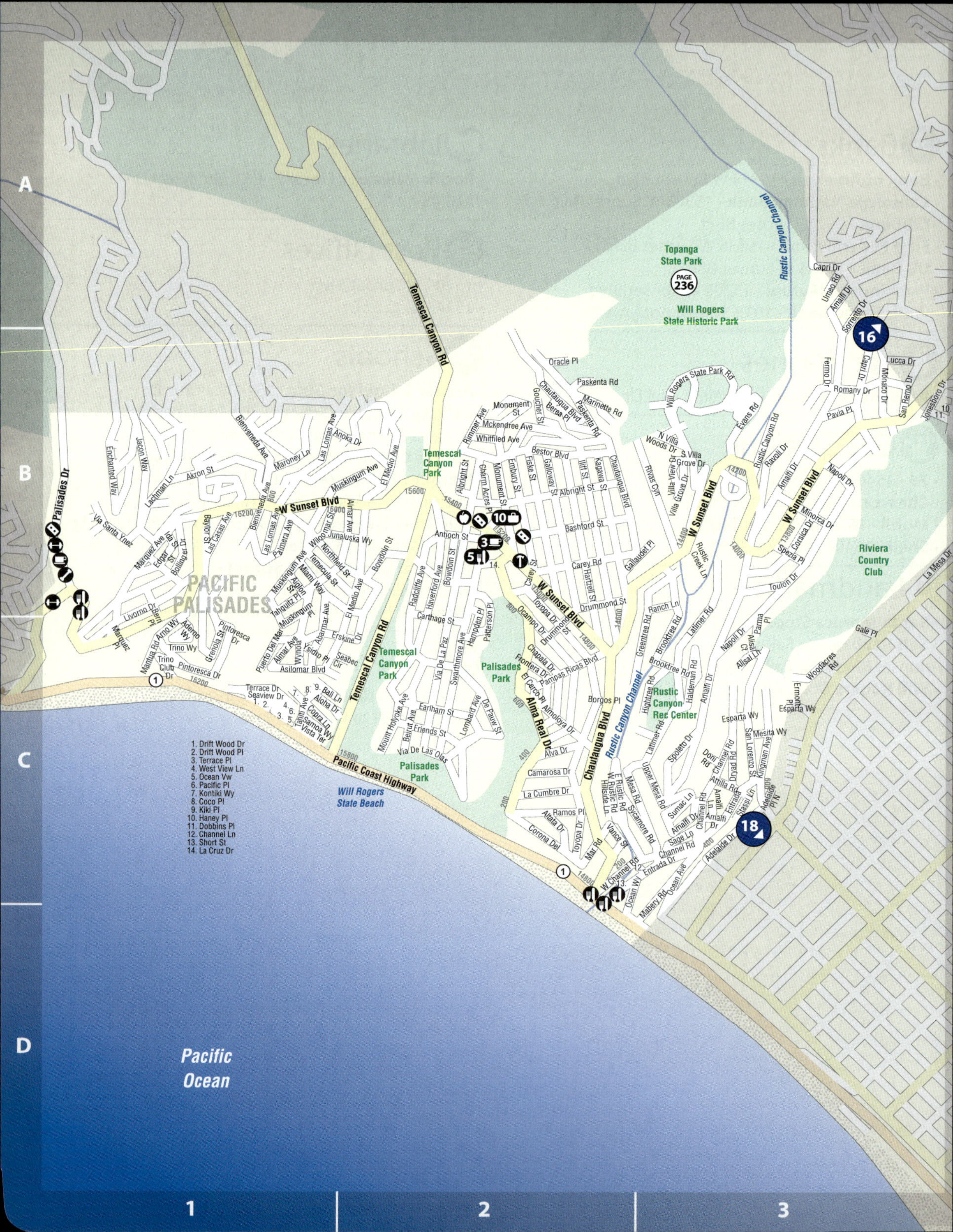

A
B
C
D

1
2
3

Pacific
Ocean

Topanga
State Park
PAGE
236
Will Rogers
State Historic Park

Rustic Canyon Channel

Capri Dr
Umeo Rd
Amalfi Dr
Sorrento Dr
16
Fermo Dr
Lucca Dr
Romany Dr
Moreno Dr
San Remo Dr
Pavia Pl
Riviera
Country
Club
La Mesa Dr
Gale Pl
Woodacres Rd

Oracle Pl
Paskenta Rd
Marinette Rd
Will Rogers State Park Rd
Evans Rd
Rustic Canyon Rd

Monument St
Mckendree Ave
Whitfiled Ave
Bestor Blvd
Chautauqua Blvd
Berea Blvd
Goucher St
Paskenta Rd
Rimmer Ave
Monument Ave

Temescal
Canyon
Park

W Sunset Blvd
Albright St
Charm Acres Pl
Embury St
Fiske St
Galloway
Iliff St
Albright St
Kagawa Ave
Chautauqua Blvd
Rivas Cyn
N Villa Woods Dr
S Villa Grove Dr
Villa View Dr
Villa Grove Dr
Bashford St

Antioch St
Carey Rd
Hartzell St
Drummond St
Gallaudet Pl
Carey Dr
Toyopa Dr
Drummond St

PACIFIC
PALISADES

W Sunset Blvd
Rustic Creek Ln
Greentree Rd
Ranch Ln
Brooktree Rd
Latimer Rd
Brooktree Rd
Haldeman Rd
Amalfi Dr
Napoli Dr
Alisal Ln
Parma
Alisai Ln
Toulon Dr
Spezia Pl
Corsica Dr
Minorca Dr
Napoli Dr

Ermonta Ave
Kingman Ave
Mesita Wy
Esparta Wy
Esparta Wy
San Lorenzo St

Jacon Way
Enchanted Way
Palisades Dr
Via Santa Ynez
Lachman Ln
Akron St
Las Lomas Anoka Dr
Bienveneda Ave
Maroney Ln
Muskingum Ave
El Medio Ave
Almar Ave
Bollinger Dr
Las Casas Ave
Las Lomas Ave
Palmera Ave
Bienveneda Ave
Marquez Ave
Edgar St
Bashford

W Sunset Blvd
Northfield St
Junaluska Wy
Muskingum Ave
Temescal Wy
Miami Way
Tahquitz Pl
Aderno
Erskine
El Medio Ave
Bowdoin St
Radcliffe Ave
Haverford Ave
Bowdoin Ave
Antioch St
Via De La Paz
Swarthmore Ave
Hampden Pl
Paterson Pl
Ocampo Dr
Ocampo Dr
Frontera Dr
Chapala Dr
Las Pulgas Rd
Pampas Ricas Blvd

Temescal
Canyon
Park

Livorna Dr
Bienn Pl
Marquez Pl
Trino Wy
Pintoresca Dr
Almar Ave
Wynola
Ysidro Pl
Asilomar Blvd
Seabec
Cir
Vista Ter

Mamua Rd
Arno Wy
Grenola St
Puerto Del Mar
Abarimar Ave
Trino Club Dr
1
Pintoresca Dr
Terrace Dr
Seaview Dr
Aloha Dr
Copra Ln
Samoa Ter

1. Drift Wood Dr
2. Drift Wood Pl
3. Terrace Pl
4. West View Ln
5. Ocean Vw
6. Pacific Pl
7. Kontiki Wy
8. Coco Pl
9. Kiki Pl
10. Haney Pl
11. Dobbins Pl
12. Channel Ln
13. Short St
14. La Cruz Dr

9. Ball Ln

Mount Holyoke Ave
Beirut St
Friends St
Earlham St
Lombard Ave
Via De Las Olas
Carthage St

Palisades
Park

Temescal Canyon Rd

Pacific Coast Highway
Will Rogers
State Beach

Palisades
Park

El Cerco
Pampas Ricas Blvd
Almoloya Dr
Borgos Pl
Alva Dr
Camarosa Dr
La Cumbre Dr
Ramos Dr
Corona Del
Alteta Dr
Toyopa Dr
Mai Rd
W Channel Rd
Mabery Rd
Ocean Wy
Entrada Dr
Channel Rd
Adelaide Dr
Ocean Ave
Sage Ln
Amalfi Dr
Vance Dr
Sicamore Rd
Sumac Ln
Mesa Rd
E Rustic Rd
Hillside Rd
W Rustic Rd
Upper Mesa Rd
Spoleto Dr
Doni Rd
Channel Rd
Attilla Rd
Dryad Rd
Amalfi Dr
Entrada Dr
Kingman Ave
Adelaide Pl N
18
Amalfi Dr

Alma Real Dr
Chautauqua Blvd
Rustic Canyon Channel
Rustic
Canyon
Rec Center
Latimer Rd
Hightree Rd

1
1

Amenities in the Palisades are generally limited to the village, just off Sunset, along Swarthmore Ave. But Santa Monica is just a short hop down the PCH, as long as mudslides or flooding don't interfere—forcing a longer, and sometimes hazardous, drive along the more serpentine Sunset Blvd.

Coffee

- **Coffee Bean & Tea Leaf** • 15278 Antioch St
- **Coffee Cabana** • 548 Palisades Dr
- **Il Sogna** • 863 Swarthmore Ave
- **Starbucks** • 15300 W Sunset Blvd

Farmer's Markets

- **Farmers' Market** • Swarthmore Ave & W Sunset Blvd • Sun 8-1:30

Gyms

- **Beyond Fitness** • 544 Palisades Dr • 310-230-0663
- **Pacific Athletic Club** • 17383 Sunset Blvd • 310-459-2582

Hardware Stores

- **Norris Hardware** • 15140 W Sunset Blvd • 310-454-4116

Restaurants

- **Dante Palisades Restaurant** • 1032 Swarthmore Ave • 310-459-7561
- **Giorgio Baldi** • 114 W Channel Rd • 310-573-1660
- **Gladstone's for Fish** • 17351 Sunset Blvd • 310-454-3474
- **Kay 'n Dave's Cantina** • 15246 W Sunset Blvd • 310-459-8118
- **Marix Tex Mex Cafe** • 118 Entrada Dr • 310-459-8596
- **Mort's Palisades Delicatessan** • 1035 Swarthmore Ave • 310-454-5511
- **Patrick's Roadhouse** • 106 Entrada Dr • 310-459-4544
- **Pure Energy Café** • 17383 W Sunset Blvd • 310-573-4105
- **Robek's Juice** • 15280 Antioch St • 310-230-3991
- **Terry's** • 1028 Swarthmore Ave • 310-454-6467

Shopping

- **Benton's Sporting Goods** • 1038 Swarthmore Ave • 310-459-8451
- **Gelson's Market** • 15424 Sunset Blvd • 310-459-4483
- **Gift Garden Antiques** • 15266 Antioch St • 310-459-4114
- **Ivy Greene for Kids** • 1020 Swarthmore Ave • 310-230-0301
- **Palisades Playthings** • 1041 Swarthmore Ave • 310-454-8648
- **The Prince's Table** • 1051 Swarthmore Ave • 310-573-3667
- **Village Book** • 1049 Swarthmore Ave • 310-454-4063
- **Vivian's Boutique** • 970 Monument St • 310-573-1326
- **Whispers** • 1013 Swarthmore Ave • 310-454-5581
- **Yamato Nursery** • 15236 La Cruz Dr • 310-454-1224

Video Rental

- **2010 Video** • 1022 Swarthmore Ave • 310-454-9611
- **Blockbuster** • 970 Monument St • 310-230-3002
- **Palisades Video** • 542 Palisades Dr •

N

A
B
C
D

1
2
3

Crestwood Hills Park
Topanga State Park
Rustic Canyon
Sullivan Fire Rd

BRENTWOOD

Getty Center

Barrington Recreation Center

Los Angeles National Cemetery

Veterans Administration

Wadsworth Veterans Administration Medical

Riviera Country Club

Brentwood Country Club

UCLA

N Sepulveda Blvd
San Diego Frwy
S Sepulveda Blvd
405
I 405

Getty Center Dr
St Cloud Rd
N Norman Pl
Brentwood Grove Dr
Norman Pl
Azure Pl
Firth Ave
Mansela Pl
Tigertail Rd
N Bundy Dr
Kenter Ave
Inavale Pl
Travis Dr
La Casa
Lockearn St
Octagon St
Richwood Dr
Kenter Way
Hanley Ave
Bronza Ln
Claymont Dr
Leonard Rd
Bluestone Ter
Stonehill Ln
Deerbrook Ln
Rochedale Ln
Bramble Way
Broom Way
Rochedale Way
Hanley Ave
Walther Way
Olney Way
Rd Boonway
N Kenter Ave
Oakmont Dr
Boca De canon Ln
Mandeville Canyon Rd
Heard Pl
Westridge Rd
Westridge Ter
Stipa Way
Hilltop Way
Mango Way
Westridge Rd
Correa Way
Melhill Way
Kimberly Ln
Old Orchard Rd
Oakmont Dr
Reedvale Ln
Homewood Way
Elkins Rd
Haller Pl
Tuallitan Rd
Robinwood Dr
N Bonhill Rd
Renfrew Rd
Crown Dr
Greenock Ln
Altair Dr
Crestline Dr
Benmora Ter
Galvern Ave
Layton Way
Bundy Dr N
N Layton Dr
N Woodburn Dr
N Barrington Ave
Crescenda St
Chaparal St
Leven Ln
Banff Ln
N Westgate Ave
Granville Ave
Bonny Ave
N Saltair Ave
Foxboro Dr
Kearsarge St
Coyne St
Coyne Pl
Rose Marie Ln
Currituck Dr
Oceano Dr
S Westgate Ave
Loma Ct
Dunsan Way
Terryhill Pl
S Barrington Ave
Chenault St
Montana Ave
Bringham Ave
Gorham Ave
Gorham Pl
Veterans Administration
Bonsall Ave
Constitution Ave
Eisenhower Ave
Wilshire Blvd
Ashford St
Westboro St
N Rockingham Ave
Parkyns St
N Bristol Ave
N Carmelina Ave
N Cliffwood Ave
N Anita Ave
N Canyon View Dr
Homewood Rd
N Kenter Ave
N Tigertail Rd
Sunset Blvd
Highwood St
Bristol Cir
Marlboro St
Hanover St
Santa Catalina View
S Medio Rd
S Canyon View Dr
S Carmelina Ave
S Anita Ave
Shady Dr
1st Helena Dr
Saltair Ter
San Vicente Blvd
Tweed Ter
Dunoon Ln
Falkirk Ln
Shetland Ln
Paisley Ln
S Kenter Ave
S Saltair Ave
Evanston St
S Rockingham Ave
Brinkley Ave
Beckwith Ave
Longworth Dr
Chadbourne Ave
S Burlingame Ave
S Bristol Ave
Nimrod Pl
S 26th St
Allenford Ave
Lucca Dr
San Remo Dr
D Este Dr
Moraga Dr
Sorrento Dr
Amalfi Dr
Capri Dr
Casale Rd
San Onofra Dr
Alta Mura Rd
Umeo Rd
Old Ranch Rd
Riviera Ranch Rd
Old Oak Rd
Old Oak Ln
Sunset Blvd
Homewood Rd
San Remo Dr

15
17
19
20

1. Lindenwood Ln
2. Bluestone Ter
3. Bluegrass Ln
4. Bluegrass Way
5. Glenmere Way
6. Pontoon Pl
7. Castlegate Dr
8. Brentridge Ln
9. Brentridge Dr
10. Norway Ln
11. Kiel St
12. Ocean Pl
13. Stonehaven Way
14. Little Park Ln
15. Mandeville Ln
16. Haney Pl
17. Dobbins Pl

O.J. Simpson put Brentwood on most Americans' radar, but this neighborhood is once again the quiet and relatively unassuming place it once was. San Vicente Blvd. serves as a shady and pleasant place for a jog or bike ride (complete with a bicycle lane), but when driving, watch out for traffic cops. The road is somewhat notorious for being a speed trap.

$ Banks

- **Bank of America** · 11911 San Vicente Blvd
- **California National Bank** · 11777 San Vicente Blvd
- **Citibank** · 12001 San Vicente Blvd
- **Union Bank** · 11661 San Vicente Blvd
- **Washington Mutual** · 226 26th St
- **Wells Fargo Bank** · 11836 San Vicente Blvd
- **Wells Fargo Bank** · 143 S Barrington Pl

Gas Stations

- **76** · 12037 San Vicente Blvd
- **76** · 13060 San Vicente Blvd
- **Chevron** · 110 S Barrington Ave
- **Chevron** · 11852 San Vicente Blvd
- **Shell** · 11811 San Vicente Blvd

Landmarks

- **Getty Center** · 1200 Getty Center Dr

Libraries

- **Los Angeles Library** · 11820 San Vicente Blvd · 310-575-8273

Post Offices

- 200 S Barrington Ave

Schools

- **Archer School for Girls** · 11725 Sunset Blvd
- **Brentwood** · 100 S Barrington Pl
- **Brentwood Science** · 740 Gretna Green Way
- **Kenter Canyon Elementary** · 645 N Kenter Ave
- **Revere Middle School** · 1450 Allenford Ave
- **St Martin of Tours Elementary** · 11955 W Sunset Blvd

Supermarkets

- **Whole Foods Market** · 11737 San Vicente Blvd

N

BRENTWOOD

Crestwood Hills Park

Topanga State Park

Rustic Canyon

Riviera Country Club

Brentwood Country Club

Barrington Recreation Center

Veterans Administration

Los Angeles National Cemetery

UCLA

Wadsworth Veterans Administration Medical

Sunset Blvd

San Vicente Blvd

N Sepulveda Blvd

S Sepulveda Blvd

San Diego Frwy

Wilshire Blvd

Constitution Ave

Eisenhower Ave

405

17

15

19

20

1. Lindenwood Ln
2. Bluestone Ter
3. Bluegrass Ln
4. Bluegrass Way
5. Glenmere Way
6. Pontoon Pl
7. Castlegate Dr
8. Brentridge Ln
9. Brentridge Dr
10. Norway Ln
11. Kiel St
12. Ocean Pl
13. Stonehaven Way
14. Little Park Ln
15. Mandeville Ln
16. Haney Pl
17. Dobbins Pl

San Vicente Blvd. seems to have an outpost of every major chain restaurant, from Chin Chin to Ben & Jerry's, but few independent restaurants that are worth noting. We love the pastas at Pizzicotto. However, Brentwood is home to one of L.A.'s best independent booksellers, Dutton Books (11975 San Vicente Blvd.). They have an impressive selection and an atmosphere geared toward serious readers.

# Coffee

- **Arrosto Coffee** • 11652 San Vicente Blvd
- **Brew-N-Beans** • 11911 San Vicente Blvd
- **Coffee Bean & Tea Leaf** • 11698 San Vicente Blvd
- **Peet's Coffee & Tea** • 11750 San Vicente Blvd
- **Starbucks** • 11700 Barrington Ct
- **Starbucks** • 11703 San Vicente Blvd
- **Starbucks** • 13050 San Vicente Blvd

# Farmer's Markets

- **Brentwood** • Chayote St & Barrington Ave • Wed 3:30-7

# Gyms

- **Great Shape** • 11980 San Vicente Blvd • 310-820-6602

# Liquor Stores

- **Briggs Wines & Spirits** • 13038 San Vicente Blvd

# Pet Stores

- **Petspot** • 11720 Barrington Ct • 310-471-8169

Restaurants

- **A Votre Sante** • 13016 San Vicente Blvd • 310-451-1813
- **Brentwood Restaurant & Lounge** • 148 S Barrington Ave • 310-476-3511
- **Cheesecake Factory** • 11647 San Vicente Blvd • 310-826-7111
- **Chin Chin** • 11740 San Vicente Blvd • 310-826-2525
- **Daily Grill** • 11677 San Vicente Blvd • 310-442-0044
- **Gaucho Grill** • 11695 San Vicente Blvd • 310-447-7898
- **La Scala Presto** • 11740 San Vicente Blvd • 310-826-6100
- **Lamonica's NY Pizza** • 11678 San Vicente Blvd • 310-820-6636
- **Le Pain Quotidien** • 11702 Barrington Ct • 310-476-0969
- **Pizzicotto** • 11758 San Vicente Blvd • 310-442-7188
- **Reddi Chick BBQ** • 225 26th St • 310-393-5238
- **Toscana** • 11633 San Vicente Blvd • 310-820-2448
- **Vincenti** • 11930 San Vicente Blvd • 310-207-0127
- **Zax** • 11604 San Vicente Blvd • 310-571-3800

Shopping

- **Dutton's Brentwood Books** • 11975 San Vicente Blvd • 310-476-6263
- **Falconhead** • 11911 San Vicente Blvd • 310-471-7075
- **Maison Sud** • 11677 San Vicente Blvd • 310-207-5669
- **PJ London** • 11661 San Vicente Blvd • 310-826-4649
- **Porta Bella** • 11711 Gorham Ave • 310-820-2550
- **Terra Cotta** • 11922 San Vicente Blvd • 310-826-7878
- **Whole Foods Market** • 11737 San Vicente Blvd • 310-826-4433

Video Rental

- **Blockbuster** • 11770 San Vicente Blvd • 310-207-3837
- **Euro Video** • 11695 San Vicente Blvd • 310-442-4683

Map 17 • Bel Air / Holmby Hills
N
Stone Canyon Reservoir
A
B
C
D
1
2
3
405
N Sepulveda Blvd
N Sepulveda Blvd
E Sepulveda Fire Rd
San Diego Freeway
405
16
20
Quito Ln
Bel Air Rd
Rial Ln
Hebron Ln
Rial Ln
Corfu Ln
Larned Ln
N Beverly Glen Blvd
Sandall Ln
Levico Way
Vestone Way
Taranto Way
Fontenelle Way
Isadora Ln
Mars Ln
Bel Air Rd
Ottone Way
Dolcedo Way
Bel Air Ct
Fernbush Ln
Stradella Rd
Via Verona
Vicenza Way
Portofino Pl
Verano Rd
Roberto Ln
Somera Rd
Stradella Ct
Rocca Ct
Rocca Pl
Hollybush Ln
Angelo Rd
Anzio Rd
Somma Way
Nimes Rd
Montine Ln
Greendale Dr
Brooklawn Dr
Linda Flora Dr
Orum Rd
Roscomare Rd
Somera Rd
Chantilly Rd
Stradella Rd
Airole Way
Capello Way
Stone Canyon Rd
Strada Vecchia Rd
Tortuoso Way
Nimes Pl
Bel Air Rd
Saint Cloud Rd
Parkwood Dr
N Mapleton Dr
Baroda Dr
Delfern Dr
Moraga Ln
Vista Moraga
Moraga Dr
Spiros Spiros Dr
Bel Ter
Acanto Pl
Castano Rd
Montego Dr
Lausanne Dr
Chalon Rd
Doto Way
Cuesta Way
Bel Air Rd
Madrono Ln
Angola Ln
St Pierre Rd
St Pierre Rd
Bel Air Rd
Sunset Blvd
Linda Flora Dr
Bellagio Rd
Chalon Rd
Tarcuto Way
Stradella Rd
Sarbonne Rd
Carcassonne Rd
Siena Way
Magio Rd
Copa De Oro Rd
Bellagio Rd
Revuelta Way
S Stone Canyon Dr
S Beverly Glen Blvd
The Los A Country
Estrellita Way
Bellagio Rd
Cascata Way
Levico Pl
Bellagio Pl
Funchal
N Bentley Ave
Perugia Way
Bel Air Country Club
Barnaby Rd
Bellagio Rd
Bel Air Country Club
Strada Corta Rd
Udine Way
Marymount Pl
Acanto St
Ovida Pl
Thurston Pl
N Thurston Ave
Ashdale Ave
Ashdale Pl
Glenroy Pl
Glenroy Ave
Bentley
Bellagio Rd
W Sunset Blvd
Groverton Pl
Thurston Cir
S Thurston Ave
Bronwood Ave
Barlock Ave
De Neve Dr
Circle Dr N
UCLA
PAGE 216
BEL AIR ESTATES
1. S Sepulveda Blvd
2. Taro Way
3. Cecina Way
4. Tione Rd
5. Duluth Ln

Both of these neighborhoods are almost completely residential. Bel Air is home to former President Ronald Reagan, while Holmby Hills' most famous resident may be Hugh Hefner and his notorious Playboy Mansion. The roads are confusing and it's easy to get lost in Bel Air. But the homes are so stunning to look at that you may not mind.

Gas Stations

- **Chevron** · 670 N Sepulveda Blvd
- **Shell** · 800 N Sepulveda Blvd

Schools

- **Bellagio Road Newcomer Center Elementary** · 11301 Bellagio Rd
- **John Thomas Dye** · 11414 Chalon Rd
- **Marymount High School** · 10643 W Sunset Blvd

Stone Canyon Reservoir
Quito Ln
Hebron Ln
Bel Air Rd
Rial Ln
Rial Ln
Corfu Ln
Larned Ln
N Beverly Glen Blvd
Sandall Ln
Isadera Ln
Bel Air Mesa Ln
Levico Way
Vistone Way
Fontenelle Way
Taranto Way
Ottone Way
Bel Air Rd
Bel Air Pl
Bel Air Ct
Dolcedo Way
Savona Rd
Stradella Rd
Via Verona
Vicenza Way
Portofino Pl
Roberto Ln
Somera Rd
Verano Rd
Linda Flora Dr
Anzio Rd
Stradella Ct.
Rocca Pl
Rocca Ct.
Somma Way
Fernbush Ln
Hollybush Ln
Angelo Rd
Nimes Rd
Modline Ln
Orum Rd
Roscomare Rd
Somera Rd
Chantilly Rd
Stradella Rd
Airole Way
Capello Way
Stone Canyon Rd
Strada Vecchia Rd
Tortuoso Way
Nimes Pl
Green Gate Dr
Brooklawn Dr
BEL AIR ESTATES
Moraga Ln
Vista Moraga
Moraga Dr
Bel Ter
Acanto Pl
Casiano Rd
Spiros Pt
Spiros Dr
Chalon Rd
Chalon Rd
Chalon Rd
Tarcuto Way
Chalon Rd
Stradella Rd
Sarbonne Rd
Dolo Way
Lausanne Dr
Chalon Rd
Carcassonne Rd
Saint Cloud Rd
Cuesta Way
Madrono Ln
Bel Air Rd
St Pierre Rd
Amapola Ln
Bel Air Rd
St Pierre Rd
N Mapleton Dr
Parkwood Dr
N Faring Rd
Baroda Dr
Dalfern Dr
Sunset Blvd
Montego Dr
Linda Flora Dr
Cascada Way
Bellagio Rd
Bellagio Rd
Bellagio Rd
Ledo Way
Funchal Rd
Bel Air Country Club
Sarbonne Rd
Barnaby Rd
Bellagio Rd
Perugia Way
Siena Way
Bellagio Rd
Bel Air Country Club
Copa De Oro Rd
Bellagio Rd
S Stone Canyon Dr
Strada Corta Rd
Revuelta Way
Bel Air Rd
Baroda Dr
Sunset Blvd
S Beverly Glen Blvd
The Los A
Country
16
20
Estrellita Way
Ovada Pl
Bellagio Rd
Jai Ln
N Bentley Ave
Ashdale Ave
Ashdale Pl
Glenroy Pl
Glenroy Ave
Bentley Pl
Bellagio Rd
Marymount Pl
Udine Way
Groverton Pl
W Sunset Blvd
W Sunset Blvd
De Neve Dr
Circle Dr N
Acanto St
Thurston Pl
Thurston Cir
N Thurston Ave
S Thurston Ave
Bronwood Ave
Barlock Ave
UCLA
PAGE 216
N Sepulveda Blvd
E Sepulveda Fire Rd
San Diego Freeway
Bellagio Rd
405
405
16
20
1. S Sepulveda Blvd
2. Taro Way
3. Cecina Way
4. Tione Rd
5. Duluth Ln

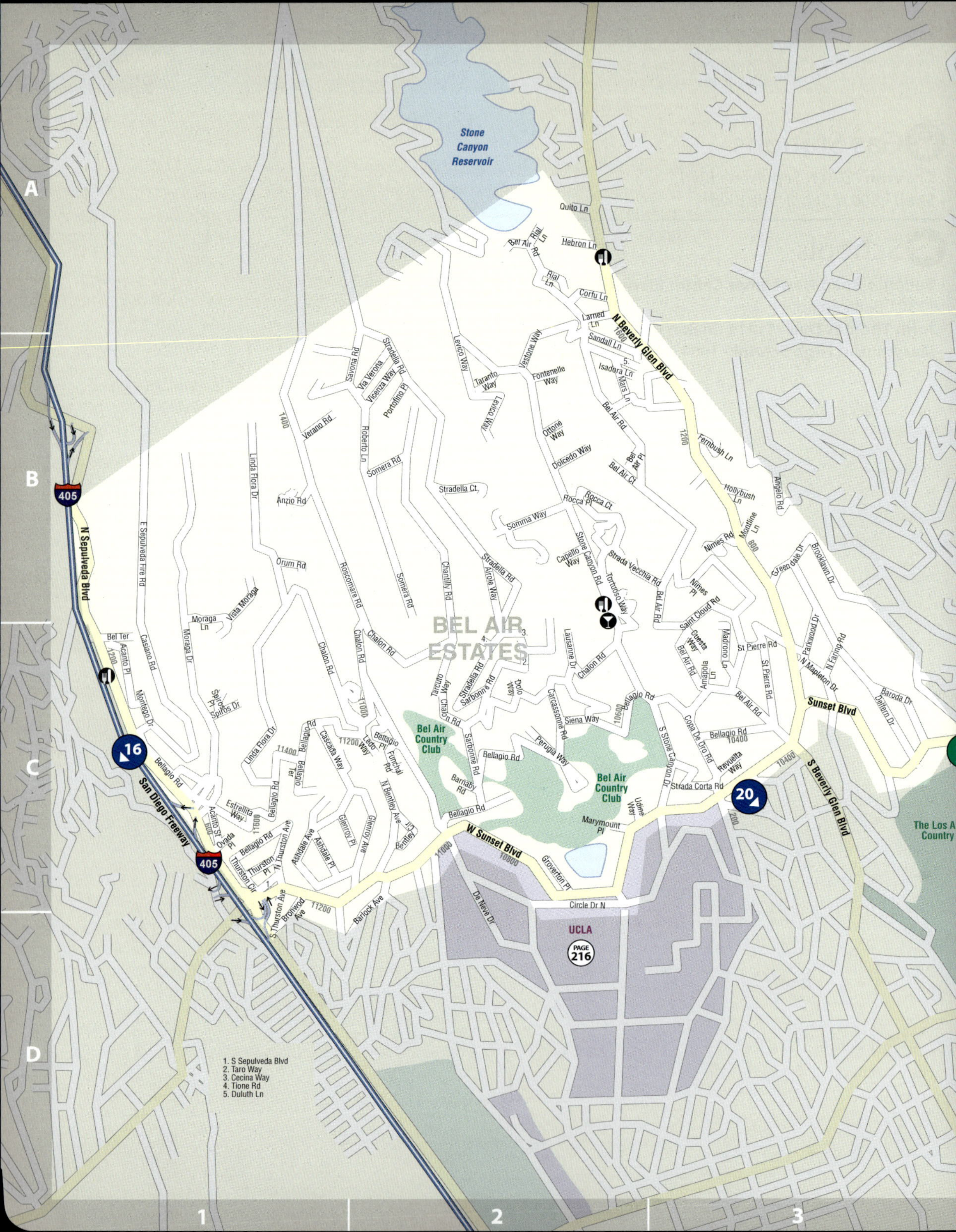

The Hotel Bel Air might be Los Angeles County's most beautiful hotel. The grounds are exquisitely maintained, and it's easy to understand why so many couples opt to hold their weddings alongside the hotel's Swan Lake, which is, as advertised, home to several swans.

Clubs

- **Hotel Bel Air Lounge** · 701 Stone Canyon Rd · 310-472-1211

Restaurants

- **Bel Air Bar & Grill** · 662 N Sepulveda Blvd · 310-440-5544
- **Four Oaks** · 2181 N Beverly Glen Blvd · 310-470-2265
- **Hotel Bel Air** · 701 Stone Canyon Rd · 310-472-1211

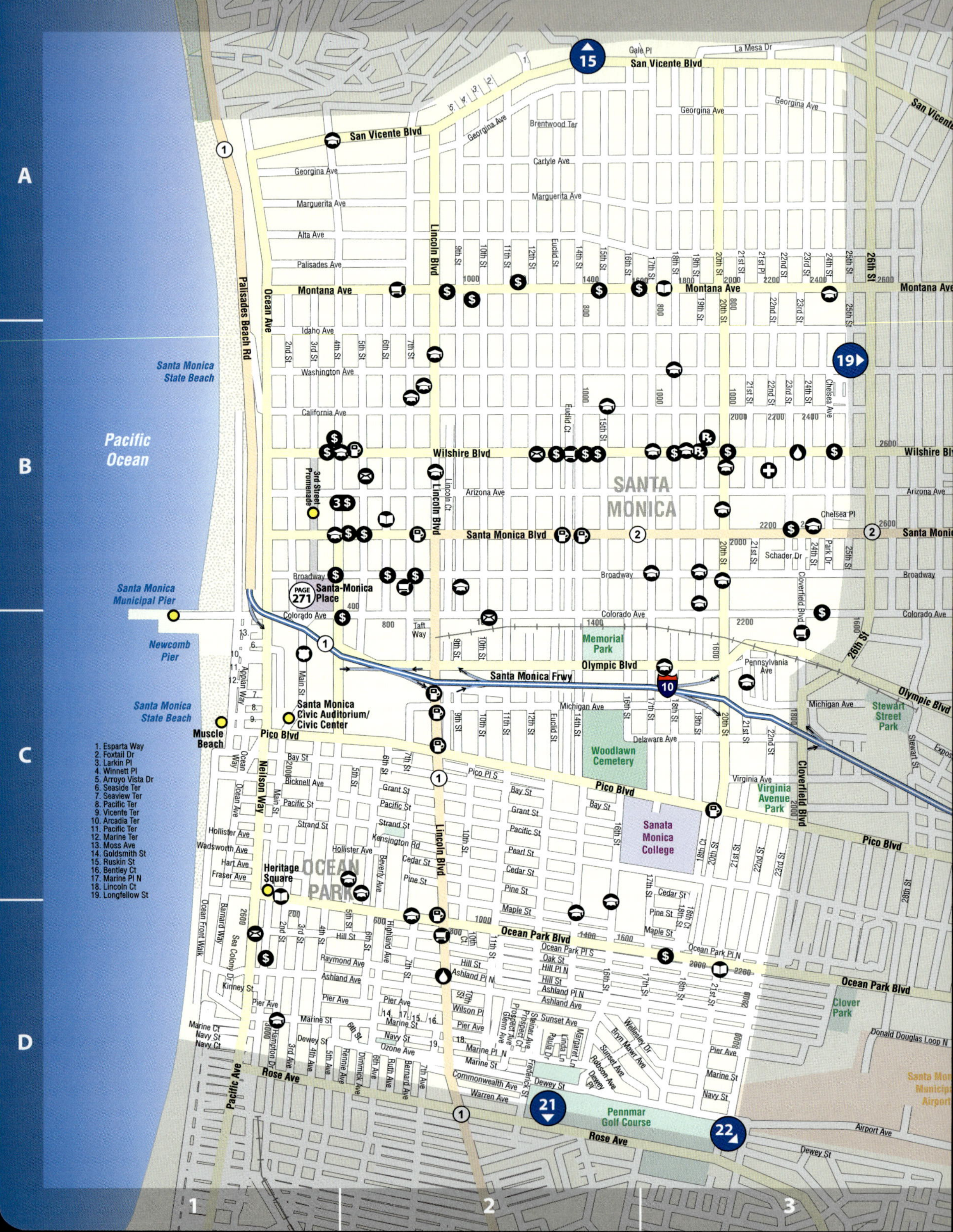
Santa Monica
Pacific Ocean
Santa Monica State Beach
Santa Monica Municipal Pier
Newcomb Pier
Muscle Beach
Palisades Beach Rd
Ocean Ave
Gale Pl
La Mesa Dr
San Vicente Blvd
Georgina Ave
Brentwood Ter
Carlyle Ave
Marguerita Ave
Georgina Ave
Alta Ave
Palisades Ave
Montana Ave
Idaho Ave
Washington Ave
California Ave
Wilshire Blvd
Arizona Ave
Santa Monica Blvd
Broadway
Colorado Ave
Olympic Blvd
Santa Monica Frwy
Lincoln Blvd
Lincoln Ct
3rd Street Promenade
Santa Monica Place
Memorial Park
Pennsylvania Ave
Chelsea Ave
Chelsea Pl
Schader Dr
Cloverfield Blvd
Park Dr
Olympic Blvd
Stewart Street Park
Michigan Ave
Woodlawn Cemetery
Delaware Ave
Virginia Ave
Santa Monica College
Virginia Avenue Park
Pico Blvd
Santa Monica Civic Auditorium/ Civic Center
Pico Blvd
Bay St
Bicknell Ave
Grant St
Pacific St
Strand St
Hollister Ave
Wadsworth Ave
Hart Ave
Fraser Ave
Ocean Park
Heritage Square
Main St
Neilson Way
Appian Way
Ocean Way
Ocean Ave
Bay St
Grant St
Pacific St
Pearl St
Cedar St
Pine St
Maple St
Ocean Park Blvd
Ocean Park Pl S
Oak St
Hill St
Ashland Pl N
Ashland Ave
Sunset Ave
Marine St
Clover Park
Pier Ave
Pier Ave
Marine St
Dewey St
Navy St
Pennmar Golf Course
Rose Ave
Airport Ave
Dewey St
Santa Monica Municipal Airport
Donald Douglas Loop N
Hampton Dr
Rennie Ave
Dimmick Ave
Ruth Ave
Bernard Ave
Barnard Way
Sea Colony
Ocean Front Walk
Pacific Ave
Rose Ave
Marine Ct
Navy St
Navy Ct
Kinney St
Ozone Ave
Commonwealth Ave
Warren Ave
Dewey St
1. Esparta Way
2. Foxtail Dr
3. Larkin Pl
4. Winnett Pl
5. Arroyo Vista Dr
6. Seaside Ter
7. Seaview Ter
8. Pacific Ter
9. Vicente Ter
10. Arcadia Ter
11. Pacific Ter
12. Marine Ter
13. Moss Ave
14. Goldsmith St
15. Ruskin St
16. Bentley Ct
17. Marine Pl N
18. Lincoln Ct
19. Longfellow St
PAGE 271
15
19
21
22
10
2nd St
3rd St
4th St
5th St
6th St
7th St
9th St
10th St
11th St
12th St
14th St
15th St
16th St
17th St
18th St
19th St
20th St
21st St
21st Pl
22nd St
23rd St
24th St
25th St
26th St
Euclid St
Euclid Ct
Euclid St
Michigan Ave
16th St
17th St
18th St
19th St
20th St
21st St
22nd St
1000
1400
800
1800
2000
2200
2400
2600
Wilshire Blvd
Santa Monica Blvd
Broadway
Taft Way
Main St

Santa Monica consists of a series of neighborhoods, each with its own distinct personality. Ocean Park is artsy, North of Montana is glitzy, Sunset Park is almost suburban, while downtown caters to a large tourist population. Parking in downtown Santa Monica can be an absolute nightmare, and private lots can be overpriced. Don't even bother looking for street parking—go right to any of the municipal lots along 2nd and 4th Streets, which have reasonable rates and a generous grace period.

$ Banks

- **Bank of America** · 1301 4th St
- **Bank of America** · 1430 Wilshire Blvd
- **Bank of the West** · 407 Colorado Ave
- **California Bank & Trust** · 100 Wilshire Blvd
- **Citibank** · 1505 Montana Ave
- **Citibank** · 501 Santa Monica Blvd
- **City National Bank** · 1801 Wilshire Blvd
- **First Federal Bank** · 1630 Montana Ave
- **First Federal Bank** · 1750 Ocean Park Blvd
- **First Federal Bank** · 2827 Main St
- **First Federal Bank** · 401 Wilshire Blvd
- **First Professional Bank** · 606 Broadway
- **First Regional Bank** · 501 Santa Monica Blvd
- **Jackson Federal Bank** · 1101 Montana Ave
- **Union Bank** · 2001 Wilshire Blvd
- **Union Bank** · 900 Montana Ave
- **US Bank** · 1401 Wilshire Blvd
- **US Bank** · 2221 Santa Monica Blvd
- **US Bank** · 2450 Colorado Ave
- **US Bank** · 400 Wilshire Blvd
- **Washington Mutual** · 1333 4th St
- **Wells Fargo Bank** · 1300 4th St
- **Wells Fargo Bank** · 1311 Wilshire Blvd
- **Wells Fargo Bank** · 2444 Wilshire Blvd
- **Wells Fargo Bank** · 710 Broadway
- **World Savings & Loan** · 729 Montana Ave

Car Washes

- **Bonus Car Wash & Auto Detail** · 2800 Lincoln Blvd
- **Wilshire West Detail & Car Wash** · 2320 Wilshire Blvd

Gas Stations

- **76** · 1402 Santa Monica Blvd
- **76** · 1944 Pico Blvd
- **Arco** · 2555 Lincoln Blvd
- **Chevron** · 1330 Santa Monica Blvd
- **Chevron** · 1732 Lincoln Blvd
- **Chevron** · 432 Wilshire Blvd
- **Exxon** · 1801 Lincoln Blvd
- **Mobil** · 731 Santa Monica Blvd
- **Shell** · 1866 Lincoln Blvd

Hospitals

- **St John's Hospital & Health** · 1328 22nd St · 310-829-5511

Landmarks

- **3rd Street Promenade** · 3rd St between Broadway & Wilshire
- **Heritage Square** · Main St & Ocean Park Blvd
- **Muscle Beach** · 1817 Ocean Front Walk
- **Santa Monica Civic Auditorium/Civic Center** · 1855 Main St
- **Santa Monica Pier** · Ocean Ave & Colorado Ave

Libraries

- **Santa Monica Fairview Library** · 2101 Ocean Park Blvd · 310-450-0443
- **Santa Monica Montana Avenue** · 1704 Montana Ave · 310-829-7081
- **Santa Monica Public Library** · 1343 6th St · 310-458-8600
- **Santa Monica Public Library** · 2601 Main St · 310-392-3804

24-Hour Pharmacies

- **Rite-Aid** · 1808 Wilshire Blvd · 310-829-3951
- **Walgreens** · 1932 Wilshire Blvd · 310-829-6813

Police

- **Santa Monica Police Headquarters** · 1685 Main St · 310-395-9931

Post Offices

- 1020 Colorado Ave
- 1217 Wilshire Blvd
- 1248 5th St
- 2720 Neilson Way

Schools

- **Carden Santa Monica** · 958 Lincoln Blvd
- **Carlthorp** · 438 San Vicente Blvd
- **Concord High School** · 1831 Wilshire Blvd
- **Crossroads** · 1714 21st St
- **Crossroads Elementary** · 1715 Olympic Blvd
- **Franklin Elementary** · 2400 Montana Ave
- **Franklin Elementary** · 2400 Montana Ave
- **Garden of Angels** · 1009 18th St
- **John Adams Middle School** · 2425 16th St
- **John Muir Elementary** · 2526 6th St
- **Lighthouse, The FSG** · 1220 20th St
- **Lincoln Middle School** · 1501 California Ave
- **McKinley Elementary** · 2401 Santa Monica Blvd
- **New Roads** · 1238 Lincoln Blvd
- **Newpath Montessori** · 1508 17th St
- **Olympic High School** · 721 Ocean Park Blvd
- **Pilgrim Lutheran** · 1730 Wilshire Blvd
- **Pluralistic School** · 1454 Euclid St
- **Rogers Elementary** · 2401 14th St
- **Roosevelt Elementary** · 801 Montana Ave
- **Santa Monica Alternative** · 2525 5th St
- **Santa Monica College** · 1900 Pico Blvd
- **Santa Monica High School** · 601 Pico Blvd
- **Santa Monica Montessori** · 1909 Colorado Ave
- **Soledad Enrichment Action** · 161 S Fetterly Ave
- **St Anne's Catholic School** · 1519 20th St
- **St Clement's** · 204 Hampton Dr
- **St John's Child & Family Development** · 1339 20th St
- **St Monica Elementary** · 1039 7th St
- **St Monica's High School** · 1030 Lincoln Blvd
- **The Montessori Center for Children** · 1513 9th St
- **Westside Waldorf** · 1229 4th St
- **Will Rogers Elementary** · 2401 14th St
- **Wilshire West** · 1516 19th St

Supermarkets

- **Albertson's** · 2627 Lincoln Blvd
- **Pavilions** · 820 Montana Ave
- **Ralph's** · 1644 Cloverfield Blvd
- **Von's** · 710 Broadway
- **Von's** · 1311 Wilshire Blvd

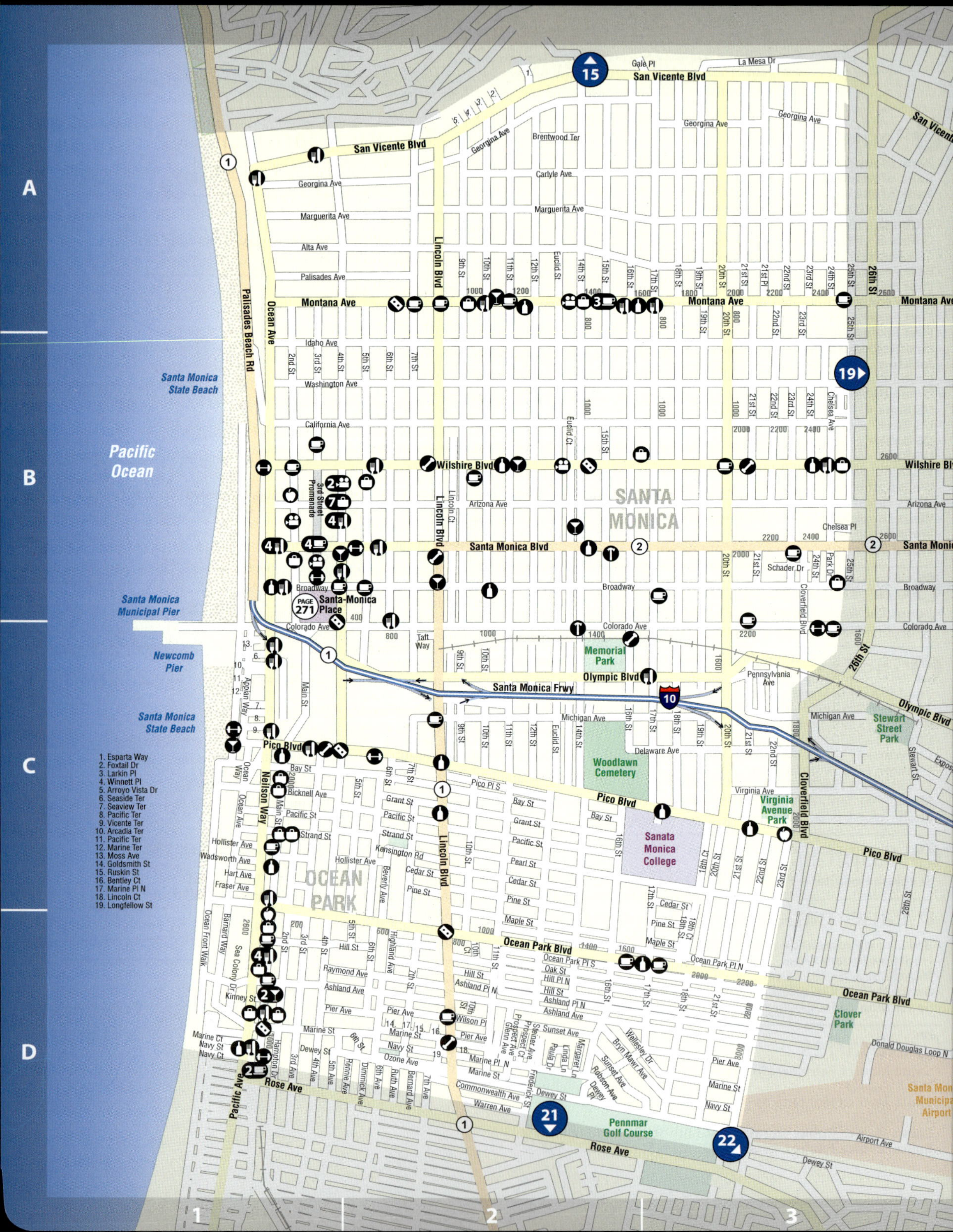

Pacific Ocean

Santa Monica State Beach

Santa Monica Municipal Pier

Newcomb Pier

Palisades Beach Rd

Ocean Ave

San Vicente Blvd

Gale Pl
La Mesa Dr
Georgina Ave
Brentwood Ter
Carlyle Ave
Marguerita Ave
Georgina Ave
San Vicente Blvd
San Vicente

Georgina Ave
Marguerita Ave
Alta Ave
Palisades Ave
Montana Ave
Idaho Ave
Washington Ave
California Ave

Lincoln Blvd
Lincoln Ct
Arizona Ave

Wilshire Blvd

Santa Monica Blvd

Broadway

Colorado Ave

3rd Street Promenade

Santa-Monica Place

PAGE 271

Taft Way

Memorial Park

Olympic Blvd

Santa Monica Frwy

Pennsylvania Ave

Michigan Ave
Delaware Ave

Woodlawn Cemetery

Pico Blvd

Bay St
Grant St
Pacific St
Strand St
Kensington Rd
Cedar St
Pine St

Ocean Way
Nielson Way
Main St
Bicknell Ave
Pacific St
Hollister Ave
Wadsworth Ave
Hart Ave
Fraser Ave

OCEAN PARK

Main St
Strand St
Hollister Ave

Beverly Ave

Highland Ave

Hill St
Ashland Ave
Pier Ave
Marine St
Ozone Ave

Barnard Way
Sea Colony Dr
Kinney St

Marine Ct
Navy St
Navy Ct
Hampton Dr
Dewey Ave
Rennie Ave
Dimmick Ave
Ruth Ave
Bernard Ave

Pacific Ave
Rose Ave
Commonwealth Ave
Warren Ave

Wilson Pl
Pier Ave
Navy Ave
Marine Pl N
Marine St

Prospect Ct
Prospect Ct
Glenn Ave
Steiner Ave
Sunset Ave
Margaret Ave
Linda Ln
Paula Dr
Robson Ave
Dewey St

Wellesley Dr
Bryn Mawr Ave
Sunset Ave

SANTA MONICA

Sanata Monica College

Chelsea Pl
Schader Dr
Cloverfield Blvd
26th St

Virginia Ave
Virginia Avenue Park

Stewart Street Park

Michigan Ave

Olympic Blvd
Stewart St
Exposi

Clover Park

Pico Blvd

Ocean Park Blvd
Ocean Park Pl S
Oak St
Hill St
Ashland Pl N
Hill St
Ashland Pl N
Ashland Ave

Ocean Park Pl N

Maple St
Cedar St
Pine St
Maple St

Pennmar Golf Course

Rose Ave

Donald Douglas Loop N

Santa Monica Municipal Airport

Airport Ave
Dewey St
Pier Ave
Marine Ave
Navy Ave
Ocean Park Blvd

Frederick St

1. Esparta Way
2. Foxtail Dr
3. Larkin Pl
4. Winnett Pl
5. Arroyo Vista Dr
6. Seaside Ter
7. Seaview Ter
8. Pacific Ter
9. Vicente Ter
10. Arcadia Ter
11. Pacific Ter
12. Marine Ter
13. Moss Ave
14. Goldsmith St
15. Ruskin St
16. Bentley Ct
17. Marine Pl N
18. Lincoln Ct
19. Longfellow St

2nd St
3rd St
4th St
5th St
6th St
7th St
9th St
10th St
11th St
12th St
14th St
15th St
16th St
17th St
18th St
19th St
20th St
21st St
21st Pl
22nd St
23rd St
24th St
25th St
26th St

Euclid St
Euclid Ct
Chelsea Ave
Arizona Ave
Park Dr

10

Sundries / Entertainment

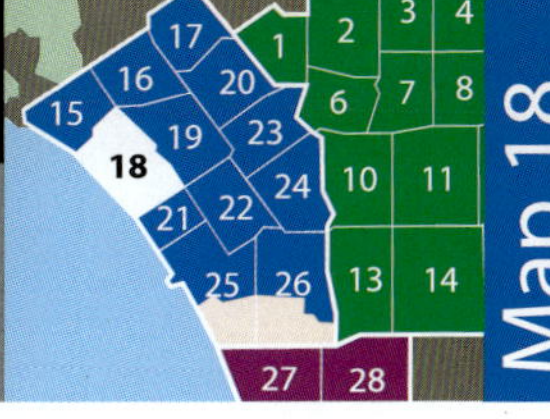

Santa Monica is home to a large number of transplants from England, so it has an impressive selection of British fare. Ye Olde King's Head is a traditional British pub, while Tudor House (1403 2nd Street) serves afternoon tea. And the Continental Shop (1619 Wilshire Blvd.) sells everything from tea cozies to sticky toffee pudding, the best thing to come out of England since the Beatles.

Clubs

- **14 Below** • 1348 14th St • 310-451-5040
- **Casa del Mar** • 1 Pico Blvd • 310-581-5533
- **Circle Bar** • 2926 Main St • 310-450-0508
- **Cock N' Bull Pub** • 2947 Lincoln Blvd • 310-399-9696
- **Father's Office** • 1018 Montana Ave • 310-393-2337
- **Harvelle's** • 1432 4th St • 310-395-1676
- **O'Brien's** • 2941 Main St • 310-396-4725
- **Rix** • 1413 5th St • 310-656-9688
- **Shutters** • 1 Pico Blvd • 310-458-0030
- **Sugar** • 814 Broadway • 310-899-1989
- **Temple Bar** • 1026 Wilshire Blvd • 310-393-6611
- **The Library Ale House** • 2911 Main St • 310-314-4855

Coffee

- **18th Street Coffee House** • 1725 Broadway
- **Arrosto Coffee** • 2002 Wilshire Blvd
- **Arrosto Coffee** • 255 Main St
- **Cafe Bolivar** • 1741 Ocean Park Blvd
- **Cafe La Mer** • 500 Broadway
- **Cafe Panini** • 225 Santa Monica Blvd
- **Charlie's Coffee** • 2425 Colorado Ave
- **Coffee Bean & Tea Leaf** • 1312 3rd St Promenade
- **Coffee Bean & Tea Leaf** • 1426 Montana Ave
- **Coffee Bean & Tea Leaf** • 1804 Lincoln Blvd
- **Coffee Bean & Tea Leaf** • 200 Santa Monica Blvd
- **Coffee Bean & Tea Leaf** • 2901 Main St
- **Coffee Bean & Tea Leaf** • 829 Wilshire Blvd
- **Coffee Cup Bakery** • 321 Santa Monica Blvd
- **Diedrich Coffee** • 732 Montana Ave
- **Infuzion Cafe** • 1149 3rd St
- **Metro Rags & Java** • 1630 Ocean Park Blvd
- **Mystic Joe** • 2311 Santa Monica Blvd
- **Peet's Coffee & Tea** • 1401 Montana Ave
- **Peet's Coffee & Tea** • 2439 Main St
- **Seattle's Best Coffee** • 1015 Montana Ave
- **Starbucks** • 1334 3rd St Promenade
- **Starbucks** • 1426 Montana Ave
- **Starbucks** • 2200 Colorado Ave
- **Starbucks** • 2671 Main St
- **Starbucks** • 3020 Lincoln Blvd
- **Starbucks** • 308 Wilshire Blvd
- **Starbucks** • 3110 Main St
- **Starbucks** • 701 Montana Ave

Farmer's Markets

- **Farmers' Market** • 2640 Main St • Sun 9:30-1
- **Farmers' Market** • Arizona Ave & 2nd St • Wed 9-2, Sat 8:30-1
- **Santa Monica** • 2300 Pico Blvd

Gyms

- **Club at MGM Plaza** • 2425 Colorado Ave • 310-829-2227
- **Club Sante** • 101 Wilshire Blvd • 310-393-4778
- **Club Sante** • 530 Pico Blvd • 310-395-0416
- **Easton Gym** • 1233 3rd St Promenade • 310-395-4441
- **Hard Body Class** • 508 Santa Monica Blvd • 310-394-3875
- **Muscle Beach** • 1817 Ocean Front Walk • 310-578-6131
- **Powerhouse Gym** • 245 Main St • 310-314-8888

Hardware Stores

- **Busy Bee Hardware** • 1521 Santa Monica Blvd • 310-395-1158
- **Fisher Lumber** • 1601 14th St • 310-395-0956

Liquor Stores

- **A & E Liquor Mart** • 2116 Pico Blvd
- **Bill's Liquor Store** • 2202 Lincoln Blvd
- **Davey Jones Liquor Locker** • 63 Navy St
- **Duck Blind** • 1102 Montana Ave
- **Ed's Liquor Store** • 825 Pico Blvd
- **Fireside Liquors** • 1421 Montana Ave
- **Frank's Liquor Store** • 115 Broadway
- **Hank's Liquor Store** • 1436 Santa Monica Blvd
- **Ladds Liquor & Deli** • 1011 Broadway
- **Marty's Liquor** • 1736 Ocean Park Blvd
- **Michael's** • 2402 Wilshire Blvd
- **Moore's Liquors** • 1713 Pico Blvd
- **Santa Monica Liquor** • 1001 Wilshire Blvd
- **Star Liquors** • 1929 Main St
- **Surf Liquor** • 2522 Main St

Movie Theaters

- **Aero Theatre** • 1328 Montana Ave
- **AMC Santa Monica 7 Plex** • 1310 3rd St Promenade
- **Broadway Cinemas 4** • 1441 3rd St Promenade
- **Laemmle's Monica 4** • 1332 2nd St
- **Mann Criterion 6** • 1313 3rd St Promenade
- **Nu Wilshire Theatre** • 1314 Wilshire Blvd

Pet Stores

- **Animal Kingdom** • 300 Pico Blvd • 310-392-4074
- **Aquarium & Pet Ctr** • 826 Wilshire Blvd • 310-395-1009
- **Cat Co** • 1637 16th St • 310-450-2287
- **Centinela Feed & Pet Supplies** • 1448 Lincoln Blvd • 310-451-7140
- **Pet Affaire** • 3013 Lincoln Blvd • 310-396-0804
- **Pets of Wilshire** • 2102 Wilshire Blvd • 310-453-7676

Restaurants

- **17th Street Café** • 1610 Montana Ave • 310-453-2771
- **Babalu** • 1002 Montana Ave • 310-395-2500
- **Back on the Beach** • 445 Pacific Coast Hwy • 310-393-8282
- **Blueberry** • 510 Santa Monica Blvd • 310-394-7766
- **Border Grill** • 1445 4th St • 310-451-1655
- **Broadway Deli** • 1457 3rd St Promenade • 310-451-0616
- **Buffalo Club** • 1520 Olympic Blvd • 310-450-8600
- **Cafe Montana** • 1534 Montana Ave • 310-829-3990
- **California Chicken Café** • 2401 Wilshire Blvd • 310-453-0477
- **Cha Cha Chicken** • 1906 Ocean Ave • 310-581-1684
- **Chaya Venice** • 110 Navy St • 310-396-1179
- **Chez Jay** • 1657 Ocean Ave • 310-395-1741
- **Chinois on Main** • 2709 Main St • 310-392-9025
- **Dhaba** • 2104 Main St • 310 399 9452
- **Falafel King** • 1315 3rd St Promenade • 310-587-2551
- **Finn McCool's** • 2700 Main St • 310-452-1734
- **Fritto Misto** • 601 Colorado Ave • 310-458-2829
- **JR Seafood** • 102 Santa Monica Pl • 310-260-8855
- **Kau-aina** • 119 Broadway • 310-394-0100
- **Library Alehouse** • 2911 Main St • 310-314-4855
- **Lobster, The** • 1602 Ocean Ave • 310-458-9294
- **Lula** • 2722 Main St • 310-392-5711
- **Mani's** • 2507 Main St • 310-396-7700
- **Michael D's Café & Catering** • 234 Pico Blvd • 310-452-8737
- **Newsroom Café** • 530 Wilshire Blvd • 310-319-9100
- **Ocean Ave Seafood** • 1401 Ocean Ave • 310-394-5669
- **Ocean Park Omelette Parlor** • 2732 Main St • 310-399-7892
- **Reel Inn** • 1220 3rd St Promenade • 310-395-5538
- **Sushi Roku** • 1401 Ocean Ave • 310-458-4771
- **Trastavere** • 1360 3rd St Promenade • 310-319-1985
- **World Café** • 2820 Main St • 310-392-1661
- **Ye Olde King's Head** • 116 Santa Monica Blvd • 310-451-1402

Shopping

- **Acorn Store** • 1220 5th St •
- **Continental Shop** • 1619 Wilshire Blvd • 310-453-8655
- **Eames Office** • 2665 Main St • 310-396-5991
- **Hear Music** • 1429 3rd St Promenade • 310-319-9527
- **Helen's Cycles** • 2501 Broadway • 310-829-1836
- **Herb King** • 2305 Main St • 310-399-4470
- **Horizons West** • 2011 Main St • 310-392-1122
- **Midnight Special Bookstore** • 1318 3rd St Promenade • 310-393-2923
- **Muskrat** • 1248 3rd St Promenade • 310-394-1713
- **Noteworthy** • 1427 3rd St Promenade • 310-260-9004
- **Number One Beauty Supply** • 1426 Montana Ave • 310-394-6968
- **One Life Natural Foods** • 3001 Main St • 310-392-4501
- **Palmetto** • 1034 Montana Ave • 310-395-6687
- **Pump Station** • 2415 Wilshire Blvd • 310-826-5774
- **Puzzle Zoo** • 1413 3rd St Promenade • 310-393-9201
- **Santa Monica Farms** • 2015 Main St • 310-396-4069
- **Splash Bath & Body** • 2823 Main St • 310-581-4200
- **Tao Healing Arts Center** • 2309 Main St • 310-396-4877
- **Tudor House** • 1403 2nd St • 310-451-4107

Video Rental

- **Blockbuster** • 2602 Lincoln Blvd • 310-392-3228
- **Blockbuster** • 1402 Wilshire Blvd • 310-394-7792
- **Blockbuster** • 180 Pier Ave • 310-452-4243
- **Blockbuster** • 625 Montana Ave • 310-393-5131
- **Vidiots** • 302 Pico Blvd • 310-392-8508

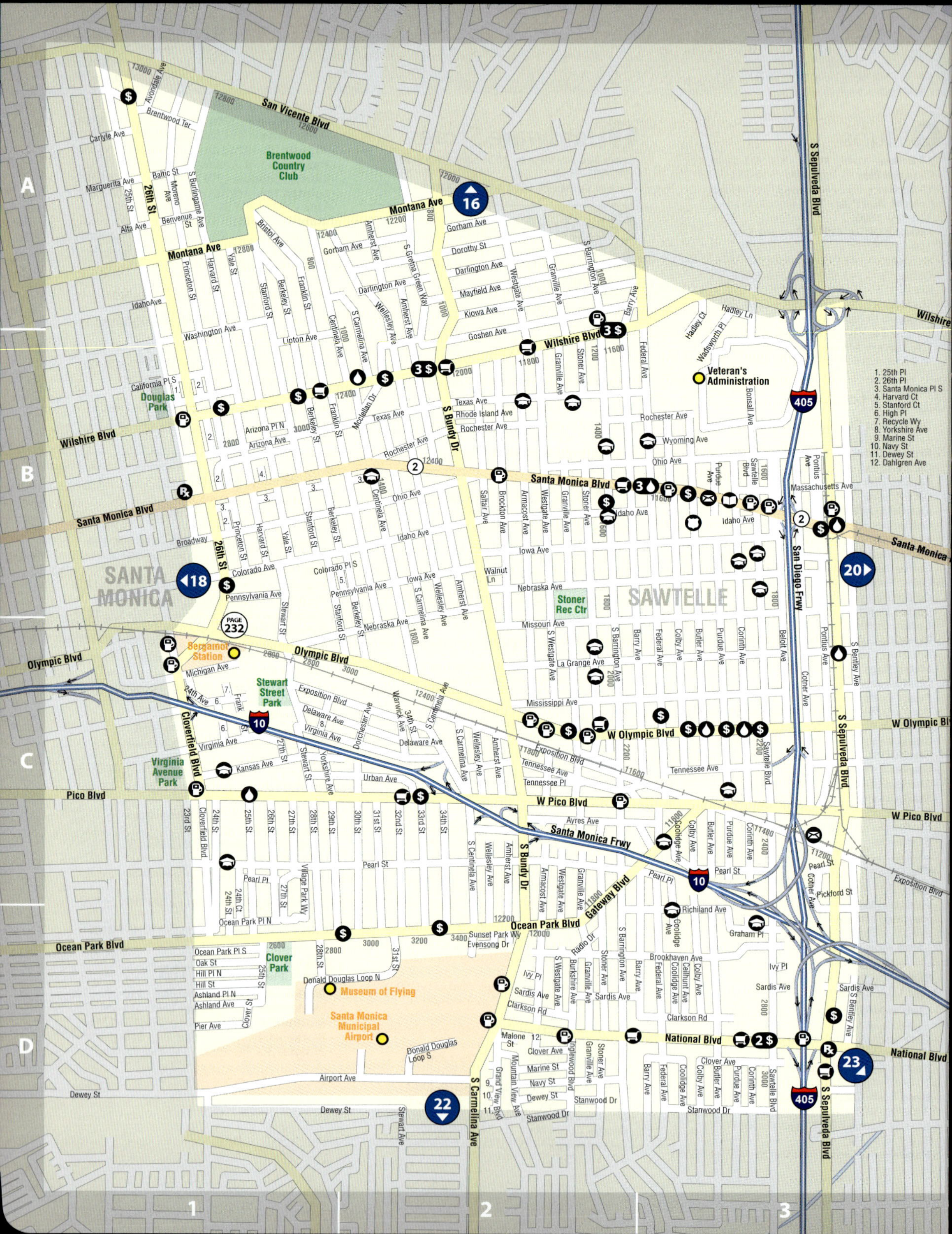

San Vicente Blvd

Brentwood Country Club

Montana Ave

16

Veteran's Administration

Wilshire Blvd

405

Wilshire

1. 25th Pl
2. 26th Pl
3. Santa Monica Pl S
4. Harvard Ct
5. Stanford Ct
6. High Pl
7. Recycle Wy
8. Yorkshire Ave
9. Marine St
10. Navy St
11. Dewey St
12. Dahlgren Ave

Santa Monica Blvd

Santa Monica

Santa Monica Blvd

SAWTELLE

Stoner Rec Ctr

20

SANTA MONICA

18

PAGE 232

Bergamot Station

Stewart Street Park

Olympic Blvd

Exposition Blvd

10

Virginia Avenue Park

Pico Blvd

W Olympic Blvd

W Pico Blvd

Santa Monica Frwy

W Pico Blvd

10

San Diego Frwy

San Diego Frwy

Ocean Park Blvd

Clover Park

Museum of Flying

Santa Monica Municipal Airport

Gateway Blvd

Richland Ave

Graham Pl

Exposition Blvd

Pickford St

National Blvd

2

23

National Blvd

405

Airport Ave

Dewey St

22

Dewey St

S Sepulveda Blvd

Often referred to as "The Westside," West LA/Santa Monica East is simultaneously a slice of "modest-LA" and young, upscale-chic. Families, couples and college students happily commingle in this eclectic neighborhood with a good residential and commercial mix.

$ Banks

- **Bank of America** · 11501 Santa Monica Blvd
- **Bank of America** · 287 26th St
- **Bank of America** · 2930 S Sepulveda Blvd
- **Bank of America** · 3320 Ocean Park Blvd
- **Bank of America Mortgage** · 3032 Wilshire Blvd
- **Bank of the West** · 11150 Santa Monica Blvd
- **California Bank & Trust** · 11345 W Olympic Blvd
- **City National Bank** · 11500 W Olympic Blvd
- **City National Bank** · 1620 26th St
- **First Bank & Trust** · 11835 W Olympic Blvd
- **First Federal Bank** · 11310 National Blvd
- **First Federal Bank** · 12401 Wilshire Blvd
- **First Professional Bank** · 11620 Wilshire Blvd
- **Guaranty Bank of California** · 12301 Wilshire Blvd
- **La Salle National Bank** · 11601 Wilshire Blvd
- **Marathon National Bank** · 11150 W Olympic Blvd
- **US Bank** · 12100 Wilshire Blvd
- **US Bank** · 3302 Pico Blvd
- **Washington Mutual** · 11285 National Blvd
- **Washington Mutual** · 12121 Wilshire Blvd
- **Washington Mutual** · 2701 Wilshire Blvd
- **Wells Fargo Bank** · 11377 W Olympic Blvd
- **Wells Fargo Bank** · 2940 Ocean Park Blvd
- **World Savings & Loan** · 11601 Wilshire Blvd

Car Washes

- **All By Hand** · 11111 Santa Monica Blvd
- **Blue Wave Car Wash** · 11602 Santa Monica Blvd
- **Brent-West Car Wash** · 11602 Santa Monica Blvd
- **Mr Detail Auto Waxing** · 11500 W Olympic Blvd
- **Santa Monica Car Wash & Detail** · 2510 Pico Blvd
- **Sepulveda West Car Wash** · 2001 S Sepulveda Blvd
- **Shell** · 11574 Santa Monica Blvd
- **Shine for Show** · 11755 Wilshire Blvd
- **West LA Car Wash** · 11350 W Olympic Blvd

Gas Stations

- **76** · 11280 National Blvd
- **76** · 11305 Santa Monica Blvd
- **76** · 11675 W Pico Blvd
- **76** · 11954 Santa Monica Blvd
- **76** · 2601 Wilshire Blvd
- **76** · 2876 S Bundy Dr
- **Arco** · 11748 W Olympic Blvd
- **Arco** · 1819 Cloverfield Blvd
- **Chevron** · 11951 W Olympic Blvd
- **Chevron** · 2328 Pico Blvd
- **Mobil** · 11666 Wilshire Blvd
- **Mobil** · 1660 S Sepulveda Blvd
- **Shell** · 11574 Santa Monica Blvd
- **Shell** · 11944 W Olympic Blvd
- **Shell** · 1802 Cloverfield Blvd
- **Texaco** · 11261 Santa Monica Blvd
- **Texaco** · 3010 S Bundy Dr

Landmarks

- **Bergamot Station** · 2525 Michigan Ave
- **Museum of Flying** · 2772 Donald Douglas Loop N
- **Santa Monica Municipal Airport** · 3223 Donald Douglas Loop S
- **Veteran's Administration** · Federal Ave & S Sepulveda Blvd

Libraries

- **West Los Angeles Regional Library** · 11360 Santa Monica Blvd · 310-575-8323

℞ 24-Hour Pharmacies

- **Sav-On** · 2505 Santa Monica Blvd · 310-828-6056
- **Sav-On** · 3010 S Sepulveda Blvd · 310- 478-9821

Police

- **Los Angeles Police Dept** · 1663 Butler Ave · 310-575-8404

Post Offices

- 11270 Exposition Blvd
- 11420 Santa Monica Blvd

Schools

- **Brockton Avenue Elementary** · 1309 Armacost Ave
- **Brooklyn Avenue Elementary** · 340 N McDonnell Ave
- **Edison Elementary** · 2425 Kansas Ave
- **Grant Elementary** · 2368 Pearl St
- **Indian Springs Continuation** · 1441 S Barrington Ave
- **New Horizon** · 1819 Sawtelle Blvd
- **Park Century** · 2040 Stoner Ave
- **Poseidon** · 11811 W Pico Blvd
- **Richland Avenue Elementary** · 11562 Richland Ave
- **Southern California Montessori** · 1430 Centinela Ave
- **St Joan of Arc Elementary** · 11561 Gateway Blvd
- **St Sebastian** · 1430 Federal Ave
- **Sterry Children's Center** · 1747 Sawtelle Blvd
- **Sterry Elementary** · 1730 Corinth Ave
- **University Senior High School** · 11800 Texas Ave
- **Webster Middle School** · 11330 W Graham Pl
- **West LA Baptist** · 1609 Barrington Ct
- **Westview** · 2000 Stoner Ave

Supermarkets

- **Albertson's** · 3105 Wilshire Blvd
- **Pavilions** · 11750 Wilshire Blvd
- **Ralph's** · 11361 National Blvd
- **Ralph's** · 11727 W Olympic Blvd
- **Ralph's** · 12057 Wilshire Blvd
- **Trader Joe's** · 3212 Pico Blvd
- **Von's** · 11674 Santa Monica Blvd
- **Von's** · 3118 S Sepulveda Blvd
- **Whole Foods Market** · 11666 National Blvd

Brentwood Country Club

SANTA MONICA

SAWTELLE

Douglas Park

Stoner Rec Ctr

Bergamot Station

Stewart Street Park

Virginia Avenue Park

Clover Park

Museum of Flying

Santa Monica Municipal Airport

PAGE 232

Street / place labels:

San Vicente Blvd, Brentwood Ter, Carlyle Ave, Marguerita Ave, Alta Ave, Idaho Ave, Montana Ave, Washington Ave, Wilshire Blvd, Santa Monica Blvd, Broadway, Colorado Ave, Pennsylvania Ave, Olympic Blvd, Michigan Ave, Pico Blvd, Ocean Park Blvd, Dewey St, Airport Ave

Arcadia Ave, Baltic St, 25th St, 26th St, Moreno Ave, S Burlingame Ave, Benevue St, Princeton St, Harvard St, Stanford St, Berkeley St, Franklin St, Lipton Ave, Centinela Ave, S Carmelina Ave, Bristol Ave, Yale St, Gorham Ave, Darlington Ave, Amherst Ave, Wellesley Ave, McClellan Dr, Texas Ave, Rochester Ave, Ohio Ave, Idaho Ave, Iowa Ave, Nebraska Ave, Missouri Ave

Gorham Ave, Dorothy St, Darlington Ave, Mayfield Ave, Kiowa Ave, Goshen Ave, Texas Ave, Rhode Island Ave, Rochester Ave

Westgate Ave, Granville Ave, Stoner Ave, S Barrington Ave, Federal Ave, Bay St, Gorham Ave, Hadley Ln, Hadley Ct, Wadsworth Pl

Wilshire Blvd, S Bundy Dr, Saltair Ave, Brockton Ave, Armacost Ave, Walnut Ln

Bonsall Ave, Rochester Ave, Wyoming Ave, Ohio Ave, Purdue Ave, Sawtelle Blvd, Massachusetts Ave, Idaho Ave

Stoner Ave, Granville Ave, Barry Ave, Colby Ave, Butler Ave, Corinth Ave, Pontius Ave, S Bentley Ave, Beloit Ave, Cotner Ave, S Sepulveda Blvd, S Diego Frwy / San Diego Frwy

La Grange Ave, Mississippi Ave, S Westgate Ave, S Barrington Ave

W Olympic Blvd, Tennessee Ave, Tennessee Pl, Exposition Blvd, Warwick Ave, Dorchester Ave, Delaware Ave, Virginia Ave, Kansas Ave, Frank, 24th Ave, Cloverfield Blvd, Virginia Ave, 27th St, Yorkshire Ave, Stewart St

W Pico Blvd, Ayres Ave, Santa Monica Frwy, Coolidge Ave, Pearl St, Pearl Pl, Richland Ave, Graham Pl, Pickford St, Exposition Blvd

23rd St, 24th St, 25th St, 26th St, 27th St, 28th St, 29th St, 30th St, 31st St, 32nd St, 33rd St, 34th St, S Centinela Ave, Amherst Ave, Wellesley Ave, S Bundy Dr, Armacost Ave, Granville Ave

Pearl St, Pearl Pl, Village Park Wy, 24th Ct, 24th St, 27th St, Ocean Park Pl N, Ocean Park Pl S, Oak St, Hill Pl N, Hill St, Ashland Pl N, Ashland Ave, Pier Ave, Donald Douglas Loop N, Donald Douglas Loop S

Sunset Park Wy, Evensong Dr, Radio Dr, S Barrington Ave, S Burkshire Ave, S Westgate Ave, Granville Ave, Stoner Ave, Ivy Pl, Sardis Ave, Clarkson Rd, Malone St, Clover Ave, Marine St, Navy St, Dewey St, Stanwood Dr, Grand View Blvd, Mountain View Ave, S Carmelina Ave, Stewart Ave

National Blvd, Inglewood Blvd, Barry Ave, Federal Ave, Coolidge Ave, Colby Ave, Purdue Ave, Corinth Ave, Sawtelle Blvd, Sardis Ave, Ivy Pl, Brookhaven Ave, Cadmium Ave, Coolidge Ave, Clarkson Rd, Richland Ave, Gateway Blvd

S Sepulveda Blvd, S Bentley Ave, Cotner Ave, Pontius Ave

Route markers: 16, 18, 20, 22, 23

I-405 / I-10 freeway shields

Santa Monica Blvd

1. 25th Pl
2. 26th Pl
3. Santa Monica Pl S
4. Harvard Ct
5. Stanford Ct
6. High Pl
7. Recycle Wy
8. Yorkshire Ave
9. Marine St
10. Navy St
11. Dewey St
12. Dahlgren Ave

Grid labels: A, B, C, D (rows); 1, 2, 3 (columns)

For services, your best bets are along the east-west arteries. Starbucks is conveniently apparent, if not unavoidable, while a great variety of restaurants and cuisines illustrate the neighborhood's diversity. The independent movie theater reigns in this neighborhood, where both the Nuart and Royal Theatres are very popular. The many high-end private gyms are the sanctuary for the fatigued and the fit—and if the workout doesn't "do you in," your monthly membership dues certainly will.

Clubs

- **Liquid Kitty** · 11780 W Pico Blvd · 310-473-3707
- **McCabe's** · 3101 Pico Blvd · 310-828-4403
- **Q's Billiards** · 11835 Wilshire Blvd · 310-477-7550

Coffee

- **Balcony** · 12431 Rochester Ave
- **Cacao Coffee House** · 11609 Santa Monica Blvd
- **Coffee Bean & Tea Leaf** · 3150 Ocean Park Blvd
- **Seattle's Best Coffee** · 12222 Wilshire Blvd
- **Starbucks** · 11155 Santa Monica Blvd
- **Starbucks** · 11280 W Olympic Blvd
- **Starbucks** · 11705 National Blvd
- **Starbucks** · 12001 Wilshire Blvd
- **Starbucks** · 12100 Santa Monica Blvd
- **Starbucks** · 2525 Wilshire Blvd
- **Starbucks** · 2901 Ocean Park Blvd
- **Unurban** · 3301 Pico Blvd

Gyms

- **24-Hour Fitness** · 2929 31st St · 310-450-4464
- **Bally Total Fitness** · 1914 S Bundy Dr · 310-820-7571
- **Bodies in Motion** · 2730 Santa Monica Blvd · 310-264-0777
- **Elio's Fitness for Success** · 12424 Wilshire Blvd · 310-479-7677
- **Elite Fitness Training Systems** · 12401 Wilshire Blvd · 310-979-6404
- **Joe's Gym** · 11601 Wilshire Blvd · 310-966-1999
- **LA Woman** · 11650 Santa Monica Blvd · 310-207-2279
- **Power House Gym** · 11400 W Olympic Blvd · 310-914-5120
- **Spectrum Club** · 2425 Olympic Blvd · 310-829-4995
- **Sports Club LA** · 1835 S Sepulveda Blvd · 310-473-1447
- **Trident Fitness** · 11355 W Olympic Blvd · 310-231-5195
- **Winsor Fitness West** · 12231 Wilshire Blvd · 310-442-1030

Hardware Stores

- **BC Door & Hardware** · 2109 Stoner Ave · 310-268-7700
- **George's Hardware & Garden Supply** · 2060 Sawtelle Blvd · 310-479-1280
- **Orchard Supply Hardware** · 2020 S Bundy Dr · 310-571-3838
- **Tool Power** · 2828 Santa Monica Blvd · 310-453-2012

Liquor Stores

- **Barrington Market & Liquor** · 1166 S Barrington Ave
- **Brockton Liquor** · 11932 Santa Monica Blvd
- **Hai's Liquor** · 11701 W Pico Blvd
- **In & Out Liquor** · 2130 Sawtelle Blvd
- **J & H Liquors** · 2717 Ocean Park Blvd
- **J & M Liquor Store** · 11306 Santa Monica Blvd
- **Jerry's Liquor Store** · 2923 Wilshire Blvd
- **Kings Liquors** · 3100 Santa Monica Blvd
- **Mark's International Wines** · 2311 Cotner Ave
- **Sunset Plaza Liquor** · 2602 Pico Blvd
- **Wine Expo** · 2933 Santa Monica Blvd

Movie Theaters

- **Laemmle Theatres** · 11523 Santa Monica Blvd
- **Leammle's Royal Theatre** · 11523 Santa Monica Blvd
- **Nuart Theatre** · 11272 Santa Monica Blvd

Pet Stores

- **Holiday Hotel for Cats** · 2327 Cotner Ave · 310-479-1440
- **Katie's Pet Depot** · 2919 Wilshire Blvd · 310-828-4545
- **LA Aquarium & Pet Supplies** · 11662 W Pico Blvd · 310-477-1928
- **Lange Foundation** · 2106 S Sepulveda Blvd · 310-473-5585
- **Petco** · 2910 Wilshire Blvd · 310-586-1963
- **Pets Salon** · 12243 Santa Monica Blvd · 310-207-0838
- **Town & Country Mobile Pet Service** · 1850 S Sepulveda Blvd · 310-479-6886

Restaurants

- **Asakuma** · 11701 Wilshire Blvd · 310-826-0013
- **Bandera** · 11700 Wilshire Blvd · 310-477-3524
- **Bombay Café** · 12021 W Pico Blvd · 310-473-3388
- **Chez Mimi** · 246 26th St · 310-393-0558
- **Hide Sushi** · 2040 Sawtelle Blvd · 310-477-7242
- **Il Forno** · 2901 Ocean Park Blvd · 310-450-1241
- **Il Moro** · 11400 W Olympic Blvd · 310-575-3530
- **Javan** · 11500 Santa Monica Blvd · 310-207-5555
- **Josie's Restaurant** · 2424 Pico Blvd · 310-581-9888
- **Kay 'n Dave's** · 262 26th St · 310-260-1355
- **LA Farm Restaurant** · 3000 Olympic Blvd · 310-449-4000
- **La Bottega Marino** · 11363 Santa Monica Blvd · 310-477-7777
- **Lares** · 2911 Pico Blvd · 310-829-4550
- **Le Saigon** · 11611 Santa Monica Blvd · 310-312-2929
- **Mishima Restaurant** · 11819 Wilshire Blvd · 310-966-1062
- **Rae's Restaurant** · 2901 Pico Blvd · 310-828-7937
- **Royal Star Seafood** · 3001 Wilshire Blvd · 323-692-5606
- **Sushi Sabasune** · 11300 Nebraska Ave · 310-268-8380
- **Tlapazola Grill** · 11676 Gateway Blvd · 310-477-1577
- **Typhoon** · 3221 Donald Douglas Loop S · 310-390-6565
- **Valentino** · 3115 Pico Blvd · 310-829-4313
- **Vito** · 2807 Ocean Park Blvd · 310-450-4999
- **Yabu** · 11820 W Pico Blvd · 310-473-9757
- **Zabies** · 3003 Ocean Park Blvd · 310-392-9036

Shopping

- **Any Occasion Balloons** · 12009 W Pico Blvd · 310-473-9963
- **California Map & Travel** · 3312 Pico Blvd
- **Graphaids** · 12400 Santa Monica Blvd · 310-820-0445
- **Hiromi Paper International** · Bergamot Station, 2525 Michigan Ave · 310-998-0098
- **McCabe's Guitar Shop** · 3001 Pico Blvd · 310-828-4427
- **Record Surplus** · 11609 W Pico Blvd · 310-478-4217

Video Rental

- **20-20 Video** · 11550 Santa Monica Blvd · 310-478-2020
- **20-20 Video** · 3000 S Sepulveda Blvd · 310-836-2020
- **A Video Store Named Desire** · 11631 Santa Monica Blvd · 310-444-0079
- **Blockbuster** · 11700 National Blvd · 310-391-8233
- **Blockbuster** · 12112 Santa Monica Blvd · 310-447-2481
- **Cinefile Video** · 11280 Santa Monica Blvd · 310-312-8836
- **Galaxy Video & 28-Minute Photo** · 2901 Ocean Park Blvd · 310-450-0900
- **Odyssey Video** · 11910 Wilshire Blvd · 310-477-2523
- **Video Addict (Asian)** · 1818 Sawtelle Blvd · 310-312-5083
- **Video Ya** · 2051 Sawtelle Blvd · 310-477-5488

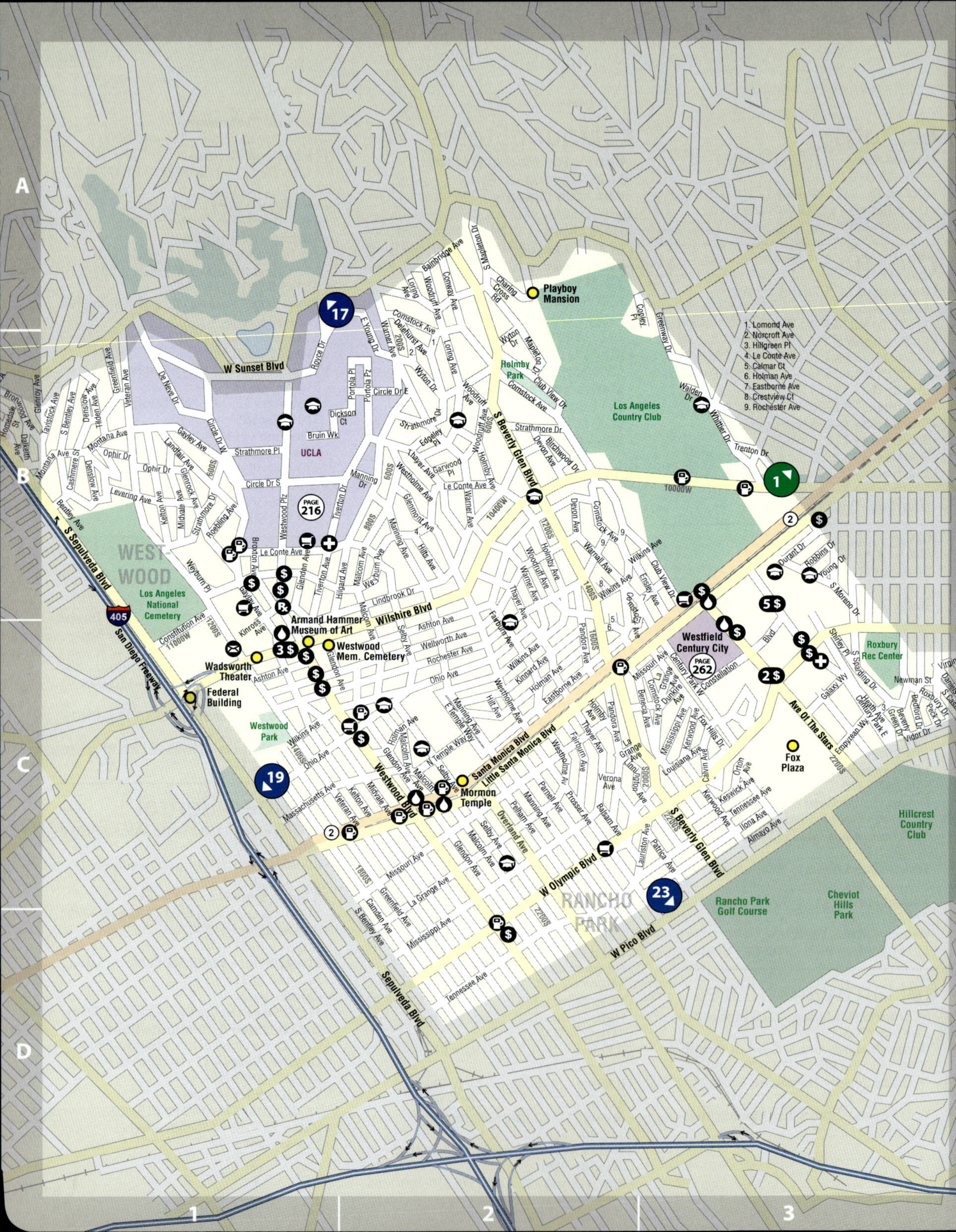
N
A
B
C
D
1
2
3
1. Lomond Ave
2. Norcroft Ave
3. Hillgreen Pl
4. Le Conte Ave
5. Calmar Ct
6. Holman Ave
7. Eastborne Ave
8. Crestview Ct
9. Rochester Ave
Playboy Mansion
Holmby Park
Los Angeles Country Club
UCLA
PAGE 216
WEST WOOD
Los Angeles National Cemetery
Armand Hammer Museum of Art
Westwood Mem. Cemetery
Wadsworth Theater
Federal Building
Westwood Park
Mormon Temple
Westfield Century City
PAGE 262
Roxbury Rec Center
Fox Plaza
Hillcrest Country Club
Rancho Park Golf Course
Cheviot Hills Park
RANCHO PARK
405
San Diego Freeway
S Sepulveda Blvd
Sepulveda Blvd
W Sunset Blvd
Wilshire Blvd
Santa Monica Blvd
Little Santa Monica Blvd
Westwood Blvd
S Beverly Glen Blvd
W Olympic Blvd
W Pico Blvd
Ave Of The Stars
Century Park E
Constellation
Overland Ave
Le Conte Ave
Strathmore Pl
Gayley Ave
Hilgard Ave
Tiverton Dr
Glendon Ave
Veteran Ave
Massachusetts Ave
Tennessee Ave
Missouri Ave
Ohio Ave
Wellworth Ave
Ashton Ave
Rochester Ave
Lindbrook Dr
Manning Ave
Beverly Glen Blvd
Comstock Ave
Bainbridge Ave
Charing Cross Rd
Mapleton Dr
Greenway Dr
Whittier Dr
Walden Dr
Trenton Dr
Durant Dr
Robbins Dr
Young Dr
S Moreno Dr
17
19
23
1
2
5
2

Century City, which is almost completely made up of office buildings, becomes a virtual ghost town at night—with the exception of the Century City Mall and ABC Entertainment Center, both of which feature top-of-the-line movie theatres. Westwood, however, always seems to be busy, probably because of the constant stream of UCLA students. Street parking is a game of chance and a test of one's patience for circling the same streets again and again. There are pay lots, but the area would definitely be better served by at least one more municipal lot—preferably toward the eastern end of Westwood.

$ Banks

- **Bank of America** · 10960 Wilshire Blvd
- **Bank of America** · 2049 Century Park E
- **Bank of America** · 930 Westwood Blvd
- **Bank of the West** · 10929 Wilshire Blvd
- **California Bank & Trust** · 1940 Century Park E
- **California Commerce Bank** · 2029 Century Park E
- **California Credit Union** · 2215 Westwood Blvd
- **California National Bank** · 1800 Ave of the Stars
- **Citibank** · 1072 Westwood Blvd
- **Citibank** · 1801 Ave of the Stars
- **City National Bank** · 1800 Century Park E
- **City National Bank** · 1950 Ave of the Stars
- **City National Bank** · 2029 Century Park E
- **City National Bank** · 2049 Century Park E
- **Comerica Bank** · 10900 WIlshire Blvd
- **First Regional Bank** · 1801 Century Park E
- **First Republic Bank** · 1888 Century Park E
- **Preferred Bank** · 1801 Century Park E
- **Union Bank** · 1310 Westwood Blvd
- **Union Bank** · 1901 Ave of the Stars
- **US Bank** · 1013 Broxton Ave
- **US Bank** · 10866 Wilshire Blvd
- **Washington Mutual** · 10901 Wilshire Blvd
- **Washington Mutual** · 1550 Westwood Blvd
- **Washington Mutual** · 1925 Century Park E
- **Wells Fargo Bank** · 10920 Wilshire Blvd
- **Wells Fargo Bank** · 1801 Ave of the Stars

◐ Car Washes

- **Blue Wave Car Wash** · 10854 Santa Monica Blvd
- **Century City** · 1800 Ave of the Stars
- **Mario's Hand Car Wash** · 10940 Wilshire Blvd
- **Mr Polish** · 1901 Ave of the Stars
- **Speedway Car Wash** · 10850 Santa Monica Blvd

℗ Gas Stations

- **76** · 10389 Santa Monica Blvd
- **76** · 9988 Wilshire Blvd
- **Arco** · 10801 Santa Monica Blvd
- **Chevron** · 10867 Santa Monica Blvd
- **Chevron** · 10984 Le Conte Ave
- **Exxon** · 10991 Santa Monica Blvd
- **Mobil** · 10857 Santa Monica Blvd
- **Mobil** · 10863 W Olympic Blvd
- **Mobil** · 1465 Glendon Ave
- **Shell** · 900 Gayley Ave

✚ Hospitals

- **Century City Hospital** · 2070 Century Park E · 310-553-6211
- **University of California-Medical Center** · 10833 Le Conte Ave · 310-825-7271

● Landmarks

- **Armand Hammer Museum of Art** · 10889 Wilshire Blvd
- **Federal Building** · Wilshire Blvd & Sepulveda Blvd
- **Fox Plaza (AKA the "Die Hard" building)** · 2121 Ave of the Stars
- **Mormon Temple** · 10777 Santa Monica Blvd
- **Playboy Mansion** · 10236 Charing Cross Rd
- **Wadsworth Theater** · 11000 Wilshire Blvd
- **Westwood Memorial Cemetery** · 1218 Glendon Ave

℞ 24-Hour Pharmacies

- **Rite-Aid** · 1101 Westwood Blvd · 310-209-0708

✉ Post Offices

- 11000 Wilshire Blvd

⚊ Schools

- **Beverly Hills High School** · 241 S Moreno Dr
- **Beverly Hills Montessori** · 1105 N Laurel Ave
- **El Rodeo Elementary** · 605 N Whittier Dr
- **Emerson Middle School** · 1650 Selby Ave
- **Fairburn Avenue Elementary** · 1403 Fairburn Ave
- **Moreno High School** · 214 Moreno Dr
- **Sinai Akiba Academy** · 10400 Wilshire Blvd
- **St Paul the Apostle** · 1536 Selby Ave
- **UCLA** · 405 Hilgard Ave
- **UCLA Neuropsychiatric Hospital** · 760 Westwood Plz
- **Warner Avenue Elementary** · 615 Holmby Ave
- **Westwood Charter** · 2050 Selby Ave

⛟ Supermarkets

- **Bristol Farms** · 1515 Westwood Blvd
- **Gelson's Markets** · 10250 Santa Monica Blvd
- **Ralph's** · 10309 W Olympic Blvd
- **Ralph's** · 10861 Le Conte Ave
- **Whole Foods Market** · 1050 S Gayley Ave

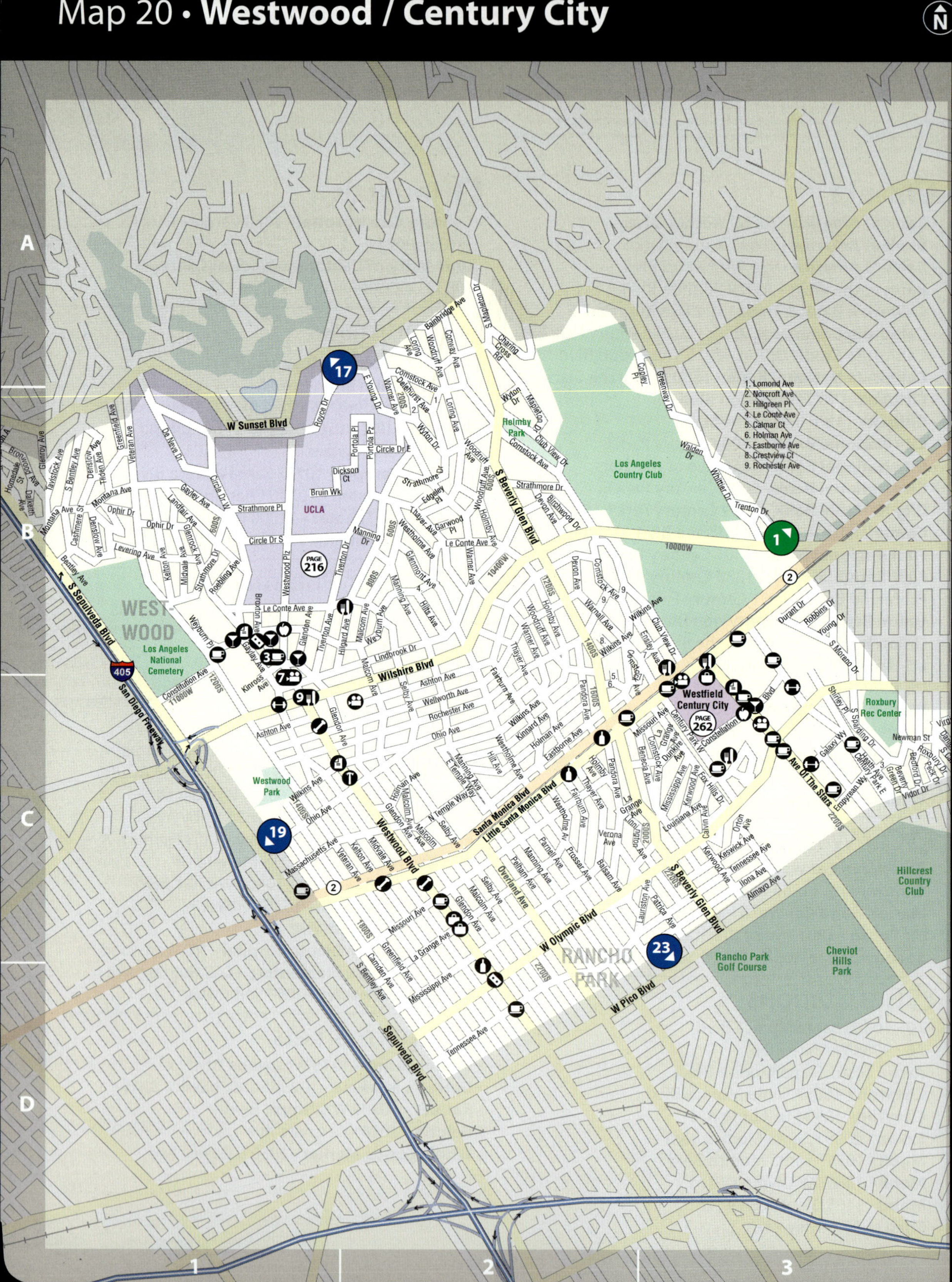
N
A
B
C
D
1
2
3
W Sunset Blvd
UCLA
WEST-WOOD
Los Angeles National Cemetery
Wilshire Blvd
Westwood Plz
PAGE 216
S Sepulveda Blvd
San Diego Freeway
405
Santa Monica Blvd
Little Santa Monica Blvd
Westwood Blvd
Westwood Park
Sepulveda Blvd
RANCHO PARK
W Olympic Blvd
W Pico Blvd
Rancho Park Golf Course
Cheviot Hills Park
Hillcrest Country Club
Roxbury Rec Center
Westfield Century City
PAGE 262
Ave Of The Stars
S Beverly Glen Blvd
Los Angeles Country Club
Helmby Park
17
1
19
23
1. Lomond Ave
2. Norcroft Ave
3. Hillgreen Pl
4. Le Conte Ave
5. Calmar Ct
6. Holman Ave
7. Eastborne Ave
8. Crestview Ct
9. Rochester Ave
10000W
10400W
Charing Cross Rd
W Sunset Blvd
Stone Dr
E Young Dr
Warner Ave
Comstock Ave
Dalehurst Ave
Loring Ave
Conway Ave
Woodruff Ave
Bainbridge Ave
Midvale Ave
Hilgard Ave
Glendon Ave
Malcolm Ave
Selby Ave
Veteran Ave
Gayley Ave
Kelton Ave
Ophir Dr
Montana Ave
Levering Ave
Bentley Ave
Greenfield Ave
Glenroy Ave
Homedale St
Kinross Ave
Ashton Ave
Wellworth Ave
Rochester Ave
Ohio Ave
Wilkins Ave
Kinnard Ave
Holman Ave
Eastborne Ave
Missouri Ave
La Grange Ave
Greenfield Ave
Camden Ave
Mississippi Ave
Tennessee Ave
Overland Ave
Manning Ave
Pelham Ave
Purnell Ave
Prosser Ave
Balsam Ave
Verona Ave
Club View Dr
Comstock Ave
Warnall Ave
Wilkins Ave
Thayer Ave
Eastborne Ave
Beverly Glen Blvd
S Beverly Glen Blvd
Pandora Ave
Fairburn Ave
Westholme Ave
Fox Hills Dr
Constellation Blvd
Century Park
Galaxy Wy
Shirley Pl
Durant Dr
Robbins Dr
Young Dr
S Moreno Dr
Newman St
Keswick Ave
Tennessee Ave
Ilona Ave
Almayo Ave
W Pico Blvd

Because of the symbiotic relationship Westwood has with UCLA, there are many unhealthy, inexpensive, but utterly delicious places to eat. Stan's Donuts is an L.A. institution; Diddy Riese Cookies can be had for a quarter apiece; and Falafel King deserves its name, serving some of the best baba ghanoush in town. With some of the best and oldest remaining one-screen movie houses in town, Westwood is a great place to take in a movie. But plan carefully; you don't want to show up on the night of the many film premieres that take place there.

24-Hour Copy Centers
- **Kinko's** • 10924 Weyburn Ave • 310-443-5502
- **Kinko's** • 1520 Westwood Blvd • 310-475-0789
- **Kinko's** • 1875 Century Park E • 310-277-0686

Clubs
- **The Century Club** • 10131 Constellation Blvd • 310-553-6000
- **W** • 930 Hilgard Ave • 310-208-8765
- **Westwood Brewing Company** • 1097 Glendon Ave • 310-209-2739

Coffee
- **Bolee's Gourmet** • 10100 Santa Monica Blvd
- **City Bean Coffee** • 2121 Ave of the Stars
- **City Bean Coffee** • 10911 Lindbrook Dr
- **Coffee Bean & Tea Leaf** • 1001 Gayley Ave
- **Coffee Bean & Tea Leaf** • 10401 Santa Monica Blvd
- **Coffee Bean & Tea Leaf** • 11049 Santa Monica Blvd
- **Coffee Bean & Tea Leaf** • 1940 Century Park E
- **Coffee Bean & Tea Leaf** • 950 Westwood Blvd
- **Java City Bakery Cafe** • 2020 Ave of the Stars
- **Kelly's Coffee & Fudge** • 10250 Santa Monica Blvd
- **Starbucks** • 10955 Weyburn Ave
- **Starbucks** • 1161 Westwood Blvd
- **Starbucks** • 1875 Century Park E
- **Starbucks** • 1898 Westwood Blvd
- **Starbucks** • 1999 Ave of the Stars
- **Starbucks** • 2049 Century Park E
- **Starbucks** • 2215 Westwood Blvd

Farmer's Markets
- **Farmers' Market** • Constellation Blvd & Ave of the Stars • Thu 11:30-3
- **Westwood** • Weyburn Ave & Westwood Blvd • Thu 2-7

Gyms
- **Bodies In Motion** • 1950 Century Park E • 310-836-8000
- **LA Fitness Sports Clubs** • 10921 Wilshire Blvd • 310-209-5002
- **Meridian Sports Club** • 2040 Ave of the Stars • 310-788-0288

Hardware Stores
- **Boulevard Hardware** • 1456 Westwood Blvd • 310-475-0795

Liquor Stores
- **Bel Air Wine Merchant** • 10421 Santa Monica Blvd
- **Frank's Liquor Mart** • 10559 Santa Monica Blvd
- **Wally's Wines & Liquors** • 2107 Westwood Blvd

Movie Theaters
- **AMC Avco Center Cinemas** • 10840 Wilshire Blvd
- **AMC Century 14** • 10250 Santa Monica Blvd
- **Century Plaza Cinemas 4** • 2040 Ave of the Stars
- **Landmark Regent Theatre** • 1045 Broxton Ave
- **Majestic Crest Theatre** • 1262 Westwood Blvd
- **Mann Bruin** • 948 Broxton Ave
- **Mann Festival 1 Theatres** • 10887 Lindbrook Dr
- **Mann National Theatre** • 10925 Lindbrook Dr
- **Mann Plaza Theatre** • 1067 Glendon Ave
- **Mann Village Theatre Westwood** • 961 Broxton Ave

Pet Stores
- **Katie's Pet Depot** • 1278 Westwood Blvd • 310-441-4122
- **Petco** • 1873 Westwood Blvd • 310-475-0303
- **Tender Loving Care Center** • 10948 Santa Monica Blvd • 310-479-4319

Restaurants
- **Big Chill** • 10850 Olympic Blvd • 310-441-0643
- **Clementine** • 1751 Ensley Ave • 310-552-1080
- **Diddy Riese Cookies** • 926 Broxton Ave • 310-208-0448
- **Earth, Wind & Flour** • 1176 Westwood Blvd • 310-470-2499
- **Falafel King** • 1059 Broxton Ave • 310-208-4444
- **Gardens on Glendon** • 1139 Glendon Ave • 310-824-1818
- **Johnnie's NY Pizzeria** • 10251 Santa Monica Blvd • 310-553-1188
- **La Bruschetta** • 1621 Westwood Blvd • 310-477-1052
- **La Cachette** • 10506 Little Santa Monica Blvd • 310-470-4992
- **Matteo's Hoboken** • 2323 Westwood Blvd • 310-474-1109
- **Mojo** • 930 Hilgard Ave • 310-443-7820
- **Napa Valley Grille** • 1100 Glendon Ave • 310-824-3322
- **Stan's Donuts** • 10948 Weyburn Ave • 310-208-8660
- **Tengu** • 10853 Lindbrook Dr • 310-209-0071

Shopping
- **Bristol Farms** • 1537 Westwood Blvd • 310-481-0100
- **Rhino Records** • 2028 Westwood Blvd • 310-474-8685
- **The Writer's Store** • 2040 Westwood Blvd • 310-441-5151
- **Three Dog Bakery** • 10250 Santa Monica Blvd • 310-557-1254

Video Rental
- **Blockbuster** • 10917 Weyburn Ave • 310-824-5235
- **Hollywood Video** • 2201 Westwood Blvd • 310-475-0636

N

Penmar
Golf Course
Penmar
Playground
Rose Ave

Glenavon Ave
Glenton Ave
Morningside Wy
Louella Ave
Glyndon Ave
Walnut Ave
Appleton Wy
Preston Way
Palms Blvd
Vienna Wy

1. The Grand Canal
2. Canal St
3. Alberta Ave
4. Meade Pl
5. Carroll Ave
6. Linnie Ave
7. Howland Ave
8. Sherman Ave
9. Nowita Ct
10. Brenta Pl

Courtland St
Indiana Ave
Appleby St
Valita St
Sunset Ave
Vernon Ct
Vernon Ave
Indiana Ave
Indiana Ave
Lake St
Dillon St
Frederick St
Elkgrove Ave
Elkgrove Cir
Elkhart Pl
Doreen Pl
Elkland Pl
Carlton Wy
Victoria Ave

Warren Ave
18
1
300

Rose Ave
Rose Ct
Flower Ct
Flower Ave
Sunset Ct
Sunset Ave
Renne Ave
3rd Ave
Vernon Ave
Vernon Ave
Vernon Ave
700
Lincoln Blvd
1400
Lincoln Ct

22
187

Chiat-Day
Building
Pacific Ave
Ozone Ct
Rose Ave
Rose Ct
Dudley Ave
Paloma Ave
Paloma Ave
Sunset Ct
200
Ocean Front Walk

Indiana Ave
Indiana Ct
Brooks Ave
Broadway Ave
Broadway Ct
Westminster Ave
4th Ave
5th Ave
6th Ave
7th Ave
San Miguel Ave
Norfolk Ave
Pleasant View Ave
Oakwood Ave
Linden Ave
Linden Ave
Nowita Pl
Superba Ave
Marco Pl
Amoroso Pl
Prospect Ave
Lucille Ave
10
Superior Ave
Victoria Ave
Penmar Ave
Walnut Ct
Walnut Ave
Penmar Ave
2400
Nelrose Ave
800
Glyndon Ave
Louella Ave
Glencoe Ave
Zanja St
Elm St

Oakwood
Rec Center
Thornton Ave
Thornton Pl
Vista Pl
Douglas Pl
Hampton Dr
Park Pl
Main St
San Juan Ave
San Juan Ct
Santa Clara Ct
Santa Clara Ct
California Ave
California Ct
Millwood Ct
Palms Blvd
Rialto Ave
Shell Ave
Shell Ct
Shell Ave
Crescent Ave
Electric Ct
Electric Ave
Narcissus Ct
Venezia Ave
Shell Ave
Venezia Ct
Victoria Ave
Zeno Pl
Boccaccio Ave
Woodlawn Ave
Oakwood Ave
Crestmoore Pl
Angelus Pl
Grand View Ave
Padua Pl
Hardin
Naples Ave
Coeur D'Alene Ave
Garfield Ave
Grant Ave
Van Buren Ave
Harrison Ave
Thatcher Ave
Lincoln Blvd
Beach Ave
Carter Ave
1
Stanford Ave
Yale Ave
400

Abbot Kinney Blvd
Alhambra Ct
Cabrillo Ave
San Juan Ave
Horizon Ave
Toledo Ct
Market St
Cadiz Ct
Altair Pl
Navarre Ct
Andalusia Ave
Cordova Ave
Rialto Ave
Seville Ct
Grand Blvd
Electric Ave
Breeze Ave
Brooks Ct
Wave Crest Ct
Club House Ave
Club House Ave
Westminster Ave
Horizon Ave
Horizon Ct

VENICE

Washington Wy
Abbot Kinney Blvd
Marr St
Mildred Ave
Clark Ave
Clement Ave
Olive Ave
Harbor St
Beach Ave
Ocean Beach Ct
McKinley Ave
Wilson Ave
Bryan Ave
Frey Ave
Coy Ave
Boone Ave
Oxford Ave
Olive Ave
Howard St
700
700
Marr St

Windward
Circle
Zephyr Ct
Windward Ave
Windward Ct
Venice Wy
17th Ave
17th Pl
18th Ave
18th Pl
19th Ave
19th Pl
20th Ave
20th Pl
Center St
Virginia Ave
Canal Ct
21st Ave
23rd Ave
23rd Pl
24th Ave
24th Pl
25th Ave
25th Pl
26th Ave
26th Pl
27th Ave
28th Ave
29th Ave
30th Ave
N Venice Blvd
S Venice Blvd
S Venice Blvd 300
Mildred Ave
Alberta Ave
Eastern Ct
Virginia Ct
Carroll Canal Ct
Linnie Canal Ct
Howland Canal Ct
Sherman Canal Ct
Grand Canal
28th Del Ave
Sanborn Ave
Ocean Ave
Ciluna Ave
Grayson Ave
Beach Ave
Ocean Ave
500
400

Venice
Canals

Venice
Boardwalk
Venice
City
Beach
PAGE
244

Venice
Pier
Anchorage St
Strongs Dr

Washington Blvd
25

Pacific
Ocean

Marina
Del Rey
PAGE
248

A
B
C
D
1
2
3

Venice has evolved with the times, from the smuggling of alcohol from the basements of beachfront hotels during prohibition, to the economic devastation of the Depression, to oil development, to the return of tourism and the introduction of the bohemian subculture. To arrive in Venice is to experience its complexities as well as its grace. The constant flow of creativity and philosophical idealism thrive to exist in harmony with modern day struggles and changes of every day urban life.

$ Banks

- **Bank of America** · 121 Windward Ave
- **Downey Savings Bank** · 13401 Washington Blvd
- **Downey Savings Bank** · 8824 S Sepulveda Blvd
- **First Coastal Bank** · 3206 Washington Blvd
- **First Federal Bank** · 13405 Washington Blvd
- **Washington Mutual** · 1415 Lincoln Blvd
- **Wells Fargo Bank** · 13400 Washington Blvd
- **Wells Fargo Bank** · 480 Washington Blvd

Car Washes

- **Marina Car Wash** · 2305 Lincoln Blvd

Gas Stations

- **76** · 300 Lincoln Blvd
- **Arco** · 251 Lincoln Blvd
- **Chevron** · 2400 Lincoln Blvd
- **Chevron** · 811 Washington Blvd
- **Shell** · 1020 Venice Blvd

Landmarks

- **Chiat-Day Building** · 340 Main St
- **Venice Boardwalk** · Ocean Front Walk
- **Venice Canals** · Venice Blvd & Pacific Ave
- **Venice Pier** · Far west end of Washington Blvd
- **Windward Circle** · Main St & Windward

Libraries

- **Venice Public Library** · 501 S Venice Blvd · 310-821-1769

Post Offices

- 1601 Main St
- 313 Grand Blvd

Schools

- **Broadway Elementary** · 1015 Lincoln Blvd
- **Coeur D'Alene Avenue Elementary** · 810 Coeur D'Alene Ave
- **First Lutheran** · 815 Venice Blvd
- **St Mark's Elementary** · 912 Coeur D'Alene Ave
- **Venice Adult Learning Center** · 1020 Victoria Ave
- **Venice Skills Center** · 611 5th Ave
- **Westminster Avenue Elementary** · 1010 Abbot Kinney Blvd

Supermarkets

- **Albertson's** · 13401 Washington Blvd
- **Ralph's** · 910 Lincoln Blvd

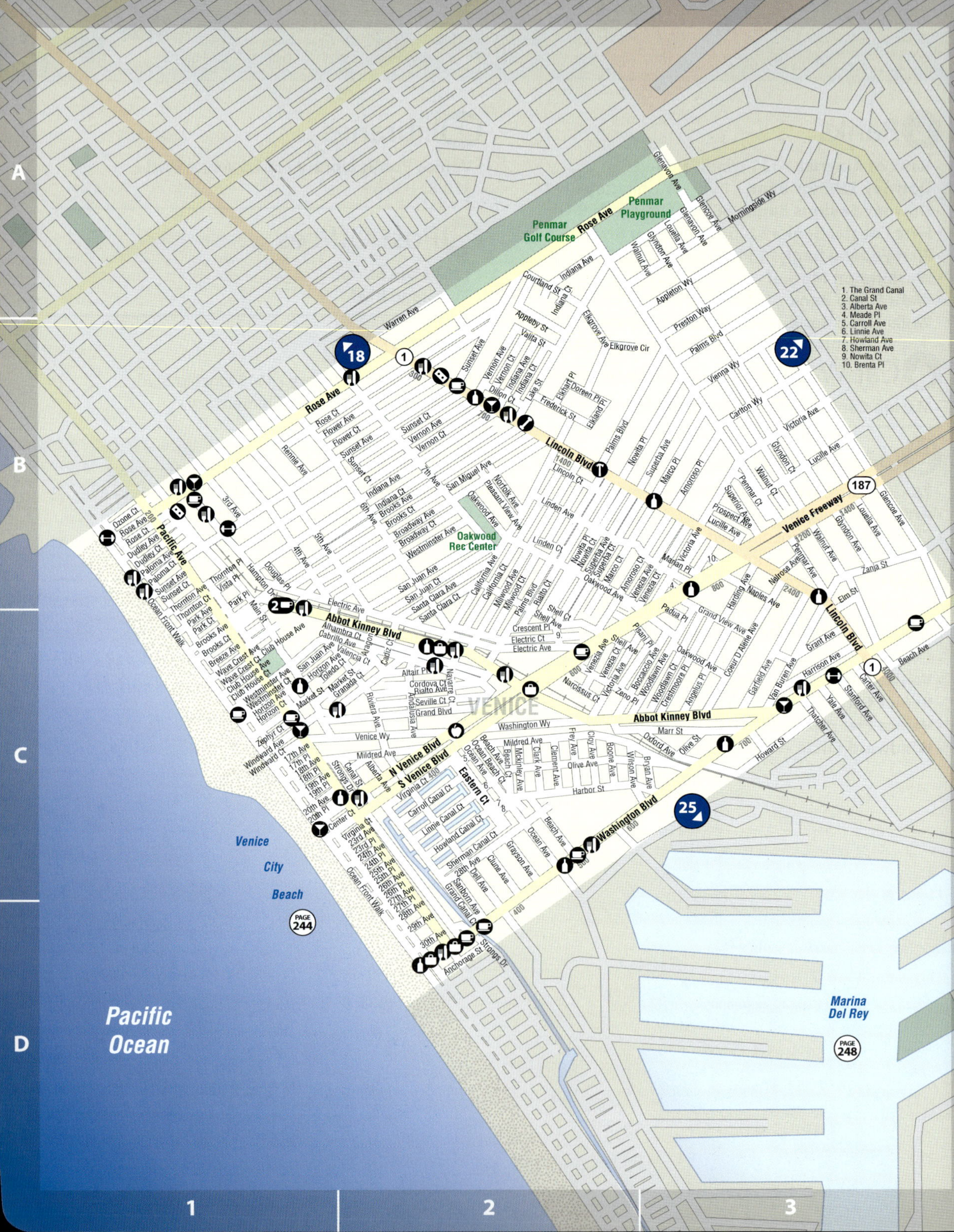

N
Map 21 • Venice

1. The Grand Canal
2. Canal St
3. Alberta Ave
4. Meade Pl
5. Carroll Ave
6. Linnie Ave
7. Howland Ave
8. Sherman Ave
9. Nowita Ct
10. Brenta Pl

Penmar Golf Course
Penmar Playground
Rose Ave

18
22
25
187

Pacific Ocean
Venice City Beach
Marina Del Rey

VENICE

Oakwood Rec Center

Rose Ave
Warren Ave
Pacific Ave
Ocean Front Walk
Lincoln Blvd
Abbot Kinney Blvd
N Venice Blvd
S Venice Blvd
Eastern Ct
Washington Blvd
Venice Freeway

Courtland St
Indiana Ave
Appleby St
Yalta St
Vernon Ave
Vernon Ct
Sunset Ave
Sunset Ct
Indiana Ave
Indiana Ct
Lake St
Dillon Ct
Frederick St
Doreen Pl
Elkhart Pl
Elkland Pl
Elkgrove Ave
Elkgrove Cir
Preston Way
Palms Blvd
Vienna Wy
Carlton Wy
Glenavon Ave
Glencoe Ave
Ouilla Ave
Morningside Wy
Appleton Wy
Walnut Ave
Gjirdon Ave
Lincoln Ct
Lincoln Blvd
Nowita Pl
Superba Ave
Marco Pl
Amoroso Pl
Penmar Ave
Walnut Ct
Victoria Ave
Lucille Ave
Zania St
Elm St
Beach Ave
Stanford Ave
Carter Ave
Harrison Ave
Thatcher Ave
Yale St
Van Buren Ave
Garfield Ave
Grant Ave
Flower Ave
Flower Ct
Rose Ct
Rennie Ave
Indiana Ave
Indiana Ct
Brooks Ave
Broadway Ct
Westminster Ave
San Miguel Ave
Pleasant View Ave
Norfolk Ave
Linden Ave
Linden Ct
California Ave
Milwood Ave
Milwood Ct
Palms Ave
Rialto Ct
Shell Ave
Shell Ct
Crescent Pl
Electric Ct
Electric Ave
San Juan Ave
Santa Clara Ave
Santa Clara Ct
3rd Ave
4th Ave
5th Ave
6th Ave
7th Ave
Ozone Ct
Rose Ave
Rose Ct
Dudley Ave
Dudley Ct
Paloma Ave
Paloma Ct
Sunset Ave
Sunset Ct
Thornton Ave
Thornton Ct
Park Ave
Park Ct
Brooks Ave
Brooks Ct
Breeze Ave
Wave Crest Ct
Club House Ave
Club House Ct
Westminster Ave
Horizon Ave
Horizon Ct
Zephyr Ct
Windward Ave
Windward Ct
Venice Way
Mildred Ave
Alberta Ave
Canal St
Abbot Kinney Blvd
Alhambra Ct
Cabrillo Ave
Navarre Ct
Cadiz Ct
Altair Pl
Cordova Ct
Rialto Ave
Seville Ct
Grand Blvd
Andalusia Ave
Riviera Ave
San Juan Ave
Valencia Ct
Market St
Granada Ct
Toledo Ct
Vista Pl
Thornton Ct
Hampton Dr
Douglas Ct
Park Pl
Main St
Electric Ave
17th Ave
18th Ave
19th Ave
19th Pl
20th Ave
20th Pl
Center Ct
22nd Ave
23rd Ave
24th Ave
24th Pl
25th Ave
25th Pl
26th Ave
26th Pl
27th Ave
27th Pl
28th Ave
28th Pl
30th Ave
Virginia Ct
Virginia Ave
Carroll Canal Ct
Linnie Canal Ct
Howland Canal Ct
Sherman Canal Ct
Grand Canal Ct
Grand Canal Ct
Dell Ave
Sanborn Ave
Anchorage St
Strongs Dr
Mildred Ave
Clark Ave
Clement Ave
Olive Ave
McKinley Ave
Harbor St
Beach Ave
Ocean Ave
Grayson Ave
Wilson Ave
Bryan Ave
Oxford Ave
Olive St
Boone Ave
Cloy Ave
Frey Ave
Marr St
Howard St
Pisani Ct
Zeno Ct
Narcissus Ct
Venezia Ave
Woodlawn Ave
Crestmoore Pl
Angelus Pl
Coeur D Alene Ave
Oakwood Ct
Boccaccio Ave
Woodlawn Ct
Vanada Ct
Veneda Ave
Pacua Pl
Grand View Ave
Naples Ave
Harding Ave
Superior Ave
Prospect Ave
Lucille Ave
Vienna Wy
Amoroso Ct
Oakwood Ave
Veneta Ave
Victoria Ct
Mapan Pl
Nowita Pl
Nowita Ct
Superba Ct
Victoria Ave
Washington Wy
Ocean Beach Ct
Walnut Ave
Glencoe Ave
Ouilla Ave

PAGE 244
PAGE 248

When Abbot Kinney conceived of Venice, CA, he envisioned it as an American replica of Venice, Italy—complete with canals. But the canals proved to be impractical after the automobile gained popularity, so most of the canals were filled in and turned to roads in 1929. Just six canals are still remaining, and they were refurbished in 1994. The houses that line the canals are gorgeous in their own right, and the area is definitely worth a visit.

 Clubs

- **Firehouse** • 213 Rose Ave • 310-396-6810
- **James' Beach** • 60 Venice Blvd • 310-823-5396
- **Scruffy O'Shea's** • 822 Washington Blvd • 310-821-0833
- **The Brig** • 1515 Abbot Kinney Blvd • 310-399-7537

 Coffee

- **Arrosto On Wheels** • 360 Hampton Dr
- **Gourment Coffee Warehouse** • 3 Westminster Ave
- **Hydrant Café** • 1202 Abbot Kinney Blvd
- **Java Roca** • 620 Lincoln Blvd
- **Ocean Breeze Cafe** • 507 Washington Blvd
- **Red Room Café** • 1604 Pacific Ave
- **Starbucks** • 100 Washington Blvd
- **Starbucks** • 13431 Washington Blvd
- **The Cow's End** • 34 Washington Blvd
- **Tucker** • 1029 Abbot Kinney Blvd

 Farmer's Markets

- **Venice** • Venice Blvd & Venice Way • Fri 7-11

 Gyms

- **Gold's Gym Enterprises** • 360 Hampton Dr • 310-392-6004
- **Optimum Boot Camp** • 26 Rose Ave • 310-664-7015
- **World Gym Fitness Center** • 3205 Washington Blvd • 310-827-8019

Hardware Stores

- **Lincoln Hardware** • 1609 Lincoln Blvd • 310-821-1027

Liquor Stores

- **Bob's Liquor Store** • 727 Lincoln Blvd
- **Day & Night Liquor & Market** • 1002 Venice Blvd
- **Joe's Liquor** • 1901 Lincoln Blvd
- **Lincoln Liquor Locker** • 2498 Lincoln Blvd
- **Lucky Stop** • 1360 Abbot Kinney Blvd
- **Marina Del Rey Liquormart** • 753 Washington Blvd
- **Munis Liquor** • 2022 Pacific Ave
- **Nick's Liquor Store** • 11 Washington Blvd
- **Trading Post Liquor Store** • 1313 Main St
- **Wolf's Liquor** • 536 Washington Blvd

Pet Stores

- **Allan's Aquarium & Pet Ctr** • 845 Lincoln Blvd • 310-399-5464

Restaurants

- **Abbot's Pizza** • 1407 Abbot Kinney Blvd • 310-314-2777
- **C&O Trattoria** • 31 Washington Blvd • 310-823-9491
- **Café 50's** • 838 Lincoln Blvd • 310-399-1955
- **Canal Club** • 2025 Pacific Ave • 310-823-3878
- **Casa Blanca Restaurant** • 220 Lincoln Blvd • 310-392-5751
- **Figtree's Café** • 429 Ocean Front Walk • 310-392-4937
- **Hal's Bar & Grill** • 1349 Abbot Kinney Blvd • 310-396-3105
- **Hama Sushi** • 213 Windward Ave • 310-396-8783
- **Joe's** • 1023 Abbot Kinney Blvd • 310-399-5811
- **Killer Shrimp** • 523 Washington Blvd • 310-578-2293
- **La Cabana Restaurant and Bar** • 738 Rose Ave • 310-392-7973
- **Rose Café** • 220 Rose Ave • 310-399-0711
- **The Brick House** • 826 Hampton Dr • 310-581-1639
- **Wabi-Sabi** • 1635 Abbot Kinney Blvd • 310-314-2229

Shopping

- **Johnny B Wood** • 1409 Abbot Kinney Blvd • 310-314-1945
- **Samy's Camera** • 585 Venice Blvd • 310-450-4551
- **The Starting Line** • 114 Washington Blvd • 310-827-3035
- **Venice Bike & Skate** • 21 Washington Blvd • 310-301-4011

Video Rental

- **Jungle Video** • 423 Lincoln Blvd • 310-314-7777
- **Main Street Video** • 1600 Main St • 310-821-7838

N
Map 22 • Mar Vista

1. Coolidge Pl
2. Craigview Ave
3. Corinth Ave
4. Rurdue Ave
5. S Barrington Ave
6. Butler Ave
7. Vienna Way
8. Marco Pl
9. Francis Pl
10. Regent St
11. Westminster Pl
12. Bradson Pl
13. Patrae St
14. Verdi St

Santa Monica Municipal Airport

Mar Vista Rec Center

MAR VISTA

Mar Vista Gardens

Culver West Park

Marina Del Rey

San Diego Freeway
405
I-405

Venice Blvd
187

Washington Blvd
Washington Pl

S Centinela Ave
S Centinela Ave

Sepulveda Channel

Marina Expressway
Marina Expressway
Marina Freeway
Centinela Creek

Ballona Creek

La Villa Marina

Culver Blvd

90
1

19
21
23
24
26

Federal Ave
Purdue Ave
Colby Ave
Butler Ave
Coolidge Ave
Corinth Ave
Sawtelle Blvd
Barry Ave
Kingsland St
Colbert Ave
Rose Ave
Woodbine St
Thermo St
Stanwood Dr
Rose Ave
S Barrington Ave
Granville Ave
Stoner Ave
Mountain View Ave
Keeshen Dr
Lawler St
Everglade St
Palms Blvd
Westminster Ave
Stoner Ave
Woodbine St
Barry Ave
Federal Ave
Purdue Ave
Corinth Ave
Tabor St
Globe Ave
Victoria Ave
McCune Ave
Biona Dr
Biona Dr
Berryman Ave
Coolidge Ave
Charnock Rd
Wildwood Ave
Modoska St
Woodward Ave
Grand View Blvd
Ocean View Blvd
Appleton Way
Woodbine St
Everglade St
Stewart Ave
Indianapolis St
Rose Ave
Stanwood Pl
Dewey St
Stanwood Dr
Warren Ave
Rose Ave
Matewood Ave
Rosewood Ave
Lake St
Psomas Ave
Morningside Way
Appleton Way
Greenwood Ave
Westwood Ave
Rosa Ave
Brooklake St
Cabrillo Blvd
Wade St
Meier St
Preston Blvd
Palms Blvd
Woodgreen St
Woodglen St
Colonial Ave
Westminster Ave
Francis Ave
Weaton Ave
Boice Ave
Wasatch Ave
Victoria Ave
Stewart Ave
Moore St
Meier St
Wade St
Marco Ave
Mc Cune Ave
Greenwood Ave
Beethoven St
Halldram St
Rosewood Ave
Ashwood Ave
Redwood Ave
Walgrove Ave
Victoria Ave
Lucille Ave
Ferndale Ave
Pacific Ave
Frances Ave
Barbara Ave
Caswell Ave
Matteson Ave
Caswell Ave
Mitchell Ave
Boise Ave
Colonial Ave
Manor Ln
Zania St
Wade St
Mc Connell Blvd
Mildred Ave
Neosho Ave
Chase Ave
Louise Ave
Westlawn Ave
Harding Ave
Campbell Ave
Grand View Dr
Lindblade Dr
East Blvd
South Park Ave
Herbert St
Sylvester St
Herbert St
Sawtelle St
Sawtelle St
Aiminda St
Marcasel Ave
Inglewood Blvd
Keeshen Dr
Pacific Ave
North Park Ave
Herbert St
Way
Victoria Ave
Venice Blvd
12400
12600
12800
Lindblade Dr
Courtleigh Dr
Avon Way
Atlantic Ave
Herbert St
Wagner St
Lindblade Dr
Braddock Dr
Marionwood Dr
Farias Ave
Sanford
Lindblade Dr
Marshall St
Allin St
Havelock Ave
Inglewood Blvd
Marshall Ct
Marshall Dr
Campbell Dr
Allin St
Culver Dr
Russo St
Culver Dr
McDonald St
Weir St
Bray St
Randall
Lindblade Dr
Selmaraine Dr
Mesmer Ave
Emporia Ave
Ethelda Ave
Stauson Ave
Dawes Ave
Coolidge Ave
S Stauson Ave
Berryman Ave
Barman Ave
Dawes Ave
Corinth Ave
Purdue Ave
Berryman Ave
Sawtelle Blvd
Grosvenor Blvd
Centinela Ave
Huntley Ave
Nurmid
Tepino Ave
Globe Ave
Sawtelle Ave
Minerva Ave
Bledsoe Ave
Abbott Ave
Matteson Ave
McLaughlin Ave
Palms Blvd
Short Ave
Gilmore Ave
Greene Ave
Walsh Ave
Mindanao Way
Glencoe Ave
Bonaparte Ave
Admiral Ave
Rubens Ave
Panama St
Alla Rd
Alla Rd
Short Ave
Sunnyside Ave
Hanger Ave
Maxella Ave
Michael Ave
Ashwood Ave
Beach Ave
Ida Ave
Moore St
Beethoven St
Greenwood Ave
Maxella Ave
Maxella Ave
Mc Connell Blvd
Mandan St
Westlawn Ave
Stewart Ave
Del Rey Blvd
Wagner Ave
Westlawn Ave
Braddock Dr
Allin St
Heavlock Ave
Mandan St
Presnell St
Milton St
Kelly St
Rosy Cir
Sanford St
Beatrice St
Baverta
Edel
Keil
Port Rd
Culver Dr
Coral Tree Pl
Beethoven St
Bay St
Grosvenor Blvd
Jandd Pl
Westlawn Ave
90

During rush hours, Venice Blvd., which runs right through Mar Vista, may be the fastest east-west alternative to the 10 Freeway.

 Banks

- **Citibank** · 4375 Glencoe Ave
- **Union Bank** · 4032 S Centinela Ave
- **Washington Mutual** · 12335 Venice Blvd
- **Wells Fargo Bank** · 4365 Glencoe Ave

 Car Washes

- **Car Wash Coin Op** · 12415 Venice Blvd
- **Handy J Car Wash** · 12681 W Washington Blvd

 Gas Stations

- **Arco** · 12000 Culver Blvd
- **Arco** · 12332 W Washington Blvd
- **Chevron** · 3500 S Centinela Ave

 Libraries

- **Mar Vista Branch Library** · 12006 Venice Blvd · 310-390-3454

 Police

- **Los Angeles Police Dept** · 12312 Culver Blvd · 310-202-4502

 Post Offices

- 3865 Grand View Blvd

 Schools

- **Beethoven Street Elementary** · 3711 Beethoven St
- **Braddock Drive Elementary** · 4711 Inglewood Blvd
- **Bradley Environmental Science and Humanities** · 3875 Dublin Ave
- **Culver Christian School** · 11312 Washington Blvd
- **Culver City Adventist School** · 11828 W Washington Blvd
- **Grand View Boulevard Elementary** · 3951 Grand View Blvd
- **Mar Vista Elementary** · 3330 Granville Ave
- **Marina Del Rey Middle School** · 12500 Braddock Dr
- **Mark Twain Middle School** · 2224 Walgrove Ave
- **Montessori Academy** · 12606 Culver Blvd
- **Montessori Learning Center** · 11363 Washington Blvd
- **Phoenix Continuation** · 12971 Zanja St
- **Shining Path Montessori** · 11500 Culver Blvd
- **Short Avenue Elementary** · 12814 Maxella Ave
- **St Gerard Majella Elementary** · 4415 Inglewood Blvd
- **Stoner Avenue Elementary** · 11735 Braddock Dr
- **Venice Senior High School** · 13000 Venice Blvd
- **Walgrove Avenue Elementary** · 1630 Walgrove Ave
- **Wildwood** · 12201 Washington Pl
- **Windward** · 11350 Palms Blvd

Supermarkets

- **Von's** · 4030 S Centinela Ave
- **Von's** · 4365 Glencoe Ave

Map 22 • Mar Vista
N
405
23
19
24
21
26
1
90

1. Coolidge Pl
2. Craigview Ave
3. Corinth Ave
4. Purdue Ave
5. S Barrington Ave
6. Butler Ave
7. Vienna Way
8. Marco Pl
9. Francis Pl
10. Regent St
11. Westminster Pl
12. Bradson Pl
13. Patrae St
14. Verdi St

Santa Monica Municipal Airport
Mar Vista Rec Center
MAR VISTA
Marina Del Rey
Culver West Park
Mar Vista Gardens
Sepulveda Channel
Ballona Creek
Centinela Creek
San Diego Freeway
Marina Expressway
Marina Freeway
La Villa Marina

Venice Blvd
Washington Blvd
Washington Pl
S Centinela Ave
Culver Blvd
Centinela Ave
187
90

What is there to do for fun in Mar Vista? Go bowling! The Mar Vista Bowl (12125 Venice Blvd.) is a throwback to the 60s, decorated with a psychedelic galaxy theme. Do wear your sharpest bowling shirt.

Clubs

- **Dear John's** · 11208 Culver Blvd · 310-397-0276

Coffee

- **Panini Coffee & Cafe** · 4325 Glencoe Ave

Hardware Stores

- **B & B Hardware** · 12450 W Washington Blvd · 310-390-9413
- **D & D Hardware Company** · 4943 McConnell Ave · 210-827-5555
- **Dick's True Value Hardware** · 12216 Venice Blvd · 310-397-3220

Liquor Stores

- **A & M Liquor** · 11700 Washington Pl
- **Beverage Warehouse** · 4935 McConnell Ave
- **Bill's Liquor** · 11700 Culver Blvd
- **Dicoteca Licorerea La Mexicana** · 4513 Inglewood Blvd
- **Happy Corner Liquors** · 4584 S Centinela Ave
- **Hillcrest Liquors** · 11300 Venice Blvd
- **Janet's Liquor** · 12333 Allin St
- **Jay's Liquor** · 11305 Washington Pl
- **Joe's Liquor** · 12701 Venice Blvd
- **Los Angeles Wine Company** · 4935 McConnell Ave
- **Lucky 7 Liquor** · 12408 W Washington Blvd
- **Rajmohan's Liquors** · 12815 Venice Blvd
- **Super Liquor & Deli Mart** · 4704 Inglewood Blvd
- **U S Liquors** · 12403 W Washington Blvd
- **Westside Liquor** · 3501 S Centinela Ave

Movie Theaters

- **United Artists Cinemas** · 4335 Glencoe Ave

Pet Stores

- **Aquarium** · 12807 Venice Blvd · 310-398-9920
- **Centilena Food & Pet Supplies** · 12553 Venice Blvd · 310-390-3232
- **Centinela Feed & Pet Supplies** · 3860 S Centinela Ave · 310-398-2134
- **Dogromat** · 12926 Venice Blvd · 310-306-8885
- **Petville Pet Shop** · 12112 Venice Blvd · 310-313-1801
- **Tsavo Pet Supplies & Dog Wash** · 12958 W Washington Blvd · 310-821-6449

Restaurants

- **Aunt Kizzy's Back Porch** · 4325 Glencoe Ave · 310-578-1005
- **Empanada's Place** · 3811 Sawtelle Blvd · 310-391-0888
- **Paco's Tacos** · 4141 Centinela Ave · 310-391-9616
- **Pepy's Galley** · 12125 Venice Blvd · 310-390-0577
- **Venus of Venice** · 12034 Venice Blvd · 310-391-7674

Shopping

- **Prebica Coffee** · 4325 Glencoe Ave · 310-823-4446
- **Record Rover** · 12204 Venice Blvd · 310-390-3132
- **The Los Angeles Wine Company** · 4935 McConnell Ave · 310-306-9463

Video Rental

- **America's Video Exhibition** · 12200 Venice Blvd · 310-737-0053
- **First Video** · 12131 Washington Pl · 310-391-5488
- **La Mexicana Video Rental (Mexican)** · 12612 W Washington Blvd · 310-390-9691

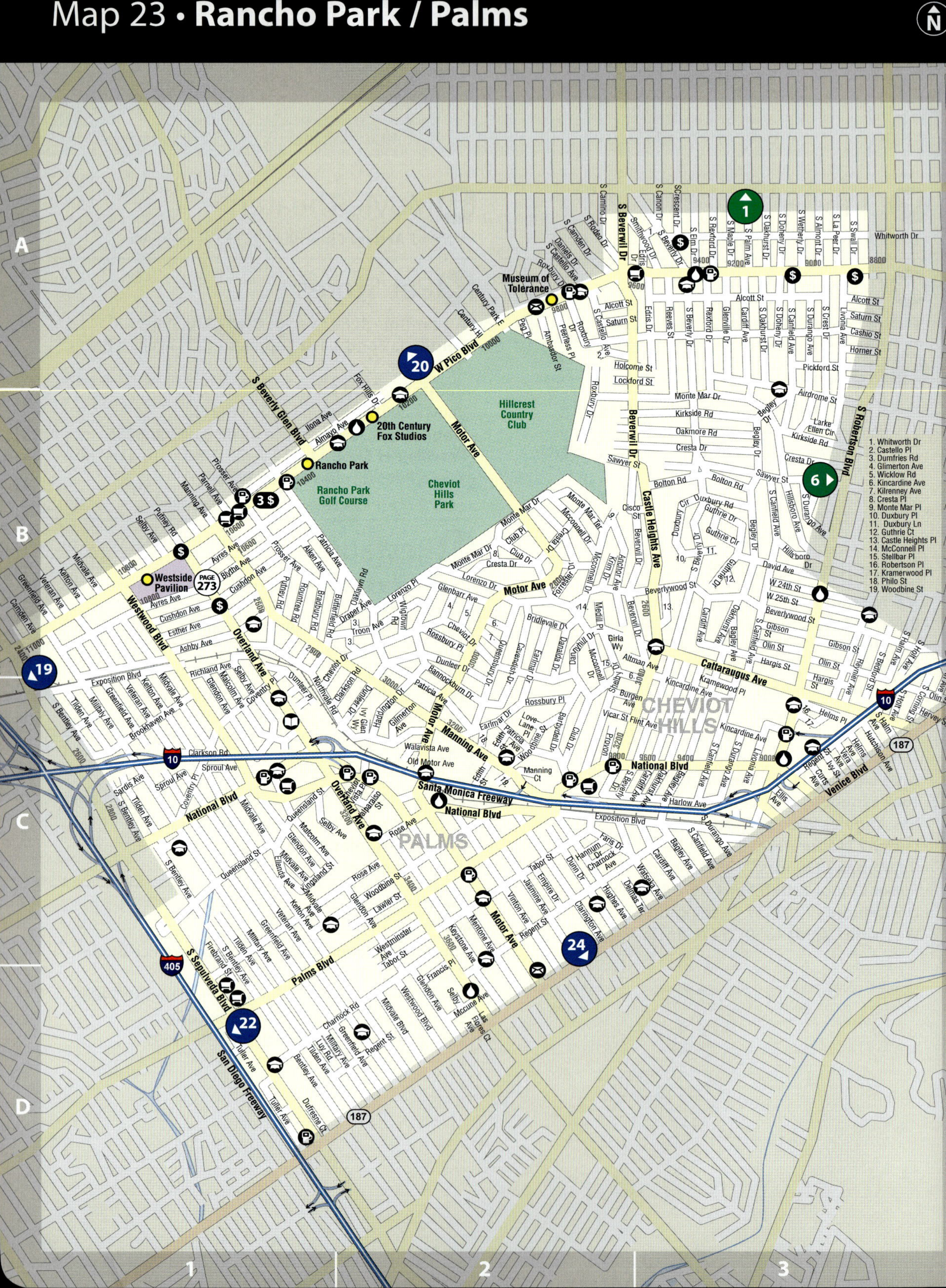

N
Museum of Tolerance
20th Century Fox Studios
Rancho Park
Hillcrest Country Club
Rancho Park Golf Course
Cheviot Hills Park
Westside Pavilion
PAGE 273
CHEVIOT HILLS
PALMS
W Pico Blvd
S Beverly Glen Blvd
S Beverwil Dr
Beverwil Dr
Motor Ave
Manning Ave
Overland Ave
Westwood Blvd
National Blvd
Santa Monica Freeway
Exposition Blvd
Palms Blvd
Venice Blvd
Cattaraugus Ave
Castle Heights Ave
S Robertson Blvd
San Diego Freeway
S Sepulveda Blvd
Whitworth Dr
Alcott St
Saturn St
Cashio St
Horner St
Pickford St
Monte Mar Dr
Kirkside Rd
Oakmore Rd
Cresta Dr
Bolton Rd
Sawyer St
Airdrome St
Larke Ellen Cir
David Ave
W 24th St
W 25th St
Beverlywood St
Gibson St
Olin St
Hargis St
Kincardine Ave
National Blvd
Exposition Blvd
Harlow Ave
Ellis Ave
1. Whitworth Dr
2. Castello Pl
3. Dumfries Rd
4. Glimerton Ave
5. Wicklow Rd
6. Kincardine Ave
7. Kilrenney Ave
8. Cresta Pl
9. Monte Mar Pl
10. Duxbury Pl
11. Duxbury Ln
12. Guthrie Ct
13. Castle Heights Pl
14. McConnell Pl
15. Stellbar Pl
16. Robertson Pl
17. Krameroad Pl
18. Philo St
19. Woodbine St
405
10
187
273
1
2
3
6
19
20
22
24

The Rancho Park Golf Course is reportedly the busiest in the world. It's located at the Cheviot Hills Recreation Center, which also contains tennis courts, basketball hoops, ball diamonds, and more. This is really an amazing public park.

$ Banks

- **Bank of America** · 10732 W Pico Blvd
- **Citibank** · 10680 W Pico Blvd
- **Citibank** · 1180 S Beverly Dr
- **Citibank** · 2566 Overland Ave
- **Washington Mutual** · 10701 W Pico Blvd
- **Washington Mutual** · 9080 W Pico Blvd
- **Wells Fargo Bank** · 10789 W Pico Blvd
- **Wells Fargo Bank** · 8901 W Pico Blvd

Car Washes

- **Bob Geco's Auto Appearance** · 3728 Overland Ave
- **Century West Car Wash** · 9500 W Pico Blvd
- **Crown Car Wash** · 10399 W Pico Blvd
- **Mr. Polish** · 10309 National Blvd
- **National Robertson Mobil Carwash** · 3071 S Robertson Blvd
- **Robertson Car Wash** · 2460 S Robertson Blvd

Gas Stations

- **76** · 9779 W Pico Blvd
- **76** · 9930 National Blvd
- **Arco** · 10612 National Blvd
- **Arco** · 3479 Motor Ave
- **Chevron** · 3029 S Robertson Blvd
- **Chevron** · 3775 S Sepulveda Blvd
- **Chevron** · 9819 National Blvd
- **Exxon** · 10691 W Pico Blvd
- **Mobil** · 10611 National Blvd
- **Mobil** · 9448 W Pico Blvd
- **Shell** · 10564 Pico Blvd
- **Shell** · 10815 National Blvd

Landmarks

- **20th Century Fox Studios** · 10201 Pico Blvd
- **Museum of Tolerance** · 9786 W Pico Blvd
- **Rancho Park**
- **Westside Pavilion** · 10800 W Pico Blvd

Libraries

- **Los Angeles Public Library** · 2920 Overland Ave · 310-840-2142

Post Offices

- 3751 Motor Ave
- 9911 W Pico Blvd

Schools

- **Canfield Avenue Elementary** · 9233 Airdrome St
- **Castle Heights Elementary** · 9755 Cattaraugus Ave
- **Charnock Road Elementary** · 11133 Charnock Rd
- **Cheviot Hills Continuation** · 9200 Cattaraugus Ave
- **Clover Avenue Elementary** · 11020 Clover Ave
- **First Lutheran** · 3732 Veteran Ave
- **Global Village** · 10524 W Pico Blvd
- **Hamilton Senior High School** · 2955 Robertson Blvd
- **Iskcon International Gurukula** · 3745 Watseka Ave
- **Julia Ann Singer Center** · 3321 Edith Ave
- **Le Lycee Francais De LA** · 3261 Overland Ave
- **New World Montessori** · 10520 Regent St
- **Newbridge** · 3754 Dunn Dr
- **Notre Dame Academy** · 2851 Overland Ave
- **Notre Dame Academy Elementary** · 2911 Overland Ave
- **Overland Avenue Elementary** · 10650 Ashby Ave
- **Palms Elementary** · 3520 Motor Ave
- **Palms Middle School** · 10860 Woodbine St
- **Redeemer Baptist Elementary** · 10792 National Blvd
- **Shalom Hebrew Academy** · 1419 S Beverly Dr
- **St Timothy's** · 10479 W Pico Blvd
- **Temple Isaiah Day** · 10345 W Pico Blvd
- **Vista** · 3200 Motor Ave
- **Yeshiva University High School** · 9760 W Pico Blvd

Supermarkets

- **Albertson's** · 3443 S Sepulveda Blvd
- **Ralph's** · 9616 W Pico Blvd
- **Trader Joe's** · 10850 National Blvd
- **Trader Joe's** · 3456 S Sepulveda Blvd
- **Von's** · 10800 W Pico Blvd
- **Von's** · 9860 National Blvd

N

Legend Index (S Robertson Blvd area)

1. Whitworth Dr
2. Castello Pl
3. Dumfries Rd
4. Glimerton Ave
5. Wicklow Rd
6. Kincardine Ave
7. Kilrenney Ave
8. Cresta Pl
9. Monte Mar Pl
10. Duxbury Pl
11. Duxbury Ln
12. Guthrie Ct
13. Castle Heights Pl
14. McConnell Pl
15. Stellbar Pl
16. Robertson Dr
17. Kramerwood Pl
18. Philo St
19. Woodbine St

Parks and Places

Hillcrest Country Club
Rancho Park Golf Course
Cheviot Hills Park
Westside Pavilion
PAGE 273
CHEVIOT HILLS
PALMS

Major Streets

W Pico Blvd
S Beverly Glen Blvd
Motor Ave
Overland Ave
Westwood Blvd
National Blvd
Santa Monica Freeway
Exposition Blvd
Manning Ave
Palms Blvd
S Sepulveda Blvd
San Diego Freeway
Venice Blvd
Century Park E
Castle Heights Ave
Beverwil Dr
Cattaraugus Ave
S Robertson Blvd

405

10

187

Grid references

A B C D

1 2 3

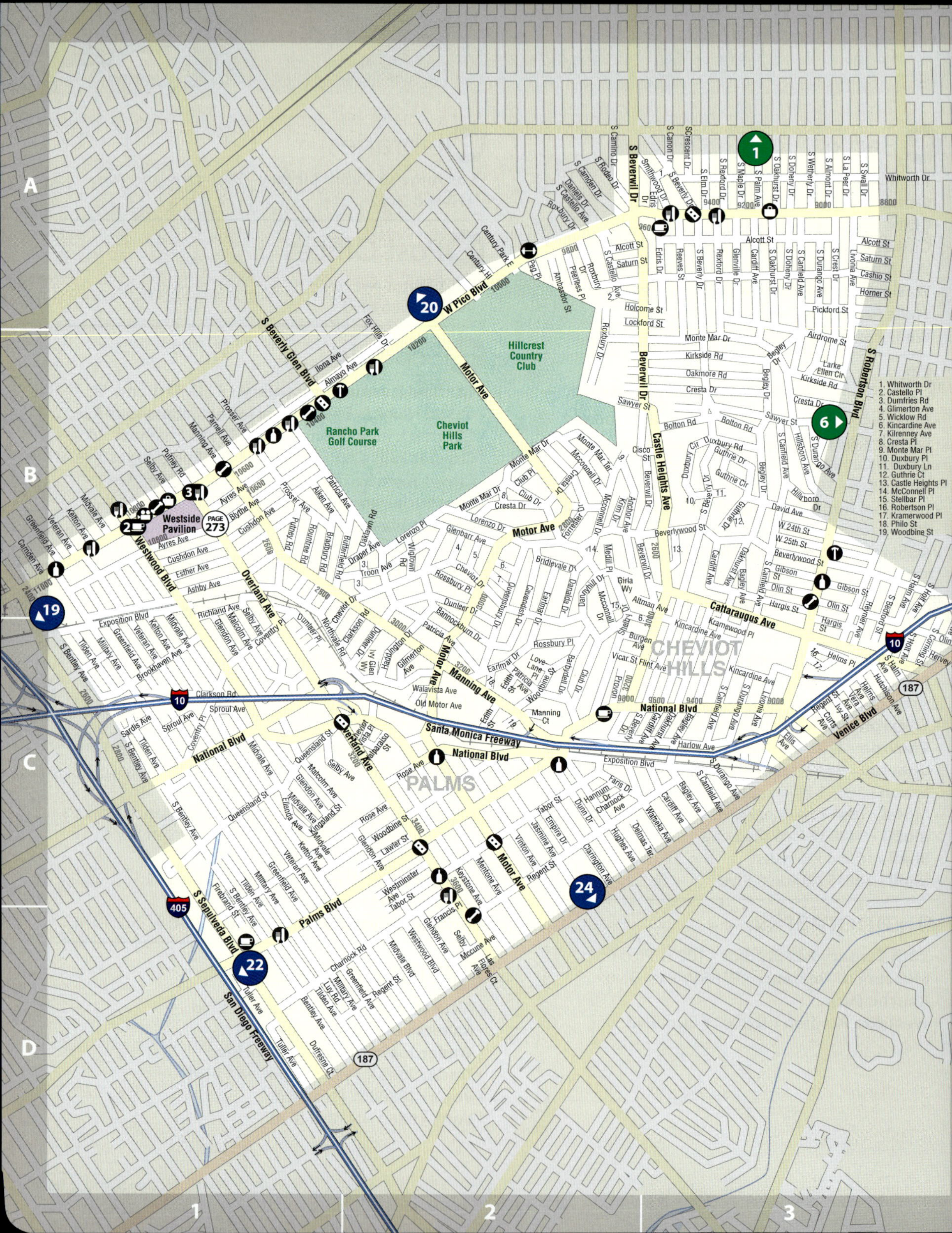

The Apple Pan, on Pico Blvd., is an L.A. institution and an intense dining experience. There are never enough seats to go around, and it's a Darwinian struggle to finagle a place at the counter and order your food. The hickory burger is messy, but well worth the trip. And since you're there, go ahead and finish the meal with a slice of the apple pie. Just pretend it's healthy.

 Coffee

- **Coffee Bean & Tea Leaf** • 10897 W Pico Blvd
- **Coffee Bean & Tea Leaf** • 3470 S Sepulveda Blvd
- **Starbucks** • 10911 W Pico Blvd
- **Starbucks** • 9618 W Pico Blvd
- **Starbucks** • 9824 National Blvd

Gyms

- **24-Hour Fitness** • 9911 W Pico Blvd • 310-553-7600

 Hardware Stores

- **Anawalt Lumber** • 11060 W Pico Blvd • 310-478-0324
- **Emil's Hardware** • 2525 S Robertson Blvd • 310-839-8571

Liquor Stores

- **Bob's Food Mart & Liquors** • 10000 National Blvd
- **Dave's Liquor Store** • 2704 S Robertson Blvd
- **Hillis Liquors** • 3308 Motor Ave
- **Joseph Liquor** • 11304 W Pico Blvd
- **Overland Liquor** • 3585 Overland Ave
- **Rancho Park Liquors** • 10526 W Pico Blvd

Movie Theaters

- **West Pavilion Cinemas** • 10800 W Pico Blvd

Pet Stores

- **Centinela Feed & Pet Supplies** • 11055 W Pico Blvd • 310-473-5099
- **Many Paws** • 2730 S Robertson Blvd • 310-837-1710
- **Westside Pet Shop** • 10588 W Pico Blvd • 310-202-1076

Restaurants

- **Apple Pan** • 10801 W Pico Blvd • 310-475-3583
- **Bourbon Street Shrimp** • 10928 W Pico Blvd • 310-474-0007
- **Delmonico's Seafood Grille** • 9320 W Pico Blvd • 310-550-7737
- **Factor's Famous Deli** • 9420 W Pico Blvd • 310-278-9175
- **Guelaguetza** • 11127 Palms Blvd • 310-837-1153
- **Gyu-kaku** • 10925 W Pico Blvd • 310-234-8641
- **Hop Li** • 10974 W Pico Blvd • 310-441-3708
- **Jack Sprat's** • 10668 W Pico Blvd • 310-837-6662
- **John O'Groat's** • 10516 W Pico Blvd • 310-204-0692
- **Junior's Deli** • 2379 Westwood Blvd • 310-475-5771
- **La Serenata Gourmet** • 10924 W Pico Blvd • 310-441-9667
- **Milky Way** • 9108 W Pico Blvd • 310-859-0004
- **Overland Café** • 3601 Overland Ave • 310-559-9999

Shopping

- **Adventure 16** • 11161 Pico Blvd • 310-473-4574
- **Delmarus Lox** • 9340 W Pico Blvd • 310-273-3004

Video Rental

- **Blockbuster** • 9618 W Pico Blvd • 310-858-3822
- **Blockbuster** • 3101 Overland Ave • 310-842-9110
- **Laser Blazer** • 10587 W Pico Blvd • 310-475-4788
- **New Wave Video** • 3500 Overland Ave • 310-838-2058
- **Pro Video** • 10403 Tabor St • 310-202-1508

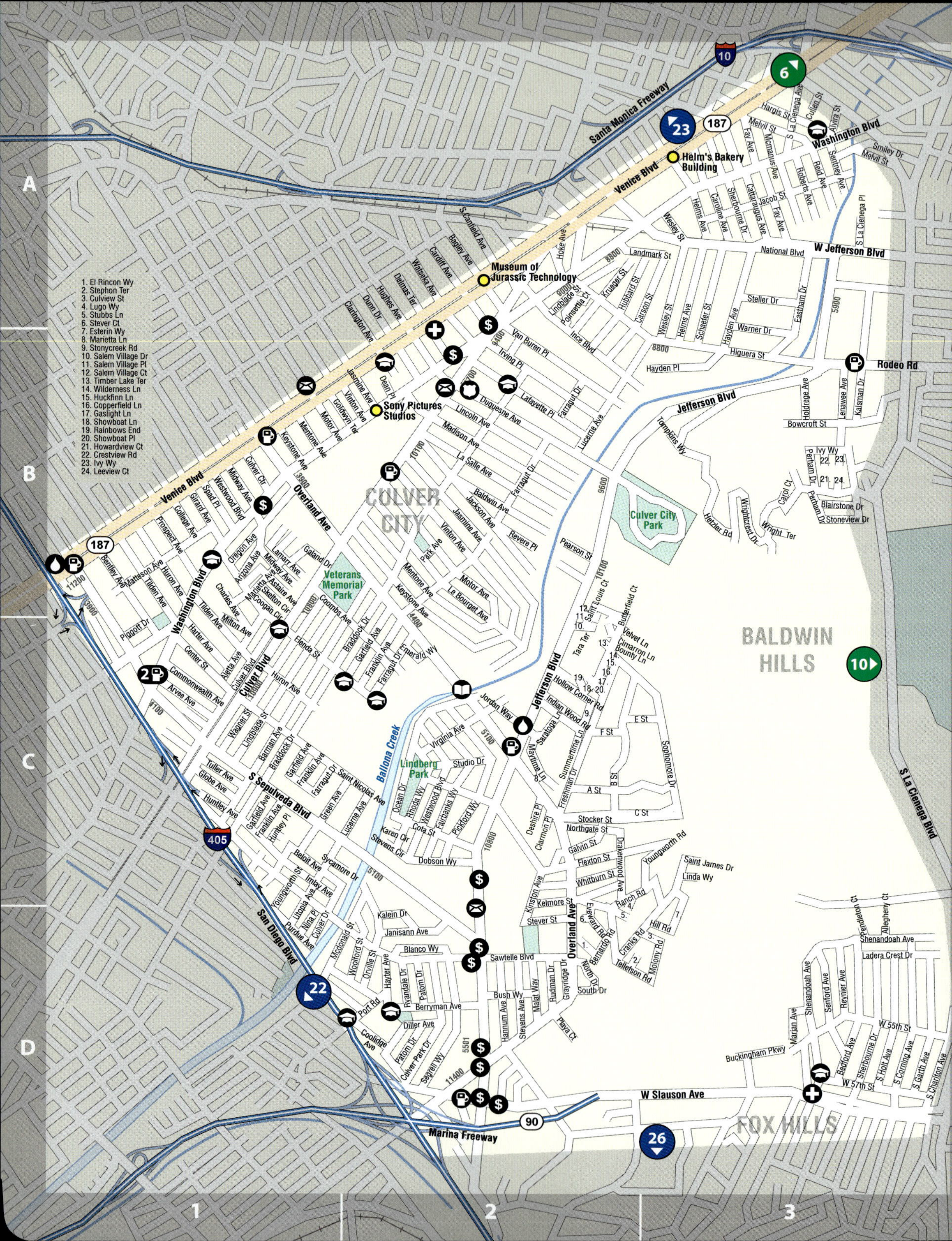

1. El Rincon Wy
2. Stephon Ter
3. Culview St
4. Lugo Wy
5. Stubbs Ln
6. Stever Ct
7. Esterin Wy
8. Marietta Ln
9. Stonycreek Rd
10. Salem Village Dr
11. Salem Village Pl
12. Salem Village Ct
13. Timber Lake Ter
14. Wilderness Ln
15. Huckfinn Ln
16. Copperfield Ln
17. Gaslight Ln
18. Showboat Ln
19. Rainbows End
20. Showboat Pl
21. Howardview Ct
22. Crestview Rd
23. Ivy Wy
24. Leeview Ct

CULVER CITY

BALDWIN HILLS

FOX HILLS

Santa Monica Freeway
Venice Blvd
Washington Blvd
W Jefferson Blvd
Jefferson Blvd
Rodeo Rd
Overland Ave
Culver Blvd
S Sepulveda Blvd
San Diego Blvd
Marina Freeway
W Slauson Ave
S La Cienega Blvd

Museum of Jurassic Technology
Sony Pictures Studios
Helm's Bakery Building
Veterans Memorial Park
Lindberg Park
Culver City Park
Ballona Creek

They used to make bread and baked goods at the Helms Bakery Building, but it's now home to an assortment of furniture stores—both high end and relatively affordable. The art deco-style building also houses the Jazz Bakery, a non-profit performance space that has hosted Woody Allen and Mose Allison. And yes, you can order dessert at the Bakery.

$ Banks

- **Bank of America** · 3809 Culver Ctr
- **Bank of America** · 5541 S Sepulveda Blvd
- **Bank of America** · 9453 Culver Blvd
- **Bank of the West** · 9735 Washington Blvd
- **Citibank** · 5700 S Sepulveda Blvd
- **First Federal Bank** · 10784 Jefferson Blvd
- **First Federal Bank** · 5573 S Sepulveda Blvd
- **US Bank** · 5399 S Sepulveda Blvd
- **Washington Mutual** · 5670 Sepulveda Blvd
- **Washington Mutual** · 9801 Washington Blvd
- **Wells Fargo Bank** · 11030 Jefferson Blvd

Car Washes

- **Bubble Machine Car Wash** · 10649 Jefferson Blvd
- **Shine & Brite Hand Car Wash** · 11166 Venice Blvd

Gas Stations

- **Arco** · 10646 Venice Blvd
- **Arco** · 11181 W Washington Blvd
- **Arco** · 5851 Rodeo Rd
- **Arco** · 6300 W Slauson Ave
- **Chevron** · 10649 Jefferson Blvd
- **Chevron** · 11197 Washington Pl
- **Shell** · 10332 Culver Blvd
- **Shell** · 3801 Sepulveda Blvd

Hospitals

- **Brotman Medical Center** · 3828 Delmas Ter · 310-836-7000

Landmarks

- **Helm's Bakery Building** · 3233 Helms Ave
- **Museum of Jurassic Technology** · 9341 Venice Blvd
- **Sony Pictures Studios** · 10202 W Washington Blvd

Libraries

- **Culver City Library** · 4975 Overland Ave · 310-559-1676

Police

- **Culver City Police Dept** · 4040 Duquesne Ave · 310-837-1221

Post Offices

- 11111 Jefferson Blvd
- 9942 Culver Blvd

Schools

- **Culver City Independent Study** · 11450 Port Rd
- **Culver City Middle School** · 4601 Elenda St
- **Culver City Senior High School** · 4401 Elenda St
- **Culver Park Continuation High School** · 5303 Berryman Ave
- **El Marino Language** · 11450 Port Rd
- **El Rincon Elementary** · 11177 Overland Ave
- **Extraordinary Place** · 5707 Shenandoah Ave
- **Farragut Elementary** · 10820 Farragut Dr
- **Howe Elementary School** · 4100 Irving Pl
- **La Ballona Elementary** · 10915 Washington Blvd
- **Play Mountain Place** · 6063 Hargis St
- **St Augustine's Catholic** · 3819 Clarington Ave

Supermarkets

- **Albertson's** · 8985 Venice Blvd
- **Pavilions** · 11030 Jefferson Blvd
- **Ralph's** · 10772 Jefferson Blvd
- **Ralph's** · 3827 Culver Ctr
- **Trader Joe's** · 10011 Washington Blvd

1. El Rincon Wy
2. Stephon Ter
3. Culview St
4. Lugo Wy
5. Stubbs Ln
6. Stever Ct
7. Esterin Wy
8. Marietta Ln
9. Stonycreek Rd
10. Salem Village Dr
11. Salem Village Pl
12. Salem Village Ct
13. Timber Lake Ter
14. Wilderness Ln
15. Huckfinn Ln
16. Copperfield Ln
17. Gaslight Ln
18. Showboat Ln
19. Rainbows End
20. Showboat Pl
21. Howardview Ct
22. Crestview Rd
23. Ivy Wy
24. Leeview Ct

CULVER CITY

BALDWIN HILLS

FOX HILLS

Santa Monica Freeway

Venice Blvd

Washington Blvd

W Jefferson Blvd

Jefferson Blvd

Rodeo Rd

Culver City Park

Veterans Memorial Park

Lindberg Park

Ballona Creek

Overland Ave

Jefferson Blvd

Washington Blvd

Culver Blvd

S Sepulveda Blvd

San Diego Blvd

Overland Ave

S La Cienega Blvd

W Slauson Ave

Marina Freeway

The Museum of Jurassic Technology is a bizarre place, and some think that the less you know about it when you get there, the better. Suffice it to say that the museum does not take science very seriously. It is designed not specifically to educate, but to make its visitors think.

 Clubs

- **Jazz Bakery** • 3238 Helms Ave • 310-271-9039

 Coffee

- **Starbucks** • 10705 W Washington Blvd
- **Starbucks** • 8985 Venice Blvd
- **Starbucks** • 9718 Washington Blvd
- **Tanner's Coffee** • 4342 Sepulveda Blvd

 Farmer's Markets

- **Culver City** • Culver Blvd & Main St • Tue 2-7

 Gyms

- **Bally Total Fitness** • 3844 Culver Ctr • 310-204-2030

Hardware Stores

- **A-1 Hardware** • 11119 Washington Blvd • 310-559-9594
- **Alvin Metals** • 8794 National Blvd • 310-559-8470
- **Anderson Plywood Sales** • 4020 Sepulveda Blvd • 310-397-8229
- **Culver City Hardware** • 5429 Sepulveda Blvd • 310-398-1251
- **Stellar's True Value** • 3833 Main St • 310-558-4507
- **The Kitchen Store** • 6322 W Slauson Ave • 310-839-5215
- **Tools To Go** • 10248 Culver Blvd • 310-815-8555

Liquor Stores

- **Al's Liquors** • 6142 Washington Blvd
- **Albert's Liquors** • 5565 Sepulveda Blvd
- **Big Seven Liquors** • 10217 Venice Blvd
- **Champion Liquor Mart** • 10891 Venice Blvd
- **Culver Liquor** • 10548 Culver Blvd
- **Liquor Barrel** • 3923 Sepulveda Blvd
- **Palm Tree Liquor Store** • 10425 Venice Blvd
- **R & Z Liquor** • 8582 Washington Blvd
- **Studio Village Liquor** • 10725 Jefferson Blvd
- **Taylor Liquors** • 11156 Washington Blvd

 Movie Theaters

- **Mann Culver Plaza Six** • 9919 Washington Blvd

Pet Stores

- **Petco** • 5347 S Sepulveda Blvd • 310-390-7255

Restaurants

- **Bamboo** • 10835 Venice Blvd • 310-287-0668
- **Café Brasil** • 10831 Venice Blvd • 310-837-8957
- **Natalee Thai** • 10101 Venice Blvd • 310-202-7003
- **Petrelli's Steakhouse** • 5615 S Sepulveda Blvd • 310-397-1438
- **Sagebrush Cantina** • 9523 Culver Blvd • 310-836-5321
- **Tito's Tacos** • 11222 Washington Pl • 310-391-5780
- **Versailles** • 10319 Venice Blvd • 310-558-3168

Shopping

- **Allied Model Trains** • 4411 Sepulveda Blvd • 310-313-9353
- **Civilization** • 8884 Venice Blvd • 310-202-8883
- **Culver City Home Brewing Supply** • 4358 1/2 Sepulveda Blvd • 310-397-3453
- **Dovetail** • 8918 Venice Blvd • 310-559-9431
- **Surfas** • 8825 National Blvd • 310-559-4770

Video Rental

- **Blockbuster** • 5359 Sepulveda Blvd • 310-915-1192
- **Blockbuster** • 9201 Venice Blvd • 310-837-1286
- **Hollywood Video** • 8985 Venice Blvd • 310-559-4942
- **Video Depot** • 10746 Jefferson Blvd • 310-202-6223

Map 25 • Marina Del Rey / Westchester West

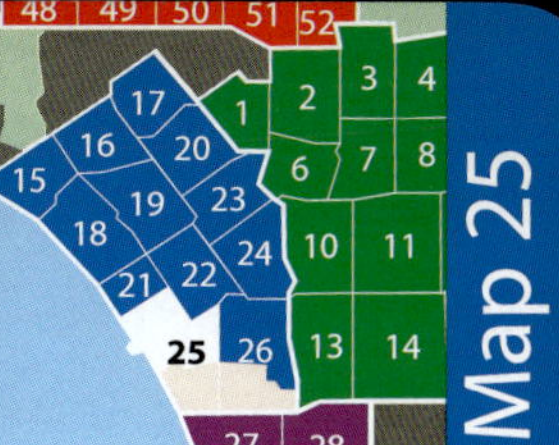

Built around the largest man-made harbor in the world, Marina del Rey is home to over 6,000 boats (yachts too!). The marina provides L.A. with an easily accessible port for amateur and professional sailors alike (not to mention a great view for drinks at sunset!).

Banks

- **Bank of America** · 4754 Admiralty Way
- **Downey Savings & Loan** · 4311 Lincoln Blvd
- **First Bank & Trust** · 4519 Admiralty Way
- **US Bank** · 4700 Lincoln Blvd
- **Washington Mutual** · 4676 Admiralty Way
- **Wells Fargo Bank** · 4676 Admiralty Way

Car Washes

- **Mr Polish** · 4333 Admiralty Way

Gas Stations

- **76** · 8300 Lincoln Blvd
- **Chevron** · 4680 Lincoln Blvd
- **Shell** · 4770 Lincoln Blvd
- **Texaco** · 8126 Lincoln Blvd

Landmarks

- **Ballona Wetlands** · Around Ballona Creek
- **Fisherman's Village** · 13755 Fiji Way
- **Marina City Towers** · 4333 Admiralty Way

24-Hour Pharmacies

- **Sav-On** · 13171 Mindanao Way · 310-821-8908

Post Offices

- 215 Culver Blvd
- 4748 Admiralty Way

Schools

- **Del Rey Continuation** · 8701 Park Hill Dr
- **Loyola Marymount University** · 7900 Loyola Blvd
- **Loyola Village Elementary** · 8821 Villanova St
- **Otis College of Art & Design** · 9045 Lincoln Blvd
- **Paseo Del Rey Elementary** · 7751 Paseo Del Rey
- **St Anastansia Elementary** · 8631 S Stanmoor Dr
- **St Bernard High School** · 9100 Falmouth Ave
- **Toibb Pacific Hebrew Academy** · 311 Culver Blvd
- **Westchester Senior High School** · 7400 W Manchester Ave

Supermarkets

- **Albertson's** · 8448 Lincoln Blvd
- **Gelson's Markets** · 13455 Maxella Ave
- **Ralph's** · 4311 Lincoln Blvd
- **Ralph's** · 4700 Admiralty Way
- **Ralph's** · 8701 Lincoln Blvd

Map 25 • Marina Del Rey / Westchester West
N

1. Burrell Pl
2. Burrell St
3. Viola Pl
4. Schooner Ave
5. Fowling St
6. Campdell St

21
22
26
27
42
90

Glencoe Ave
Center Ave
Stanford Ave
Yale Ave
Del Rey Ave
Maxella Ave
Dickson St
Berkeley Dr
Oxford Ave
Princeton Dr
Marina Point Dr
Thatcher Ave

Admiralty Park
Marina City Dr
Promenade Way
Via Riata
Admiralty Way
Palawan Way
Bali Way
La Villa Marina Ave
Marina Expy
Admiral Ave

Anchorage St
Buccaneer St
Catamaran St
Driftwood St
Eastwind St
Fleet St
Galleon St
Hurricane St
Ironsides St
Jib St
Ketch St
Lighthouse St
Northstar St
Outrigger St
Privateer St
Quarterdeck St
Reef St
Spinnaker St
Topsail St
Union Jack St
Voyage St
Westwind St
Yawl St

Via Marina
Del Ali
Via Dolce
Pacific Ave
Canal Ct
Roma Ct
Katch Ct
Northstar Ct
Outrigger Ct
Privateer Ct
Reef Ct
Reef Mall
Spinnaker Ct
Topsail Ct
Union Jack Mall
Voyage Ct
Westwind Ct
Pointe Ct
Via Marina Ct

Panay Way
Marquesas Way
Tahiti Way
Bora Bora Way
NW Passage
Captains Row Dr
Old Harbor Lane
Channel Walk

Marina Del Rey
PAGE 248

Burton Chase Park

Fiji Way

MARINA DEL REY

Mindanao Way

Bolona Creek

Venice County Beach

Del Ray Lagoon Park

PLAYA DEL REY

Nicholson St
Culver Blvd
Cabora Dr
Sunset Ave
Surf St
Convoy St
Montreal St
Fowling St
Rees St
Sunridge
62nd Ave
63rd Ave
64th Ave
65th Ave
66th Ave
Ocean Front Walk
Vista Del Mar
Trolley Pl
Trolleyway
Argonaut St
Culver Pl

Veraqua Dr
Guiana Dr
Sunnysea Dr
Falmouth Ave
Calabat Ave
Tuscany Ave
Billowvista Dr
Rees Wk
W 79th St
Hulbert Ave
W 80th St
W 81st St
W 82nd St
W 83rd St
W 85th St
Berger Pl
Hastings Ave
Siran Dr
Berger Ave

Talbert St
Redlands St
Manitoba St
Waterview St
Sandpiper St
Delgany Ave
Falmouth Ave
Paseo Del Rey
Saint Bernardo
W 87th St
W 88th St
W 88th Pl
W 89th St
W 91st St
W 90th St
W 92nd St
Park Hill Dr
Cum. Laude Ave
Waist Pl
Flax Pl
Bella Vista St

W Manchester Ave
7600
Northside Pkwy
Airport Service Rd

Dockweiler State Beach

Pacific Ocean

Vista Del Mar
Pershing Drive
World Way West
Airport Service Rd

Los Angeles International Airport
PAGE 274

W Jefferson Blvd
Lincoln Blvd
Bay St
Bria Way
Fountain Park Dr
Alla Rd
Pacific Promenade
Villosa Dr
Playa Vista Dr
Crescent Pk W
Cabora Dr
LMU Dr

McConnell Ave
Beethoven St
Celedon Creek
Discovery Creek
Runway Rd
12800
W 78th St
W 80th St
Cabora Dr
Colgin Dr
Raiford Dr

Loyola Marymount University

Westlawn Ave
Ignatian Cir
Georgetown Ave
Holy Cross Pl
Loyola Blvd
Regis Way
Gonzaga Ave
Fordham Rd
Campion Dr
Alzaran Ave
Nardian Way

42
1
7200
Westchester Rec Center

Westchester Golf Co

Northside Pkwy

27
West Imperial Highway

1
2
3

Sundries / Entertainment

Because of a large storm drain that flows throughout the year, Mothers Beach has not always gotten a high score when local water has been tested for bacterial pollution. But Mothers Beach was singled out as a "Best Beach for Kids" by Sunset Magazine. There are no waves—the beach lies in a quiet cove—and lifeguards are especially attentive. We guess it's a trade-off.

24-Hour Copy Centers

- **Kinko's** • 4350 Lincoln Blvd • 310-827-2297

Clubs

- **Brennan's** • 4089 Lincoln Blvd • 310-821-6622
- **Marina Lounge at the Furama Hotel** • 8601 Lincoln Blvd • 310-670-8111

Coffee

- **Coffee Bean & Tea Leaf** • 13420 Maxella Ave
- **Johnnie's Coffee** • 4720 1/2 Admiralty Way
- **Starbucks** • 4264 Lincoln Blvd
- **Tanner's Coffee** • 200 Culver Blvd

Gyms

- **Fitness Forum** • 4144 Glencoe Ave • 310-578-2272
- **LA Fitness Sports Clubs** • 13455 Maxella Ave • 310-827-0904
- **Marina City Club** • 4333 Admiralty Way • 310-822-0611
- **Marina Fitness Center** • 14045 Panay Way • 310-821-1662

Hardware Stores

- **Gerald's Home Decorating Ctr** • 7280 W Manchester Ave • 310-670-0652
- **Home Depot** • 12975 W Jefferson Blvd • 310-822-3330

Liquor Stores

- **Century Marina Liquors** • 8526 Lincoln Blvd
- **Del Rey Liquors** • 8367 W Manchester Ave
- **Marina Liquor Mart** • 4148 Via Marina
- **Sandune Liquor Store** • 317 Culver Blvd

Movie Theaters

- **Marina Marketplace Cinemas** • 13455 Maxella Ave

Pet Stores

- **Doggone Gourmet** • 8707 Falmouth Ave • 310-306-7217
- **Pet Stuff** • 4722 Admiralty Way • 310-301-2105

Restaurants

- **Alejo's** • 4002 Lincoln Blvd • 310-822-0095
- **Alejo's** • 8343 Lincoln Blvd • 310-822-0095
- **Antica Pizzeria** • 13455 Maxella Ave • 310-577-8182
- **Ballona Fish Market** • 13455 Maxella Ave • 310-822-8979
- **Café Del Rey** • 4451 Admiralty Way • 310-823-6395
- **Caffe Pinguini** • 6935 Pacific Ave • 310-306-0117
- **Casa Escobar** • 14160 Palawan Way • 310-822-2199
- **Chan Darette** • 13490 Maxella Ave • 310-301-1004
- **Paco's Tacos** • 8329 Lincoln Blvd • 310-670-5466
- **Shanghai Red's** • 13813 Fiji Way • 310-823-4522
- **The Shack** • 185 Culver Blvd • 310-823-6222
- **The Warehouse** • 4499 Admiralty Way • 310-823-5451

Video Rental

- **Odyssey Video** • 4240 Lincoln Blvd • 310-823-2780

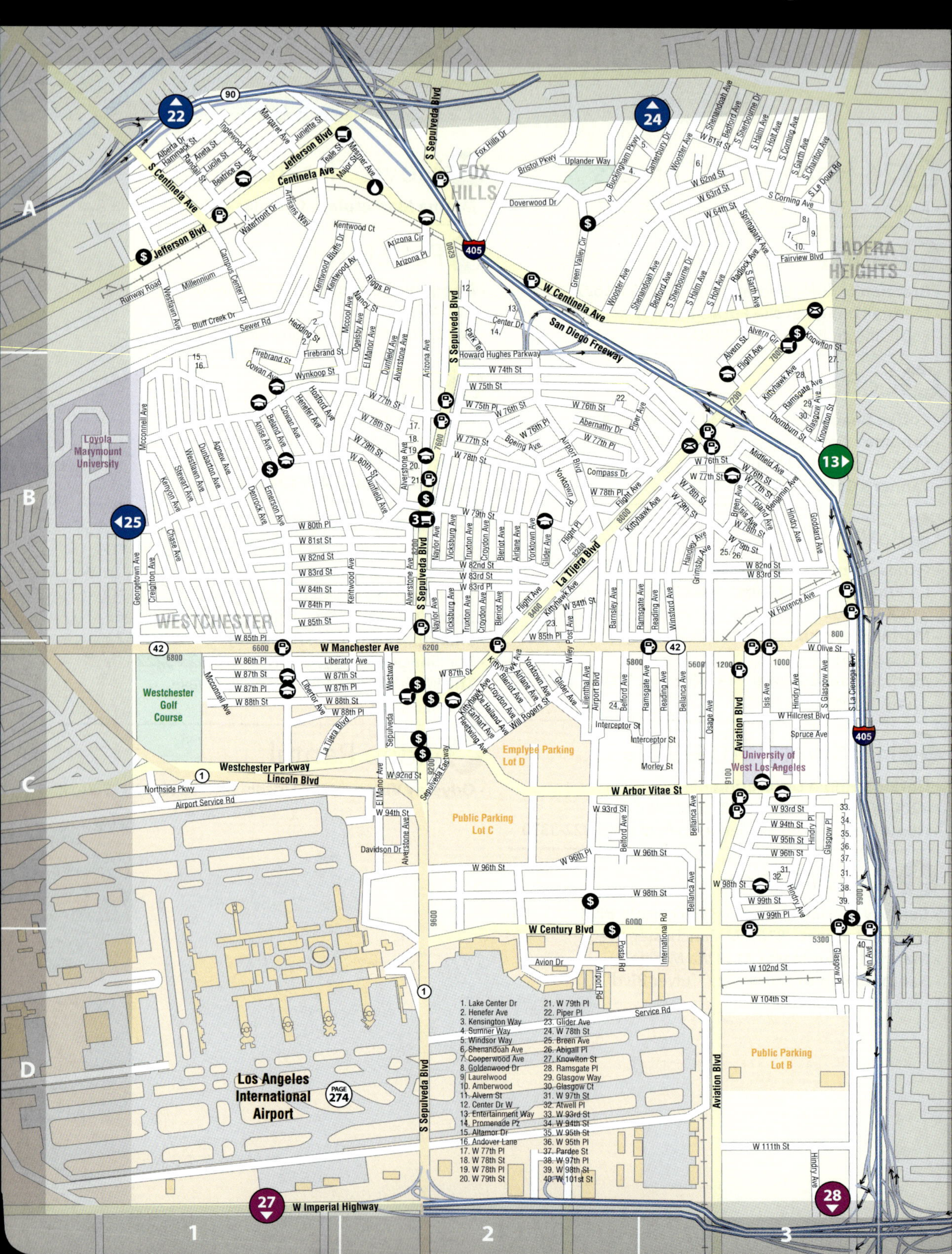
22
24
90
S Sepulveda Blvd
Fox Hills Dr
Bristol Pkwy
Uplander Way
FOX HILLS
Buckingham Pkwy
Cantorbury Dr
Shenandoah Ave
S 61st St
Bedford Ave
S Sherbourne Dr
S Halm Ave
S Holt Ave
S Corning Ave
S La Doux Rd
S Garth Ave
S Charlton Rd
Alberta Dr
Hammack St
Inglewood Blvd
Margaret Ave
Juniette St
Teale St
Mesmer Ave
Major Ave
Doverwood Dr
W 62nd St
W 63rd St
W 64th St
S Corning Ave
Springpark Ave
LADERA HEIGHTS
Fairview Blvd
Aneta St
Lucile St
Beatrice St
Jefferson Blvd
Centinela Ave
Artesians Way
S Centinela Ave
S Sherbourne Dr
Green Valley Cir
Shenandoah Ave
Bedford Ave
S Halm Ave
S Holt Ave
Radlock Ave
S Garth Ave
Jefferson Blvd
Watertront Way
Kentwood Ct
Arizona Cir
Arizona Pl
W Centinela Ave
Alvern Cir
Alvern Ave
Knowlton St
Campus Center Dr
Westlawn Ave
Millennium
Kentwood Bluffs Dr
Kentwood Ave
Riggs Pl
S Sepulveda Blvd
W Howard Hughes Parkway
San Diego Freeway
Flight Ave
Kirthhawk Ave
Ramsgate Ave
Thornburn St
Glasgow Ave
Knowlton St
Runway Road
Bluff Creek Dr
Sewer Rd
Hedding St
Nancy St
Oglesby Ave
Duntfield Ave
Alverstone Ave
Arizona Ave
W 74th St
W 75th St
W 76th St
Abernathy Dr
Piper Ave
Midtield Ave
W 76th St
Green Ave
W 77th Pl
Hindry Ave
Goddard Ave
Firebrand St
Firebrand St
El Manor Ave
Cowan Ave
Wynkoop St
W 75th Pl
W 77th St
Boeing Ave
Airport Blvd
W 77th Pl
Compass Dr
Toland Ave
W 76th St
W 77th St
Loyola Marymount University
McConnell Ave
Hasford Ave
Henefer Ave
Anise Ave
Beland Ave
Cowan Ave
W 77th St
W 78th St
W 79th St
W 80th St
W 78th Pl
W 77th St
W 78th St
W 78th St
Yorktown Pl
Flight Ave
W 78th St
Kirthhawk Ave
W 79th St
Handley Ave
W 78th St
W 79th St
25
26
WESTCHESTER
25
Dunbarton Ave
Westlawn Ave
Stewart Ave
Agnew Ave
Duntield Ave
Alverstone Ave
S Sepulveda Blvd
W 79th St
Naylor Ave
Vicksburg Ave
Truxton Ave
Croydon Ave
Yorktown Ave
Airlane Ave
Glider Ave
La Tijera Blvd
Kirthhawk Ave
Grimsby Ave
W 82nd St
W 83rd St
Georgetown Ave
Creighton Ave
Chase Ave
Emerson Ave
Derrick Ave
Kentwood Ave
W 80th Pl
W 81st St
W 82nd St
W 83rd St
W 84th St
W 84th Pl
W 85th St
Naylor Ave
Vicksburg Ave
Truxton Ave
Croydon Ave
Bleriot Ave
Flight Ave
Kirthhawk Ave
W 84th St
W 85th Pl
Winstord Ave
Barnsley Ave
Ramsgate Ave
Reading Ave
W Florence Ave
800
W Olive St
W 85th Pl
42
6800
McConnell Ave
Liberator Ave
W 86th Pl
W 87th St
W 87th St
W 88th St
W Manchester Ave
6200
Kirtyha Ave
Yorktown Ave
Airlane Ave
Glider Ave
Lillenthal Ave
Airport Blvd
Belford Ave
Ramsgate Ave
Reading Ave
Bellanca Ave
5800
1200
Isis Ave
Hindry Ave
S Glasgow Ave
1000
W Olive St
S La Cienega Blvd
Westchester Golf Course
Sepulveda
Westway
Bleriot Ave
W 87th St
W 88th St
W 88th Pl
La Tijera Blvd
W 87th St
Croydon Ave
Holland Ave
Earhart Ave
Will Rogers
Airport Blvd
Interceptor St
Osage Ave
Aviation Blvd
W Hillcrest Blvd
Spruce Ave
405
Westchester Parkway
Lincoln Blvd
Northside Pkwy
Airport Service Rd
El Manor Ave
W 92nd St
Sepulveda Freeway
Employee Parking Lot D
Interceptor St
Morley St
University of West Los Angeles
W Arbor Vitae St
9100
W 93rd St
W 94th Pl
W 95th Pl
W 96th St
W 98th Pl
W 99th Pl
33.
34.
35.
36.
37.
31.
38.
39.
Public Parking Lot C
W 94th St
Davidson Dr
Alverstone Ave
9600
W 96th St
W 96th St
Belford Ave
W 96th St
Bellanca Ave
W 93rd St
W 94th St
W 95th St
W 96th St
32
W 98th St
W 99th St
W 99th Pl
40
W Century Blvd
6000
Postal Rd
International Rd
W 102nd St
W 104th St
5300
Glasgow Pl
Avion Dr
Airport Rd
Los Angeles International Airport
PAGE 274
S Sepulveda Blvd
Service Rd
Public Parking Lot B
Aviation Blvd
W 111th St
Hindry Ave
27
28
W Imperial Highway
1. Lake Center Dr
2. Henefer Ave
3. Kensington Way
4. Sumner Way
5. Windsor Way
6. Shenandoah Ave
7. Cooperwood Ave
8. Goldenwood Dr
9. Laurelwood
10. Amberwood
11. Alvern St
12. Center Dr W
13. Entertainment Way
14. Promenade Pz
15. Altamor Dr
16. Andover Lane
17. W 77th Pl
18. W 78th St
19. W 78th St
20. W 79th St
21. W 79th Pl
22. Piper Pl
23. Glider Ave
24. W 78th St
25. Breen Ave
26. Abigall Pl
27. Knowlton St
28. Ramsgate Pl
29. Glasgow Way
30. Glasgow Ct
31. W 97th Pl
32. Atwell Pl
33. W 93rd St
34. W 94th St
35. W 95th Pl
36. W 95th Pl
37. Pardee St
38. W 97th Pl
39. W 98th Pl
40. W 101st St
13
3
405
A
B
C
D
1
2
3

La Tijera Blvd, which runs through this neighborhood, is the best shortcut to LAX that we know. It's accessible from La Cienega Blvd., and is never congested. Just don't tell anyone else about it…

$ Banks

- **Bank of America** · 8946 S Sepulveda Blvd
- **Citibank** · 8800 S Sepulveda Blvd
- **Citibank** · 9841 Airport Blvd
- **City National Bank** · 12555 W Jefferson Blvd
- **City National Bank** · 6033 W Century Blvd
- **Comerica Bank** · 9920 S La Cienega Blvd
- **First Federal Bank** · 8750 S Sepulveda Blvd
- **Washington Mutual** · 8950 S Sepulveda Blvd
- **Wells Fargo Bank** · 5899 Green Valley Cir
- **Wells Fargo Bank** · 6571 W 80th St
- **Wells Fargo Bank** · 6921 La Tijera Blvd
- **Wells Fargo Bank** · 8814 S Sepulveda Blvd

Car Washes

- **Playa Vista Car Care** · 6900 S Centinela Ave

Gas Stations

- **76** · 7550 S Sepulveda Blvd
- **76** · 8525 S Sepulveda Blvd
- **76** · 8600 Aviation Blvd
- **Arco** · 1100 W Manchester Blvd
- **Arco** · 5201 Century Blvd
- **Arco** · 7370 La Tijera Blvd
- **Arco** · 9200 Aviation Blvd
- **Chevron** · 5156 W Century Blvd
- **Chevron** · 5975 W Centinela Ave
- **Chevron** · 6101 W Manchester Ave
- **Chevron** · 6900 S Centinela Ave
- **Chevron** · 7360 La Tijera Blvd
- **Exxon** · 9131 Aviation Blvd
- **Mobil** · 6100 Sepulveda Blvd
- **Mobil** · 6600 W Manchester Ave
- **Mobil** · 7601 S Sepulveda Blvd
- **Mobil** · 8307 S La Cienega Blvd
- **Shell** · 12313 Jefferson Blvd
- **Shell** · 804 W Manchester Blvd
- **Texaco** · 5551 W Century Blvd
- **Texaco** · 5800 W Manchester Ave

Post Offices

- 6824 La Tijera Blvd
- 7381 La Tijera Blvd

Schools

- **98th Street Elementary** · 5431 W 98th St
- **Amino Leadership High School** · 1155 Arbor Vitae St
- **Cowan Avenue Elementary** · 7615 Cowan Ave
- **Escela De Montessori** · 8820 Sepulveda Eastway
- **Kentwood Elementary** · 8401 Emerson Ave
- **Living World Christian Academy** · 6520 Arizona Ave
- **Los Angeles Open Charter School** · 5540 W 77th St
- **Orville Wright Middle School** · 6550 W 80th St
- **Playa Del Rey Elementary** · 12221 Juniette St
- **St Jerome Catholic School** · 5570 Thornburn St
- **University of West Los Angeles** · 1155 W Arbor Vitae St
- **Visitation Elementary** · 8740 Emerson Ave
- **Westchester Lutheran** · 7831 S Sepulveda Blvd
- **Westchester Lutheran Middle School** · 6705 W 77th St
- **Westchester Neighborhood School** · 5520 Arbor Vitae St
- **Westport Heights Elementary** · 6011 W 79th St

Supermarkets

- **Albertson's** · 5750 Mesmer Ave
- **Ralph's** · 8824 S Sepulveda Blvd
- **Trader Joe's** · 8645 S Sepulveda Blvd
- **Von's** · 6571 W 80th St
- **Von's** · 6921 La Tijera Blvd

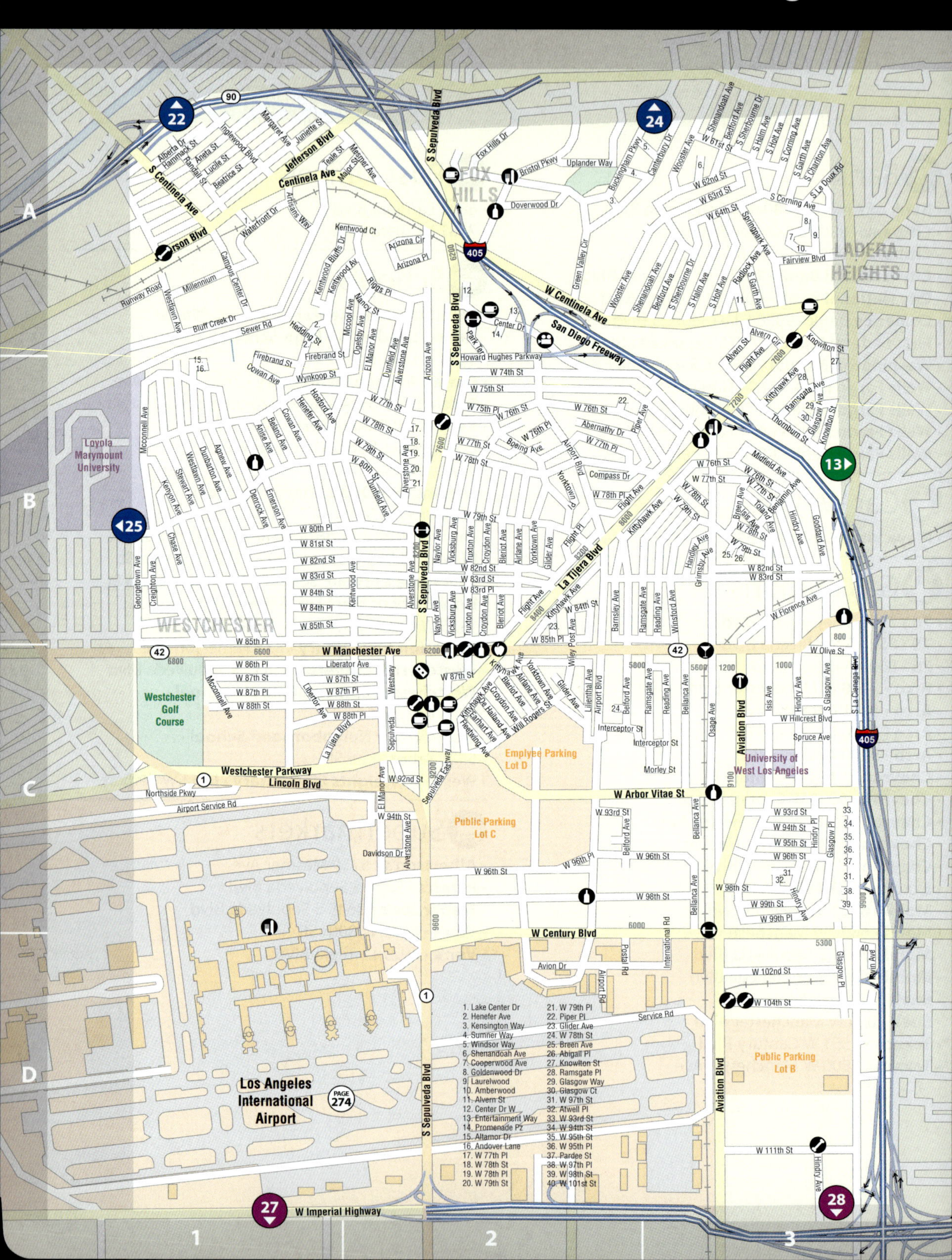
22
24
25
13
27
28
42
42
90
405
405
Loyola Marymount University
FOX HILLS
LADERA HEIGHTS
WESTCHESTER
Westchester Golf Course
University of West Los Angeles
Los Angeles International Airport
PAGE 274
Westchester Parkway
Lincoln Blvd
Northside Pkwy
Airport Service Rd
Public Parking Lot C
Public Parking Lot B
Emplyee Parking Lot D
W Imperial Highway
San Diego Freeway
S Sepulveda Blvd
S Centinela Ave
Centinela Ave
W Centinela Ave
Jefferson Blvd
S Sepulveda Blvd
Howard Hughes Parkway
W Manchester Ave
W Arbor Vitae St
W Century Blvd
Aviation Blvd
La Tijera Blvd
La Cienega Blvd

1. Lake Center Dr
2. Henefer Ave
3. Kensington Way
4. Sumner Way
5. Windsor Way
6. Shenandoah Ave
7. Cooperwood Ave
8. Goldenwood Dr
9. Laurelwood
10. Amberwood
11. Alvern St
12. Center Dr W
13. Entertainment Way
14. Promenade Pz
15. Altamor Dr
16. Andover Lane
17. W 77th Pl
18. W 78th St
19. W 78th Pl
20. W 79th Ave
21. W 79th Pl
22. Piper Pl
23. Glider Ave
24. W 78th St
25. Breen Ave
26. Abigall Pl
27. Knowlton St
28. Ramsgate Pl
29. Glasgow Way
30. Glasgow Ct
31. W 97th Pl
32. Atwell Pl
33. W 93rd St
34. W 94th St
35. W 95th St
36. W 95th Pl
37. Pardee Pl
38. W 97th Pl
39. W 98th St
40. W 101st St

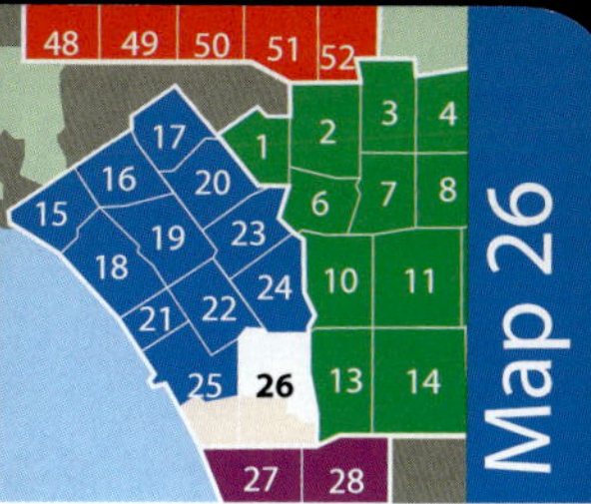

LAX may be the bane of many Westchester residents' existence, but thanks to the airport, they've been the beneficiaries in recent years of several coffee shops and a Trader Joe's. The 405 makes it easy to go to points north and south for more upscale shopping and dining experiences, so the area's amenities tend to be more in the vein of creature comforts for the locals.

24-Hour Copy Centers

- **Kinko's** • 5855 W Century Blvd • 310-665-5955

Clubs

- **Westchester Sports Grill** • 5630 W Manchester Ave • 310-670-2366

Coffee

- **Coffee Co** • 8751 La Tijera Blvd
- **L'Aroma Espress** • 8901 Sepulveda Eastway
- **Starbucks** • 294 Fox Hills Mall
- **Starbucks** • 5301 W Centinela Ave
- **Starbucks** • 6081 Center Dr
- **Starbucks** • 8817 S Sepulveda Blvd

Farmer's Markets

- **Westchester** • 6200 W 87th St • Wed 8:30-1

Gyms

- **24-Hour Fitness** • 5711 W Century Blvd • 310-410-9909
- **Spectrum Club** • 6833 Park Ter • 310-216-3060
- **Westchester Family YMCA** • 8015 S Sepulveda Blvd • 310-568-2077

Hardware Stores

- **Southland Lumber & Supply** • 8710 Aviation Blvd • 323-776-3530

Liquor Stores

- **A & A Liquors** • 6200 W Manchester Ave
- **Kentwood Mini Market** • 7923 Emerson Ave
- **Purdy Liquor** • 5919 W 98th St
- **Regal Liquor** • 6295 Bristol Pkwy
- **Sear's Liquor Store** • 5206 Arbor Vitae St
- **Stan's Liquor** • 842 W Manchester Blvd
- **Stewart's Liquor** • 7411 La Tijera Blvd

Movie Theaters

- **The Bridge: Cinema de Lux** • 6081 Center Dr

Pet Stores

- **Aquarium Arts** • 11160 Hindry Ave • 310-649-1517
- **Centinela Feed & Pet Supplies** • 7600 S Sepulveda Blvd • 310-216-9261
- **Drexler Marine Fish** • 5420 W 104th St • 310-410-1662
- **Eco-Pet** • 6955 La Tijera Blvd • 310-645-8892
- **Exclusively Reptiles** • 6218 W Manchester Ave • 310-649-4963
- **House Cat Premiere Services** • 12505 W Jefferson Blvd • 310-577-9956
- **Petco** • 8801 S Sepulveda Blvd • 310-645-7198
- **Sea Dwelling Creatures** • 5515 W 104th St • 310-676-9697

Restaurants

- **Buggy Whip** • 7420 La Tijera Blvd • 310-645-7131
- **Encounter** • 209 World Way • 310-215-5151
- **Nick's Little Place** • 6251 Bristol Pkwy • 310-670-2920
- **Paco's Tacos** • 6212 W Manchester Ave • 310-634-8692

Video Rental

- **Blockbuster** • 8813 S Sepulveda Blvd • 310-649-3699

Map 27 • El Segundo / Manhattan Beach

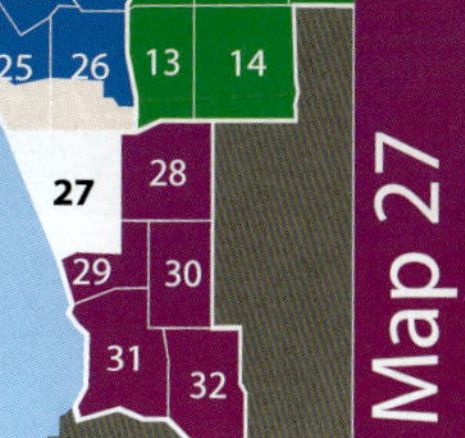

The area continues to grow, and has hit the big time with the opening of Raleigh Studios Manhattan Beach, where shows like "Boston Public" and "The Practice" now film. Traffic on the 405 used to lighten up just past LAX, but the new businesses that have opened along El Segundo Blvd. and Rosecrans Ave have, unfortunately, extended the congestion farther south.

$ Banks

- **Bank of America** · 3016 Sepulveda Blvd
- **Bank of America** · 835 N Sepulveda Blvd
- **Bank of the West** · 3500 Aviation Blvd
- **Citibank** · 2710 Sepulveda Blvd
- **Comerica Bank** · 2121 Rosecrans Ave
- **First Coastal Bank** · 275 Main St
- **Union Bank** · 2910 N Sepulveda Blvd
- **Union Bank** · 400 Manhattan Beach Blvd
- **US Bank** · 3300 N Sepulveda Blvd
- **Washington Mutual** · 130 E Grand Ave
- **Washington Mutual** · 201 Manhattan Beach Blvd
- **Washington Mutual** · 550 N Sepulveda Blvd
- **Washington Mutual** · 700 S Sepulveda Blvd
- **Wells Fargo Bank** · 3110 N Sepulveda Blvd
- **Wells Fargo Bank** · 500 N Sepulveda Blvd

Car Washes

- **Auto Magic** · 1717 N Sepulveda Blvd
- **Manhattan Car Wash** · 300 S Sepulveda Blvd
- **Red Carpet Hand Wash** · 2414 N Sepulveda Blvd

Gas Stations

- **76** · 3410 Aviation Blvd
- **76** · 603 N Sepulveda Blvd
- **76** · 770 N Sepulveda Blvd
- **Arco** · 1002 Manhattan Beach Blvd
- **Chevron** · 2301 N Aviation Blvd
- **Chevron** · 232 Main St
- **Chevron** · 3633 N Sepulveda Blvd
- **Chevron** · 601 Vista Del Mar
- **Manhattan Beach Fuel** · 1100 Manhattan Beach Blvd
- **Mobil** · 1865 Manhattan Beach Blvd
- **Mobil** · 765 N Sepulvdea Blvd
- **Shell** · 1129 N Sepulveda Blvd

Landmarks

- **Chevron Oil Refinery** · East of Sepulveda Blvd, north of Rosecrans Ave
- **Manhattan Beach State Pier** · West of Manhattan Beach Blvd

Libraries

- **El Segundo Public Library** · 111 W Mariposa Ave · 310-322-4121
- **Manhattan Beach Library** · 1320 Highland Ave · 310-545-8595

Police

- **El Segundo City Police Dept** · 348 Main St · 310-524-2200
- **Manhattan Beach Police Dept** · 420 15th St · 310-802-5100

Post Offices

- 1007 N Sepulveda Blvd
- 200 Main St
- 425 15th St

Schools

- **American Martyrs** · 1701 Laurel Ave
- **Center Street Elementary** · 700 Center St
- **Dana Intermediate School** · 13500 Aviation Blvd
- **El Segundo High School** · 640 Main St
- **El Segundo Middle School** · 332 Center St
- **Grandview Elementary** · 455 25th St
- **Manhattan Beach Middle School** · 1501 Redondo Ave
- **Meadows Avenue Elementary** · 1200 N Meadows Ave
- **Mira Costa High School** · 701 S Peck Ave
- **Montessori** · 315 S Peck Ave
- **Pacific Elementary** · 1214 Pacific Ave
- **Pennekamp Elementary** · 110 S Rowell Ave
- **Richmond Street Elementary** · 615 Richmond St
- **Robinson Elementary** · 80 Morningside Dr
- **St Anthony Catholic School** · 233 Lomita St
- **Via Pacifica School** · 1700 Manhattan Beach Blvd

Supermarkets

- **Bristol Farms** · 1570 Rosecrans Ave
- **Ralph's** · 2700 N Sepulveda Blvd
- **Ralph's** · 500 N Sepulveda Blvd
- **Trader Joe's** · 1800 Rosecrans Ave
- **Trader Joe's** · 1821 Manhattan Beach Blvd
- **Von's** · 410 Manhattan Beach Blvd

N
Map 27 • El Segundo / Manhattan Beach

PAGE 274
Los Angeles International Airport
W Imperial Hwy
Glenn Anderson Freeway
105
25
26
28
29

Dockweiler State Beach
El Segundo Beach
Pacific Ocean
Manhattan County Beach
Vista Del Mar

EL SEGUNDO
EL PORTO
MANHATTAN BEACH

Washington Park
El Segundo Recreation Park
Library Park
The Lakes at El Segundo Golf Course
Sand Dune Park
Live Oak Park
Plaza Golf Course
Marine Ave Sport Park
Polliwog Park
Valley Park

W Imperial Ave
W Acacia Ave
W Walnut Ave
W Sycamore Ave
W Maple Ave
W Oak Ave
W Palm Ave
W Elm Ave
W Mariposa Ave
W Pine Ave
W Holly Ave
Grand Ave
W Franklin Ave
W El Segundo Blvd
Binder Pl

E Acacia Ave
E Walnut Ave
E Sycamore Ave
E Maple Ave
E Oak Ave
E Palm Ave
E Elm Ave
E Mariposa Ave
E Pine Ave
E Holly Ave
Grand Ave
E El Segundo Blvd

Dune St
Hillcrest St
Yucca St
Loma Vista St
Bayonne St
Virginia St
Whiting St
Loma Vista St
Valley St
Hillcrest St

Cedar St
Pepper St
Concord St
Main St
Eucalyptus St
Cypress St
Sheldon St
McCarthy Ct
Lomita St
Richmond St
Standard St
Arena St
Concord St
Virginia St

Maryland St
Bungalow Dr
Penn St
Sierra St
Center St
Nevada St
Oregon St
California St
Kansas St
Illinois St
Washington St
Indiana St
Lairport St
Illinois St
California St

Continental Blvd
N Nash St
Duley Rd
N Douglas St
Hornet Way
Aviation Blvd
Judah St

S Sepulveda Blvd
N Sepulveda Blvd
S Hughes Way
S Allied Way
Chapman Way
Coral Cir
S Douglas St
Utah Ave
Alaska Ave
Hawaii St
Park Pl
Apollo St
Continental Way
Rosecrans Ave

36th Pl
36th St
35th Pl
35th St
34th St
33rd Pl
33rd St
31st Pl
31st St
30th St
29th St
27th St
25th St
24th St

Bell Ave
Blanche Rd
Agnes Rd
Laurel Ave
Pacific Ave
Palm Ave
Maple Ave
N Poinsettia Ave
N Walnut Ave
Pine Ave
Elm Ave
Oak Ave

Park View Ave
Park Pl
Fairway Dr
Westport
Village Cir
Marine Ave

23rd St
22nd St
21st St
20th St
19th St
18th St
17th St
15th St
12th St

N Meadows Ave
N Rowell Ave
N Peck Ave
N Herrin Ave
N Redondo Ave
Manzanita Ln
Lynngrove Dr
Faymont Ave
Harkness St
Wendy Way
N Aviation Blvd

Manhattan Beach Blvd
Chestnut Ave
Magnolia Ave

11th St
10th St
8th St
6th St
5th St
3rd St
2nd St
1st St

John St
Pacific Pl
Johnson St
N Poinsettia Ave
Larsson St
N Dianthus St
Anderson St
S Sepulveda Blvd

Carriage Pl
S Redondo Ave
Gates Ave
Curtis Ave
Voorhees Ave
Ruhland Ave
Nelson Ave
Mathews Ave

Duncan Ave
Boundary Pl
Longfellow Ave
Francisco St
Homer St
N Inglewood Dr
Palm Dr
Terraza
Prospect Ave
Alma Ave
Ardath Dr
S Meadows Ave
S Herrin Ave
S Peck Ave
Tennyson St
Shelley St
Keats St

1. E Elsey Pl
2. Bridgeport
3. Chatham
4. Stratford
5. Cambridge
6. Santa Cruz Ct
7. San Miguel Ct
8. Evergreen Ln
9. Grenada Ct
10. Catalina Ct
11. Laguna Ct
12. Malaga Pl
13. Malaga Wy
14. Gateway Dr
15. Bermuda Ct
16. Dover Pl
17. Nantucket Pl
18. Cayman Ct
19. Coronado Ct
20. Monterey Ct
21. Marin Ct
22. Tiburon Ct
23. Bryant Pl
24. Villa Escuela
25. Arbolado Ct
26. Center Pl
27. Deegan Pl
28. Church St
29. Fisher Ave
30. Railroad Pl
31. La Carlita Pl
32. Braeholm Pl
33. Hermosa View Dr

PAGE 246

Highland Ave
Ocean Dr
N Valley Dr
N Ardmore Ave
N Ardmore Ave
N Valley Dr
The Strand

1
2
3
A
B
C
D

It would be very easy to survive for an indefinite time without ever leaving Rosecrans Ave., which boasts several supermarkets, movie theatres, and a camping/wilderness store. But make your way closer to the ocean in Manhattan Beach, and you'll find much quirkier shops and restaurants that all have a personality of their own.

 Coffee

- **Blue Butterfly Coffee** · 351 Main St
- **Coffee Bean & Tea Leaf** · 3008 N Sepulveda Blvd
- **Coffee Bean & Tea Leaf** · 321 Manhattan Beach Blvd
- **Manhattan Coffee** · 350 N Sepulveda Blvd
- **Our Daily Grind** · 503 Main St
- **Peet's Coffee & Tea** · 328 Manhattan Beach Blvd
- **Starbucks** · 2231 Rosecrans Ave
- **Starbucks** · 233 Manhattan Beach Blvd
- **Starbucks** · 530 N Sepulveda Blvd

 Farmer's Markets

- **Farmers' Market** · Main St at City Hall · Thu 3-7

Gyms

- **24-Hour Fitness** · 1500 Rosecrans Ave · 310-536-9300
- **4 Star Gym** · 436 Main St · 310-414-9696
- **Club at Pacific Corporate Towers** · 200 N Sepulveda Blvd · 310-563-1442
- **Manhattan Beach Cross Training** · 3701 Highland Ave · 310-545-4982
- **Spectrum Club** · 2250 Park Pl · 310-643-6878

Hardware Stores

- **Ace Hardware** · 203 E Grand Ave · 310-322-4545
- **Manhattan Hardware** · 1005 N Aviation Blvd · 310-372-2402

Liquor Stores

- **El Porto Market & Deli** · 4103 Highland Ave
- **Jon's Liquor** · 3508 Aviation Blvd
- **Leonard's Liquor Store** · 630 N Sepulveda Blvd
- **Lindy's Liquor & Deli** · 11720 Aviation Blvd
- **Mac's Liquor** · 2201 Highland Ave
- **Moon's Market** · 3307 Highland Ave
- **Mr D's Liquor Marts** · 1100 N Sepulveda Blvd
- **Village Liquor** · 506 Center St

Movie Theaters

- **Mann Manhattan Village Theatre** · 3560 N Sepulveda Blvd
- **Pacific Theatres Beach Cities** · 831 S Nash St

Pet Stores

- **Critter Corral Pet Shop** · 118 W Grand Ave · 310-322-3077
- **We Love Pets** · 815 Manhattan Ave · 310-372-1212

 Restaurants

- **Cozymel's** · 2171 Rosecrans Ave · 310-606-5464
- **Houston's** · 1550 Rosecrans Ave · 310-643-7211
- **Il Fornaio** · 1800 Rosecrans Ave · 310-725-9555
- **The Spot** · 110 2nd St · 310-376-2355
- **Uncle Bill's Pancake House** · 1305 Highland Ave · 310-545-5177

Shopping

- **GeoDecor** · 113 Shelton St · 310-322-4043

Video Rental

- **Blockbuster** · 2200 N Sepulveda Blvd · 310-545-0202
- **Imperial Video Store** · 958 Main St · 310-322-8042
- **Main Street Video** · 239 Main St · 310-322-8700
- **Title Wave Video** · 3215 Highland Ave · 310-545-4777

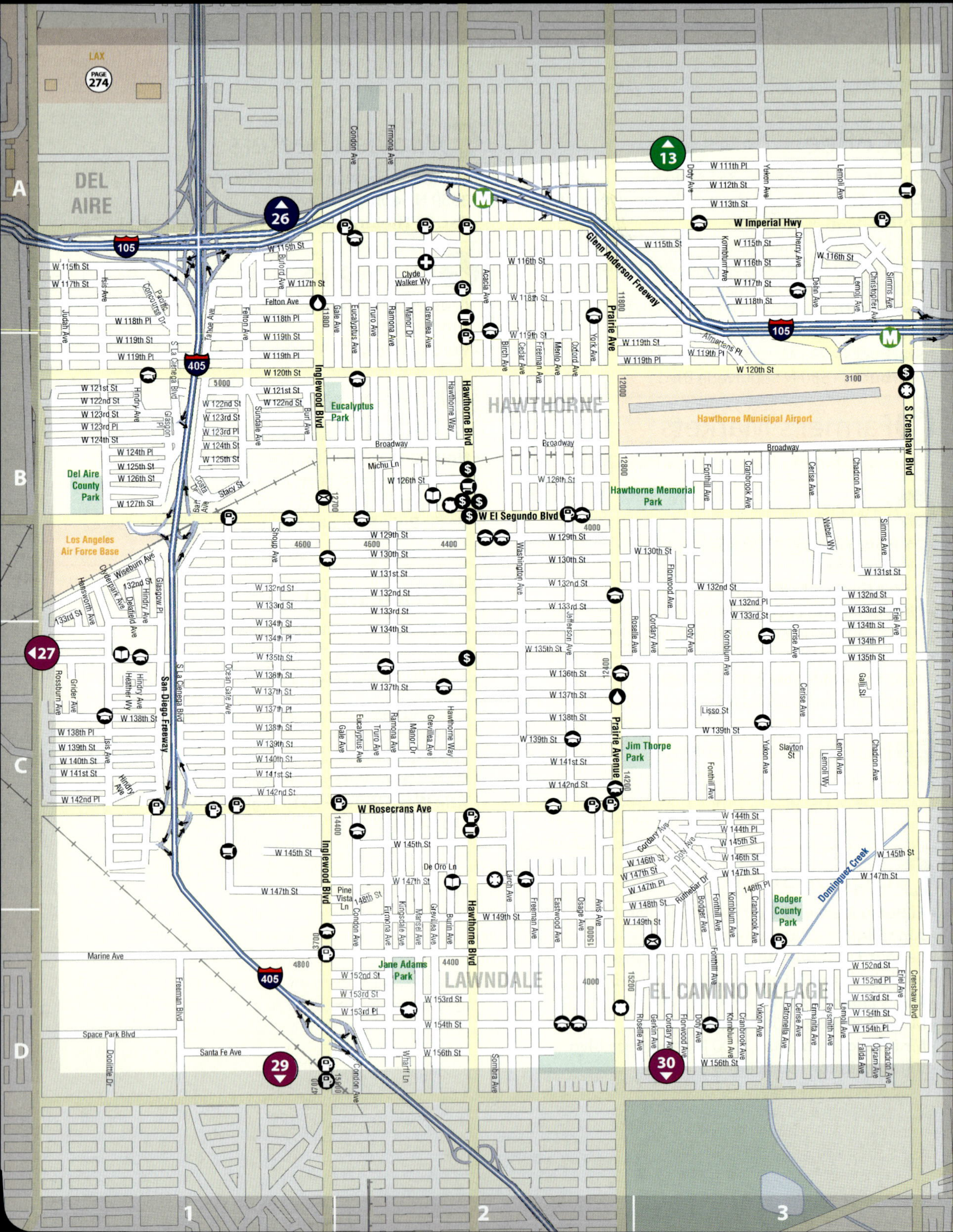

N

Place names / Areas

DEL AIRE

HAWTHORNE

LAWNDALE

EL CAMINO VILLAGE

Los Angeles Air Force Base

LAX PAGE 274

Hawthorne Municipal Airport

Eucalyptus Park

Del Aire County Park

Hawthorne Memorial Park

Jim Thorpe Park

Bodger County Park

Jane Adams Park

Freeways / Routes

105

405

Glenn Anderson Freeway

San Diego Freeway

Pacific Concourse Dr

13

26

127

29

30

Streets

Condon Ave
Firmona Ave
W 111th Pl
W 112th St
W 113th St
Doty Ave
Yukon Ave
Lemoli Ave
W Imperial Hwy
Kornblum Ave
W 115th St
W 116th St
W 117th St
W 118th St
Cherry Ave
Dehn Ave
Lemoli Ave
Christopher Ave
Simms Ave
Clyde Walker Wy
W 115th St
W 117th St
Isis Ave
Judah Ave
W 118th Pl
W 119th St
W 119th Pl
Felton Ave
Tahoe Ave
Buford Ave
W 117th St
Felton Ave
W 118th Pl
W 119th St
W 119th Pl
W 120th St
Gale Ave
Eucalyptus Ave
Truro Ave
Ramona Ave
Manor Dr
Grevillea Ave
Acacia Ave
W 116th St
W 118th St
W 119th St
Birch Ave
Cedar Ave
Freeman Ave
Menlo Ave
Oxford Ave
York Ave
Prairie Ave
11800
Glenn Anderson Freeway
Almertens Pl
W 119th St
W 119th Pl
W 120th St
3100
3000
S Crenshaw Blvd
S La Cienega Blvd
Inglewood Blvd
Hindry Ave
W 121st St
W 122nd St
W 123rd St
W 123rd St
W 124th St
W 124th Pl
W 125th St
W 126th St
W 127th St
Glasgow Pl
W 121st St
W 122nd St
W 123rd St
W 123rd Pl
W 124th St
W 125th St
5000
Sundale Ave
Burl Ave
Hawthorne Way
Hawthorne Blvd
Broadway
Michu Ln
W 126th St
Broadway
Broadway
12000
12800
Fonthill Ave
Cranbrook Ave
Cerise Ave
Chadron Ave
Stacy St
Bart Ave
Bern Ave
W 129th St
W 130th St
W 131st St
W 132nd St
W 133rd St
W 134th St
Shoup Ave
4600
4600
4400
Washington Ave
W 129th St
W 130th St
W 132nd St
W 133rd St
4000
W El Segundo Blvd
W 130th St
Florwood Ave
Roselle Ave
Cordary Ave
Doty Ave
Kornblum Ave
W 132nd St
W 133rd St
Cerise Ave
Simms Ave
Weber Wy
W 131st St
W 132nd St
W 133rd St
W 134th St
Eriel Ave
W 134th Pl
W 135th St
Ocean Gate Ave
W 134th St
W 134th Pl
W 135th St
W 136th St
W 137th St
W 137th Pl
W 138th St
W 139th St
W 140th St
W 141st St
W 142nd St
Gale Ave
Eucalyptus Ave
Truro Ave
Ramona Ave
Manor Dr
Grevillea Ave
Hawthorne Way
W 137th St
Jefferson Ave
12000
W 135th St
W 136th St
W 137th St
W 138th St
W 139th St
W 141st St
W 142nd St
Prairie Avenue
14200
Jim Thorpe Park
Lisso St
W 139th St
Kornblum Ave
Yukon Ave
Fonthill Ave
Cerise Ave
Slayton St
Lemoli Ave
Lemoli Wy
Chadron Ave
Galli St
San Diego Freeway
S La Cienega Blvd
Rossburn Ave
Grider Ave
Isis Ave
Hindry Ave
Heather Wy
W 138th Pl
W 139th St
W 140th St
W 141st St
W 142nd Pl
Hindry Ave
W Rosecrans Ave
14400
W 144th St
W 144th St
W 145th St
W 146th St
W 147th St
Cordary Ave
Doty Ave
W 145th St
W 146th St
W 147th St
W 147th Pl
W 148th Pl
Ruthelen St
Bodger St
Avis Ave
Osage Ave
Eastwood Ave
Fonthill Ave
Kornblum Ave
Cranbrook Ave
Bodger County Park
Dominguez Creek
W 145th St
W 147th St
Inglewood Blvd
W 145th St
W 147th St
De Oro Ln
Pine Vista Ln
148th St
W 147th St
Larch Ave
Freeman Ave
W 148th St
W 149th St
Condon Ave
Firmona Ave
Kingsdale Ave
Marsel Ave
Grevillea Ave
Burin Ave
Hawthorne Blvd
3700
Marine Ave
405
4800
Jane Adams Park
W 152nd St
W 153rd St
W 153rd Pl
W 154th St
W 156th St
4400
Somera Ave
4000
15200
Roselle Ave
Gerkin Ave
Cordary Ave
Doty Ave
Florwood Ave
Kornblum Ave
Cranbrook Ave
Yukon Ave
Patronella Ave
Cerise Ave
Ermanita Ave
Crenshaw Blvd
Eriel Ave
Lemoli Ave
Feysmith Ave
W 152nd St
W 153rd St
W 154th St
W 154th Pl
Chadron Ave
Ogram Ave
Falda Ave
W 156th St
Freeman Blvd
Space Park Blvd
Santa Fe Ave
Doolittle Dr
Condon Ave
4700
Wharff Ln
Hindy Ave
Wiseburn Ave
132nd St
Hansworth Ave
Clydesdale Ave
Delafield Ave
Glasgow Pl
133rd St
Hindry Ave
Delafield Ave
Hindry Ave
Hawthorne Way

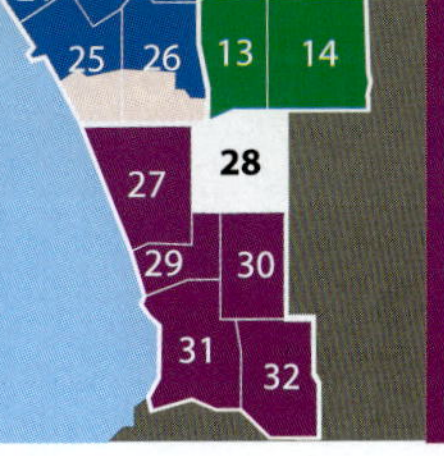

Hawthorne's municipal airport, also known as Jack Northrop Field, is home to the Western Museum of Flight. The Museum's collection is mainly devoted to one of Hawthorne's largest businesses, the Northrop Grumman Corp., which helped boost the city's reputation as the "cradle of aviation."

$ Banks

- **Bank of America** · 11525 Crenshaw Blvd
- **Bank of America** · 12547 S Hawthorne Blvd
- **Citibank** · 12710 Hawthorne Blvd
- **Union Bank** · 12801 Hawthorne Blvd
- **Washington Mutual** · 12645 Hawthorne Blvd
- **Wells Fargo Bank** · 13545 Hawthorne Blvd

Car Washes

- **Astro Finish Car Waxing** · 13762 Prairie Ave
- **E-Z Self Svc Car Wash** · 11817 Inglewood Ave

Gas Stations

- **76** · 3101 W Imperial Hwy
- **76** · 4008 W Rosecrans Ave
- **76** · 5105 W Rosecrans Ave
- **Arco** · 11402 Hawthorne Blvd
- **Arco** · 11890 S Hawthorne Blvd
- **Arco** · 2730 Marine Ave
- **Arco** · 4009 W Rosecrans Ave
- **Arco** · 4015 W El Segundo Blvd
- **Arco** · 5038 El Segundo Blvd
- **Arco** · 5230 Rosecrans Ave
- **Chevron** · 14305 Hawthorne Blvd
- **Mobil** · 3705 Inglewood Ave
- **Mobil** · 4500 W Imperial Hwy
- **Mobil** · 4750 Inglewood Ave
- **Shell** · 11741 Hawthorne Blvd
- **Shell** · 4750 W Rosecrans Ave
- **Shell** · 4755 W Imperial Hwy
- **Shell** · 5035 W Rosecrans Ave
- **Texaco** · 15606 Inglewood Ave

Hospitals

- **Robert F Kennedy Medical Center** · 4500 W 116th St · 310-973-1711

Libraries

- **Hawthorne Public Library** · 12700 Grevillea Ave · 310-679-8193
- **Lawndale Library** · 14615 Burin Ave · 310-676-0177
- **Wiseburn Library** · 5335 W 135th St · 310-643-8880

Police

- **Hawthorne City Police Service** · 4440 W 126th St · 310-970-7976
- **Lawndale Sheriff Service Center** · 15331 Prairie Ave · 310-219-2750

Post Offices

- 12700 Inglewood Ave
- 4320 Marine Ave

Schools

- **Acacia Baptist School** · 4712 W El Segundo Blvd
- **Addams Elementary** · 4535 W 153rd Pl
- **Al-Huda Islamic School** · 12209 Hawthorne Way
- **Anderson Elementary** · 4110 W 154th St
- **Anza Elementary** · 5234 W 120th St
- **Bennett-Kew Elementary** · 11710 Cherry Ave
- **Bud Carlson Middle School** · 13838 Yukon Ave
- **Burnett** · 5403 W 138th St
- **Cabrillo Elementary** · 5309 W 135th St
- **CBC Christian School** · 4475 W 137th St
- **Environmental Charter** · 4234 W 147th St
- **Eucalyptus Elementary** · 12044 Eucalyptus Ave
- **Fun Ship Childrens Center** · 4141 W El Segundo Blvd
- **Hawthorne Academy** · 12500 Ramona Ave
- **Hawthorne High School** · 4859 W El Segundo Blvd
- **Hawthorne Middle School** · 4366 W 129th St
- **Jefferson Elementary** · 4091 W 139th St
- **Jefferson Elementary** · 4091 W 139th St
- **Kornblum Elementary** · 3620 El Segundo Blvd
- **Lawndale High School** · 14901 Inglewood Ave
- **Leuzinger High School** · 4118 W Rosecrans Ave
- **Light and Life Christian School** · 14204 Prairie Av
- **Lloyde High School** · 14901 Inglewood Ave
- **Mitchell Elementary** · 14429 Condon Ave
- **Mt Cavalry Christian Academy** · 13253 S Hawthorne Blvd
- **Nellieo Wonderland Preschool** · 4720 W Imperial Hwy
- **Prairie Vista Middle School** · 13600 Prairie Ave
- **Ramona Elementary** · 4617 W 136th St
- **Rogers Middle School** · 4110 W 154th St
- **South Bay Lutheran High School** · 3600 W Imperial Hwy
- **St Joseph's Elementary** · 11886 Acacia Ave
- **Trinity Lutheran** · 4783 W 130th St
- **Twain Elementary** · 3728 W 154th St
- **Vine Christian Academy** · 3210 W 155th St
- **Washington Elementary** · 4339 W 129th St
- **Will Rogers Intermediate School** · 4110 W 154th St
- **Williams Elementary** · 13434 Yukon Ave
- **York Elementary** · 11838 York Ave
- **Yukon Middle School** · 13838 Yukon Ave
- **Zela Davis Elementary** · 13435 S Yukon Ave

Supermarkets

- **Albertson's** · 12630 Hawthorne Blvd
- **Food 4 Less** · 14500 Ocean Gate Ave
- **Ralph's** · 11202 Crenshaw Blvd
- **Ralph's** · 11873 Hawthorne Blvd
- **Ralph's** · 14310 Hawthorne Blvd
- **Von's** · 4001 Inglewood Ave

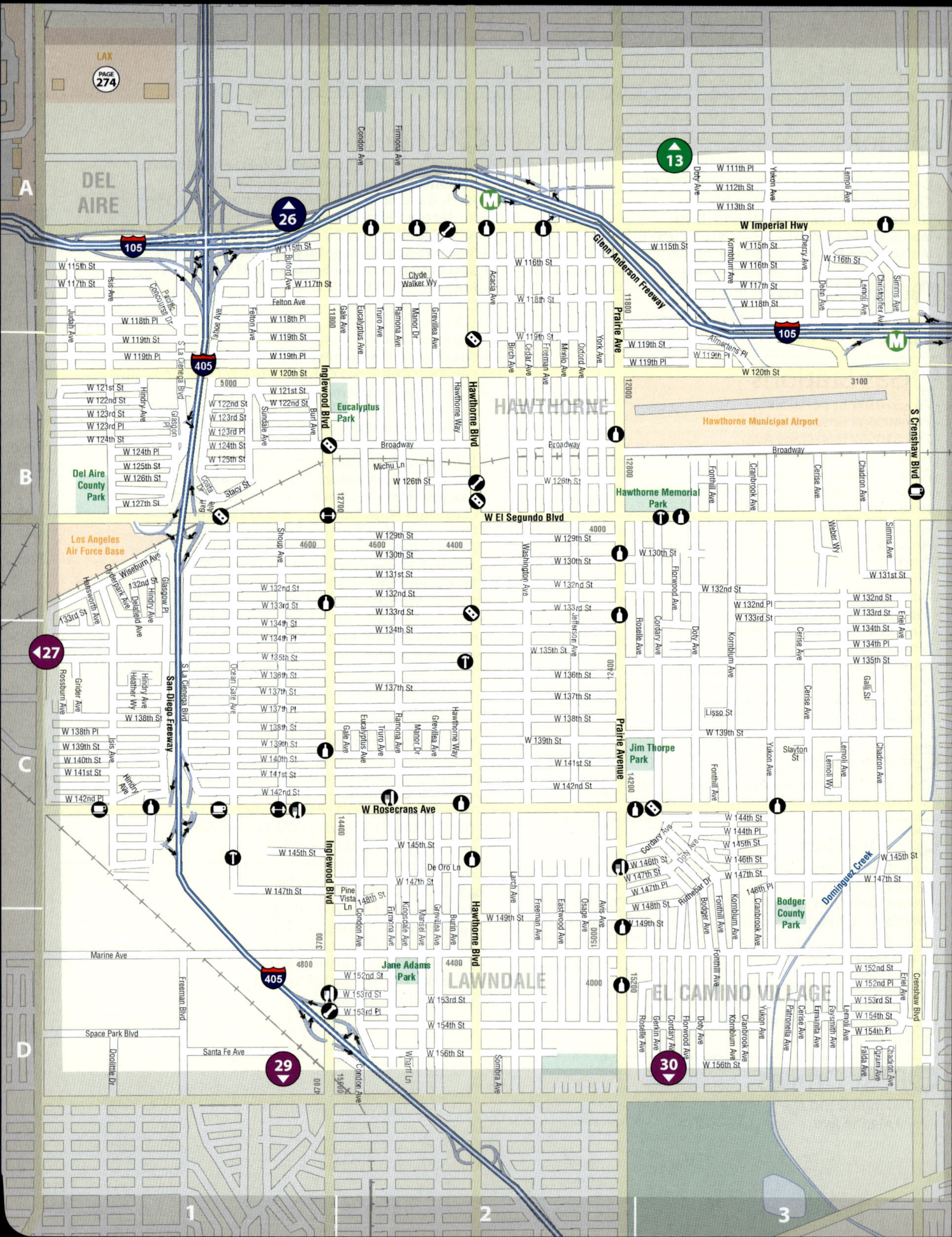

LAX
PAGE
274

DEL AIRE

HAWTHORNE

LAWNDALE

EL CAMINO VILLAGE

Del Aire
County
Park

Los Angeles
Air Force Base

Eucalyptus
Park

Hawthorne Municipal Airport

Hawthorne Memorial
Park

Jim Thorpe
Park

Bodger
County
Park

Jane Adams
Park

Glenn Anderson Freeway

San Diego Freeway

Dominguez Creek

Streets and avenues:

Condon Ave, Firmona Ave, W 111th Pl, W 112th St, W 113th St, Doty Ave, Yukon Ave, Lemoli Ave

W Imperial Hwy

W 115th St, W 116th St, W 117th St, W 118th St, W 119th St, W 120th St

Kornblum Ave, Cherry Ave, Dahn Ave, Lemoli Ave, Christopher Av, Simms Ave

Almertens Pl

Prairie Ave

Acacia Ave, Birch Ave, Cedar Ave, York Ave, Oxford Ave, Menlo Ave, Freeman Ave

Buford Ave, Felton Ave, Gale Ave, Eucalyptus Ave, Truro Ave, Ramona Ave, Manor Dr, Grevillea Ave

W 115th St, W 117th St, W 118th Pl, W 119th St, W 119th Pl, W 120th St

Clyde Walker Wy

Hawthorne Way, Hawthorne Blvd

Tahoe Ave, S La Cienega Blvd, Pacific Concourse Dr

Judah Ave, Isis Ave

W 115th St, W 117th St, W 118th Pl, W 119th St, W 119th Pl

W 121st St, W 122nd St, W 123rd St, W 123rd Pl, W 124th St

Hindry Ave, Glasgow Pl

W 121st St, W 122nd St, W 123rd St, W 123rd Pl, W 124th Pl, W 125th St, W 126th St, W 127th St

Sundale Ave, Burl Ave

Inglewood Blvd

Broadway, Michu Ln, W 126th St

W El Segundo Blvd

Stacy St, Burr Ave, Cota Ave

Shoup Ave, Ocean Gate Ave

W 129th St, W 130th St, W 131st St, W 132nd St, W 133rd St, W 134th St, W 134th Pl, W 135th St, W 136th St, W 137th St, W 137th Pl, W 138th St, W 139th St, W 140th St, W 141st St, W 142nd St

Washington Ave, Jefferson Ave

W 129th St, W 130th St, W 132nd St, W 133rd St, W 135th St, W 136th St, W 137th St, W 138th St, W 139th St, W 141st St, W 142nd St

Flotwood Ave, Roselle Ave, Cordary Ave, Doty Ave, Kornblum Ave, Cerise Ave, Simms Ave

Webel Wy

W 131st St, W 132nd St, W 133rd St, W 134th St, W 134th Pl, W 135th St

Galli St, Lisso St, Slayton St

Yukon Ave, Fonthill Ave, Lemoli Ave, Lemoli Wy, Cerise Ave, Chadron Ave, Eriel Ave

Hindry Ave, Heather Wy, Grider Ave, Rossburn Ave, Isis Ave

W 138th Pl, W 139th St, W 140th St, W 141st St, W 142nd Pl

Gale Ave, Eucalyptus Ave, Truro Ave, Ramona Ave, Manor Dr, Grevillea Ave, Hawthorne Way

W Rosecrans Ave

Larch Ave, Freeman Ave, Eastwood Ave, Osage Ave, Avis Ave

Cordary Ave, Ruthebar Dr, Fonthill Ave, Kornblum Ave, Cranbrook Ave

W 144th St, W 144th Pl, W 145th St, W 146th St, W 147th St, W 147th Pl, W 148th St, W 149th St

De Oro Ln, W 145th St, W 147th St, W 147th St

Pine Vista Ln, Condon Ave, Firmona Ave, Kingscale Ave, Mansel Ave, Grevillea Ave, Burn Ave

W 146th St, W 147th Pl, W 148th St, W 149th St

Prairie Avenue

Marine Ave, Space Park Blvd, Santa Fe Ave

Freeman Blvd, Doolittle Dr

W 152nd St, W 153rd St, W 153rd Pl, W 154th St, W 156th St

Wharff Ln, Sombra Ave

W 152nd St, W 152nd Pl, W 153rd St, W 154th St, W 154th Pl, W 156th St

Roselle Ave, Gerkin Ave, Cordary Ave, Flotwood Ave, Doty Ave, Kornblum Ave, Cranbrook Ave, Yukon Ave, Cerise Ave, Ermanita Ave, Gerysmith Ave, Patronella Ave, Falda Ave, Ogram Ave, Chadron Ave, Eriel Ave, Crenshaw Blvd

S Crenshaw Blvd

Broadway

Wiseburn Ave, Clyterpark Ave, Delafield Ave, 132nd St, Hansworth Ave, 133rd Ave

Interstate/Route markers: 105, 405, 26, 13, 27, 29, 30

11800, 11900, 12000, 12800, 14400, 13700, 4800, 4400, 4000, 5000, 5200, 4600, 12700, 12200, 14200, 2400, 5500, 3100, 3700, 15200, 4000

A B C D

1 2 3

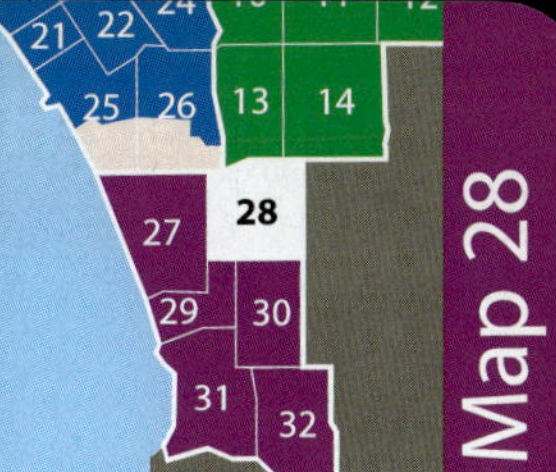

Thanks in part to rising South Bay real estate prices and an active city council, this older, blue collar-flavored "City of Good Neighbors" is on the rise. Hawthorne is home to the Blue Bird Liquor Store, the luckiest place in L.A. to buy a lottery ticket. There's a line around the block when the jackpot gets big!

Coffee

- **South Coast Refreshments** · 12597 Crenshaw Blvd
- **Starbucks** · 5030 W Rosecrans Ave
- **Starbucks** · 5378 W Rosecrans Ave

Gyms

- **Bally Total Fitness** · 5001 El Segundo Blvd · 310-263-7520
- **Los Angeles Rock Gym** · 4926 W Rosecrans Ave · 310-973-3388

Hardware Stores

- **Hawthorne Hardware** · 13532 Hawthorne Blvd · 310-676-2253
- **Home Depot** · 14603 Ocean Gate Ave · 310-644-9600
- **Seers Lumber** · 3856 W El Segundo Blvd · 310-676-5497

Liquor Stores

- **Art's Rite Liquor** · 14000 Inglewood Ave
- **Avenue Liquor** · 13305 Inglewood Ave
- **Blue Bird Liquor** · 13746 Hawthorne Blvd
- **BMW Liquor Mart** · 4533 W Imperial Hwy
- **Bob's Liquor & Delicatessen** · 3127 W Imperial Hwy
- **Frank's Liquor** · 12329 Prairie Ave
- **Mel & Leo's Liquor Store** · 14245 Hawthorne Blvd
- **Mr B's Mini Mart** · 3500 W Rosecrans Ave
- **Pound Penny Liquor & Market** · 13353 Prairie Ave
- **Ramp West Market & Liquor** · 5221 W Rosecrans Ave
- **S & D Liquor** · 3910 W Rosecrans Ave
- **SK Liquor Mart** · 15202 Prairie Ave
- **S & P Liquor Store** · 13007 Prairie Ave
- **Snappy Food Mart** · 4172 W Imperial Hwy
- **Variety Liquor** · 4669 W Imperial Hwy
- **Young's Liquor Mart** · 3800 W El Segundo Blvd

Pet Stores

- **Petco** · 3901 Inglewood Ave · 310-355-1370
- **Su Aquarium** · 12625 Hawthorne Blvd · 310-675-8652

Restaurants

- **Café Cabana** · 14605 S Prairie Ave · 310-675-7323
- **Chicken Madras** · 4850 W Rosecrans Ave · 310-675-5533
- **Daphne's** · 3901 Inglewood Ave · 310-676-9165
- **Piggies** · 4601 W Rosecrans Ave · 310-679-6326

Video Rental

- **Alex Video** · 13339 Hawthorne Blvd · 310-675-6536
- **Blockbuster** · 3909 W Rosecrans Ave · 310-644-1970
- **Hollywood Video** · 12750 Hawthorne Blvd · 310-679-5797
- **Video Town** · 12404 Inglewood Ave · 310-675-5747
- **Video Vision** · 5051 W El Segundo Blvd · 310-679-5976
- **Videomax** · 11911 Hawthorne Blvd · 310-644-7345

405

A

$

28

Manhattan Beach Blvd

Doolittle Dr

Warfield Ave
Dufour Ave
Bataan Rd
Farrell Ave

Sebald Ave
Burritt Ave
Spurgeon Ave
Thomas Ave
Hawkins Ave
Johnston Ave

Dow Ave
159th St
160th St

McBain Ave
Vargas Wy
Phelan Blvd
Faber St

W 159
W 160
W 161
W 162

Ernest Ave
Perry Ave
Plant Ave

Glenn
Anderson
Park

White Clr
Pinckard Ave
Mary Ave
Timothy

Carlsbad St
Blaisdell Ave
Gibson Pl

W 163
W 164
W 165

Rindge Ln
Vail Ave

Robinson St
Graham Ave
Gates Ave
Curtis Ave
Voorhees Ave
Ruhland Ave
Nelson Ave
Mathews Ave

Barkley Ln
Perkins Ln
Felton Ln
Phelan Ln
Mackay Ln

Perkins Ln

W 166
W 167
W 168
W 169
W 170

Inglewood Ave

REDONDO BEACH

W 173

1. Circle Dr
2. Circle Ct
3. Oak St
4. Mira St
5. Campana St
6. Joy St
7. 15th Pl
8. Aubrey Park Ct
9. Montgomery Dr
10. Massey Ave
11. Hall Ct
12. Margaret Ct

1

B

30

27

91

Artesia Blvd   91

Gould Ave
28th Ct
27th Ave
Gould Ter
Gould Ave
Valley
Park
Porter Ln

El Oeste
Vanderbilt Ln
Carnegie Ln
Rockefeller Ln

26th St
25th St
24th Pl
24th St

Silverstone
Morningside
Dl
Park Ave

25th St
24th Pl
24th St

Wylie
Goodman Ave
Steinhart Ave
Reed St
Herrin St
Carver St
Dixon St
Wollacott St
Axenty Way

Aviation Way

Slauson Ln

Carnegie Ln

24th St
23rd St
22nd

Manhattan Ave
Loma Dr
Power St

21st St
20th St
Valley
Park Ave
19th St

20th Pl
20th St
19th St

Carnegie Ave
Harper Ave
Stanford Ave
Silver St
Ormond St
Ford Ave
Carnegie Ln

Ormond St

Grant Ave
Huntington Ln
Harriman Ln
Clark Ln
Marshallfield Ln
Pullman Ln

Blossom Ln
Rindge Ln
Green Ln

Mackay Ln
Phelan Ln
Felton Ln

Perkins Ln

Springfield Ave
Rhodes St
Hillcrest St
18th St
17th St
16th St

Golden Ave
Pacific Coast Hwy

21st St
20th St
19th St
18th St

Palm St

Aviation Blvd

Prospect Ave

182nd St
182nd Pl

Ava Ave
Ardmore Ave

Raymond
16th St
15th St

Corona St

Hadley Ln
Ives Ln
Hill Ln

183rd St
184th St
185th St

Felton Ave

**HERMOSA
BEACH**

18th St
17th St
16th St
15th St
14th St
13th St

Palm Dr
Loma Dr

Bonnie Brae St
Owosso Ave

Clark Ln
Goodman Ave

Belmont Ln
Speyer Ln
Speyer Ln
Morgan Ln

Carmalita Ave

Fisher Ct
Naramore
Wy

Alvord Ln
Fisk Ln

Ripley Ave
Earle Ln
11.
12.
Amy Ln

Prult Dr
Lilienthal Ln
High Ln

Ralston Ln
Alvord Ln
Fisk Ln
Spreckels Ln
Armour Ln

*Hermosa
Beach*

Hermosa Beach
Fishing Pier

Pier Ave
Cypress Ave
11th St

Valley Dr
11th Pl
10th St
9th St

8th St

Haynes Ln
Morgan Ln
Havemeyer Ave
Carlson Ln
Spreckels Ln
Armour Ln
Van Horne Ln
Lomax Ln

Havemeyer Ln

Rindge Ln
Earle Ln
Glick Ct
Earle Ct

Meyer Ln

$ $

PAGE
245

11th St
10th St
9th St
8th St
7th St
6th St
5th St
4th St

Hermosa Ave
Monterey Blvd
Sunset Dr
Loma Dr

Clark
Park
Bard St
Gravley

8th St
7th St
6th St
5th St
4th St
3rd St

7th Pl
6th Pl
Genty

10.

Reynolds Ln

Blossom
Ct
Cluster Ln

$

190th St

R $

South
Park

Greenbelt
Park

Bayview Dr
Manhattan Ave
Culpepper Ct
Hill St

Ocean
View Ln
Pine St
Hopkins St

2nd St
1st Pl
Barney Ct
Meyer Ct
1st St
3rd St

Anita St

Agate St

31

Dominguez
Park

Anza Ave

C

*Pacific
Ocean*

1

Herondo St
Lyndon St
1st St
1st Ct

N Maria Ave

Prospect Ave

TORRANCE

D

*King
Harbor*

1   2   3

You'll know you've reached Hermosa Beach when you begin to notice its distinctive street signs, which are brown with an almost antique typeface. This community has a small town feel, making it no surprise that at one point, Ozzie and Harriet called Hermosa their home.

 Banks

- **Bank of America** • 90 Pier Ave
- **Citibank** • 81 Pier Ave
- **Comerica Bank** • 2015 Manhattan Beach Blvd
- **Washington Mutual** • 4840 190th St

Car Washes

- **Aviation Auto Spa** • 1616 Aviation Blvd
- **Hermosa Beach Car Wash** • 1000 Pacific Coast Hwy
- **Pacific Auto Cleaning** • 1421 Aviation Blvd

 Gas Stations

- **76** • 5404 W 190th St
- **Arco** • 1131 Pacific Coast Hwy
- **Arco** • 15922 Inglewood Ave
- **Arco** • 1800 W Artesia Blvd
- **Arco** • 1890 Pacific Coast Hwy
- **Mobil** • 2714 Artesia Blvd
- **Shell** • 1700 Artesia Blvd

Landmarks

- **Hermosa Beach Fishing Pier** • End of Pier Ave

Libraries

- **Hermosa Beach Public Library** • 550 Pier Ave • 310-379-8475
- **Redondo Beach North Library** • 2000 Artesia Blvd • 310-318-0677

24-Hour Pharmacies

- **Sav-On** • 5020 W 190th St • 310-370-5607

Police

- **Hermosa Beach Police Dept** • 540 Pier Ave • 310-318-0360

Post Offices

- 2215 Artesia Blvd
- 565 Pier Ave

Schools

- **Adams Middle School** • 2600 Ripley Ave
- **Birney Elementary** • 1600 Green Ln
- **Coast Christian School** • 525 Earle Ln
- **Coast Christian School** • 850 Inglewood Ave
- **Hermosa Valley Elementary** • 1645 Valley Dr
- **Jefferson Elementary** • 600 Harkness Ln
- **Lincoln Elementary** • 2223 Plant Ave
- **Madison Elementary** • 2200 Mackay Ln
- **Our Lady of Guadalupe** • 340 Massey St
- **St Lawerence Martyr Elementary** • 1950 S Prospect Ave
- **Washington** • 1150 Lilienthal Ln
- **Washington Elementary** • 1100 Lilienthal Ln

Supermarkets

- **Albertson's** • 2115 Artesia Blvd
- **Albertson's** • 2510 Pacific Coast Hwy
- **Ralph's** • 1100 Pacific Coast Hwy
- **Von's** • 715 Pier Ave

1. Circle Dr
2. Circle Ct
3. Oak St
4. Mira St
5. Campana St
6. Joy St
7. 15th Pl
8. Aubrey Park Ct
9. Montgomery Dr
10. Massey Ave
11. Hall Ct
12. Margaret Ct

REDONDO BEACH

HERMOSA BEACH

Hermosa Beach

Pacific Ocean

King Harbor

TORRANCE

Valley Park

Glenn Anderson Park

Clark Park

South Park

Greenbelt Park

Dominguez Park

Manhattan Beach Blvd
Warfield Ave
Dufour Ave
Bataan Rd
Farrell Ave
Ernest Ave
Perry Ave
Plant Ave
Robinson St
Graham Ave
Gates Ave
Curtis Ave
Voorhees Ave
Ruhland Ave
Nelson Ave
Mathews Ave
Artesia Blvd

Sebald Ave
Burritt Ave
Spurgeon Ave
Thomas Ave
Hawkins Ave
159th St
160th St
W 159th
W 160th
W 161st
W 164th
W 165th
W 166th
W 167th
W 168th
W 169th
W 170th
W 173rd

Doolittle Dr
Green Ln
Blossom Ln
Ridge Ln
Vail Ave
Mackay Ln
Phelan Ln
Felton Ln
Perkins Ln
Inglewood Ave

Dow Ave
McBain Ave
Gibson Pl
Vargas Wy
Phelan Blvd
Johnston Ave
White Cir
Pinckard Ave
May Ave
Timothy
Barkley Ln
Carlsbad Dr
Blaisdell
Faber

Vanderbilt Ln
Carnegie Ln
Rockefeller Ln
Grant Ave
Huntington Ln
Harriman Ln
Clark Ln
Marshallfield Ln
Pullman Ln
Hadley Ln
Ives Ln
Hill Ln
High Ln
Fisher Ct
Naramore Wy
Alvord Ln
Fisk Ln
Glick Ct
Earle Ct
190th St

Slauson Ln
Blossom Ln
Rindge Ln
Mackay Ln
Phelan Ln
Felton Ln
Perkins Ln

182nd St
183rd St
184th St
185th St
Ralston Ln
Alvord Ln
Fisk Ln
Spreckels Ln
Armour Ln
Felton Ave
Lilienthal Ln
Pruitt Dr

Aviation Way
Aviation Blvd
Belmont Ln
Speyer Ln
Morgan Ln
Havemeyer Ln
Carson Ln
Spreckels Ln
Armour Ln
Van Horne Ln
Lomax Ln

Carmelita Ave
Speyer Ln
Haynes Ln
Morgan Ln
Havemeyer Ln
Carlson Ln
Spreckels Ln

Blossom Ct
Ripley Ave
Rindge Ln
Earle Ln
Amy Ct
Cluster Ln

Anita St
Agate St
Prospect Ave
N Maria Ave
Anza Ave

28th Ct
27th Ct
26th St
25th St
24th St
23rd St
22nd
21st St
20th St
19th St
18th St
17th St
16th St
15th St
14th St
13th St
11th St
10th St
9th St
8th Pl
7th St
6th St
5th St
4th St
3rd St

Gould Ave
Gould Ter
Gould Ave
Porter Ln
Valley Dr
El Oeste Dr
Ardmore Ave
Borden Ave
Rhodes St
Hillcrest Dr
Springfield Ave

Pacific Coast Hwy
Prospect Ave
Aviation Blvd

Hermosa Ave
Monterey Blvd
Bard St
Valley Dr

Herondo St
Lyndon St

91

Gould Ave
Morningside Dr
Silverstrand Ave
Manhattan Ave
Loma Dr
Power St
Palm Dr
The Strand
Beach Dr
Cypress Ave
Loma Dr
Sunset Dr

Reed St
Dixon St
Herrin St
Carver St
Wollacott St
Axenty Way
Harkness Ln
Flagler Ln
Steinhart Ave
Stanford Ave
Goodman Ave
Carnegie Ln
Harper Ave
Silver Ave
Ford Ave
Ormond Ln
Palm Ln
Golden Ave
Raymond Ave
Ocean Dr
Bonnie Brae St
Gates Ave
Corona St
Gentry St
Pine St
Gravley
Ocean View Ave
Hopkins St
Meyer Ct
Barney St
Culper Ct
Hill St

PAGE 245

Wylie
Reynolds Ln
Goodman Ave
Clark Ln

Belmont Ln
Speyer Ln
Morgan Ln

Reynolds Ln
8th St
7th Pl
6th Pl
Holdwell Ln
Carnelita Ave

Sundries / Entertainment

Pier Avenue is the place to go for a night out. Don't miss Ragin' Cajun, which features great N'awlins style cooking and Dixie Beer.

24-Hour Copy Centers

- **Kinko's** • 1139 Artesia Blvd • 310-379-7433

Clubs

- **The Lighthouse Café** • 30 Pier Ave • 310-372-6911
- **The Pitcherhouse** • 142 Pacific Coast Hwy • 310-374-0626

Coffee

- **Coffee Bean & Tea Leaf** • 1133 Artesia Blvd
- **Coffee Bean & Tea Leaf** • 1227 Hermosa Ave
- **Espresso Wash** • 509 Pier Ave
- **Expresso Coffee** • 1700 Artesia Blvd
- **Java Man** • 157 Pier Ave
- **Starbucks** • 1100 Pacific Coast Hwy
- **Starbucks** • 1303 Hermosa Ave
- **Starbucks** • 1904 Artesia Blvd
- **Starbucks** • 5050 W 190th St

Farmer's Markets

- **Farmers' Market** • Valley Dr between 10th St & 8th St • Fri 2-4

Gyms

- **Bally Total Fitness** • 1133 Artesia Blvd • 310-372-0068

Hardware Stores

- **Anza True Value Hardware** • 2441 190th St • 310-376-0852
- **Kurt True Value Hardware** • 2404 Artesia Blvd • 310-376-3494
- **Triangle Hardware** • 403 Pacific Coast Hwy • 310-372-2414
- **Westwood Building Materials** • 15708 Inglewood Ave • 310-643-9158

Liquor Stores

- **Abe's Liquor** • 240 Pier Ave
- **B & K Liquor** • 16210 Inglewood Ave
- **Manhattan Liquors** • 1157 Artesia Blvd
- **McNamara's Liquor** • 4703 Artesia Blvd
- **Mr B's Liquor Marts** • 2433 190th St
- **No 1 Liquor Mart** • 1520 Aviation Blvd
- **Paul's Liquor** • 2218 Artesia Blvd
- **Robert's Liquor** • 74 Pier Ave

Pet Stores

- **Bow Wow Boutique** • 433 Pier Ave • 310-372-7722

Restaurants

- **El Burrito Jr** • 919 Pacific Coast Hwy • 310-316-5058
- **Havana Mania** • 3615 Inglewood Ave • 310-725-9075
- **Hennessey's Tavern** • 8 Pier Ave • 310-372-5759
- **Il Boccaccio** • 39 Pier Ave • 310-376-0211
- **Le Beaujolais** • 522 Pacific Coast Hwy • 310-543-5100
- **Martha's 22nd Street Grill** • 25 22nd St • 301-376-7786
- **Ragin' Cajun** • 422 Pier Ave • 310-376-7878
- **Reel Inn** • 2533 Pacific Coast Hwy •
- **The Tea House** • 2533 Pacific Coast Hwy • 310-326-5420

Shopping

- **Splash Bath & Body** • 132 Pier Ave • 310-376-7270

Video Rental

- **Blockbuster** • 709 Pier Ave • 310-379-1834
- **Disc Is It** • 2301 Artesia Blvd • 310-921-9993
- **Hollywood Video** • 2101 Artesia Blvd • 310-921-3102
- **Movies N You** • 2123 Artesia Blvd • 310-793-2216

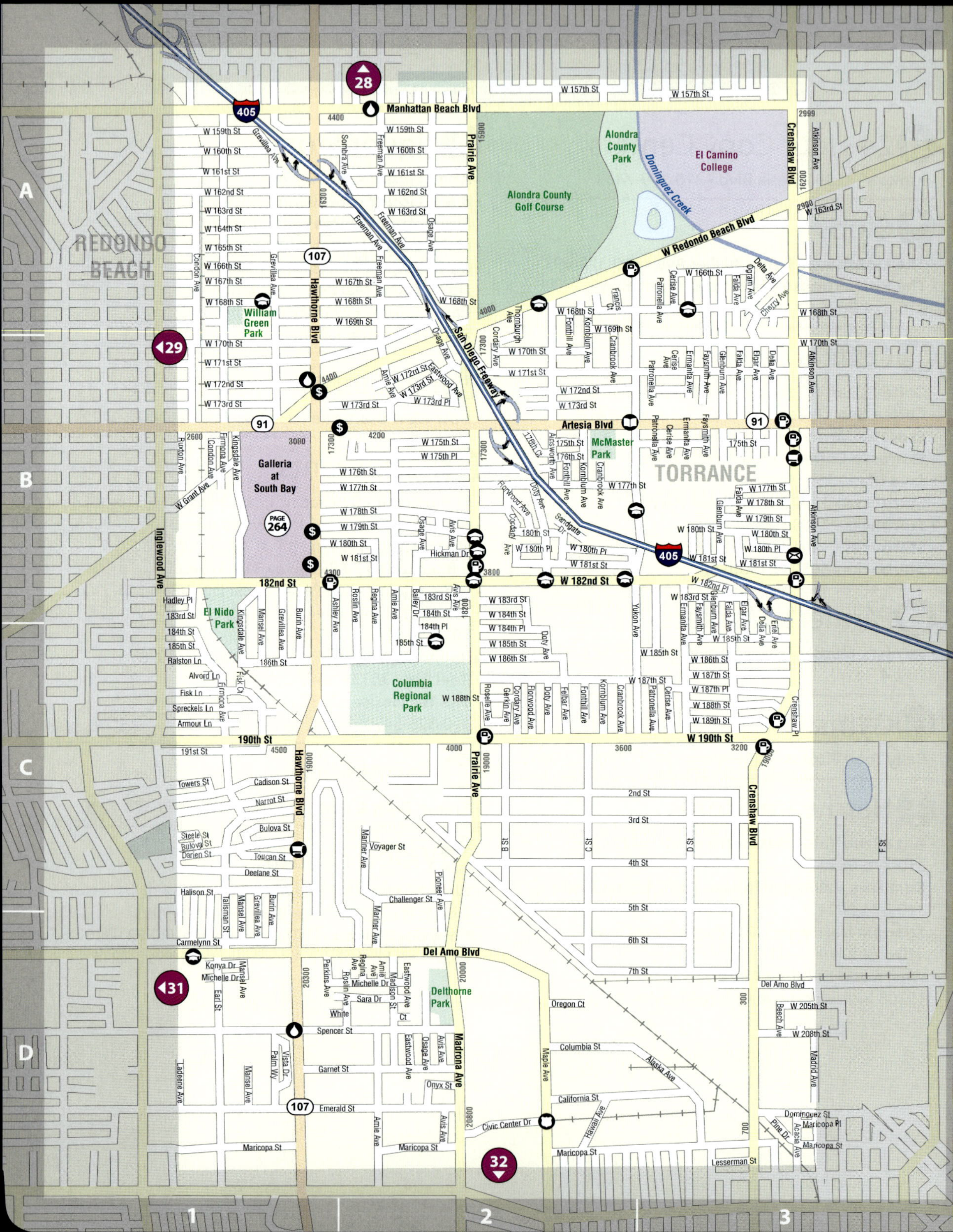

28
Manhattan Beach Blvd
405
W 157th St
W 157th St
2999
W 159th St
W 159th St
4400
Prairie Ave
13900
Alondra County Park
Crenshaw Blvd
Atkinson Ave
W 160th St
W 160th St
Sonbra Ave
Freeman Ave
2991
El Camino College
W 161st St
W 161st St
W 162nd St
W 162nd St
Osage Ave
Alondra County Golf Course
2900
W 163rd St
A
W 163rd St
Freeman Ave
W 163rd St
W 164th St
REDONDO
BEACH
W 165th St
Condon Ave
Grevillea Ave
107
Dominguez Creek
W Redondo Beach Blvd
W 166th St
Delta Ave
W 166th St
Ogram Ave
Cerise Ave
Falda Ave
Cherry Ave
W 167th St
W 167th St
Hawthorne Blvd
Francis Ct
Patronella Ave
W 168th St
William Green Park
W 168th St
Thornburgh Ave
W 168th St
Kornblum Ave
Fonthill Ave
W 168th St
Glenburn Ave
Elgar Ave
Delta Ave
W 169th St
4000
W 169th St
29
W 170th St
W 169th St
Cranbrook Ave
Patronella Ave
Cerise Ave
Ermanita Ave
Faysmith Ave
Falda Ave
Atkinson Ave
W 170th St
W 171st St
San Diego Freeway
W 170th St
W 170th St
W 172nd St
4400
Cordary Ave
W 171st St
Amie Ave
Eastwood Ave
W 172rd St
W 173rd St
W 172nd St
W 173rd St
91
W 173rd St
W 173rd Pl
W 173rd St
Artesia Blvd
91
2600
3000
4200
W 175th St
McMaster Park
175th St
Ruxton Ave
Condon Ave
Kingsdale Ave
Firmona Ave
17300
W 175th Pl
Ainsworth Ave
175th St
Cerise Ave
Ermanita Ave
Faysmith Ave
B
W Grant Ave
Galleria at South Bay
W 176th St
176th St
Fonthill Ave
Kornblum Ave
Cranbrook Ave
TORRANCE
Patronella Ave
Falda Ave
W 177th St
W 177th St
Flaxwood Ave
Doty Ave
W 177th St
Glenburn Ave
W 177th St
W 178th St
W 178th St
W 178th St
PAGE 264
W 179th St
Osage Ave
Avis Ave
Cordary Ave
W 179th St
180th St
Sandgate Dr
W 179th St
405
W 180th St
Hickman Dr
180th St
W 180th Pl
W 180th Pl
W 180th St
W 180th Pl
W 181st St
Atkinson Ave
182nd St
Ashley Ave
4400
3800
W 181st St
W 181st St
W 182nd St
W 182nd Pl
Hadley Pl
El Nido Park
Roslin Ave
Regina Ave
Amie Ave
183rd St
Bailey Dr
Avis Ave
W 183rd St
Yukon Ave
W 183rd St
Ermanita Ave
Faysmith Ave
Glenburn Ave
Elgar Ave
Delta Ave
Entel Ave
183rd St
184th St
184th St
W 184th St
W 185th St
184th St
Mansel Ave
Grevillea Ave
Burin Ave
184th Pl
W 184th Pl
185th St
Ralston Ln
185th St
Doty Ave
W 185th St
Alvord Ln
Fisk Ct
186th St
W 186th St
W 185th St
Fisk Ln
Firmona Ave
Columbia Regional Park
W 188th St
Roselle Ave
Gerkin Ave
Cordary Ave
Flaxwood Ave
Doty Ave
W 186th St
W 187th St
W 187th St
Spreckels Ln
Fonthill Ave
Felbar Ave
Kornblum Ave
Cranbrook Ave
Patronella Ave
Cerise Ave
W 187th Pl
Armour Ln
W 188th St
Crenshaw Pl
W 189th St
190th St
W 190th St
191st St
4500
Hawthorne Blvd
19000
4000
Prairie Ave
19000
3600
3200
19000
Crenshaw Blvd
Towers St
Cadison St
2nd St
C
Narrot St
3rd St
F St
Steele St
Bulova St
Mariner Ave
Voyager St
IS B
IS C
IS D
Bulova St
Darien St
Toucan St
4th St
Deelane St
Halison St
Pioneer Ave
Challenger St
5th St
Mansel Ave
Grevillea Ave
Burin Ave
Talisman St
Mariner Ave
6th St
Carmelynn St
Del Amo Blvd
7th St
31
Konya Dr
Mansel Ave
Earl St
Michelle Dr
Perkins Ave
Regina Ave
Amie Ave
Madison Ave
Michelle Dr
Eastwood Ave
20800
Del Amo Blvd
Roslin Ave
Sara Dr
Madison Ct
Delthorne Park
Oregon Ct
W 205th St
300
Beech Ave
White
Spencer St
Columbia St
W 208th St
Madrid Ave
Vista Dr
Palm Wy
Maple Ave
Alaska Ave
D
Ladeene Ave
Garnet St
Avis Ave
Eastwood Ave
Osage Ave
Madrona Ave
California St
Dominguez St
Maricopa Pl
Acacia Ave
107
Emerald St
Onyx St
20800
Civic Center Dr
Pine Dr
202
Maricopa St
Amie Ave
Maricopa St
Avis Ave
Maricopa St
32
Lesserman St
Maricopa St

This is primarily a suburban area characterized by tract homes and large chain stores. The main social hub of this area is the South Bay Galleria, which although not as large as its rival down the road, Del Amo Mall, is decidedly more upscale, boasting the only Nordstrom in the entire South Bay.

$ Banks

- **Bank of America** · 1603 Hawthorne Blvd
- **Union Bank** · 1413 Hawthorne Blvd
- **Washington Mutual** · 17200 Hawthorne Blvd
- **Wells Fargo Bank** · 4340 Artesia Blvd

Car Washes

- **Bay Cities Carwash** · 4457 Manhattan Beach Blvd
- **Del Amo Car Wash** · 20505 Hawthorne Blvd
- **Lawndale Car Wash** · 17111 Hawthorne Blvd

Gas Stations

- **76** · 3975 W 190th St
- **76** · 4373 W 182nd St
- **Arco** · 18180 Prairie Ave
- **Chevron** · 17405 Crenshaw Blvd
- **Mobil** · 18200 Crenshaw Blvd
- **Mobil** · 19009 Crenshaw Blvd
- **Shell** · 18910 Crenshaw Blvd
- **Shell** · 3101 Artesia Blvd

Libraries

- **North Torrance Library** · 3604 Artesia Blvd · 310-323-7200

Police

- **Torrance Police Dept** · 3300 Civic Center Dr N · 310-328-3456

Post Offices

- 18080 Crenshaw Blvd

Schools

- **ABC Playhouse** · 18213 Prairie St
- **Ascension Luthern Elementary** · 17910 S Prairie Ave
- **Carr Elementary** · 3404 W 168th St
- **Edison Elementary** · 3800 W 182nd St
- **El Camino College** · 16007 Crenshaw Blvd
- **Green Elementary** · 4520 W 168th St
- **Magruder Middle School** · 4100 W 185th St
- **North High School** · 3620 W 182nd St
- **School of Life** · 18090 Prairie Ave
- **South Bay Junior Academy** · 4400 Del Amo Blvd
- **St Catherine's Laboure** · 3846 Redondo Beach Blvd
- **Yukon Elementary** · 17815 Yukon Ave

Supermarkets

- **Ralph's** · 1413 Hawthorne Blvd
- **Ralph's** · 17500 Crenshaw Blvd
- **Trader Joe's** · 19720 Hawthorne Blvd

Map 30 · Torrance North

The Galleria at South Bay couldn't be more opposite from its neighbor down the road, Del Amo. While Del Amo is the larger mall, it's big and gloomy and devoid of personality. The Galleria, largely because of its glass roof, feels airier and brighter, making for an infinitely more pleasurable shopping experience.

Coffee

- **Starbucks** · 17400 Hawthorne Blvd
- **Starbucks** · 1815 Hawthorne Blvd
- **Starbucks** · 3931 W Artesia Blvd

Gyms

- **Bally Total Fitness** · 20040 Hawthorne Blvd · 310-542-3511
- **West End Racquet & Health Club** · 4343 Spencer St · 310-542-7373

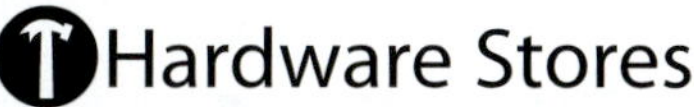Hardware Stores

- **Ace Hardware** · 4868 W 190th St · 310-542-3526

Liquor Stores

- **ABC Liquors** · 3709 W 190th St
- **Lawndale Liquors** · 16201 Hawthorne Blvd
- **M & M Liquor** · 4015 W 182nd St
- **Mr J's Liquor Marts** · 15734 Hawthorne Blvd
- **Yukon Liquor** · 3615 Artesia Blvd

Movie Theaters

- **AMC Galleria-South Bay Cinema 16** · 1815 Hawthorne Blvd
- **Redondo Beach Cinema 3** · 1509 Hawthorne Blvd

Pet Stores

- **Pet City** · 18305 Hawthorne Blvd · 310-542-6442
- **Pets Plus** · 17440 Crenshaw Blvd · 310-719-7088

Restaurants

- **Flossie's Restaurant** · 3566 W Redondo Beach Blvd · 310-352-4037
- **Pizza Show** · 4567 Artesia Blvd · 310-542-6966

Video Rental

- **Blockbuster** · 17124 Hawthorne Blvd · 310-371-5498
- **Video Entertainment Center** · 16216 Hawthorne Blvd · 310-371-6306
- **Video For You** · 3594 Redondo Beach Blvd · 310-217-0258

A map of Redondo Beach. Major labeled features and streets include:

Parks and landmarks: Dominguez Park, Entradero Park, La Romeria Park, Paradise Park, Alta Vista Park, El Retiro Park, Walteria Park, Palos Verdes Golf Club, Portofino Marina, King Harbor, Redondo Beach Marina, Redondo Beach Pier, Redondo County Beach, Del Amo Fashion Center.

Water/regions: Pacific Ocean, Malaga Cove, REDONDO BEACH, TORRANCE, HOLLYWOOD RIVIERA.

Major streets: Beryl St, Del Amo Blvd, Torrance Blvd, Sepulveda Blvd, Palos Verdes Blvd, Pacific Coast Hwy, Anza Ave, Lomita Blvd, Hawthorne Blvd, N Pacific Coast Hwy, S Pacific Coast Hwy, Camino Real, N Prospect Ave, S Prospect Ave, N Catalina Ave, S Catalina Ave, Palos Verdes Dr N, Palos Verdes Dr W.

Adjacent map references: 29, 30, 32, 9, PAGE 247, PAGE 249, PAGE 263.

Street index (numbered list):

1. Francisca Ave
2. Helberta Ave
3. Harkness Ln
4. Deelane St
5. Cadison St
6. Flavian Ave
7. Bartlett Dr
8. Halison Pl
9. Jeffrey Dr
10. Felker Dr
11. Maricopa St
12. Colony Ct
13. Talisman St
14. Evalyn Ave
15. Cathann Pl
16. Elmo Ave
17. Tiffany Ct
18. Audrey Ave
19. 228th Pl
20. 229th St
21. 230th St
22. Moresby Dr
23. Biak Ct
24. Paul Ave
25. Bernice Ave
26. Dewey Ave
27. Charlotte Dr
28. Lupine Dr
29. Rockview Dr
30. Crosshill Ave
31. Massena Ave
32. Albert Ave
33. Glenn Pl
34. Barbara St
35. Scannel Ave
36. Sierra Vista Dr
37. Vista Del Mar
38. Via El Prado
39. S Camino De La Costa
40. S Elena Ave
41. Via Estrelita
42. Via Bonita
43. Via Del Puente
44. Paseo De Los Reyes
45. Avd De Jose
46. Calle De Castellana
47. Via Los Miradores
48. Paseo De Las Estrellas
49. Calle cabrillo
50. El Chico
51. Via Los Miradores
52. Greenmeadows St
53. Highgrove St
54. Via Las Vegas
55. Via Ardilla
56. Via Adarme
57. Vista Del Vegas
58. Harrlee Ln
59. Nancylee Ln
60. Theo Ave
61. Mayor Dr
62. Meadow Park Ln
63. Los Codona Ave
64. Walnut St
65. Cl De Primera

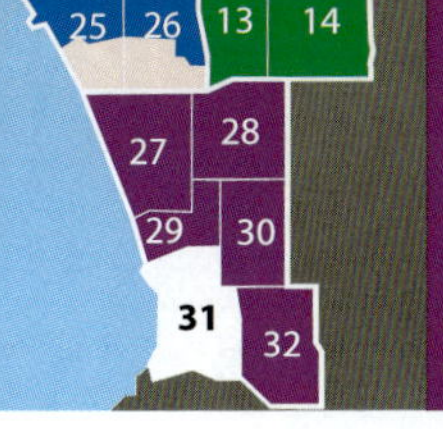

Redondo has evolved from a sleepy little bedroom/beach community into a very diverse area. It's hard to beat living, working, or playing by the beach. Areas like King Harbor Pier (a typical beach boardwalk experience) and Riviera Village, with its cool boutiques and hip restaurants, ensure that there is something for everyone.

$ Banks

- **Bank of America** • 1601 S Pacific Coast Hwy
- **Bank of America** • 21700 Hawthorne Blvd
- **Bank of America** • 22 Malaga Cove Plz
- **Bank of America** • 222 S Catalina Ave
- **Bank of America** • 4206 Pacific Coast Hwy
- **Bank of the West** • 23865 Hawthorne Blvd
- **Bank of the West** • 23865 Hawthorne Blvd
- **Bay Cities National Bank** • 1333 S Pacific Coast Hwy
- **Bay Cities National Bank** • 23550 Hawthorne Blvd
- **Bay Cities National Bank** • 811 N Catalina Ave
- **California Bank & Trust** • 21515 Hawthorne Blvd
- **California National Bank** • 24020 Hawthorne Blvd
- **Cathay Bank** • 23228 Hawthorne Blvd
- **Comerica Bank** • 21535 Hawthorne Blvd
- **East West Bank** • 23670 Hawthorne Blvd
- **Fidelity Federal Bank** • 24020 Hawthorne Blvd
- **First Bank & Trust** • 23133 Hawthorne Blvd
- **First Bank & Trust** • 650 Palos Verdes Blvd
- **Fremont Investment & Loan** • 21842 Hawthorne Blvd
- **Malaga Bank** • 2514 Via Tejon
- **Pacific Union Bank** • 21838 Hawthorne Blvd
- **Union Bank** • 1401 Pacific Coast Hwy
- **Union Bank** • 21201 Hawthorne Blvd
- **Union Bank** • 24030 Hawthorne Blvd
- **US Bank** • 1217 N Catalina Ave
- **Washington Mutual** • 1600 S Pacific Coast Hwy
- **Washington Mutual** • 21660 Hawthorne Blvd
- **Wells Fargo Bank** • 301 S Pacific Coast Hwy
- **Wells Fargo Bank** • 1212 Beryl St
- **Wells Fargo Bank** • 1701 S Elena Ave
- **Wells Fargo Bank** • 21323 Hawthorne Blvd
- **Western Financial Bank** • 21705 Hawthorne Blvd

Car Washes

- **Hollywood Riviera Car Wash** • 1500 S Pacific Coast Hwy

Gas Stations

- **76** • 1870 S Elena Ave
- **Arco** • 300 S Pacific Coast Hwy
- **Arco** • 4205 Pacific Coast Hwy
- **Chevron** • 1500 S Pacific Coast Hwy
- **Chevron** • 1630 S Elena Ave
- **Chevron** • 21130 Anza Ave
- **Chevron** • 4135 Pacific Coast Hwy
- **Mobil** • 20306 Anza Ave
- **Mobil** • 246 Pacific Coast Hwy
- **Mobil** • 4202 Pacific Coast Hwy
- **Shell** • 20305 Anza Ave
- **Shell** • 23140 Hawthorne Blvd
- **Shell** • 4530 Torrance Blvd

Hospitals

- **Little Co of Mary Hospital** • 4101 Torrance Blvd • 310-540-7676

Libraries

- **El Retiro Library** • 126 Vista Del Parque • 310-375-0922
- **Isabel Henderson Library** • 4805 Emerald St • 310-371-2075
- **Malaga Cove Library** • 2400 Via Campesina • 310-377-9584
- **Redondo Beach Public Library** • 303 N Pacific Coast Hwy • 310-318-0675
- **Walteria Library** • 3815 W 242nd St • 310-375-8418

Police

- **Redondo Beach Police Dept** • 401 Diamond St • 310-379-2477

Post Offices

- 1201 N Catalina Ave
- 2516 Via Tejon
- 3856 Sepulveda Blvd
- 4216 Pacific Coast Hwy

Schools

- **Alta Vista Elementary** • 815 Knob Hill Ave
- **Anza Elementary** • 21400 Ellenwood Dr
- **Arnold Elementary** • 4100 W 227th St
- **Beryl Heights** • 920 Beryl St
- **Bishop Montgomery High School** • 5430 Torrance Blvd
- **Bishop Mora Salesian High School** • 960 S Soto St
- **Calle Mayor Middle School** • 4800 Calle Mayor
- **Carden Dominion School** • 320 Knob Hill
- **Day Treatment Center** • 410 Camino Real
- **Jefferson Middle School** • 21717 Talisman St
- **Menorah Community Day School** • 1101 Camino Real
- **Parras Middle School** • 200 N Lucia
- **Redondo High School** • 631 Vincent Park
- **Redondo Shores High School** • 1000 Del Amo St
- **Richardson Middle School** • 23751 Nancylee Ln
- **Riveria Hall Lutheran** • 330 Palos Verdes Blvd
- **Riviera Elementary** • 365 Paseo De Arena
- **Seaside Elementary** • 4651 Sharynne Ln
- **Sigma** • 23800 Hawthorne Blvd
- **South Bay High School** • 4025 W 226th St
- **South High School** • 4801 Pacific Coast Hwy
- **St James Elementary** • 4625 Garnet St
- **Towers Elementary** • 5600 Towers St
- **Tulita Elementary** • 1520 S Prospect Ave
- **Victor Elementary** • 4820 Spencer St
- **West High School** • 20401 Victor St

Supermarkets

- **Albertson's** • 1516 S Pacific Coast Hwy
- **Albertson's** • 21035 Hawthorne Blvd
- **Albertson's** • 615 N Pacific Coast Hwy
- **Bristol Farms** • 1700 Pacific Coast Hwy
- **Pavilions** • 4705 Torrance Blvd
- **Ralph's** • 5035 Pacific Coast Hwy
- **Trader Joe's** • 1761 S Elena Ave
- **Von's** • 1212 Beryl St
- **Von's** • 245 Palos Verdes Blvd
- **Whole Foods Market** • 405 N Pacific Coast Hwy

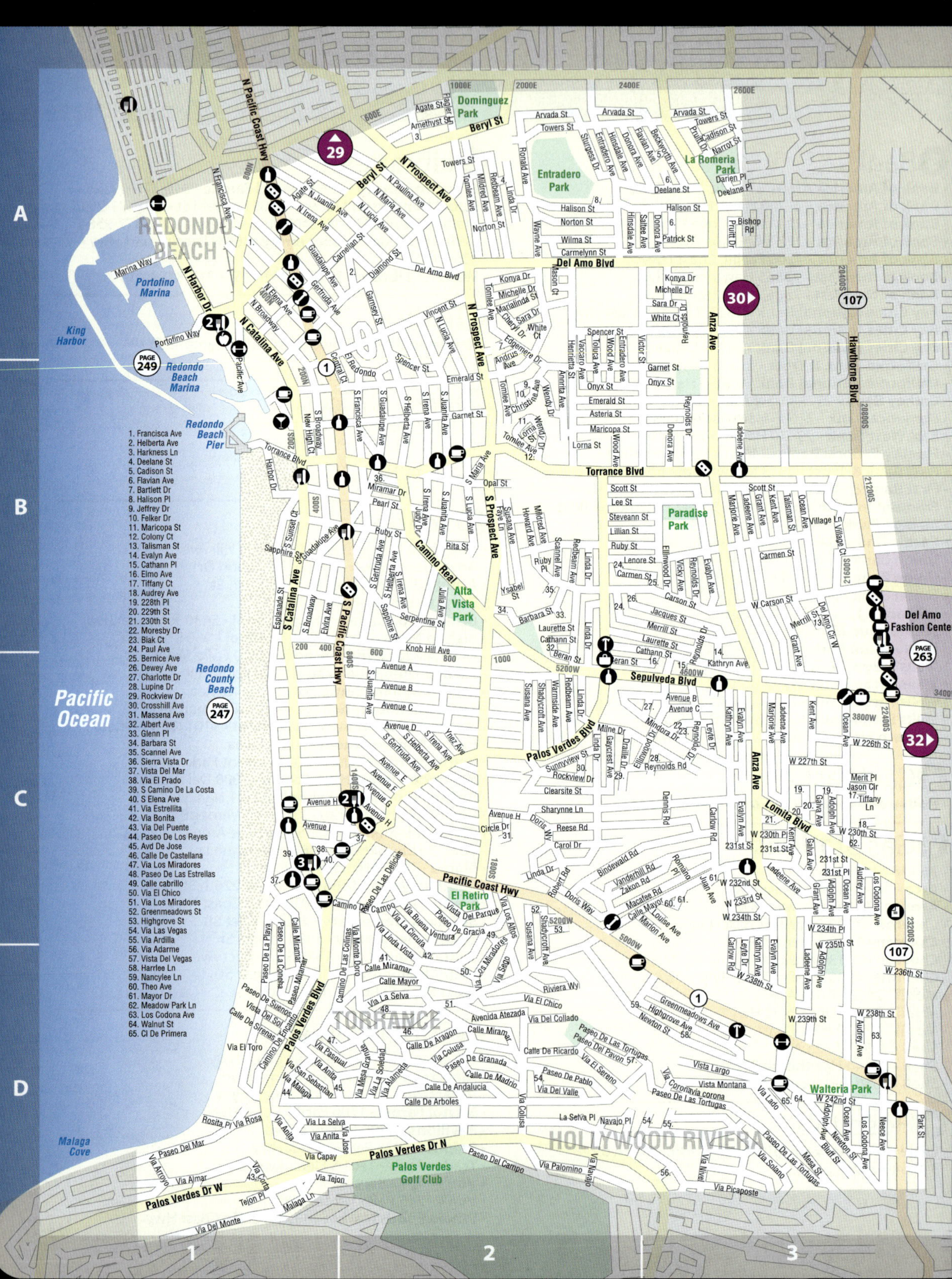

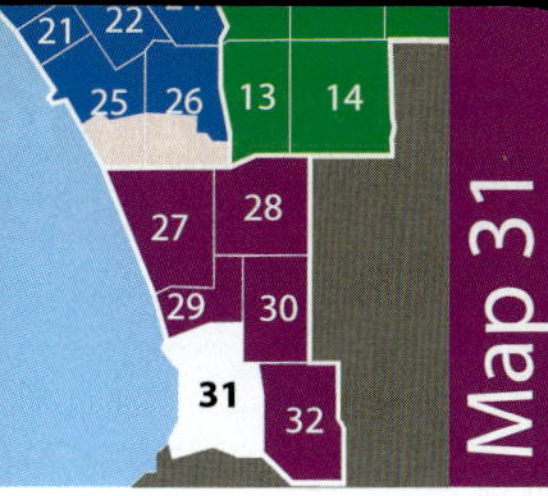

El Retiro Park, just off the PCH at Prospect Ave., is known to the locals as "Rocketship" Park and offers one of the community's loveliest views of the ocean. While their kids climb on the jungle gyms, parents can take a load off and enjoy the sunset just off the coast.

24-Hour Copy Centers
- **Kinko's** • 23325 Hawthorne Blvd • 310-373-2530

Clubs
- **Starboard Attitude** • 202 The Pier • 310-379-5144

Coffee
- **Carissimo Bakery** • 1611 S Catalina Ave
- **Catalina Coffee Company** • 126 N Catalina Ave
- **Coffee Bean & Tea Leaf** • 1617 S Elena Ave
- **Coffee Bean & Tea Leaf** • 21300 Hawthorne Blvd
- **Coffee Beanery** • Del Amo Fashion Square
- **Coffee Cartel** • 1820 S Catalina Ave
- **Coffee Merchant** • 407 N Pacific Coast Hwy
- **Gloria Jean's Gourmet Coffees** • 275 Del Amo Fashion Ctr
- **Lizzie's Cup of Joe** • 800 Torrance Blvd
- **Polonez Kaffee** • 24002 Vista Montana
- **Starbucks** • 1749 S Elena Ave
- **Starbucks** • 21209A Hawthorne Blvd
- **Starbucks** • 300 N Pacific Coast Hwy
- **Starbucks** • 3737 Pacific Coast Hwy
- **Starbucks** • 5005 Pacific Coast Hwy
- **Starbucks** • Del Amo Fashion Square

Farmer's Markets
- **Redondo Beach-Harbor Dr** • South of King Harbor Pier • Thu 7-11
- **Redondo Pier** • Redondo Pier

Gyms
- **Bally Total Fitness** • 4230 Pacific Coast Hwy • 310-375-9612
- **Gold's Gym** • 200 N Harbor Dr • 310-374-5522
- **Sportcenter Fitness** • 819 N Harbor Dr • 310-376-9443

Hardware Stores
- **Orchard Supply Hardware** • 4340 Pacific Coast Hwy • 310-375-3077
- **Woods Hardware** • 22217 Palos Verdes Blvd • 310-540-5355

Liquor Stores
- **Ajaxx Liquor Store** • 715 N Pacific Coast Hwy
- **Chateau Liquor Store** • 4545 Sepulveda Blvd
- **House of Cigars & Liquor** • 400 S Pacific Coast Hwy
- **King's Liquor & Gourmet** • 4435 Torrance Blvd
- **OK Liquor Store** • 22216 Palos Verdes Blvd
- **Party House** • 1817 S Catalina Ave
- **Pierside Liquors** • 310 Torrance Blvd
- **Pony Square Liquors** • 1882 S Pacific Coast Hwy
- **Prince Liquor** • 4425 Calle Mayor
- **Ruby's Liquor** • 443 S Pacific Coast Hwy
- **VIP Liquor & Market** • 604 Torrance Blvd
- **Walteria Country Liquor** • 24212 Hawthorne Blvd

Pet Stores
- **Animal Lovers Pet Shop** • 5141 Calle Mayor • 310-378-3052
- **Centinela Feed & Pet** • 413 N Pacific Coast Hwy • 310-318-2653
- **Petco** • 537 N Pacific Coast Hwy • 310-374-7969
- **Petsmart** • 3855 Sepulveda Blvd • 310-316-9047

Restaurants
- **Bluewater Grill** • 665 N Harbor Dr • 310-318-3474
- **Captain Kidd's** • 209 N Harbor Dr • 310-372-7703
- **Chez Melange** • 1716 S Pacific Coast Hwy • 310-540-1222
- **Christine** • 24530 Hawthorne Blvd • 310-373-1952
- **Collet Tea** • 320 S Catalina Ave • 310-372-0348
- **El Torito Grill** • 21321 Hawthorne Blvd • 310-543-1896
- **HT Grill** • 1710 S Catalina Ave • 310-316-6658
- **Hennessey's Tavern** • 1712 S Catalina Ave • 310-540-8443
- **Splash** • 350 N Harbor Dr • 310-798-5348
- **The Banyan Water Garden Café** • 600 S Pacific Coast Hwy • 310-316-0316
- **The Original Pancake House** • 1756 S Pacific Coast Hwy • 310-543-9875
- **Zazou** • 1810 S Catalina Ave • 310-540-4884

Shopping
- **Cookin Stuff** • 22217 Palos Verdes Blvd • 310-371-2220
- **Lindbergh Nutrition** • 3804 Sepulveda Blvd •

Video Rental
- **20-20 Video** • 705 N Pacific Coast Hwy • 310-376-2020
- **Blockbuster** • 1900 S Pacific Coast Hwy • 310-316-8957
- **Blockbuster** • 21841 Hawthorne Blvd • 310-540-6373
- **Blockbuster** • 417 N Pacific Coast Hwy • 310-798-2833
- **Hollywood Video** • 21149 Hawthorne Blvd • 310-316-9306
- **Hollywood Video** • 633 N Pacific Coast Hwy • 310-318-0564
- **Movies N You** • 4641 Torrance Blvd • 310-370-8280
- **Premieres Video** • 725 S Pacific Coast Hwy • 310-316-9336

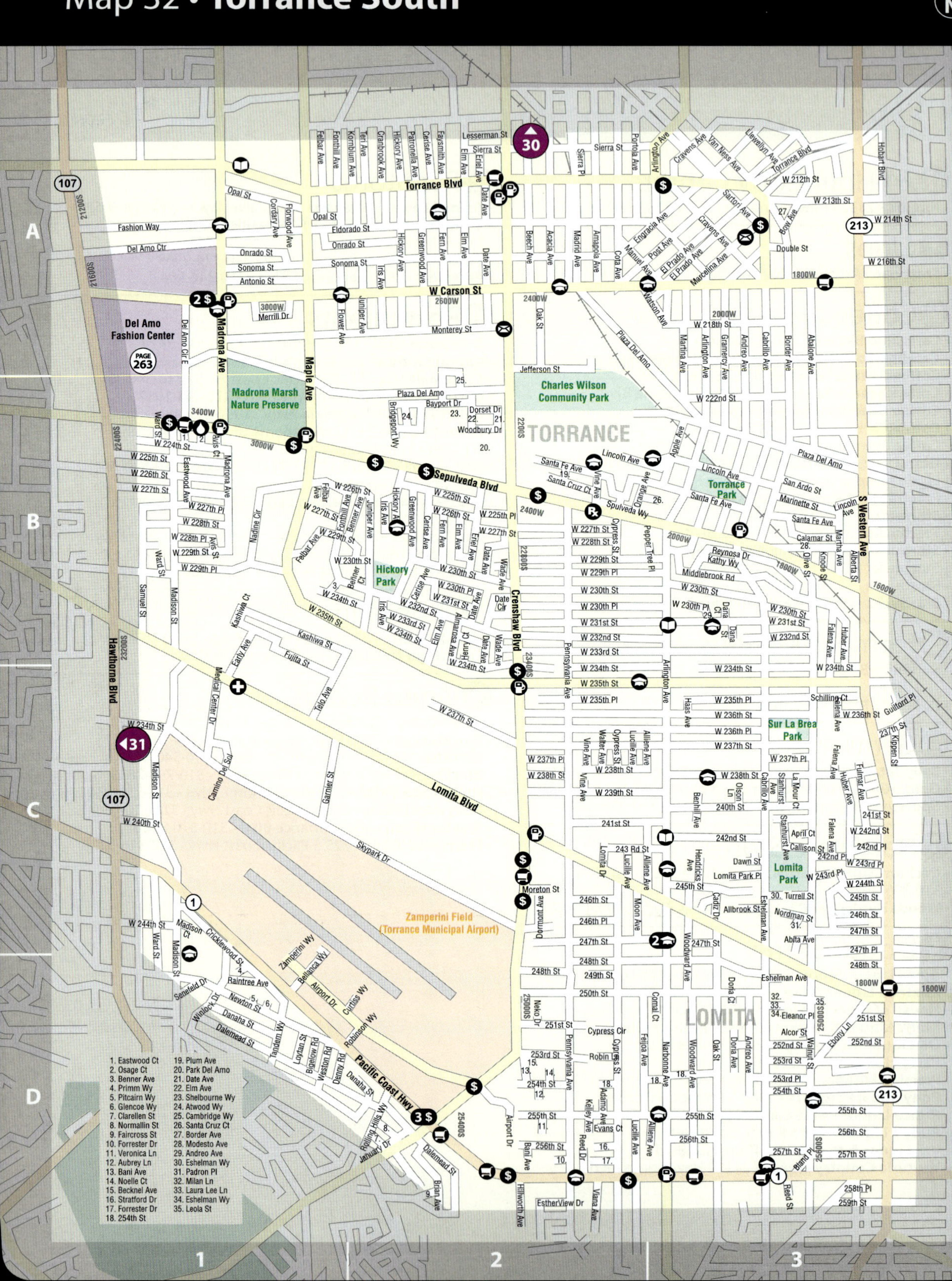
107
213
TORRANCE
LOMITA
Del Amo Fashion Center
PAGE 263
Madrona Marsh Nature Preserve
Charles Wilson Community Park
Torrance Park
Lincoln Ave
Hickory Park
Sur La Brea Park
Lomita Park
Zamperini Field (Torrance Municipal Airport)
Hawthorne Blvd
Madrona Ave
Maple Ave
Crenshaw Blvd
S Western Ave
Torrance Blvd
W Carson St
Sepulveda Blvd
Lomita Blvd
Pacific Coast Hwy
Fashion Way
Del Amo Ctr
Del Amo Cir E
Opal St
Eldorado St
Onrado St
Sonoma St
Antonio St
Merrill Dr
Ward St
W 224th St
W 225th St
W 226th St
W 227th St
W 227th Pl
W 228th St
W 228th Pl
W 229th St
W 229th Pl
W 230th St
Eastwood Ave
Madrona Ave
Nadine Cir
Axis Ct
Samuel St
Madison St
Ward St
Kashiwa Ct
Earту Ave
Kashiwa St
Fujita St
Telo Ave
Gramercy St
Medical Center Dr
Camino Del Sol
Madison St
Madison Ct
Cricklewood St
Senefeld Dr
Winlock Dr
Raintree Ave
Newton St
Danaha St
Dalemead St
Zamperini Wy
Bellanca Wy
Airport Dr
Curtiss Wy
Robinson Wy
Lydian St
Bigelow Rd
Weston Rd
Danny Rd
Tandem Wy
Skypark Dr
Jefferson St
Plaza Del Amo
Bayport Dr
Dorset Dr
Bridgeport Wy
Woodbury Dr
Felbar Ave
Fonthill Ave
Juniper Ave
Greenwood Ave
Centae Ave
Fern Ave
Elm Ave
Date Ave
Iris Ave
Hickory Ave
Benner Ave
W 226th St
W 227th St
W 228th St
W 229th St
W 230th St
W 231st St
W 232nd St
W 233rd St
W 234th St
W 235th St
W 237th St
W 238th St
Wade Ave
Date Cir
Almansa Ave
Pennsylvania Ave
Santa Fe Ave
Lincoln Ave
Vine Ave
Santa Cruz Ct
Spulveda Wy
Pepper Tree Ln
Cypress St
W 227th St
W 228th St
W 229th St
W 229th Pl
W 230th St
W 230th Pl
W 231st St
W 232nd St
W 233rd St
W 234th St
W 235th St
W 235th Pl
W 236th St
W 237th St
W 237th Pl
W 238th St
W 239th St
Reynosa Dr
Kathy Wy
Middlebrook Rd
Dana Ct
Arlington Ave
Haas Ave
Alliene Ave
Lucille Ave
Water Ave
Vine Ave
Berkhill Ave
Olson Ln
240th St
241st St
242nd St
243 Rd St
Lucille Dr
Allbrook Ln
San Ardo St
Marinette St
Santa Fe Ave
Calamar St
Olive St
Knode St
Martha Ave
Alberta St
Lincoln Ave
Schilling Ct
Selena Ave
Hulber Ave
Falena Ave
Sur La Brea Park
La Mour Ct
Stanhurst Ave
Cabrillo Ave
Stanhurst Ave
April Ct
Callison
Dawn St
Hendricks Ave
Lomita Park Pl
245th St
Cadiz Dr
Eshelman Ave
Doria Ct
Eshelman Ave
Abita Ave
Fulmar Ave
Huber Ave
Falena Ave
Kippen St
Guilford Pl
W 234th St
W 235th St
W 236th St
237th St
W 242nd St
W 243rd St
W 244th St
245th St
246th St
247th St
248th St
Moreton St
246th St
246th Pl
247th St
248th St
249th St
250th St
251st St
253rd St
254th St
255th St
256th St
257th St
258th St
259th St
Lomita Dr
Moon Ave
Comal Ct
Neko Dr
Pennsylvania Ave
Cypress Cir
Cypress St
Robin St
Adamo Ave
Kelley Ave
Reed St
Evans Ave
Bani Ave
Narbonne Ave
Woodward Ave
Feijoa Ave
Lucille Ave
Alliene Ave
Oak St
Andreo Ave
Doria Ave
Walnut St
Ebony Ln
Alcor Ct
Eleanor Pl
251st St
252nd St
253rd St
253rd Pl
254th St
255th St
256th St
257th Pl
258th Pl
259th St
Brand St
Reed St
Hillworth Ave
EstherView Dr
Brian St
Dalemead St
January Dr
Bani Ave
Sierra St
Portola Ave
Cravens Ave
Van Ness Ave
Llewellyn Ave
Torrance Blvd
Hobart Blvd
W 212th St
W 213th St
W 214th St
W 215th St
W 216th St
W 218th St
W 222nd St
Engracia Ave
Post Ave
El Prado Ave
Marcelina Ave
Sartori Ave
Manuel Ave
Cota Ave
Amapola Ave
Madrid Ave
Acacia Ave
Beech Ave
Oak St
Watson Ave
Plaza Del Amo
Martina Ave
Arlington Ave
Gramercy Ave
Andreo Ave
Cabrillo Ave
Border Ave
Abalone Ave
Double St
Bow Ave
Fashion Way
Felbar Ave
Fonthill Ave
Kornblum Ave
Jeft Ave
Cranbrook Ave
Hickory Ave
Patronella Ave
Carlise Ave
Faysmith Ave
Elm Ave
Eriel Ave
Date Ave
Sierra Pl
Lesserman St
Madrona Ave
Opal St
Cordary Ave
Florwood Ave
Onrado St
Monterey St
Fern Ave
Iris Ave
Flower Ave
Juniper Ave
30
31
1
2
3
1. Eastwood Ct
2. Osage Ct
3. Benner Ave
4. Primm Wy
5. Pitcairn Wy
6. Glencoe Wy
7. Clarellen St
8. Normallin St
9. Faircross St
10. Forrester Dr
11. Veronica Ln
12. Aubrey Ln
13. Bani Ave
14. Noelle Ct
15. Becknel Ave
16. Stratford Dr
17. Forrester Dr
18. 254th St
19. Plum Ave
20. Park Del Amo
21. Date Ave
22. Elm Ave
23. Shelbourne Wy
24. Atwood Wy
25. Cambridge Wy
26. Santa Cruz Ct
27. Border Ave
28. Modesto Ave
29. Andreo Ave
30. Eshelman Wy
31. Padron Pl
32. Milan Ln
33. Laura Lee Ln
34. Eshelman Wy
35. Leola St
A
B
C
D

Considering its humble beginnings as a rather milquetoast, suburban area, Torrance has morphed into quite a diverse community. Torrance boasts several fine restaurants, a good farmers market, and several cultural events throughout the year. Western Avenue has several interesting Japanese markets and restaurants; "Old Town" Torrance has a charm all its own.

$ Banks

- **Bank of America** · 25435 Crenshaw Blvd
- **California Center Bank** · 2742 W Sepulveda Blvd
- **Citibank** · 2700 Pacific Coast Hwy
- **City National Bank** · 3424 W Carson St
- **First Federal Bank** · 2177 Pacific Coast Hwy
- **First Federal Bank** · 23415 Crenshaw Blvd
- **First Federal Bank** · 3422 W Carson St
- **Jackson Federal Bank** · 25345 Crenshaw Blvd
- **Nara Bank** · 3030 Sepulveda Blvd
- **Preferred Bank** · 3501 Sepulveda Blvd
- **US Bank** · 2270 Pacific Coast Hwy
- **US Bank** · 2860 Sepulveda Blvd
- **Washington Mutual** · 2121 Torrance Blvd
- **Washington Mutual** · 2750 Pacific Coast Hwy
- **Wells Fargo Bank** · 1403 Sartori Ave
- **Wells Fargo Bank** · 24325 Crenshaw Blvd
- **Wells Fargo Bank** · 24439 Crenshaw Blvd
- **Western Financial Bank** · 2424 Sepulveda Blvd

Car Washes

- **Madrona Car Wash** · 3405 Sepulveda Blvd
- **Torrance Auto Spa** · 1751 Crenshaw Blvd

Gas Stations

- **Arco** · 1210 Crenshaw Blvd
- **Chevron** · 1700 Crenshaw Blvd
- **Chevron** · 23420 Crenshaw Blvd
- **Chevron** · 2761 Cabrillo Ave
- **Chevron** · 3405 Sepulveda Blvd
- **Mobil** · 1640 Crenshaw Blvd
- **Mobil** · 25808 Narbonne Ave
- **Mobil** · 3006 Sepulveda Blvd
- **Mobil** · 3328 W Carson St
- **Shell** · 2477 Lomita Blvd
- **Shell** · 2504 Torrance Blvd

Hospitals

- **Torrance Memorial Medical Center** · 3330 Lomita Blvd · 310-325-9110

Libraries

- **Lomita Public Library** · 24200 Narbonne Ave · 310-539-4515
- **Southeast Torrance Library** · 23115 Arlington Ave · 310-530-5044
- **Torrance Public Library** · 3301 Torrance Blvd · 310-618-5959

Rx 24-Hour Pharmacies

- **Rite-Aid** · 2240 W Sepulveda Blvd · 310-325-0868

Post Offices

- 1433 Marcelina Ave
- 2510 Monterey St
- 25131 Narbonne Ave

Schools

- **Adams Elementary** · 2121 W 238th St
- **Adams Learning Academy** · 4501 S Wadsworth Ave
- **Advanced Education** · 25533 Narbonne Ave
- **Branch of Hope** · 2370 W Carson St
- **Bravo Medical Magnet High School** · 1200 N Cornwell St
- **Fern Elementary** · 1314 Fern Ave
- **First Lutheran & Early** · 2900 W Carson St
- **Fleming Middle School** · 25425 Walnut St
- **Harbour Church Schools** · 1716 W 254th St
- **Hickory Elementary** · 2800 W 227th St
- **Hickory Tree** · 21720 Madrona Ave
- **Lomita Elementary** · 2211 247th St
- **Madrona Middle School** · 21364 Madrona Ave
- **Maimonides Torah Academy** · 24412 Narbonne Ave
- **Nativity** · 2371 W Carson St
- **Pacific Coast Montessori** · 2342 Pacific Coast Hwy
- **Shery High School** · 2600 Vine St
- **St Margaret Mary** · 25515 Eshelman Ave
- **Switzer Center** · 1110 Satori Ave
- **Torrance Elementary** · 2125 Lincoln Ave
- **Torrance High School** · 2200 Carson St
- **Walteria Elementary** · 24456 Madison St
- **Wood Elementary** · 2250 W 235th St

Supermarkets

- **Albertson's** · 2130 Pacific Coast Hwy
- **Albertson's** · 2515 Torrance Blvd
- **Ralph's** · 1770 Carson St
- **Ralph's** · 24911 Western Ave
- **Ralph's** · 3455 Sepulveda Blvd
- **Trader Joe's** · 2545 Pacific Coast Hwy
- **Von's** · 24325 Crenshaw Blvd
- **Whole Foods Market** · 2655 Pacific Coast Hwy

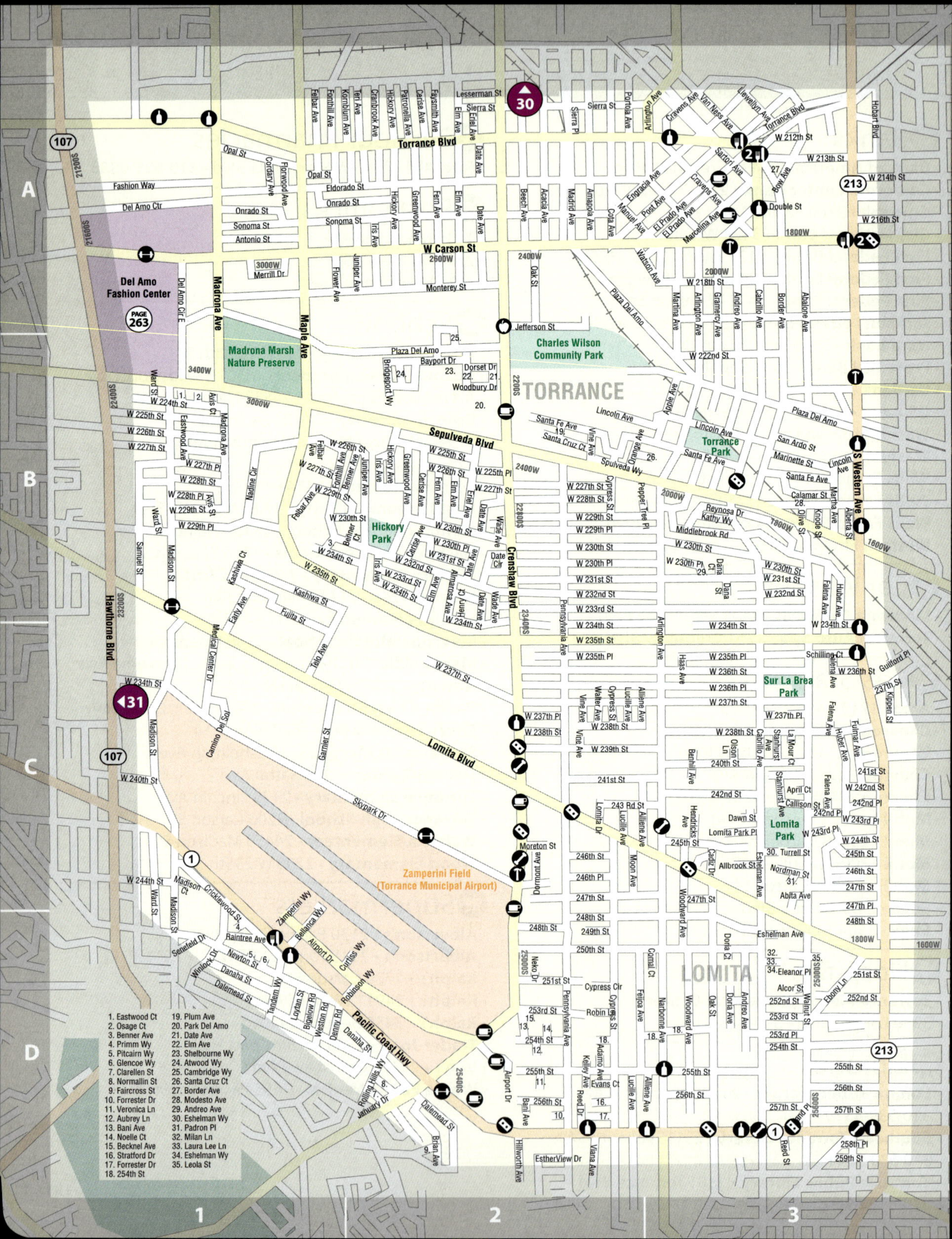

Del Amo Fashion Center
PAGE 263

Madrona Marsh Nature Preserve

Charles Wilson Community Park

TORRANCE

Torrance Park

Hickory Park

Sur La Brea Park

Lomita Park

LOMITA

Zamperini Field
(Torrance Municipal Airport)

1. Eastwood Ct
2. Osage Ct
3. Benner Ave
4. Primm Wy
5. Pitcairn Wy
6. Glencoe Wy
7. Clarellen St
8. Normaillin St
9. Faircross St
10. Forrester Dr
11. Veronica Ln
12. Aubrey Ln
13. Bani Ave
14. Noelle Ct
15. Becknel Ave
16. Stratford Dr
17. Forrester Dr
18. 254th St
19. Plum Ave
20. Park Del Amo
21. Date Ave
22. Elm Ave
23. Shelbourne Wy
24. Atwood Wy
25. Cambridge Wy
26. Santa Cruz Ct
27. Border Ave
28. Modesto Ave
29. Andreo Ave
30. Eshelman Wy
31. Padron Pl
32. Milan Ln
33. Laura Lee Ln
34. Eshelman Wy
35. Leola St

Torrance is home to an annual Oktoberfest, which is held at the Alpine Village on Torrance Blvd. every autumn. There you can enjoy Bavarian pretzels, sausage and, after some really good German beer, a chorus or two of the Chicken Dance. Enjoy!

Coffee

- **Bechamel Bakery** • 1616 Cravens Ave
- **Downtown Grounds** • 1341 El Prado Ave
- **Hot Bagels** • 24200 Crenshaw Blvd
- **Kelly's Coffee & Fudge** • 2595 Airport Dr
- **Starbucks** • 2370 Crenshaw Blvd
- **Starbucks** • 24427 Crenshaw Blvd
- **Starbucks** • 25348 Crenshaw Blvd

Farmer's Markets

- **Wilson Park** • Crenshaw Blvd & Jefferson St • Tue 8-12, Sat 8-1

Gyms

- **24-Hour Fitness** • 2685 Pacific Coast Hwy • 310-534-5100
- **LA Fitness Sports Club** • 3550 W Carson St • 310-921-9890
- **Rolling Hills Athletic Club** • 3601 Lomita Blvd • 310-791-2700
- **South End Racquet & Health Club** • 2800 Skypark Dr • 310-530-0630

Hardware Stores

- **Home Depot** • 24451 Crenshaw Blvd • 310-325-9600
- **Lovelady Hardware** • 1967 W Carson St • 310-328-4274
- **Lowe's Home Improvement Warehouse** • 22255 S Western Ave • 310-787-1469

Liquor Stores

- **Ace Hi Liquors** • 25511 Narbonne Ave
- **Bottle Shop** • 2087 Torrance Blvd
- **Brite Spot Liquor Store** • 1725 Pacific Coast Hwy
- **Eldorado Liquor Mart** • 23421 S Western Ave
- **Frank's Liquor Store** • 1601 Cabrillo Ave
- **J & S Liquor** • 23804 Crenshaw Blvd
- **Lomita Liquor & Deli** • 2022 Pacific Coast Hwy
- **McCowan Liquor** • 22802 S Western Ave
- **Moran's Liquor** • 2354 Pacific Coast Hwy
- **Mr K's Liquor Marts** • 3405 Torrance Blvd
- **One Stop Liquor Market** • 22540 S Western Ave
- **Royal Liquor** • 3114 Pacific Coast Hwy

Pet Stores

- **7 Dog Heaven** • 1960 Pacific Coast Hwy • 310-325-4947
- **A Paw-Fect World** • 23916 Crenshaw Blvd • 310-326-8881
- **Lomita Feed Store** • 24411 Narbonne Ave • 310-326-4738
- **Pet Centre USA** • 1747 Pacific Coast Hwy • 310-325-2002
- **Petco** • 24413 Crenshaw Blvd • 310-530-5945

Restaurants

- **Aioli** • 1261 Cabrillo Ave • 310-320-9200
- **Beijing Islamic** • 3160 Pacific Coast Hwy • 310-784-0846
- **Breadstix** • 1261 Cabrillo Ave • 310-320-9500
- **Depot** • 1250 Cabrillo Ave • 310-787-7501
- **Koji BBQ Buffet** • 1725 W Carson St • 310-787-1820

Video Rental

- **Blockbuster** • 1929 Pacific Coast Hwy • 310-534-2933
- **Blockbuster** • 24329 Crenshaw Blvd • 310-325-0757
- **Hollywood Video** • 2549 Pacific Coast Hwy • 310-539-5508
- **J T Video** • 2146 Lomita Blvd • 310-539-9748
- **James South Bay Entertainment** • 23910 Crenshaw Blvd • 310-539-4573
- **Sakura Video (Japanese)** • 2383 Lomita Blvd • 310-325-0306
- **Super Movies N You** • 2113 Pacific Coast Hwy • 310-539-9088
- **Tri-Video** • 1658 W Carson St • 310-212-5358
- **Video Access** • 2746 Cabrillo Ave • 310-533-8049
- **Video Japan Number 2 (Japanese)** • 1735 W Carson St • 310-787-1131

EAGLE ROCK

HIGHLAND PARK

MOUNT WASHINGTON

Occidental College

Eagle Rock Community Cultural Center

League of Latin American Citizens

Eagle Rock Rec Center

Builder's Club

Judson Studios

Freeways and major roads:
134 Ventura Freeway
123
47
34
2
36
38
110
Glendale Freeway
Pasadena Freeway
Ventura Freeway
Colorado Blvd
Eagle Rock Blvd
York Blvd
N Figueroa St
La Loma Rd
N Avenue 54

Streets:
Summer Ave
Lockhaven Dr
Sierra Villa Dr
Live Oak View Ave
Collage View Ave
Ellenwood Pl
Windermere Ave
El Rio Ave
Brockland Ave
Caspar Ave
N Maywood Ave
Hill Dr
Neal Dr
Estes Rd
W Hill Dr
Argus Dr
Hermosa Ave
La Roda Ave
Mount Royal Dr
Vincent Ave
Townsend Ave
Dahlia Dr
Loleta Ave
Kinchelloe Dr
Blue Hill Rd
Wiemada Ave
Kincheloe Dr
Hartwick St
Mount Helena Ave
Mount Bonito Dr
Monte Bonito Dr
Kiplin Ave
Linsford Dr
Cedaredge Ave
Waldo Pl
Genevieve Ave
Los Robles
Linda Rosa Ave
Saginaw St
Wiota St
Neola St
Ruth Ave
Glacier St
Colorado Blvd
Bampton Rd
Brixton Rd
Sycamore Gln
Elmwood Dr
Redwood Dr
Glenover Dr
Malcolm Dr
Aluta Dr
Sequoia Dr
Tamarac Dr
Jacaranda Dr
Kaweah Dr
Gernillen Dr
Capinero Dr
Arvin Ave
Glen Hoyt
Poppy Peak Dr
Marianna Rd
Washburn Rd
Doremus Rd
Langria Pl
Oleander Dr
E View Dr
Marie Ave
Cresthaven Dr
Lamanda Ter
N Avenue 62
N Avenue 63
N Avenue 64
N Avenue 66
Elgin St
Newland St
Hamlet St
Branch St
Ruby Ave
Meridian
Weaver Ave
Milwaukee Ave
Fayette St
Toledo St
Nolden St
N Ave 57
N Ave 56
N Ave 55
Le Gray Ave
Stratford Rd
Range View Ave
Meridian
Almaden Dr
Fallston St
Eaton St
Delphi St
La Prada St
Oak Crest Wy
Springvale Dr
Roy St
Savin Dr
Lewis St
Vista Pl
Fisher St
Kilby St
N Avenue 60
N Avenue 61
Burwood Ave
Hillandale Dr
Raser St
Tehama St
Upperton Ave
Nordyke St
Buena Vista Ter
Annan Way
Tipton Wy
Crestwood Wy
N Figueroa St
Wildwood Dr
Oak Grove Dr
Hepner Ave
Avoca Ave
Wicopee Ave
Yosemite St
Lanark St
Glen Arbor Ave
Poppy Ters
Eucalyptus Ln
Silverwood Dr
Upperton Pl
Townsend Ave
Vincent Ave
Ray Ct
Floristan Ave
Lick Ave
Grandola Ave
Waldran Ave
Holbrook St
Wista St
Neola St
Ward St
Rosmary Dr
La Roda Ave
Olson St
Escarpa Dr
Delrosa Dr
Chicksaw Ave
Oak Tree Dr
Shearin Ave
Glen Iris Ave
Las Flores Dr
Colorado Blvd
Yosemite Dr
Addison Wy
Laverna Ave
Norwalk Ave
Resthaven Pl
Las Colinas Ave
Ridgeview Ave
Ridgeview Ave
Westdale Ave
Campus Rd
Coons Rd
Baxter Rd
Bird Rd
Emmons Rd
Corliss St
Corliss St
Paulhan Ave
Alumni Ave
Weller Rd
Bird Rd
N Ave 46
N Ave 47
Hazelwood Ave
Armadale Ave
Campus Rd
N Ave 49
N Ave 50
N Ave 51
York Blvd
Charters Ave
Mendota Ave
Farnam St
Dexter St
Lincoln Ave
Buchanan St
Baltimore St
Hub St
Irvington Ter
Irvington Pl
Miriam St
Raphael St
San Rafael Ave
Banks Court Dr
Charters Ave
Coringa Dr
Eaton Ave
N Ave 52
Barker Dr
Phillips Wy
Raser St
Wildwood Dr
Silverwood Dr
Abbott St
Abbott Pl
Granada St
Monte Vista St
Ash St
Marmion Way
Stoll Dr
Terraca Dr
El Mio Dr
Aldama St
Mesa Ave
Outlook Ave
Piedmont Ave
N Avenue 54
S Ave 52
S Ave 53
S Ave 57
S Ave 58
S Ave 59
S Ave 60
S Ave 61
S Ave 63
S Ave 64
S Ave 66
Echo St
Meridian
Benner St
Omaha St
Carlota Blvd
Bertha St
Thorne St
Marmion Wy
Arroyo Dr
Arroyo Glen St
Hayes Ave
Shults St
Roble Ave
Longfellow St
Roselawn Pl
Leslie Wy
Omaha St
Pasadena Freeway

Legend/index (1–105):

1. El Canto Dr	36. Cherry Dr
2. Kerwin Dr	37. Shelby Pl
3. Janet Pl	38. Minden Pl
4. Castle Crest Dr	39. Juniper Dr
5. Rodin Pl	40. Cheviotdale Pl
6. Zaca Pl	41. Cheviotdale Dr
7. Prismo Dr	42. Evergreen Dr
8. Dicturn St	43. Pleasant Wy
9. Banbury Pl	44. Pine Grove Ave
10. Lytelle Pl	45. Poppy Peak Dr
11. York Hill Pl	46. Strickland Ave
12. College View Pl	47. Burwood Ter
13. Westdale Ave	48. Cheviotdale Pl
14. Eagle View Cir	49. Jacqueline Pl
15. Montiflora Ave	50. Rosswood Ter
16. Linda RosaAve	51. Highgrove Ter
17. Algoma Ave	52. Palm View Dr
18. Glen Aylsa Ave	53. Adelaide Pl
19. Tenshaw Pl	54. Planada Ave
20. Frackelton Pl	55. Crescent St
21. Rockview Ter	56. Ruby St
22. Upton Pl	57. Salonica St
23. Upton Ct	58. Garvanza Ave
24. Eagle Vista Dr	59. Weaver Ln
25. Hillmont Ave	60. Aldama St
26. Cedaredge Ct	61. Myosotis St
27. Hillmont Ave	62. Albans St
28. Highcrest Ave	63. La Prada Ter
29. Maison Ave	64. Highgate Ave
30. Genevieve Ave	65. Eaton Ter
31. Kipling Ave	66. Dogwood Pl
32. Colorado Al	67. Onarga Ave
33. Glengarry Al	68. Farrington Ln
34. Melrose Al	69. Crestwood Wy
35. Melrose Ave	70. Crestwood Ter

71. Annan Ter	
72. Manantonga Ter	
73. Betty Pl	
74. Rice St	
75. High St	
76. Beconia Ave	
77. Brevis St	
78. Silverwood Ln	
79. Loleta Pl	
80. Loleta Ave	
81. Oak Grove Pl	
82. Silver Oak Ter	
83. Ellita Pl	
84. Gracita Pl	
85. Longfellow St	
86. Roselawn Pl	
87. Leslie Wy	
88. S Ave 59	
89. Hayes Ave	
90. Shults St	
91. S Ave 61	
92. S Ave 63	
93. S Ave 83	
94. Arroyo Glen St	
95. S Ave 64	
96. La Riba Wy	
97. Roble Ave	
98. S Ave 66	
99. Stowe ter	
100. Livermore Ter	
101. Mount Angelus Dr	
102. La Follette Dr	
103. Wayland St	
104. Lamont Dr	
105. Garrison Dr	

The area hasn't changed much over the years, and many residents have banded together to prevent over-development. But Eagle Rock has been deemed a "hot" market in local real estate circles, so they may not be able to hold off the major chain stores forever.

$ Banks

- **Bank of America** · 2263 Colorado Blvd
- **Bank of America** · 5515 N Figueroa St
- **Citibank** · 5015 Eagle Rock Blvd
- **Citibank** · 5053 York Blvd
- **Jackson Federal Bank** · 6301 N Figueroa St
- **Washington Mutual** · 5700 N Figueroa St
- **Wells Fargo Bank** · 7311 N Figueroa St

Car Washes

- **Glen-Rock Car Wash** · 2711 Colorado Blvd
- **JJ's Hand Car Wash** · 7320 N Figueroa St
- **Laser Coin Car Wash** · 1707 Colorado Blvd

Gas Stations

- **76** · 2711 Colorado Blvd
- **76** · 4755 Eagle Rock Blvd
- **Chevron** · 6405 York Blvd
- **Chevron** · 7368 N Figueroa St
- **Mobil** · 2207 Colorado Blvd
- **Mobil** · 6174 York Blvd
- **Shell** · 2200 Colorado Blvd
- **Shell** · 5404 York Blvd

Landmarks

- **Builder's Club** · 1269 Hill Dr
- **Eagle Rock Community Cultural Center** · 2225 Colorado Blvd
- **Judson Studios** · 200 S Ave 66
- **League of United Latin-American Citizens** · 4512 Eagle Rock Blvd

Libraries

- **Los Angeles Library** · 5027 Caspar Ave · 323-258-8078

Post Offices

- 5132 York Blvd
- 5930 N Figueroa St
- 7435 N Figueroa St

Schools

- **ABC Child Development** · 5443 Ash St
- **American Montessori Preschool-Kindergarten** · 4817 Eagle Rock Blvd
- **American Montessori Preschool-Elementary** · 4475 Eagle Rock Blvd
- **Annandale Elementary** · 6125 Poppy Peak Dr
- **Buchanan Street Elementary** · 5024 Buchanan St
- **Burbank Middle School** · 6460 N Figueroa St
- **Central High School** · 1560 N Ave 53
- **Dahlia Heights Elementary** · 5063 Floristan Ave
- **Delevan Drive Elementary** · 4168 W Ave 42
- **Eagle Rock Elementary** · 2057 Fair Park Ave
- **Eagle Rock Junior High School** · 1750 Yosemite Dr
- **Eagle Rock Montessori** · 1439 W Colorado Blvd
- **Franklin Community Adult School** · 820 N Ave 54
- **Franklin Senior High School** · 820 N Ave 54
- **Garvanza Elementary** · 317 N Ave 62
- **Good Shepherd Lutheran** · 6338 N Figueroa St
- **Harvest Christian Academy** · 5066 Ellenwood Dr
- **Highland Park Continuation** · 928 N Ave 53
- **Highland Park HeadStart/ABC Child Development** · 5443 Ash St
- **Luther Burbank Middle School** · 6460 N Figueroa St
- **Meridian Early Education Center** · 6124 Ruby Pl
- **Monte Vista Street Elementary** · 5423 Monte Vista St
- **Montessori Children's World Private** · 1439 Colorado Ave
- **Occidental College** · 1600 Campus Rd
- **Optimist High School** · 6957 N Figueroa St
- **Rockdale Elementary** · 1303 Yosemite Dr
- **St Dominic Elementary** · 2005 Merton Ave
- **St Ignatius Elementary** · 6025 Monte Vista St
- **Westminster Academy** · 1495 Colorado Blvd
- **Yorkdale Elementary** · 5657 Meridian St

Supermarkets

- **Albertson's** · 4211 Eagle Rock Blvd
- **Super A Foods** · 2245 Yosemite Dr
- **Super A Foods** · 5250 York Blvd
- **Trader Joe's** · 1566 Colorado Blvd
- **Von's** · 7311 N Figueroa St

EAGLE ROCK

HIGHLAND PARK

MOUNT WASHINGTON

Occidental College

Eagle Rock Rec Center

Ventura Freeway
Glendale Freeway
Pasadena Freeway

Colorado Blvd
York Blvd
Eagle Rock Blvd
N Figueroa St
La Loma Rd

1. El Canto Dr
2. Kerwin Dr
3. Janet Pl
4. Castle Crest Dr
5. Rodin Pl
6. Zaca Pl
7. Prismo Dr
8. Dicturn St
9. Banbury Pl
10. Lytelle Pl
11. York Hill Pl
12. College View Pl
13. Westdale Ave
14. Eagle View Cir
15. Montiflora Ave
16. Linda Rosa Ave
17. Algoma Ave
18. Glen Aylsa Ave
19. Tenshaw Pl
20. Frackelton St
21. Rockview Ter
22. Upton Pl
23. Upton Ct
24. Eagle Vista Dr
25. Hillmont Ave
26. Cedaredge Ct
27. Hillmont Ave
28. Highcrest Ave
29. Maison Ave
30. Genevieve Ave
31. Kipling Ave
32. Colorado Al
33. Glengarry Rd
34. Melrose Al
35. Melrose Ave

36. Cherry Dr
37. Shelby Pl
38. Minden Pl
39. Juniper Dr
40. Cheviotdale Pl
41. Cheviotdale Dr
42. Evergreen Dr
43. Pleasant Wy
44. Pine Grove Ave
45. Poppy Peak Dr
46. Strickland Ave
47. Burwood Ter
48. Cheviotdale Pl
49. Jacqueline Pl
50. Rosswood Ter
51. Highgrove Ter
52. Palm View Dr
53. Adelaide Pl
54. Planada Ave
55. Crescent St
56. Ruby St
57. Salonica St
58. Garvanza Ave
59. Weaver Ln
60. Aldama St
61. Myosotis St
62. Albans St
63. La Prada Ter
64. Highgate Ave
65. Eaton Ter
66. Dogwood Pl
67. Onarga Ave
68. Farrington Ln
69. Crestwood Wy
70. Crestwood Ter

71. Annan Ter
72. Manantonga Ter
73. Betty Pl
74. Rice St
75. High St
76. Beconia Ave
77. Brevis St
78. Silverwood Ln
79. Loleta Pl
80. Loleta Ave
81. Oak Grove Pl
82. Silver Oak Ter
83. Ellita Pl
84. Gracita Pl
85. Longfellow St
86. Roselawn Pl
87. Leslie Wy
88. S Ave 59
89. Hayes Ave
90. Shults St
91. S Ave 61
92. S Ave 63
93. S Ave 83
94. Arroyo Glen St
95. S Ave 64
96. La Riba Wy
97. Roble Ave
98. S Ave 66
99. Stowe ter
100. Livermore Ter
101. Mount Angelus Dr
102. La Follette Dr
103. Wayland St
104. Lamont Dr
105. Garrison Dr

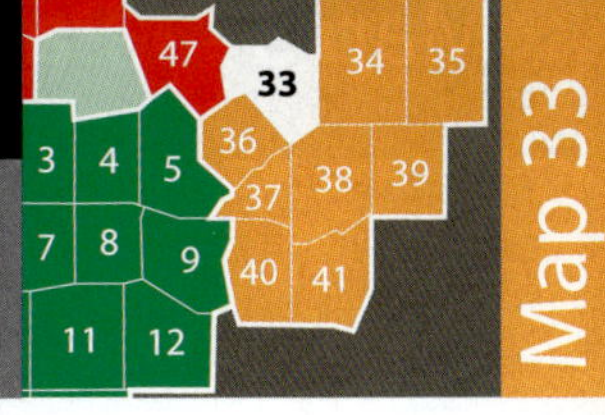

Even Starbucks has failed to penetrate the area, which relies mainly upon independent, mom-and-pop establishments. For serious shopping (as well as nightlife), residents are advised to hop on the 110 and head for Old Town in Pasadena.

Clubs

- **Mr T's Bowl** • 5621 1/2 N Figueroa St • 323-256-4850

Coffee

- **Beaujolais Boulangerie** • 1661 Colorado Blvd
- **Fatty's** • 1627 Colorado Blvd
- **Mocha Express** • 2700 Colorado Blvd
- **Oxy Café** • 4862 Eagle Rock Blvd
- **Pat and Lorraine's Coffee Shop** • 4720 Eagle Rock Blvd
- **Swork Coffee** • 2160 Colorado Blvd

Farmer's Markets

- **Eagle Rock Farmer's Market** • 2100 Merton Ave • Fri 5-8:30

Hardware Stores

- **Do It Best Hardware** • 5040 York Blvd • 323-254-6843
- **Eagle Rock Lumber & Hardware** • 2223 Fair Park Ave • 323-255-1451
- **Garvanza Hardware** • 6324 York Blvd • 323-256-3211
- **Sam's Ace Hardware** • 5031 York Blvd • 323-256-1001
- **Tritch Hardware** • 1620 Colorado Blvd • 323-255-8222

Liquor Stores

- **Amigos Liquor** • 5611 N Figueroa St
- **Annandale Liquors** • 1414 W Colorado Blvd
- **Bert's Liquor Store** • 4604 York Blvd
- **Beverage Liquor Shop** • 1605 Colorado Blvd
- **Chic's Liquor Store** • 1954 Colorado Blvd
- **Dan's Liquors** • 5711 York Blvd
- **Eagle Rock Market** • 4729 Eagle Rock Blvd
- **JC's Liquor** • 5326 York Blvd
- **Liquor Azteca de Oro** • 5049 York Blvd
- **Mario's Liquor Store** • 5421 York Blvd
- **One's Liquor** • 1664 Colorado Blvd
- **York Square Liquors** • 6312 York Blvd

Movie Theaters

- **Highland Theater** • 50604 N Figueroa St

Pet Stores

- **Birdman Pet Shop** • 5926 N Figueroa St • 323-344-0696
- **Julie's Dog Grooming** • 1803 Colorado Blvd • 323-258-5548
- **KB Aquarium & Pets** • 2108 Colorado Blvd • 323-255-7372
- **Verdugo Pet Shop** • 5022 York Blvd • 323-255-2327

Restaurants

- **Auntie Em's Kitchen** • 4616 Eagle Rock Blvd • 323-255-0800
- **Café Beaujolais** • 1712 Colorado Blvd • 323-255-5111
- **Capri Restaurant** • 4604 Eagle Rock Blvd • 323-257-3225
- **Casa Bianca** • 1650 Colorado Blvd • 323-256-9617
- **Classic Thai Restaurant** • 1708 Colorado Blvd • 323-478-0530
- **Colombo's** • 1833 Colorado Blvd • 323-254-9138
- **Eagle Rock Italian Bakery & Deli** • 1726 Colorado Blvd • 323-255-8224
- **El Arco Iris** • 5684 York Blvd • 323-254-3401
- **El Huarache Azteca** • 5225 York Blvd • 323-478-9572
- **Galco's** • 5700 York Blvd • 323-255-7115
- **Pete's Blue Chip** • 1701 Colorado Blvd • 323-478-9022
- **Sicha Siam** • 4403 Eagle Rock Blvd • 323-344-8285
- **Villa Sombrero** • 6101 York Blvd • 323-256-9014

Shopping

- **Country Pickin's** • 2477 Colorado Blvd • 323-256-8132
- **Galco's Soda Pop Stop** • 5702 York Blvd • 323-255-7115

Video Rental

- **Best Video** • 6473 N Figueroa St • 323-257-8586
- **Blockbuster** • 6312 N Figueroa St • 323-259-5980
- **Blockbuster** • 2175 Colorado Blvd • 323-255-2445
- **Planet Video** • 5445 N Figueroa St • 323-982-9064
- **Video 808** • 1608 Colorado Blvd • 323-259-8282
- **Video Street 56** • 5544 York Blvd • 323-349-0622
- **York Video** • 5001 York Blvd • 323-256-0882

Map 34 • Pasadena

The Rose Bowl draws thousands of people to Pasadena on any given weekend for sporting events, but the monthly Swap Meet (on the second Sunday of each month) is really not to be missed. Serious shoppers (including a number of Hollywood production designers) line up just after dawn and pay extra for early admission. But some of the best bargains end up going to those people who sleep in and only begin to haggle as merchants are packing it in late in the afternoon.

$ Banks

- **Bank of America** · 145 W California Blvd
- **Bank of America** · 532 E Colorado Blvd
- **Bank of America** · 880 E Colorado Blvd
- **Bank of America** · 929 Fair Oaks Ave
- **Bank of the West** · 587 E Colorado Blvd
- **Bank One** · 1111 S Arroyo Pkwy
- **Citibank** · 161 W California Blvd
- **Citibank** · 201 N Garfield Ave
- **Citibank** · 285 S Lake Ave
- **Citizens Business Bank** · 225 E Colorado Blvd
- **City National Bank** · 215 N Marengo Ave
- **Community Bank** · 100 Corson St
- **Community Bank** · 505 E Colorado Blvd
- **East West Bank** · 1001 Fair Oaks Ave
- **Far East National Bank** · 301 N Lake Ave
- **First Professional Bank** · 55 E California Blvd
- **Union Bank** · 70 S Lake Ave
- **United Commercial Bank** · 199 S Los Robles Ave
- **Washington Mutual** · 860 E Colorado Blvd
- **Wells Fargo Bank** · 1000 Fair Oaks Ave
- **Wells Fargo Bank** · 155 W California Blvd
- **Wells Fargo Bank** · 350 W Colorado Blvd
- **Wells Fargo Bank** · 655 N Fair Oaks Ave
- **Wells Fargo Bank** · 82 S Lake Ave

Car Washes

- **Arroyo-California Car Wash** · 605 S Arroyo Pkwy
- **Pasadena Auto Wash** · 164 W Del Mar Blvd

Gas Stations

- **76** · 155 E Glenarm St
- **76** · 2601 Mission St
- **76** · 911 E Washington Blvd
- **Arco** · 208 E Orange Grove Blvd
- **Arco** · 445 E Walnut St
- **Arco** · 736 Mission St
- **Arco** · 885 E California Blvd
- **Chevron** · 1200 Fair Oaks Ave
- **Chevron** · 160 E California Blvd
- **Chevron** · 666 N Lake Ave
- **Independent** · 2507 Mission St
- **Mobil** · 290 S Arroyo Pkwy
- **Mobil** · 474 S Lake Ave
- **Shell** · 1050 S Fair Oaks Ave
- **Shell** · 200 N Fair Oaks Ave
- **Shell** · 631 N Garfield Ave
- **Shell** · 632 N Garfield Ave

Hospitals

- **Huntington Memorial Hospital** · 100 W California Blvd · 626-397-5000

Landmarks

- **Gamble House** · 4 Westmoreland Pl
- **Old Town** · Fair Oaks Ave & Colorado Blvd
- **Pasadena City Hall** · 100 N Garfield Ave
- **Pasadena Civic Auditorium** · 300 E Green St
- **Pasadena Playhouse** · 37 S El Molino Ave
- **Rose Bowl** · 991 Rosemont Ave
- **Wrigley Mansion** · 391 S Orange Grove Blvd

Libraries

- **Allendale Branch Library** · 1130 S Marengo Ave · 626-799-2519
- **La Pintoresca Branch Library** · 1355 N Raymond Ave · 626-797-1873
- **Pasadena Public Library** · 285 E Walnut St · 626-744-4052
- **San Rafael Library** · 1240 Nithsdale Rd · 626-795-7974
- **South Pasadena Library** · 1100 Oxley St · 626-403-7330
- **Villa Parke Library** · 363 F Villa St · 626-744-6510

Police

- **Pasadena Police Dept** · 207 N Garfield Ave · 626-744-4501
- **South Pasadena Police Dept** · 1422 Mission St · 626-403-7270

Post Offices

- 1001 Fremont Ave
- 1355 N Mentor Ave
- 281 E Colorado Blvd
- 600 Lincoln Ave
- 870 S Raymond Ave
- 99 W California Blvd

Schools

- **Allendale Elementary** · 1135 S Euclid Ave
- **Arroyo Vista Elementary** · 335 El Centro St
- **Blair High School** · 1201 S Marengo Ave
- **Chandler** · 1005 Armada Dr
- **Highland Child Care Center & Preschool** · 840 N Ave 66
- **Hillsides Education Center** · 940 Ave 64
- **Lake Ave Christian School** · 393 N Lake Ave
- **Linda Vista Elementary** · 1259 Linda Vista Ave
- **Madison Elementary** · 515 E Ashtabula St
- **Mayfield Junior** · 405 S Euclid Ave
- **Mayfield Senior** · 500 Bellefontaine St
- **New Horizon** · 626 Cypress Ave
- **Oak Knoll Montessori** · 140 N Oak Knoll Ave
- **Pacific Oaks Children's School** · 714 W California Blvd
- **Roosevelt Elementary** · 315 N Pasadena Ave
- **Rose City High School** · 325 S Oak Knoll Ave
- **San Pascual Ave Elementary** · 815 San Pascual Ave
- **San Rafael Elementary** · 1090 Nithsdale Rd
- **Sequoyah** · 535 S Pasadena Ave
- **Southwestern Academy-Veronda** · 2800 Monterey Rd
- **St Andrews Elementary** · 42 Chestnut St
- **Star Children Academy** · 1143 N Lake Ave
- **Waverly** · 396 S Pasadena Ave
- **Westgate Palms** · 480 Westgate St
- **Westridge School for Girls** · 324 Madeline Dr

Supermarkets

- **Bristol Farms** · 606 Fair Oaks Ave
- **Food 4 Less** · 1329 N Lake Ave
- **Gelson's Markets** · 245 E Green St
- **Pavilions** · 1213 Fair Oaks Ave
- **Pavilions** · 845 E California Blvd
- **Ralph's** · 160 N Lake Ave
- **Ralph's** · 320 W Colorado Blvd
- **Trader Joe's** · 610 S Arroyo Pkwy
- **Trader Joe's** · 613 Mission St
- **Von's** · 1129 Fair Oaks Ave
- **Von's** · 155 W California Blvd
- **Von's** · 655 N Fair Oaks Ave
- **Wild Oats** · 603 S Lake Ave

N

1. Linda Vista Way
2. Banyan St
3. Rancheros Pl
4. Pine Oak Ln
5. Belday Rd
6. Mira Vista Ter
7. La Vereda Rd
8. La Cumbre Dr
9. El Circulo Dr
10. El Portolo
11. Camino Silvoso
12. Las Palmas Rd
13. Arroyo Dr
14. Solita Rd
15. Wotkyns Dr
16. Richland Pl
17. Manzanita Ave
18. Rosewalk Wy
19. Cypress Ave
20. Prospect Ter
21. Prospect Cres
22. Mayview Ln
23. Winona Wy
24. Hickory Ln
25. Ridgewood Ln
26. Rosewood Ln
27. Longwood Ln
28. Prospect So
29. Westmoreland Pl
30. Kensington Pl
31. Continental Ct
32. Live Oaks Ave
33. Maple St
34. W Washington Pl
35. Florence Dr
36. Banbury Alley
37. Chapman Ave
38. Brooks Ave
39. W Eureka St
40. Orange Grove Pl
41. Champlain Ave
42. Holland Alley
43. Progress Ln
44. Birge Alley
45. Eucalyptus Ln
46. Birch Ln
47. Elm Ln
48. Poplar Ln
49. Spruce Ln
50. Glorieta St
51. La Pintoresca Dr
52. Crystal Ln
53. Linville Alley
54. Cowgill Alley
55. Jackson St
56. Adena St
57. Ashtabula St
58. Barnhart Alley
59. Thompson Dr
60. Elgin Alley
61. N Oakland Av
62. N Madison Ave
63. Leighton Alley
64. Mountain Pl
65. Heather Sq
66. Johnson Alley
67. Wright Ave
68. Boylston St
69. Carter Alley
70. Michener Alley
71. Townsend Pl
72. Pearl Pl
73. Cottage Pl
74. N Euclid Ave
75. Reinway Ct
76. Garden Village Ct
77. Maple Wy
78. Rosita Ln
79. Annandale Ter
80. Court Ter
81. Linda Vista Ave
82. California Ter
83. Terrace Dr
84. Gordon Ter
85. Havendale Dr
86. Buckingham Pl
87. San Rafael Ter
88. Mesa Verde Rd
89. Romney Wy
90. Romney
91. Bellefontaine Pl
92. Mayfield HS
93. Westover Pl
94. Garden Ln
95. Busch Pl
96. Stoneridge Dr
97. Orange Grove Cir
98. Busch Garden Dr
99. Busch Ct
100. Busch Garden Ln

101. Christiansen Aly
102. Leonard Pieroni Aly
103. S De Lacey Ave
104. Central Ct
105. Baker Aly
106. Gertrude Ct
107. Herr Aly
108. Tenhaeff aly
109. Concordia Ct
110. Drexel Pl
111. Alessandro Pl
112. Kendall Aly
113. Townsend Pl
114. Ninde Pl
115. N Garfield Ave
116. Garfield Ave
117. N Arroyo Pkwy
118. Legge Aly
119. Weight Aly
120. Metcalf Aly
121. Evanston Pl
122. Picher aly
123. Parker Aly
124. Converse Aly
125. Gibbs Aly
126. Mira Monte Pl
127. Boston Ct
128. Market Aly
129. Palm View Pl
130. Granite Dr
131. Oakwood Pl
132. Lakewood
133. Oak Knoll Gardens Dr
134. Arboleda Dr
135. Chestnut Ave
136. Brookmere Rd
137. Hillside Rd
138. Hermosa Pl
139. Orange Grove Ter
140. Prospect Ln
141. Five Oaks Dr
142. Arroyo Vista Pl
143. Pico Aly
144. Indiana Ct
145. Doran St
146. Cawston St
147. Jacobs Ln
148. Hawthorne Ln
149. Throop Aly
150. Orange Grove Pl
151. McCament Aly
152. Glendon Ln
153. Loma Vista Ct
154. Glendon Ct
155. Glendon Wy
156. Prospect St
157. Beacon Ave
158. Prospect Cir
159. Highland St
160. Columbia Aly
161. Brocadero Pl
162. Grace Ter
163. Grace Wk
164. Alarcon Pl
165. Columbia Pl
166. Fremont Ln
167. Oaklawn Pl
168. Ozmun Ct
169. Mound Ave
170. Hope Ct
171. Hopewell Ln
172. Central Aly
173. Fair Oaks Ave
174. Mockingbird Ln
175. Raymond Hill Rd
176. Cedarcrest Ave
177. Raymondale Dr
178. Ellincourt Dr
179. Foothill St
180. Hardison Pl
181. Hardison Aly
182. Virginia Pl
183. Oxley Aly
184. Donaldo Ct
185. Marengo Aly
186. Pico Aly
187. Montrose Ln
188. North Aly
189. South Aly
190. Old Mill Rd
191. Oak Knoll Cir
192. Huntington Cir
193. Huntington Garden Dr
194. Straats
195. Ardmore Rd
196. Bonita Dr

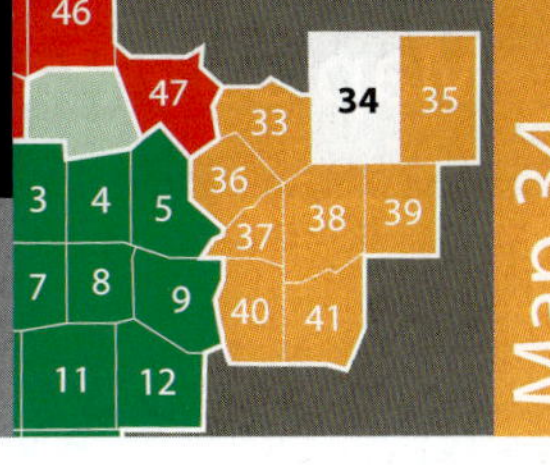

Jan and Dean sang about the "Little Old Lady From Pasadena," but this is not your parents' Pasadena anymore. Old Town is now a thriving shopping and entertainment district, and the crowds are thick on Saturday nights.

24-Hour Copy Centers
- **Kinko's** • 855 E Colorado Blvd • 626-793-6336

Clubs
- **Club 41** • 41 S De Lacey Ave • 626-795-4141
- **Freddie's 35er Bar** • 12 E Colorado Blvd • 626-356-9315
- **Jake's Billiards** • 38 W Colorado Blvd • 626-568-1602
- **The Muse** • 54 E Colorado Blvd • 626-793-0608

Coffee
- **African Coffee Import** • 1272 N Lake Ave
- **Coffee Bean & Tea Leaf** • 18 S Fair Oaks Ave
- **Coffee Bean & Tea Leaf** • 415 S Lake Ave
- **Coffee Bean & Tea Leaf** • 700 S Fair Oaks Ave
- **Cyber Caffe** • 107 S Fair Oaks Ave
- **Equator Coffee House** • 22 Mills Pl
- **House of Coffee** • 620 Mission St
- **Kaldi Coffee & Tea** • 1019 El Centro St
- **La Luce Cafe & Deli** • 62 W Union St
- **Peet's Coffee & Tea** • 605 S Lake Ave
- **Second Cup** • 84 S Fair Oaks Ave
- **Starbucks** • 1000 Fair Oaks Ave
- **Starbucks** • 117 W Colorado Blvd
- **Starbucks** • 408 E Colorado Blvd
- **Starbucks** • 454 Fair Oaks Ave
- **Starbucks** • 556 S Fair Oaks Ave
- **Starbucks** • 575 S Lake Ave
- **Starbucks** • 671 N Fair Oaks Ave
- **Starbucks** • 82 S Lake Ave
- **Tiffany's Coffee** • 263 E Colorado Blvd

Farmer's Markets
- **Pasadena** • 363 E Villa St • Tue 8:30-12:30

Gyms
- **24-Hour Fitness** • 202 The Plaza Pasadena • 626-568-3785
- **24-Hour Fitness** • 525 E Colorado Blvd • 626-795-7121
- **Athletic Garage** • 121 Waverly Dr • 626-229-9769
- **Bally Total Fitness** • 45 S Arroyo Pkwy • 626-577-8588
- **Body Image** • 350 S Lake Ave • 626-449-8115
- **Break Thru Fitness** • 87 Fraser Alley • 626-396-1700
- **LA Fitness Sports Clubs** • 201 S Lake Ave • 626-568-3598
- **Le Studio Fitness** • 236 W Mountain St • 626-792-9866
- **Pasadena Athletic Club** • 25 W Walnut St • 626-793-8161

Hardware Stores
- **Orchard Supply Hardware** • 452 Fair Oaks Ave • 626-403-8115
- **Pasadena True Value Hardware** • 409 N Fair Oaks Ave • 626-792-2196

Liquor Stores
- **Andy's Liquors** • 124 E Orange Grove Blvd
- **Antonio's Liquor Store** • 15 E Holly St
- **Cal-Oaks Liquors** • 32 W California Blvd
- **Foremost Liquor Stores** • 301 Monterey Rd
- **Liquor Box** • 1445 Lincoln Ave
- **Milt's Liquor Store** • 400 E Orange Grove Blvd

Movie Theaters
- **AMC Old Pasadena 8** • 42 Miller Alley
- **Laemmle Playhouse 7** • 673 E Colorado Blvd
- **Pacific Paseo Stadium 14** • 336 E Colorado Blvd
- **Rialto Theatre** • 1023 Fair Oaks Ave
- **UA Marktplace** • 64 W Colorado Blvd

Pet Stores
- **Pat McKay Animal Nutrition** • 396 W Washington Blvd • 626-296-1120
- **Pet's Delight** • 725 Fair Oaks Ave • 626-799-2935
- **Petco** • 845 S Arroyo Pkwy • 626-577-2600
- **Protect Your Pets** • 537 S Raymond Ave • 626-795-1058
- **Three Dog Bakery** • 24 Smith Alley • 626-440-0443

Restaurants
- **Akbar** • 44 N Fair Oaks Ave • 626-577-9916
- **Arroyo Chop House** • 536 S Arroyo Pkwy • 626-577-7463
- **Burger Continental** • 535 S Lake Ave • 626-792-6634
- **Café Bizou** • 91 N Raymond Ave • 626-792-9923
- **Cafe Med** • 260 E Colorado Blvd • 626-793-0600
- **Celestino** • 141 S Lake Ave • 626-795-4006
- **De Lacey's Club 41** • 41 S De Lacey Ave • 626-795-4141
- **EuroPane** • 950 E Colorado Blvd • 626-577-1828
- **Five Sixty-One** • 561 E Green St • 626-405-1561
- **Gordon Biersch** • 41 Hugus Alley • 626-569-5240
- **Hop Li** • 526 Alpine St • 213-680-3939
- **Julienne** • 2649 Mission St • 626-441-2299
- **Maison Akira** • 713 E Green St • 626-796-9501
- **Marston's** • 151 E Walnut St • 626-796-2459
- **Pho 79** • 29 S Garfield Ave • 626-289-0239
- **Radhika's** • 140 Shoppers Ln • 626-744-0994
- **Raymond, The** • 1250 S Fair Oaks Ave • 626-441-3136
- **Roscoe's Chicken & Waffles** • 830 N Lake Ave • 626-791-4890
- **Twin Palms** • 101 W Green St • 626-577-2567
- **Yujean Kang's** • 67 N Raymond Ave • 626-585-0855

Shopping
- **Paperwhites** • 956 Mission St • 626-441-2196
- **Three Dog Bakery** • 24 Smith Alley • 626-440-0443

Video Rental
- **Blockbuster** • 151 W California Blvd • 626-440-7074
- **Blockbuster** • 1100 Fair Oaks Ave • 626-441-8112
- **Blockbuster** • 320 S Lake Ave • 626-568-9874
- **Hollywood Video** • 25 E California Blvd • 626-304-9340
- **Ito Video** • 41 E Orange Grove Blvd • 626-683-9503
- **Luigi's Video** • 544 N Fair Oaks Ave • 626-796-9645
- **Pasadena Video** • 453 E Orange Grove Blvd • 626-744-9698
- **Pepe's Video Store** • 313 E Orange Grove Blvd • 626-792-7127
- **Q Video** • 1279 N Lake Ave • 626-398-8686
- **Rio Video** • 633 S Arroyo Pkwy • 626-792-7090
- **Video Plus** • 811 Fair Oaks Ave • 626-441-6643

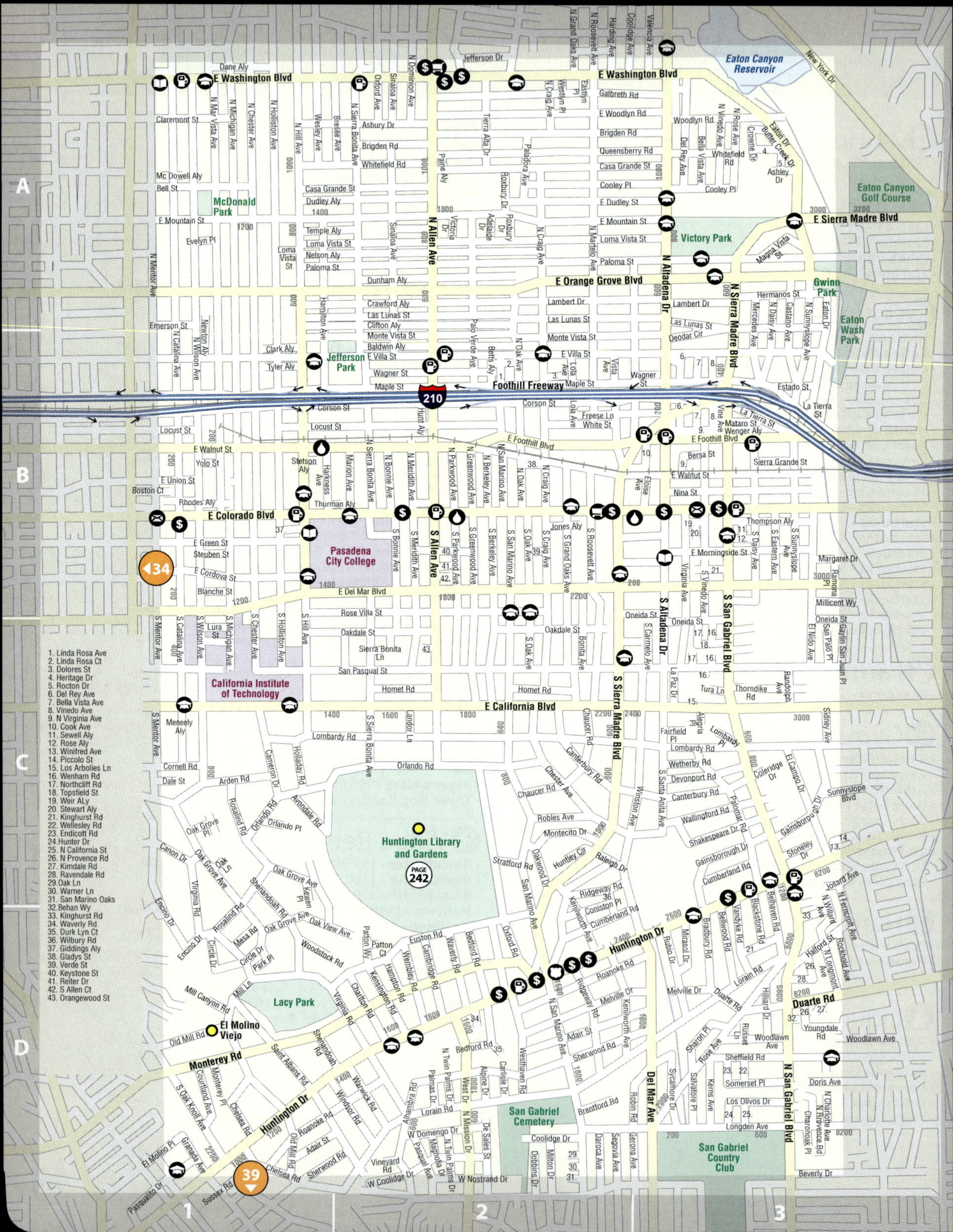

N

1. Linda Rosa Ave
2. Linda Rosa Ct
3. Dolores St
4. Heritage Dr
5. Rocton Dr
6. Del Rey Ave
7. Bella Vista Ave
8. Vinedo Ave
9. N Virginia Ave
10. Cook Ave
11. Sewell Aly
12. Rose Aly
13. Winifred Ave
14. Piccolo St
15. Los Arbolies Ln
16. Wenham Rd
17. Northcliff Rd
18. Topsfield St
19. Weir ALy
20. Stewart Aly
21. Kinghurst Rd
22. Wellesley Rd
23. Endicott Rd
24. Hunter Dr
25. N California St
26. N Provence Rd
27. Kimdale Rd
28. Ravendale Rd
29. Oak Ln
30. Warner Ln
31. San Marino Oaks
32. Behan Wy
33. Kinghurst Rd
34. Waverly Rd
35. Durk Lyn Ct
36. Wilbury Rd
37. Giddings Aly
38. Gladys St
39. Verde St
40. Keystone St
41. Reiter Dr
42. S Allen Ct
43. Orangewood St

This area is the home of Cal Tech, the institution of higher learning to which Angelenos turn whenever the ground shakes. It is the Cal Tech seismograph that provides the official Richter Scale reading for any earthquake, and it is the school's experts who serve as reassuring voices through each subsequent aftershock.

$ Banks

- **Bank of America** · 1687 E Colorado Blvd
- **Bank of America** · 2180 Huntington Dr
- **Bank of the West** · 2395 Huntington Dr
- **Bank of the West** · 2500 E Colorado Blvd
- **China Trust Bank USA** · 2956 Huntington Dr
- **Citizens Business Bank** · 1010 E Colorado Blvd
- **United National Bank** · 2090 Huntington Dr
- **Washington Mutual** · 1845 E Washington Blvd
- **Washington Mutual** · 2675 E Colorado Blvd
- **Wells Fargo Bank** · 1830 E Washington Blvd
- **Wells Fargo Bank** · 1390 N Allen Ave
- **Wells Fargo Bank** · 2355 E Colorado Blvd
- **Wells Fargo Bank** · 2355 Huntington Dr

Car Washes

- **Chevron Car Wash** · 1400 E Colorado Blvd
- **Sparkle Car Wash** · 2400 E Colorado Blvd
- **Walnut-Hill Hand Car Wash** · 1465 E Walnut St

Gas Stations

- **76** · 1816 E Villa St
- **Arco** · 1010 E Washington Blvd
- **Arco** · 2800 E Foothill Blvd
- **Chevron** · 1400 E Colorado Blvd
- **Chevron** · 2155 Huntington Dr
- **Chevron** · 233 N Altadena Dr
- **Exxon** · 2995 Huntington Dr
- **Mobil** · 1813 E Colorado Blvd
- **Mobil** · 210 N Sierra Madre Blvd
- **Mobil** · 475 N Allen Ave
- **Shell** · 2716 E Colorado Blvd
- **Shell** · 8204 Huntington Dr
- **Texaco** · 1600 E Washington Blvd

Landmarks

- **El Molino Viejo** · 1120 Old Mill Rd
- **Huntington Library and Gardens** · 1151 Oxford Rd

Libraries

- **Hill Avenue Branch Library** · 55 S Hill Ave · 626-796-1276
- **Lamanda Park Library** · 140 S Altadena Dr · 626-793-5672
- **Santa Catalina Library** · 999 E Washington Blvd · 626-794-1219

Police

- **San Marino Police Dept** · 2200 Huntington Dr · 626-300-0720

Post Offices

- 2609 E Colorado Blvd
- 967 E Colorado Blvd

Schools

- **Assumption Elementary** · 2660 E Orange Grove Blvd
- **California Institute of Technology** · California Blvd & Hill Ave
- **California Academy for Liberal Studies** · 3838 Eagle Rock Blvd
- **Calvary Christian School** · 1555 E Colorado Blvd
- **Carver Elementary** · 1300 San Gabriel Blvd
- **Coombs Elementary** · 2600 Paloma St
- **Frostig Center of Education Therapy** · 971 N Altadena Dr
- **Grace Christian School** · 73 N Hill Ave
- **Hamilton Elementary** · 2089 Rose Villa St
- **Huntington Middle School** · 1700 Huntington Dr
- **Jefferson Elementary** · 1500 E Villa St
- **Living Way Christian Academy** · 2495 E Mountain St
- **Longfellow Elementary** · 1065 E Washington Blvd
- **Oddessy Charter School** · 1555 E Colorado Blvd
- **Pasadena City College** · 1570 E Colorado Blvd
- **Pasadena High School** · 2925 E Sierra Madre Blvd
- **Pasadena Towne Country** · 200 S Sierra Madre Blvd
- **Polytechnic** · 1030 E California Blvd
- **San Marino High School** · 2701 Huntington Dr
- **San Marino Montessori** · 444 S Sierra Madre Blvd
- **St Gregory Church Am** · 2215 E Colorado Blvd
- **St Philip's the Apostle** · 171 S Hill Ave
- **Stoneman** · 1560 Pasqualito Dr
- **Sts Felicitas and Perpetua** · 2955 Huntington Dr
- **Valentine Elementary** · 1650 Huntington Dr
- **Villa Esperanza** · 2116 E Villa St
- **Walden** · 74 S San Gabriel Blvd
- **Washington Elementary** · 300 N San Marino Ave
- **Webster Elementary** · 2101 E Washington Blvd
- **Wilson Elementary** · 8317 Sheffield Rd

Supermarkets

- **Von's** · 1390 N Allen Ave
- **Von's** · 2355 E Colorado Blvd

N

E Washington Blvd
Jefferson Dr
Eaton Canyon Reservoir
New York Dr

McDonald Park
Eaton Canyon Golf Course
E Sierra Madre Blvd
Victory Park
Gwinn Park
Eaton Wash Park
Jefferson Park

E Orange Grove Blvd
Foothill Freeway
I-210
Colorado Blvd
Pasadena City College
E Del Mar Blvd
California Institute of Technology
E California Blvd
Huntington Library and Gardens
PAGE 242
Lacy Park
Monterey Rd
Huntington Dr
Duarte Rd
San Gabriel Cemetery
San Gabriel Country Club

34
39

Street index (left column):

1. Linda Rosa Ave
2. Linda Rosa Ct
3. Dolores St
4. Heritage Dr
5. Rocton Dr
6. Del Rey Ave
7. Bella Vista Ave
8. Vinedo Ave
9. N Virginia Ave
10. Cook Ave
11. Sewell Aly
12. Rose Aly
13. Winifred Ave
14. Piccolo St
15. Los Arbolies Ln
16. Wenham Rd
17. Northcliff Rd
18. Topsfield St
19. Weir Aly
20. Stewart Ave
21. Kinghurst Rd
22. Wellesley Rd
23. Endicott Rd
24. Hunter Dr
25. N California St
26. N Provence Rd
27. Kimdale Rd
28. Ravendale Rd
29. Oak Ln
30. Warner Ln
31. San Marino Oaks
32. Behan Wy
33. Kinghurst Rd
34. Waverly Rd
35. Durk Lyn Ct
36. Wilbury Rd
37. Giddings Aly
38. Gladys St
39. Verde St
40. Keystone St
41. Reiter Dr
42. S Allen Ct
43. Orangewood St

Though San Marino is fairly residential, it's home to the Huntington Library and Gardens, a lovely place to spend a weekend afternoon—and an offbeat place to take visiting relatives from out of town.

Coffee

- **Coffee Beanery** · 1225 E Washington Blvd
- **Espress Y'Self** · 1359 N Altadena Dr
- **Ragtime Gourmet Tea Coffee** · 975 E Green St
- **Starbucks** · 161 N Hill Ave
- **Starbucks** · 1830 E Washington Blvd
- **Starbucks** · 2265 Huntington Dr
- **Starbucks** · 3007 Huntington Dr
- **X-Presso Speciality Sales** · 2341 E Foothill Blvd

Farmer's Markets

- **Pasadena** · Paloma St & Sierra Madre Blvd · Sat 8:30-12:30

Gyms

- **Gold's Gym** · 39 S Altadena Dr · 626-304-1133
- **Long Term Muscle** · 2370 E Colorado Blvd · 626-793-5353

Hardware Stores

- **Berg Hardware** · 495 N Altadena Dr · 626-793-6161
- **Crown City Hardware** · 1047 N Allen Ave · 626-794-1188
- **Davis Lumber** · 1787 E Walnut St · 626-792-7104

Liquor Stores

- **Allen Villa Beverage** · 490 N Allen Ave
- **Foothill Liquor** · 2547 E Foothill Blvd
- **Golden Liquor Mart** · 2897 E Colorado Blvd
- **Liquor Mart** · 2044 E Colorado Blvd
- **Mission Liquor Store** · 1801 E Washington Blvd
- **Pat's Liquors** · 1072 E Colorado Blvd

Movie Theaters

- **Academy 6** · 1003 E Colorado Blvd

Pet Stores

- **Pasadena Tropical Fish** · 2982 E Colorado Blvd · 626-449-4987

Restaurants

- **Bistro 45** · 45 S Mentor Ave · 626-795-2478
- **Halie** · 1030 E Green St · 626-440-7067
- **Mijas** · 2506 Huntington Dr · 626-287-1021
- **San Marino Grill** · 2494 Huntington Dr · 626-286-2500
- **Sushi Bar Yoshida** · 2026 Huntington Dr · 626-281-9292
- **Zankou Chicken** · 1415 E Colorado Blvd · 818-244-1937

Video Rental

- **Blockbuster** · 1830 E Washington Blvd · 626-345-9136
- **Blockbuster** · 900 Huntington Dr · 626-289-9931
- **Laser Library** · 1190 E Colorado Blvd · 626-577-7035
- **Plaza Video** · 1832 E Colorado Blvd · 626-793-2451
- **Star Video** · 1878 E Washington Blvd · 626-791-9708
- **Video Grand** · 376 N Allen Ave · 626-578-1640
- **Video Horizons** · 2423 E Colorado Blvd · 626-304-0304

N

Forest Lawn Memorial Park (Glendale)

GLASSELL PARK

MOUNT WASHINGTON

CYPRESS PARK

Glassell Park & Rec Center

Glassell Park

Bicentennial Park

Mount Washington Hotel/Self-Realization

Southwest Museum

The Lummis Home

Ernest E Debs Regional Park

Elysian Park

Los Angeles River

Glendale Freeway

Golden State Freeway

Pasadena Freeway

Eagle Rock Blvd

York Blvd

N San Fernando Rd

N Figueroa St

Cypress Ave

Verdugo Rd

Petrita Ave

W Ave 40

1. Charters Ave
2. W Ave 44
3. Verdugo Vista Ter
4. Division Pl
5. Cleland Pl
6. Holyoke Dr
7. Isabel Cir
8. Knob Dr
9. Kemper St
10. Kemper Ct
11. Tacuba St
12. Beauvais Ave
13. Clermont St
14. Shanley Ave
15. N Ave 49
16. N Ave 48
17. Sonata Ln
18. Montezuma Ct
19. Pasadena Ave Ter
20. Theresa St
21. Shelburn Ct
22. Andalusia Ave
23. Vista Gloriosa Dr
24. American Pl
25. Glenalbyn Dr
26. Beech St
27. Seymour St
28. Gay St

PAGE 233

Most residents of Mt. Washington love the fact that after they turn off the area's main drag, Figueroa St., it's as if they've left Los Angeles altogether. Neighboring areas have had problems with gangs, but Mt. Washington remains a remote hideaway.

Car Washes

- **Highland Car Wash** · 5128 N Figueroa St
- **Zeavy Car Wash** · 4000 N Figueroa St

Gas Stations

- **76** · 2250 N Figueroa St
- **Arco** · 105 N Ave 52
- **Arco** · 2135 San Fernando Rd
- **Arco** · 2251 N Figueroa St
- **Arco** · 4380 Eagle Rock Blvd
- **Chevron** · 2601 N Figueroa St
- **Chevron** · 4005 Eagle Rock Blvd
- **Chevron** · 4419 N Figueroa St
- **Shell** · 4236 Eagle Rock Blvd
- **Shell** · 5137 N Figueroa St

Landmarks

- **Mount Washington Hotel/Self-Realization** · 3880 San Rafael Ave
- **Southwest Museum** · 234 Museum Dr
- **The Lummis Home** · 200 E Ave 43

Libraries

- **Cypress Park Branch Library** · 1150 Cypress Ave · 323-224-0039

Post Offices

- 3950 Eagle Rock Blvd

Schools

- **Aldama Elementary** · 632 N Ave 50
- **Aragon Avenue Elementary** · 1118 Aragon Ave
- **Arroyo Seco** · 4805 Sycamore Ter
- **California State University - Los Angeles** · 5151 State University Dr
- **Divine Saviour** · 624 Cypress Ave
- **Dorris Place Elementary** · 2225 Dorris Pl
- **Glassell Park Elementary** · 2211 W Ave 30
- **Loreto Street Elementary** · 3408 Arroyo Seco Ave
- **Mount Washington Elementary** · 3981 San Rafael Ave
- **Nightingale Middle School** · 3311 N Figueroa St
- **Ribet Academy** · 2911 San Fernando Rd
- **St Bernard Elementary** · 3254 Verdugo Rd
- **Sycamore Grove** · 4900 N Figueroa St
- **Toland Way Elementary** · 4545 Toland Way

Supermarkets

- **Albertson's** · 133 W Ave 45
- **Food 4 Less** · 5100 N Figueroa St
- **Ralph's** · 2716 N San Fernando Rd
- **Super A Foods** · 2925 Division St

N
Forest Lawn Memorial Park (Glendale)
GLASSELL PARK
MOUNT WASHINGTON
CYPRESS PARK
Elysian Park
Ernest E Debs Regional Park
Glassell Park & Rec Center
Glassell Park
Bicentennial Park
Los Angeles River
Glendale Freeway
Golden State Freeway
Pasadena Freeway
Eagle Rock Blvd
York Blvd
N Figueroa St
N San Fernando Rd
Eagle Rock Blvd
Riverside Dr
W Ave 40
W Ave 40
Delay Dr
Bushwick Ave
Estara Ave
Edward Ave
Moss Ave
Hallett Ave
Verdugo Pl
Big Oak Dr
Perlita Ave
Blimp St
Gail St
Forney St
Lads St
Dallas St
Cabot St
Birkdale St
Altman St
Dorris St
Glover Pl
Riverdale Ave
Meadowvale Ave
Shortdale Ave
Blake Ave
Gatewood St
Fernleaf St
Elmgrove Ave
Duvall St
Oros St
Barclay St
Crystal St
Harwood St
W Avenue 33
W Avenue 32
W Avenue 31
W Avenue 30
W Ave 32
Moss Ave
Cazador Ct
Carlyle Pl
Cazador Pl
Carlyle St
Division St
Cypress Ave
Macon St
Silver St
Frederick St
Futura St
Elm St
Asbury St
Chaucer St
Arvia St
Granada St
Alice St
Roseview Ave
Granada St
Alice St
Roseview Ave
Loosmore Ave
Maceo St
Thorpe Ave
Carleton Ave
Merced St
Pepper Ave
W Avenue 27
Drew St
Idell St
Jeffries Ave
Ruby St
Huron St
N Ave 22
Cresmore Rd
Mimosa Dr
Inglis Dr
Canada St
El Rosa Dr
Paseo Dr
Kinney St
Kinney Ct
Lavell Dr
The Paseo
Lavell Dr
Parrish Ave
Shire Dr
Baysh
Hines Dr
Richardson St
Cazador St
Panamint Dr
Camorilla Dr
Loma Lada Dr
Rome Dr
Gassen Pl
Wollam St
Isabel Dr
Burnell St
Kilbourn St
Fillmore Pl
Future Pl
Tatum St
Division St
Scarboro St
Wollam St
Winmar Dr
Bridgeport Dr
Randall Ct
Killarney Ave
Cliff St
Tacoma Ave
Roseview Ave
San Rafael Dr
Mayfair Dr
Del Rio Ave
Tacoma Ave
Cliff Dr
Altamont St
Loosmore St
Isabel St
Cypress Ave
Aragon Ave
Etta St
Montalvo St
Ulysses St
James St
Cedar St
Locust St
Romulo St
Isabel St
Shirleff Ct
N Figueroa St
Marmion Wy
Arroyo Seco Ave
French St
Carlota Blvd
Sunbeam Dr
Ackerman Dr
Ackerman Dr
College Crest Dr
Barryknoll Dr
Barryknoll Dr
Verdugo View Dr
Verdugo View Dr
Verdugo View Dr
Panamint St
Toland Way
Scandia Way
Verdugo View Dr
W Ave 42
W Ave 43
W Ave 43
Toland Pl
Mont Eagle Pl
El Paso Dr
Scandia Wy
Cazador St
Brilliant Dr
Loveland Dr
Marcopa Dr
Brittnell Dr
Cazador Ct
Division St
Alder Dr
Annette St
N Figueroa St
Lincoln Ave
Alumni Ave
N Ave 45
N Ave 46
Hazelwood
Toland Way
Mendota Ave
N Ave 49
Farnam Ave
Banks Court Dr
El Paso Dr
San Rafael Ave
Terrace 49
Terrace 49
Aldama St
San Marcos St
Eldred St
Granada St
Cross St
Cross Ave
Crane Blvd
Lynn St
Malta St
Monte Vista St
Hackett Pl
Sycamore Ter
Oak Terrace Dr
Echo St
S Avenue 50
S Avenue 51
S Avenue 51
N Avenue 51
N Avenue 50
N Avenue 49
Marmion Wy
Mayo St
Palmero Dr
Nordica Dr
Jessica Dr
Otay Dr
Cleland Ave
Nob Hill Dr
Cynthia Av
San Andreas Ave
Sea View Dr
Sea View Ln
Sea View Ave
El Cedro Ave
Atajo St
Sano Dr
San Rafael
Primavera Ave
Primavera Wy
Sunny Heights Dr
Rome Dr
Karella St
Danforth Dr
Pheasant Dr
Quail St
Glenalbyn Dr
Dove Rd
Milton St
Wren Dr
Rustic Dr
Dummick Dr
Sunnyhill Dr
Moon Ave
Crane Blvd
Museum Dr
Lasey Wy
Crane Blvd
Disbin Pl
Furness Ave
Sycamore Ter
Rainbow Ave
Frontenac Ave
Rome Ct
Elyria Dr
Mt Washington Dr
W Avenue 37
San Rafael Dr
Camino Real
Monterey
Glenwood Ave
Glenmuir Ave
W Ave 41
Glenalbyn Wy
Canyon Vista Dr
W Avenue 44
ACanon Crest Dr
W Avenue 46
Starling Wy
Glenalbyn Dr
Maria Dr
Museum Dr
Woodside Dr
N Figueroa St
Mt Washington Dr
Glenalbyn Dr
West Point Dr
Del Norte St
W Ave 42
W Ave 43
W Ave 45
E Ave 41
E Ave 40
E Ave 39
E Ave 38
E Ave 37
E Ave 36
Midland St
Monument St
Sycamore Pk Dr
Oban Dr
Latin Wy
Division St
Alegria St
Olancha Dr
Oneonta Dr
Nob Hill Dr
Oneonta Dr
Friends Dr
Cleland Ave
Terrace 49
Division St
Hasterhill Dr
Flaterhill Dr
Latin
Wy
Oban Dr
Mendota Ave
N Ave 49
Toland Way
Hazelwood Ave
N Ave 46
N Ave 45
York Blvd
4400
4600
4800
5000
5200
4200
4000
3800
3600
3400
3800
4200
2600
2800
200
400
600
1200
2800
2500
Eagle Rock Blvd
47
33
33
37
5
5
110
110
PAGE 233
GLASSELL PARK
W Avenue 35
W Avenue 34
Arthur St
Arthur St
Eshra Ave
Bank St
W Ave 30
W Ave 30
W Ave 31
Cazador Pl
Gassen Pl
Wollam St

1. Charters Ave
2. W Ave 44
3. Verdugo Vista Ter
4. Division Pl
5. Cleland Pl
6. Holyoke Dr
7. Isabel Cir
8. Knob Dr
9. Kemper St
10. Kemper Ct
11. Tacuba St
12. Beauvais Ave
13. Clermont St
14. Shanley Ave
15. N Ave 49
16. N Ave 48
17. Sonata Ln
18. Montezuma Ct
19. Pasadena Ave Ter
20. Theresa St
21. Shelburn Ct
22. Andalusia Ave
23. Vista Gloriosa Dr
24. American Pl
25. Glenalbyn Dr
26. Beech St
27. Seymour St
28. Gay St

A
B
C
D
1
2
3

The trade-off to living off the beaten path is that Mt. Washington residents are completely dependent upon the freeway for even the most basic necessities. The neighborhood lacks many amenities and has few major chains, but Old Town Pasadena is just a few exits away on the 110.

Coffee

- **Rock Rose Cafe** · 4108 N Figueroa St

Hardware Stores

- **Home Depot** · 2055 N Figueroa St · 323-441-1310
- **Verdugo Hardware** · 3516 Eagle Rock Blvd · 323-255-5191

Liquor Stores

- **Barney's Liquors & Market** · 5001 Monte Vista St
- **Cypress Liquor** · 1207 Cypress Ave
- **Golden Liquor Store** · 3924 N Figueroa St
- **Highland Plaza Liquors** · 5012 N Figueroa St
- **L & M Liquor** · 4010 Eagle Rock Blvd
- **Mike's Liquor** · 3192 Verdugo Rd
- **S & J Liquor Store** · 925 Cypress Ave
- **Sun Liquor & Mini Mart** · 204 E Ave 42

Pet Stores

- **Hal's Eagle Rock Pet Shop** · 4374 Eagle Rock Blvd · 323-255-5714

Restaurants

- **Chico's** · 100 N Ave 50 · 323-254-2445
- **La Abeja** · 3700 N Figueroa St · 323-221-0474

Video Rental

- **21 Video** · 2211 N San Fernando Rd · 323-221-1793
- **Big J Video** · 4157 Eagle Rock Blvd · 323-254-5740
- **Gina's Video** · 1008 1/2 Cypress Ave · 323-441-1250
- **Jae's Video** · 2933 Division St · 323-223-5525
- **Landmark Video (Filipino)** · 3756 W Ave 40 · 323-256-0969
- **Max Video** · 4319 N Figueroa St · 323-222-7572
- **Video Club of LA** · 3756 W Ave 40 · 323-255-9883

N

1. Pagoda Ct
2. Pagoda Pl
3. E Avenue 41
4. E Avenue 35
5. Idylwild Ave
6. E Avenue 32
7. Montecito St
8. Augustine Ct
9. Fonda Wy
10. Prewett St
11. Two Tree Ave
12. Abrigo Ave
13. Ashland Ave
14. Lincoln High Pl
15. Lincoln High Ct
16. Metzler Dr
17. Chile St
18. Mallard St
19. Superior Ct
20. Supreme Ct
21. Canto Dr
22. Beryl St
23. Duke St
24. Manitou Pl
25. Park Heights
26. North Pl
27. S Ave 16
28. Savoy St
29. Stadium Wy
30. Aurora St

Ernest E Debs Regional Park
Elysian Park
PAGE 233
Los Angeles River
Heritage Square Museum
MONTECITO HEIGHTS
LINCOLN HEIGHTS
Lincoln Park
Hazard Park

110
5
36
38
40
5
9

Griffin Ave
Mosher Ave
Montecito Dr
Evandale Dr
Paige St
Elderbank Dr
E Avenue 43
Montecito Dr
Sinova St
Lafona Ave
Latrobe St
Berenice Ave
Berenice Pl
Montecito Dr
Montecito Dr
Roberta St
Avenue 39
Griffin Ave
Victorine St
Luther St
Mercury Ave
Borel St
Raynol St
Rolle St
Turquoise St
W Rose Hill Dr
Pasadena Freeway
Arroyo Seco
Cardota Blvd
Lupin Ter
Radio Dr
Gillig Ave
Sierra St
Eva Ter
Telluride St
Radium
Forest Park Dr
W Ave 34
W Ave 33
W Ave 31
W Ave 30
W Ave 29
W Ave 28
Smith St
E Avenue 33
E Avenue 31
Fenn St
Johnston St
E Avenue 28
Clifton St
Alta Pl
Flora Ave
Amethyst St
Paradise Dr
Rising Dr
Forest Park Dr
Onyx St
Commodore St
E Rose Hill Pl
Lacy St
Artesian St
Humboldt St
Pasadena Ave
Thomas St
Pomona
Minnesota St
Terry Pl
George St
Emma Ave
Lincoln Park Ave
Lincoln High Dr
Golden State Freeway
N Ave 22
Lacy St
Humboldt St
Barranca St
N Avenue 26
N Avenue 25
N Avenue 23
N Avenue 19
E Avenue 26
Sichel St
Griffin Ave
Johnston St
Aylesworth Pl
Altura St
Gates St
Alta St
Lincoln Park Ave
Holgate Sq
Buena Vista View Dr
S Ave 24
Street Clock
Daly St
N Broadway
Thomas St
Alta St
Prince St
Coral St
Amador St
S Avenue 22
Workman St
Manitou Ave
Eastlake Ave
Manitou Ave
N Mission Rd
N Soto St
Solano Ave
Casanova St
Park Row Dr
S Avenue 20
Vallejo St
Carr Ln
Hancock Ave
Baldwin St
Baldwin St
Alta St
Keith St
Bishops Rd
Baker St
S Avenue 18
S Avenue 19
Barbee St
Johnston St
Barbee St
Selig Pl
N Broadway
Abbot St
Naud St
Willardt St
Mesnager St
S Avenue 17
Mozart St
S Avenue 21
Darwin Ave
Hatfield
N Spring St
N Main St
S Avenue 21
N Main St
Abner St
Pasadena Ave

Montecito Heights may be an L.A. birdwatcher's paradise. The area is home to a chorus of songbirds, numerous hawks, and the occasional Great White Owl. So vast is the local avian population that the Audobon Society has recently established a presence here and is considering the creation of a bird sanctuary in Ernest E. Debs Regional Park.

$ Banks

- **Bank of America** · 2400 N Broadway
- **East West Bank** · 2601 N Broadway
- **Wells Fargo Bank** · 2511 Daly St

Gas Stations

- **76** · 2001 N Broadway
- **Arco** · 2214 N Broadway
- **Arco** · 2829 N Broadway
- **Shell** · 3130 N Broadway

○ Landmarks

- **Heritage Square Museum** · 3800 N Homer St
- **Street Clock** · 2423 Broadway

Libraries

- **Lincoln Heights Branch Library** · 2530 Workman St · 323-226-1692

Schools

- **Albion Street Elementary** · 322 S Ave 18
- **Boyle Heights Continuation** · 544 E Mathews St
- **Cathedral High School** · 1253 Bishop Rd
- **Crittenton High School** · 234 E Ave 33
- **Gates Street Elementary** · 3333 Manitou Ave
- **Glen Alta Elementary** · 3410 Sierra St
- **Griffin Avenue Elementary** · 2025 Griffin Ave
- **Hillside Elementary** · 120 E Ave 35
- **Latona Ave Elementary** · 4312 Berenice Ave
- **Lincoln Adult** · 3501 N Broadway
- **Lincoln Senior High School** · 3501 N Broadway
- **Montecito Park Baptist** · 333 E Ave 43
- **Our Lady Help of Christians** · 2024 Darwin Ave
- **Pubelo de Los Angeles Continua** · 2506 Alta St
- **Sacred Heart High School** · 2111 Griffin Ave

Supermarkets

- **Von's** · 2511 Daly St

N

1. Pagoda Ct
2. Pagoda Pl
3. E Avenue 41
4. E Avenue 35
5. Idylwild Ave
6. E Avenue 32
7. Montecito St
8. Augustine Ct
9. Fonda Wy
10. Prewett St
11. Two Tree Ave
12. Abrigo Ave
13. Ashland Ave
14. Lincoln High Pl
15. Lincoln High Ct
16. Metzler Dr
17. Chile St
18. Mallard St
19. Superior Ct
20. Supreme Ct
21. Canto Dr
22. Beryl St
23. Duke St
24. Manitou Pl
25. Park Heights
26. North Pl
27. S Ave 16
28. Savoy St
29. Stadium Wy
30. Aurora St

Ernest E Debs
Regional Park

MONTECITO
HEIGHTS

LINCOLN HEIGHTS

Elysian
Park

Lincoln
Park

Hazard
Park

Los Angeles River

Pasadena Freeway
Golden State Freeway
Arroyo Seco

110
5
36
38
40
5
9

PAGE
233

N Broadway
N Main St
N Spring St
N Mission Rd
N Soto St
Daly St
Pasadena Ave
Griffin Ave
Mosher Ave
Montecito Dr
Carlota Blvd

E Avenue 43
E Avenue 39
E Avenue 33
E Avenue 31
E Avenue 26

Manitou Ave
Baldwin Ave
Eastlake Ave
Barbee St
Darwin Ave
Abner St
Hatfield
Selig Pl

Amador St
Solano Ave
Cassanova St
Baker St
Bishops Rd
Buena Vista View Dr
Park Row Dr

Lincoln Park Ave
Lincoln High Dr
Alta St
Thomas St
Prince St
Coral St
Holgate Sq
Parkside Ave
Keith St

Victorine St
Luther St
Mercury Ave
Borel St
Rolle St
Gillig Ave
Raynol St
Reynolds Ave
Sierra St
Eva Ter
Turquoise St
Telluride St
Tourmaline St
Amethyst St
Radium
Onyx St
Commodore St
Paradise Dr
Rising Dr
Forest Park Dr
W Rose Hill Pl
E Rose Hill Pl
Evandale Dr
Paige St
Elderbank Dr
Sinova St
Latona Ave
Berenice Ave
Berenice Pl
Roberta St
Radio Dr
Lupin Ter
Fenn St
Johnston St
Clifton St
Pomona
Flora Ave
Alta Pl
Emma Ave
Minnesota St
Terry Pl
George St
Aylesworth Pl
Altura St
Sichel St
Hancock St
Johnston St
Workman St
Carr Ln
Vallejo
Barbee St
Mozart St
Naud St
Willard St
Messenger
Albion St
Humboldt St
Artesian St
Lacy St
Barranca St
Montecito Dr

W Ave 34
W Ave 33
W Ave 31
W Ave 30
W Ave 29
W Ave 28
W Avenue 26

N Ave 22
N Avenue 25
N Avenue 23
N Avenue 19
S Ave 24
S Avenue 22
S Avenue 20
S Avenue 19
S Avenue 18
S Avenue 17
S Avenue 21

Lincoln Heights is home to the San Antonio Winery, Los Angeles' last remaining winery. Tours are available, along with dinner at the winery's restaurant and live music on the weekends.

Coffee

- **Super Snack Stand** • 2700 N Broadway

Hardware Stores

- **5 Points Hardware** • 2615 Pasadena Ave • 323-225-6423

Liquor Stores

- **Mandala Liquor Store** • 2920 N Broadway
- **Royal Liquors** • 2501 Pasadena Ave

Pet Stores

- **Jack's Pet Shop** • 2634 Pasadena Ave • 323-225-6315
- **Pete's Pet Supply** • 2828 N Broadway • 323-227-5019

Video Rental

- **Best Video** • 2924 N Broadway • 323-222-3276
- **Hollywood Video** • 3030 N Broadway • 323-221-3201
- **Star Video** • 112 E Ave 26 • 323-222-9046

1. Hardison Wy
2. Warwick Pl
3. South Ln
4. Hill Dr
5. Los Laureles
6. Oak Crest Ave
7. Mtn View Ave
8. Indiana
9. Martos Dr
10. Gates Pl
11. Alta Vista Cir
12. La Portada
13. Indiana Pl
14. Indiana Ter
15. Portola Ter
16. Temple Ter
17. Cabrillo Villas St
18. Hulbert Ave
19. Los Alisos
20. Hawley Ave
21. Stanford Ter
22. Austin Ter
23. Wilson Summit St
24. Fremont Villas St
25. Catalina ter
26. Marshall Villas St
27. Drake Ter
28. Vallejo Villas St
29. Pacific Aly
30. El Cerrito Cir
31. Hill Ln
32. Meridian Ln
33. Camino Cerrado
34. La Bellorita
35. Glen Pl
36. Spruce St
37. Hunt Ln
38. Gillette Cres
39. Hopewell Ln
40. Beech St
41. Wolford St
42. Huntingdon Ln
43. El Tesorito
44. Maple St
45. Maple Wy
46. Elmpark St
47. Hill Ln
48. Valley View Rd
49. Crestlake Ave
50. Garden Homes Ave
51. Richard Circle Dr
52. Remstoy Dr
53. Moffatt St
54. Berkshire Ave
55. Cambridge Pl
56. Atlas St
57. Placer Pl
58. Berkshire
59. Manchester Ave
60. Randolph St
61. Yoakum St
62. Carnegie St
63. Renovo St
64. Hillview Pl
65. Browne Ave
66. Hillsdale Dr
67. Academy St
68. Rosemead Ave
69. Sardon St
70. Beryl St
71. Yorba St
72. Amethyst St
73. Topaz St
74. Dudley Dr
75. Ferntop Dr
76. Cato Wy
77. Waldo Ct
78. Kenneth Dr
79. Jasper St
80. Lynnfield St
81. Carter Dr
82. Betty Dr
83. Edloft St
84. Twining St
85. Grey Dr
86. Minto Ct
87. Paola Ave
88. Fithian Ave
89. Thelma Ave
90. Butterfly Ln
91. Templeton St
92. Castalia Ave
93. Okell St
94. Wadena St
95. Hall St
96. Lowell Ave
97. Stockbridge Ave
98. Lakewood Ave
99. Glenridge Ave
100. W Commonwealth Ave
101. Patio Pl
102. Somerset St
103. Copeland Pl
104. Hyde St
105. Chadwick Cir
106. Chester St
107. Lynnfield Cir
108. Ballard St
109. Martin St
110. Far Pl
111. Budau Ave
112. Delor Dr
113. Haven St
114. Budau Pl
115. Adkins Ave
116. Newark Ave
117. Mallory St
118. Harmony Ln
119. McPherson Pl
120. Belleglade Ave
121. La Calandria Wy
122. N Dittman Ave
123. Abner St
124. Jade St
125. Del Paso Ave
126. Del Paso Ct
127. Abner St
128. Ronda Dr
129. Adkisson Ave
130. Attrdge Ave
131. Middle Rd
132. Farquhar St
133. Seldner St
134. Marney Ave
135. Drucker St
136. Tim Ave
137. Beatie Pl
138. Lafler Rd
139. Bohlig Rd
140. Cavanagh Cir
141. Shaw Pl
142. Tuller Rd
143. Block Pl
144. Levanda Ave
145. Dobbs St
146. Warwick Ave
147. College Sq Dr
148. Vandalia Ave
149. Terrace Ave
150. Alta Vista Dr
151. Glen View Dr
152. Danzig Pl
153. Jurich St
154. Julep St
155. Avondale Dr

It should come as no surprise that in 1997, Cal State L.A.—located at the intersection of two major freeways, the 10 and 710, in one of the most car-oriented cities in the nation—brought home the gold for its student-built, solar-powered car in Sunrayce 97, a famed North American solar car race.

$ Banks

- **Bank of America** · 2400 W Commonwealth Ave
- **Washington Mutual** · 1305 Fair Oaks Ave
- **Washington Mutual** · 4887 Huntington Dr N

Gas Stations

- **76** · 2551 W Main St
- **76** · 475 S Ave 60
- **Arco** · 3201 W Valley Blvd
- **Arco** · 4860 S Huntington Dr
- **Chevron** · 1535 N Eastern Ave
- **Chevron** · 2500 W Hellman Ave
- **Chevron** · 2600 W Valley Blvd
- **Mobil** · 1600 N Eastern Ave
- **Mobil** · 2601 W Main St
- **Shell** · 4590 Huntington Dr

Libraries

- **Los Angeles Library** · 4990 Huntington Dr S · 323-225-9201

Post Offices

- 3316 N Eastern Ave
- 4875 Huntington Dr

Schools

- **All Saints Catholic School** · 3420 Portola Ave
- **Bushnell Way Elementary** · 5507 Bushnell Way
- **Busy Bees Wonderland School** · 1851 W Imperial Hwy
- **California State University - Los Angeles** · 5151 State University Dr
- **California Technical High School** · 1717 1/2 W Century Blvd
- **El Sereno Elementary** · 3838 Rosemead Ave
- **El Sereno Middle School** · 2839 N Eastern Ave
- **Emery Park Elementary** · 2821 W Commonwealth Ave
- **Farmdale Elementary** · 2660 Fithian Ave
- **Fremont Elementary** · 2001 S Elm St
- **Fremont Elementary** · 3320 Las Palmas Ave
- **Holy Family** · 1301 Rollin St
- **Huntington Drive Elementary** · 4435 Huntington Dr N
- **Institute for Redesign of Learning** · 1955 Fremont Ave
- **LA County High School for the Arts** · 5151 State University Dr
- **Monterey Hills Elementary** · 1624 Via del Rey
- **Multnomah Street Elementary** · 2101 N Indiana St
- **Our Lady of Guadalupe** · 4504 Browne Ave
- **Pacific Christian High School** · 625 Coleman Ave
- **Sierra Park Elementary** · 3170 Budau Ave
- **Sierra Vista Elementary** · 4342 Alpha St
- **South Pasadena Middle School** · 1600 Oak St
- **South Pasadena Senior High School** · 1401 Fremont Ave
- **Stancliff** · 1101 Arroyo Verde Rd
- **Sugar Cone Castle Educational Center** · 3044 W Main St
- **Wilson Senior High School** · 4500 Multnomah St

Supermarkets

- **Albertson's** · 2400 W Commonwealth Ave
- **Food 4 Less** · 4910 Huntington Dr S

1. Hardison Wy
2. Warwick Pl
3. South Ln
4. Hill Dr
5. Los Laureles
6. Oak Crest Ave
7. Mtn View Ave
8. Indiana
9. Martos Dr
10. Gates Pl
11. Alta Vista Cir
12. La Portada
13. Indiana Pl
14. Indiana Ter
15. Portola Ter
16. Temple Ter
17. Cabrillo Villas St
18. Hulbert Ave
19. Los Alisos
20. Hawley Ave
21. Stanford Ter
22. Austin Ter
23. Wilson Summit St
24. Fremont Villas St
25. Catalina ter
26. Marshall Villas St
27. Drake Ter
28. Vallejo Villas St
29. Pacific Aly
30. El Cerrito Cir
31. Hill Ln
32. Meridian Ln
33. Camino Cerrado
34. La Bellorita
35. Glen Pl
36. Spruce St
37. Hunt Ln
38. Gillette Cres
39. Hopewell Ln
40. Beech St
41. Wolford Ln
42. Huntingdon Ln
43. El Tesorito
44. Maple St
45. Maple Wy
46. Elmpark St
47. Hill Ln
48. Valley View Rd
49. Crestlake Ave
50. Garden Homes Ave
51. Richard Circle Dr
52. Remstoy Dr
53. Moffatt St
54. Berkshire Ave
55. Cambridge Pl
56. Atlas St
57. Placer Pl
58. Berkshire
59. Manchester Ave
60. Randolph St
61. Yoakum St
62. Carnegie St
63. Renovo St
64. Hillview Pl
65. Browne Ave
66. Hillsdale Dr
67. Academy St
68. Rosemead Ave
69. Sardon St
70. Beryl St
71. Yorba St
72. Amethyst St
73. Topaz St
74. Dudley Dr
75. Ferntop Dr
76. Cato Wy
77. Waldo Ct
78. Kenneth Dr
79. Jasper St
80. Lynnfield St
81. Carter Dr
82. Betty Dr
83. Edloft St
84. Twining St
85. Grey Dr
86. Minto Ct
87. Paola Ave
88. Fithian Ave
89. Thelma Ave
90. Butterfly Ln
91. Templeton St
92. Castalia Ave
93. Okell Dr
94. Wadena St
95. Hall St
96. Lowell Ave
97. Stockbridge Ave
98. Lakewood Ave
99. Glenridge Ave
100. W Commonwealth Ave
101. Patio Pl
102. Somerset Pl
103. Copeland Pl
104. Hyde St
105. Chadwick Cir
106. Chester St
107. Lynnfield Cir
108. Ballard St
109. Martin St

110. Far Pl
111. Budau Ave
112. Delor Dr
113. Haven St
114. Budau Pl
115. Adkins Ave
116. Newark Ave
117. Mallory St
118. Harmony Ln
119. McPherson Pl
120. Belleglade Ave
121. La Calandria Wy
122. N Dittman Ave
123. Abner St
124. Jade St
125. Del Paso Ave
126. Del Paso Ct
127. Abner St
128. Ronda Dr
129. Adkisson Ave
130. Attrdge Ave
131. Middle Rd
132. Farquhar St
133. Seldner St
134. Marney Ave
135. Drucker St
136. Tim Ave
137. Beatie Pl
138. Lafler Rd
139. Bohlig Rd
140. Cavanagh Cir
141. Shaw Pl
142. Tuller Rd
143. Block Pl
144. Levanda Ave
145. Dobbs St
146. Warwick Ave
147. College Sq Dr
148. Vandalia Ave
149. Terrace Ave
150. Alta Vista Ave
151. Glen View Dr
152. Danzig Pl
153. Jurich Pl
154. Julep Pl
155. Avondale Dr

Among the eclectic group of alumni who have passed through the gates of Cal State University Los Angeles (CSULA) are Billie Jean King, Joseph Wambaugh, Los Angeles District Attorney Steve Cooley, and the famed, diminutive actor Billy Barty.

Coffee

- **Coffee Tea or Me** • 2945 Budau Ave

Hardware Stores

- **Atlas Building Supply** • 4207 Whiteside St • 323-263-3871
- **Newland Hardware** • 4938 Huntington Dr S • 323-227-1933
- **Valley Hardware** • 4757 Valley Blvd • 323-222-9670

Liquor Stores

- **Mickey's Liquor** • 4904 Huntington Dr S
- **Nate's Friendly Liquor Store** • 4412 Huntington Dr S
- **Pete's Liquor Store** • 2639 W Valley Blvd
- **Tropic Liquor** • 210 N Huntington Dr

Pet Stores

- **David's Pet Shop** • 4913 Huntington Dr N • 323-226-9007
- **Petsmart** • 2568 W Commonwealth Ave • 626-284-3390

Video Rental

- **Blockbuster** • 2581 W Commonwealth Ave • 626-576-4550
- **Eastern Video** • 3108 N Eastern Ave • 323-221-3301
- **Legend Entertainment** • 4960 Huntington Dr S • 323-225-9833
- **Neighborhood Video of Alhambra** • 2146 S Fremont Ave • 626-282-6146
- **Rene's Video** • 5380 Huntington Dr S • 323-221-7771
- **Video 4U** • 1689 N Eastern Ave • 323-262-8850

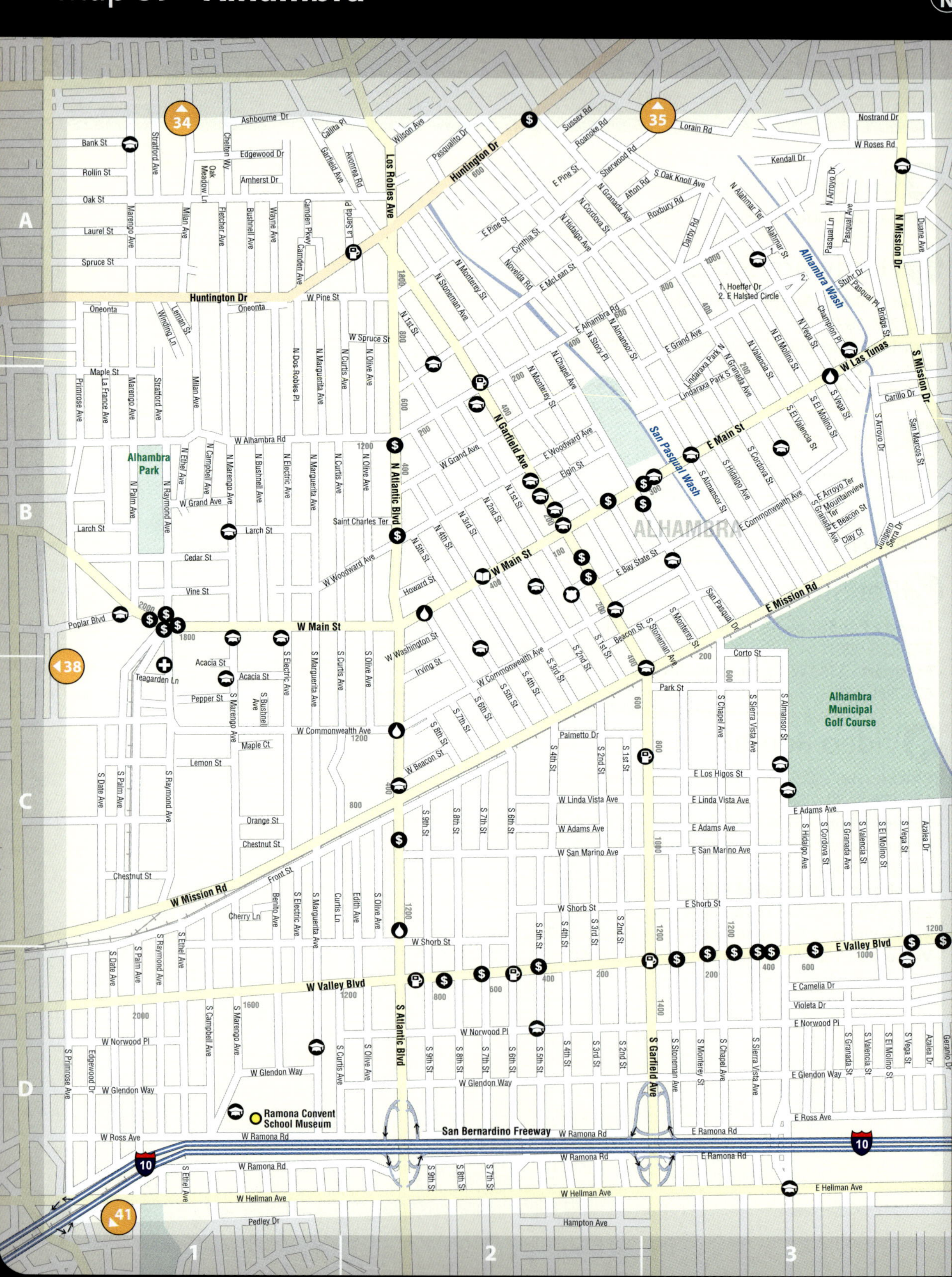

Map 39 • Alhambra
N
34
35
38
41
Alhambra Park
Alhambra Municipal Golf Course
ALHAMBRA
Ramona Convent School Museum
San Bernardino Freeway
Alhambra Wash
San Pasqual Wash

1. Hoeffer Dr
2. E Halsted Circle

Bank St
Rollin St
Oak St
Laurel St
Spruce St
Stratford Ave
Oak Meadow Ln
Chelten Wy
Edgewood Dr
Amherst Dr
Ashbourne Dr
Callita Pl
Garfield Ave
Avonnea Rd
La Senda Pl
Camden Pkwy
Camden Ave
Wayne Ave
Bushnell Ave
Fletcher Ave
Milan Ave
Wilson Ave
Huntington Dr
Los Robles Ave
Pasqualito Dr
Sussex Rd
Roanoke Rd
Sherwood Rd
S Oak Knoll Ave
Afton Rd
Roxbury Rd
Kendall Dr
Lorain Rd
Nostrand Dr
W Roses Rd
N Mission Dr
N Arroyo Dr
Pasqual Ave
Pasqual Ln
Stuhr Dr
N Pasqual Pl Bridge St
Champion Pl
Duane Ave

Huntington Dr
Oneonta
W Pine St
W Spruce St
Oneonta
Leman St
Winding Ln
Maple St
La France Ave
Marengo Ave
Stratford Ave
Milan Ave
Primrose Ave
N Ethel Ave
N Palm Ave
N Campbell Ave
N Raymond Ave
N Marengo Ave
N Bushnell Ave
N Electric Ave
N Marguerita Ave
N Curtis Ave
N Olive Ave
N Dos Robles Pl
N 1st St
N Stoneman Ave
N Monterey St
E Pine St
Cynthia St
Novelda Rd
E McLean St
N Cordova St
N Hidalgo Ave
N Granada Ave
E Alhambra Rd
E Grand Ave
E Woodward Ave
N Story Pl
N Chapel Ave
N Almansor St
N Monterey St
Elgin St
Lindaraxa Park N
Lindaraxa Park S
N El Molino St
N Valencia St
N Granada Ave
N Vega St
Alahmar St
Alahmar Ter
W Las Tunas
S Vega St
S El Molino St
S Hidalgo Ave
S Cordova St
E Main St
E Commonwealth Ave
E Arroyo Ter
Mountainview Ter
E Granada Ave
E Beacon St
Clay Ct
Carillo Dr
S Arroyo Dr
San Marcos St
S Mission Dr
Junipero Serra Dr

Alhambra Park
W Alhambra Rd
W Grand Ave
W Grand Ave
Larch St
Larch St
Saint Charles Ter
Cedar St
Vine St
Poplar Blvd
Teagarden Ln
Acacia St
Pepper St
W Main St
W Woodward Ave
W Main St
Howard St
Irving St
S Electric Ave
S Marguerita Ave
S Curtis Ave
S Olive Ave
S Bushnell Ave
S Marengo Ave
Acacia St
Maple Ct
Lemon St
Orange St
Chestnut St
W Commonwealth Ave
W Washington St
W Beacon St
S 9th St
S 8th St
S 7th St
S 6th St
N 5th St
N 4th St
N 3rd St
N 2nd St
N 1st St
N Garfield Ave
N Atlantic Blvd
W Commonwealth Ave
W Main St
E Bay State St
S 1st St
S 2nd St
S 3rd St
S 4th St
S 5th St
Beacon St
S Stoneman Ave
S Monterey St
San Pasqual Dr
E Mission Rd
Corto St
Park St
Palmetto Dr
S Chapel Ave
S Sierra Vista Ave
S Almansor St
E Los Higos St
E Linda Vista Ave
E Adams Ave
E San Marino Ave
W Linda Vista Ave
W Adams Ave
W San Marino Ave
S 4th St
S 2nd St
S 1st St
Alhambra Municipal Golf Course
S Hidalgo Ave
S Cordova St
S Granada Ave
S Valencia St
S El Molino St
S Vega St
Azalea Dr
E Adams Ave
E Shorb St
W Shorb St
W Shorb St
W Valley Blvd
E Valley Blvd
S Garfield Ave
S Stoneman Ave
S Monterey St
S Chapel Ave
S Sierra Vista Ave
E Camelia Dr
Violeta Dr
E Norwood Pl
E Glendon Way
E Ross Ave
S Granada Ave
S Valencia St
S El Molino St
S Vega St
Azalea Dr
Geraino Dr
Front St
Benito Ave
Cherry Ln
W Mission Rd
S Date Ave
S Palm Ave
S Raymond Ave
S Ethel Ave
S Electric Ave
S Marguerita Ave
Curtis Ln
Edith Ave
S Olive Ave
S Atlantic Blvd
W Valley Blvd
S Campbell Ave
S Marengo Ave
W Norwood Pl
W Glendon Way
W Glendon Way
S Curtis Ave
S Olive Ave
W Norwood Pl
W Glendon Way
S 9th St
S 8th St
S 7th St
S 6th St
S 5th St
S 4th St
S 3rd St
S 2nd St
S Date Ave
S Primrose Ave
Edgewood Dr
W Norwood Pl
W Ross Ave
W Ramona Rd
W Ramona Rd
San Bernardino Freeway
W Ramona Rd
E Ramona Rd
E Ramona Rd
W Hellman Ave
Hampton Ave
Pedley Dr
S Ethel Ave
S 9th St
S 8th St
S 7th St
W Hellman Ave
E Hellman Ave
E Ross Ave

Alhambra is considered the "Gateway to the San Gabriel Valley." The city is essentially a subdivision, having once comprised part of a massive ranch belonging to Don Benito Wilson. The rest of Wilson's humble abode included Pasadena, South Pasadena, and San Marino.

$ Banks

- **American International Bank** · 1881 W Main St
- **Bank of America** · 160 E Main St
- **Bank of America** · 300 N Atlantic Blvd
- **Bank of America** · 444 E Valley Blvd
- **Bank of the West** · 100 S Garfield Ave
- **Bank of the West** · 1833 N Atlantic Blvd
- **Bank of the West** · 331 N Atlantic Blvd
- **Bank of the West** · 855 W Valley Blvd
- **California Bank & Trust** · 230 E Valley Blvd
- **Cathay Bank** · 601 N Atlantic Blvd
- **China Trust Bank USA** · 726 E Valley Blvd
- **Citibank** · 1 W Bay State St
- **East West Bank** · 1881 W Main St
- **East West Bank** · 403 W Valley Blvd
- **East West Bank** · 805 Huntington Dr
- **Far East National Bank** · 105 E Valley Blvd
- **Far East National Bank** · 809 S Atlantic Blvd
- **International Bank of California** · 711 W Valley Blvd
- **Preferred Bank** · 325 E Valley Blvd
- **United Commercial Bank** · 1211 E Valley Blvd
- **Washington Mutual** · 401 E Valley Blvd
- **Wells Fargo Bank** · 123 S Chapel Ave
- **Wells Fargo Bank** · 1421 E Valley Blvd
- **Wells Fargo Bank** · 1910 W Main St
- **Wells Fargo Bank** · 345 E Main St

Car Washes

- **Alhambra Car Wash** · 707 W Main St
- **Atlantic Self-Serve Car Wash** · 1271 S Atlantic Blvd
- **Boulevard Hand Car Wash** · 389 S Atlantic Blvd
- **Butch's Beauty Shine** · 1200 E Main St

Gas Stations

- **76** · 2140 Huntington Dr
- **76** · 601 W Valley Blvd
- **76** · 848 S Garfield Ave
- **Exxon** · 600 N Garfield Ave
- **Mobil** · 1000 W Valley Blvd
- **Shell** · 1401 S Garfield Ave

Hospitals

- **Alhambra Hospital** · 100 S Raymond Ave · 626-570-1606

Landmarks

- **Ramona Convent School Museum** · 1701 W Ramona Rd

Libraries

- **Alhambra Library** · 410 W Main St · 626-570-5008

Police

- **Alhambra Police Dept** · 211 S 1st St · 626-570-5107

Schools

- **A+ Math** · 27 W Main St
- **Alhambra Children Learning Center** · 210 E Main St
- **Alhambra High School** · 101 S 2nd St
- **All Souls Parish School** · 29 S Electric Ave
- **Baldwin Elementary** · 900 S Almansor Ave
- **Brighttood Elementary** · 15 W Alhambra Rd
- **Century High School** · 20 S Marengo Ave
- **Children Montessori Center** · 150 N Garfield Ave
- **Childtime Child Care** · 1418 S Vega St
- **Coolidge Elementary** · 421 N Mission Dr
- **Emmaus Lutheran Church & School** · 840 S Almansor St
- **First Christian Church Education Center** · 220 S 5th St
- **Garfield Adult Education Ctr** · 217 N Garfield Ave
- **Garfield Elementary** · 110 W McLean St
- **Granada Elementary** · 100 S Granada Ave
- **Independence High School** · 217 N Garfield Ave
- **Kumon Math & Reading Center** · 330 S Garfield Ave
- **Leeway School** · 9-1/2 Almansor Ave
- **Love & Care Christian Education Center** · 115 S Marengo Ave
- **Marengo Elementary** · 1400 Marengo Ave
- **Marguerita Elementary** · 1603 S Marguerita Ave
- **Mark Keppel High School** · 501 E Hellman Ave
- **Northrup Elementary** · 409 S Atlantic Blvd
- **Oneonta Montessori** · 2221 Poplar Blvd
- **Park Elementary** · 301 N Marengo Ave
- **Payke Gymnastics Academy** · 107 S Garfield Ave
- **Ramona Convent Secondary** · 1701 W Ramona Rd
- **Ramona Elementary** · 509 W Norwood Pl
- **San Gabriel Valley Academy** · 354 E Main St
- **San Marino Educational Center** · 1300 E Main St
- **St Therese** · 515 N Vega St
- **Triumph Education Center** · 29 N Garfield Center
- **Wonder World Preschool** · 220 S Chapel Ave

Supermarkets

- **Ralph's** · 1745 Garfield Ave
- **Ralph's** · 345 E Main St
- **Super A Foods** · 300 W Main St

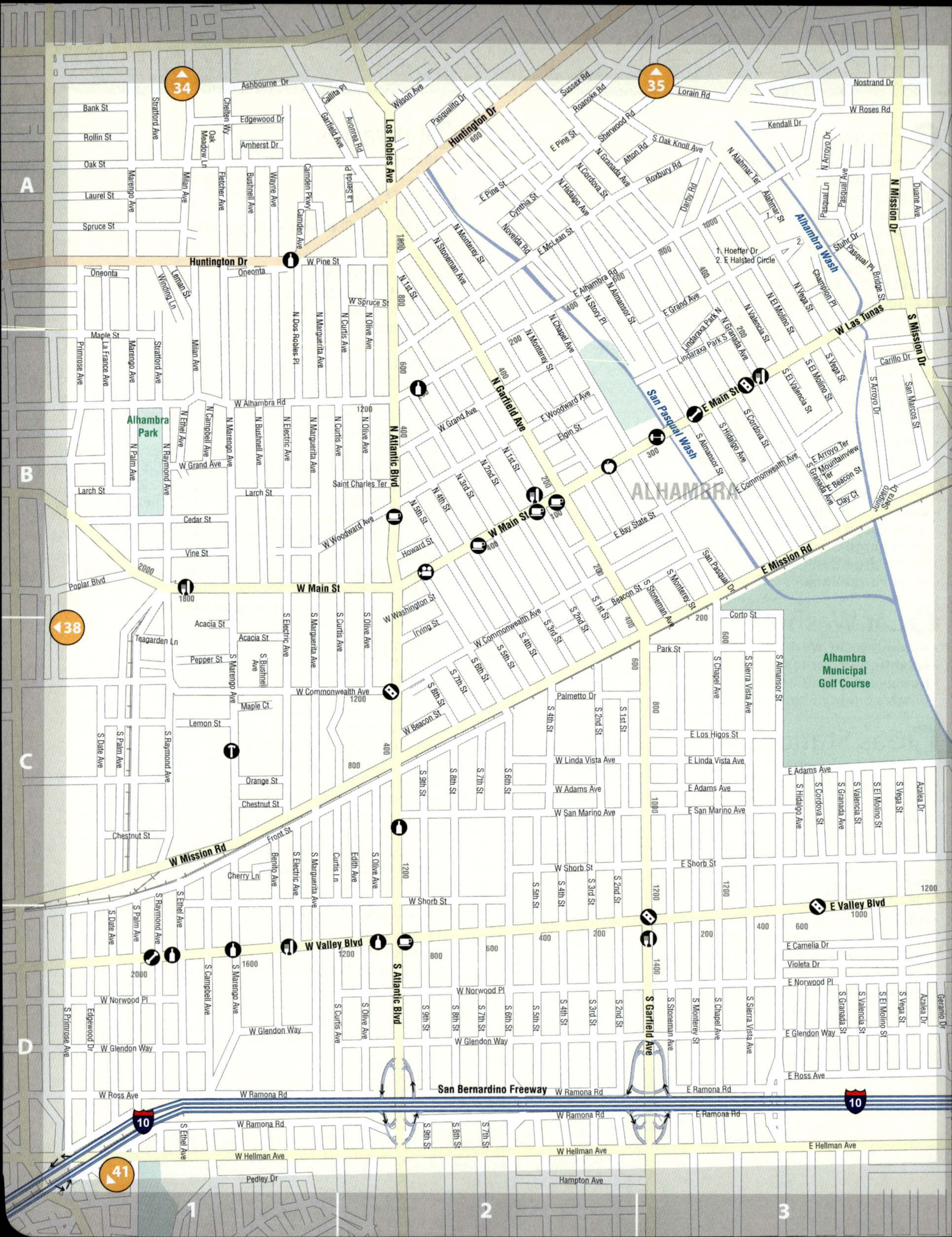

34

35

Ashbourne Dr
Callita Pl
Wilson Ave
Pasqualito Dr
Huntington Dr
Sussex Rd
Roanoke Rd
Lorain Rd
Nostrand Dr

Bank St
Stratford Ave
Chelten Wy
Edgewood Dr
Garfield Ave
Avonrea Rd
La Senda Dr
600
E Pine St
Sherwood Rd
S Oak Knoll Ave
Kendall Dr
W Roses Rd

Rollin St
Oak Meadow Ln
Amherst Dr
Los Robles Ave
E Pine St
N Granada Ave
Afton Rd
Roxbury Rd
Darby Rd
N Arroyo Dr
Pasqual Ter

Oak St
Marengo Ave
Milan Ave
Wayne Ave
Bushnell Ave
Fletcher Ave
Camden Pkwy
Camden Ave
Cynthia St
N Hidalgo Ave
N Cordova St
1000
N Alahmar Ter
Alahmar St
Stuhr Dr
N Mission Dr

A
Laurel St
E McLean St
N Vega St
Alhambra Wash
Duane Ave

Spruce St
Novelda Rd
800
Champion Pl
N Granada Ave
Pasqual Pl Bridge Rd

Oneonta
Huntington Dr
W Pine St
Oneonta
W Spruce St
N 1st St
N Monterey St
N Stoneman Ave
E Alhambra Rd
600
N Story Pl
N Almansor St
E Grand Ave
N Valencia St
N El Molino St
W Las Tunas
S Mission Dr

Lenan St
Winding Ln
N Dos Robles Pl
N Olive Ave
N Curtis Ave
N Marguerita Ave
1800
800
200
N Chapel Ave
400
N Almansor St
Lindaraxa Park N
Lindaraxa Park S
N Granada Ave
200
S El Molino St
Carillo Dr

Maple St
La France Ave
Marengo Ave
Stratford Ave
Milan Ave
400
N Monterey St
E Woodward Ave
E Main St
S El Valencia St
S Vega St
San Marcos St

1. Hoefter Dr
2. E Halsted Circle

Primrose Ave
N Ethel Ave
N Campbell Ave
N Marengo Ave
N Bushnell Ave
N Marguerita Ave
N Curtis Ave
N Olive Ave
1200
W Alhambra Rd
W Grand Ave
N 2nd St
N 1st St
200
Elgin St
E Main St
S Almansor St
S Cordova St
E Arroyo Ter
Mountainview Ter
S Arroyo Dr

B
Alhambra Park
N Palm Ave
N Raymond Ave
W Grand Ave
Larch St
Saint Charles Ter
N 3rd St
N 4th St
200
100
S Hidalgo Ave
E Commonwealth Ave
S Granada Ave
E Beacon St
Clay Ct
Juniperro Serra Dr

Larch St
Cedar St
W Woodward Ave
N 5th St
Howard St
400
W Main St
ALHAMBRA
E Bay State St
San Pasqual Wash

Vine St
2000
S Electric Ave
S Marguerita Ave
S Curtis Ave
S Olive Ave
W Washington St
200
S 2nd St
S 1st St
400
S Monterey St
San Pasqual Dr
E Mission Rd

Poplar Blvd
1800
W Main St
Irving St
W Commonwealth Ave
S 3rd St
S 4th St
Beacon St
S Stoneman Ave
200
Corto St

38
Teagarden Ln
Acacia St
Acacia St
S Marengo Ave
S Bushnell Ave
S 5th St
S 6th St
600
Park St
S Chapel Ave
S Sierra Vista Ave
S Almansor St
Alhambra Municipal Golf Course

Pepper St
Maple Ct
S 7th St
S 8th St
W Commonwealth Ave
1200
W Beacon St
Palmetto Dr
S 4th St
S 2nd St
S 1st St
800
E Los Higos St

Lemon St
S Date Ave
S Palm Ave
S Raymond Ave
400
800
W Linda Vista Ave
E Linda Vista Ave
E Adams Ave
S Hidalgo Ave
S Cordova Ave
S Granada Ave
S Valencia St
S El Molino St
S Vega St
Azalea St

C
Orange St
Chestnut St
S 9th St
S 8th St
S 7th St
S 6th St
W Adams Ave
E Adams Ave
W San Marino Ave
E San Marino Ave

Chestnut St
Front St
W Mission Rd
Benito Ave
S Electric Ave
S Marguerita Ave
Curtis Ln
Edith Ave
S Olive Ave
1200
W Shorb St
E Shorb St

Cherry Ln
W Shorb St
S 5th St
S 4th St
S 3rd St
S 2nd St
1200
1200
E Valley Blvd
1000
1200

S Date Ave
S Palm Ave
S Ethel Ave
S Raymond Ave
W Valley Blvd
1200
1400
200
400
600
E Camelia Dr

2000
1600
S Campbell Ave
S Marengo Ave
800
600
400
200
200
Violeta Dr
E Norwood Pl

W Norwood Pl
W Glendon Way
S Curtis Ave
S Olive Ave
W Norwood Pl
S 9th St
S 8th St
S 7th St
S 6th St
S 5th St
S 4th St
S 3rd St
S 2nd St
S Garfield Ave
S Stoneman Ave
S Monterey St
S Chapel Ave
S Sierra Vista Ave
S Granada St
S Valencia St
S El Molino St
S Vega St
E Glendon Way

D
S Primrose Ave
Edgewood Dr
W Glendon Way
E Ross Ave

W Ross Ave
W Ramona Rd
San Bernardino Freeway
W Ramona Rd
E Ramona Rd
Geranio Dr

I-10
S Ethel Ave
W Ramona Rd
S 9th St
S 8th St
S 7th St
W Ramona Rd
E Ramona Rd
I-10

W Hellman Ave
W Hellman Ave
E Hellman Ave

41
Pedley Dr
Hampton Ave

1
2
3

Don't miss Fosselman's Ice Cream Parlor. Their ice cream has been made in a back room on the premises for more than seventy years. What's Fosselman's secret? 16 percent butterfat. Yikes! But every calorie is worth it.

 ## Coffee

- **Coffee Bean & Tea Leaf** • 9 E Main St
- **I Browse Coffee** • 11 W Main St
- **Starbucks** • 101 W Main St
- **Starbucks** • 141 N Atlantic Blvd
- **Valley Tea & Coffee** • 1101 W Valley Blvd

 ## Farmer's Markets

- **Alhambra** • S Monterey St & Main St • Sun 8:30-1

Gyms

- **LA Fitness Sports Clubs** • 412 E Main St • 626-299-5980

Hardware Stores

- **Home Depot** • 500 S Marengo Ave • 626-458-9800

Liquor Stores

- **Lee's Liquor Store** • 1152 W Valley Blvd
- **Marengo Liquor** • 1700 W Valley Blvd
- **Mitchell's Liquor Store** • 2020 W Valley Blvd
- **Ocean Liquor Store** • 2005 Huntington Dr
- **Super Store** • 320 W Alhambra Rd

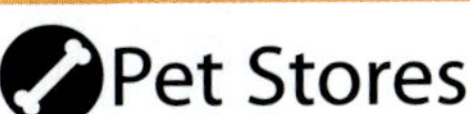 ## Movie Theaters

- **Edwards Atlantic Cinemas** • 700 W Main St

Pet Stores

- **McCormick's Pet Emporium** • 644 E Main St • 626-289-4393

Restaurants

- **Angelo's Italian Restaurant** • 1540 W Valley Blvd • 626-282-6533
- **Cuban Bistro** • 28 W Main St • 626-308-3350
- **Fosselman's Ice Cream Parlor** • 1824 W Main St • 626-282-6533
- **MPV Seafood** • 1412 S Garfield Ave • 626-289-3018
- **Wahib's Middle East** • 910 E Main St • 626-576-1048

Video Rental

- **99 Thai Video** • 24 W Valley Blvd • 626-300-8361
- **Hollywood Video** • 701 E Main St • 626-308-3427
- **Video 101** • 1100 W Commonwealth Ave • 626-308-3883

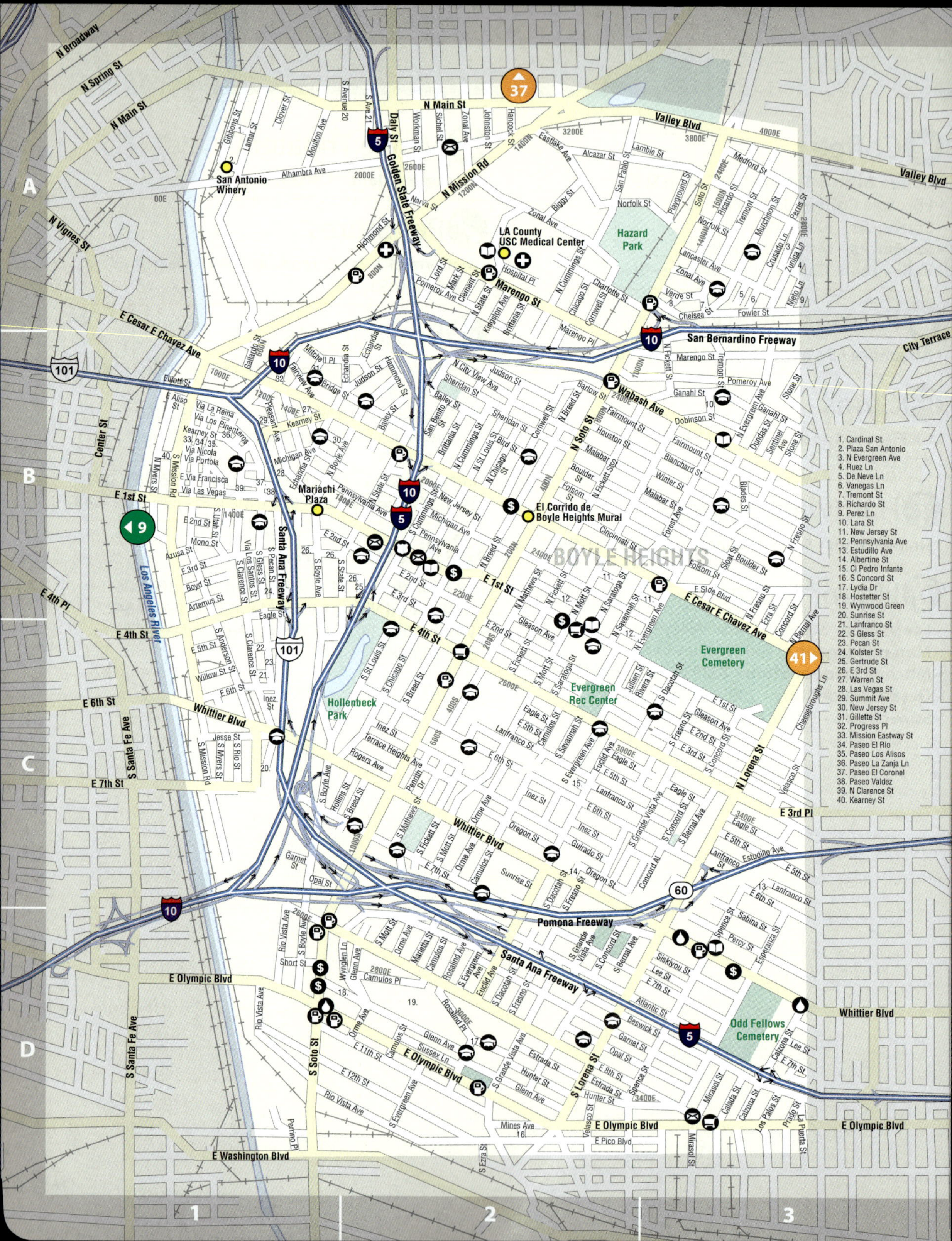

BOYLE HEIGHTS
San Antonio Winery
LA County USC Medical Center
Hazard Park
Mariachi Plaza
El Corrido de Boyle Heights Mural
Evergreen Cemetery
Evergreen Rec Center
Hollenbeck Park
Odd Fellows Cemetery
Los Angeles River
Golden State Freeway
San Bernardino Freeway
Santa Ana Freeway
Pomona Freeway
N Main St
Valley Blvd
N Mission Rd
Marengo St
E Cesar E Chavez Ave
Wabash Ave
E 1st St
E 4th St
Whittier Blvd
E Olympic Blvd
E Washington Blvd
N Lorena St
S Soto St
N Soto St
E 3rd Pl
City Terrace
1. Cardinal St
2. Plaza San Antonio
3. N Evergreen Ave
4. Ruez Ln
5. De Neve Ln
6. Vanegas Ln
7. Tremont St
8. Richardo St
9. Perez Ln
10. Lara St
11. New Jersey St
12. Pennsylvania Ave
13. Estudillo Ave
14. Albertine St
15. Cl Pedro Infante
16. S Concord St
17. Lydia Dr
18. Hostetter St
19. Wynwood Green
20. Sunrise St
21. Lanfranco St
22. S Gless St
23. Pecan St
24. Kolster St
25. Gertrude St
26. E 3rd St
27. Warren St
28. Las Vegas St
29. Summit Ave
30. New Jersey St
31. Gillette St
32. Progress Pl
33. Mission Eastway St
34. Paseo El Rio
35. Paseo Los Alisos
36. Paseo La Zanja Ln
37. Paseo El Coronel
38. Paseo Valdez
39. N Clarence St
40. Kearney St
A
B
C
D
1
2
3

Mariachi Plaza is exactly what its name implies: a public gathering place where mariachis can show off their stuff and book future performances. This is the place to come if you're looking for authentic entertainment for your next fiesta. It's also worth checking out some of the murals near the corner of Cesar Chavez Ave. and Soto Street.

$ Banks

- **Bank of America** · 1308 S Soto St
- **Bank of America** · 2305 E Cesar E Chavez Ave
- **Bank of America** · 3475 Whittier Blvd
- **US Bank** · 2708 E 1st St
- **Washington Mutual** · 1350 S Soto St
- **Washington Mutual** · 2301 E 1st St

Car Washes

- **Bob's Hand Car Wash** · 3629 Whittier Blvd
- **Olympic Car Wash** · 2740 E Olympic Blvd
- **Tio Car Wash** · 3442 Whittier Blvd

Gas Stations

- **76** · 1171 S Soto St
- **76** · 1848 Marengo St
- **Arco** · 3401 Whittier Blvd
- **Arco** · 401 S Soto St
- **Chevron** · 1101 N Mission Rd
- **Exxon** · 2740 E Olympic Blvd
- **Exxon** · 2925 E Cesar E Chavez Ave
- **Mobil** · 1010 N Soto St
- **Mobil** · 1166 S Soto St
- **Shell** · 1203 N Soto St
- **Shell** · 1410 S Soto St
- **Shell** · 1900 E Cesar E Chavez Ave
- **Texaco** · 3154 E Olympic Blvd

Hospitals

- **LA County USC Medical Center** · 1200 N State St
- **Los Angeles County Women's Hospital** · 1240 N Mission Rd · 323-226-3054

Landmarks

- **El Corrido de Boyle Heights Mural** · 2336 E Cesar E Chavez Ave
- **LA County USC Medical Center** · 1200 N State St
- **Mariachi Plaza** · Boyle Ave & First St
- **San Antonio Winery** · 737 Lamar St

Libraries

- **Benjamin Franklin Library** · 2200 E 1st St · 323-263-6901
- **Hinomoto Library** · 129 N Saratoga St · 323-261-3300
- **Los Angeles Library** · 803 Spence St · 323-268-4710
- **Malabar Library** · 2801 Wabash Ave · 323-263-1497
- **Nursing Library** · 1200 N State St · 323-226-4923

Police

- **Los Angeles Police Dept** · 2111 E 1st St · 213-485-2949

Post Offices

- 2016 E 1st St
- 2425 Alhambra Ave
- 3641 E 8th St

Schools

- **1st Street Elementary** · 2820 E 1st St
- **Assumption** · 3016 Winter St
- **Breed Street Elementary** · 2226 E 3rd St
- **Bridge Street Elementary** · 605 N Boyle Ave
- **Dacotah Street Combination Ctr** · 3142 Lydia Dr
- **Dena Elementary** · 1314 Dacotah St
- **Dolores Mission Elementary** · 170 S Gless St
- **East LA Light and Life School** · 207 Dacotah St
- **Euclid Ave Elementary** · 806 Euclid Ave
- **Evergreen Avenue Elementary** · 2730 Ganahl St
- **First Street Elementary** · 2820 E 1st St
- **Hollenbeck Middle School** · 2510 E 6th St
- **Lorena St Elementary** · 1015 S Lorena St
- **Malabar St Elementary** · 3200 Malabar St
- **Murchison Street Elementary** · 1501 Murchison St
- **Our Lady of the Rosary of Talp** · 411 S Evergreen Ave
- **Resurrection** · 3360 E Opal St
- **San Antonio De Padua** · 1500 Bridge St
- **Santa Isabel Elementary** · 2424 Whittier Blvd
- **Santa Teresita** · 2646 Zonal Ave
- **Second St Elementary** · 1942 E 2nd St
- **Sheridan St Elementary** · 416 Cornwell St
- **Soto Street Children's Ctr** · 2616 E 7th St
- **Soto Street Elementary** · 1020 S Soto St
- **St Mary's Catholic Elementary** · 416 S St Louis St
- **Sunrise Elementary** · 2821 E 7th St
- **Theodore Roosevelt Senior High School** · 456 S Mathews St
- **Utah Street Elementary** · 255 N Clarence St
- **White Memorial Adventist** · 1605 New Jersey St

Supermarkets

- **Food 4 Less** · 2750 E 1st St
- **Food 4 Less** · 3654 E Olympic Blvd
- **Super A Foods** · 425 S Soto St

BOYLE HEIGHTS

1. Cardinal St
2. Plaza San Antonio
3. N Evergreen Ave
4. Ruez Ln
5. De Neve Ln
6. Vanegas Ln
7. Tremont St
8. Richardo St
9. Perez Ln
10. Lara St
11. New Jersey St
12. Pennsylvania Ave
13. Estudillo Ave
14. Albertine St
15. Cl Pedro Infante
16. S Concord St
17. Lydia Dr
18. Hostetter St
19. Wynwood Green
20. Sunrise St
21. Lanfranco St
22. S Gless St
23. Pecan St
24. Kolster St
25. Gertrude St
26. E 3rd St
27. Warren St
28. Las Vegas St
29. Summit Ave
30. New Jersey St
31. Gillette St
32. Progress Pl
33. Mission Eastway St
34. Paseo El Rio
35. Paseo Los Alisos
36. Paseo La Zanja Ln
37. Paseo El Coronel
38. Paseo Valdez
39. N Clarence St
40. Kearney St

There may be no better area for Mexican food in all of L.A. Be sure to visit some of the local bakeries for pan dulce, and dinner at La Serenata de Garibaldi alone is worth the trip.

Hardware Stores

- **Eastside Hardware Supply** · 3008 Whittier Blvd · 323-261-3357
- **Mena's Plumbing & Hardware** · 3109 Wabash Ave · 323-262-3879
- **Moe's Hardware Store** · 3044 Wabash Ave · 323-268-0824

Liquor Stores

- **Amigo Liquor** · 3124 E 4th St
- **B & G Liquors** · 1529 E 1st St
- **Beverage Center** · 2121 Whittier Blvd
- **Brooklyn Liquor Store** · 2101 E Cesar E Chavez Ave
- **J T Ramirez Market** · 736 S Soto St
- **Major Liquor Stores** · 2335 E 1st St
- **Regency Liquor** · 1260 S Soto St
- **S & M Liquor Store** · 3000 N Main St
- **Triple M Liquor & Delicatessen** · 2910 Marengo St

Pet Stores

- **E & M Pet Shop** · 2011 E 1st St · 323-728-8390
- **Elias Pet Shop** · 2500 E Cesar E Chavez Ave · 323-263-3138
- **Happy Pets** · 2011 E 1st St · 323-265-3614
- **VIP Pet Shop** · 305 N Soto St · 323-266-1166

Restaurants

- **Barbara's at the Brewery** · Brewery Art Complex, 620 Moulton Ave · 323-221-9204
- **El Tepeyac** · 812 N Evergreen Ave · 323-267-8668
- **La Parrilla** · 2126 E Cesar E Chavez Ave · 323-262-3434
- **La Serenata de Garibaldi** · 1842 E 1st St · 323-265-2887

Video Rental

- **66 Video** · 2916 E Cesar E Chavez Ave · 323-260-7415
- **John Juan Video** · 1405 Murchison St · 323-222-4853
- **Joyce's Videos** · 2830 Wabash Ave · 323-261-5385
- **S & S Video (Spanish)** · 3358 E Olympic Blvd · 323-780-3981
- **Sixty Six Video** · 2609 N Main St · 323-225-2876
- **Tele-Video** · 2191 Whittier Blvd · 323-262-3735
- **Video Century** · 919 S Soto St · 323-262-5003
- **Video Express** · 305 N Soto St · 323-261-3383
- **Wabash Video** · 3083 Wabash Ave · 323-526-9956

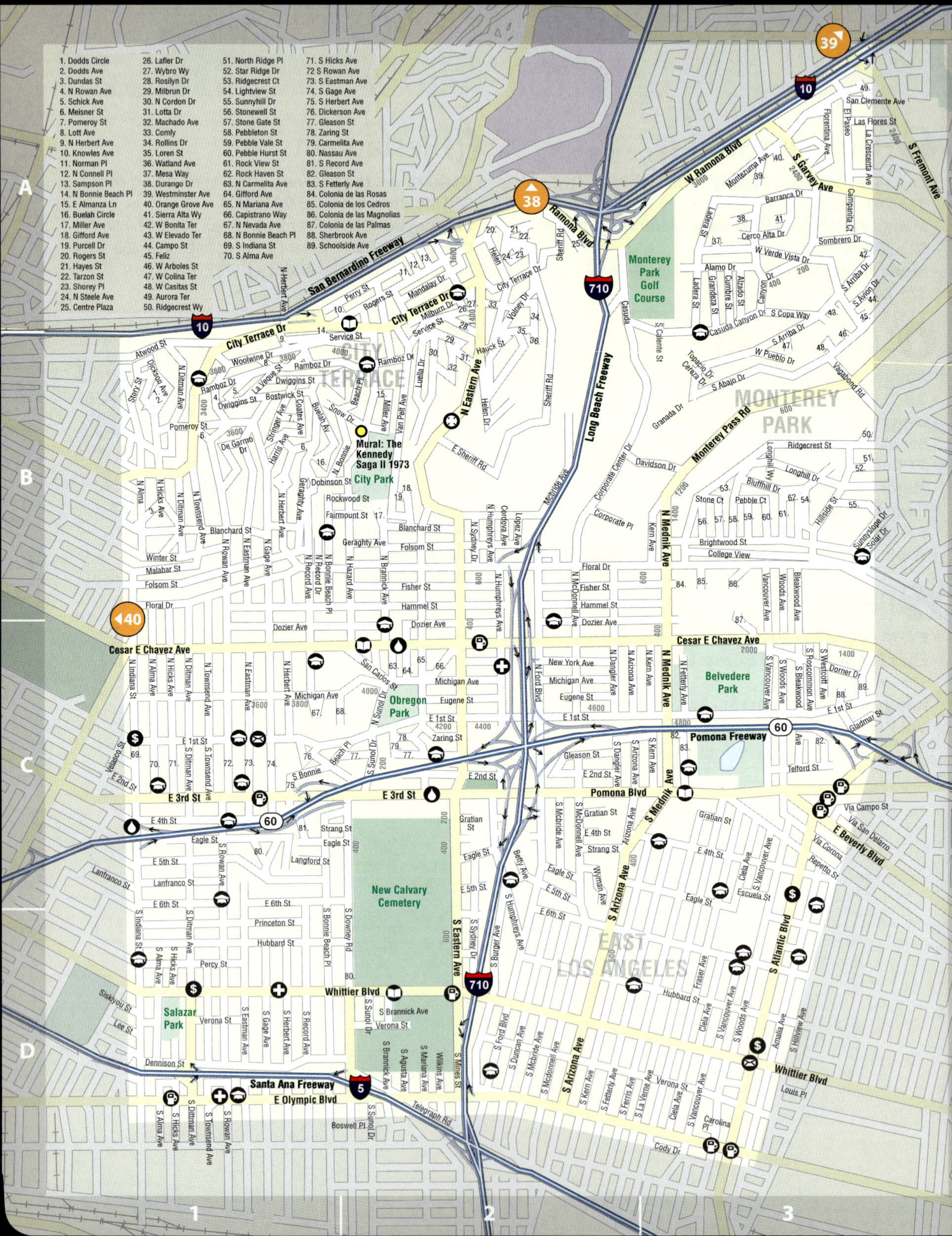
1. Dodds Circle
2. Dodds Ave
3. Dundas St
4. N Rowan Ave
5. Schick Ave
6. Meisner St
7. Pomeroy St
8. Lott Ave
9. N Herbert Ave
10. Knowles Ave
11. Norman Pl
12. N Connell Pl
13. Sampson Pl
14. N Bonnie Beach Pl
15. E Almanza Ln
16. Buelah Circle
17. Miller Ave
18. Gifford Ave
19. Purcell Dr
20. Rogers St
21. Hayes St
22. Tarzon St
23. Shorey Pl
24. N Steele Ave
25. Centre Plaza
26. Lafler Dr
27. Wybro Wy
28. Rosilyn Dr
29. Milbrun Dr
30. N Cordon Dr
31. Lotta Dr
32. Machado Ave
33. Comly
34. Rollins Dr
35. Loren St
36. Watland Ave
37. Mesa Way
38. Durango Dr
39. Westminster Ave
40. Orange Grove Ave
41. Sierra Alta Wy
42. W Bonita Ter
43. W Elevado Ter
44. Campo St
45. Feliz
46. W Arboles St
47. W Colina Ter
48. W Casitas St
49. Aurora Ter
50. Ridgecrest Wy
51. North Ridge Pl
52. Star Ridge Dr
53. Ridgecrest Ct
54. Lightview St
55. Sunnyhill Dr
56. Stonewell St
57. Stone Gate St
58. Pebbleton St
59. Pebble Vale St
60. Pebble Hurst St
61. Rock View St
62. Rock Haven St
63. N Carmelita Ave
64. Gifford Ave
65. N Mariana Ave
66. Capistrano Way
67. N Nevada Ave
68. N Bonnie Beach Pl
69. S Indiana St
70. S Alma Ave
71. S Hicks Ave
72. S Rowan Ave
73. S Eastman Ave
74. S Gage Ave
75. S Herbert Ave
76. Dickerson Ave
77. Gleason St
78. Zaring St
79. Carmelita Ave
80. Nassau Ave
81. S Record Ave
82. Gleason St
83. S Fetterly Ave
84. Colonia de las Rosas
85. Colonia de los Cedros
86. Colonia de las Magnolias
87. Colonia de las Palmas
88. Sherbrook Ave
89. Schoolside Ave
CITY TERRACE
MONTEREY PARK
EAST LOS ANGELES
San Bernardino Freeway
Long Beach Freeway
Pomona Freeway
Santa Ana Freeway
City Terrace Dr
Cesar E Chavez Ave
E 3rd St
Pomona Blvd
Whittier Blvd
E Olympic Blvd
W Ramona Blvd
S Garvey Ave
Monterey Pass Rd
N Eastern Ave
S Eastern Ave
S Atlantic Blvd
E Beverly Blvd
S Arizona Ave
N Mednik Ave
Monterey Park Golf Course
City Park
Mural: The Kennedy Saga II 1973
Obregon Park
Belvedere Park
New Calvary Cemetery
Salazar Park
A
B
C
D
1
2
3

The Anthony Quinn Library may be the only public library in the world with an extensive collection of memorabilia pertaining to the late actor, whose childhood home once stood on the ground the library now occupies. Quinn may have been best known for "Zorba the Greek," but the Mexican-born actor was a transplant to East L.A.

$ Banks

- **Bank of America** · 941 S Atlantic Blvd
- **Citibank** · 3479 E 1st St
- **Washington Mutual** · 459 S Atlantic Blvd
- **Wells Fargo Bank** · 3800 Whittier Blvd

Car Washes

- **Al's Auto Spa Car Wash** · 3585 E 4th St
- **Ricky's Hand Car Wash** · 4247 E 3rd St
- **Romero Car Wash** · 4141 E Cesar E Chavez Ave

Gas Stations

- **76** · 300 S Atlantic Blvd
- **76** · 3860 E 3rd St
- **76** · 5200 E Olympic Blvd
- **Chevron** · 250 S Atlantic Blvd
- **Exxon** · 5050 E Olympic Blvd
- **Mobil** · 301 S Atlantic Blvd
- **Shell** · 326 S Atlantic Blvd
- **Shell** · 3965 E Olympic Blvd
- **Shell** · 4357 E Cesar E Chavez Ave
- **Shell** · 4411 Whittier Blvd

Hospitals

- **East LA Doctors Hospital** · 4060 Whittier Blvd · 323-268-5514
- **Los Angeles Community Hospital** · 4081 E Olympic Blvd · 323-267-0477
- **Santa Marta Hospital** · 319 N Humphreys Ave · 323-266-6500

Landmarks

- **Mural: The Kennedy Saga II 1973 (City Terrace Park)** · 1126 N Hazard Ave

Libraries

- **Anthony Quinn Library** · 3965 E Cesar E Chavez Ave · 323-264-7715
- **East Los Angeles Library** · 4801 E 3rd St · 323-264-0155
- **El Camino Real Library** · 4264 Whittier Blvd · 323-269-8102
- **Los Angeles County Library** · 4025 City Terrace Dr · 323-261-0295

Post Offices

- 3729 E 1st St
- 975 S Atlantic Blvd

Schools

- **An-An Child Care** · 2725 W Ramona Rd
- **Apostolic Christian Academy** · 4818 E Hubbard St
- **Belvedere Elementary** · 3724 E 1st St
- **Belvedere Middle School** · 312 N Record Ave
- **Bene Preschool** · 2421 W Jefferson Blvd
- **Brightwood Elementary** · 1701 Brightwood St
- **City Terrace Elementary** · 4350 City Terrace Dr
- **Eastman Ave Elementary** · 4112 E Olympic Blvd
- **Ford Boulevard Elementary** · 1112 S Ford Blvd
- **Fourth Street Elementary** · 420 Amalia Ave
- **Garfield Community Adult** · 5101 E 6th St
- **Garfield Community Adult** · 831 N Bonnie Beach Pl
- **Garfield Senior High School** · 5101 E 6th St
- **Griffith Middle School** · 4765 E 4th St
- **Hamasaki Elementary** · 4865 E 1st St
- **Hammel Street Elementary** · 438 N Brannick Ave
- **Harrison Street Elementary** · 3529 City Terrace Dr
- **Humphreys Ave Elementary** · 500 S Humphreys Ave
- **Kennedy Elementary** · 4010 E Ramboz Dr
- **Marianna Ave Elementary** · 4215 Gleason St
- **Monterey Continuation** · 466 S Fraser St
- **Monterey Highlands Elementary** · 400 Casuda Canyon Dr
- **Our Lady of Lourdes** · 315 S Eastman Ave
- **Our Lady of Soledad** · 4545 Dozier St
- **Ramona High School** · 231 S Alma Ave
- **Rowan Ave Elementary** · 600 S Rowan Ave
- **Soledad Enrichment Action** · 204 Hampton Dr
- **Soledad Enrichment Action** · 3763 E 4th St
- **St Alphonsus** · 552 Amalia Ave
- **Stevenson Middle School** · 725 S Indiana St

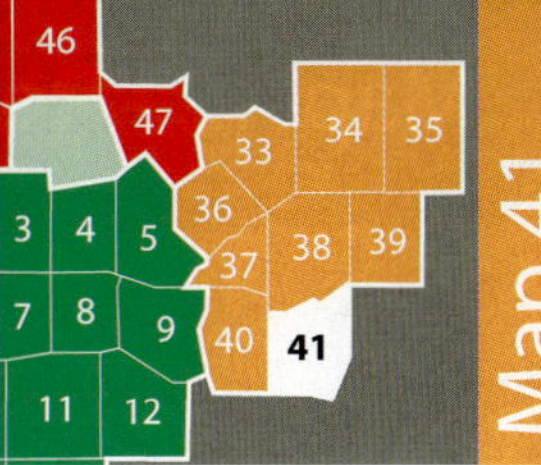

Feel like goin' fishin'? Look no further than the pond at Belvedere Park, located just north of Pomona Blvd. on Vancouver Avenue.

Clubs

- **Hi D Hi** · 4952 Whittier Blvd · 323-266-3821

Hardware Stores

- **Brooklyn Hardware** · 3734 E Cesar E Chavez Ave · 323-264-6260
- **DJK Hardware** · 1012 S Atlantic Blvd · 323-269-8375
- **Don's Hardware & Plumbing** · 4655 E Olympic Blvd · 323-261-5166
- **Eddie Dillen Hardware** · 4615 Whittier Blvd · 323-269-3126
- **Indiana Home Supply** · 944 S Indiana St · 323-265-2008
- **Laguna Park Hardware** · 3948 Whittier Blvd · 323-263-1044
- **Loveday Lumber** · 500 N Ford Blvd · 323-269-9591

Liquor Stores

- **Andy's Liquor** · 4312 E Cesar E Chavez Ave
- **Atlantic Liquors** · 1010 S Atlantic Blvd
- **Ayutla Liquor** · 3548 E 1st St
- **Eddie's Drive-In Liquor Store** · 5024 Whittier Blvd
- **Green Mill Liquor** · 3812 Whittier Blvd
- **John's Liquor** · 405 S Indiana St
- **Lim Fung Liquor** · 3563 E Cesar E Chavez Ave
- **Paco's Liquor** · 5048 E 3rd St
- **Pueblo Liquor** · 4600 Whittier Blvd
- **Safety Liquor Stores** · 4635 Whittier Blvd
- **Salud Market** · 625 N Mednik Ave
- **Sam's Liquor Store** · 3984 Whittier Blvd
- **Sportsman Liquor Store** · 3918 1/4 City Terrace Dr
- **T & H Liquor** · 460 S Atlantic Blvd
- **T & S Liquor** · 4530 Whittier Blvd
- **Victoria's Liquor Market** · 3882 E 1st St
- **Winn's Liquor Store** · 4048 E Olympic Blvd
- **Zozaya Market & Liquor** · 116 N Rowan Ave

Pet Stores

- **Bob's Tropical Fish** · 234 S Atlantic Blvd · 323-261-6675
- **Gonzalez's Pet Shop** · 4131 E Cesar E Chavez Ave · 323-262-1008
- **Jesse's Pet Shop** · 3875 Whittier Blvd · 323-262-7947
- **Lorena's Pet Shop** · 3536 E Cesar E Chavez Ave · 323-261-7556
- **Pet Shop Casa Galleros** · 4516 E Cesar E Chavez Ave · 323-780-5811

Video Rental

- **20-20 Video** · 4975 Whittier Blvd · 323-266-0202
- **AJ Video** · 3864 E Cesar E Chavez Ave · 323-268-3539
- **Cool Video** · 3545 E 1st St · 323-269-4122
- **Ecumex Video** · 3757 E 1st St · 323-269-2972
- **JC Video Superstore** · 283 S Atlantic Blvd · 323-266-1055
- **Nancy's Video** · 715 1/2 S Atlantic Blvd · 323-268-5849
- **Sonia's Fashions & Video Rents** · 4308 E Cesar E Chavez Ave · 323-268-5785
- **Video Camacho** · 710 N Eastern Ave · 323-268-5057
- **Video Vision** · 5209 E Olympic Blvd · 323-268-1722
- **Videoland** · 3857 Whittier Blvd · 323-266-2553
- **Videopolis** · 3918 E Olympic Blvd · 323-264-0366

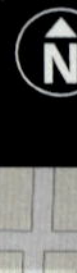

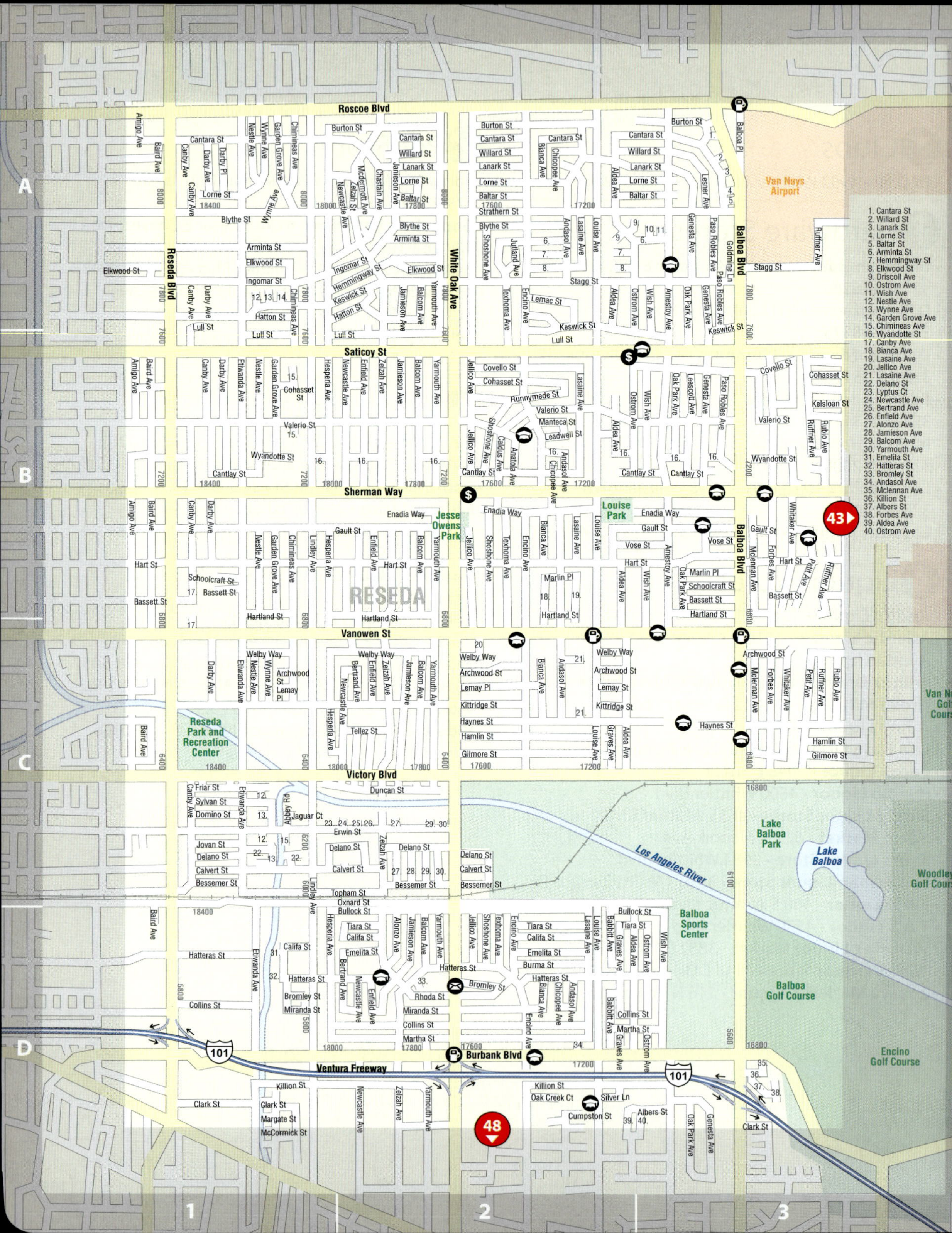

A B C D
1 2 3

Reseda lies in the heart of the San Fernando Valley. Tom Petty sang of the neighborhood in "Free Fallin'," its biggest claim to fame and what most endears it to the locals—at least, those locals who listen to classic rock.

 Banks

- **Nara Bank** · 17639 Sherman Way
- **Washington Mutual** · 17204 Saticoy St

Gas Stations

- **76** · 17300 Vanowen St
- **Shell** · 17660 Burbank Blvd
- **Shell** · 6801 Balboa Blvd
- **Texaco** · 16930 Roscoe Blvd

Post Offices

- 5805 White Oak Ave

Schools

- **Anatola Avenue Elementary** · 7364 Anatola Ave
- **Balboa Pre-School and Kindergarten** · 16836 Sherman Way
- **Bethel Lutheran Elementary** · 17500 Burbank Blvd
- **Beverly Christian School** · 345 S Woods Ave
- **Birmingham Senior High School** · 17000 Haynes St
- **Emelita Elementary** · 17931 Hatteras St
- **Gault Street Elementary** · 17000 Gault St
- **Independence Continuation** · 6501 Balboa Blvd
- **Lemay Street Elementary** · 17520 Vanowen St
- **Mulholland Middle School** · 17120 Vanowen St
- **St Bridget of Sweden** · 16711 Gault St
- **Stagg Street Elementary** · 7839 Amestoy Ave
- **The Community School** · 17216 Saticoy St
- **The Fairfield School** · 16945 Sherman Way
- **Valley Magnet School** · 6701 Balboa Blvd
- **Westmark School** · 5461 Louise Ave

Supermarkets

- **Ralph's** · 17250 Saticoy St
- **Trader Joe's** · 17640 Burbank Blvd

N

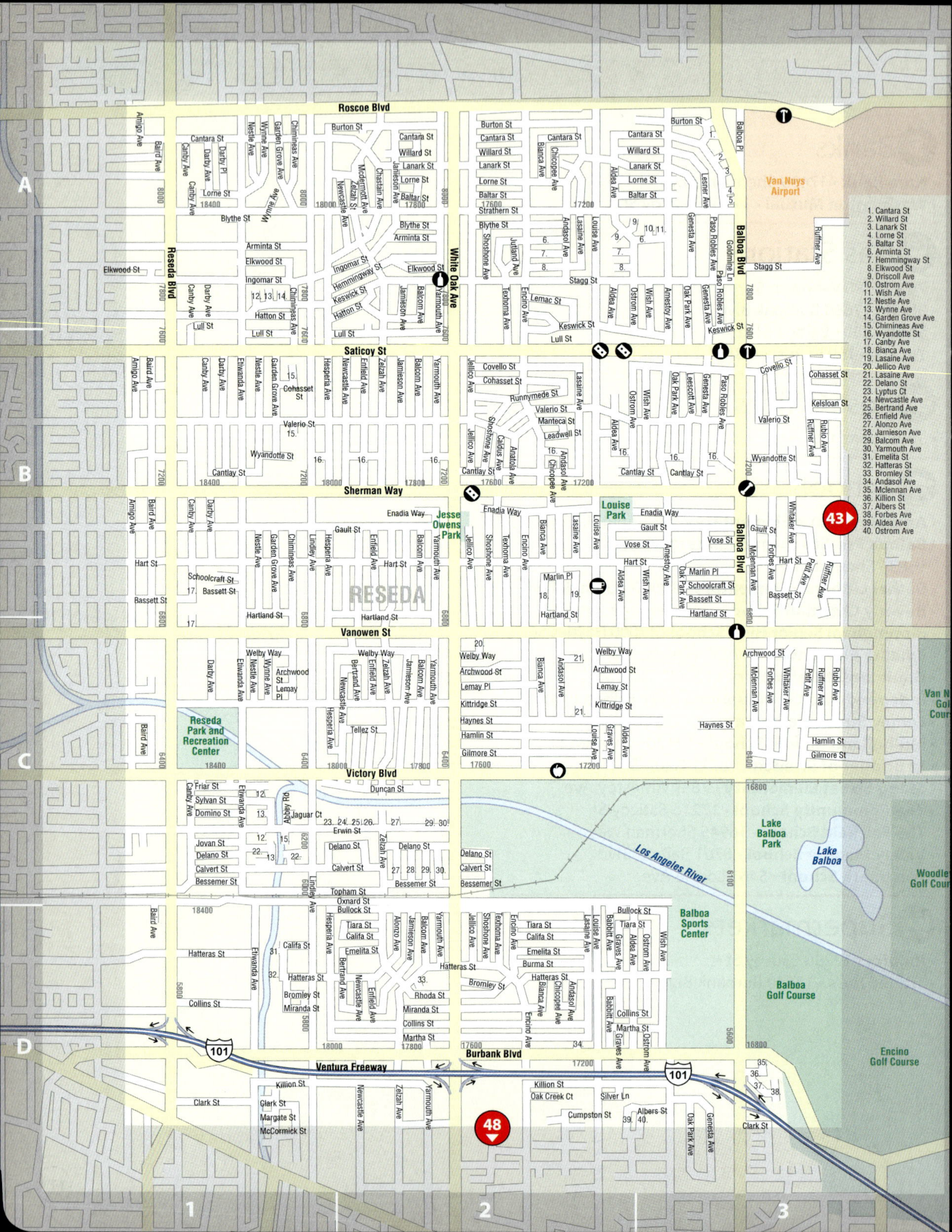

Van Nuys Airport

Roscoe Blvd
Saticoy St
Sherman Way
Vanowen St
Victory Blvd
Ventura Freeway
Burbank Blvd

Reseda Blvd
White Oak Ave
Balboa Blvd
Amigo Ave
Baird Ave

RESEDA

Jesse Owens Park
Louise Park
Reseda Park and Recreation Center
Balboa Sports Center

Los Angeles River
Lake Balboa Park
Lake Balboa
Balboa Golf Course
Van Nuys Golf Course
Woodley Golf Course
Encino Golf Course

101

1. Cantara St
2. Willard St
3. Lanark St
4. Lorne St
5. Baltar St
6. Arminta St
7. Hemmingway St
8. Elkwood St
9. Driscoll Ave
10. Ostrom Ave
11. Wish Ave
12. Nestle Ave
13. Wynne Ave
14. Garden Grove Ave
15. Chimineas Ave
16. Wyandotte St
17. Canby Ave
18. Bianca Ave
19. Lasaine Ave
20. Jellico Ave
21. Lasaine Ave
22. Delano St
23. Lyptus Ct
24. Newcastle Ave
25. Bertrand Ave
26. Enfield Ave
27. Alonzo Ave
28. Jamieson Ave
29. Balcom Ave
30. Yarmouth Ave
31. Emelita St
32. Hatteras St
33. Bromley St
34. Andasol Ave
35. Mclennan Ave
36. Killion St
37. Albers St
38. Forbes Ave
39. Aldea Ave
40. Ostrom Ave

43
48

Lake Balboa Park makes for a lovely place to spend a weekend day. Rent a paddleboat and work your way across the lake; or grab a fishing rod—the lake is stocked regularly by the Department of Fish and Game. The park is surrounded by three golf courses, and is home to the Valley Jazz Festival.

Coffee
- **Kona Specialties** · 6956 Louise Ave

Farmer's Markets
- **Encino** · 17400 Victory Blvd · Sun 8-1

Hardware Stores
- **Home Depot** · 16810 Roscoe Blvd · 818-786-9600
- **Spectra Paint Center** · 7615 Balboa Blvd · 818-786-5610

Liquor Stores
- **Dale's Junior Stores** · 16925 Vanowen St
- **Wine & Liquor Depot** · 16938 Saticoy St

Pet Stores
- **Quality Pet Shop** · 7225 Balboa Blvd · 818-343-7211

Restaurants
- **Amber's Chicken Kitchen** · 16900 Burbank Blvd · 818-995-3200

Video Rental
- **Blockbuster** · 17288 Saticoy St · 818-342-8835
- **Western Video (Korean)** · 17639 Sherman Way · 818-708-2496

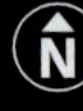

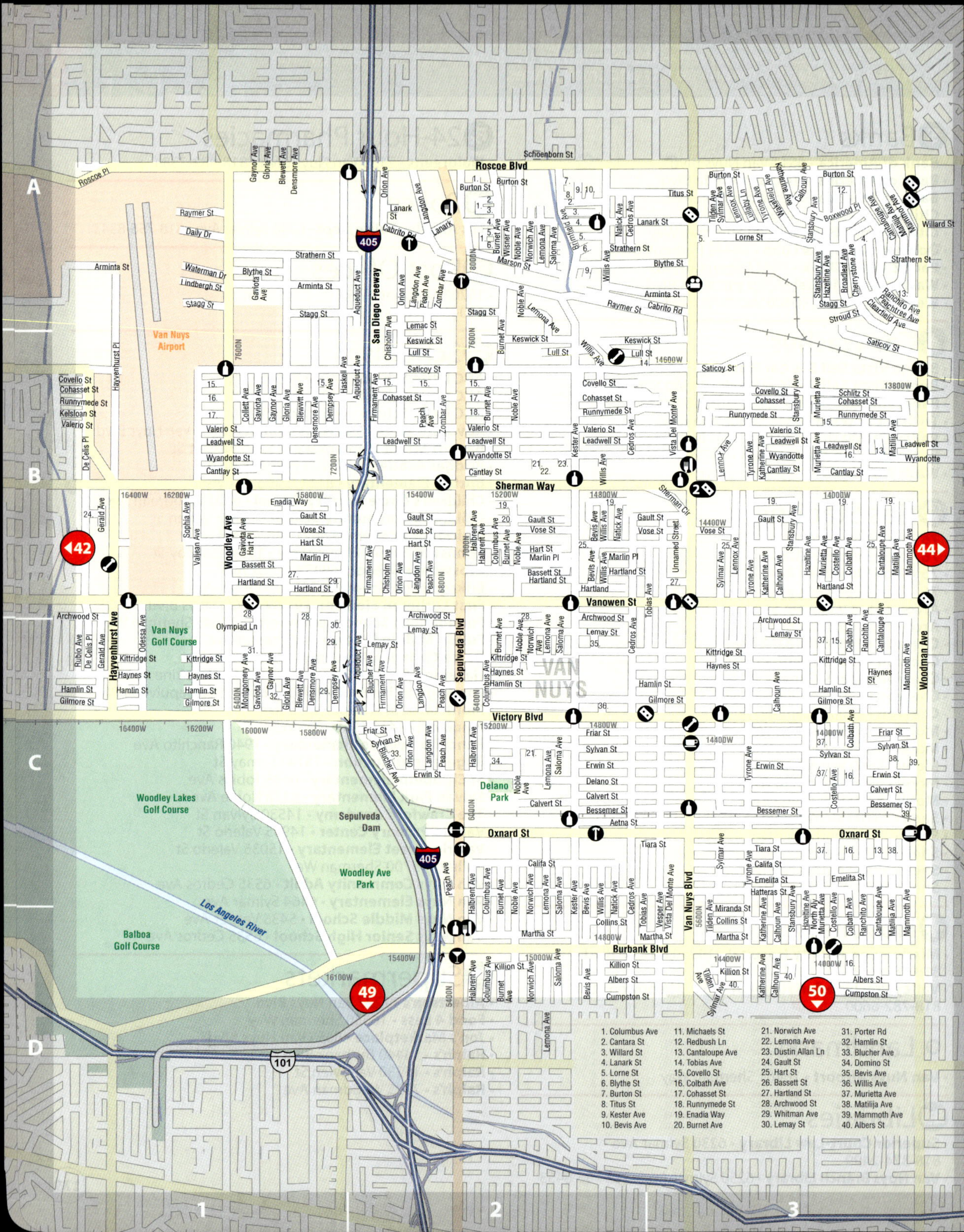
N
Roscoe Blvd
Roscoe Pl
Schoenborn St
San Diego Freeway
405
Van Nuys Airport
Woodley Ave
Sepulveda Blvd
Sherman Way
Vanowen St
Victory Blvd
Oxnard St
Burbank Blvd
Van Nuys Blvd
Woodman Ave
Haynvenhurst Ave
Van Nuys Golf Course
Woodley Lakes Golf Course
Sepulveda Dam
Woodley Ave Park
Balboa Golf Course
Los Angeles River
Delano Park
VAN NUYS
101
42
44
49
50
A
B
C
D
1
2
3
1. Columbus Ave
2. Cantara St
3. Willard St
4. Lanark St
5. Lorne St
6. Blythe St
7. Burton St
8. Titus St
9. Kester Ave
10. Bevis Ave
11. Michaels St
12. Redbush Ln
13. Cantaloupe Ave
14. Tobias Ave
15. Covello St
16. Colbath Ave
17. Cohasset St
18. Runnymede St
19. Enadia Way
20. Burnet Ave
21. Norwich Ave
22. Lemona Ave
23. Dustin Allan Ln
24. Gault St
25. Hart St
26. Bassett St
27. Hartland St
28. Archwood St
29. Whitman Ave
30. Lemay St
31. Porter Rd
32. Hamlin St
33. Blucher Ave
34. Domino St
35. Bevis Ave
36. Willis Ave
37. Murietta Ave
38. Matilija Ave
39. Mammoth Ave
40. Albers St

Sundries / Entertainment

One of the most convenient areas for shopping is The Plant, at 7800 Van Nuys Blvd., a former General Motors assembly plant, which now houses a Home Depot, Babies R Us, a 16-plex movie theatre, and more.

Coffee

- **Cafe De Hollywood** · 6322 Van Nuys Blvd
- **Kyffin Coffee** · 6000 Woodman Ave

Gyms

- **LA Fitness Sports Clubs** · 5990 Sepulveda Blvd · 818-988-7411

Hardware Stores

- **Coast To Coast Store** · 15430 Cabrito Rd · 818-901-1602
- **CWH** · 7910 Sepulveda Blvd · 818-787-0525
- **Orchard Supply Hardware** · 5960 Sepulveda Blvd · 818-779-7292
- **Peterson Lumber & Supply** · 7610 Woodman Ave · 818-782-9320
- **Valley Sash & Door** · 14829 Oxnard St · 818-785-8628

Liquor Stores

- **Adam's Liquor** · 14556 Vanowen St
- **Allan's Liquor & Junior Market** · 16060 Vanowen St
- **At Express Liquor** · 5658 Sepulveda Blvd
- **Casino Liquors** · 14900 Victory Blvd
- **Confetti Liquors** · 13674 Oxnard St
- **D & K Liquor Store** · 15245 Saticoy St
- **Dale's Van Nuys** · 14055 Burbank Blvd
- **George's Liquor** · 14102 Oxnard St
- **Gigi's Liquor** · 14038 Victory Blvd
- **Jay's Liquor** · 14411 Victory Blvd
- **Lloyd's Liquor Market** · 7219 Kester Ave
- **Michael's Market & Liquor** · 7510 Woodman Pl
- **One Stop Liquor & Market** · 14521 Sherman Way
- **Pat's Liquor & Junior Market** · 6020 Kester Ave
- **R & D Liquors** · 6073 Van Nuys Blvd
- **Sam's Liquor** · 15717 Vanowen St
- **Stark Liquor** · 14915 Vanowen St
- **Tori Liquor & Junior Market** · 7300 Sepulveda Blvd
- **Valley Liquor** · 7357 Van Nuys Blvd
- **Woodley Liquors** · 7550 Woodley Ave

Movie Theaters

- **Plant Sixteen Theatres** · 7876 Van Nuys Blvd

Pet Stores

- **Birds Plus** · 14041 Burbank Blvd · 818-901-1187
- **Falcon Labs** · 14737 Lull St · 714-630-6342
- **Pat's Bird Connection** · 6363 Van Nuys Blvd · 818-786-2730
- **Poodle Puff** · 14046 Burbank Blvd · 818-780-1600

Restaurants

- **Dr. Hogly Wogly's Tyler Texas BBQ** · 8136 Sepulveda Blvd · 818-780-6701
- **Krispy Kreme** · 7249 Van Nuys Blvd · 818-908-9113
- **Zankou Chicken** · 5658 Sepulveda Blvd · 818-781-0615

Video Rental

- **20-20 Video** · 6440 Sepulveda Blvd · 818-780-2020
- **Hollywood Video** · 7221 Van Nuys Blvd · 818-997-0706
- **J & R Video** · 14048 Vanowen St · 818-994-8552
- **Prael (Thai)** · 8205 Woodman Ave · 818-376-1976
- **Speed Video** · 16065 Vanowen St · 818-785-3051
- **Video City** · 8245 Woodman Ave · 818-786-4950
- **Video Japan (Japanese)** · 15355 Sherman Way · 818-786-0850
- **Video Rose** · 14655 Victory Blvd · 818-989-4050
- **Video Supermart Valley (Korean)** · 7130 Van Nuys Blvd · 818-997-7410
- **Video World** · 8111 Van Nuys Blvd · 818-780-8124
- **Videomen** · 14522 Vanowen St · 818-786-3561

NORTH HOLLYWOOD

VALLEY GLEN

Los Angeles Valley College

Erwin park

Valley Plaza Park

Sun Valley Park Rec Center

Victory Vineland Park

North Hollywood Park and Recreation Center

Hollywood Freeway

Tujunga Wash

1. Stagg St
2. Wixom St
3. Keswick St
4. Wortser Ave
5. Morse Ave
6. Goodland Ct
7. Goodland Ave
8. Goosfold Ave
9. Bonfield Ave
10. Daha Pl
11. Armita St
12. Elkwood St
13. Divan Pl
14. Solvang St
15. Covello St
16. Todd Ct
17. Milldale Ct
18. Doran Pl
19. Jolene Ct
20. Eloise Ave
21. Morse Ave
22. Mary Ellen Ave
23. Ortley Pl

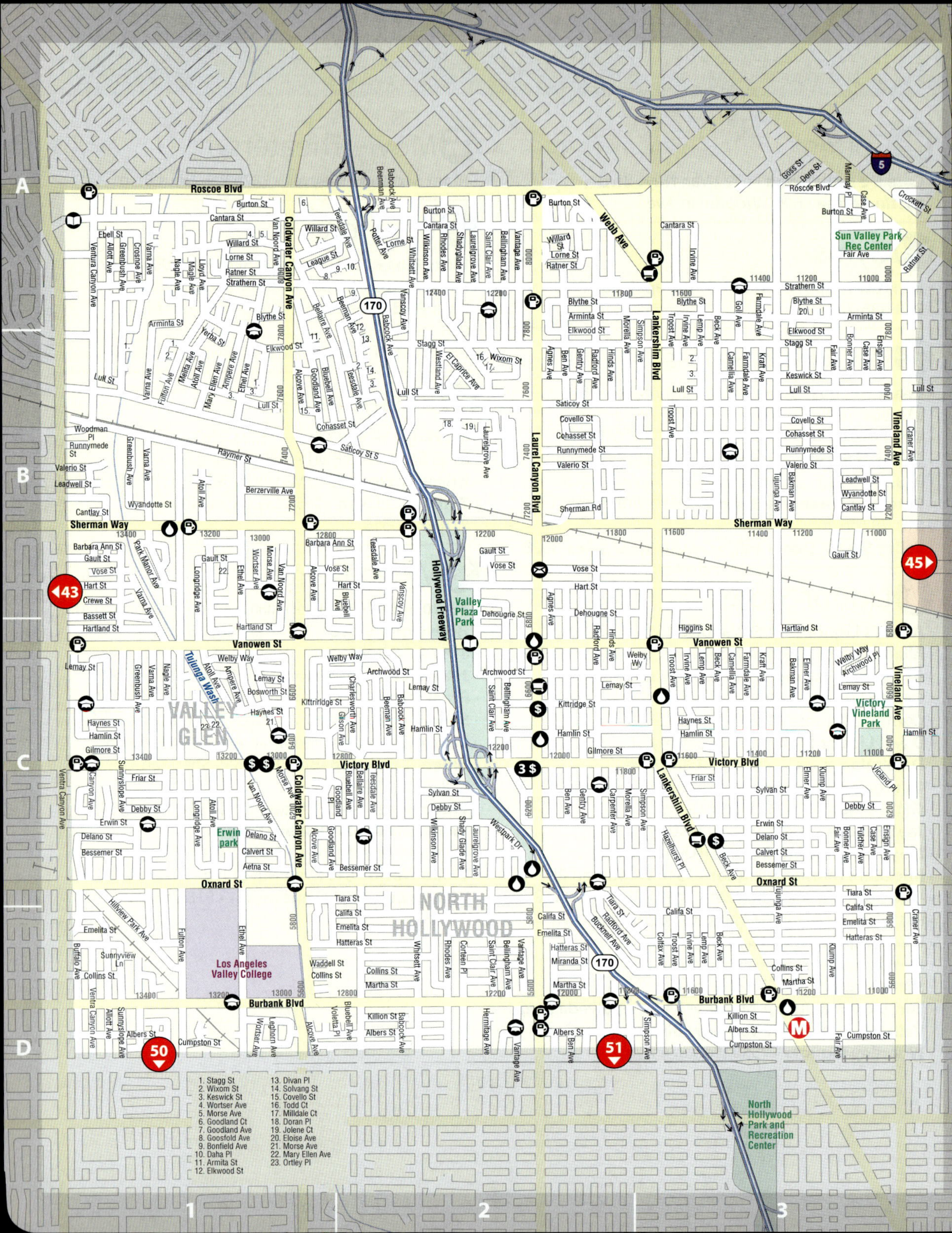

Locals hope that the recent opening of a subway station in North Hollywood will be a boon to the ever-growing NoHo Arts District, which boasts over thirty theatres at last count. The subway is also proving attractive to people trying to leave the area, providing a convenient and fast way of traveling from North Hollywood to Universal City and Downtown without having to sit in traffic.

$ Banks

- **Bank of America** · 13051 Victory Blvd
- **Bank of America** · 6600 Laurel Canyon Blvd
- **California National Bank** · 6350 Laurel Canyon Blvd
- **Citibank** · 13003 Victory Blvd
- **Washington Mutual** · 6400 Laurel Canyon Blvd
- **Wells Fargo Bank** · 12160 Victory Blvd
- **Wells Fargo Bank** · 6140 Lankershim Blvd

Car Washes

- **Buena Vista Self-Svc Car Wash** · 6809 Laurel Canyon Blvd
- **Lankershim Car Wash** · 6622 Lankershim Blvd
- **National Car Wash** · 5950 Laurel Canyon Blvd
- **Oxnard Car Wash** · 12119 Oxnard St
- **Plaza Car Wash** · 6462 Laurel Canyon Blvd
- **Sherman Way Car Wash** · 13310 Sherman Way
- **Tujunga Car Wash** · 5553 Tujunga Ave

Gas Stations

- **76** · 11407 Burbank Blvd
- **76** · 11705 Victory Blvd
- **76** · 12856 Sherman Way
- **76** · 13650 Vanowen St
- **76** · 7955 Laurel Canyon Blvd
- **Arco** · 13260 Sherman Way
- **Arco** · 6757 Laurel Canyon Blvd
- **Arco** · 6800 Lankershim Blvd
- **Arco** · 6804 Vineland Ave
- **Arco** · 8004 Lankershim Blvd
- **Chevron** · 11000 Victory Blvd
- **Chevron** · 12950 Victory Blvd
- **Chevron** · 5544 Laurel Canyon Blvd
- **Chevron** · 7214 Whitsett Ave
- **Chevron** · 8263 Laurel Canyon Blvd
- **Mobil** · 11680 Burbank Blvd
- **Mobil** · 12500 Sherman Way
- **Mobil** · 401 S Robertson Blvd
- **Mobil** · 7004 Laurel Canyon Blvd
- **Shell** · 11680 Victory Blvd
- **Shell** · 13606 Roscoe Blvd
- **Shell** · 5555 Laurel Canyon Blvd
- **Shell** · 5957 Vineland Ave
- **Texaco** · 13666 Victory Blvd

Libraries

- **Kaiser Permanente Medical Library** · 13652 Cantara St · 818-375-3000
- **Valley Plaza Library** · 12311 Vanowen St · 818-765-0805

Police

- **Los Angeles Police Dept** · 11640 Burbank Blvd · 818-623-4016

Post Offices

- 6535 Lankershim Blvd
- 7035 Laurel Canyon Blvd

Schools

- **Adat Ari El Day School** · 12020 Burbank Blvd
- **Arminta Street Elementary** · 11530 Strathern St
- **Burbank Boulevard Elementary** · 12215 Albers St
- **Camellia Avenue Elementary** · 7451 Camellia Ave
- **Coldwater Canyon Ave Elementary** · 6850 Coldwater Canyon Ave
- **Erwin Street Elementary** · 13400 Erwin St
- **Fair Avenue Elementary** · 6501 Fair Ave
- **Gentle Shepherd Education Center** · 12120 Strathern St
- **Grant Senior High School** · 13000 Oxnard St
- **Kittridge Street Elementary** · 13619 Kittridge St
- **Laurel Hall** · 11919 Oxnard St
- **Laurence 2000 School** · 13639 Victory Blvd
- **London Continuation** · 12924 Oxnard St
- **Los Angeles Valley College** · 5800 Fulton Ave
- **Lowman Elementary** · 12827 Saticoy St
- **Madison Middle School** · 13000 Hart St
- **Maud Booth Family Center** · 11243 Kitteridge St
- **Monlux Elementary** · 6155 Bellaire Ave
- **New School for Child Development** · 13130 Burbank Blvd
- **North Hollywood Montessori** · 11849 Burbank Blvd
- **Princeton College Preparatory** · 13440 Crewe St
- **Saticoy Elementary** · 7850 Ethel Ave
- **St Jane Frances de Chantal** · 12950 Hamlin St
- **Strathern Street Elementary** · 7939 Saint Clair Ave
- **Victory Boulevard Elementary** · 6315 Radford Ave

Supermarkets

- **Food 4 Less** · 8035 Webb Ave
- **Ralph's** · 6657 Laurel Canyon Blvd
- **Von's** · 6140 Lankershim Blvd

Map 44 • North Hollywood

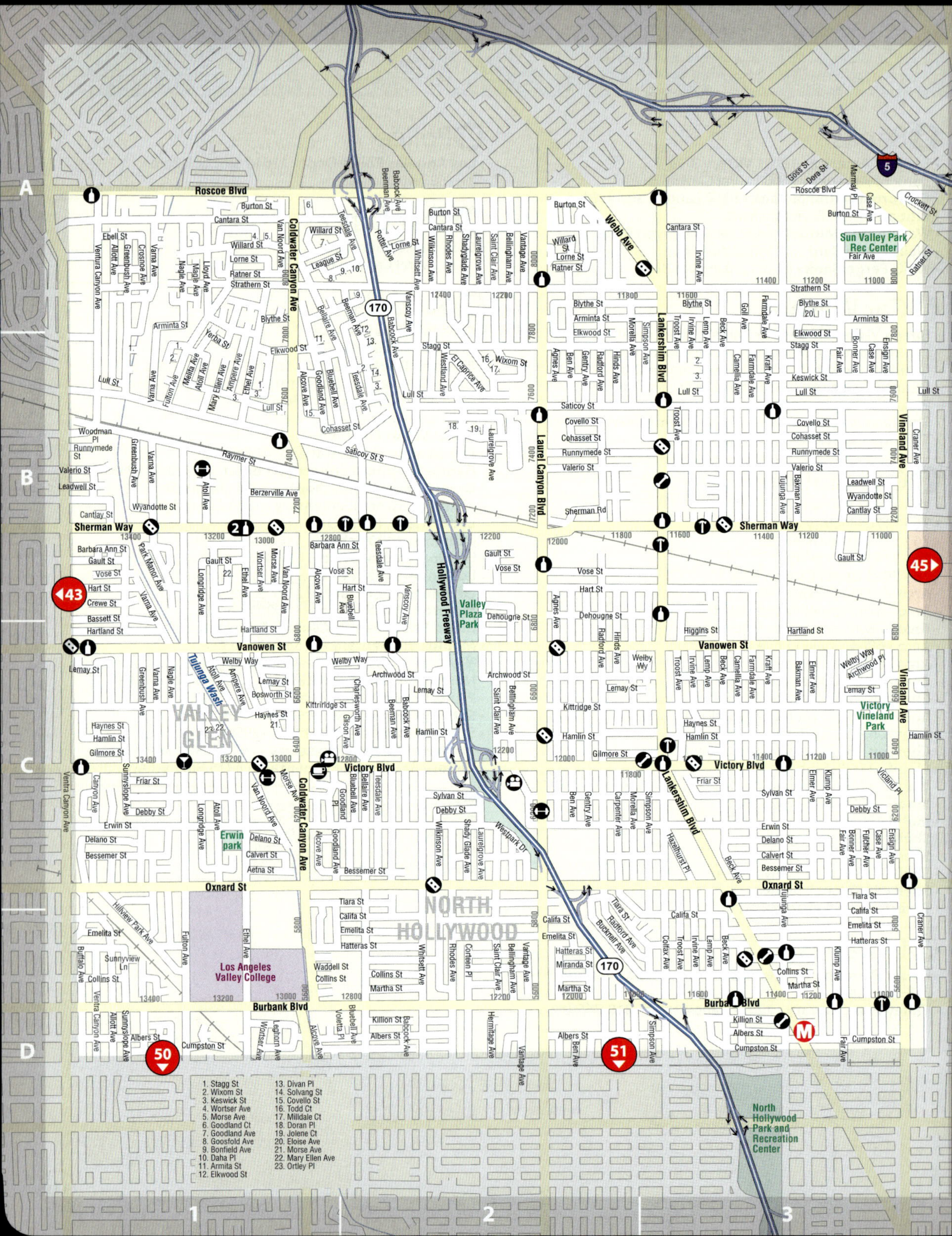

Roscoe Blvd
Sherman Way
Vanowen St
Victory Blvd
Oxnard St
Burbank Blvd
Coldwater Canyon Ave
Laurel Canyon Blvd
Lankershim Blvd
Vineland Ave
Hollywood Freeway
Webb Ave
Raymer St
Saticoy St S
Tujunga Wash
VALLEY GLEN
NORTH HOLLYWOOD
Valley Plaza Park
Erwin park
Los Angeles Valley College
Sun Valley Park Rec Center
Victory Vineland Park
North Hollywood Park and Recreation Center
170
5
43
45
50
51
A
B
C
D
1
2
3
1. Stagg St
2. Wixom St
3. Keswick St
4. Wortser Ave
5. Morse Ave
6. Goodland Ct
7. Goodland Ave
8. Goosfold Ave
9. Bonfield Ave
10. Daha Pl
11. Arminta St
12. Elkwood St
13. Divan Pl
14. Solvang St
15. Covello St
16. Todd Ct
17. Milldale Ct
18. Doran Pl
19. Jolene Ct
20. Eloise Ave
21. Morse Ave
22. Mary Ellen Ave
23. Ortley Pl

One of the most famous people who have called North Hollywood home is Amelia Earhardt. A statue honoring the aviatrix stands at "Five Points," the busy intersection of Lankershim, Camarillo, and Vineland streets.

Clubs

- **McRed's** • 13235 Victory Blvd • 818-980-2845
- **Rawhide** • 10937 Burbank Blvd • 818-760-9798

Coffee

- **Starbucks** • 12848 Victory Blvd

Gyms

- **Bally Total Fitness** • 13069 Victory Blvd • 818-506-4208
- **Chin Gym** • 7373 Atoll Ave • 818-982-1170
- **Gold's Gym** • 6233 Laurel Canyon Blvd • 818-506-4600

Hardware Stores

- **Alema** • 12547 Sherman Way • 818-982-4000
- **Anawalt Lumber True Value** • 11000 Burbank Blvd • 818-769-4421
- **Home Base** • 12727 Sherman Way • 818-503-9082
- **Home Depot** • 11600 Sherman Way • 818-764-9600
- **Moulding Center** • 6501 Lankershim Blvd • 818-985-5376
- **Riverside Contractors Supply** • 5621 Fulton Ave • 818-785-5178
- **Terry Lumber** • 7151 Lankershim Blvd • 818-982-6046

Liquor Stores

- **7 & 7 Liquor Junior Mart** • 13654 Victory Blvd
- **A & S Liquor Store** • 5745 Tujunga Ave
- **Ash Dod Market** • 12650 Sherman Way
- **Carmel Liquor** • 12516 Vanowen St
- **Chivalry Liquors** • 7552 Laurel Canyon Blvd
- **Circus Liquor** • 5600 Vineland Ave
- **Circus Liquors** • 6417 Lankershim Blvd
- **D & R Liquors** • 6917 Lankershim Blvd
- **Danny's Liquor & Market** • 7202 Lankershim Blvd
- **Dorose Liquors** • 13560 Roscoe Blvd
- **Fair House Liquor** • 12903 Sherman Way
- **Gip Liquor** • 13100 Sherman Way
- **Golden Arrow Liquors** • 13231 Victory Blvd

- **Handy Mart Liquors** • 8012 Laurel Canyon Blvd
- **Imperial Liquors** • 13324 Vanowen St
- **Joe's Liquor & Deli** • 11228 Burbank Blvd
- **K-1 Liquor Market** • 13056 Sherman Way
- **Kim Liquor Store** • 5940 Lankershim Blvd
- **Lankershim Mini-Market** • 7614 Lankershim Blvd
- **Metro's Liquor** • 6400 Tujunga Ave
- **Phil's Liquor Deli** • 11510 Burbank Blvd
- **Saticoy Liquor Store** • 11415 Saticoy St
- **Sunrise Liquors** • 12931 Saticoy St
- **Tom's Liquor Market** • 12861 Vanowen St
- **Urban Liquors** • 8323 Lankershim Blvd
- **Vineland Wine Cellar** • 6012 Vineland Ave

Movie Theaters

- **Century 8 Theatres** • 12827 Victory Blvd
- **United Artists Theatres** • 6355 Bellingham Ave

Pet Stores

- **Aquarium Village** • 11734 Victory Blvd • 818-985-3813
- **Bird House** • 5742 Lankershim Blvd • 818-766-4269
- **Deep Sea Aquarium** • 7355 Lankershim Blvd • 818-764-0875
- **Pet Stop** • 5505 1/2 Tujunga Ave • 818-760-7387

Video Rental

- **Another Video 4U (Spanish)** • 11539 Sherman Way • 818-255-3930
- **Blockbuster** • 6507 Laurel Canyon Blvd • 818-509-8802
- **Hollywood Video** • 8065 Webb Ave • 818-504-6438
- **Planet Video** • 13041 Victory Blvd • 818-508-9429
- **Video 94** • 13648 Vanowen St • 818-994-5878
- **Video Center** • 5751 Lankershim Blvd • 818-760-4722
- **Video Citi** • 11650 Victory Blvd • 818-980-1505
- **Video Citi** • 12051 Vanowen St • 818-982-0414
- **Video Market** • 13434 Sherman Way • 818-982-8488
- **Video Star** • 12455 Oxnard St • 818-762-1283
- **Video Swan** • 7455 Lankershim Blvd • 818-982-2243
- **Video Universe** • 12937 Sherman Way • 818-764-8842

N

1. Glenhill Ave
2. Glencrest Dr
3. Via Pavia
4. Via Nola
5. Via Udine
6. Via Siena
7. Via Genova
8. Via Catalina
9. Via Zibello
10. Via Sorrento
11. Via Napoli
12. Scott Rd
13. Scott Wy
14. Via Rimini
15. Via Bernard
16. Via Milano
17. Rosa Maria
18. Via Ronaldo
19. Via Foggia
20. Via Tivoli
21. Wyandotte St
22. N Valley St
23. Jannetta Ave
24. Kittridge St
25. W Chestnut St
26. Riverton Ave

SUN VALLEY
Stagg St
Wixom St
Keswick St
Lull St
Saticoy St
Cohasset St
Cantlay St
Sherman Wy
Sherman Pl

Burbank-Glendale-Pasadena Airport
PAGE 278

San Fernando Blvd
Golden State Freeway
Woodbury University
Scott Rd

N Glenoaks Blvd
Washington Cir
Floyd St
Maria St

Vanowen St
W Empire Ave
W Vanowen Pl
W Vanowen St
W Valhalla Dr
Gross Park
Pierce Valhalla Cemetery
Pacific Park
W Pacific Ave
Ralph Foy Park
W Monterey Ave
Vickroy Park

Victory Vineland Park
Dubnoff Way
Monterey Ave
W Victory Blvd
W Jeffries Ave
W Wyoming Ave
Friar St
Sylvan St
Erwin St
Calvert St
NORTH HOLLYWOOD

44
46

Oxnard St
Edison Way
Tiara St
Valley Park
Califa St
W Allan Ave
W Hatteras Ave
N Whitnall Hwy
Collins St
Willowcrest Ave
Cumpston St
W Burbank Blvd
W Chandler Blvd
W Magnolia Blvd

Margate St
Weddington St
Mccormick St
Chandler Blvd
Myrna St
Griffith Manor Park
Whitnall Park

Hartsook St
Hesby St
Morrison St
Huston St
Peachgrove St
La Maida St
Camarillo Pl
Forman Ln
Woodland Ave
Warner Ranch
W Verdugo Ave
Jacaranda Ave
NBC Television Studios

51
52

Blix St
Kling St
Hortense St
Sarah St
Ventura Freeway
W Alameda Ave
Lankershim Blvd

134
134

N Hollywood Way
N Buena Vista St
N Keystone St
N Lincoln St
N Brighton St
N Myers St
N Lamer St
N Parish Pl
W Magnolia Blvd
Izay Park

1   2   3
A   B   C   D

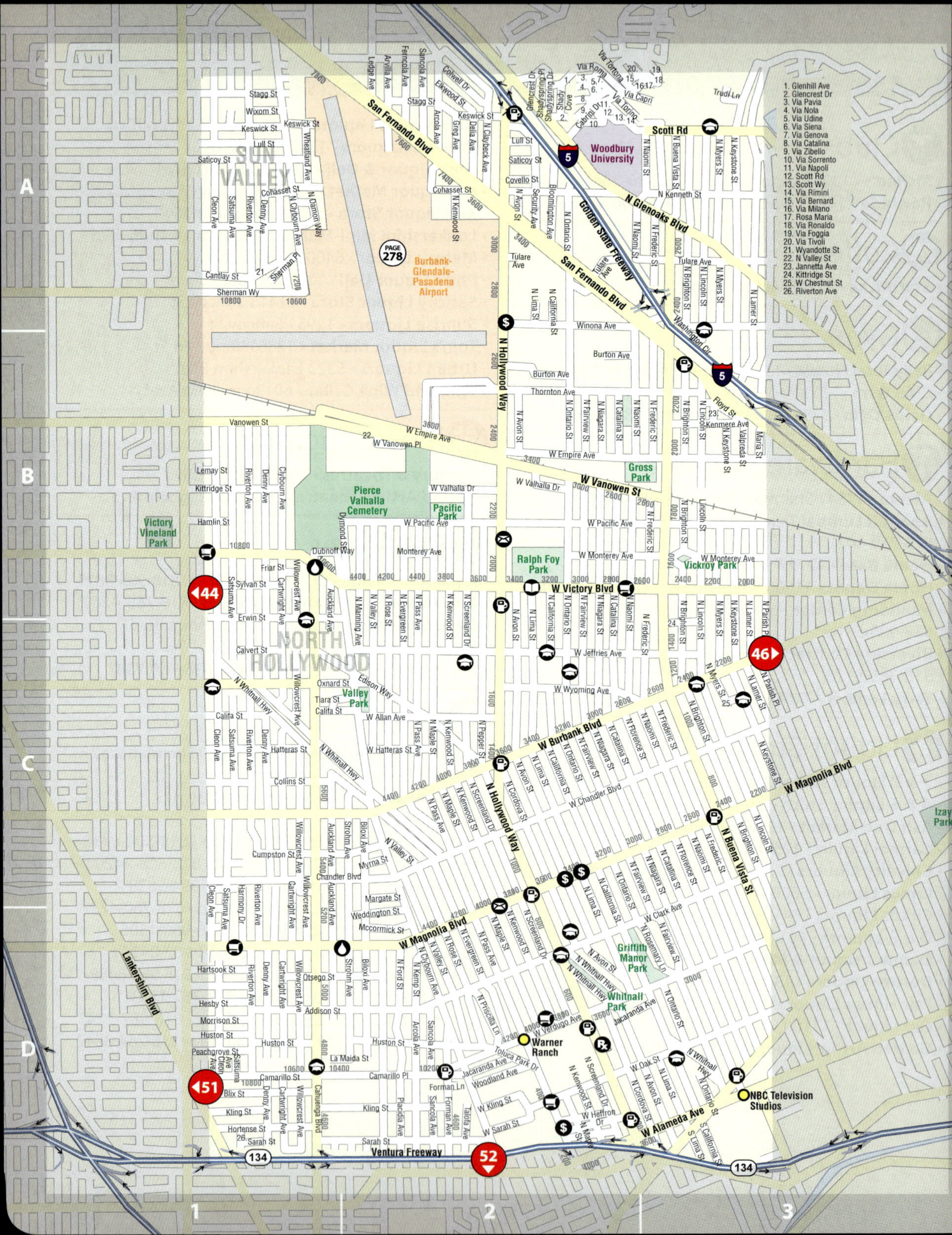

When Johnny Carson came to you "live from beautiful downtown Burbank!" he was actually at the corner of Alameda and Olive. Though both "downtown" and "beautiful" are disputable, it's still fun to drive by the NBC studios and see the scores of tourists who show up to watch the nightly taping of "The Tonight Show."

$ Banks

- **Bank of America** · 255 N Pass Ave
- **Bank of America** · 3400 W Magnolia Blvd
- **Community Bank** · 2800 N Hollywood Way
- **Washington Mutual** · 3521 W Magnolia Blvd

Car Washes

- **In-N-Out Car Wash** · 10505 Victory Blvd
- **Toluca Lake Car Wash** · 10515 Magnolia Blvd

Gas Stations

- **76** · 1401 N Hollywood Way
- **76** · 200 N Hollywood Way
- **76** · 3701 W Magnolia Blvd
- **Exxon** · 2417 N San Fernando Blvd
- **Mobil** · 1951 N Hollywood Way
- **Mobil** · 2500 W Magnolia Blvd
- **Mobil** · 3020 W Olive Ave
- **Shell** · 11339 Camarillo St
- **Shell** · 550 N Hollywood Way
- **Shell** · 7710 N Hollywood Way

Landmarks

- **NBC Television Studios** · 3000 W Alameda Ave
- **Warner Ranch** · Verdugo Ave & Pass Ave

Libraries

- **Northwest Library** · 3323 W Victory Blvd · 818-238-5640

Rx 24-Hour Pharmacies

- **Sav-On** · 511 Hollywood Way · 818-841-0710

Post Offices

- 2140 N Hollywood Way
- 3810 Magnolia Blvd

Schools

- **American Lutheran Elementary** · 755 N Whitnall Hwy
- **Bret Harte Children's Ctr** · 1421 N Ontario St
- **Burlington** · 242 N Burlington Ave
- **Edison Elementary School** · 2110 W Chestnut St
- **Harte Elementary School** · 3200 W Jeffries Ave
- **Luther Burbank Middle School** · 3700 W Jeffries Ave
- **Monterey High School** · 1915 W Monterey Ave
- **Options for Youth-Burbank Charter** · 2309 W Burbank Blvd
- **Oxnard Street Elementary** · 10912 Oxnard St
- **Providencia Elementary** · 1919 N Ontario St
- **Roosevelt Elementary** · 850 N Cordova St
- **St Francis Xavier** · 3601 Scott Rd
- **St Patrick's Catholic** · 10626 Erwin St
- **Stevenson Elementary** · 3333 W Oak St
- **Toluca Lake Elementary** · 4840 Cahuenga Blvd
- **Washington Elementary School** · 2322 N Lincoln St
- **Woodbury University** · 7500 Glenoaks Blvd

Supermarkets

- **Albertson's** · 3830 W Verdugo Ave
- **Ralph's** · 10900 Magnolia Blvd
- **Ralph's** · 10911 Victory Blvd
- **Ralph's** · 2600 W Victory Blvd
- **Von's** · 301 N Pass Ave

SUN VALLEY
NORTH HOLLYWOOD
Woodbury University
Burbank-Glendale-Pasadena Airport
PAGE 278

San Fernando Blvd
Golden State Freeway
Ventura Freeway
Lankershim Blvd
N Hollywood Way
N Glenoaks Blvd
W Magnolia Blvd
W Burbank Blvd
W Victory Blvd
W Vanowen St
W Empire Ave
W Alameda Ave
W Magnolia Blvd
N Buena Vista St
Scott Rd

1. Glenhill Ave
2. Glencrest Dr
3. Via Pavia
4. Via Nola
5. Via Udine
6. Via Siena
7. Via Genova
8. Via Catalina
9. Via Zibello
10. Via Sorrento
11. Via Napoli
12. Scott Rd
13. Scott Wy
14. Via Rimini
15. Via Bernard
16. Via Milano
17. Rosa Maria
18. Via Ronaldo
19. Via Foggia
20. Via Tivoli
21. Wyandotte St
22. N Valley St
23. Jannetta Ave
24. Kittridge St
25. W Chestnut St
26. Riverton Ave

Victory Vineland Park
Pierce Valhalla Cemetery
Pacific Park
Ralph Foy Park
Gross Park
Vickroy Park
Valley Park
Griffith Manor Park
Whitnall Park
Izay Park

Stagg St
Wixom St
Keswick St
Lull St
Saticoy St
Cohasset St
Cantlay St
Sherman Wy
Vanowen St
Lemay St
Kittridge St
Hamlin St
Friar St
Sylvan St
Erwin St
Calvert St
Oxnard St
Tiara St
Califa St
W Allan Ave
W Hatteras St
Collins St
Cumpston St
Chandler Blvd
Margate St
Weddington St
Mccormick St
Hartsook St
Heshy St
Morrison St
Huston St
Peachgrove St
Camarillo St
Kling St
Hortense St
Sarah St

134
52

From dollar t-shirts at the Salvation Army to fifty-dollar suits worn by your favorite TV star, the shopping along Magnolia Blvd., offers a vast array of choices. Peppered with unique antique and book stores and old-school restaurants, this area makes for a nice contrast to the overcrowded mall and cookie-cutter chain stores a few blocks away in downtown Burbank.

Clubs

- **Dimples** • 3413 W Olive Ave • 818-842-2336
- **The Blue Saloon** • 4657 Lankershim Blvd • 818-766-4644
- **Tinhorn Flats** • 2623 Magnolia Blvd • 818-567-2470

Coffee

- **Starbucks** • 347 N Pass Ave

Gyms

- **World Gym Fitness Center** • 2010 N Hollywood Way • 818-563-4203

Hardware Stores

- **California Do-It Ctr** • 3221 W Magnolia Blvd • 818-845-8301
- **Estrada Hardware** • 3110 N Damon Way • 818-840-8029
- **Reno Hardware & Supply** • 2901 Thornton Ave • 818-842-3667

Liquor Stores

- **A & O Liquor Store** • 3117 W Olive Ave
- **Aero Liquor Store** • 2527 W Burbank Blvd
- **Bamford Liquor & Delicatessen** • 10575 Magnolia Blvd
- **Hermawam Meiling** • 2415 N San Fernando Blvd
- **Jet Stream Liquor** • 10922 Vanowen St
- **La Paz Liquor** • 4101 W Magnolia Blvd
- **Magnolia Liquor Market** • 3801 W Magnolia Blvd
- **Nelson's Liquor** • 4420 W Victory Blvd
- **Riverton Liquors** • 10800 Magnolia Blvd
- **Royal Liquor** • 5600 Cahuenga Blvd
- **Starlite Liquor** • 3510 W Victory Blvd
- **Tip Top Liquor** • 2501 W Victory Blvd

Pet Stores

- **Pet Emporium** • 923 N Hollywood Way • 818-848-0123
- **Pet Mania** • 353 N Pass Ave • 818-848-5512
- **Petco** • 3525 W Victory Blvd • 818-566-8528

Restaurants

- **Chili John's** • 2108 Burbank Blvd • 818-846-3611
- **Full of Life** • 2515 Magnolia Blvd • 818-845-8343
- **Pinocchio's** • 3103 Magnolia Blvd • 818-845-3517
- **Poquito Mas** • 10651 Magnolia Blvd • 818-994-8226
- **Santa Fe Tacos** • 353 N Pass Ave • 818-563-4324

Shopping

- **Arte de Mexico** • 5356 Riverton Ave • 818-769-5090
- **Atomic Records** • 3812 W Magnolia Blvd • 818-848-7090
- **Fry's** • 2311 N Hollywood Way • 818-526-8100
- **It's a Wrap** • 3315 W Magnolia Blvd • 818-567-7366
- **Lady Peter's Whimsey** • 2922 W Magnolia Blvd • 818-842-1947
- **Pinocchio's** • 3103 Magnolia Blvd • 818-845-3517
- **The Train Shack** • 1030 Hollywood Way • 818-842-3330

Video Rental

- **Blockbuster** • 2420 W Burbank Blvd • 818-566-1193
- **Hollywood Video** • 2484 W Victory Blvd • 818-559-2560
- **Lakeside Video** • 353 N Pass Ave • 818-848-2001
- **Twisted Video** • 10530 Burbank Blvd • 818-508-0559
- **Victory Video** • 2501 W Victory Blvd • 818-846-2585
- **Video 91** • 10723 Burbank Blvd • 818-766-0684

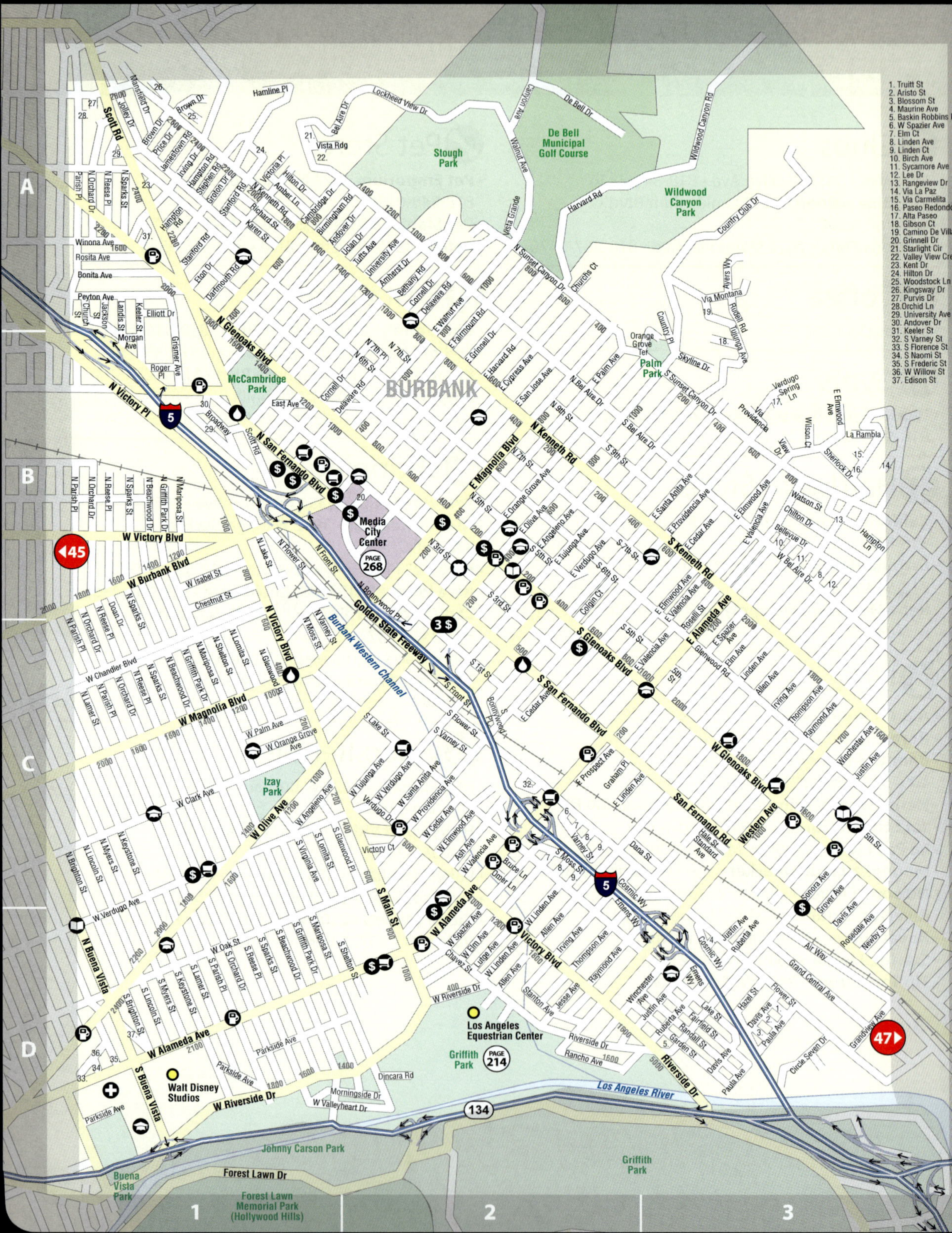

N

1. Truitt St
2. Aristo St
3. Blossom St
4. Maurine Ave
5. Baskin Robbins
6. W Spazier Ave
7. Elm Ct
8. Linden Ave
9. Linden Ct
10. Birch Ave
11. Sycamore Ave
12. Lee Dr
13. Rangeview Dr
14. Via La Paz
15. Via Carmelita
16. Paseo Redondo
17. Alta Paseo
18. Gibson Ct
19. Camino De Villa
20. Grinnell Dr
21. Starlight Cir
22. Valley View Cres
23. Kent Dr
24. Hilton Dr
25. Woodstock Ln
26. Kingsway Dr
27. Purvis Dr
28. Orchid Ln
29. University Ave
30. Andover Dr
31. Keeler St
32. S Varney St
33. S Florence St
34. S Naomi St
35. S Frederic St
36. W Willow St
37. Edison St

BURBANK

Stough Park
De Bell Municipal Golf Course
Wildwood Canyon Park
Orange Grove Ter.
Palm Park
McCambridge Park
Media City Center
PAGE 268
Golden State Freeway
Burbank Western Channel
Izay Park
Walt Disney Studios
Los Angeles Equestrian Center
Griffith Park
PAGE 214
Johnny Carson Park
Buena Vista Park
Forest Lawn Memorial Park (Hollywood Hills)
Forest Lawn Dr
Los Angeles River
Griffith Park

45
47

Scott Rd
N Victory Pl
N Glenoaks Blvd
N San Fernando Blvd
W Victory Blvd
W Burbank Blvd
W Magnolia Blvd
W Olive Ave
N Victory Blvd
N Buena Vista
S Buena Vista
W Alameda Ave
W Riverside Dr
S Main St
W Alameda Ave
Victory Blvd
S San Fernando Blvd
S Glenoaks Blvd
N Kenneth Rd
E Magnolia Blvd
N Sunset Canyon Dr
S Sunset Canyon Dr
E Alameda Ave
S Kenneth Rd
W Glenoaks Blvd
San Fernando Rd
Western Ave
Riverside Dr
134

The area surrounding the equestrian center on Riverside Drive is a great place to spend the day. Within a city block, there's a bowling alley where you can bowl to black lights and rock and roll, an ice skating rink that offers lessons and public skating hours, and trail rides that end with a relaxing margarita when you get to the bottom of the hill.

$ Banks

- **Bank of America** · 142 E Olive Ave
- **Bank of America** · 6400 San Fernando Rd
- **California National Bank** · 240 N San Fernando Blvd
- **Citibank** · 360 E Magnolia Blvd
- **Citibank** · 400 W Alameda Ave
- **Jackson Federal Bank** · 601 S Glenoaks Blvd
- **Washington Mutual** · 100 N 1st St
- **Washington Mutual** · 1110 W Alameda Ave
- **Washington Mutual** · 840 N San Fernando Blvd
- **Wells Fargo Bank** · 141 N Glenoaks Blvd
- **Wells Fargo Bank** · 1011 N San Fernando Blvd
- **Wells Fargo Bank** · 116 E Olive Ave
- **Wells Fargo Bank** · 1820 W Verdugo Ave
- **Wells Fargo Bank** · 900 N San Fernando Blvd

Car Washes

- **Classic Hand Car Wash** · 506 S San Fernando Blvd
- **In-N-Out Service Center** · 1420 N San Fernando Blvd
- **Magnolia Car Wash** · 910 W Magnolia Blvd

Gas Stations

- **76** · 2128 N Glenoaks Blvd
- **76** · 901 N San Fernando Blvd
- **Arco** · 201 W Alameda Ave
- **Arco** · 250 S Glenoaks Blvd
- **Chevron** · 100 S Glenoaks Blvd
- **Chevron** · 140 E Alameda Ave
- **Chevron** · 1501 W Glenoaks Blvd
- **Chevron** · 1655 Victory Blvd
- **Chevron** · 2501 W Olive Ave
- **Chevron** · 439 W Alameda Blvd
- **Mobil** · 1700 W Glenoaks Blvd
- **Mobil** · 349 S Glenoaks Blvd
- **Mobil** · 520 S Verdugo Dr
- **Sevan** · 1638 N San Fernando Blvd
- **Shell** · 181 W Alameda Ave
- **Shell** · 1919 W Alameda Ave

Hospitals

- **Providence St Joseph Medical** · 501 S Buena Vista St · 818-843-5111

Landmarks

- **Los Angeles Equestrian Center** · 480 Riverside Dr
- **Walt Disney Studios** · 500 S Buena Vista

Libraries

- **Buena Vista Library** · 401 N Buena Vista St · 818-238-5620
- **Burbank Central Library** · 110 N Glenoaks Blvd · 818-238-5600
- **Grandview Library** · 1535 5th St · 818-548-2049

Police

- **Burbank Police Dept** · 200 N 3rd St · 818-238-3333

Post Offices

- 135 E Olive Ave
- 1634 N San Fernando Blvd
- 6444 San Fernando Rd

Schools

- **Balboa Elementary** · 1844 Bel Aire Dr
- **Bellarmine-Jefferson High School** · 465 E Olive Ave
- **Burbank High School** · 902 N 3rd St
- **Burroughs High School** · 1920 Clark Ave
- **Clearview** · 1930 W Glenoaks Blvd
- **Disney Elementary School** · 1220 W Orange Grove Ave
- **Emerson Elementary** · 720 E Cypress Ave
- **First Lutheran School** · 1001 S Glenoaks Blvd
- **Franklin Child Care Center** · 1610 Lake St
- **Franklin Elementary** · 1610 Lake St
- **Jefferson Elementary** · 1540 5th St
- **Jefferson Elementary** · 1900 N 6th St
- **John Muir Middle School** · 1111 N Kenneth Rd
- **Jordan Middle School** · 420 S Mariposa St
- **McKinley Elementary** · 349 W Valencia Ave
- **Miller Elementary** · 720 E Providencia Ave
- **Providence High School** · 511 S Buena Vista St
- **St Finbar Catholic School** · 2120 W Olive Ave
- **St Robert Bellarmine Catholic School** · 154 N 5th St

Supermarkets

- **Albertson's** · 1855 W Glenoaks Blvd
- **Jon's Marketplace** · 1717 W Glenoaks Blvd
- **Pavilions** · 1110 W Alameda Ave
- **Ralph's** · 1100 N San Fernando Blvd
- **Ralph's** · 25 E Alameda Ave
- **Trader Joe's** · 345 S Lake Blvd
- **Von's** · 1110 W Alameda Ave
- **Von's** · 1011 N San Fernando Blvd
- **Von's** · 1820 W Verdugo Ave

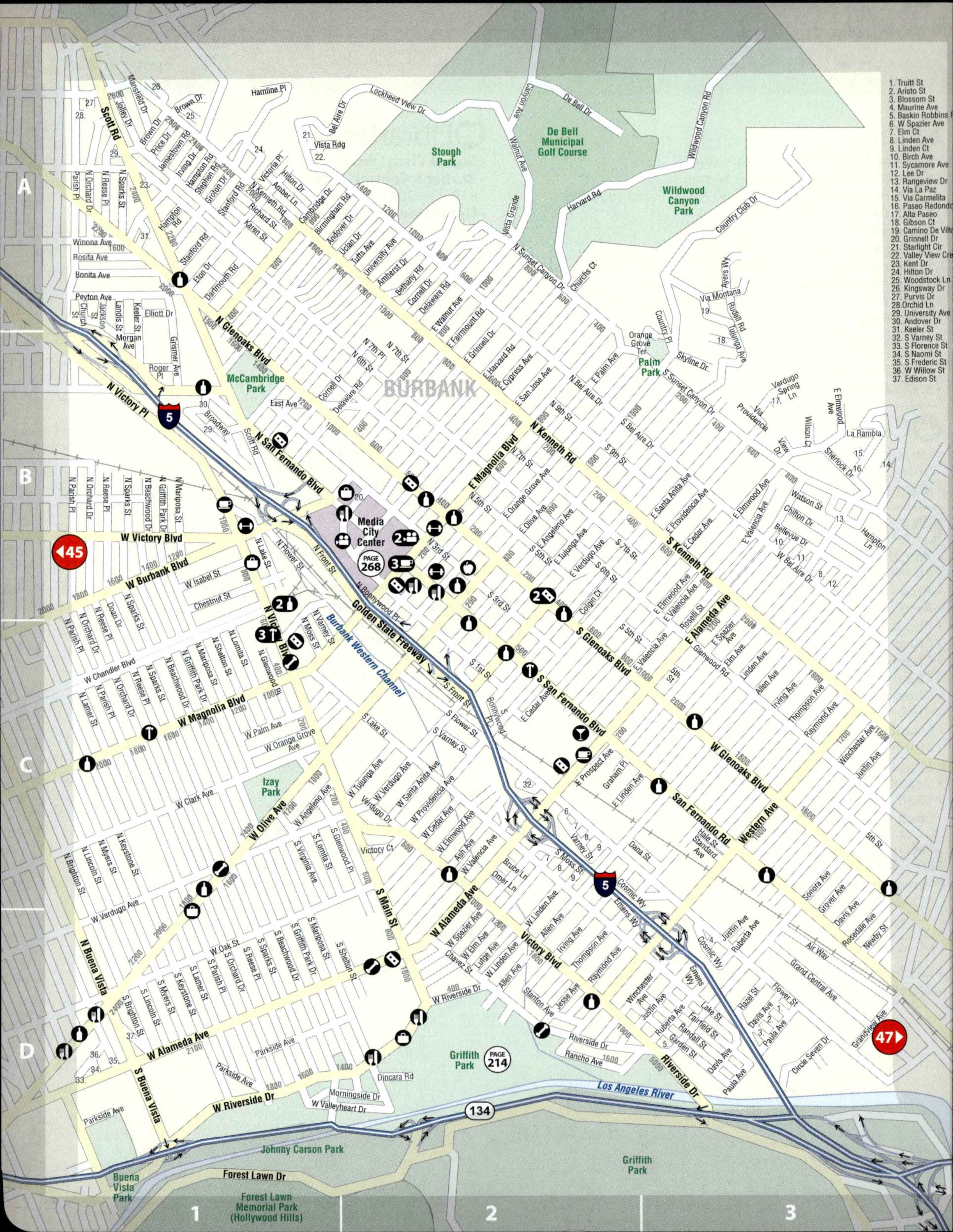

BURBANK

Parks & Landmarks

Stough Park
De Bell Municipal Golf Course
Wildwood Canyon Park
McCambridge Park
Media City Center — PAGE 268
Izay Park
Palm Park
Orange Grove Ter
Griffith Park — PAGE 214
Johnny Carson Park
Buena Vista Park
Forest Lawn Memorial Park (Hollywood Hills)
Griffith Park

Street Index

1. Truitt St
2. Aristo St
3. Blossom St
4. Maurine Ave
5. Baskin Robbins Pl
6. W Spazier Ave
7. Elm Ct
8. Linden Ave
9. Linden Ct
10. Birch Ave
11. Sycamore Ave
12. Lee Dr
13. Rangeview Dr
14. Via La Paz
15. Via Carmelita
16. Paseo Redondo
17. Alta Paseo
18. Gibson Ct
19. Camino De Villas
20. Grinnell Dr
21. Starlight Cir
22. Valley View Cres
23. Kent Dr
24. Hilton Dr
25. Woodstock Dr
26. Kingsway Dr
27. Purvis Dr
28. Orchid Ln
29. University Ave
30. Andover Dr
31. Keeler St
32. S Varney St
33. S Florence St
34. S Naomi St
35. S Frederic St
36. W Willow St
37. Edison St

Major Roads & Highways

Golden State Freeway (I-5)
Burbank Western Channel
Los Angeles River
San Fernando Rd
N Glenoaks Blvd
S Glenoaks Blvd
W Glenoaks Blvd
N San Fernando Blvd
S San Fernando Blvd
E Magnolia Blvd
W Magnolia Blvd
W Burbank Blvd
N Victory Pl
W Victory Blvd
Victory Blvd
W Olive Ave
W Alameda Ave
W Riverside Dr
Riverside Dr
N Kenneth Rd
S Kenneth Rd
E Alameda Ave
Western Ave
Scott Rd
N Buena Vista
S Buena Vista
N Brighton St
Forest Lawn Dr
Cosmic Way
Grand Central Ave

Route 134

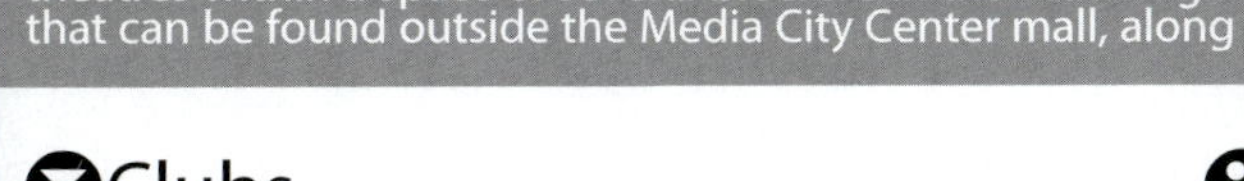

Burbank's Media District continues to grow. It sometimes seems as if every major chain restaurant and store has an outpost there, and the area boasts three major movie theatres within a space of several blocks. But the hidden gems are the used bookstores that can be found outside the Media City Center mall, along San Fernando Road.

Clubs

- **The Blue Room** · 916 S San Fernando Blvd · 323-849-2779

Coffee

- **Coffee Bean & Tea Leaf** · 340 N San Fernando Blvd
- **Coffee Beanery** · 201 E Magnolia Blvd
- **Starbucks** · 113 E Alameda Ave
- **Starbucks** · 1711 N Victory Pl
- **Starbucks** · 300 N San Fernando Blvd

Farmer's Markets

- **Burbank** · 3rd St & Orange Grove Ave · Sat 8-12:30

Gyms

- **Burbank YMCA** · 321 E Magnolia Blvd · 818-845-8551
- **Los Angeles Lifting Club** · 1031 N Victory Pl · 818-846-5438
- **World Gym Fitness Center** · 226 E Palm Ave · 818-954-0021

Hardware Stores

- **Burbank Paint** · 548 S San Fernando Blvd · 818-845-2684
- **Designer Door & Window** · 1701 W Magnolia Blvd · 818-841-3181
- **Orchard Supply Hardware** · 641 N Victory Blvd · 818-557-2755
- **Payless Tools** · 509 N Victory Blvd · 818-843-2140
- **Terry Lumber** · 640 N Victory Blvd · 818-842-2177

Liquor Stores

- **ABC Liquor & Deli** · 2112 W Magnolia Blvd
- **Ace Liquors** · 1740 Victory Blvd
- **Alameda Liquor** · 929 S Victory Blvd
- **Burbank Liquor & Market** · 500 S Glenoaks Blvd
- **Castle Liquors** · 6808 San Fernando Rd
- **Favorite Liquor & Deli** · 533 S Victory Blvd
- **Glenmar Liquors** · 2000 N Glenoaks Blvd
- **K & K Liquor Store** · 515 N Victory Blvd
- **M & M Liquors** · 1951 W Glenoaks Blvd
- **Roy's Liquor** · 1627 N San Fernando Blvd
- **Star Express Market** · 539 N Glenoaks Blvd
- **Thirst Quencher Liquors** · 440 N Glenoaks Blvd
- **UM Liquor** · 401 N Victory Blvd
- **Village Liquor & Market** · 211 E Olive Ave

Movie Theaters

- **AMC Burbank 14 Theatres** · 140 E Palm Ave
- **Media Center 8** · 210 E Magnolia Blvd
- **Media Center North** · 770 N 1st St

Pet Stores

- **Burbank Pet Plaza** · 1080 W Alameda Ave · 818-557-0144
- **Millennium Pets** · 409 N Victory Blvd · 818-845-7305
- **Pets R Us** · 839 W Glenoaks Blvd · 818-553-8060
- **Scales 'N' Tails** · 1720 W Verdugo Ave · 818-842-6496
- **Stephens Hay & Grain** · 1840 Riverside Dr · 818-242-4540

Restaurants

- **Gordon Biersch Brewing** · 145 S San Fernando Blvd · 818-569-5240
- **Market City Caffe** · 164 E Palm Ave · 818-840-7036
- **Mi Piace** · 801 N San Fernando Blvd · 818-843-1111
- **Poquito Mas** · 2635 W Olive Ave · 818-563-2252
- **Ribs USA** · 2711 W Olive Ave · 818-841-8872
- **Riverside Café** · 1221 W Riverside Dr · 818-563-3567
- **Viva Fresh** · 900 W Riverside Dr · 818-845-2425

Shopping

- **Book City** · 308 N San Fernando Blvd · 818-848-4417
- **Creature Features** · 1802 W Olive Ave · 818-842-9383
- **Pickwick Center** · 1001 Riverside Dr · 818-845-5300
- **Valley Dealer Exchange** · 825 N Victory Blvd · 818-767-1800

Video Rental

- **20-20 Video** · 600 S Glenoaks Blvd · 818-559-2300
- **Blockbuster** · 1212 N San Fernando Blvd · 818-558-5292
- **Blockbuster** · 324 S Glenoaks Blvd · 818-972-9292
- **GM Video Rentals** · 511 N Victory Blvd · 818-843-2182
- **Goodtime Video** · 520N Glenoaks Blvd · 818-558-5618
- **Hollywood Video** · 105 E Alameda Ave · 818-845-0553
- **Plaza Video** · 1040 W Alameda Ave · 818-846-5005

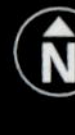

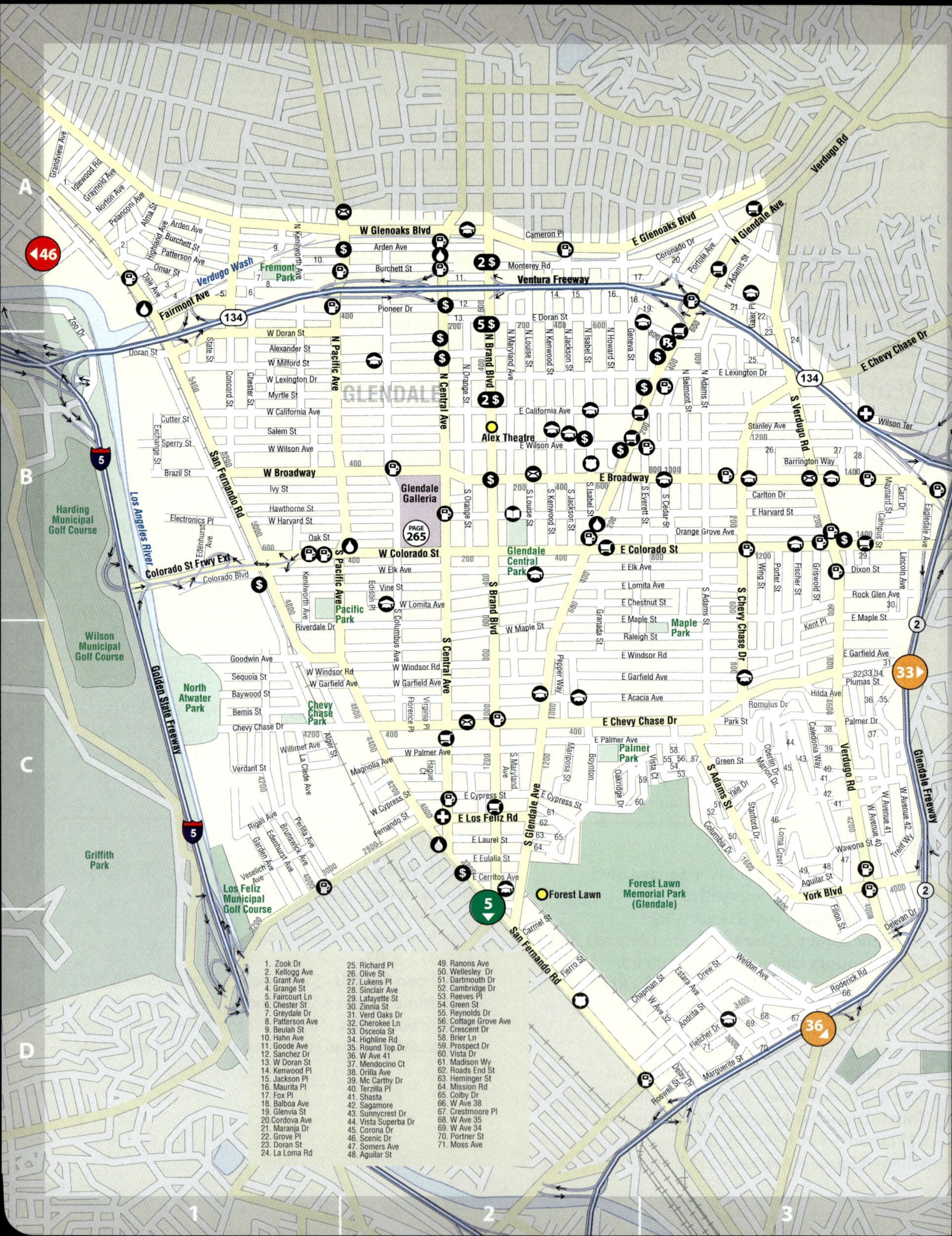
N
GLENDALE
Glendale Galleria
PAGE 265
Alex Theatre
Forest Lawn
Forest Lawn Memorial Park (Glendale)
Fremont Park
Pacific Park
Glendale Central Park
Maple Park
Palmer Park
Chevy Chase Park
North Atwater Park
Harding Municipal Golf Course
Wilson Municipal Golf Course
Los Feliz Municipal Golf Course
Griffith Park
Los Angeles River
Verdugo Wash
Golden State Freeway
Glendale Freeway
Ventura Freeway
W Glenoaks Blvd
E Glenoaks Blvd
W Broadway
E Broadway
W Colorado St
E Colorado St
E Chevy Chase Dr
E Los Feliz Rd
N Brand Blvd
S Brand Blvd
N Central Ave
S Central Ave
N Pacific Ave
S Pacific Ave
San Fernando Rd
S Glendale Ave
N Glendale Ave
S Verdugo Rd
Verdugo Rd
S Chevy Chase Dr
S Adams St
York Blvd
Colorado St Frwy Ext
Fairmont Ave
1. Zook Dr
2. Kellogg Ave
3. Grant Ave
4. Grange St
5. Faircourt Ln
6. Chester St
7. Greydale Dr
8. Patterson Ave
9. Beulah St
10. Hahn Ave
11. Goode Ave
12. Sanchez Dr
13. W Doran St
14. Kenwood Pl
15. Jackson Pl
16. Maurita Pl
17. Fox Pl
18. Balboa Ave
19. Glenvia St
20. Cordova Ave
21. Maranja Dr
22. Grove Pl
23. Doran St
24. La Loma Rd
25. Richard Pl
26. Olive St
27. Lukens Pl
28. Sinclair Ave
29. Lafayette St
30. Zinnia St
31. Verd Oaks Dr
32. Cherokee Ln
33. Osceola St
34. Highline Rd
35. Round Top Dr
36. W Ave 41
37. Mendocino Ct
38. Orilla Ave
39. Mc Carthy Dr
40. Terzilla Pl
41. Shasta
42. Sagamore
43. Sunnycrest Dr
44. Vista Superba Dr
45. Corona Dr
46. Scenic Dr
47. Somers Ave
48. Aguilar St
49. Ranons Ave
50. Wellesley Dr
51. Dartmouth Dr
52. Cambridge Dr
53. Reeves Pl
54. Green St
55. Reynolds Dr
56. Cottage Grove Ave
57. Crescent Dr
58. Brier Ln
59. Prospect Dr
60. Vista Dr
61. Madison Wy
62. Roads End St
63. Heminger St
64. Mission Rd
65. Colby Dr
66. W Ave 38
67. Crestmoore Pl
68. W Ave 35
69. W Ave 34
70. Portner St
71. Moss Ave

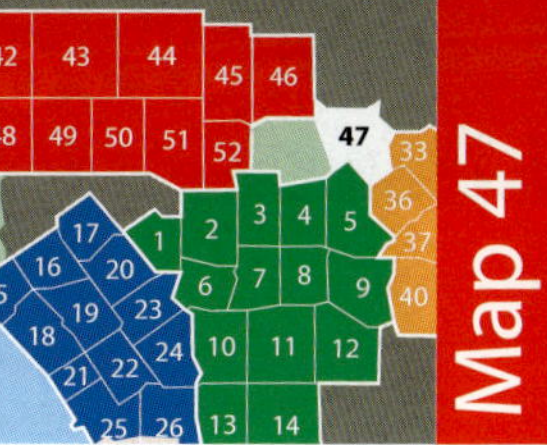

You might not see many stars out and about in Glendale these days, but Forest Lawn has become the final resting place for quite a bunch. George Burns, Jimmy Stewart, and novelist Louis L'Amour are among the rich and famous buried at Forest Lawn. This cemetery is something of a spectacle, and might be worth a trip while you're still around to enjoy it.

$ Banks

- **Bank of America** • 203 N Glendale Ave
- **Bank of America** • 345 N Brand Blvd
- **Bank of America** • 3812 San Fernando Rd
- **Bank of the West** • 400 N Glendale Ave
- **Citibank** • 414 N Central Ave
- **Citibank** • 700 N Brand Blvd
- **City National Bank** • 550 N Brand Blvd
- **Community Bank** • 100 N Brand Blvd
- **East West Bank** • 520 N Central Ave
- **Fidelity Federal Bank** • 4565 Colorado Blvd
- **Fidelity Federal Bank** • 600 N Brand Blvd
- **First Regional Bank** • 655 N Central Ave
- **Nara Bank** • 831 N Pacific Ave
- **Union Bank** • 330 N Brand Blvd
- **US Bank** • 701 N Brand Blvd
- **Washington Mutual** • 500 N Glendale Ave
- **Washington Mutual** • 620 N Brand Blvd
- **Wells Fargo Bank** • 1416 E Colorado St
- **Wells Fargo Bank** • 535 N Brand Blvd
- **Western Financial Bank** • 611 E Wilson Ave

Car Washes

- **Antique Car Wash** • 236 S Glendale Ave
- **Broadway Car Wash** • 361 W Broadway
- **California Car Wash** • 3940 San Fernando Rd
- **California Detail Shop** • 453 W Colorado St
- **Doherty's Unocal** • 901 N Central Ave
- **Galleria Car Wash** • 5720 San Fernando Rd

Gas Stations

- **76** • 200 N Glendale Ave
- **76** • 200 S Central Ave
- **76** • 901 N Central Ave
- **Arco** • 144 N Verdugo Rd
- **Arco** • 4103 Verdugo Rd
- **Arco** • 501 W Colorado St
- **Arco** • 5800 San Fernando Rd
- **Chevron** • 1101 E Colorado Blvd
- **Chevron** • 2960 W Broadway
- **Chevron** • 3100 N San Fernando Rd
- **Chevron** • 466 W Broadway
- **Chevron** • 501 E Glenoaks Blvd
- **Mobil** • 1028 S Brand Blvd
- **Mobil** • 1324 S Central Ave
- **Mobil** • 250 S Glendale Ave
- **Mobil** • 301 S Verdugo Rd
- **Mobil** • 700 N Glendale Ave
- **Mobil** • 800 N Pacific Ave
- **Mobil** • 825 N Central Ave
- **Shell** • 1401 E Colorado St
- **Shell** • 4067 Verdugo Rd
- **Shell** • 501 W Colorado Blvd
- **Shell** • 625 N Pacific Ave
- **Texaco** • 401 N Glendale Ave

Hospitals

- **Glendale Adventist Medical Center** • 1509 Wilson Ter • 818-409-8000
- **Glendale Memorial Hospital** • 1420 S Central Ave • 818-502-1900

Landmarks

- **Alex Theatre** • 216 N Brand Blvd
- **Forest Lawn** • 1712 S Glendale Ave

Libraries

- **Glendale Central Library** • 222 E Harvard St • 818-548 2020

24-Hour Pharmacies

- **Rite-Aid** • 531 N Glendale Ave • 818-241-9770

Police

- **Glendale Police Dept** • 140 N Isabel St • 818-548-4840
- **Los Angeles Police Dept** • 3353 N San Fernando Rd • 213-485-2563

Post Offices

- 1009 N Pacific Ave
- 101 N Verdugo Rd
- 120 E Chevy Chase Dr
- 313 E Broadway

Schools

- **Cerritos Elementary** • 120 E Cerritos Ave
- **Columbus Elementary** • 425 W Milford St
- **Daily High School** • 220 N Kenwood Pl
- **Edison Elementary** • 440 W Lomita Ave
- **First Lutheran School and Art Academy** • 1300 E Colorado St
- **Fletcher Drive Elementary** • 3350 Fletcher Dr
- **Glendale Alternative High School** • 223 N Jackson St
- **Glendale Senior High School** • 1440 E Broadway
- **Holy Family Elementary** • 400 S Louise St
- **Holy Family High School** • 400 E Lamita Ave
- **Horace Mann Elementary** • 501 E Acacia Ave
- **Hoskins Center** • 1479 E Broadway
- **Incarnation Elementary** • 123 W Glenoaks Blvd
- **Irving Middle School** • 3010 Estara Ave
- **John Marshall Elementary** • 1201 E Broadway
- **Muir Elementary** • 912 S Chevy Chase Dr
- **Roosevelt Middle School** • 1017 S Glendale Ave
- **Tobinworld** • 920 E Broadway
- **White Elementary** • 744 E Doran St
- **Wilson Middle School** • 1221 Monterey Rd
- **Zion Lutheran** • 301 N Isabel St

Supermarkets

- **Albertson's** • 1000 S Central Ave
- **Jon's Marketplace** • 600 E Colorado St
- **Ralph's** • 1010 N Glendale Ave
- **Ralph's** • 1416 E Colorado St
- **Ralph's** • 211 N Glendale Ave
- **Trader Joe's** • 130 N Glendale Ave
- **Von's** • 311 W Los Feliz Rd
- **Von's** • 561 N Glendale Ave
- **Whole Foods Market** • 826 N Glendale Ave

Map 47 · Glendale South
N

46

134

5

GLENDALE

Verdugo Wash
Fremont Park
Los Angeles River
Harding Municipal Golf Course
Wilson Municipal Golf Course
North Atwater Park
Griffith Park
Los Feliz Municipal Golf Course
Golden State Freeway
Pacific Park
Chevy Chase Park
Glendale Galleria
PAGE 265
Glendale Central Park
Maple Park
Palmer Park
Forest Lawn Memorial Park (Glendale)

W Glenoaks Blvd
E Glenoaks Blvd
Arden Ave
Burchett St
Ventura Freeway
Cameron Pl
Monterey Rd
Coronado Dr
Portola Ave
N Glendale Ave
W Adams St
E Doran St
E Lexington Dr
E Chevy Chase Dr
Verdugo Rd
Wilson Ter
Stanley Ave
Barrington Way
Carlton Dr
E Harvard St
Orange Grove Ave
Dixon St
Rock Glen Ave
E Maple St
E Garfield Ave
Plumas St
Hilda Ave
Romulus Dr
Palmer Dr
Caledonia Way
Green St
S Adams St
Loma Crest
Wawona St
Aguilar St
York Blvd
Delevan Dr
Glendale Freeway
33
36
2

Grandview Ave
Idlewood Rd
Graynold Ave
Alma St
Arden Ave
Norton Ave
Palanconi Ave
Highland Ave
Burchett St
Patterson Ave
Omar St
Dale Ave
Fairmont Ave
Zoo Dr
Doran St
State St
Chester St
Concord St
Cutter St
Exchange St
Sperry St
Brazil St
Electronics Pl
San Fernando Rd
Edenhurst Ave
Colorado St Frwy Ext
Colorado Blvd
Kenilworth Ave
Riverdale Dr
Goodwin Ave
Sequoia St
Baywood St
Bemis St
Chevy Chase Dr
Verdant St
Willimet Ave
Auga St
La Clede Ave
Magnolia Ave
Rigali Ave
Perlita Ave
Brunswick Ave
Edenhurst Ave
Garden Ave
Veselich Ave
Fernando Ct
W Cypress St
E Los Feliz Rd
E Laurel St
E Eulalia St
E Cerritos Ave
San Fernando Rd
Carmel St
Fierro St

W Doran St
Alexander St
W Milford St
W Lexington Dr
Myrtle St
W California Ave
Salem St
W Wilson Ave
W Broadway
Ivy St
Hawthorne St
W Harvard St
Oak St
W Colorado St
W Elk Ave
Vine St
W Lomita Ave
Edison Pl
W Windsor Rd
W Garfield Ave
Florence Pl
Virginia Pl
Hague Ct
W Palmer Ave
S Central Ave
S Pacific Ave
S Columbus Ave
S Brand Blvd

N Pacific Ave
N Central Ave
N Brand Blvd
N Orange St
N Maryland Ave
N Louise St
N Jackson Ave
N Kenwood St
N Isabel St
N Howard St
Geneva St
E Doran St
E California Ave
E Wilson Ave
E Broadway
S Orange St
S Louise St
S Jackson St
S Kenwood St
S Isabel St
S Everett St
S Cedar St
E Colorado St
E Elk Ave
E Lomita Ave
E Chestnut St
E Maple St
Granada St
Raleigh St
E Windsor Rd
E Garfield Ave
E Acacia Ave
E Chevy Chase Dr
Pepper Way
S Maryland Ave
Mariposa Dr
Boynton
E Cypress St
S Glendale Ave
E Palmer Ave
Vista Ct
Oakridge Dr
Columbia Dr
S Adams St
Stanford Dr
Marton Dr
Obelrin Dr
Caledonia Way

N Kenworth Pl
Pioneer Dr

Belmont St
N Adams St
Carr St
Maynard Campus St
Eagledale
Lincoln Ave
Griswold St
Fischer St
Porter St
Wing St
S Chevy Chase Dr
Kent Pl
Park St
Yale Dr
Green St

W Avenue 42
W Avenue 41
W Avenue 40
W Avenue 38
W Avenue 35
W Avenue 34
Trent Wy
Filson St
Chapman St
Estara Ave
Drew St
Weldon Ave
Andrita St
W Ave 22
Fletcher Dr
Roswell Ave
Delay Dr
Marguerite St
Roderick Rd
Crestmoore Pl

1. Zook Dr
2. Kellogg Ave
3. Grant Ave
4. Grange St
5. Faircourt Ln
6. Chester St
7. Greydale Dr
8. Patterson Ave
9. Beulah St
10. Hahn Ave
11. Goode Ave
12. Sanchez Pl
13. W Doran St
14. Kenwood Pl
15. Jackson Pl
16. Maurita Pl
17. Fox Pl
18. Balboa Ave
19. Glenvia St
20. Cordova Ave
21. Maranja Dr
22. Grove Pl
23. Doran St
24. La Loma Rd
25. Richard Pl
26. Olive St
27. Lukens Pl
28. Sinclair Ave
29. Lafayette St
30. Zinnia St
31. Verd Oaks Dr
32. Cherokee Ln
33. Osceola St
34. Highline Rd
35. Round Top Dr
36. W Ave 41
37. Mendocino Ct
38. Orilla Ave
39. Mc Carthy Dr
40. Terzilla Pl
41. Shasta
42. Sagamore
43. Sunnycrest Dr
44. Vista Superba Dr
45. Corona Dr
46. Scenic Dr
47. Somers Sove
48. Aguilar St
49. Ranons Ave
50. Wellesley Dr
51. Dartmouth Dr
52. Cambridge Dr
53. Reeves Pl
54. Green St
55. Reynolds Dr
56. Cottage Grove Ave
57. Crescent Dr
58. Brier Ln
59. Prospect Dr
60. Vista Dr
61. Madison Wy
62. Roads End St
63. Heminger St
64. Mission Rd
65. Colby Dr
66. W Ave 38
67. Crestmoore Pl
68. W Ave 35
69. W Ave 34
70. Portner St
71. Moss Ave

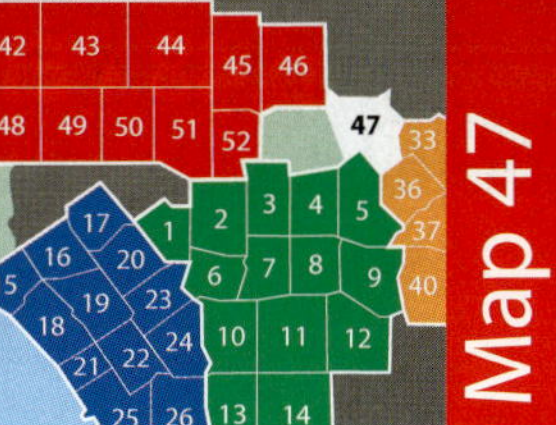

It all happens in and around the Glendale Galleria, one of the biggest shopping malls the Valley has to offer.

24-Hour Copy Centers
- **Kinko's** • 225 N Brand Blvd • 818-500-1811

Clubs
- **Jax Bar and Grill** • 339 N Brand Blvd • 818-500-1604

Coffee
- **Brand Coffee** • 701 N Brand Blvd
- **Coffee Express** • 742 N Glendale Ave
- **Edna's Coffee & Grocery** • 420 S Glendale Ave
- **La Goccia Espresso Bar** • 101 N Brand Blvd
- **Starbucks** • 130 S Brand Blvd
- **Starbucks** • 469 Burchett St
- **Tiffany's Coffee** • 900 N Pacific Ave

Farmer's Markets
- **Farmers' Market** • 100 N Brand Blvd • Thu 9:30-1:30

Gyms
- **24-Hour Fitness** • 240 N Brand Blvd • 818-240-5111
- **Bally Total Fitness** • 623 S Central Ave • 818-240-2425
- **World Gym** • 1001 E Colorado Blvd • 818-243-1600
- **YWCA of Glendale** • 735 E Lexington Dr • 818-242-4155

Hardware Stores
- **Home Depot** • 5040 San Fernando Rd • 818-246-9600
- **Virgil's Hardware Home & Garden** • 520 N Glendale Ave • 818-242-1104

Liquor Stores
- **A-1 Liquor** • 1145 E Colorado St
- **Adams Square Liquor** • 1021 E Chevy Chase Dr
- **B & C Liquor** • 102 W Colorado St
- **Broadway Liquors** • 465 W Broadway
- **Cavalier Liquor** • 1307 W Glenoaks Blvd
- **Colorado Liquor** • 468 W Colorado St
- **Eco Wines & Spirits** • 3235 N San Fernando Rd
- **Esquire Liquor** • 5300 San Fernando Rd
- **Glendale House of Liquor** • 420 S Glendale Ave
- **Golden Jug Liquors** • 1311 E Colorado St
- **Gourmet Liquors** • 715 S Central Ave
- **House of Liquor** • 1008 E Colorado St
- **Liquor Zone** • 424 S Central Ave
- **Ma's Market** • 4106 San Fernando Rd
- **Michall's Liquor** • 333 N Verdugo Rd
- **Old Green Mill Liquor House** • 4520 San Fernando Rd
- **Red Carpet Wines & Spirits** • 400 E Glenoaks Blvd
- **Rodeo Liquor & Deli** • 205 S Glendale Ave
- **Windsor Liquor** • 801 S Glendale Ave

Movie Theaters
- **AMC Center Cinema** • 501 N Orange St
- **Mann 4 Glendale Marketplace** • 144 S Brand Blvd
- **Mann Exchange 10** • 128 N Maryland Ave

Pet Stores
- **Pets R Us** • 1315 E Colorado St • 818-246-2923
- **Pretty Bird** • 1247 E Colorado St • 818-265-0566
- **Tropical Imports Unlimited** • 1134 E Colorado St • 818-240-9356

Restaurants
- **Blue Pyramid** • 1000 E Broadway • 818-548-1000
- **Cinnabar** • 933 S Brand Blvd • 818-551-1155
- **Damon's Steakhouse** • 317 N Brand Blvd • 818-507-1510

Video Rental
- **20-20 Video** • 1023 S Brand Blvd • 818-240-2020
- **ABCVideo (Asian)** • 4108 Verdugo Rd • 323-257-7225
- **Blockbuster** • 306 N Glendale Ave • 818-547-1146
- **Blockbuster** • 900 E Colorado St • 818-549-0801
- **Blockbuster** • 900 N Pacific Ave • 818-507-4392
- **Chaterian** • 1022 E Broadway • 818-242-6928
- **Glendale Video Shop (Korean)** • 1100 S Central Ave • 818-240-9880
- **Glendale Videograph** • 620 S Glendale Ave • 818-240-5463
- **Happy Nights Video** • 725 S Glendale Ave • 818-507-0988
- **Interhome Video** • 519 S Verdugo Rd • 818-956-6031
- **Mundo Latino (Spanish)** • 401 W Los Feliz Rd • 818-241-2263
- **Q Video** • 1144 E Broadway • 818-244-8228
- **Video Station** • 1112 1/2 W Glenoaks Blvd • 818-242-6512

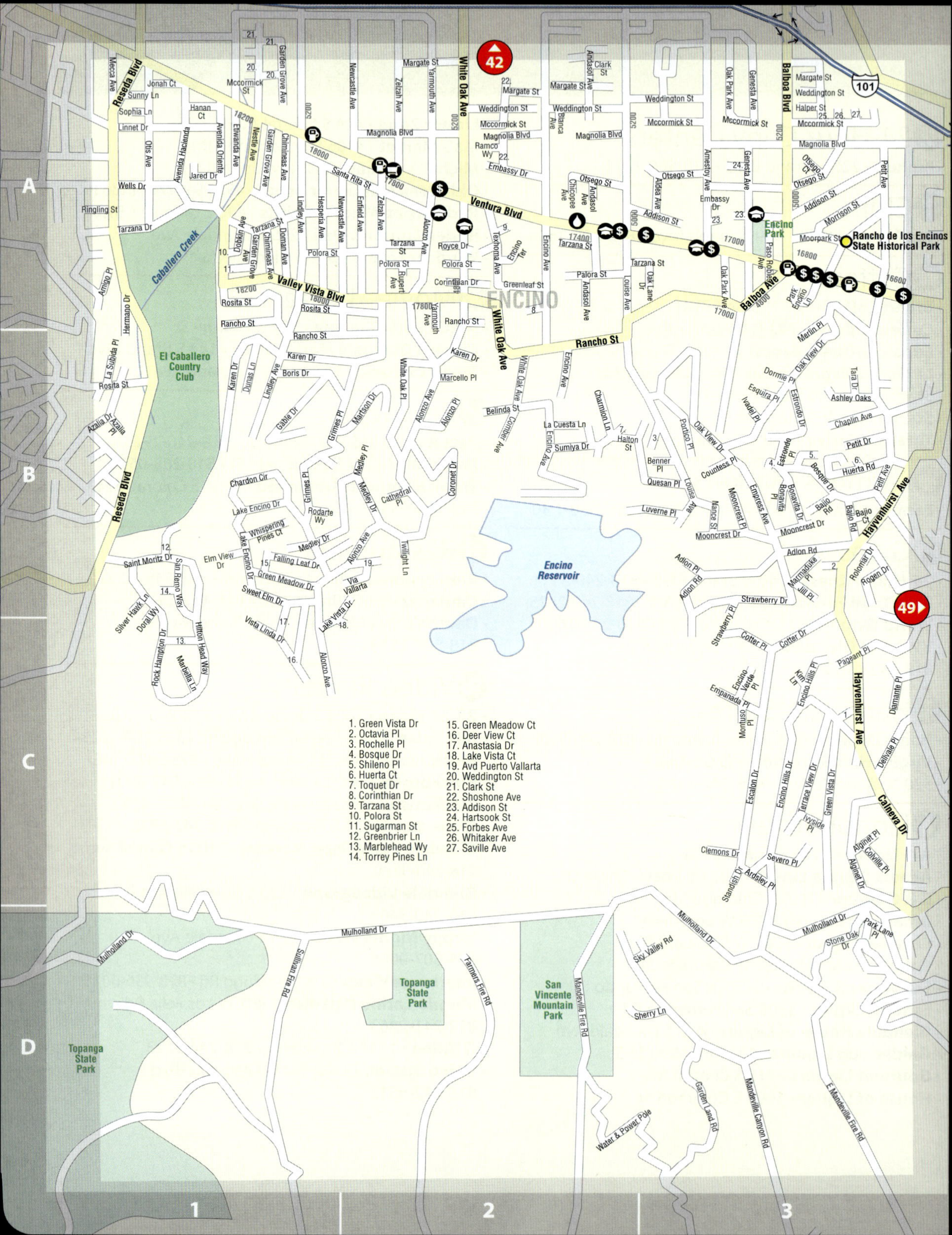

1. Green Vista Dr
2. Octavia Pl
3. Rochelle Pl
4. Bosque Dr
5. Shileno Pl
6. Huerta Ct
7. Toquet Dr
8. Corinthian Dr
9. Tarzana St
10. Polora St
11. Sugarman St
12. Greenbrier Ln
13. Marblehead Wy
14. Torrey Pines Ln
15. Green Meadow Ct
16. Deer View Ct
17. Anastasia Dr
18. Lake Vista Ct
19. Avd Puerto Vallarta
20. Weddington St
21. Clark St
22. Shoshone Ave
23. Addison St
24. Hartsook St
25. Forbes Ave
26. Whitaker Ave
27. Saville Ave

Ten miles from Hollywood and 20 miles from downtown L.A., this 42,500-person community is a meld of the two worlds—mixing just about anything you'd ever need from L.A., with a little entertainment, and a few celebrities—Encino offers it all in the San Fernando Valley!

$ Banks

- **Bank of America** · 16640 Ventura Blvd
- **California National Bank** · 16820 Ventura Blvd
- **California National Bank** · 16830 Ventura Blvd
- **Downey Savings & Loan** · 17250 Ventura Blvd
- **First Bank & Trust** · 17777 Ventura Blvd
- **First Regional Bank** · 16830 Ventura Blvd
- **Union Bank** · 16633 Ventura Blvd
- **Washington Mutual** · 17107 Ventura Blvd
- **Western Financial Bank** · 17323 Ventura Blvd

Car Washes

- **Premier Car Wash** · 17432 Ventura Blvd

Gas Stations

- **76** · 16900 Ventura Blvd
- **76** · 17849 Ventura Blvd
- **Chevron** · 18081 Ventura Blvd
- **Shell** · 16801 Ventura Blvd

Landmarks

- **Rancho de los Encinos State Historical Park** · 16756 Moorpark St

Post Offices

- 4930 Balboa Blvd

Schools

- **Crespi Carmelite High School** · 5031 Alonzo Ave
- **Encino Elementary** · 16941 Addison St
- **Los Encinos Elementary** · 17114 Ventura Blvd
- **Morning Star Christian Academy** · 17327 Ventura Blvd
- **Our Lady of Grace** · 17720 Ventura Blvd
- **Our Lady of Grace** · 5011 White Oak Ave

Supermarkets

- **Ralph's** · 17840 Ventura Blvd

N

Major roads/features:
Reseda Blvd, White Oak Ave, Balboa Blvd, Ventura Blvd, Valley Vista Blvd, Rancho St, Mulholland Dr, Hayvenhurst Ave, Caineva Dr

101 · 42 · 49

ENCINO

Encino Reservoir

Caballero Creek

El Caballero Country Club

Encino Park

Topanga State Park

San Vincente Mountain Park

Street index:

1. Green Vista Dr
2. Octavia Pl
3. Rochelle Pl
4. Bosque Dr
5. Shileno Pl
6. Huerta Ct
7. Toquet Dr
8. Corinthian Dr
9. Tarzana St
10. Polora St
11. Sugarman St
12. Greenbrier Ln
13. Marblehead Wy
14. Torrey Pines Ln
15. Green Meadow Ct
16. Deer View Ct
17. Anastasia Dr
18. Lake Vista Ct
19. Avd Puerto Vallarta
20. Weddington St
21. Clark St
22. Shoshone Ave
23. Addison St
24. Hartsook St
25. Forbes Ave
26. Whitaker Ave
27. Saville Ave

A
Mecca Blvd, Reseda Blvd, Sunny Ln, Sophia Ln, Linnet Dr, Otis Ave, Jonah Ct, Hanan Ct, Avenida Oriente, Avenida Hacienda Eqnway, Jared Dr, Wells Dr, Ringling St, Tarzana Dr, McCormick St, Garden Grove Ave, Chimineas Ave, Newcastle Ave, Lindley Ave, Hesperia Ave, Santa Rita St, Enfield Ave, Zelzah Ave, Yarmouth Ave, Margate St, Magnolia Blvd, White Oak Ave, Weddington St, Margate St, Embassy Dr, Andasol Ave, Clark St, Weddington St, Bianca Ave, Magnolia Blvd, Ramco Wy, Otsego St, Chicopee Ave, Andasol Ave, Addison St, Weddington St, Oak Park Ave, Genesta Ave, McCormick St, Amestoy Ave, Embassy Dr, Margate St, Weddington St, Halper St, McCormick St, Magnolia Blvd, Otsego Ct, Petit Ave, Addison St, Morrison St, Moorpark St

Ventura Blvd

B
Reseda Blvd, Amigo Pl, Hermano Dr, Azalia Dr, Azalia Pl, La Subida Pl, Rosita St, Tarzana Dr, Garden Grove Ave, Donan Ave, Chimineas Ave, Newcastle Ave, Polora St, Rosita St, Rancho St, Karen Dr, Lindley Ave, Boris Dr, Grimes Pl, Grimes Pl, Gable Dr, Martson Dr, Medley Pl, Chardon Cir, Lake Encino Dr, Rodarte Wy, Whispering Pines Ct, Medley Dr, Elm View Dr, Falling Leat Dr, Green Meadow Dr, Alonzo Ave, Coronado Dr, Twilight Ln, Cathedral Pl, White Oak Pl, Marcello Pl, Marc. Alonzo Ave, Alonzo Pl, Royce Dr, Polora St, Rupert Ave, Corinthian Dr, Greenleaf Ave, Yarmouth Ave, Rancho St, Karen Dr, Belinda St, Conner Ave, Encino Ave, La Cuesta Ln, Sumiya Dr, Halton St, Charmion Ln, Benner Pl, Quesan Pl, Luverne Pl, Louise Ave, Portico Pl, Oak View Dr, Countess Pl, Nance Dr, Empress Ave, Mooncrest Pl, Mooncrest Dr, Bonavita Dr, Bonavita Pl, Bosque Dr, Huerta Rd, Mooncrest Dr, Adlon Rd, Merlin Pl, Dormie Dr, Esquira Pl, Ivadel Pl, Estrondo Dr, Oak View Dr, Tara Dr, Ashley Oaks, Chaplin Ave, Petit Dr, Estrondo Dr, Bajio Rd, Bajio Rd, Petit Ave, Hayvenhurst Ave

El Caballero Country Club

C
Saint Moritz Dr, San Remo Way, Silver Hawk Ln, Doral Wy, Rock Hampton Dr, Hilton Head Way, Marbella Ln, Elm View Dr, Lake Encino Dr, Green Meadow Dr, Sweet Elm Dr, Vista Linda Dr, Via Vallarta, Lake Vista Dr, Alonzo Ave, Encino Reservoir, Adlon Rd, Adlon Pl, Strawberry Dr, Marmaduke, Jill Pl, Strawberry Pl, Cotter Pl, Cotter Pl, Rolomar Dr, Rogen Dr, Pageant Pl, Encino Verde Pl, Empanada Pl, Montoro Rd, Encino Hills Dr, Kim Ln, Encino Hills Dr, Terrace View Dr, Green Vista Dr, Ivyside Pl, Delnate Pl, Diamante Pl, Hayvenhurst Ave, Clemons Dr, Severo Pl, Alginet Pl, Colville Pl, Alginet Dr, Caineva Dr, Standish Dr, Ardsley Pl

49

D
Topanga State Park, Mulholland Dr, Sullivan Fire Rd, Farmers Fire Rd, Topanga State Park, San Vincente Mountain Park, Mandeville Fire Rd, Sky Valley Rd, Sherry Ln, Mulholland Dr, Mulholland Dr, Stone Oak Dr, Park Lane Pl, Garden Land Rd, E Mandeville Fire Rd, Mandeville Canyon Rd, Water & Power Pole

1 · 2 · 3

Called home by the Tongva Indians in 1769, Encino today is a multicultural mecca, with Persians, Asians, Israelis, Russians, and even movie stars residing in the area. This vast array of cultures makes for a unique and varied community boasting both elegant and offbeat shopping, plenty of recreation, and delectable dining that will delight any palate.

Coffee

- **Cafe De Gourmets** · 17233 Ventura Blvd
- **Nuts Landing** · 17028 Ventura Blvd
- **Starbucks** · 17308 Ventura Blvd

Gyms

- **Bally Total Fitness** · 17401 Ventura Blvd · 818-382-6060
- **Bodies In Motion** · 17031 Ventura Blvd · 818-995-7700

Liquor Stores

- **C & C Liquor** · 18089 Ventura Blvd
- **Encino Park Liquor** · 18001 Ventura Blvd

Movie Theaters

- **Town Center 5** · 17200 Ventura Blvd

Pet Stores

- **Petco** · 17919 Ventura Blvd · 818-343-1124

Restaurants

- **Bagel Nosh Deli & Restaurant** · 17271 Ventura Blvd · 818-995-4545
- **Baklava Factory** · 17141 Ventura Blvd · 818-728-1600
- **Buca di Beppo** · 17500 Ventura Blvd · 818-995 3288
- **California Wok** · 16656 Ventura Blvd · 818-386-0561
- **Catch 21** · 17316 Ventura Blvd · 818-789-3474
- **Cha Cha Cha Encino** · 17499 Ventura Blvd · 818-789-3600
- **Chili My Soul** · 4928 Balboa Blvd · 818-981-7685
- **Jerry's Famous Deli** · 16650 Ventura Blvd · 818-906-1800
- **Jerusalem Pizza** · 17942 Ventura Blvd · 818-758-9595
- **Johnny Rocket's** · 16901 Ventura Blvd · 818-981-5900
- **Kaiten Sushi** · 17302 Ventura Blvd · 818-986-7003
- **Mulberry Street Pizza** · 17040 Ventura Blvd · 818-906-8881
- **Versailles Restaurant** · 17410 Ventura Blvd · 818-906-0756
- **Vittorio's Italian Cucina** · 17644 Ventura Blvd · 818-986-9074

Shopping

- **A Rodin Art** · 17015 Ventura Blvd · 818-396-9148
- **Antik Shop** · 4909 Genesta Ave · 818-990-5990
- **Encino Newsstand** · 16720 Ventura Blvd ·
- **Encino Park & Community Center Map** · 4900 Genesta Ave · 818-995-1690
- **Herbalogics** · 17200 Ventura Blvd · 818-990-9990
- **Hopscotch** · 16740 Ventura Blvd
- **Ragg Tatoo** · 17245 Ventura Blvd · 818-990-7244
- **Sneaker Warehouse** · 16736 Ventura Blvd · 818-995-8999

N

SHERMAN OAKS

Sepulveda Dam Recreational Area

Sepulveda Dam

Burbank Blvd
Ventura Freeway
Ventura Blvd

Upper Stone Canyon Reservoir

Ahh's Discount Store

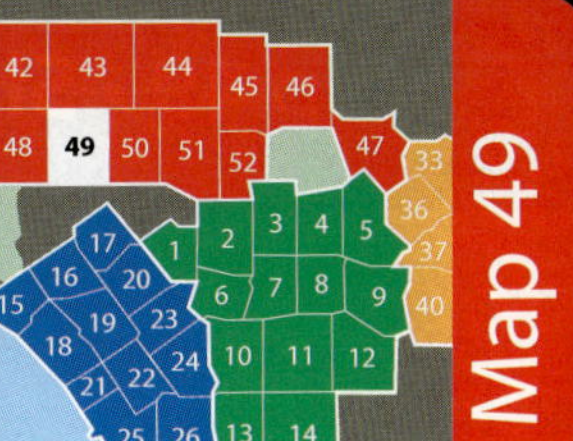

When Moon Zappa sang of Valley girls, this was the area she was referencing. The newly renovated Sherman Oaks Galleria is a far cry from what it was when featured in the "Valley Girl" movie, but the new incarnation has much to offer. With a giant Tower Records, a brand new Burke Williams Spa, a Magic Johnson 24-Hour Fitness Gym, a state-of-the-art movie theater, and restaurants to boot! It's not a bad place to duck into and beat the summer valley heat. This busy strip of Ventura Blvd. is a banking mecca of the valley.

$ Banks

- **Bank Leumi Le Israel** · 16530 Ventura Blvd
- **Bank of America** · 14701 Ventura Blvd
- **Bank of the West** · 15165 Ventura Blvd
- **Bank of the West** · 16027 Ventura Blvd
- **California Bank & Trust** · 16130 Ventura Blvd
- **Citibank** · 15233 Ventura Blvd
- **Citibank** · 15840 Ventura Blvd
- **Citibank** · 16601 Ventura Blvd
- **Citibank** · 3812 Sepulveda Blvd
- **City National Bank** · 15260 Ventura Blvd
- **City National Bank** · 16133 Ventura Blvd
- **Comerica Bank** · 15303 Ventura Blvd
- **Downey Savings Bank** · 16325 Ventura Blvd
- **Manufacturers Bank** · 16255 Ventura Blvd
- **National Bank of California** · 14724 Ventura Blvd
- **US Bank** · 15910 Ventura Blvd
- **Washington Mutual** · 15260 Ventura Blvd
- **Washington Mutual** · 15821 Ventura Blvd
- **Washington Mutual** · 16437 Ventura Blvd
- **Wells Fargo Bank** · 14855 Ventura Blvd

Car Washes

- **Encino Auto Wash** · 16300 Ventura Blvd
- **Sherman Oaks Car Wash** · 15150 Ventura Blvd

Gas Stations

- **76** · 15410 Ventura Blvd
- **Mobil** · 4528 Sepulveda Blvd

Hospitals

- **Encino Hospital** · 16237 Ventura Blvd · 818-995-5000

o Landmarks

- **Ahh's Discount Store (former El Reina Theatre)** · 14622 Ventura Blvd

Post Offices

- 14900 Magnolia Blvd

Schools

- **Curtis School Foundation** · 15871 Mulholland Dr
- **Emek Hebrew Academy** · 15365 Magnolia Blvd
- **Kester Avenue Elementary** · 5353 Kester Ave
- **Lanai Road Elementary** · 4241 Lanai Rd
- **Milken Community High School** · 15800 Mulholland Dr
- **Mirman School for Gifted Children** · 16180 Mulholland Dr
- **Roscomare Road Elementary** · 2425 Roscomare Rd
- **Sherman Oaks Elementary** · 14755 Greenleaf St
- **St Cyril's Catholic School** · 4548 Haskell Ave
- **Stephen S Wise Temple Elementary** · 15500 Stephen S Wise Dr
- **Valley Beth Shalom Day School** · 15739 Ventura Blvd
- **Westland** · 16200 Mulholland Dr

Supermarkets

- **Gelson's Markets** · 16450 Ventura Blvd
- **Pavilions** · 14845 Ventura Blvd
- **Ralph's** · 16325 Ventura Blvd
- **Whole Foods Market** · 4520 Sepulveda Blvd

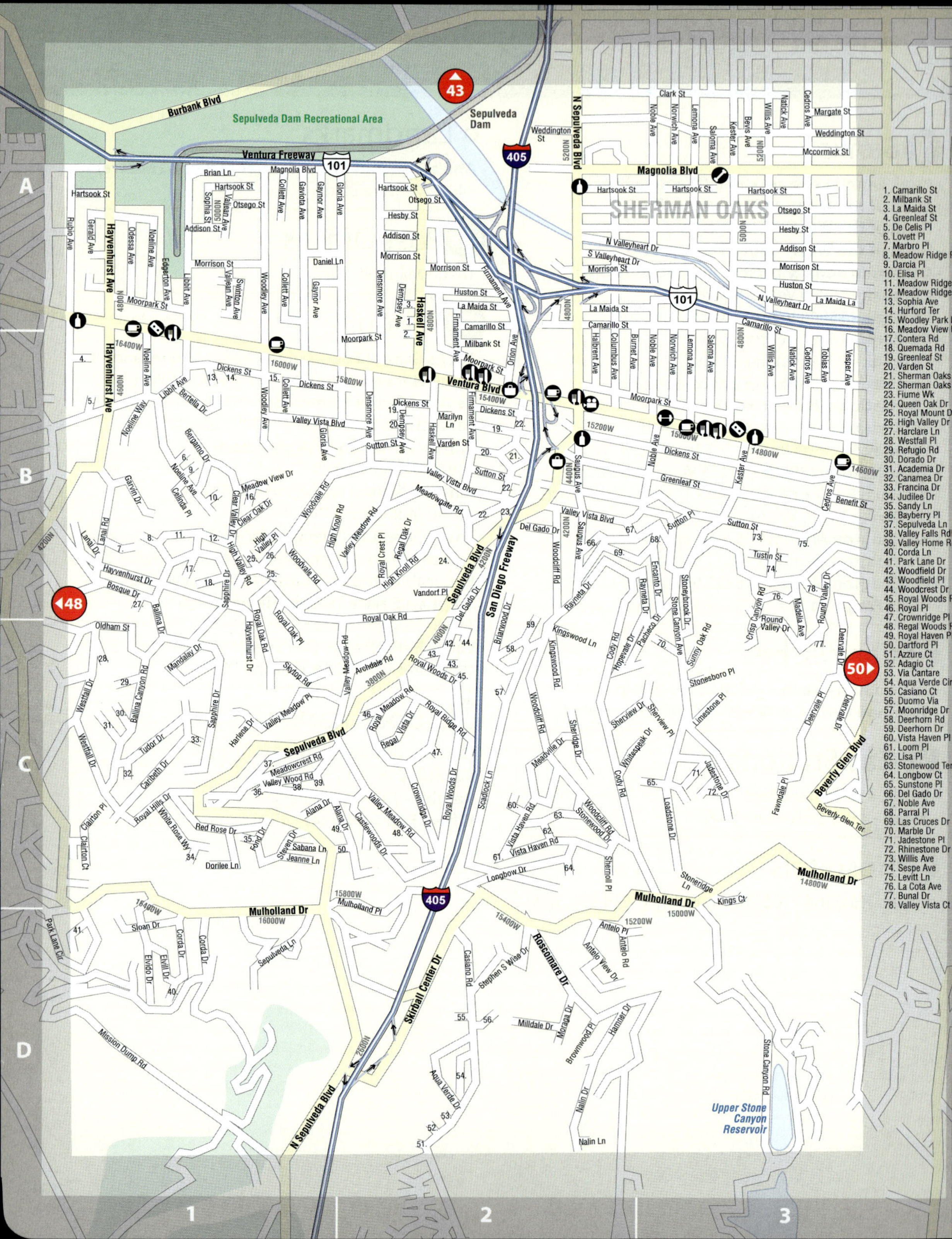

N
43
48
50
A
B
C
D
1
2
3
Sepulveda Dam Recreational Area
Sepulveda Dam
SHERMAN OAKS
Upper Stone Canyon Reservoir
Burbank Blvd
Ventura Freeway
101
405
San Diego Freeway
N Sepulveda Blvd
Sepulveda Blvd
Magnolia Blvd
Ventura Blvd
Mulholland Dr
Skirball Center Dr
Roscomare Rd
Beverly Glen Blvd
Haskell Ave
Havvenhurst Ave
Valley Vista Blvd
Moorpark St
Dickens St
Hartsook St
Morrison St
Camarillo St
Royal Oak Rd
Royal Woods Dr
Valley Meadow Rd
Woodcliff Rd
Stone Canyon Rd
Mission Dump Rd
16400W
16000W
15800W
15400W
15200W
15000W
14800W
14600W
1. Camarillo St
2. Milbank St
3. La Maida St
4. Greenleaf St
5. De Celis Pl
6. Lovett Pl
7. Marbro Pl
8. Meadow Ridge
9. Darcia Pl
10. Elisa Pl
11. Meadow Ridge
12. Meadow Ridge
13. Sophia Ave
14. Hurford Ter
15. Woodley Park
16. Meadow View
17. Contera Rd
18. Quemada Rd
19. Greenleaf St
20. Varden St
21. Sherman Oaks
22. Sherman Oaks
23. Fiume Wk
24. Queen Oak Dr
25. Royal Mount D
26. High Valley Dr
27. Harclare Ln
28. Westfall Pl
29. Refugio Rd
30. Dorado Dr
31. Academia Dr
32. Canamea Dr
33. Francina Dr
34. Judilee Dr
35. Sandy Ln
36. Bayberry Pl
37. Sepulveda Ln
38. Valley Falls Rd
39. Valley Home R
40. Corda Ln
41. Park Lane Dr
42. Woodfield Dr
43. Woodfield Pl
44. Woodcrest Dr
45. Royal Woods
46. Royal Pl
47. Crownridge Pl
48. Regal Woods
49. Royal Haven P
50. Dartford Pl
51. Azzure Ct
52. Adagio Ct
53. Via Cantare
54. Aqua Verde Cir
55. Casiano Ct
56. Duomo Via
57. Moonridge Dr
58. Deerhorn Rd
59. Deerhorn Dr
60. Vista Haven Pl
61. Loom Pl
62. Lisa Pl
63. Stonewood Ter
64. Longbow Ct
65. Sunstone Pl
66. Del Gado Dr
67. Noble Ave
68. Parral Pl
69. Las Cruces Dr
70. Marble Dr
71. Jadestone Pl
72. Rhinestone Dr
73. Willis Ave
74. Sespe Ave
75. Levitt Ln
76. La Cota Ave
77. Bunal Dr
78. Valley Vista Ct

Many folks think that Rubin's Red Hots (15322 Ventura Blvd.) has some of the best Chicago-style franks around. But they face strong competition from hot dog purveyors on the other side of the hill, like West Hollywood's Tail O' the Pup and L.A.'s institution, Pink's.

Coffee

- **Coffee Bean & Tea Leaf** · 16101 Ventura Blvd
- **Starbucks** · 14622 Ventura Blvd
- **Starbucks** · 15030 Ventura Blvd
- **Starbucks** · 15303 Ventura Blvd
- **Starbucks** · 16461 Ventura Blvd

Gyms

- **24-Hour Fitness** · 15301 Ventura Blvd · 818-728-6777

Liquor Stores

- **Oaks Liquor** · 5148 Sepulveda Blvd
- **Rubio Liquor & Grocery Market** · 16573 Ventura Blvd
- **Valley Beverage** · 14901 Ventura Blvd
- **Wines of the World** · 4534 Saugus Ave

Movie Theaters

- **Galleria Stadium** · 15301 Ventura Blvd

Pet Stores

- **Animal Affaire** · 14921 Magnolia Blvd · 818-789-3723

Restaurants

- **California Chicken Café** · 15601 Ventura Blvd · 818-789-8056
- **Delmonico's Lobster House** · 16358 Ventura Blvd · 818-986-0777
- **Fuddrucker's** · 15301 Ventura Blvd · 818-995-4552
- **Posto** · 14928 Ventura Blvd · 818-784-4400
- **Prego** · 15301 Ventura Blvd · 818-905-7004
- **Rubin's Red Hots** · 15322 Ventura Blvd · 818-905-6515
- **The Weiner Factory** · 14917 Ventura Blvd · 818-789-2676

Shopping

- **Sherman Oaks Castle Park** · 4899 Sepulveda Blvd · 818-756-9459
- **Tower Records-Video-Books Video** · 15301 Ventura Blvd · 818-995-7373

Video Rental

- **Blockbuster** · 14936 Ventura Blvd · 818-788-6162
- **Blockbuster** · 16403 Ventura Blvd · 818-784-5396

N

43
44
49
51

Clark St
Margate St
Circle Dr
Tilden Ave
Sylmar Ave
Tyrone Ave
Chandler Blvd
Hazeltine Ave
Margate St
Weddington St
Magnolia Blvd
Hartsook St
Otsego St
Hesby St
Morrison St
Huston St
Peach Groove St
La Maida St
Murietta Ave
Rancho Ave
Stern Ave
Matilija Ave
Mammoth Ave
Woodman Ave
Buffalo Ave
Ventura Canyon Ave
Allott Ave
Hesby St
Sunnyslope Ave
Greenbush Ave
Varna Ave
Nagle Ave
Fulton Ave
Chandler Blvd
Margate St
Weddington St
Mccormick St
Hartsook St
Otsego St
Hesby St
Addison St
Morrison St
Huston St
Kuen Pl
Weddington St
Van Noord Ave
Coldwater Canyon Ave
Tujunga Wash
Leghorn Ave
Chandler Blvd
Wortser Ave
Morse Ave
Van Noord Ave
Alcove Ave
La Maida St

Vista Del Monte Ave
Van Nuys Blvd
Van Nuys - Sherman Oaks Park
Addison St
Huston St
Tilden Ave
Sylmar Ave
Lennox Ave
Tyrone Ave
Katherine Ave
Calhoun Ave
Stansbury Ave

Westfield Shoppingtown Fashion Square
PAGE 272

Ventura Freeway
101
Hortense St
Valleyheart Dr
Kling St
Sarah St
Ethel Ave
Riverside Dr
Kling St
Hortense St
Sarah St
Milbank St
Landale St
Studio City Recreation Center

Los Angeles River
Valleyheart Dr N
Varna Ave
Nagle Ave
Fulton Ave
Longridge Ave
Atoll Ave
Mary Ellen Ave
Wortser Ave
Morse Ave
Van Noord Ave

Rye St
Moorpark St
Bloomfield St
Valleyheart Dr
Woodbridge St
Alcove Ave

Benefit St
Dunbar Pl
Dickens St
Greenleaf St
Roblar Pl
Ventura Blvd
Costello Ave
Hazeltine Ave
Stansbury Ave
Calhoun Ave
Katherine Ave
Murietta Ave
Colbath Ave
Stern Ave
Matilija Ave
Mammoth Ave
Milbank St
Studio City Golf and Tennis

SHERMAN OAKS

Milbrook Dr
Knobhill Dr
Roblar Rd
Valley Vista Blvd
Murietta Ave
Davana Ter
Davana Rd
Woodman Ave
Ventura Canyon Ave
Allott Ave
Sunnyslope Ave
Greenbush Ave
Dixie Canyon Ave
Nagle Ave
Fulton Ave
Longridge Ave
Mary Ellen Ave
Dickens St
Greenleaf St
Galewood St
Blairwood Dr
Coldwater Canyon Ave

Beverly Glen Blvd
Longvalley Valley Rd
Sunset Dr
Beverly Ridge
Camino De La Cumbre
Oakfield Dr
Glorietta Dr
Hollyline Ave
Witzel Dr
Sherwood Pl
Davana Rd
Wieslin Ave
Contour Dr
Galewood St
Chettenham Dr
Inwood Dr
Newcomb Dr
Ethel Ave
Galewood St
Longridge Ave
Van Noord Ave
Alcove Ave
Halkirk St

Beresford Rd
Aubrey Rd
Clevendon Rd
Durham Rd
Benedict Canyon Ln
Fire Rd
Benedict Canyon Dr
Glenridge Dr
Bodega Dr
Dixie Canyon Park
Beverly Ranch Rd
Dixie Canyon Ave
Chettenham Dr
Dixie Canyon Av
Alomar Dr
Longridge Ave
Potosi Ave
Oeste Ave
Haciénda Dr

Cov Dr
Beverly Glen Blvd
Mulholland Dr
Deep Canyon Dr
Mulholland Dr
Java Dr
Sumatra Dr
Coldwater Canyon Ln

Nicada Dr
Greentree Ct
Clearwood
Tiffany Ctr
Windtree Dr
Colina Wy
Raybet Rd
Woodmeadow Dr
Hollow Glen Cir
Benedict Canyon Dr
Deep Canyon Dr
Gloucester Dr
Hythe Ct
Royston Pl
Denbigh Dr
Cardigan Pl
Liebe Dr
Wallingford Dr
Deep Canyon Dr
Hutton Dr
Toppington Dr
Abington Dr
Hutton Pl
Blantyre Dr
Melinda Dr
Arby Dr
Beverly Park Ct
Beverly Park Ln
Summitridge Dr
Upper Franklin Canyon Reservoir

Nicada Dr
Bottlebush Dr
Claray Ln
Beverly Glen Blvd
Brianwood Park
Angelo Dr
Oak Pass Rd
Hutton Dr
Ellison Dr
Hensal Rd

1. Camino De La Solana
2. Camino De La Ronda
3. De La Cumbre Pl
4. Glorietta Pl
5. Westpark Rd
6. Beverly Glen Cir
7. Autumn Leaf Cir
8. Summer Holly Cir
9. Clusterberry Ct
10. Clematis Ct
11. Mossy Rock Cir
12. Almaden Ct
13. Deep Canyon Pl
14. Aldbury Ct
15. Tottenham Ct
16. Burnley Pl
17. Moorgate Rd
18. Royce Ct
19. Whitwell Dr
20. Suffolk Dr
21. Donington Pl
22. Firth Dr
23. Gibraltar Dr
24. Trudy Dr
25. Drake Ln
26. Kirkland Ct
27. Beverly Park Wy
28. Van Noord Ave
29. Alomar Dr
30. Stoneridge Pl
31. Rand Dr
32. Rand Ct
33. Oleander Ln
34. Oak Canyon Ave
35. Woodman Canyon Av
36. Deer Ave
37. Koster Ave
38. Debstone Ave
39. Stoneview Dr
40. Stone Hill Pl
41. Mammoth Pl
42. Buffalo Ave
43. Costello Ave
44. Branton Pl
45. Fulton Ct
46. Atoll Ave
47. Oak Park Ln

1
2
3
A
B
C
D

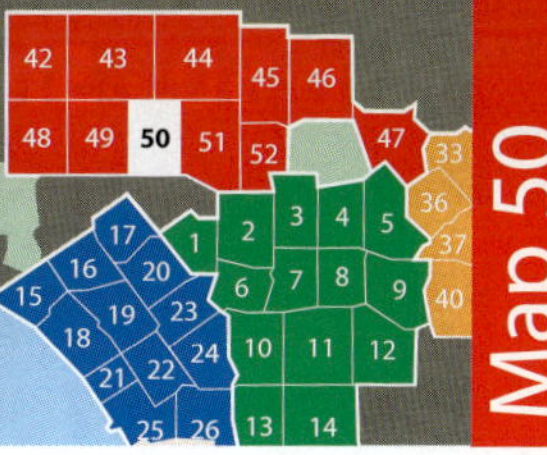

Realtors love to talk up this neighborhood's proximity to the Westside, and they have a point. Beverly Glen Blvd. and Coldwater Canyon are both solid alternatives to the congested 405. But once you make the commitment to a route, you're basically stuck. If they're backed up, Beverly Hills can be almost an hour away.

$ Banks

- **Bank of America** · 13700 Riverside Dr
- **Citibank** · 4474 Van Nuys Blvd
- **Downey Savings & Loan** · 13701 Riverside Dr
- **Downey Savings & Loan** · 4520 Van Nuys Blvd
- **First Federal Bank** · 2920 N Beverly Glen Cir
- **Washington Mutual** · 13949 Ventura Blvd

Car Washes

- **Handy J Car Wash** · 14311 Ventura Blvd
- **Rob's Car Wash** · 5300 Van Nuys Blvd
- **Ventura Car Wash** · 13320 Ventura Blvd

Gas Stations

- **76** · 12863 Ventura Blvd
- **76** · 14478 Ventura Blvd
- **76** · 4804 Coldwater Canyon Ave
- **Arco** · 4359 Coldwater Canyon Ave
- **Chevron** · 12860 Riverside Dr
- **Chevron** · 14505 Ventura Blvd
- **Mobil** · 12904 Ventura Blvd
- **Mobil** · 13272 Moorpark St
- **Mobil** · 4715 Van Nuys Blvd
- **Shell** · 4404 Woodman Ave
- **Shell** · 4441 Van Nuys Blvd
- **Shell** · 5161 Van Nuys Blvd

Hospitals

- **Sherman Oaks Hospital & Health** · 4929 Van Nuys Blvd · 818-981-7111

Libraries

- **Sherman Oaks Library** · 14245 Moorpark St · 818-981-7850

Rx 24-Hour Pharmacies

- **Rite-Aid** · 13333 Riverside Dr · 818-907-1431

Schools

- **Buckley** · 3900 Stansbury Ave
- **CE Merdinian Armenian Evangelical Elementary** · 13330 Riverside Dr
- **Chandler Elementary** · 14030 Weddington St
- **Dixie Canyon Avenue Elementary** · 4220 Dixie Canyon Ave
- **East Valley Academy** · 13351 Riverside Dr
- **Harvard-Westlake** · 3700 Coldwater Canyon Ave
- **Millikan Middle School** · 5041 Sunnyslope Ave
- **Notre Dame High School** · 13645 Riverside Dr
- **Riverside Drive Elementary** · 13061 Riverside Dr
- **St Francis Desales Elementary** · 13368 Valleyheart Dr
- **St Michael All Angels Parish School** · 3646 Coldwater Canyon Ave

Supermarkets

- **Beverly Glen Market Place** · 2964 Beverly Glen Cir
- **Gelson's Markets** · 4520 Van Nuys Blvd
- **Ralph's** · 12842 Ventura Blvd
- **Ralph's** · 12921 Magnolia Blvd
- **Ralph's** · 14049 Ventura Blvd
- **Trader Joe's** · 14119 Riverside Dr
- **Whole Foods Market** · 12905 Riverside Dr

N

43

44

Clark St
Margate St
Circle Dr
Tilden Ave
Sylmar Ave
Tyrone Ave
Vista Del Monte Ave
Chandler Blvd
Chandler Blvd
Margate St
Weddington St
Hazeltine Ave
Magnolia Blvd
Van Nuys - Sherman Oaks Park
Hartsook St
Addison St
Otsego St
Hesby St
Morrison St
Huston St
Peach Groove St
La Maida St
Murietta Ave
Ranchito Ave
Stern Ave
Matilija Ave
Mammoth Ave
Woodman Ave
Hartsook St
Hesby St
Sunnyslope Ave
Greenbush Ave
Varna Ave
Nagle Ave
Fulton Ave
Margate St
Weddington St
Mccormick St
Kuen Pl
Chandler Blvd
Hartsook St
Otsego St
Hesby St
Addison St
Morrison St
Huston St
Riverside Dr
Van Noord Ave
Morse Ave
Wortser Ave
Ethel Ave
La Maida St
Alcove Ave
Coldwater Canyon Ave
Tujunga Wash
Katherine Ave
Calhoun Ave
Stansbury Ave
Lennox Ave
Tilden Ave
Sylmar Ave
Van Nuys Blvd
Vista Del Monte Ave
Westfield Shoppingtown Fashion Square
PAGE 272
Ventura Freeway
101
Kling St
Hortense St
Sarah St
Milbank St
Landale St
Studio City Recreation Center
Hortense St
Valleyheart Dr
Los Angeles River
Valleyheart Dr N
Kling St
Sarah St
Varna Ave
Nagle Ave
Fulton Ave
Longridge Ave
Atoll Ave
Mary Ellen Ave
Wortser Ave
Morse Ave
Van Noord Ave
Milbank St
Murietta Ave
Colbath Ave
Stern Ave
Matilija Ave
Mammoth Ave
Rye St
Moorpark St
Benefit St
Dickens St
Dunbar Pl
Greenleaf St
Roblar Pl
Ventura Blvd
Bloomfield St
Woodbridge St
Valleyheart Dr
Valleyheart Dr
Alcove Ave
Studio City Golf and Tennis
49
51
SHERMAN OAKS
Knobhill Dr
Longview Valley Rd
Oakfield Dr
Millbrook Dr
Beverly Glen Blvd
N Beverly Glen Blvd
Stansbury Ave
Hazeltine Ave
Costello Ave
Davana Ter
Davana Rd
Roblar Rd
Valley Vista Blvd
Murietta Ave
Hollyline Ave
Witzel Dr
Sherwood Pl
Woodman Ave
Ventura Canyon Ave
Allott Ave
Sunnyslope Ave
Greenbush Ave
Dixie Canyon Ave
Nagle Ave
Fulton Ave
Longridge Ave
Mary Ellen Ave
Ethel Ave
Galewood St
Dickens St
Greenleaf St
Galewood St
Blairwood Dr
Van Noord Ave
Coldwater Canyon Ave
Hacienda Dr
Potosi Ave
Oeste Ave
Halkirk St
Westlin Ave
Contour Dr
Cheltenham Dr
Inwood Dr
Newcomb Dr
Alomar Dr
Dixie Canyon Park
Barcarry Ranch Rd
Claywood Dr
Simatra Dr
Coldwater Canyon Ln
Beverly Glen Blvd
Mulholland Dr
Mulholland Dr
Nicada Dr
Greentree Ct
Clearwood Ct
Tiffany Cir
Raybet Rd
Windtree Dr
Colina Wy
Nicada Dr
Bottlebrush Dr
Bassi Dr
Hollow Glen Cir
Woodvale Rd
Angelo Dr
Benedict Canyon Dr
Liebe Dr
Deep Canyon Dr
Royston Dr
Denbigh Dr
Cardigan Pl
Wallingford Dr
Hutton Dr
Gloucester Dr
Hythe Ct
Saye Dr
Torpington Dr
Abington Dr
Hutton Pl
Blantyre Dr
Melinda Dr
Arby Dr
Oak Pass Rd
Ellison Dr
Hensal Rd
Beverly Park Ct
Beverly Park Ln
Summitridge Dr
Upper Franklin Canyon Reservoir
Brianwood Park
Java Dr
Mulholland Dr
Fire Rd
Benedict Canyon Ln
Davana Dr
Glennridge Dr
Bosque Dr

1. Camino De La Solan
2. Camino De La Ronda
3. De La Cumbre Pl
4. Glorietta Pl
5. Westpark Rd
6. Beverly Glen Cir
7. Autumn Leaf Cir
8. Summer Holly Cir
9. Clusterberry Ct
10. Clematis Ct
11. Mossy Rock Cir
12. Almaden Ct
13. Deep Canyon Pl
14. Aldbury Ct
15. Tottenham Ct
16. Burnley Pl
17. Moorgate Rd
18. Royce Ct
19. Whitwell Dr
20. Suffolk Dr
21. Donington Pl
22. Firth Dr
23. Gibraltar Dr
24. Trudy Dr
25. Drake Ln
26. Kirkland Dr
27. Beverly Park Wy
28. Van Noord Ave
29. Alomar Dr
30. Stoneridge Pl
31. Rand Dr
32. Rand Ct
33. Oleander Ln
34. Oak Canyon Ave
35. Woodman Canyon Ave
36. Deer Ave
37. Koster Ave
38. Debstone Ave
39. Stoneview Dr
40. Stone Hill Pl
41. Mammoth Ave
42. Buffalo Ave
43. Costello Ave
44. Branton Pl
45. Fulton Ct
46. Atoll Ave
47. Oak Park Ln

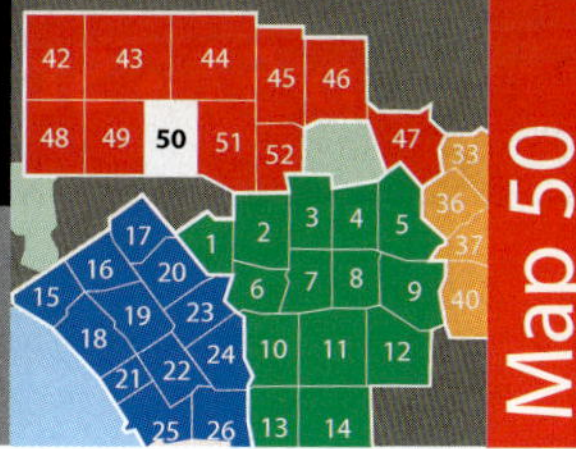

Our biggest beef about the Valley is that there just aren't enough places to get a decent breakfast. But Sherman Oaks may be the exception. It is home to both the neighborhood favorite, Jinky's, and a transplant from over the hill, Hugo's. Expect long lines at both places on the weekends, but trust us—they're worth it.

Clubs

- **Cozy's** • 14058 Ventura Blvd • 818-986-6000

Coffee

- **Arrosto Coffee** • 4566 Van Nuys Blvd
- **Coffee Bean & Tea Leaf** • 12930 Ventura Blvd
- **Coffee Bean & Tea Leaf** • 14006 Riverside Dr
- **Coffee Roaster** • 13567 Ventura Blvd
- **Lulu's Beehive** • 13203 Ventura Blvd
- **Pane Dolce** • 13608 Ventura Blvd
- **Starbucks** • 12824 Ventura Blvd
- **Starbucks** • 13351 Riverside Dr
- **Starbucks** • 13535 Ventura Blvd
- **Starbucks** • 2952 N Beverly Glen Cir

Gyms

- **Dare To Be Fit** • 14330 Ventura Blvd • 818-788-6070
- **LA Fitness Sports Clubs** • 5300 Coldwater Canyon Ave • 818-505-0772

Hardware Stores

- **Checker Paint** • 14434 Ventura Blvd • 818-784-0192
- **GD Builders Hardware & Plumbing** • 13241 Ventura Blvd • 818-784-6274

Liquor Stores

- **F & M Liquors** • 14230 Ventura Blvd
- **Fulton Square Liquors & Market** • 4824 Fulton Ave
- **Metro Liquors** • 14431 Magnolia Blvd
- **Party House Liquors** • 13302 Moorpark St
- **Silver Liquor** • 4405 Woodman Ave
- **Tony's Liquor Store** • 13368 Ventura Blvd
- **Tropicana Liquors** • 4346 Van Nuys Blvd
- **Wine N' Liquor Basket** • 4454 Van Nuys Blvd

Movie Theaters

- **Sherman Oaks Cinemas** • 4500 Van Nuys Blvd

Pet Stores

- **Aquarium Center** • 14255 Ventura Blvd • 818-501-3544
- **Pets Naturally** • 13459 Ventura Blvd • 818-784-1233
- **Pets of Belair** • 2924 Beverly Glen Cir • 310-475-7977

Restaurants

- **Bistro Garden at Coldwater** • 12950 Ventura Blvd • 818-501-0202
- **Bistro Gardens** • 12950 Ventura Blvd • 818-501-0202
- **Café Bizou** • 14016 Ventura Blvd • 818-788-3536
- **Carnival Restaurant** • 4356 Woodman Ave • 818-784-3469
- **Casa Vega** • 13301 Ventura Blvd • 818-788-4868
- **Diwan** • 13045 Ventura Blvd • 818-501-6015
- **Genmai** • 4454 Van Nuys Blvd • 818-986-7060
- **Hugo's** • 12851 Riverside Dr • 818-761-8985
- **Iroha** • 12953 Ventura Blvd • 818-990-9559
- **Jinky's** • 14120 Ventura Blvd • 818-981-2250
- **Le Chine Wok** • 2958 Beverly Glen Cir • 310-475-1146
- **Le Petit Bistro** • 13360 Ventura Blvd • 818-501-7999
- **Maria's Italian Kitchen** • 13353 Ventura Blvd • 818-906-0783
- **Max** • 13355 Ventura Blvd • 818-784-2915
- **Mazzarino's** • 12920 1/2 Riverside Dr • 818-788-5050
- **Mistral Brasserie** • 13422 Ventura Blvd • 818-981-6650
- **Mulholland Grill** • 2932 Beverly Glen Cir • 310-470-6223
- **Pinot Bistro** • 12969 Ventura Blvd • 818-990-0500
- **Rive Gauche** • 14106 Ventura Blvd • 818-990-3573
- **Stanley's** • 13817 Ventura Blvd • 818-986-4623
- **Sushi Ko** • 2932 1/2 Beverly Glen Cir • 310-475-8689
- **The Great Greek** • 13362 Ventura Blvd • 818-905-5250

Shopping

- **Baxter Northrup Music** • 14534 Ventura Blvd • 323-872-0756
- **Doll Shoppe** • 13300 Riverside Dr • 818-784-3655
- **Juvenile Shop** • 13356 Ventura Blvd • 818-986-6214
- **Mark's Garden** • 13838 Ventura Blvd • 818-906-1718
- **Pajama Party** • 14006 Riverside Dr • 818-788-2470
- **Pink Cheeks** • 14562 Ventura Blvd • 818-906-8225
- **Second Spin Records** • 14564 Ventura Blvd • 818-986-6866
- **Vera's Retreat** • 2980 Beverly Glen Cir • 310-440-6362
- **Western Bagel** • 12930 Ventura Blvd • 818-567-0413

Video Rental

- **Beverly Glen Film Festival** • 2950 N Beverly Glen Cir • 310-475-2269
- **Blockbuster** • 4560 Van Nuys Blvd • 818-990-1695
- **Blockbuster** • 13303 Riverside Dr • 818-501-8335
- **Hollywood Video** • 14525 Ventura Blvd • 818-986-1874
- **Video Hut** • 13713 Moorpark St • 818/385-0067

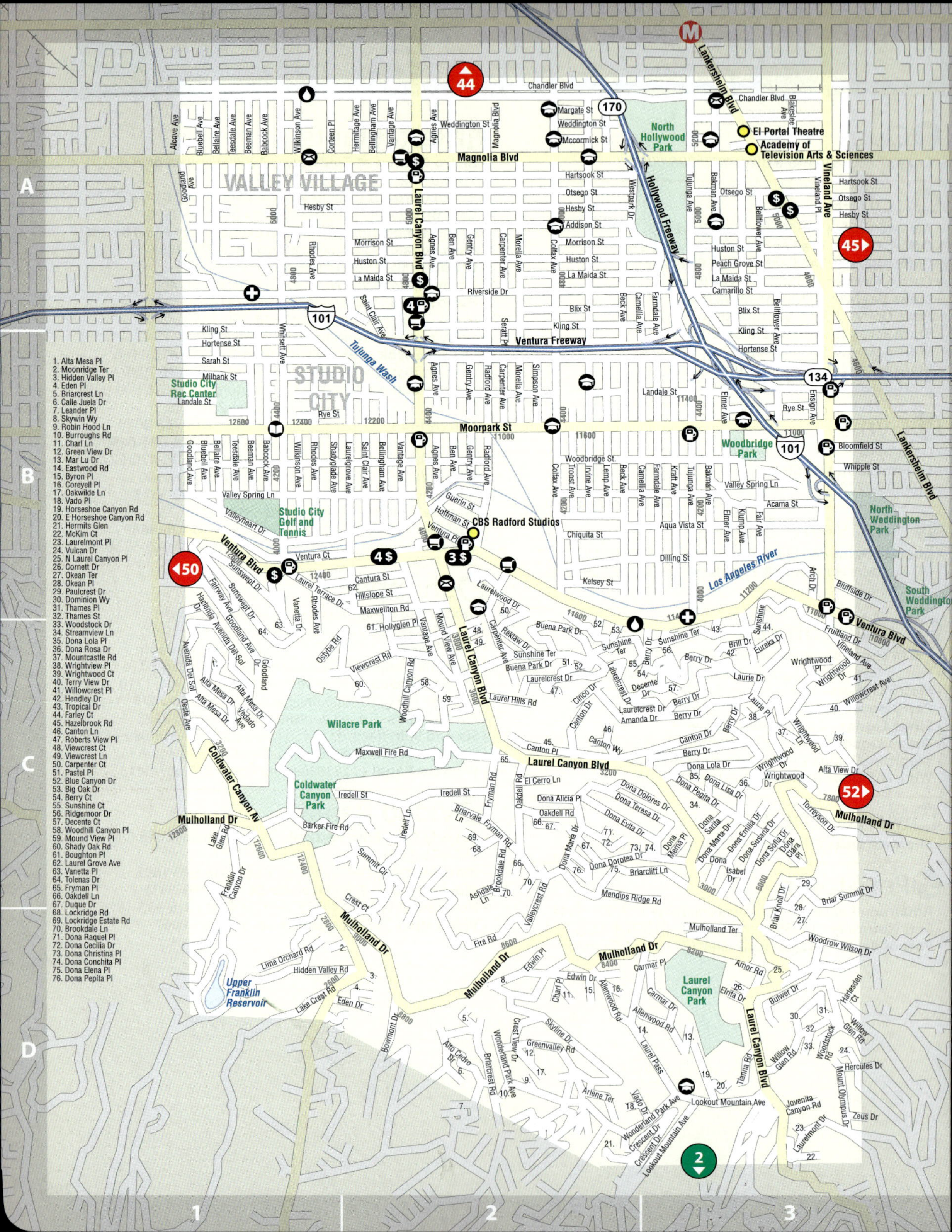

VALLEY VILLAGE
STUDIO CITY
Chandler Blvd
Magnolia Blvd
Laurel Canyon Blvd
Ventura Freeway
Hollywood Freeway
Moorpark St
Ventura Blvd
Lankershim Blvd
Vineland Ave
Coldwater Canyon Av
Mulholland Dr
Tujunga Wash
Los Angeles River
North Hollywood Park
El Portal Theatre
Academy of Television Arts & Sciences
Studio City Rec Center
Studio City Golf and Tennis
CBS Radford Studios
Woodbridge Park
North Weddington Park
South Weddington Park
Wilacre Park
Coldwater Canyon Park
Laurel Canyon Park
Upper Franklin Reservoir
Lookout Mountain Ave
101
134
170
44
45
50
52
2
A
B
C
D
1
2
3
1. Alta Mesa Pl
2. Moonridge Ter
3. Hidden Valley Pl
4. Eden Pl
5. Briarcrest Ln
6. Calle Juela Dr
7. Leander Pl
8. Skywin Wy
9. Robin Hood Ln
10. Burroughs Rd
11. Charl Ln
12. Green View Dr
13. Mar Lu Dr
14. Eastwood Rd
15. Byron Pl
16. Coreyell Pl
17. Oakwilde Ln
18. Vado Pl
19. Horseshoe Canyon Rd
20. E Horseshoe Canyon Rd
21. Hermits Glen
22. McKim Ct
23. Laurelmont Pl
24. Vulcan Dr
25. N Laurel Canyon Pl
26. Cornett Dr
27. Okean Ter
28. Okean Pl
29. Paulcrest Dr
30. Dominion Wy
31. Thames Pl
32. Thames St
33. Woodstock Dr
34. Streamview Ln
35. Dona Lola Pl
36. Dona Rosa Dr
37. Mountcastle Rd
38. Wrightview Pl
39. Wrightwood Ct
40. Terry View Dr
41. Willowcrest Pl
42. Hendley Dr
43. Tropical Dr
44. Farley Ct
45. Hazelbrook Rd
46. Canton Ln
47. Roberts View Pl
48. Viewcrest Ct
49. Viewcrest Ln
50. Carpenter Ct
51. Pastel Pl
52. Blue Canyon Dr
53. Big Oak Dr
54. Berry Ct
55. Sunshine Ct
56. Ridgemoor Dr
57. Decente Ct
58. Woodhill Canyon Pl
59. Mound View Pl
60. Shady Oak Rd
61. Boughton Pl
62. Laurel Grove Ave
63. Vanetta Pl
64. Tolenas Dr
65. Fryman Pl
66. Oakdell Ln
67. Duque Dr
68. Lockridge Rd
69. Lockridge Estate Rd
70. Brookdale Ln
71. Dona Raquel Pl
72. Dona Cecilia Dr
73. Dona Christina Pl
74. Dona Conchita Pl
75. Dona Elena Pl
76. Dona Pepita Pl

Aficionados of Los Angeles car culture will want to take note of Studio City Car Wash. The giant hand holding a pink convertible atop a sponge was a subject of much debate in Studio City. One faction wanted the "eyesore" torn down; one wanted to preserve the "example of car culture at its best." In the end, a compromise was made; the hand may remain, but is currently being downsized and moved back from the street front.

$ Banks

- **Bank of America** · 12223 Ventura Blvd
- **Bank of America** · 5025 Lankershim Blvd
- **Bank of America** · 5201 Laurel Canyon Blvd
- **Citibank** · 12191 Ventura Blvd
- **Citibank** · 4821 Laurel Canyon Blvd
- **Citibank** · 5077 Lankershim Blvd
- **City National Bank** · 12001 Ventura Pl
- **City National Bank** · 12515 Ventura Blvd
- **First Republic Bank** · 12070 Ventura Blvd
- **Union Bank** · 12185 Ventura Blvd
- **Washington Mutual** · 12051 Ventura Blvd
- **Wells Fargo Bank** · 12251 Ventura Blvd

Car Washes

- **Galaxy Car Wash** · 12444 Chandler Blvd
- **Studio City Car Wash** · 11514 Ventura Blvd

Gas Stations

- **76** · 10974 Ventura Blvd
- **76** · 10984 Riverside Dr
- **76** · 4388 Tujunga Ave
- **76** · 4654 Laurel Canyon Blvd
- **Arco** · 12500 Ventura Blvd
- **Arco** · 5158 Laurel Canyon Blvd
- **Chevron** · 10960 Moorpark St
- **Chevron** · 4757 Laurel Canyon Blvd
- **Mobil** · 11001 Ventura Blvd
- **Mobil** · 4359 Laurel Canyon Blvd
- **Mobil** · 4377 Vineland Ave
- **Mobil** · 4801 Laurel Canyon Blvd
- **Shell** · 12007 Ventura Blvd
- **Shell** · 4647 Laurel Canyon Blvd

Landmarks

- **Academy of Television Arts & Sciences** · 5220 Lankershim Blvd
- **CBS Radford Studios** · 4024 Radford Ave
- **El Portal Theatre** · 5269 Lankershim Blvd

Libraries

- **North Hollywood Regional LIbrary** · 5211 Tujunga Ave · 818-766-7185
- **Studio City Branch** · 12511 Moorpark St · 818-755-7873

Post Offices

- 11304 Chandler Blvd
- 12450 Magnolia Blvd
- 3950 Laurel Canyon Blvd

Schools

- **Beth Meier** · 11728 Moorpark St
- **Campbell Hall** · 4533 Laurel Canyon Blvd
- **Carpenter Avenue Elementary** · 3909 Carpenter Ave
- **Colfax Avenue Elementary** · 11724 Addison St
- **Country School** · 5243 Laurel Canyon Blvd
- **Earhart Continuation** · 5355 Colfax Ave
- **Lankershim Elementary** · 5250 Bakman Ave
- **North Hollywood High School** · 5231 Colfax Ave
- **Oakwood Elementary** · 11230 Moorpark St
- **Oakwood Secondary School** · 11600 Magnolia Blvd
- **Reed Middle School** · 4525 Irvine Ave
- **San Fernando Valley Profession** · 12034 Riverside Dr
- **St Paul's First Lutheran** · 11330 McCormick St
- **Wonderland Avenue Elementary** · 8510 Wonderland Ave

Supermarkets

- **Gelson's Markets** · 4738 Laurel Canyon Blvd
- **Jon's Marketplace** · 12122 Magnolia Blvd
- **Trader Joe's** · 11976 Ventura Blvd
- **Von's** · 4033 Laurel Canyon Blvd

1. Alta Mesa Pl
2. Moonridge Ter
3. Hidden Valley Pl
4. Eden Pl
5. Briarcrest Ln
6. Calle Juela Dr
7. Leander Pl
8. Skywin Wy
9. Robin Hood Ln
10. Burroughs Rd
11. Charl Ln
12. Green View Dr
13. Mar Lu Dr
14. Eastwood Rd
15. Byron Pl
16. Coreyell Pl
17. Oakwilde Ln
18. Vado Pl
19. Horseshoe Canyon Rd
20. E Horseshoe Canyon Rd
21. Hermits Glen
22. McKim Ct
23. Laurelmont Pl
24. Vulcan Dr
25. N Laurel Canyon Pl
26. Cornett Dr
27. Okean Ter
28. Okean Pl
29. Paulcrest Dr
30. Dominion Wy
31. Thames Pl
32. Thames St
33. Woodstock Dr
34. Streamview Ln
35. Dona Lola Pl
36. Dona Rosa Dr
37. Mountcastle Rd
38. Wrightview Pl
39. Wrightwood Ct
40. Terry View Dr
41. Willowcrest Pl
42. Hendley Dr
43. Tropical Dr
44. Farley Ct
45. Hazelbrook Rd
46. Canton Ln
47. Roberts View Pl
48. Viewcrest Ct
49. Viewcrest Ln
50. Carpenter Ct
51. Pastel Pl
52. Blue Canyon Dr
53. Big Oak Dr
54. Berry Ct
55. Sunshine Ct
56. Ridgemoor Dr
57. Decente Ct
58. Woodhill Canyon Pl
59. Mound View Pl
60. Shady Oak Rd
61. Boughton Pl
62. Laurel Grove Ave
63. Vanetta Pl
64. Tolenas Dr
65. Fryman Pl
66. Oakdell Ln
67. Duque Dr
68. Lockridge Rd
69. Lockridge Estate Rd
70. Brookdale Ln
71. Dona Raquel Dr
72. Dona Cecilia Dr
73. Dona Christina Pl
74. Dona Conchita Pl
75. Dona Elena Pl
76. Dona Pepita Pl

It has been said that one can find anything in the world on this fertile strip of Ventura Boulevard, and we sure aren't going to be the first to dispute that. There's a "transformation specialist" who will turn an average businessman into a dancing showgirl in a matter of hours. Of course, those less brave can just go watch the female impersonators next door at The Queen Mary.

24-Hour Copy Centers
- **Kinko's** • 12101 Ventura Blvd • 818-980-2679

Clubs
- **Clear** • 11916 Ventura Blvd • 818-980-4811
- **Firefly** • 11720 Ventura Blvd • 818-762-1833
- **Fox & Hounds** • 11100 Ventura Blvd • 818-763-7976
- **Residuals** • 11042 Ventura Blvd • 818-761-8301
- **The Queen Mary** • 12449 Ventura Blvd • 818-506-5619

Coffee
- **Aroma Coffee and Tea** • 4360 Tujunga Ave
- **Caffe Neo** • 11239 Ventura Blvd
- **Coffee Bean & Tea Leaf** • 12050 Ventura Blvd
- **Eagle's Cafe** • 5231 Lankershim Blvd
- **Java Joy** • 11288 Ventura Blvd
- **Jennifer's Coffee Connection** • 4397 Tujunga Ave
- **Peet's Coffee & Tea** • 12215 Ventura Blvd
- **Seattle's Best Coffee** • 12229 Ventura Blvd
- **Starbucks** • 10965 Ventura Blvd
- **Starbucks** • 12170 Ventura Blvd
- **Starbucks** • 4800 Laurel Canyon Blvd

Farmer's Markets
- **Ventura Place** • NE of the Laurel Canyon/ Ventura intersection • Sun 8-1

Gyms
- **Bally's Total Fitness** • 11315 Ventura Blvd • 818-760-7800
- **Cardio Barre** • 12530 Riverside Dr • 818-761-4525
- **Noho Gym** • 5126 Lankershim Blvd • 818-766-8888
- **Reel Fitness** • 12215 Ventura Blvd • 818-508-0690
- **Studio City Fitness** • 12733 Ventura Blvd • 818-506-1436

Hardware Stores
- **Mother of Pearl & Sons Trading** • 12328 Ventura Blvd • 818-505-8057
- **North Hollywood Hardware** • 11847 Ventura Blvd • 818-980-2453
- **Steven Nurseries & Hardware** • 12000 Riverside Dr • 818-763-6296

Liquor Stores
- **Colfax Liquors** • 11710 Riverside Dr
- **Flask Liquor & Wine** • 12194 Ventura Blvd
- **Hughie's Liquor** • 12121 Magnolia Blvd
- **J & J Wines & Spirits** • 11312 Ventura Blvd
- **Jaby's Liquor Junior Market** • 5144 Colfax Ave
- **Laurel Park Liquors** • 4407 Laurel Canyon Blvd
- **Oasis Liquor** • 4800 Whitsett Ave
- **Ringside Liquors Jr Market** • 12500 Moorpark St
- **Sam's Liquor Store** • 4832 Lankershim Blvd
- **Sauce & Such Liquor Mart** • 4803 Whitsett Ave
- **Valley Stores Liquor Dept** • 11418 Moorpark St
- **Vendome Liquor & Wine Shops** • 11555 Ventura Blvd

Pet Stores
- **It's A Dog's Life** • 11305 Ventura Blvd • 818-509-3930
- **Kool Kats & Hot Dawgs** • 11440 Ventura Blvd • 818-753-2744
- **Mark's Pet Supplies** • 12069 Ventura Pl • 818-760-4300
- **Mark's Tropical Fish** • 12063 Ventura Pl • 818-762-7700
- **Petco** • 12800 Ventura Blvd • 818-506-6416

Restaurants
- **Art's Deli** • 12224 Ventura Blvd • 818-762-1221
- **Caioti** • 4346 Tujunga Ave • 818-761-3588
- **Du-Par's** • 12036 Ventura Blvd • 818-766-4437
- **Firefly** • 11720 Ventura Blvd • 818-762-1833
- **Henry's Tacos** • 11401 Moorpark St • 818-769-0343
- **Katsu-ya** • 11680 Ventura Blvd • 818-985-6976
- **Killer Shrimp** • 4000 Colfax Ave • 818-508-1570
- **La Loggia** • 11814 Ventura Blvd • 818-985-9222
- **Matsuda** • 11837 Ventura Blvd
- **Mexicali** • 12161 Ventura Blvd • 818-985-1744
- **Out Take Café** • 12159 Ventura Blvd • 818-760-1111
- **Sushi Dan Rockin' Sushi** • 11056 Ventura Blvd • 818-985-2254
- **Sushi Nozawa** • 11288 Ventura Blvd • 818-508-7017
- **Suzanne's Country Deli** • 11273 Ventura Blvd • 818-762-9494
- **Teru Sushi** • 11940 Ventura Blvd • 818-763-6201
- **Tokyo Delve's Sushi Bar** • 5239 Lankershim Blvd • 818-766-3868
- **Vitello's** • 4349 Tujunga Ave • 818-769-0905

Shopping
- **Dari** • 12184 Ventura Blvd • 818-762-3274
- **Dovetail** • 12336 Ventura Blvd • 818-752-6531
- **Iliad Bookstore** • 4820 Vineland Ave • 818-509-2665
- **La Knitterie Parisienne** • 12642 Ventura Blvd • 818-766-1515
- **Marie et Cie** • 11704 Riverside Dr • 818-508-5049
- **Studio City Camera Exchange** • 12174 Ventura Blvd • 818-762-4749

Video Rental
- **20-20 Video** • 12113 Ventura Blvd • 818-762-2020
- **Blockbuster** • 11978 Ventura Blvd • 818-505-9753
- **Blockbuster** • 4821 Lankershim Blvd • 818-505-1800
- **Eddie Brandt Saturday Matinee** • 5006 Vineland Ave • 818-506-4242
- **Odyssey Video** • 4810 Vineland Ave • 818-769-2001
- **Video Club** • 4811 Whitsett Ave • 818-766-2388
- **Video Saloon** • 5202 Vineland Ave • 818-985-9582
- **Video West** • 11376 Ventura Blvd • 818-760-0096

TOLUCA LAKE

Toluca Lake

Warner Bros Studios

Forest Lawn Memorial Park

Weddington Park North

Weddington Park South

Lakeside Country Club

Los Angeles River

Campo de Cahuenga

Universal Studios

PAGE 234

MOUNT OLYMPUS

Hollywood Reservoir

Runyon Canyon Park

Bob's Big Boy

Streets and places (labels):

W Alameda Ave · W Olive Ave · Riverside Dr · Moorpark St · Bloomfield St · Woodbridge St · Whipple St · Landale St · Cartwright Ave · Placidia Ave · Forman Ave · Talofa Ave · Mariota Ave · Ponca Ave · Clybourn Ave · Mc Farlane Ave · N Valley St · N Rose St · N Pass Ave · N Maple Dr · N Kenwood Ave · N Cordova St · S Avon St · S California St · S Fairview St · Valley Heart Dr · W Warner Blvd · Warner Blvd · Toluca Lake Ave · S Valley St · S Rose St · Franklin Ave · Hood Ave · W Lakeside Dr · Forest Lawn Dr · Barham Blvd

Lankershim Blvd · Cahuenga Blvd · Denny Ave · Riverton Ave · Satsuma Ave · Acama St · Aqua Vista St · Chiquita St · Brookview Dr · Cartwright Ave · Valleyheart Dr · Willowcrest Ave · Bluffside Dr · Toluca Estates Dr · Toluca Rd · Valley Spring Ln · Arcola Ave · Navajo Ave

Ventura Blvd · Fruitland Dr · Vineland Ave · Willowcrest Pl · Lankershim Blvd · Fredonia Dr · Universal City Plz · Coral Dr · Universal Center Dr · Buddy Holly Dr

Skyhill Dr · Regal Pl · Cahuenga Blvd · Alta View Dr · Bellfield Way · Wrightwood Ln · Multiview Dr · Broadlawn Dr · Oakley Dr · Ione Dr · Ione Pl · Bonnie Hill Dr · Adina Dr · Oak Glen Dr · Blair Dr · Troy Dr · Floyd Ter · Ellis Dr · Lindo St · Craig Dr · Hilloak Dr · Primera Ave · Lake Hollywood Dr · La Suvida Dr · N Knoll Dr · Wonder View Dr

Mulholland Dr · Torreyson Dr · Torreyson Pl · Firve Dr · Sunnywood Ln · Chandelle Rd · Kimdale Dr · Lolina Ln · Nichols Canyon Pl · Montcalm Ave · Passmore Dr · Oakshire Dr · Bennett Dr · Dos Palos Dr · Barbara Ct · Cadet Ct · Oakcrest Dr · Ellington Dr · Hollycrest Dr · Benda St · Tareco Dr · Wonder View Dr · Lakeridge Rd · Lake Hollywood Dr

Firenze Ave · Seattle Dr · Woodrow Wilson Dr · Westbrook Ave · Rue De Valle · Montcalm Ave · La Cuesta Dr · Caverna Dr · Pacific View Dr · Pyramid Pl · Sunday Tr · Valevista Tr · Sunnydip Tr · Padwood Tr · Woodrow W · Treasure Tr · Woody Tr · Vanland Tr · Visa Dr · Sunny Cv · Cahuenga Blvd E · Cahuenga Blvd W

Cardwell Pl · Cardwell Dr · Hercules Dr · Venus Dr · Apollo Dr · Hermes Dr · Achilles Dr · Oceanus Dr · Jupiter Dr · Zorada Dr · Jalmia Pl · Jalmia Dr · Jalmia Wy · Willow Glen Rd · Zorada Ct · Devista Dr · N Nichols Canyon · Del Zuro Dr · Lisco Pl · Astral Dr · Astral Pl · Solar Dr · Carob Dr · Mulholland Dr · Sunnydell Trl · Outpost Cove Dr · Dresden Dr · Runyon Canyon Rd · Outpost Dr · Larmar Rd · Carman Crest Dr · Chelan Wy · Chelan Dr · Malaga Rd

These neighboring communities couldn't be more different. Universal City amounts to little more than the Studio and the Theme Park, while Toluca Lake is a true neighborhood with a wide variety of residences and the aforementioned lake, which is stocked for fishing, boating, and swimming.

 Banks

- **Bank of America** · 110 Universal City Plz
- **Bank of America** · 255 N Pass Ave
- **Bank of America** · 4123 W Olive Ave
- **California Credit Union** · 3330 Cahuenga Blvd W
- **City National Bank** · 3500 W Olive Ave
- **First Entertainment Credit Union** · 6735 Forest Lawn Dr
- **Union Bank** · 3900 W Alameda Ave
- **Washington Mutual** · 4455 Lankershim Blvd
- **World Savings & Loan** · 10064 Riverside Dr

 Car Washes

- **Ecco** · 3500 W Olive Ave
- **Lakeside Car Wash** · 3700 W Riverside Dr

Gas Stations

- **Arco** · 3704 Cahuenga Blvd
- **Arco** · 4506 Lankershim Blvd
- **Chevron** · 3701 W Riverside Dr
- **Chevron** · 3780 Cahuenga Blvd
- **Mobil** · 10570 Riverside Dr
- **Mobil** · 3240 Cahuenga Blvd W

 Landmarks

- **Bob's Big Boy** · 4211 Riverside Dr
- **Campo de Cahuenga** · 3912 Lankershim Blvd
- **Forest Lawn Memorial Park** · 6300 Forest Lawn Dr
- **Hollywood Reservoir** · East of Hwy 101
- **Universal Studios** · 100 Universal Center Dr
- **Warner Brothers Studios** · 4000 Warner Blvd

Post Offices

- 10063 Riverside Dr
- 4029 Lankershim Blvd

Schools

- **Rio Vista Elementary** · 4243 Satsuma Ave
- **St Charles Borromeo Catholic School** · 10850 Moorpark St
- **Valley View Elementary** · 6921 Woodrow Wilson Dr

Supermarkets

- **Ralph's** · 10901 Ventura Blvd
- **Trader Joe's** · 10130 Riverside Dr

TOLUCA LAKE

Warner Bros Studios

Toluca Lake

Lakeside Country Club

Los Angeles River

Weddington Park North

Weddington Park South

Universal Studios

PAGE 234

MOUNT OLYMPUS

Hollywood Reservoir

Runyon Canyon Park

Streets (numbered index):

1. Toluca Lake Ln
2. Velma Dr
3. De Witt Dr
4. Charleston Wy
5. Blair Cres
6. Winnie Dr
7. La Sombra Dr
8. La Falda Pl
9. Wonder View Pl
10. Hollycrest Pl
11. Benda Pl
12. Primera Pl
13. Wonder View Pz
14. Kentucky Dr
15. Terry View Dr
16. Oakley Dr
17. Carse Dr
18. Hild Tr
19. Springlet Tr
20. Sycamore Tr
21. Goodview Tr
22. Oak Point Dr
23. Pyramid Dr
24. Las Alturas St
25. Vista Crest Dr
26. Cahuenga Park Tr
27. Park Center Dr
28. Palo Vista Dr
29. Soper Dr
30. Nichols Canyon Rd
31. Chandelle Pl
32. Flynn Ranch Rd
33. Firenze Pl
34. Seattle Pl
35. La Castana Dr
36. Bantam Pl

Street names (map labels):

Riverside Dr, Moorpark St, Landale St, Cartwright Ave, Bloomfield St, Whipple St, Satsuma Ave, Riverton Ave, Denny Ave, Lankershim Blvd, Cahuenga Blvd, Bloomfield Ave, Woodbridge St, Strohm Ave, Edge Ave, Arcola Ave, Valley Spring Ln, Toluca Estates Dr, Toluca Rd, Toluca Lake Ave, Placidia Ave, Forman Ave, Talofa Ave, Mariota Ave, Ponca Ave, Chilborn Ave, Mc Farlane Ave, Navajo Ave, N Valley St, N Rose St, Warner Blvd, S Valley St, S Rose St, Franklin Ave, Hood Ave, Toluca Lake Ave, N Pass Ave, N Maple St, N Kenwood Blvd, W Olive Ave, W Warner Blvd, W Alameda Ave, S Cordova St, S Axon St, S California St, S Fairview St, Valley Heart Dr, Forest Lawn Dr, W Lakeside Dr, Barham Blvd, N Coyote Canyon Dr, Dark Canyon Dr, S Coyote Canyon Dr, Craig Dr, Hillock Dr, Troy Dr, Blair Dr, Troy Pl, Floyd Ter, Ellis Pl, Floyd Dr, Primera Ave, Lake Hollywood Dr, La Suvida Dr, N Knoll Dr, Wonder View Dr, Lindo St, Primera Ave, Lake Hollywood Dr, Lakeridge Rd, Benda St, Tareco Dr, N Knoll Dr, Hollycrest Dr, Cahuenga Blvd E, Barbara Dr, Cadel Ct, Oakcrest Dr, Bennett Dr, Dos Palos Dr, Woodrow Wilson Dr, Treasure Tr, Pacific View Ter, Woody Tr, Vanland Tr, Viso Dr, Pacific View Dr, Sunny Cv, Sunnydell Trl, Mulholland Dr, Cahuenga Blvd W

Acama St, Aqua Vista St, Chiquita St, Brookview Dr, Denny Pl, Cartwright Ave, Valleyheart Ave, Bluffside Dr, Ventura Blvd, Fruitland Dr, Vineland Ave, Willowcrest Pl, Willowcrest Ave, Lankershim Blvd, Fredonia Dr, Fredonia Dr, Regal Pl, Fredonia Dr, Skyhill Dr, Alta View Dr, Bellfield Way, Wrightwood Ln, Mulholland Dr, Torreyson Dr, Torreyson Pl, Universal City Plz, Coral Dr, Cahuenga Blvd, Buddy Holly Dr, Multiview Dr, Broadlawn Dr, Oakley Dr, Ione Dr, Ione Pl, Bonnie Hill Dr, Bonnie Hill Dr, Adina Dr, Oakshire Dr, Oakglen Dr, Oak Glen Dr, Blair Dr, Floye Dr, Sunnywood Ln, Kirndale Ln, Lolina Ln, Nichols Canyon Rd, Firenze Ave, Seattle Pl, Woodrow Wilson Dr, Westbrook Ave, Rue De Valle, Montcalm Ave, Woodrow Wilson Dr, Montcalm Ave, La Cuesta Dr, Caverna Dr, Pacific View Dr, Pyramid Pl, Mulholland Dr, N Nichols Canyon Rd, Del Zuro Dr, Lisbo Pl, Zorada Dr, Jalmia Pl, Jalmia Dr, Jalmia Wy, Devista Dr, Willow Glen Rd, Zorada Ct, Esperanza, Astral Dr, Astral Pl, Solar Dr, Carob Dr, Cardwell Pl, Cardwell Pl, Apollo Dr, Hercules Dr, Venus Dr, Achilles Dr, Oceanus Dr, Dresden Dr, Jupiter Dr, Larmar Ave, Chelan Dr, Chelan Wy, Outpost Dr, Outpost Cove Dr, Carmen Crest Dr, Malaga Rd, Runyon Canyon Rd, Sunjal Tr, Valevista Tr, Sunnydip Tr, Pacific View Ter, Passmore Dr, Ellington Dr, Bennett Dr, Bennett Dr

Priscilla's Coffee on Riverside Drive has successfully hung in there against major chains like the Coffee Bean & Tea Leaf and Starbucks, which opened an outpost right across the street several years ago. But Priscilla's has its loyalists who appreciate the shop's homey atmosphere—and darned good coffee.

24-Hour Copy Centers

- **Kinko's** • 4100 W Riverside Dr • 818-567-1044

Clubs

- **BB King's Blues Club** • 100 Universal Center Dr • 818-622-5464
- **Rumba Room** • 100 Universal Center Dr • 818-622-1227
- **The Baked Potato** • 3787 Cahuenga Blvd • 323-582-0748
- **The Casting Office** • 3256 Cahuenga Blvd • 323-851-4300
- **Timmy Nolan's** • 10111 Riverside Dr • 818-985-3359

Coffee

- **Cinema Café** • 4444 Lankershim Blvd
- **Coffee Bean & Tea Leaf** • 10121 Riverside Dr
- **Geri's World Coffee & Bagels** • 3425 Cahuenga Blvd
- **Igloo Cafe** • 171 N Maple St
- **Priscilla's Coffee Tea & Gifts** • 4150 W Riverside Dr
- **Romancing The Bean** • 4301 W Riverside Dr
- **Starbucks** • 100 Universal City Plz
- **Starbucks** • 1000 Universal Center Dr
- **Starbucks** • 3800 W Alameda Ave
- **Starbucks** • 4207 W Riverside Dr
- **Upstart Crow Bookstore & Coffee House** • 1000 Universal Center Dr

Gyms

- **Sports Center** • 6711 Forest Lawn Dr • 323-851-9376

Hardware Stores

- **Rick's Hardware** • 4382 Lankershim Blvd • 818-508-7948

Liquor Stores

- **House of Ambrose** • 3331 Barham Blvd
- **Maple Liquor** • 4001 W Riverside Dr
- **Spirit Cellar** • 3278 Cahuenga Blvd W
- **Universal Liquors** • 3797 Cahuenga Blvd
- **Vendome Liquor & Wine Shops** • 10600 Riverside Dr

Movie Theaters

- **Cineplex Odeon** • 100 Universal City Plz
- **Universal City Imax Theatre** • 100 Universal City Plz

Pet Stores

- **Four Paws Only of Toluca Lake** • 10214 Riverside Dr • 818-760-3366

Restaurants

- **Barsac Brasserie** • 4212 Lankershim Blvd • 818-760-7081
- **Buca di Beppo** • 100 Universal Center Dr • 818-509-9463
- **Ca' del Sole** • 4100 Cahuenga Blvd • 818-985-4669
- **California Canteen** • 3311 Cahuenga Blvd • 323-876-1702
- **Dalt's Grill** • 3500 W Olive Ave • 818-953-7750
- **La Scala Presto** • 3821 Riverside Dr • 818-846-6800
- **Miceli's** • 3655 Cahuenga Blvd • 323-851-3344
- **Mo's** • 4301 Riverside Dr • 818-845-3009
- **Paty's** • 10001 Riverside Dr • 818-761-0041
- **Priscilla's Coffee** • 4150 Riverside Dr • 818-843-5707
- **Prosecco Restaurant** • 10144 Riverside Dr • 818-505-0930
- **Roma Via Paris** • 3413 Cahuenga Blvd • 323-882-6965
- **Smoke House Restaurant** • 4420 W Lakeside Dr • 323-849-3641
- **Versailles** • 100 Universal Center Dr • 818-505-0093
- **Wolfgang Puck Café** • 100 Universal Center Dr • 818-985-9653
- **Yamakawa** • 10118 Riverside Dr • 818-763-8355

Shopping

- **Cinema Secrets Beauty Supply** • 4400 W Riverside Dr • 818-846-0579
- **Geographia Map & Book Store** • 4000 W Riverside Dr • 818-848-1414
- **Pergolina** • 10139 Riverside Dr • 818-508-7708
- **Steel Casey** • 10624 Ventura Blvd • 818-763-5667

Video Rental

- **Blockbuster** • 10911 Ventura Blvd • 818-762-9257

MAP 46
MAP 52
MAP 47
MAP 3
MAP 4
MAP 5
BURBANK
GLENDALE
HOLLYWOOD HILLS
LOS FELIZ
N Buena Vista St
W Olive Ave
S Buena Vista St
W Alameda Ave
Victory Blvd
S Main St
W Alameda Ave
Western Ave
W Glenoaks Blvd
San Fernando Rd
W Glenoaks Bl
Disney Studios
NBC Studios
Buena Vista Park
Riverside Dr
Riverside Dr
Riverside Dr
Ventura Freeway
Los Angeles River
Los Angeles Equestrian Center
Forest Lawn Dr
Zoo Dr
Travel Town Museum
Los Angeles Live Streamers Inc.
Zoo Dr
Soccer Fields
San Fernando Rd
W Broadway
Mount Sinai Memorial Park
Griffith Park Dr
Los Angeles Zoo
Zoo Dr
Autry Museum of Western Heritage
Forest Lawn Memorial Park (Hollywood Hills)
Mount Hollywood Dr
Griffith Park Boys Camp
Harding Municipal Golf Course
Colorado St Freeway Exit
Cahuenga Peak 1820 ft (555 m)
Vista Del Valle
Griffith Park Dr
Crystal Springs Dr
Golden State Freeway
Wilson Municipal Golf Course
North Atwater Park
Mt. Lee 1680 ft (512 m)
Mount Lee Dr
Play Ground
Park HQ
Visitor Center
Hollywood Sign
Crystal Springs Picnic Grounds
Mulholland Hwy
Mt. Hollywood 1625 ft (496 m)
Cedar Tree Picnic Grounds
Crystal Springs Dr
Griffith Park Dr
N Beachwood Dr
Vermont Canyon Rd
Bird Sanctuary
Vista Del Valle
Los Feliz Municipal Golf Course
Los Feliz Blvd
Tennis Courts
Pony and Train Rides
Azalea Gardens
Western Canyon Rd
Picnic Grounds
Vermont Canyon Rd
Commonwealth Canyon Dr
Hollywood Reservoir
Observation Rd
Greek Theater
Roosevelt Municipal Golf Course
Griffith Rec Ctr
Fern Dell Dr
Griffith Observatory
Glendale Blvd
N Beachwood Dr
N Western Ave
Los Feliz Blvd
Rowena Ave
N Cahuenga Blvd
Hillhurst Ave
N Commonwealth Canyon Ave
Franklin Ave
Hollywood Blvd
W Sunset Blvd
W Silver Lake
Griffith Park

4730 Crystal Springs Drive
Los Angeles, CA 90027
Phone: 213-485-5501 or 323-913-4688
NFT Map: 4

Overview

Named after its former owner, Colonel Griffith Jenkins Griffith, the park has over 4,107 acres of natural terrain covered with California oak trees, wild sage, and manzanita. Griffith Park is the largest municipal park and urban wilderness area in the United States. Although a large portion of the park remains almost unchanged, a number of attractions have been built within the park, including recreation areas, horse riding trails, a Greek Theater, Griffith Observatory, Travel Town Museum, and the Los Angeles Zoo. Colonel Griffith J. Griffith's gift of five square miles was given as a Christmas gift to the city of Los Angeles almost unconditionally. Griffith specified that, "It must be made a place of recreation and rest for the masses, a resort for the rank-and-file, for the plain people." So to all you plain, rank-and-filers out there, if what you're after is a break from the hustle and bustle of LA life, Griffith Park is a nice place to head for a day out.

Practicalities

Griffith Park is open to the public from 6 am to 10 pm daily. Bridle trails, hiking paths, and mountain roads are closed at sunset.

Located northwest of downtown LA, Griffith Park is easily reached from either the I-5 or the SR-134. Freeway off-ramps leading to the park from I-5 are Los Feliz Boulevard, Griffith Park (direct entry), and Zoo Drive. Approaching the park on SR-134 eastbound, take either the Forest Lawn Drive or Victory Boulevard off-ramps. From SR-134 westbound, take Zoo Drive or Forest Lawn Drive. After leaving the freeways, handy signs will guide you right into the park. Just a little note of warning: the speed limit on all park roads is 25 mph and is strictly enforced.

Activities

Located within the park are facilities for golf (Harding, Roosevelt, and Wilson Municipal Golf Courses), swimming (the Plunge Pool open in summer months), hiking, jogging, horse-riding, tennis (Griffiths Riverside Pay, Vermont Pay, and the free Griffith Park Drive Courts), soccer (John Ferraro Athletic Fields at the northeast corner of the park), camping, and picnicking at one of the five main picnic areas. In most developed areas of the park, games and sports are permitted to be played and there are special areas set aside for soccer, badminton, baseball, and softball. Children's playgrounds can be found at various locations in the park, usually near picnic grounds. Among the various playgrounds is Shane's Inspiration, a "boundless playground" designed to allow children with disabilities to play alongside their able-bodied peers. Bicycles can be rented from the Travel Town Museum if you'd like to ride through Griffith Park.

Barbecues

If you're planning on having a relaxing barbecue in the park, you need to be particularly careful between spring and early fall when brush fires present a definite safety hazard since the underbrush is very dry. Open fires are prohibited, but public barbecue pits are provided free of charge at picnic areas. In case of emergency in the park, notify the ranger station at 213-913-4688 or dial 911.

Griffith Observatory

The observatory closed in January 2002 for a much needed three-year renovation. When it reopens, it will have doubled in size and will be home to a state-of-the-art planetarium. In the meantime, a temporary facility has opened just south of the LA Zoo and the Autry Museum. The temporary site features modest exhibits and a telescope, but seems mainly intended for astronomy buffs who simply hate to miss out on a meteor shower. The satellite facility is open Tuesday through Friday from 1 pm until 10 pm, and from 10 am until 10 pm on Saturdays and Sundays.

Autry Museum of Western Heritage

The museum opening hours are Tuesday through Sunday from 10 am until 5 pm. It is also open late on Thursdays, until 8 pm. Admission is $7.50 for adults, $5 for students and seniors, and $3 for children under 12. On Thursdays between 4 pm and 8 pm, admission is free. The Autry Museum is home to stories of the people, cultures, and events that have shaped the legacy of this region. Step back in time and take a look at the lives of the Spanish explorers, explore the western myths of radio, movies, and television, and view western art from Remington, Russell, and others. If you find that immersing yourself in all the gun-toting camaraderie works up your appetite, try the Golden Spur Cafe, which is open for breakfast and lunch.

Greek Theater

Built with funds left to the city by Griffith J. Griffith, the Greek Theater was officially dedicated on September 25, 1930. Today it features a 6,162-seat capacity and, after an artist has sold 100,000 seats, he has his handprint and signature cemented into the Wall of Fame. If you're wondering which greats may have achieved that honor, they include Johnny Mathis, Harry Belafonte, and Santana. Call 323-665-1927 for concert schedules. See page 321 for more information.

Los Angeles Zoo

The Los Angeles Zoo is located in Griffith Park at the junction of Ventura (134) and Golden State (5) Freeways. The zoo is open daily from 10 am until 5 pm except December 25th, and in the summer (July 1 to Sept 3), the zoo stays open an extra hour until 6 pm. Entrance fees are $8.25 adults, $5.25 seniors, and $3.25 children 2 to 12. If you're an AAA member, take your card for a $2 discount for adults and $1 for children (up to 2 adults and 2 kids).
Phone: 323-644-6400 Fax 323-662-9786.

Travel Town Museum

The Travel Town Museum is located at 5200 Zoo Drive, at the northwest corner of Griffith Park. Exit Forest Lawn Drive, Ventura Freeway (134). The museum is open Monday through Friday, 10 am to 4 pm, Sunday and Saturday, 10 am to 5 pm. Closing time is one hour later in summer and the museum is closed on December 25th. And guess what? Entrance is free! Not only that, there's lots of public parking available. This is also the place to go if you would like to rent a bike to ride around Griffith Park.
Phone: 323-662-5874.

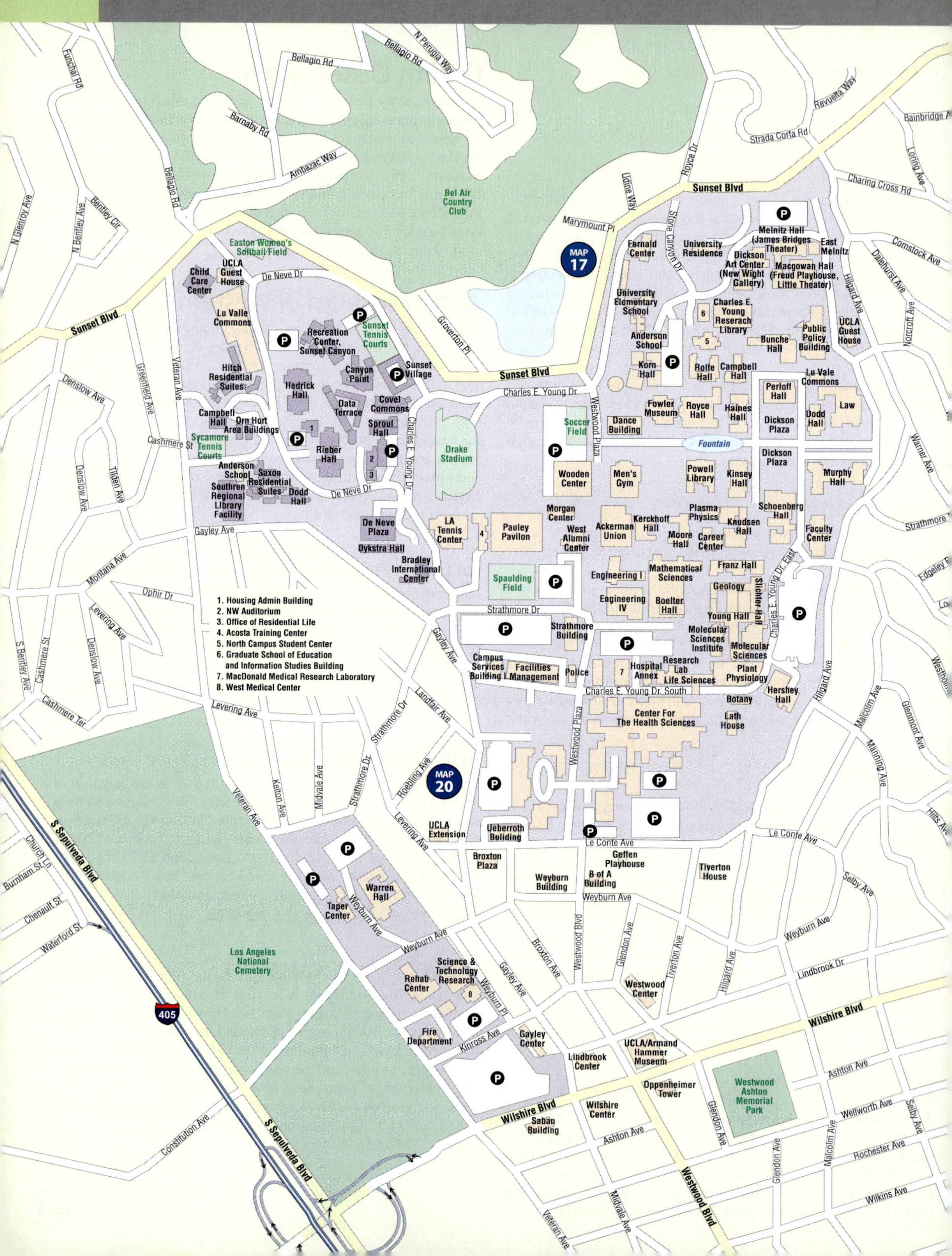

1. Housing Admin Building
2. NW Auditorium
3. Office of Residential Life
4. Acosta Training Center
5. North Campus Student Center
6. Graduate School of Education and Information Studies Building
7. MacDonald Medical Research Laboratory
8. West Medical Center

Mailing Address: 405 Hilgard Avenue, Box 951361,
Los Angeles, CA 90095-1361
Location: 405 Hilgard Avenue at Sunset Boulevard
Phone: 310-825-4321   Website: www.ucla.edu
Opened: August 29th, 1882
Present Number of Students: 36,900
Type of School: Public
NFT Map: 20

Overview

Located in Westwood, UCLA is a large educational institution catering to undergraduate students, graduate scholarship, research, and public service. Known in the US and around the world for its academic excellence, UCLA has also consistently produced champion sports teams and athletes.

UCLA's Extension Program is extremely popular and offers continuing education for adults in topics ranging from architecture to screenwriting to wine tasting. The courses are offered quarterly and are popular with people considering a career change, as well as those with simply a general interest in a topic.

Tuition

For the 2002-03 academic year, annual registration fees were $4,878 for residents of California. Living expenses (including books and supplies) were estimated by the university at around $8,000 for those living with relatives and around $14,000 for students living in residence halls or off-campus apartments. If you're not a resident of California, you can add a non-resident tuition of just over $12,279 to your fees. In effect, this means that a resident student living with relatives can expect one year of study to cost around $13,300 ($19,400 on-campus) while a non-resident living on campus will pay around $32,000.

Facilities

The UCLA campus is like a small city, with its own police department and fire marshal and a range of services including shops, restaurants, post offices, and banks. If you are a visitor to UCLA and you need to find parking, there are 11 Parking and Information booths located around the campus where you can park and obtain a handy map for your visit. UCLA's circular drive loops around the entire campus and is extremely easy to navigate. If you're just popping in, metered parking is available for 25¢ per 8 minutes (take lots of quarters) or $7 for the entire day. Student parking (granted quarterly through application) is assigned by a need-based point system, which takes into consideration class standing, employment/academic obligations, and commuter distance when granting permits.

Cultural Events

UCLA also provides the community with a wide variety of cultural programs. The university is affiliated with the Geffen Playhouse in Westwood (10886 Le Conte Ave., 310-208-5454), which has been the LA stop for Broadway plays such as *The Weir* and *Wit*. On campus, Royce Hall has hosted a wide variety of music and dance programs, from the Los Angeles Philharmonic to Elvis Costello. And each April, UCLA is home to the Los Angeles Times' Festival of Books, *the* literary event of the year.

Sports

You don't need to be a UCLA student, staff member, or alumnus to appreciate the vast talents of UCLA's athletes. Top-ten nationally ranked teams at UCLA include men's water polo, women's soccer, women's volleyball, and football. For up-to-date information, scores, and schedules, check out the official athletics website at www.uclabruins.com. For tickets, call 310-UCLA-WIN.

Department Contact Information

Undergraduate Admissions 310-835-3101
Graduate Admissions 310-206-6086
College of Letters and Science 310-825-9009
Anderson School of Management 310-825-6121
Graduate School of Education
    and Information Studies 310-825-8326
School of the Arts and Architecture 310-206-6465
The Henry Samueli School of
    Engineering and Applied Science 310-825-2826
School of Dentistry .310-825-2337
School of Law 310-825-4841
School of Medicine .310-825-6373
School of Nursing 310-825-7181
School of Public Health 310-825-5140
School of Public Policy and 310-206-7568
    Social Research
School of Theater, Film and Television . . .310-825-5761

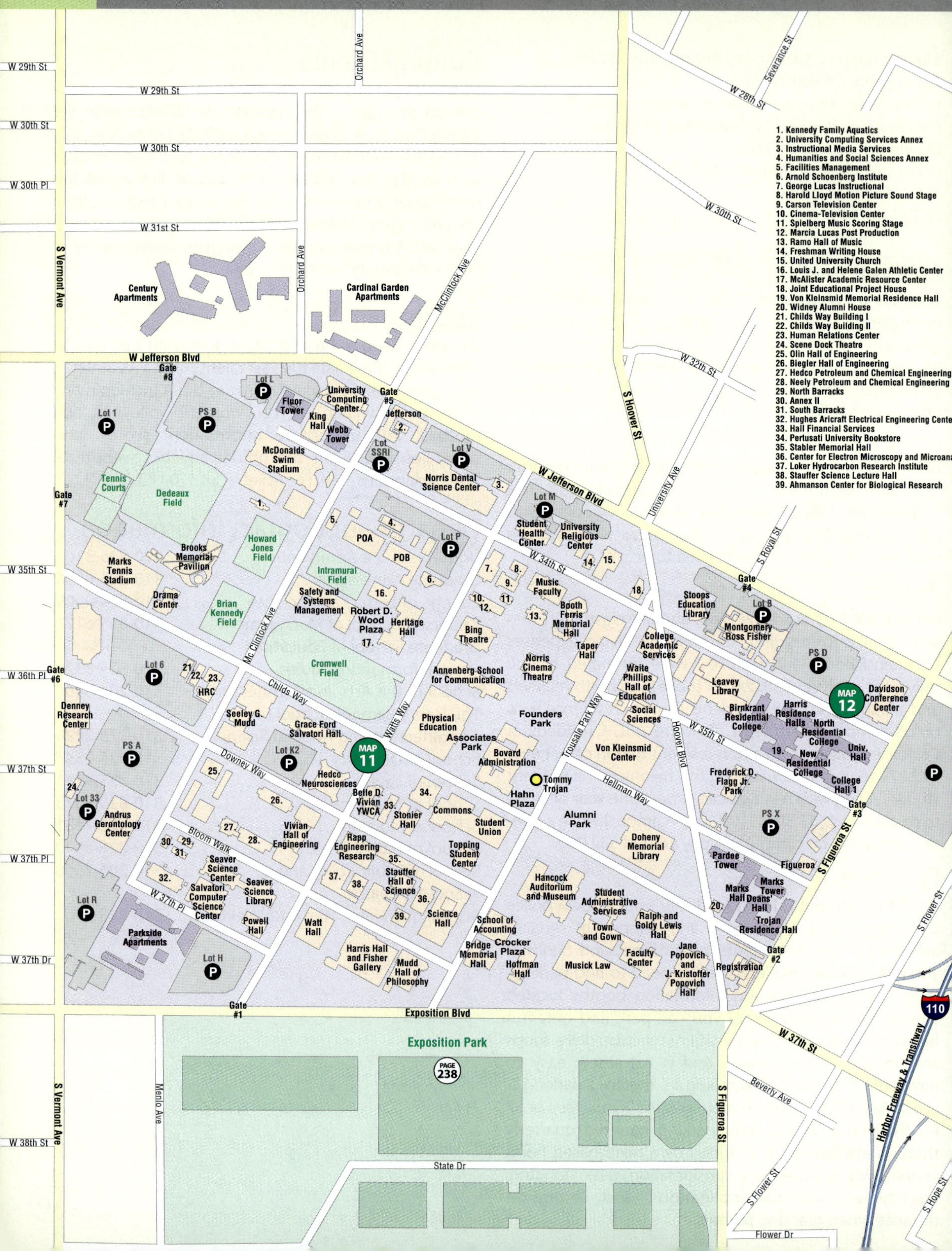
1. Kennedy Family Aquatics
2. University Computing Services Annex
3. Instructional Media Services
4. Humanities and Social Sciences Annex
5. Facilities Management
6. Arnold Schoenberg Institute
7. George Lucas Instructional
8. Harold Lloyd Motion Picture Sound Stage
9. Carson Television Center
10. Cinema-Television Center
11. Spielberg Music Scoring Stage
12. Marcia Lucas Post Production
13. Ramo Hall of Music
14. Freshman Writing House
15. United University Church
16. Louis J. and Helene Galen Athletic Center
17. McAlister Academic Resource Center
18. Joint Educational Project House
19. Von Kleinsmid Memorial Residence Hall
20. Widney Alumni House
21. Childs Way Building I
22. Childs Way Building II
23. Human Relations Center
24. Scene Dock Theatre
25. Olin Hall of Engineering
26. Biegler Hall of Engineering
27. Hedco Petroleum and Chemical Engineering
28. Neely Petroleum and Chemical Engineering
29. North Barracks
30. Annex II
31. South Barracks
32. Hughes Aricraft Electrical Engineering Center
33. Hall Financial Services
34. Pertusati University Bookstore
35. Stabler Memorial Hall
36. Center for Electron Microscopy and Microanalysis
37. Loker Hydrocarbon Research Institute
38. Stauffer Science Lecture Hall
39. Ahmanson Center for Biological Research

W 29th St
Orchard Ave
Severance St
W 28th St
W 29th St
W 30th St
W 30th St
W 30th St
W 30th St
W 30th Pl
W 31st St
S Vermont Ave
Orchard Ave
McClintock Ave
Century Apartments
Cardinal Garden Apartments
W Jefferson Blvd
S Hoover St
W 32nd St
Gate #8
Lot L
University Computing Center
Gate #5
Jefferson
Lot 1
PS B
Fluor Tower
King Hall
Webb Tower
Lot SSRI
Lot V
University Ave
McDonalds Swim Stadium
Norris Dental Science Center
W Jefferson Blvd
Tennis Courts
Dedeaux Field
Lot M
Student Health Center
University Religious Center
S Royal St
Gate #7
Howard Jones Field
POA
Lot P
POB
W 34th St
Music Faculty
Gate #4
Marks Tennis Stadium
Brooks Memorial Pavilion
Intramural Field
Booth Ferris Memorial Hall
Stoops Education Library
Lot B
W 35th St
Drama Center
Brian Kennedy Field
Safety and Systems Management
Robert D. Wood Plaza
Heritage Hall
Bing Theatre
Taper Hall
Montgomery Ross Fisher
PS D
Lot 6
HRC
Cromwell Field
Childs Way
Annenberg School for Communication
Norris Cinema Theatre
College Academic Services
Leavey Library
Harris Residence Halls
MAP 12
Davidson Conference Center
W 36th Pl
Gate #6
Seeley G. Mudd
Physical Education
Founders Park
Waite Phillips Hall of Education
Birnkrant Residential College
North Residential College
Univ. Hall
Denney Research Center
PS A
Grace Ford Salvatori Hall
Associates Park
Social Sciences
Von Kleinsmid Center
W 35th St
New Residential College
College Hall 1
W 37th St
Lot K2
Downey Way
MAP 11
Bovard Administration
Hoover Blvd
Frederick D. Flagg Jr. Park
Gate #3
Lot 33
Hedco Neurosciences
Tommy Trojan
Hellman Way
PS X
Andrus Gerontology Center
Belle D. Vivian YWCA
Hahn Plaza
Alumni Park
Pardee Tower
Figueroa
Bloom Walk
Stonier Hall
Commons
Student Union
Doheny Memorial Library
Marks Hall
Marks Tower Deans' Hall
Vivian Hall of Engineering
Rapp Engineering Research
Topping Student Center
Trojan Residence Hall
W 37th Pl
Seaver Science Center
Salvatori Computer Science Center
Seaver Science Library
Stauffer Hall of Science
Hancock Auditorium and Museum
Student Administrative Services
Ralph and Goldy Lewis Hall
Lot R
W 37th Pl
Powell Hall
Watt Hall
Science Hall
School of Accounting
Town and Gown
Faculty Center
Jane Popovich and J. Kristoffer Popovich Hall
Registration
Parkside Apartments
Lot H
Harris Hall and Fisher Gallery
Mudd Hall of Philosophy
Bridge Memorial Hall
Crocker Plaza
Hoffman Hall
Musick Law
Gate #2
Gate #1
Exposition Blvd
S Figueroa St
S Flower St
Exposition Park
PAGE 238
S Vermont Ave
Menlo Ave
S Figueroa St
Beverly Ave
Harbor Freeway & Transitway
W 37th St
110
W 38th St
State Dr
S Flower St
S Hope St
Flower Dr

Mailing Address: *University Park Campus (UPC):*
         USC, Los Angeles CA 90089
Mailing Address: *Health Sciences Campus (HSC):*
         USC, Los Angeles CA 90033
Location (UPC):   *University Park, between Figueroa St,*
         Exposition Park and Jefferson Blvd
Location (HSC):   *San Pablo*
Phone: 213-740-2311   Website: www.usc.edu
Opened: 1880
Present Number of Students: 28,000
Type of School: Private, non-denominational
NFT Map: 11-12

Overview

The University Park Campus, home to USC's College of Letters, Arts and Sciences, the Graduate School, and 14 professional schools, is located three miles south of downtown Los Angeles. Located seven miles from the University Park Campus, the Health Sciences Campus provides an environment for students, patients, and scientists from around the world. The 31-acre campus hosts the medical and pharmacy schools, as well as programs in occupational therapy, physical therapy, and nursing. USC's film school boasts an especially impressive pedigree. Its founding faculty included Douglas Fairbanks and D.W. Griffith, and it has churned out equally famous alumni, such as George Lucas and Robert Zemeckis. A shuttle service between the campuses runs approximately every hour throughout the week.

Tuition

For the 2002-03 academic year, annual undergraduate tuition and fees were $28,692 (based on 20 units of tuition). Some of the specialized professional programs also carry additional fees. Annual living expenses (including books and supplies) are estimated by the university at around $12,000 for the Fall and Spring semesters. Because USC is a private university, there is no additional tuition charged for out-of-state or out-of-country students.

Parking

Parking on campus is $6. A small number of one-hour metered parking spaces are also available. Four-hour and two-hour metered parking is available on Figueroa and Jefferson. $3-a-day lots are available Mon-Fri across the street from the campus on Figueroa (next to the Sizzler restaurant) and on Jefferson (next to the Shrine Auditorium). Parking rates for these lots may vary for special events.

Sports

Formerly known as the Methodists or Wesleyans, the Trojans were renamed in 1912 after the fighting spirit the teams displayed against stronger and better equipped opponents. Top-ten nationally ranked teams at USC include women's volleyball, men's water polo, women's golf, and men's golf. For up-to-date information, scores and schedules, check out the official athletics website at www.usctrojans.com. For tickets, call 213-740-GO SC.

Department Contact Information

Undergraduate Admission 213-740-8899
Graduate Admission 213-740-5868
College of Letters, Arts and Sciences 213-740-5930
Leventhal School of Accounting 213-740-4838
School of Architecture 213-740-2723
Marshall School of Business 213-740-8885
School of Cinema-Television 213-740-2911
Annenberg School for Communication .213-821-0768
School of Dentistry 213-740-2800
Rossier School of Education 213-740-7296
School of Engineering 213-740-7832
School of Fine Arts 213-740-2787
Leonard Davis School of Gerontology ...213-740-6060
Independent Health Professions 323-442-2890
The Law School 213-740-2523
Keck School of Medicine 323-442-1842
School of Pharmacy 323-442-1369
School Policy, Planning 213-740-6842
    and Development
School of Social Work 213-740-2711
School of Theater 213-740-1286

Overview

When outsiders fantasize about Southern California, it's not the smog-filled sky of downtown LA that runs through their minds. It's the sandy beaches and sunny skies of Malibu—the city that inspired a coconutty rum and perhaps the most famous Barbie Doll ever.

The area's first settlers were the Chumash Indians. The names of some of their villages are still a part of local culture—Ojai, Mugu, and Zuma, to name just a few. Malibu's current residents are a very different tribe. For instance, The Colony, a gated community, is home to a wide array of celebrities, businessmen, and anyone else who can spare the $1 million-plus that it takes to buy a parcel of beachfront land.

Depending upon weather and acts of God (like the fires and mudslides that frequently strike this beautiful stretch of coastline), Malibu lies about 45 minutes from downtown LA, or approximately 35 miles.

The best thing about Malibu is its remoteness. You feel as though you've left LA and gone somewhere else. The worst thing about Malibu is...its remoteness. You feel as though you've left LA and gone somewhere else. Somewhere very far away.

Getting There

With few exceptions, it's difficult to go anywhere in Malibu without encountering the Pacific Coast Highway for at least some of the trip. From the southern half of LA, the easiest option is to take the 10 Freeway to the PCH and head north. On summer weekends, the PCH becomes a virtual parking lot, but at least you can enjoy the smell of the ocean and the view of the waves.

From the Valley and points north, your best bet is to hop on the 101 Freeway and head north, toward Ventura. Exit at Las Virgenes and follow the signs for Las Virgenes Road/Malibu Canyon; then take Malibu Canyon Road right to the PCH. If you're planning on going even further north into Malibu, you can also exit the 101 at Kanan Road, which becomes Kanan Dume Road and terminates at the PCH.

The Beaches

These are the main attraction in Malibu, and you have a number of public beaches from which to choose. Keep in mind that dogs are not allowed on any public beach, and parking is a challenge. There are three options: 1) Pay whatever the day's going rate is at any number of parking lots conveniently located at each Malibu beach. 2) Find street parking in any of Malibu's residential areas—which then entails hiking down to the beach, often with the added challenge of crossing the PCH (Malibu's answer to the video game "Frogger.") Or 3) Get all of the planets to align just so, allowing you to score that perfect parking spot on the beach side of PCH, right outside the entrance to your chosen beach. We grudgingly admit that option #1 may be your best bet.

Many of Malibu's private beaches are accessible to the public via causeways or public gates. These are some of Malibu's more popular public beaches:

- **Topanga State Beach.** Located along PCH at Topanga Canyon Blvd. Popular for surfing.
- **Malibu Lagoon State Beach.** Located just west of the Malibu Pier. Also features a bird sanctuary.
- **Malibu Surfrider Beach.** Home of the Malibu Pier, located along the 23000 block of PCH. This is one of the most famous surfing beaches in the world.
- **Dan Blocker Beach.** Named for the actor who played "Hoss" on the TV series *Bonanza*. He was one of the original owners of this stretch of beach, along with his co-stars, Lorne Greene and Michael Landon, who donated it to the state after Blocker's death. This beach is on the PCH between Puerco Canyon and Corral Canyon.
- **Point Dume State Beach.** This state-owned beach is accessed from Westward Beach Road. One of the area's most beautiful beaches, it features nearby hiking trails, reefs for scuba diving, and tidepools.
- **Zuma Beach.** This very popular beach is located on the PCH, just west of Heathercliff Drive. It's expansive, is home to a number of volleyball courts, and tends to be very crowded in the summer.
- **Robert H. Meyer Memorial State Beach.** This is actually a grouping of three small beaches—El Pescador, La Piedra, and El Matador. They are located about 10 miles west of Malibu proper.
- **Nicholas Canyon Beach.** Located at 33850 Pacific Coast Highway. Lots of room for laying out in the sun or a game of Frisbee.

The Adamson House

Located at Malibu Lagoon State Beach, the Adamson House was the home of Rhoda Rindge Adamson, whose family, the Rindges, once owned the Malibu Spanish Land Grant (as the area was originally known), and her husband, Merritt Huntley Adamson. The house features liberal use of the ceramic tile manufactured by the then-famed Malibu Potteries. The Adamson House and Museum are open Wed. to Sat., from 11 am to 3 pm, while the grounds are open daily from 8 am until sunset. The property is also available for weddings and other special events. Call 310-456-8432 for more information.

Malibu Creek State Park

What is now a 7000-acre state park once belonged to motion picture studio Twentieth Century Fox, which used the park to double for Korea in the TV series *M*A*S*H*. The park is home to some 30 miles of hiking and riding trails, as well as a campground featuring 60 campsites, along with barbecues, showers, and toilet facilities. The park's entrance is located along Las Virgenes/Malibu Canyon Road, just south of Mulholland Highway. For camping and other information, please call 818-880-0367.

Pepperdine University

It's hard to imagine getting any studying done on a campus just a few hundred yards from the ocean, but Pepperdine students manage to pull it off (well, sometimes). The campus may be best known as the location for the 1970's TV spectacular, *The Battle of the Network Stars*, but Pepperdine is represented by 14 NCAA Division I athletic teams in sports ranging from men's water polo to women's golf. The university's Center for the Arts typically hosts an eclectic lineup of events such as piano recitals, modern dance, and children's theatre. Visit Pepperdine's website (www.pepperdine.edu) or call 310-506-4000 for additional details.

Where to Eat

Malibu relies upon the PCH as its Main Street and most of the town's dining establishments are located along either side. Dining experiences in Malibu tend to be one extreme or the other—either ultra-casual or ultra-pricey. Here are some restaurants that we recommend at either end of the spectrum:

- **Coogies.** Malibu Colony Plaza, 23755 W. Malibu Road, 310-317-1444. Upscale diner fare. This unpretentious restaurant is healthier than the typical diner and is a great bet for breakfast by the beach.
- **Neptune's Net.** 42505 PCH, 310-457-3095. Seafood. Though it's almost at the Ventura county line, this place is worth the drive. Very "beachy," Neptune's Net serves up a variety of seafood, either steamed or fried.
- **Duke's Malibu.** 21150 PCH, 310-317-0177. California-Hawaiian. Lots of seafood dishes served amidst a fun, surfer theme.
- **Marmalade Café.** 3894 Cross Creek Road, 310-317-4242. California-style sandwiches and salads. If you want a nice lunch in a nice setting, this is the place to go. But their food travels well as take-out, and they have a great catering business, as well.
- **Taverna Tony.** Malibu Country Mart, 23410 Civic Center Way, 310-317-9667. Greek. Delicious food in a fun, festive setting that includes live music.
- **Granita.** Malibu Colony Plaza, 23725 W. Malibu Road, 310-456-0488. California-Mediterranean. Wolfgang Puck's restaurant by the beach, the food is good but the décor is better.
- **Geoffrey's.** 27400 PCH, 310-457-1519. California-eclectic. Pronounced "Joffrey's," this restaurant actually serves delicious food that merits the snooty attitude you may occasionally encounter here. This is one of the most beautiful and romantic restaurants in LA.

Additional Information

Beach hours and surf reports:
http://beaches.co.la.ca.us/BandH/Beaches/main.htm
General Malibu info: www.ci.malibu.ca.us/

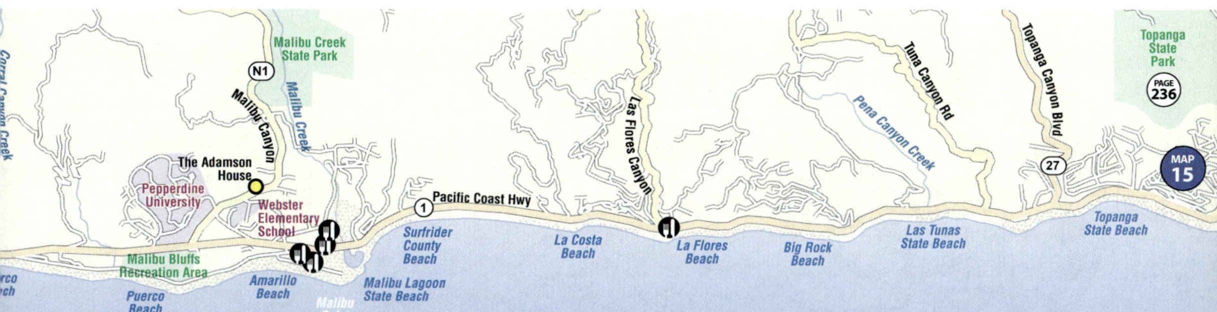

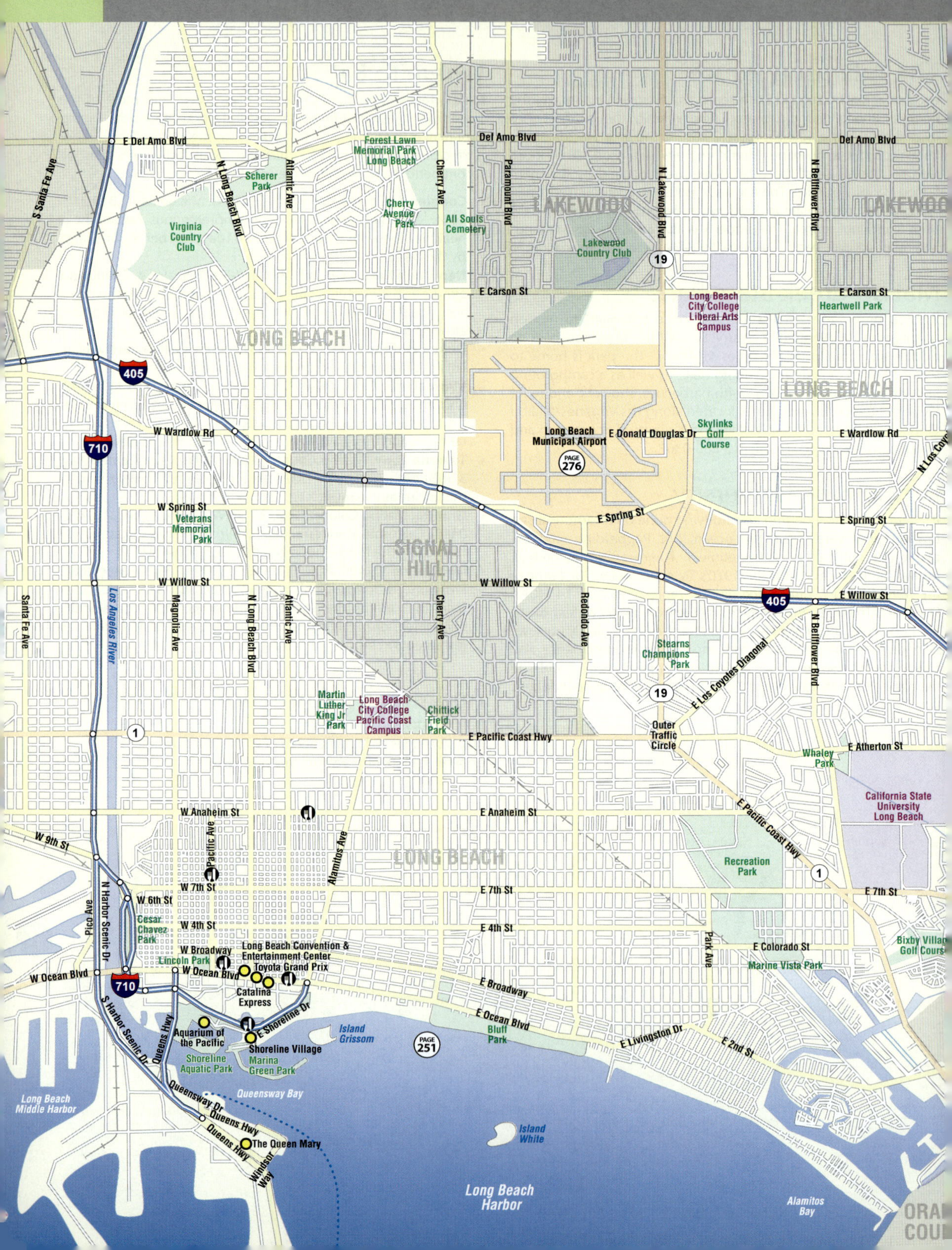
E Del Amo Blvd
S Santa Fe Ave
Scherer Park
N Long Beach Blvd
Atlantic Ave
Forest Lawn Memorial Park Long Beach
Del Amo Blvd
Cherry Ave
Paramount Blvd
LAKEWOOD
N Lakewood Blvd
N Bellflower Blvd
LAKEWOOD
Del Amo Blvd
Virginia Country Club
Cherry Avenue Park
All Souls Cemetery
Lakewood Country Club
19
LONG BEACH
E Carson St
Long Beach City College Liberal Arts Campus
E Carson St
Heartwell Park
LONG BEACH
LONG BEACH
405
710
W Wardlow Rd
Long Beach Municipal Airport
E Donald Douglas Dr
Skylinks Golf Course
PAGE 276
E Wardlow Rd
W Spring St
Veterans Memorial Park
E Spring St
E Spring St
Santa Fe Ave
Los Angeles River
W Willow St
Magnolia Ave
N Long Beach Blvd
Atlantic Ave
SIGNAL HILL
W Willow St
Cherry Ave
Redondo Ave
405
E Willow St
N Los Coyotes
E Willow St
N Bellflower Blvd
Stearns Champions Park
19
E Los Coyotes Diagonal
1
Martin Luther King Jr Park
Long Beach City College Pacific Coast Campus
Chittick Field Park
E Pacific Coast Hwy
Outer Traffic Circle
Whaley Park
E Atherton St
E Pacific Coast Hwy
California State University Long Beach
W Anaheim St
E Anaheim St
Recreation Park
1
W 9th St
Pacific Ave
LONG BEACH
E 7th St
E 7th St
N Harbor Scenic Dr
W 7th St
Alamitos Ave
E 7th St
W 6th St
Cesar Chavez Park
W 4th St
E 4th St
Park Ave
E Colorado St
Bixby Village Golf Course
W Broadway
Lincoln Park
W Ocean Blvd
Long Beach Convention & Entertainment Center Toyota Grand Prix
Marine Vista Park
Pico Ave
710
W Ocean Blvd
Catalina Express
E Broadway
S Harbor Scenic Dr
Queens Hwy
Aquarium of the Pacific
E Shoreline Dr
Island Grissom
E Ocean Blvd
Bluff Park
E Livingston Dr
E 2nd St
Shoreline Village
Shoreline Aquatic Park
Marina Green Park
PAGE 251
Long Beach Middle Harbor
Queensway Dr
Queens Hwy
Queensway Bay
Island White
Queens Hwy
The Queen Mary
Windsor Way
Long Beach Harbor
Long Beach Harbor
Alamitos Bay
ORANGE COUNTY

Overview

Most Angelenos tend to visit Long Beach only when they're on their way to someplace else, like Orange County or Catalina. But they might be interested to learn that Long Beach is actually California's fifth-largest city, with a population of over 400,000 and diverse areas ranging from the somewhat touristy Shoreline Village to the much hipper Belmont Shore.   And, with its own beaches, an eleven-mile coastline, and relative proximity to downtown Los Angeles (25 miles), Long Beach is a destination in its own right.

Getting There

From Los Angeles, driving to Long Beach couldn't be easier. Simply find your way to the 405 or the 5 freeways and head south, and take either freeway to the 710 S. The 10 freeway also intersects with the 710 east of downtown, so this is a viable option as well.

The Metro Blue Line travels to downtown Long Beach from approximately 5 am until 11:45 pm. For a roundtrip fare of $2.70, you can board the Blue Line at the 7th Street/Metro Center or the Pico Blvd. stop (near the Los Angeles Convention Center). The train makes several stops in Long Beach, including one at the Transit Mall on 1st Street, between Pine and Pacific. For additional information about the Blue Line, visit www.wgn.net/~elson/larail/blue.html on the web, or call 213-620-RAIL.

Once in Long Beach, another option for getting around is the AquaBus. This 40-foot-long water taxi costs just $2 and will ferry you to a number of Long Beach's coastal attractions. There are stops at the Aquarium, the Queen Mary, the Catalina Express, and Shoreline Village.   For more information and schedules, please call 800-995-4386.

Attractions

The Queen Mary

Once a vessel that carried movie stars and heads of state across the Atlantic Ocean, the Queen Mary is now a floating hotel and museum, available for weddings, bar mitzvahs, and rubber stamp conventions. (We kid you not.) But in all seriousness, the ship is awesome in scope and its historical significance to the way we used to travel. There are several restaurants on board the ship as well as other diversions, including the former Russian submarine, *Scorpion*, a "Ghosts & Legends" tour that examines rumors that the ship is haunted, and a special tour that covers the Queen Mary's stint as a troop transport during World War II.

Admission: A "First Class Passage" that includes admission to all of these attractions costs $24.95 for each adult and $12.95 for kids 5-11. Smaller packages are also available.

Directions: The Queen Mary is located at 1126 Queens Highway, at the south end of the 710 freeway.

Call 562-435-3511 for more details, or visit http://www.queenmary.com on the web.

Aquarium of the Pacific

Opened with much fanfare in 1998, the Aquarium of the Pacific's mission is to educate Californians about the wildlife indigenous to our own Pacific Ocean, so don't come here looking to see Atlantic salmon or Maine lobsters. While Sea World, farther south in San Diego, relies heavily upon flashy acts like Shamu to draw visitors, the Aquarium of the Pacific is all about the animals.

Admission: Adult admission packages start at $18.75. The aquarium is open every day from 9 am until 6 pm. It's closed on Christmas and for the entire weekend of the Toyota Grand Prix, which is typically in April.

Directions: Take the 405 S to the 710 S, and follow the signs to Downtown Long Beach and the Aquarium. The Aquarium is located at 100 Aquarium Way, off of Shoreline Drive. Parking is available at a municipal lot located just a few feet from the Aquarium. The cost is $6 with an Aquarium ticket stub, $7 without.

For more information, call 562-590-3100 or visit http://www.aquariumofpacific.org

Long Beach Convention & Entertainment Center

This complex is home to an eclectic assortment of events. Long Beach's professional hockey team, the Ice Dogs, play their home games at the Long Beach Arena; the Terrace Theatre hosts a variety of plays and musical performances; and the Convention Center includes a large ballroom that serves as the site for many a senior prom.

Directions: Take the 405 S to the 710 S and head for the Downtown exits. The 710 turns into Shoreline Drive. Follow this to Linden and turn into the parking lot.

Additional information and a calendar of events is available at www.longbeachcc.com, or by calling 562-436-3661.

The Ice Dogs, who play from October until early April, are part of the West Coast Hockey League. You can check their schedule at www.icedogshockey.com, and tickets are available through Ticketmaster.

Catalina Express

This ferry service makes regular crossings between mainland California and Catalina Island, a pleasant getaway for a day or a weekend. There isn't a whole lot to do on Catalina, but that's basically the point of going. The Catalina Express leaves Long Beach for Catalina three times daily and the boat ride is approximately one hour long. Bring sunscreen, a beach towel, and Dramamine—the boat ride is often a rough one.

One-way adult tickets cost $21.50 and reservations are recommended. Call 800-481-3470 for more details.

North Pine
East Village Arts District
11th St
10th St
9th St
8th St
7th St
6th St
5th St
4th St
3rd St
1st St
Broadway
Long Beach Plaza
Museum of Latin American Art
Golden Shore Ave
Maine Ave
Daisy Ave
Magnolia Ave
Chestnut Ave
Cedar Ave
Pacific Ave
Pine Ave
Long Beach Blvd
Elm Ave
Atlantic Ave
Lime Ave
Olive Ave
Alamitos Ave
Cerritos Ave
Bonito Ave
Broadway
1st St
West Gateway
Long Beach Freeway
Pine Avenue
Edison Theatre
World Trade Center/
Long Beach Area
Convention &
Visitors Bureau
W Ocean Blvd
Seaside Way
Maine Way
Long Beach Convention &
Entertainment Center
Shoreline Dr
Shoreline Park
Marina Green Park
Catalina
Landing
Shoreline
Village
Aquarium of
the Pacific
N Harbor Scenic Dr
Queen's WY Bridge
710
Island
Grissom
Queensway Bay
Catalina Express
Terminal
Queen Mary
Seaport
Harbor Scenic Dr

Shoreline Village

Designed to look like an old-fashioned fishing village, Shoreline Village is a collection of shops, restaurants, and amusements that might best be described as "quaint." Don't get us wrong—there's always a time and a place for skee-ball, and sometimes Shoreline Village might prove to be that place. There are also less cheesy things to do—in-line skate rental and sailing lessons, to name just a few. Add to this a number of restaurants and snack shops, and Shoreline Village might just merit a visit.

Directions: Take the 710 S and follow signs for the Aquarium. Continue past the Aquarium and Pine Avenue, and turn right onto Shoreline Village Drive. Parking is free with any purchase.

Hours: Shoreline Village is open seven days a week from 10 am until 9 pm. In the summer, the closing time is pushed back until 10 pm. More questions? Check http://www.shorelinevillage.com or 562-435-2668 for additional info.

Toyota Grand Prix

Every April the streets of downtown Long Beach turn into Daytona. The Grand Prix is actually a series of races, run by professional racecar drivers. But the real draw is the Pro/Celebrity Race, which actually draws a fairly impressive roster for its celeb race. The 2003 race included such heavy hitters as Buzz Aldrin, Angie Everhart, and the guy who plays Bo on *Days of Our Lives*.

Tickets are available on-line, at www.longbeachgp.com, or by calling 888-82-SPEED. A three-day adult pass is $51, while a "Superphoto" ticket (which includes pit access!) will set you back $238.

Where to Eat

Pine Avenue, in downtown Long Beach, is the center of Long Beach's nightlife. The bars tend to be a bit overrun by students from nearby Cal State Long Beach.

Where to Shop

Each of Long Beach's diverse neighborhoods has its own personality, and its businesses reflect that.

- **Pine Avenue**, in the downtown area, is a fairly trendy shopping district, featuring lots of chains.
- **Belmont Shore**, along 2nd Street between Livingston and Bayshore Drives, is home to more upscale shops.
- **Midtowne**, the Fourth Street Corridor between Cherry and Junipero, is the place to go for vintage wear and antiques.
- **Shoreline Village** caters to the tourist market.

But our favorite place for shopping in Long Beach is the monthly swap meet, which is held on the third Sunday of each month at Veteran's Stadium, just off of Lakewood Blvd. near the Long Beach Airport. An overwhelming number of antiques dealers show up regularly, and the sale is open to the public from 6:30 am to 3 pm. Admission is $5. Early birds are welcome to show up at 5:30 for the higher rate of $10.

$ Banks

- **ACI Automated Collection** • 235 E Broadway
- **Bank of America** • 150 Long Beach Blvd
- **California Bank** • 444 W Ocean Blvd
- **Citibank** • 601 W Ocean Blvd
- **City National Bank** • 11 Golden Shore St
- **Comerica Bank** • 301 E Ocean Blvd
- **Export-Import** • 1 World Trade Center
- **Farmers & Merchants Bank** • 302 Pine Ave
- **First Bank & Trust** • 100 Oceangate
- **Generations Trust** • 111 W Ocean Boulevard
- **International City** • 249 E Ocean Blvd
- **International City** • 550 Elm Avenue
- **Peoples Bank of California** • 525 E Ocean Boulevard
- **Unicon Financial** • 200 Pine Ave
- **Union Bank** • 400 Oceangate
- **United California Bank** • 200 Oceangate
- **Washington Mutual** • 1 World Trade Ctr
- **Washington Mutual** • 401 E Ocean Blvd
- **Wells Fargo Bank** • 111 W Ocean Blvd
- **Western Bank** • 1 World Trade Ctr

○ Landmarks

- **Aquarium of the Pacific** • 100 Aquarium Way
- **Catalina Express Terminal** • Berth 95, San Pedro
- **Catalina Landing** • 330 Golden Shore St
- **Edison Theater** • 213 E Broadway
- **Long Beach Convention & Visitor's Bureau** • 1 World Trade Ctr
- **Museum of Latin American Art** • 628 Alamitos Ave
- **Queen Mary Seaport** • 1126 Queens Hwy
- **Shoreline Village** • 419 Shoreline Village Dr

Y Clubs

- **Blue Café** • 210 Promenade • 562-983-7111

Movie Theaters

- **AMC Theatres Pine Square 16** • 245 Pine Ave • 562-435-4262

Restaurants

- **555 East** • 555 E Ocean Blvd • 562-437-0626
- **Alegria** • 115 Pine Ave • 562-436-3388
- **Baja Sonora Grille** • 70 Atlantic Ave • 562-437-4583
- **Cha Cha Cha** • 762 Pacific Ave • 562-436-3900
- **George's Greek Deli** • 318 Pine Ave • 562-437-1184
- **Joe's Crab Shack** • 655 S Marina Dr • 562-594-6551
- **King's Fish House** • 100 W Broadway • 562-432-7463
- **L'Opera** • 101 Pine Ave • 562-491-0066
- **La Traviata** • 301 Cedar Ave • 562-432-8022
- **Long Beach Café** • 615 E Ocean Blvd • 562-436-6037
- **Madison** • 102 Pine Ave • 562-628-8866
- **Mamma Tina Cucina** • 329 Pacific Ave • 562-432-9718
- **Mum's Restaurant** • 144 Pine Ave • 562-437-7700
- **Parker's Lighthouse** • 435 Shoreline Village Dr • 562-432-6500
- **Sir Winston's** • 1126 Queen's Hwy • 562-435-3511
- **Sky Room** • 40 S Locust Ave • 562-983-2722
- **Uncle Al's Seafood** • 400 E First St • 562-436-2553
- **Utopia** • 445 E First St • 562-432-6888
- **Wasabi Japanese Restaurant** • 200 Pine Ave • 562-901-0300
- **Yard House** • 401 Shoreline Village Dr • 562-628-0466

Shopping

- **Acres of Books** • 240 Long Beach Blvd • 562-437-6980
- **City Place** • 275 E 4th St • 562-432-8325
- **Crate & Barrel** • 240 Pine Ave • 562-435-6577
- **Mood Swings** • 455 E Ocean Blvd • 562-437-6250
- **Pike at Rainbow Harbor** • Pine Ave & Shoreline Dr • 562-432-8325
- **Z Gallerie** • 230 Pine Ave • 562-491-0766

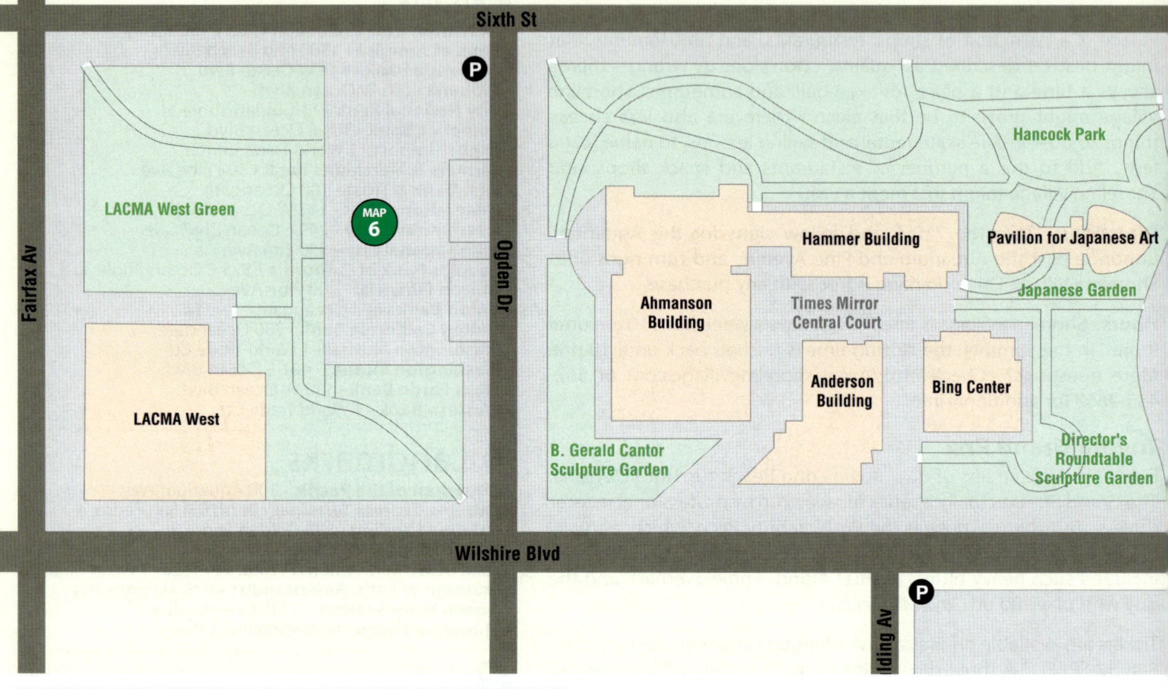

General Information

Address:	*5905 Wilshire Blvd.,*
	Los Angeles, CA 90036
Telephone:	*323-857-6000*
Website:	*www.lacma.org*
NFT Map:	*6*

Overview

LACMA is like that old sweater hanging in the back of your closet. You forget that it's there, sometimes for years at a time, but when you do finally put it on again, you wonder why it's been so long. A return visit to LACMA almost always triggers this reaction, if only because there's just so much there to do. In addition to the Art Museum, the LACMA grounds are also home to a lovely park, the Page Museum, and the rather anticlimactic La Brea Tar Pits.

But the powers-that-be at LACMA are apparently aware that the museum has taken a back seat in recent years to flashier arts complexes designed by famed architects, like Richard Meier's Getty or the nearly finished Disney Concert Hall, designed by Frank Gehry. In 2001, plans were announced to tear down LACMA's four main buildings—the last of which was only opened in 1986—and replace them with a single building designed by another superstar architect, Rem Koolhaas. While Koolhaas' design has been met with overwhelming praise—his single building is more open and has a far better flow than the current layout—some residents have expressed outrage over the decision to tear down four perfectly good buildings, and many art lovers would rather see the $200 million budget spent on new paintings and sculptures. This major construction project will be done in stages, so at least part of the museum will remain open throughout the entire process.

Practicalities

With the opening of LACMA West in the old May Company building in 1994, the museum extended its reach on Wilshire Blvd. as far west as Fairfax Avenue. The main buildings can be entered just east of Ogden Drive.

LACMA is open Monday, Tuesday, and Thursday from 12 noon until 8 pm. The museum stays open late on Fridays, until 9 pm. On weekends, the hours are 11 am until 8 pm. LACMA is closed on Wednesdays.

Admission is $7 for adults, $5 for seniors and students, and $1 for children aged 6-17. But if that's too steep for your budget, visit the museum on the second Tuesday of any month, when admission is free. Annual membership packages start at $65, and allow unlimited admission for two adults and children under 17.

Getting There

From the 10 freeway: Take the 10 freeway to Fairfax Ave. and drive north. Turn right at Wilshire Blvd. The museums will be on your left.

From the San Fernando Valley: Take the 101 S to Highland, and head south to Franklin. Turn right and take Franklin to La Brea. Make a left onto La Brea, and continue south to Wilshire Blvd. Turn right on Wilshire, and the museum will be on your right.

MTA buses 20, 21, 217, and 720 all stop near the museum, on either Wilshire Blvd. or Fairfax Ave.

There are parking lots on Wilshire, just across from the museum at Spaulding Avenue and at Ogden Drive. You must pay to park here during the day, but they're free after 7 pm. If you can time your visit accordingly, however, there are meters behind the museum, along 6th Street, that allow for 4-hour parking from 8 am until 6 pm. Bring lots of quarters, and this move may ultimately save you some money.

L.A. County Museum of Art

The museum's collection is housed mainly in four buildings. The Anderson Building is home to LACMA's collection of modern and contemporary art. The permanent collection includes David Hockney's "Mulholland Drive The Road to the Studio," one of the most LA paintings that we know. Inside the Ahmanson Gallery, you'll find European paintings and sculpture from the 12th to 20th centuries, as well as American art from the colonial period to World War II. The Hammer Building tends to hold temporary exhibitions, while the Pavilion for Japanese Art is a freestanding building that holds Japanese works from 3000 B.C. to the 20th Century.

LACMA is also a great destination on weekend evenings. On Fridays, the museum is open late—until 9 pm—and there's live jazz on the Times Mirror Central Court from 5:30 until 8:30. You can also hear live chamber music every Sunday at 6 pm in the Bing Theatre. Both of these weekly concerts are free. The Bing Theatre is also home to regular screenings of classic films, occasionally with a guest speaker. Movie tickets include an admission to all of the galleries, and cost $7 to the public, $5 to members. Screenings are every Friday and Saturday at 7:30.

LACMA West

In 1998, the art deco May Company department store reopened as LACMA West. The building has hosted special exhibits, like 1999's Van Gogh show. But LACMA West is now the place in LA to view Latin American art. The building houses the Bernard and Edith Lewin Latin American Art Galleries, a collection dominated by Mexican modern masters. The collection rotates, but Diego Rivera and David Alfaro Siqueiros are among the artists whose work has been displayed here. Young art enthusiasts may enjoy the Boone Children's Gallery, which frequently incorporates works from the main museum's permanent collection. Admission is included along with your regular museum ticket.

The George C. Page Museum

Located just east of LACMA, the Page Museum is best known as the home of the La Brea Tar Pits. Almost everyone who moves to Los Angeles has heard of the Tar Pits in some context, and most make a pilgrimage at some point, hoping to see something dynamic, something bubbling, something interesting. What you end up seeing, however, is a large pool of tar. It's about as anticlimactic as it gets. The Tar Pits become exponentially more interesting, however, during the eight to ten-week period, usually in July and August, when excavation takes place. It's at this time that museumgoers can watch paleontologists sift through the tar. The process is painstaking and oddly fascinating, even if it's hard to escape the feeling that everything cool has already been unearthed.

Inside the Page Museum, it's possible to view over one million specimens of fossils recovered from the Tar Pits. Among them are saber-toothed cats and mammoths. Sadly, there are no dinosaurs; but many a child has been riveted by the exhibit of the 9000-year old La Brea Woman, whose fossil is still the only human remains ever found in the Tar Pits.

The Museum is open Monday through Friday from 9:30 am until 5 pm, and from 10 am until 5 pm on Saturdays and Sundays. Adult admission is $6, seniors and students get in for $3.50, and children 5-12 are just $2. Admission is free on the first Tuesday of every month. Since LACMA is free on the second Tuesday, there are two days every month that make it possible to do both museums for the price of one.

For additional information on the Page Museum, call 323-934-PAGE or visit www.tarpits.org.

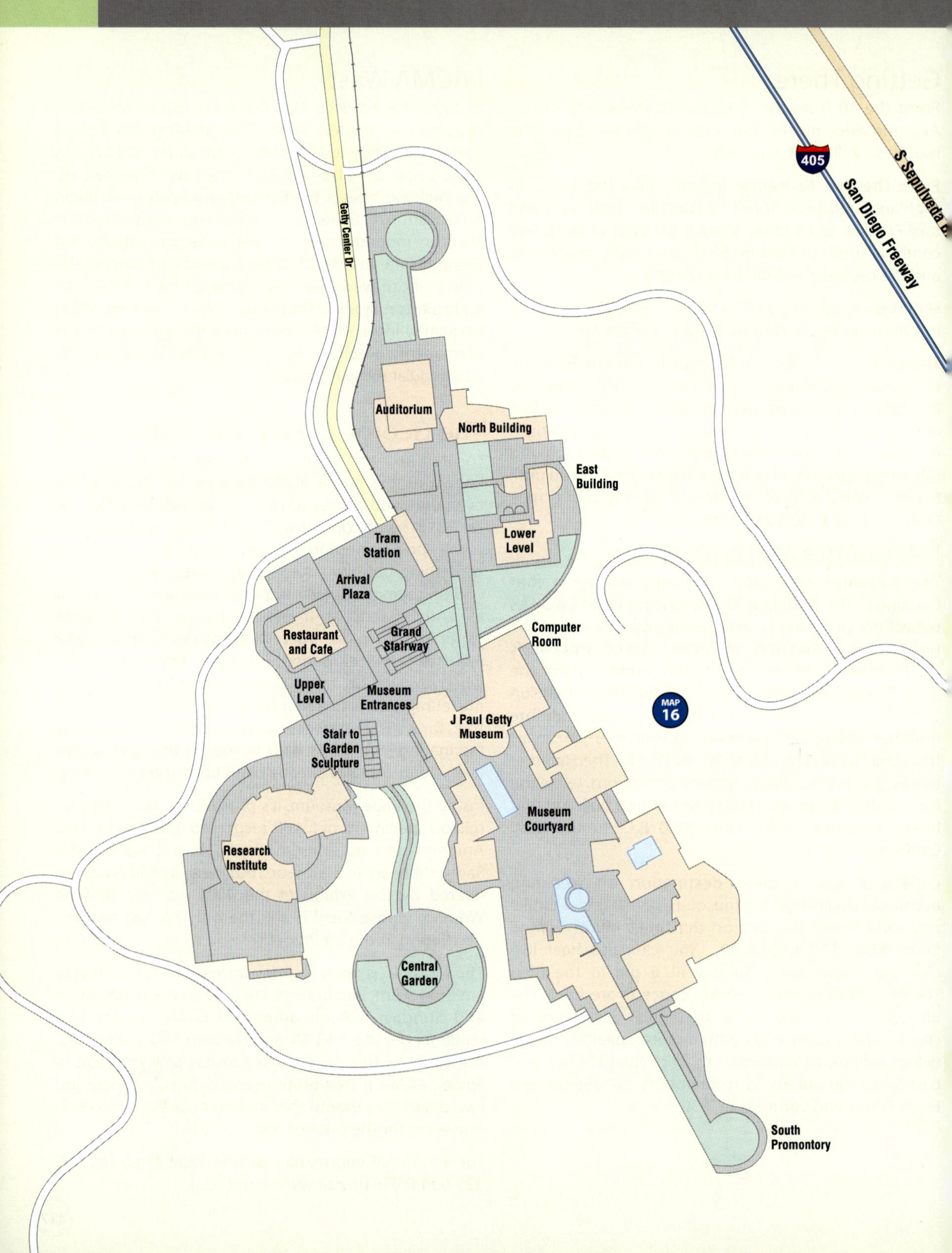
405
San Diego Freeway
S Sepulveda Bl
Getty Center Dr
Auditorium
North Building
East Building
Tram Station
Lower Level
Arrival Plaza
Restaurant and Cafe
Grand Stairway
Computer Room
Upper Level
Museum Entrances
MAP 16
Stair to Garden Sculpture
J Paul Getty Museum
Research Institute
Museum Courtyard
Central Garden
South Promontory

General Information

Address: 1200 Getty Center Dr,
              Los Angeles, CA 90049
Phone: 310-440-7300
Website: www.getty.edu
NFT Map: 16

Overview

The Getty Center is cool. In fact, the Getty Center is so cool that you can visit and come away completely satisfied, even if you never enter the museum and look at the art—though that would be a terrible mistake. Designed by Richard Meier, the J. Paul Getty Center moved in 1997 to its stunning new location high atop the Santa Monica Mountains. The Getty was hardly slumming it in its former Malibu location, but almost everything about the new facility is breathtaking. Though best known for the museum, there is so much more to the complex than that. The Getty is a multi-sensory experience, from the feel of the building's travertine marble façade, to the sound of water flowing through the garden, to the taste of the food served in the Getty's restaurant, fresh from that day's farmers market.

What to See

Oh, and there's art, too. The original Getty Museum began as a place for oilman J. Paul Getty to hang his astonishing collection of art. Though he never lived to see the museum, he left behind a staggering trust fund that has allowed the Getty to aggressively add to the collection over the years. The permanent collection includes several Van Goghs, including what might be the Getty's highest profile acquisition, "Irises". There are also Rembrandts, Cezannes, and a rare collaboration between Rubens and Brueghel. In addition to the mostly pre-20th- century paintings, the Getty also has an extensive collection of antiquities. These works will eventually be on display at the old Getty Museum in Malibu, which will be renamed the Getty Villa.

It may be impossible to see the entire collection in one visit—three hours is the absolute minimum you should plan on spending at the museum—and then there is the rest of the Getty Center. The Central Garden, designed by Robert Irwin, is intended to be (and most definitely *is*) a work of art on its own. The garden's benches and chairs invite visitors to relax and enjoy the view, which includes the entire Santa Monica Bay. Meier's building design is also worth much more than a cursory look. The travertine marble used in the construction comes from the same source as the Coliseum in Rome and, if you look closely, you can sometimes spot fossils that are trapped inside the stone. Some of the better examples of these are spotlighted throughout the Central Garden. The travertine was intended to reflect light and we should warn you that it can be extremely bright at the Getty. Do not leave home without your sunglasses!

Practicalities

One of the biggest misconceptions about the Getty is that it's still hard to get in. That isn't the case at all, and parking reservations are only required on weekdays before 4 pm. But if you don't like to plan ahead, the Getty's hours are more than accommodating. The museum is open Tuesday to Thursday, from 10 am until 6 pm, and these operating hours apply to Sundays as well. But Friday and Saturday, the Getty stays open late, until 9 pm, and it's one of the classier dates you can take someone on. Best of all, admission is free—you only have to pay for parking, which is $5. The museum also thoughtfully provides umbrellas, free of charge, for protection from either rain or sun.

How to Get There

The easiest way to get to the Getty is to make your way to the 405 freeway and exit at Getty Center Drive. Follow the signs into the parking garage. Parking is $5. Elevators for the parking garage are all color-coded, making it easy to remember where you've parked.

Two bus lines also stop at the Getty, MTA Bus 561 and Santa Monica Big Blue Bus 14.

There is also a free parking and shuttle service at the corner of Sepulveda Blvd. and Constitution Avenue (just north of Wilshire). Reservations are not required for this lot, which makes your visit to the Getty absolutely free.

Once you do arrive in the parking garage, you have two options for getting to the Getty Center. You can take the tram, which runs frequently, or you can walk to the top of the hill. But bear in mind that this is about a mile and completely uphill.

Where to Eat

The remote location means that you're basically limited to the Getty Center's dining facilities, but luckily the options here are many and all quite good. At the high end, The Restaurant is open for lunch every day the Center is open and serves dinner from 5 pm until 9 pm on Fridays and Saturdays. Their menu is market-driven, so it changes frequently, but serves healthy, California-style fare. Reservations are suggested and can be made by e-mail or by calling 310-440-7300. Same-day reservations are sometimes available through the Visitor Information Desk.

The Café is run by the same management as the restaurant, making the same high-quality food available in a more casual setting. The Café is open on weekdays from 11:30 until 3:30, and on Friday and Saturday evenings until 8:30.

Additionally, the Garden Terrace Café is a self-serve dining facility that overlooks the Central Garden and there are also several coffee carts around the complex that carry lunch items and snacks. Should you opt to brown bag it, a picnic area is located at the lower tram station and is open until thirty minutes before closing time every day the Getty Center is open.

General Information

Address: 6333 W. Third Street, Los Angeles, CA 90036
Phone: 323-933-9211
Website: www.farmersmarketla.com
NFT Map: 2

Overview

The Farmers Market began in the 1930s, as a dirt lot where farmers would park their trucks and sell produce right out of the tailgates. It grew into the bizarre grouping of souvenir shops and food stalls that still stand today. In recent years, the Farmers Market has scaled back, as the north half of the market was razed to make room for The Grove, a new shopping mall, in a move that displaced numerous merchants and angered many loyal customers. Time hasn't stopped at the Farmers Market—it's now home to a Starbucks and features karaoke every Saturday evening. But the Farmers Market still feels like it's in an LA of another era, from the handcrafted wooden shopping baskets to the motherly waitresses at DuPar's Restaurant.

Practicalities

The Farmers Market is open to the public Monday through Friday from 9 am to 9 pm, Saturdays from 9 am until 8 pm, and Sundays from 10 am until 7 pm.

To drive to the Farmers Market from almost anywhere south of the Valley or north of LAX, your best bet is to just take surface streets. The Grove's opening has made Third Street slower going than it used to be, but Beverly Blvd. isn't going to be much better. From points east, there is no quicker shortcut than 6th Street. Take whichever east-west thoroughfare you choose until you hit Fairfax Ave., and head north. You can't miss the Farmers Market at the corner of Third and Fairfax. If you're coming from the Westside or South Bay, you might hop on the 10 freeway and exit at Fairfax, and head north. And Valley residents can hop on the 101 and exit at Highland. Take Highland to Third Street and turn right. Continue on Third until you reach Fairfax, and the Farmers Market will be on your right.

Before the opening of The Grove, parking at the Farmers Market was a challenge, but at least it was free. To discourage mall patrons from hogging the smallish parking lot, however, the Farmers Market now charges for parking. With validation, you get two hours of free parking and the third hour is just $1.

Where to Shop

There are two kinds of shops at the Farmers Market—the kind that sell food, and the kind that don't. You can't really go wrong with any of the former. Mr. Marcel's Gourmet Market has an extensive selection of imported cheese, while you can watch the whole candy-making process at Littlejohn's English Toffee House. Magee's House of Nuts has been in operation at the Farmers Market since it opened and will open your eyes to a world of nut butters that goes far beyond peanuts. And The Fruit Company always offers a wide variety of fruits that are always fresher and more reasonably priced than any local supermarket.

The Farmers Market's other businesses are a bit more eclectic, and can be somewhat hit or miss. By Candlelight has an impressive selection of candles, and Light My Fire sells bottled hot sauce that ranges from mild to downright combustible. But many shops cater to the tourist crowd and sell cheap, Hollywood-themed souvenirs. If you're hoping to do some serious shopping, hop on the trolley and head over to The Grove.

Where to Eat

There may be no better place for breakfast in all of LA than Kokomo, one of the Farmers Market's few sit-down dining establishments. This extremely casual café has an eclectic breakfast and lunch menu and, best of all, their egg dishes can all be accompanied by coffeecake. DuPar's has its loyal fans, mainly for the pie, but the food court may be a better option. The Gumbo Pot serves up the best Gumbo YaYa this side of the Mississippi, and Bob's Coffee and Donuts is considered by many to have the best donuts in LA. For a more elegant Farmers Market experience, check out the newly opened wine bar at Mr. Marcel's. C'est magnifique.

General Information

Address:	1201 S. Figueroa
	Los Angeles, CA 90015
Telephone:	213-741-1151
Website:	www.lacclink.com
NFT Map:	9

Given the diverse line-up of events held at the Convention Center, it stands to reason that every Los Angeles resident will find him- or herself there at least once, whether for a convention, a trade show, or a bridal fair. In 2002 alone, the Convention Center is scheduled to play host to the ShowBiz Expo (a kind of nirvana for film geeks who actually understand the difference between THX and SDDS sound), a meeting of Tupperware reps, and the American College of Obstetricians and Gynecologists' Convention. From the outside, the Convention Center can appear daunting. But once inside, its halls and facilities are surprisingly user-friendly.

The Convention Center is impossible to miss from the street, and its glass-and-girder exterior is clearly visible from both the 10 and 110 freeways. The building's design allows for a maximum amount of natural light to flood the lobbies and concourses, in stark contrast to the windowless exhibit halls and meeting rooms, where it's easy to lose track of time. The Convention Center has three major exhibit halls: West Hall, South Hall, and Kentia Hall (located beneath South Hall), as well as 54 meeting rooms. It's possible to book a small, intimate meeting for fewer than 20 people or a large-scale event for over 20,000. The really big shows, like the Auto Show, tend to be held in either the South or West Halls—or sometimes both.

How to Get There—Driving & Parking

Located just a stone's throw from Staples Center, the Los Angeles Convention Center is easily reached from any part of LA The Convention Center lies at the intersection of the Santa Monica Freeway (the 10) and the Harbor Freeway (the 110). The simplest option is to exit the 110 at Pico Blvd. and head north. But if you're coming from the Westside or Central Los Angeles area, you may be better off skipping the freeways altogether and using either Olympic or Pico Boulevards to get to downtown. The Convention Center's cross street is Figueroa.

There are five parking structures available to patrons of the Convention Center, all of which charge just $7 per day. Parking for the West Hall is located just north of Pico Blvd. Make a right turn at the intersection of Cherry and 12th Street into the parking garage. To park for the South Hall, look for Convention Center Drive, just off of Venice Blvd. on the Convention Center's south side.

How to Get There—Public Transportation

The Metro Blue Line stops on Pico Blvd. for both the Convention Center and Staples Center. This is a convenient alternative from the Valley, as well as the South Bay.

Buses 30, 31, 81, 442, 444, 445, 446, 447, 439, LX 422, LX423, LX448, and LX419 also stop near the Convention Center.

Where to Eat

Of course, the fastest and most convenient way to refuel at the Convention Center is to dine at any one of its own restaurants or snack bars. The Galaxy Café, in the lobby of the West Building, is probably the center's nicest. It offers the option of outdoor seating and boasts a full bar, though it's only open for breakfast and lunch. Inside the South Building, there is the more casual Compass Cafe, which offers a variety of sandwiches, salads, and beverages. And if you're really on the run, there are concession stands inside both the West and South exhibit halls, stocked with hot dogs, sodas, and the usual lunch counter fare.

But if you have time to venture out into the Convention Center's neighborhood, you'll find an eclectic variety of restaurants just a short walk (or cab ride) away. Here are some nearby restaurants that might be worth a visit:

- **Philippe's the Original**, 1001 North Alameda Street, 213-628-3781. Deli fare. They supposedly invented the French Dip sandwich. Would you ever even think of ordering anything else?
- **Original Pantry Café**, 877 S. Figueroa Street, 213-627-6879. American/Comfort food. The restaurant never closes. It's basic and dependable.
- **Langer's**, 704 S. Alvarado Street, 213-483-8050. Deli fare. Their pastrami sandwich is legendary.
- **Ciudad**, 445 S. Figueroa Street, 213-486-5171. Latin food. The chefs/owners of Santa Monica's Border Grill take their act downtown. After a long day of meetings and exhibits, check out their rum sampler.
- **Pacific Dining Car**, 1310 Sixth Street, 213-483-6000. Steaks and chops. This meat-and-potatoes restaurant is an LA institution and is open 24-hours. After 11 pm, take your choice of dinner or breakfast.

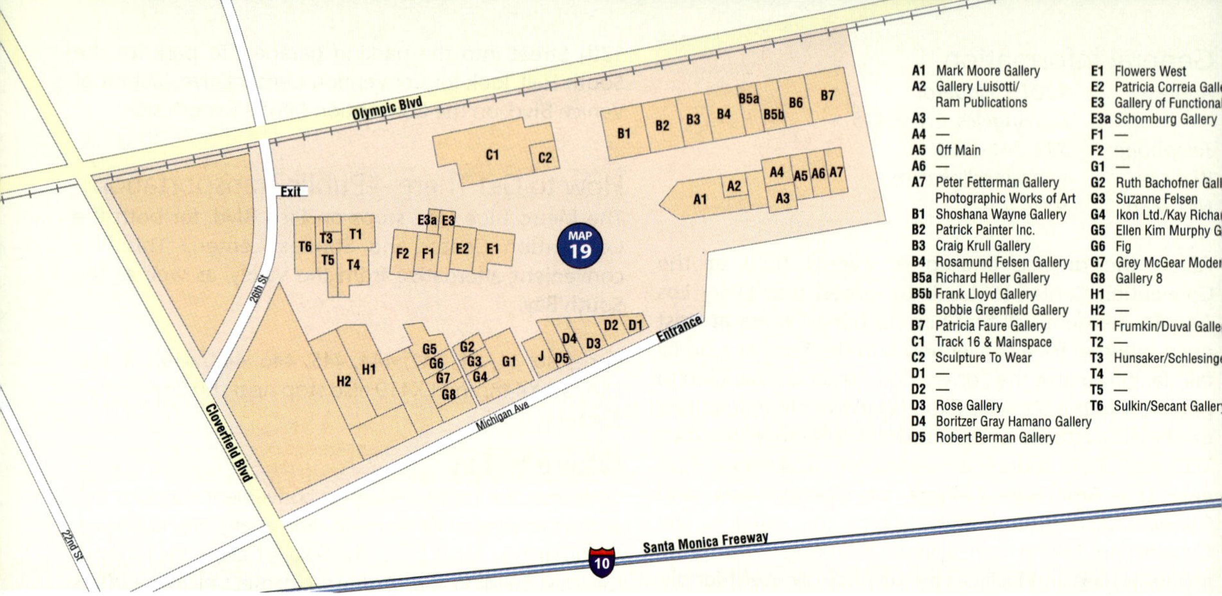

General Information

Address: 2525 Michigan Avenue, Santa Monica, CA 90404
Phone: 310-586-6488
Website: www.bergamotstation.com
NFT Map: 19

Overview

Without a doubt, Bergamot Station is the best one-stop art experience you can have in Los Angeles. Originally a stop on the Red Line trolley in the 1800s, Bergamot Station spent most of the last fifty years in a variety of incarnations, from celery-packing facility to ice-making plant. But after it had been abandoned, the City of Santa Monica wisely saw the area's potential and asked developer Wayne Black to find an artistic use for the property. By 1994, Bergamot Station was up and running as a destination for art lovers, who could simply park their cars and actually spend their day looking at art, rather than driving all over the city from one gallery to the next.

Practicalities

Most of the galleries at Bergamot Station are open Tuesday through Saturday, from 11 am until 6 pm. The shops and galleries are generally closed Sundays and Mondays, but this does vary from gallery to gallery.

The complex is located on Michigan Avenue in Santa Monica, just east of Cloverfield Blvd. Bergamot Station is easily accessed from the 10 freeway. Simply exit at Cloverfield/26th Street. Turn right at the first traffic light, Michigan Avenue, and stay on Michigan until it dead ends. The entrance to Bergamot Station will be on your left.

If you're taking surface streets, Olympic Blvd. is usually your best bet. Take Olympic to Cloverfield and turn left, then turn left again on Michigan Avenue. Bergamot Station is at the end of the street, on the left-hand side.

What to See

Bergamot Station is home to almost forty galleries, each of which has its own personality. Rose Gallery deals in photographs and has shown a diverse line-up of artists from Manuel Alvarez Bravo to Wim Wenders. Track 16 focuses on modern and contemporary art and has featured artists like Karen Finley and Man Ray. The Gallery of Functional Art definitely shows art—but that art often doubles as furniture or lighting. Suzanne Felsen's unique jewelry is art by any definition of the word. There is an eclectic variety to be seen at Bergamot Station and our advice is to use the complex as it was intended—park and simply stroll from one gallery to the next. If you keep a brisk pace, you can get through everything in an hour or two. But to get the most out of Bergamot Station, we would suggest spending an entire afternoon there.

In addition to the galleries, Bergamot Station has several other tenants of note, including The Santa Monica Museum. Admission is free and this non-collecting museum always features exhibits like no other museum in LA. Santa Monica Auctions features live art auctions of works by major artists. And Hiromi Paper International is a retail shop that sells just one thing—paper. Hiromi's exquisite papers range from offbeat to exquisite, and most are so gorgeous that it would be a shame to write on them.

Where to Eat

The Gallery Café remains the complex's only option for breakfast or lunch. It's open Monday from 9 am until 4 pm, Tuesday through Friday from 9 am until 5 pm, and on Saturday from 10 am until 5 pm. They mainly serve sandwiches and salads.

There are also some excellent restaurants in the area for a more leisurely lunch or a post-gallery dinner.

- **Il Moro**, 11400 W. Olympic Blvd., 310-575-3530, offers delicious pastas and Italian entrees.
- **LA Farm**, 3000 W. Olympic Blvd., 310-449-4000, serves California-style cuisine in a beautiful patio setting.
- **JR Seafood**, 11901 Santa Monica Blvd., 310-268-2463, features all of your favorite Chinese dishes, with an emphasis on fish and seafood.

Overview

Aptly nicknamed "The Happiest Place on Earth," it's difficult to visit Disneyland and not have fun—unless, of course, your trip happens to coincide with school vacation time or a major holiday, in which case you'll spend more of your day in lines than on rides. If you're visiting Disneyland without kids, you might want to go to the park on weekdays during school semesters. But in the summer, you can avoid at least some of the crowds by taking advantage of Disneyland's later operating hours. By arriving around 4 or 5 pm, even on a Saturday, you'll still have a good eight hours to ride the Matterhorn—and the lines will almost disappear after the last parade, when the families and small children begin to clear out of the park. Lines for the most popular rides, like Splash Mountain and Indiana Jones' Adventure, are shortest at the beginning and end of the day, and also during the parades. The same is true for Grizzly River Run, Soarin' Over California, and California Screamin' at the adjacent California Adventure. Opt for a Fastpass at any ride, and you can take a ticket, return to the ride at the allocated time, and join the less congested Fastpass line—which is a great idea, unless the park is really, really busy and they run out of Fastpass tickets! There's good news and bad news at Disneyland in 2004 (and you decide which is which!): a new ride, the Many Adventures of Winnie the Pooh, has opened at the site of the old Country Bear Jamboree, while Space Mountain has closed for redesign and will reopen in 2005. The best advice we can offer is to take lots of money, for the Happiest Place on Earth is also one of the Most Expensive, and wear comfy shoes.

How to Get There—Driving & Parking

Traveling southbound on I-5 (Golden State/Santa Ana freeway): Exit at Disneyland Drive and turn left (south). Follow the signs to the Mickey & Friends Parking Structure entrance.

Traveling northbound on I-5 (Santa Ana freeway): Exit on Katella Avenue and turn left (west). Proceed west to Harbor Boulevard. Turn right on Harbor and look for the Mickey & Friends Parking Structure entrance on the left at Disney Way.

Traveling eastbound or westbound on the 22 (Garden Grove) freeway: Exit on Harbor Boulevard and head northbound. Continue north on Harbor for approximately 4 miles. The Mickey & Friends Parking Structure entrance will be on the left just past Katella Avenue at Disney Way.

Once in the parking lot, head to the escalators, which take you directly to the Mickey & Friends Loading Zone. Trams collect visitors and drop them off at the Mickey & Friends Tram Station, located within walking distance of both theme parks. Parking costs $8 for cars, $10 for oversized vehicles, campers and motor homes, and $15 for buses.

How to Get There—Mass Transit

All of the LA area airports have shuttle services to the Disneyland Resort. Bus 460 goes somewhere near the park, but we really recommend driving a car!

Hours of Operation

The hours of operation for both parks vary, depending on what time of the year you visit. Summer time, school vacation, and holiday hours are usually 8 am until 11 pm for Disneyland and 10 am until 10 pm for California Park. In the off-season, Disneyland is open from 10 am until 8 pm and California Park opens its gates from 10 am until 6 pm. Check the website or call for more accurate times for the days you plan to visit. Disneyland's website is also useful for checking out what rides might be closed for maintenance on a given day. There's nothing more disappointing than finding out that Pirates of the Caribbean is closed on the day you've decided to visit the park.

Entrance Fees

There are not many places that you will visit where the child entrance fee only covers children 3 to 9 years of age—Disneyland is one of them. One-day general admission tickets to Disneyland or California Adventure Park will set you back $47 for regular admission and $37 for children (3–9), with children under 3 free. If you're planning on staying a few days and visiting both of the parks, the Park Hopper Ticket is what you need. The 2-day ticket costs $99 regular and $79 for children 3-9. They sometimes have special deals on their website, so make sure you check it before you buy tickets—it also saves having to wait in line at the entrance. And if you plan on being a frequent Disneyland guest, you might consider investing in an Annual Passport, which has varying rates, depending on how many restrictions you're willing to accept.

Lockers

If you're on the move and you have some valuables you'd rather not leave in your car, lockers located outside the main entrances to Disneyland and California Adventure are available for use. Locker rentals are $3, $4, or $5 per day, depending on the size required.

Package Express

If you purchase more mouse ears that you can carry while inside the park, a free Package Express service can arrange for your parcels to be waiting for you to retrieve outside the park.

Kennels

Traveling with your pooch can create problems, and orchestrating a trip to Disneyland is no exception. None of the hotels in the downtown Disneyland area allow pets, but if you're passing through and plan on staying elsewhere overnight, indoor kennel facilities are available for a charge of $10. The kennel is located to the right of the Main Entrance of Disneyland.

First Aid

Should you develop an ailment while enjoying your time in the parks, a first aid station is located at the end of Main Street, U.S.A. across from Central Plaza in Disneyland and next to the Mission Tortilla Factory in the Pacific Wharf area at California Adventure.

ATMs

Within Disneyland, ATMs are located at the Main Entrance, Main Street, U.S.A., Frontierland, Fantasyland, and Tomorrowland. They are at the Main Entrance, Bay Area, Pacific Wharf, and Hollywood Pictures Backlot at California Park.

Practical Information

Location: 1313 S. Harbor Blvd.
      Anaheim, CA 92803-3232
Website: www.disneyland.com
Disneyland Info (recorded): 714-781-4565
Disneyland Info (operator): 714-781-7290
Disneyland Travel Packages: 800-225-2024 or 714-520-5060
Disneyland Resort Hotels: 714-956-6425

Overview

Depending on your tastes, Universal Studios can be either a fun-filled experience or a nauseating nightmare. In addition to cheesy live shows like the Wild, Wild West Stunt Show, you can take an interesting 45-minute tour of the studio backlot where tram passengers come face to face with *King Kong* and the shark from *Jaws*. If thrills are what you're after, try Waterworld, Shrek 4D or the Back to the Future ride, which is housed in the world's tallest (13 stories) Omnimax Theater. Just outside the theme park gates is City Walk, an LA-themed complex featuring shops, restaurants, and other diversions, like a bowling alley and a blues club. City Walk can be a shock to the senses. It's always crowded, it's extremely noisy, and it's packed with cheesy shops that cater to tourists. But the 18-screen Universal City Cinemas is a great place to catch a movie. Allow a full day to take in all the park has to offer.

How to Get There—Driving & Parking

Universal Studios Hollywood is located between Hollywood and the San Fernando Valley, just off the 101 Hollywood/Ventura Freeway. Exit at Universal Center Drive or Lankershim Boulevard and follow the signs to the parking areas.

Preferred parking ($13) is located in the Rocky & Bullwinkle Lot and is one of the closest parking lots to Universal Studios Theme Park. If you would prefer to park your car yourself, general parking is located in the Curious George Garage, Jurassic Parking Garage, Frankenstein, and the Woody Woodpecker Lot. All are within walking distance to any Universal destination and cost $8 for the day.

How to Get There—Mass Transit

There is a Red Line Metro rail station at Universal City. MTA Buses 96, 150, 156, 163, 166, 240, and 426 also run to Universal City Station.

Hours of Operation

Universal Studios is open from 9 am until 10 pm on weekends during peak times and 9 am until 9 pm during busy weeks. During the slower months, operation hours are from 10 am until 6 pm. Call 1-800-UNIVERSAL the day you are going to confirm opening hours or check the website in advance.

Entrance Fees

One-day tickets cost $47 for adults and $37 for children aged 3-11. But for $45, Universal also offers a Deluxe Celebrity Annual Pass. For this price, you get entry, 15% discount on entry for up to 6 friends, discounts on food and merchandise throughout the park, and $100 in savings at Universal restaurants and shops. If money is no object, consider purchasing the Front of the Line Pass ($79), which allows you to cut the line for rides and snag the best seats in the house for any performance. Check www.universalstudios.com for additional packages and deals.

Lockers

Coin-operated lockers are located just inside the park and cost $1 or $1.50 depending on their size. Since they're inside the park, you can keep adding junk as the day goes by.

Package Delivery

If you buy merchandise within the park, there's a handy delivery service that has your parcels waiting when you leave. The pickup point is located near the exit at Universal Film Co.

Kennels

If you can't bear to leave your pet at home or if you're passing through on a longer journey, Universal provides a complimentary kennel service for park guests. You need to visit the Guest Services window at the entrance to the park, and your pet will be escorted by one of the Guest Service Representatives

First Aid

There are two first aid stations at Universal Studios, located in the Upper Lot next to Animal Planet Live! and in the Jurassic Park Visitors Center in the Lower Lot.

ATMs

Cash machines are located at the main entrance to the right of the ticket booths and in the Lower Lot near the Jurassic Cove Café.

Practical Information

Location: 100 Universal City Plaza,
      Universal City, CA 91608
Website: www.universalstudios.com
Prices, Directions and Park Info: 1-800-UNIVERSAL
Special Events: 818-622-3036
Group Sales: 800-959-9688 ext 2
NFT Map: 52

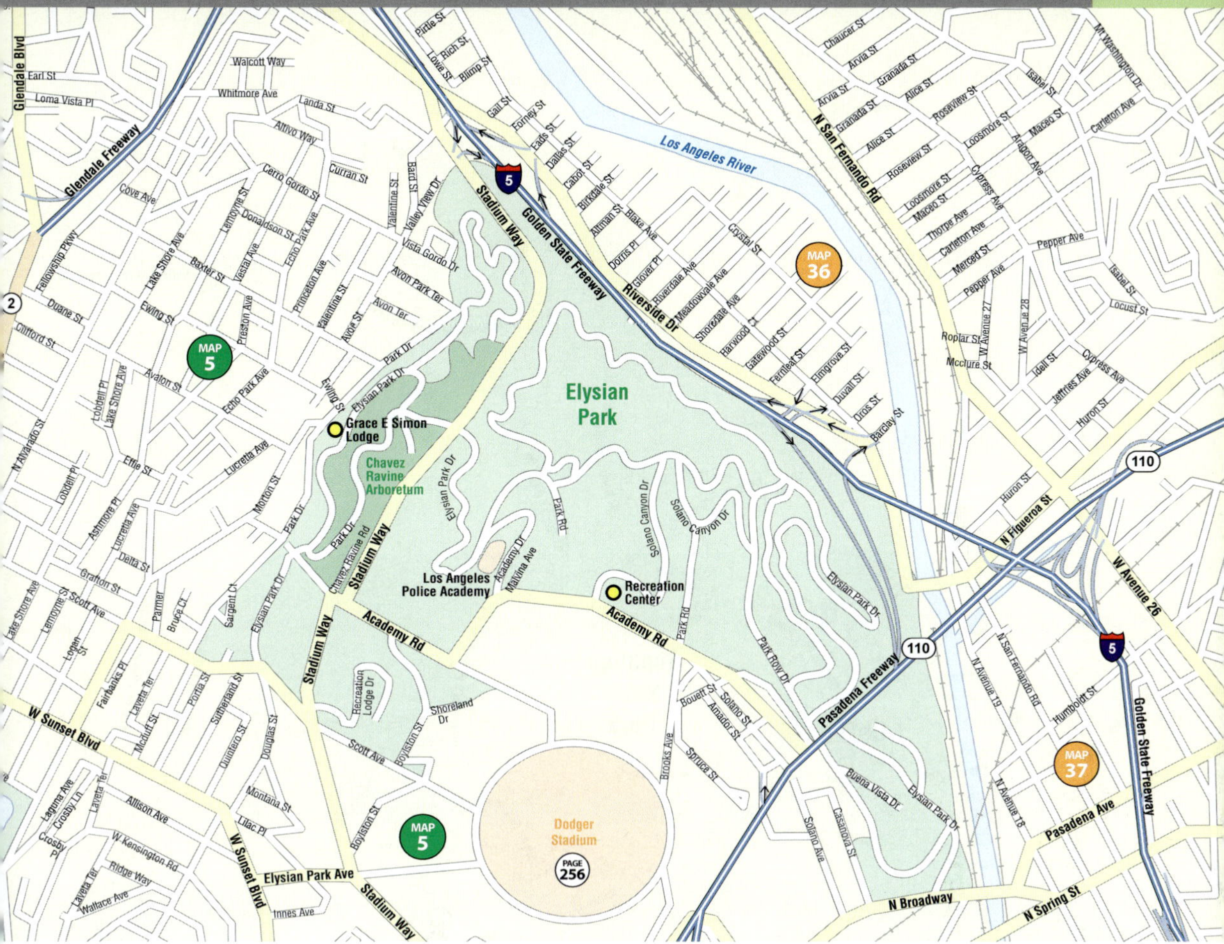

1880 Academy Dr, Los Angeles, CA
Phone: 213-485-5054
NFT Map: 5

Overview

When Los Angeles was founded in 1781, more than 600 acres of parkland was set aside for public use, and today Elysian Park is the second-largest park in the Los Angeles area. The majority of the park has been maintained in its original state and is crisscrossed with hiking trails. The status of the oldest park in LA has not always remained stable, with a "Citizens Committee to Save Elysian Park" convening in 1965 to organize public support to preserve Elysian Park lands as public open space. More than 30 years later, the park has seen none of the planned redevelopment and the committee continues to "arouse public and official awareness of the value of saving the last of these Pueblo lands set aside two centuries ago." Don't let the fault line running underneath Elysian Park dissuade you from a relaxing visit!

Practicalities

Admission to the park and arboretum is free. Elysian Park is located next to Dodger Stadium and the Police Academy and can be reached from the 5 or 110 freeways (exit Stadium Way). The Chavez Ravine Arboretum is on the west side of Stadium Way near the Grace E. Simon Lodge.

Central Picnic Area

The central picnic area (along Stadium Way) houses barbeque pits, a small human-made lake and a children's play area. A café at the Police Academy opens to the public weekdays from 6 am until 3 pm. Keep your eye open for the Chinatown 10K Run that passes through the park each year, usually in February!

Chavez Ravine Arboretum

In 1893, the Los Angeles Horticultural Society established the arboretum and extensive botanical gardens in Elysian Park. The Chavez Ravine Arboretum was declared "City Historical-Cultural Monument Number 48" in 1967, and today Los Angeles Beautiful sponsors the arboretum. Many of the trees are the oldest and largest of their kind in California or even the United States, and there are over 1,000 tree species from around the world that can be grown at the arboretum due to its moderate climate. The Los Angeles Beautiful Arbor Day is held annually at the Chavez Ravine Arboretum: call for more information. Admission to the arboretum is free. Phone: 213-485-5054.

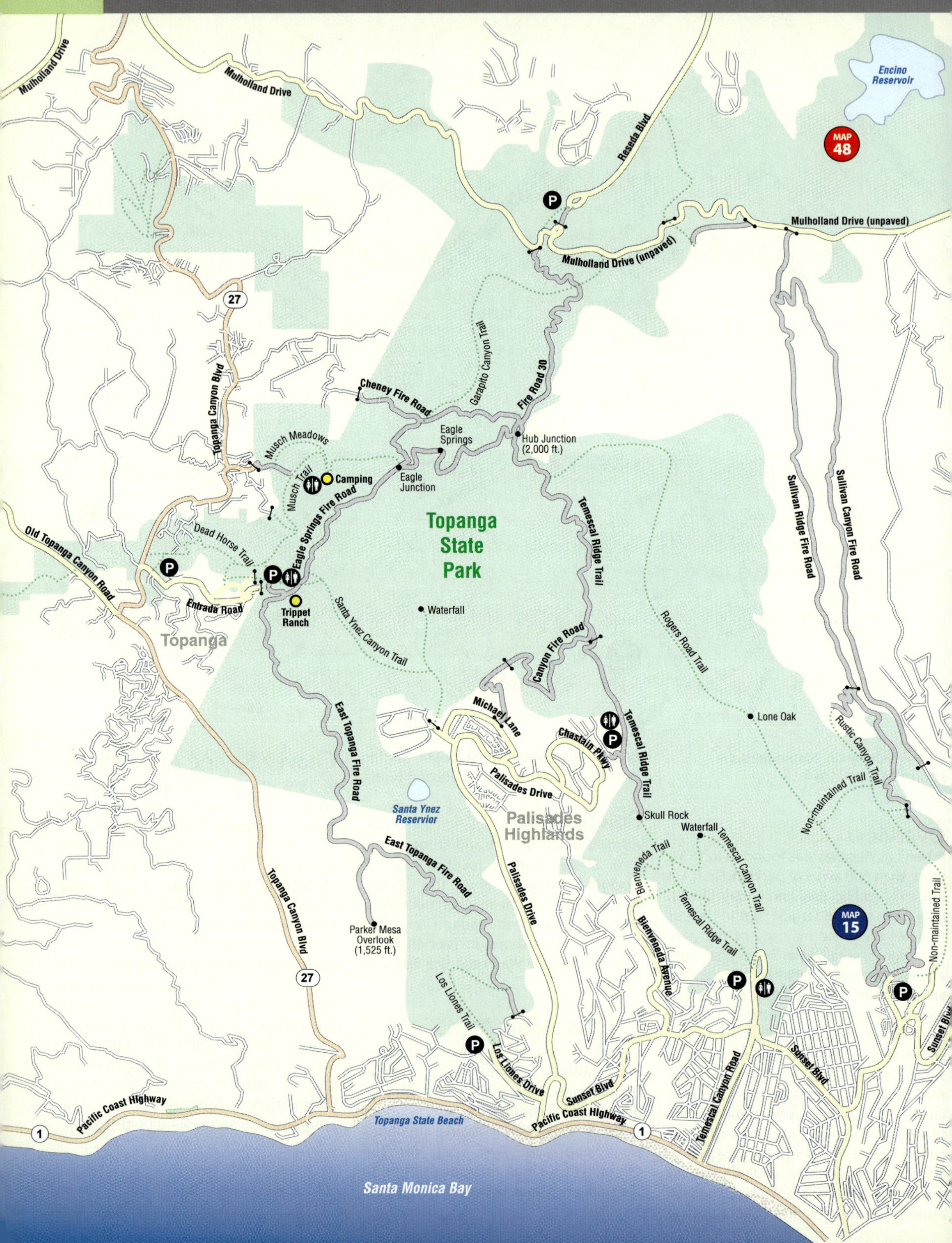
Mulholland Drive
Mulholland Drive
Encino Reservoir
MAP 48
Reseda Blvd
Mulholland Drive (unpaved)
Mulholland Drive (unpaved)
27
Topanga Canyon Blvd
Cheney Fire Road
Garapito Canyon Trail
Fire Road 30
Musch Meadows
Eagle Springs
Hub Junction (2,000 ft.)
Musch Trail
Camping
Eagle Junction
Eagle Springs Fire Road
Sullivan Ridge Fire Road
Sullivan Canyon Fire Road
Dead Horse Trail
Topanga State Park
Temescal Ridge Trail
Old Topanga Canyon Road
P
P
Entrada Road
Trippet Ranch
Waterfall
Santa Ynez Canyon Trail
Canyon Fire Road
Rogers Road Trail
Topanga
Lone Oak
Rustic Canyon Trail
East Topanga Fire Road
Michael Lane
Chastain Pkwy
Temescal Ridge Trail
P
Palisades Drive
Santa Ynez Reservoir
Palisades Highlands
Skull Rock
Waterfall
Non-maintained Trail
East Topanga Fire Road
Bienveneda Trail
Temescal Canyon Trail
Temescal Ridge Trail
Topanga Canyon Blvd
Parker Mesa Overlook (1,525 ft.)
Bienveneda Avenue
MAP 15
27
Palisades Drive
Los Liones Trail
P
P
Non-maintained Trail
P
Pacific Coast Highway
Los Liones Drive
Sunset Blvd
Sunset Blvd
Temescal Canyon Road
Sunset Blvd
1
Topanga State Beach
Pacific Coast Highway
1
Santa Monica Bay

Address: 1501 Will Rogers State Park Road,
            Pacific Palisades, CA 90272
Phone: 310-454-8212
California State Parks Website: http://cal-parks.ca.gov
NFT Map: 15

Located entirely within the Los Angeles City limits, Topanga is considered the world's largest wildland located within the boundaries of a big city. More than 11,000 acres of land are preserved in the park with 36 miles of trails available for recreation. The park is bound on the south by Pacific Palisades and Brentwood, on the west by Topanga Canyon and on the east by Rustic Canyon. On fine days you can experience magnificent views of the Pacific Ocean while on smoggy days you may struggle to breathe as you hike or run the trails.

Practicalities

Open from dawn until dusk (approximately 8 am until 6 pm), the day use of the park is $5 on weekends. From Pacific Coast Highway (1), travel north on Topanga Canyon Boulevard, pass the post office at the center of "town," then turn right on Entrada Road. Keep to the left at every opportunity until you reach the park's main parking lot (about one mile). From the Ventura Freeway (101), exit at Topanga Canyon Boulevard, drive south over the crest of the mountains and proceed three miles to Entrada Road and turn left. Follow the above directions.

Activities

With 36 miles of trails, Topanga is ideal for uninterrupted walking, running, cycling, and horse riding. Mountain bikers are meant to be restricted to the fire roads but keep an eye out as they often go flying around the pedestrian roads. There are many marked trails for hikers, most of which can be accessed from Trippet Ranch (off Entrada Road), once a "gentleman's ranch" for a weekend escape from the city. In addition to the Park Office, Trippet Ranch accommodates parking facilities, picnic areas, toilets and drinking fountains, and a great little visitors center that offers guided walking tours on Sunday mornings. If you're looking for a low-impact interaction with nature, you can take yourself along the self-guided nature trail using a trail guide (25¢ and available at the parking lot) or join one of the Sunday guided walks with experts well-versed in the flora and fauna of the area. Call the park for more information about guided walk schedules.

You'll find it difficult to believe that these spectacular canyons, cliffs, rock formations, and waterfalls exist within the LA city limits. Another visual highlight of the park is the blooming flowers that attract thousands of avid gardeners and photographers each year. For information on flowers blooming in the park call 818-768-3533.

Hiking Trails

Many of the park's trails can be accessed from Trippet Ranch. The Musch Trail leads north to Musch Trail Campground.

Just under two miles from Trippet is Eagle Junction, where the Eagle Springs loop trail begins. Climbing Eagle Rock on the northern section of the loop will give you a panoramic view of the park. At the eastern end of the Eagle Springs loop, you will come to the Hub Junction. From there you can take the Temescal Ridge Trail south or the fire road north or circle back and complete the Eagle Springs loop to Trippet Ranch.

Going north from Hub Junction, take the fire road for 2 miles through chaparral to reach unpaved Mulholland Drive. If you head south on Temescal Ridge Trail, you will find yourself high above the canyons with sycamore and oak riparian forests below.

Another option from Trippet Ranch is to walk east to the Topanga Fire Road and then north for a short distance to the Santa Ynez Trail. As you descend into the Santa Ynez Canyon, look out for the crumbly sandstone formations with pockets where moisture collects—you'll notice tiny cliff gardens dwelling in those pockets. Near the bottom of the trail is a short 0.8 mile trail leading to a lovely waterfall.

Shorter hikes can be done from other parking lots in Topanga State Park. From the Los Liones Dr parking lot, you can complete a 1.7 mile loop hike on the Los Liones Trail or, for a longer hike, take the East Topanga Fire Road to the Parker Mesa Overlook for stunning views of the canyon.

If you park in the first lot on Entrada Road (if you hit Trippet Ranch, you've gone too far), you can take the 1.1 mile Dead Horse Trail to Trippet Ranch.

To access the Caballero Canyon Trail or the Bent Arrow Trail, take Reseda Blvd into the Caballero Canyon Park lot.

Camping

Camping facilities are available on a first-come first-served basis, and you will need to contact the park directly for information. There are a campground and bathrooms located off the Musch Trail.

Downey Way
Childs Way
College
University of
Southern
California
PAGE
218
W 37th Pl
Watts Way
W 37th St
Trousdale Pkwy
Exposition Blvd
37th St
37th Place
Natural History
Museum of LA County
Rose
Garden
Kinsey Dr
Armory
Buliding
Aerospace
Hall
IMAX
Theater
State Dr
California
Science
Center
Technology
Hall
Kinsey Hall
of Health
Kinsey
Aud.
California
African
American
Museum
38th St
State Dr
Museum Dr
W 39th St
N Coliseum Dr
Museum Dr
S Vermont Ave
Menlo Ave
Los Angeles
Memorial
Coliseum
MAP
11
N Coliseum Dr
Figueroa Street
39th St
S Coliseum Dr
Leighton Ave
Los Angeles
Sports Arena
Exposition Park
South
S Coliseum Dr
Harbor Freeway & Transitway
110
W Martin Luther King Jr Blvd
Hoover St
W 40th Pl
W 40th Pl
W 40th Pl

NFT Maps: 11-12

Overview

Exposition Park is bounded by Figueroa to the east, Martin Luther King Jr. to the south, Menlo to the west, and Exposition Boulevard to the north. Originally called Agricultural Park, the area was developed in 1876 as a showground for agricultural and horticultural fairs. In June 1923, the Los Angeles Memorial Coliseum, named in honor of those who died in World War I, was completed. The stadium was enlarged for the 1932 Olympics and also hosted the 1984 Olympics. Today Exposition Park houses the Natural History Museum, Armory Building, IMAX Theatre, Rose Garden, California Museum of Science and Industry, California African American Museum, LA Memorial Coliseum, and the indoor Los Angeles Sports Arena.

Practicalities

From the north, take 101 south to 110 south, exit at Martin Luther King Jr. Boulevard west, and enter on Hoover. From the south, take 405 north to 110 north, exit at Martin Luther King Jr. Boulevard west, and enter on Hoover. From the west, take 10 east to the 110 south and follow the above directions. From the east, take 10 west to 110 south and follow the above directions. If you're taking public transport, take the Metro Rail Red Line to the 7th Street/Metro Center Station. Catch the Dash F bus at the corner of Seventh and Flower. The bus will stop in front of the University of Southern California across the street from the Natural History Museum on Exposition Boulevard.

Parking

There are parking spaces located at various places within the park. Parking rates and availability will vary for special events. Four-hour and two-hour metered parking is available on Figueroa and Jefferson. There are a number of lots on the streets surrounding the park, and the usual weekly day rate is $3. Rates vary when special events are in progress, and the average cost of parking in a lot is $10.

Los Angeles Memorial Coliseum & Los Angeles Sports Arena

The history of the Coliseum/Sports Arena complex spans eight decades. It is the only arena in the world to play host to two Olympiads (10th and 23rd), two Super Bowls (1st and 7th), and one World Series (1959). In the past, the complex has played host to the Rams, the Dodgers, and the Lakers and was the expansion home of the San Diego Chargers and the Kings. Today, the Coliseum is home to the University of Southern California's Trojan football team (call 213-740-GOSC for tickets) and various other special events. Check the website (www.lacoliseum.com) for event details. The main box office switchboard is open from 10 am to 6 pm and can be reached at 213-748-6131.

Rose Garden

The 7.5-acre Rose Garden was completed in 1928 and there were 15,793 roses in full bloom for the opening. Today the sunken garden contains more than 20,000 rose bushes representing 190-plus varieties. In Southern California, roses bloom from March to November. The garden is open daily, is free to the public, and is located within Exposition Park at 701 State Drive (310-548-7675).

Natural History Museum of LA County

The Natural History Museum is located at 900 Exposition Boulevard in Exposition Park, across from the University of Southern California (USC). Parking is available off Menlo Avenue. Cost for parking will run between $5 and $10, depending on events in the Exposition Park area. The Museum's opening hours are 9 am until 5 pm Monday to Friday and 10 am until 5 pm Saturday and Sunday. Adults can expect to pay $8 for entry, seniors and students are $5.50, and children 5–12 are $2. But if you schedule your visit on the first Tuesday of the month, it won't cost you a cent! Although the museum is open during USC football games, we highly recommend that you avoid the Exposition Park area at all costs on those days unless you're attending the football game. Museum phone: 213-763-DINO. Website: www.nhm.org.

California Science Center & IMAX

The Science Center is open is open daily from 10 am until 5 pm and admission to Science Center exhibition halls is free. The IMAX is open daily and admission is $7.50 adults, $5.50 seniors and students, and $4.50 children. Check the website (www.casciencectr.org) or call 213-744-7400 for show information. Parking is $6 per car, $10 for buses or oversize vehicles, and the entrance to the visitor parking lot is on Figueroa at 39th Street.

California African American Museum

The California African American Museum researches, collects, preserves, and interprets the art, history, and culture of African Americans with emphasis on California and the western United States. The museum is open Wednesdays through Saturdays, from 10 am until 4 pm. Admission is free.

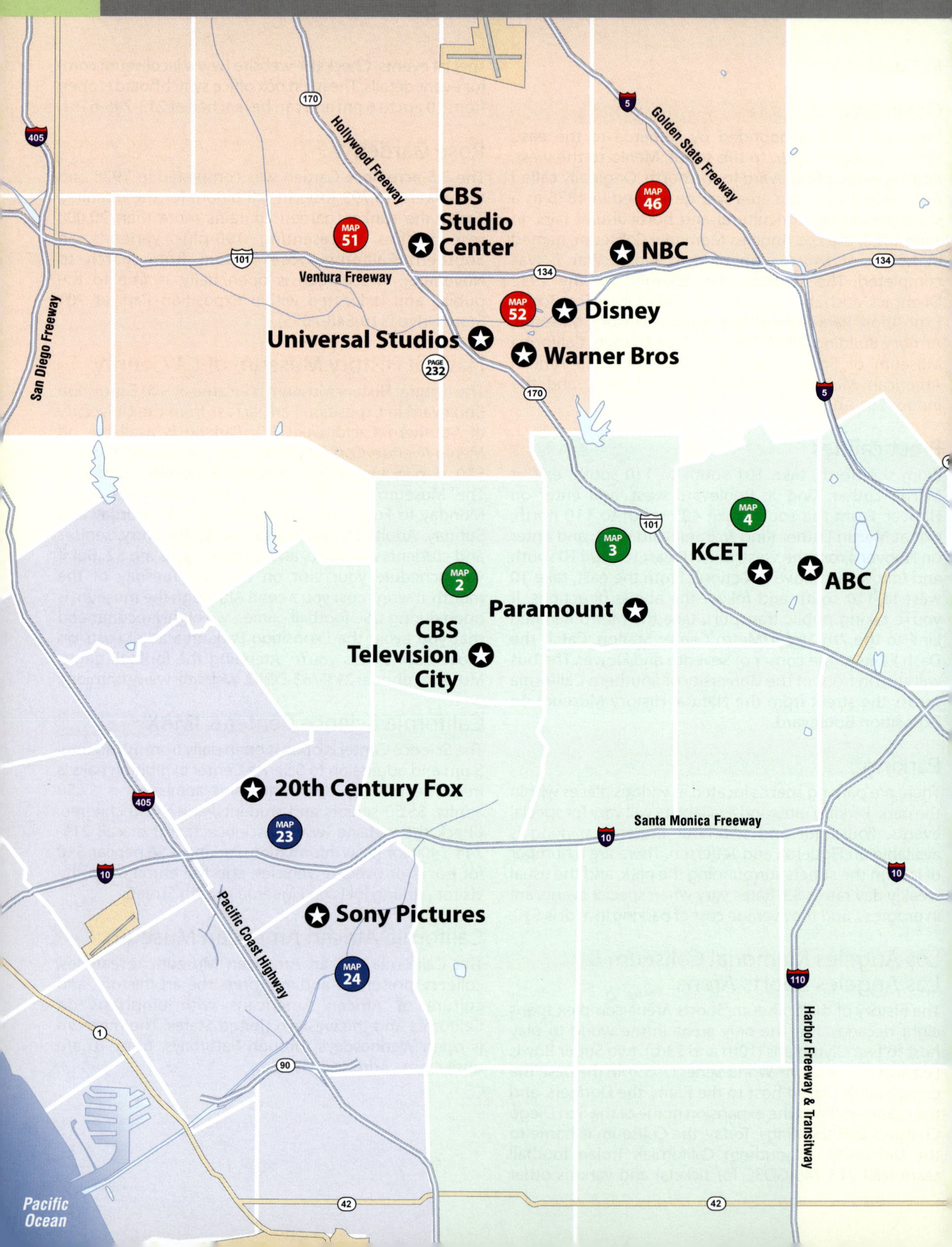
170
5
Golden State Freeway
405
Hollywood Freeway
MAP 46
CBS Studio Center
MAP 51
NBC
101
134
Ventura Freeway
134
MAP 52
Disney
Universal Studios
Warner Bros
San Diego Freeway
PAGE 232
170
5
MAP 4
MAP 3
KCET
MAP 2
ABC
Paramount
CBS Television City
20th Century Fox
MAP 23
Santa Monica Freeway
10
10
10
Pacific Coast Highway
Sony Pictures
MAP 24
1
Harbor Freeway & Transitway
90
42
42
Pacific Ocean

Overview

Whether you're a visitor to LA or a long-time resident, it can be interesting to get a glimpse of what happens behind the cameras. Many of the movie studios and some of the television studios offer tours for a fee, and all of the TV studios need audiences for show tapings, giving out free tickets to those willing to give up their time. An excellent website for the lowdown on movie and television studios, as well as a host of other "star-related" information is the Seeing Stars website: www.seeing-stars.com.

Warner Bros. Studio

4000 Warner Blvd, Burbank,
818-954-1744 or 818-954-1008, www.studio-tour.com
A small tram that makes many stops will take you on a tour of Warner Bros. Studios. One of the better studio tours, it is also one of the most expensive. Expect to hand over $32 for this intimate 110-acre backlot tour. You can take photos when they allow you to, but only stills. Tours are given weekdays every half hour from 9 am until 3 pm and reservations are required. The tour office is located at the studio's Gate 4 entrance at Olive Avenue and Hollywood Way. Shows that tape here include *Friends*, *Everybody Loves Raymond*, and the *Drew Carey Show*.

Paramount Pictures Studio

Entrance at 5555 Melrose Ave, Hollywood,
323-956-1777, www.paramount.com
In the past, Paramount has run two-hour guided walking tours through the lot every half-hour from 9 am until 2 pm weekdays. However, that tour has been suspended, due to heightened security concerns. But if you'd like some free entertainment, you can go along and see a taping of one of the shows such as *Becker*, *Frasier*, or *Dr. Phil*. For show taping schedules, check the website for the dates you plan on visiting or call Show Information at 323-956-5575.

Sony Pictures Studio (Columbia/Tristar Pictures)

10202 W Washington Blvd, Culver City,
310-244-4000, www.spe.sony.com
In 1990, Sony Entertainment of Japan purchased the old MGM Studio in Culver City where *The Wizard of Oz* was filmed. More recently, *The Hollow Man* and *Charlie's Angels* were filmed there. If you'd like to see the workings of a modern film studio, you can take a two-hour guided walking tour of the studio for $20. You pay for the tickets at the Sony Plaza building across Madison Street from the main gate. Make reservations in advance by phoning 323-520-TOUR. All guests on the tour must be at least 12 years old.

NBC Studios

3000 West Alameda Ave (at Bob Hope Dr), Burbank,
818-840-3537 or 818-840-4444
The tour of NBC Studios gives you an insight into the inner workings of television. Apart from KCET, the local public television station, NBC is the only television studio in LA to offer tours. It is also one of the cheapest tours in town at $7, and it consists of a 70-minute indoor walking tour. Tours run weekdays between 9 am and 3 pm and on holiday weekends—call ahead to make reservations and check opening times. If you're interested in seeing a taping of *The Tonight Show with Jay Leno*, tickets are available in-person from the ticket counter on the actual day of taping or in advance by mail. To pick up your tickets in person, first phone to check availability.

CBS Studio Center

4024 Radford Ave, Studio City, 818-655-5000
The titles currently being shot at the studio include *Will & Grace*, *Two Guys & a Girl*, *Just Shoot Me*, *Spin City*, *Malcolm in the Middle*, *That 70's Show*, *Yes Dear*, and the soap opera *Passions*. Although there are no tours of this studio, members of the public who wish to be audience members can contact Audiences Unlimited (see end of page).

CBS Television City

7800 Beverly Blvd, Los Angeles,
323-575-2458 (tickets), www.cbs.com
Not to be confused with CBS Studio Center, Television City films such gems as *The Price is Right*, *Hollywood Squares*, *According to Jim*, and *Politically Incorrect*. If you want to see a taping and you don't care what it is, you can walk up to the studio's ticket office (near the corner of Beverly & Fairfax) and pick up tickets of shows that require audiences. If you're after tickets for a specific show, you will need to call 323-575-2458 (live) or 323-575-2449 (*The Price is Right* recorded hotline) in advance.

ABC TV

4151 Prospect Ave, Los Angeles,
310-557-7777, kabctv7@aol.com
There are no public tours of ABC studios, but tickets to some shows can be obtained through Audiences Unlimited or by calling the ABC Show Ticket Hotline on 310-520-1ABC. You can also try writing to ABC Guest Services, 4151 Prospect Ave, Los Angeles, CA 90027.

Disney Studios

500 S Buena Vista Street, Burbank, 818-560-1000
Not open to the public apart from the taping of such shows as *8 Simple Rules* and *My Wife and Kids*, audiences can secure tickets through Audiences Unlimited (see end of page).

20th Century Fox

10201 W Pico, Century City, www.fox.com
Tickets for show tapings are available through Audiences Unlimited (see end of page).

KCET Studio

4401 Sunset Blvd, Hollywood,
323-953-5289, www.kcet.org
This one is free!! KCET, local public television (PBS) station Channel 28, offers free tours of its studio on Fridays, but you'll need to book three weeks in advance if you want to participate in the 90-minute tour.

Audiences Unlimited

Audiences Unlimited is an agency that distributes free tickets to the tapings of television shows. Call 818-753-3470, or go to www.audiencesunlimited.com. Tickets can also be obtained by mail (include SASE) by writing to Audiences Unlimited, 100 Universal City Plaza, Building 153, Universal City, CA 91608. You need to specify the name of the show, date, and number in your party. For a recording of show schedules and ticket information call 818-771-7195.

Location:	1151 Oxford Road, San Marino, CA 91108
Phone:	626-405-2100
Website:	www.huntington.org
NFT Map:	35

Overview

The private and non-profit Huntington was founded in 1919 by railroad and real estate developer Henry Edwards Huntington and has since grown into an institution which contains a library, three galleries, and a magnificent 150-acre garden featuring 14,000 different species of plants. The Huntington was opened to the public in 1928, and visitors today can walk freely through the gardens and gallery. But be warned: you need to be an approved scholar and apply in writing before you can get your hands on the extensive, dated library collection. The complex is also home to a lovely tea room, making your visit to Huntington a thoroughly refined affair.

How to Get There—Driving

The Huntington is located adjacent to Pasadena, in the city of San Marino, which is about twelve miles northeast of downtown Los Angeles. The Huntington has two entrance gates: one on Oxford Road and a second entrance at Allen Avenue, just south of California Boulevard.

Harbor or Pasadena Freeway 110: Head north towards Pasadena where 110 will end, becoming Arroyo Parkway. Turn right on California Blvd. Travel along California for about 3 miles. At Allen Avenue, turn right and proceed two blocks to the gates of the Huntington.

Foothill Freeway 210: If you're coming from the east, exit at the Allen Avenue off-ramp in Pasadena. Turn left and go south for two miles to the Huntington's gate. If you're coming from the west into Pasadena, take the Hill Avenue exit and continue straight alongside the freeway for 3 blocks. At Allen Avenue, turn right and head south for two miles to the Huntington's entrance gates.

Santa Monica Freeway 10: From Santa Monica, LAX, or the West Side, take the 10 freeway eastbound to the 110 freeway north and follow the directions for the 110.

How to Get There—Mass Transit

The Huntington is located in a residential area, and the closest bus stops are about one mile away. Take MTA Bus lines 79/379, 401, 188, or 264 or Foothill Transit line 187. For buses 79, 379, and 401, disembark at San Marino Avenue. For bus 188 and Foothills line 187, get off at the corner of Colorado Boulevard and Allen Avenue. For line 264, get off at Huntington Drive and Sierra Madre Boulevard.

Opening Hours

Tuesday–Friday: 12 noon to 4:30 pm. Saturday & Sunday: 10:30 am to 4:30 pm. Summer Hours (June through August): Tuesday–Sunday 10:30 am to 4:30 pm.

Entrance Fees

$10 adult, $8.50 senior (age 65 and over), $7 student (age 12-18 or with full-time student I.D.), $4 youth (ages 5-11). Free for children under 5. Groups of 10 or more, $8 per person. Admission is free to all visitors on the first Thursday of every month.

The Library

The Huntington Library contains approximately 5 million items available for research by scholars, mainly in the fields of British and American history and literature. It also has works in the fields of 15th-century books, history of science, and maritime history. A selection of items are displayed in the Library Exhibition Hall where the general public can view the progress of Anglo-American development over the past 1,000 years. You need to be a qualified scholar before you're allowed to touch any of the collection, and even then you need to apply for "reading privileges" through the Reader Services Department.

The Art Collections

The Huntington Gallery mainly displays British and French art of the 18th and 19th centuries. The Virginia Steele Scott Gallery of American Art brings together American paintings from the 1730s to the 1930s. In addition, there are changing exhibitions and special events so you should check the website for current and future exhibitions.

The Botanic Gardens

The highlight of a visit to Huntington is the sweeping gardens covering 150 acres and dotted with various statues, benches, and fountains. The different landscapes include the Australian Garden, Japanese Garden, Shakespeare Garden, Desert, Herb, Jungle, Lilly, Palm, Camellia, and Subtropical Gardens. There are also garden talks and sales throughout the year so check the website for specific events.

Overview

Housing an amusement park on its pier, Santa Monica Beach is one of the widest and most popular beaches in the Los Angeles area, playing host to 3 million visitors each year. The pier originally began as two piers, built side by side in 1909 and 1921, that were going to be torn down after years of deterioration, until local residents rallied to save them. In 1988, a new concrete substructure was built, adding strength and stability to a pier that would be able to withstand violent storms. (www.santamonicapier.org)

Practicalities

There is a parking lot located north of the pier at 1550 PCH, which costs $6 weekdays and $7 weekends, during the off-season, and $7 weekdays and $8 weekends during the summer months. There is also metered parking along Ocean Avenue north and south of the pier. Pier Info: 310-458-8900. Beach info: 310-396-3266. A visitor information stand is located on Ocean Avenue and Santa Monica Boulevard.

Restrooms

There are restrooms located on the pier.

Amusement Park

Located right on the Santa Monica Pier, Pacific Park Amusement Center offers a nine-story Ferris wheel that provides its riders with a terrific view of the coastline and the city. There is also a 1920s-vintage carousel, rollercoaster, skeeball, air hockey, pinball, and video games to keep visitors amused. (www.pacpark.com)

Camera Obscura

One of the most unusual things to do at Santa Monica Beach is the Camera Obscura, located just north of the Pier at 1450 Ocean Avenue. Enter this darkened room, and you will see images from the outside cast onto a table by a long-focus camera lens. The Camera Obscura has been housed inside the Santa Monica Senior Recreation Center since 1955, and is free. You simply have to leave your driver's license at the Rec Center's office in exchange for the key. It may not be as exciting as the nearby roller coaster, but it's a lot more unique. Call (310) 458-8644 for more information.

UCLA Ocean Discovery Center

This facility is a hands-on aquarium/learning center focusing on the study of underwater sea life. It is a chance to "learn about the Santa Monica Bay in a whole new way." Labor Day to June 30, the center is open to the public from 11 am until 5 pm weekends. In the summer, the center is open Tuesday through Friday 3 pm–6 pm, Saturday 11 am–5 pm, and Sunday 11 am–6 pm. Admission is $3 and children under 2 are free. Check out their website for further information: www.odc.ucla.edu (Ph: 310-393-6149)

Shopping

The best shopping to be had is two blocks east of Ocean Avenue along the Third Street Promenade. This three-block pedestrian mall is lined with restaurants, bars, movie theaters, and retail stores including everything from bookstores to swimwear shops. On Wednesday, California farmers sell their produce on Arizona Avenue in the mall, between Second and Fourth.

Restaurants and Cafes

- **17th Street Café** · 1610 Montana Ave
- **Babalu** · 1002 Montana Ave
- **Chez Jay** · 1657 Ocean Ave
- **El Cholo** · 1025 Wilshire Blvd
- **Fritto Misto** · 601 Colorado Ave
- **Library Alehouse** · 2911 Main St
- **Lula** · 2722 Main St
- **Newsroom Café** · 530 Wilshire Blvd
- **Reel Inn** · 1220 Third St. Promenade
- **World Café** · 2820 Main St
- **Ye Olde King's Head** · 116 Santa Monica Blvd

Overview

With funky shops, sports courts, street performers, and Muscle Beach, where fanatic bodybuilders pump iron in a public show of strength, there's definitely something for everyone here! Street performers aid in creating the unique atmosphere, and on any given day you're almost guaranteed to catch a glimpse of the shirtless, roller-skating, turban-wearing, guitar-playing artist Harry Perry. Numerous street vendors also sell everything from silver jewelry and personal art to massages and psychic readings.

Practicalities

The beach area is closed from 10:30 pm until 5 am. The parking lot is located where North Venice intersects with Ocean Front Walk and is open 7 am to 8 pm weekdays ($5) and closes at 9 pm weekends ($6.50). Before 9 am, parking is just $3. Be prepared to pay up to $10 on holidays (310-399-2775). In addition to the public parking lots, free parking is available on nearby side streets if you don't mind a sometimes-lengthy hunt for a spot. However, the area surrounding Venice Beach can be a bit dicey after dark, so exercise caution when walking around on foot.

Restrooms

A recently renovated restroom is located next to Muscle Beach and there is also a restroom on the Venice Pier.

Sports

Considering the sunny, seaside location, it is no surprise that surfing, skating, cycling, and basketball are popular recreation activities in the Venice Beach area. One of Venice Beach's main sporting attractions is Muscle Beach, built at a cost of $500,000, which attracts weightlifters and spectators from all over the world. For a measly $5 you can buy a day pass and pump iron with the best of them (310-399-2775). On a strong south swell, you will find some decent surfing waves at the breakwater—the waves hit the breakwater rocks then wrap around to the right. You can break a sweat in the free paddle tennis courts or, if yoga is more your speed, there is a class on the beach in front of the Breakwater for a donation on Saturday at 10:30 am (bring a towel). There are also basketball courts, handball courts, a roller rink, skate park, legal graffiti area, punching bag hookups, rings, parallel bars, and a rope to climb. Finally, it's also possible to rent bicycles, roller skates, and in-line skates at several vendors along the boardwalk. A bike path that begins in Redondo Beach (and runs north to Malibu) runs parallel to Venice Beach, and is a perfect place to try out your rented wheels.

Venice Pier

The pier is open from 8 am to 10 pm and the parking lot is located at Washington Boulevard and Ocean Walk Front. Parking costs $5 weekdays and $6.50 weekends (310-457-2525). The pier is stronger than ever after being recently rebuilt and is a popular spot for local anglers. Restrooms are available on the pier.

Venice Rose

The beach is closed from midnight to 5 am. The parking lot is located where Ocean Front Walk crosses Rose Avenue and costs $5 weekdays and $6.50 weekends (310-399-2775). There is also some free street parking on Rose Avenue, which is where the Venice Boardwalk begins. It is an ideal place for skating, bike riding, or just relaxing and people-watching. Rose Avenue has a nice playground surrounded by palm trees, and the sand beach is long and wide, making it an ideal spot for families.

Shopping

From cheap t-shirts and sunglasses to surfboards and jewelry, Venice beach offers a bevy of shopping opportunities in a unique bohemian environment. In addition to the fixed shop fronts along the boardwalk, many street vendors also set up along the main strip to sell their wares.

Restaurants and Cafes

- **Abbot's Pizza** · 1407 Abbott Kinney Blvd
- **C&O Tratorria** · 31 Washington Blvd
- **Canal Club** · 2025 Pacific Ave
- **Joe's** · 1023 Abbott Kinney Blvd
- **Rose Café** · 220 Rose Ave
- **Washington Street Bar & Grill** · 3016 Washington Blvd

Overview

The word "hermosa" means "beautiful" in Spanish and is an appropriate name for the area surrounding Hermosa Beach and Pier. Hermosa Beach has never permitted cheap amusements along its Strand, and the most popular forms of recreation in the area are surfing, playing volleyball, fishing, and sunbathing.

Practicalities

Hermosa Beach is open from sunrise to sunset. There is metered street parking for 25¢ per 30 minutes and a 3-story parking lot on 13th St., which costs 50¢ per hour with a maximum fee of $8 per day. Phone 310-372-2166.

Restrooms

There are restrooms located on the Pier and at 2nd St., 11th St., 14th St., and 22nd St.

Sports

Like it's northern neighbors, Venice and Santa Monica, Hermosa Beach is home to surfers, skaters, joggers, walkers, and volleyball players. Hermosa's claim to fame is an annual volleyball tournament, which is televised nationally, and the Annual Surf Festival, a sports event that draws lifeguard participants from all over California and as far away as Australia. Surfing and volleyball lessons are available right on the beach, and if you don't have your own boogie board, surfboard, or skates, you can always rent them. Pier Surf (25 Pier Ave 310-372-2012), located just up from the Hermosa Beach Pier, rents surfboards for $10 an hour ($18 a day). Hermosa Cyclery (20 13th St. 310-376-2720) has a nice selection of bikes and skates at affordable prices; rates start at $7 an hour ($21 a day) for both bikes and rollerblades.

Fishing

Located at the west end of Pier Avenue, the Hermosa Beach Pier is 1,228 feet long and offers year-round fishing. The Pier houses a tackle shop that rents equipment and sells bait (310-372-2124). Alternatively you can visit Just Fishing, located at 21 Pier Avenue (310-374-9388).

Shopping

There is a multitude of shopping opportunities within walking distance of the beach along Pier Avenue, Manhattan Avenue, Artesia Boulevard, and the Pacific Coast Highway, where you'll find an abundance of clothing, jewelry, sunglasses, and shoe stores. If you're after fresh produce, eggs, honey, or flowers, the Farmers' Market, located on Valley Drive (between 8th and 10th Streets), is open every Friday from 12 noon until 4 pm, rain or shine.

Restaurants and Cafes

- **Hennessey's Tavern** • 8 Pier Ave
- **Il Bocaccio** • 39 Pier Ave
- **Martha's 22nd Street Grill** • 25 22nd St
- **Ragin' Cajun** • 422 Pier Ave

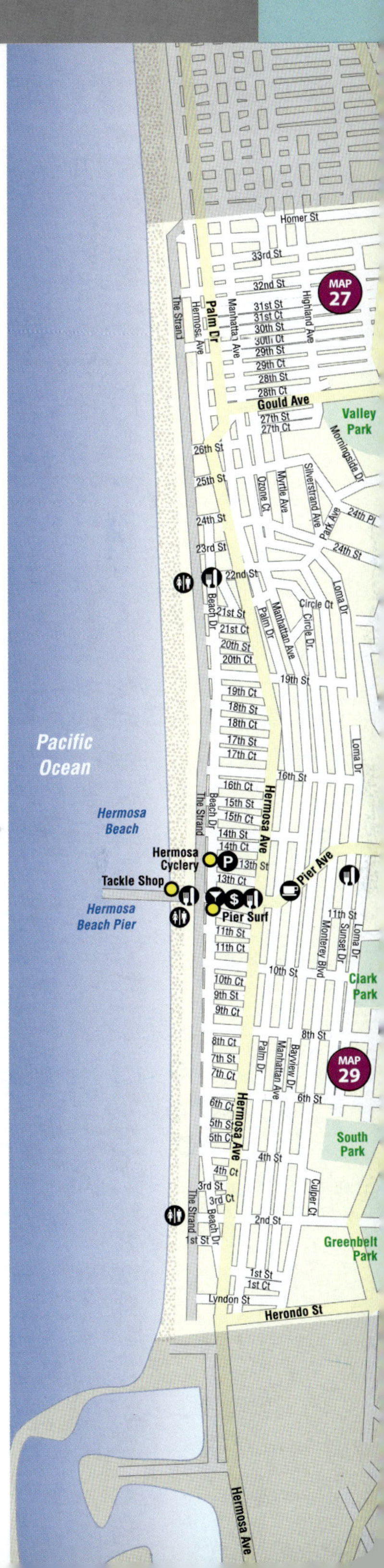

Overview

Manhattan Beach is famous for being the location from which the Beach Boys drew inspiration for their surf music. The beach is indeed a prime location for surfing, boogie boarding, and body surfing, as well as swimming, diving, and fishing. Manhattan's upscale accommodations and restaurants mean that the neighborhood attracts a more affluent clientele and that restaurants here are a little more expensive than those in neighboring Hermosa and Redondo Beaches.

Practicalities

Manhattan Beach is open from sunrise until midnight. There are two metered parking lots with 5-hour limits. One quarter buys only fifteen minutes, so make sure you stock up on quarters before you leave home. Metered street parking is also available at the same rates.

Restrooms

Clean restrooms with showers are located at the base of the pier, as well as at 8th St, Manhattan Beach Boulevard, Marine, and Rosecrans.

Sports

If you're a surfer, boogie boarder, or body surfer, you'll find decent waves at Manhattan Beach. Other popular sports include volleyball, cycling, and skating.

Manhattan Pier

Though it has much more of a "no-frills" atmosphere than Venice or Santa Monica Piers, the pier at Manhattan Beach is one of LA County's nicest. It is home to the Oceanographic Teaching Station, which is equipped with a marine laboratory and aquarium. The Aquarium and Teaching Station is open from 3 pm until sunset during the week and 10 am until sunset on the weekends and entry is FREE! (310-379-8117) There are also telescopes located on the pier that give terrific views of Palos Verdes, Catalina, and the northern beaches.

Shopping

For those born to shop, Manhattan Beach is a treasure trove of eclectic shops and boutiques. The Manhattan Village Mall is an intimate shopping spot and you will find a variety of shops and boutiques along Sepulveda Boulevard.

Restaurants and Cafes

- **Cozymels** • 2171 Rosecrans Ave
- **Houstons** • 1550 Rosecrans Ave
- **Il Fornaio** • 1800 Rosecrans Ave
- **Soleil** • 1142 Manhattan Ave
- **Versailles** • 1000 N Selpulveda Blvd
- **Uncle Bill's** • 1305 Highland Ave

Overview

The Redondo Beach Harbor Enterprise occupies over 150 acres of land and water area including the beach, parks, pier, boardwalk, and arcade. Redondo Beach is an historic beach town that reflects the best of the Southern Californian lifestyle. Cleaner and less visited than some of the more northern LA beaches, Redondo offers an array of recreational activities and is family-friendly. Even though the water is fairly clean, it is a good idea not to swim too close to storm water drains, especially after it rains—luckily, it doesn't rain too often! From the beach, you get a beautiful view of the Palos Verdes Peninsula, and if you wait around until dusk, you will be rewarded with a magnificent Southern Californian sunset.

Practicalities

Like most of the other South Bay beaches, Redondo is open from sunrise to sunset. You can still walk along the beach after sunset but swimming is not permitted. The parking lot is located on the corner of Pacific Coast Hwy and Torrance Blvd and has a capacity of over 900 spaces. The hours are 11 am–7 pm and it costs $3 to park all day on weekdays, $5 on weekends in the winter, and $5 weekdays and $7 weekends in the summer months. If you shop along the pier, you can even have your parking validated. There is additional parking at the Plaza Parking Structure at 180 N. Harbor Drive at Pacific Avenue, which has the same rates at the Pier Parking Lot. Bus parking is $10 at both lots. Metered street parking is also available in surrounding streets.

Restrooms

You will find clean restrooms located throughout the pier, and there's also one midway down the beach for bathers.

Sports

The big activity in this area, apart from the usual swimming, skating, and cycling, is boating. Whether you're launching your own or paying for an excursion boat, the Redondo Pier is a good departure point. Sport fishing is popular and Redondo hosts a Halibut Derby each year (310-372-2111). There is a nice beach break for surfers and a lovely park directly behind the beach for playing games.

Redondo Pier

The pier, boardwalk, and arcade combine to provide a smorgasbord of entertainment and dining pleasure. The pier is shaped like a horseshoe and holds a couple of nice restaurants. Nestled next to the pier, the boardwalk also provides restaurants, bars, and a variety of retail stores.

Seaside Lagoon

The Seaside Lagoon is located at 200 Portofino Way in Redondo Beach's King Harbor. From 190th Street, go west toward the beach until the street ends, then turn left onto Harbor Drive, and proceed for about one mile. Parking is available at the Redondo Beach Marina and can be validated at the Lagoon. The large saltwater lagoon is heated by a nearby steam-generating plant and provides trained lifeguards. Besides swimming, the lagoon offers a large sand area for sunbathing, children's play equipment, snack bar facilities provided by Ruby's Restaurant, and volleyball courts. Open from 10 am until 5:45 pm in the summer months, the cost of admission is $3.75 for adults and $2.75 children aged 2 to 17. Phone: 310-318-0681

Redondo Fun Factory

Located under the pier, the Fun Factory is open seven days a week and features over 300 arcade and prize-redemption games, as well as a Tilt-A-Whirl and kiddie rides. Open 10 am until 10 pm, Monday to Thursday and Sunday; until midnight on Friday and Saturday. Phone: 310-374-9982

Shopping

In addition to the shopping opportunities on the pier and boardwalk, the Riviera Village is an eclectic shopping area situated in South Redondo between Pacific Coast Highway and Catalina Avenue south of Avenue I. It contains many one-of-a-kind boutiques, galleries, cafes, and restaurants. If you're looking for something fresh, try the Market at Veteran's Park, which operates every Thursday morning from 8 pm until noon.

Restaurants and Cafes

- **Coyote Cantina** · 531 N. Pacific Coast Highway
- **El Pollo Inka** · 23705 Hawthorne Blvd
- **Gina Lee's Bistro** · 211 Palos Verdes Dr
- **Kincaid's Bay House** · 500 The Pier
- **Zazou** · 1810 S. Catalina Ave

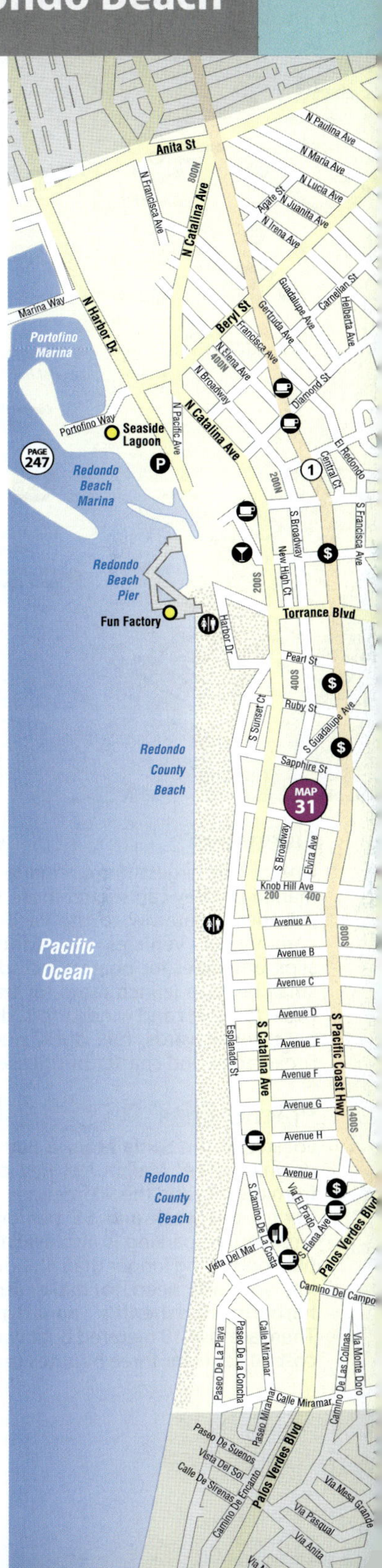

Overview

One of the largest human-made marinas in the world, Marina Del Rey can shelter more than 6,000 vessels and provides a gateway to the Pacific for recreational and commercial vehicles. In addition to 6,100 boat slips, amenities for boaters include beach-launching for small boats, a launch ramp for trailered boats, a sailing basin for boats and windsurfers, dry storage, a Sea Scout base, repair yards, fuel dock, pump-out stations, boat brokerages, and charter businesses.

Practicalities

Located in the Santa Monica Bay 15 miles southwest of downtown LA, Marina Del Rey can be easily accessed from the 405 and the 90 freeways. Parking is $2 per entry during the week and $5 per entry on the weekend. Limited free parking is also available on Dock 52. If you plan on staying longer than 48 hours in the large parking lot, you will need to make arrangements with the harbormaster/sheriff's department (310-823-7762). There are also 18 metered boat washdown spaces, which cost 50 cents for three minutes (requires quarters).

Launch Ramp & Fuel Dock

Hand-carried small boats such as kayaks and tin boats are easily launched at the public beach in Basin D, also known as Mother's Beach because of the absence of surf, making it a safer swimming beach for children. There is a public launch ramp at the head of the first finger at Mindanao Way on the east side of the channel. The eight-lane ramp can get very busy, especially on the weekends and during summer months, so be prepared to wait. The fee is $5 for one launch and recovery. The fuel dock is on the west side of the channel just inside the bend.

Harbor Info

The entrance to the marina is located between two jetties (north and south) that sit inside of the breakwater that runs parallel to the shore. The north and south ends of the breakwater and the ends of both jetties are marked with lights which can be distinguished by their color and length between flashes. This information is especially important during darkness and foggy weather. North Breakwater Light, 1 flashes WHITE every six seconds. South Breakwater Light, 2 flashes RED every six seconds. North Jetty Light, 3 flashes WHITE every five seconds and South Jetty Light, 4 flashes RED every four seconds.

Guest Slips

The Los Angeles County Department of Beaches and Harbors offers boat slips to guests. There is a 4-hour tie-up dock between H and G basins on the east side of the main channel, and overnight docking (up to 7 days) can be arranged at the Community Building in the park. To obtain an overnight slip, you will need to produce your registration papers and identification. Overnight facilities include electricity, water, showers, and restrooms. If you are a yacht club member, try contacting the yacht clubs in the area to see if they offer reciprocal guest slips.

Harbor Patrol & Anchorage

The Harbor Patrol is run by the Los Angeles County Sheriff's Department and located on the east side of the main channel. They are on call 24 hours per day and can be reached on Channel 16 with 12 as the working channel (310-823-7762). During storms or other emergencies, anchoring is allowed in the north end of the entrance channel.

No Boat?

If you don't have your own water craft, commercial vehicles leave from Dock 52 and provide all of the gear you will need for a great day of fishing, including rods, reels, and bait. If pier fishing is more your style, head down Fiji Way to Fisherman's Village and you can throw a line in from the docks. If you get tired of that, there is an array of souvenir shops and restaurants to keep you entertained.

Restrooms

There are restrooms at Fisherman's Village and next to the launch ramp. There is also a portable restroom at Dock 52.

Overview

Redondo Beach is home to four marinas—King Harbor, Port Royal, Portofino, and Redondo Beach—and together they combine to provide 1,400 boat slips of various sizes. Whether you're an avid angler or you like eating seafood by the water, Redondo is a great place to spend a day or five.

Practicalities

There are several double-spaced parking spots within Redondo Beach Marina for parking vehicles with boat trailers. In the summer months the marina gets very busy, so it's a good idea to make an early start to ensure you get a parking space. You can expect to pay between $3 and $7 per day for parking.

Boat Hoist & Fuel Docks

Unlike most other marinas, the Redondo Beach Marina has a boat hoist instead of a launch ramp. Skilled hoist operators launch boats mechanically via slings using the two five-ton hoists, which are capable of launching boats up to 10,000 pounds and 30 feet in length. The boat hoist is open in winter from 7 am until 5 pm on weekdays and from 6 am to 6 pm on weekends. The extended summer hours (6 am until 6 pm weekdays, 6 am until 8 pm weekends) begin Memorial Day weekend. The round-trip hoist fee is $8 for a hand-launch size boat, $18 for personal watercraft, $30 for 18 ft to 24 ft, and $40 for 25 ft and over. If you want to stay out late or overnight, arrangements can be made for a fee (310-374-3481). If you're a local resident with proof of boat registration, you can obtain a book of boat hoist coupons from City Hall, Door E for $7.50. If you're launching a boat by hand, you can do so behind the Seaside Lagoon via the Redondo Beach Marina parking lot or along Portofino Way. There are two fuel docks, one at the commercial basin and one across from the Harbor Patrol office.

Harbor Info

The entrance to the marina is at the south end of the harbor between two lighted jetties with a lighted buoy to the SSW of the exterior jetty to guide you into the marina.

Guest Slips

King Harbor Marina offers guest boat slips and docking accommodations for one or more days. 208 Yacht Club Way, 310-376-6926. The yacht clubs offer reciprocal overnight stays so check there first if you're a yacht club member.

Harbor Patrol

The Harbor Patrol office is located at the west end of Marina Way, adjacent to Moonstone Park (310-318-0632).

No Boat?

Not to worry. You can hire fishing rods and tackle and purchase bait and salt water fishing licenses right on the Redondo Sport Fishing Pier. If you'd rather be out on the water, fishing trips range from $23 ($18 kids) for a half-day to $750 for a 15-person charter boat for the day. Whale watching is another option with excursions on the Voyager at 10 am and 1:30 pm. Tours run for three to three-and-a-half hours and the whale watch season runs from mid-December to March each year. For something a little racier, try sailing classes or a high-speed tour of the coast on the Ocean Racer.

Restrooms

There are many restrooms located in and around the harbor, including on Redondo Pier and along the beach areas.

Overview

A wind current known as "Hurricane Gulch," just outside the Cabrillo Marina means that the area provides good sailing weather all year long.

Practicalities

Cabrillo Marina is easy to reach from the I-5 or the 405 to 110 South and exit at Harbor Boulevard. There is plenty of free parking at the Cabrillo Marina and amenities include restrooms, water, electricity, showers, and lockers.

Launch Ramp & Fuel Dock

Run by the LA County Department of Recreation and Parks, the boat ramp is open 24 hours a day and has nearby space for trailer parking and boat washing, as well as restroom facilities. You will find fuel at the Cabrillo Marine Fuel Dock, which is located at Berth 31, 210 Whaler's Walk.

Harbor Info

The breakwater entrance to the western end of San Pedro Bay is Angel's Gate, which is marked by the Los Angeles Lighthouse (33°42.5'N - 118°15.0'W). This marina has a lot of traffic, including huge ships and other commercial vehicles, so boat owners should study their charts in order to navigate the waters appropriately.

Guest Slips

Guest end-ties are available for overnight docking for boats up to 55 feet long for up to three days. Four mooring buoys are offered in the inner harbor for vessels up to 40 feet long, and in the outer harbor 14 mooring buoys are available for boats up to 50 feet long. Overnight mooring will cost between $8.50 and $12.40 a foot, depending on the location and amenities provided.

Harbor Patrol

The Port Warden and staff of the Los Angeles Harbor Department monitor the harbor. They are located at 425 S. Palos Verdes Street, San Pedro.

No Boat?

Fishing is permitted from the Cabrillo Pier. During grunion season, the silvery fish emerge twice a month, like clockwork, to lay their eggs under a full or new moon. During part of the season, it is legal to catch these fish—but only by hand! If you want to participate you will need to take a flashlight. If you don't fancy getting wet, it's almost as much fun to watch. The Cabrillo Marine Aquarium is nearby and costs a mere donation of $5 for adults and $1 for children, and the beach and bathhouse are also enjoyable playgrounds.

Overview

Boaters using the Long Beach Marina will find that it is well-protected due to its location in a natural bay and the series of offshore breakwaters nearby. As a result, sailing is a popular recreational activity out of Long Beach, which is also the home of the Congressional Cup, Transpac, and Olympic trial races. The 3,800-slip marina is run by the City of Long Beach.

Practicalities

Daily parking is available close to the marina. Boaters wishing to leave their vehicles and trailer in the launch parking lot longer than one day need to visit the Alamitos Bay office and pay in advance for a parking pass. Side ties are also available for 50 cents per foot per night.

Launch Ramp & Fuel Dock

Given the size of Long Beach Marina, it is not surprising that four launch ramps exist in the area. The Granada Launch Ramp is at Granada Avenue and Ocean Boulevard. Granada Launch Ramp is open from 8 am until sunset and is only for catamarans, sailboards, and jet-powered personal watercraft. Claremont Launch Ramp is located at Claremont and Ocean Blvd. and only takes sailing craft. Marine Stadium (Appian Way between Second and Colorado) is open year-round. Boats must travel counter-clockwise within the stadium and, if pulling a skier, must have an observer. Boats in the stadium must be 20 feet or less and have a reverse gear. If skiers go down, a red flag must be raised as a signal to other craft. There is another launch ramp across the stadium named Davies Ramp. All launch ramps cost $8.

There are two fuel docks in Long Beach—one in Downtown Shoreline Marina and one in Alamitos Bay. The hours in Alamitos Bay are 8 am to 5 pm in the winter and 7 am to 6 pm from May 31 to Labor Day. The fuel docks not only supply gas and diesel fuels, but also stock propane, snacks, beer, ice, and frozen bait. They accept Union 76 credit cards or cash (562-594-0888). Downtown Shoreline (562-436-4430).

Guest Slips

Guest moorings are available year-round and the rental fee is 60¢ per foot per night. Visiting boaters need to visit one of the two offices and rent a mooring or you can call and make advance reservations. Reservations are usually only required for holiday weekends.

Harbor Patrol

The Harbor Patrol secures the waters of the city and the Marine Patrol ensures that everything on the adjoining land is as it should be. The Marine Patrol is a 24-hour security service that can be called upon at any time. All Lifeguard/Harbor Patrol boats are run by trained, professional lifeguards and are also equipped for emergencies such as fire, boats sinking, or pumpouts. If you happen to need your boat towed, the Harbor Patrol/Rescue Boats will oblige but keep in mind that if it's not an emergency, you will be charged a towing fee.

No Boat?

If you're on a budget but you'd like a piece of the action, a free family attraction is the Belmont Pier at Ocean and 39th Place, which has free public fishing. No license is required as long as you stay on the pier (562-434-6781). Just remember that if you decide to fish from the beach or jetties, you need a salt-water fishing license. If you get tired of the salt and sand, you may opt for the Belmont Plaza Olympic Pool (4000 Olympic Plaza Drive, 562-438-0389).

City of LA Tennis Courts

There are two types of courts run by the city: Open Play, which are free and available on a first-come first-serve basis, and Reservation/Pay Tennis, where hourly fees apply per court and reservations are required. Courts cost $3 per hour weekdays from 7 am until 4 pm, $6 per hour all other times. Call 213-625-1010 for Pay Tennis schedules, registration and reservations, or download the tennis card application from *www.cityofla.org/RAP/dos/tennis/permits.htm*. Lit courts are open from 7 am to 10 pm. Unlit courts are open from dawn to dusk.

Reservation/Pay	Address	# courts	Phone	Map
Balboa	17015 Burbank Blvd	16	818-995-6570	42
Cheviot Hills	2551 Motor Ave	14	310-836-8879	51
Pacific Palisades	851 Alma Real Dr	8	310-454-3905	15
Griffith-Riverside	3401 Riverside Dr	12	323-661-5318	5
Van Nuys	14201 Huston	8	818-756-8400	50
Griffith-Vermont Canyon*	2715 Vermont Canyon	12	323-664-3521	4
Westchester	7000 W Manchester Ave	8	310-670-5510	26
Westwood	1350 Sepulveda Blvd	8	310-575-8299	19

Open Play/Free	Address	Phone	Map
Algin Sutton Rec Ctr	8800 S Hoover St	323-753-5808	14
Aliso Pico Rec Ctr	370 S Clarence St	323-264-5261	40
Arroyo Seco Park	5566 Via Marisol St	N/A	38
Arthur Ashe Ctr	5001 Rodeo Rd	323-290-3141	10
Barrington Rec Ctr	333 S Barrington Ave	310-476-4866	16
Daniels Field Sports Ctr	845 W 12th St	310-548-7728	
Eagle Rock Rec Ctr*	1100 Eagle Vista Dr	323-257-6948	33
Echo Park Rec	1632 Bellevue Ave	213-250-3578	5
El Sereno Rec Ctr	4721 Klamath Place	323-225-3517	38
Elysian Park Therapeutic	929 Academy Rd	323-226-1402	5
Encino Park	16953 Ventura Blvd	818-995-1690	48
Glassell Park Rec Ctr	3650 Verdugo Rd	323-257-1863	36
Glen Alla Park	4601 Alla Rd	N/A	22
Harvard Rec Ctr	1535 W 62nd St	323-778-2579	14
Hazard Rec Ctr	2230 Norfolk St	213-485-6839	40
Hollenbeck Rec Ctr	415 S Saint Louis St	323-261-0113	40
Jim Gilliam Rec Ctr	4000 S La Brea Ave	323-291-5928	10
Lafayette Community Ctr	625 S Lafayette Pk Pl	213-387-9426	8
Lanark Rec Ctr	5301 Tujunga Ave	818-883-1503	
Lincoln Park Rec Ctr	3501 Valley Blvd	213-237-1726	40
Loren Miller Rec Ctr	2717 Halldale Ave	323-734-1302	11
Mar Vista Rec Ctr	11430 Woodbine Ave	310-398-5982	22
Montecito Heights Rec Ctr	4545 Homer St	213-485-5148	37
North Hollywood Rec Ctr	5301 Tujunga Ave	818-763-7651	51
Oakwood Rec Ctr	767 California St	310-452-7479	21
Penmar Rec Ctr	1341 Lake St	310-396-8735	21
Queen Anne Rec Ctr	1240 West Blvd	323-934-0130	7
Reseda Rec Center	18411 Victory Blvd	818-881-3882	42
Ross Snyder Rec Ctr	1501 E 41st St	213-847-3255	12
Rustic Canyon Rec Ctr	601 Latimer Rd	310-454-5734	15
Sepulveda Rec Ctr	8801 Kester Ave	818-893-3700	
Shatto Rec Ctr	3191 W 4th St	213-386-8877	8
South Park	345 E 51st St	213-847-6746	12
St Andrews Rec Ctr	8701 St Andrews	213-485-1751	14
Stoner Rec Ctr	1835 Stoner Ave	310-479-7200	19
Studio City Rec Ctr	12621 Rye St	818-769-4415	51
Sycamore Grove Park	4702 N Figueroa St	N/A	36
Valley Plaza Rec Center	12240 Archwood St	818-765-5885	44
Van Ness Rec Ctr	5720 2nd Ave	323-296-1559	11
Van Nuys Rec Ctr	14301 Vanowen St	818-756-8131	43
Victory-Vineland Rec Ctr	11112 Victory Blvd	818-985-9516	44
Yosemite Rec Ctr	1840 Yosemite Dr	213-257-1644	33

* unlit

LA County Tennis Courts

	Address	Phone	Map
Belvedere Park	4914 E Cesar E Chavez Ave	323-260-2342	41
City Terrace Park	1126 N Hazard Ave	323-260-2371	41
Ruben F Salazar Park	3864 Whittier Blvd	323-260-2330	41
Ladera Park	6027 Ladera Park Ave	310-217-8361	13
Jesse Owens Park	9651 S Western Ave	310-217-8361	14

Parks and Recreation Contact Info

City of LA Parks	323-586-6543 213-978-0066 213-473-7055	County of LA Parks	323-291-0199 213-738-2965

Public Pools

Public Pools	Address	Phone	Map
Downey Pool	1775 N Spring St, Los Angeles	323-226-1671	37
EG Roberts Pool	4526 W Pico Blvd, Los Angeles	323-936-8483	7
Glassell Pool	3704 Verdugo Rd, Los Angeles	323-226-1669	36
Highland Park Pool	6150 Piedmont Ave, Los Angeles	323-226-1669	33
Los Angeles Swimming Pools	3401 Riverside Dr, Los Angeles	323-906-7953	5
Recreation Center Stoner Pool	1831 Stoner Ave, Los Angeles	310-477-7207	19
Seaside Lagoon	200 Portofino Way, Redondo Beach	310-318-0681	25
Victor E Bernstead Plunge Pool	3331 Torrance Blvd, Torrance	310-781-7113	32
Westchester Pool	9100 Lincoln Blvd, Los Angeles	310-840-2129	25
Yosemite Recreation Canter	1840 Yosemite Dr, Los Angeles	323-257-1644	33

Bowling Alleys

Bowling Alleys	Address	Phone	Map
All Star Bowling Lanes	4459 Eagle Rock Blvd	323-254-2579	33
AMF El Dorado Lanes	8731 Lincoln Blvd	310-670-0688	25
AMF Mar Vista Lanes	12125 Venice Blvd	310-391-5288	22
AMF Midtown Bowling Center	4645 Venice Blvd	323-933-7171	7
AMF Southbay Lanes	1515 Hawthorne Blvd	310-371-7521	30
AMF Santa Monica Bay Shore Lanes	234 Pico Blvd	310-399-7731	18
AMF Van Nuys Bowlerland	7501 Van Nuys Blvd	818-989-1610	43
Bowl-O-Drome	21915 S Western Ave	310-328-0133	32
Gable House	22501 Hawthorne Blvd	310-378-2265	31
Lucky Strike Lanes	Hollywood & Highland Mall	323-467-7776	4
Jewel City Bowl	135 S Glendale Ave	818-243-1188	47
Pickwick Bowling	921 W Riverside Dr	818-845-5300	46
Shatto 39 Lanes	3255 W Fourth St	213-385-9475	8

Public Golf Courses

Public Golf Courses	Address	Phone	Fee	Map
Alhambra Municipal Golf Course	630 S Almansor St, Alhambra	626-570-5059	$24	39
Alonda Park Golf Course	16400 S Prairie Ave	310-217-9915	$21-27	30
Arroyo Seco Golf Course	1055 Lohman Ln, S Pasadena	323-255-1506	$12	34
Brookside Golf Club	1133 Rosemount Ave, Pasadena	626-796-0177	$40	34
Chester Washington Golf Course	1930 W 120th St, Hawthorne	323-756-6975	$21-27	25
De Bell Municipal Golf Course	1500 E Walnut Ave, Burbank	323-845-5052	$20-25	46
Sepulveda/Encino Golf Course	16821 Burbank Blvd, Encino	818-995-1170	$25	42
Harding Municipal Golf Course	4730 Crystal Springs Dr, Los Feliz	323-663-2555	$23	4
Los Feliz Golf Course	3207 Los Feliz Blvd, Los Feliz	323-663-7758	$5	5
Penmar Golf Course	1233 Rose Ave, Venice	310-396-6228	$12	21
Rancho Park Golf Course	10460 W Pico Blvd, West LA	323-838-7373	$23	23
Roosevelt Municipal Golf Course	2650 N Vermont Ave, Los Feliz	323-665-2011	$13	4
Van Nuys Golf Course	6550 Odessa Ave, Van Nuys	818-785-3685	$18	43
Westchester Golf Course	6900 W Manchester Ave, Westchester	310-670-5110	$17	26
Wilson Municipal Golf Course	4730 Crystal Springs Dr, Los Feliz	323-663-2555	$21-25	4

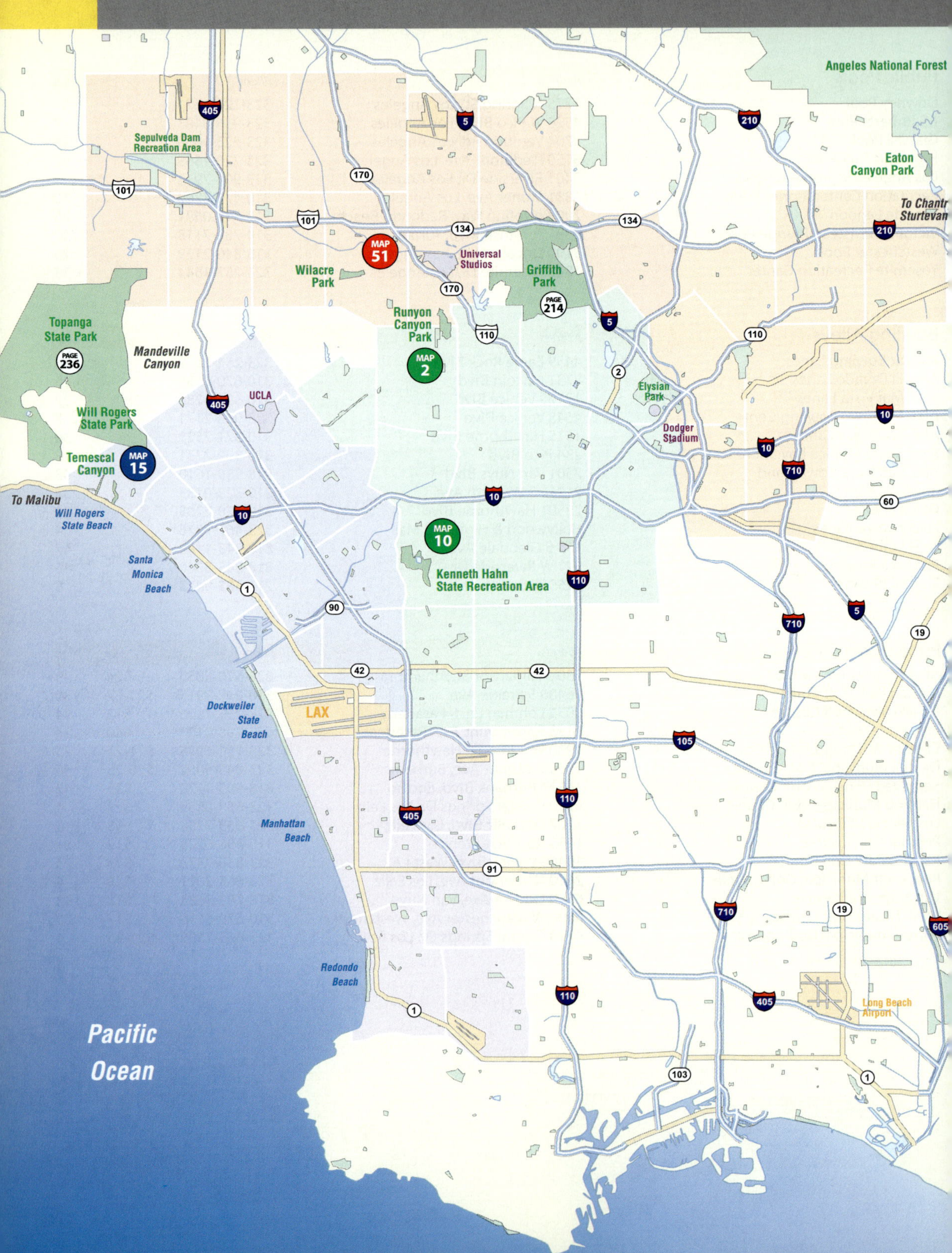
Angeles National Forest
Sepulveda Dam Recreation Area
Eaton Canyon Park
To Chantr Sturtevan
Wilacre Park
MAP 51
Universal Studios
Griffith Park
PAGE 214
Runyon Canyon Park
MAP 2
Topanga State Park
PAGE 236
Mandeville Canyon
Elysian Park
Dodger Stadium
Will Rogers State Park
UCLA
Temescal Canyon
MAP 15
To Malibu
Will Rogers State Beach
Santa Monica Beach
MAP 10
Kenneth Hahn State Recreation Area
Dockweiler State Beach
LAX
Manhattan Beach
Redondo Beach
Long Beach Airport
Pacific Ocean

Overview

Johnny Carson once said that you know it's springtime in Burbank when they replace the brown plastic shrubbery with green plastic shrubbery. In reality, however, Los Angeles does have its fair share of nature—unfortunately, you often have to drive to it. But you don't always have to drive very far and, depending on where you live, there just might be a hiking trail in your own backyard. Literally. From the beachside cliffs of Malibu to the snow-capped mountains of the Angeles National Forest, there is a path for everyone, whether you're looking for a relatively quick way to unwind after a long day of work or you're prepared to spend an entire day pushing yourself to the top of the mountain.

An excellent source of information about various trails is the book, *Afoot and Afield in Los Angeles County*, by Jerry Schad (Wilderness Press). The Sierra Club also sponsors a series of regularly scheduled hikes around the greater Los Angeles area, which can be a great way to meet other hikers and learn the terrain. Check their website, *http://www2.angeles.sierraclub.org/angelestrips/rtrips.htm*, for schedules and more information. In the meantime, here are just some of the walks that we recommend:

West Hollywood

Runyon Canyon Park
Enter from either Fuller or Vista Streets, just north of Franklin Ave. Parking is available on neighboring streets, but check the signs for restrictions. This is the perfect early morning or after-work hike—it's only 1 to 2 miles and can be done in an hour. If the main path isn't enough of a workout for you, veer left just after the gates near the Vista entrance. This challenging, mostly uphill climb will give you a solid workout. Runyon Canyon also gets extra points for its off-leash policy for canine hikers.

Hollywood

Mount Lee (AKA, the Hollywood Sign)
Drive up Beachwood Canyon to Hollyridge Drive. Hollyridge Trail will take you up to the summit of Mount Lee, where you can look down from behind (and just above) the letters of the Hollywood sign. The round trip is approximately three miles. Parking is free, but be courteous to the area's residents.

Griffith Park

Fern Dell/Mt. Hollywood
Enter Griffith Park from Los Feliz Blvd. by turning left at Fern Dell Drive. As you might expect from its name, Fern Dell is rich in plant life. The area gets a lot of shade and its relatively flat terrain makes it a popular choice for families out hiking. But continue across the observatory road and you will soon find your way to the top of Mount Hollywood, which offers a lovely view of the Hollywood sign, as well as the smog over downtown. Ah, nature. Expect to spend about two hours, as long as you keep up a brisk pace.

Dante's View
Begin this dog-friendly hike in the parking lot for the Griffith Park Observatory, and you will eventually (the entire hike is only 2.25 miles) reach Dante's View, a garden originally planted by Dante Orgolini, who reportedly began the garden in 1964 after a failed marriage. Mr. Orgolini has passed on, but his garden is still tended by volunteers.

Baldwin Hills

Kenneth Hahn State Recreation Area
This park, located at 4100 S. La Cienega Blvd., features 7 miles of trails for hiking, from the Bowl Loop (just 0.8 miles) to the 2.6-mile Ridge Trail.

Pacific Palisades

Will Rogers State Park
The most popular walk at this park, located just north of Sunset Blvd., is to the idyllic sounding Inspiration Point. The hike is easy—almost too easy—and can be done in one hour, round trip. But the view—to Catalina, on a clear day—is lovely and makes for a nice change of pace.

Temescal Canyon
Head north at the intersection of Sunset Blvd. and Temescal Canyon Road, and park at Gateway Park. Once inside, you have the option of two trails—Canyon or Ridge—but be sure to follow the trail markers for the appropriately named Skull Rock, which is this hike's must-see. This is a moderate hike, and the round trip is approximately 5 miles.

Brentwood

Mandeville Canyon
From Sunset Blvd., go north on Mandeville Canyon until you reach Garden Land Road, and find street parking. A fire road takes you to the Nike Missile Site, which has been turned into a park, with restrooms and drink machines. The hike starts off as a challenge but eventually levels off a bit. It can be done in its entirety in just under two hours.

Pasadena/San Gabriel Valley

Chantry Flat/Sturtevant Falls
Take the 210 to Santa Anita Avenue and head north. Follow the road up the mountain and use the parking lot at Chantry Flat. From the parking lot, the 3.4-mile round trip to Sturtevant Falls takes approximately 90 minutes. In addition to the novelty of the actual waterfalls—which are actually pretty cool—your walk will take you past some private cabins nestled in the woods. These buildings look like something out of a fairy tale.

Eaton Canyon Falls
Exit the 210 at Altadena and travel north to the Eaton Canyon Natural Area (just past New York Drive). This hike will also take you to a waterfall, and it's especially friendly for dogs (on leashes) and kids, because of its relatively easy level of difficulty. The trail crosses over a creek several times during the 3.3-mile round trip so you may get wet. Dress accordingly.

Studio City

Wilacre Park
This short but still exhausting hike (2.7 miles) can be finished in about an hour, and is another great walk to save for the end of the day (especially in the hot summer months) or to do with a canine friend (on a leash, unfortunately). Park in the gravel lot at the corner of Laurel Canyon Blvd. and Fryman, and travel up the Dearing Mountain Trail. You will eventually emerge from the canyon in the midst of a residential neighborhood, on Iredell Lane. But follow this street back out to Fryman Road, and turn left to return to the parking lot.

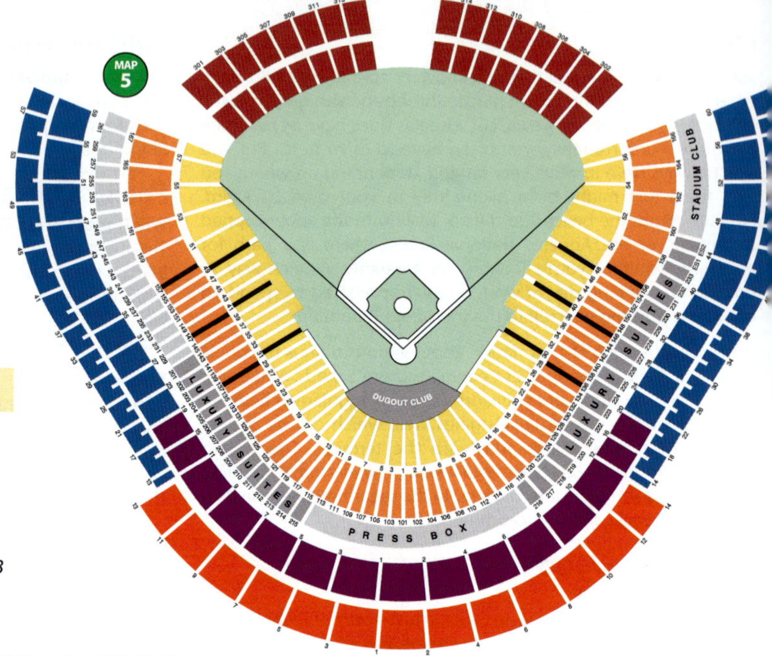

■ Top Deck	■ Loge Level	♿ Top Deck Aisles 3 to 5, 4 to 6
■ Inner Reserved Level	■ Field Level	Reserved Level Aisles 1 to 11, 2 to 12
■ Outer Reserved Level	■ Left and Right Field Pavillion	Loge Level Aisles 143 to 167, 142 to 166
■ Club Level	■ Sold Out	

Practical Information

Location: 1000 Elysian Park Avenue,
Los Angeles, CA 90012
Information and Tickets: 323-224-1HIT
Website: www.dodgers.mlb.com
Season tickets: 1-800-6-DODGER
Dugout Club and Luxury Suites: 323-224-1320
Hearing Disabilities TTY/TDD Line: 323-224-1833
Lost and Found: 323-224-1509
Blue Crew Fan Club: 323-224-1315
NFT Map: 5

How to Get Tickets

You can order Dodgers tickets by phone, through the box office at Dodger Stadium (Monday through Saturday, 8:30 am to 5:30 pm and during all Dodger games), and on the Internet through the Dodgers' website.

Overview

It's been a long time since the Dodgers have won a pennant, but Dodger Stadium remains one of the simplest and most beautiful places to watch a ballgame. One can almost excuse Walter O'Malley for moving the team out of Brooklyn in 1957. Located just a stone's throw from the Police Academy, Dodger Stadium lacks the bells and whistles of some of today's newer stadiums or the history of Fenway Park or Yankee Stadium. The rolling hills and palm trees of Chavez Ravine are particularly lovely at sunset. Top off the view with a Dodger Dog and an It's It ice cream sandwich—the chocolate-covered oatmeal cookie/ice cream concoction that replaced the much beloved Cool-A-Coo several seasons ago—and another loss by the Dodgers doesn't seem so bad.

How to Get There—Driving

From the 101 freeway: Exit Alvarado, go north, then turn right on Sunset. Go approximately one mile and turn left on Elysian Park Avenue. You will run into Dodger Stadium.
From the 110 freeway: Take the Dodger Stadium exit and go straight off the off-ramp.
From the 5 freeway (south): Exit Stadium Way, then turn left and follow the baseball signs until you enter Dodger Stadium off of Academy Road.
From the 5 freeway (north): Exit Stadium Way and turn left on Riverside Drive. Turn left onto Stadium Way and follow the baseball signs until you enter Dodger Stadium off of Academy Road.
From LAX: Take the 105 freeway (east) to the 110 freeway (north). Take the Dodger Stadium exit and go straight off the off-ramp.

From Burbank Airport: Get on the 5 freeway (south). Exit Stadium Way, then turn left and follow the baseball signs until you enter Dodger Stadium off of Academy Road.

Whenever possible, use surface roads. Sunset Boulevard is particularly convenient and will take you from as far west as the Pacific Ocean right to Elysian Park Avenue. Beverly Boulevard is often less congested—and more direct—than the sometimes-curving Sunset Blvd. Take Beverly to Alvarado, then head north on Alvarado until you reach Sunset Blvd., then turn right and take Sunset to Elysian Park Ave.

Parking

General parking for cars and motorcycles is $8 and parking is permitted in any unreserved parking area. Parking for large vehicles, including buses, motor homes, limousines, and other oversized vehicles is $25. Those vehicles are required to park in Lot 7.

How to Get There—Mass Transit

Mass transit is really not a great option for getting to Dodger Stadium. If you really have no other way of getting there, take bus line 2, 3 or 4 and get off at Sunset/Innes. The best part of the journey is the last leg—a three-quarter mile walk to the stadium up a steep hill! Look on the bright side though, you'll be walking downhill on the way home...

If you take a cab to the game and you plan to depart from the stadium by cab, a taxi service is available in Lot 3 on the western side of the stadium or at the Union 76 Service Station near Lot 37 beyond the center field wall.

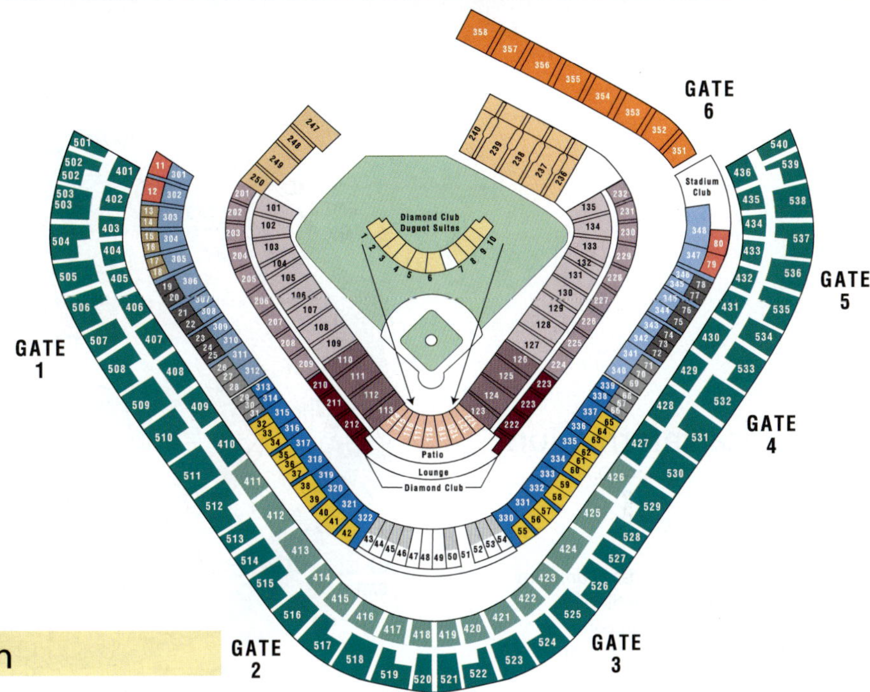

Practical Information

Location: 200 Gene Autry Way,
Anaheim, CA 92806
Individual Tickets: 714-663-900
Package Tickets: 1-800-796-HALO
Website: www.angels.mlb.com

Overview

We NFT editors have to give the Angels their props—not only did they finally make it to the World Series in 2002, but they won, beating our beloved New York Yankees in the process. And how has the Angels' parent company, Disney, rewarded their team for such greatness? By selling them, of course. Truth be told, Disney lost interest in the Angels years ago, after springing for a much needed (and well received) refurbishment of Anaheim Stadium that turned the outfield into something that looks like it's been relocated from Disneyland's Critter Country. Few Angels fans will be sorry to see Disney go. Now if only they could do something about that Rally Monkey...

How to Get There—Driving

From downtown: Take 605 south, take the CA-91/Artesia Freeway east, and take the I-5/Santa Ana Fwy. exit on the right towards Santa Ana. Merge onto I-5 south, take the exit on the right towards Anaheim Blvd./Haster St./Katella Ave. Turn left onto W. Freedman Way, turn right onto S. Anaheim Blvd., and turn left onto E. Katella Ave.

Parking

The parking lot opens two-and-a-half hours prior to the start of the scheduled first pitch, and since there are only three entrances to the Edison Field parking lot, (via Douglass Road, State College Boulevard, and Orangewood Avenue), we suggest you get there early. Parking staff will direct you towards vacancies. Day-of-game parking is $8 and oversized vehicles (greater than 20 feet in length) are $16.

The bus parking lot is located by the Orangewood Avenue entrance. Season ticket holders with parking coupons can use the Express Entry Lane on Orangewood Avenue.

How to Get There—Mass Transit

If you can get yourself to Union Station (Metro Red Line), you can take the Amtrak Surf Line bound for San Diego, which stops not too far from the Big Ed at Anaheim Station. A one-way fare will set you back $8, and the Orange County Transportation Authority has a bus service to the ballpark. Call 800-636-RIDE for more information on bus schedules.

But unless you're watching a pitchers' duel or a complete blowout, the train may not be an option for most night games. The last train back to LA leaves Anaheim just after 10 pm, making an overnight stay in beautiful downtown Anaheim a definite possibility.

Patrons that require a taxi service from Edison Field can swing by the Guest Relations Center and ask a concierge to call them a taxi.

How to Get Tickets

You can purchase tickets in person at the Box Office, which is open Monday through Saturday from 9:00 am to 5:30 pm and Sundays (game days only) 9:00 am to 5:30 pm, by phoning the box office or online through Ticketmaster, which can be reached from the Angels' website or at *www.ticketmaster.com.*

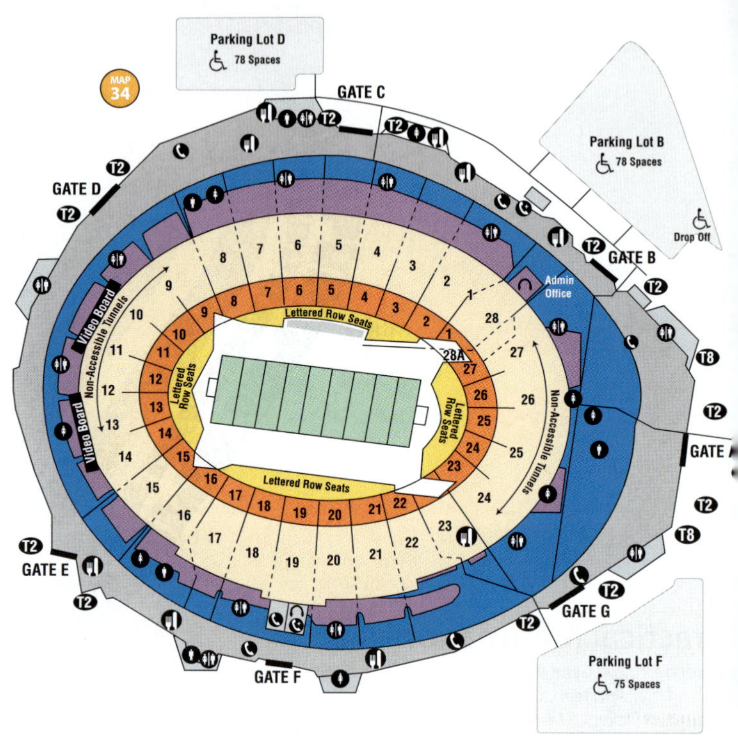

Practical Information

Location: 1001 Rose Bowl Drive,
Pasadena, CA 91103
Phone: 626-577-3100
Suites: 626-577-3171
Website: www.rosebowlstadium.com
Tournament of Roses website:
www.tournamentofroses.com
Rose Bowl Tickets: 213-365-3550
Rose Parade Grandstand Tickets:
626-795-4171
LA Galaxy Soccer website: www.lagalaxy.com
LA Galaxy Soccer tickets: 1-877-3GALAXY
UCLA website: www.uclabruins.com
UCLA tickets: 310-825-2101
Flea Market: 323-560-7469
NFT Map: 34

Overview

The Rose Bowl Stadium is the largest stadium in Southern California, seating almost 100,000, and is most famous for the New Year's Day face-off between the Big 10 and Pac 10 champs. The stadium is also home to the Galaxy soccer team and the UCLA Bruins football team, along with the occasional Eagles concert or Lilith Fair. But it's possible that the Rose Bowl's most popular event is the monthly swap meet, held on the second Sunday of each month. This flea market takes over the entire complex, with new products (like beef jerky and household goods) sold within the stadium's gates, while an adjacent parking lot turns into the world's largest garage sale. Serious shoppers arrive at dawn, and few go home empty-handed.

How to Get There—Driving

There is one major consideration you need to take into account when driving to the Rose Bowl—AVOID the Pasadena Freeway 110. The best approaches to the stadium are the Pasadena 210 Freeway. Take the Mountain/Seco/Arroyo Blvd./Windsor exit and follow signs to the stadium. If you approach on the 134 freeway, exit at Linda Vista and follow signs. A less congested alternative if you're coming from the west is to take 134 to Glendale Freeway (2) north then take 210 freeway east to Pasadena and exit at Mountain/Seco/Arroyo Blvd./Windsor.

Parking

There are 20,000 parking spaces available at the Rose Bowl Stadium. Parking for UCLA games is $5 for cars, $10 for motor homes/limousines and no charge for buses. At Galaxy soccer games, it's $5 for cars, $20 for motor homes/limousines and $20 for buses. The cost of parking for cars at the Rose Bowl is $15 and $30 on game day. For limo and bus parking information call 626-397-4220. For RV parking prior to day of game call 626-577-3101. For the Rose Parade, paid parking is available on a first-come, first-served basis at various lots and parking structures near the parade route, including locations at Boston Court/Mentor, Union/El Molino, Euclid/Union, Raymond/Union, 40 North Mentor/Lake, 465 East Union near Los Robles, 44 South Madison near Green, 462 East Green near Los Robles, and Colorado/Los Robles.

How to Get There—Mass Transit

There are no city buses or trains that stop near the stadium.

How to Get Tickets

Tickets to the Rose Bowl, Rose Parade, UCLA games, and Galaxy soccer games are all available online through the individual websites and phone numbers listed above.

Practical Information

*Location: 1111 S Figueroa Street,
Los Angeles, CA 90015
Website: www.staplescenter.com
Staples Center Box Office: 213-742-7340
Staples Center Parking: 213-742-7275
LA Sparks website: www.lasparks.com
LA Sparks phone: 877-44-SPARKS
LA Lakers website: www.lakers.com
LA Lakers phone: 213-480-3232
LA Clippers website: www.clippers.com
LA Clippers phone: 213-742-7555
LA Kings website: www.lakings.com
LA Kings phone: 1-888-KINGS-LA
LA Avengers website: www.laavengers.com
LA Avengers phone: 888-AVENGERS
NFT Map: 9*

Overview

The Staples Center is located in downtown Los Angeles near the intersection of the 10 (Santa Monica) and 110 (Harbor) freeways. The Los Angeles Convention Center's North Hall was demolished in 1998 to make room for construction of the Staples Center, and an astounding 98% of the former building was recycled for other uses rather than being used in landfill. On September 4, 2001, the Los Angeles City Council approved a development plan for the LA Sports & Entertainment District (LASED) adjacent to Staples Center. The proposed development, which includes four million square feet next to the Staples arena, will incorporate two hotels, shops, restaurants, live theatre, housing, an open air plaza, and an expansion of the Convention Center.

Though Staples Center was named "Arena of the Year" in January 2001, it's actually an illustration of LA's class struggle at its ugliest. The arena has been criticized by sports fans and concertgoers for its somewhat elitist layout. The hall features a large number of luxury "sky boxes" that are actually located just behind the first tier of seats, making a good seat hard to come by for the average ticket holder—who typically winds up in the nosebleed seats. But since the Lakers, Clippers, Kings, Sparks, and Avengers all call Staples Center home, most LA sports fans are forced to make the best of the situation. Love it or hate it, Staples is quickly becoming a catalyst for a revitalization of the downtown area.

How to Get There—Driving

The best advice we can offer is to get off of the freeway as soon as possible and make your way to Olympic Boulevard. If you're coming from the north, take I-5 S (or 101 S) to 110 S (Harbor Fwy/Los Angeles). Exit at Olympic Boulevard and turn left onto 11th Street. Continue past Cherry Street and Georgian Street and the Staples Center is on the right. From the south, take the 110 N and exit at Adams Boulevard. Turn left onto Figueroa Street, then make another left at 11th Street.

Parking

Parking Lot 2 opens at 8 am for guests visiting the Box Office, Fox Sports Sky Box, or Team LA store. Parking Lots 1 & 3 open two-and-a-half hours prior to the start of an event. The remaining lots open 90 minutes prior to the start of an event. However, the lots at Staples Center are overpriced, and many are available only to VIPs and season ticket holders. If you're willing to arrive a little early for an event and walk a few blocks, there is a fair amount of parking available on neighboring streets. Easy in, easy out, and best of all—it's free!

How to Get There—Mass Transit

The best form of public transport to the Staples Center is the Metro Rail. Take the Blue Line to Pico and the stadium is just a block away. Buses 27, 28, 30, 31, 33, 81, 333, 434, 439, 442, 444, 445, 446, and 447 also stop near the stadium.

How to Get Tickets

Tickets for the Sparks (WNBA), Lakers (NBA), Clippers (NBA), Kings (NHL), and Avengers (Arena) can all be purchased online through Ticketmaster at www.ticketmaster.com (213-480-3232) or through the individual websites and phone numbers listed above.

Practical Information

Location: 2695 East Katella Avenue,
 Anaheim, CA 92806
Admin Phone: 714-704-2400
Box Office Phone: 714-704-2500
Group Sales: 714-704-2420
Website: www.arrowheadpond.com
Email: contactus@arrowheadpond.com
Might Ducks Website: www.mightyducks.com

Overview

Located in Anaheim, Arrowhead Pond is home to the NHL Mighty Ducks of Anaheim and regularly hosts a variety of sporting, music, and family shows throughout the year, including the Expanets John R. Wooden Classic and Fight Night, World Wrestling, circuses, and the Harlem Globetrotters.

How to Get There—Driving

From Los Angeles, take 405 South to 22 East to 57 North. Exit on Katella Avenue, turn right, then turn left on Douglas St. If you're approaching on I-5 South, exit on Katella Avenue. Turn left onto Katella Avenue then left on Douglas St. From I-10 head east to 57 South and exit on Katella Avenue. Turn left then turn left on Douglas St.

From Orange County, take 405 North to I-5 North to 57 North. Exit on Katella Avenue and turn right, then make a left on Douglas St. From the 22 East/West take 57 North. Exit on Katella Avenue, turn right, then left on Douglas St. Take the 55 North to 22 West to 57 North. Exit on Katella Avenue and turn right. Turn left on Douglas St.

Parking

Parking for Ducks home games is $8 day-of-game, $8 per game for season parking, and $12 per game for preferred parking (sold on a season basis only). The costs for other events at the Pond vary, but generally the fees are $10 for general parking, $16 preferred parking (if available), $16 limos & RVs, $20 bus, and $25 bus shuttle (unlimited drop-off and pick-up for an event). Call 714-704-2400 (Ogden) for accurate fees for each event.

How to Get There—Mass Transit

The Orange County Transit Authority provides transport to Arrowhead Pond. Check www.octa.net for schedules or phone 714-636-RIDE or 1-800-636-RIDE from South Orange County, Riverside, and Corona. In addition to OCTA, there is also an Amtrak station located within walking distance of the arena in the parking lot at Edison International Field. But do consult a schedule before taking Amtrak down to Anaheim. Their trains are somewhat limited, particularly at night, when a hockey game or event might be letting out.

How to Get Tickets

You can get tickets from the box office, Ticketmaster outlets, or online at ticketmaster.com. The box office is open Monday to Friday 10 am until 6 pm and Saturday 10 am until 4 pm. It is also open Sunday 3 hours prior to an event, but only selling tickets for that event. A "wristband lottery" for any remaining tickets to popular events takes place the morning of the event with line-ups beginning at 7 am, wristband distribution at 8 am, number drawing at 9:45 am, and on-sale beginning at 10 am. This system was put in place to stop scalping and to give everyone a fair chance to be first in line.

There is something quintessentially Los Angeles about the Beverly Center. It is probably the best known and (as the crow flies) most centrally located mall in town. There is also a feeling of upbeat Hollywood professionalism about it, probably because many film/TV/video stylists and wardrobe persons shop it for work. Since The Grove opened its doors just a little ways down the street, the Beverly Center has become something of a ghost town. But as long as there are Angelenos who shop, there will always be—for better or worse—a Beverly Center.

Shopping

The Beverly Center serves mid- to upper-mid-range shoppers with fairly tony clothing and housewares options. But despite the cushiness of Pottery Barn, Williams-Sonoma, and Bang & Olufsen, the mall really has an all-girls clubhouse feel to it. The major aspects of girly enterprise are well covered: make-up (in addition to the department store cosmetic counters, there are M.A.C. and stila boutiques); lingerie (Atmosphere, Victoria's Secret); two-piece bathing suits (Everything But Water); and flirty dresses (Betsey Johnson, Shaya, Laundry). It also delivers with some help from some off-the-beaten-path mall players: the Armani Exchange, D&G, Diesel, and Hugo Boss. It is a great place to buy presents for anyone, including yourself. It is hard not to be inspired by See's and Godiva Chocolates, the Mont Blanc and Aveda stores, or Jennifer Kaufman (jewelry) and the Belgravia Collection.

Food

The eighth floor features a small collection of adequate options. Rubio's Baja Grill and A&W add variety to the usual food court line-up. Outside seating is plentiful, non-smoking, and features an almost-panoramic eastern view of the city. For a more neighborhoody feel, head on foot to Who's On Third (8369 W. Third, near Kings Road), a friendly breakfast and lunch joint with good eggs and a handful of sidewalk tables.

Drawbacks

This is a popular mall in a busy part of town; it is bordered by another mall (the Beverly Connection), and a huge medical center (Cedars-Sinai). That's why it's a good idea to enter from the San Vicente (westernmost and least-congested) side of the building. And although traffic flows well inside the mall, traffic in the parking lot does not. Stay cool, knowing the good stuff's waiting upstairs. The Cineplex Odeon now shows those movies rejected by the theaters at The Grove, and the theaters here are tiny. And no matter how spectacular the view from the rooftop seating, the food court choices just aren't very tempting.

How to Get There

From the 10 in either direction, exit La Cienega Blvd. Head north on La Cienega approximately two-and-a-quarter miles, and you will see the behemoth just ahead on your left. Cross Third Street, and turn left into the mall at the next signal.

From the 101 in either direction, exit Highland Blvd. and head south on Highland approximately 2 miles until Beverly Blvd. Turn right onto Beverly, and head west about two miles to La Cienega. Make a left onto La Cienega, and an immediate right into the mall.

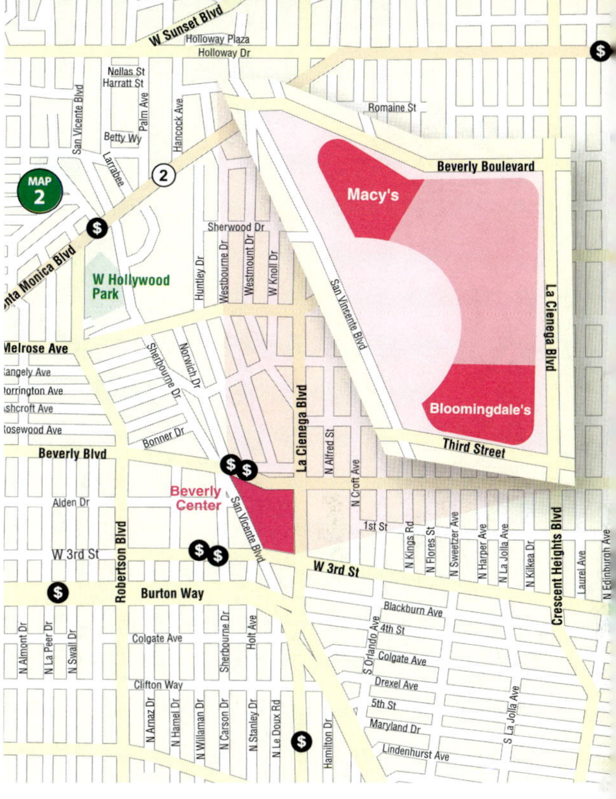

Department Stores

- Bloomingdale's
- Macy's

Apparel

General
- AIX Armani Exchange
- Banana Republic
- Club Monaco
- D&G
- Diesel
- DKNY
- Everything But Water
- French Connection
- Gap
- Guess?
- Lucky Brand Jeans
- Timberland
- Tommy Hilfiger
- Wilsons Leather

Men's
- B2
- Bernini
- Bernini Sport
- BOSS Hugo Boss
- HUGO Hugo Boss
- Macy's Men's Store
- Politix
- Traffic
- Y.M.L.A.

Women's
- Ann Taylor
- Arden B
- Atmosphere Lingerie
- bebe
- Betsey Johnson
- Cache
- Express
- Fitelle
- Here
- Issi
- Max Studio
- Obzee
- Politix Women
- Privilege
- Rampage
- Shaya
- Traffic Studio
- Vertigo
- Victoria's Secret
- Wet Seal
- What Lies Beneath
- XXI Forever

Shoes

- Agatha Paris
- Aldo
- Charles David
- Foot Locker
- Lady Footlocker
- Louis Vuitton
- Nine West
- Skechers
- Steve Madden
- Timberland

Jewelry & Accessories

- Adrienne Vittadini
- Agatha Paris
- Bailey, Banks & Biddle
- Belgravia Collection
- Eldorado Watch Company
- Jacqueline Jarrot
- Jennifer Kaufman
- Le Cadeau
- Swatch
- Watch Station

Children's & Toys

- Baby Gap
- Brooks Shoes for Kids
- Gap Kids
- Guess? Kids
- Gymboree
- Sanrio

Electronics & Entertainment

- Bang & Olufsen
- Bose
- Nextel

Home Furnishings

- Bed, Bath & Beyond
- Breaking the Mold Candle Co.
- Pottery Barn
- Restoration Hardware
- William-Sonoma Grande Cuisine
- Z Gallerie

Health & Beauty

- Aveda
- Bath & Body Works
- Carlton Hair International
- General Nutrition Center
- H2O Plus
- Kristy-The Beauty Store
- M.A.C.
- stila cosmetics
- The Body Shop
- Victoria's Secret Beauty

Gifts/Cards/Books

- Brentano's
- Brookstone
- Mont Blanc
- Papyrus

Specialty

Eyewear
- Occhiali da Sole
- Optical Fashion Center
- Optometric Options
- SEE Eyewear
- Solstice
- Sunglass Hut

Luggage
- LeSportsac
- Louis Vuitton
- Sylvie & J
- Tumi

Sporting Goods
- Brooks Shoes for Kids
- Champs Sports
- Everything But Water
- Foot Locker

Miscellaneous
- Bose
- Coach
- Nextel
- Pet Love
- The Discovery Channel Store

Food

- Food Court
  - California Crisp
  - de Euro Cafe
  - Hibachi-San
  - Panda Express
- Rubio's Fresh Mexican Grill
- Sbarro
- The Great Steak & Fry Company
- Tommie's Hamburgers

Restaurants
- California Pizza Kitchen
- Chipotle Mexican Grill
- Grand Lux Cafe
- Hard Rock Cafe
- P.F. Chang's China Bistro
- Rubio's Baja Grill
- Todai
- Ubon
- Vie de France
- Wave

Specialty
- Auntie Anne's
- Coffee Bean & Tea Leaf
- Godiva Chocolatier
- Mrs. Field's Cookies
- Neuhaus Chocolates
- See's Candies
- Starbuck's
- Surf City Squeeze

Services

- Airport Shuttle Service
- California Welcome Center
- Cash Machine
- Guest Services
- Hand Car Wash
- Ritz Camera
- Security Office
- Taxi Service

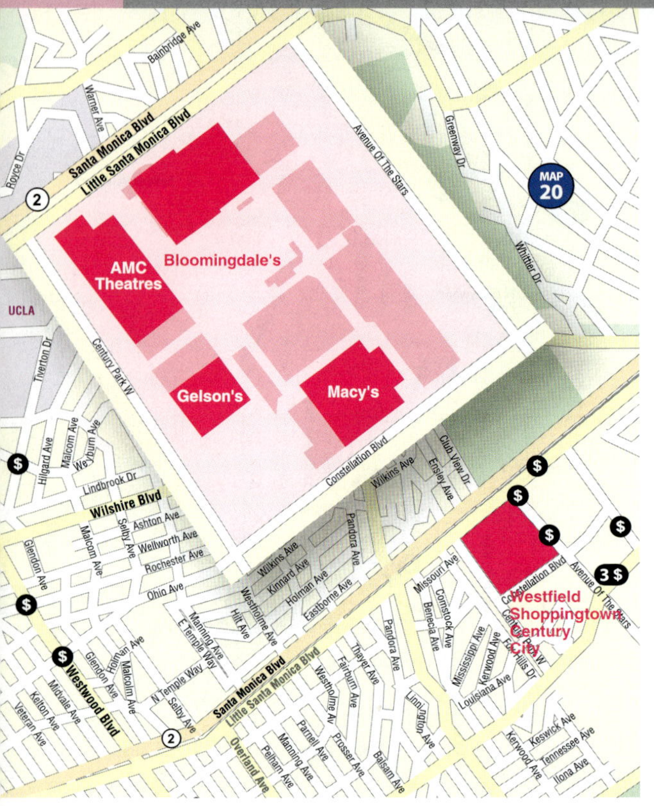

Traffic, smog, earthquakes, and gigantic billboards for bloated action films: these are am[ong] the prices we pay for living in Los Angeles. But the Westfield Shoppingtown Century C[ity] manages to make them all worthwhile. An outdoor, upscale mall blessed with particula[rly] temperate weather, a 14-screen movie theater, and discerning retail, one is hard-presse[d] find a better place to shop or simply to lose oneself for the day. Though the mall may now [be] part of a large corporation, in our hearts and minds it will always be the Century City Shoppin[g] Mall.

Shopping

Set around a gleaming Bloomingdale's, the mall is bright, cheerful, and feels freshly paint[ed]. Even the most familiar mall denizens (Express, Hold Everything, Ann Taylor) have an add[ed] glossy sheen. The Italians have an impressive toehold here: Cottura offers beautiful ha[nd] painted pottery; Occhiali da Sole, high-end sunglasses; and MaxMara is famous for its coa[ts]. Tiffany's offers jewelry and a few sterling silver novelty items—for their full line, go to [the] Beverly Hills store. Brooks Brothers and Cole-Haan strike a nice patrician chord. Shaya is a sm[all] women's boutique with one-of-a-kind accessories and clothes. Between Restoration Hardw[are], Crate & Barrel, and the Bloomingdale's housewares department, bridal registries are cover[ed]. Recently arrived is the Wolford store, home of fabulous hosiery. Brentano's Books is thorou[gh], highly browsable, and features weekly readings and book signings.

Food

Lots of outdoor seating and a nice variety of cuisines await you. Gulen's Mediterranean a[nd] Tacone wraps are both good. The teriyaki chicken bowls are always popular at Kisho-An, a[nd] Johnny Rockets may be the most reliable, albeit the greasiest, place to take the kids. The cof[fee] cart near the Discovery Channel store has good coffee and kind service. Houston's is great [for] a before- or after-movie dinner, but keep an eye on the time (see "Drawbacks" below), as th[ere] is often a long wait.

Drawbacks

The Macy's is smallish and in need of cheering up. Go for the seasonal sales and the mensw[ear], and while you're at that end of the mall, go to the Metropolitan Museum of Art store. Weeke[nd] parking is a beast. Period. Arrive by noon, or consider valet parking (at Gelson's, if you will [be] spending at least $25 there, or on the Santa Monica Blvd. side). Another option is to have y[our] car washed at Walker Detail while you shop: $12 including tip and worth every penny. They[']re on parking Level B. Once the free parking limit is exceeded (three hours free; four with A[MC] Theater validation), the parking fees start racking up quickly and can result in considera[ble] sticker-shock.

How to Get There

From the 405 in either direction, exit Santa Monica Blvd. and head east on Santa Mon[ica] Blvd. past Sepulveda, make a slight jog right onto Little Santa Monica Blvd., and follo[w] approximately one-and-a-half miles to the mall. The entrance is on your right just past Cen[tury] Park.

From Olympic Blvd in either direction, head north on Avenue of the Stars to Constellat[ion]. Turn left on Constellation and look for the parking entrance 150 yards down on your right[.]

Department Stores
Bloomingdale's
Macy's

Apparel
Men
  Banana Republic Men
  Bernini
  BOSS Hugo Boss
  Dunhill
  Gingiss Formalwear
  Politix
  Structure
General
  Abercrombie & Fitch
  Benetton
  Brooks Brothers
  Gap
  Guess?
  J. Crew
  Speedo Authentic Fitness
  Urban Leather
  Wolford
Women's
  Ann Taylor
  Allen Allen
  Banana Republic Women
  BCBG Max Azria
  Cache
  Eileen Fisher
  Express
  Kimono-Ya
  Lane Bryant
  Laura Ashley
  Louis Vuitton
  M. Cole
  MaxMara
  Mimi Maternity
  Shaya
  Talbots
  Talbots Petites
  Vencci
  Victoria's Secret

Shoes
Charles David
Cole Haan
Foot Locker
Johnston & Murphy
Kenneth Cole
Via Spiga

Jewelry & Accessories
Arva Jewelers
Aura Shop
Connections
Glamour Gear
Landau Costume Jeweller
Mel & Di
Swatch
Tiffany & Co.
Tourneau
ZYL Collections

Children's & Toys
Gap Kids
Kids Music Box
Mille Petites Fleurs
Petit Jardin Children's
  Shoes
Puzzle Zoo Toys
Riginals
Spotlight Tween
The Disney Store
Tutto Bimbi Italy

Electronics & Entertainment
EBX
FYE

Home Furnishings
Casanova Accessories
Cottura
Crate & Barrel
Pottery Barn
Restoration Hardware

Health & Beauty
Aveda
Century Nail Design
Crabtree & Evelyn
Glamour Gear
Great Earth Vitamins
Horton & Converse
  Pharmacy
Kristy Beauty Supply
L'Occitane
Origins
The Body Shop

Gifts/Cards/Books
Gifts
  Discovery Channel Store
  Get Personal
  Illuminations
  Metropolitan Museum of
    Art Store
Cards
  Card Fever
  Morrow Luxury Stationers
Books
  Brentano's
  Century City News
  Rand McNally

Specialty
Eyewear
  Century City Optometry
  Occhiali da Sole
  Optical Fashion Center
  Shades of LA
  Sunglass Hut
Luggage
  Bag n' Baggage
  Dooney & Burke
  El Portal Luggage
  J. Hambleton, Ltd.
  Toscani
  Tumi

Sporting Goods
All Pro Sport
Foot Locker
Miscellaneous
  Antiqua
  Casanova Accessories
  Coach
  Flight Centre
  Fortune & Co.
  Get Personal
  Heaven Scent
  Kimono-Ya
  Nature's Touch
  Pashmina by Tina
  Photallica
  ProSports
  Safe Talk
  Shape Up USA
  Stamp, Stamp, Stamp
  The Woofery
  Three Dog Bakery

Movie Theater
AMC Century 14 Theatres

Food
Restaurants
  59th & Lex Café
  Corner Café and Bakery
  Europa Steak and Subs
    Grill
  Great Kahn's Mongolian
    Festival
  Gulen's Mediterranean
    Cuisine
  Gulf Stream Restaurant
  Houston's
  Johnny Rockets
  La Cucina di Capri
  Pasta Bene
  Stage Deli of New York
  Stir Crazy

Fast Food
Baja Fresh
California Crisp
California Roasters
Jody Maroni's
Khyber Express
Panda Express
Tacone Wraps
Wetzel's Pretzels
Specialty
  All American Kosher De[li]
  Ben & Jerry's Ice Cream
  Corner Café and Bakery
  Courtyard Café & Yogur[t]
    Place
  Gelson's Market
  Godiva Chocolatier
  Kelly's Coffee & Fudge
    Factory
  Kisho-An
  See's Candies
  Sorabol
  South Seas
  Yin Yang

Services
Any Time Cleaners
Bank of America ATM
Customer Service
On-Site Car Wash
Parking Office
Raul's Shoe Shine
Security Office
Show Wiz Instant Repai[r]
U.S. Postal Service
Watch Repair/Key Make[r]

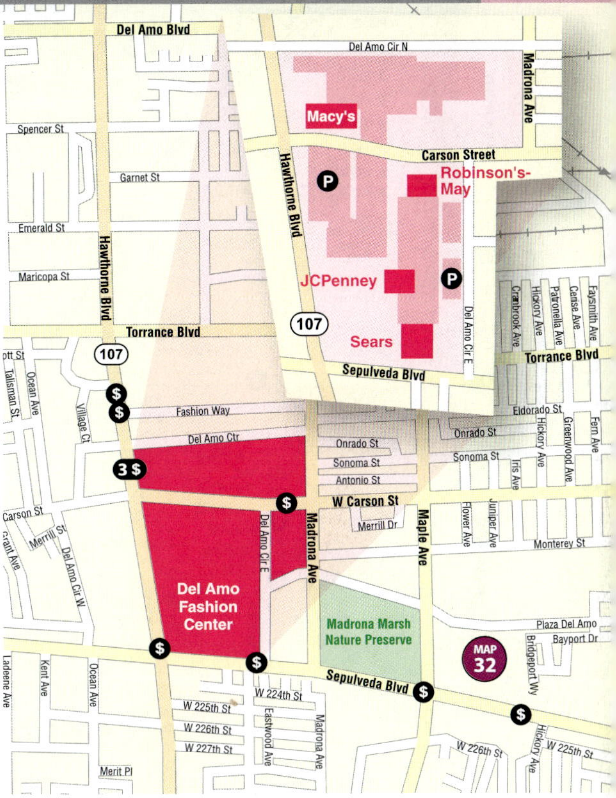

Every mall has a critical mass—a point where its size and its volume of offerings exactly matches the average shopper's ability to absorb them without being crushed under the weight of too many choices. Having exceeded critical mass, the Del Amo Fashion Center in Torrance invites comparisons to black holes and all-you-can-eat shrimp specials. Getting what you need out of it—or simply getting too close to it—may push you past the point of no return.

Shopping

It's easy to pick on the Del Amo Fashion Center just because it's big. But in fairness, Del Amo offers things other malls don't. Most often, discount retailers such as TJ Maxx and Marshall's and Burlington Coat Factory are not found alongside the department stores that sell the same name-brand clothing. Few have Old Navy, Gap, and Banana Republic under one roof. But on this scale, the mall illustrates a larger truth: despite the best efforts of retailers, redundancy is inevitable. Though only one has an auto center, Sears and JC Penney actually offer up a fair amount of overlapping product. So do Robinsons-May and Macy's, Forever 21 and Charlotte Russe, Zu-Topia and Rave Girl, Foot Locker and FootAction. This is where critical mass enters: is this volume worth the physical effort and mental concentration required to tap it? Del Amo is best approached with very comfortable shoes, an open mind, and an extra cup of coffee—from whomever you buy it: Dairy Queen, Starbucks, the Coffee Bean & Tea Leaf, the Universal Coffee Company, or Gloria Jean's Coffee. Shoppers seeking a smaller venue should consider the Galleria at South Bay as an alternate venue.

Food

The International Café is centrally located, and features Mexican, Mediterranean, and Pacific Rim cuisines in addition to fast food offerings such as Chick-Fil-A and Hot Dog On A Stick. The area is clean, brightly lit, and well attended. Vie-de-France offers a quieter alternative if you need to escape the crowd for a few moments. To break up a long expedition, consider going outside the mall. Black Angus and Lucille's Smokehouse BBQ, both adjacent to the mall, offer a chance to protein-load in relatively quieter surroundings.

Drawbacks

Even more than its glandular problem, Del Amo suffers from an often labyrinthine floor plan that makes it hard to see what's ahead. An excess of tile and a lack of natural light give some of the corridors a bunker-like feel. And a mall of this size deserves a full-service, great bookstore: B. Dalton hardly does the job.

How to Get There

From the 405 South, exit Redondo Beach, head east to Prairie Avenue, and take Prairie approximately three miles. Turn right on Carson to enter the parking lot.

From the 405 North, exit Artesia Blvd. and head west on Artesia to Prairie Avenue. Make the left at Prairie and continue on Prairie approximately three miles. Turn right on Carson to enter the parking lot.

From the 110 in either direction, exit Carson, and proceed west three miles on Carson to the Del Amo Fashion Center.

Department Stores

Burlington Coat Factory
JC Penney
Jo-Ann-Etc
Macy's
Macy's Home & Furniture Gallery
Marshall's
Robinsons-May
Sears
TJ Maxx

Apparel

Men
Alfa Moda
Burton's
Caracci for Men
Domani
Gingiss Formal Wear
Mani Gi Italy
Men's Wearhouse
Metropolis
Mr. Big Mr. Tall

General
Aeropostale
American Eagle Outfitters
Banana Republic
Beyond the Beach
Dive N Surf
Gap
Guess?
Old Navy
Liberty Leather
Pacific Sunwear
Wilsons Suede & Leather

Women's
Ames
Ann Taylor
AVENUE
Casual Corner
Charlotte Russe
Express
Forever 21
Frederick's of Hollywood
Lady Bug
Lafayette
Lane Bryant
Lerner New York
Liza Fashions
Mimi Maternity
Motherhood Maternity
Petite Sophisticate
Rampage
Silhouette
St. Michel
Studio Moda
Styles
Tempest
Victoria's Secret
Wet Seal
Windsor Fashion

Shoes

Bakers
Bostonian
Cathy Jean
Famous Footwear
Florsheim Shoes
Foot Locker
FootAction USA
Jarman
Johnston & Murphy
Kids Foot Locker
Lady Foot Locker
Leeds
Naturalizer
Payless Shoe Source
Robert Wayne Footwear
Salvatory
Signature Italia
Stride Rite
Van's
Waltz

Jewelry & Accessories

Crescent Jewelers
Del Time
Fred Meyer Jewelers
Gold & Silver Plus
Kay Jewelers
Kevin Jewelers
Michael's Jewelers
Precise Jewelers
Rain Dance
Robert's Jewelers
Samuel's Jewelers
Sing's Jewelry
Valalan's Jewelers
Watch City
Whitehall Jewelers
Zales Jewelry

Children's & Toys

All Our Children
Anchor Blue kids
Gap Kids
Gymboree
K B Toys
Kids Foot Locker
Limited Too
Old Navy
The Children's Place

Electronics & Entertainment

Aladdin's Castle
Radio Shack
Sam Goody
SunCoast Motion Picture Co.
The Good Guys!

Home Furnishings

Golden Fine Art
Hayes Furniture
Prints Plus

Health & Beauty

Bath & Body Works
Blooming Beauty Supply & Salon
Confetti Hair Place
Del Amo Fashion Wigs
Fifth Avenue Nails
General Nutrition Center
GNC Live Well
MasterCuts
Merle Norman Cosmetics
Michael David and Company
Salon Vivace
The Body Shop
Upstairs Hair D'Sign
Victoria's Secret Body
Vitamin World

Gifts/Cards/Books

Aahs
Barnes & Noble
Carlton Cards
Charlotte's Room
Gift Connection
Lee's Hallmark
Sparrow's Hallmark Shop
Things Remembered

Specialty

Brookstone
Carimar
Claire's Boutique
The Coffee Beanery
Copeland's Sports
The Disney Store
The Franklin Mint
The Game Keeper
Gloria Jean's Coffee Beans
Kensington Luggage
Just Sports
Liberty Leather
Luxury Perfumes
Monogram With Us
Nations Travelstore
P.O.S.E.
Pin City USA
Poetic License
Sanrio Surprises
Starbuck's
Sunglass Hut Watch Station
Topkapi
Travelex
Universal Coffee & Tea Co.

Carts

AT&T Wireless
Bags Galore
Brasco Int.
GameStop
Hair Art
Heavenly Blooms
Heavenly Scents
Home Aromas
I Massage

Kareen's Silver
Kopenhagen Chocolate
LA Fitness
Leather Collection
MCI Worldcom
Memory Lane
Oriental Gifts
Photo Fun
Poetic License
Power Cell
Sun Shades
Total Wireless

Food

Acapulco
Black Angus Restaurant
Burger King
Carl's Jr.
Chick-Fil-A
China Inn
Cinnabon
Dairy Queen/Orange Julius
Del Amo Steak House
Denny's
East Wind
Gengis Khan
Grandma's Old Fashioned Ice Cream
Hometown Buffet
Hot Dog On A Stick
Hot Dogs, Etc.
International House of Pancakes
King Potato
Koo Koo Roo
Lucille's Smoke House BBQ
Mahalo Teriyaki
Mammas Pizzeria of New York
McDonald's
Mediterranean Delight
Mexican Express
Mrs. Fields Cookies
Nacho Fast
Outback Steakhouse

Oven Fresh Pasco Cafe
Pretzel Maker
Sbarro
See's Candies
Sunny's Grille
Sushi Boy
Sweet Factory
Tokyo Grill
Vie De France

Services

Airline Ticket Center
American Express Travel
American Red Cross
Bank of America
Bank of America ATM Center
Continental Airlines
Del Amo Optometry, P.C.
Del Amo Tailors & Alterations
Dr. Robert Weinstein, O.D.
Flight Centre
Fremont Investment
LensCrafters
Lottery Booth
Pacific Union Bank
Pearle Vision
Ritz Camera One Hour Photo
Shoe Doctor
Dr. I.R. Title, Optometrist
Ronald J. Tom, D.D.s. & Assoc.
Torrance Police Comminity
Uni-Foto 1 Hour Photo
United States Post Office
Verizon Wireless
Vogue Shoe Repair
Washington Mutual
Dr. Robert Weinstein, O.D.

All the malls that bear the name "Galleria" are modeled, in theory at least, on the Galleria Vittorio Emmanuele in Milan, a four-story shopping center with a greenhouse-like glass roof that fills the space with light. The Galleria at South Bay is blessed with just such a glass roof. What is more, both Gallerias are pleasant places to spend time, even if you don't have much shopping to do. But only one of them has a Sharper Image, a Skechers store, a 16-theater multiplex, and a Dairy Queen. Along with the high price of transatlantic tickets, these are just a few of the reasons why the Galleria at South Bay is such a solid bet.

Shopping

The anchor stores—Mervyn's, Robinsons-May, and Nordstrom—accurately describe the price range available at the Galleria. The mall manages to strike a nice balance of retail offerings. It is an excellent place to bring your Christmas shopping list or a friend you'd like to treat to something special. Ann Taylor, Lane Bryant, Motherhood Maternity, and Reference serve women in all different sizes, walks of life, and life-stages. (Men in need of suits and serious office attire are best served at Nordstrom and Robinsons-May, and for formalwear, Gary's Tux). Between Abercrombie & Fitch and Up Against The Wall, young hipsters should have their needs meet. Rounding out the mix are a good variety of sporting good and athletic shoe stores, including a Vans store, Champs, and Foot Locker.

Food

The Galleria's food court, the Picnic Place, is a winner. Take the express escalator from the main floor, and grab a table overlooking the fountain in center court. There is a nice range of food options, from Great Khan Mongolian BBQ, to Johnny Rockets, to Napoli Pizza. The place is clean and well tended, though located perilously close to KB Toys. With children regularly going AWOL during the course of lunch, it gets hectic. Be careful as you carry your tray. For table service in a less ricochet-prone setting, eat downstairs at California Pizza Kitchen (CPK) or at Red Robin. For a break off-premises, consider heading to South Bay Bowl (a block south of Mervyn's) to throw some rocks and eat some dogs.

Drawbacks

As with practically everywhere, weekend parking is a hassle. It is five dollars to valet and worth it (valets are near CPK on the east side, and adjacent to Nordstrom on the west). A mall this nice cries out for a more serious bookstore than the B. Dalton presently in place. And, apart from Nordstrom, there isn't a women's shoe store to satisfy serious shoe shoppers. This already pleasant place could be made even more so, if water fountains and restrooms were easier to find.

How to Get There

From the 405 south, exit Redondo Blvd. and head west on Redondo three-quarters of a mile to Hawthorne Blvd. Turn left on Hawthorne; the mall entrance is on your right.
From the 405 north, exit Redondo Blvd. and head west on Artesia approximately three-quarters of a mile to Hawthorne Blvd. Turn left on Hawthorne; the mall entrance is on your right.

Department Stores

Mervyn's
Nordstrom
Robinsons-May

Apparel

Men
Gary's Tux Shop
Mr. Rags
Resari Men's Clothing
Urban Leather
General
Abercrombie & Fitch
Anchor Blue
Banana Republic
Eddie Bauer
Gap
Pacific Sunwear
Up Against the Wall
Women's
Ann Taylor
bebe
Cache
EX Apparel
Express
Forever 21
Lane Bryant
Limited
Motherhood Maturity
Planet Funk
Reference
Victoria's Secret
Windsor Fashion

Shoes

Baker's Shoes
Cassidy's Shoes
Easy Spirit
Enzo Angiolini
Foot Locker
FootAction USA
Journeys
Lady Foot Locker
Milano Shoes
Nine West
Payless Shoe Source
Reflection
Shoe Wiz - Shoe Repair
Skechers
Vans
Walking Company
Walking Store

Jewelry & Accessories

Jewelry
Afterthoughts
Ben Bridge Jewelers
Derano Jewelers
Fast Fix Jewelry Repair
Icing
Jewelry Box
Moonlight
Redondo Beach Watch Company
Silver-R-Us
Tic Time
White Diamond Jewelers
Zales
Watches
The Watch Station

Children's & Toys

The Children's Store
The Disney Store
Gap Kids/Baby Gap
Gymboree
K-B Toys
Kids Foot Locker
Limited Too
Teddy Bear Stuffers
TomKid
Train Dreams

Electronics

Comp USA
Electronics Boutique
Let's Talk Cellular
Phonex Communications
Powercell
Radio Shack
Sam Goody
The Sharper Image
Suncoast Motion Picture Co.
T-Mobile

Home Furnishings

EXPO Design Center
House of Décor
Prints Plus
Select Comfort
Yankee Candle

Health & Beauty

Bath & Body Works
Glamour Beauty Supply & Salon
Glamour Shots
Hair Diamond
Happy Nails & Spa
Luxury Perfumes
ProActiv
Regis Hairstylists
Rite Aid Pharmacy
Vitamin World

Gifts/Cards/Books

American Greetings
B. Dalton Bookseller
Gift World
Sparrow's Hallmark
Spencer Gifts

Specialty

Eyewear
Butterfly Sunshade
Lenscrafters
Sunglass Hut
Sunglass Hut International
Sporting Goods
Champs Sporting Goods
Sports Stop
Sports Treasures
Miscellaneous
Cigar Guy
Custom Sticker Factory
Folks for Folks (folk art)
Heena Boutique
John Robert Powers (modeling)
Leather Collection
Lids
Picture People
Rose Depot
Sticker Photo Booth
Summer Looks
The General Store

Food

Restaurants
California Pizza Kitchen
Great Khan's Mongolian Festival
Johnny Rockets
Red Robin
Tokyo Grill
Fast Food
Arby's
Café Nordstrom
Chck-fil-A
El Pollo Loco
H. Salt Fish & Chips
Hot Dog on a Stick
Kelly's Cajun Grill
McDonald's
Napoli Pizza
Panda Express
Steak Escape
Specialty
Bakker's Cookies
Boba Loca Tea & Coffee
Cinnabon
The Crepe House
Dairy Queen/Orange Julius
Frosty Bites
Godiva Chocolatier
Rocky Mountain Chocolate Factory
Starbucks
Surf City Squeeze
The Sweet Factory
Wetzel's Pretzels

Services

Automatic Phone Booth
Bank of America ATM
Beneficial Financial
California Federal ATM
Consumer Pulse
First Federal Bank ATM
Galleria Alterations
Galleria Dental
Infoplace ATM
Dr. Ivor Meyerson, O.D.
Nordstrom FSB ATM
Ritz Cameras & 1 Hour Photo
Dr. Rojo, O.D.
South Bay Bowling Center
Things Remembered
U.S. Post Office
US Bank ATM

The Glendale Galleria is a very accommodating mall. Not sure what you want? No problem. Know exactly what you want? No problem. On a budget? On a bender? No problem. All are welcome. It serves a broad range of shoppers—families, singles, youngsters, hipsters, and oldsters—and serves them at all different price-points. Whoever you are, odds are that you will find what you need.

Shopping

The Glendale Galleria delivers all the retail food groups, with a few welcome surprises. Make-up and perfume junkies mix with fellow addicts at Sephora. Everything But Water has great women's swimwear (and the Macy's swimwear department is pretty good, too). If you need a dress for the Oscars and Valentino isn't offering you a freebie, check out the formal gowns at Carraz. Solstice has seriously fun sunglasses, and you can pick up an I-Pod and some tunes at the newly opened Apple store. The mall is also peppered with carts selling those things that those carts sell. The best of them is Cactus Graphics (near JC Penney). Turn to them for "Mafia Staff Car" license plate brackets and "Women Want Me/Fish Fear Me" bumperstickers.

Food

The food court meets a variety of needs—Hot Dog On A Stick, La Salsa, Panda Express. Diners are advised to stick with what they know (e.g., slightly puzzling is "LA Italian"—a claim which makes as much sense as "NYC Mexican"). Lisa's Tea Treasures serves a pleasant high tea for those who prefer a leisurely pace. Nordstrom's coffee bar can be a welcomely civil place to take a load off. Glendale has a large Armenian community, and when in the vicinity, it would be a shame not to go to Carousel (340 N. Brand at California) for satisfying Middle Eastern food at friendly prices in a baroque setting.

Drawbacks

The Glendale Galleria is lit like an aquarium—with natural light only available at the entrances. Big as it is, it has neither a movie theater nor a grocery store. The mall is very popular, and foot traffic on the second floor can get bottlenecked, especially on weekends. The layout is long from north to south, making it worth planning ahead to park. If you are visiting only the shops on the Broadway side (Mervyn's, Nordstrom, Macy's), enter the smaller parking lot on Orange south of Broadway. Otherwise, use the main mall parking lot as indicated below. The entrance near McDonald's is almost mid-mall, if you are looking for a parking equidistant from both ends.

How to Get There

From the 5 in either direction, exit Colorado and take Colorado east about a mile-and-a-half. The entrance to the mall parking lot is at a light on the left a hundred or so yards before you get to the intersection at Central.

From the 134 in either direction, exit Central/Brand Blvd. and head south on Brand about a mile-and-a-half. Turn right on Broadway, and head west an eighth of a mile. The entrance to the mall parking lot is at a light on the left about a hundred or so yards after Central. It is marked "Galleria."

Department Stores
JC Penney
Macy's
Mervyn's
Nordstrom
Robinsons-May

Apparel
Men
Bachrach
Gingiss Formal Wear
Jimmy Au's for Men 5'8 & Under
Le Prestige
Quake Sportswear
Structure
General
Abercrombie & Fitch
American Eagle Outfitters
Anchor Blue
Artistic Wear
Banana Republic
Boarder's Sports
Eddie Bauer
Fabiani Leather
Gap
Guess?
Hot Topic
Lids
Lucky Brand Jeans
Mr. Rags
Pro Images
Speedo Authentic Fitness
The Rag Factory
Timberland
Upscale Space
Wilson's The Leather Experts
Women's
Ann Taylor
Arden B
bebe
Cache
Carraz
Casual Corner
Charlotte Russe
Devon Becke
Everything But Water
Express
Forever 21
Fredrick's of Hollywood
J. Jill
Jessica McClintock
Lane Bryant
Lerner New York
Ligali
Motherhood Maternity
Nine West
Privilege
Rampage
Red Eye
Talbots
The Whitehouse & Black Market
Victoria's Secret
Wet Seal
Windsor Fashions

Shoes
Aerosoles
Bakers
Cathy Jean
Charles David
Dominic's
Easy Spirit
Foot Locker
Footaction USA
J. Stephens
Johnston & Murphy
Lady Foot Locker
Naturalizer
Nine West
Nunn Bush Brass Boot
Payless Shoesource
Sam & Libby
Skechers
Steve Madden Shoes
The Athlete's Foot
The Scream Shop
The Walking Company
Vans
Zaza Shoes

Jewelry & Accessories
Afterthoughts
Bailey Banks & Biddle
Ben Bridge Jewelers
Claire's Accessories
Classic Designs Fine Jewelers
Fast Fix Jewelry
Fred Meyer's Jewelry
Helzberg Diamonds
Keeping Time
Landau Collection
McClave Jewelers
Moonlight Silver Jewelry & Accessories
Nothing But Silver
Romano's Jewelers
Solstice
Sunglass Hut
Swatch
Urban America
Whitehall Company Jewelers
Zales

Children's & Toys
Baby Gap
Build-A-Bear Workshop
Gap Kids
Guess? Kids
Gymboree
Janie & Jack
K-B Toys
Kids Foot Locker
Limited Too
Pencil Club
Stride Rite
The Children's Place
The Disney Store
The Right Start
Timberland
Zutopia

Electronics & Entertainment
Apple
Bose
Games Workshop
Planet X
Radio Shack
Renaissance Gallery
Ro's Gallery
Sam Goody
Star Images
Suncoast Motion Picture Company
The Game Keeper
The Wherehouse
Verizon

Home Furnishings
Prints Plus
Select Comfort
The Bombay Company
Williams Sonoma

Health & Beauty
Amore
Aveda
Bath & Body Works
Carlton Hair Int'l
Crabtree & Evelyn
General Nutrition Center
H2O Plus
L'Occitane
Linear Hair
MAC Cosmetics
Sephora
The Body Shop
Victoria's Secret Beauty

Gifts/Cards/Books
Brookstone
Discovery Channel Store
Illuminations
Landau
Mont Blanc
New Wing
Papyrus
Personal Touch
Rand McNally
Rosy's Hallmark
Ruggle's Hallmark
Sanrio Surprises
Successories
Swarovski
The Franklin Mint
The Museum Company
The San Francisco Music Box Company
The Sharper Image
Things Remembered
Thomas Kinkade at Glendale Galleria
Utopia

Specialty
Eyewear
Insight Optometry
Lenscrafters
Optical Fashion Center
Luggage
Kensington Luggage
Sporting Goods
Champs Sports
Miscellaneous
Coach
Custom Images
Pet Love
The Picture People

Food
Food Court
Auntie Anne's Pretzels
Cinnabon
Edo Japan
Fresh Connection
Hawaiian BBQ Express
Hot Dog on a Stick
International Grill
La Cucina By Sbarro
LA Italian Kitchen
La Salsa
McDonald's
Mrs. Fields Cookies
Orange Julius
Pacific Seafood Grill
Panda Express
Pop Thai
Surf City Squeeze
The Steak Escape
Wetzel's Pretzels Juice It Up
Restaurants
Asia Noodle Café
Carl's Jr. Restaurant
Cleo & Cucci
Daphne's Greek Café
Great Kahn's
Red Robin Burger & Spirits Emporium
Todai Restraunt 50 W. Broadway

Specialty
Blue Chip Cookies
Gloria Jean's Coffee Bean
Godiva Chocolatier
Häagen-Dazs
Kelly's Coffee & Fudge Factory
Lisa's Tea Treasures
Muscle Beach Lemonade
See's Candies
Sweet Factory
The Bread Winner

Services
Fast Fix Jewelry Repair
Galleria Shoe Care
Glamour Shots
Glendale Police Substation
JCPenney Hair Salon
JCPenney Optical
JCPenney Photography
Kits Camera One Hour Photo
Mall Security
Photo Perfections
Ritz Camera One Hour Photo
Street Corner News
Tailor Town
Teagle Optometry
Tender Sender Postal Center
Thomas Cook Foreign Exchange

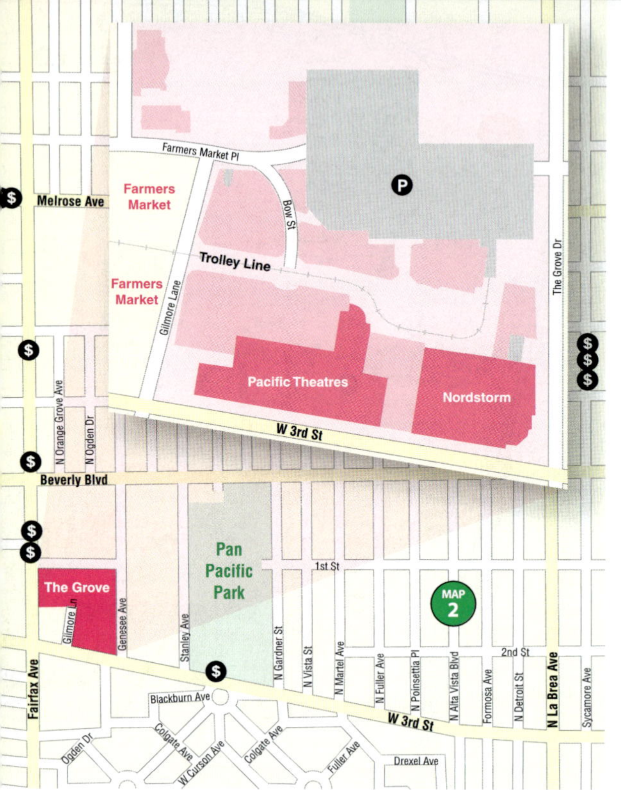

Many of us were outraged when a large section of the 65-year old Farmer's Market was leveled to make way for another shopping mall and vowed to boycott the new mall. But when the Grove opened in March 2002, it was beautiful—and many of its most vocal detractors had to sheepishly admit they were wrong. The Grove is beautiful in that pristine, otherworldly way that only exists in make-believe places like Oz or Las Vegas, to which it has aptly been compared. The mall offers a little something for everyone—eclectic shops, a 14-screen movie theatre, and an old fashioned trolley linking The Grove to the adjacent Farmers Market. The trolley is mainly for atmosphere, but it works on that level. And trust us—the kids love it.

Shopping

The Grove is fairly restrained, with just one anchor store—Nordstrom—and a small one at that. The emphasis here is on high-end specialty stores. Nike Goddess carries fitness wear for women, while Hawk Skateboarding appeals to the extreme sports crowd. This family-friendly mall houses the area's only Pottery Barn Kids and FAO Schwartz. The usual suspects—The Gap and its brethren—are well represented but The Grove also houses the unexpected—Bodega Chocolates, Amadeus Spa, and what might be the mall's most beautifully designed retail store, Anthropologie. And if none of these stores fit your mood there's always Barnes & Noble, which carries books in everyone's size.

Food

We've got good news and bad news. The good news is that the food court doesn't tempt you with typical mall fare. The bad news is that there is no food court at all—only full service restaurants. Lunch or dinner at The Grove is going to cost you. The Farm of Beverly Hills offers American comfort food, while the Wood Ranch BBQ & Grill is a carnivore's paradise. Other sit-down establishments include Madame Wu's Bistro (Chinese) and Maggiano's Little Italy (Italian), and there are a handful of specialty kiosks, like Haägen-Dazs and Surf City Squeeze. Our advice: Head for the Farmers Market and its eclectic food court. The Gumbo Pot features the best muffelata this side of N'awlins and there's no better place for breakfast than Kokomo.

Drawbacks

The lack of affordable places to eat can be a drag, and traffic has indeed been a problem. Third Street gets congested, and the traffic light at Beverly Blvd. and The Grove Drive is so poorly timed that two cars are lucky to advance on a green light.

How to Get There

From the 10 in either direction: Exit at Fairfax and head north approximately three miles. Go through the intersection at Third and Fairfax and turn right at Farmers Market Way. Drive past the Farmers Market and enter The Grove's parking structure.

From the 101 in either direction: Exit at Highland and head south toward Franklin Avenue. Turn right onto Franklin, and continue until you hit La Brea Ave. Make a left turn and continue south on La Brea, to Third Street. Turn right onto Third Street, and continue until you reach The Grove Drive. Make a right turn into the mall.

Parking at The Grove is $1 for the first three hours.

Apparel

General
- Abercrombie & Fitch
- Banana Republic
- Gap
- J. Crew
- Lucky Brand Dungarees
- Max Nugus Haute Couture
- Pacific Sunwear
- Tommy Bahama

Women's
- Anthropologie
- Arden B.
- Chico's
- M. Frederic
- Reference
- Victoria's Secret

Shoes

- Nike Goddess
- Nordstrom

Jewelry & Accessories

- Ice Accessories
- Paragon Watch Company
- Siany

Children's & Toys

- Baby Gap/Gapkids
- FAO Schwartz
- Janie & Jack
- Pottery Barn Kids

Electronics & Entertainment

- Apple Computers
- The Grove Pacific Theatre

Home Furnishings

- Anthropologie
- Banana Republic
- Crate & Barrel
- Lucy Zahran & Co

Health & Beauty

- Amadeus Spa
- L'Occitane
- Victoria's Secret

Gifts/Cards/Books

- Barnes & Noble

Specialty

Eyewear
- Optical Fashion Center

Luggage
- The Sak Elliot Lucca

Miscellaneous
- Hawk Skate
- Quicksilver Boardriders Club
- Wentworth Gallery

Food

Restaurants
- Corner Bakery
- Madame Wu's Asian BIstro
- Maggiano's Little italy
- Morels French Steakhouse
- The Farm of Beverly Hills
- Wood Ranch BBQ and Grill

Specialty

- All American Sausage C
- Bodega Chocolates
- Haägen-Dazs
- Nordstrom Café
- Olivers & Co.
- Surf City Squeeze
- Wetzel's Pretzels

Services

- ATMs
- Concierge Desk
- Parking Office
- Security Office
- Transportation
- Valet Parking

More than just a mall, Hollywood & Highland opened in late 2001 to much fanfare. Compared regularly to both the Strip in Las Vegas and the "new" Times Square, it is shiny, well-lit, and family- and pedestrian-friendly. So how does it rate? It's okay. Its state-of-the-art Kodak Theater is home to the Oscars. Much is made about the Oscars "coming back" to Hollywood. (The first Oscars were held across the street in the Roosevelt Hotel. But we digress.) Ultimately, Hollywood & Highland is a gajillion-dollar environment in which tourists can shop and take pictures of each other. So why include it in a book that is specifically not for tourists? Because eventually we all have out-of-town guests on our hands, and it can be hard to convince them that this isn't one of Los Angeles' must-see attractions. It may also be hard to convince those same guests that Halle and Julia don't spend all their free time hanging out there in the off-season.

Shopping
Curiosity seekers will enjoy browsing Louis Vuitton, Celine, and Versace (though buyers of same know to do so in Beverly Hills, where it's nicer). Luxury goods emporium DFS Galleria gets you all the fun of a duty-free shop without an international airline ticket. The Build-A-Bear workshop is a mandatory stop for both plushies and children under 13. And, in the sigh-of-relief category, representation by the Republics of Banana, Gap, and Ann Taylor mean that no man, woman, or child need go a moment longer without a clean tee or flat-front khakis.

Food
There are two food groups at Hollywood & Highland: dessert and everything else. The best desserts are at Cafe Mozart, featuring coffee and sweets in the Viennese style. For everything else, take your out-of-towner to the CPK. It's good people-watching. A clever (and discreet) visitor might be tempted to ride the elevators in the adjacent Renaissance Marriott up to the hotel's rooftop pool, so as to enjoy a spectacular view and a cool drink. This same clever visitor will also feign innocence (or illiteracy) when faced with the "For Hotel Guests Only" signs.

Drawbacks
Once you accept that Hollywood & Highland for what it is (a place to baby-sit children and out-of-towners) there are actually few drawbacks. Except of course, all the other children and out-of-towners who are also visiting and the mind-boggling traffic in the area surrounding the complex. The streets surrounding the place—Highland, Franklin, Orange, and Hollywood—can all get distressingly tangled on weekends. The entrance to the Chinese 6 Theaters (not to be confused with the Chinese Theater next-door) is not well-marked.

How to Get There
Without a car: take the Red Line to the Hollywood & Highland station. Exit the station. Thumb your nose at the traffic all around you.
From the 101 South: exit at Highland Ave./Hollywood Bowl; merge onto Cahuenga Boulevard. Cahuenga becomes N. Highland Avenue. Stay on Highland until Hollywood Boulevard.
From the 101 North: exit at Highland Ave./Hollywood Bowl exit. Keep right at the fork in the ramp. Merge onto Odin Street, then turn left onto Highland Avenue.
From 405 in either direction: exit Santa Monica Blvd. Head east on Santa Monica Blvd. through Beverly Hills, West Hollywood, and into Hollywood. Turn left on Highland.

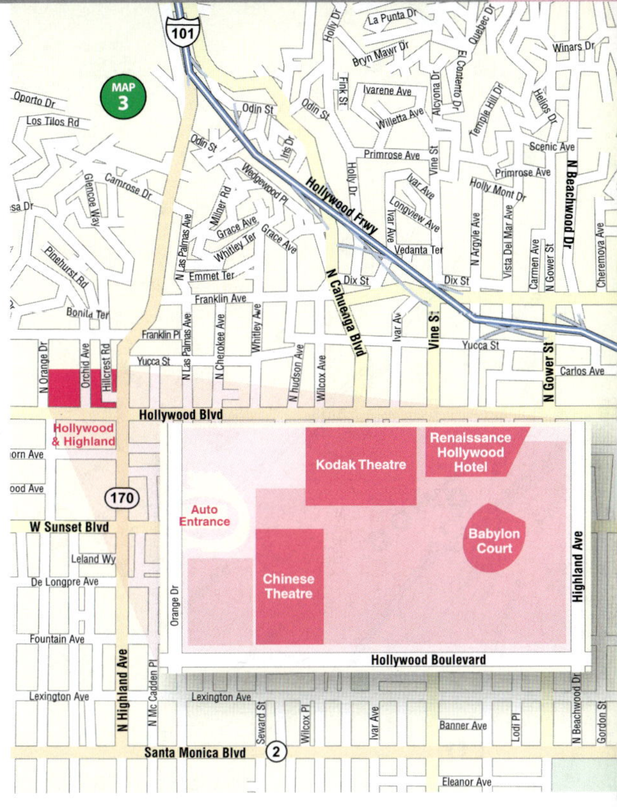

Apparel
General
4 You
Banana Republic
Gap
Hot Topic
Oakley
Sisley
Studio
Tommy Hilfiger
Versace Classic

Women's
Ann Taylor Loft
bebe
Benetton
Express
Luxe Lingerie
Planet Funk
Seventeen
Victoria's Secret

Shoes
ALDO Shoes
Nine West
O' My Sole

Jewelry & Accessories
Agatha
Argenti
Dejaun Jewelers
Red Diamond Jewelers
Swarovski
Swatch

Health & Beauty
Aveda
Lather
MAC Cosmetics
Neutrogena
Origins
Sephora

Gifts/Cards/Books
Backstage at the Chinese
Book City
Brookstone
Build-A-Bear Workshop
Neuhaus Chocolatier

Specialty
Eyewear
Oakley
Optique Vivendi
Sun's Up
Miscellaneous
DFS Galleria
Louis Vuitton

Food
Eateries
Auntie Anne's Pretzels
Baja Hollywood
Burger King
Cold Stone Creamery
Cupid's Hot Dogs
Elixir Tonics & Teas
Hollywood Mongolian Grill
Great Steak & Potato
Green Earth Café
Johnny Rockets
Nestle's Toll House
Starbucks
Surf City Squeeze

Restaurants
Bice Mercato
California Pizza Kitchen
The Grill on Hollywood
The Highlands Restaurant
Koji's Sushi & Shabu Shabu Restaurant
Loggia at the Highlands
Trastevere Ristorante Italiano
Vert - A Brasserie by Wolfgang Puck

Services
Kodak Image Center Solutions
Kodak Theatre Guided Tour
U.S. Post Office/Postal Rental Store
Visitor's Information Center

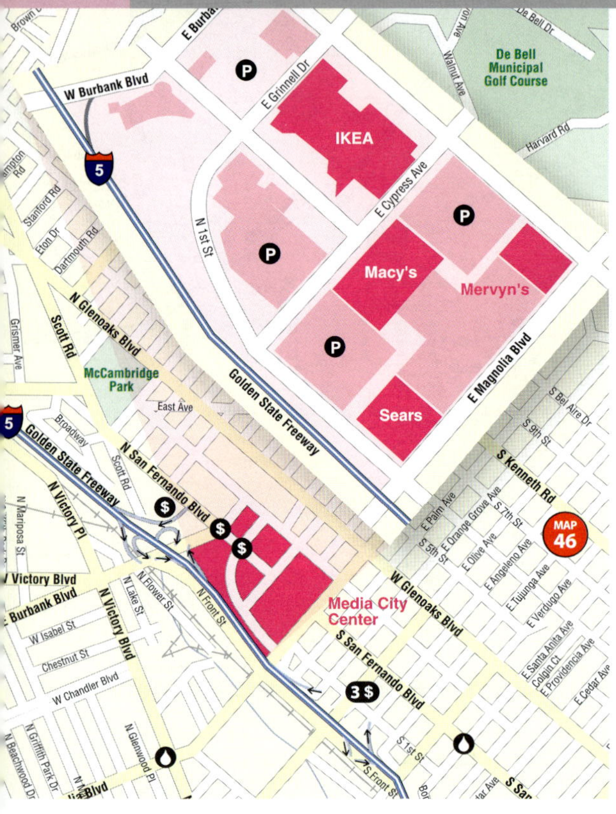

All new arrivals to the city pass through the portals of IKEA at some point in their assimilation, making the Media City Center in Burbank the Ellis Island of Los Angeles. But to see the Media City Center only for its Sten shelving, Billy bookcases, and Ringum area rugs would be to miss the point. The Media City Center also has a full-service, mid-range mall (with its own carousel), a boatload of movie theaters, and access to a quaint stretch of San Fernando Blvd. that gives a glimpse of the pre-megaplex "beautiful downtown Burbank" celebrated on *Laugh-In*.

Shopping

The mall itself is for moderate shoppers and has the reliable fare you'd expect from anchors Mervyn's, Macy's, and Sears. The Sport Chalet is fun and well-stocked. Women's clothing outlets (Georgiou, Lerner, Express) outnumber men's (Corsine, Structure) by nearly five to one. Fortunately, the whole family can shop at The Gap. The carousel is beautiful, and the calliope music will drive you less crazy than you'd have thought. Not to be missed is home accessories curiosity Elegante. There may be no other place in the hemisphere to find both a toddler-sized red velvet chaise longue and a five-foot tall fiberglass sculpture of dolphins leaping in formation. Outside the mall, the Virgin Megastore is a good place to lose yourself if the calliope music does start to drive you crazy. Exhausted fathers and sons seek asylum at Circuit City, particularly on Sundays during football season.

Food

The food court is upstairs on the Magnolia Blvd. side of the mall, offering up the basics (McDonald's, Panda Express), as well as a good dose of natural light. Johnny Rockets has some good family-sized tables away from the fray. Out on strollable San Fernando Blvd., there are a number of places to eat and drink. Market City Caffe (164 East Palm Avenue, at San Fernando) specializes in Italian antipasti and inspired martinis. On the Burbank Blvd. side of the Center are three Southern California institutions: Baja Fresh, Koo Koo Roo, and In-N-Out.

Drawbacks

There are several AMC Theaters here, including one in the mall. Be sure which one you are going to. As with everywhere, parking gets complicated on weekends. Enter the parking lot on First Street across from IKEA at your own risk. A far easier and less congested option is to park in the East Garage, on Third between San Jose and Magnolia.

How to Get There

From the 5 in either direction, exit at Burbank Blvd., and head east on Burbank to North Third Street. Turn right on Third and head down four blocks. The East Parking Garage is on your right, the block after IKEA.

Department Stores

IKEA
Macy's
Mervyn's
Sears

Apparel

General
  Anchor Blue
  Concrete Jungle
  Fabriani Leather
  Gap
  Leathermode
  Pacific Sunwear
Men's
  Corsine
  Flamingo Ties
  Structure
Women's
  Design Clothes
  Express
  Expression Plus
  Forever 21
  Georgiou
  June's Fashions
  Lane Bryant
  Lerner
  Styles For Less
  Victoria's Secret

Shoes

Foot Locker
FootAction USA
Lady Foot Locker
Payless Shoe Source
Red Zone Footwear
Two Lips
Wild Pair

Jewelry & Accessories

Afterthoughts
All That Glitters
Claire's Accessories
Mandarin Gems
Maola's Silver Imports
Media Time Watch & Clock
Timepiece Network
Young's Art Box

Children's & Toys

Gameland
JF Kids
K-B Toys
Sweet Little Faces

Electronics & Entertainment

All Amusement
AMC Theatres (Media 6)
AMC Theatres (Media 8)
Circuit City
Colony Theatre
CompUSA
Historic Carousel
Office Depot
Radio Shack
Sam Goody
Suncoast Motion Picture Co.
Sure Call Wireless
Virgin Megastore

Home Furnishings

Bally's Furniture & Décor
Elegant Creations
Elements
Graphics Gallery
Home Again Crafts
Pretty Choice
Sleep N' Dream
The Bombay Company
Tradewinds

Health & Beauty

Bath & Body Works
Candles & Creations
Carlton Hair International
GNC
Perfume Corner
Queen Nails
Trends LA
Vitamin World

Gifts/Cards/Books

Barnes & Noble
Dice
Ruggles Hallmark
Sanrio Surprises
Simply Personalized
Vera's Carlton Cards
Vicki's Gifts
Waldenbooks

Specialty

Eyewear
  Stein Optical
  Sunglass Hut
Luggage
  Luggage Man
Sporting Goods
  All Pro Sports
  Sport Chalet

Food

Fast Food
  Dairy Queen/Orange Julius
  El Pollo Loco
  Freezy Dizzy
  Hot Dog On A Stick
  Ice Cream Paradise
  In-N-Out Burger
  Johnny Rockets
  Koo Koo Roo
  McDonald's
  Mediterranean Delight
  Mr. Hot Dog
  Mrs. Fields
  Panda Express
  Pretzelmaker
  Rapido Fresh Grill
  Sbarro Pizza
  Surf City Squeeze
  Teriyaki Tokyo
Restaurants
  Baja Fresh Mexican Grill
  California Pizza Kitchen
  Catch 21
  Chevy's Mexican Restaurant
  Crabby Bob's
  Mi Piace
  Mongolian Grill
  Zono Sushi
Specialty
  Candy Station
  Coffee Beanery
  See's Candies

Services

Heel 2 Toe Shoe Repair
Media 1 Hour Photo
Ritz Camera
Simply Personalized
Suburban Associates

The Northridge Fashion Center has a lot going for it. The physical plant is well laid-out and features a pleasant outdoor pedestrian area. It has an affordable range of retail, three mid-range department stores, and two big toy stores, one for kids (K-B) and one for adults (Cost Plus). With all that going for it, it's a shame that it is tucked just far enough out of the way not to merit a visit. However, if you are going to Sears anyway for a fridge or new tires, or are fairly deep in the West San Fernando Valley, there is no reason not to go check it out. Except perhaps, for the parking during the summer (see "Drawbacks" below).

Shopping

The Northridge Fashion Center is popular and bustling. It succeeds by clothing, outfitting, and entertaining families at all stages, from "Will you marry me?" to "Don't make me pull this car over." You can find an outpost of Frederick's of Hollywood, engagement rings (McClave's Jeweler is very nice, as is Kristof's), formal wear (Gary's Tux Shop), and department store bridal registries (Robinsons May and Macy's). A million affordable and fun things to go in a new home—or to spruce up the old one—are at housewares-furniture-coffee-etc. importer Cost Plus. Kids clothing and shoes are available in quantity at Old Navy, The Children's Place, Payless Kids, and Kids Foot Locker. Readers of all ages will find something good at Borders (note: it's okay for the whole family to sit, or lay down, on the floor of their children's department, if a time-out is called for). The only family member that might get short-changed at Northridge is the suit-wearing male. The selections are pretty thin in the mall. Macy's offsets this a little. But a sharp-dressed man is better served at the Fashion Square in Sherman Oaks.

Food

The NFC Cafés are clean and well lit, and offer access to outside seating. There is a nice variety of cuisines, ranging in nutritional value from low (Cinnabon) to relatively high (California Fresh Foods). The line for Donatello's Pizza is long but moves fairly fast. La Salsa, Sansei, and Surf City Squeeze hold down the middle ground. There are a number of sit-down restaurants in the complex. For a break (weather permitting), sit outside on the patio at Wood Ranch BBQ and take in some good food and better people-watching.

Drawbacks

Whether you come from the 101 or the 118, the drive along Tampa can be slow. The parking lot fills up quickly, and in summer you may be in for a long, hot (100 degrees, anyone?) walk to and from the mall. There is a beautiful Gelson's supermarket nearby. It is far enough away from the main mall to require moving your car, yet close enough to make you feel guilty for doing so.

How to Get There

From the 101 in either direction, exit Tampa Blvd. and head north on Tampa approximately four miles to Plummer. Mall entrance is on left.

From the 118 in either direction, exit Tampa Blvd. and head south on Tampa approximately four miles to Plummer. Mall entrance is on right.

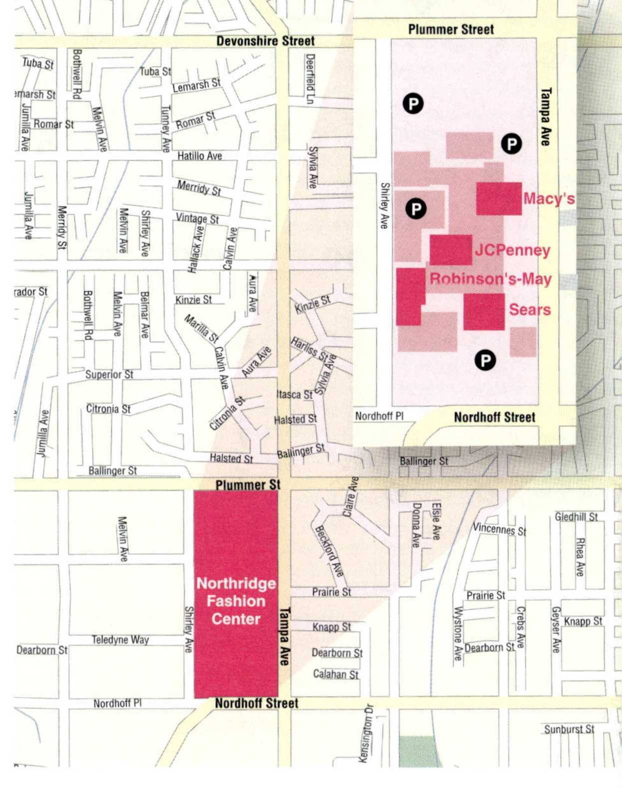

Department Stores

- J C Penney
- Macy's
- Robinsons-May South
- Sears

Apparel

Men
- Gary's Tux Shop
- Metropolis
- Mr Rags
- Structure
- White Sands

General
- Anchor Blue
- Banana Republic
- Beyond The Beach
- Eddie Bauer
- Gap
- Guess?
- Hot Topic
- Lids
- Life Uniforms
- Old Navy Clothing Company
- Pacific Sunwear Of California
- Wilson's House Of Suede

Women's
- 5-7-9 Shop
- Afterthoughts Boutique
- Ann Taylor Loft
- Casual Corner
- Charlotte Russe
- Claire's Accessories
- Contempo Casuals
- Express
- Forever 21
- Frederick's of Hollywood
- Icing
- L'Patricia
- Lane Bryant
- Mode Plus
- Motherhood Maternity
- Reference
- Reflection
- This Is It by Macy's
- Victoria's Secret
- Wet Seal
- Windsor Fashions

Shoes

- Basix Footwear
- Cathy Jean
- Daisy
- Easy Spirit
- Family Shoe Center
- Finish Line
- Florsheim Shoes
- Foot Connection
- Foot Locker
- FootAction USA
- Jarman Shoes
- Journey's
- Kids Foot Locker
- Lady Foot Locker
- Naturalizer Shoes
- Payless Shoesource/Payless Kid
- Shiekh
- Stride Rite
- Vans

Jewelry & Accessories

- Moonlight Accessory Gallery
- On Time
- Watch Station
- Ben Bridge Jewelry
- Crescent Jewelers
- Daniel's Jewelers
- Helzberg Diamonds
- Intrigue Jewelers
- Kay Jewelers
- Kevin Jewelers
- Kristof's Jewelers
- McClave Jewelers
- Na Hoku Jewelers
- Whitehall Co Jewelers
- Zales Jewelers

Children's & Toys

- Children's Place
- Disney Store
- Game Keeper
- Gap Kids/Baby Gap
- Gymboree
- Kay-Bee Toys
- Limited Too
- QT Kids

Electronics & Entertainment

Electronics
- Apple Store
- Circuit City
- Radio Shack
- Sam Goody's Musicland
- Software Etc
- Suncoast Pictures
- Verizon Wireless

Home Furnishings

- Bombay Company
- Prints Plus
- Select Comfort
- Thomas Kinkade Gallery

Health & Beauty

- A Touch Of Beauty
- Bath & Body Works
- Body Shop
- Clinique (Macy's)
- Fashion Nails
- Gap Body
- H2O Plus
- Image Hair Salon
- Look Out Perfume
- Merle Norman Cosmetics
- ProfessioNail
- Regis Hairstylists
- Skinmarket
- Victoria's Secret Beauty

Gifts/Cards/Books

- Amber's Hallmark
- B Dalton Booksellers
- Borders Books & Music
- Caprice
- Jay's Luggage & Gifts
- Paolo Biacci
- San Francisco Music Box
- Sanrio Surprises
- Spencer Gifts
- Things Remembered
- Wicks 'N Sticks
- Yankee Candle Company

Specialty

Eyewear
- Lenscrafters
- Sunglass Hut

Sporting Goods
- Champs Sports
- Just Sports

Miscellaneous
- Cost Plus World Market
- Firestone
- Pet World
- Sears Auto Center

Food

Fast Food
- A & W Hot Dogs & More
- Auntie Anne's
- California Fresh Foods
- Cinnabon
- Mrs Field's Cookies
- Orange Julius/Dairy Queen
- Pretzel 'N' Cheese
- San Francisco Cookie
- Steak Escape
- Topz

Food Court

- Boardwalk Fries
- Chinese Gourmet Express
- Donatello's Pizza
- La Salsa
- Sansei
- Surf City Squeeze
- Tommie's

Restaurants
- Big Apple Deli
- Claim Jumper
- Don Ricardo's Restaurant
- On The Border Mexican Cafe
- Romano's Macaroni Grill
- Sushi Factory
- Wood Ranch BBQ & Grill

Specialty
- Ben & Jerry's
- Daily Grind
- General Nutrition Center
- Gloria Jean's Gourmet Coffee
- Great Earth Vitamins
- Harry & David
- Ice Cool
- See's Candies
- Sweet Factory
- Vitamin World

Services

- Cunningham Field & Research
- Gymboree Play And Music
- LA Radio Listening Service
- Photomakers
- Ritz Camera One Hour Photo

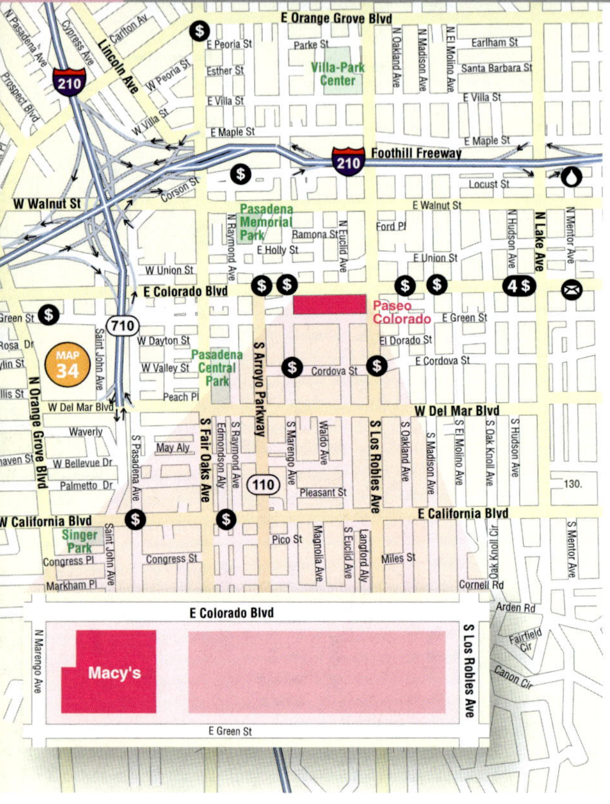

Paseo Colorado, a brand new live-work-retail complex in the heart of downtown Pasadena, is off to an impressive start. Built to encourage strolling, its layout and architecture echo both colonial Mexican and classic California craftsman styles. An outdoor, pedestrian-friendly place to congregate, shop, eat, and amble, it also presents a nice alternative—or addition—to Old Town (just west on Colorado Blvd.), which at peak hours can push maximum density.

Shopping

The Paseo is just as good a place to come and shop with a list as it is to wander aimlessly. In addition to a solid Macy's (which bore up during the Paseo's construction with quiet dignity), it features some strong and unexpected offerings for Southern California mall retail. These stores may well become the new favorites of some shoppers. Interesting options include Japanese Weekend Maternity Wear, B. Luu women's wear, J. Jill, Tommy Bahama, Elements Furniture, and April Cornell. The Bombay Company, Eddie Bauer, Ann Taylor Loft, Brookstone, and K-B Toys are all on hand for those who crave more standard mall fare. It should be noted that apart from Macy's, however, the children's clothing options—such as Jacadi—are limited and pricey.

Food

There is not a centrally located food court, but a variety of good things to eat are available on the second floor. Sit-down restaurants include Los Angeles favorites Islands and P.F. Chang's. Having the Border Grill on this side of town is a real luxury (the original is in Santa Monica) and worth a visit if you've never tried their delicious and innovative Mexican food. It was nothing short of a genius maneuver to put the Cold Stone Creamery within sight of the Pacific Theaters. Summer evenings in Pasadena were made for post-movie strolling with an ice cream cone in hand.

Drawbacks

There is plenty of parking available in the vicinity, though the garage under the Paseo is to be avoided. It's too popular for its own good. Our directions steer you to a less chaotic option. The restaurants are all on the second floor of the Paseo, but there is not one contiguous second floor, making finding what you want an up-and-down-the-stairs project. Check the Paseo directory before you head up.

How to get there

From the 134 in either direction, exit Marengo and head south on Marengo a half-mile to Colorado Blvd. Parking is available in the structure on the right just past Colorado.

From the 110 North, exit Fair Oaks Blvd and head north on Fair Oaks to Colorado Blvd. Turn right and head approximately a half-mile to Marengo. Turn right at Marengo to enter parking. There is also parking on the Green Street side of the Paseo. Remember to have your ticket validated!

Department Stores

Macy's

Apparel

General
A Snail's Pace Running Shop
Eddie Bauer
Epic Sports
Lucky Brand Dungarees
Quiksilver Board Riders
Tommy Bahama

Women's
Ann Taylor Loft
April Cornell
B. Luu
Betsey Johnson
Flutter
Gossip
J. Jill
Jaloux/Zalu
Japanese Weekend Maternity
Max Studio
Planet Funk
Reference
Therapy
White House/Black Market

Shoes

Cole Haan
DSW Shoe Warehouse

Children's & Toys

Jacadi
K-B Toys

Electronics & Entertainment

Cingular Wireless
Pacific 14 Theatres
Sam Goody/Suncoast

Home Furnishings

April Cornell
Arabesque
Bombay Company
Elements Furniture & Gifts

Health & Beauty

M.A.C. Cosmetics
Sephora

Gifts/Cards/Books

Brookstone
Following Sea
Sam Goody/Suncoast
The Museum Company
Yankee Candle Company

Specialty

Luggage
El Portal

Miscellaneous
Brighton Collectibles
Coach
Leather Town

Food

Restaurants
Bice
Border Grill
Café Med
California Crisp
Chinese Gourmet Café
Cold Stone Creamery
Island's Fine Burgers & Drinks
Juice it Up!
P.F. Chang's China Bistro
Rubio's Baja Grill
Tokyo Wako

Specialty
Gelson's The Super Market
Harry and David
Starbucks Coffee Company

Services

Amadeus Day Spa
Equinox Fitness Clubs

The Santa Monica Place is a perfectly average mall in a spectacular location—barely a quarter-mile from the beach and adjacent to the Third Street Promenade. The location, combined with no-surprises store offerings, make it hard to justify a visit. There are simply better places in the neighborhood to be. Better places, of course, unless it's raining. (And it does—eventually—rain in Southern California.) Since preparedness is everything, keep this description and a collapsible umbrella handy. Just in case.

Shopping

This is not a mall for serious shoppers—again, the location just doesn't encourage it, and the shops are too mid-range to do serious damage. Unless you know that what you want is already at one of the stores (Victoria's Secret, Brookstone, Williams Sonoma, etc.), the best bets are to enjoy any accidental finds you might make and to take advantage of the mall's strengths. For instance: the Santa Monica Place skews very young. So bring your teen-aged niece and watch her flirt with boys as she heads for the Macy's Junior Dept., and then on to Wet Seal and Forever 21. Or better still, leave the kids at home and go to Frederick's of Hollywood. You get all the fun without having to brave Hollywood Blvd. And since you're at the beach anyway, you may as well buy a bathing suit at Pacific Sunwear, or the Speedo Store, and then find some new shades at Sun Shade or Sunglass Hut (both have good sales, making it worth at least a drive-by).

Food

The food court is bustling and cacophonous. Hot Dog On A Stick and Charlie Burgers will put you in a good-time mood, provided you can find a table. Don't hesitate to make those orders "to go." If it is raining, consider hiding out on the "quiet" side of the mall (near Colorado Blvd.) and grab a seat at Tanner's Coffee Co. No trip to the area is complete without a trip to Bay Cities, Los Angeles' best classic Italian deli (1517 Lincoln Blvd. at Broadway): it's the closest thing Los Angeles has to Mulberry Street. Fresh bread, dizzyingly good sandwiches, tasty mozzarella, meatballs, lasagna, and all manner of antipasti. Did we say fresh bread?

Drawbacks

This particular area of Santa Monica can get congested on weekends. Pedestrians, some on roller blades, will more than test your patience. Once inside the mall, clientele consists of teens and tourists; foot traffic can be erratic and loud, particularly on the Broadway side of the mall. And a warning: many patrons don't make it to the second and third floors of Santa Monica Place. Rather than the upper floors evoking a sense of peace and quiet, it ends up feeling more like a ghost town, or The Day After.

How to Get There

From the 10 west, head north on Lincoln a quarter-mile to Colorado. Head west on Colorado and enter the parking lot from that side.
From PCH heading east, exit Ocean Avenue, go left on Ocean and right on Colorado.

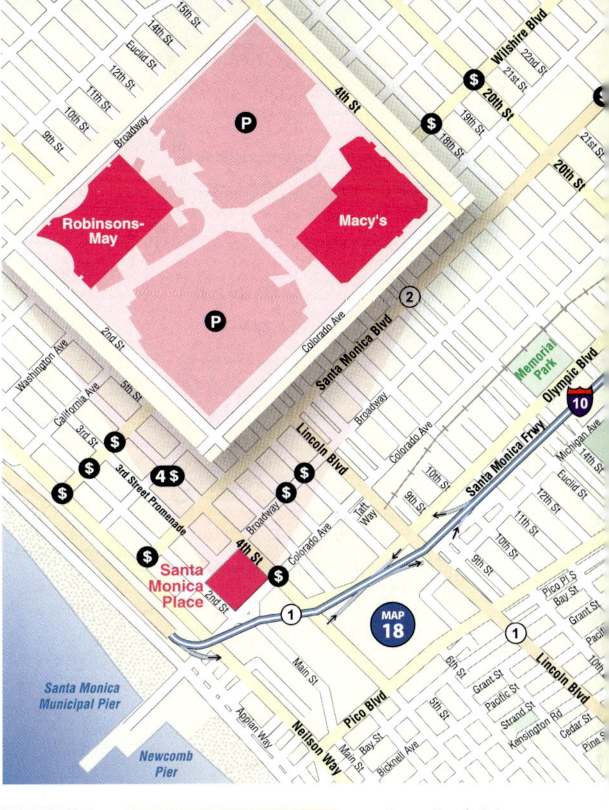

Department Stores
- Macy's
- Robinsons-May

Apparel

Men
- Gallini
- Matrix
- Structure

General
- Anchor Blue
- Eddie Bauer
- Hot Topic
- Leather Expo
- Pacific Sunwear
- Reflex
- Speedo Authentic Fitness

Women's
- Ann Taylor
- Arden B
- Baly's
- BCBG
- Deena Hahn
- Diva
- Express
- Forever 21
- Frederick's of Hollywood
- Image
- Kimono-Ya
- Limited
- M. Cole
- Maje
- Motherhood Maternity
- Parallel
- Planet Funk
- Victoria's Secret
- Wet Seal

Shoes
- Charles David
- Easy Spirit
- Foot Locker
- FootAction USA
- Kenneth Cole
- Lady Footlocker
- Nine West
- Payless Shoe Source

Jewelry & Accessories
- Antiqua
- Argenti
- Bubar's Jewelers
- Fast Fix Jewelry
- Icing
- Kenneth Cole
- Tic Time
- Watch World
- Whitehall Jewelers
- Zales

Children's & Toys
- Gap Kids/Baby Gap
- Gymboree
- K-B Toys
- Sanrio Surprises
- Wizards of the Coast

Electronics & Entertainment
- Electronics Boutique
- Nextel
- Radio Shack
- Ritz Camera
- Sam Goody
- Suncoast Motion Picture Co.

Home Furnishings
- Bombay Company

Health & Beauty
- Bath & Body Works
- Body Shop
- Carlton Hair
- General Nutrition Center
- Nail Elite
- Natura Beauty Emporio
- Perfumeria International
- Salon Vivace

Gifts/Cards/Books
- Bordados
- Brookstone
- Carlton Cards
- Hiland Tobacco & Collectibles
- Indian Arts
- Moonlight Candles
- Things Remembered
- Williams-Sonoma

Specialty

Eyewear
- LensCrafters
- Optometric Options
- Sun Shade Optique
- Sunglass Hut Sport

Luggage
- Kensington Luggage
- Tumi

Sporting Goods
- All Pro Sports
- Foot Locker
- Lady Foot Locker
- Speedo Authentic Fitness

Food

Fast Food
- Auntie Annie's Soft Pretzels
- Blue Forest Bakery
- Burger King
- Dairy Queen/Orange Julius
- Godiva Chocolates
- Mrs. Fields Cookies
- Sweet Factory
- Tanner's Coffee Co.

Food Court
- California Squeeze
- Charlie Burgers
- Charlie Kabob
- Charly Temmel
- China Inn
- Fiesta Fresh
- Garden Gourmet
- Great Khan's Mongolian Festival
- Great Steak & Potato
- Hot Dog on a Stick
- Kelly's Cajun Grill
- Khyber Express
- Memphis Rotisserie Chicken
- Tokyo Kitchen
- Villa Italian

Restaurants
- JR Seafood
- Tilly's Terrace

Specialty
- Godiva

Services
- Community Room
- H.I.S. Tours
- Management Office
- Mid-America Research
- Santa Monica Visitor Center
- Security Office
- Shoe Care
- U.S. Bank

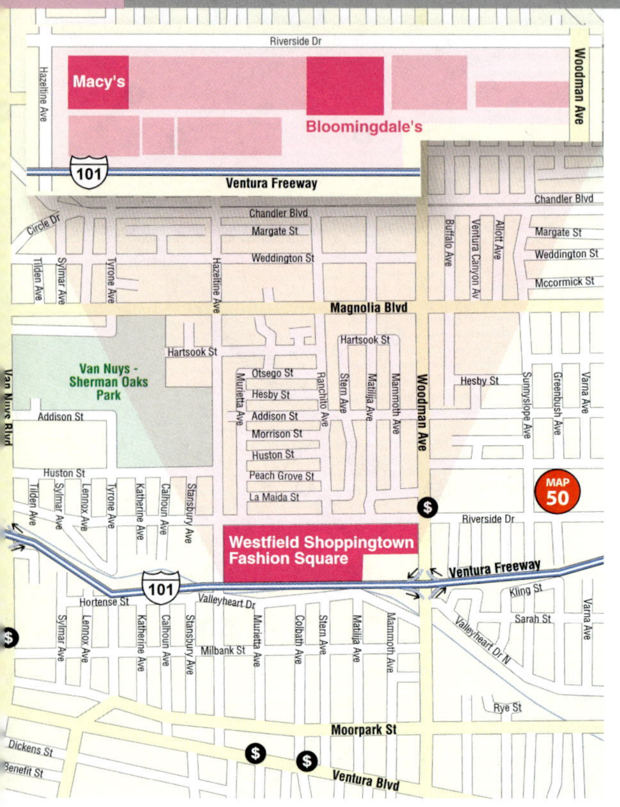

Many take great pleasure in decrying the Valley's lack of charm, interest, and substance. These people, much like their brethren who insist that happiness cannot be bought, simply do not know where to shop. The quickest way to turn a Valley detractor into a Valley booster, fer shure, is to take them to the Fashion Square in Sherman Oaks. This well-designed, upper-mid-range retail venue with marble floors, good light, and nice muzak has the power to change both minds and wardrobes.

Shopping

Anchored by Macy's and Bloomingdale's (the former is particularly thorough and upscale-feeling; the latter's shoe, cosmetics, and housewares departments go the distance), the Fashion Square is a must-go for well-dressed families and their equally well-dressed homes. J. Jill, J. Crew, and 818 Freight offer a break from retail-as-usual (though the Fashion Square has that, too). Denise Carolyn and Siany both have impressive accessories that are more colorful, and just plain more fun, than what's on the beaten path. Whether you like them baby doll, flannel, and or just artfully draped across a chair, Pajama Party has great sleepwear. Even the wholly unwhimsical Walking Co., home of sensible footwear, has some surprisingly fun options (though sadly none with stilettoes). With Restoration Hardware, Williams Sonoma, Z Gallerie, Pottery Barn, and the Bloomingdale's housewares department under one roof, all manner of home needs are covered, and in high style. The Fashion Square is also blessed with two particularly nice jewelers, Polachek and De Aguiar. The feather in Fashion Square's cap is Brentano's, a not-too-big book store with a good selection.

Food

The Garden Café Food Court features mall standards—Sbarro, Subway, Great Steak & Potato—but places like Sansei and Massis Kabob are a nice reminder that you are in Los Angeles. The tables are always full, so follow the signs upstairs to the additional seating. Tables, chairs, and quiet await. The line for the Coffee Bean & Tea Leaf is always long—the Ice Blended appears to be the official beverage of the Fashion Square. 59th and Lex, the café on Bloomingdale's third floor is a great get-away-from-it-all, even if the food isn't great value for the dollar. It's worth it just to watch your fellow shoppers disappear as they step onto the "down" escalator that runs adjacent to the cafe.

Drawbacks

Weekends, the parking lot traffic is deceptively crowded and hostile. Once shoppers are out of their cars and inside the mall, both hostility and density drop dramatically. So don't let the megalomaniacs in the 10 mpg land-barges and the dive bombers in the convertibles deter you. Also, the Fashion Square has neither a movie theater nor a grocery store (though there is a Trader Joe's at the corner of Hazeltine and Riverside).

How to get there

From the 101 in either direction, exit Woodman. Head north on Woodman one block, and go left onto Riverside. The parking lot can be entered on both the Riverside and the Hazeltine sides of the mall. Bloomingdale's shoppers will want to enter on Hazeltine.

Department Stores

Bloomingdale's
Macy's

Apparel

Men
  Dakota Blue
  Gary's Tux
  Prestigio
  Structure
General
  American Eagle
   Outfitters
  Abercrombie & Fitch
  Banana Republic
  De Aguiar Designs
  Guess
  J. Crew
  Pacific Sunwear
  Pajama Party
  Speedo Authentic
   Fitness
Women's
  818 Freight
  A Pea In The Pod
  Ann Taylor
  Arden B.
  bebe
  Betsey Johnson
  Bisou Bisou
  Casual Corner
  Coldwater Creek
  Contempo Casuals
  Express
  Georgiou
  Hepburns
  Here
  J. Jill
  Lane Bryant
Macy's Swimwear
Max Studio
Planet Funk
Rampage
Victoria's Secret
Wet Seal

Shoes

Cathy Jean
Enzo Angiolini
Erik's Shoes
Foot Locker
Journeys
Lady Foot Locker
Nine West
Silvano Shoes
The Walking Company

Jewelry & Accessories

De Aguiar Designs
Dejaun Jewelers
Denise Carolyn
Jacqueline Jarrot
Polachek's Jewelers
Zales
Accessories
  Claire's Boutique
  Tic Time
  Watch Station

Children's & Toys

Brooks Shoes For Kids
Gap Kids/Baby Gap
Gymboree
Kids Foot Locker
Limited Too
Oh, Baby!

Electronics & Entertainment

Radio Shack

Home Furnishings

Brighton Collectibles
Hold Everything
Home Shops
Mission Renaissance
Pottery Barn Design
 Studio
Restoration Hardware
Siany
The Bombay Company
Williams-Sonoma
Z Gallerie

Health & Beauty

General
  OSIM
Health
  GNC Live Well
Beauty
  Bath & Body Works
  Beauty Essentials
  Carlton Hair
  Chayo Salon
  Gap/Gap Body
  Hair Make-Over
  Macy's Hair Salon
  Sephora
  The Body Shop
  Victoria's Secret Beauty

Gifts/Cards/Books

Gifts
  Brentano's
  Brookstone
  Discovery Channel Store
  Edmund's Unique Gifts
  Old Pro Gallery
  Sanrio Surprises
  The Disney Store
  Things Remembered
  Yankee Candle
   Company
Stationery
  Lavenders Hallmark
  Papyrus

Specialty

Eyewear
  LensCrafters
  Maison d'Optique
  Sunglass Hut
  Urban Sunglasses
Luggage
  Coach
  Kensington Luggage
  Kipling
  Tumi
Sporting Goods
  Old Pro Gallery
Miscellaneous
  It's A Blooming Business

Food

Restaurant
  59th & Lexington Café
   (Bloomingdale's)
  Cleo & Cucci
Food Court
  California Crisp
  Carl's Jr.
  Great Steaks & Patato
  La Salsa
  Massis Kabob
  Mrs. Fields/Pretzelmak
  Panda Express
  Sansei
  Sbarro
  Subway
  Surf City Squeeze
Specialty
  Coffee Bean & Tea Leaf
  See's Candles
  Sweet Sue

Services

Adept Research
Concierge Services
Fashion Square
 Management
Mission Renaissance A
 School
Ritz Camera
Security Office
Shoe Doctor

Well-located near both the 10 and the 405 freeways, the Westside Pavillion balances airiness with reasonable size (compared to the energy required to take on the Beverly Center or the Glendale Galleria) and good variety of retail. In addition to Nordstrom and Robinsons-May (both well-stocked), the usual suspects—Banana, Gap, Victoria's Secret, Nine West, Express, Rampage, Foot Locker, et al—are all in attendance. Even on busy Saturdays, foot traffic manages to flow nicely. Somebody had the right idea when they put the kids' stores (Gap Kids, Right Start, Gymboree) within shouting distance of each other.

Shopping

This mall was made for women of all ages in need of shoes or something to wear to a wedding, prom, or formal event. First and foremost: Nordstrom's shoe sales are high holidays on the retail calendar. This much is known. And in true egalitarian spirit, the footwear offerings run the gamut from Payless Shoe Source to Charles David, with Aldo and Nine West in between.

Both wedding guests and members of the bridal party are well served here. Splendiferous offers one-of-a-kind handmade dresses and accessories. Emphasis is on beading and personal service. They sell bridal gowns, too. Lili's of Beverly Hills can outfit any M.O.B. or M.O.G., while bridesmaids can find classy evening gowns at BCBG. And if you are looking for an off-the-registry gift for the bride and groom, U-Topia and Anthology have many unique home items, mostly on the Shabby Chic side.

Food

The food court hits the major food groups and is surprisingly clean. Tables do get bussed regularly. Not to be missed is Hot Dog On A Stick, with fresh lemonade and the best-dressed counter staff on the planet. The best food, however, is just outside the mall: the Apple Pan (10801 Pico) is a Los Angeles institution, serving old-school hickory burgers in a lunch-counter setting.

Drawbacks

On the downside: though Robinsons-May gets an "A" for effort, serious housewares shoppers are better served elsewhere (see the Century City Shopping Center). The Westside Pavillion's parking lot is possibly the most confusingly laid-out in the county. Also, the Westside Pavillion Cinemas offer current indie, foreign, and art house films on irritatingly small screens. Sub-titles can be hard to read in such close quarters, and popular movies can sell out quickly.

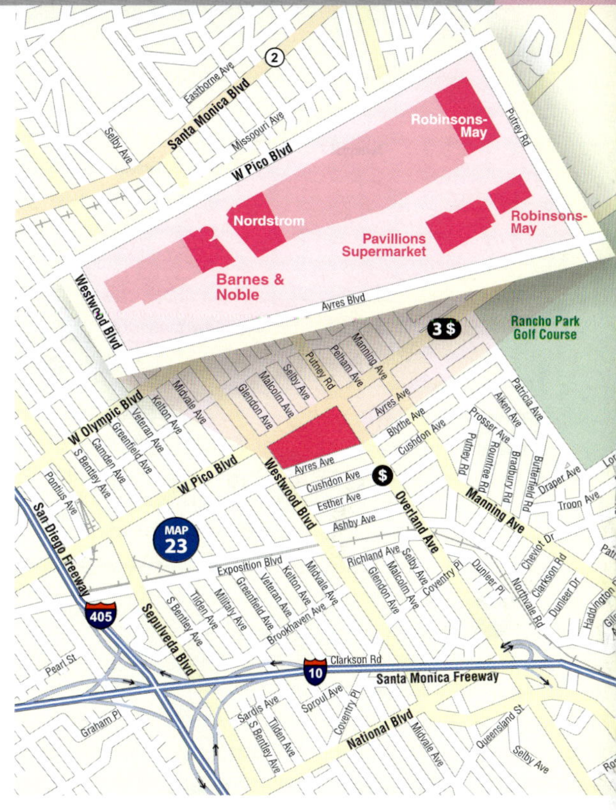

Department Stores

Nordstrom
Robinsons-May

Apparel

Men's Apparel
  Banana Republic Men
General
  American Eagle
   Outfitters
  Gap
  Guess
  Pacific Sunwear
  Xtreme Board Shop
Women's
  Ann Taylor
  Baly's
  Banana Republic
   Women
  Barami Studio
  BCBG Dresses
  bebe
  Canyon Beachwear
  Express
  H2
  Image
  Lane Bryant
  Lili's of Beverly Hills
  Limited
  Morgan De Toi
  Motherhood Maternity
  Parallel
  Planet Funk
  Privilege
  Rampage
  Shapes
  Splendiferous

Victoria's Secret
Wilson's Leather
Windsor Fashion

Shoes

Aldo Shoes
Brooks Shoes for Kids
Cathy Jean
Charles David
Easy Spirit
Foot Locker
Journeys
Lady Foot Locker
Nine West
Payless ShoeSource
Steve Madden
The Walking Company
Vans

Jewelry & Accessories

Afterthoughts
Claire's Accessories
Elza Jewelers
Jewelry Collection
Servis & Taylor
Silver Island
Watch Collection
Westime
Whitehall Jewelers
Zales Jewelry

Children's & Toys

Baby Genius
Build-A-Bear Workshop
Disney Store
Game Keeper
Gap Kids

Gymboree
K-B Toys
Limited Too
Music N Me
Right Start
TomKid

Electronics & Entertainment

All State Cellular
Cingular PCS Express
Electronics Boutique
Laptopmania
MCI Worldcom
Ritz Camera
Suncoast Video
T-Mobile
Westside One Hour
  Photo

Movie Theater

Westside Pavilion
  Cinemas

Home Furnishings

Anthology
Select Comfort
Utopia
Village Art Gallery

Health & Beauty

Bare Escentuals
Bath & Body Works
Carlton Hair
  International
Hair Makeover
LA Nails
Linear Hair
Lisa's Beauty Supplies
Merle Norman

Perfume Gallery
Regis Hairstylists
The Body Shop

Gifts/Cards/Books

Gifts
  It's a Fancy World
  Natural Wonders
Cards
  Hallmark Gold Crown
  Papyrus
  Things Remembered
Books
  Barnes & Noble
  Hallmark Gold Crown
  Waldenbooks

Specialty

Eyewear
  Lencrafters
  Optometric Options
  Sunglass Chalet
  Sunglass Hut
Luggage
  Peninsula Luggage

Food

Fast Food
  Baja Buds
  California Crisp
  California Steak and
   Fries
  Catch 21
  Cinnabon
  Coffee Bean & Tea Leaf

East Wind
Hana Grill
Hot Dog on a Stick
Ice N Cream
La Salsa
McDonald's
Mrs. Field's Cookies
New York Deli
Panda Express
Pretzel Time
Sbarro
Sisley Italian Kitchen
Restaurants
  Tony Roma's
Specialty
  Barnes & Noble Cafe
   Starbucks
  GNC
  Nordstrom Espresso Bar
  See's Candies
  Tasties

Services

Beverly Hills Fencers
Dance Studio No. 1
Fast Fix Jewelry Repair
Field Management
Shoe Care
SPCALA Pet Adoption
U.S. Post Office
West LA Chamber

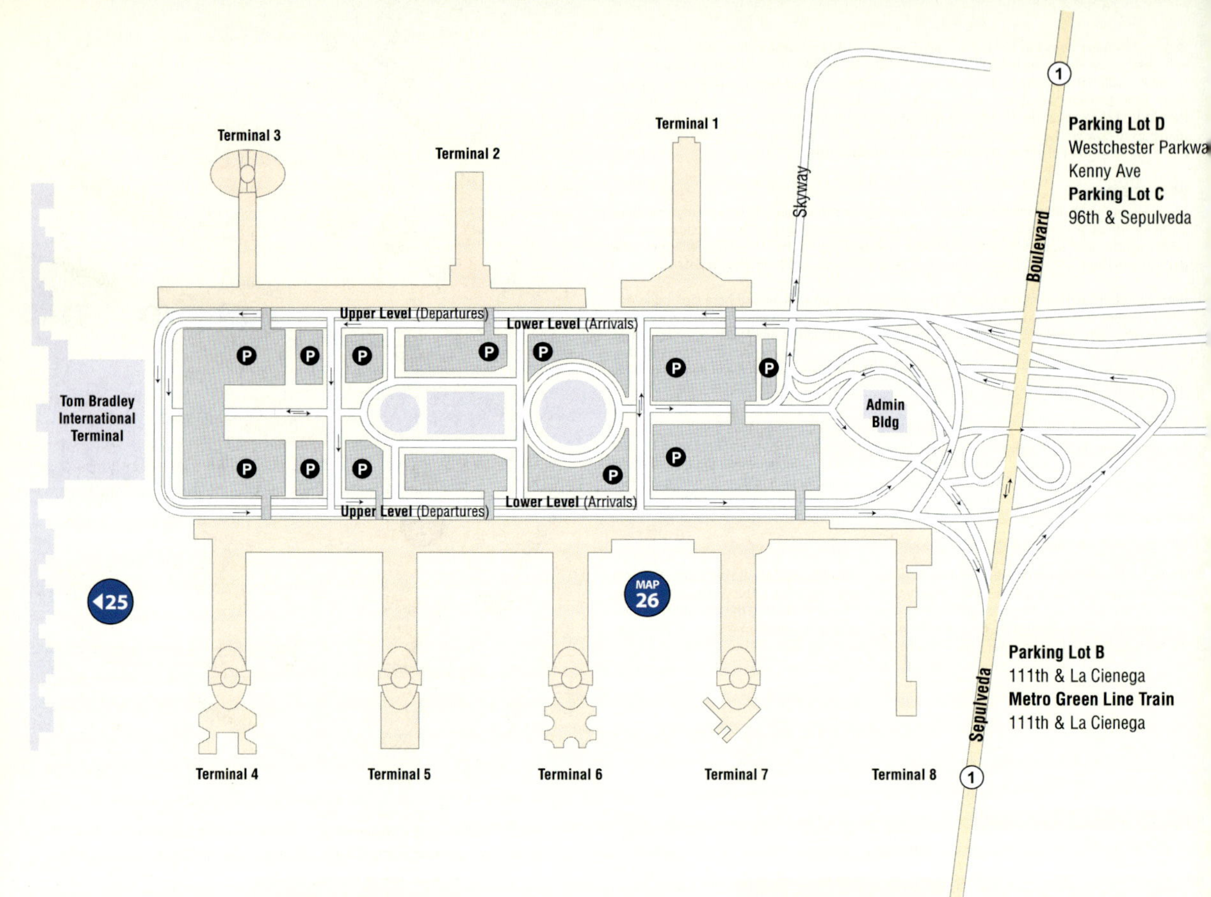

Airline	Terminal	Airline	Terminal	Airline	Terminal
Aer Lingus	TBIT	Cathay Pacific Airways	TBIT	Miami Air	2
Aero California	TBIT	Champion Air	2	Midwest Express	3
Aeroflot	TBIT	China Airlines	TBIT	National Airlines	6
Aeromexico	5	China Eastern	TBIT	Northwest Airlines	2
Air Canada/Canadian	2	China Southern	5	Omni Air International	2
Air China	2	Continental Airlines	6	Philippine Airlines	TBIT
Air France	TBIT	Copa Airlines (Panama)	6 & TBIT	QANTAS	TBIT
Air Jamaica	5	Corsair	TBIT	Singapore Airlines	TBIT
Air Mobility Command (AMC)	2	Delta Airlines	5	Skywest Airlines	6
Air New Zealand	2	Egypt Air	TBIT	Southwest Airlines	1
Air Pacific	TBIT	El Al Israel Airlines	TBIT	Spirit	5
Air Tahiti Nui	5	EVA Air	TBIT	Sun Country Airlines	5
Alaska Airlines	3 & TBIT	Frontier	3	Swissair	TBIT
Alitalia	TBIT	Hawaiian Airlines	2	TACA International Airlines	TBIT
All Nippon Airways (ANA)	TBIT	Horizon	3	Thai Airways	TBIT
America West Airlines	1	Japan Air Lines	TBIT	Trans World Airlines	3
American Airlines	3, 4	KLM Royal Dutch Airlines	2	United Airlines	6 & 7
American Eagle	4	Korean Airlines	TBIT	United Shuttle	7 & 8
American Trans Air	2	LACSA Airlines	TBIT	United Express	7
AOM French Airlines	TBIT	LAN Chile	TBIT	US Airways	1
Asiana Airlines	TBIT	LTU International Airways	TBIT	Vanguard	3
Avianca	2	Lufthansa German Airlines	TBIT	Varig Brazilian Airlines	TBIT
British Airways	TBIT	Malaysia Airline System	TBIT	Virgin Atlantic Airways	2
Canada 3000	TBIT	Mexicana Airlines	TBIT	World Airlines	2

Overview

Traditionally as congested and confusing as the freeway system that surrounds it, LAX is trying to become a more aesthetically pleasing place to while away hours spent waiting for a flight. The city recently unveiled its "Enhancement Project," a ring of 100-foot high neon pylons and the letters, "LAX"—seemingly a modern take on Stonehenge, if envisioned by a kindergarten class with a Lite Brite. The good news is that food at LAX has improved in recent years. The airport now features two Wolfgang Puck Cafes, an outpost of the Gordon Biersch Brewery, and a Daily Grill, allowing you to avoid airplane food altogether. But you may still have a hard time locating these establishments within LAX's vast and unconnected ring of terminals. Picking up and dropping off can be a nightmare, due to poorly labeled parking lots and overzealous traffic cops. Sadly, Angelenos have few alternatives to LAX (which is ranked fourth worldwide for number of passengers handled) and consider the airport's long lines a necessary evil. Besides, there's nothing like that moment upon takeoff, when the airplane clears the smog and gives way to that rare LA sight—blue sky.

How to Get There—Driving

The easiest way to drive to LAX is typically not the fastest. The most direct route to the airport is to take the Santa Monica Freeway (405) to the Century Freeway (105), which leads you right into the airport. But the 405 is almost always congested, so it's possible to exit at Century Blvd. or Imperial Highway to shave a few minutes off the trip. But as the cab drivers know, surface roads are the preferable way to access LAX whenever possible. From the northern beach cities (Santa Monica, etc.), take Lincoln Blvd. south until it joins Sepulveda Blvd. This will lead you right to LAX, but be prepared to make a sudden right turn into the airport. From the South Bay, Sepulveda is also the preferred route, but this time the airport will be on your left. The quickest route to LAX from Central LA is La Cienega Blvd. South of Rodeo Road, La Cienega becomes a mini-freeway that rarely becomes congested. Take La Cienega to La Tijera Blvd., and go east on La Tijera until you reach Sepulveda. Hang a left onto Sepulveda and drive just a few blocks south until you hit the airport.

How to Get There—Mass Transit

In a word: Don't. Though many buses will take you to LAX, the trip may last longer than your actual flight. Sure, you're getting a lot of bang out of your $1.35 fare, but this is the way to go only if you have time for a "leisurely" ride to the airport. City buses deposit passengers at the LAX Transit Center, where a free shuttle travels to each of the airport's terminals. Another free shuttle connects LAX to the Metro Green Line Aviation Station, where LA's Light Rail system ferries travelers from outlying areas like Redondo Beach (to the south) and Norwalk (to the east).

How to Get There—Really

If you're at all clever, convince a friend to drive you. But if that's not an option, car services and taxis are truly the best way to go. Super Shuttle's (800-258-3826) rates start at under $20 and increase with distance from LAX. Most local cab companies also offer a flat rate to LAX that can be economical if more than one person is traveling. Average costs for a one-way trip to LAX are $16 from Redondo Beach, $18 from Santa Monica, $27 from downtown, $40 from Van Nuys, and $50 from Pasadena. Some taxi services are: Beverly Hills Cab Co. (310-273-6611), L.A. Taxi/United Checker Cab (213-627-7000), and Valley Cab (818-787-1900).

Parking

For quick trips to pick someone up, two-hour metered parking is available on LAX's Lower/Arrival area opposite Terminals 1, 2A, 2B, 3, 4, 6, and 7. 25¢ gets you fifteen minutes, so bring plenty of quarters. But these lots can be hard to spot, and you may find yourself in one of the pricier structures opposite each of the terminals. Parking for up to two hours in these lots costs $4, with a $30 maximum. For long-term parking it's best to use Lots B and C, but be sure to allow an extra half-hour in your schedule for dealing with the parking lot shuttle bus. Lot C is at Sepulveda Blvd. and 96th Street, and rates are $10 for each 24 hours. Lot B is further away, at La Cienega and 111th Street, but less expensive at just $8 per day.

General Information	
Website:	www.los-angeles-lax.com
Email:	Infoline@airports.ci.la.ca.us
Phone:	1-888-544-9444
Baggage Storage:	310-646-0222
Lost and Found:	310-417-0440
Police:	310-646-7911
First Aid:	310-215-6000
Customs Information:	310-215-2415
Los Angeles MTA:	800-266-6883

Car Rental	
Alamo	310-649-2245
Avis	310-342-9208
Budget	310-642-4555
Dollar	310-410-5454
Enterprise	310-215-6856
Fox	888-332-4369
Hertz	310-568-3434
National	909-937-7555
Ritz	800-641-3222
Thrifty	310-645-1880
U-Save	310-649-5806

Hotels

Best Western Airpark Hotel
640 W Manchester Blvd, 310-673-5550
Comfort Inn and Suites
4922 W Century Blvd, 310-671-7213
Days Inn Airport Center
901 W Manchester Blvd, 310-646-3478
Los Angeles Airport Hilton
5711 W Century Blvd, 310-410-4000
Los Angeles Airport Marriott
5855 W Century Blvd, 310-215-1355
Motel 6
5101 W Century Blvd, 310-419-1234
Travelodge LAX Century Blvd
5547 W Century Blvd, 310-649-4000

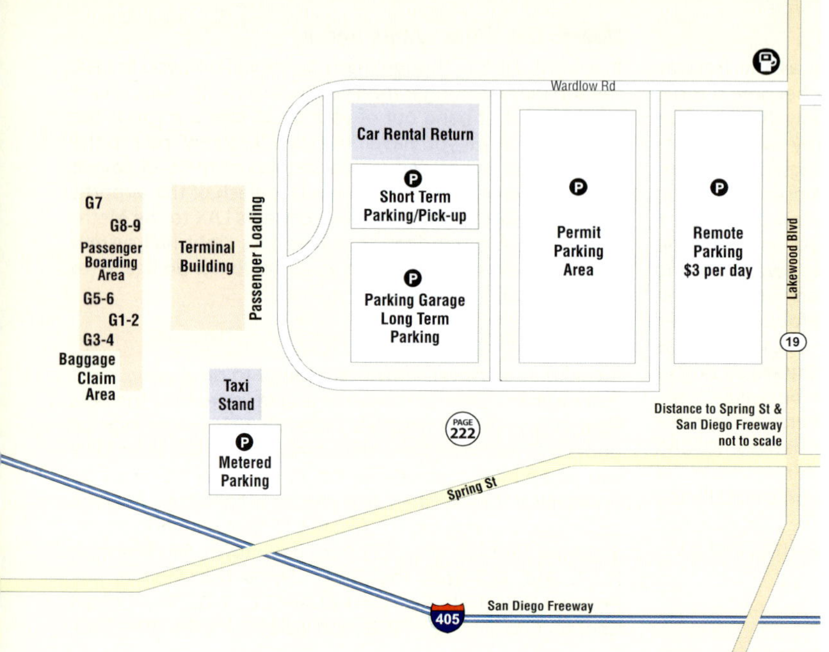

Parking

Long Beach Airport has the lowest parking rates of any airport in the Los Angeles basin. The first twenty minutes are free. Each hour after that will clock up $1. The maximum daily rate in the long-term parking is $12. There is a 2 hour maximum for short-term parking. There is also a $6 per day "Park and Walk" lot at the main airport entrance on the corner of Donald Douglas Drive and Lakewood Boulevard.

Overview

If the Long Beach Airport offered flights to more destinations, it might be the best airport in the world. But then again, if it offered more options, it would be that much busier and would probably lose some of its appeal. A trip to the Long Beach Airport feels like a throwback to the 1940s, when the art deco style terminal was built. The airport is tiny, with an outdoor baggage claim area, making it impossible to get lost. Sadly, however, Long Beach Airport only offers flights to Dallas (on American Airlines), to Seattle (on Horizon Air), and to Phoenix (on America West). However, bargain start-up JetBlue has recently begun offering several low-priced, non-stop flights to New York out of Long Beach, making the airport a definite option for East Coast travel.

History

When you visit Long Beach Airport, it's not just an airport that you're looking at, but a valuable piece of Los Angeles history. During the 1920s, landings and take-offs were performed on the city's huge crescent-shaped beach at low tides. In 1923, a 150-acre piece of land was set aside on the site where the airport now resides. By 1941, the airfield had increased to 500 acres and the airport's art deco style terminal building was completed. Relics and photos of times past can be viewed at the Long Beach Airport Historical Aviation Exhibit, opened in 1991 at the airport's 50th anniversary.

How to Get There—Driving

Long Beach Airport can be reached easily from just about anywhere in the Los Angeles basin. From the 405, take the Lakewood Boulevard exit northbound. Proceed past Spring Street to the next stop light, which is Donald Douglas Drive. Turn left into the main entrance to the airport. From the 91 freeway, take the Lakewood Boulevard exit and proceed southbound approximately four miles. Make a right at Donald Douglas Drive into the main airport entrance.

How to Get There—Mass Transit

If you really must take public transport, for 90 cents the Long Beach Transit bus Route 111 runs from Broadway to South Street via Lakewood Boulevard and makes a stop right at the airport. You can take the Blue Line train from downtown LA to the Transit Mall Station in Long Beach to connect with the Route 111 bus. Visit the Long Beach Transit website at www.lbtransit.com or call 562-591-2301 for schedule information. Visit the Los Angeles MTA website at www.mta.net for Blue Line schedules or dial 800-commute.

If you're in the Long Beach area, you don't have a car, and you don't wish to take public transport, your best bet is going to be a Long Beach Yellow Cab. Alternatively, if you would like to employ an airport van, shuttle, or limousine you can call 562-570-2600 for current listings.

Airlines

America West
American Airlines
JetBlue Airways
Horizon Air

General Information

Website: www.lgb.org
Email: lgbarpt@ci.long-beach.ca.us
Phone: 562-570-2678
Fax: 562-570-2603
Safety Hotline: 877-723-3542
Public Affairs: 562-570-2640
Long Beach Yellow Cab: 562-549-6900
Long Beach Transit Bus: 562-591-2301
Long Beach Transit Website
www.lbtransit.com

Car Rental

Avis   800-831-2847
Budget   800-221-1203
Enterprise   800-325-8007
Hertz   800-654-1120
National   800-227-7368

Hotels

Holiday Inn Long Beach Airport
    2640 Lakewood Blvd., 562-597-4401
Long Beach Airport Marriott
    4700 Airport Plaza Drive, 562-425-5210
Residence Inn by Marriott
    4111 E. Willow Street, 562-595-0909

Overview

Though most Angelenos associate John Wayne with Hollywood westerns rather than air travel, Orange County has seen fit to name its only commercial airport after the actor, a longtime O.C. resident, and honor the Duke with a nine-foot bronze statue, complete with cowboy hat and spurs. Located well behind the "Orange Curtain," John Wayne Airport is a trek from LA (approximately fifty miles), but airlines can sometimes make it worth your while with slightly lower fares to and from Orange County. Unlike LAX's often confusing loop of terminals and parking lots, John Wayne is much more user-friendly, even without trendy bars and restaurants. Aesthetically, the airport makes a real effort, featuring rotating art exhibits on the departure level. John Wayne boasts just two terminals, compared to LAX's eight, and parking is predictably easier as well. Probably the best thing we can say about John Wayne Airport is that it isn't LAX.

How to Get There—Driving

Sadly, most paths from LA County to John Wayne Airport at some point lead to the 405 Freeway—one of LA's more congested routes. But the 405 will also bring you closest to John Wayne, which lies just a short distance from the MacArthur Blvd. Exit (CA-73). The most direct route from many parts of LA is to take the San Diego Freeway (405 S) to CA-73 South, then take the exit towards Irvine Avenue/Campus Drive/John Wayne Airport and follow the signs into the airport from there. From downtown or the eastern part of Los Angeles, however, there is another option. You can take the Santa Ana Freeway (5 S) to the Costa Mesa Freeway (55 S), exiting at the ramp marked "I-405 S to San Diego/John Wayne Airport" and follow the signs from there.

How to Get There—Mass Transit

From LA? You've got to be kidding. But if you're determined to go this route, you'd better have a lot of free time. There are no direct bus routes that connect Los Angeles County with John Wayne Airport. However, for just $3.35, the MTA can get you as far as Disneyland! After the two-hour bus ride from LA, you might enjoy a few rides down Space Mountain or the Matterhorn. When you're through, board Bus #43 heading south toward Costa Mesa, and take this to the corner of Harbor and MacArthur Blvds. From here, transfer to Bus #76 heading east toward Newport Beach, which will take you right past the airport.

How to Get There—Car Services

This may also not be the most attractive option for most people. A taxi ride from Los Angeles to John Wayne Airport starts from about $75 to $80. Some companies to consider are L.A. Taxi, 213-627-7000, and the Beverly Hills Cab Company, 310-273-6611. Returning from John Wayne offers fewer alternatives. The John Wayne Airport Yellow Cab Service, 800-535-2211, is the only company authorized to pick up fares at John Wayne Airport. They'll charge around $90 from the airport to downtown. Supershuttle, 800-258-3826, is a veritable bargain, at $50 from downtown to John Wayne.

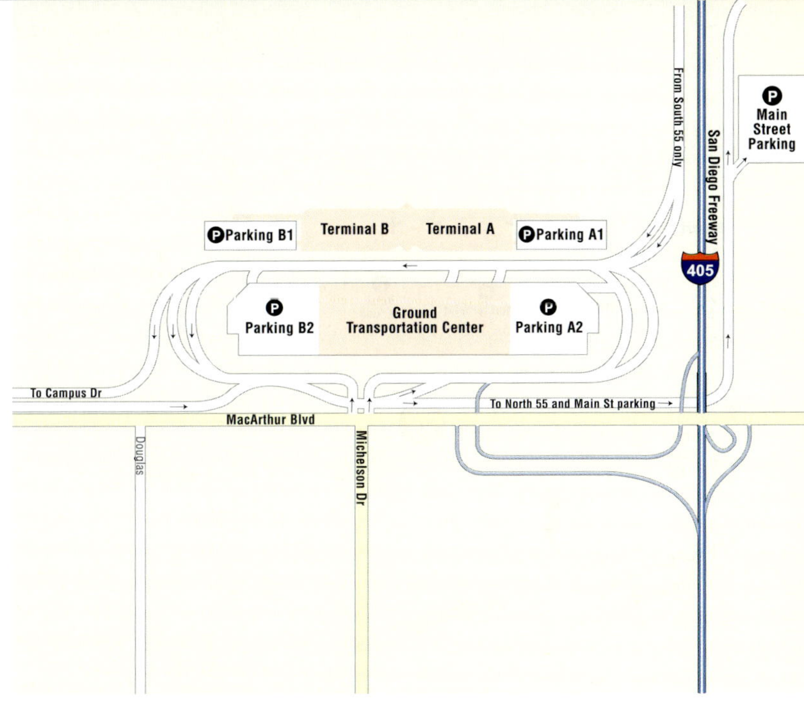

How to Get There-Really

Honestly, you're better off driving yourself. Most of your friends will make themselves scarce when you hit them up for a ride and, in the long run, long-term parking may end up being much cheaper than a car service.

Parking

Valet parking is available at John Wayne for $20 per day. But if you leave a few extra minutes before your flight, you can save a fair amount of money by parking your own car. Short-term lots (A2, A2, B1, and B2) charge $1 per hour, with a $17 maximum for the first and second 24-hour periods. Long-term parking lots (the only slightly more distant Main Street Lot) max out at $12 per day, and a courtesy shuttle to the terminal is available every 15 minutes. Selected parking spaces are available in Lots A1 and B1 for a two-hour maximum, and are ideal for dropping people off and picking up.

Airlines	Terminal
Alaska	A
Aloha	B
American	A
American Eagle	A
America West	B
America West Express	B
Continental	A
Delta	A
Delta Connection (Skywest)	A
Northwest	B
Southwest	B
United	B
United Express (Skywest)	B
US Airways	B

General Information

Website:	www.ocair.com
Email:	amccarley@ocair.com
Phone:	949-252-5200
American Taxi:	888-482-9466
Airport Bus:	800-772-5299
Airport Tours:	949-252-5168

Car Rental

On-Site:

Alamo	800-327-9633
Avis	800-230-4898
Budget	800-221-1203
Enterprise	800-736-8222
Hertz	800-654-3131
National	800-227-7368
Thrifty	800-847-4389

Off-Site:

Advantage	800-777-5500
Fox	800-225-4369
Ritz	800-641-3222
United	866-878-6483

Hotels

Best Western
 2700 Hotel Terrace Dr, 800-432-0053
Embassy Suites
 1325 E Dyer Rd, 714-241-3800
Holiday Inn
 2726 South Grand Ave, 800-888-5540
Quality Suites
 2701 Hotel Terrace Dr, 714-957-9200
Ramada Plaza
 2726 S Grand Ave, 800-707-6375
Travelodge
 1400 SE Bristol Street, 714-557-8700

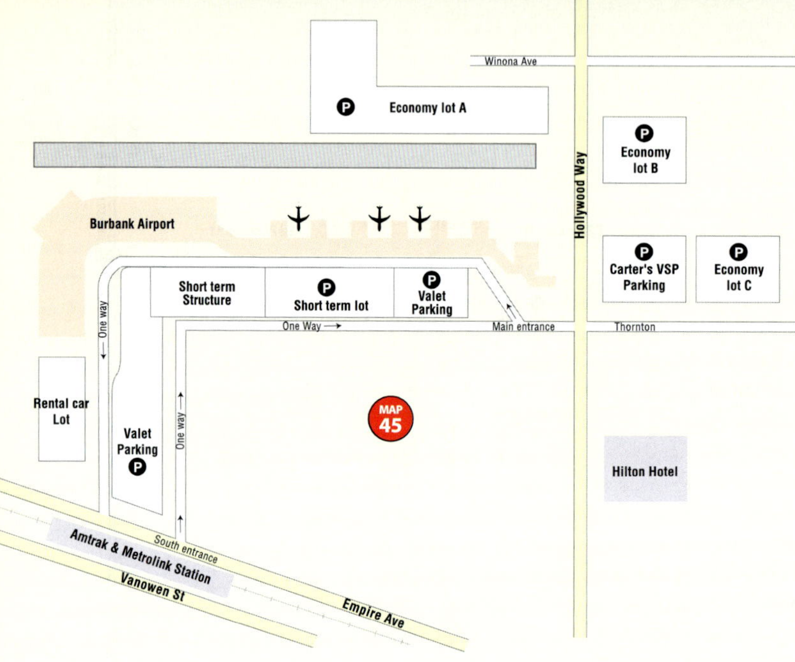

Overview

Burbank Airport is a great deal smaller and more user-friendly than LAX, and is a smart alternative for residents of the San Fernando and San Gabriel Valleys. Like many parts of the Valley itself, the airport doesn't have a great deal of personality, but what it lacks in ambience it makes up for in convenience—although it lacks the selection of airlines, flights, and amenities found at the behemoth LAX. But the Burbank Airport is planning a new and improved terminal building to replace the existing structure. While still maintaining the same number of gates, the interior of the building will become significantly roomier, allowing for more concession and lounge areas for the 5 million people who use it each year.

How to Get There—Driving

The airport is just off I-5, so if you're approaching from the north or south, take I-5 and exit at the Lincoln Street/Burbank Airport Exit. Head north on San Fernando Boulevard, turn left onto N. Lincoln Street, make a right onto Thornton Avenue and another right onto N. Hollywood Way.

If you're approaching from the south on 101 N, take the Vineland Avenue exit, go north on Vineland for approx. 2.7 miles, turn right onto Victory Boulevard and then make a left onto N. Hollywood Way.

Approaching from the west, take 101 S to CA-134 E, then take the Vineland Avenue exit and follow the above directions.

From the east, take CA-134 west to I-5 and follow the directions given for I-5 above.

It's also possible—and often preferable—to drive to Burbank Airport from parts of the Valley by taking any number of surface roads. Sherman Way is a fairly direct route to the airport from the western end of the Valley. From all other directions, it's best to choose your favorite non-freeway route to Hollywood Way and take that right into the airport.

How to Get There—Mass Transit

If you're a fan of taking public transport, you are in luck! Similar to the rail systems in Europe and Japan, Metrolink and Amtrak trains both go right to the airport—well almost! The terminals are just a short walk or a free shuttle bus away.

The Burbank Airport station is on the yellow line of the Metrolink service and, depending on where you're coming from, during peak hours it will cost between $4 one-way (if you're traveling in the same zone) and $10.25 (if you're starting from the very end of the Orange County Line). If you're making your journey outside of peak traveling times, you can expect to pay between $3 and $7.75, www.metrolink.com, 800-371-LINK.

Amtrak's Pacific Surfliner Train (which runs from San Diego to San Luis Obispo) also makes a stop at the Burbank Airport Rail Station and Amtrak's Motor Coach Service to the San Joaquin trains in Bakersfield stops nearby, www.amtrakwest.com, 800-USA-RAIL.

MTA buses are slower and cheaper, but will also get you there. Numbers 94, 163, 165, and 394 all make stops at Burbank Airport. For schedules and fare information, check out the MTA website at www.mta.net or give them a call at 800-COMMUTE.

Parking

Most people who regularly opt for Burbank over LAX admit that the latter has one advantage over its Valley alternative—parking at Burbank Airport is definitely more expensive. An hour in the short-term parking will cost you $1.82, an additional $3.64 for the second hour, and another $5.45 for the third hour. If you stay longer than that, the price increases significantly. Four hours will set you back $10.91, five hours and the maximum daily rate is $15.45. If you're planning on parking for longer than a day, a better option is the Economy Parking Lot, which operates a free shuttle to the terminal building and starts at $1.82 per hour with the maximum daily cost set at $4.55. Travelers coming from nearby Warner Brothers and Disney Studios are among those who rave about Burbank Airport's valet parking option—its flashiest and most LA feature—but be prepared to stay more than one day, at a rate of $11.82 per day.

Airlines

Alaska	Aloha
American	America West
Southwest	United

Car Rental

On-Site:

Alamo	800-327-9633
Avis	800-331-1212
Hertz	800-654-3131
National	800-227-7368

Off-Site:

Budget	800-527-0700
Dollar	800-800-4000
Enterprise	818-558-7336
Horizon	800-472-8661
Thrifty	800-843-7376

General Information

Website: www.bur.com
Email: answers@bur.org
Phone: 818-840-8840
Parking Information: 818-840-8837

Hotels

Anabelle Hotel   2011 W Olive Ave, 818-845-7800
Hilton Burbank
        2500 Hollywood Way, 800-468-3576
Hilton Universal City
        555 Universal Terrace Pkwy, 800-727-7110
Ramada Inn Burbank
        2900 N San Fernando Blvd, 818-843-5955
Safari Inn   1911 W Olive Ave, 818-845-8586
Sheraton Universal
        333 Universal Terrace Pkwy, 818-980-1212
Travelodge Burbank
        1112 N Hollywood Way, 818-845-2408

Airline	Phone	LAX	John Wayne	Burbank	Long Beach
Aer Lingus	800-474-7424	●			
Aero California	800-428-2163	●			
Aeroflot	888-340-6400	●			
Aeromexico	800-237-6639	●			
Air Canada/Canadian	888-247-2262	●			
Air China	800-882-8122	●			
Air France	800-232-2747	●			
Air Jamaica	800-523-5585	●			
Air Mobility Command (AMC)	310-363-0715	●			
Air New Zealand	800-262-1234	●			
Air Pacific	310-227-0290	●			
Air Tahiti Nui	877-824-4846	●			
Alaska Airlines	800-426-0333	●	●	●	
Alitalia	800-223-5730	●			
All Nippon Airways (ANA)	800-235-9262	●			
Aloha Airlines	800-367-5250		●	●	
America West Airlines	800-235-9292	●	●	●	●
American Airlines	800-433-7300	●	●	●	●
American Trans Air	800-225-2995	●			
Asiana Airlines	800-227-4262	●			
Avianca	800-284-2622	●			
British Airways	800-247-9297	●			
Canada 3000	310-338-2201	●			
Cathay Pacific Airways	800-233-2742	●			
Champion Air	800-922-2606	●			
China Airlines	800-227-5118	●			
China Eastern	626-583-1500	●			
China Southern	888-338-8988	●			
Continental Airlines	800-525-0280	●	●		
Copa Airlines (Panama)	800-359-2672	●			
Corsair	800-677-0720	●			
Delta Airlines	800-221-1212	●	●		
Egypt Air	800-334-6787	●			
El Al Israel Airlines	800-223-6700	●			
EVA Air	800-695-1188	●			
Frontier	800-432-1359	●			
Hawaiian Airlines	800-367-5320	●			
Horizon	800-547-9308	●			●
Japan Air Lines	800-525-3663	●			
JetBlue Airways	800-538-2583				●
KLM Royal Dutch Airlines	800-556-9000	●			
Korean Airlines	800-438-5000	●			
LACSA Airlines	800-225-2272	●			
LAN Chile	800-735-5526	●			
LTU International Airways	800-888-0200	●			
Lufthansa German Airlines	800-645-3880	●			
Malaysia Airline System	800-552-9264	●			
Mexicana Airlines	800-531-7921	●			
Miami Air	305-871-8001	●			
Midwest Express	800-452-2022	●			
National Airlines	888-757-5387	●			
Northwest Airlines	800-225-5252	●	●		
Omni Air International	310-646-1930	●			
Philippine Airlines	800-435-9725	●			
QANTAS	800-227-4500	●			
Singapore Airlines	800-742-3333	●			
Skywest Airlines	800-241-6522	●		●	
Southwest Airlines	800-435-9792	●	●	●	
Spirit	800-772-7117	●			
Sun Country Airlines	800-359-6786	●			
Swissair	800-221-4740	●			
TACA International Airlines	800-535-8780	●			
Thai Airways	800-426-5204	●			
United Airlines	800-241-6522	●	●	●	
United Shuttle	800-748-8853	●			
US Airways	800-428-4322	●	●		
Vanguard	800-826-4827	●			
Varig Brazilian Airlines	800-468-2744	●			
Virgin Atlantic Airways	800-862-8621	●			
World Airlines	800-967-5395	●			

Overview

Thousands of buses make up the majority of LA's public transport network, covering more than 300 routes throughout the city. Although most of the buses are administered by the Metropolitan Transportation Authority (MTA), not all of them are, and fares and procedures vary between services. The websites for the services are an excellent resource for getting route and schedule information and trip planning. Fares for seniors, the disabled, and students can be as low as 25% of the full fare and differ for each service. While discounts for seniors and the disabled can be paid as individual fares or using discounted monthly passes, students are usually required to purchase monthly tickets—more information can be obtained from each student's school, as the cost of fares can vary between schools. On all services, children under the age of five ride free. Be aware that you should have the correct fare (and documentation if necessary) ready when you board each bus. Most of the fare machines take $1 notes but do not give change. If you're planning a journey that will incorporate multiple services including buses, rail, and even Amtrak, the Metro Trip Planner website will tell you how to get from point A to point B in a matter of seconds and it will conveniently detail times, fares and directions (for details, see the Metro Trip Planner section on the next page).

Metropolitan Transportation Authority (MTA)

www.mta.net 1-800-COMMUTE

MTA buses are distinguished by their white color and distinctive orange and red stripes. Bus stops have a big orange M on a white, rectangular sign. A single fare on an MTA bus costs $1.35 (45¢ senior/disabled). If your journey involves changing buses, you can purchase a 25¢ transfer (10¢ senior/disabled) from the driver when you board. If you're changing buses again, buy another transfer from the driver when you hand in the first transfer. Transfers are good for approximately one hour after you receive them. If you plan to switch to the Metro Rail, the same transfers are valid. (If you're transferring from the Metro Rail to Bus Lines 20, 21, 22, 320, or 322, make sure you ask for your free transfer).

If you're planning on using the bus at least ten times, it is much cheaper to purchase a bag of 10 tokens at a local store or supermarket for $9, effectively making each journey only 90¢. If you're a regular bus user, you might consider buying a weekly pass ($11), semi-monthly pass ($21), or regular monthly pass ($42, and $12 senior/disabled). You can't just buy the semi-monthly and monthly passes anytime, though. They begin from the 25th or the 9th of the current month and can be bought in person from Metro Customer Centers or ordered through the mail and delivered to your home or office. MTA passes are valid on Commuter Express, DASH Downtown LA, Community Connection Routes 142, 147, 203, 208, and all Metro MTA rail and bus routes. However, LADOT passes are not valid on MTA services.

Los Angeles Department of Transportation (LADOT)

www.ladottransit.com 213, 310, 323 or 818-808-2273

DASH (Downtown Area Short Hop) shuttle system operates buses A, B, C, D, E, and F throughout downtown LA. This reliable service runs every 5 to 15 minutes, depending on the time of day and route, and costs only 25¢. The buses not only service downtown, but also stop at the city's major landmarks and sites, including Union Station, the Convention Center, USC, Exposition Park, and the Garment District. DASH also runs services to many parts of west LA including Venice, Hollywood, West Hollywood, Beverly Hills, Studio City and Watts, Wilmington, Northridge, Chatsworth, and Crenshaw.

The **Commuter Express** is mainly a service for people traveling to and from work between downtown LA and suburbs such as Culver City, Westwood, Brentwood, Encino, Glendale, Burbank, Redondo Beach, and the San Fernando Valley. Each journey costs between $1.10 and $3.10, depending on your departure and destination points and how long you travel on the freeways. Seniors/disabled pay half the regular fare.

Community Connection serves the needs of city neighborhoods including San Pedro, Terminal Island, Long Beach Transit Mall, Griffith Park, and Beachwood Canyon. LADOT also operates an electric trolley in San Pedro, which runs solely on battery power and departs every 15 minutes. One-way fares on the regular bus routes costs 90¢, 45¢ disabled/senior, and the electric trolley is 25¢ per ride.

Municipal Buses

Santa Monica Bus Lines serves Santa Monica, Malibu, and Venice, and it will cost you a mere 75¢ to race between the beach towns. They also operate an express bus (Line 10) to downtown LA that costs $1.75 (60¢ seniors, 25¢ disabled). If you buy a "Little Blue Card," you'll save pennies per ride. The big blue buses are instantly recognizable, and the stops are identified by a blue triangle on a light pole marked "Big Blue Bus," www.bigbluebus.com, 310-451-5444.

The **West Hollywood CityLine** is a shuttle service that covers 18 locations in West Hollywood and costs 50¢ per ride, 800-447-2189.

Foothill Transit serves primarily the San Gabriel and Pomona Valleys, and fares cost between $1.10 for local trips and $3.35 for the most expensive express journey. Monthly passes cost between $45 for a local pass and up to $133 for a joint Foothills/MTA pass on the most expensive express route, www.foothilltransit.org, 626-967-4147.

Culver CityBus costs 75¢ (50¢ student, 35¢ senior/disabled) and covers Culver City, Venice, Mar Vista, LAX, and Westwood/UCLA. www.culvercity.org/depts_bus.html, 310-253-6500.

Orange County Transit Authority (OCTA)

www.octa.net, 714-636-RIDE for Central and North Orange County, 800-636-RIDE for South Orange County, Riverside and Corona.

The regular fare on OCTA buses is $1, with senior and disability fares a mere 25¢. A day pass entitles you to unlimited use of all local routes (excluding express routes 701 & 721) on the day it is purchased and costs $2.50 (50¢ senior/disabled). A local monthly pass for OCTA services is $37.50 ($10 senior/disabled). The express monthly pass (includes daily service to Los Angeles aboard routes 701 and 721) is $107. Individual journeys on the 701 and 721 express routes to LA cost $3 and $2 if you have a day pass for that day. (Metrolink monthly passes are now valid on local OCTA services.)

Ventura Intercity Service Transit Authority (VISTA)

www.goventura.org/vista/vista.htm, 800-438-1112

Fixed bus routes will set you back $1 per ride (50¢ senior/disability). Santa Paula and Fillmore dial-a-rides cost $1.50 (75¢ senior/disability), and the Conejo Connection/Coastal Express is $2 ($1 senior/disability). Monthly passes vary from between $40 and $75, depending on the routes you plan to take.

Metro Trip Planner — http://mtaweb6.mta.net

The search engine website is one of the best public transport facilities we've ever seen. The search engine covers more than 45 of Southern California's transport networks including MTA buses and trains, OCTA and VISTA buses, Amtrak, Metrolink, MAX, and dozens of municipal services across Southern California.

Using the search facility, you enter your start point, end point, the day you'd like to travel, the time you need to arrive at your destination, fare category, special accommodations such as wheelchairs and bicycles, and then you submit your requirements. What you get in return is a detailed description of the journey you need to take, including the type of transport, where it leaves from, the times it departs and arrives, the fare for each sector, and where you need to transfer. For example, if you were going from Universal Studios to Disneyland, leaving your departure point at 12 noon, you would take the Red Metro Line at Universal City Station (12:16 pm—$1.60, get MTA transfer), get off at 7th Street Metro Center and exit at Figueroa (12:37 pm) and take MTA Bus #460 Anaheim/Disneyland (12:43 pm, show driver transfer and pay $2). Get off at Disneyland at 2:39 pm and the entire journey will have cost you $3.60.

Start and end points can be addresses (including residential), intersections, or landmarks, and you can also decide whether you want the fastest itinerary, fewest transfers, or shortest walking distance. It's a good idea to try all three, as often the travel times are very similar and the cost difference is significant. The other thing to remember is that it doesn't recognize neighborhoods, so if you're traveling to or from somewhere like Venice, make sure you use "Los Angeles" as the city or it won't recognize the input. It also works best if you use abbreviated versions of roads (Rd, St, Dr, Bl). If it doesn't recognize an intersection, try reversing the street names and see if that helps. A terrific system to employ should you be planning to use the public transport network, it's too bad the public transport system itself is not quite so clever and efficient.

Union Station

Union Station, built in 1939, is located in downtown Los Angeles on 800 N. Alameda St., between the Santa Ana Freeway (US 101) and Cesar E. Chavez Avenue (Formerly Macy St.). Union Station services three rail networks—the local Metro Rail Red Line, Amtrak (including the Pacific Sunliner and Coast Starlight Lines), and Southern California's Metrolink. A plan to extend the Blue Line, linking Union Station with Chinatown, Highland Park, and Pasadena, was scheduled to open in May 2001, but has been delayed until July 2003.

Amtrak

Amtrak, America's intercity national rail network, has five major lines that depart from LA's Union Station. Pacific Surfliner (formerly the San Diegans) runs between San Diego, LA, and Santa Barbara and on to San Luis Obispo and Paso Robles. This is the train to take if you want beautiful ocean views! A one-way trip from San Diego to LA will set you back just under $25 and will get you there in under three hours—traveling the length of the line costs $62. Amtrak no longer offers transportation to Las Vegas via train since the Desert Wind line closed down, but they do provide a bus service, which takes 5 to 6 hours depending on what time you leave, and it costs $34.50. Shuttle service to Bakersfield connects the Pacific Surfliner with the San Joaquin trains, which run from Bakersfield through Fresno to Oakland. The Coast Starlight runs the length of the coast from LA through Oakland and Portland to Seattle. The LA-to-Oakland fare is $66, and if you go all the way to Seattle, it will cost you $145. If you're trying to get to San Francisco, take the train to Oakland and then Amtrak's motor connection to San Francisco, which takes roughly an hour ($74). If you're heading east, the Sunset Limited line is the train you need. It runs from LA through Tucson–(Phoenix)–San Antonio–Houston–New Orleans–Jacksonville and Orlando. The Texas Eagle has a similar first leg and covers Los Angeles–Tucson–San Antonio–Dallas–Little Rock–St. Louis–Chicago. The Southwest Chief goes from LA to Kansas City to Chicago. Check the Amtrak website or call to check schedules on the days you wish to travel.
Website: www.amtrak.com and www.amtrakwest.com
Phone: 800-USA-RAIL
Email: service@sales.amtrak.com

Metrolink

Not to be confused with the MTA's Metro Rail, Metrolink is an aboveground rail network which primarily services Southern California, including Los Angeles County, Ventura County, San Bernadino County, Orange County, Riverside County, and San Diego County. The lines run as far south as Oceanside in San Diego County and as far north as Montalvo in Ventura County and Lancaster in LA County. Fares are calculated according to the number of zones you cross during your journey. A peak hour one-way fare can cost between $4 and $10.25, and it is definitely cheaper to purchase a round-trip ticket ($6.50 peak one zone) at the beginning of your journey rather than two one-way fares. If you're planning on taking a few trips, the 10-trip pass is a good purchase at $27.00 for one zone ($2.70 for each fare), up to $92 for seven zones. There are discounts for seniors/disabled at all times and for youth during off-peak hours. Monthly passes are also available ($86.50–$294.25) for daily train users.
Website: www.metrolinktrains.com Phone: 800-371-LINK

Metro Rail

The Metro Rail network is ever-expanding as the city of LA realizes the importance of having an effective rail network. Parts of the system run underground, but the majority of the tracks have been laid above ground. Whatever the case, taking the Metro Rail is much faster than sitting on slow, crowded city buses, with the only downfall being somewhat limited coverage.

It takes a lot to get LA residents out of their cars, but Metro Rail is becoming a popular alternative, particularly for people heading for destinations like the Wiltern, Staples Center, or Universal City—all of which are located just steps from a subway stop.

You don't need to swipe your ticket or hand it to station supervisors when you use Metro Rail. Police check tickets for validity onboard trains, and if you fail to produce a valid ticket, you will receive a fine worth well more than the fare. So it's a good idea to purchase a ticket before you board.

The new modern light-rail will extend the Blue Line from Union Station in downtown LA out to Pasadena in an attempt to ease traffic on the Pasadena (110) and Foothill (I-210) Freeways, and should be finished in a couple of years. Talks are still underway about access to the west side, but, as Metro Rail's popularity grows, this seems to be a more viable possibility.

To take your bike on a train, you have to apply for a free metro permit available through the mail. Call 1-800-COMMUTE and ask for Metro Cycle Express and they will send you a permit application. Bicycles are allowed onboard Metro Rail trains during non-peak times and are excluded from boarding weekdays from 6-9 am and 3-7 pm. Bicycle racks and lockers are available for use at select Metro stations. Bicycle racks are available on a first-come, first-serve basis free of charge, and lockers may be leased through Cycle Express.

North Hollywood
Universal City
Hollywood/Highland
Hollywood/Vine
Hollywood/Western
Vermont/Sunset
Vermont/Santa Monica/City College
Vermont/Beverly
Wilshire/Western
Wilshire/Normandie
Wilshire/Vermont
Westlake/MacArthur
7th Street/Metro Center
Civic Center/Tom Bradley
Union Station/Gateway Transit Center
Pershing Square
Pico
Grand
San Pedro
Washington
Vernon
Slauson
Florence
Firestone
103rd St/Kenneth Hahn
Hawthorne
Aviation
Mariposa/Nash
El Segundo/Nash
Douglas/Rosecrans
Marine/Redondo
Vermont
Crenshaw
Harbor Freeway
Avalon
Imperial/Wilmington/Rosa Parks
Long Beach
Lakewood
I 605/I 105
Compton
Artesia
Del Amo
Wardlow
Willow
Pacific Coast Highway
Anaheim
Pacific
Transit Mall
5th Street
1st Street
Pacific Ocean

"Turn the world over on its side and everything loose will land in Los Angeles."
—Frank Lloyd Wright

Useful Phone Numbers

Emergencies	**911**
Los Angeles City Hall	(213) 485-2121
Pacific Bell	(800) 310-BELL
CalTrans	(213) 897-3656
DWP	(800) 342-5397
Southern California Edison	(800) 655-4555
The Gas Company	(800) 427-2200

Websites

- **www.notfortourists.com** — The most comprehensive L.A. site there is.
- **www.lacity.org** — The city's official home on the web.
- **traffic.info.lacity.org** — Real time traffic information.
- **www.losangelesalmanac.com** — Anything you could ever need to know about L.A.
- **www.lausd.k12.ca.us** — Contact info and report cards for schools in your neighborhood.

Less Practical Information

- Los Angeles averages 329 days of sunshine each year. Yet we still whine about the other 36.
- The longest street in Los Angeles is Sepulveda Boulevard, which runs 76 miles from the San Fernando Valley to Long Beach.
- With few exceptions, L.A. bars are legally prohibited from serving alcohol between the hours of 2 am and 6 am.
- The Library Tower (633 W. Fifth Street) is Los Angeles' tallest building (and was spectacularly taken out by aliens in the 1997 blockbuster, "Independence Day").
- The city boasts more stage theaters (80+) and museums (300) than any other city in the U.S. And New Yorkers say we have no culture.
- There are 527 miles of freeway and 382 miles of conventional highway in Los Angeles County. Bette Midler is determined to clean up all of them.
- Angelenos drive 92 million vehicle miles every day. Giving them ample time to admire the amber hues of our smog-riddled sunsets.
- Annually, L.A. residents consume over one billion pounds of red meat, over 300 billion pounds of ice cream, and absolutely no carbs whatsoever.

Essential L.A. Movies

Sunset Boulevard (1950)
Singin' in the Rain (1952)
Rebel Without a Cause (1955)
Chinatown (1974)
Shampoo (1975)
10 (1979)
Blade Runner (1982)
Valley Girl (1983)
Down and Out in Beverly Hills (1986)
L.A. Story (1991)
Grand Canyon (1991)
The Player (1992)
Short Cuts (1993)
Volcano (1997)
L.A. Confidential (1997)

Essential L.A. Songs

"Hooray for Hollywood" — Various, written by Johnny Mercer & Richard A. Whiting (1937)
"There's No Business Like Show Business" —Ethel Merman, written by Irving Berlin (1954)
"California Girls" — The Beach Boys (1965)
"Ladies of the Canyon" — Joni Mitchell (1970)
"L.A. Woman" — The Doors (1971)
"I Am… I Said" — Neil Diamond (1971)
"You're So Vain" — Carly Simon (1972)
"Eggs and Sausage" — Tom Waits (1975)
"Hotel California" — The Eagles (1976)
"The Pretender" — Jackson Browne (1976)
"Valley Girl" — Frank and Moon Unit Zappa (1982)
"I Love L.A." — Randy Newman (1983)
"My Life is Good" — Randy Newman (1983)
"Sunset Grill" — Don Henley (1984)
"Paradise City" — Guns N Roses (1987)
"F—- Tha Police" — N.W.A. (1988)
"Free Fallin'" — Tom Petty (1989)
"Neighborhood" — Los Lobos (1990)
"All I Wanna Do" — Sheryl Crow (1993)
"Californication" — Red Hot Chili Peppers (1999)

Los Angeles Timeline

1781	El Pueble de Nuestra Senora de la Reina de Los Angeles de Porciuncula — AKA, Los Angeles — is founded.
1822	Los Angeles becomes a Mexican City when Mexico wins its independence from Spain.
1842	Gold rush hits Southern California.
1850	L.A. County is established, City of L.A. is incorporated.
1880	USC is founded.
1881	Rail lines between L.A. and the East Coast are completed.
1881	The L.A. Times begins printing.
1882	Electricity comes to downtown L.A.
1890	First Tournament of Roses Parade.
1891	CalTech opens its doors
1892	Abbott Kinney stakes his claim in Venice.
1894	Labor rioting breaks out in L.A. during national railroad strike.
1896	Griffith J.Griffith donates land that will become Griffith Park.
1899	L.A. Stock Exchange opens
1902	City's first movie theater opens for business.
1909	Construction on L.A. aqueduct begins.
1910	Alice Stebbins Wells appointed to L.A. police force as the nation's first female policewoman.
1913	The Los Angeles Aqueduct brings water from the Owens Valley.
1915	Universal Studios opens.
1915	San Fernando Valley annexed by City of L.A.
1919	UCLA is formed.
1922	Hollywood Bowl opens.
1923	The Hollywood Sign is erected.
1932	Tenth Olympic Games are held in L.A.
1939	Union Station opens.
1940	Pasadena Freeway (later the 110) is L.A.'s first freeway.
1946	KTLA is L.A.'s first commercial television station.
1947	Black Dahlia murder. The case is never solved.
1953	The famed "four-level" opens, linking the 101 and 110 freeways.
1954	Completion of the Watts Towers.
1955	Disneyland opens.
1958	The Dodgers relocate from Brooklyn.
1960	The Lakers leave Minneapolis for L.A.
1964	The Music Center opens Downtown.
1965	LACMA opens its door.
1965	The Watts Riots
1968	Robert Kennedy assassinated at Ambassador Hotel
1969	Manson Murders.
1971	Sylmar Earthquake
1974	J. Paul Getty Museum opens in Pacific Palisades.
1980	Screen Actors Guild Strike
1984	The 23rd Olympiad is held in L.A.
1989	Mayor Tom Bradley elected to an unprecedented fifth term.
1991	Rodney King is beaten by four police officers
1992	Verdict in King case leads to citywide rioting.
1992	Landers Earthquake
1993	Menendez Murder Trial #1
1994	O.J. Simpson arrested after slow speed chase.
1994	Northridge Earthquake
1995	Departure of Rams and Raiders leaves L.A. without a football team.
1997	The Getty Center opens in Brentwood.
2002	Anaheim Angels win their first World Series.

January

Event	Location	Description
Tournament of Roses Parade	Pasadena. Just follow the crowds.	A Southern California tradition. (January 1)
Rose Bowl	The Rose Bowl, of course	"The Granddaddy of All Bowl Games." (January 1)
Japanese New Year "Oshogatsu" Celebration	Little Tokyo	Soothe your New Year's hangover with the sound of Taiko drums. (January 1)
Greater LA Auto Show	LA Convention Center	Cars, cars, and, yes, more cars.
Golden Globe Awards	Beverly Hilton Hotel	Better than the Oscars because they let the stars drink. (Third Sunday in January)
Martin Luther King Day Parade	Inglewood. Manchester Blvd. @ Grevillea Park	
Chinese New Year	Chinatown	Features a parade, a street fair, and even a golf tournament. (January or February)

February

Event	Location	Description
Aztec New Year Celebration	Eagle Rock Community Cultural Center	Ring in the Aztec New Year with pre-Columbian style music.
Lunar New Year Parade and Festival	Valley Blvd., Alhambra	Yet one more New Year's celebration…
Firecracker Run 5K/10K	N. Broadway and College Street, Chinatown	Race celebrating Chinese New Year.
Pan African Film & Arts Festival	Magic Johnson Theaters, 3650 Martin Luther King Jr. Blvd.	One of America's largest festivals of black films and fine arts.
Mardi Gras	El Pueblo Historical Monument, 125 Paseo de la Plaza	Celebrate "Fat Tuesday" on Olvera Street.
Brazilian Carnaval	Hollywood Palladium, Sunset & Vine	Samba your way down the Walk of Fame.
Nissan Open	Riviera Country Club, Pacific Palisades	The PGA tour comes to the Westside. (February 14-22)
Scottish Festival	Queen Mary, Long Beach	Wear a kilt, eat some haggis.
American Film Market	Loew's Santa Monica Beach Hotel	Made a movie? Here's where you sell it.
Academy Awards	Kodak Theatre, Hollywood Blvd & Highland Ave	More revered as an LA holiday than Presidents' Day. (February 29)

March

Event	Location	Description
Los Angeles Marathon	Throughout LA	The one day a year we choose not to drive.
West Week	Pacific Design Center, WeHo	An interior design fest!
Cesar E. Chavez Day	Olvera Street	Honors the Mexican American farm labor leader. (March or April)
Spring Fling	LA Zoo	Kiddie crafts and photo ops with "Big Bunny."

April

Event	Location	Description
Blessing of the Animals	Olvera Street	If your pet needs more than pampering…
Bunka Sai Japanese Cultural Festival	Ken Miller Rec. Center, Torrance	Japanese culture, from judo to origami.
Garifuna Street Festival	Avalon Ave., South Central LA	Celebrates largest Black ethnic group in Central America.
Jimmy Stewart Relay	Griffith Park	Like running a marathon, but with help.
Eco Maya Mother Earth Day Festival	Los Angeles City College	Ecology and the cooking of the Largest Tamal in the World.
50+ Fitness Jamboree & Health Expo	Griffith Park	Includes 1K & 5K walks with celebrity seniors.
Toyota Grand Prix of Long Beach	Downtown Long Beach	Auto racing.
Los Angeles Times Book Fair	UCLA campus	The city's biggest and coolest literary event.
Blooming of the Roses	Exposition Park Rose Garden	Stop and smell the roses. Literally.
Annual Arbor Day Festival	Woodley Park, Van Nuys	Trees aren't just for hugging.
Fiesta Broadway	Downtown LA	Celebrate Cinco de Mayo a little early.
Dolo Coker Scholarship Benefit Jazz Concert	Founder's Church, 3281 W 6th St	Supports young jazz hopefuls.

May

Event	Location	Description
Cinco de Mayo Celebration	Olvera Street	Celebrates Mexican independence. Que bueno!
LA Asian Pacific Film & Video Festival	DGA, Japan American Theatre, David Henry Hwang Theatre	Showcases works by Pacific-American and international artists.
Los Angeles Antiques Show	Santa Monica Airport, Barker Hangar	Antiques galore.
Revlon Run/Walk for Women	LA Memorial Coliseum at Exposition Park	5K race raises money for women's cancers.
Avenues of Art and Design	West Hollywood	Art walk.
Family FunFest and Kodomo-no-Hi, Children's Day Celebration	Japanese American Cultural & Community Center, Little Tokyo	Celebrate kids the Japanese way.
Israeli Festival	Woodley Park, Van Nuys	Annual commemoration of Israel's Independence Day
Annual Country Garden Faire	Sepulveda Garden Center, Encino	For those with who have green thumbs, and those who want one.
NOHO Theater and Arts Festival	Lankershim Blvd. & Magnolia, North Hollywood	Performances scattered throughout the NOHO arts district
Affaire in the Gardens	Beverly Gardens Park, Beverly Hills	Art show.
John Anson Ford Amphitheatre Season	Ford Amphitheatre, Hollywood	Dance programs, films, and music galore. (through September)

June

Event	Location	Description
Life Cycle	San Francisco to Los Angeles	600-mile bicycle ride for AIDS-related charities.
Kids' Nature Festival	Temescal Gateway Park, Pacific Palisades	Lets kids interact with nature.
IFP Los Angeles Film Festival	DGA, 7920 Sunset Blvd.	A breath of cinematic fresh air.
JMP Jazz & Blues Festival	Leimert Park Village	Performances by jazz & blues greats, as well as their protégés.

- Great American Irish Fair & Music Festival — Woodley Park, Encino — Like St. Patrick's Day in June.
- Playboy Jazz Festival — Hollywood Bowl — Almost more jazz than you can handle.
- Van Nuys Air Show — Van Nuys Airport — Fancy flying.
- Mariachi-USA Festival — Hollywood Bowl — Traditional mariachi music, as well as Ballet Foklorico.
- Christopher Street West — West Hollywood Park — Celebrates gay pride.
- ArtWallah Festival of South Asian Arts — Art Share, 801 East 4th Place, Downtown — Showcases South Asian Diaspora through the arts.

July

- At the Beach, LA Black Pride Festival — Westin Airport Hotel, Pt. Dume Beach in Malibu — Largest annual gathering of African-American lesbians and gay men in the world.
- Mercedes-Benz Cup — LA Tennis Center, UCLA — Tennis.
- Outfest — DGA, 7920 Sunset Blvd. — Gay and lesbian film festival.
- Lotus Festival — Echo Park Lake — Celebrates Asian and Pacific cultures.
- Central Avenue Jazz Festival — Central Ave. between 42nd and 43rd Streets — Remembers Central Ave. as the hot spot it was from the 1920s–50s.

August

- Long Beach Renaissance Fair — Queen Mary, Long Beach — When the modern world becomes too much to bear…
- Long Beach Jazz Festival — Queen Mary, Long Beach — Jazz by the sea.
- LA International Short Film Festival — Hollywood — For movie lovers with short attention spans.
- Nisei Week Japanese Festival — Little Tokyo — Don't miss the Tofu Festival!
- LA Greek Fest — Mormandy Ave. at Pico — Eat a gyro, break a plate, have some ouzo…
- Marcus Garvey Day Parade and Festival — Elegant Manor, 3115 W. Adams Blvd. — Invites all to celebrate "Africa for the Africans at home or abroad."
- Sunset Junction Street Faire — 3600 to 4600 Sunset Blvd., LA — One of LA's funkiest neighborhoods puts on a fair.

September

- Long Beach Blues Festival — Cal State Long Beach — Spend Labor Day weekend with Blues heavyweights.
- Emmy Awards — Shrine Auditorium — TV's night to shine.
- Lobster Festival — Seaside Lagoon, Redondo Beach — Great food, good music, family fun.
- Los Angeles City Birthday Celebration — El Pueblo Historical Monument, 125 Paseo de la Plaza — Happy Birthday, dear LA-ay, Happy Birthday to you!
- Salvadoran Parade and Festival — LA City College — All things Salvadoran.
- Mexican Independence Celebration — Olvera Street — Traditional Mexican foods and entertainment.
- LA County Fair — Fairplex in Pomona — Livestock, rides, and food on a stick.
- Brazilian Street Carnaval — Downtown Long Beach Promenade Theatre — Rio Brazilian fun.
- Thai Cultural Day — Barnsdall Art Park or LA City College — Day-long celebration of Thailand.
- Oktoberfest — Alpine Village, Torrance — German music, German beer, American hangover.

October

- Asian American Jazz Festival — Luckman Fine Arts Comples, CSULA — Spotlights Asian-American jazz musicians.
- Halloween Carnival — Santa Monica Blvd., WeHo — Fun for kids, more fun for adults. (October 31)
- AIDS Walk — West Hollywood Park — 10K walkathon raises money for AIDS-related organizations.
- Affaire in the Gardens — Beverly Gardens Park, Beverly Hills — Twice-yearly art show.
- Feria de los Ninos Celebration — Hollenbeck Park, East LA — Ethnic food and entertainment with an emphasis on family-friendly activities.
- Echo Park Arts Festival — Various — One of LA's artiest communities' time to shine.
- Harvest Festival of the ARTS — Pico Union Alvarado Terrace Park — Tries to raise children's self-esteem through art.
- KTLA KIDS Day LA Celebration — Exposition Park and Recreation Center — Forget the kids. We want to hang out with Jennifer York.
- International Festival of Masks — LA Craft & Folk Art Museum — Celebrates mask making all around the world.
- Autumn in the Japanese Garden — Japanese Garden, 6100 Woodley Ave., Van Nuys — Learn origami or just stroll through the garden.

November

- Dia de los Muertos Celebration — Olvera Street — Traditional celebration of Mexico's Day of the Dead.
- AFI LA International Film Festival — Various locations — Not as cool as Sundance, but it'll do.
- Los Angeles Mariachi Festival — Mariachi Plaza, Boyle Heights — Spotlights traditional music and food from Mexico.
- Arroyo Arts Collective Discovery Tour — Tour begins at Lummis Home, 200 E Ave 43 — Local artists kindly open up their homes and studios.
- Three Stooges Big Screen Event — Alex Theatre, 216 Brand Blvd, Glendale — Surely this will only interest true cinephiles.
- Doo Dah Parade — Colorado Blvd., Pasadena — Irreverent spoof of the more stately Rose Parade.
- Beverly Hills Flower & Garden Festival — Greystone Estate
- Blockbuster Hollywood Spectacular — Hollywood Blvd., from Grauman's Chinese Theatre to Vine Street — We still like to think of it as the Hollywood Christmas Parade. (Thanksgiving weekend)
- Downtown on Ice, Winter Wonderland Skating Rink — Pershing Square — Pretend you're at a tiny version of Rockefeller Center. (November-December)

December

- KROQ Acoustic Christmas — Universal Amphitheatre — Spotlights hot alternative bands.
- Griffith Park Light Festival — Crystal Springs Road, Griffith Park — Drive-thru tour of impressive lighting displays.
- Marina del Rey Holiday Boat Parade — Main Channel, Marina del Rey — Imaginatively lit boats.
- Navidad en la Calle Ocho — 8th Street at Normandie Ave — 8th Street's answer to the Hollywood Christmas Parade.
- Las Posadas — Olvera Street — Candlelit reenactment of Mary & Joseph's journey to Bethlehem.

The average Los Angeles resident spends an unhealthy amount of time in his or her car, and a large percentage of that time is spent sitting in traffic. There are at least a few ways to pass that time safely and legally. For those of us who aren't lucky enough to have 6-disc CD changers hidden in the trunk, here is what you might find on the LA airwaves.

AM Stations

Freq	Call	Format	Noteworthy Programs
570	KLAC	Talk	Lakers games and music so old it's cool.
600	KOGO	Talk	Talk with a conservative slant. Home of Dr. Laura, Art Bell, and, of course, Rush.
640	KFI	Talk	NFT editors love the Phil Hendrie show. It's classic talk radio with a twist.
690	XETRA	Sports/Talk	UCLA basketball & football, as well as the Jim Rome show.
710	KDIS	Radio Disney	Mickey Mouse and 'N Sync.
740	KBRT	Religious	
790	KABC	News/Talk	Larry Elder, Bill O'Reilly, et al.
830	KPLS	Talk	"Radio on the Right"—Don Imus, Laura Ingraham.
870	KRLA	Talk	Lots of shows about health.
900	KALI	Spanish/Religious	
930	KHJ	Spanish/News	Regional Mexican music.
980	KFWB	News	Their traffic reports are a must-listen for commuters.
1020	KTNQ	News/Talk (Spanish)	Galaxy soccer games.
1070	KNX	News	All news, all the time.
1110	KSPN	Sports	ESPN radio.
1150	KXTA	Sports/Talk	Fox' radio affiliate. Dodger games are heard here.
1190	KEZY	Variety/Foreign Language	
1230	KYPA	Korean programming	Radio Korea.
1260	KJAZ	Jazz	
1280	KFRN	Religious	"Family Radio."
1300	KAZN	Chinese programming	
1330	KWKW	Talk (Spanish)	News, talk, sports, and Laker games en espanol.
1390	KLTX	Religious	
1430	KALI	Spanish	
1460	KTYM	Religious/Foreign language	
1510	KMSL	Sports	"The Muscle"
1540	KMPC	Sports	The Phil Jackson Show, The Sporting News
1650	KFOX	Korean	

FM Stations

Freq	Call	Format	Noteworthy Programs
88.1	KLON	Jazz & Blues	
88.5	KCSN	Eclectic	Their diverse line-up includes a Sunday morning commercial-free Beatles show.
88.7	KSPC	Alternative	College radio at its most bizarre.
88.9	KXLU	Eclectic	More college radio. Sample as you like.
89.3	KPCC	Eclectic/NPR	Lots of radio gameshows, and the often-fascinating "Airtalk" with Larry Mantle.
89.9	KCRW	Eclectic/NPR	NFT editors love "Morning Becomes Eclectic" for music and Harry Shearer's "Le Show" for its satiric look at LA.
90.7	KPFK	Eclectic/Political	Talk radio with a very liberal slant.
91.5	KUSC	Classical	
92.3	KHHT	R&B Oldies	Smokey Robinson spins the oldies on Sundays.
92.7	KLIT	Adult Contemporary	
93.1	KCBS	Classic Rock	Listen long enough and we guarantee you'll start playing the air guitar.
93.5	KFSG	Religious	Pat Boone!
93.9	KZLA	Country	
94.3	KMXN	Adult Contemporary	Like VH1, only softer.
94.7	KTWV	Smooth Jazz	For fans of Kenny G and John Tesh.
95.1	KFRG	Country	"K-Frog" takes its amphibious theme very seriously.
95.5	KLOS	Classic Rock	Mark & Brian in the morning, and old fashioned rock-and-roll all day.
95.9	KFSH	Contemporary Christian	Ultra clean-cut Christian pop and rock music.
96.3	KXOL	Spanish	Spanish pop and dance music.
96.7	KWIZ	Spanish	Spanish programming.
97.1	KLSX	Talk	"Alternative", male-oriented talk. Howard Stern and Tom Leykis are found here.
97.5	KSSE	Spanish Pop/Rock	Modern Spanish hits.
97.9	KLAX	Mexican	Regional Mexican.
98.3	KRCV	Spanish	
98.7	KYSR	Adult Contemporary	Star 98.7. Danny Bonaduce is their morning man. Adult Album Alternative the rest of the day.
99.1	KGGI	Urban Contemporary	
99.5	KKLA	Religious	Religious talk radio.
99.9	KOLA	Rock Oldies	
100.3	KKBT	Urban Contemporary	Hip-hop and R&B.
101.1	KRTH	Oldies	It's always a kinder, gentler time on K-Earth.
101.9	KSCA	Spanish	Regional Mexican.
102.3	KJLH	R&B	Urban contemporary.
102.7	KIIS	Top 40	Rick Dees in the morning.
103.5	KOST	Adult Contemporary	Dedications all night with "Love Songs on the KOST".
103.9	KRCD	Spanish	Shares a signal with 98.3 KRCV.
104.3	KBIG	Adult Contemporary	Music from the 70s, 80s, and 90s. And occasionally the 00s.
105.1	KMZT	Classical	"K-Mozart."
105.9	KPWR	Dance/Urban	Hip-Hop.
106.3	KALI	Vietnamese	
106.7	KROQ	Modern Rock	This influential station breaks new bands all the time.
107.1	KLYY	Spanish	
107.5	KLVE	Spanish	Spanish adult contemporary.
107.9	KWVE	Religious	

These days, the hottest accessory in L.A. isn't an iPod or a Louis Vuitton Murakami bag. It's a kid. And just when you think you've learned to navigate L.A. in your previously unencumbered form, you suddenly find yourself stumbling through a new maze of Baby Gaps, Mommy & Me's, and indoor gyms. There are two awesome things about parenting in L.A.: We drive almost everywhere, so there's no need to figure out how to fit your Combi Twin Savvy Double Stroller down the narrow aisle of a public bus. And even better—no snowsuits or mittens. Ever. That alone makes dealing with the smog that much more bearable. We'd need an entire book to point out every store or playground to make your rugrat's life richer, but here is a sampling of information that will hopefully make your life a little easier.

Essentials

Kids come into the world with nothing, yet by their first birthdays their stuff fills up at least a room and a half of your house. Where does all of this stuff come from? Here are some of our favorite places for both necessities and the more frivolous (but no less fun) purchases.

Map	Store	Address	Phone	
1	Auntie Barbara's Antiques	238 S Beverly Dr, Beverly Hills	310-285-0873	Vintage children's furnishings.
2	Storyopolis	116 N Robertson Blvd, West Hollywood	310-358-2500	Children's literature and art.
2	Ga Ga	8362 W 3rd St, Los Angeles	323-653-3388	High-end toys and clothes.
2	Wound & Wound Toy Co	7374 Melrose Ave, Los Angeles	323-653-6703	All things wind-up.
7	Flicka	204 N Larchmont Blvd, Los Angeles	323-466-5822	Upscale kids' clothes.
15	Littlebits	15301 Antioch St, Pacific Palisades	310-459-0011	Fancy children's apparel.
15	Ivy Greene for Kids	1020 Swarthmore Ave, Pacific Palisades	310-230-0301	Kids' formalwear.
15	Palisades Playthings	1041 Swarthmore Ave, Pacific Palisades	310-454-8648	Toys galore.
16	Bellini Juvenile Designer Furniture	11980 San Vicente Blvd, Brentwood	310-371-5579	Nursery furniture.
18	Acorn Store	1220 5th St, Santa Monica	310-451-5845	Wooden toys.
18	Pump Station	2415 Wilshire Blvd, Santa Monica	310-826-5774	For nursing moms and tots.
18	Puzzle Zoo	1413 3rd St Promenade, Santa Monica	310-393-9201	Awesome toy store
18	This Little Piggy Wears Cotton	309 Wilshire Blvd, Santa Monica	310-260-2727	Comfy kids' clothes.
18	Every Picture Tells A Story	1318 Montana Ave, Santa Monica	310-451-2700	Art gallery and bookstore.
18	Imagine That	927 Montana Ave, Santa Monica	310-395-9553	Upscale furnishings.
18	Oohs & Oz	1700 Ocean Park Blvd, Santa Monica	310-392-7160	Resale that seems new.
19	Malina Children's Store	3314 Pico Blvd, Santa Monica	310-395-5965	High-end clothes.
20	Riginals	10250 Santa Monica Blvd, Century City	310-557-2532	High-end clothes.
20	Peanut Butter Playground	2042 Westwood Blvd, Westwood	310-475-5354	Upscale clothes and toys.
20	Traveling Tikes	10461 Santa Monica Blvd, Century City	310-234-9554	Strollers, bikes, and more.
23	Needles N' Tees	9223 W Pico Blvd, Los Angeles	310-276-2531	Personalized items.
25	Sid & Me	8338 Lincoln Blvd, Playa del Rey	310-874-1787	Everything for baby's room.
27	Bassinets & Blueberries	2403 N Sepulveda Blvd, Manhattan Beach	310-802-0412	High-end kids' stuff.
27	Baby A	1108 Manhattan Ave, Manhattan Beach	310-798-8086	Upscale gifts for tikes.
27	Babystyle (retail store)	3200 Sepulveda Blvd, Manhattan Beach	310-802-0224	Website comes to life.
31	Little Moon	1813 S Catalina Ave, Redondo Beach	310-373-3766	Fancy frocks and the like.
35	Saturday's Child	2529 Mission St, San Marino	626-441-8888	High-end kids' stuff.
48	Gregory's Toys	16101 Ventura Blvd, Encino	818-906-2212	Toys, toys, toys.
48	Harry Harris Children's Shoes	16766 Ventura Blvd, Encino	818-981-2641	First footwear.
48	Hopscotch Kids	16740 Ventura Blvd, Encino	818-783-4080	Kids' clothing.
48	Encino Kid	17157 Ventura Blvd, Encino	818-990-4510	Kids' clothing.
49	Rebel Elle	16101 Ventura Blvd, Encino	818-981-6200	Trendy kids' clothes.
49	A Mother's Haven	15928 Ventura Blvd, Encino	818-380-3111	Nursing products and support.
50	Juvenile Shop	13356 Ventura Blvd, Sherman Oaks	818-986-6214	One-stop baby shopping.
50	Doll Shoppe	13300 Riverside Drive, Sherman Oaks	818-784-3655	Dolls and their accessories.
51	Safer Baby	12420 Ventura Blvd, Studio City	818-766-4866	One-stop babyproofing.
51	M Fredric Kids	12128 Ventura Blvd, Studio City	818-985-9445	Cute and comfy clothes.
51	Moms The Word	12182 1/2 Ventura Blvd, Studio City	818-760-7192	Maternity and nursing wear.
52	One Hot Mama Maternity	3246 Cahuenga Blvd W	323-969-0790	Maternity wear.

The Bestest of the Best

Most Kid-Friendly Mall: *The Grove, Third Street & Fairfax Ave, (Map 10).* They've got a trolley, a musical water fountain, FAO Schwartz, and arts and crafts hour every Thursday morning at 11 am. Oh, and there are shops and restaurants for parents as well.

Coolest Bookstore: *Storyopolis, 116 N Robertson Blvd, 310-358-2500 (Map 6).* Looking for the Hillary Clinton biography? Look somewhere else. This store sells only the most beautiful and beloved children's books, along with the artwork found within. Toddler story time Tuesdays at 10 am.

Best Playground: *Shane's Inspiration, Griffith Park. (Map 5).* The playground was designed to allow handicapped children to play alongside their able-bodied peers. But the equipment is colorful, innovative, and appealing to all. For a similar playground, check out Aidan's Place in Westwood, on Sepulveda Blvd. just south of Wilshire Blvd.

Restaurant Most Welcoming to Kids: *Angeli, 7274 Melrose Ave, 323-936-9086 (Map 2).* Sure, you could go to Shakey's or Chuck E. Cheese, but would you want to if you didn't have kids? Angeli is moderately priced, serves delicious pizzas and pastas, and provides young diners with their own ball of pizza dough to mold, shape, or fling at each other.

Most Surprising Place For Parents To Network: *Petting Zoo, Studio City Farmers Market. Ventura Place between Laurel Canyon and Ventura Blvd, Sundays, 8 am–1 pm. (Map 51).* Overall, the Studio City Farmers Market is a Sunday morning kids' paradise. There are pony rides, a moon bounce, face painting, and a small train. But stand in the petting zoo long enough and you will encounter every person you have ever met in L.A. who has a child under the age of five. The animals are docile and the pen is kept as clean as is realistically possible. And the pig loves to have his belly rubbed.

Best Resource for New Mothers: *The Pump Station, 2415 Wilshire Blvd, Santa Monica, 310-826-5774 (Map 8).* From breast pumps to nursing bras to high end baby clothes, the Pump Station carries everything you need to get through the first few months of parenthood. Even more useful, however, are the new mother support groups, where lactation consultants/R.N.'s Corky and Wendy can talk any nervous new mother down from their ledge.

Most Enjoyable Rainy Day Activity: *Boone Children's Gallery at LACMA East, Wilshire Blvd & Fairfax Ave, 323-857-6000 (Map 6).* This exhibit, which changes annually, introduces kids to art by letting them do what kids do best: climb, feel, mold, and explore. Wear them out here, then take them next door to see the Hockneys.

Handiest Phone Number: *The Babysitters' Guild, (323) 938-8372.* Give them 24 hours notice, and they'll send you a competent, CPR-trained sitter with at least one year's experience working in childcare.

Fun in the Sun

What makes for an excellent public park? In our opinion, any combination of the following: ample shade, well maintained (and appealing or innovative) equipment, and an indefinable, overall good vibe. Most L.A. neighborhood parks feature at least a strip of grass and a slide or two, but these are some of the parks that are worth venturing out of your own neighborhood to explore:

- **Coldwater Canyon Park**, *Coldwater Canyon Dr & N Beverly Dr, Beverly Hills (Map 1).* The signs may say "No wading," but on any given day dozens of kids splash through the man-made stream that runs through this park.
- **Roxbury Park**, *Olympic Blvd & Roxbury Dr, Beverly Hills (Map 1).* Not one, but two sizeable playgrounds with a wide variety of obstacles to climb on or slide down. Steam emanates from the dinosaur area every ten minutes or so.
- **West Hollywood Park**, *San Vicente Blvd between Melrose Ave & Santa Monica Blvd, West Hollywood (Map 2).* Run of the mill equipment, but a shady canopy covers the toddler play area. Great weekday "Tiny Tots" program.
- **Shane's Inspiration**, *Griffith Park (Map 4).* This colorful playground was designed to accommodate handicapped and able-bodied children alike.
- **Echo Park**, *Between Glendale Blvd & Echo Park Ave, just south of Sunset Blvd (Map 5).* Lively crowds and a small lake, with paddleboats available for rental.
- **La Cienega Park**, *La Cienega Blvd & Olympic Blvd (Map 6).* Excellent music and dance classes for the smallest kids; colorful playground and chess players almost all day.
- **MacArthur Park**, *6th St & Alvarado St (Map 8).* Small lake with paddleboats, as well as the chance to visit the park that inspired the epic '60s song.
- **Kenneth Hahn State Recreational Area**, *La Cienega Blvd south of Rodeo Rd. (Map 10).* Hiking trails and a terrific play area for the kids.
- **Douglas Park**, *Wilshire Blvd & 25th St, Santa Monica (Map 19).* Lots of grass and a water area that is home to several live ducks.
- **Westwood Park**, *Sepulveda Blvd between Wilshire Blvd. & Santa Monica Blvd (Map 20).* Features Aidan's Place, a playground designed to accommodate both handicapped and able-bodied children.
- **Penmar Playground**, *Marine St & 16th St, Santa Monica (Map 21).* Brand new playground and piñata pole, suitable for kids' birthday parties.
  Culver City Park, *Jefferson Blvd & Duquesne Ave (Map 24).* Features a 5000-square foot skateboard park. Helmets required.
- **Polliwog Park**, *Redondo Ave & Manhattan Beach Blvd (Map 27).* Park contains a pond, as well as a playground area featuring a large, wooden, sunken galleon.

- **Seaside Lagoon**, *200 Portofino Way, Redondo Beach (Map 31)*. Beach playground with a large, heated, saltwater swimming pool.
- **Garfield Park**, *Stratford Ave & Mission Ave, South Pasadena (Map 34)*. Lots of shade & rolling green hills.
- **Lacey Park**, *Monterey Rd & Virginia Rd, San Marino (Map 35)*. Includes a stroller/bicycle loop for fitness-minded moms and traveling tikes.
- **Lake Balboa Park**, *Balboa Blvd & Victory Blvd (Map 42)*. Ducks to feed, a lake to walk around, and a great playground to boot.
- **Johnny Carson Park**, *400 S Bob Hope Dr & Riverside (Map 46)*. Picturesque park is home to numerous community events and festivals.
- **Encino Park**, *Ventura Blvd & Genesta Ave (Map 48)*. Two shady playgrounds, at least one of which keeps the little ones fenced in.
- **Studio City Recreation Center (AKA Beeman Park)**, *Beeman Ave & Rye St (Map 51)*. Play in some sand, swing on a swing, and stop inside the park office to greet Beeman the Bunny.

Rainy Day Alternatives— Indoor Playgrounds

Because wet weather is such an anomaly in Southern California, LA parents tend to lose it a little when forced to seek shelter indoors with the kids for a day or two. The kids, however, are perfectly happy, especially when exposed to some of LA's indoor playgrounds, where the temperature is always a pleasant 72 degrees and there's always padding or a cushion to break their fall.

Bright Child, 1415 4th St, Santa Monica, 310-393-4844 (Map 18)

Child's Play, 2299 Westwood Blvd, Westwood, 310-470-4997 (Map 23)

Gymboree, Westside Pavilion, 10800 W Pico Blvd, West LA, 310-470-7780 (Map 19)

Gymboree, 14801 Ventura Blvd, Sherman Oaks, 818-905-6225 (Map 49)

Gymboree, 443 E Irving Dr, Suite F, Burbank, 818-955-8964 (Map 46)

Gymboree, 435 S Fair Oaks, South Pasadena, 626-445-1122 (Map 34)

Gymboree, 220 Aviation Blvd, Manhattan Beach, 310-798-8996 (Map 27)

Under the Sea, 2424 W Victory Blvd, Burbank, 818-567-9945 (Map 45)

Rainy Day Alternatives—Classes

Most of the play facilities listed above emphasize open play, allowing for parental spontaneity and the fickle nature of young children. But with a little planning and structure (as counterintuitive as that might be), LA kids have a variety of classes available to them that rivals that of most Ivy League universities.

My Gym, *numerous locations around the LA area*. Visit www.my-gym.com for addresses. Gymnastics, circle time, and other traditionally kid-like activity.

Creative Space, *6325 Santa Monica Blvd, Hollywood, 323-462-4600, (Map 23)*. An eclectic line-up of classes that includes Storybook Cooking for toddlers, knitting and breakdancing for the 'tweens, and yoga and scrapbooking for adults.

Baby Geniuses, *Westside Pavilion, 10800 W Pico Blvd, 310-441-5222, (Map 19)*. Art and language classes for kids from 10 months to 12 years.

Creative Kids, *11301 W Olympic Blvd, West LA, 310-473-6090, (Map 34)*. Their diverse schedule includes art classes for toddlers, dance and cooking for slightly older kids, and children's theatre for ages 3-18.

Dance & Jingle, *1900 W Mountain St, Glendale, 818-845-3925*. Very sought after music and movement class.

L.A. Zoo, *Zoo Drive, Griffith Park, 323-644-6400, (Map 5)*. The zoo's classes range from "Toddler Totes," which involves singing, an animal guest, and a backpack filled with educational goodies, to "Wild Planet," a more sophisticated program for adolescent zookeepers-in-training.

Music Together, *numerous locations around LA*. Visit www.musictogether.com for more info. Teaches young children the fundamentals of rhythm and music through the modeling of parents and caregivers, while exposing them to a wide array of music from diverse cultures and time periods.

Library

Where to go for additional information:

- www.gocitykids.com
- www.at-la.com/@la-kid.htm
- www.local.thedaisychain.com/Los_Angeles__CA/

- Fun and Educational Places to Go With Kids and Adults in Southern California - Susan Peterson, Sunbelt Publications, 2001.

Websites

- **LA Gay and Lesbian Center: www.laglc.org**
  If you're in trouble, looking for support, or need advice, this is the place to go. LA Gay and Lesbian Center is a community resource offering legal, medical, outreach, and education services, among many others.
- **Circuit Noize: www.circuitnoize.com**
  The premier source of circuit party information, parties, events, music, tickets, gay travel, and dancing.
- **Gay.com: www.gay.com**
  If you're looking for love online, this is the place to visit. Gay.com has hundreds of chat rooms for people around the country, with eight devoted to LA, two to Long Beach, and two to Orange County.
- **Friendster: www.friendster.com**
  A website to find dates/friends/activity partners online based on the idea that you're less likely to find psychos online if the person you meet is a friend of a friend of a friend.
- **A Different Light Bookstore: www.adlbooks.com/wh.html**
  This store has an excellent selection of lesbian and gay books, magazines, cards, and videos and holds special activities almost nightly.
- **West Hollywood: www.westhollywood.com**
  Comprehensive online guide to West Hollywood, featuring music, arts, videos, nightlife, circuits, classifieds, buzz, photos, and shopping.
- **QV Magazine: www.qvmagazine.com/menu.html**
  Online edition of LA's gay Latino magazine.
- **Power Up: www.power-up.net**
  As their website states, "The mission of this 'girls' club' is to promote, encourage, and support the visibility and integration of women in the entertainment industry though career-building resources, including a resume bank, networking events, roundtables, seminars, mentors, and grants for filmmaking."
- **Los Angeles Tennis Association: www.lataweb.com**
  With over 400 members, this is the largest gay and lesbian tennis club in the world.
- **Greater Los Angeles Softball Association: www.lagaysoftball.com**
  This exclusively gay and lesbian league has men's and women's divisions with over 30 teams participating.
- **Gay Men's Chorus of Los Angeles: www.gmcla.com**
  If you fancy yourself as a choral singer, or you would like to hear and see the chorus in action, check out their site for a rehearsal schedule and performance dates.
- **Metropolitan Community Church: www.mccla.org**
  This popular church is gay- and lesbian-friendly and offers multi-denominational services.

Publications

Pick up a copy of the following publications to find out what's happening around town, from the current political headlines to the most happening clubs. They can be found in gay-friendly bookstores, cafes, bars, and various shops.

Circuit Noize. 818-769-9390, www.circuitnoize.com
Frontiers. 323-848-2222, www.frontiersnewsmagazine.com
QV Magazine. 818-766-0023, www.qvmagazine.com/menu.html
The Lesbian News. 310-787-8658, www.lesbiannews.com
The Advocate. 323-871-1225, www.advocate.com
West Hollywood Independent. 323-932-6397

Bookstores

A Different Light Bookstore, 8853 Santa Monica Boulevard (at San Vicente Boulevard), West Hollywood 310-854-6601 - www.adlbooks.com, 10 am until midnight daily.

Circus of Books (two locations), 8230 Santa Monica Boulevard (between Harper and LaJolla Avenues), West Hollywood, 323-656-6533; and 4001 Sunset Boulevard (at Sanborn Avenue), Silver Lake, 323-666-1304, www.circusofbooks.com, 6am until 2am daily.

Health Center and Support Organizations

LAMBDA
McDonald Wright Building, 1625 N. Schrader Blvd, Los Angeles, CA 90028
Phone toll-free: 877-4-LAMBDA lambdamedical@laglc.org
Due to financial considerations, LAMBDA's Museum Square location was closed down in the middle of 2002. The McDonald Wright Building location is still operational and offers the following services:
- Pedro Zamora Youth HIV Program - 323-993-7571, healthservices@laglc.org
- Counseling services including general, addiction recovery, stop domestic violence and HIV/AIDS - 323-993-7640, mentalhealth@laglc.org
- HIV Testing - 323-993-7500, healthservices@laglc.org
- Lesbian Health Clinic - 8240 Santa Monica Boulevard (at Harper Ave), West Hollywood - 323-650-1508.

AIDS Project Los Angeles. *323-992-1600*
Provides assistance for people living with AIDS and an information hotline. *www.apla.org*

HIV LA. *www.hivla.org*
An online resource to find services available for those in Los Angeles County with HIV/AIDS in both English and Spanish.

Anti-Gay Bashing Resources. *323-848-6414*

GLAAD Los Angeles. *5455 Wilshire Blvd. #1500, Los Angeles, CA 90036 -- 323-933-2240 – www.glaad.org*

Gay and Lesbian Youth Talk Line. *818-508-1802*

Gay

Akbar: 4356 Sunset Blvd, Silverlake, 323-665-6810
Arena: 6655 Santa Monica Blvd, West Hollywood, 323-462-0714
Club 7969: 7969 Santa Monica Blvd (b/w Fairfax and Crescent Heights), West Hollywood, 323-654-0280
The Factory: 652 N La Peer Dr (at Robertson), West Hollywood, 877-447-5252
Faultline: 4216 Melrose Ave, Silverlake, 323-660-0889
FuBar: 7994 Santa Monica Blvd, West Hollywood, 323-654-0396
Gauntlet: 4219 Santa Monica Blvd, Silverlake, 323-669-9472
Here: 696 N Robertson Blvd, West Hollywood, 310-360-8455
House of Blues: 8430 Sunset Blvd, West Hollywood, 323-692-5657
Hump @ 66 Wednesdays: 6266 Sunset Blvd, West Hollywood, 213-926-9536
Micky's Bar: 8857 Santa Monica Blvd, West Hollywood, 310-657-1176
Motherlode: 8944 Santa Monica Blvd (at San Vicente), West Hollywood, 310-659-9700
Probe: 836 North Highland Ave (b/w Waring and Willoughby), Hollywood, 323-461-8301
Rage: 8911 Santa Monica Blvd, (b/w Larrabee and San Vicente), West Hollywood, 310-652-7055
Revolver: 8851 Santa Monica Blvd /9 at Larrabee), West Hollywood, 310-659-8851
Roosterfish: 1302 Abbot Kinney Blvd, Venice Beach, 310-392-2123
Spike: 7746 Santa Monica Blvd, West Hollywood, 323-656-9343
Wonder Bar: 2692 La Cienega, Los Angeles, 310-837-7443
Woody's: 2810 Hyperion Ave, 213-660-1503

Lesbian

Club 7969 (Michelle's XXX Review Tuesday): 7969 Santa Monica Blvd (b/w Fairfax and Crescent Heights), West Hollywood, 323-654-0280
Echo: ("Milk" Thursday): 1822 Sunset Blvd, Echo Park Here (Fuse Thursday): 696 N Robertson Blvd, 310-360-8455
Jewels Catch One: 4067 W Pico Blvd (at Crenshaw), Mid-City, 323-734-8849
Normandie Room: 8737 Santa Monica Blvd (b/w La Cienega and San Vicente), West Hollywood, 310-659-6204
The Factory (Girl Bar Friday): 652 N La Peer Dr (at Robertson), West Hollywood, 877-447-5252
The Palms: 8572 Santa Monica Blvd (at La Cienega), West Hollywood, 310-652-6188
The Plush Pony: 5261 Alhambra Ave, Los Angeles, 323-224-9488

Both

Abbey: 692 N Robertson Blvd, 310-855-9977
Dreams: 1717 Silverlake Blvd, Los Angeles, 323-661-4380
The Echo : 1822 Sunset Blvd, Echo Park, 213-413-8200
Felt (Girls Tuesday, Boys Thursday): 8279 Santa Monica Blvd, West Hollywood, 323-822-3888
The Falcon (Beige, Tuesdays): 7213 Sunset Blvd, Hollywood, 323-850-5350
JJ's Pub: 2692 S. La Cienega Blvd, Los Angeles, 310-837-7443
Marix Tex-Mex Café: 1108 North Flores St, West Hollywood, 323-656-8800
Parlor Club: 7702 Santa Monica Blvd, West Hollywood: 323-650-7968
Redhead Bar: 2218 E First St, Los Angeles, 323-263-2995

Library	Address	Phone	Map
Alhambra Library	410 W Main St	626-570-5008	39
Anthony Quinn Library	3965 E Cesar Chavez Ave E	323-264-7715	41
Art Research Library	5905 Wilshire Blvd	323-857-6118	6
Atwater Library	3379 Glendale Blvd	323-664-1353	5
Baldwin Hills Library	2906 S La Brea Ave	323-733-1196	10
Benjamin Franklin Library	2200 E 1st St	323-263-6901	40
Beverly Hills Public Library	444 N Rexford Dr	310-288-2220	1
Braille Institute Library	4205 Melrose Ave	323-660-3880	4
Buena Vista Library	401 N Buena Vista St	818-238-5620	46
Burbank Central Library	110 N Glenoaks Blvd	818-238-5600	46
Cahuenga Library	4591 Santa Monica Blvd	323-664-6418	4
California Department-Justice	300 S Spring St	213-897-2342	9
California State Dept of Corporations	3700 Wilshire Blvd	213-736-3632	8
Chinatown Branch Library	536 W College St	213-620-0925	9
City Attorney's Library	200 N Main St	213-485-5400	9
Culver City Library	4975 Overland Ave	310-559-1676	24
Cypress Park Branch Library	3320 Pepper Ave	213-612-0460	36
Defense Technical Information Ctr	222 N Sepulveda Blvd	310-335-4170	27
East Los Angeles Library	4801 E 3rd St	323-264-0155	41
Echo Park Library	1410 W Temple St	213-250-7808	9
El Camino Real Library	4264 Whittier Blvd	323-269-8102	41
El Retiro Library	126 Vista Del Parque	310-375-0922	31
El Segundo Public Library	111 W Mariposa Ave	310-322-4121	27
Exposition Park Library	3665 S Vermont Ave	323-732-0169	11
Fairfax Branch Library	161 S Gardner St	323-936-6191	2
Felipe De Neve Branch-LA Library	2820 W 6th St	213-384-7676	8
Frances Howard Goldwyn Library	1623 Ivar Ave	323-467-1821	3
Franklin D Murphy Library	244 S San Pedro St	213-628-2725	9
General Hospital Medical Library	1200 N State St	323-226-7006	40
Glendale Central Library	222 E Harvard St	818-548-2020	47
Goethe Institute-Los Angeles	5750 Wilshire Blvd	323-525-3388	6
Grandview Library	1535 5th St	818-548-2049	46
Hermosa Beach Public Library	550 Pier Ave	310-379-8475	29
Hill Avenue Branch Library	55 S Hill Ave	626-796-1276	35
Hinomoto Library	129 N Saratoga St	323-261-3300	40
Howrey & Simon Law Library	550 S Hope St	213-892-1800	9
Hyde Park Branch Library	6527 Crenshaw Blvd	323-750-7241	14
Inglewood City Library	101 W Manchester Blvd	310-412-5380	13
Inglewood Library	3202 W 85th St	310-412-5400	14
Isabel Henderson Library	4805 Emerald St	310-371-2075	31
Jefferson Library	2211 W Jefferson Blvd	323-734-8573	11
John C Fremont Library	6121 Melrose Ave	323-962-3521	3
John Muir Library	1005 W 64th St	323-789-4800	14
Kaiser Permanente Medical Library	13652 Cantara St	818-375-3000	44
LA County Law Library	301 W 1st St	213-629-3531	9
La Pintoresca Branch Library	1355 N Raymond Ave	626-797-1873	34
LACMA Visual Resource Center	5905 Wilshire Blvd	323-857-6116	6
Lamanda Park Library	140 S Altadena Dr	626-793-5672	35
Lawndale Library	14615 Burin Ave	310-676-0177	28
Lennox LA County Library	4359 Lennox Blvd	310-674-0385	13
Lincoln Heights Branch Library	2530 Workman St	323-226-1692	37
Little Tokyo Library	244 S Alameda St	213-612-0525	9
Lomita Public Library	24200 Narbonne Ave	310-539-4515	32
Los Angeles Central Library	630 W 5th St	213-228-7000	9
Los Angeles City Library	2700 W 52nd St	323-292-4328	11
Los Angeles City Library	8946 Sepulveda Eastway	310-645-6082	26
Los Angeles County Library	4025 City Terrace Dr	323-261-0295	41
Los Angeles County Library	12700 Grevillea Ave	310-679-8193	28
Los Angeles Library	4504 S Central Ave	323-234-9106	12
Los Angeles Library	803 Spence St	323-268-4710	40
Los Angeles Library	4990 Huntington Dr S	323-225-9201	38
Los Angeles Library	2801 Wabash Ave	323-268-0874	40
Los Angeles Library	4607 S Main St	323-234-1685	12
Los Angeles Library	5027 Caspar Ave	323-258-8078	33
Los Angeles Library	1403 N Gardner St	323-876-2741	2
Los Angeles Library	1636 W Manchester Ave	323-778-8062	14
Los Angeles Library	11820 San Vicente Blvd	310-575-8273	16
Los Angeles Public Library	1340 W 106th St	323-757-9373	14
Los Angeles Public Library	2920 Overland Ave	310-838-2157	23
Los Feliz Branch Library	1874 Hillhurst Ave	323-913-4710	4
Malaga Cove Library	2400 Via Campesina	310-377-9584	31
Manhattan Beach Library	1320 Highland Ave	310-545-8595	27
Memorial Branch Library	4625 W Olympic Blvd	323-938-2732	7
MPA Library	1 Gateway Plz	213-922-4859	9
North Torrance Library	3604 Artesia Blvd	310-323-7200	30
Northwest Library	3323 W Victory Blvd	818-238-5640	45
Nursing Library	1200 N State St	323-226-4923	40
Pacific Palisades Library	861 Alma Real Dr	310-459-2754	15
Parral	1925 W Temple St	213-484-0818	9
Pasadena City Library	1130 S Marengo Ave	626-799-2519	34
Pasadena Public Library	285 E Walnut St	626-744-4052	34
Pio Pico Koreatown Library	695 S Serrano Ave	213-368-7282	8
Redondo Beach North Library	2000 Artesia Blvd	310-318-0677	29
Redondo Beach Public Library	303 N Pacific Coast Hwy	310-318-0675	31
Regional Family Planning Library	3600 Wilshire Blvd	213-386-5614	8
Robertson Library	1719 S Robertson Blvd	310-840-2147	6
San Rafael Library	1240 Nithsdale Rd	626-795-7974	34
Santa Catalina Library	999 E Washington Blvd	626-794-1219	35
Santa Monica Fairview Library	2101 Ocean Park Blvd	310-450-0443	18
Santa Monica Montana Avenue	1704 Montana Ave	310-829-7081	18
Santa Monica Public Library	1343 6th St	310-458-8600	18
Santa Monica Public Library	2601 Main St	310-392-3804	18
Sherman Oaks Library	14245 Moorpark St	818-981-7850	50
South Pasadena Library	1100 Oxley St	626-403-7330	34
Southeast Torrance Library	23115 Arlington Ave	310-530-5044	32
Studio City Branch	12511 Moorpark St	818-755-7873	51
Superior Court-Law Library	6230 Sylmar Ave	818-374-2499	43
Torrance Public Library	3301 Torrance Blvd	310-618-5959	32
Valley Plaza Library	12311 Vanowen St	818-765-0805	44
Van Nuys Branch Library	6250 Sylmar Ave	818-756-8453	43
Venice Public Library	501 S Venice Blvd	310-821-1769	21
Vermont Square Branch Library	1201 W 48th St	323-290-7405	11
View Park Library	3854 W 54th St	323-293-5371	10
Villa Parke Library	363 E Villa St	626-744-6510	34
Walteria Library	3815 W 242nd St	310-375-8418	31
Washington Irving Branch Library	4117 W Washington Blvd	323-734-6303	7
Water & Power Library	111 N Hope St	213-367-1995	9
West Hollywood Public Library	715 N San Vicente Blvd	310-652-5340	2
West Los Angeles Regional Library	11360 Santa Monica Blvd	310-575-8323	19
Wilshire Library	149 N St Andrews Pl	323-957-4550	7
Wiseburn Library	5335 W 135th St	310-643-8880	28

Police Stations

	Address	Phone	Map
Alhambra Police Dept	211 S 1st St	626-570-5107	39
Beverly Hills Police	464 N Rexford Dr	310-550-4951	1
Burbank Police Dept	200 N 3rd St	818-238-3333	46
Culver City Police Dept	4040 Duquesne Ave	310-837-1221	24
El Segundo City Police Dept	348 Main St	310-524-2200	27
Glendale Police Dept	140 N Isabel St	818-548-4840	47
Hawthorne City Police Service	4440 W 126th St	310-970-7976	28
Hermosa Beach Police Dept	540 Pier Ave	310-318-0360	29
Inglewood Police Dept	1 W Manchester Blvd	310-412-5210	13
Lawndale Sheriff Service Center	15331 Prairie Ave	310-219-2750	28
Los Angeles County Park Police	2101 N Highland Ave	323-845-0080	3
Los Angeles Police Dept	1358 Wilcox Ave	213-485-4302	3
Los Angeles Police Dept	4861 Venice Blvd	213-485-4022	6
Los Angeles Police Dept	2710 W Temple St	213-485-4061	8
Los Angeles Police Dept	150 N Los Angeles St	213-485-2121	9
Los Angeles Police Dept	251 E 6th St	213-485-3294	9
Los Angeles Police Dept	1546 W M L King Jr Blvd	213-485-2582	11
Los Angeles Police Dept	3400 S Central Ave	323-846-6547	12
Los Angeles Police Dept	1663 Butler Ave	310-575-8404	19
Los Angeles Police Dept	12312 Culver Blvd	310-202-4502	22
Los Angeles Police Dept	2111 E 1st St	213-485-2949	40
Los Angeles Police Dept	6240 Sylmar Ave	818-756-8343	43
Los Angeles Police Dept	11640 Burbank Blvd	818-623-4016	44
Los Angeles Police Dept	3353 N San Fernando Rd	213-485-2563	47
Manhattan Beach Police Dept	420 15th St	310-802-5100	27
Pasadena Police Dept	207 N Garfield Ave	626-744-4501	34
Redondo Beach Police Dept	401 Diamond St	310-379-2477	31
San Marino Police Dept	2200 Huntington Dr	626-300-0720	35
Santa Monica Police Headquarters	1685 Main St	310-395-9931	18
South Pasadena Police Dept	1422 Mission St	626-403-7270	34
Torrance Police Dept	3300 Civic Center Dr N	310-328-3456	30

Important Phone Numbers

Life-Threatening Emergencies:	**911**
Non-Emergency Police Service:	877-ASK-LAPD (275-5273)
Wanted Persons:	213-485-2603
Rape Victims Hotline:	800-793-3385
Crime Victims Hotline:	213-485-6976
Domestic Violence Hotline:	800-978-3600
Missing Persons Unit:	213-485-5381
Sex Crimes Report Line:	213-485-2883
Noise Complaints (NET):	213-473-7840
Complaints (Internal Affairs):	213-485-4152
County-Wide Resources:	323-686-0950
Website:	www.lapdonline.org

Statistics

	2001	2000	1999
Uniformed Personnel	8,906	9,436	9,668
Murders	476	548	424
Rapes	1,139	1,413	1,152
Robberies	13,814	15,481	14,184
Felony Assaults	15,722	15,690	16,410
Burglaries	20,943	24,306	21,195
Larcenies	64,788	62,018	72,068
Auto Theft	25,204	29,518	25,730

Hospitals

	Address	Phone	Map
Alhambra Hospital	100 S Raymond Ave	626-570-1606	39
Brotman Medical Center	3828 Delmas Ter	310-836-7000	24
California Hospital Medical	1338 S Hope St	213-742-5555	9
California Hospital Medical	1401 S Grand Ave	213-748-3855	9
Cedars-Sinai Medical Ctr	8700 Beverly Blvd	310-423-3277	2
Centinela Hospital Medical Center	555 E Hardy St	310-673-4660	13
Century City Hospital	2070 Century Park E	310-553-6211	20
Children's Hospital	4650 W Sunset Blvd	323-660-2450	4
City of Angels Medical Center	1711 W Temple St	213-989-6100	9
Daniel Freeman Memorial Hospital	333 N Prairie Ave	310-674-7050	13
East LA Doctors Hospital	4060 Whittier Blvd	323-268-5514	41
Encino Hospital	16237 Ventura Blvd	818-995-5000	49
Glendale Adventist Medical Center	1509 Wilson Ter	818-409-8000	47
Glendale Memorial Hospital	1420 S Central Ave	818-502-1900	47
Good Samaritan Hospital	1225 Wilshire Blvd	213-977-2121	9
Hollywood Community Hospital	6245 De Longpre Ave	323-462-2271	3
Huntington Memorial Hospital	100 W California Blvd	626-397-5000	34
Kaiser Foundation Hospital	4867 W Sunset Blvd	323-783-4011	4
Kaiser Foundation Hospital	6041 Cadillac Ave	323-857-2201	6
LA County USC Medical Center	1200 N State St	323-226-2622	40
Little Co of Mary Hospital	4101 Torrance Blvd	310-540-7676	31
Los Angeles Community Hospital	4081 E Olympic Blvd	323-267-0477	41
Los Angeles County Women's Hospital	1240 N Mission Rd	323-226-3054	40
Midway Hospital	5925 San Vicente Blvd	323-938-3161	6
Mission Community Hospital	14850 Roscoe Blvd	818-787-2222	43
Pacific Alliance Medical Center	531 W College St	213-624-8411	9
Providence St Joseph Medical	501 S Buena Vista St	818-843-5111	46
Queen Of Angels Hospital	1300 N Vermont Ave	213-413-3000	4
Robert F Kennedy Medical Center	4500 W 116th St	310-973-1711	28
Santa Marta Hospital	319 N Humphreys Ave	323-266-6500	41
Sherman Oaks Hospital & Health	4929 Van Nuys Blvd	818-981-7111	50
St John's Hospital & Health	1328 22nd St	310-829-5511	18
Torrance Memorial Medical Center	3330 Lomita Blvd	310-325-9110	32
University California-Medical Center	10833 Le Conte Ave	310-825-7271	20
Valley Presbyterian Hospital	15107 Vanowen St	818-782-6600	43

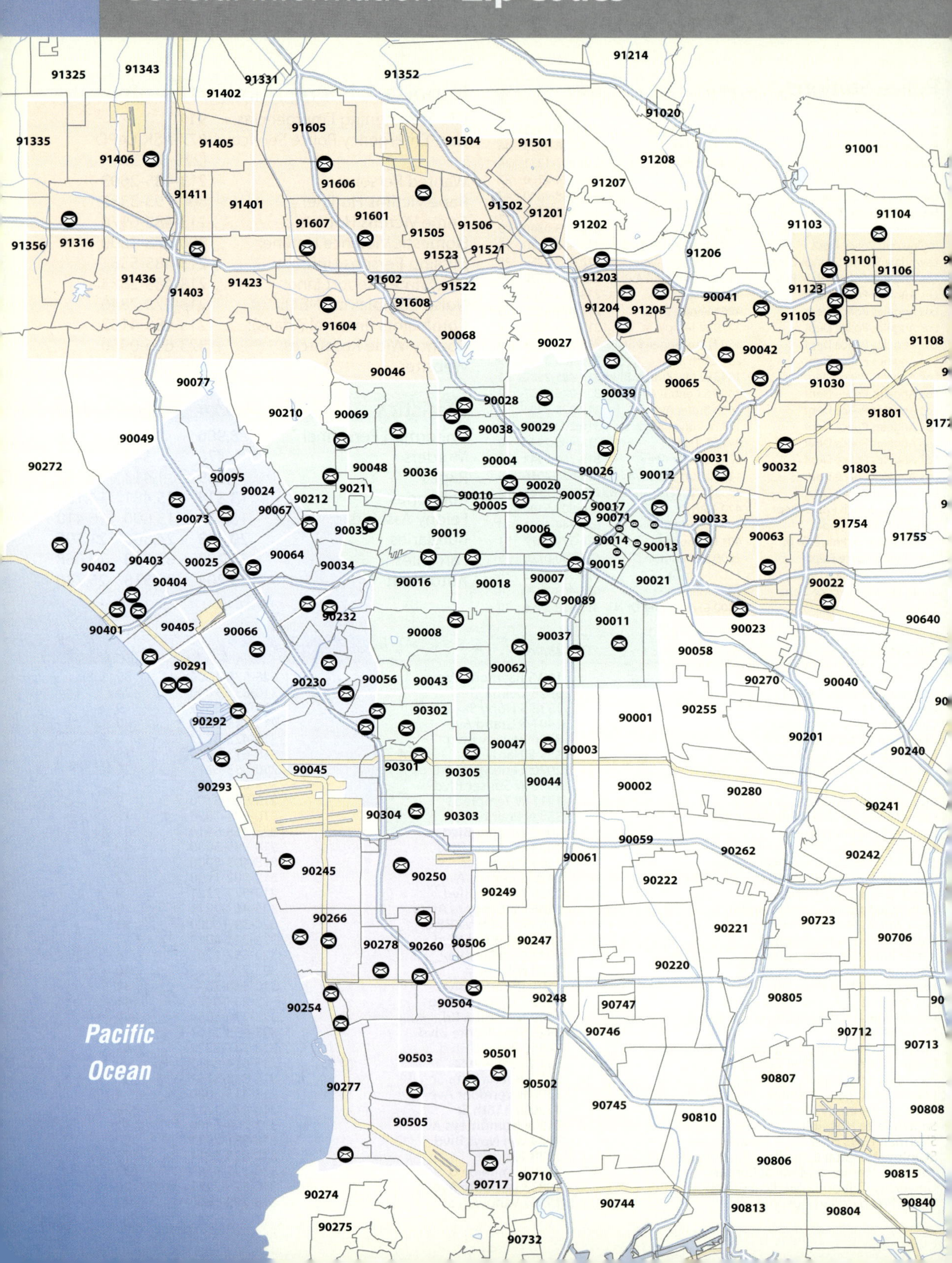

91325
91343
91331
91352
91214
91402
91020
91605
91335
91405
91504
91501
91001
91208
91406
91207
91411
91401
91606
91502
91201
91202
91103
91104
91607
91601
91505
91506
91203
91206
91101
91106
91523
91521
91204
91205
91041
91123
91436
91423
91602
91522
91105
91108
91403
91608
91204
91205
91042
91030
91356
91316
91604
90068
90027
90065
91801
90077
90046
90039
91803
90049
90210
90069
90028
90031
91754
90272
90095
90048
90036
90004
90026
90012
90032
91755
90024
90211
90038
90029
90057
90033
90022
90067
90212
90010
90020
90017
90063
90073
90035
90005
90071
90015
90640
90025
90064
90019
90006
90014
90013
90023
90402
90403
90034
90016
90018
90007
90021
90058
90040
90404
90232
90008
90037
90089
90011
90405
90066
90056
90043
90062
90270
90401
90291
90230
90302
90047
90003
90255
90201
90292
90045
90301
90305
90044
90001
90240
90293
90304
90303
90002
90280
90241
90059
90262
90242
90245
90250
90249
90061
90222
90266
90278
90260
90506
90247
90221
90723
90706
90254
90504
90248
90220
90277
90503
90501
90747
90805
90502
90746
90712
90713
90505
90745
90807
90810
90808
90806
90815
90274
90744
90813
90804
90840
90275
90717
90710
90732
Pacific Ocean

Map	Address	Zip	Map	Address	Zip	Map	Address	Zip
1	312 S Beverly Dr	90212	14	2200 W Century Blvd	90047	33	5132 York Blvd	90042
	323 N Crescent Dr	90210		3212 W 85th St	90305		5930 N Figueroa St	90042
	325 N Maple Dr	90210		8200 S Vermont Ave	90044		7435 N Figueroa St	90041
2	1125 N Fairfax Ave	90046	15	15209 W Sunset Blvd	90272	34	1001 Fremont Ave	91030
	7610 Beverly Blvd	90048		15243 La Cruz Dr	90272		1355 N Mentor Ave	91104
	820 N San Vicente Blvd	90069	16	200 S Barrington Ave	90049		281 E Colorado Blvd	91101
3	1425 N Cherokee Ave	90028	18	1020 Colorado Ave	90401		600 Lincoln Ave	91103
	1615 Wilcox Ave	90028		1217 Wilshire Blvd	90403		870 S Raymond Ave	91105
	6457 Santa Monica Blvd	90038		1248 5th St	90401		99 W California Blvd	91105
4	1825 N Vermont Ave	90027		2720 Neilson Way	90405	35	2609 E Colorado Blvd	91107
5	1525 N Alvarado St	90026	19	11270 Exposition Blvd	90064		967 E Colorado Blvd	91106
	3370 Glendale Blvd	90039		11420 Santa Monica Blvd	90025	36	3950 Eagle Rock Blvd	90065
6	1270 S Alfred St	90035	20	11000 Wilshire Blvd	90024	38	3316 N Eastern Ave	90032
	4960 W Washington Blvd	90016	21	1601 Main St	90291		4875 Huntington Dr	90032
	5350 Wilshire Blvd	90036		313 Grand Blvd	90291	40	2016 E 1st St	90033
7	4040 W Washington Blvd	90018	22	3865 Grand View Blvd	90066		2425 Alhambra Ave	90031
8	2390 W Pico Blvd	90006	23	3751 Motor Ave	90034		3641 E 8th St	90023
	265 S Western Ave	90004		9911 W Pico Blvd	90035	41	3729 E 1st St	90063
	3751 W 6th St	90020	24	11111 Jefferson Blvd	90230		975 S Atlantic Blvd	90022
9	100 W Olympic Blvd	90015		9942 Culver Blvd	90232	42	5805 White Oak Ave	91316
	1808 W 7th St	90057	25	215 Culver Blvd	90293	43	15701 Sherman Way	91406
	300 N Los Angeles St	90012		4748 Admiralty Way	90292		6200 Van Nuys Blvd	91401
	350 S Grand Ave	90071	26	6824 La Tijera Blvd	90045	44	6535 Lankershim Blvd	91606
	505 S Flower St	90071		7381 La Tijera Blvd	90045		7035 Laurel Canyon Blvd	91605
	508 S Spring St	90013	27	1007 N Sepulveda Blvd	90266	45	2140 N Hollywood Way	91505
	760 N Main St	90012		200 Main St	90245		3810 Magnolia Blvd	91505
10	3650 W M L King Jr Blvd	90008		425 15th St	90266	46	135 E Olive Ave	91502
	3894 Crenshaw Blvd	90008	28	12700 Inglewood Ave	90250		1634 N San Fernando Blvd	91504
11	1515 W Vernon Ave	90062		4320 Marine Ave	90260		6444 San Fernando Rd	91201
	3585 S Vermont Ave	90007	29	2215 Artesia Blvd	90504	47	1009 N Pacific Ave	91202
	5472 Crenshaw Blvd	90043		565 Pier Ave	90254		101 N Verdugo Rd	91206
	5832 S Vermont Ave	90044	30	18080 Crenshaw Blvd	90504		120 E Chevy Chase Dr	91205
12	4352 S Central Ave	90011	31	1201 N Catalina Ave	90277		313 E Broadway	91205
	819 W Washington Blvd	90015		2516 Via Tejon	90274	48	4930 Balboa Blvd	91316
13	300 E Hillcrest Blvd	90301		3856 Sepulveda Blvd	90505	49	14900 Magnolia Blvd	91403
	4443 Lennox Blvd	90304		4216 Pacific Coast Hwy	90505	51	11304 Chandler Blvd	91601
	811 N La Brea Ave	90302	32	1433 Marcelina Ave	90501		12450 Magnolia Blvd	91607
				2510 Monterey St	90503		3950 Laurel Canyon Blvd	91604
				25131 Narbonne Ave	90717	52	10063 Riverside Dr	91602
							4029 Lankershim Blvd	91604

Pick-up time, p.m.

Map 1 • Beverly Hills *

Drop box	100 N Crescent Dr	4:00
Mail Boxes Etc	269 S Beverly Dr	5:00
Drop box	301 N Canon Dr	4:45
Drop box	312 S Beverly Dr	5:00
Drop box	325 N Maple Dr	5:00
Drop box	345 N Maple Dr	5:00
Mail Box Exchg	369 S Doheny Dr	4:00
Drop box	421 N Rodeo Dr	5:00
Drop box	433 N Camden Dr	4:30
Drop box	8899 Beverly Blvd	5:00
Drop box	8920 Wilshire Blvd	5:15
Service Center	8950 W Olympic Blvd	6:00
Drop box	8981 W Sunset Blvd	5:00
Drop box	9000 W Sunset Blvd	5:00
Drop box	9033 Wilshire Blvd	5:30
Drop box	9060 Santa Monica Blvd	5:00
Drop box	9171 Wilshire Blvd	6:00
Mail Services	9190 W Olympic Blvd	5:00
Service Center	9201 W Sunset Blvd	5:45
Drop box	9220 W Sunset Blvd	5:00
Drop box	9229 W Sunset Blvd	4:45
Drop box	9255 W Sunset Blvd	5:00
Drop box	9292 Wilshire Blvd	4:00
Drop box	9300 Wilshire Blvd	5:00
Drop box	9301 Wilshire Blvd	5:00
Kinko's	9334 Wilshire Blvd	5:00
Drop box	9350 Wilshire Blvd	5:00
Drop box	9401 Wilshire Blvd	5:00
Drop box	9420 Wilshire Blvd	4:00
Drop box	9440 Santa Monica Blvd	5:30
Drop box	9454 Wilshire Blvd	5:00
Drop box	9460 Wilshire Blvd	5:00
Mail Box Times	9461 Charleville Blvd	5:30
Drop box	9465 Wilshire Blvd	5:00
Drop box	9560 Wilshire Blvd	4:45
Drop box	9595 Wilshire Blvd	5:00
Drop box	9601 Wilshire Blvd	5:00
Mail Boxes Etc	9663 Santa Monica Blvd	5:00
Drop box	9665 Wilshire Blvd	5:00
Service Center	9680 Santa Monica Blvd	5:00
Drop box	9701 Wilshire Blvd	5:00
Drop box	9720 Wilshire Blvd	5:00
Drop box	9777 Wilshire Blvd	5:00
Beverly Hills	9899 Santa Monica Blvd	4:00
Beverly Hills Mail Box		
	9903 Santa Monica Blvd	4:30

Map 2 • West Hollywood *

Drop box	1011 N Fuller Ave	4:45
Russian Universal Svc		
	1123 N Fairfax Ave	5:00
Drop box	116 N Robertson Blvd	5:15
The Box Depot	119 N Fairfax Ave	5:00
Drop box	145 S Fairfax Ave	5:00
Drop box	200 N Robertson Blvd	4:45
Drop box	250 N Robertson Blvd	4:45
Beverly Hills US Mail		
	311 N Robertson Blvd	4:00
Drop box	444 S San Vicente Blvd	4:45
Miracle Mail	5850 W 3rd St	4:30
Drop box	7060 Hollywood Blvd	5:00
CnC Mail Box Services		
	7070 Sunset Blvd	5:00
Mail Boxes Etc	7095 Hollywood Blvd	5:30
Box Brothers	7162 Beverly Blvd	5:00
Drop box	7250 Beverly Blvd	5:00
Box and Ship	7304 Beverly Blvd	5:00
Mail Boxes Pmb	7336 Santa Monica Blvd	5:00
Mister Mail	7510 W Sunset Blvd	5:15
Drop box	7551 W Sunset Blvd	5:30

Drop box	7610 Beverly Blvd	5:15
Kinko's	7630 W Sunset Blvd	5:15
Drop box	7753 Santa Monica Blvd	5:15
Drop box	7920 W Sunset Blvd	5:00
West Hollywood Mail & Msg		
	7985 Santa Monica Blvd	5:00
E & G Mail Boxes	8023 Beverly Blvd	4:00
Drop box	8060 Melrose Ave	5:00
Drop box	8075 W 3rd St	5:00
Drop box	811 N La Brea Ave	4:30
Box & Ship	8172 W Sunset Blvd	5:00
Drop box	820 N San Vicente Blvd	4:30
Postal Center & More		
	8205 Santa Monica Blvd	5:00
Drop box	8221 Melrose Ave	5:00
Banner Pkg	8231 W 3rd St	4:30
Drop box	8242 W 3rd St	5:00
Drop box	8265 W Sunset Blvd	5:15
Drop box	8322 Beverly Blvd	4:00
Postal Plus	836 N La Cienega Blvd	5:00
Box Brothers	8365 Santa Monica Blvd	4:30
Mail Boxes Etc	8391 Beverly Blvd	4:30
Mail Boxes & Things		
	8424 Santa Monica Blvd	5:00
Drop box	8436 W 3rd St	4:00
Drop box	8439 W Sunset Blvd	5:00
Kinko's	8471 Beverly Blvd	4:00
Boxes & More	8491 W Sunset Blvd	5:00
Drop box	8500 Melrose Ave	5:00
Mail Boxes Etc	8581 Santa Monica Blvd	4:45
Drop box	8635 W 3rd St	5:00
Drop box	8687 Melrose Ave	5:00
Mail Service Ctr	8721 Santa Monica Blvd	3:45
Drop box	8730 W Sunset Blvd	5:00
Drop box	8914 Santa Monica Blvd	5:00
Box to Go	901 N Fairfax Ave	5:00

Map 3 • Hollywood *

Drop box	1040 N Las Palmas Ave	5:45
Drop box	1149 N Gower St	5:00
Highland Postal Center		
	1304 N Highland Ave	5:00
Kinko's	1440 Vine St	5:00
Rex Mail Co	1608 N Cahuenga Blvd	5:15
Drop box	1615 Wilcox Ave	4:30
Drop box	1645 Vine St	5:00
Drop box	1680 Vine St	5:15
Drop box	1800 Vine St	5:00
Drop box	306 N Larchmont Blvd	4:00
Village Mail Call	419 N Larchmont Blvd	5:15
Drop box	5300 Melrose Ave	5:00
Trans-Caucuses Shipping		
	6051 Hollywood Blvd	4:30
Drop box	6255 W Sunset Blvd	5:30
Drop box	6430 W Sunset Blvd	5:00
Staples	6450 W Sunset Blvd	5:15
Drop box	6464 W Sunset Blvd	5:30
Drop box	6565 W Sunset Blvd	5:00
Shipping & Mailboxes		
	6660 W Sunset Blvd	4:30
Service Center	6666 Lexington Ave	6:00
Drop box	6671 W Sunset Blvd	5:15
Drop box	6777 Hollywood Blvd	4:45
Drop box	6801 Hollywood Blvd	5:00
Drop box	6922 Hollywood Blvd	5:30
Drop box	846 N Cahuenga Blvd	5:15

Map 4 • Los Feliz *

Drop box	1300 N Vermont Ave	4:30
Kingston Mail & Gift Mart		
	1555 N Vermont Ave	4:00
Drop box	1825 N Vermont Ave	5:00

Box Brothers	1954 Hillhurst Ave	5:00
Copycat/Pack'n'Fly	2046 Hillhurst Ave	4:00
Drop box	4021 Rosewood Ave	5:00

Map 5 • Silver Lake/Echo Park/Atwater *

Drop box	1525 N Alverado St	5:00
Drop box	1910 W Sunset Blvd	5:00
Drop box	2512 Hyperion Ave	4:30
Box and Ship	2590 Glendale Blvd	4:15
Postalworks	2658 Griffith Park Blvd	5:00
Drop box	3370 Glendale Blvd	4:30
Speedco Fax & Pack		
	3371 Glendale Blvd	4:00

Map 6 • Miracle Mile/Mid-City *

Coast To Coast	1109 S La Cienega Blvd	4:30
Drop box	1270 S Alfred St	4:30
Adore Freight/Shipping Etc		
	1494 S Robertson Blvd	4:00
Drop box	1833 S La Cienega Blvd	5:00
Drop box	195 S Robertson Blvd	5:00
Mailbox Express	289 S Robertson Blvd	4:00
Drop box	50 N La Cienega Blvd	3:45
Drop box	5350 Wilshire Blvd	5:00
Staples	5425 Wilshire Blvd	5:00
Drop box	5455 Wilshire Blvd	5:00
Mail Boxes Etc	5482 Wilshire Blvd	5:00
Kinko's/Svc Ctr	5500 Wilshire Blvd	6:00
The Box Store	5657 Wilshire Blvd	5:00
Drop box	5670 Wilshire Blvd	5:00
Drop box	5700 Wilshire Blvd	5:00
Drop box	5750 Wilshire Blvd	5:00
Drop box	5757 Wilshire Blvd	5:00
Drop box	5900 Wilshire Blvd	5:15
Mailcom Services	5939 W Pico Blvd	3:30
Drop box	6100 Wilshire Blvd	5:00
Box Depot	6230 Wilshire Blvd	4:30
Drop box	6300 Wilshire Blvd	5:00
Drop box	6310 San Vicente Blvd	4:30
Service Center	6361 Wilshire Blvd	6:00
Drop box	640 S San Vicente Blvd	4:45
Drop box	6404 Wilshire Blvd	5:00
Drop box	6500 Wilshire Blvd	5:00
Beverly Hills Postal Center		
	8306 Wilshire Blvd	3:30
Drop box	8383 Wilshire Blvd	5:30
Drop box	8447 Wilshire Blvd	4:00
Drop box	8484 Wilshire Blvd	5:30
Drop box	8500 Wilshire Blvd	5:00
Drop box	8730 Wilshire Blvd	5:00
Drop box	9100 Wilshire Blvd	5:30
Drop box	9107 Wilshire Blvd	5:00

Map 7 • Hancock Park *

Mail Boxes Etc	137 N Larchmont Blvd	5:00
Drop box	3780 Wilshire Blvd	5:00
Charlie Chan Printing		
	3974 Wilshire Blvd	4:20
Drop box	4055 Wilshire Blvd	5:00
Drop box	4201 Wilshire Blvd	5:00
Drop box	4221 Wilshire Blvd	5:00
Drop box	4601 Wilshire Blvd	4:30
Drop box	4751 Wilshire Blvd	5:00
Drop box	4929 Wilshire Blvd	5:00
Wilshire Mail Boxes		
	5042 Wilshire Blvd	5:00
Drop box	5055 Wilshire Blvd	5:00

Map 8 • Korea Town *

Drop box	2500 Wilshire Blvd	5:00
Drop box	2510 Wilshire Blvd	4:30
Mail Plus	269 S Western Ave	4:45
Drop box	3055 Wilshire Blvd	5:00

Pick-up time, p.m.

Plus One Shipping	3191 1/2 W Olympic Blvd	3:30
Drop box	3200 Wilshire Blvd	5:00
Drop box	3250 Wilshire Blvd	5:00
Drop box	3255 Wilshire Blvd	5:00
Copy Express LA	3321 Wilshire Blvd	4:00
Service Center	3345 Wilshire Blvd	6:00
Drop box	3435 Wilshire Blvd	5:00
Drop box	3450 Wilshire Blvd	5:00
Drop box	3530 Wilshire Blvd	5:00
Drop box	3550 Wilshire Blvd	5:00
Drop box	3600 Wilshire Blvd	5:00
Drop box	3660 Wilshire Blvd	5:00
Drop box	3699 Wilshire Blvd	5:00
Drop box	3700 Wilshire Blvd	5:00
Drop box	3731 Wilshire Blvd	5:00
Drop box	3751 W 6th St	5:00
Drop box	520 S La Fayette Park Pl	5:00
Drop box	520 S Virgil Ave	5:00
Drop box	672 S Lafayette Park Pl	5:00

Map 9 • Downtown *

Drop box	1000 Wilshire Blvd	5:00
Drop box	1010 Wilshire Blvd	5:00
Drop box	1055 W 7th St	5:00
Drop box	1055 Wilshire Blvd	5:15
Drop box	1100 S San Pedro St	5:00
Drop box	112 W 9th St	5:15
Drop box	1150 S Olive St	5:15
Drop box	117 W 9th St	5:15
Drop box	1200 Santee St	5:00
Drop box	1200 Wilshire Blvd	5:00
Drop box	1201 S Figueroa St	5:15
Drop box	1201 W 5th St	4:30
Drop box	1318 E 7th St	4:00
Drop box	1545 Wilshire Blvd	5:05
Drop box	1601 E Olympic Blvd	5:00
Drop box	1625 W Olympic Blvd	5:00
Drop box	201 N Figueroa St	5:00
Drop box	2010 Wilshire Blvd	4:45
Drop box	207 S Broadway	5:10
Drop bos	225 E 9th St	5:00
Drop box	255 E Temple St	5:00
Drop box	261 S Figueroa St	5:00
Drop box	300 N Los Angeles St	5:15
Drop box	300 S Spring St	4:45
Drop box	312 N Spring St	5:10
Drop box	315 W 9th St	5:15
Service Center	330 S Hope St	6:15
Drop box	333 S Beaudry Ave	4:45
Drop box	333 S Hope St	5:30
Drop box	350 S Figueroa St	5:15
Drop box	420 Boyd St	4:45
Drop box	420 E 3rd St	5:00
Drop box	444 S Flower St	5:30
Drop box	445 S Figueroa St	5:00
Service Center	505 S Flower St	6:00
Drop box	510 W 6th St	5:00
Drop box	515 S Figueroa St	5:00
Drop box	515 W 6th St	5:00
Drop box	550 S Hope St	5:00
Service Center	554 S Grand Ave	6:00
Drop box	555 W 5th St	5:30
Drop box	600 Wilshire Blvd	5:15
Drop box	601 S Figueroa St	5:00
Drop box	601 W 5th St	5:00
Drop box	606 S Olive St	5:00
Drop box	624 S Grand Ave	5:15
Drop box	626 Wilshire Blvd	4:50
Drop box	627 S Central Ave	5:00
Drop box	633 W 5th St	4:45
Drop box	634 S Spring St	4:30
Drop box	650 S Hill St	5:00
Drop box	660 S Figueroa St	5:00
Drop box	700 S Flower St	5:10
Drop box	707 Wilshire Blvd	5:10
Drop box	714 W Olympic Blvd	5:00
Service Center	735 S Figueroa St	6:00
Drop box	760 N Main St	4:45
Drop box	800 E 12th St	5:15
Drop box	800 N Alameda St	5:00
Drop box	800 S Figueroa St	4:45
Drop box	800 W 6th St	5:15
Drop box	800 Wilshire Blvd	4:45
Drop box	801 S Figueroa St	5:00
Drop box	801 S Grand Ave	5:00
Drop box	810 N Alameda St	5:00
Drop box	811 W 7th St	4:45
Drop box	818 W 7th St	5:00
Drop box	819 Santee St	5:00
Kinko's/Svc Ctr	835 Wilshire Blvd	6:00
Drop box	860 S Los Angeles St	5:00
Drop box	865 S Figueroa St	5:00
Drop box	888 S Figueroa St	5:00
Drop box	900 Wilshire Blvd	5:00
Drop box	911 Wilshire Blvd	5:15
Drop box	977 N Broadway	4:45

Map 10 • Baldwin Hills *

Drop box	3650 W M L King Jr Blvd	4:30
My Mailbox	3717 S La Brea Ave	4:30
Drop box	3870 Crenshaw Blvd	5:00
Drop box	5100 W Goldleaf Circle	5:00
Drop box	5120 W Goldleaf Circle	5:00

Map 11 • South Central West *

Drop box	4401 Crenshaw Blvd	4:00
Drop box	840 Childs Way	4:30
Drop box	900 Exposition Blvd	5:00

Map 12 • South Central East *

Drop box	1631 S Alameda St	5:00
Staples	1701 S Figueroa St	5:15
Drop box	1933 S Broadway	5:00
Kinko's	2723 S Figueroa St	5:00
Service Center	3333 S Grand Ave	5:30

Map 13 • Inglewood *

Drop box	101 N La Brea Ave	5:30
Drop box	1050 S Prairie Ave	4:30
Drop box	111 N La Brea Ave	5:30
Drop box	333 N Prairie Ave	5:00
Drop box	401 S Prairie Ave	5:00
The Mail Connection	6709 La Tijera Blvd	5:00

Map 14 • Inglewood East *

Drop box	2200 W Century Blvd	4:45

Map 15 • Pacific Palisades *

Drop box	15209 W Sunset Blvd	4:00
The Office Supplier	15237 W Sunset Blvd	3:30
Mail Boxes Etc	15332 Antioch St	4:00
Drop box	860 Via De La Paz	4:00
Palisadus Letter Shop	865 Via De La Paz	3:30
Drop box	881 Alma Real Dr	4:00

Map 16 • Brentwood *

Drop box	11611 San Vicente Blvd	5:00
Drop box	11661 San Vicente Blvd	5:00
Brentwood Mail Box	11693 San Vicente Blvd	4:00
Mail Boxes Etc	11718 Barrington Court	4:30
Drop box	11726 San Vicente Blvd	5:00
Drop box	11777 San Vicente Blvd	4:45
Drop box	11812 San Vicente Blvd	5:00
Drop box	11911 San Vicente Blvd	5:00
Drop box	11999 San Vicente Blvd	4:00
Drop box	12011 San Vicente Blvd	4:00
Drop box	200 S Barrington Ave	5:15

Map 17 • Bel Air/Holmby Hills *

Drop box	1007 N Sepulveda Blvd	5:00
Drop box	110 Westwood Plaza	4:00
The Pulse	308 Westwood Plaza	5:00
Drop box	612 N Sepulveda Blvd	4:30
Drop box	630 N Sepulveda Blvd	5:15

Map 18 • Santa Monica *

Drop box	100 Wilshire Blvd	5:00
Mail & Photo	1007 Montana Ave	3:45
Drop box	120 Broadway	5:00
Drop box	1245 16th St	5:00
The Mail House	1247 Lincoln Blvd	4:30
Drop box	1250 4th St	5:00
Drop box	1250 6th St	5:00
Drop box	1299 Ocean Ave	5:00
Drop box	1401 Ocean Ave	5:00
Drop box	1422 2nd St # 24	4:30
Drop box	1437 7th St	5:00
Drop box	1542 15th St	4:30
Drop box	1601 Cloverfield Blvd	4:30
Drop box	1601 Main St	5:00
Drop box	1630 17th St	5:00
Drop box	1640 5th St	5:00
Drop box	1661 Lincoln Blvd	5:00
Executive Express	1700 Ocean Ave	4:00
Ocean Park Mail & Bus	171 Pier Ave	5:30
Drop box	1717 4th St	5:00
Drop box	1750 Ocean Park Blvd	4:30
Drop box	1821 Wilshire Blvd	5:00
Drop box	1919 Santa Monica Blvd	5:00
Drop box	200 Main St	5:00
Drop box	2001 Santa Monica Blvd	4:30
Drop box	2001 Wilshire Blvd	5:00
Drop box	201 Wilshire Blvd	4:45
Drop box	2020 Santa Monica Blvd	5:00
Drop box	2040 Broadway	4:30
Box Brothers	2113 Wilshire Blvd	4:30
Posttel Business Center	2118 Wilshire Blvd	4:30
Drop box	2120 Colorado Ave	4:30
Drop box	2121 16th St	4:30
Drop box	221 Hampton Dr	4:30
Drop box	233 Wilshire Blvd	5:00
Drop box	2415 Main St	5:00
Drop box	2425 Colorado Ave	5:00
Drop box	2444 Wilshire Blvd	4:30
Drop box	2450 Colorado Ave	4:30
Aim Mail Center	2461 Santa Monica Blvd	4:30
Main Street Printing	2629 Main St	4:45
Drop box	2720 Neilson Way	5:00
Drop box	401 Wilshire Blvd	5:00
Drop box	425 15th St	4:30
Drop box	429 Santa Monica Blvd	5:00
Drop box	501 Colorado Ave	5:00
Drop box	501 Santa Monica Blvd	5:00
Drop box	520 Broadway	5:00
Drop box	530 Wilshire Blvd	4:45
Drop box	565 Pier Ave	5:00
Kinko's	601 Wilshire Blvd	5:00
Drop box	725 Arizona Ave	5:00
Box Brothers	825 Wilshire Blvd	3:00
Drop box	902 Colorado Ave	5:00
Service Center	925 Wilshire Blvd	5:00

Pick-up time, p.m.

Map 19 • West LA/Santa Monica East *

Drop box	11111 Santa Monica Blvd	5:00
Drop box	11150 Santa Monica Blvd	5:00
Drop box	11150 W Olympic Blvd	5:00
Boxes Plus	11209 National Blvd	5:00
Drop box	11340 W Olympic Blvd	5:00
Drop box	11377 W Olympic Blvd	5:00
Drop box	11400 W Olympic Blvd	5:00
Drop box	11420 Santa Monica Blvd	4:30
Drop box	11440 San Vicente Blvd	4:00
Drop box	11500 W Olympic Blvd	5:00
Mail Boxes Etc	1158 26th Street	5:00
Drop box	11601 Wilshire Blvd	5:00
Drop box	11620 Wilshire Blvd	5:00
Drop box	11628 Santa Monica Blvd	4:30
National Mailbox Center		
	11664 National Blvd	4:30
Box Brothers	11701 Wilshire Blvd	4:30
Drop box	11755 Wilshire Blvd	5:00
Drop box	11766 Wilshire Blvd	5:00
Kinko's	11819 Wilshire Blvd	4:00
Drop box	11845 W Olympic Blvd	5:00
Drop box	11859 Wilshire Blvd	5:00
Drop box	11900 W Olympic Blvd	5:00
Boxes & More	11901 Santa Monica Blvd	4:30
Drop box	12100 Wilshire Blvd	5:00
Drop box	12121 Wilshire Blvd	5:00
Drop box	12233 W Olympic Blvd	5:00
Drop box	12300 Wilshire Blvd	5:00
Drop box	12301 Wilshire Blvd	5:00
Drop box	12304 Santa Monica Blvd	5:00
VIP Postal Svcs	12335 Santa Monica Blvd	3:45
Drop box	12400 Wilshire Blvd	5:00
Drop box	12424 Wilshire Blvd	5:00
Drop box	1620 26th St	4:45
Drop box	1640 S Sepulveda Blvd	5:00
Drop box	1815 Centinela Ave	5:00
Drop box	1849 Sawtelle Blvd	5:00
Drop box	1950 Sawtelle Blvd	5:00
Drop box	1990 S Bundy Dr	5:00
Drop box	2001 S Barrington Ave	5:00
Staples	2052 S Bundy Dr	5:00
Drop box	2100 Sawtelle Blvd	4:15
Kinko's	2139 S Bundy Dr	4:00
Drop box	2215 S Sepulveda Blvd	4:00
Drop box	2400 S Barrington Ave	5:00
Drop box	2425 Olympic Blvd	5:00
Drop box	2440 S Sepulveda Blvd	4:30
Drop box	2525 Michigan Ave	4:45
Brentwood Shipping & Mail		
	253 26th St	4:00
Drop box	2530 Wilshire Blvd	4:45
Drop box	2701 Ocean Park Blvd	4:30
Drop box	2716 Ocean Park Blvd	4:30
Drop box	2730 Wilshire Blvd	5:00
Drop box	2800 28th St	5:00
National Mailbox Center		
	2801 Ocean Park Blvd	5:00
Drop box	2811 Wilshire Blvd	5:00
Drop box	2850 Ocean Park Blvd	5:00
Drop box	3000 Olympic Blvd	5:00
Drop box	3130 Wilshire Blvd	5:00
Service Center	3210 Ocean Park Blvd	5:00
Drop box	3223 D. Douglas Loop S	5:00

Map 20 • Westwood/Century City *

Drop box	1000 Veteran Ave	4:30
Drop box	10100 Santa Monica Blvd	5:30
Drop box	10250 Santa Monica Blvd	5:00
Drop box	10351 Santa Monica Blvd	5:00
Drop box	10390 Santa Monica Blvd	5:00
Drop box	10474 Santa Monica Blvd	5:00
Drop box	10585 Santa Monica Blvd	5:00
Drop box	10635 Santa Monica Blvd	5:00
Drop box	10780 Santa Monica Blvd	4:45
Drop box	10850 Wilshire Blvd	5:00
Drop box	10866 Wilshire Blvd	4:30
Drop box	10877 Wilshire Blvd	5:00
Service Center	10880 Wilshire Blvd	6:00
Drop box	10920 Wilshire Blvd	5:00
Kinko's	10924 Weyburn Ave	5:00
Drop box	10940 Wilshire Blvd	5:00
Drop box	10960 Wilshire Blvd	5:00
Drop box	10990 Wilshire Blvd	5:00
Drop box	1100 Glendon Ave	5:00
Drop box	11000 Wilshire Blvd	5:00
Mail Boxes Box & Ship		
	11041 Santa Monica Blvd	4:45
Drop box	11050 Santa Monica Blvd	5:00
Box Brothers	1351 Westwood Blvd	5:00
Kinko's	1520 Westwood Blvd	5:00
Drop box	1800 Ave of the Stars	5:00
Drop box	1801 Century Park E	5:30
Drop box	1840 Century Park E	5:00
Mail Boxes Etc	1875 Century Park E	5:00
Drop box	1880 Century Park E	5:00
Drop box	1888 Century Park E	5:00
Drop box	1900 Ave of the Stars	5:30
Drop box	1901 Ave of the Stars	5:00
Service Center	1925 Century Park E	6:30
Drop box	1999 Ave of the Stars	5:00
Drop box	2029 Century Park E	5:00
Drop box	2049 Century Park E	5:00
Box City	2056 Westwood Blvd	4:45
Drop box	2080 Century Park E	5:00
Service Center	2121 Ave of the Stars	6:00
Box & Ship	2180 Westwood Blvd	4:30
The Pulse	398 Portola Plaza	4:00
Drop box	500 S Sepulveda Blvd	4:30
Mail Boxes Etc	914 Westwood Blvd	5:00
Drop box	924 Westwood Blvd	5:00

Map 21 • Venice *

Staples	1501 Lincoln Blvd	5:00
Drop box	330 Washington Blvd	5:00
USA Mail & Business Center		
	520 Washington Blvd	4:30
Drop box	636B Venice Blvd	5:00

Map 22 • Mar Vista *

Drop box	11965 Venice Blvd	5:00
Drop box	12910 Culver Blvd	5:30
Drop box	13323 W Washington Blvd	4:45
Drop box	3826 Grand View Blvd	5:30
Drop box	4501 Glencoe Ave	5:00
Drop box	4551 Glencoe Ave	5:00

Map 23 • Rancho Park/Palms *

24/7 Postal Ctr	10008 National Blvd	4:00
Drop box	10801 National Blvd	5:00
Drop box	10951 W Pico Blvd	5:00
Drop box	11270 Exposition Blvd	5:15
Drop box	1180 S Beverly Dr	5:00
Drop box	2566 Overland Ave	5:00
Drop box	3000 S Robertson Blvd	5:00
Drop box	3415 S Sepulveda Blvd	5:00
Drop box	3751 Motor Ave	5:00
The Box Store	8918 W Pico Blvd	4:30
Von's Shopping Center		
	9854 National Blvd	4:00
Drop box	9911 W Pico Blvd	5:00

Map 24 • Culver City *

Drop box	100 Corporate Pointe	5:00
Drop box	10768 Venice Blvd	4:30
Drop box	11111 Jefferson Blvd	5:00
Drop box	11144 Washington Blvd	5:00
Drop box	301 Corporate Pointe	5:00
Drop box	3700 S Robertson Blvd	6:00
Drop box	400 Corporate Pointe	5:00
Box City	4220 Lincoln Blvd	4:30
Kinko's	5575 Sepulveda Blvd	4:30
Drop box	5601 W Slauson Ave	5:00
Drop box	5701 W Slauson Ave	5:00
Drop box	600 Corporate Pointe	4:15
CopyMax	8985 Venice Blvd	5:30
Drop box	9696 Culver Blvd	5:00
Drop box	9942 Culver Blvd	5:00

Map 25 • Marina Del Rey *

Drop box	13160 Mindanao Way	5:00
Mail Boxes Etc	13428 Maxella Ave	4:00
Drop box	322 1/2 Culver Blvd	4:00
Service Center	4170 Del Rey Ave	5:30
Box and Ship	4242 Lincoln Blvd	4:30
Drop box	4333 Admiralty Way	5:00
Kinko's	4350 Lincoln Blvd	5:00
Drop box	4640 Admiralty Way	5:00
Drop box	4676 Admiralty Way	5:00
Marina Mail Ctr	4712 Admiralty Way	4:30
Drop box	4720 Lincoln Blvd	5:00
Drop box	5419 McConnell Ave	5:00
Drop box	7001 World Way W	4:45
Drop box	7301 World Way W	4:30
Drop box	8055 W Manchester Ave	4:30
Playa Postal Ctr	8117 W Manchester Ave	4:00

Map 26 • Westchester/Fox Hills/LAX *

Service Center	11221 S Hindry Ave	6:45
Drop box	11222 S La Cienega Blvd	5:30
Drop box	12555 W Jefferson Blvd	5:00
Drop box	419 Hindry Ave	5:00
Drop box	420 Hindry Ave	5:00
Drop box	5200 W Century Blvd	5:00
Drop box	5250 W Century Blvd	5:00
Drop box	5757 W Century Blvd	5:30
Drop box	5777 W Century Blvd	5:15
Kinko's	5855 W Century Blvd	4:30
Drop box	5933 W Century Blvd	5:15
Drop box	5959 W Century Blvd	5:15
Drop box	6053 W Century Blvd	5:00
Drop box	6060 Center Dr	5:00
Drop box	6080 Center Dr	5:00
Drop box	6101 W Centinela Ave	5:00
Drop box	6133 Bristol Pkwy	5:00
Drop box	6151 W Century Blvd	5:00
Service Center	6167 Bristol Pkwy	6:00
Drop box	6225 W Century Blvd	5:00
Drop box	6601 Center Dr W	5:00
Drop box	6701 Center Dr W	5:15
Drop box	6801 Park Ter	4:30
Drop box	7381 La Tijera Blvd	5:00
Drop box	8616 La Tijera Blvd	4:45
Staples	8704 S Sepulveda Blvd	4:30
Mail Call	8726 S Sepulveda Blvd	4:45
Drop box	8901 S La Cienega Blvd	5:30
Drop box	8939 S Sepulveda Blvd	5:00
Drop box	9133 S La Cienega Blvd	5:30
Drop box	9800 S La Cienega Blvd	5:30
Drop box	9841 Airport Blvd	5:15
Drop box	9920 S La Cienega Blvd	5:30

Map 27 • El Segundo/Manhattan Beach *

Drop box	100 N Sepulveda Blvd	5:30
Drop box	101 Continental Blvd	5:15
Current Events	1140 Highland Ave	4:00
Drop box	1230 Rosecrans Ave	5:00

** Pick-up time, p.m.*

Drop box	130 E Grand Ave	5:15
Drop box	1334 Park View Ave	5:45
Drop box	14500 Aviation Blvd	4:30
Drop box	1600 Rosecrans Ave	4:30
Mail Boxes Etc	1601 N Sepulveda Blvd	4:00
Drop box	1700 E Walnut Ave	4:30
Drop box	1960 E Grand Ave	5:30
Drop box	201 N Douglas St	5:15
Drop box	2041 Rosecrans Ave	5:00
Drop box	2101 E El Segundo Blvd	5:30
Drop box	2101 Rosecrans Ave	5:30
Drop box	2121 Park Pl	5:30
Drop box	2121 Rosecrans Ave	5:30
Mail Boxes Etc	214 Main St	4:45
Drop box	2141 Rosecrans Ave	5:30
Drop box	222 N Sepulveda Blvd	5:30
Drop box	2221 Rosecrans Ave	5:30
Drop box	225 S Sepulveda Blvd	5:15
Drop box	2361 Rosecrans Ave	5:00
Drop box	2401 E El Segundo Blvd	4:30
Manhattan Postal Center	2905 N Sepulveda Blvd	4:00
Drop box	300 Continental Blvd	5:45
Drop box	300 N Sepulveda Blvd	5:45
Drop box	3601 N Aviation Blvd	4:45
Drop box	505 N Sepulveda Blvd	5:00
Drop box	550 Continental Blvd	5:15
Drop box	645 S Allied Way	5:00
Drop box	818 Manhattan Beach Blvd	4:00
Drop box	831 S Douglas St	5:30
Drop box	840 Apollo St	5:30
Drop box	880 Apollo St	5:30
Drop box	898 N Sepulueda Blvd	4:00

Map 28 • Hawthorne *

Service Center	12600 S Prairie Ave	6:45
Mail Box & Stuff	14402 Hawthorne Blvd	4:30
Drop box	3690 Redondo Beach Ave	5:30
Postal Page	3918 W Rosecrans Ave	4:30
Kinko's	5201 W Rosecrans Ave	5:00
Drop box	5220 Pacific Concourse Dr	5:00
Drop box	5230 Pacific Concourse Dr	5:00
Drop box	5245 Pacific Concourse Dr	5:00

Map 29 • Hermosa Beach *

Drop box	1102 Aviation Blvd	4:30
Kinko's	1139 Artesia Blvd # A	4:30
Drop box	1426 Aviation Blvd	4:45
Drop box	1620 Aviation Blvd	4:45
Postal Boxes Etc	17252 Hawthorne Blvd	4:45
Postal Plus	17528 Hawthorne Blvd	4:15
Drop box	2200 Pacific Coast Hwy	4:45
Box Brothers	2302 Artesia Blvd	4:00
Drop box	2447 Pacific Coast Hwy	4:00
Drop box	2601 Manhattan Beach Blvd	5:00
Beach Mailbox	2629 Manhattan Ave	4:30
Drop box	2908 Oregon Court	5:30
Drop box	3 W 190th St	5:15
Drop box	3547 Voyager St	5:00
Drop box	3625 Del Amo Blvd	5:30
Drop box	3880 Del Amo Blvd # 3914	5:30

Map 30 • Torrance North *

Drop box	119 W Torrance Blvd	3:30
Packaging Store	1207 S Pacific Coast Hwy	4:15
Drop box	1611 S Pacific Coast Hwy	4:30
Postal Plus	17528 Hawthorne Blvd	4:30
Kinko's	1770 S Pacific Coast Hwy	4:15
Drop box	18080 Crenshaw Blvd	5:00
Drop box	18411 Crenshaw Blvd	5:00
Drop box	200 S Pacific Coast Hwy	4:30
Service Center	21023 Hawthorne Blvd	5:45
Drop box	21250 Hawthorne Blvd	5:30

Drop box	21307 Hawthorne Blvd	5:15
Drop box	21515 Hawthorne Blvd	5:30
Drop box	22750 Hawthorne Blvd	5:00
Drop box	22819 Hawthorne Blvd	4:45
Kinko's	23325 Hawthorne Blvd	5:30
Drop box	23326 Hawthorne Blvd	5:30
Drop box	23430 Hawthorne Blvd	5:00
Drop box	23456 Hawthorne Blvd	5:30
My Express Mail	3025 Artesia Blvd	4:00
Drop box	3838 W Carson St	5:00
Postal Solutions	4455 Torrance Blvd	5:00
Postal Annex Plus	553 N Pacific Coast Hwy	4:30
Mail Stop Extra	817 Torrance Blvd	4:30

Map 31 • Redondo Beach *

Mail Boxes Etc	21143 Hawthorne Blvd	5:00
Drop box	22529 Hawthorne Blvd	5:00
Drop box	4216 Pacific Coast Hwy	5:00

Map 32 • Torrance South *

Drop box	1433 Marcelina Ave	5:00
Drop box	1815 W 213th St	5:00
Box Brothers	1827 1/2 Pacific Coast Hwy	5:00
Mail Boxes Galore	1880 W Carson St	4:45
Drop box	1919 Torrance Blvd	5:00
Lomita Mail Car	2017 Lomita Blvd	4:30
Drop box	2216 Sepulveda Blvd	4:30
Drop box	23545 Crenshaw Blvd	5:30
Drop box	2377 Crenshaw Blvd	4:30
Drop box	24050 Madison St	5:00
Postal Annex	24325 Crenshaw Blvd	4:30
Drop box	2501 W 237th St	5:30
Drop box	2510 Monterey St	5:00
Drop box	25131 Narbonne Ave	5:00
Drop box	25200 Crenshaw Blvd # 2	5:00
Drop box	2535 W 237th St	5:30
The Postal Mart	2537 Pacific Coast Hwy	4:45
Drop box	2601 Airport Dr	5:00
Drop box	2720 Monterey St	4:45
Drop box	2780 Skypark Dr	5:00
Drop box	3305 Fujita St	5:30
Drop box	3400 Torrance Blvd	5:00
Drop box	3424 W Carson St	5:00
Drop box	3440 Lomita Blvd	5:00
Drop box	3528 Torrance Blvd	5:00
Drop box	3665 Pacific Coast Hwy	4:30

Map 33 • Eagle Rock/Highland Park *

Eaglerock Mailing Ctr	2272 Colorado Blvd	4:00
Drop box	7435 N Figueroa St	4:30

Map 34 • Pasadena *

Drop box	1001 Fremont Ave	5:00
Drop box	101 S Marengo Ave	5:00
Drop box	1111 S Arroyo Pkwy	5:00
Post Pack & Ship	115 W California Blvd	4:30
Drop box	117 E Colorado Blvd	5:00
Drop box	123 S Marengo Ave	4:45
Drop box	125 S Grand Ave	4:00
Drop box	130 N Marengo Ave	4:30
Service Center	135 N Los Robles Ave	5:45
Drop box	140 S Lake Ave	4:30
Drop box	145 Pasadena Ave	5:00
Drop box	150 E Colorado Blvd	5:00
Drop box	150 S Los Robles Ave	5:00
Drop box	155 N Lake Ave	4:30
Drop box	199 S Los Robles Ave	5:00
Drop box	2 N Lake Ave	5:00
Drop box	200 E Del Mar Blvd	4:45
Drop box	200 S Los Robles Ave	5:00
Drop box	201 S Lake Ave	5:00
Drop box	210 S De Lacey Ave	5:00

Drop box	221 E Walnut St	5:00
Mail Box Plus	235 E Colorado Blvd	4:00
Drop box	2600 Mission St	4:30
Drop box	273 S Lake Ave	5:00
Drop box	281 E Colorado Blvd	4:30
Cal Oaks Box & Ship	30 W California Blvd	4:00
Drop box	300 N Lake Ave	5:00
Service Center	300 S Grand Ave	6:15
Drop box	301 N Lake Ave	5:00
Drop box	35 N Lake Ave	5:00
Drop box	35 S Raymond Ave	5:00
Drop box	350 S Grand Ave	4:30
Drop box	350 W Colorado Blvd	5:00
Drop box	46 Smith Aly	4:45
Kinko's	460 Fair Oaks Ave	4:00
Mail Box Planet	530 S Lake Ave	4:30
Drop box	55 S Lake Ave	5:00
Drop box	600 S Lake Ave	5:00
Packaging Store	620 S Raymond Ave	4:30
Drop box	625 Fair Oaks Ave	5:00
Drop box	70 S Lake Ave	4:30
Drop box	719 Mission St	5:00
OfficeMax	721 E Colorado Blvd	4:00
Drop box	800 E Colorado Blvd	5:00
Kinko's/Svc Ctr	855 E Colorado Blvd	5:30
Post & Package Center	920 E Colorado Blvd	4:30
Drop box	937 E Green St	4:45
Drop box	99 W California Blvd	5:00

Map 35 • Pasadena East/San Marino *

Drop box	1010 E Union St	4:45
Drop box	1201 N Catalina Ave	4:30
Drop box	1224 E Green St	5:00
The Postmaster	2245 E Colorado Blvd	4:45
Drop box	2500 E Foothill Blvd	5:00
Drop box	2540 Huntington Dr	5:00
Drop box	2609 E Colorado Blvd	4:30
Drop box	2960 Huntington Dr	5:00
Drop box	967 E Colorado Blvd	5:00

Map 36 • Mt. Washington *

Drop box	2000 N San Fernando Rd	5:30

Map 37 • Lincoln Heights *

Drop box	1900 N Main St	5:00

Map 38 • El Sereno *

Monterey Business Ctr	5902 Monterey Rd	4:00

Map 39 • Alhambra *

Drop box	1603 W Valley Blvd	5:15
Box-All Parcel Ctr	2107 W Commonwealth Ave	5:00
Drop box	419 N Atlantic Blvd	4:45
Drop box	428 S Atlantic Blvd	4:30
Staples	610 E Valley Blvd	4:00
Broad Solutions	630 E Main St	4:00
Drop box	801 S Garfield Ave	5:00

** Pick-up time, p.m.*

Map 40 • Boyle Heights　*

Drop box	1200 N State St	5:00
Drop box	1240 N Mission Rd	4:45
Drop box	2010 Zonal Ave	4:45

Map 41 • City Terrace/East LA　*

Drop box	1000 Corporate Center Dr	5:00
Drop box	1255 Corporate Center Dr	5:00
Drop box	2540 Corporate Pl	5:00

Map 42 • Reseda/Encino West　*

Mail Boxes Etc	17216 Saticoy St	4:00
Drop box	5535 Balboa Blvd	4:30
Drop box	5805 White Oak Ave	4:00
Drop box	6345 Balboa Blvd	4:30

Map 44 • North Hollywood　*

West Coast Mail Centers		
	13659 Victory Blvd	4:00

Map 45 • Burbank　*

Drop box	1016 N Hollywood Way	5:15
Drop box	2140 N Hollywood Way	4:45
Drop box	2740 W Magnolia Blvd	4:45
Drop box	2924 W Magnolia Blvd	4:15
Abs Zone	3106 W Magnolia Blvd	4:00
Mail Boxes Etc	3727 W Magnolia Blvd	4:30
Drop box	4116 W Magnolia Blvd	5:00
Drop box	4605 Lankershim Blvd	5:30
Drop box	4640 Lankershim Blvd	5:30
Drop box	5503 Cahuenga Blvd	5:00
Mail Boxes & Accessories		
	859 N Hollywood Way	4:15

Map 46 • Burbank East/Glendale West　*

Drop box	100 N 1st St	5:15
Kinko's/Svc Ctr	101 N San Fernando	5:30
Drop box	101 N Victory Blvd	4:45
Drop box	1060 W Alameda Ave	4:00
Drop box	1213 Flower St	4:45
Mail Boxes Etc	1317 N San Fernando Blvd	5:00
Central Pak & Mail		
	145 S Glenoaks Blvd	4:30
Drop box	1700 Victory Blvd	5:00
Box Brothers	1806 W Olive Ave	4:45
Drop box	1918 W Magnolia Blvd	5:00
Drop box	217 E Alameda Ave	4:15
Drop box	221 W Alameda Ave	4:30
Drop box	2300 W Olive Ave	5:00
Drop box	303 N Glenoaks Blvd	5:00
Drop box	333 N Glenoaks Blvd	4:30
Mail Boxes & More		
	355 S Flower St	5:00
Drop box	601 S Glenoaks Blvd	5:00

Map 47 • Glendale South　*

Drop box	101 N Brand Blvd	5:00
Drop box	101 N Verdugo Rd	4:30
Drop box	1010 N Central Ave	4:30
Mail Boxes Etc	1147 E Broadway	4:00
Drop box	130 N Brand Blvd	4:30
Box Brothers	133 1/2 S Brand Ave	4:45
Drop box	1400 S Central Ave	5:00
Drop box	144 N Glendale Ave	5:00
Kinko's	225 N Brand Blvd	5:00
Drop box	230 N Maryland Ave	5:00
Mail Boxes Etc	249 N Brand Blvd	4:00
Drop box	300 W Glenoaks Blvd	4:30
Drop box	315 Arden Ave	5:00
Service Center	330 N Brand Blvd	5:30
Drop box	425 E Colorado St	5:00
Drop box	425 W Broadway	5:00
Drop box	4820 San Fernando Rd	5:00
Drop box	500 N Brand Blvd	4:45
Drop box	500 N Central Ave	5:00
ABC Mailbox	501 W Glenoaks Blvd Ste 10	4:00
Drop box	505 N Brand Blvd	5:00
Drop box	517 E Wilson Ave	4:45
Drop box	550 N Brand Blvd	12:00
Drop box	655 N Central Ave	4:00
Drop box	700 N Brand Blvd	5:00
Drop box	700 N Central Ave	5:00
Drop box	801 N Brand Blvd	5:00

Map 48 • Encino　*

Drop box	14141 Covello St	4:45
Drop box	15107 Vanowen St	4:00
Drop box	15701 Sherman Way	5:00
Box City	16113 Sherman Way	4:30
Box Brothers	16227 Victory Blvd	4:00
Drop box	16380 Roscoe Blvd	5:00
Drop box	16461 Sherman Way	4:30
Drop box	16600 Sherman Way	5:00
Drop box	16633 Ventura Blvd	5:00
Kinko's	16652 Ventura Blvd	4:00
Drop box	16830 Ventura Blvd	5:00
Drop box	17000 Ventura Blvd	4:45
Drop box	17200 Ventura Blvd	4:30
PostNet	17328 Ventura Blvd	4:30
Drop box	17337 Ventura Blvd	5:00
Drop box	17547 Ventura Blvd	4:45
Mail Boxes Etc	18034 Ventura Blvd	4:45
Encino Mail Boxes		
	4924 Balboa Blvd	4:30
Drop box	4930 Balboa	4:00
B & E Postal Ctr	5632 Van Nuys Blvd	4:00
Drop box	5805 Sepulveda Blvd	4:30
Kinko's/Svc Ctr	5810 Sepulveda Blvd	5:45
Drop box	5990 Sepulveda Blvd	5:00
Drop box	6200 Van Nuys Blvd	4:45
Drop box	6230 Van Nuys Blvd	4:30
Drop box	6454 Van Nuys Blvd	4:15
Drop box	7100 Hayvenhurst Ave	4:45
Drop box	7120 Hayvenhurst Ave	5:00

Map 49 • Sherman Oaks West　*

Drop box	14724 Ventura Blvd	5:00
Drop box	14900 Magnolia Blvd	4:45
Drop box	14900 Ventura Blvd	5:00
Drop box	15000 Ventura Blvd	4:45
Blvd Postal Stop & Service		
	15030 Ventura Blvd	4:00
Drop box	15060 Ventura Blvd	4:30
Drop box	15130 Ventura Blvd	5:00
Drop box	15165 Ventura Blvd	5:15
Drop box	15206 Ventura Blvd	4:30
Drop box	15233 Ventura Blvd	5:15
Drop box	15250 Ventura Blvd	5:00
Drop box	15300 Ventura Blvd	4:30
Drop box	15303 Ventura Blvd	5:15
Drop box	15315 Magnolia Blvd	4:30
Drop box	15456 Ventura Blvd	4:30
Service Center	15720 Ventura Blvd	5:00
Drop box	15760 Ventura Blvd	5:00
Drop box	15821 Ventura Blvd	5:00
Drop box	15910 Ventura Blvd	5:00
Drop box	15915 Ventura Blvd	5:00
Drop box	15928 Ventura Blvd	4:30
Drop box	16000 Ventura Blvd	4:45
Drop box	16027 Ventura Blvd	5:00
Drop box	16030 Ventura Blvd	5:00
Drop box	16055 Ventura Blvd	4:45
Bizzy Box	16060 Ventura Blvd	4:00
Drop box	16130 Ventura Blvd	5:00
Drop box	16133 Ventura Blvd	4:45
All Boxed In	16161 Ventura Blvd Ste C	4:30

Map 49 (continued)

Drop box	16200 Ventura Blvd	5:00
Drop box	16255 Ventura Blvd	4:45
Drop box	16311 Ventura Blvd	4:45
Drop box	16400 Ventura Blvd	5:00
Drop box	16501 Ventura Blvd	4:45
Drop box	16530 Ventura Blvd	5:15
Telepostalcom	4528 Saugas Ave	4:00

Map 50 • Sherman Oaks East　*

Mail Boxes & Things		
	12930 Ventura Blvd	4:30
Post Masters	13351 Riverside Dr	5:00
Drop box	13400 Riverside Dr	5:15
Personally Yours Mail Box		
	13547 Ventura Blvd	4:00
Drop box	13701 Riverside Dr	5:15
Box Brothers	13824 Ventura Blvd	5:00
Drop box	14011 Ventura Blvd	4:30
Drop box	14140 Ventura Blvd	4:30
Mail Boxes & More		
	14320 Ventura Blvd	4:00
Mail Box Svcs Plus		
	14431 Ventura Blvd	4:00
Dickens Box	4335 Van Nuys Blvd	4:00
Drop box	4400 Coldwater Canyon Ave	5:00
Kinko's	4556 Van Nuys Blvd	4:30
Federal Mailbox Center		
	4570 Van Nuys Blvd	4:30
Drop box	4730 Woodman Ave	4:45
Drop box	5000 Van Nuys Blvd	5:00

Map 51 • Studio City/Valley Village　*

Pack N Mail	11054 Ventura Blvd	4:30
Mail Boxes Etc	11271 Ventura Blvd	5:00
Postal & Packing Emporium		
	11288 Ventura Blvd	4:30
Drop box	11304 Chandler Blvd	4:30
American Post and Parcel		
	11333 Moorpark St	5:00
Drop box	11846 Ventura Blvd	4:30
Drop box	12001 Ventura Pl	5:00
Kinko's/Svc Ctr	12101 Ventura Blvd	5:30
Universal Mail & Business		
	12400 Ventura Blvd	4:30
Drop box	12450 Magnolia Blvd	4:30
Drop box	12605 Ventura Blvd	4:15
Drop box	12650 Riverside Dr	4:30
Drop box	12711 Ventura Blvd	5:00
Studio City Postal Ctr		
	3940 Laurel Canyon Blvd	4:00
Drop box	4370 Tujunga Ave	5:00
Mail Box & Photo	4821 Lankershim Blvd Ste F	4:15
Drop box	5200 Lankershim Blvd	5:00
EZ Pack & Ship	5424 Laurel Canyon Blvd	4:30

Map 52 • Universal City/Toluca Lake　*

Drop box	10 Universal City Plaza	5:30
The Mail Box	10153 1/2 Riverside Dr	4:15
Packaging Store	10218 Riverside Dr	4:00
Drop box	3151 Cahuenga Blvd W	5:15
Drop box	3330 Cahuenga Blvd	5:15
Drop box	3365 Barham Blvd	5:15
Drop box	3400 W Riverside Dr	5:00
Drop box	3500 W Olive Dr	5:00
Drop box	3800 Barham Blvd	5:00
Service Center	3817 Riverside Dr	5:30
Drop box	3900 W Alameda Ave	5:00
Drop box	4029 Lankershim Blvd	5:00
Drop box	4100 W Alameda Ave	5:00
Kinko's	4100 W Riverside Dr	5:15
Drop box	4450 W Lakeside Dr	5:00
Drop box	6711 Forest Lawn Dr	5:00
Drop box	6735 Forest Lawn Dr	5:00
Drop box	6767 Forest Lawn Dr	5:00

Map 1 • Beverly Hills

Academy of Motion Picture Arts & Sciences	8949 Wilshire Blvd	310-278-8990	Brake for red carpets and klieg lights! Many premieres are held here.
Beverly Hills Civic Center	Rexford Dr & Santa Monica Blvd	310-550-4654	Infrastructure for the rich and famous.
Beverly Hills Hotel	9641 Sunset Blvd	310-276-2251	Legends have stayed at the Pink Palace.
Greystone Park	905 Loma Vista Dr	310-786-1000	Formerly the Doheny Mansion, now a lovely public park.
Museum of Television and Radio	465 N Beverly Dr	310-275-5200	Where reruns of old sitcoms are considered art.
Regent Beverly Wilshire Hotel	9500 Wilshire Blvd	310-275-5200	

Map 2 • West Hollywood

CBS Television City	Beverly Blvd & N Fairfax Ave	323-852-2624	Wanna be on *Price is Right*? Come on down.
Pacific Design Center	Melrose Ave & San Vicente Blvd	310-657-0800	Nicknamed "The Blue Whale" for obvious reasons.
Pan Pacific Park	7600 Beverly Blvd	323-939-8874	It's a storm drain! We mean, it's a park!
Rock Walk	7435 Sunset Blvd	323-874-1060	Mann's Chinese has John Wayne, the Rock Walk has Slash.
Runyon Canyon Park	Franklin Ave & Fuller Dr	n/a	Once Errol Flynn's estate, now an off-leash hiking trail.
Santa Monica Blvd	Between La Cienega Blvd & Robertson Blvd	n/a	The heart of gay West Hollywood.
Schindler House	833 N Kings Rd	323-651-1510	A desert camp inspired this creation by architect Rudolph Schindler.
Silent Movie Theatre	611 N Fairfax Ave	323-655-2520	Only the ticket prices will remind you that it's the 21st century.
Sunset Strip	Sunset Blvd between N Doheny Dr & N Fairfax Ave	n/a	Its clubs and restaurants are still the center of LA's nightlife.

Map 3 • Hollywood

Capitol Records Building	1750 N Vine St	323-462-6252	Designed to look like a stack of records.
Hollywood Bowl	2301 N Highland Ave	323-850-2000	Eclectic music and picnicking under the stars.
Hollywood Forever Cemetery	6000 Santa Monica Blvd	323-469-1181	The only place in LA where you can still see Douglas Fairbanks and Tyrone Power.
Hollywood Walk of Fame	Hollywood Blvd from N Gower St to LaBrea Ter	323-469-8311	Tourists love this shrine to often mediocre celebs.
Hollywood Wax Museum	6767 Hollywood Blvd	323-462-5991	
Mann's Chinese Theatre	6925 Hollywood Blvd	323-464-8111	See how your shoe size measures up against Sylvester Stallone's.
Pantages Theatre	6233 Hollywood Blvd	323-410-1062	LA's very weak answer to Broadway.
Paramount Pictures	5555 Melrose Ave	323-956-5575	The last movie studio actually in Hollywood.

Map 4 • Los Feliz

American Film Institute	2021 N Western Ave	323-856-7600	The next David Lynch might be honing his craft here right now. Or not.
Ennis-Brown House	2607 Glendower Ave	323-660-0607	Frank Lloyd Wright's version of a Mayan temple.
Greek Theatre	2700 N Vermont Ave	323-468-1767	The venue is usually more impressive than its line-up of musical acts.
Hollyhock House	4800 Hollywood Blvd	323-485-4580	Another Frank Lloyd Wright design, open for public tours.

Map 5 • Silver Lake/Echo Park/Atwater

Dodger Stadium	1000 Elysian Park Ave	323-224-1400	With a view like this, who needs luxury boxes?
Echo Park	Glendale Blvd & Park Ave	n/a	The paddle boats alone are worth a trip.
Richard Neutra houses	2200 Silver Lake Blvd	n/a	A don't-miss for architecture buffs.
Silver Lake Reservoir	Silverlake Blvd & Duane St	n/a	Take a jog, a stroll, and a dog! There is an off-leash dog park at the reservoir's base.

Map 6 • Miracle Mile/Mid-City

Craft & Folk Art Museum	5800 Wilshire Blvd	323-937-5544	If you like that sort of thing…
George C. Page Museum of LaBrea Discoveries	5801 Wilshire Blvd	323-936-2230	Don't miss the La Brea Woman exhibit.
LA Country Museum of Art	5905 Wilshire Blvd		
LaBrea Tar Pits	Wilshire Blvd & S Curson Ave	323-934-7243	It's just a big pool of tar, yet it continues to fascinate us.
LACMA West (former May Co Building)	6067 Wilshire Blvd	323-933-4510	This art deco building used to be home to the May Co. Department Store.
Lula Washington Dance Theatre	5041 W Pico Blvd	323-936-6519	Renowned African-American dance company with classes and residencies.
Petersen Automotive Museum	6060 Wilshire Blvd	323-930-2277	

Map 7 • Hancock Park

Getty House (Mayor's official residence)	605 S Irving Blvd	323-930-6430	The home that LA's mayors use to par-tay.
Los Altos Apartments	4121 Wilshire Blvd	323-464-0600	There is a waiting list for apartments in this historic Spanish-style building.
Wilshire Ebell Theatre & Club	4401 W 8th St	323-939-1128	Renaissance style buildings used mainly for private events.
Wiltern Theatre	3780 Wilshire Blvd	323-380-5005	Cool art deco building attracts equally cool, eclectic musical acts.

Map 8 • Korea Town

MacArthur Park	Wilshire Blvd & S Alvarado St	n/a	No longer the safest of public parks, but definitely one of the oldest.
Southwestern Law School	3050 Wilshire Blvd	213-738-6700	Art Deco department store turned law school.

Map 9 · Downtown

Angel's Flight	W 4th St & Hill St	213-626-1901	Due to a tragic accident, funicular is now simply a walkway.
Chinatown	700-1000 N Broadway	n/a	It may not sound like much, but the slippery shrimp at Yang Chow can't be missed.
City Hall	200 N Spring St	213-485-2121	Got a gripe? Here's the place to start.
Grand Central Market	317 S Broadway	213-624-2378	Mexican specialties and more.
Instituo Cultural Mexicano	125 Paseo de la Plaza	213-624-3660	Dedicated to cultural exchange between American and Mexican cultures.
Japanese American National Museum	369 E 1st St	213-625-0414	Chronicling the Japanese experience in the U.S.
LA Convention Center	1201 S Figueroa St	213-741-1151	The building's green glass exterior is visible for miles.
MOCA	250 S Grand Ave	213-626-6222	Received much well-deserved attention for its wildly popular Andy Warhol retrospective.
MOCA at the Geffen Contemporary	152 N Central Ave	213-626-6222	Formerly known as the "Temporary Contemporary", the museum is still going strong.
Museum of Neon Art	501 W Olympic Blvd	213-489-9918	
Music Center	135 N Grand Ave	213-972-7211	Angelenos are still waiting for Frank Gehry's Disney Hall to open.
Olvera Street	Olvera St	n/a	An authentic Mexican marketplace in the heart of downtown LA.
Staples Center	1111 S Figueroa St	213-742-7333	If the Staples folk could find a way to play baseball inside the arena, they'd lure the Dodgers too.
Union Station	800 N Alameda St	213-625-5865	Makes you wish people still traveled by train.
World Trade Center	350 S Figueroa St	213-489-3337	Far less impressive than its former NY namesake, but a vital part of downtown nonetheless.

Map 10 · Baldwin Hills

Baldwin Hills Village Oil Wells			There's really oil in LA?
Kenneth Hahn State Recreation Area	4100 S La Cienega Blvd	323-298-3660	Most people only think of this park as they're driving to LAX. That's a mistake.

Map 11 · South Central West

Exposition Park	Menlo Ave & S Park Dr	213-765-5369	Forget the Coliseum and check out the Rose Garden. Or not.
LA County Museum of Natural History	900 Exposition Blvd	213-744-3466	Kids just love the dinosaur fossils.
Museum of Science & Industry	700 State Dr	213-744-7400	The IMAX theatre is the best part of the museum experience.

Map 12 · South Central East

LA Memorial Coliseum	3911 S Figueroa St	213-747-7111	We're still waiting for that LA football team…
Shrine Auditorium	665 W Jefferson Blvd	213-748-5116	The mosque design makes it one of the neighborhood's most visible buildings.
Sports Arena	3939 S Figueroa St	213-748-6131	It's been pretty lonely here since the Clippers left.

Map 13 · Inglewood

Hollywood Park	1050 S Prairie Ave	213-419-1500	When you've just got to play the ponies…
The Forum	Manchester Ave & Prairie Ave	213-419-3100	The Lakers' and Kings' former home is now the Faithful Central Bible Church. There's irony for you.

Map 15 · Pacific Palisades

Santa Monica Steps	4th St & Adelaide Dr	n/a	Climbing these is the most LA workout you can ever hope to have.
Self Realization Fellowship Lake Shrine Temple	Sunset Blvd near Palisades Dr	310-454-4114	Stunning gardens.
Will Rogers State Park	Sunset Blvd	310-454-8282	Hiking, picnicking, and polo. Yes, polo.

Map 16 · Brentwood

Getty Center	1200 Getty Center Dr	310-440-7300	

Map 18 · Santa Monica

3rd Street Promenade	3rd St between Broadway & Wilshire	n/a	Day or night, there's always something going on.
Heritage Square	Main St & Ocean Park Blvd	310-392-8537	A taste of 19th century life amidst Starbucks and bagel shops.
Muscle Beach	1817 Ocean Front Walk	310-578-6131	
Santa Monica Civic Auditorium/ Civic Center	1855 Main St	310-393-9961	Bizarre mix of cool rock concerts and antique sales.
Santa Monica Pier	Ocean Ave & Colorado Ave	310-458-8900	Like Coney Island, but with less character. Much less character.

Map 19 · West LA/Santa Monica East

Bergamot Station	2525 Michigan Ave	310-829-5854	The best one-stop art experience you can have in LA.
Museum of Flying	2772 Donald Douglas Loop N	310-392-8822	
Santa Monica Municipal Airport	3223 Donald Douglas Loop S	310-458-8591	Home to lots of small planes and private jets. And an annual Barneys NY sale.
Veteran's Administration	Federal Ave & S Sepulveda Blvd	213-809-7229	Non-veterans may wind up parking here when the UCLA lots are full.

Map 20 • Westwood/Century City

Armand Hammer Museum of Art	10889 Wilshire Blvd	310-443-7000	Its office building location makes it easy to forget about.
Federal Building	Wilshire Blvd & Sepulveda Blvd		Picketers of any and all causes seem magnetically drawn to this building.
Fox Plaza (AKA The "Die Hard" Building)	2121 Ave of the Stars	310-277-2121	Known to locals as "the Die Hard building" for its role in the Bruce Willis actioner of the same name.
Mormon Temple	10777 Santa Monica Blvd	310-474-1549	Always one of the more festively lit buildings at Christmastime.
Playboy Mansion	10236 Charing Cross Rd	unavailable	We'd tell you all about it if only Hef would send us an invitation.
Wadsworth Theater	11000 Wilshire Blvd	310-478-7578	They offer free jazz concerts on the first Sunday of every month.
Westwood Memorial Cemetery	1218 Glendon Ave	310-272-2484	Marilyn Monroe and Natalie Wood are among the famous residents.

Map 21 • Venice

Chiat-Day Building	340 Main St	310-305-5000	Frank Gehry's design features a large statue of binoculars marking its entrance.
Venice Boardwalk		n/a	A freak show to some, while others thrive on the eclectic crowds that are drawn here.
Venice Canals	Venice Blvd & Pacific Ave	n/a	There used to be more than six, but they were deemed impractical and turned into roads.
Venice Pier	Far west end of Washington Blvd	n/a	It's been a casualty to weather conditions at least twice.
Windward Circle	Main St & Windward	n/a	A great meeting place for those looking to spend the day at the beach.

Map 23 • Rancho Park/Palms

20th Century Fox Studios	10201 Pico Blvd	310-277-2121	Check out the Star Wars mural. It's way cool.
Museum of Tolerance	9786 W Pico Blvd	310-553-8403	A humbling experience that is worth a visit.
Rancho Park		310-839-7750	Its golf course is supposedly the busiest public course in the world.
Westside Pavilion	10800 W Pico Blvd	310-474-6255	We defy you to find your car at the end of any shopping expedition.

Map 24 • Culver City

Helm's Bakery Building	3233 Helms Ave	n/a	They used to make bread, now they sell furniture.
Museum of Jurassic Technology	9341 Venice Blvd	310-836-6131	
Sony Pictures Studios	10202 W Washington Blvd	310-244-4000	No tours, no trams, just Sony's foothold in the entertainment business.

Map 25 • Marina Del Rey/Westchester West

Ballona Wetlands	Around Ballona Creek	n/a	The city is encroaching upon these Wetlands, so their days may sadly be numbered.
Fisherman's Village	13755 Fiji Way	310-823-5411	"Quaint" shopping and dining are, geared to resemble an East Coast fishing town.
Marina City Towers	4333 Admiralty Way	310-822-0611	Massive condo complex that has even turned up on shows like *Melrose Place*.

Map 27 • El Segundo/Manhattan Beach

Chevron Oil Refinery	East of Sepulveda Blvd, North of Rosecrans Ave		It ain't pretty, but it's definitely noticeable.
Manhattan Beach State Pier	West of Manhattan Beach Blvd	n/a	Don't miss the Roundhouse Marine Studies Lab and Aquarium at the end of the pier!

Map 29 • Hermosa Beach

Hermosa Beach Fishing Pier	End of Pier Ave	n/a	Just bring your pole. There are bait and tackle shops right on the pier.

Map 33 • Highland Park

Builder's Club	1269 Hill Dr		
Eagle Rock Community Cultural Center	2225 Colorado Blvd	323-226-1617	Classes, performances, and exhibitions for the local community.
Judson Studios	200 S Ave 66	323-255-0131	Stained glass like you've never seen before.
League of United Latin-American Citizens	4512 E Rock Blvd		Helps to improve conditions for Latin-American citizens nationally.

Map 34 • Pasadena

Gamble House	4 Westmoreland Pl	626-793-3334	Pasadena's Craftsman style, at its best.
Old Town	Fair Oaks Ave & Colorado Blvd	n/a	A fine example of urban regentrification at work.
Pasadena City Hall	100 N Garfield Ave	626-744-4000	A lovely building with even lovelier gardens.
Pasadena Civic Auditorium	300 E Green St	626-793-2122	Home to both the Pasadena Symphony and the People's Choice Awards.
Pasadena Playhouse	37 S El Molino Ave	626-356-7529	Back in the day, the Playhouse's now defunct acting school turned out many a movie star.
Rose Bowl	991 Rosemont Ave	626-577-3100	UCLA football, Galaxy soccer games, and a swap meet every month.
Wrigley Mansion	391 S Orange Grove Blvd	626-449-7673	Check out the Mission-style architecture.

Map 35 • Pasadena East/San Marino

El Molino Viejo	1120 Old Mill Rd	626-449-5450	Southern California's first water-powered gristmill. Who needs Disneyland?
Huntington Gardens and Library	1151 Oxford Rd	626-405-2100	A perfect place to bring relatives from out of town.

Map 36 • Mt. Washington

Mount Washington Hotel/ Self-Realization Institute	3880 San Rafael Ave	323-225-2471	Beautiful gardens, which are open to the public.
Southwest Museum	234 Museum Dr	323-221-2164	An underrated collection of Native American art.
The Lummis Home	200 E Ave 43	323-222-0546	An original home conceived by an original man.

Map 37 • Lincoln Heights

Heritage Square Museum	3800 N Homer St	626-449-0193	A cluster of buildings that have been saved from demolition through relocation to Heritage Square.
Street Clock	2423 Broadway	n/a	Art Deco timepiece.

Map 39 • Alhambra

Ramona Convent School Museum	1701 W Ramona Rd	626-282-4151	Some of the campus' buildings have been here since the 19th century.

Map 40 • Boyle Heights

El Corrido de Boyle Heights Mural	2336 E Cesar E Chavez Ave	n/a	Public art at its most colorful.
LA County USC Medical Center	1200 N State St	323-226-2622	The façade may look familiar to viewers of TV's *General Hospital*.
Mariachi Plaza	Boyle Ave & First St	n/a	Need a mariachi? Look no further!

Map 41 • City Terrace/East LA

Mural: The Kennedy Saga II 1973 (City Terrace Park)	1126 N Hazard Ave	n/a	Located inside the City Terrace Park social hall.

Map 43 • Van Nuys

Van Nuys Airport	16461 Sherman Way	818-785-8838	The world's busiest general aviation airport.

Map 45 • Burbank

NBC Television Studios	3000 W Alameda Ave	818-840-4444	The line forms early for crowds hoping to view the daily *Tonight Show* taping.
Warner Ranch	Verdugo Ave & Pass Ave	818-954-6000	That NY fountain where TV's *Friends* dance in the opening credits? Right here on the ranch.

Map 46 • Burbank East/Glendale West

Los Angeles Equestrian Center	480 Riverside Dr	818-840-9066	Polo, dressage, and the Los Angeles Gay Rodeo.
Walt Disney Studios	500 S Buena Vista	818-560-1000	The quirkiest architecture of all of the major motion picture studios.

Map 47 • Glendale South

Alex Theatre	216 N Brand Blvd	818-243-2539	
Forest Lawn	1712 S Glendale Ave	800-204-3131	The Ponderosa of LA cemeteries.

Map 48 • Encino

Rancho de los Encinos State Historical Park	16756 Moorpark St	818-784-4849	The rancho was damaged in the Northridge quake, but the park is still open.

Map 49 • Sherman Oaks West

Ahh's Discount Store (former El Reina Theatre)	14622 Ventura Blvd	818-990-2951	Once glamorous movie palace turned novelty store.

Map 51 • Studio City/Valley Village

Academy of Television Arts & Sciences	5220 Lankershim Blvd	818-754-2825	Where else can you see a 20-foot tall Emmy award?
CBS Radford Studios	4024 Radford Ave	818-655-5000	*Seinfeld*'s NY sensibilities were actually found here, in the heart of the Valley.
El Portal Theatre	5269 Lankershim Blvd	818-508-4234	Former Vaudeville/Silent Movie house now anchors the NoHo Arts District.

Map 52 • Universal City/Toluca Lake

Bob's Big Boy	4211 Riverside Dr	818-843-9334	The original Bob's Big Boy, as if the giant "Big Boy" out front didn't tip you off.
Campo de Cahuenga	3912 Lankershim Blvd	818-763-7651	This historic park is not regularly open to the public.
Forest Lawn Memorial Park	6300 Forest Lawn Dr	800-204-3131	It's the Disneyland of cemeteries.
Hollywood Reservoir		n/a	Jog or stroll around lovely "Lake Hollywood."
Universal Studios	100 Universal Center Dr	818-777-1000	New Yorkers scoff at the Studio's diminutive "tower." Entering City Walk is like walking through the glitzy gates of mega franchise Hell.
Warner Brothers Studios	4000 Warner Blvd	818-954-1744	The studio's water tower serves as a beacon for much of downtown Burbank.

Map 1 · Beverly Hills

Avalon Hotel Of Beverly Hills	9400 W Olympic Blvd	310-277-5221	225	
Beverly Crescent Hotel	403 N Crescent Dr	310-247-0505		
Beverly Hills Hotel	9641 Sunset Blvd	310-276-2251	410	★★★★★
Beverly Hills Reeves Hotel	120 S Reeves Dr	310-271-3006	69	
Beverly Hilton	9876 Wilshire Blvd	310-274-7777		
Del Flores Hotel	409 N Crescent Dr	310-274-5115	85	
L'Ermitage Hotel	9291 Burton Way	310-278-3344	325	★★★★★
Maison 140	140 S Lasky Dr	310-271-2145	169	
Mosaic Hotel	125 S Spalding Dr	310-278-0303	225	★★★★
Peninsula Beverly Hills	9882 Santa Monica Blvd	310-551-2888		
Radisson Beverly Pavillion Hote	9360 Wilshire Blvd	310-273-1400		
Regent Beverly Wilshire Hotel	9500 Wilshire Blvd	310-275-5200	310	★★★★
Summit Hotel Rodeo Drive	360 N Rodeo Dr	310-273-0300	179	★★★★

Map 2 · West Hollywood

Argyle	8358 Sunset Blvd	323-654-7100		
Bel Age	1020 N San Vicente Blvd	310-854-1111		
Beverly Croft Towers	8455 Beverly Blvd	323-658-5300		
Beverly Inn	7701 Beverly Blvd	323-931-8108	55	
Beverly Laurel Motor Hotel	8018 Beverly Blvd	323-651-2441	84	
Beverly Plaza Hotel	8384 W 3rd St	323-658-6600	139	★★★
Beverly Terrace Motor Hotel	469 N Doheny Dr	310-274-8141	115	★★
Bevonshire Lodge Motel	7575 Beverly Blvd	323-936-6154	55	
Chateau Marmont	8221 W Sunset Blvd	323-656-1010	295	
Days Inn	7023 W Sunset Blvd	323-464-8344	99	★★★★★
Elan Hotel Modern	8435 Beverly Blvd	323-658-6663	165	★★★
Fairfax Motel	913 N Fairfax Ave	323-654-5570	31	
Farmer's Daughter Hotel	115 S Fairfax Ave	323-937-3930	99	★★★
Grafton on Sunset	8462 Sunset Blvd	323-654-4600	159	★★★★
Guest House Inn	7721 Beverly Blvd	323-692-1777	60	
Highland Gardens Hotel	7047 Franklin Ave	323-850-0536	65	★★★
Holiday Inn Express	1520 N La Brea Ave	323-464-3243	129	
Hollywood Seven Star Motel	1730 N La Brea Ave	323-876-2714		
Hollywood-La Brea Motel	7110 Hollywood Blvd	323-876-8000	54	
Hotel Sofitel	8555 Beverly Blvd	310-278-5444	185	★★★★
Hyatt on Sunset	8401 Sunset Blvd	323-656-1234	126	★★★
Kerry Club Hotels	8019 1/2 Melrose Ave	323-951-0386		
Le Meridien At Beverly Hills	465 S La Cienega Blvd	310-247-0400	164	★★★★
Le Parc	733 N W Knoll Dr	310-855-8888	139	★★★★
Mondrian	8440 Sunset Blvd	323-650-8999	270	
Orbit Hotel	7950 Melrose Ave	323-655-1510	67	
Park Plaza Lodge	6001 W 3rd St	323-931-1501	68	2.5
Saharan Motel	7212 W Sunset Blvd	323-874-6700	55	
Standard	8300 Sunset Blvd	323-650-9090	135	
Sunset Marquis Hotel	1200 N Alta Loma Rd	310-657-1333	285	★★★★
Sunset Palms Motel	7160 W Sunset Blvd	323-874-6660	49	
Travel Inn Hollywood	7370 W Sunset Blvd	323-876-0330	50	
Travelodge	7051 W Sunset Blvd	323-462-0905	85	

Map 3 · Hollywood

Best Inn	1822 N Cahuenga Blvd	323-467-2252	45	
Budget Inn	6826 W Sunset Blvd	323-465-7186	70	
Dunes Sunset Motel & Coffee	5625 W Sunset Blvd	323-467-5171		
Econo Lodge	777 Vine St	323-463-5671	64	
French Cottage	6757 W Sunset Blvd	323-464-9144	45	
Galaxyinn	1057 Vine St	323-462-6351		
Guest House international Inn	6700 W Sunset Blvd	323-467-6137	59	
Holiday Inn	2005 N Highland Ave	323-850-5811	139	★★★
Holiday Inn	5625 Hollywood Blvd	323-466-2342	129	★★★
Hollywood Celebrity Hotel	1775 Orchid Ave	323-850-6464	79	★★★
Hollywood Downtowner Motel	5601 Hollywood Blvd	323-464-7193		
Hollywood Hills Hotel	6141 Franklin Ave	323-464-5181	99	★★★
Hollywood Hills Hotel Apts	1999 N Sycamore Ave	323-850-1909	79	
Hollywood Hills Inn	6830 W Sunset Blvd	323-466-9053	45	
Hollywood International Hotel	1921 N Highland Ave	323-876-6544		
Hollywood International Youth	6820 Hollywood Blvd	323-463-0797		

Map 3 · Hollywood — continued

Hollywood Orchid Suites Hotel	1753 Orchid Ave	323-969-9829		
Hollywood Plaza Inn	2011 N Highland Ave	323-851-1800	109	
Hollywood Roosevelt Hotel	7000 Hollywood Blvd	323-466-7000	159	★★★
Hollywood Towne House Motel	6055 W Sunset Blvd	323-462-3221		
La Mirage Inn	6020 Franklin Ave	323-464-1824	74.1	
Las Palmas Hotel	1738 N Las Palmas Ave	323-464-9236	45	
Liberty Hotel	1770 Orchid Ave	323-962-1788		
Magic Hotel of Hollywood	7025 Franklin Ave	323-851-0800	79	
Mark Twain Hotel	1622 Wilcox Ave	323-463-2111	45	
Motel 6 Hollywood	1738 Whitley Ave	323-464-6006	51.99	
Oban Hotel	6364 Yucca St	323-466-0524	50	
St Moritz Hotel	5849 W Sunset Blvd	323-467-2174	45	
Sunset-8 Motel	6516 W Sunset Blvd	323-461-2748		
Trylon Hotel	6515 Franklin Ave	323-851-7036	55	
Vagabond Inn	1133 Vine St	323-466-7501	72	★★
Vine Lodge Hotel	1818 Vine St	323-464-9661	40	
Vista Hotel	1611 Vista Del Mar St	323-460-6000	50	
Western Plaza Motel	1066 N Wilton Pl	323-871-1126	45	

Map 4 · Los Feliz

Bon-Air Motel	1727 N Western Ave	323-464-4154	55	
Comfort Inn	321 N Vermont Ave	323-665-0344	80	★★
Coral Sand Hotel	1730 N Western Ave	323-467-5141	72	
Days Inn	5410 Hollywood Blvd	323-463-7171	109	
Economy Inn	5308 W Sunset Blvd	323-466-9191	52	
Gerschwin Hotel	5533 Hollywood Blvd	323-464-1131		
Harvard House Motel	5251 Hollywood Blvd	323-463-3238	55	
Holiday Inn	250 Silver Lake Blvd	213-387-5737	89	★★★
Hollywood City	1615 N Western Ave	323-469-2700	50	
Hollywood Inn Express	5131 Hollywood Blvd	323-663-1243	50	
Hollywood Premiere Motel	5333 Hollywood Blvd	323-466-1691	55	
Hollywood Roxy Hotel	1655 N Western Ave	323-463-3106	95	
Hollywood Stars Inn	5435 W Sunset Blvd	323-462-0062	50	
Oak Tree Motel	5265 W Sunset Blvd	323-466-8521	45	
Palm Motel	5435 W Sunset Blvd	323-462-0212		
Ramada Inn	1160 N Vermont Ave	323-660-1788	79.99	★★★
Super 8 Motel	1536 N Western Ave	323-467-3131	60	
Travelodge	1401 N Vermont Ave	323-665-5735	80	★★
Tropicana Inn Motel	5444 Fountain Ave	323-469-4999		
Value Inn	5200 W Sunset Blvd	323-666-0692	55	

Map 5 · Silver Lake/Echo Park/Atwater

Comfort Inn	2717 W Sunset Blvd	213-413-8222	65	★★★
Holiday Lodge Motel	811 N Alvarado St	213-413-0050	55	
Los Feliz Motel	3101 Los Feliz Blvd	323-667-2567	79	★★★
Olive Motel	2751 W Sunset Blvd	213-413-0300	75	
Super 8 Motel	1341 W Sunset Blvd	213-250-2233	67	

Map 6 · Miracle Mile/Mid-City

Anne's Motel	1755 S La Cienega Blvd	310-837-5173	55	
Best Motel	5350 W Olympic Blvd	323-936-6966		
Carlyle Inn	1119 S Robertson Blvd	310-275-4445	129	★★★
Cinema Motel	5274 W Washington Blvd	323-935-1526	35	
Grand Motel	1479 S La Cienega Blvd	310-652-3644	40	
Happy Times Guest House	5022 W Washington Blvd	323-954-0963	25	
Mansfield Motel	5000 W Washington Blvd	323-935-4060	40	
Melody Motel	5062 W Washington Blvd	323-935-3410	45	
Olympic Motor Lodge	5850 W Olympic Blvd	323-936-1625	60	
Park Cienega Motor Hotel	1777 S La Cienega Blvd	310-837-5366	45	
Relax Inn	1269 S La Brea Ave	323-939-3772		
Reno Motel	5136 W Washington Blvd	323-932-8251	45	
Royal Hawaiian Motel	1632 S La Brea Ave	323-937-2049	45	
Sea Way Motel	5961 Venice Blvd	323-933-2467	55	
Wilshire Crest Hotel	6301 Orange St	323-936-5131	98	
Wilshire Orange Hotel	6060 W 8th St	323-931-9533	57	

Map 7 · Hancock Park

Dunes Wilshire Motor Hotel	4300 Wilshire Blvd	323-938-3616	67.5	
Friendship Motor Inn	1148 Crenshaw Blvd	323-937-1600	50	
Gem Motel	4915 W Washington Blvd	323-934-3027	45	
Ramada Inn	3900 Wilshire Blvd	213-736-5222		
Rotex Hotel	3411 W Olympic Blvd	323-734-7373	89	

Map 8 · Korea Town

Alexandria Lodge Motel	300 S Alexandria Ave	213-385-6015	65	
Alvarado Inn Towner Motel	1212 S Alvarado St	213-383-4774	45	
Alvarado Palms Motel	931 S Alvarado St	213-480-8867	40	
Best Western Inn	603 S New Hampshire Ave	213-385-4444	89	
Catalina 8 Inn	812 S Catalina St	213-739-8681	60	
Chancellor Hotel	3191 W 7th St	213-383-1183		
Days Inn	457 S Mariposa Ave	213-380-6910	79.95	★★
East West Hotel	3206 W 8th St	213-389-6711		
Econo Lodge	3400 W 3rd St	213-385-0061	69	
Garden Suites Hotel	681 S Western Ave	213-383-3344	84.7	
Golden Tower Motel	501 S Alexandria Ave	213-385-9129	50	
Howard Johnson Plaza Hotel	2619 Wilshire Blvd	213-387-5311		
JJ Grand Hotel	620 S Harvard Blvd	213-383-3000	108	★★★
LA Hamilton Tourist Hotel	3170 W 8th St	213-384-7768	50	
La Fayette Hotel	2731 Beverly Blvd	213-383-3182		
Mariposa Motel	518 S Mariposa Ave	213-388-1433	45	
Motel Inn	2787 W 8th St	213-487-0197	45	
Normandie Tourist Hotel	605 S Normandie Ave	213-383-1351	50	
Oasis Motel	2200 W Olympic Blvd	213-385-4191	55	
Olympic Hotel	725 S Westlake Ave	213-413-3900		
Oxford Palace Hotel	745 S Oxford Ave	213-389-8000	114	★★★
Radisson Wilshire Plaza Hotel	3515 Wilshire Blvd	213-381-7411		
Vermont Motel	1717 S Vermont Ave	323-730-1578	55	
Western Inn	921 S Western Ave	323-733-5166	71	
Westwood Inn	906 S Alvarado St	213-388-3137		

Map 9 · Downtown

Alexandria Hotel	501 S Spring St	213-626-7484	50	
Baltimore Hotel	501 S Los Angeles St	213-627-5941	33	
Best Western Dragon Gate Inn	818 N Hill St	213-617-3077		
Best Western Mayfair Hotel	1256 W 7th St	213-484-9789	109	★★★
Bixby Hotel	433 Wall St	213-620-1374	30	
Bristol Hotel	423 W 8th St	213-627-0124	37	
Cecil Hotel	640 S Main St	213-624-4545	36	
City Center Motel	1135 W 7th St	213-628-7141	55	
Comfort Inn	1710 W 7th St	213-616-3000	64.99	★★
Delux Inn	355 S Alvarado St	213-484-1883	40	
Holiday Inn	1020 S Figueroa St	213-748-1291	139.95	★★★
Holiday Inn	750 Garland Ave	213-628-5242	79	★★★
Hollywood Express	141 N Alvarado St	213-413-6699	60	
Hotel Oviatt	1315 S Flower St	213-749-2227	40	
Hyatt Hotels & Resorts	711 S Hope St	213-683-1234	109	★★★★
Inn Towne Hotel	913 S Figueroa St	213-628-2222	79	
Jerry's Motel	285 Lucas Ave	213-481-8181	60	
Kawada Hotel	200 S Hill St	213-621-4455	109	★★★
Keio Plaza Intercontl	523 W 6th St	213-680-0024		
King Edward Hotel	121 E 5th St	213-626-6107	23	
Little Tokyo Hotel	327 1/2 E 1st St	213-617-0128	40	
Marriott Hotels & Resorts	333 S Figueroa St	213-617-1133	169	★★★★
Metro Plaza Hotel	711 N Main St	213-680-0200	85	
Millennium Biltmore	506 S Grand Ave	213-624-1011		
Milner Hotel	813 S Flower St	213-627-6981	69	
Miyako Inn & Spa	328 E 1st St	213-617-2000	79	★★★★
Motel De Ville	1123 W 7th St	213-624-8474	45	
New Otani Hotel & Garden	120 S Los Angeles St	213-629-1200	143	★★★★
Nutel Hotel	1906 W 3rd St	213-483-6681	49	
Omni Los Angeles Hotel	251 S Olive St	213-617-3300	230	★★★
Paradise Motel	1116 W Sunset Blvd	213-250-9094	55	
Prince Hotel LA	1255 W Temple St	213-250-8925	62	
Ramada Inn	611 S Westlake Ave	213-483-8606	72	★★★
Royal Pagoda Motel	995 N Broadway	323-223-3381	51	

Map 9 · Downtown — continued

Royal Viking Motel	2025 W 3rd St	213-353-0619	35	
Stuart Hotel	718 S Union Ave	213-413-2556	45	
Westin Bonaventure Hotel	404 S Figueroa St	213-624-1000	204	★★★★
Wilshire Grand Hotel & Centre	930 Wilshire Blvd	213-688-7777		
Wyndham Checkers Hotel	535 S Grand Ave	213-624-0000	199	★★★

Map 10 · Baldwin Hills

Adams Motel	4905 W Adams Blvd	323-731-2165	40	
Baldwin Hills Motor Inn	3020 S La Brea Ave	323-732-0864	65	
Expo Inn	4523 Exposition Blvd	323-731-9293	45	
Jet Inn Motor Hotel	4542 W Slauson Ave	323-295-2544	40	

Map 11 · South Central West

24 Hour Motel	5857 Crenshaw Blvd	323-295-9400	45	
Comfort Inn	4122 S Western Ave	323-294-5200	70	★★
Deluxe Inn	4721 S Vermont Ave	323-234-2430		
Harvard Motor Inn	1574 W Martin Luther King Jr Blvd	323-298-1018		
Mustang Motel	4121 S Western Ave	323-298-0351	75	
Raymona Motel	3211 W Jefferson Blvd	323-735-9077	48	
Sahara Inn	4501 S Vermont Ave	323-235-1904	40	
Santa Barbara Motel	1758 W Martin Luther King Jr Blvd	323-296-2576		
Snooty Fox Motor Inn	4120 S Western Ave	323-294-0083	75	
Y-Tell Motel	5501 S Western Ave	323-290-3563	45	

Map 12 · South Central East

Broadway Motel	301 W 49th St	323-231-4303	50	
City Motel	4731 S Figueroa St	323-232-4200	40	
Crown Inn	4760 S Broadway	323-232-2011	40	
Eastsider Motel	2133 S Central Ave	213-748-1048	30	
Radisson Hotel Midtown Los Angeles	3540 S Figueroa St	213-748-4141		
Sandpiper Motel	4112 S Central Ave	323-231-0249	60	
Vagabond Inn	3101 S Figueroa St	213-746-1531	89	

Map 13 · Inglewood

Adventurer All Suite Hotel	4200 W Century Blvd	310-419-0999	59	
Airport Motel	4054 W Century Blvd	310-671-0104	45	
Airport Park View Hotel	3900 W Century Blvd	310-677-8899	36	
Best Western Air Park Hotel	640 W Manchester Blvd	310-677-7378	79	★★★
Best Western Inn	1730 Centinela Ave	310-568-0071	69.3	★★
Best Western Inn	5005 W Century Blvd	310-677-7733	99	★★★
Caesars Motor Hotel	4652 W Century Blvd	310-671-6161	40	
Comfort Inn & Suites	4922 W Century Blvd	310-671-7213	79	★★
Econo Lodge	4123 W Century Blvd	310-672-7285	50	
Econo Lodge	439 W Manchester Blvd	310-674-8596	55	
Geneva Budget Motel	321 W Manchester Blvd	310-677-9171	50	
Guest House Inn Intl	11025 S Prairie Ave	310-412-7100		
Holly Crest Hotel	4027 W Century Blvd	310-673-8612	30	
Hollywood Park Motel	823 S Prairie Ave	310-673-1919		
La Brea Hotel	524 N La Brea Ave	310-672-1333	29	
Lotus Motel	437 W Manchester Blvd	310-672-5586	51.3	
Marletta's Motel	4849 W Century Blvd	310-677-7500	39.9	
Motel 6	5101 W Century Blvd	310-419-1234	55.99	
Ramada Inn	4300 W Century Blvd	310-419-1011	58	★★★
Rodeway Inn	3940 W Century Blvd	310-672-4570	55	
Royal Century Hotel	4330 W Century Blvd	310-673-2400	45	
Royal Comfort Motel Budget Inn	4230 W Century Blvd	310-419-8041		
Sea Breeze Inn	4307 W Century Blvd	310-674-5444	45	
Super 8 Motel	4238 W Century Blvd	310-672-0740	54	
Tivoli Motor Hotel	4861 W Century Blvd	310-677-9181	59	
Topper Motel	4331 W Century Blvd	310-671-0424	50	
Travel King Motel	6220 S La Brea Ave	323-295-6666		
Wel-Come Inn	11125 S Prairie Ave	310-672-5052	40	

Map 14 • Inglewood East/Morningside Park

Anand Motel	10210 S Western Ave	323-418-8488	45	
Atlas Motel	7322 S Western Ave	323-752-7542	45	
Celestial Motel	7410 S Vermont Ave	323-778-3117	45	
Cornett Motel	6345 Crenshaw Blvd	323-751-3227	40	
Hoover Motel	9710 S Hoover St	323-755-9272	45	
Hyde Park Motel	6340 Crenshaw Blvd	323-752-0355	45	
Look Motor Inn	7827 Crenshaw Blvd	323-759-1623	45	
Paradise Inn	10641 S Vermont Ave	323-777-3841	50	
Ricky Motel	2125 W Manchester Ave	323-758-9252	65	
Vermont Motel	9823 S Vermont Ave	323-755-5533	35	
Western Motel	10411 S Vermont Ave	323-755-2596	52	

Map 15 • Pacific Palisades

Channel Road Inn	219 W Channel Rd	310-459-1920	185	

Map 16 • Brentwood

Brentwood Motor Hotel	12200 W Sunset Blvd	310-476-9981	119	
Holiday Inn	170 N Church Ln	310-476-6411	98.95	★★★
Luxe Summit	11461 W Sunset Blvd	310-476-6571	149	★★★★

Map 17 • Bel Air/Holmby Hills

Hotel Bel Air	701 Stone Canyon Rd	310-472-1211	385	★★★★

Map 18 • Santa Monica

American Motel	1243 Lincoln Blvd	310-458-1411	65	
Bayside Hotel	2001 Ocean Ave	310-396-6000	109	
Best Western Ocean View	1447 Ocean Ave	310-458-4888	159	
Cal Mar Hotel Suites	220 California Ave	310-395-5555	149	
Casa Del Mar	1910 Ocean Way	310-581-5533	295	★★★★
Doubletree Guest Suites	1707 4th St	310-395-3332	179.55	
Embassy Suites Hotel	1001 3rd St	310-394-1279		
Four Point Sheraton	530 Pico Blvd	310-399-9344	174	★★★
Georgian Hotel	1415 Ocean Ave	310-395-9945	197	3.5
Holiday Inn	120 Colorado Ave	310-451-0676	159.95	★★★
Holiday Motel	1102 Pico Blvd	310-450-9666	55	
Hotel California	1670 Ocean Ave	310-393-2363	169	★★★
Hotel Carmel	201 Broadway	310-451-2469	109	2.5
Hotel Ocenana	849 Ocean Ave	310-393-0486		
Le Merigot Santa Monica Beach	1740 Ocean Ave	310-395-9700		
Loews Santa Monica Hotel	1700 Ocean Ave	310-458-6700	255	★★★
Ocean Lodge	1667 Ocean Ave	310-451-4146	99	
Ocean Park Inn	2452 Lincoln Blvd	310-392-3966	60	
Pacific Sands Motel	1515 Ocean Ave	310-395-6133	85	
Palm Motel	2020 14th St	310-452-3861	70	
Radisson Hotel Huntley	1111 2nd St	310-394-5454	159	
Rest Haven Motel	815 Grant St	310-452-3977	55	
Santa Monica Gateway Hotel	1920 Santa Monica Blvd	310-829-9100		
Santa Monica Motel	2102 Lincoln Blvd	310-392-6806	60	
Sea Shore Motel & Apartments	2637 Main St	310-392-2787		
Shangri-La Hotel	1301 Ocean Ave	310-394-2791	153	★★★
Shutters on the Beach	1 Pico Blvd	310-458-0030	325	★★★★
Travelodge	1525 Ocean Ave	310-451-0761	165	
Viceroy	1819 Ocean Ave	310-260-7500		

Map 19 • West LA/Santa Monica East

Best Western Inn	11250 Santa Monica Blvd	310-478-1400	119	
Best Western Inn	2528 S Sepulveda Blvd	310-477-9066	90	
Brooks Hotel	1541 Sawtelle Blvd	310-479-9404	25	
Comfort Inn	2815 Santa Monica Blvd	310-828-5517	99	★★★
Days Inn	3007 Santa Monica Blvd	310-829-6333	89.1	
Edwardian Hotels	1853 S Bentley Ave	310-473-8377		
Ocean Park Hotel	2680 32nd St	310-452-1469	60	
Pavilions Motel	2338 Ocean Park Blvd	310-450-4044	60	
Travelodge	3102 Pico Blvd	310-450-5766	71.95	
Village Motel	2624 Santa Monica Blvd	310-828-0515	75	
West End Hotel	1538 Sawtelle Blvd	310-444-8990		
Wilshire Motel	12023 Wilshire Blvd	310-478-3545	75	

Map 20 • Westwood/Century City

Century Plaza Hotel	2025 Ave of the Stars	310-551-3334		
Century Wilshire Hotel	10776 Wilshire Blvd	310-474-4506		
Claremont Hotel	1044 Tiverton Ave	310-208-5957	56	
Courtyard By Marriott	10320 W Olympic Blvd	310-556-2777	139	
Doubletree Hotel	10740 Wilshire Blvd	310-475-8711	134.1	
Hilgard House Hotel	927 Hilgard Ave	310-208-3945	149	
Holiday Inn	10330 W Olympic Blvd	310-553-1000	105.4	★★★
Hotel Del Capri	10587 Wilshire Blvd	310-474-3511	110	★★★
Little Inn	10604 Santa Monica Blvd	310-475-4422	55	
Park Hyatt Los Angeles	2151 Ave of the Stars	310-277-1234		
Royal Palace Westwood	1052 Tiverton Ave	310-208-6677	89	
Royal Santa Monica Motel	10811 Santa Monica Blvd	310-475-3536	55	
Stars Inn	10269 Santa Monica Blvd	310-556-3076	62.7	
Travelodge	10740 Santa Monica Blvd	310-474-4576	71.4	
W Hotel	930 Hilgard Ave	310-208-8765	299	

Map 21 • Venice

Cadillac Hotel	8 Dudley Ave	310-399-8876	99	
Encore Motel	13432 Washington Blvd	310-823-5066	50	
Golden Star Motel	710 Rose Ave	310-399-1208	60	
Holiday Inn	737 Washington Blvd	310-821-4455	89	★★★
Inn at Venice Beach	327 Washington Blvd	310-821-2557	139	★★★
Jolly Roger Hotel	2904 Washington Blvd	310-822-2904	70	
Lincoln Inn	2447 Lincoln Blvd	310-822-0686	65	
Marina Pacific Hotel & Suites	1697 Pacific Ave	310-452-1111		
Ramada Inn	3130 Washington Blvd	310-821-5086	71.2	★★★
Rose Inn	2435 Lincoln Blvd	310-301-7073	89	
Venice Beach Hotel	1515 Pacific Ave	310-452-3052		
Venice Beach House	15 30th Ave	310-823-1966	130	
Venice Beach Suites	1305 Ocean Front Walk	310-396-4559	99	

Map 22 • Mar Vista

Baldwin Motel	12823 W Washington Blvd	310-301-0687	45	
Culver Motel	11162 Culver Blvd	310-558-9769	35	
Econo Lodge	11933 W Washington Blvd	310-398-1651	55	
Paradise Motel	11750 W Washington Blvd	310-390-4044	50	
Sunbay Motels	12841 W Washington Blvd	310-306-7081	60	
Super 8 Motel	12660 W Washington Blvd	310-306-8243	75	

Map 23 • Rancho Park/Palms

Crowne Plaza	1150 S Beverly Dr	310-553-6561		
Loews Beverly Hills	1224 Beverwil Dr	310-277-2800	199	★★★★
Residence Inn	1177 S Beverly Dr	310-277-4427	109	
Royal Westwood	2352 Westwood Blvd	310-475-4551	68.5	

Map 24 • Culver City

Astro Motel	3850 Sepulveda Blvd	310-398-3815	43	
Circle K Motel	5329 Sepulveda Blvd	310-391-9309	35	
Culver Hotel	9400 Culver Blvd	310-838-7963	99	
Deano's Motel	3868 Sepulveda Blvd	310-390-3511	45	
Half Moon Motel	3958 Sepulveda Blvd	310-391-5279	45	
Holiday Inn	3930 Sepulveda Blvd	310-390-2189	89	★★★
Metro Motel	8846 National Blvd	310-838-4554	50	
Sunburst Motel	3900 Sepulveda Blvd	310-398-7523	69	
Travelodge	11180 Washington Pl	310-839-1111	71.1	
Vista Motel	4900 Sepulveda Blvd	310-390-2014	52	

Map 25 • Marina Del Rey/Westchester West

Foghorn Beachfront Hotel	4140 Via Marina	310-823-4626	109	★★
Furama Hotel	8601 Lincoln Blvd	310-670-8111	59	★★★
Inn at Playa Del Rey	435 Culver Blvd	310-574-1920	145	★★★
Jamaica Bay Inn	4175 Admiralty Way	310-823-5333	159	★★★
La Vista Motel	8035 Lincoln Blvd	310-670-0224	47	
Marina Beach Marriott Resort	4100 Admiralty Way	310-301-3000		
Marina Del Rey Courtyard	13480 Maxella Ave	310-822-8555	139	
Marina Del Rey Hotel	13534 Bali Way	310-301-1000	109	★★★
Marina International Hotel	4200 Admiralty Way	310-301-2000	89	★★★
Ritz Carlton Hotel	4375 Admiralty Way	310-823-1700	229	★★★★

Map 26 • Westchester/Fox Hills/Ladera Heights

Crowne Plaza Los Angeles Arprt	5985 W Century Blvd	310-642-7500		
Days Inn	901 W Manchester Blvd	310-649-0800	51.75	
Embassy Suites Hotel	9801 Airport Blvd	310-215-1000	149	
Extended Stayamerica	6531 S Sepulveda Blvd	310-568-9337	84	
Four Points Barcelo Hotel	5990 Green Valley Cir	310-641-7740	105	★★★
Four Points Hotel by Sheraton	9750 Airport Blvd	310-645-4600		
Hampton Inn	10300 S La Cienega Blvd	310-846-3200	85	
Hilton	5711 W Century Blvd	310-410-4000	71	
Holiday Inn	9901 S La Cienega Blvd	310-649-5151	61.8	★★★
Howard Johnson	8620 Airport Blvd	310-645-7700	59	
Marriott Los Angeles Airport	5855 W Century Blvd	310-641-5700		
Quality Inn	5249 W Century Blvd	310-645-2200	69.95	
Radisson Hotel Los Angeles West	6161 W Centinela Ave	310-649-1776		
Ramada Inn	6333 Bristol Pkwy	310-484-7000	53.1	★★★
Renaissance Los Angeles Hotel	9620 Airport Blvd	310-337-2800		
Sandman Motel	850 W Manchester Blvd	310-649-6500	49	
Sheraton	6101 W Century Blvd	310-642-1111	139	★★★
Super 8 Motel	9250 Airport Blvd	310-670-2900	60	
Travelodge	5547 W Century Blvd	310-649-4000	59.95	
Westin Los Angeles Airport	5400 W Century Blvd	310-216-5858	169	★★★

Map 27 • El Segundo/Manhattan Beach

Comfort Inn	850 N Sepulveda Blvd	310-318-1020	95	★★★
Concord Hotel	221 Concord St	310-322-6116	75	
Courtyard by Marriott	2000 E Mariposa Ave	310-322-0700	79	
Doubletree Hotel	1985 E Grand Ave	310-322-0999	53.1	
El Camino Motel	3301 N Sepulveda Blvd	310-546-5464	58	
Embassy Suites Hotel	1440 E Imperial Ave	310-640-3600	189	
Hacienda Hotel-LA Airport	525 N Sepulveda Blvd	310-615-0015	59	
Hi View Motel	100 S Sepulveda Blvd	310-374-4608	59	
Hilton	2100 E Mariposa Ave	310-726-0100	139	
Holiday Inn	900 N Sepulveda Blvd	310-318-6132	76.91	★★★
Homestead Village	1910 E Mariposa Ave	310-607-4000	89.99	
LAX Suites	11838 Aviation Blvd	310-643-9905	49.95	
Manhattan Beach Motel	4017 Highland Ave	310-545-9020		
Marriott Manhattan Beach	1400 Park View Ave	310-546-7511	109	
Residence Inn	1700 N Sepulveda Blvd	310-546-7627	89	
Sea View Inn at the Beach	3400 Highland Ave	310-545-1504	95	★★
Seahorse Inn	233 N Sepulveda Blvd	310-376-7951	62	
Summerfield Suites El Segundo	810 S Douglas St	310-725-0100		
Travelodge-LAX South	1804 E Sycamore Ave	310-615-1073	54	
Twin Towers Motel	11706 Aviation Blvd	310-643-5384	40	

Map 28 • Hawthorne

Acacia Inn	4307 W Imperial Hwy	310-674-3110	50	
Best Western South Bay Hotel	15000 Hawthorne Blvd	310-973-0998		
Budget Inn Motel	14815 Hawthorne Blvd	310-675-8523	45	
Days Inn	15636 Hawthorne Blvd	310-676-7378	51.75	
Del Aire Inn	4610 W Imperial Hwy	310-673-4141	50	
Deluxe Motel	13640 Hawthorne Blvd	310-644-1154	54	
Diamond Inn	3735 W Imperial Hwy	310-674-1278	51	
Dream Inn	3201 W Imperial Hwy	310-412-0912	40	
El Rancho Inn	3900 W El Segundo Blvd	310-973-3522	45	
El Segundo Inn	4930 W El Segundo Blvd	310-644-4944	56	
Hawthorne Plaza Inn	12043 Hawthorne Blvd	310-973-3432	60	
Holiday Inn	14814 Hawthorne Blvd	310-676-1111	73.06	★★★
Hollypark Motel	3928 W Imperial Hwy	310-674-3433	45	
Imperial Motel	4709 W Imperial Hwy	310-671-7700	45	
Kings Motel	3505 W Imperial Hwy	310-674-2196	45	
LA Mirage Inn	4501 W Imperial Hwy	310-671-6017	62	
Manor Motel	4191 W El Segundo Blvd	310-675-9179	40	
Palm Inn	3301 W Imperial Hwy	310-674-2794	39.99	
Prairie Motel	15125 Prairie Ave	310-679-6850	50	
Ramada Inn	5250 W El Segundo Blvd	310-536-9800	59	★★★
Tourist Lodge	3649 W Imperial Hwy	310-677-0112	50	
Travelers Inn	14808 Hawthorne Blvd	310-675-5228	55	

Map 29 • Hermosa Beach

Hotel	Address	Phone	Price	Stars
Beach House Inn at Hermosa	1300 The Strand	310-374-3001		
Best Western Galleria Inn	2740 Artesia Blvd	310-370-4353	75	
Grand View Motor Hotel	55 14th St	310-374-8981	119	
Hotel Hermosa	2515 Pacific Coast Hwy	310-318-6000	79	★★★
Quality Inn & Suites	901 Aviation Blvd	310-374-2666	109	
Sea Side Motel	1935 Artesia Blvd	310-376-0430	55	
Sea Sprite Ocean Front Motel	1016 The Strand	310-376-6933		

Map 30 • Torrance North

Hotel	Address	Phone	Price	Stars
Del Amo Inn	20534 Hawthorne Blvd	310-542-9417	65	
Hawthorne Suites	370 Crenshaw Blvd	310-787-7795	99	
Summerfield Suites	19901 Prairie Ave	310-371-8525	149	

Map 31 • Redondo Beach

Hotel	Address	Phone	Price	Stars
Best Western Inn	1850 S Pacific Coast Hwy	310-540-3700	89	
Best Western Sunrise	400 N Harbor Dr	310-376-9715	119	
Budget 9 Motel	711 S Pacific Coast Hwy	310-540-1888	47	
Crowne Plaza	300 N Harbor Dr	310-318-8888	159	★★★★
Days Inn	4111 Pacific Coast Hwy	310-378-8511	48	
Driftwood Motel	3960 Pacific Coast Hwy	310-375-0511	48	
East West Inn Motel	435 S Pacific Coast Hwy	310-540-5998	55	
Milano Luxury Rentals	20900 Anza Ave	310-370-6333		
Moonlite Inn	625 S Pacific Coast Hwy	310-540-4058	55	
Palos Verdes Inn	1700 S Pacific Coast Hwy	310-316-4211	98	
Portofino Hotel & Yacht Club	260 Portofino Way	310-379-8481		
Redondo Pier Lodge	206 S Pacific Coast Hwy	310-318-1811	69	★★
Starlite Motel	716 S Pacific Coast Hwy	310-316-4314	62	
Torrance Hilton at South Bay	21333 Hawthorne Blvd	310-540-0500		
Vagabond Inn	6226 S Pacific Coast Hwy	310-378-8555	82	

Map 32 • Torrance South

Hotel	Address	Phone	Price	Stars
Bartlett Motel	2364 Pacific Coast Hwy	310-325-0302	45	
Courtyard by Marriott	2633 Sepulveda Blvd	310-533-8000	109	
Eldorado Coast	2037 Pacific Coast Hwy	310-534-0700	49	
Extended Stayamerica	3525 Torrance Blvd	310-540-5442	80	
Leo's Motel	1879 Lomita Blvd	310-326-0445	40	
Lomita Motel	2237 Pacific Coast Hwy	310-326-7530	45	
Plaza Hotel	1720 Cabrillo Ave	310-328-4671	48.79	
Ramada Inn	2880 Pacific Coast Hwy	310-325-0660	52.5	★★★
Ramada Inn	3673 Torrance Blvd	310-316-5570	56.25	★★★
Residence Inn	3701 Torrance Blvd	310-543-4566	139	
Travelodge	2448 Sepulveda Blvd	310-539-9888	56.25	

Map 33 • Highland Park

Hotel	Address	Phone	Price	Stars
Casa Lu-An Motel	1045 Colorado Blvd	323-257-6341	45.6	
Comfort Inn	2300 Colorado Blvd	323-256-1199	65	★★
Eagle Rock Motel	7041 N Figueroa St	323-256-5106	50	
Highland Park Motel	4855 York Blvd	323-258-8444	50	
Islander Motel	1460 Colorado Blvd	323-257-8926	40	
Regency Inn	2378 Colorado Blvd	323-257-8168	59	
Rose Bowl Motel	1533 Colorado Blvd	323-258-8033	40	
Welcome Inn	1840 Colorado Blvd	323-256-1673	57	
York Motel	4722 York Blvd	323-257-4863	42	

Map 34 • Pasadena

Hotel	Address	Phone	Price	Stars
Bissell House Bed & Breakfast	201 Orange Grove Ave	626-441-3535		
Hilton Pasadena	168 S Los Robles Ave	626-577-1000	179	
Livingstone Hotel & Apartments	139 S Los Robles Ave	626-795-3311		
Pasadena Courtyard by Marriot	180 N Fair Oaks Ave	626-403-7600		
Pasadena Inn	400 S Arroyo Pkwy	626-795-8401	79	
Ritz Carlton Huntington Hotel	1401 S Oak Knoll Ave	626-568-3900		
Sheraton Pasadena	303 Cordova St	626-449-4000	169	★★★
Westin Pasadena Hotel	191 N Los Robles Ave	626-792-2727	179	★★★★

Map 35 • Pasadena East/San Marino

Astromotel Pasadena	2818 E Colorado Blvd	626-449-3370	45	
Best Western Inn	2156 E Colorado Blvd	626-793-9339	75	
Comfort Inn	2462 E Colorado Blvd	626-405-0811	77	★★
Econo Lodge	2860 E Colorado Blvd	626-792-3700	59	
Pasadena Motor Inn	2097 E Colorado Blvd	626-796-3122	45	
Saga Motor Hotel	1633 E Colorado Blvd	626-795-0431	82	
Super 8 Motel	2863 E Colorado Blvd	626-449-3020	58.99	
Swiss Lodge	2800 E Colorado Blvd	626-449-1122	43	
Travelodge	2131 E Colorado Blvd	626-796-3121	60	
Vagabond Inn	1203 E Colorado Blvd	626-449-3170	61	
Westway Inn-Pasadena	1599 E Colorado Blvd	626-304-9678	59	

Map 39 • Alhambra

Days Inn	15 N 1st St	626-308-0014	55.8	
Fremont Inn	2221 W Commonwealth Ave	626-300-0003		
Lanai Motel	1749 W Valley Blvd	626-282-8421	39	

Map 40 • Boyle Heights

Chicago Hotel	323 N Soto St	323-266-4006		
Hotel Antonio	229 N Soto St	323-264-5574	35	
Marengo Inn	2050 Marengo St	323-223-2080	50	
Soto Hotel	402 N Soto St	323-264-3388	30	

Map 41 • City Terrace/East LA

Com-On Inn	1560 Monterey Pass Rd	323-263-9888	45	
Vista Motel	4180 City Terrace Dr	323-260-7880	45	

Map 43 • Van Nuys

Airtel Plaza Hotel	7277 Valjean Ave	818-997-7676	149	★★★★
Arrow Hotel	6945 Sepulveda Blvd	818-786-6966		
Best Western Inn	5525 Sepulveda Blvd	818-787-2300	135	
Cabana Motel	5764 Sepulveda Blvd	818-780-8413	55	
Cinema Motel	6242 Sepulveda Blvd	818-786-3606	48	
El Cortez Motel	5746 Sepulveda Blvd	818-994-1900	53	
Holiday Inn	8244 Orion Ave	818-989-5010	87.2	★★★
Hyland Motel	7041 Sepulveda Blvd	818-781-2780	57	
Le Rendezvous Motel	6501 Sepulveda Blvd	818-786-1564	45	
Panorama Motel	8209 Sepulveda Blvd	818-786-4434	50	
Starlight Cottage	5450 Sepulveda Blvd	818-786-4722	55	
Tangiers Motel	7615 Sepulveda Blvd	818-994-8547	45	
Town House Motel	6957 Sepulveda Blvd	818-782-8800	45	
Travelodge	6909 Sepulveda Blvd	818-787-5400	58.5	

Map 44 • North Hollywood

Camino Motel & Apartments	13561 Sherman Way	818-780-0558		
Cinema Spa Motel	6147 Lankershim Blvd	818-769-3380	60	
Pepper Tree Motel	5909 Lankershim Blvd	818-763-6959	50	
Ritz Motel	6021 Lankershim Blvd	818-769-7520	50	
Silver Saddle Motel	6235 Lankershim Blvd	818-766-5285	55	
Studio Lodge	11254 Vanowen St	818-760-1194	34.99	
Village Inn Motel	7833 Lankershim Blvd	818-764-6007	40	

Map 45 • Burbank

Econo Inn	10750 Magnolia Blvd	818-769-8434	49	
Hilton	2500 N Hollywood Way	818-843-6000	189	
Quality Inn	2255 N Buena Vista St	818-848-1680	82	
Ramada Inn	2900 N San Fernando Blvd	818-843-5955	78.75	★★★
Travelodge	1112 N Hollywood Way	818-845-2408	62.1	

Map 46 • Burbank East/Glendale West

99 Palms Motel	1012 Winchester Ave	818-244-0788	40	
Anabelle Hotel	2011 W Olive Ave	818-845-7800	129	★★★
Burbank Inn & Suites	180 W Alameda Ave	818-842-1114	85	
Glen Capri Motel	6700 San Fernando Rd	818-244-8434	60	
Griffith Park Motel	1634 Victory Blvd	818-244-5071	45	
Holiday Inn	150 E Angeleno Ave	818-841-4770	114	★★★
Homestead Guest Studios	1377 W Glenoaks Blvd	818-956-6665	99.99	

Overview

Given the size of Los Angeles, there are relatively few areas designated as dog-friendly spaces where dogs can run and play without the restraints of a leash. There are a handful of parks and beaches in the greater LA area that have space allocated for dogs and an equal or greater number of volunteer groups lobbying for increased pooch playgrounds. Most of the parks listed below prohibit dogs in heat, aggressive dogs, and dogs without inoculations. But these parks are also unsupervised, so pet owners should act responsibly and keep an eye on their own dogs. Some do not allow toys such as balls and Frisbees, and most of them require you to scoop after your dogs! Rules will be different at each park, so it's a good idea to carefully read the posted signs before you enter. A great website to check out is www.dogfriendly.com, which not only lists dog-friendly parks, but also has information on dog-friendly accommodations, attractions, restaurants, and even retail stores.

Laurel Canyon Park

8260 Mulholland Drive (nearest crossroad Laurel Canyon Boulevard), Studio City (818-756-8060). Features 3 acres of off-leash space in a fenced area. Off-leash hours are 6 am until 10 am and 3 pm until dusk. Dogs have to be leashed between 10 am and 3 pm. Available resources include parking for 35 cars, public phones, a small fenced-in children's play area, and a hot dog stand!

This is a fairly spacious dog park, but it does have drainage problems and can get rather muddy. Be prepared for your dog to come home fairly filthy. But this is an extremely popular place for dog lovers, attracting a fair number of celebrity pet owners. You're more likely to have a star sighting here than at Moomba.

Silverlake Recreation Center

1850 W. Silverlake Drive, Los Angeles (323-644-3946). Open from 6 am until 10 pm, this park features 1.25 acres of off-leash area covered with some grassy areas and some dirt areas and plenty of room to run. The only parking available is street parking. Silverlake Recreation Center is well-renowned as a meeting place for pooch owners, so if you're after company, take your dog down for a run.

Runyon Canyon Park

2001 N. Fuller (north of Franklin Ave.), Hollywood (no phone). Located in Hollywood, Runyon Canyon Park is almost completely undeveloped. While it doesn't have a fenced-in dog play area, dogs are permitted to walk the hiking trails unleashed with their owners. Of the 160-acre park, 90 acres are designated as off-leash areas. There are three entrances to the park on Fuller, Vista, and Mulholland, with limited street parking at each entrance and dirt parking available on Mulholland.

Unlike most of LA's dog parks, Runyon Canyon offers the opportunity for pet owners to get a workout alongside their pooches. Runyon has several hiking trails of varying difficulties, depending upon the dog and his or her owner.

Westminster Senior Citizens Center

1234 Pacific Avenue, Venice (310-392-5566). This park features 0.8 acres of off-leash space and a small (50' x 25') area for small dogs. Open from 6 am until 10 pm, there is limited on-site parking.

Sepulveda Basin Off-Leash Dog Park

17550 Victory Boulevard, Encino (818-756-8190). Featuring a 5-acre off-leash area with half an acre for small pooches, this park is open daily from sunrise to sunset except Friday mornings when it is closed until 11 am for maintenance. There is on-site parking available for 100 cars and, whatever you do, avoid parking at any time on Whiteoak or Victory, as the ticketing agents there are vigilant about giving tickets, and you will almost certainly receive one. Check out Randy's Sepulveda Basin Dog Park page at www.dog-park.com.

Griffith Park

There are various places within Griffith Park that allow dogs to be off-leash. The trails across from the observatory are dog-friendly, and you can even take your dog to the roof of the observatory via the outside stairs as long as it is on a leash. The short 1-mile train ride off Crystal Springs allows dogs to ride (accompanied by an adult, of course), so you can make the journey with your four-pawed friend. We suggest that you pick up a map at the Ranger's Station (Crystal Spring and Griffith Park Drive) to check which trails allow dogs.

Beaches

While places like Venice Beach and the Ocean Front Walk are completely off-limits to dogs, whether leashed or not, there are still some dog-friendly beaches and a core group of volunteers fighting hard to keep it that way. Huntington Dog Beach (PCH and Golden West Street) is a beautiful, one-mile stretch of beach that allows dogs on leashes as long as their owners pick up after them. The only place they are allowed off-leash is in the water under supervision. Leo Carillo State Beach (PCH 30 miles north of Malibu) also allows dogs on a leash, and there are restrictions about where dogs can play—they are not allowed between towers 2 and 3, the busiest part of the beach, and they are not allowed in tide pools. Check the signs carefully before embarking on a beach adventure with your dog. Redondo Beach Dog Park is located away from the foreshore next to Dominguez Park (Flagler Lane and 190th St.). A fenced area, Redondo Beach Dog Park has play spaces for large and small dogs. Long Beach Dog Park is located at 7th St. and Federation Drive behind the Casting Pond, and dogs are allowed to run leash-free in this area.

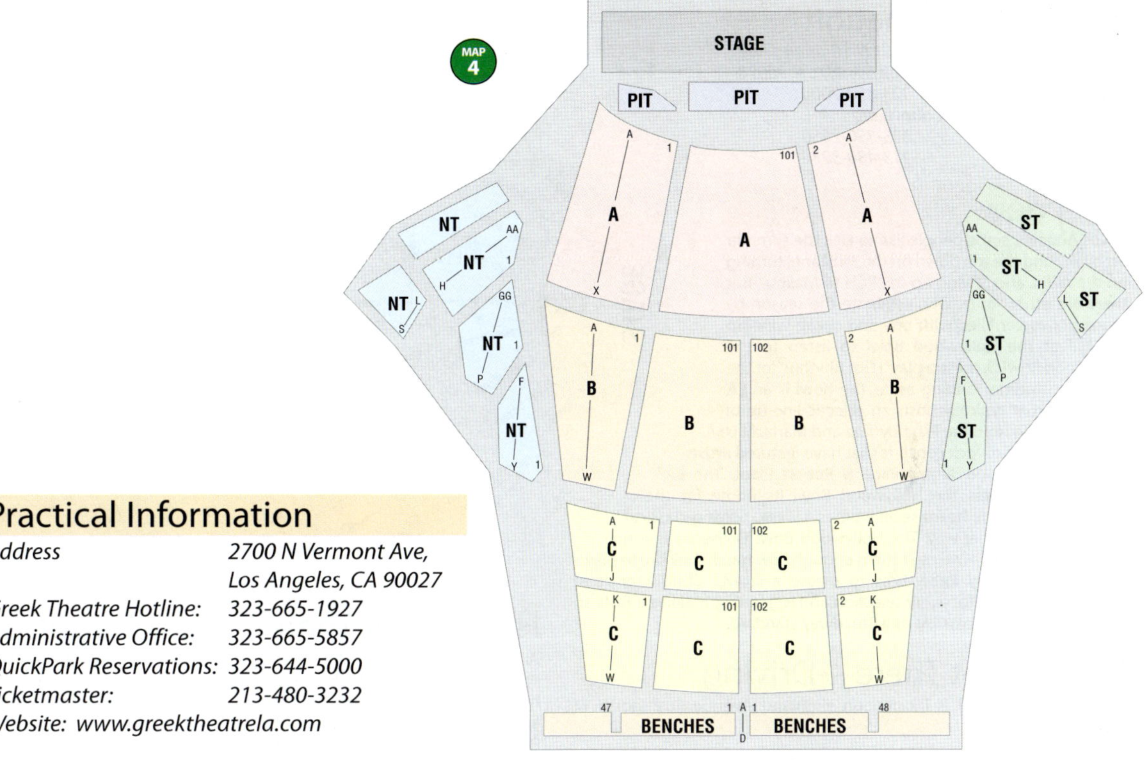

Practical Information

Address	2700 N Vermont Ave, Los Angeles, CA 90027
Greek Theatre Hotline:	323-665-1927
Administrative Office:	323-665-5857
QuickPark Reservations:	323-644-5000
Ticketmaster:	213-480-3232
Website:	www.greektheatrela.com

Overview

It was Neil Diamond himself who once referred to the Greek Theatre as "the place that God made for performers when they die." He made this statement on a "Hot August Night" in 1972, and the series of concerts that spawned Neil's live album of that name remain some of the most legendary in Greek Theatre history. Sadly, Mr. Diamond showed some prescience in making that observation, for the Greek's current line-up typically contains a large number of reunion tours and "together at last" combinations like Kenny Loggins and America. But it would be a shame to write off the Greek altogether. If you look carefully through the Greek's annual schedule, you will find some cool acts—the Gipsy Kings and Los Lobos usually play there, and Sting and Macy Gray have also performed at the Greek in recent years. And the Greek's setting, just inside Griffith Park, makes it a spectacular place to see a concert—at 6,150 seats, the Greek is about one-third the size of LA's only other outdoor venue, the Hollywood Bowl.

How to Get Tickets

The Greek Theatre's box office only sells tickets in person. But tickets to all events are available through Ticketmaster, at either 213-480-3232 or at www.ticketmaster.com.

How to Get There

Via surface streets: Make your way to Franklin Avenue. Take Franklin to Vermont, and head north. The Greek Theatre will be inside Griffith Park, on your left.

From the 10 freeway: Exit at Vermont, and drive north.

From the 101 freeway, heading north: Exit at Vermont Avenue. Turn right onto Vermont and follow it into Griffith Park.

From the 101 freeway, heading south: Exit at Vine Street. Go straight under the underpass, and you will be going east on Franklin Ave. When you reach Western Avenue, turn left. Western will curve to the right and turn into Los Feliz Blvd. Turn left at Vermont, and follow it into Griffith Park.

Parking

The Greek Theatre uses stacked parking, so you can't leave until everyone around you does. This is the $10 option. But if you feel like spending $40, you can use QuickPark, which allows you to leave whenever the heck you want to. Advance reservations are required, and all major credit cards are accepted.

Practical Information

Address: 2301 N. Highland Ave
    Hollywood, CA 90078
Information Box Office: 323-850-2000
Website: www.hollywoodbowl.org
Group Sales: 323-850-2050
Ticketmaster: 213-480-3232

Overview

In Los Angeles, some people like to kick the summer off by putting the top down on the Mustang, turning up the radio, and driving up the PCH to Malibu. But there are others of us who celebrate the season by lugging a cooler filled with brie and cheap wine up the hill at the Hollywood Bowl to listen to the Hollywood Bowl Orchestra play "I Got Rhythm" for the fifty-seventh time. Kidding aside, the Bowl is an LA institution that typically hosts an eclectic line-up of events ranging from the Playboy Jazz and Mariachi USA Festivals in June to rock concerts that have featured artists like the Beatles and Jimmy Page & Robert Plant. The LA Philharmonic makes the Hollywood Bowl its home for the summer and can be heard several times a week, playing classical music the traditional way. The Hollywood Bowl Orchestra is much more pop-oriented—we can't stress enough how much they like to play Gershwin—but they know how to please a crowd. Conductor John Mauceri has a story for every selection and is gifted at making a Russian symphony feel as accessible as a Broadway standard.

How to Get There—Driving

The Hollywood Bowl is located on Highland Avenue, just north of Franklin Avenue.

From the 10 freeway: Exit at La Brea, and drive north. Turn right at Franklin, and head east until you reach Highland Avenue. Make a left turn, and the Bowl will be just ahead on your left.

From the 101 freeway: Exit at Highland Avenue, and follow the signs to the bowl.

Parking

Once you reach the Hollywood Bowl, your adventure has only just begun, since the Bowl only offers 2,800 parking spots for 18,000 seats. However, you have several parking options. If you plan ahead, you can reserve a parking spot in the Bowl Lower Terrace Lot (for $12), the Upper Terrace Lot ($11), or the Odin Street Lot (also $11). If spots remain (and they often do, at least if you arrive early), these lots are available without reservations for $13 (Lower Terrace and Upper Terrace) and $12 (Odin Street and Fairfield lots across the street from the Bowl). But keep in mind, the Hollywood Bowl lots use stacked parking—once you're in, you're in until everyone around you decides it's time to leave. So you'll have plenty of time to check in with Mom, Dad, Greg, Marsha, and the rest of your family.

The Hollywood Bowl also operates four off-site parking lots, from which you can catch a shuttle to the Bowl's main entrance. These lots are located at Hollywood & La Brea, the LA Zoo, and there are two lots on Ventura Blvd. between Vineland and Lankershim. Parking at these lots is free, but the shuttle costs $3 per person. Shuttle tickets are available through either Ticketmaster or the Hollywood Bowl.

We recommend that you check out some of the private parking lots adjacent to the bowl. Many of the Hollywood Bowl's neighbors, from the VFW Hall on Highland to the Hollywood United Methodist Church on Franklin, have realized that there is money to be made by opening their parking lots to Bowl patrons (!). You might ultimately end up paying more at some of these lots ($15-20, on average), but as you drive toward the 101, past the lots filled with stacked cars, you'll think this is the best investment you've made since Enron…er, Microsoft.

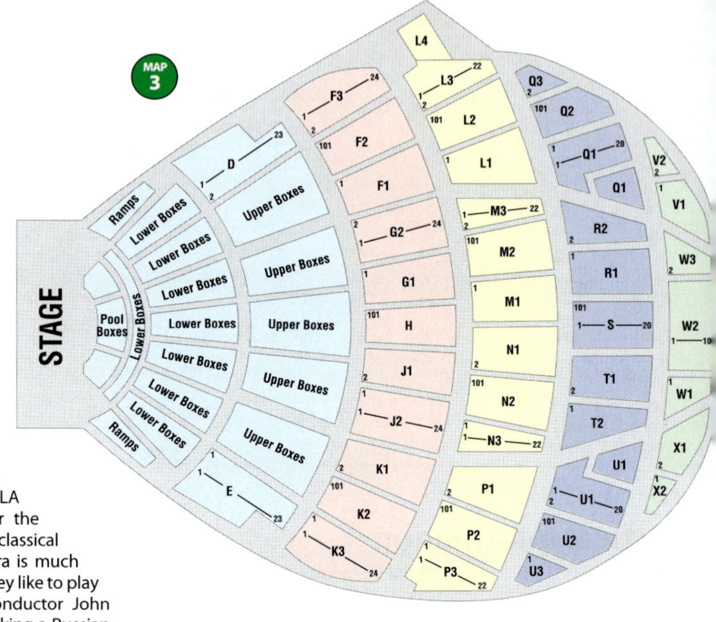

How to Get There—Mass Transit

Another attractive option for traveling to and from the Bowl is to use their Park & Ride service. This lets you leave your car at a parking lot near your home and ride a shuttle bus from there to the Bowl's main entrance. There are fifteen Park & Ride locations. For the location nearest you, as well as Park & Ride tickets, call Ticketmaster or the Hollywood Bowl box office. Tickets can also be purchased at the Hollywood Bowl's website.

The MTA operates a Hollywood Bowl Shuttle (Line 163) from the corner of Hollywood Blvd. and Argyle, just steps away from the Metro Rail station at Hollywood and Vine, starting three hours before scheduled performances. The Bowl is also a regularly scheduled stop on MTA Line 420 Local.

Where to Eat

Picnicking is a huge part of the Hollywood Bowl experience. Restaurants in and around LA are aware of this fact and devise special menus comprised of foods that travel well and can be eaten cold. The Hollywood Bowl also offers its own Picnic Box Menu, which can either be brought to your seat (if you're in a box) or picked up at a counter (if you're in the cheaper seats). Staccato, located between the first and second promenades, also provides a wide variety of picnic food at their counter.

There are picnic areas outside the Hollywood Bowl (which open four hours before a performance), but people tend to make their own picnic area wherever they can—walkways, concrete walls, etc.—or just eat at their seats.

If you can't make the picnic thing happen, there are many places to eat inside the Bowl. The Rooftop provides a view of the Bowl and surrounding hillside, while Patina at the Pool is the Bowl's outpost of one of LA's trendiest high-end restaurants. At the other end of the scale, there are refreshment stands throughout the Hollywood Bowl, selling hot dogs, popcorn, and beverages (including wine and beer).

Tickets

Tickets for individual shows are available either through Ticketmaster or the Hollywood Bowl box office. It's also possible to subscribe to series (like Wednesday Jazz or Classical Thursdays) by contacting the Hollywood Bowl, either by phone or through their website.

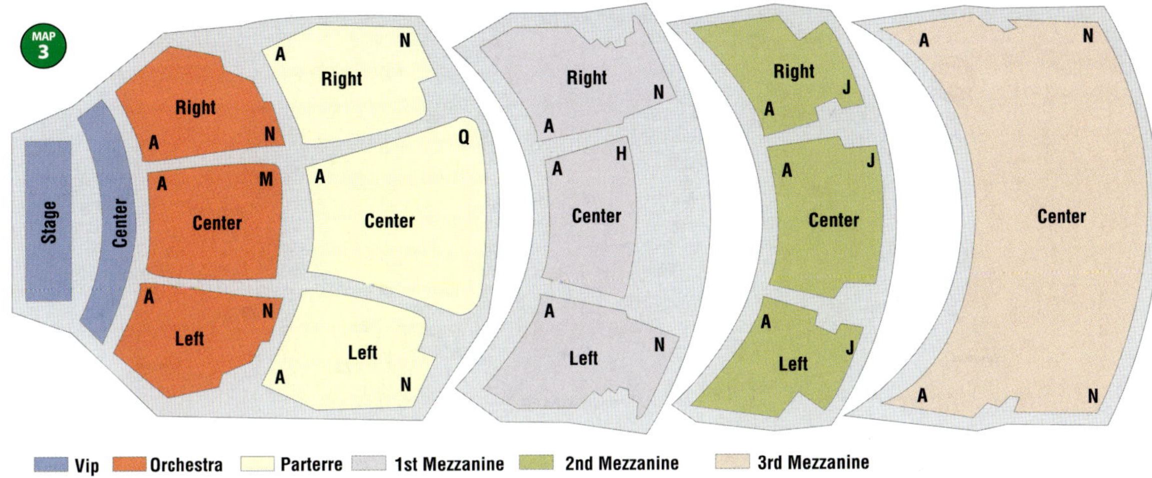

Practical Information

Address: 6801 Hollywood Blvd, Suite 180
Hollywood, CA 90028
Phone: 323-308-6300
Website: www.kodaktheatre.com
Ticketmaster: 213-480-3232
NFT Map: 3

Overview

Most media-savvy Americans are already familiar with the Kodak Theatre, which has been the home of the Academy Awards since opening in November of 2001. Without a doubt, the Kodak looks fabulous on TV. But unless you're Jack Nicholson, a Coen Brother, or the recipient of the Jean Hersholt Humanitarian Award, you may be less than thrilled with the view from your seat. Seats at the Kodak are raked at an alarmingly high angle, potentially providing spectators in the upper levels with a nosebleed and a swell view of the tops of the performers' heads.   The first three levels (through the first mezzanine) aren't bad, however, and the Kodak features an eclectic lineup that ranges from Russian ballet to kids' fare to the BET Awards Show. The Kodak Theatre is located within the large Egyptian-style sarcophagus known as Hollywood & Highland, so there are plenty of overpriced, mediocre places to eat before or after the show. We suggest forgoing the fancier establishments and just making a meal out of the chocolate chip cookies at the Nestle Tollhouse Café.

How to Get Tickets

The box office at the Kodak Theatre is open Monday through Saturday from 10 am to 6 pm, and on Sundays from 10 am until 2 pm. The box office phone number is 323-308-6363. Groups of 20 or more can arrange for discounted tickets by calling 1-866-LAGROUP.

Tickets are also available through Ticketmaster, 213-480-3232, or at www.ticketmaster.com.

How to Get There

The Kodak Theatre is part of the Hollywood & Highland complex, which predictably can be found at the corner of Hollywood & Highland. From most parts of Los Angeles, the easiest way to reach this behemoth is via the 101 freeway. Exit the freeway at Highland Avenue and head south. Enter the parking garage via Highland, next to the Renaissance Hollywood Hotel.

From the South, you may want to avoid significant traffic downtown by taking the 10 freeway to La Brea Avenue and heading north. Take La Brea all the way up to Franklin Avenue and turn right, then make another right onto Highland Avenue. Drive south until you reach the entrance for the parking garage.

How to Get There—Mass Transit

The Metro Red Line stops at the Hollywood & Highland Station. This may actually be the easiest option for people coming from the Valley, especially when Highland Avenue backs up during Hollywood Bowl season.

The 212, 217, 163, 180, 181, and 380 buses also stop in the immediate vicinity of the Kodak.

Parking

The closest parking facility for the Kodak is the Hollywood & Highland parking garage. Escalators from said garage will deliver you virtually to the Kodak Theatre's doorstep, and any merchant in the mall will validate your parking, making it a bargain at just $2 for four hours. But as you circle lower and lower into the parking garage, journeying ever closer to the Earth's core, you become increasingly aware of how precious life is and what a colossal bummer it would be to be stuck in this garage in the event of an earthquake. That said, when you're late for Sesame Street Live and the kids are screaming in the backseat for Elmo, you may want to let Fate roll the dice.

If you've got a little extra time, however, there are numerous lots that can be entered from Hollywood Boulevard that cater to the tourists who have come to see the Walk of Fame. Rates vary but are relatively inexpensive, rarely setting you back more than $6 for the evening.

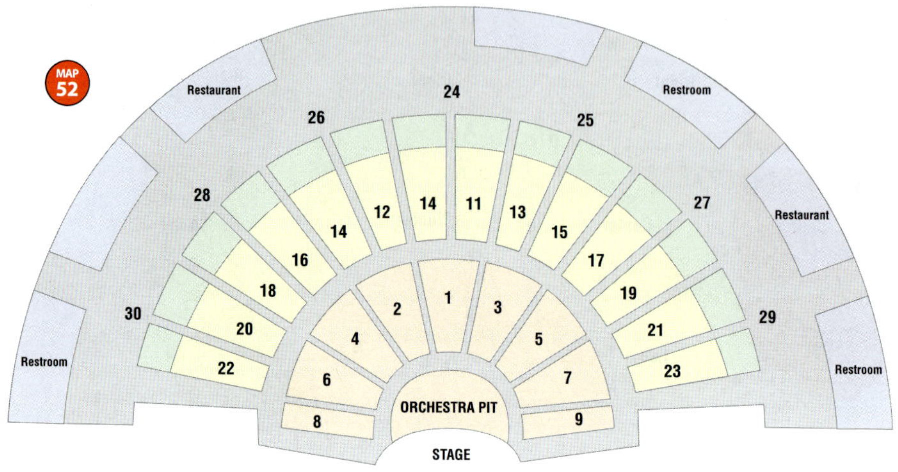

Practical Information

Address: 100 Universal City Plaza
               Universal City, CA 91608
Phone: 818-622-4440
Ticketmaster: 213-480-3232

Overview

Probably the worst thing we can say about the Universal Amphitheatre is that it lacks personality. But that shortcoming may be a good thing, for it allows it to take on the personality of the act it is hosting, whether that act is a Nine Inch Nails concert, a large-scale charity benefit, or the MTV Movie Awards. Probably the best thing we can say about the 6,000-seat Universal Amphitheatre is that there isn't a bad seat in the house, which is why it remains one of LA's most popular venues for concerts and special events. Another reason for the Amphitheatre's popularity is its location, just off of Universal City Walk. Though definitely an assault to the senses, City Walk provides ample opportunities for pre-concert dinners or post-show dessert or drinks without having to get in your car and drive.

How to Get Tickets

You can reach the concert hotline and receive additional box office info by calling 818-622-4440. Tickets for most events are available through Ticketmaster or through box offices located at the Universal Amphitheatre or on City Walk. Tickets may also be charged by phone by calling 213-252-TIXS.

How to Get There—Driving

The Universal Amphitheatre is located right outside the gates of the Universal Studios Hollywood theme park, just off of the 101 freeway. If you are coming from the north, exit the 101 South at Lankershim Blvd. and turn left onto Cahuenga Blvd. Make a left turn onto Universal Center Drive, and drive up the hill to the parking facilities.

From the 101 North, exit at Universal Center Drive. Turn right at the first traffic light, and drive up the hill to the parking facilities.

How to Get There—Mass Transit

There is a Metro Red Line stop just across Lankershim Blvd. from the Universal Studios entrance. If you cross the street from the subway station, a free shuttle will take you up the hill to the theme park and Amphitheatre.

MTA buses 96, 150, 156, 166, 240, and 426 also run to the Universal City Station.

Parking

Parking at Universal Studios Hollywood costs $8 for the general parking lots, $13 for preferred parking, and $17.50 for valet. The "Frankenstein" and "Curious George" parking lots are closest to the Amphitheatre.

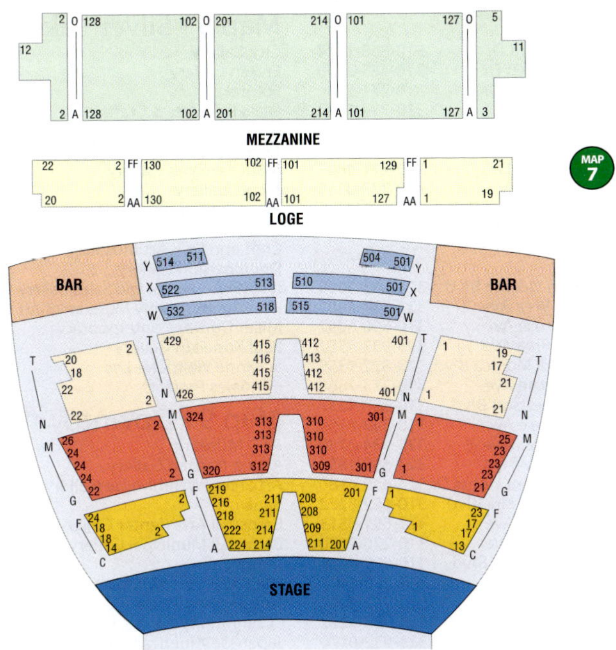

Practical Information

Address:	*3790 Wilshire Blvd.*
	Los Angeles, CA 90010
Phone:	*213-388-1400*
Ticketmaster:	*213-480-3232*

Overview

Its name comes from the intersection where it stands—Wilshire Blvd. and Western Ave.—and the Wiltern is widely known for its Art Deco architecture. The theater was opened in 1931 as a movie house and underwent a major renovation in 1985 that turned the venue into one of the best places in LA to see a musical act. But in 2002, the theater was dramatically reconfigured, to the dismay of many concertgoers. The lower level's 1,200 fixed seats were removed, allowing for several different seating configurations, none of which are especially appealing. Depending on what kind of act you're seeing, you may spend an evening sitting on an uncomfortable folding chair, or you may end up standing all night, wishing you were sitting on an uncomfortable folding chair. The venue has always featured an eclectic lineup that ranged from Hootie and the Blowfish to Lou Reed to Eddie Izzard in 2003 alone. When buying tickets for a show at the Wiltern, keep in mind that the balcony seats have not changed and might be an attractive option for folks too old for the mosh pit. You may be further from the stage, but at least you'll be comfortable.

How to Get There—Driving

Any number of east-west streets will take you to Western Avenue. The Wiltern is at the corner of Western and Wilshire.

From the 10 Freeway: Exit at Western Avenue and drive north, until you reach Wilshire Blvd. The Wiltern will be on your right.

From the 101 Freeway: Use the Santa Monica Blvd./Western Ave. exit and take Western south to Wilshire.

How to Get There—Mass Transit

The Metro Rail Red Line stops just across Wilshire from the Wiltern, at Western Avenue. A number of buses also access the theater. Bus 720 runs along Wilshire Blvd., while buses 207 and 357 run on Western Avenue. Routes 18 and 426 also stop near the theater.

Parking

There are a number of parking lots in the area and limited street parking on and around Wilshire Blvd. A large parking structure is available right behind the theater, which can be accessed off of Oxford or Western.

Map 1 • Beverly Hills

Anderson Galleries	354 N Bedford Dr	310-858-1644
Christie's Los Angeles	360 N Camden Dr	310-385-2600
Gagosian Gallery	456 N Camden Dr	310-271-9400
Galerie Michael	430 N Rodeo Dr	310-273-3377
Galerie Yoram Gil	319 N Canon Dr	310-275-8130
Grant Selwyn Fine Art	341 N Canon Dr	310-777-2400
Latin American Masters	264 N Beverly Dr	310-271-4847
Martin Lawrence Gallery	460 N Rodeo Dr	310-777-0365
McLean Gallery	23410 Civic Center Way	310-456-2226
Steve Turner Gallery	275 S Beverly Dr	310-271-3721

Map 2 • West Hollywood

Adamson-Duvannes	484 S San Vicente Blvd	323-653-1015
Apex Fine Art	152 N La Brea Ave	323-634-7887
Chac Mool Gallery	8920 Melrose Ave	310-550-6792
Couturier Gallery	166 N La Brea Ave	323-933-5557
Dirt	7906 Santa Monica Blvd	323-822-9359
Don O'Melveny Gallery	9009 Melrose Ave	310-273-7868
Earl McGrath Gallery	454 N Robertson Blvd	310-657-4257
Edenhurst Gallery	8920 Melrose Ave	310-247-8151
Fahey/Klein Gallery	148 N La Brea Ave	323-934-2250
Forum Gallery Los Angeles	8069 Beverly Blvd	323-655-1550
G Ray Hawkins Gallery	300 N Crescent Hghts Dr	323-655-4180
Gallery 825, LA Art Association	825 N La Cienega Blvd	310-652-8272
Gemini G.E.L.	8365 Melrose Ave	323-651-0513
George Stern Fine Arts	8920 Melrose Ave	310-276-2600
Glass Garage Fine Art Gallery	414 N Robertson Blvd	310-659-5228
Herbert Palmer Gallery	9003 Melrose Ave	310-278-6407
Iturralde Gallery	116 S La Brea Ave	323-937-4267
Jack Rutberg Fine Arts	357 N La Brea Ave	323-938-5222
Jan Baum Gallery	170 S La Brea Ave	323-932-0170
Jerry Solomon Art Centre/ ArtTerritory	960 N La Brea Ave	323-512-0124
Johnson Art Collection	8304B Melrose Ave	323-655-5738
Kantor Gallery	8642 Melrose Ave	310-659-5388
Kiyo Higashi Gallery	8332 Melrose Ave	323-655-2482
Koplin Gallery	464 N Robertson Blvd	310-657-9843
Lacy Primitive & Fine Art	8448 Melrose Pl	323-653-1655
Louis Stern Fine Arts	9002 Melrose Ave	310-276-0147
Mak Center for Art & Architecture	835 N Kings Rd	323-651-1510
Manny Silverman Gallery	619 N Almont Dr	310-659-8256
Margo Leavin Gallery	812 N Robertson Blvd	310-273-0603
Michael Hittleman Gallery	8797 Beverly Blvd	323-655-5364
Michael Kihzner Fine Art	1010 Palm Ave	310-659-5222
Michael Kohn Gallery	8071 Beverly Blvd	323-658-8088
Morseburg Galleries	9089 Santa Monica Blvd	310-273-5207
Muriel Kretchner Gallery	8908 Melrose Ave	310-858-8566
Regen Projects	629 N Almont Dr	310-276-5424
Remba Gallery- Mixografia Workshop	462 N Robertson Blvd	310-657-1101
Riskpress Gallery	8533 Melrose Ave	213-300-3005
Robert Rootenberg Gallery	7918 Santa Monica Blvd	323-822-1114
Roth Horowitz Anderson	8446A Melrose Pl	323-782-8446
Silk Roads Design Gallery	8590 Melrose Ave	310-855-0585
Stephen Cohen Gallery	7358 Beverly Blvd	323-937-5523
Tasende Gallery	8808 Melrose Ave	310-276-8686
Tobey C Moss Gallery	7321 Beverly Blvd	323-933-5523
White Room Gallery	8810 Melrose Ave	310-859-2402
William A Karges Fine Art	9001 Melrose Ave	310-276-8551

Map 3 • Hollywood

Los Angeles Contemporary Exhibitions	6522 Hollywood Blvd	323-957-1777
Michael Dawson Gallery	535 N Larchmont Blvd	323-469-2186
Newspace Gallery	5241 Melrose Ave	
T Studio Contemporary Art	1615 N Cahuenga Blvd	323-465-8525
The Advocate Gallery, LA Gay and Lesbian Center	1125 N McCadden Pl	323-860-7337

Map 4 • Los Feliz

Circle Elephant Art	4634 Hollywood Blvd	323-662-3279
LA City College Da Vinci Art Gallery	855 N Vermont Ave	323-953-4118
Living Room Gallery	524 N Hoover St	323-428-5700
Orbetello Gallery	679 Berendo St	213-840-7897

Map 5 • Silver Lake/Echo Park/Atwater

City Gallery	3165 Los Feliz Blvd	323-663-992
Enisen Gallery	3419 Glendale Blvd	323-660-378
Fototeka	1549 Echo Park Ave	213-250-468
Ojala Fine Arts & Crafts	1547 Echo Park Ave	213-250-415

Map 6 • Miracle Mile/Mid-City

A Shenere Velt Gallery	1525 S Robertson Blvd	310-552-341
Alcott Gallery	1439 A S Robertson Blvd	310-552-077
Artbrokering.com/Strategic Fine Arts	8621 Wilshire Blvd	323-939-353
Craft and Folk Art Museum	5814 Wilshire Blvd	323-937-423
Doublevision Gallery	5820 Wilshire Blvd	323-936-155
LACMA Art Rental and Sales Gallery	5905 Wilshire Blvd	323-857-6500
Los Angeles County Museum of Art	5905 Wilshire Blvd	323-857-6000
Miller Durazo Contemporary	8720 1/2 W Pico Blvd	310-338-288
Paul Kopeikin Gallery	6150 Wilshire Blvd	323-937-076
Susanne Vielmeter Los Angeles Projects	5363 Wilshire Blvd	323-933-211

Map 9 • Downtown

A+D Museum	304 S Broadway	213-620-996
Acuna-Hansen Gallery	427 Bernard St	323-441-162
Art Share-Warehouse Gallery	801 E 4th Pl	213-687-732
Bank	400 S Main St	323-839-298
Barnsdall Arts Center Gallery	433 S Spring St	213-473-845
Barnsdall Municipal Gallery	433 S Spring St	213-473-843
Cirrus Gallery	542 S Alameda St	213-680-347
Hollyhock House Gallery	433 S Spring St	213-473-845
Japanese American Cultural and Community Center, George Doizaki Gallery	244 S San Pedro St	213-628-272
Japanese American National Museum	369 E 1st St	213-625-0414
Junior Arts Center Gallery	433 S Spring St	213-473-843
L.A.Artcore	120 Judge John Aiso St	213-617-327
Lman Gallery	949 Chung King Rd	213-628-388
Museum of Neon Art	501 W Olympic Blvd	213-489-991
Odyssey IV Gallery	1308 Factory Pl	213-689-779
Post Gallery	1904 E 7th Pl	213-488-337
The Project	962B East 4th St	213-620-069
Transport Gallery	1308 Factory Pl	213-623-409
Tropico de Nopal Gallery-Art Space	1665 Beverly Blvd	213-481-811
Zone 9: Art-Flatfile Gallery	453 S Spring St	213-622-241

Map 10 • Baldwin Hills

FDG Gallery	4470 W Adams Blvd	323-737-498

Map 11 • South Central West

USC–Fisher Gallery, University of Art Galleries	823 Exposition Blvd	213-740-456

Map 13 • Inglewood

INSYNC Media	550 N Oak St	310-680-244

Map 15 • Pacific Palisades

David Jacobs Atelier	201 Entrada Dr	310-573-141
Heritage Gallery	1300 Chautauqua Blvd	310-230-434

Map 16 • Brentwood

Del Mano Gallery	11981 San Vicente Blvd	310-476-850
J Paul Getty Museum at The Getty	1200 Getty Center Dr	310-440-730
Leslie Sacks Fine Art	11640 San Vicente Blvd	310-820-944
Mount St Mary's College - Jose Drudis-Biada Gallery	12001 Chalon Rd	310-954-436

Map 18 • Santa Monica

18th Street Arts Complex	1639 18th St	310-453-371
Angles Gallery	2230 Main St	310-369-501
Bronson Fine Arts	1410 2nd St	310-587-257
Christopher Grimes Gallery	916 Colorado Ave	310-587-337
Dorothy Goldeen Art Advisory	185 Pier Ave	310-399-448
Eames Office Gallery & Store	2665 Main St	310-396-599
Fidelity Arts	1410 2nd St	310-587-257
Hamilton Galleries	1431 Ocean Ave	310-451-998
LA Foto	806 Pico Blvd	310-664-156

atin American Contemporary Gallery (LACG) — 1431 Ocean Ave — 310-395-6001
owe Gallery — 2034 Broadway — 310-449-0184
 Hanks Gallery — 3008 Main St — 310-392-8820
anta Monica College, Pete & Susan Barrett Art Gallery — 11th St & Santa Monica Blvd — 310-434-3434
xth Street Gallery — 1414 6th St — 310-395-4404
lvia White Gallery — 2022B Broadway — 310-828-6200
rrence Rogers Fine Art — 1231 5th St — 310-394-4999

Map 19 • West LA/Santa Monica East
rt Source LA — 2801 Ocean Park Blvd — 310-452-4411
ackstreet Galleries — 11618 W Exposition Blvd — 310-479-6262
rnie Wolfe Gallery — 1653 Sawtelle Blvd — 310-473-1645
AG, The Artists' Gallery — 2903 Santa Monica Blvd — 310-829-9556
ergamot Station Galleries, 2525 Michigan Ave:
  Art Concepts — 310-315-9772
  Bobbie Greenfield Gallery — 310-264-0640
  Fig Gallery — 310-829-0345
  Flowers West — 310-586-9200
  Frank Lloyd Gallery — 310-264-3866
  Frumkin/Duval Gallery — 310-453-1850
  Gail Harvey Gallery — 310-829-9125
  Gallery 825/LAAA Annex — 310-652-8272
  Hunsaker/Schlesinger Fine Art — 310-828-1133
  Ikon Ltd., Kay Richards Contemporary — 310-828-6629
  JKD Gallery — 310-998-5888
  Patricia Correia Gallery — 310-264-1760
  Patricia Faure Gallery — 310-449-1479
  Richard Heller Gallery — 310-453-9191
  Robert Berman Gallery — 310-315-9506
  Rosamund Felsen Gallery — 310-828-8488
  Ruth Bachofner Gallery — 310-829-3300
  Santa Monica Museum of Art — 310-586-6488
  Schomburg Gallery — 310-453-5757
  Sculpture to Wear, a division of the Berman Gallery — 310-829-9960
  Shoshana Wayne Gallery — 310-453-7535
  Track 16 Gallery — 310-264-4678

Map 20 • Westwood/Century City
oswell-Crowe Gallery — 10215 Santa Monica Blvd — 213-445-5200
alian Culture Institute - Spazio Italia — 1023 Hilgard Ave — 310-443-3250
CLA Fowler Museum — UCLA Campus, west of Royce Hall — 310-825-4361
CLA Hammer Museum — 10899 Wilshire Blvd — 310-443-7000

Map 21 • Venice
riffin Contemporary — 55 N Venice Blvd — 310-578-2280
 Louver Galleries — 45 N Venice Blvd — 310-822-4955
ght Space Gallery — 1732 Abbot Kinney Blvd — 310-301-6969
ff-Rose, The Secret Studio-Gallery of Venice — 841 Flower Ave — 310-664-8977
KG, Stark-Kikuchi Gallery — 1423 Abbot Kinney Blvd — 310-452-7936
apbox — 701 Venice Blvd — 310-305-9145
parc Art Gallery — 685 Venice Blvd — 310-822-9560
he Sandbox — 1327 Abbot Kinney Blvd — 310-399-4164

Map 22 • Mar Vista
est Side Art — 3793 Boise Ave — 310-313-2346

Map 24 • Culver City
esh Paint Art Advisors — 9355 Culver Blvd — 310-558-9355
arylin Pink/Master Prints & Drawing/Fine Arts — 4129 Sepulveda Blvd — 310-391-3883
est LA College Art Gallery — 4800 Freshman Dr — 310-287-4200

Map 25 • Marina Del Rey/Westchester West
en Maltz Gallery, Otis College of Art and Design — 9045 Lincoln Blvd — 310-665-6906
oyola Marymount University - Laband Gallery — 7900 Loyola Blvd — 310-338-2880

Map 27 • El Segundo/Manhattan Beach
anhattan Beach Creative — 1560 Manhattan Beach Blvd — 310-802-5440

Map 28 • Hawthorne
Soicher Marin Gallery — 12824 Cerise Ave — 310-679-5000

Map 30 • Torrance North
El Camino College Art Gallery — 16007 Crenshaw Blvd — 310-660-3010
Joslyn Fine Arts Gallery — 3320 Civic Center Dr — 310-781-7159

Map 33 • Highland Park
Eagle Rock Community Cultural Center — 2225 Colorado Blvd — 323-226-0949
Judson Gallery of Contemporary and Traditional Art — 200 S Ave 66 — 323-255-0131
Weingart and Mullin Galleries - Occidental College — 1600 Campus Rd — 323-259-2749

Map 34 • Pasadena
Armory Northwest — 965 N Fair Oaks Ave — 626-792-5101
DNFA Gallery — 41 N Fair Oaks Ave — 626-792-5031
Kelley Gallery — 696 E Colorado Blvd — 626-577-5657
Krueger Gallery — 826 E California Blvd — 626-793-5724
Norton Simon Museum of Art — 411 W Colorado Blvd — 626-449-6840
Pacific Asia Museum — 46 N Los Robles Ave — 626-449-2742
Pasadena Museum of California Art — 490 E Union St — 626-568-3665
The Folk Tree — 217 S Fair Oaks Ave — 626-795-8733
The Folk Tree Collection — 199 S Fair Oaks Ave — 626-793-4828
The Museum of Contemporary Art — 250 S Grand Ave — 213-626-6222

Map 35 • Pasadena East/San Marino
California Art Club Gallery — 1120 Old Mill Rd — 626-449-5458
Huntington Library Art Collection — 1151 Oxford Rd — 626-449-6840
Pasadena City College Art Gallery — 1570 E Colorado Blvd — 626-568-3674

Map 36 • Mt. Washington
LA River Li'l Frogtown Gallery — 1625 Blake Ave — 323-226-0356
Southwest Museum — Marmion Way & Museum Dr — 323-221-2164

Map 37 • Lincoln Heights
Plaza de la Raza, Boathouse Gallery — 3540 N Mission Rd — 323-223-2475

Map 38 • El Sereno
CSU Los Angeles-Luckman Gallery — 5151 State University Dr — 323-343-6604
Harriet and Charles Luckman Fine — Cal State — 323-343-6604

Map 40 • Boyle Heights
At The Brewery Project — 676 S Ave 21 — 323-222-0222
East Los Angeles College, Vincent Price Gallery — 1301 E Cesar E Chavez Ave — 323-265-8841
I-5 Gallery at Brewery Art Colony — 2100 N Main St — 323-342-0717
Raid Projects Gallery — 602 Moulton St — 323-441-9553

Map 41 • City Terrace/East LA
Galeria Otra-Vez — 3802 E Cesar E Chavez Ave — 323-881-6444

Map 46 • Burbank East/Glendale West
Creative Arts Center Gallery — 1100 W Clark Ave — 818-238-5397

Map 49 • Sherman Oaks West
Skirball Cultural Center — 2701 N Sepulveda Blvd — 310-440-4500
University of Judaism-Platt and Borstein Galleries — 15600 Mulholland Dr — 310-476-9777

Map 51 • Studio City/Valley Village
Lankershim Art Center — 5108 Lankershim Blvd — 818-760-1278

Map 52 • Universal City/Toluca Lake
A Studio Gallery — 4260 Lankershim Blvd — 818-980-9100
Martin Lawrence Gallery — Universal Citywalk — 818-508-7867

Long Beach
Rio Hondo College Art Gallery — 3600 Workman Mill Rd — 562-692-0921

Anyone can, and everybody does, go to the Getty, to LACMA, and to MOMA. Why not beat the crowds and hit the smaller museums? They will scratch itches you never knew you had. Local wonders include: the Museum of TV & Radio, the Autry Museum of Western Heritage, the Petersen Automotive Museum, the Norton Simon Museum, and the mind-bending Museum of Jurassic Technology.

Museum	Address	Phone	Map
African-American Firefighter	1401 S Central Ave	213-744-1730	47
Afro-American Museum	600 State Dr	213-744-7432	11
Alhambra Historical Society	1550 W Alhambra Rd	626-300-8845	39
American Friends-Israel Museum	270 N Canon Dr	310-858-8890	1
American Society of Military	1816 S Figueroa St	213-746-1776	12
Angels Attic	516 Colorado Ave	310-394-8331	18
Armand Hammer Museum	10889 Wilshire Blvd	310-443-7000	20
Armory Center for the Arts	145 N Raymond Ave	626-792-5101	34
Art Mural	8131 Naylor Ave	310-215-0215	26
Autry Museum of Western Heritage	4700 Western Heritage Way	323-667-2000	
Black Fax & Wax Museum	3742 W M L King Jr Blvd	323-299-8835	10
Blitzstein Museum of Art	428 N Fairfax Ave	323-852-4830	2
Bonnie Brae House Museum	216 N Bonnie Brae St	213-484-6690	9
California Heritage Museum	2612 Main St	310-392-8537	18
Geffen Contemporary	152 N Central Ave	213-621-2766	47
Grier-Musser Museum	403 S Bonnie Brae St	213-413-1814	9
Hermosa Beach Historical	710 Pier Ave	310-318-9421	29
Hollywood Entertainment Museum	7021 Hollywood Blvd	323-465-7900	3
Hollywood Guiness Museum	6764 Hollywood Blvd	323-463-6433	3
Hollywood History Museum	1660 N Highland Ave	323-464-7776	3
Hollywood Studio Museum	2100 N Highland Ave	323-874-2276	3
Hollywood Wax Museum	6767 Hollywood Blvd	323-462-5991	3
Holyland Exhibition	2215 Lake View Ave	323-664-3162	5
Huntington Library Art	1151 Oxford Rd	626-405-2141	35
J Paul Getty Museum	1200 Getty Center Dr	310-440-7360	16
Japanese American National Museum	369 E 1st St	213-625-0414	9
Jurassic	131 Broadway	310-899-2992	18
Kidspace-An Interactive Museum	480 N Arroyo Blvd	626-449-9143	34
LA County Museum of Art	5905 Wilshire Blvd	323-857-6000	6
L Ron Hubbard Life Exhibition	6331 Hollywood Blvd	323-960-3511	3
LA County Museum-Natural Hstry	900 Exposition Blvd	213-763-3466	11
Los Angeles Craft & Folk Art	5814 Wilshire Blvd	323-937-4230	6
Los Angeles Museum-Holocaust	6006 Wilshire Blvd	323-761-8170	6
Los Angeles Police Society	6045 York Blvd	323-344-9445	33
Mak Center Mackey House	1137 S Cochran Ave	323-939-9420	6
Manhattan Beach Historical	1601 Manhattan Beach Blvd	310-374-7575	27
Moca at the Pacific Design Center	8687 Melrose Ave	213-621-1741	2
Mona-Museum of Neon Art	501 W Olympic Blvd	213-489-9918	9
Museum In Black	4331 Degnan Blvd	323-292-9528	11
Museum of African American Art	4005 Crenshaw Blvd	323-294-7071	10
Museum of Contemporary Art	250 S Grand Ave	213-621-2766	34
Museum of Death	6340 Hollywood Blvd	323-466-8011	3
Museum of Flying	2772 Donald Douglas Loop N	310-392-8822	19
Museum of Jurassic Technology	9341 Venice Blvd	310-836-6131	24
Museum of Television & Radio	465 N Beverly Dr	310-786-1000	1
Norton Simon Museum of Art	411 W Colorado Blvd	626-449-6840	34
Pacific Asia Museum	46 N Los Robles Ave	626-449-2742	34
Page Museum at the La Brea Pits	5801 Wilshire Blvd	323-934-7243	19
Pasadena Historical Museum	470 W Walnut St	626-577-1660	34
Petersen Automotive Museum	6060 Wilshire Blvd	323-930-2277	6
Santa Monica Historical Museum	1539 Euclid St	310-395-2290	18
Santa Monica Museum of Art	2525 Michigan Ave	310-586-6488	19
Simon Wiesenthal Center's Museum of Tolerance	9786 W Pico Blvd	310-553-8403	23
Skirball Cultural Ctr	2701 N Sepulveda Blvd	310-440-4500	49
Southwest Museum of the American Indian	234 Museum Dr	323-221-2164	36
Torrance Historical Society	1345 Post Ave	310-328-5392	32
Travel Town Museum	5200 Zoo Dr	323-662-5874	
Venice Oceanarium	330 Market St	310-396-7974	9
Western Museum of Flight	12016 Prairie Ave	310-644-6778	28
Zimmer Children's Museum	6505 Wilshire Blvd	323-761-8989	6

Map 1 · Beverly Hills

Avalon Hotel Bar	9400 W Olympic Blvd	310-277-5221	Hip young crowd at hotel bar.
Coconut Club	9876 Wilshire Blvd	310-285-1358	Hotel nightclub.
Good Bar	9229 Sunset Blvd	310-271-8355	Sunset Strip hotspot.
Joya	242 N Beverly Dr	310-888-8811	Drinks & fondue.
Peninsula Hotel	9882 Santa Monica Blvd	310-551-2888	Classy hotel bar.
Regent Beverly Wilshire	9500 Wilshire Blvd	310-275-5200	Hotel bar with clubby feel.
Trader Vic's	9876 Wilshire Blvd	310-276-6345	Paper umbrellas & people watching.

Map 2 · West Hollywood

Bar Marmont	8221 W Sunset Blvd	323-650-0575	Trendy spot for dining & drinking.
Barfly	8730 Sunset Blvd	310-360-9490	European style nightclub.
Barney's Beanery	8447 Santa Monica Blvd	323-654-2287	A low rent (but fun) LA institution.
Bel Age Hotel	1020 N San Vicente Blvd	310-854-1111	Hotel bar.
Chateau Marmont	8221 Sunset Blvd	323-656-1010	Coolest hotel bar on the Strip.
Dominick's	8715 Beverly Blvd	310-652-7272	Entertainment industry hangout.
Dublins	8240 Sunset Blvd	323-656-0100	Popular (but cavernous) faux Irish pub.
El Carmen Tequila & Taco Bar	8138 W 3rd St	323-852-1552	Among the best margaritas in LA.
El Coyote	7312 Beverly Blvd	323-939-2255	Go for the drinks, not the food.
Farmer's Market Bars	Corner 3rd St and Fairfax Ave	323-933-9211	Saturday evening karaoke!
Fenix Lounge	8385 W Sunset Blvd	323-654-7100	Super elegant hotel bar.
Formosa Café	7156 Santa Monica Blvd	323-850-9050	A throwback to Old Hollywood.
Garden of Eden	7080 Hollywood Blvd	323-465-3336	
Genghis Cohen	740 N Fairfax Ave	323-653-0640	Acoustic music & Chinese food.
House of Blues	8430 Sunset Blvd	323-848-5100	Venue attracts major musical acts.
Jones	7205 Santa Monica Blvd	323-850-1727	A place to be seen.
Largo	432 N Fairfax Ave	323-852-1073	Most eclectic musical lineup in LA.
Lava Lounge	1533 N La Brea Ave	323-876-6612	Mini-mall tiki bar.
Lola's	945 N Fairfax Ave	213-736-5652	Birthplace of the apple martini.
Louis XIV	606 N La Brea Ave	323-394-5102	Can be a Eurotrashy crowd.
Max's	442 N Fairfax Ave	323-651-4421	A truly great "divey" bar.
Molly Malone's	575 S Fairfax Ave	323-935-1577	The ultimate neighborhood pub.
North	8029 W Sunset Blvd	323-654-1313	Supper club.
Rage	8911 Santa Monica Blvd	310-652-7055	Still the most popular bar in Boys' Town.
Roxy	9009 Sunset Blvd	310-276-2222	A bastion of the Sunset Strip.
Saddle Ranch Chop House	8371 W Sunset Blvd	323-656-2007	Two words: mechanical bull.
Snake Pit Ale House	7529 Melrose Ave	323-852-9390	Fairfax District neighborhood bar.
The Bar at the Four Season Hotel	300 S Doheny Dr	310-273-2222	Elegant hotel bar.
The Factory/Ultra Suede	661 N Robertson Blvd	310-724-8181	Wildly popular gay dance club.
The Gate	643 N La Cienega Blvd	310-289-8808	Nightclub resembles an English manor.
The Lounge	9077 Hollywood Blvd	323-228-4830	The new "in" place.
The Rainbow	9015 Sunset Blvd	310-278-4232	Many hair bands got their start here.
The Ruby	7070 Hollywood Blvd	323-467-7070	Popular dance club with a young crowd.
The Skybar	8440 W Sunset Blvd	323-650-8999	Still hard to get on the list.
The Standard Hotel Lobby	8300 W Sunset Blvd	323-654-2800	Funkier than the Sky Bar.
The Troubadour	9081 Santa Monica Blvd	310-276-6168	Attracts a lot of singer-songwriters.
Viper Room	8852 Sunset Blvd	310-358-1880	Still hot after all these years.
Whiskey Bar	1200 N Alta Loma Rd	310-657-0612	Lively music industry hangout.
Whisky A Go Go	8901 Sunset Blvd	310-652-4202	A rock n' roll institution.

Map 3 · Hollywood

AD	836 N Highland Ave	323-467-3000	Dance club.
Beauty Bar	1638 N Cahuenga Blvd	323-464-7676	Martinis and manicures.
Birds	5925 Franklin Ave	323-465-0175	One of Hollywood's more neighborhoody bars.
Blue	1642 Las Palmas Ave	323-462-7442	Goth & techno club.
Boardner's	1642 N Cherokee Ave	323-462-9621	Quiet watering hole becomes dance club.
Burgundy Room	1621 1/2 Cahuenga Blvd	323-465-7530	Faux divey neighborhood bar.
Cat & Fiddle	6530 W Sunset Blvd	323-468-3800	English pub.
Catalina Bar & Grill	1640 N Cahuenga Blvd	323-466-2210	Jazz VIPs play here.
Cinespace	6356 Hollywood Blvd	323-228-4830	It's about movies here, not music.
Daddy's	1610 N Vine St	323-463-7777	Cozy cocktail lounge.
Deep	1707 N Vine St	323-462-1144	Ultra trendy dance club.
El Floridita	1253 N Vine St	323-871-8612	Salsa club (with lessons!).
For Stars Shoes	6364 Hollywood Blvd	323-462-6448	
Frolic Room	6245 Hollywood Blvd	323-462-5890	Hollywood neighborhood bar.
Goldfinger's	6423 Yucca St	323-962-2913	Comfortable but cool cocktail lounge.
Hollywood Athletic Club	6525 Sunset Blvd	323-462-6262	Old style gym is now a dance hall.
Joseph's	1775 Ivar Ave	323-462-8697	Justin & Britney might be seen here.
Knitting Factory	7021 Hollywood Blvd	323-463-0204	Eclectic acoustic lineup.
La Palmas Supper Club	1714 N Las Palmas Ave	323-464-0171	Hot Mexican restaurant & dance club.
Musso & Frank Grill Bar	6667 Hollywood Blvd	323-467-5123	Hollywood's oldest bar.
Nacional	1645 N Wilcox Ave	323-962-7712	Cuban-themed bar/lounge.
Sunset Room	1430 N Cahuenga Blvd	323-463-0004	Prepare to wait behind the velvet ropes.
The Baked Potato Hollywood	6266 Sunset Blvd	323-461-6400	Jazz club.
The Cinegrill	7000 Hollywood Blvd	323-466-7000	Cabaret.
The Highlands	6801 Hollywood Blvd	323-461-9800	Club within the Hollywood & Highland complex.
The Larchmont	5657 Melrose Ave		New dance club with outdoor patio.
the room	1626 N Cahuenga Blvd	323-462-7196	Neighborhood bar with DJs.
The Well	6255 W Sunset Blvd	323-467-9355	Understated entertainment industry meeting place.
Three of Clubs	1123 N Vine St	323-462-6441	Low key Hollywood hangout.
White Lotus	1743 N Cahuenga Ave	323-463-0060	Hottest, newest club.

Map 4 • Los Feliz

Akbar	4356 W Sunset Blvd	323-665-6810	"Sexually diverse" crowd.
Bar Vermont	1712 N Vermont ave	323-661-6163	Hot DJs and cool cocktails.
Tantra Bar	3705 W Sunset Blvd	323-663-9090	Indian food & awesome dancing.
The Derby	4500 Los Feliz Blvd	323-663-8979	The swing renaissance began here.
The Dresden Room	1760 N Vermont Ave	323-665-4294	Home of the famed "Marty & Elayne."
The Garage	4519 Santa Monica Blvd	323-662-6166	Neighborhood rock n' roll bar.
The Good Luck Bar	1514 Hillhurst Ave	323-666-3524	Asian-themed cocktail lounge.
Tiki Ti	4427 W Sunset Blvd	323-669-9381	Zombies, anyone?
Ye Rustic Inn	1831 Hillhurst Ave	323-662-5757	Total neighborhood bar.

Map 5 • Silver Lake/Echo Park/Atwater

Bigfoot Lounge	3172 Los Feliz Blvd	323-662-9227	Bar decked out like hunting lodge.
Silverlake Lounge	2906 Sunset Blvd	323-663-9636	As eclectic and colorful as the surrounding neighborhood.
Spaceland	1717 Silver Lake Blvd	323-661-4380	Alternative music venue.
The Red Lion Tavern	2366 Glendale Blvd	323-662-5337	German bar. Oktoberfest all year long.
The Roost	3100 Los Feliz Blvd	323-664-7272	Neighborhood bar.
The Short Stop	1455 W Sunset Blvd	213-250-5902	LAPD hangout turned hotspot.
The Tam O'Shanter	2980 Los Feliz Blvd	323-664-0228	Irish pub.

Map 6 • Miracle Mile/Mid-City

Conga Room	5364 Wilshire Blvd	323-938-1696	Latin music, dining, and dancing.
El Rey	5515 Wilshire Blvd	323-936-4790	Diverse musical lineup.
The Joint	8771 W Pico Blvd	310-275-2619	Jazz bar.
The Mint	6010 Pico Blvd	323-954-9630	Blues bar.
Tom Bergin's Tavern	840 S Fairfax Ave	323-936-7151	Neighborhood Irish pub.

Map 7 • Hancock Park

Jewel's Catch One	4067 W Pico Blvd	323-737-1159	Attracts "sexually diverse" crowd.
Mixed Nuts Comedy Club	4000 W Washington Blvd	323-735-6622	
Voodoo	4120 W Olympic Blvd	323-930-9600	Tiki décor, techno music.

Map 8 • Korea Town

Atlas Bar & Grill	3760 Wilshire Blvd	213-380-8400	Jazz in an art deco setting.
La Fonda De Los Camperos	2501 Wilshire Blvd	213-380-5055	Traditional Latin music.

Map 9 • Downtown

Downtown LA Standard	550 S Flower St	213-892-8080	Bar with best view of LA.
Mayan	1038 S Hill St	213-746-4287	Dance club with strict dress code.
Stock Exchange	618 S Spring St	213-487-3877	Upscale art deco dance club.

Map 10 • Baldwin Hills

Café Club Fais Do-Do	5257 W Adams Blvd	323-954-8080	Cajun food, eclectic music.
The Living Room	2636 Crenshaw Blvd	323-735-8748	Blues bar.

Map 11 • South Central West

Babe's Ricky Inn	4339 Leimert Blvd	323-295-9112	Blues music.

Map 17 • Bel Air/Holmby Hills

Hotel Bel Air Lounge	701 Stone Canyon Rd	310-472-1211	Out of the way hotel bar.

Map 18 • Santa Monica

14 Below	1348 14th St	310-451-5040	Neighborhoody rock n' roll bar.
Casa del Mar	1 Pico Blvd	310-581-5533	High end hotel bar.
Circle Bar	2926 Main St	310-450-0508	Once divey, now trendy.
Cock N' Bull Pub	2947 Lincoln Blvd	310-399-9696	Irish pub.
Father's Office	1018 Montana Ave	310-393-2337	Impressive selection of beers.
Harvelle's	1432 4th St	310-395-1676	Blues by the beach.
O'Brien's	2941 Main St	310-396-4725	Neighborhood Irish pub.
Rix	1413 5th St	310-656-9688	Upscale supper club.
Shutters	1 Pico Blvd	310-458-0030	One of the "beachiest" Santa Monica hotel bars.
Sugar	814 Broadway	310-899-1989	Hip Westside dance spot.
Temple Bar	1026 Wilshire Blvd	310-393-6611	Food, martinis, & good local music.
The Library Ale House	2911 Main St	310-314-4855	No books, lots of beer.

Map 19 • West LA/Santa Monica East

Liquid Kitty	11780 W Pico Blvd	310-473-3707	Westside DJ club.
McCabe's	3101 Pico Blvd	310-828-4403	Famed LA haunt for live acoustic music.
Q's Billiards	11835 Wilshire Blvd	310-477-7550	Pool, pool, beer, and pool.

Map 20 • Westwood/Century City

The Century Club	10131 Constellation Blvd	310-553-6000	Upscale rock club for the VH1 set.
W	930 Hilgard Ave	310-208-8765	Modern, trendy hotel bar.
Westwood Brewing Company	1097 Glendon Ave	310-209-2739	Microbrewery with comedy upstairs.

Map 21 • Venice

Firehouse	213 Rose Ave	310-396-6810	Neighborhood bar.
James' Beach	60 Venice Blvd	310-823-5396	Outdoor patio bar with ocean view.
Scruffy O'Shea's	822 Washington Blvd	310-821-0833	Irish pub.
The Brig	1515 Abbot Kinney Blvd	310-399-7537	Artsy neighborhood's trendy bar.

Map 22 • Mar Vista

Dear John's	11208 Culver Blvd	310-397-0276	Old school piano bar.

Map 24 • Culver City

Jazz Bakery	3238 Helms Ave	310-271-9039	Live theatre-style jazz and yes, dessert.

Map 25 • Marina Del Rey/Westchester West

Brennan's	4089 Lincoln Blvd	310-821-6622	Irish pub with turtle-racing.
Marina Lounge at the Furama Hotel	8601 Lincoln Blvd	310-670-8111	Hotel bar near LAX.

Map 26 • Westchester/Fox Hills/Ladera Heights

Westchester Sports Grill	5630 W Manchester Ave	310-670-2366	All things sports.

Map 29 • Hermosa Beach

The Lighthouse Café	30 Pier Ave	310-372-6911	Jazz by the beach.
The Pitcherhouse	142 Pacific Coast Hwy	310-374-0626	Rock n' roll bar with 50 years of history.

Map 31 • Redondo Beach

Starboard Attitude	202 The Pier	310-379-5144	South Bay's oldest blues bar.

Map 33 • Highland Park

Mr T's Bowl	5621 1/2 N Figueroa St	323-256-4850	Bowling alley turned rock club.

Map 34 • Pasadena

Club 41	41 S De Lacey Ave	626-795-4141	100 year-old bar.
Freddie's 35er Bar	12 E Colorado Blvd	626-356-9315	Neighborhood bar.
Jake's Billiards	38 W Colorado Blvd	626-568-1602	Pool hall and bar.
The Muse	54 E Colorado Blvd	626-793-0608	Dance club with Salsa Thursdays.

Map 41 • City Terrace/East LA

Hi D Hi	4952 Whittier Blvd	323-266-3821	

Map 44 • North Hollywood

McRed's	13235 Victory Blvd	818-980-2845	Local bands and cheap drinks.
Rawhide	10937 Burbank Blvd	818-760-9798	Gay bar features country music & line dancing.

Map 45 • Burbank

Dimples	3413 W Olive Ave	818-842-2336	Claims to be the "first karaoke club in America."
The Blue Saloon	4657 Lankershim Blvd	818-766-4644	Intimate music club.
Tinhorn Flats	2623 Magnolia Blvd	818-567-2470	Karaoke Thursday nights.

Map 46 • Burbank East/Glendale West

The Blue Room	916 S San Fernando Blvd	323-849-2779	Somewhat upscale neighborhood bar.

Map 47 • Glendale South

Jax Bar and Grill	339 N Brand Blvd	818-500-1604	Jazz club.

Map 50 • Sherman Oaks East

Cozy's	14058 Ventura Blvd	818-986-6000	Ventura Blvd. blues club.

Map 51 • Studio City/Valley Village

Clear	11916 Ventura Blvd	818-980-4811	Transparent décor, trendy crowd.
Firefly	11720 Ventura Blvd	818-762-1833	Good food, excellent cocktails.
Fox & Hounds	11100 Ventura Blvd	818-763-7976	English pub.
Residuals	11042 Ventura Blvd	818-761-8301	Low key entertainment industry hangout.
The Queen Mary	12449 Ventura Blvd	818-506-5619	Female impersonator shows.

Map 52 • Universal City/Toluca Lake

BB King's Blues Club	100 Universal Center Dr	818-622-5464	
Rumba Room	100 Universal Center Dr	818-622-1227	City Walk Salsa club.
The Baked Potato	3787 Cahuenga Blvd	323-582-0748	Jazz club.
The Casting Office	3256 Cahuenga Blvd	323-851-4300	Divey neighborhood strip mall bar.
Timmy Nolan's	10111 Riverside Dr	818-985-3359	Irish pub.

New Yorkers who say there is no serious book culture in Los Angeles are merely envious of our weather and our deep, golden tans. Our seriously fine bookstores prove just how wrong they are. Be sure to check out Vroman's, Skylight Books (excellent readings), Dutton's, Book Soup, Midnight Special, Brentano's, Bookzone in the UCLA Student Union, Hennessy+Ingalls (art and architecture books), and—hello, theater people!—Samuel

Map 2 • West Hollywood

A Different Light Bookstore	8853 Santa Monica Blvd	310-854-6601	Gay/lesbian.
Audobon Society Bookstore	7377 Santa Monica Blvd	323-876-0202	Books on nature.
Barnes & Noble	189 The Grove Dr	323-525-0270	Chain
Bodhi Tree Bookstore	8585 Melrose Ave	310-659-1733	New Age, spiritual.
Book Soup	8818 W Sunset Blvd	310-659-3110	Great independent bookstore.
Borders Books & Music	330 S La Cienega Blvd	310-659-4046	Chain.
Brentano's	8500 Beverly Blvd	310-652-8024	Chain owned by Borders.
Circus of Books	8230 Santa Monica Blvd	323-656-6533	Gay.
Cook's Library	8373 W 3rd St	323-655-3141	Cookbooks.
Golden Apple Comics	7711 Melrose Ave	323-658-6047	Comics.
Heritage Classics	8980 Santa Monica Blvd	310-657-9699	Rare books and bindery.
Illiterature	456 S La Brea Ave	323-937-3506	Books and gifts—great shop.
Kovcheg Russian Bookstore	7508 W Sunset Blvd	323-876-2749	Russian books.
Lumiere Books on Photography	7461 Beverly Blvd	323-549-9808	Photography books.
Samuel French Theatre & Film	7623 W Sunset Blvd	323-876-0570	Theater & film books.
Storyopolis	116 N Robertson Blvd	310-358-2500	Great children's bookstore.
Talking Book World	7164 Beverly Blvd	323-932-8111	Audio books.
Traveler's Bookcase	8375 W 3rd St	323-655-0575	Excellent shop for travelers.
Unicorn Bookstore	8940 Santa Monica Blvd	310-652-6253	

Map 3 • Hollywood

Back Lot Books & Movie Posters	6309 Hollywood Blvd	323-460-6020	Movie books and posters.
Book City Collectables	6631 Hollywood Blvd	323-466-0120	
Daily Planet	5931 1/2 Franklin Ave	323-957-0061	
Hollywood Magic	6614 Hollywood Blvd	323-464-5610	
Joshua Tree Bookstore	1308 N Cahuenga Blvd	323-464-2665	
Larry Edmunds Cinema & Theatre	6644 Hollywood Blvd	323-463-3273	Cinema and theatre books.
Opamp Technical Books	1033 N Sycamore Ave	323-464-4322	
Wise International Bookstore	1680 Vine St	323-469-6510	

Map 4 • Los Feliz

Circus of Books	4001 W Sunset Blvd	323-666-1304	Gay books and magazines.
Siam Books Ctr	5178 Hollywood Blvd	323-665-4236	Thai books.
Soap Plant	4633 Hollywood Blvd	323-663-0122	Eclectic selection.

Map 5 • Silver Lake/Echo Park/Atwater

Book Bound-Eclectic & Edgy	1545 Echo Park Ave	213-481-0802	Eclectic selection.
CM Bookshop In Silverlake	2388 Glendale Blvd	323-913-9677	
Libreria Mexico De Sunset	1632 W Sunset Blvd	213-250-4835	

Map 6 • Miracle Mile/Mid-City

New Mastodon German Books	5820 Wilshire Blvd	323-525-1948	German books.

Map 7 • Hancock Park

Chevalier's Books	126 N Larchmont Blvd	323-465-1334	General.
Educational Book Store	3959 Wilshire Blvd	213-387-3184	Educational books and school supplies.
Jeong Eum Sa	3921 Wilshire Blvd	213-738-9140	Korean books.

Map 8 • Korea Town

8th Street Book Land	3068 W 8th St	213-384-5995
Bohemia Books	2122 W 7th St	213-387-4187
Chong No Book Ctr	2785 W Olympic Blvd	213-739-8107
Dong-A Book Plaza	3460 W 8th St	213-382-7100
Jeong Eum Korea Book Ctr	928 S Western Ave	213-387-0234
Korea One America Branch	170 S Western Ave	213-388-0914
Libreria Hispanoamerica	2502 W 6th St	213-384-6084
Orange Comics	3500 W 8th St	
Pathfinder Books	4229 S Central Ave	323-233-9372
Shin Jin Books	356 S Western Ave	213-386-0222
Smart Book	170 S Western Ave	213-388-3338
Spanish Bookstore	3102 Wilshire Blvd	213-739-8899
Springwater Book Imports Omc	3003 W Olympic Blvd	213-380-0212
Student Books	244 S Oxford Ave	213-387-1582
Sung Ji Book Ctr	2852 W Olympic Blvd	213-388-2839

Map 9 • Downtown

Asahiya Book Stores	333 S Alameda St	213-626-5650	
B Dalton	201 N Los Angeles St	213-687-3050	Chain.
China Book Store	652 N Broadway	213-680-9230	
China Cultural Ctr	970 N Broadway	213-489-3827	
Great Wall Books & Art	970 N Broadway	213-617-2817	
Happyland	685 N Spring St	213-687-3721	
Hongwanji Place	311 E 1st St	213-680-0364	
Kinokuniya Book Stores-America	123 Astronaut Onizuka St E	213-687-4480	Japanese books.
Koma Bookstore	548 S Spring St	213-622-0501	Countercultural books.
Legal Book Store	316 W 2nd St	213-626-2139	
Libros Revolucion	312 W 8th St	213-488-1303	
Niming Books	969 N Hill St	213-687-9817	
Thai Books & Music Dokya	1100 N Main St	323-342-9982	
Thang Long Bookstore	767 N Hill Pl	213-628-1644	
US Government Bookstore	505 S Flower St	213-239-9844	
Waldenbooks	700 W 7th St	213-624-5137	

Map 10 • Baldwin Hills

Baha'i Bookshop	5755 Rodeo Rd	323-933-8297	Books about the Baha'i faith.
Eso Won Books	3655 S La Brea Ave	323-294-0324	
Waldenbooks	3650 W Martin Luther King Jr Blvd	323-295-5905	

Map 11 • South Central West

Libreria Azteca	1429 W Adams Blvd	323-733-4040	
Step 2 Bookstore	4309 Leimert Blvd	323-291-5843	
Third World Ethnic Books	3617 Montclair St	323-737-3292	

Map 12 • South Central East

Imix Books	3655 S Grand Ave	213-765-0827	Spanish books.
Theosophy	245 W 33rd St	213-748-7244	

Map 14 • Inglewood East/Morningside Park

Bright Lights Children's Book	8461 S Van Ness Ave	323-971-1296	
Express Yourself Books	1425 W Manchester Ave	323-750-4114	General.

Map 15 • Pacific Palisades

Village Books	1049 Swarthmore Ave	310-454-4063	

Map 16 • Brentwood

Dutton's Brentwood Bookstore	11975 San Vicente Blvd	310-476-6263	
Follett Campus Bookstore	12001 Chalon Rd		

Map 17 • Bel Air/Holmby Hills

UCLA Bookzone	308 Westwood Plz	310-206-4041	

Map 18 • Santa Monica

A & R Textbooks	1703 Pico Blvd	310-314-4361	
Angel City Bookstore & Gallery	218 Pier Ave	310-399-8767	
Arcana Books on the Arts	1229 3rd St Promenade	310-458-1499	Excellent art and architecture. Hard to find.
B Dalton Bookseller	106 Santa Monica Pl	310-451-8419	Chain.
Barnes & Noble Booksellers	1201 3rd St Promenade	310-260-9110	Chain.
Barry R Levin Science Fiction	720 Santa Monica Blvd	310-458-6111	
Borders Books & Music	1415 3rd St Promenade	310-393-9290	Chain.
Form Zero Architectural Books	811 Traction Ave	213-620-1920	
Hennessey & Ingalls Art Books	1254 3rd St Promenade	310-458-9074	Superb art and architecture.
Midnight Special Bookstore	1318 3rd St Promenade	310-393-2923	
Thunderbolt Books	512 Santa Monica Blvd	310-899-9279	
Wilshire Books	3018 Wilshire Blvd	310-828-3115	Used books.

Map 19 • West LA/Santa Monica East

California Map & Travel Ctr	3312 Pico Blvd	310-396-6277	Map and travel.
Gene De Chene Bookseller	11556 Santa Monica Blvd	310-477-8734	
Sawtelle Books & Music	2105 Sawtelle Blvd	310-477-8686	
Talk of the Town News	11203 National Blvd	310-312-0405	

Map 20 • Westwood/Century City

Borders Books & Music	1360 Westwood Blvd	310-475-3444	Chain.
Brentano's	10250 Santa Monica Blvd	310-785-0204	Chain in Century City Mall.
Dehkhoda Persian Book Store	1387 Westwood Blvd	310-477-0044	Persian books.
Nashr-E, Ketab	1413 Westwood Blvd	310-444-7788	Persian books.
Pettler & Lieberman Bookseller	2345 Westwood Blvd	310-474-2479	Contemporary literature.
Rand McNally Map & Travel	10250 Santa Monica Blvd	310-556-2202	Chain in Century City Mall.
Shar-E-Keta	1434 Westwood Blvd	310-470-4700	Persian books.
Technical Book	2056 Westwood Blvd	310-475-5711	Technical books.

Map 21 • Venice

Beyond Baroque Foundation	681 Venice Blvd	310-822-3006	
Mystery Annex	1407 Ocean Front Walk	310-399-2360	Mystery.
Small World Books	1407 Ocean Front Walk	310-399-2360	General.

Map 22 • Mar Vista

Ashahiya Bookstores	3760 S Centinela Ave	213-626-5650	
Libreria La Mexicana	12618 W Washington Blvd	310-391-9467	
Rick Benzel Book Dealers	3431 McLaughlin Ave	310-397-1367	
Sam Johnson's Bookshop	12310 Venice Blvd	310-391-5047	

Map 23 • Rancho Park/Palms

Ambrosia Books & Collectibles	10679 W Pico Blvd	310-475-5825	
Barnes & Noble Booksellers	10850 W Pico Blvd	310-475-4144	Chain.
Children's Book World	10580 1/2 W Pico Blvd	310-559-2665	Children's books.
Waldenbooks	10800 W Pico Blvd	310-474-6550	Chain.

Map 24 • Culver City

Bookstar	11000 Jefferson Blvd	310-391-0818	Owned by B&N—chain.
Follett Campus Bookstore – Pepperdine	400 Corporate Pointe	310-568-5741	Chain.

Map 25 • Marina Del Rey/Westchester West

Barnes & Noble Booksellers	13400 Maxella Ave	310-306-3213	Chain.
Follet Campus Bookstore - Loyola Marymount University	7900 Loyola Blvd	310-338-2889	

Map 26 • Westchester/Fox Hills/Ladera Heights

Borders Books & Music	6081 Center Dr	310-215-3720	Chain
University-West LA Bookstore	1155 W Arbor Vitae St	310-670-8949	
Waldenbooks	124 Fox Hills Mall	310-313-9352	

Map 27 • El Segundo/Manhattan Beach

B Dalton Bookseller	3200 N Sepulveda Blvd	310-546-5514	Chain.
Barnes & Noble Booksellers	1800 Rosecrans Ave	310-725-7025	Chain.
Catch Our Rainbow Books	3132 Pacific Coast Hwy	310-325-1081	Children's bookstore.
Dave's Old Book Shop	350 N Sepulveda Blvd	310-376-0879	
Nations Travel Store	1590 Rosecrans Ave	310-318-9915	Travel books and maps.
Richard Upton & Sons Book	917 Hillcrest St	310-322-7202	Publishes and sells books on American West.

Map 29 • Hermosa Beach

Book Value	2535 Pacific Coast Hwy	310-530-5343	Japanese books.
Bookstar	2730 Pacific Coast Hwy	310-326-8722	Chain owned by B&N.
Information Guides	32 18th St	310-379-1094	

Map 30 • Torrance North

B Dalton Bookseller	1815 Hawthorne Blvd	310-371-8737	Chain.
Comic Vendor	17430 Crenshaw Blvd	310-515-2676	
Kaede Shobo Japanese Bookstore	2147 W 182nd St	310-324-9892	
Nations Travel Stores	287 Del Amo Fashion Ctr	310-921-2242	
Talking Book World	18605 Hawthorne Blvd	310-793-2333	Audio books.

Map 31 • Redondo Beach

Accessories To Murder	903 S Pacific Coast Hwy	310-792-0972	Murder.
Barnes & Noble	21500 Hawthorne Blvd	310-370-5552	Chain.
Book Again	5039 Torrance Blvd	310-542-1156	Used.
Encore Books	1704 S Pacific Coast Hwy	310-540-1106	Used and rare.
Jimmy B's Audiobooks	1632 S Pacific Coast Hwy	310-792-1718	Audio books.
Psychic Eye Bookshops	3902 Pacific Coast Hwy	310-378-7754	New Age.
Sandpiper Books	4665 Torrance Blvd	310-371-2002	Used.
Super Crown Books	21217 Hawthorne Blvd	310-316-0522	

Map 32 • Torrance South

B Dalton Bookseller	3525 W Carson St	310-370-5735	Chain.
Borders Books & Music	3700 Torrance Blvd	310-540-7000	Chain.
Step'n Stones	1327 Post Ave	310-618-1171	
Torrance Book Buddy	1328 Sartori Ave	310-328-1134	

Map 33 • Highland Park

Another World Comics & Books	1615 Colorado Blvd	323-257-7757	

Map 34 • Pasadena

Barnes & Noble Booksellers	111 W Colorado Blvd	626-585-0362	Chain.
Book Em Mysteries	1118 Mission St	626-799-9600	Mystery.
Borders Books & Music	475 S Lake Ave	626-304-9773	Chain.

Bungalow News	746 E Colorado Blvd	626-795-9456	Magazines and paperbacks.
Cliff's Books	630 E Colorado Blvd	626-449-9541	Used.
Crown Books	127 S Lake Ave	626-568-9488	Chain.
Distant Lands Travel Bookstore & Outfitter	56 S Raymond Ave	626-449-3220	Maps and travel books.
Gamble House Bookstore	4 Westmoreland Pl	626-449-4178	Design, art and architecture.
Norton Simon Museum of Art	411 W Colorado Blvd	626-449-6840	Museum shop.
Rudolf Steiner Library Book	110 Martin Aly	626-578-7513	Library and small bookstore.
Vroman Museum Collection	340 S Lake Ave	626-396-1670	
Vroman's Bookstore	695 E Colorado Blvd	626-449-5320	Great independent bookstore.

Map 35 • Pasadena East/San Marino

Cal-Gold Enterprises	2569 E Colorado Blvd	626-792-6161	Gold miners.

Map 38 • El Sereno

Legal Books Distributing	4247 Whiteside St	323-526-7110	
Student Book Mart & Copy Ctr	1725 N Eastern Ave	323-262-5511	

Map 39 • Alhambra

Chase Book Store	210 E Main St	626-300-8666	
Chinese Book Store	1436 S Atlantic Blvd	626-282-6980	
Jilie	1283 E Valley Blvd	626-308-1466	
Kingston Culture Plaza	228 W Valley Blvd	626-570-1277	

Map 40 • Boyle Heights

Alpha & Omega Book Shop	807 Euclid Ave	323-261-5381	Spanish books.
Sears Book Ctr	2650 E Olympic Blvd	323-265-3153	

Map 43 • Van Nuys

Bargain Books	14426 Friar St	818-782-2782	
Russian Book	13757 Victory Blvd	818-781-7533	

Map 45 • Burbank

Aero & Automobile Books	3524 W Magnolia Blvd	323-849-1294	Auto & air.
American Opinion Books & Flags	5653 Cahuenga Blvd	818-769-4019	
Dutton's Books	3806 W Magnolia Blvd	818-840-8003	Independent.
Last Grenadier	820 Hollywood Way	818-848-9144	

Map 46 • Burbank East/Glendale West

A & S Bargain Books	301 N San Fernando Blvd	818-713-8172	Bargain books.
Barnes & Noble Booksellers	731 N San Fernando Blvd	818-558-1383	Chain.
Best Seller Book Shop	130 N San Fernando Blvd	818-955-8243	General used.
Creature Features	1802 W Olive Ave	818-842-9383	
Psychic Eye Book Shops	1011 W Olive Ave	818-845-8831	Metaphysical, self-help.

Map 47 • Glendale South

Barnes & Noble Booksellers	245 N Glendale Ave	818-246-4677	Chain.
Berj Armenian Bookstore	422 S Central Ave	818-244-3830	Armenian books.
Borders Books & Music	100 S Brand Blvd	818-241-8099	Chain.
Sardarabad Book Svc	1111 S Glendale Ave	818-500-0790	Iranian books.
Young Scholar	233 N Central Ave	818-246-7063	Children's and teacher's books.

Map 49 • Sherman Oaks West

Barnes & Noble Booksellers	16461 Ventura Blvd	818-380-1636	Chain.
Borders Books & Music	14651 Ventura Blvd	818-728-6593	Chain

Map 50 • Sherman Oaks East

Brentano's	14006 Riverside Dr	818-788-8661	Chain owned by Borders.
Crown Books	4454 Van Nuys Blvd		
Dangerous Visions	13563 Ventura Blvd	818-886-6963	Science, fantasy, horror.
Psychic Eye Book Shops	13435 Ventura Blvd	818-906-8263	Metaphysical, self-help

Map 51 • Studio City/Valley Village

A & S Bargain Books	12050 Ventura Blvd	818-238-0371	Bargain books.
Bookstar	12136 Ventura Blvd	818-505-9528	Owned by B&N— chain.
Dutton's Books	5146 Laurel Canyon Blvd	818-769-3866	Great independent bookstore.
Iliad Book Shop	4820 Vineland Ave	818-509-2665	
Laurel Park Newsstand	4346 Laurel Canyon Blvd	818-769-8583	
Paris Bookstore	4820 Laurel Canyon Blvd	818-762-7557	
Portrait of a Bookstore	4360 Tujunga Ave	818-769-3853	
Raven's Flight	5050 Vineland Ave	818-985-2944	
Samuel French's Theatre & Film	11963 Ventura Blvd	818-762-0535	Theater and film books.

Map 52 • Universal City/Toluca Lake

Geographia Map & Travel Bookstore	4000 W Riverside Dr	818-848-1414	Maps and travel.
Upstart Crow	1000 Universal Center Dr	818-763-1811	General interest.

Arts & Entertainment • Restaurants

Key: $: Under $10 / $$: $10–$20 / $$$: $20–$30 / $$$$: $30+   * : Does not accept credit cards. / † : Accepts only American Express.

Map 1 • Beverly Hills

Baja Fresh	475 N Beverly Dr	310-858-6690	$*	Cheap Mexican.
Barney Greengrass	9570 Wilshire Blvd	310-777-5877	$$$*	An LA icon.
Belvedere, The	9882 Little Santa Monica Blvd	310-788-2306	$$$$	Upscale hotel dining.
Blue on Blue	9400 W Olympic Blvd	310-277-5221	$$$	Funky hotel dining.
Brighton Coffee Shop	9600 Brighton Way	310-276-7732	$	Comfort food.
Cafe Talesai	9198 W Olympic Blvd	310-271-9345	$$$	Thai specialties with a twist.
Crustacean	9646 Santa Monica Blvd	310-205-8990	$$$$*	High-end Vietnamese.
Da Pasquale	9749 Santa Monica Blvd	310-859-3884	$$*	Neighborhood Italian.
El Torito Grill	9595 Wilshire Blvd	310-550-1599	$$	Okay food, better drinks.
Farm of Beverly Hills	439 N Beverly Dr	310-273-5578	$$$	Fresh California fare.
Ginza Sushi-Ko	218 N Rodeo Dr	310-247-8939	$$$$	Very high-end sushi.
Grill, The	9560 Dayton Way	310-276-0615	$$$$	Hollywood power lunch spot.
Joss	9255 Sunset Blvd	310-276-1886	$$$	Haute Chinese cuisine.
Kate Mantilini	9101 Wilshire Blvd	310-278-3699	$$$*	Late-night stargazing.
La Scala	410 N Canon Dr	310-275-0579	$$$*	Classic Italian.
Le Pain Quotidien	9630 Little Santa Monica Blvd	310-859-1100	$	Classy French sandwich shop.
Mandarin, The	430 N Camden Dr	323-272-0267	$$$	Upscale Cantonese-Mandarin food.
Maple Drive	345 N Maple Dr	310-274-9800	$$$$	Comfort food for the entertainment industry.
Mastro	246 N Canon Dr	310-888-8782	$$$$	Great steaks, upstairs piano bar is a don't miss.
Mulberry Street Pizzeria	347 N Canon Dr	310-247-8988	$*	Thin-crust pizza.
Mulberry Street Pizzeria	240 S Beverly Dr	310-247-8100	$*	Thin-crust pizza.
Nate 'n Al's	414 N Beverly Dr	310-274-0101	$$*	New York style deli.
Nic's	453 N Canon Dr	310-550-5707	$$$$	Oysters and martinis, need we say more?
Polo Lounge	9641 Sunset Blvd	310-276-2251	$$$$	The Grande Dame of hotel dining.
Regent Beverly Wilshire	9500 Wilshire Blvd	310-275-5200	$$$$	For the "Pretty Woman" in us all.
Trader Vic's	9876 Wilshire Blvd	310-276-6345	$$$$	Old school Polynesian-themed restaurant; fruity drinks and fried appetizers.
Xi'an	362 N Canon Dr	310-275-3345	$$	Healthy Chinese food that tastes delicious.

Map 2 • West Hollywood

Ago	8478 Melrose Ave	323-655-6333	$$$	High-end Italian.
Amici	469 N Doheny Dr	310-858-0271	$$$*	Pacific Italian chain.
Angeli Caffe	7274 Melrose Ave	323-936-9086	$$	Starch-tastic bread and tasty pastas.
Angelini Osteria	7313 Beverly Blvd	323-297-0070	$$$$	Upscale Italian.
Authentic Café	7605 Beverly Blvd	323-939-4626	$$*	Eclectic.
Balboa	The Grafton Hotel, 8462 W Sunset Blvd	323-650-8383	$$$$	Steaks on the Sunset Strip.
Barefoot Bar & Grill	8722 W 3rd St	310-276-6223	$$$	The California cuisine always draws crowds.
Basix Cafe	8333 Santa Monica Blvd	323-848-2460	$$	Popular breakfast spot.
Bistro 21	846 N La Cienega Blvd	310-967-0021	$$$$	French-Asian bistro with a cult following.
Bossa Nova	685 N Robertson Blvd	310-657-5070	$*	Paradise for meat lovers.
Cadillac Café	359 N La Cienega Blvd	310-657-6591	$$*	An eclectic scene.
Café Angelino	8735 W 3rd St	310-246-1177	$$	Flaky thin-crust pizzas.
Cafe Med	8615 Sunset Blvd	310-652-0445	$$	Low key Sunset Plaza Italian.
Café Pranzo	8514 W 3rd St	310-652-7755	$$	A little Italian gem in a nondescript strip mall
Campanile	624 S La Brea Ter	323-938-1447	$$$$*	Romantic Medierranean.
Canter's Deli	419 N Fairfax Ave	323-651-2030	$*	Classic deli.
Chaya Brasserie	8741 Alden Dr	310-859-8833	$$$$	Great food in a schmoozy setting.
Chianti	7383 Melrose Ave	323-653-8333	$$$$	An Italian classic.
Chianti Cucina	7383 Melrose Ave	323-653-8333	$$$	More casual than Chianti, just as good.
Cynthia's	8370 W 3rd St	323-658-7851	$$$*	American favorites. Order the cobbler—trust us.
Doughboys	8136 W 3rd St	323-651-4202	$*	Popular sandwiches and salads.
East India Grill	345 N La Brea Ter	323-936-8844	$$*	Indian with a California twist.
Ed's Coffee Shop	460 N Robertson Blvd	310-659-8625	$	Home-cookin'.
Farm of Beverly Hills	189 The Grove Dr	323-525-1699	$$$	Fresh California fare.
Fish Grill	7226 Beverly Blvd	323-937-7162	$*	No-frills, super-fresh fish
Flora Kitchen	460 S La Brea Ave	323-931-9900	$$	Dine inside a flower shop.
Genghis Cohen	740 N Fairfax Ave	323-653-0640	$$*	Chinese with live music.
Gumbo Pot	6333 W 3rd St	323-933-0358	$	Best Cajun in LA.
Hirozen	8385 Beverly Blvd	323-653-0470	$$$*	Great mini-mall sushi.
House of Blues	8430 Sunset Blvd	323-848-5100	$$$	
Hugo's	8401 Santa Monica Blvd	323-654-3993	$$*	Power brunches.
Ivy, The	113 N Robertson Blvd	310-274-8303	$$$$	Where celebs and power brokers eat.
Jar	8225 Beverly Blvd	323-655-6566	$$$$	Upscale comfort food.
King's Road Cafe	8361 Beverly Blvd	323-655-9044	$$	Strongest coffee you'll ever drink.
Kokomo	inside Farmer's Market, at 3rd St & Fairfax Ave	323-933-0773	$*	Standard American fare.

Le Pain Quotidien	8607 Melrose Ave	310-854-3700	$	Classy French sandwich shop.
Lucques	8474 Melrose Ave	323-655-6277	$$$$	Chez Panisse-style cooking in an LA setting.
Mandarette	8386 Beverly Blvd	323-655-6115	$$$*	Chinese fusion.
Manhattan Won Ton Company	151 S Doheny Dr	310-888-2804	$$$	Modern Chinese, check out the Buddha bar.
Newsroom Café	120 N Robertson Blvd	310-652-4444	$$*	Star-laden vegetarian.
Noura Café	8479 Melrose Ave	323-651-4581	$$*	Middle Eastern with belly-dancing.
Pig, The	612 N La Brea Ave	323-935-1116	$$	Messy southern BBQ joint. Yum.
Pink's Famous Chili Dogs	709 N La Brea Ave	323-931-4223	$*	The name says it all.
Quality Food & Beverage	8030 W 3rd St	323-658-5959	$*	Dog-friendly brunch hangout.
Real Food Daily	414 N La Cienega Blvd	310-289-9910	$$	One of the healthiest tasting restaurants in town.
Saddle Ranch Chop House	8371 Sunset Blvd	323-656-2007	$$$	Chophouse with a mechanical bull.
Sweet Lady Jane	8360 Melrose Ave	323-653-7145	$$	Decadent desserts to die for
Swingers	8020 Beverly Blvd	323-653-5858	$*	Classic late-night diner.
Tail o' the Pup	329 N San Vicente Blvd	310-652-4517	$*	Famous hot dog stand.
The Standard	8300 Sunset Blvd	323-650-9090	$$*	Late-night star watching.
Urth Caffé	8565 Melrose Ave	310-659-0628	$*	People-watching coffee shop.
Yabu	521 N La Cienega Blvd	310-854-0400	$$$	Hip sushi and noodles.

Map 3 · Hollywood

Ammo	1155 N Highland Ave	323-871-2666	$$	Trendy California comfort food.
Cat N' Fiddle Pub & Restaurant	6530 W Sunset Blvd	323-468-3800	$$	Irish pub with a large outdoor patio for star-gazing. Try the fish and sticks. Moderately priced.
Chan Dara	310 N Larchmont Blvd	323-467-1052	$$*	Thai.
Hola	1807 N Cahuenga Blvd	323-466-0000	$*	Super cheap Mexican restaurant that some locals say is tastier than its larger, more expensive counterparts. Free delivery.
Hollywood & Vine Diner	6263 Hollywood Blvd	323-461-2345	$$$	Great 20's style interior and large bar serving California cuisine and specialty drinks.
House, The	5750 Melrose Ave	323-462-4687	$$$$	Only organically grown produce is used here.
Les Deux Cafes	1638 N Las Palmas Ave	310-465-0509	$$$$*	First-class French with the stars.
Miceli's	1646 N Las Palmas Ave	323-466-3438	$$	Miceli's is the place to get Italian/Sicilian food, hands down! Singing waiters and reasonable prices make this a Hollywood favorite.
Musso & Frank	6667 Hollywood Blvd	301-467-7788	$$$*	Old-fashioned American.
Off Vine	6263 Leland Way	301-962-1900	$$$*	Romantic Californian.
Patina	5955 Melrose Ave	310-467-1108	$$$$*	French-Californian fusion.
Roscoe's Chicken & Waffles	1514 N Gower St	323-466-7453	$$$*	Southern fried bonanza.
Sunset Room	1430 N Cahuenga Blvd	323-463-0004	$$$$	
The Pig & Whistle	6714 Hollywood Blvd	323-463-0000	$$$	An old time establishment in Hollywood that recently reopened. Food is so-so, but there is a cool back room with several beds... Good vibe.
Yamakasa	1900 N Highland Ave	323-882-6524	$$	Newly renovated, if you're looking for a quick sushi-fix check out this moderately priced Japanese restaurant.
Yamashiro	1999 Sycamore Ave	323-466-5125	$$$	A perfect choice for a romantic evening, the Japanese restaurant Yamashiro is a bit pricey, but the service is excellent and it has an unbeatable view of LA.
Zumaya	5722 Melrose Ave	323-464-0624	$$	Authentic Mexican.

Map 4 · Los Feliz

Café Stella	3932 Sunset Blvd	323-666-0265	$$$*	Trendy French bistro.
Cha Cha Cha	656 N Virgil Ave	323-664-7723	$	Caribbbean fare, Sangria, different breakfast, festive atmosphere
El Conquistador	3701 Sunset Blvd	323-666-5136	$$	Mole Ole!
Electric Lotus	4656 Franklin Ave	323-953-0040	$$*	Hip Indian disco.
Fred 62	1850 N Vermont Ave	323-667-0062	$$*	Asian fusion diner.
Mexico City	2121 Hillhurst Ave	323-661-7227	$$*	Arty Tex-Mex cantina.
Millie's	3524 Sunset Blvd	323-664-0404	$*	Devil Mess is the best reason to be bad.
Palermo	1858 N Vermont Ave	323-663-1178	$$*	Traditional Southern Italian.
Shin	1972 Hillhurst Ave	323-664-1891	$$	Japanese food, sushi, good salads.
Trattoria Farfalla	1978 Hillhurst Ave	323-661-7365	$$*	Inexpensive reliable Italian.
Vida	1930 Hillhurst Ave	323-660-4446	$$$*	Hip, creative Californian.
Vito's Pizza	814 N Vermont Ave	323-667-2723	$	Home-made everything.
Zankou Chicken	5065 W Sunset Blvd	323-665-7845	$*	Cheap Armenian chain.

Map 5 · Silver Lake/Echo Park/Atwater

Chameau	2520 Hyperion Ave	323-953-1973	$$$	BYOB Moroccan.
Les Freres Taix	1911 W Sunset Blvd	213-484-1265	$$*	Traditional French bistro.
Osteria Nonni	3219 Glendale Blvd	323-666-7133	$$	Tasty Italian in a pleasant room.
Police Academy Café	1880 Academy Dr		$$*	Dine with the cadets.
Tam O'Shanter	2980 Los Feliz Blvd	323-664-0228	$$$*	Scottish-English pub.

Key: $: Under $10 / $$: $10–$20 / $$$: $20–$30 / $$$$: $30+ *: Does not accept credit cards. / † : Accepts only American Express.

Map 6 • Miracle Mile/Mid-City

Brasserie Des Artistes	8300 Wilshire Blvd	323-655-6196	$$$	This French bistro located on a corner in front of a mini-mall is excellent from the décor to the food. Karaoke Wednesdays.
Caffé Latte	6254 Wilshire Blvd	323-936-5213	$$*	California-style coffee-breakfast shop.
Crazy Fish	9105 W Olympic Blvd	310-550-8547	$$*	Insanely popular sushi joint.
La Boca del Conga Room	5370 Wilshire Blvd	323-938-1696	$$$	Located next to the Conga Room for Cuban cuisine dining before heading next door for Salsa dancing.
Lucy's	1371 S La Brea Ave	323-938-4337	$*	A 24-hour drive-through taco stand that also sells chili dogs, burgers, and anything else bad for you.
Mo Better Meatty Meat Burgers	5855 W Pico Blvd	323-938-6558	$$*	Known for the vegetarian hot dogs and burgers used with pure vegetables (no tofu allowed in this joint), but serves real meat cooked better than most carnivores could do.
Natalee Thai	998 S Robertson Blvd	310-855-9380	$$	Popular Thai food.
Nyala	1076 S Fairfax Ave	323-936-2486	$$	One of the more high-end Ethiopian establishments when it comes to décor, but the $4.95 vegetarian lunch buffet is the most popular aspect.
Rosalind's	1044 S Fairfax Ave	323-936-2486	$$	One of the first Ethiopian businesses to open on this stretch of Fairfax, and an old favorite of the locals.
Roscoe's Chicken & Waffles	5006 W Pico Blvd	323-934-4405	$*	Cheap Southern soul food chain.
Temple	14 N La Cienega Blvd	310-360-9460	$$$$	A swanky Korean place with ultra modern interior. Home delivery service and private parties with DJs are very popular.
Versailles	1415 S La Cienega Blvd	310-289-0392	$$*	Cheap Cuban chain.
Wi Jammin	5103 Pico Blvd	323-965-9809	$	A tiny hole-in-the-wall Caribbean restaurant where the local hairdressers hang out.

Map 7 • Hancock Park

Kiku Sushi	246 N Larchmont Blvd	323-464-1294	$$	Sushi here is good and moderately priced. There's all you can eat at both lunch and dinner.
La Luna	113 N Larchmont Blvd	323-962-2130	$$$*	Cauual Italian trattoria.
Larchmont Village Pizzeria	131 N Larchmont Blvd		$*	Might be LA's best NY-style pizza.
Le Petit Greek	127 N Larchmont Blvd	323-464-5160	$$	Gyros, anyone?
Prado	244 N Larchmont Blvd	323-467-3871	$$$*	Spicy Latin-Caribbean.

Map 8 • Korea Town

Atlas Bar & Grill	3760 Wilshire Blvd	213-380-8400	$$$*	Elegant dance club with food.
El Cholo	1121 S Western Ave	323-734-2773	$$*	Long time favorite Mexican chain.
El Farolito	2737 W Pico Blvd	323-731-4329	$*	Chicken enchiladas.
LA Farm	3000 W Olympic Blvd	310-449-4000	$$$*	Hip California-French fusion.
Soot Bull Jeep	3136 W 8th St	213-387-3865	$$	Korean BBQ.
Taylor's Prime Steaks	3361 W 8th St	213-382-8449	$$$*	Old fashioned steak house.
Tommy's	2575 Beverly Blvd	213-389-9060	$	Their burgers are renowned.
Woo Lae Oak	623 S Western Ave	213-384-2244	$$$*	You cook Asian BBQ.

Map 9 • Downtown

Brooklyn Bagel	2217 Beverly Blvd	213-413-4114	$*	The only place that makes their own bagels in the neighborhood, everyday. Has been in business for over 47 years.
California Roll & Sushi Fish	727 W 7th St	213-489-0238	$$	Good Japanese food. They serve sushi a la carte, bento box for lunch, and sushi combination plates.
Checkers	535 S Grand Ave	213-624-0000	$$$$	Upscale, downtown, pre-theater dining.
Cicada	617 S Olive St	213-488-9488	$$$$	California-Italian.
Ciudad	445 S Figueroa St	213-486-5171	$$	Pan-Latino.
El Cholo	1025 Wilshire Blvd	310-417-1910	$$*	Popular Mexican chain.
Emerson's	606 S Olive St	213-623-3006	$*	Specialty salads, sandwiches and coffees.
Emerson's	862 S Los Angeles St	213-623-8807	$*	Specialty salads, sandwiches and coffees.
Empress Pavillion	988 N Hill St	213-617-9898	$$*	Lively chinese dim sum.
Engine Co No 28	644 S Figueroa St	213-624-6996	$$	Great salads, soups, pastas and entrees. Vegetarian friendly.
Mrs Beasley's	735 S Figueroa St	213-228-0227	$	Cakes, muffins, cookies, bars, soups, sandwiches, coffee, juice, etc. Also does gift baskets.
Nick & Stef's Steakhouse	330 S Hope St	213-680-0330	$$$$	Old fashioned steaks in an ultra modern downtown setting.
NY Pizza	518 W 6th St	213-614-1100	$*	Best pizza in the neighborhood.

Original Pantry	877 S Figueroa St	213-972-9279	$*	Long time old-fashioned diner.
Original Pantry Cafe	877 S Figueroa St	213-972-9279	$$	An LA institution.
Pacific Dining Car	1310 W 6th St	213-483-6000	$$$$*	Steak all day, all night.
Philippe, the Original	1001 N Alameda St	213-628-3781	$*	The best French dips in town.
Seoul Jung Korean	930 Wilshire Blvd	213-888-7777	$$$	Upscale Korean BBQ. Fresh ingredients. Meat and fish dishes, vegetarian-friendly.
Soul Folks Café	714 Traction Ave	213-613-0381	$$	Great Southern food. Vegetarian is offered.
Yang Chow	819 N Broadway	213-625-0811	$$*	Popular chinese chain.

Map 10 • Baldwin Hills

Leo's BBQ	2619 Crenshaw Blvd	323-733-1186	$$*	Down-home favorites.

Map 11 • South Central West

Harold & Belle's	2920 W Jefferson Blvd	323-735-9023	$$$$*	Great Cajun food.
La Barca	2414 S Vermont Ave	323-758-7433	$$	Mexican.

Map 15 • Pacific Palisades

Dante Palisades Restaurant	1032 Swarthmore Ave	310-459-7561	$$$	Italian food (closed from 3-5pm).
Giorgio Baldi	114 W Channel Rd	310-573-1660	$$$$	Memorable Tuscan cooking.
Gladstone's for Fish	17351 Sunset Blvd	310-454-3474	$$$	Touristy seafood with great view.
Kay 'n Dave's Cantina	15246 W Sunset Blvd	310-459-8118	$	Mexican food.
Marix Tex Mex Cafe	118 Entrada Dr	310-459-8596	$$*	Mexican, but all about the margaritas.
Mort's Palisades Delicatessan	1035 Swarthmore Ave	310-454-5511	$	Breakfast, lunch, dinner, sandwiches $8, Mexican food.
Patrick's Roadhouse	106 Entrada Dr	310-459-4544	$$	Quintessential place for breakfast at the beach.
Pure Energy Café	17383 W Sunset Blvd	310-573-4105	$	Healthy Mexican food.
Robek's Juice	15280 Antioch St	310-230-3991	$	Juice, salads, sandwiches.
Terry's	1028 Swarthmore Ave	310-454-6467	$$	Breakfast, lunch, dinner, sandwich, salads, omelettes.

Map 16 • Brentwood

A Votre Sante	13016 San Vicente Blvd	310-451-1813	$$*	Vegetarian health food.
Brentwood Restaurant & Lounge	148 S Barrington Ave	310-476-3511	$$$	California-style comfort food.
Cheesecake Factory	11647 San Vicente Blvd	310-826-7111	$$*	American comfort food—and of course, cheesecake.
Chin Chin	11740 San Vicente Blvd	310-826-2525	$$*	Chinese chain.
Daily Grill	11677 San Vicente Blvd	310-442-0044	$$*	Home cooking.
Gaucho Grill	11695 San Vicente Blvd	310-447-7898	$$	Argentine cuisine with lots of meat.
La Scala Presto	11740 San Vicente Blvd	310-826-6100	$$*	Classic Italian.
Lamonica's NY Pizza	11678 San Vicente Blvd	310-820-6636	$*	New York pizza by the slice.
Le Pain Quotidien	11702 Barrington Ct	310-476-0969	$	Classy French sandwich shop.
Pizzicotto	11758 San Vicente Blvd	310-442-7188	$$$*	Pizza and pasta.
Reddi Chick BBQ	225 26th St	310-393-5238	$$	Chicken with a cult following.
Toscana	11633 San Vicente Blvd	310-820-2448	$$$*	Tuscan with great pizzas.
Vincenti	11930 San Vicente Blvd	310-207-0127	$$$$	Fine Italian food & wine.
Zax	11604 San Vicente Blvd	310-571-3800	$$$$	High-end neighborhoody feel.

Map 17 • Bel Air/Holmby Hills

Bel Air Bar & Grill	662 N Sepulveda Blvd	310-440-5544	$$$*	Californian with quick Getty access.
Four Oaks	2181 N Beverly Glen Blvd	310-470-2265	$$$$	Intimate spot with excellent food and plenty of star sightings.
Hotel Bel Air	701 Stone Canyon Rd	310-472-1211	$$$$*	Nouvelle Californian/French.

Map 18 • Santa Monica

17th Street Café	1610 Montana Ave	310-453-2771	$$*	California casual.
Babalu	1002 Montana Ave	310-395-2500	$$*	Caribbean—don't skip dessert.
Back on the Beach	445 Pacific Coast Hwy	310-393-8282	$$	California food, California beach, California experience.
Blueberry	510 Santa Monica Blvd	310-394-7766	$*	Cheap homecooking.
Border Grill	1445 4th St	310-451-1655	$$$	Mexican restaurant run by popular TV chefs.
Broadway Deli	1457 3rd St Promenade	310-451-0616	$$$	Overpriced but popular deli food.
Buffalo Club	1520 Olympic Blvd	310-450-8600	$$$$	Exclusive clubby dining.
Cafe Montana	1534 Montana Ave	310-829-3990	$$$	A neighborhood staple.
California Chicken Café	2401 Wilshire Blvd	310-453-0477	$	Good rotisserie chicken & sides. Cheap & fast.
Cha Cha Chicken	1906 Ocean Ave	310-581-1684	$*	Caribbean chicken.
Chaya Venice	110 Navy St	310-396-1179	$$$	Slightly upscale place to meet or experience but not imposed upon ambience.
Chez Jay	1657 Ocean Ave	310-395-1741	$$$*	California seafood.
Chinois on Main	2709 Main St	310-392-9025	$$$$	Wolfgang Puck does Chinese—brilliantly.
Dhaba	2104 Main St	310 399 9452	$$	Visit India with a Dhaba Dinner.
Falafel King	1315 3rd St Promenade	310-587-2551	$*	One of the cheapest, best meals on the Promenade.
Finn McCool's	2700 Main St	310-452-1734	$$*	Neighborhood comfort food.

Key: $: Under $10 / $$: $10–$20 / $$$: $20–$30 / $$$$: $30+   * : Does not accept credit cards. / † : Accepts only American Express.

Map 18 • Santa Monica — continued

Fritto Misto	601 Colorado Ave	310-458-2829	$$*	Inexpensive California-Italian.
JR Seafood	102 Santa Monica Pl	310-260-8855	$$	Chinese with an emphasis on seafood.
Kau-Aina	119 Broadway	310-394-0100	$	Nicer than Fatburger with a lot more variety.
Library Alehouse	2911 Main St	310-314-4855	$$	Beer and classy pub fare.
Lobster, The	1602 Ocean Ave	310-458-9294	$$$$	Definitely order the lobster.
Lula	2722 Main St	310-392-5711	$$*	Inexpenisve Mexican with strong margaritas.
Mani's	2507 Main St	310-396-7700	$	Bakery, café, juices, sugarless cookies—oh my!
Michael D's Café & Catering	234 Pico Blvd	310-452-8737	$	Next to bowling alley—scarf 'n' score!
Newsroom Café	530 Wilshire Blvd	310-319-9100	$$*	Inexpensive healthfood.
Ocean Ave Seafood	1401 Ocean Ave	310-394-5669	$$$$	Upscale seafood by the beach.
Ocean Park Omelette Parlor	2732 Main St	310-399-7892	$	Home of well-stuffed, three-egg omelettes
Reel Inn	1220 3rd St Promenade	310-395-5538	$$*	Speedy fresh seafood.
Sushi Roku	1401 Ocean Ave	310-458-4771	$$$$	Sushi by the beach.
Trastavere	1360 3rd St Promenade	310-319-1985	$$$	Their gnocchi and olive dip rate a trip.
World Café	2820 Main St	310-392-1661	$$*	Outdoor people-watching.
Ye Olde King's Head	116 Santa Monica Blvd	310-451-1402	$$*	Traditional English fare and beer.

Map 19 • West LA/Santa Monica East

Asakuma	11701 Wilshire Blvd	310-826-0013	$$$	More than just sushi.
Bandera	11700 Wilshire Blvd	310-477-3524	$$$	Dimly lit; Yuppy-ish. Reliable New-American cuisine.
Bombay Café	12021 W Pico Blvd	310-473-3388	$$*	Inspired Indian Cuisine.
Chez Mimi	246 26th St	310-393-0558	$$$	Onion soup and other French staples.
Hide Sushi	2040 Sawtelle Blvd	310-477-7242	$$$	Not for the sushi-phobic.
Il Forno	2901 Ocean Park Blvd	310-450-1241	$$	Northern Italian cuisine. Great pastas & NYC-style pizzas.
Il Moro	11400 W Olympic Blvd	310-575-3530	$$$	Creative Italian specialties.
Javan	11500 Santa Monica Blvd	310-207-5555	$	Persian cuisine. Huge portions of tasty charbroiled meats.
Josie's Restaurant	2424 Pico Blvd	310-581-9888	$$$	Reputable chef. Great interior. New American cuisine.
Kay 'n Dave's	262 26th St	310-260-1355	$$	Healthy Mexican with a family-friendly atmosphere.
LA Farm Restaurant	3000 Olympic Blvd	310-449-4000	$$$	Relaxed, beautiful patio. Cal-French cuisine. Excellent service.
La Bottega Marino	11363 Santa Monica Blvd	310-477-7777	$$	Italian deli-restaurant. Affordable. Charming setting.
Lares	2911 Pico Blvd	310-829-4550	$$	Rich, authentic Mexican meals—and potent margaritas.
Le Saigon	11611 Santa Monica Blvd	310-312-2929	$*	Great Korean food.
Mishima Restaurant	11819 Wilshire Blvd	310-966-1062	$	Cheap Japanese noodles and basic sushi. Clean and bright.
Rae's Restaurant	2901 Pico Blvd	310-828-7937	$*	Neighborhood hangout—they line up for breakfast!
Royal Star Seafood	3001 Wilshire Blvd	323-692-5606	$$	Dim sum and then some seafood.
Sushi Sasabune	11300 Nebraska Ave	310-268-8380	$$$$	No California Roll, no menu. Trust the chef.
Tlapazola Grill	11676 Gateway Blvd	310-477-1577	$$	Southern Mexican.
Typhoon	3221 Donald Douglas Loop S	310-390-6565	$$$	Eclectic Pan-Asian. Aviation motif. Cool & chic.
Valentino	3115 Pico Blvd	310-829-4313	$$$$	Classy Italian. Flawless. Dazzling wine list.
Vito	2807 Ocean Park Blvd	310-450-4999	$$$	Reliable Italian.
Yabu	11820 W Pico Blvd	310-473-9757	$$$	Hip sushi and noodles.
Zabies	3003 Ocean Park Blvd	310-392-9036	$	Neighborhood café. Friendly. Cheap. Good breakfast and lunch.

Map 20 • Westwood/Century City

Big Chill	10850 Olympic Blvd	310-441-0643	$*	Best frozen yogurt in LA!
Clementine	1751 Ensley Ave	310-552-1080	$$	True American cuisine with a modern flair.
Diddy Riese Cookies	926 Broxton Ave	310-208-0448	$*	25¢ cookies and ice cream sandwiches.
Earth, Wind & Flour	1176 Westwood Blvd	310-470-2499	$$	"Boston-style" pizzas and pastas.
Falafel King	1059 Broxton Ave	310-208-4444	$*	Fast food Middle Eastern.
Gardens on Glendon	1139 Glendon Ave	310-824-1818	$$$*	Californian favorites.
Johnnie's NY Pizzeria	10251 Santa Monica Blvd	310-553-1188	$*	New York style pizza.
La Bruschetta	1621 Westwood Blvd	310-477-1052	$$$	Classic Italian—their bruschetta is delicious.
La Cachette	10506 Little Santa Monica Blvd	310-470-4992	$$$$	High-end French.
Matteo's Hoboken	2323 Westwood Blvd	310-474-1109	$$*	Southern Italian fare.
Mojo	930 Hilgard Ave	310-443-7820	$$$$	Nuevo Latino cuisine.
Napa Valley Grille	1100 Glendon Ave	310-824-3322	$$$$	Upscale dining.
Stan's Donuts	10948 Weyburn Ave	310-208-8660	$*	Try a Reese's Peanut Butter Cup donut.
Tengu	10853 Lindbrook Dr	310-209-0071	$$$	Hip Asian fare.

Map 21 • Venice

Abbot's Pizza	1407 Abbot Kinney Blvd	310-314-2777	$*	Bagel crust pizza.
C&O Trattoria	31 Washington Blvd	310-823-9491	$$*	Cheap Italian.
Café 50's	838 Lincoln Blvd	310-399-1955	$*	All-American food without pretense.
Canal Club	2025 Pacific Ave	310-823-3878	$$$*	Chinese-Cuban fusion.
Casa Blanca Restaurant	220 Lincoln Blvd	310-392-5751	$$$	Nice evening out guaranteed.
Figtree's Café	429 Ocean Front Walk	310-392-4937	$$	Great service, take in the ocean view!
Hal's Bar & Grill	1349 Abbot Kinney Blvd	310-396-3105	$$$	Pub food.
Hama Sushi	213 Windward Ave	310-396-8783	$$$*	Hip Japanese.
Joe's	1023 Abbot Kinney Blvd	310-399-5811	$$$*	Nouveau Californian.
Killer Shrimp	523 Washington Blvd	310-578-2293	$$	An exotic option to seafood dining.
La Cabana Restaurant and Bar	738 Rose Ave	310-392-7973	$$	Very festive atmosphere and diverse meeting place.
Rose Café	220 Rose Ave	310-399-0711	$$*	Trendy eclectic Californian.
The Brick House	826 Hampton Dr	310-581-1639	$$	Definitely a local hangout. Lunch and breakfast only.
Wabi-Sabi	1635 Abbot Kinney Blvd	310-314-2229	$$	Sushi.

Map 22 • Mar Vista

Aunt Kizzy's Back Porch	4325 Glencoe Ave	310-578-1005	$$*	Southern comfort food.
Empanada's Place	3811 Sawtelle Blvd	310-391-0888	$*	The name says it all.
Paco's Tacos	4141 Centinela Ave	310-391-9616	$*	Cheap Tex-Mex.
Pepy's Galley	12125 Venice Blvd	310-390-0577	$*	Unpretentious bowling alley diner.
Venus of Venice	12034 Venice Blvd	310-391-7674	$	Tex-Mex vegan.

Map 23 • Rancho Park/Palms

Apple Pan	10801 W Pico Blvd	310-475-3583	$*	Hamburger joint.
Bourbon Street Shrimp	10928 W Pico Blvd	310-474-0007	$$*	Cajun and seafood.
Delmonico's Seafood Grille	9320 W Pico Blvd	310-550-7737	$$$	Dependable old school seafood.
Factor's Famous Deli	9420 W Pico Blvd	310-278-9175	$	Traditional delicatessen fare.
Guelaguetza	11127 Palms Blvd	310-837-1153	$	Authentic Oaxacan dishes.
Gyu-kaku	10925 W Pico Blvd	310-234-8641	$$$	Japanese style Korean BBQ.
Hop Li	10974 W Pico Blvd	310-441-3708	$$	Cantonese cuisine.
Jack Sprat's	10668 W Pico Blvd	310-837-6662	$$*	Healthy.
John O'Groats	10516 W Pico Blvd	310-204-0692	$*	Breakfast hang-out.
Junior's Deli	2379 Westwood Blvd	310-475-5771	$$*	New York diner/deli.
La Serenata Gourmet	10924 W Pico Blvd	310-441-9667	$$*	Mexican with seafood specialties.
Milky Way	9108 W Pico Blvd	310-859-0004	$$$	Kosher dairy restaurant.
Overland Café	3601 Overland Ave	310-559-9999	$$	Great California cuisine and atmosphere.

Map 24 • Culver City

Bamboo	10835 Venice Blvd	310-287-0668	$$*	Cheap Caribbean.
Café Brasil	10831 Venice Blvd	310-837-8957	$$	The fresh-squeezed juices are amazing!
Natalee Thai	10101 Venice Blvd	310-202-7003	$$	Popular Pad Thai and curries.
Petrelli's Steakhouse	5615 S Sepulveda Blvd	310-397-1438	$$$	Meat and potato lovers' paradise.
Sagebrush Cantina	9523 Culver Blvd	310-836-5321	$$	Great southwestern food in an upscale, soulful groove.
Tito's Tacos	11222 Washington Pl	310-391-5780	$*	Cheap taco stand.
Versailles	10319 Venice Blvd	310-558-3168	$*	Cuban fusion.

Map 25 • Marina Del Rey/Westchester West

Alejo's	8343 Lincoln Blvd	310-822-0095	$*	Classic cheap Italian.
Alejo's	4002 Lincoln Blvd	310-822-0095	$	Italian for bargain hunters.
Antica Pizzeria	13455 Maxella Ave	310-577-8182	$$$	Classic Neapolitan pizzas and pastas.
Ballona Fish Market	13455 Maxella Ave	310-822-8979	$$	Hans Rockenwagner does fish.
Café Del Rey	4451 Admiralty Way	310-823-6395	$$$*	Eclectic seafood.
Caffe Pinguini	6935 Pacific Ave	310-306-0117	$$$*	Italian on the beach.
Casa Escobar	14160 Palawan Way	310-822-2199	$$	Great quesadillas and chimichangas!
Chan Darette	13490 Maxella Ave	310-301-1004	$$*	Trendy Thai.
Paco's Tacos	8329 Lincoln Blvd	310-670-5466	$*	Inexpensive Tex-Mex.
Shanghai Red's	13813 Fiji Way	310-823-4522	$$$	Lovely Victorian-style restaurant with incredible brunch.
The Shack	185 Culver Blvd	310-823-6222	$$$*	Cheap burgers and more.
The Warehouse	4499 Admiralty Way	310-823-5451	$$$	Romantic enough to ask someone to marry you.

Map 26 • Westchester/Fox Hills/Ladera Heights

Buggy Whip	7420 La Tijera Blvd	310-645-7131	$$	Go for the piano bar more than the food.
Encounter	209 World Way	310-215-5151	$$$$	Neon martinis in a Jetsons-style setting.
Nick's Little Place	6251 Bristol Pkwy	310-670-2920	$	Dog friendly restaurant serving sandwiches and salads.
Paco's Tacos	6212 W Manchester Ave	310-634-8692	$*	Inexpensive Tex-Mex.

Key: $: Under $10 / $$: $10–$20 / $$$: $20–$30 / $$$$: $30+   * : Does not accept credit cards. / † : Accepts only American Express.

Map 27 • El Segundo/Manhattan Beach

Name	Address	Phone	Price	Description
Cozymel's	2171 Rosecrans Ave	310-606-5464	$$*	Tex-Mex.
Houston's	1550 Rosecrans Ave	310-643-7211	$$*	Casual upscale American favorites.
Il Fornaio	1800 Rosecrans Ave	310-725-9555	$$$*	Tuscan chain.
The Spot	110 2nd St	310-376-2355	$$	Vegetarian specialties.
Uncle Bill's Pancake House	1305 Highland Ave	310-545-5177	$	Breakfast by the beach.

Map 28 • Hawthorne

Name	Address	Phone	Price	Description
Café Cabana	14605 S Prairie Ave	310-675-7323	$*	A Cuban-style deli with many tempting choices!
Chicken Madras	4850 W Rosecrans Ave	310-675-5533	$$	Good vegetarian choices and great Naan!
Daphne's	3901 Inglewood Ave	310-676-9165	$	Excellent Baklava!
Piggies	4601 W Rosecrans Ave	310-679-6326	$*	Older style Greek coffee shop.

Map 29 • Hermosa Beach

Name	Address	Phone	Price	Description
El Burrito Jr	919 Pacific Coast Hwy	310-316-5058	$*	There is always a line-up outside of this unimpressive looking stand, and with good reason—authentic Mexican food.
Havana Mania	3615 Inglewood Ave	310-725-9075	$$	Cuban cuisine at it's finest!
Hennessey's Tavern	8 Pier Ave	310-372-5759	$$	Californian favorites
Il Boccaccio	39 Pier Ave	310-376-0211	$$$*	Authentic Italian.
Le Beaujolais	522 Pacific Coast Hwy	310-543-5100	$$$	Quality French food served with a very French attitude to boot.
Martha's 22nd Street Grill	25 22nd St	301-376-7786	$$$*	American fusion.
Ragin' Cajun	422 Pier Ave	310-376-7878	$$	Blackened catfish is a favorite.
Reel Inn	2533 Pacific Coast Hwy		$$*	Fresh fish.
The Tea House	2533 Pacific Coast Hwy	310-326-5420	$$*	First-class Chinese cuisine with an International/Polynesian flair.

Map 30 • Torrance North

Name	Address	Phone	Price	Description
Flossie's Restaurant	3566 W Redondo Beach Blvd	310-352-4037	$*	The fried chicken is legendary.
Pizza Show	4567 Artesia Blvd	310-542-6966	$*	This unimpressive looking little shack turns out some fine pizza (whole or slices) and good sandwiches.

Map 31 • Redondo Beach

Name	Address	Phone	Price	Description
Bluewater Grill	665 N Harbor Dr	310-318-3474	$$	Fresh fish and seafood specialties.
Captain Kidd's	209 N Harbor Dr	310-372-7703	$$*	It's not fancy, but a complete fresh seafood dinner runs from $7.99 on up to $21.99 for a whole lobster!
Chez Melange	1716 S Pacific Coast Hwy	310-540-1222	$$$	This one has attracted many foodies from all over LA. An eclectic, continental menu.
Christine	24530 Hawthorne Blvd	310-373-1952	$$$$	Eclectic California-Mediterranean food.
Collet Tea	320 S Catalina Ave	310-372-0348	$$*	They provide the hat and feather boa, while you treat yourself to a not-so-traditional English tea.
El Torito Grill	21321 Hawthorne Blvd	310-543-1896	$$	Good food, better margaritas.
HT Grill	1710 S Catalina Ave	310-316-6658	$$*	Innovative, eclectic bistro food at reasonable prices.
Hennessey's Tavern	1712 S Catalina Ave	310-540-8443	$*	Bar food at it's finest, and yes, a great place to watch the game and drink hearty.
Splash	350 N Harbor Dr	310-798-5348	$$$	Mediterranean bistro food; interesting and creative—with a glass enclosed kitchen so that you can watch the chef at work.
The Banyan Water Garden Café	600 S Pacific Coast Hwy	310-316-0316	$*	Authentic Indonesian cuisine without having to board a plane !
The Original Pancake House	1756 S Pacific Coast Hwy	310-543-9875	$*	Come join the throngs for a weekend breakfast…bring patience (the wait can be long) and your appetite.
Zazou	1810 S Catalina Ave	310-540-4884	$$$	Mediterranian-Italian fusion.

Map 32 • Torrance South

Name	Address	Phone	Price	Description
Aioli	1261 Cabrillo Ave	310-320-9200	$$	A bistro featuring eclectic, inspired dishes from all over the globe—including a huge selection of tapas.
Beijing Islamic	3160 Pacific Coast Hwy	310-784-0846	$$*	Delicious, quality Chinese food at bargain prices.
Breadstix	1261 Cabrillo Ave	310-320-9500	$	Fresh baked breads, excellent sandwiches, salads, and other goodies.
Depot	1250 Cabrillo Ave	310-787-7501	$$$	Chef Michael Shafer's culinary creations range from Classical to ethnic to good old American and beyond.
Koji BBQ Buffet	1725 W Carson St	310-787-1820	$$	Cook your own Korean-style BBQ. There are also Japanese and Chinese specialties at this buffet-style restaurant featuring about 100 items.

Map 33 • Highland Park

Auntie Em's Kitchen	4616 Eagle Rock Blvd	323-255-0800	$	Homemade soup and chili.
Café Beaujolais	1712 Colorado Blvd	323-255-5111	$$	Dinner only.
Capri Restaurant	4604 Eagle Rock Blvd	323-257-3225	$$*	Some of the best pizzas and pastas in Eagle Rock since 1963.
Casa Bianca	1650 Colorado Blvd	323-256-9617	$$*	Italian.
Classic Thai Restaurant	1708 Colorado Blvd	323-478-0530	$$*	Yummy Thai.
Colombo's	1833 Colorado Blvd	323-254-9138	$$	Incredible Continental cuisine at reasonable prices.
Eagle Rock Italian Bakery & Deli	1726 Colorado Blvd	323-255-8224	$	Famous rum cake and amazing deli sandwiches.
El Arco Iris	5684 York Blvd	323-254-3401	$	Mexican.
El Huarache Azteca	5225 York Blvd	323-478-9572	$*	The best tacos, huaraches, tortas, and sopes in town.
Galco's	5700 York Blvd	323-255-7115	$	Only soda shop in LA.
Pete's Blue Chip	1701 Colorado Blvd	323-478-9022	$*	Diner food.
Sicha Siam	4403 Eagle Rock Blvd	323-344-8285	$$	Thai.
Villa Sombrero	6101 York Blvd	323-256-9014	$$	Mexican.

Map 34 • Pasadena

Akbar	44 N Fair Oaks Ave	626-577-9916	$$	Creative Indian cooking.
Arroyo Chop House	536 S Arroyo Pkwy	626-577-7463	$$$*	Hip, expensive steakhouse.
Burger Continental	535 S Lake Ave	626-792-6634	$*	Burgers and more.
Café Bizou	91 N Raymond Ave	626-792-9923	$$$*	BYOB French bistro.
Cafe Med	260 E Colorado Blvd	626-793-0600	$$	Reliable Italian specialties.
Celestino	141 S Lake Ave	626-795-4006	$$$*	Italian.
De Lacey's Club 41	41 S De Lacey Ave	626-795-4141	$$$	For carnivores and cocktail connoisseurs.
EuroPane	950 E Colorado Blvd	626-577-1828	$*	European bakery.
Five Sixty-One	561 E Green St	626-405-1561	$$$$	Culinary arts students show off their stuff.
Gordon Biersch	41 Hugus Alley	626-569-5240	$$*	Basic American brewpub.
Hop Li	526 Alpine St	213-680-3939	$$*	Inexpensive Chinese.
Julienne	2649 Mission St	626-441-2299	$$*	California/French/Bistro
Maison Akira	713 E Green St	626-796-9501	$$$$	Light, French-Japanese cooking.
Marston's	151 E Walnut St	626-796-2459	$$	Awesome breakfasts and traditional American dinners.
Pho 79	29 S Garfield Ave	626-289-0239	$*	Cheap Vietnamese noodle shop.
Radhika's	140 Shoppers Ln	626-744-0994	$$	Tikka Masala and live jazz.
Raymond, The	1250 S Fair Oaks Ave	626-441-3136	$$$$	Romantic, special occasion dining.
Roscoe's Chicken & Waffles	830 N Lake Ave	626-791-4890	$$*	Cheap Southern chain.
Twin Palms	101 W Green St	626-577-2567	$$$*	Hip, casual Californian.
Yujean Kang's	67 N Raymond Ave	626-585-0855	$$$*	Chinese fusion.

Map 35 • Pasadena East/San Marino

Bistro 45	45 S Mentor Ave	626-795-2478	$$$$	High-end gourmet food and wine.
Halie	1030 E Green St	626-440-7067	$$$$	Reasonably priced gourmet California-French food.
Mijas	2506 Huntington Dr	626-287-1021	$*	Everything but the tortillas are homemade.
San Marino Grill	2494 Huntington Dr	626-286-2500	$*	Retro dining experience—only breakfast and lunch.
Sushi Bar Yoshida	2026 Huntington Dr	626-281-9292	$$$	San Marino's only place for raw fish and dim sum.
Zankou Chicken	1415 E Colorado Blvd	818-244-1937	$*	Cheap Armenian chain.

Map 36 • Mt. Washington

Chico's	100 N Ave 50	323-254-2445	$	Mexican seafood.
La Abeja	3700 N Figueroa St	323-221-0474	$$	Mexican.

Map 39 • Alhambra

Angelo's Italian Restaurant	1540 W Valley Blvd	626-282-6533	$	Pizzas and lasagna.
Cuban Bistro	28 W Main St	626-308-3350	$$$	Cuban comfort food and unorthodox cocktails that would make Fidel want to defect.
Fosselman's Ice Cream Parlor	1824 W Main St	626-282-6533	$*	Treats and novelties.
MPV Seafood	1412 S Garfield Ave	626-289-3018	$$*	Seafood with an Asian twist.
Wahib's Middle East	910 E Main St	626-576-1048	$$	Very traditional Middle Eastern cooking.

Map 40 • Boyle Heights

Barbara's at the Brewery	Brewery Art Complex, 620 Moulton Ave	323-221-9204	$$	Bar food and drinks for the art crowd.
El Tepeyac	812 N Evergreen Ave	323-267-8668	$$	Burritos the size of chihuahuas.
La Parrilla	2126 E Cesar E Chavez Ave	323-262-3434	$$*	Better than average Mexican chain.
La Serenata de Garibald	1842 E 1st St	323-265-2887	$$$*	Creative Mexican seafood.

Map 42 • Reseda

Amber's Chicken Kitchen	16900 Burbank Blvd	818-995-3200	$$	Chicken! Donuts and bagels for breakfast.

Key: $: Under $10 / $$: $10–$20 / $$$: $20–$30 / $$$$: $30+ * : Does not accept credit cards. / † : Accepts only American Express.

Map 43 • Van Nuys

Dr Hogly Wogly's Tyler Texas BBQ	8136 Sepulveda Blvd	818-780-6701	$$*	Texas BBQ.
Krispy Kreme	7249 Van Nuys Blvd	818-908-9113	$*	Hot doughnut chain.
Zankou Chicken	5658 Sepulveda Blvd	818-781-0615	$*	Cheap Armenian chain.

Map 45 • Burbank

Chili John's	2108 Burbank Blvd	818-846-3611	$*	Best chili this side of the Mississippi.
Full of Life	2515 Magnolia Blvd	818-845-8343	$$	Health food store/restaurant.
Pinocchio's	3103 Magnolia Blvd	818-845-3517	$	Super-cheap, great Italian deli.
Poquito Mas	10651 Magnolia Blvd	818-994-8226	$*	Cheap, fresh Mexican chain.
Santa Fe Tacos	353 N Pass Ave	818-563-4324	$	Great, cheap Mexican.

Map 46 • Burbank East/Glendale West

Gordon Biersch Brewing	145 S San Fernando Blvd	818-569-5240	$$*	Basic American brewpub.
Market City Caffe	164 E Palm Ave	818-840-7036	$$*	Inexpensive Italian chain.
Mi Piace	801 N San Fernando Blvd	818-843-1111	$$$$*	Italian chain with outdoor tables.
Poquito Mas	2635 W Olive Ave	818-563-2252	$*	Cheap, fresh Mexican chain.
Ribs USA	2711 W Olive Ave	818-841-8872	$*	Cheap, casual BBQ.
Riverside Café	1221 W Riverside Dr	818-563-3567	$$*	Casual dining with a British flair.
Viva Fresh	900 W Riverside Dr	818-845-2425	$$	Mexican restaurant/lounge.

Map 47 • Glendale South

Blue Pyramid	1000 E Broadway	818-548-1000	$$$	Creative Mediterranean.
Cinnabar	933 S Brand Blvd	818-551-1155	$$$$	Pacific Rim cuisine in an industrial setting.
Damon's Steakhouse	317 N Brand Blvd	818-507-1510	$$	Lots of red meat and cheesy tropical drinks.

Map 48 • Encino

Bagel Nosh Deli & Restaurant	17271 Ventura Blvd	818-995-4545	$$	Bagels, sandwiches, salads, hamburgers.
Baklava Factory	17141 Ventura Blvd	818-728-1600	$	European and Eastern pastries.
Buca di Beppo	17500 Ventura Blvd	818-995-3288	$$*	Lively traditional Italian chain—dinner only.
California Wok	16656 Ventura Blvd	818-386-0561	$$	Healthy Chinese food.
Catch 21	17316 Ventura Blvd	818-789-3474	$	Seafood, chicken, ribs, salads.
Cha Cha Cha Encino	17499 Ventura Blvd	818-789-3600	$$$*	Caribbean party atmosphere.
Chili My Soul	4928 Balboa Blvd	818-981-7685	$*	Chili.
Jerry's Famous Deli	16650 Ventura Blvd	818-906-1800	$$	They serve almost everything, from pizza and pasta to Mexican, burgers, salads, and Jewish food.
Jerusalem Pizza	17942 Ventura Blvd	818-758-9595	$	Pizza!
Johnny Rockets	16901 Ventura Blvd	818-981-5900	$	
Kaiten Sushi	17302 Ventura Blvd	818-986-7003	$	Sushi.
Mulberry Street Pizza	17040 Ventura Blvd	818-906-8881	$*	Thin-crust NY-style pizza.
Versailles Restaurant	17410 Ventura Blvd	818-906-0756	$$	Cuban food.
Vittorio's Italian Cucina	17644 Ventura Blvd	818-986-9074	$$	Pasta, chicken, seafood.

Map 49 • Sherman Oaks West

California Chicken Café	15601 Ventura Blvd	818-789-8056	$*	Cheap, fresh chicken in every way.
Delmonico's Lobster House	16358 Ventura Blvd	818-986-0777	$$$	Upscale seafood.
Fuddruckers	15301 Ventura Blvd	818-995-4552	$$	Build-your-own burger joint.
Posto	14928 Ventura Blvd	818-784-4400	$$$$*	Home-style Italian.
Prego	15301 Ventura Blvd	818-905-7004	$$$	Hearty Italian dining.
Rubin's Red Hots	15322 Ventura Blvd	818-905-6515	$	Best Chicago style franks around. Classic hot dog stand.
The Weiner Factory	14917 Ventura Blvd	818-789-2676	$*	Custom-blended dogs, knockwurst, and sausage. Casual setting.

Map 50 • Sherman Oaks East

Bistro Garden at Coldwater	12950 Ventura Blvd	818-501-0202	$$$$	Long-time Studio City favorite. Take your parents!
Café Bizou	14016 Ventura Blvd	818-788-3536	$$$*	Popular French bistro.
Carnival Restaurant	4356 Woodman Ave	818-784-3469	$$	Lebanese food.
Casa Vega	13301 Ventura Blvd	818-788-4868	$$	Very popular restaurant and bar. Good food, even better margaritas.
Diwan	13045 Ventura Blvd	818-501-6015	$$	Lovely ambience. California-Continental cuisine.
Genmai	4454 Van Nuys Blvd	818-986-7060	$$	A health-food Japanese restaurant that offers some vegan choices.

Hugo's	12851 Riverside Dr	818-761-8985	$$	Neighborhood restaurant and tea house, good food.
Iroha	12953 Ventura Blvd	818-990-9559	$$$	Great sushi and ambience.
Jinky's	14120 Ventura Blvd	818-981-2250	$	Neighborhood diner known for breakfast.
Le Chine Wok	2958 Beverly Glen Cir	310-475-1146	$$*	Fancy Chinese.
Le Petit Bistro	13360 Ventura Blvd	818-501-7999	$$$$*	Busy French bistro.
Maria's Italian Kitchen	13353 Ventura Blvd	818-906-0783	$$*	Casual family Italian.
Max	13355 Ventura Blvd	818-784-2915	$$$	Eclectic California bistro menu.
Mazzarino's	12920 1/2 Riverside Dr	818-788-5050	$$*	Southern Italian pizza and more.
Mistral Brasserie	13422 Ventura Blvd	818-981-6650	$$$	French bistro with cozy atmosphere.
Mulholland Grill	2932 Beverly Glen Cir	310-470-6223	$$$*	Neighborhood Northern Italian.
Pinot Bistro	12969 Ventura Blvd	818-990-0500	$$$$$*	Creative California-French bistro.
Rive Gauche	14106 Ventura Blvd	818-990-3573	$$$	French bistro with courtyard setting.
Stanley's	13817 Ventura Blvd	818-986-4623	$$	Excellent salads, casual neighborhood restaurant and bar.
Sushi Ko	2932 1/2 Beverly Glen Cir	310-475-8689	$$	This sushi restaurant is a frequent meeting place for those looking for a halfway spot between the Valley and Hollywood.
The Great Greek	13362 Ventura Blvd	818-905-5250	$$$*	Lively, fun Greek.

Map 51 • Studio City/Valley Village

Art's Deli	12224 Ventura Blvd	818-762-1221	$*	New York-style deli.
Caioti	4346 Tujunga Ave	818-761-3588	$$*	Trendy, creative Italian.
Du-Par's	12036 Ventura Blvd	818-766-4437	$*	Cheap breakfast joint.
Firefly	11720 Ventura Blvd	818-762-1833	$$	Gourmet bistro bood in a cozy, clubby atmosphere.
Henry's Tacos	11401 Moorpark St	818-769-0343	$*	Late-night taco stand.
Katsu-ya	11680 Ventura Blvd	818-985-6976	$$$	Great sushi; gets crowded on weekends. Try the baked crab roll in soy paper.
Killer Shrimp	4000 Colfax Ave	818-508-1570	$$*	Inexpensive shrimp only.
La Loggia	11814 Ventura Blvd	818-985-9222	$$$*	Homestyle Italian.
Matsuda	11837 Ventura Blvd		$$	Yes, yet another decent mini-mall sushi experience.
Mexicali	12161 Ventura Blvd	818-985-1744	$$*	Lively California-Mexican.
Out Take Café	12159 Ventura Blvd	818-760-1111	$$	Excellent eclectic fare.
Sushi Dan Rockin' Sushi	11056 Ventura Blvd	818-985-2254	$$$	Excellent sushi on a budget. Fun atmosphere.
Sushi Nozawa	11288 Ventura Blvd	818-508-7017	$$$*	Extreme sushi storefront.
Suzanne's Country Deli	11273 Ventura Blvd	818-762-9494	$	Great salads & sandwiches—bright and cheery.
Teru Sushi	11940 Ventura blvd	818-763-6201	$$	Basic—but delicious—sushi.
Tokyo Delve's Sushi Bar	5239 Lankershim Blvd	818-766-3868	$$$	Sushi.
Vitello's	4349 Tujunga Ave	818-769-0905	$$	Traditional Italian fare, opera on weekends. Unfortunately, site of Robert Blake and Bonnie Lee Blakely's last meal together.

Map 52 • Universal City/Toluca Lake

Barsac Brasserie	4212 Lankershim Blvd	818-760-7081	$$$	French-California.
Buca di Beppo	100 Universal Center Dr	818-509-9463	$$*	Lively traditional Italian chain—dinner only.
Ca' del Sole	4100 Cahuenga Blvd	818-985-4669	$$$*	Italian with garden tables.
California Canteen	3311 Cahuenga Blvd	323-876-1702	$$$	French.
Dalt's Grill	3500 W Olive Ave	818-953-7750	$$$	American favorites.
La Scala Presto	3821 Riverside Dr	818-846-6800	$$*	Casual Italian chain.
Miceli's	3655 Cahuenga Blvd	323-851-3344	$$*	Lively, fun Italian known for its singing waiters.
Mo's	4301 Riverside Dr	818-845-3009	$$*	Hamburger haven.
Paty's	10001 Riverside Dr	818-761-0041	$$	American classics.
Priscilla's Coffee	4150 Riverside Dr	818-843-5707	$*	All sorts of coffee.
Prosecco Restaurant	10144 Riverside Dr	818-505-0930	$$$	Northern Italian.
Roma Via Paris	3413 Cahuenga Blvd	323-882-6965	$$$	French.
Smoke House Restaurant	4420 W Lakeside Dr	323-849-3641	$$$	Steakhouse.
Versailles	100 Universal Center Dr	818-505-0093	$$*	Cheap Cuban fast-food chain.
Wolfgang Puck Café	100 Universal Center Dr	818-985-9653	$$*	Casual California chic.
Yamakawa	10118 Riverside Dr	818-763-8355	$$$	Across the board Japanese.

Map 1 • Beverly Hills

Caviarteria	158 S Beverly Dr	310-285-9773	Caviar and other gourmet specialties.
Cheese Store of Beverly Hills	419 N Beverly Dr	310-278-2855	High-quality cheese, even better olives.
Fishland	9150 W Olympic Blvd	310-271-2553	Restaurant-quality seafood at take-home prices.
Mrs Beasley's/Miss Grace Lemon Cake Co	255 1/2 S Beverly Dr	310-281-8096	How most Hollywood assistants' holiday weight is gained.

Map 2 • West Hollywood

Book Soup	8818 Sunset Blvd	310-659-3110	One of LA's coolest bookstores.
Button Store	8344 W 3rd St	323-658-5473	Every button you could possibly need.
Centerfold Newsstand	716 N Fairfax Ave	323-651-4822	A terrific selection of magazines and papers.
Chado Tea Room	8422 1/2 W 3rd St	323-655-2056	Where tea lovers go when they die.
Chateau Marmutt	8128 W 3rd St	323-653-2062	If you love your pet—and money is no object.
Denim Doctor	8044 W 3rd St	323-852-0171	They'll sell you vintage jeans or fix the ones you've already got.
Fred Segal	8100 Melrose Ave	323-651-4129	The place to shop in LA for trendy clothes and accessories.
Golden Apple	7711 Melrose Ave	323-658-6047	Shangri-la for comic book lovers.
Guitar Center	7425 Sunset Blvd	323-874-1060	Their walk of fame alone is worth the trip.
I Martin	8330 Beverly Blvd	323-653-6900	They cater to both serious racers and the training wheels crowd.
Illume	8302 W 3rd St	800-245-5863	High-end candles in a variety of divine scents and sizes.
Kbond	7257 Beverly Blvd	323-939-8866	Men's clothes. Would you expect any less than cool from a store by a man named James Bond?
Malia Mills	7972 Melrose Ave	323-655-4709	They take all of the trauma out of buying a bathing suit.
Mani's Bakery	519 S Fairfax Ave	323-938-8800	Desserts so delicious you'll never know they're sweetened with fruit juice.
Mr Marcel's	6333 W 3rd St (Farmers Market)	323-935-9451	Gourmet French cheeses and wine bar.
Plastica	8405 W 3rd St	323-655-1051	All things trendy and plastic.
Pleasure Chest	7733 Santa Monica Blvd	323-650-1022	Popular sex shop with something for everyone, in a discreet setting.
Pulp	456 S La Brea Ave	323-937-3506	For people who still write letters (or wish they did).
Restoration Hardware	131 N La Cienega Blvd	310-360-9651	
Sam Ash Music	8000 Sunset Blvd	323-654-4922	Like the nearby Guitar Center, but far less intimidating.
Samy's Camera	431 S Fairfax Ave	323-938-4400	The only place to go to for cameras in LA.
Solomon's	447 N Fairfax Ave	323-653-9045	Everything from seder plates to menorahs.
Soolip	8646 Melrose Ave	310-360-0545	Cards, wrapping paper, and gifts you'd like to give to yourself.
Splash Bath & Body	8934 Santa Monica Blvd	310-657-7627	Their soaps and bath bombs turn your tub into your own personal spa.
Storyopolis	116 N Robertson Blvd	310-358-2500	You can get lost in here for hours amidst the Dr. Seuss and Maurice Sendak.
The Cook's Library	8373 W 3rd St	310-665-3141	Books on food for amateur chefs and professional eaters.
Trashy Lingerie	402 La Cienega Blvd	310-652-4543	Trashy, but they also sell high-quality custom-fitted lingerie.
Traveler's Bookcase	8375 W 3rd St	310-665-0575	A must-visit before any trip.
Zipper	8316 W 3rd St	323-662-9463	Upscale gifts and funky home furnishings.

Map 3 • Hollywood

Amoeba Music	6400 Sunset Blvd	310-245-6400	The largest used records store in LA.
Blest Boutique	1634 Cahuenga Blvd	323-467-0180	Hip clothing boutique with punk/alternative fashion at prices ranging from "That's it?!" to "That's not too bad!"
Cahuenga World News	1652 N Cahuenga Blvd	323-465-4357	If this place doesn't carry it, chances are it's not in circulation.
Conservatory Florist	1900 N Highland Ave	323-851-6290	Gorgeous, minimalist floral creations.
Definitive Music	1628 N Cahuenga Blvd	323-728-4345	Hard-to-find DJ beats and house music.
Hollywood Hills Beauty Center and Spa	1915 N Highland Ave	323-874-5159	Deceptively large, unassuming spot offers cheap good massages.
Larry Edmunds Cinema and Theater Bookshop	6644 Hollywood Blvd	323-463-3273	Need to find a movie still from the 30s? It's here.
Ray the Retoucher	1330 N Highland Ave	323-463-0555	Headshot help.
Vine American Party Store	5969 Melrose Ave	323-467-7124	Decorations and party favors for parties from New Year's to Hannukah.

Map 4 • Los Feliz

Eastside Records	1813 Hillhurst Ave	323-913-7461	Lots of used vinyl, hard-to-find music.
LS	2120 Hillhurst Ave		One-of-a-kind necklaces, bracelets, and earrings made of eclectic gemstones.
Naturemart & Bulk Bin	2080 Hillhurst Ave	323-667-1677	Neighborhood health food store.
Squaresville	1800 N Vermont Ave	323-669-8464	An awesome collection of vintage clothing, including high-end labels like Gucci and Pucci.
Uncle Jer's	4459 W Sunset Blvd	323-662-6710	They sell everything from funky clothes to incense.
Wacko	4633 Hollywood Blvd	323-663-0122	Every kind of book, tchotchkes, "party favors," and obscure tee.

Map 5 • Silver Lake/Echo Park/Atwater

Rockaway Records	2395 Glendale Blvd	323-664-3232	5000 square feet of used vinyl and CDs.

Map 6 • Miracle Mile/Mid-City

Ace Gallery	5514 Wilshire Blvd	323-935-4411	Established in 1940, this up-and-down gallery showcases mostly local Los Angeles artists.
Albertson Wedding Chapel	5318 Wilshire Blvd	323-937-4919	Wanna get married *now*? Civil and Catholic services available.
Bang a Drum	1255 S La Brea Ave	800-495-1109	Hand drums, from Native American to Middle Eastern.
City Spa	5325 Pico Blvd	323-933-5954	Body wraps, massages, and steam rooms galore.
Feldmar Watch	9000 W Pico Blvd	310-272-1196	From Timex to Rolex, they've got it all.
Hansen's Cakes	1072 S Fairfax Ave	323-936-4332	Wedding cake central & imaginative birthday creations.
Kitson	115 S Robertson Blvd	310-859-2652	It's the place to shop for the person who has everything.
Marinello Beauty School	6111 Wilshire Blvd	323-938-2005	A full-service beauty school with facials at half the going rate.
Miauhaus	1201 S La Brea Ave	323-933-6150	Art gallery spotlighting emerging and contemporary artists.
Oh My Nappy Hair!	805 S La Brea Ave	323-939-3999	Specializes in braids, locks, and extensions.
Up Health Merchants	1017 S Fairfax Ave	323-935-3020	Vitamins, holistic remedies, and all that crunchy granola head stuff.

Map 7 • Hancock Park

Landis Department Store	138 N Larchmont Blvd	323-465-7998	A little bit of EVERTHING. The stationary department is especially good.
Larchmont Beauty Center	208 N Larchmont Blvd	323-466-6859	Arguably the best beauty supply store in the city.
Larchmont News Stand	230 N Larchmont Blvd		Good selection of newspapers and magazines.

Map 9 • Downtown

7 + Fig at Ernst & Young Plaza	735 S Figueroa St	213-955-7150	Downtown's only real shopping mall.
California Market Center	110 E 9th St	866-746-7262	Gift and home accent showrooms, as well as nine restaurants.
LA Flower Market	766 Wall St	213-622-1966	Say it with flowers—cheaply.
Moskatel's	738 S Wall St	213-689-4590	They carry everything you need for a party. Except for the guests.
Santee Alley	Between Santee and Maple, from 12th St to Olympic Blvd		The perfect place to find convincing "Kate Spate" or "Prado" handbags.
Thomas Bros Map Store	521 W 6th St	213-627-4018	Place to pick up the latest edition of the Thomas Guide.

Map 10 • Baldwin Hills

Graphaids	3030 S La Cienega Blvd	310-204-1212	If you're not an artist, this store will make you wish you were.

Map 15 • Pacific Palisades

Benton's Sporting Goods	1038 Swarthmore Ave	310-459-8451	Beach clothing and equipment.
Gelson's Market	15424 Sunset Blvd	310-459-4483	Fancy groceries.
Gift Garden Antiques	15266 Antioch St	310-459-4114	Fine gifts.
Ivy Greene for Kids	1020 Swarthmore Ave	310-230-0301	Kids' clothes.
Palisades Playthings	1041 Swarthmore Ave	310-454-8648	Toy store.
The Prince's Table	1051 Swarthmore Ave	310-573-3667	Gifts.
Village Book	1049 Swarthmore Ave	310-454-4063	Books.
Vivian's Boutique	970 Monument St	310-573-1326	Clothing.
Whispers	1013 Swarthmore Ave	310-454-5581	Women's clothing.
Yamato Nursery	15236 La Cruz Dr	310-454-1224	Fancy flora and fauna.

Map 16 • Brentwood

Dutton's Brentwood Books	11975 San Vicente Blvd	310-476-6263	Fantastic collection of books, outdoor reading area.
Falconhead	11911 San Vicente Blvd	310-471-7075	Cowboy's one-stop boots, buckles, and belts.
Maison Sud	11677 San Vicente Blvd	310-207-5669	French provincial accessories.
PJ London	11661 San Vicente Blvd	310-826-4649	Women's fashions, mostly resale.
Porta Bella	11711 Gorham Ave	310-820-2550	Antique wood furniture—armchairs to armoirs.
Terra Cotta	11922 San Vicente Blvd	310-826-7878	Furniture in warm earthen colors.
Whole Foods Market	11737 San Vicente Blvd	310-826-4433	Fresh produce and groceries—Brentwood's hippie corner.

Map 18 • Santa Monica

Acorn Store	1220 5th St		Unique toy store, handmade dolls and puppets.
Continental Shop	1619 Wilshire Blvd	310-453-8655	One stop shopping for everything from AbFab tapes to tea cozies.
Eames Office	2665 Main St	310-396-5991	Who'd think that a desk chair could be fun?
Hear Music	1429 3rd St Promenade	310-319-9527	Knowledgable staff that lets you listen before you buy.
Helen's Cycles	2501 Broadway	310-829-1836	Bikes sold by people who know what they're talking about.
Herb King	2305 Main St	310-399-4470	One stop for herbs and homeopathic remedies.
Horizons West	2011 Main St	310-392-1122	Everything for the surf-and-skate crowd.
Midnight Special Bookstore	1318 3rd St Promenade	310-393-2923	Get lost for hours reading about any and everything.

Map 18 • Santa Monica — continued

Muskrat	1248 3rd St Promenade	310-394-1713	Vintage clothing—poodle skirts to denim shirts.
Noteworthy	1427 3rd St Promenade	310-260-9004	Classy cards and quirky gifts.
Number One Beauty Supply	1426 Montana Ave	310-394-6968	A high-end Montana Ave selection at un-Montana Ave prices.
One Life Natural Foods	3001 Main St	310-392-4501	Produce, groceries, herbs, everything organic.
Palmetto	1034 Montana Ave	310-395-6687	Bath supplies, soap, natural beauty products.
Pump Station	2415 Wilshire Blvd	310-826-5774	Where new mothers turn for helpful advice and swell baby products.
Puzzle Zoo	1413 3rd St Promenade	310-393-9201	Toy store caters to the sci-fi geek and child within us all.
Santa Monica Farms	2015 Main St	310-396-4069	Organic produce, groceries, juices, sandwiches to go.
Splash Bath & Body	2823 Main St	310-581-4200	Creatively scented soaps and bath goods that are fun to use.
Tao Healing Arts Center	2309 Main St	310-396-4877	Learn to give a massage or just have one yourself.
Tudor House	1403 2nd St	310-451-4107	British souvenirs and afternoon tea.

Map 19 • West LA/Santa Monica East

Any Occasion Balloons	12009 W Pico Blvd	310-473-9963	Every size balloon, in every shape and color imaginable.
California Map & Travel	3312 Pico Blvd		Great map warehouse.
Graphaids	12400 Santa Monica Blvd	310-820-0445	They appeal to both serious artists and doodlers.
Hiromi Paper International	Bergamot Station, 2525 Michigan Ave	310-998-0098	Handcrafted paper so gorgeous you won't want to write on it.
McCabe's Guitar Shop	3001 Pico Blvd	310-828-4427	Geared more toward the fledgling Bob Dylan than Eddie Van Halen.
Record Surplus	11609 W Pico Blvd	310-478-4217	No glitz, no pizzazz. For serious music lovers only.

Map 20 • Westwood/Century City

Bristol Farms	1537 Westwood Blvd	310-481-0100	Upscale grocery. Newest and biggest of it's kind.
Restoration Hardware	10250 Santa Monica Blvd	310-551-4995	
Rhino Records	2028 Westwood Blvd	310-474-8685	Unique new and used record store. Don't miss the parking lot sales.
The Writer's Store	2040 Westwood Blvd	310-441-5151	Seminars, books, and computer software for writing.
Three Dog Bakery	10250 Santa Monica Blvd	310-557-1254	Doggie "pastries" that you may want to eat yourself.

Map 21 • Venice

Johnny B Wood	1409 Abbot Kinney Blvd	310-314-1945	Vintage and collectible furniture.
Samy's Camera	585 Venice Blvd	310-450-4551	The only place to go to for cameras in LA.
The Starting Line	114 Washington Blvd	310-827-3035	If you are a serious walker or runner, this place is for you. Super-smart staff is very service-oriented.
Venice Bike & Skate	21 Washington Blvd	310-301-4011	Rentals.

Map 22 • Mar Vista

Prebica Coffee	4325 Glencoe Ave	310-823-4446	They mainly supply fine restaurants, but here they can supply you.
Record Rover	12204 Venice Blvd	310-390-3132	Extremely knowledgable staff and reasonably priced.
The Los Angeles Wine Company	4935 McConnell Ave	310-306-9463	Stemware, gift bags, and wine accessories, too.

Map 23 • Rancho Park/Palms

Adventure 16	11161 Pico Blvd	310-473-4574	Camping supplies that make city slickers want to commune with nature.
Delmarus Lox	9340 W Pico Blvd	310-273-3004	If only LA had a bagel that measured up to their lox.

Map 24 • Culver City

Allied Model Trains	4411 Sepulveda Blvd	310-313-9353	It's so much more than just Lionel.
Civilization	8884 Venice Blvd	310-202-8883	Trendy and offbeat furniture that manages to look homey.
Culver City Home Brewing Supply	4358 1/2 Sepulveda Blvd	310-397-3453	Literally everything you need to brew beer.
Dovetail	8918 Venice Blvd	310-559-9431	Solid pine furniture for every room of your house.
Surfas	8825 National Blvd	310-559-4770	For those who own a restaurant or just wish they did.

Map 27 • El Segundo/Manhattan Beach

GeoDecor	113 Shelton St	310-322-4043	Fossils. This unusual store is open only by appointment.

Map 29 • Hermosa Beach

Splash Bath & Body	132 Pier Ave	310-376-7270	Fizzy bath boms, funky soaps, and rubber duckies.

Map 31 • Redondo Beach

Cookin Stuff	22217 Palos Verdes Blvd	310-371-2220	Possibly the largest selection of cooking supplies for the layperson in all of LA County.
Lindbergh Nutrition	3804 Sepulveda Blvd		A mecca for bodybuilders and others wishing to "keep in the pink."

Map 33 • Highland Park

Country Pickin's	2477 Colorado Blvd	323-256-8132	Some of the freshest and ripest produce Eagle Rock has to offer.
Galco's Soda Pop Stop	5702 York Blvd	323-255-7115	Who knew there were so many different brands of root beer?

Map 34 • Pasadena

Paperwhites	956 Mission St	626-441-2196	Packaged cards, as well as custom invitations and announcements.
Three Dog Bakery	24 Smith Alley	626-440-0443	Fancy biscuits you'd be proud to offer man's best friend.

Map 43 • Van Nuys

The Plant	7800 Van Nuys Blvd		

Map 45 • Burbank

Arte de Mexico	5356 Riverton Ave	818-769-5090	Furniture and crafts with a Mexican flair.
Atomic Records	3812 W Magnolia Blvd	818-848-7090	Used records. An eclectic inventory at reasonable prices.
Fry's	2311 N Hollywood Way	818-526-8100	Huge electronics store with a B-movie, spaceship-themed exterior.
It's a Wrap	3315 W Magnolia Blvd	818-567-7366	Clothes previously worn by your favorite TV stars.
Lady Peter's Whimsey	2922 W Magnolia Blvd	818-842-1947	Eclectic antiques.
Pinocchio's	3103 Magnolia Blvd	818-845-3517	Authentic Italian market.
The Train Shack	1030 Hollywood Way	818-842-3330	Fun model train store.

Map 46 • Burbank East/Glendale West

Book City	308 N San Fernando Blvd	818-848-4417	Hollywood-oriented books.
Creature Features	1802 W Olive Ave	818-842-9383	Unique comic book store; specializing in B-movie/horror.
Pickwick Center	1001 Riverside Dr	818-845-5300	Bowling alley, ice rink, often hosts antique or art fairs.
Valley Dealer Exchange	825 N Victory Blvd	818-767-1800	One of the most painless used car-buying experiences you will ever have.

Map 48 • Encino

A Rodin Art	17015 Ventura Blvd	818-396-9148	Bronze statues, paintings.
Antik Shop	4909 Genesta Ave	818-990-5990	Funky antiques.
Encino Newsstand	16720 Ventura Blvd		Foreign and domestic mags.
Encino Park & Community Center Map	4900 Genesta Ave	818-995-1690	Playground, picnic tables, tennis courts, grass, and trees.
Herbalogics	17200 Ventura Blvd	818-990-9990	Herb store and acupuncture.
Hopscotch	16740 Ventura Blvd		Kids' clothing.
Ragg Tatoo	17245 Ventura Blvd	818-990-7244	Funky clothing.
Sneaker Warehouse	16736 Ventura Blvd	818-995-8999	Shoes galore!

Map 49 • Sherman Oaks West

Sherman Oaks Castle Park	4899 Sepulveda Blvd	818-756-9459	Excellent batting cages and miniature golf.
Tower Records-Video-Books	15301 Ventura Blvd	818-995-7373	Giant music store.

Map 50 • Sherman Oaks East

Baxter Northrup Music	14534 Ventura Blvd	323-872-0756	Great selection of sheet music. Also instrument sales.
Doll Shoppe	13300 Riverside Dr	818-784-3655	A leading source for dolls, miniatures and doll houses, as well as a "doll hospital."
Juvenile Shop	13356 Ventura Blvd	818-986-6214	A civilized alternative to Babies R Us.
Mark's Garden	13838 Ventura Blvd	818-906-1718	Florist.
Pajama Party	14006 Riverside Dr	818-788-2470	Pajamas. Some are sexy, some are comfy.
Pink Cheeks	14562 Ventura Blvd	818-906-8225	Spa. Claims to have invented the famous "playboy" bikini wax.
Second Spin Records	14564 Ventura Blvd	818-986-6866	Reasonably priced used CDs.
Vera's Retreat	2980 Beverly Glen Cir	310-440-6362	Well known day spa frequented by ladies who lunch, as well as celebrities.
Western Bagel	12930 Ventura Blvd	818-567-0413	Local favorite.

Map 51 • Studio City/Valley Village

Dari	12184 Ventura Blvd	818-762-3274	One of the Valley's outposts for trendy women's clothes.
Dovetail	12336 Ventura Blvd	818-752-6531	Sturdy pine furniture made to order.
Iliad Bookstore	4820 Vineland Ave	818-509-2665	Used and new books; specializing in literature and art.
La Knitterie Parisienne	12642 Ventura Blvd	818-766-1515	The best knitting store around.
Marie et Cie	11704 Riverside Dr	818-508-5049	Coffee, home furnishings, and gifts all in one.
Studio City Camera Exchange	12174 Ventura Blvd	818-762-4749	Great local camera store. Very knowledgeable staff.

Map 52 • Universal City/Toluca Lake

Cinema Secrets Beauty Supply	4400 W Riverside Dr	818-846-0579	Fabulous selection, including film makeup.
Geographia Map & Book Store	4000 W Riverside Dr	818-848-1414	This is an amazing travel store. They have thought of everything.
Pergolina	10139 Riverside Dr	818-508-7708	Gifts and items for home.
Steel Casey	10624 Ventura Blvd	818-763-5667	Popular seller of retro office furniture.

Do not miss an opportunity to go to the Mark Taper Forum and the Geffen Playhouse. *The Lion King* will play at the Pantages Theater long after the polar ice caps melt. But Los Angeles supports literally dozens of theater companies, many of which are represented in the annual Edge of the World Theater Festival held each November. Be sure to check out productions by A Noise Within, the Actor's Gang, and the Open Fist Theater.

Theater	Address	Phone	Map
18th Street Art Complex	1629 18th St	310-829-9789	18
2100 Square Feet	5615 San Vicente Blvd	323-936-6818	6
24th Street Theatre	1117 W 24th St	323-667-0417	11
A Noise Within	5151 State University Dr	323-224-6420	38
ASK Theater Projects	11845 W Olympic Blvd	310-478-9275	19
ACME Comedy Theater	135 N La Brea Ave	323-525-0202	2
Actor Workspace	5654 Cahuenga Blvd	818-505-9154	45
Actor's Gang	6201 Santa Monica Blvd	323-465-0566	3
Actors Art Theatre	6128 Wilshire Blvd	323-969-4953	6
Actors Circle Theater	7313 Santa Monica Blvd	323-882-8043	2
Actors Workout Studio	4735 Lankershim Blvd	323-225-9924	51
Ahmason Theater	135 S Grand Ave	213-628-2772	34
Alex Theatre	216 N Brand Blvd	818-243-2539	47
Alliance Theatre	3204 W Magnolia Blvd	818-566-7935	45
Alterknit Lounge	7021 Hollywood Blvd	323-463-0204	3
Ambassador Auditorium	300 E Green St	626-304-6106	34
American Renegade Theater	11136 Magnolia Blvd	818-506-7550	51
Attic Theatre Ctr	8663 Chalmers Dr	323-462-9720	6
Back Parlor Theater	4378 Lankershim Blvd	818-752-3786	52
Bang Improv Studio	457 N Fairfax Ave	323-653-6886	2
Beverly Garland Theater	4222 Vineland Ave	213-683-3422	51
Beverly Hills Playhouse	254 S Robertson Blvd	310-855-1556	6
Black Box	12420 Santa Monica Blvd	310-979-7078	19
Black Dahlia Theatre	5453 W Pico Blvd	323-525-0070	6
Blank Theatre Company	6500 Santa Monica Blvd	323-662-7734	3
Brick Box	1608 Cosmo St	323-461-7300	3
Calabas Actors' Space	25000 W Mureau Rd	818-705-2690	
Candlefish Theatre Company	1540 Cahuenga Blvd	323-460-2080	3
Canon Theatre Box Office	205 N Canon Dr	310-859-2830	1
Cara a Cara Theater	4534 Fountain Ave	323-669-3970	4
Cast Theatre	804 N El Centro Ave	323-957-2343	3
Celebration Theater	7051 Santa Monica Blvd	323-957-1884	3
Center Theater	300 E Ocean Blvd	562-436-4610	
Century City Playhouse	10508 W Pico Blvd	310-204-4440	23
Chandler Studio	12443 Chandler Blvd	818-786-1045	51
Chesley Playhouse	5131 Chesley Ave	323-293-3138	11
City Garage	1340 1/2 4th St	310-319-9939	18
Civic Light Opera of South Bay	2226 Artesia Blvd	310-372-4477	29
Civic Light Opera-South Bay	710 Pier Ave	310-379-1979	29
Coast Playhouse	8325 Santa Monica Blvd	800-595-4849	2
Coleman Smith Artistic Co	6448 Santa Monica Blvd	323-467-6057	3
Colony Studio Theatre	1944 Riverside Dr	323-665-3011	5
Colony Theatre Co Data Line	555 N 3rd St	818-558-7118	46
Company of Angels Theater	2106 Hyperion Ave	323-883-1717	5
Complex East Theater	6468 Santa Monica Blvd	818-508-8253	3
Coronet Theatre	366 N La Cienega Blvd	310-657-7377	2
Court Theatre	722 N La Cienega Blvd	310-652-4035	2
Deaf West Theatre	5112 Lankershim Blvd	818-762-2998	51
Dorie Theater	6474 Santa Monica Blvd	310-358-2969	3
Ebell Theatre	4401 W 8th St	323-939-0126	7
Edgewater Entertainment	1925 Century Park E	310-226-6757	20
Egyptian Arena Theater	1625 N Las Palmas Ave	323-960-4441	3
Electric Lodge	1416 Electric Ave	310-281-6299	21
Elephant Asylum Theater	6320 Santa Monica Blvd	877-642-0227	3
Elephant Performance Lab	1078 N Lilian Way	310-250-7279	3
Elephant Theater	6322 Santa Monica Blvd	323-769-5842	3
Falcon Theatre Box Office	4252 W Riverside Dr	818-955-8101	52
Fine Arts Theatre	8556 Wilshire Blvd	310-652-1330	6
Fountain Theater	5060 Fountain Ave	323-663-1525	4
Frida Kahlo Theater	2332 W 4th St	213-382-8133	8
Gascon Center Theatre Live	8737 Washington Blvd	310-204-3126	24
Geffen Playhouse	10886 Le Conte Ave	310-208-5454	20
Gene Bua Acting for Life Theatre	3435 W Magnolia Blvd	818-547-3268	45
Gene Bua Theater	3435 W Magnolia Blvd	818-628-0688	45
Glendale Center Theatre	324 N Orange St	818-244-8481	47
Globe Theatre	1107 N Kings Rd	323-654-5623	2
Greenway Arts Alliance	544 N Fairfax Ave	323-655-4402	2
Groundling Theater	7307 Melrose Ave	323-934-9700	2
Henri Fonda Theatre	6126 Hollywood Blvd	213-365-3500	3
Highways	1651 18th St	310-453-1755	18
Hollywood Court Theatre	6537 Santa Monica Blvd	310-289-2999	3
Hudson Avenue Theater	6539 Santa Monica Blvd	323-769-5858	3
Hudson Guild Theater	6543 Santa Monica Blvd	323-960-7774	3
Imagination Co	318 Lincoln Blvd	310-392-4911	21
Improv Olympic West	6366 Hollywood Blvd	323-962-7560	3
Inglewood Playhouse	740 Warren Lane	323-962-7560	13
Iranian Performing Arts Ctr	10508 W Pico Blvd	310-204-5959	23
Ivar Theatre	1605 Ivar Ave	323-461-7300	3
Jewel Box Theatre Center	1951 Cahuenga Blvd	323-469-4343	3
Knightsbridge Theatre	35 S Raymond Ave	626-440-0821	34

Theater	Address	Phone	Map
LA Jewish Theater	1528 Gordon St	310-967-1352	3
LA Repertory Company	6560 Hollywood Blvd	323-769-5794	3
Lehman Engel Musical Theatre	335 N Brand Blvd	818-502-3309	47
Lex Theater	6760 Lexington Ave	323-957-5782	3
Lilian Theater	1076 Lilian Way	323-816-0002	3
Magicopolis	1418 4th St	310-451-2241	18
Malibu Stage	29243 Pacific Coast Hwy	310-589-1998	
Mark Taper Forum	135 N Grand Ave	213-628-2772	9
Masquer's Cabaret	8334 W 3rd St	323-653-4848	2
McCadden Theater	1157 N McCadden Pl	323-860-6503	3
Met Theatre	1089 N Oxford Ave	323-957-1152	4
Mexican Cultural Institute	125 Paseo De La Plz	213-624-3660	9
Miracle Theater	226 S Market St	310-671-4665	13
Morgan-Wixxon Theatre	2627 Pico Blvd	310-828-7519	19
Moving Arts	514 S Spring St	213-622-8906	9
National Comedy Theater	733 Seward St	323-856-4796	3
New Attic Studios	5429 W Washington Blvd	310-470-3560	6
Next Stage Theatre	1523 N La Brea Ave	213-444-6621	2
Odyssey Theatre Ensemble	2055 S Sepulveda Blvd	310-477-2055	19
Open Fist Theatre Co	1625 N La Brea Ave	323-882-6912	2
Open Stage West	14366 Ventura Blvd	818-206-4000	50
PAC Theatre	1108 Seward St	323-957-9556	3
Pacific Resident Theatre	705 1/2 Venice Blvd	310-306-3943	9
Palm Canyon Theatre	538 N Palm Canyon Dr	760-323-5123	
Pantages Theater	6233 Hollywood Blvd	213-365-3500	3
Pasadena Center	300 E Green St	626-793-2122	34
Pasadena Playhouse State Theater	39 S El Molino Ave	626-792-8672	34
Playhouse West School and Repertory Theater	4250 Lankershim Blvd	818-971-7191	52
Playhouse West Studio	10634 Magnolia Blvd	818-955-7013	45
Playwright Kitchen	366 N La Cienega Blvd	310-652-9602	2
Powerhouse Theater	3116 2nd St	310-396-3680	18
Rachel Rosenthal Co	2847 S Robertson Blvd	310-839-0661	23
Redondo Beach Performing Arts	1935 Manhattan Beach Blvd	310-318-0644	27
Robert Frost Performing Arts Center	4401 Elenda St	310-839-6800	24
Robert Stein Group	12178 Ventura Blvd	818-766-0660	51
Rose Theater	318 Lincoln Blvd	310-392-6963	21
Ruby Theatre Complex	6476 Santa Monica Blvd	323-960-4330	3
Saint Genesius Theatre	1047 N Havenhurst	310-285-4646	
Santa Monica Playhouse & Group	1211 4th St	310-394-9779	18
Second City Studio Theater	8156 Melrose Ave	310-372-4477	2
Secret Rose Theater	11246 Magnolia Blvd	818-766-3691	51
Shakespeare Festival LA	1238 W 1st St	213-481-2273	9
Sidewalk Studio Theater	4150 Riverside Dr	818-846-3403	52
Sierra Stage	1444 N Sierra Bonita Ave	323-932-1161	
Skirball Cultural Center	2701 N Sepulveda Blvd	310-440-4500	49
Skylight Theatre	1816 N Vermont Blvd	310-855-1556	4
Stage 52	5299 W Washington Blvd	213-480-3232	6
Steam Salon	314 N Harper Ave	323-822-1170	2
Stella Adler Theater	6773 Hollywood Blvd	323-465-4446	3
Taber Theatre	4301 N Cahuenga Blvd	818-508-7084	52
Tamarind Theater	5919 Franklin Ave	323-692-9455	3
The Company Rep	5269 Lankershim Blvd	818-508-4200	51
The Complex	6470 Santa Monica Blvd	323-668-0071	3
The Evidence Room Theater	2220 Beverly Blvd	213-381-7118	9
The Ford	2580 Cahuenga Blvd	323-314-6332	3
Theater of NOTE	1517 Cahuenga Blvd	323-856-8611	3
Theatre 150	918 E Ojai Ave	805-646-4300	
Theatre 40	241 S Moreno Dr	310-556-9040	20
Theatre Palisades	941 Temescal Canyon Rd	310-454-1970	15
Theatre / Theater	6425 Hollywood Blvd	323-937-6911	3
Third Stage	2811 W Magnolia Blvd	818-842-4755	45
Third Street Theatre	8140 W 3rd St	323-852-0615	2
Tiffany Theaters Box Office	8532 W Sunset Blvd	310-289-2999	2
Torrance Cultural Arts Ctr	3330 Civic Center Dr N	310-781-7150	30
Tracy Roberts Theatre	12265 Ventura Blvd	818-623-9500	51
Victory Theatres	3326 W Victory Blvd	818-843-9253	45
We Tell Stories	2100 Panamint Dr	323-256-2336	36
West Coast Ensemble	3151 Cahuenga Blvd	323-876-9337	52
Westchester Playhouse	8301 Hindry Ave	310-645-5156	26
Westwood Playhouse	10886 Le Conte Ave	310-208-5454	20
Whitmore Lindley Theatre Ctr	11006 Magnolia Blvd	818-761-0704	51
Working Stage	1516 N Gardner St	323-851-2603	2
Zephyr Theater	7456 Melrose Ave	323-871-0750	2
ZJU Theater Group	4850 Lankershim Blvd	818-202-4120	51
Zoo Theater	1611 N Cahuenga Blvd	323-460-4233	3

Must go: with its stadium seating and good coffee, the Laemmle Playhouse 7 in Pasadena is your best bet for indie and foreign film-going. The Egyptian (home of the American Cinematheque) programs for true cinephiles. Every weekend, LACMA screens rare and classic gems. The New Beverly is a classic, old-school rep house. For classic, restored movie palaces, hit the Vista and El Capitan. Must miss: stay away from the Beverly Center, the Hollywood Galaxy, and the Beverly Connection Cinemas.

Theater	Address		Map
Academy 6	1003 E Colorado Blvd	626-229-9400	35
Aero Theatre	1328 Montana Ave	310-395-4990	18
AMC Avco Center Cinemas	10840 Wilshire Blvd	310-475-0711	20
AMC Beverly Connection	100 N La Cienega Blvd		2
AMC Burbank 14 Theatres	140 E Palm Ave	818-953-9800	46
AMC Center Cinema	501 N Orange St	818-549-9950	47
AMC Century 14	10250 Santa Monica Blvd	310-553-8900	20
AMC Galleria-South Bay Cinema 16	1815 Hawthorne Blvd	310-793-7477	30
AMC Hollywood Galaxy Cinema	7021 Hollywood Blvd	323-957-9246	3
AMC Old Pasadena 8	42 Miller Alley	626-585-8900	34
AMC Santa Monica 7 Plex	1310 3rd St Promenade	310-395-3030	18
Broadway Cinemas 4	1441 3rd St Promenade	310-458-3924	18
California Science Center IMAX	700 State Dr	213-748-6321	11
Cecchi Gori Fine Arts Theatre	8556 Wilshire Blvd		6
Century 8 Theatres	12827 Victory Blvd	818-508-6004	44
Century Plaza Cinemas 4	2040 Ave of the Stars	310-553-4291	20
Cineplex Odeon	100 Universal City Plz	818-508-0588	52
Edwards Atlantic Cinemas	700 W Main St	626-458-8663	39
Egyptian Theater	6712 Hollywood Blvd	323-466-3456	3
El Capitan	6838 Hollywood Blvd		3
Flagship University Village 3	3323 S Hoover St	213-748-6321	12
Galleria Stadium	15301 Ventura Blvd		49
Grauman's Chinese Theatre	6925 Hollywood Blvd	323-464-6266	3
Highland Theater	50604 N Figueroa St	323-256-6383	33
Laemmle Fairfax	7907 Beverly Blvd	323-653-3117	2
Laemmle Music Hall Theatre	9036 Wilshire Blvd	310-274-6869	6
Laemmle Playhouse 7	673 E Colorado Blvd	626-844-6500	34
Laemmle Sunset 5 Theatres	8000 W Sunset Blvd	323-848-3500	2
Laemmle Theatres	11523 Santa Monica Blvd	310-478-1041	19
Laemmle Grande	349 S Figueroa St	213-617-0268	9
Laemmle Monica 4	1332 2nd St	310-394-9741	18
Landmark Regent Theatre	1045 Broxton Ave	310-208-3259	20
Leammle Royal Theatre	11523 Santa Monica Blvd	310-477-5581	19
Loews Beverly Center 13	8522 Beverly Blvd	310-652-7760	2
Los Feliz 3 Theater	1822 N Vermont Ave	323-668-9004	4
Magic Johnson Theatre 15	4020 Marlton Ave	323-290-5900	10
Majestic Crest Theatre	1262 Westwood Blvd	310-474-7866	20
Mann 4 Glendale Marketplace	144 S Brand Blvd	818-241-2784	47
Mann Bruin	948 Broxton Ave	310-208-8998	20
Mann Chinese 6	6801 Hollywood Blvd		3
Mann Criterion 6	1313 3rd St Promenade	310-395-1599	18
Mann Culver Plaza Six	9919 Washington Blvd	310-841-2993	24
Mann Exchange 10	128 N Maryland Ave	818-549-0045	47
Mann Festival 1 Theatres	10887 Lindbrook Dr	310-208-4575	20
Mann Manhattan Village Theatre	3560 N Sepulveda Blvd	310-640-1075	27
Mann National Theatre	10925 Lindbrook Dr	310-208-4366	20
Mann Plaza Theatre	1067 Glendon Ave	310-208-3097	20
Mann Village Theatre Westwood	961 Broxton Ave	310-208-5576	20
Marina Marketplace Cinemas	13455 Maxella Ave	310-827-2883	25
Media Center 8	210 E Magnolia Blvd		46
Media Center North	770 N 1st St		46
New Beverly Cinema	7165 Beverly Blvd	323-938-4038	2
Nu Wilshire Theatre	1314 Wilshire Blvd	310-394-8099	18
Nuart Theatre	11272 Santa Monica Blvd	310-478-6379	19
Pacific Paseo Stadium 14	336 E Colorado Blvd		34
Pacific Theatres Beach Cities	831 S Nash St	310-607-0007	27
Pacific Theatres - The Grove Stadium 14	189 The Grove Dr	323-692-0829	2
Plant Sixteen Theatres	7876 Van Nuys Blvd	818-779-0323	43
Redondo Beach Cinema 3	1509 Hawthorne Blvd	310-370-8588	30
Regent Showcase Theatre	614 N La Brea Ave	323-934-2944	2
Rialto Theatre	1023 Fair Oaks Ave	626-799-9567	34
Sherman Oaks Cinemas	4500 Van Nuys Blvd	818-986-9660	50
The Bridge: Cinema de Lux	6081 Center Dr	310-568-3375	26
Town Center 5	17200 Ventura Blvd	818-981-9811	48
UA Marktplace	64 W Colorado Blvd	626-795-1386	34
United Artists Cinemas	4335 Glencoe Ave	310-823-3959	22
United Artists Theatres	6355 Bellingham Ave	818-766-4317	44
Universal City IMAX Theatre	100 Universal City Plz	818-760-8100	52
Vine Theatre	6321 Hollywood Blvd	323-463-6819	3
Vista Theatre	4473 Sunset Blvd	323-660-6639	4
West Pavilion Cinemas	10800 W Pico Blvd	310-475-0202	23

Connect

At the Getty Center –
where art delights and inspires

© 2003 J. Paul Getty Trust

ADMISSION IS ALWAYS FREE | OPEN TUESDAY–SUNDAY 10–6
FRIDAY AND SATURDAY UNTIL 9PM | CLOSED MONDAY. PARKING $5
THE GETTY CENTER, LOS ANGELES   310.440.7300   WWW.GETTY.EDU

GETTY

Discover the Museum that's also a Masterpiece

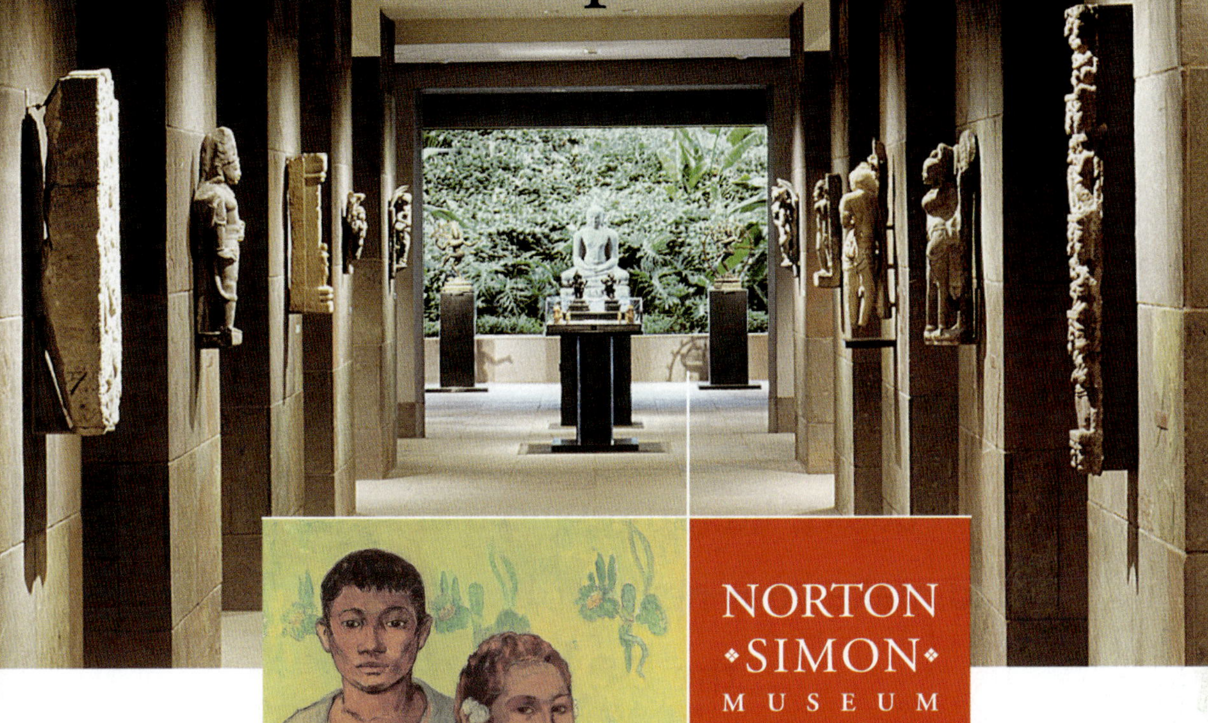

Paul Gauguin

Tahitian Woman and Boy, 1899

Masterpieces

Experience one of the world's finest private collections of European and Asian art — in light-filled galleries and tranquil garden spaces.

Open Noon – 6:00 p.m. every day except Tuesday; Friday, Noon – 9:00 p.m.

411 West Colorado Blvd. **Pasadena, CA** (626) 449-6840   www.nortonsimon.org

Planning a trip?

Traveler's Bookcase can help.

More than **15,000** travel guides,

books, literature and maps

to make your next trip

the **best ever!**

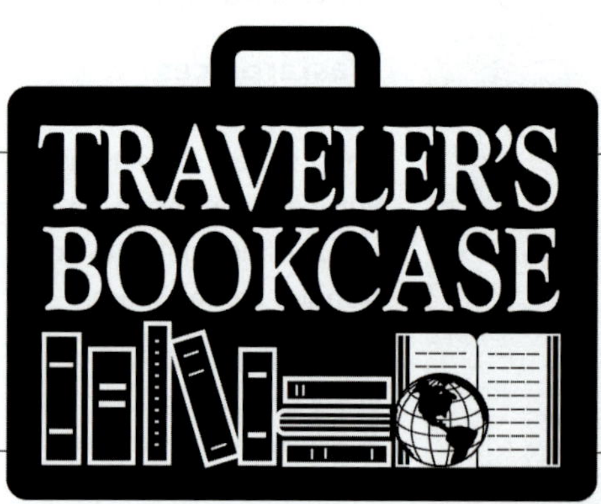

8375 West Third Street
Los Angeles, CA 90048

(800) 655-0575
travelbk@aol.com

Call or e-mail our world-traveled staff for help.

MORNING BECOMES ECLECTIC

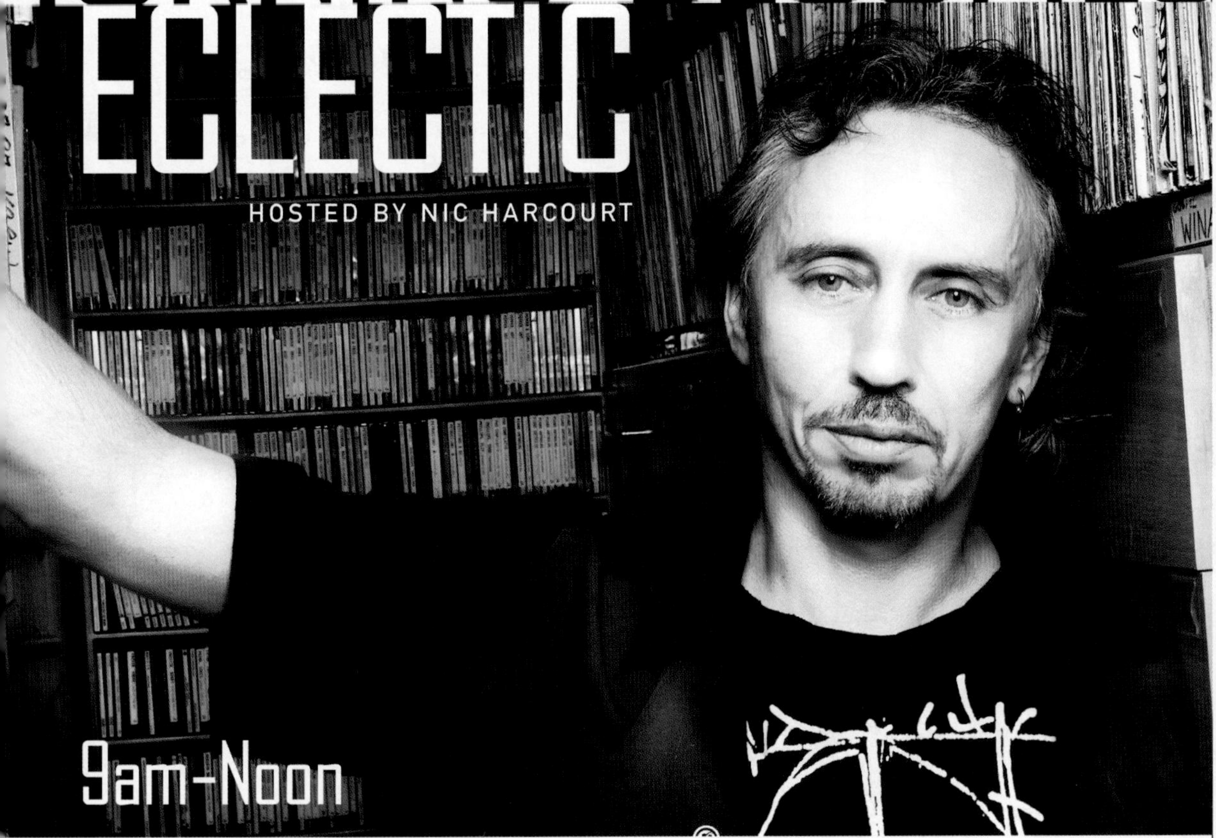

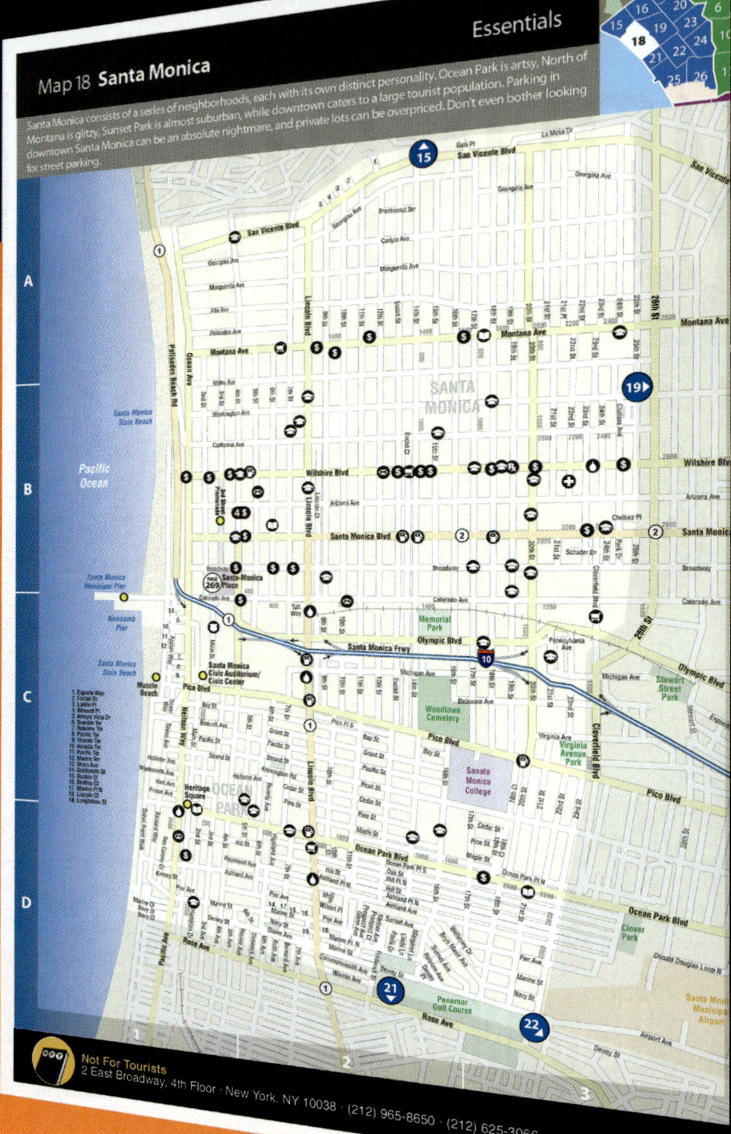

Essentials
Map 18 Santa Monica
Santa Monica consists of a series of neighborhoods, each with its own distinct personality. Ocean Park is artsy, North of Montana is glitzy, Sunset Park is almost suburban, while downtown caters to a large tourist population. Parking in downtown Santa Monica can be an absolute nightmare, and private lots can be overpriced. Don't even bother looking for street parking.
Not For Tourists
2 East Broadway, 4th Floor · New York, NY 10038 · (212) 965-8650 · (212) 625-3066 · www.notfortourists.com

Street Index

Street	Page	Grid
E 15th St	9	C1/D2/D1
W 15th St		
(100-1350)	9	C1
(1351-3023)	8	D2/D1
(3024-3598)	7	C3/C2
16th Ct	29	C1
16th Helena Dr	16	C2
16th Pl	27	C2
W 16th Pl	7	C1/D3
16th St		
(1-1199)	29	C2/C1
(101-499)	27	C2
16th St (101-3199)	18	A2/B2/C2/D2
E 16th St		
(101-1575)	9	D1/D2
(1576-1899)	12	B3
17th Ave	21	C1
17th Ct	29	C1
17th Helena Dr	16	C2
17th Pl (28-99)	21	C1
17th Pl (101-499)	27	C2
W 17th Pl	8	D2
17th St		
(1-1299)	29	C2/C1
(101-1550)	27	C2/C3
17th St (101-3399)	18	A3/B3/C3/D3/D2
E 17th St		
(101-999)	9	D1
(1301-1599)	12	B3
W 17th St		
(100-398)	9	C1/D1
(600-798)	12	A1
(800-1698)	8	D2/D3
(2600-4898)	7	C1/D1/D2/D3
18th Ave	21	C1
18th Ct (17-99)	29	C1
18th Ct (2123-2599)	18	C3
18th Helena Dr	16	C2
18th Pl (1-99)	21	C1
18th Pl (101-499)	27	C2
18th St		
(1-999)	29	C1
(101-1699)	27	C2/C3
18th St (201-3299)	18	A3/B3/C3/D3
E 18th St	12	A2/A3/B3
W 18th St		
(100-798)	12	A1/A2
(1000-2369)	8	D3/D1/D2
(2370-4898)	7	D1/D3/D2
(5700-8998)	6	C1/C2
19th Ave	21	C1
19th Ct	29	C1
19th Helena Dr	16	C2
19th Pl (1-99)	21	C1
19th Pl (101-499)	27	C2
19th St		
(1-899)	29	C1
(101-1899)	27	C2/C3
19th St (201-2099)	18	A3/B3/C3
20th Ave	21	C1
20th Ct	29	C1
20th Helena Dr	16	C2
20th Pl (1-99)	21	C1
20th Pl (101-1299)	27	C2
20th St		
(1-899)	29	C1
(101-1299)	27	C3/C2
20th St (201-2699)	18	A3/B3/C3/D3
E 20th St	12	A2/B3
W 20th St		
(500-1098)	12	A1
(1100-2157)	8	D1/D2/D3
(2158-4932)	7	D3
(4933-5298)	6	C3
21st Ct	18	C3
21st Ct (17-99)	29	C1
21st Helena Dr	16	C2
21st Pl (101-799)	18	A3
21st Pl (101-599)	27	C2
21st St		
(1-1099)	29	B1/C1
(101-1699)	27	C3/C2
21st St (201-3299)	18	A3/B3/C3/D3
E 21st St	12	A2/B2/B3
W 21st St		
(100-1198)	12	A1/A2
(1500-2155)	8	D1/D2
(2156-4979)	7	D1/D3/D2
(4980-5298)	6	C3/D3
22nd Ct	29	C1
22nd Helena Dr	16	C2
W 22nd Pl		
(1501-1599)	11	A3
(4000-4198)	7	D2
22nd St		
(1-199)	29	C1
(1101-1699)	27	C3
22nd St (201-2699)	18	A3/B3/C3/D3
E 22nd St	12	A2/B2/B3
W 22nd St		
(100-1214)	12	A1/A2
(1215-2098)	11	A2/A3
23rd Ave	21	C2
23rd Helena Dr	16	C2
23rd Pl (1-99)	21	C2
23rd Pl (101-599)	27	C2
23rd St		
(1-99)	29	B1
(101-1899)	27	C2/C3
23rd St (200-3299)	18	A3/B3/C3/D3
E 23rd St	12	A2/B2/B3
W 23rd St		
(100-1249)	12	A1/A2
(1250-3349)	11	A1/A2/A3
(3350-4998)	7	D2/D1
(5000-5098)	6	D3
24th Ave	21	C2
24th Ct	19	C1
24th Helena Dr	16	C2
24th Pl		
(1-99)	21	C2
(101-300)	27	C2
(430-799)	29	B1
W 24th Pl	27	C2
24th St		
(1-1100)	29	B1
(101-599)	27	C2
(201-1499)	18	A3/B3
(1801-2692)	19	C1
E 24th St	12	A2/B3/B2
W 24th St		
(100-1149)	12	A1/A2
(1150-3198)	11	A2/A3
(8900-9198)	23	B3
25th Ave	21	C2
25th Helena Dr	16	C2
25th Pl (30-99)	21	C2
25th Pl (101-499)	27	C2
25th St		
(1-699)	29	B1
(101-799)	27	C2
25th St	16	D1
(301-2899)	19	A1/B1/C1/D1
(801-1499)	18	A3/B3
E 25th St	12	B2/B3
W 25th St		
(100-1149)	12	A1/B2
(1150-4398)	11	A1/A2/A3
(4300-5798)	10	A3/A1
(8900-9198)	23	B3
26th Ave	21	D2
26th Pl	27	C2
W 26th Pl	11	A2
26th St		
(1-399)	29	B1
(101-799)	27	C2
26th St		
(138-239)	16	D1
(279-2699)	19	A1/B1/C1
27th Ave	21	D2
27th Ct	29	B1
27th Pl (1-99)	21	D2
27th Pl (101-499)	27	C2
27th St		
(101-1099)	27	C2/C3
(140-399)	29	B1
27th St (2001-2399)	19	C1
E 27th St	12	B1/B2/B3/C3
W 27th St		
(100-1139)	12	A1/B1
(1140-3998)	11	A1/A3/A2
28th Ave	21	C2/D2
28th Ct	29	B1
28th Pl		
(1-99)	21	D2
(101-499)	27	C2
28th St		
(101-999)	27	C2
(101-599)	29	B1
E 28th St	12	B1/B3/B2
W 28th St		
(100-1199)	12	A1/B1
(1200-4297)	11	A1/A2/A3
(4298-4798)	10	A3
29th Ave	21	D2
29th Ct		
(101-199)	29	B1
(201-599)	27	D2
29th Pl (1-99)	21	D2
29th Pl (101-499)	27	C2
W 29th Pl	12	B1
(2000-2398)	11	A1/A2
29th St (101-799)	27	C2/D2
29th St (2201-2699)	19	C2
E 29th St	12	B1/B2
W 29th St		
(400-598)	12	B1
(1100-4129)	11	A1/A3/A2
(4130-4798)	10	A3
30th Ave	21	D2
30th Pl	11	B3
30th Pl (1-99)	21	D2
30th Pl (1-598)	27	C2/D2
W 30th Pl	11	B3
30th St (101-1099)	27	C2/C3/D2/D3
30th St (2201-2699)	19	C2
E 30th St	12	B1/B2
W 30th St		
(100-1064)	12	A1/B1
(1085-3756)	11	A3/A1/A2/B3
(3757-4798)	10	A3
31st Pl	27	C2/D2
31st St (101-999)	27	C2/D2/C1
31st St (2201-2977)	19	C2
E 31st St	12	B1/B2
W 31st St		
(100-598)	12	B1
(1000-2398)	11	B1/B2/B3
32nd Pl	27	C2/D2
32nd St (101-499)	27	C2/C1
32nd St (2201-2699)	19	C2
E 32nd St	12	B1/B2/B3
W 32nd St	12	B1
33rd Pl	27	C2/C1/D2
33rd St		
(101-1099)	27	C2/C3/D2/C1
(2301-2699)	19	C2
E 33rd St	12	B1/B2/B3
W 33rd St	12	B1
34th Pl	27	C2/C1/D2
34th St (101-499)	27	C2/C1/D2
34th St (1801-2699)	19	C2
E 34th St	12	C2
W 34th St		
(600-901)	12	B1
(902-3769)	11	B3
35th Pl	27	C2/D2/C1
W 35th Pl		
(799-601)	12	B1
(1200-2098)	11	B2/B3
35th St	27	C2/C1/D2
E 35th St	12	B1/B2/C2
W 35th St		
(100-680)	12	B1
(681-2098)	11	B2/B3
36th Pl	27	C2/C1
E 36th Pl	12	B1
W 36th Pl		
(100-198)	12	B1
(1000-2098)	11	B3/B2
36th St	27	C2/C1
E 36th St	12	B1/B2
W 36th St		
(100-698)	12	B1
(1100-3556)	11	B1/B3/B2
(3557-3898)	10	B3
W 37th Dr	11	B2/B3
37th Pl	11	B3
W 37th Pl		
(101-428)	12	B1
(1100-2298)	11	B2/B1/B3
E 37th St	12	B1/C2
W 37th St		
(100-498)	12	B1
(953-1798)	11	B2/B3
38th Pl	27	C1
W 38th Pl	11	B2/B1
38th St	27	C1
E 38th St	12	B1/C1/C2
W 38th St		
(100-498)	12	B1/C1
(1000-1898)	11	B2/B3
W 39th Pl	11	B3/B2
39th St	27	B1
W 39th St		
(100-498)	12	B1/C1
(800-3551)	11	B3/B2/B1
(3552-3898)	10	B3
E 40th Pl	12	C2/C3
W 40th Pl		
(100-649)	12	C1
(650-1398)	11	C3
40th St	27	B1
W 41st Dr		
(500-649)	12	C1
(650-2598)	11	C2/C1/C3
E 41st Pl	12	C2/C1/C3
W 41st Pl		
(100-649)	12	C1
(650-2098)	11	C2/C3
41st St	27	B1
E 41st St	12	C2/C3
W 41st St		
(100-649)	12	C1
(650-3598)	11	C1/C2/C3
E 42nd Pl	12	C2/C1/C3
W 42nd Pl		
(100-649)	12	C1
(650-2098)	11	C3/C2
42nd St	27	B1
E 42nd St	12	C2/C1/C3
W 42nd St		
(100-649)	12	C1
(650-2898)	11	C3/C2/C1
E 43rd Pl	12	C2/C3/C1
W 43rd Pl		
(100-649)	12	C1
(650-3498)	11	C2/C3/C1
43rd St	27	B1
E 43rd St	12	C3/C2/C1
W 43rd St		
(100-649)	12	C1
(650-3448)	11	C1/C3/C2
44th St	27	B1
45th St	27	B1
E 45th St	12	C2/C3/C1
W 45th St		
(100-649)	12	C1
(650-1898)	11	C3/C2
E 46th St	12	C3/C2/C1
W 46th St		
(100-649)	12	C1
(650-3398)	11	C2/C3/C1
E 47th Pl	12	C1
W 47th Pl	12	C3/C2/C1
E 47th St	12	C3/C2/C1
W 47th St		
(100-649)	12	C1
(650-1898)	11	C3/C2
E 48th Pl	12	D3
E 48th St	12	C2/C3/D1/C1
W 48th St		
(100-649)	12	C1/D1
(650-3598)	11	C3/C2/C1
E 49th Pl	12	D2
W 49th Pl	12	D1
E 49th St	12	D2/D1/D3

Street	Block	Map	Grid
W 49th St			
	(100-649)	12	D1
	(650-1898)	11	D2/D3
E 50th Pl		12	D3
W 50th Pl		11	D3
E 50th St		12	D3/D2/D1
W 50th St			
	(100-649)	12	D1
	(650-3398)	11	D2/D3/D1
W 51st Pl		11	D3/D2
E 51st St		12	D2/D3/D1
W 51st St			
	(100-649)	12	D1
	(650-1898)	11	D2/D3
	(5100-5498)	24	D3
E 52nd Pl		17	D2
W 52nd Pl		12	D1
E 52nd St		12	D2/D3/D1
W 52nd St			
	(100-649)	12	D1
	(650-3574)	11	D3/D2/D1
	(3575-3798)	10	D3
E 53rd St		12	D3/D2/D1
W 53rd St			
	(100-649)	12	D1
	(650-1798)	11	D2/D3
54th St		12	D3
E 54th St		12	D3/D2/D1
W 54th St			
	(100-649)	12	D1
	(650-3574)	11	D2/D3/D1
	(3575-5298)	10	D3/D1
55th St		24	D3
E 55th St		12	D3/D2/D1
W 55th St			
	(100-649)	12	D1
	(650-1798)	11	D2/D3
	(5200-5498)	24	D3
E 56th St		12	D3/D2/D1
W 56th St			
	(100-649)	12	D1
	(650-1798)	11	D3/D2
E 57th St		12	D3/D2/D1
W 57th St			
	(100-649)	12	D1
	(650-3574)	11	D2/D3/D1
	(3575-4898)	10	D3/D2
	(5200-5501)	24	D3
E 58th Pl		12	D3/D2
W 58th Pl			
	(800-1449)	14	A3/A2
	(1450-3549)	11	D2/D1
	(3550-4498)	10	D3/D2
	(5000-5198)	13	A1
E 58th St		12	D3/D2/D1
W 58th St			
	(100-649)	12	D1
	(650-1799)	11	D3/D2
W 59th Dr		14	A3
W 59th Pl			
	(400-3549)	14	A3/A2/A1
	(3550-4598)	13	A3/A2
W 59th St			
	(500-3549)	14	A3/A2/A1
	(3550-5898)	13	A2/A3/A1
W 60th Pl		14	A2/A3
W 60th St			
	(400-3559)	14	A2/A3/A1
	(3560-4598)	13	A2/A3
W 61st St			
	(500-1698)	14	A3/A2
	(3600-4598)	13	A2/A3
	(5400-5598)	26	A3
62nd Ave		25	B1
62nd Pl		25	B1
W 62nd Pl			
	(800-998)	14	A3
	(4600-4698)	13	A2
W 62nd St			
	(400-3098)	14	A3/A1/A2
	(3600-5098)	13	A2/A1/A3
	(5300-5698)	26	A3
63rd Ave		25	B1
W 63rd Pl		14	A3
W 63rd St			
	(3100-3549)	14	A1
	(3550-5098)	13	A3/A2/A1
	(5500-5698)	26	A3
64th Ave		25	B1
E 64th Pl		13	A2
W 64th Pl		13	A1/A2
W 64th St			
	(100-5398)	13	A1/A3/A2
	(315-3098)	14	A1/A2/A3
	(5203-5698)	26	A3
65th Ave		25	B1
W 65th Pl		14	A2/A1/A3
E 65th St		13	A3/A2
W 65th St		14	A3/A2
66th Ave		25	B1/C1
W 66th Pl		14	A1
E 66th St		13	A3
W 66th St		14	A3/A1/A2
E 67th St		13	A3/A2
W 67th St		14	A3/A2/B2/B1
E 68th St		13	A3
W 68th St		14	A3/B3/B2/B1
W 69th St		14	B3/B2/B1
W 70th St		14	B3/B2/B1
W 71st St			
	(400-3546)	14	B1/B3/B2
	(3547-3598)	13	A3
W 73rd St		14	B1/B2/B3
W 74th Pl		14	B1
W 74th St			
	(400-3598)	14	B2/B1/B3
	(5600-6298)	26	B2/B3
W 75th Pl			
	(3500-3598)	14	B1
	(6055-6299)	26	B2
W 75th St			
	(400-3498)	14	B1/B2/B3
	(5700-6198)	26	B2/B3
W 76th Pl		26	B2
W 76th St			
	(404-3498)	14	B3/B2/B1
	(5400-7630)	26	B2/B3
W 77th Pl		26	B2
W 77th St			
	(400-3498)	14	B3/B2/B1
	(5400-6998)	26	B2/B1/B3
W 78th Pl			
	(1800-3598)	14	B1/B2
	(5800-6398)	26	B2
W 78th St			
	(400-3598)	14	B3/B2/B1
	(5500-6398)	26	B2/B3
	(7200-7298)	25	B3
W 79th Pl		26	B2
W 79th St			
	(416-3598)	14	B3/B2/B1
	(5500-6398)	26	B2/B3
	(7700-7998)	25	B2
W 80th Pl		26	B2/B1
W 80th St			
	(400-3598)	14	B3/B1/B2
	(6301-7014)	26	B2/B1
	(7015-7998)	25	B3/B2
W 81st Pl		14	B3
W 81st St			
	(400-3598)	14	B3/B1/B2
	(6300-6698)	26	B2/B1
	(7300-7998)	25	B3/B2
W 82nd Pl		14	B1
W 82nd St			
	(400-3598)	14	B3/B1/B2
	(5300-6698)	26	B2/B1/B3
	(7300-7798)	25	B3/B2
W 83rd Pl			
	(1250-1398)	14	B2
	(6000-6298)	26	B2
W 83rd St			
	(428-3598)	14	B3/B2/B1
	(5200-7014)	26	B2/B3/B1
	(7015-8298)	25	B3/C2
W 84th Pl			
	(400-3598)	14	B3/C3/C2/ B2/B1/C1
	(6200-6958)	26	B1/B2
W 84th St			
	(400-3398)	14	B3/B1/B2
	(5900-6519)	26	B2
	(6520-7298)	25	B3
W 85th Pl		26	B3/B2/B1
W 85th St			
	(500-3499)	14	C3/C2/C1
	(3500-7014)	26	B1/B2
	(7015-7798)	25	C3
W 86th Pl		26	C2/C1
W 87th Pl			
	(400-6499)	14	C3
	(6500-6798)	26	C1
	(7300-7498)	25	C3
W 87th St			
	(100-1898)	14	C2/C3
	(6200-6798)	26	C1/C2
	(7300-7398)	25	C3
W 88th Pl			
	(420-1898)	14	C2/C3
	(6400-6598)	26	C2/C1
	(7200-7598)	25	C3
W 88th St			
	(400-3448)	14	C2/C1/C3
	(5800-6898)	26	C2/C1
	(7300-7598)	25	C3
W 89th St			
	(400-2186)	14	C3/C2
	(2187-6284)	26	C2
	(7300-7598)	25	C3
W 90th Pl		14	C2
W 90th St			
	(400-3503)	14	C1/C2/C3
	(3504-3899)	13	C3
	(3900-7598)	25	C3
W 91st Pl			
	(400-1998)	14	C2/C3
	(7400-7698)	25	C3
W 91st St			
	(400-2174)	14	C3/C2
	(2175-7798)	25	C2/C3
W 92nd St			
	(408-2174)	14	C3/C2
	(2175-6398)	26	C2
	(7300-7798)	25	C3/C2
W 93rd St			
	(400-2198)	14	C3/C2
	(4800-4898)	13	C1
	(5200-5898)	26	C2/C3
W 94th Pl		14	C2
E 94th St		13	C2
W 94th St			
	(200-4898)	13	C2/C1
	(361-2998)	14	C2/C3/C1
	(5200-5498)	26	C2/C3
W 95th Pl		26	C3
W 95th St			
	(400-2998)	14	C3/C1/C2
	(4800-5098)	13	C1
	(5200-5898)	26	C3/C2
W 96th Pl			
	(2000-2098)	14	C2
	(5900-5998)	26	C2
W 96th St			
	(1000-2174)	14	C2/C3
	(2175-4998)	13	C1
	(5200-6423)	26	C3/C2
96th Street Brg		26	C2
W 97th Pl		26	C3
E 97th St		13	C2
W 97th St			
	(400-2198)	14	C3/C2
	(4800-4998)	13	C1
	(5200-5398)	26	C3
E 98th St		13	C2
W 98th St			
	(100-5098)	13	C1/C2
	(404-4804)	14	C3/C2
	(5200-6298)	26	C3/C2
W 99th Pl		26	C3
E 99th St		13	C2
W 99th St			
	(400-3298)	14	C1/C3/C2
	(4800-5098)	13	C1
	(5300-5498)	26	C3
E 101st St		13	A2
W 101st St			
	(400-2998)	14	C1/D3/D2/D1
	(4000-5098)	13	D2/D1
	(5100-5198)	26	D3
W 102nd St			
	(400-3098)	14	D3/D1/D2
	(3600-4498)	13	D3/D2
	(5220-5598)	26	D3
W 103rd Pl		14	D2
W 103rd St			
	(400-2198)	14	D2/D3
	(4000-4398)	13	D2
W 104th Pl		14	D3
W 104th St			
	(400-3549)	14	D3/D2/D1
	(3550-5098)	13	D3/D2/D1
	(5100-5598)	26	D3
W 105th St			
	(400-2098)	14	D3/D2
	(3600-4398)	13	D2/D3
W 106th St			
	(400-2098)	14	D3/D2
	(3600-5098)	13	D2/D1/D3
	(5100-5198)	26	D3
W 107th St			
	(400-2162)	14	D3/D2/D1
	(2163-4298)	13	D2/D3
W 108th St			
	(376-3998)	13	D2/D3
	(379-3449)	14	D1/D2/D3
W 109th Pl		14	D2/D3
W 109th St			
	(400-3449)	14	D2/D1/D3
	(3450-5098)	13	D1/D3/D2
W 110th St			
	(400-3449)	14	D1/D3/D2
	(3450-4998)	13	D1/D3/D2
W 111th Pl			
	(3100-3899)	28	A3/A2
	(3900-5098)	13	D1
W 111th St			
	(1336-3449)	14	D1/D2
	(3450-4898)	13	D3/D2/D1
	(5200-5598)	26	D3
W 112th St			
	(3100-3899)	28	A3
	(3900-5098)	13	D1
W 113th St		28	A3/A2
115th St		28	A2
W 115th St		27	A3
	(3300-5537)	28	A2/A1/A3
W 116th St		28	A2/A1/A3
W 117th Pl		28	A3
117th St		28	A2
W 117th St		27	A3
	(3300-5598)	28	A3/A2/A1
W 118th Pl		27	A3
	(3100-5598)	28	A3/A1
118th St		27	A3
W 118th St		27	A3
	(3300-5598)	28	A2/A1/A3
W 119th Pl		27	A3
	(3700-5598)	28	B3/B1
W 119th St			
	(3004-5598)	28	A3/A2/A1/B3
	(3035-3003)	27	A3
W 120th St			
	(2682-5598)	28	B1/B3/B2
W 121st St		27	B1
W 122nd St			
	(4000-5598)	28	B1/B2
W 123rd Pl		27	A3
	(4800-5598)	28	B1
W 123rd St			
	(4700-5495)	28	B1
	(5496-5598)	27	A3
W 124th Pl		28	B1
W 124th St		27	A3
	(5000-5598)	28	B1
W 125th St		28	B1
W 126th St		28	B1/B3/B2
W 127th Pl		28	B1
W 127th St		28	B1
W 129th St		28	B1/B2

Street Index

Street	Page	Grid
W 130th St	28	B2/B3/B1
W 131st St	28	B1/B2/B3
W 132nd Pl	28	C3
W 132nd St	28	B1/B2/B3/C3
W 133rd St	28	B1/C2/C3
W 134th Pl	28	C1/C3
W 134th St	28	C1/C3/C2
W 135th St		
(2994-5535)	28	C2/C1/C3
(5536-5598)	27	B3
W 136th St	28	C2/C1
W 137th Pl	28	C1/C2
W 137th St	28	C2/C1
W 138th Pl	28	C1
W 138th St		
(4000-5536)	28	C1/C2
(5537-5598)	27	B3
W 139th St	28	C3/C2/C1
W 140th St	28	C2/C1
W 141st St	28	C2/C1
142nd Pl	28	C1
W 142nd Pl	28	C1
W 142nd St	28	C1/C2
142nd Way	28	C1
W 144th Pl	28	C3
W 144th St	28	C3/C1
W 145th St	28	C2/C1/C3
W 146th St	28	C3/C1
W 147th Pl	28	C3
W 147th St	28	C3/C1/C2
W 148th Pl	28	C3
W 148th St	28	D3
W 149th St	28	D2
W 152nd Pl	28	D3
W 152nd St	28	D3/D2
W 153rd Pl	28	D2
W 153rd St	28	D2/D3
W 154th Pl	28	D3
W 154th St	28	D3/D2
W 155th St	28	D3
W 156th St	28	D2/D3
W 157th St	30	A2/A3
159th St	29	A3
W 159th St	29	A3
(4000-4798)	30	A2/A1
160th St	29	A3
W 160th St	30	A2/A1
W 161st St	30	A2/A1
162nd St	30	A1
W 162nd St	30	A2/A1
W 163rd St	30	A2/A1
W 164th St	30	A3/A1/A2
W 165th St	30	A2/A1
W 166th St	30	A1/A3/A2
W 167th St	30	A1/A2/A3
W 168th St	30	A2/A1/A3
W 169th St	30	A1/A2
W 170th St	30	B3/B1/B2
W 171st St	30	B1/B2/B3
W 172nd St	30	B2/B1/B3
W 173rd Pl	30	B2
W 173rd St	30	B2/B1
W 175th Pl	30	B2
W 175th St	30	B2/B3
W 176th Ct	30	B2
W 176th St	30	B2
W 177th St	30	B2/B3/B1
W 178th St	30	B1/B3/B2
W 179th St	30	B3/B2/B1
W 180th Pl	30	B3/B2
W 180th St	30	B3/B2
W 181st Pl	30	B3
W 181st St	30	B2/B3
182nd Pl	29	C3
W 182nd Pl	30	B3
182nd St		
(2601-2762)	29	C3
(2763-4599)	30	B1
W 182nd St	30	B3/B2
183rd St	29	C3
W 183rd St	30	B3/B2
W 184th Pl	30	C2
184th St	29	C3
W 184th St	30	B2/C2
185th St	29	C3
W 185th St	30	C3/C2
186th St	30	C1
W 186th St	30	C3/C2
W 187th Pl	30	C3
W 187th St	30	C3/C2
W 188th St	30	C2/C3
W 189th St	30	C3
190th St		
(1901-2895)	29	C3/C2
(2892-2999)	30	C1
W 190th St	30	C2/C3/C1
W 191st St	30	C1
W 205th St	30	D3
W 208th St	30	D3
W 212th St	32	A3
W 213th St	32	A3
W 214th St	32	A3
W 215th St	32	A3
W 216th St	32	A3
W 218th St	32	A3
W 219th St	32	A3
W 220th St	32	B3
W 222nd St	32	B3
W 223rd St	32	B3
W 224th St	32	B1
W 225th Pl	32	B2
W 225th St	31	
(2600-3798)	32	B1/B2
W 226th St		
(1602-4598)	31	C3
(1651-3699)	32	B1/B2
W 227th Pl	32	B1
W 227th St		
(1600-4298)	31	C3
(1650-3699)	32	B1/B2
W 228th Pl		
(3400-3698)	32	B1
(3900-4198)	31	C3
W 228th St	32	B1/B2/B3
W 229th Pl	32	B1/B2
W 229th St		
(2200-3598)	32	B1/B2
(4100-4198)	31	C3
W 230th Pl		
(2100-2798)	32	B2/B3
(4200-4398)	31	C3
W 230th St		
(1900-3749)	32	B1/B2/B3
(3750-4301)	31	C3
W 231st Pl	31	C3
W 231st St		
(1900-2698)	32	B2/B3
(3900-4598)	31	C3
W 232nd St		
(1900-2898)	32	B1/B2/B3
(3900-4498)	31	C3
W 233rd St		
(1900-2898)	32	B2/C3
(4400-4498)	31	C3
W 234th Pl	31	D3
234th St	32	C1
W 234th St		
(1700-2998)	32	B1/B2/C2/C3
(3800-4498)	31	C3
W 235th Pl	32	C2/C3
235th St	41	C3
W 235th St		
(1700-2848)	32	C2/C3
(2850-4098)	31	D3
W 236th Pl	32	C2
W 236th St		
(1700-2498)	32	C2/C3
(4000-4198)	31	D3
237th Pl	32	C3
W 237th Pl	32	C2/C3
237th St	32	C3
W 237th St	32	C2/C3
238th St	32	C3
W 238th St		
(1700-2498)	32	C2/C3
(3700-4498)	31	D3
W 239th St		
(1700-2498)	32	C3/C2
(4100-4198)	31	D3
240th St	32	C3
W 240th St	31	D3
241st St	32	C3/C2
242nd Pl	32	C3
W 242nd Pl	32	C3
242nd St	32	C3
W 242nd St		
(1700-3674)	32	C3/C1
(3675-4198)	31	D3
243rd Pl	32	C3
W 243rd Pl	32	C3
243rd St	32	C2
W 244th St		
(1700-3674)	32	C3/C1
(3675-3898)	31	D3
245th St	32	C3
246th Pl	32	C3
246th St	32	C2/C3
247th Pl	32	D3
W 247th Pl	32	D3
247th St	32	C3/C2
248th St	32	D2/D3
249th St	32	D2
W 249th St	32	D3
250th St	32	D2/D3
251st St	32	D3/D2
252nd St	32	D3
253rd Pl	32	C3
253rd St	32	D2/D3
254th St	32	D2/D3
255th St	32	D3/D2
256th St	32	D3/D2
257th St	32	D3
258th Pl	32	D3
259th St	32	D3

Street	Page	Grid
Bluff St	52	B1
Bluffhill Dr	41	B3
Bluffside Dr	51	B3
(10600-10998)	52	B1
Blythe Ave	23	B1
Blythe St		
(11200-14649)	44	A1/A2/A3
(14650-16098)	43	A2/A1
(17400-18398)	42	A1/A2
Boaz St	12	B2
S Bob Hope Dr	46	D1
Bobstone Dr	50	C2
Boca Ave	38	D1
Boca De Canon Ln	16	B1
Boccaccio Ave	21	C3/C2
Boden St	10	A1
Bodger Ave	28	C3
Bodie St	40	B1
Boeing Ave	26	B2
Boeing Pl	26	B2
Bohlig Rd	38	C2/C3
Boise Ave	22	B1/C2
Bolas St	16	C3
Bolero Ln	9	B3
Bollinger Dr	15	B1
Bolton Rd	23	B3
Bomer Dr	36	B3
Bonair Pl	3	B1
Bonaparte Ave	22	C2
Bonavita Dr	48	B3
Bonavita Pl	48	B3
Bond St	9	C1
Bonfield Ave	44	A1/A2
N Bonhill Rd	16	B2/C2
Bonita Ave		
(200-598)	35	B2/C2
(1700-2098)	46	A1
Bonita Dr		
(601-699)	34	D3
(700-998)	38	A3
Bonita Ter (1401-1499)	41	A3
Bonita Ter (6800-6998)	3	B1
Bonner Ave	44	B3/C3/D3
Bonner Dr	2	C1
N Bonnie Ave	35	B2
S Bonnie Ave	35	B2/C2
N Bonnie Beach Pl		
(101-1383)	41	B1/C1
(1384-1699)	38	D1/D2
S Bonnie Beach Pl	41	D1/C1
Bonnie Brae St	29	C2
N Bonnie Brae St		
(101-563)	9	A1
(564-1099)	5	D2/D1
S Bonnie Brae St		
(100-749)	9	A1/B1
(750-1898)	8	C3/D3
Bonnie Hill Dr	52	C2
Bonny Ln	16	C2
N Bonnywood Pl	46	B2/C2
S Bonnywood Pl	46	C2
Bonsall Ave	19	A3/B3
(1-99)	16	C3
Bonsallo Ave	11	D3
(1900-5849)	12	A1
(5850-7198)	14	A3/B3
Bonvue Ave	4	A2
Boone Ave	21	C2
Bora Bora Way	25	B1
Borden Ave	29	B1
Border Ave	32	A3/B3
Borel St	37	B3
Borgos Pl	15	C2
Boris Dr	48	B1/B2
Borland Rd	38	C2
Bosque Dr		
(16400-16589)	49	B1
(16590-16998)	48	B3
Boston Ct	35	B1
Boston St	9	A2/B2
Bostwick St	41	B1
Bosworth St	44	C1
Bottlebrush Dr	50	D1
Bouett St	5	D3
Boughton Pl	51	C2
Boulder St	40	B2/B3
Boundary Pl	27	D2/D3
Boundary St	38	B1
Bounty Ln	24	C2
Bow Ave	32	A3
Bowcroft St		
(5600-5837)	10	B1
(5838-6098)	24	B3
Bowdoin St	15	B2/B1
Bowesfield St	10	B1
N Bowling Green Way	16	B2/C2
S Bowling Green Way	16	C2
Bowman Blvd	38	C1
Bowmont Dr	51	D2
Boxwood Pl	43	A3
Boyce Ave	5	A1/A2
Boyd St		
(201-499)	9	C2
(1301-1499)	40	B1
N Boyle Ave	40	B2/B1
S Boyle Ave	40	B1/C1/D1
Boylston St	34	A3
N Boylston St		
(101-699)	9	A2/B2
(1301-1899)	5	D2
S Boylston St	9	B2/B1
Boynton St	47	C2
Bradbury Rd		
(1300-1598)	35	D3
(10500-10698)	23	B1
Braddock Dr		
(9600-11524)	24	B2/C1
(11526-12798)	22	B3/C3/C2
Bradford St	34	C1
Bradley Pl	13	A1
Bradna Dr	10	D2
Bradson Pl	22	C3
Braeburn Way	4	A3
Braeholm Pl	27	D2
Braewood Ct	38	A3
Braley Ct	34	B2
Bramble Way	16	B2
Brampton Rd	33	B3
Branch St	33	C3
N Brand Blvd	47	A2/B2
S Brand Blvd		
(104-1764)	47	B2/C2
(1766-1998)	5	A2
Branden St	5	C1/C2
N Brannick Ave	41	B2/C2
S Brannick Ave	41	D2
Branton Pl	50	A2
Brawley St	38	C2
Bray St	22	C3
Brayton Pl	33	B3
Brazil St	47	B1
Brea Crest Dr	10	D2
N Breed St	40	B2
S Breed St	40	B2/C2/C1
Breen Ave	26	B3
Breeze Ave	21	C1
Breeze Ct	21	C1
Brent Ave	34	D2
Brent Pl	47	B1
Brenta Pl	21	B3
Brentford Rd	35	D2
Brentnal Rd	34	C1
Brentridge Dr	16	A2
Brentridge Ln	16	A2
Brentwood Grove Dr	16	B2
Brentwood St	12	D1
Brentwood Ter		
(1201-1399)	18	A2
(12900-13098)	19	A1
Bresee Ave	35	A2
E Brett St	13	A3/A2
Brian Ave	32	D2
Brian Ln	49	A1
Briar Knoll Dr	51	D3
Briar Summit Dr	51	D3
Briarcliff Ln	51	C3
Briarcliff Rd	3	B3
Briarcrest Ln	51	D2
Briarcrest Rd	51	D2
Briarvale Ln	51	C2
Briarwood Dr		
(10291-10399)	50	D1
(15400-15598)	49	C2
Briarwood Ln	14	C1
Bridewell St	34	D1
Bridge St		
(101-399)	39	A3
(1401-1899)	40	B1/B2
Bridgeport	27	C3
Bridgeport Dr	36	C2
Bridgeport Way	32	B2
Bridle Ln	1	B1
Bridlevale Dr	23	B2
Brier Ave	5	B2
Brier Dr	2	A1
Brier Ln	47	C3
Brigden Rd	35	A2
Bright Ln	5	B1
Brighton Ave		
(2600-5098)	11	A2/C2/D2
(7200-7898)	14	B2
N Brighton St		
(101-400)	46	D1
(401-2999)	45	A3/B3/C3
S Brighton St	46	D1
Brighton Way	1	C2
Brightwood St	41	B3
W Brightwood St	41	B3
Brill Dr	51	C3
Brilliant Dr	36	B2
Brilliant Pl	36	B2
Brilliant Way	36	B2
Brimfield Ave	43	A2
Bringham Ave	16	C3
Brinkley Ave		
(1301-1322)	15	B3
(1323-1499)	16	C1
N Bristol Ave	16	B2/C2
S Bristol Ave		
(100-449)	16	C2/D2
(450-898)	19	A1
N Bristol Cir	16	C2
S Bristol Cir	16	C2
Bristol Pkwy	24	D2
(6000-6398)	26	A2
Brittania St	40	B2
Brixton Rd	33	B3
Broadlawn Dr	52	C1
Broadleaf Ave	43	A3
Broadview Ter	3	A1
Broadway		
(101-2550)	18	B3/B2/B1
(2551-3988)	19	B2/B1
Broadway (1001-1099)	34	C2
Broadway (1101-1599)	46	B1
Broadway (3990-4998)	28	B2/B1/B3
E Broadway	47	B2/B3
N Broadway		
(101-1011)	9	A3/B3/B2
(1012-3899)	37	C3/C2/C1/D1
N Broadway (101-599)	31	A1/B1
S Broadway		
(100-1760)	9	B2/C2/C1/D1
(1762-5799)	12	A2/A1/B1/C1/D1
S Broadway (100-798)	31	B1
W Broadway		
(100-2999)	47	B2/B1/B3
(2700-2925)	33	A1
Broadway Ct	21	B2
Broadway Pl		
(1000-1099)	9	C2
(3500-4098)	12	B1/C1
Broadway St	21	B2/B1
E Broadway St	47	B3
Brocadero Pl	34	C2
Brockton Ave	19	B2
Bromley Ct	42	D2
Bromley Ln	14	C1
Bromley St	42	D2/D1
Bronholly Dr	3	A3
N Bronson Ave	3	A3/B3/C3/D3
S Bronson Ave		
(500-2498)	7	B3/C2/D2
(2500-4298)	11	A1/B1/C1
Bronson Hill Dr	3	A3
Bronwood Ave		
(120-260)	17	D1
(261-398)	20	B1
Bronze Ln	16	B1
Brookdale Ln	51	C2
Brookdale Rd	51	C2
Brookhaven Ave		
(10800-11149)	23	C1
(11150-12198)	19	C3/D3/D2
Brooklake St	22	B1
Brooklawn Dr	17	B3
Brooklyn Pl	41	C1
Brookmere Rd	34	C2
Brooks Ave		
(1-899)	21	B2/B1/C1
(701-899)	34	A2
(1751-1822)	5	D3
Brooks Ct	21	B2/B1/C1
Brooktree Rd	15	B3/C2/C3
Brookview Dr	52	B1
Broom Way	16	B2
Brown Dr	46	A1
Browne Ave	38	B1
Browning Blvd	11	C3/C2
Brownwood Pl	49	D2
Broxton Ave	20	B1
Bruce Ct	5	D2
S Bruce Ln	46	C2
Bruna Pl	4	A1
Bruno St	9	B3
Brunswick Ave		
(1200-1398)	38	A2
(3600-3998)	5	A1/A2
(4000-4798)	47	C1
Brushton St	10	B1
Bryan Ave	21	C3
Bryant Pl	27	D3
Bryant St	34	A1
Bryn Mawr Ave	18	D3
Bryn Mawr Ct	3	A2
Bryn Mawr Dr	3	A2
Bryn Mawr Rd	4	A2
Brynhurst Ave		
(3400-5874)	11	C1/D1
(5875-7398)	14	A1/B1
Buccaneer St	25	A1
Buchanan St	33	C2/C3
Buckeye St	34	A3
Buckingham Pkwy		
(5777-5999)	24	D3
(6000-6298)	26	A2
Buckingham Pl	34	C1
Buckingham Rd		
(1600-4198)	10	B3/A3
(1700-2364)	7	C2/D1
Buckler Ave		
(1201-6398)	13	A2
(5800-5874)	10	D2
Bucknell Ave	44	D2
E Buckthorn St	13	C2
W Buckthorn St	13	C2/C1
Budau Ave	38	C2
Budau Pl	38	C2
Budlong Ave		
(2150-3970)	11	A3
(6700-8598)	14	B3/C3
S Budlong Ave		
(1900-2140)	8	D2
(2141-5824)	11	A3/B3/C3/D3
(5825-11098)	14	A3/B3/C3/D3
Buelah Ave	41	B1
Buelah Cir	41	B1
Buena Park Dr	51	C2
Buena Vista Ln	34	D2
Buena Vista St	34	D2/D3
N Buena Vista St		
(101-500)	46	D1
(501-3099)	45	A3/B3/C3
S Buena Vista St	46	D1
Buena Vista Ter	33	B3
Buena Vista View Dr	37	C1
Buenos Aires Dr	20	B1

Street	Page	Grid
Buffalo Ave		
(4601-5450)	50	A2/B2
(5451-6799)	44	C1/D1
Buford Ave		
(10000-11198)	13	D1
(11426-11798)	28	A1
Bullard Ave	38	C2
Bullock St	42	D2
Bulova St	30	C1
Bulwer Dr	51	D3
Bunal Dr	49	C3
N Bundy Dr	16	B2/C2
S Bundy Dr		
(100-749)	16	C2
(750-3198)	19	A2/B2/C2/D2
(3199-5099)	22	C3
(5100-5598)	26	A1
Bungalow Dr	27	A2/B2
Bunker Hill Ave	9	A2
N Bunker Hill Ave	9	B2
Burbank Arpt	45	B2
Burbank Blvd	46	B1
(4407-10944)	45	C2/C1
(10945-13698)	44	D3/D2/D1
(13699-16498)	43	D2/D3/D1
(16363-16668)	49	A1
(16669-18614)	42	D1/D2/D3
E Burbank Blvd	46	B1
W Burbank Blvd		
(2-1924)	46	B1
(1925-4498)	45	C3/C2
Burchard Ave	10	A1
Burchett St	47	A1/A2
Burgen Ave	23	C2/C3
Burger Ave	41	D2
Burin Ave		
(10000-11398)	13	D2
(14300-18598)	28	C2/D2
(19900-20198)	30	D1
S Burin Ave	13	D2
	28	A2
Burkshire Ave	19	D3
Burl Ave	28	B1
S Burl Ave	13	D1
Burleigh Dr	34	C1
S Burlingame Ave		
(100-498)	16	C1/C2/D2
(500-798)	19	A1
N Burlington Ave		
(101-499)	9	A1
(501-599)	5	D1
S Burlington Ave		
(100-2098)	8	D3/C3
(150-849)	9	B1
Burma St	42	D2
Burnell Dr	36	C1
Burnet Ave		
(4601-5599)	49	A2
(5601-8299)	43	A2/B2/C2
Burnham St	16	C3
Burnley Pl	50	D2
Burns Ave	4	C2
S Burnside Ave		
(300-698)	2	D3
(700-2498)	6	A3/B3/C3/C2/D2
(2500-3998)	10	A2/B2/B1
Burr St	38	B2
Burrell Pl	25	A1
Burrell St	25	A1
Burritt Ave	29	A3
Burroughs Rd	51	D2
Burton Ave	45	B2
Burton Pl	42	A2
Burton St		
(11000-13498)	44	A1/A2/A3
(13800-15298)	43	A3/A2
(17000-18098)	42	A2/A3
Burton Way		
(8500-9177)	2	D1
(9146-9399)	1	C3/C2
Burwood Ave	33	B3
Burwood Ter	33	B3
Busch Garden Ct	34	C1
Busch Garden Dr	34	C1
Busch Garden Ln	34	C1
Busch Pl	34	C2
Bush Way	24	D2
Bushnell Ave	39	A1
N Bushnell Ave	39	A1/B1
S Bushnell Ave	39	C1/D1
Bushnell Way	38	A1
Bushwick St	36	A1/B1
Butler Ave		
(1400-3274)	19	B3/C3/D3
(3275-3799)	22	A2/B2
Butter Creek Dr	35	A3
Butterfield Ct	24	C2
Butterfield Rd	23	B2/B1/C1
Butterfly Ln	38	C2
Byrd Ave	14	B1/C1
Byrd St	43	A1
Byron Pl	51	D2

C

Street	Page	Grid
C St	24	C2
Cable Pl	13	B2
Cabora Dr	26	A1
(8100-8324)	25	B3/B2
Cabot St	36	C1
Cabrillo Ave		
(1101-1699)	21	C1/C2
(1159-23998)	32	A3/B3/C3
(1400-1899)	38	C3
Cabrillo Blvd	22	B1
Cabrillo Dr	1	A2
Cabrillo Villas St	38	A1
Cabrini Dr	45	A3/A2
E Cabrini Dr	45	A3
W Cabrini Dr	45	A3
Cabrito Rd	43	A2/A3
Cadet Ct	52	C2
Cadillac Ave	6	C1/D1
Cadison St		
(4500-4749)	30	C1
(4750-5198)	31	A3
Cadiz Dr	32	C3
Cadman Dr	5	A1
Cahuenga Access Rd	52	C2
Cahuenga Blvd		
(2301-2799)	3	A1
(2751-4527)	52	A1/B1//B2/C2/C3
(4528-6399)	45	B1/C1/D1
N Cahuenga Blvd	3	A1/A2/B2/C2/D2
Cahuenga Park Trl	52	C2
Cahuenga Ter	3	A1/A2
Cairo Walk	50	C1
Calabar Ave	25	C2
Calada St	40	D3
Calamar Ave	32	B3
Caldus Ave	42	B2
W Caldwell St	40	D1
Caledonia Way	47	C3
Calhoun Ave		
(4301-5450)	50	A1/B1
(5451-8199)	43	A3/B3/C3/D3
S Caliente St	41	A3
Califa St		
(10400-13664)	44	D3/D2/D1
(10450-10914)	45	C1
(13665-15298)	43	C3/C2
(17300-18198)	42	D2/D1
California Ave		
(101-2465)	18	B3/B2/B1
(501-1099)	21	B2/C2
(2466-2599)	19	B1
E California Ave	47	B3/B2
W California Ave	47	B2/B1
E California Blvd		
(1-985)	34	C3/C2
(986-3040)	35	C1/C2/C3
W California Blvd	34	C2/C1
California Ct	21	B2
California Incline	18	B1
California Pl	18	B3
California St		
(201-2699)	27	A2
(2700-2998)	30	D2
N California St		
(101-3299)	45	A2/B2/C2/D3
(701-900)	35	D3
S California St		
(100-306)	45	D3
(307-498)	52	A3
California Ter	34	B1/C1
Calle Cabrillo	31	C2
Calle De Andalucia	31	D2
Calle De Aragon	31	D2
Calle De Arboles	31	D2/D1
Calle De Castellana	31	D2
Calle De Felipe	31	D2
Calle De Madrid	31	D2
Calle De Primera	31	D3
Calle De Ricardo	31	D2
Calle De Sirenas	31	D1
Calle Juela Dr	51	D2
Calle Mayor	31	C3/C2/D2/D1
Calle Miramar	31	C1/D1/D2
S Calle Miramar	31	C1
Calle Pedro Infante	40	C2
Calle Vista Dr	1	A2
Callison St	32	C3
Callita Pl	39	A1
Calmar Ct	20	C2
Calneva Dr		
(16500-16564)	49	C1
(16566-16698)	48	C3
Calumet Ave	5	D2
Calvert St		
(10700-10898)	45	C1
(10930-13098)	44	C1/C3/C2
(13700-15098)	43	C3/C2
(17600-18698)	42	C2/C1
Calvin Ave	20	C3
Calzona St	40	D3
Camarillo Pl	45	D2
Camarillo St		
(10104-10602)	51	A3
(10603-14549)	45	D2/D1
(14550-15798)	49	A2/B2/B3
Camarosa Dr	15	C2
Cambria St	9	B1
Cambridge	27	C3
Cambridge Dr		
(401-950)	46	A1
(951-1398)	47	C3
Cambridge Pl	38	A3
Cambridge Rd	35	D2
Cambridge St	8	D1
Cambridge Way		
(2101-2199)	32	B2
(5600-5698)	24	D3
Camden Ave	23	B1
(1400-2398)	20	C1/D2
(1710-1949)	39	A1
N Camden Dr	1	B1/C2
S Camden Dr		
(100-149)	23	A3
(150-424)	1	D2
(425-1298)	20	C3
Camden Pkwy	39	A1
Camelia Dr	39	D3
E Camelia Dr	39	D3
Camellia Ave		
(4001-7799)	44	B3/C3/D3
(4064-4799)	51	B3
Camerford Ave	3	D2
Camero Ave	4	B3
Cameron Dr	35	C1
Cameron Ln	9	C1
Cameron Pl	47	A2
Camino Cerrado	38	A2
Camino De Encanto	31	D1
Camino De La Costa	31	C1/D1
Camino De La Cumbre	50	B1/C1
Camino De La Cumbre Pl		
	50	C1
Camino De La Solana	50	C1
Camino De Las Colinas		
	31	C2/D1
Camino De Villas	46	B3
Camino Del Campo	31	C2/C1
Camino Del Cielo	38	A2
Camino Del Sol		
(200-398)	38	A.
(23763-23765)	32	C
Camino Lindo	38	A.
Camino Palmero St	2	A
Camino Real		
(358-1199)	31	B.
(4001-4299)	36	B
Camino Silvoso	34	B
Camino Verde	38	A.
Camorilla Dr	36	B.
Campana St	29	C.
Campanita Ct	41	A
N Campbell Ave	39	B
S Campbell Ave	39	D
Campbell Dr	22	C2/C
Campdell St	25	C.
Campion Dr	25	B.
Campo St	41	A
Campus Rd	41	A.
(1401-1999)	33	B2/B1/C1/C.
(1800-1998)	38	D.
Campus St	47	B.
Camrose Dr	3	A1/B
Camulos Pl	40	D2/D
Camulos St	40	C2/D.
Canada St	36	B
Canal Ct	25	A
Canal St	21	C
Cananea Dr	49	C
Canasta St	48	A
Canby Ave	42	A1/B1/C
Candace Pl	33	A
S Canfield Ave	24	A
(1400-1752)	6	B1/C
(1753-3808)	23	B3/C
Canon Crest St	36	C
Canon Dr	34	C
N Canon Dr	1	B1/B2/C
S Canon Dr	1	D
Cantaloupe Ave	43	A3/B3/C3/D
Cantara St		
(11011-13664)	44	A2/A1/A
(13665-15298)	43	A
(17000-18600)	42	A3/A2/A
Cantata Dr	2	A
Canterbury Ave	44	A
Canterbury Dr		
(5619-5937)	24	D
(5938-6298)	26	A3/A
Canterbury Rd	35	C2/C
Canterbury St	47	C
Cantlay St		
(10700-10915)	45	A
(10916-13698)	44	B3/B
(13700-16198)	43	B3/B1/B
(16600-18398)	42	B3/B2/B
Canto Dr	37	C
Canton Dr	51	C3/C
Canton Ln	51	C
Canton Pl	51	C
Canton Way	51	C
Cantura St	51	B2/B
Canyon Cv	3	A
Canyon Dr	3	A3/B
Canyon Heights Ln	3	A
Canyon Oak Dr	3	A
Canyon Ter	3	A
N Canyon View Dr	16	C
S Canyon View Dr	16	C
Canyon Vista Dr	36	C2/C
Capello Way	17	B
Capetown Ave	38	D
Capinero Dr	33	B
Capistrano Way		
(650-798)	6	A
(4201-4299)	41	C
Capri Dr		
(1201-1448)	15	B
(1449-1699)	16	C
Caprino Pl	42	B
Captains Row	25	B
Carcassone Rd	17	C

Street Index

Street	Page	Grid
Del Amo Cir		
(314-300)	31	B3/C3
(21700-21798)	32	A1/B1
Del Amo Ctr		
(383-424)	32	A1
(425-465)	31	B3
Del Amo St	31	A2
Del Gado Dr	49	B2/B3
Del Mar Ave		
(1400-1484)	3	B2
(1483-2099)	35	D2/D3
(3900-4298)	4	C3
N Del Mar Ave	35	D3
E Del Mar Blvd		
(1-931)	34	B3/C2/C3
(932-3023)	35	B3/B2/B1
W Del Mar Blvd	34	C2
Del Monte Dr	5	C1
Del Norte St	36	C2
Del Paso Ave	38	D1
Del Paso Ct	38	D1
Del Ray Ave	21	C3
Del Ray Blvd	22	C2
Del Rey Aly	35	A3
Del Rey Ave		
(201-1299)	35	A3/B3
(4018-4113)	21	C3
(4114-4298)	25	A2
Del Rey Lagoon Park	25	B1
Del Rio Ave	36	C2
Del Rosa Dr	34	B2
Del Rosa Pl	34	B2
Del Valle Dr	6	B2
Del Vina St	35	B3
Del Zuro Dr	52	D2
Delafield Ave	28	B1
Delano St		
(10600-10698)	45	C1
(11230-13698)	44	C1/C3
(14100-15098)	43	C2/C3
(17500-18598)	42	C2/C1
Delaware Ave		
(1601-2250)	18	C3
(2251-3399)	19	C2/C1
(5101-5199)	33	B1
Delaware Rd	46	A2/B2/B1
Delay Dr	47	D3
Delevan Dr		
(2600-2859)	33	B1
(2860-3098)	47	D3
Delfern Dr	17	C3
Delgany Ave		
(3382-8149)	50	C2
(8150-8798)	25	C2
Delia Ave		
(7501-7699)	45	A2
(16600-18498)	30	A3/B3/C3
Dell Aly	25	A1
Dell Ave	21	C2
Dell Oak Dr	3	A3
Della Dr	1	B1
Dellvale Pl	48	C3
Dellwood Ln	17	A2
Delmas Ter		
(3700-3798)	23	C2
(3800-3898)	24	B2
Delong St	9	C1
Delor Dr	38	C2
Delor Rd	33	B1
Deloz Ave	4	B3
Delphi St	33	C3
Delrosa Dr	33	B1
Delrosa Walk	33	B1
Delta St	5	C2
Dempsey Ave		
(4401-4999)	49	A2/B2
(6401-7499)	43	B1/C1
Denair St	16	B3
Denbigh Dr	50	D2
Denby Ave	5	B2
Denker Ave		
(3400-5820)	11	B2/C2/D2
(6500-11024)	14	A2/C2/D2
S Denker Ave		
(5822-5874)	11	D2
(5875-10898)	14	A2/B2/C2/D2
Dennis Rd	31	C3
Dennison St	41	D1
Denny Ave		
(4001-4531)	52	A1/B1
(4535-7599)	45	A1/B1/C1/D1
Denny Rd	32	D1
Denrock Ave	26	B1
Denslow Ave	20	B1
Densmore Ave		
(4301-5199)	49	A2/B2
(6401-7799)	43	B1/C1
Denver Ave	11	D3
(5820-11098)	14	C3/A3/B3/D3
Deodar Cir	35	B3
Derby Pl	47	C3
Descanso Dr		
(3200-3208)	5	C1
(3209-3498)	4	D3
Deshire Pl	24	C2
Desmond Estates Rd	52	D2
Detour Dr	3	A2
N Detroit St	2	B3/C3
S Detroit St		
(100-998)	6	B3
(150-649)	2	D3
Devista Dr	52	D1
Devista Pl	52	D1
Devlin Dr	2	B1
Devlin Pl	2	B1
Devon Ave	20	B2
Devonport Rd	35	C3
Dewap Rd	9	B2
Dewey Ave		
(940-1399)	8	C2
(1400-21898)	31	B2
Dewey Pl	18	D2
Dewey St		
(401-2242)	18	D3/D2
(2243-13298)	19	D1/D2
Dexter St	33	C2
Diamante Dr	48	C3
Diamante Pl	48	C3
Diamond Ave		
(900-1249)	34	D2
(1250-1898)	38	A3
Diamond St		
(101-1499)	31	A2/A1/B1
(900-1098)	9	B2
Diana St		
(2701-2799)	35	C3
(3250-3326)	8	A2
Diane Way	2	A1
N Dianthus St	27	C2/D3
S Dianthus St	27	D3
Dickens St		
(12900-14549)	50	B1/B3
(14550-16298)	49	B1/B2/B3
Dickerson Ave	41	C1
Dicks St	2	C1
Dickson Ave	41	B1
W Dickson Ct	20	B2
Dickson Ln	2	A2
Dickson St	25	A1/B2
Dicturn St	33	B1
Diller Ave	24	D2
Dilling St	51	B3/B2
Dillon Ct	21	B2
Dillon St	4	D3
N Dillon St		
(101-399)	8	A3
(401-899)	4	D3
(1601-1899)	5	C1
S Dillon St	8	A3
Dimmick Ave	18	D2
Dimmick Dr	36	B3
Dincara Rd	46	D2
N Ditman Ave		
(101-1399)	41	B1/C1
(1401-2499)	38	C1/D1
S Ditman Ave	41	C1/D1
Divan Pl	44	B2
Division Pl	36	A2
Division St	36	A2/B2/B1
Dix St	3	B2
Dixie Canyon Ave	50	B2/C2
Dixie Canyon Pl	50	C2
S Dixon Ave	14	D1
Dixon St		
(1401-1625)	47	B3
(1626-1899)	29	B2
N Doan Dr	46	C1
Dobbins Ave	39	A3
Dobbins Pl	16	C1
Dobbs St	38	C2/C3
Dobinson St		
(2601-3164)	40	B3
(3165-3999)	41	B1
Dobkin Ave	48	A1
Dobson Way	24	C2
Dockweiler Pl	6	C3
Dockweiler St	6	B3
(4500-5098)	7	C1/C2
Dodds Ave	41	B1
Dodds Cir	41	B1
Dogwood Pl	33	B3
N Doheny Dr		
(101-1899)	2	A1/B1/C1/D1
(1172-1444)	1	A3
S Doheny Dr		
(100-399)	2	C1/D1
(100-1598)	6	A1/B1
Doheny Rd	1	A2/A3
Dolcedo Way	17	B2
Dolo Way	17	C2
Dolores St		
(1700-3047)	47	D2
(2101-2199)	35	B2
Doman Ave	48	A1
Domingo Dr	35	D2
Dominguez St	30	D3
N Dominion Ave	35	A2
Dominion Way	51	D3
Domino St		
(15100-15198)	43	C2
(18202-18498)	42	C1
Don Alanis Pl	10	C3
Don Alberto Pl	10	C2
Don Alegre Pl	10	C2
Don Arellanes Dr	10	C3
Don Arturo Pl	10	C2
Don Carlos Dr	10	C2
Don Cota Pl	10	C2
Don Diablo Dr	10	C2
Don Diego Dr	10	C2
Don Felipe Dr	10	C3/C2
Don Ibarra Pl	10	C3
Don Jose Dr	10	C2
Don Lorenzo Dr	10	C2
Don Luis Dr	10	C3/C2
Don Mariano Dr	10	C3
Don Miguel Dr	10	C2
Don Milagro Dr	10	C2
Don Ortega Pl	10	C2
Don Pablo Pl	10	C2
Don Porfirio Pl	10	C2
Don Quixote Dr	10	C2
Don Ricardo Dr	10	C2
Don Rodolfo Pl	10	C2
Don Tapia Pl	10	C2/C3
Don Timoteo Dr	10	C2
Don Tomaso Dr	10	C2
Don Tonito Dr	10	C2
Don Valdes Dr	10	C2
Don Zarembo Dr	10	C2
Dona Alicia Pl	51	C2
Dona Cecilia Dr	51	C2
Dona Christina Pl	51	C2
Dona Clara Pl	51	C3
Dona Conchita Pl	51	C2
Dona Dolores Pl	51	C3
Dona Dorotea Dr	51	C2/C3
Dona Elena Pl	51	C2
Dona Emilia Dr	51	C3
Dona Evita Dr	51	C2/C3
Dona Isabel Dr	51	C3
Dona Lisa Dr	51	C3
Dona Lola Dr	51	C3
Dona Lola Pl	51	C3
Dona Maria Dr	51	C2
Dona Marta Dr	51	C3
Dona Mema Pl	51	C3
Dona Nenita Pl	51	C3
Dona Pegita Dr	51	C3
Dona Pepita Pl	51	C2
Dona Raquel Pl	51	C2
Dona Rosa Dr	51	C3
Dona Sarita Pl	51	C3
Dona Sofia Dr	51	C3
Dona Susana Dr	51	C3
Dona Teresa Dr	51	C2/C3
Donald Douglas Loop	19	D2
Donaldo Ct	34	D2
Donaldson St	5	C2
Doni Rd	15	C3
Donington Pl	50	D2
Donora Ave	31	B3/A3
Doolittle Dr	29	A3
Dorado Dr	49	C1
Doral Way	48	B1
Doran Pl	44	B2
Doran St		
(1000-1098)	34	D1
(4500-4598)	47	B1
E Doran St	47	A2/B3
W Doran St	47	A2/B2/A1/B1
Dorchester Ave		
(1801-2299)	19	C2
(2901-3499)	38	B3/C3
Doreen Pl	21	B2
Doremus Rd	33	B3
Doresta Rd	34	D3
Doria Ave	32	D3
Dorilee Ln	49	C1
Doris Ave	35	D3
Doris Way	31	C2
Dormie Pl	48	B3
Dormont Ave	32	C2
Dorner Dr	41	C3
W Dorner Dr	41	C3
Dorothy St	19	A2
Dorrington Ave	2	C1
Dorris Pl	36	C1
Dorset Dr	32	B2
Dorsey St	12	C3
Dos Palos Dr	52	C2
N Dos Robles Pl	39	A1/B1
Doty Ave		
(10000-11118)	13	D3
(11119-15649)	28	A3/B3/C3/D3
(15650-18998)	30	A2/B2/C2
Double St	32	A3
Douglas Aly	34	B2
Douglas Pl	21	B1
Douglas St		
(101-599)	9	A2/B2
(201-699)	34	A3/A2
(601-1499)	5	D2
N Douglas St	26	D2
(101-999)	27	A3/B3
S Douglas St	27	B3
Dove Dr	36	B3
Dover Ln	14	C1
Dover Pl		
(23-98)	27	C3
(3701-3799)	5	A1
Dover St	5	A2/A1
Doverwood Dr	26	A2
Dow Ave	29	A3
Dowlen Dr	19	B3
Downes Rd	16	B2
S Downey Rd	41	C1/D1
Doyle Pl	37	D1
Dozier Ave	41	C3/C2/C1
Dracena Dr	4	B2
Draille Dr	31	C2
Drake Ln	50	D2
Drakewood Ave	24	C2/D2
Draper Ave	23	B2
W Dresden Dr	52	D1
Drew St	47	D3
Drexel Ave	2	D2/D3
Drexel Pl	34	C2

Street Index

Street	Page	Grid
Driftwood Dr	15	C1
Driftwood Pl	15	C1
Driftwood St	25	A1
Driscoll Ave	42	A2
Drucker Ave	38	D2
Druid St	38	C1/C2
Drummond St	15	B2/C2
Drury Ln	5	B1
Dryad Rd	15	C3
Dryden Pl	8	A3
Drysdale Ave	38	B2
Duane Ave	39	A3
Duane St	5	C2
Duarte Rd	35	D3
Duarte St	12	D3
Dublin Ave	11	B1
Dubnoff Way	45	B1
Ducommun St	9	B3
Dudley Aly	35	A2
Dudley Ave	21	B1
Dudley Ct	21	B1
Dudley Dr	38	C1
E Dudley St	35	A2
Dufour St		
(1901-1999)	27	C3
(2001-2299)	29	A3
Dufresne Ct	23	D1
Duke St	37	C3
Duley Rd	27	A3
Duluth Ln	17	B2
Dumfries Rd	23	B2
Dunas Ln	48	B1
Dunbar Pl	50	B1
Dunbarton Ave	26	B1
Duncamp Pl	2	A1
Duncan Ave	27	D2/D3
S Duncan Ave	41	D2
Duncan Dr	27	D3
Duncan Pl	27	D3/D2
Duncan St	42	C1/C2
Dundas Dr	51	A3
Dundas St		
(1001-1099)	40	B3
(3201-3299)	41	B1
Dundee Dr	4	A3/A2
Dundee Pl	4	A3
Dune St	27	A1
Dunfield Ave	26	A2/B2
Dunford Ln	13	B3
Dunham Aly	35	A2
Dunkirk Ave	20	C3
Dunleer Dr	23	B2/C2
Dunleer Pl	23	B1/C1
Dunn Ave	38	D1
Dunn Dr		
(3500-3799)	23	C2
(3800-3898)	24	B2
Dunoon Ln	16	C2
S Dunsmuir Ave		
(600-3898)	10	A2/B2
(700-2498)	6	A3/B3/C3/D2
Dunstan Way	16	C3
Duomo Via St	49	D2
Duque Dr	51	C2
Duquesne Ave	24	B2/B3
Durand Dr	3	A2
S Durango Ave	24	A2
(1400-1998)	6	B1/C1
(3100-3798)	23	C3
Durango Dr	41	A3
Durant Dr	1	D2
Duray Pl	10	A2/B2
Durham Rd	50	C2
Durklyn Ct	35	D2
Dustin Allen Ln	43	B2
Dustin Dr	36	B3/C3
Duvall St	36	D1
Duxbury Cir	23	B3
Duxbury Ln	23	B3
Duxbury Pl	23	B3
Duxbury Rd	23	B3
Dwiggins St	41	B1
N Dymond St	45	B1

E

Street	Page	Grid
E St	24	C3
Eads St	36	C1
Eagle Rock Blvd		
(2901-4370)	36	A2/A1/B1
(4301-5299)	33	A1/B1/C1
Eagle St		
(1501-3599)	40	C1/C2/C3
(3601-5304)	41	C1/C2/C3/D3
Eagle View Cir	33	B1
Eagle Vista Dr	33	A3/B2
Eagledale Ave	47	B3
Earhart Ave	26	C2
Earl Ct	5	C2
Earl St	31	B3
(2200-2498)	5	C2
(20200-21198)	30	D1
Earldom Ave	25	C3
Earle Ct	29	C3
Earle Ln	29	C3
Earle St	29	C3
Earlham St		
(669-827)	34	B3
(15200-15598)	15	C2
W Earlham St	15	C2
Earlmar Dr	23	B2/C2
Early Ave	32	B1/C1
East Ave	46	B1/B2
East Blvd	22	B2/B3
N East Edgeware Rd	5	D2
N East Park Way	13	A3
East Way	26	D1
Eastborne Ave	20	B3/C3/C2
Easterly Ter	5	C1
Eastern Ave	35	B3
N Eastern Ave		
(101-1456)	41	A2/B2/C2
(1458-3499)	38	B2/C2/D2
S Eastern Ave	41	B2/C2/D2
Eastern Canal	21	C2
Eastern Ct	21	C2
Eastham Dr	24	A3/B3
Eastlake Ave		
(1401-1950)	40	A2
(1951-2598)	37	C2/D2
Eastlyn Pl	35	A2
N Eastman Ave	41	B1/C1
S Eastman Ave	41	C1/D1
Eastwind St	25	A1
Eastwood Ave		
(10800-11108)	13	D2
(11109-15398)	28	A2/C2/D2
(15700-20798)	30	A2/B2/D2
N Eastwood Ave	13	B2
Eastwood Ct	32	B1
Eastwood Rd	51	D2
Eastwood St	32	B1
Easy St	34	D1
Eaton Dr	35	B3
Eaton St	33	B2/C3/C2
Eaton Ter	33	C3
Ebell St	44	A1
Ebey Ave	38	A1
Ebony Ln	32	D3
Echandia St	40	B1
Echo Park Ave	5	C2/D2
Echo Park Ter	5	D2
Echo St		
(4901-5199)	36	B3
(5501-6299)	33	C3/D2/D1
Edelle Pl	38	C1
Eden Dr	51	D2
Eden Pl	51	D2
Edendale Pl	5	C2
Edenhurst Ave		
(3600-3998)	5	A1/A2
(4000-5099)	47	B1/C1
Edgar St	15	B1
Edgecliffe Dr	4	C3/D3
Edgehill Dr	11	A1/B1/C1
Edgeley Pl	20	B2
Edgemar Ave		
(5600-5874)	10	D2
(5875-5998)	13	A2
Edgemere Dr	31	A2/B2

Street	Page	Grid
N Edgemont St		
(101-250)	8	A2
(251-2499)	4	A2/B2/C2/D2
S Edgemont St	8	A2
Edgerton Ave	49	A1
E Edgeware Rd		
(301-524)	9	A2
(525-999)	5	D2
N Edgeware Rd	9	B2
S Edgeware Rd	9	B2
W Edgeware Rd	5	D2
Edgewater Ter	5	B2
Edgewood Dr	39	A1/D1
Edgewood Pl		
(4500-5098)	7	C1//C2
(5100-5898)	6	B2/B3
Edgewood St	13	A2/B2
N Edinburgh Ave	2	B2/C2
S Edinburgh Ave	2	D2
N Edison Blvd	45	C2
S Edison Blvd	46	D1
Edison Ln	34	D2
Edison Pl	47	B2
Edison St	38	B1/B2
Edison Walk	38	B2
Edison Way	45	C1
Edith Ave	39	D1
Edith St	23	C2
Edloft Ave	38	B1/C1
Edmondson Aly	34	C2
Edmonton Pl	13	C3
Edna St	38	C2
Edris Dr	23	A3
Edsel Ave	22	C3
Edward Ave		
(2901-2950)	5	B2
(2951-3299)	36	B1
Edward E Horton Ln	42	D3
Edwin Aly	34	B2
Edwin Dr	51	D2
Edwin Pl	51	D2
Effie Pl	5	C1
Effie St		
(1700-3549)	5	C1/C2
(3550-4398)	4	C3
Effingham Pl	5	A1
Eileen Ave		
(5400-5798)	10	D3
(6000-6398)	13	A3
Eisenhower	16	C3
El Atajo St	36	B2
El Bonito Ave	5	A2
El Camino Dr	1	C2
S El Camino Dr	1	D2
El Campo Dr	35	C3
El Canto Dr	33	B1
El Caprice Ave	44	B2
El Cedro St	36	B2
N El Centro Ave	3	B2/C2/D2
El Centro St	34	D2/D1
El Cerco Pl	15	C2
El Cerrito Cir	38	A3
El Cerrito Pl	2	A3
El Cerro Ln	51	C2
El Circulo Dr	34	B1
El Contento Dr	3	A2
El Coronado St	38	A2
El Dorado St		
(441-2168)	34	B3
(2169-2698)	32	A2
El Manor Ave	26	C2/B2
El Medio Ave	15	B1/C1
El Medio Pl	15	B1
El Mio Dr	33	C3
El Mirador Dr		
(1200-1298)	34	A1
(5200-5298)	10	B2
N El Molino Ave	34	A3/B3
S El Molino Ave		
(2-2149)	34	B3/C3/D3
(2150-2298)	39	A2
El Molino Pl	39	A2
N El Molino St	39	A3
S El Molino St	39	B3/C3/D3
El Moran St	5	C2

Street	Page	Grid
El Nido Ave	35	B3/C3
El Oeste Dr	29	B1
El Paseo	41	A3
El Paseo Dr	36	B1
El Paseo St	41	A3
El Paso Dr	36	A2/B3
El Paso Walk	11	A3
El Porto St	27	B1
El Portolo	34	B1
El Prado Ave	32	A3/A2
El Redondo Ave	31	A2/B2
El Reposo Dr	33	B1
El Retiro Way	1	A2
El Rincon Way	24	D2
El Rio Ave	33	A1
El Roble Dr	33	B1
El Rosa Dr	36	B1
E El Segundo Blvd	27	B3/B2
W El Segundo Blvd		
(100-498)	27	B1/B2
(2958-5399)	28	B3/B2/B1
El Sereno Ave	38	B2
El Tesorito St	38	A3
El Tovar Pl	2	C1
El Verano Ave	33	A1/B1
Elden Ave	8	C2
Elden Way	1	B1
Elder Ct	34	D1
Elder St	34	D1
Elderbank Dr	37	B3
Elderwood St	16	B3
Eldora Rd	34	A3
Eldorado St	32	A2/A1
Eldred St	36	B3
Eleanor Ave	3	C2/C1
Eleanor Pl	32	D3
Electra Ct	2	A2
Electra Dr	2	A2
Electric Ave	21	B1/C2
N Electric Ave	39	A1/B1
S Electric Ave	39	D1/C1
Electric Ct	21	C2
Electric Dr	34	B2
Electric St	5	B2
Electronics Pl	47	B1
N Elena Ave	31	A1
S Elena Ave	31	C1
Elenda St	24	B1/C1/C2
Elevado Ave		
(9106-9165)	2	C1
(9166-9950)	1	B3/B2/C2/C1
Elevado St		
(1401-1699)	5	C1
(9099-8901)	2	C1
Elevado Ter	41	A3
Elgar Ave	30	A3/B3
Elgin Aly	34	A3
Elgin St		
(1-299)	39	B2
(6301-6550)	33	C3
(6551-6899)	34	D1
Elisa Pl	49	B1
E Elk Ave	47	B2/B3
W Elk Ave	47	B2/B1
Elkgrove Ave	21	B2
Elkgrove Cir	21	B2
Elkhart Pl	21	B2
Elkins Rd	16	B2
Elkland Pl	21	B2
Elkwood St		
(10100-10698)	45	A1/A2
(11200-12998)	44	B2/B3/B1
(17200-18532)	42	A1/A2
Ellenda Ave	23	C1
Ellenda Pl	23	C1
Ellendale Pl		
(1900-2098)	8	D2
(2100-2898)	11	A2
Ellenwood Dr	33	A1/B3
Ellenwood Pl	33	A3
Ellett Pl	5	C2
Ellincourt Dr	34	D2
Ellington Dr	52	C2
Ellington Ln	34	C3
Ellinwood Dr	31	B3/C3/C2

Street Index

Street	Page	Grid
Farmer Fire Rd	48	D1
Farmers Fire Rd	48	D2
Farmouth Dr	4	A3
Farnam St		
(901-943)	36	A3
(945-1099)	33	C2
Farnham Ln	13	C3
Farnsworth Ave	38	B2/C2
Farquhar St	38	D2
Farragut Dr	24	B2/C2/C1
Farrell Ave		
(1901-1999)	27	D3
(2001-2299)	29	A3
Farrington Ln	33	B3
Farwell Ave	5	B2
Fashion Way	32	A1
Fawndale Pl	49	C3
Fay Ave	24	A3
Fay Pl	34	A3
Faye Ln	31	B2
Fayette St	33	C2/C3
Faymont Ave	27	C3
Faysmith Ave	32	A2
(800-18498)	30	A3/B3/D3
(1028-15549)	28	D3
Featherstone Ln	14	C1
Federal Ave		
(1200-3231)	19	C3/B3/D3
(3232-3598)	22	A2
Fedora St	8	C2
Feijoa Ave	32	D2
Felbar Ave		
(800-23098)	32	A1/B1
(18600-18998)	30	C2
Feliz St	41	A3
Felker Dr	31	B2
Fellowship Park Way	5	C2
Felton Ave		
(9500-10998)	13	C1/D1
(11400-12698)	28	A1/B1
Felton Ln	29	B3/C3
Fenn St	37	B3
Fennell Pl	2	B1
Fermo Dr	15	B3
Fern Ave	32	A2/B2
Fern Dell Dr	4	A1/B1
Fern Dell Pl	4	B1
Fern Dr	34	B1
Fern Pl	38	C1
Fernando Ct	47	C2
Fernbush Ln	17	B3
Ferncola Ave	45	A2
Ferncroft Rd	5	A1
Ferndale Ave	22	B1
Ferndale St	10	A2/A3
Fernleaf St	36	D1
Ferntop Dr	38	C1
Fernwood Ave		
(3000-3574)	5	B1/C1
(3575-5549)	4	C3/C1
(5550-5898)	3	C1
Ferrara St	34	D1
S Ferris Ave	41	C3/D3/D2
Ferrocarril Ave	32	B3
N Fetterly Ave	41	C3
S Fetterly Ave	41	C3/D2
N Fickett St	40	B3/B2
S Fickett St	40	C2/D1
Field Ave		
(1101-1399)	13	A2
(3000-3498)	10	A3
Fierro St	47	D2
Figueroa St	36	D2/C3
N Figueroa St		
(101-799)	9	B2
(2001-5360)	36	B3/C3/D2
(5361-7587)	33	A3/B3/C3/ D2/D1
S Figueroa St		
(100-1698)	9	B2/B1/C1
(1700-5898)	12	A1/B1/C1/D1
(5899-11098)	14	A3/B3/C3/D3
Figueroa Ter		
(700-949)	9	A2
(950-1198)	5	D2
Figueroa Way	12	A1
Fiji Way	25	A2/B2
Filion St	47	D3
E Fillmore St	34	C2
Fillmore St	34	C2/C3
Finch St	5	B2
Fink St	3	A2
Finley Ave	4	B2/B3
N Fir Ave	13	B2
S Fir Ave	13	B2/C2/D2
Fir St	10	A2
Fire And Service Rd	22	C3
Fire Rd	51	C2
Firebrand St		
(3300-3449)	23	C1
(3450-6598)	26	A1
Firenze Ave	52	C1
Firenze Pl	52	C1
Firmament Ave		
(4301-5199)	49	A2/B2
(6401-7599)	43	B2/C2
Firmin St	9	B2
Firmona Ave		
(549-19398)	30	A1/B1/C1
(10000-11198)	13	D2
(11200-15698)	28	A2/C2/D2
Firth Ave	16	B2
Firth Dr	50	D2
Fischer St	47	C3
Fishburn Ave	38	D1
Fisher Ave	27	C2
Fisher Ct	29	C3
Fisher St		
(301-399)	33	C3
(4001-4799)	41	B3/B2
Fisk Ct	30	C1
Fisk Ln		
(2401-2750)	29	C3
(2751-2999)	30	C1
Fiske St	15	B2
Fitch Dr	3	B1
Fithian Ave	38	B2/C2
Flag St	3	A3
Flagler Ln		
(1-338)	31	A2
(339-1999)	29	B2/C2
Flavian Ave	31	A3
Flax Pl	25	C3
Flaxton St	24	C2
Fleet St	25	A1
Fleetwing Ave	26	C2
Flemish Ln	4	C1
Fletcher Ave		
(1600-2098)	39	A1
Fletcher Dr		
(2301-2999)	5	A2/B2
(2998-3899)	47	D3/D2
(3901-3999)	36	A1
Fleur Dr	34	D3
Flight Ave	26	A3/B3/B2
Flight Pl	26	B2
Flint Ave	23	C3
Flora Ave	37	C3
Flora Dr	13	B1
Floral Ave	2	A2
Floral Dr	41	B2/B3/B1
W Floral Dr	41	B3
Floral Park Ter	34	D2
E Florence Ave	13	A3/B3/B2
W Florence Ave		
(101-3552)	13	A3/B1/B2
(398-3599)	14	B3/B2/B1
(795-1299)	26	C3/B3
Florence Dr	34	A2
Florence Pl	47	C2
N Florence St	45	C2/C3/D3
S Florence St	46	D1
Florentina Ave	41	A3
Flores Ave	13	A1
Flores De Oro	38	A3
N Flores St	2	B2/C2
S Flores St	2	D2
Floresta Ave	11	D1
Floresta Way	10	D3
Florida St	9	C1
Floristan Ave	33	B2
Florizel St	38	B1
Florwood Ave		
(1300-1598)	32	A1
(12900-15549)	28	B3/D3
(15550-18998)	30	B2/C2
Flournoy Rd	27	B2/C2
Flower Ave		
(601-1798)	32	A1
(651-999)	21	B2
Flower Ct	21	B2
Flower Dr	12	B1
Flower St		
(700-949)	47	A1
(950-1998)	46	C2/D3
N Flower St		
(301-399)	9	B2
(401-499)	13	B2
(701-999)	46	B1
S Flower St		
(100-1398)	46	C2
(200-1698)	9	B2//C1
(500-1210)	13	C2/D2
(1700-5798)	12	A1/B1/C1/D1
(5868-9998)	14	A3/B3/C3
Floyd St	45	A2/B3
Floyd Ter	52	B2/C2
Floye Dr	52	C1
Flume Walk	49	B2
Flynn Ranch Rd	52	C1
Folsom St		
(2301-3287)	40	B2/B3
(3288-4499)	41	B2/B1
Fond Dr	49	C1
Fonda Way	37	C2
Fontenelle Way	17	B2
Fonthill Ave		
(800-23098)	32	A1/B1
(12500-16899)	28	B3/C3/D3
(16900-18898)	30	B2/C2
E Foothill Blvd	35	B3/B2
Foothill Dr	3	B3
N Foothill Rd	1	B2/C2/C3
Foothill St	34	D2
Forbes Ave		
(5201-5367)	48	A3
(5368-7599)	42	B3/C3/D3
Ford Ave	29	B2/C2
N Ford Blvd	41	B2/C2
S Ford Blvd	41	B2/C2/D2
Ford Pl	34	B3
N Ford St	45	D2
Fordham Rd	25	B3/C3
Fordyce Rd	16	B2
Forest Ave		
(101-425)	47	C2
(426-999)	40	B3/B2
(600-1375)	34	A1/A2/D1/D2
Forest Knoll Dr	2	B1
Forest Lawn Dr	46	D2
(6598-6898)	52	A3
Forest Park Dr	37	C3
Forest St	13	A2
Forman Ave		
(4201-4536)	52	A2
(4537-4999)	45	D2
Forman Ln	45	D2
N Formosa Ave	2	B3/C3
S Formosa Ave	2	D3
Forney St	36	C1
Forrester Dr		
(2300-2498)	32	D2
(2700-2898)	23	B2
Fortuna St	12	D3
Fortune Pl	34	D1
Fortune Way	34	C1/D1
Foster Dr	6	B2
Fountain Ave		
(3836-5574)	4	C3/C2/C1
(5575-7062)	3	C3/C1/C2
(7063-8498)	2	B2/B3/B1
Fountain Pl	47	A2
Fowler St		
(2701-3159)	40	A3
(3160-3699)	38	D1
Fowling St	25	C2
Fox Hills Dr	24	D2
	26	A2
(1800-2343)	20	C3
(2344-6199)	23	B2
Fox Hills Mall	26	A2
Foxboro Dr	16	A2
Foxtail Dr	18	A2
Frackelton Pl	33	A2
Frances Ave	22	B1/B2/C2
Francina Dr	49	C1
Francis Ave		
(2700-2998)	8	B2
(4200-4498)	7	B2
Francis Ct		
(1100-1198)	46	D3
(16700-16798)	30	D2
Francis Pl		
(10700-10798)	23	D2
(11400-11699)	22	B2
N Francisca Ave	31	A1/B2
S Francisca Ave	31	B2/B1
Francisca St	35	B2
Francisco St		
(401-599)	27	D2
(600-998)	9	B1/C1
Frank Ct	9	C2
Frank St	19	C1
E Franklin Ave	27	A2/B2
Franklin Ave		
(101-199)	39	A3
(3700-5549)	4	B1/B3/B2
(5550-7045)	3	B3/B2/B1
(7046-10728)	2	A3/A1//B1
(10729-11298)	24	C2/C1
W Franklin Ave		
(100-4149)	27	A1/A2
(4150-4298)	52	A2
Franklin Canyon Dr		
(2479-2793)	50	D3
(2795-3099)	51	C1
Franklin Ct	47	B2
Franklin Pl	3	B1
Franklin St	19	B1/B2
Franklin Way	2	A1
Fraser Aly	34	B2
Fraser Ave		
(101-199)	18	D1
(300-1232)	41	C3/D3
N Frederic St		
(101-399)	46	D1
(401-3299)	45	A3/B3/C3
S Frederic St	46	D1
Frederick St		
(100-3199)	18	D2
(300-1098)	21	B2
(2701-2899)	36	C1
Fredonia Dr	52	B1
Freeman Ave		
(11400-15699)	28	A2/B2/C2/D2
(15700-17098)	30	A2/B2
S Freeman Ave		
(10000-11145)	13	D2
(11146-11198)	28	A2
Freeman Blvd		
(2801-2899)	29	B3
(3769-4099)	28	D1
Freemont Villas St	38	A2
Freese Ln	35	B2
Fremont Ave		
(200-2098)	38	A3
(206-1349)	34	A3
N Fremont Ave		
(1-199)	38	B3
(101-499)	9	B2
S Fremont Ave		
(2-2198)	38	B3/C3
(2100-2114)	41	A3
Fremont Dr	34	B2
Fremont Ln	34	D2
Fremont Pl	7	B2/C2
Fremont Villas St	38	A2
French Ave	36	D2
Freshman Dr	24	C2
N Fresno St	40	B3/C3

Street Index

Street	Page	Grid
Glenroy Pl	17	C1
Glensummer Rd		
(33-167)	33	B3
(168-398)	34	C1
Glenullen Dr		
(200-215)	34	C1
(216-498)	33	B3
Glenvia St	47	A3
Glenview Ave	5	B2
Glenville Dr	23	A3
Glenway Dr	13	B1
Glenwood Ave	36	C3
N Glenwood Pl	46	C1
S Glenwood Pl	46	C1
Glenwood Rd	46	C3
N Gless St	40	B1
S Gless St	40	B1/C1
Glick Ct	29	C3
Glider Ave	26	B2/C2
Globe Ave		
(3600-4198)	22	A2/B3
(4399-4201)	24	C1
Gloria Ave		
(4401-5199)	49	B1/A1
(6401-7999)	43	A1/B1/C1
Glorieta St	34	A2
Glorietta Dr	50	C1
Glorietta Pl	50	C1
Glorietta St	34	A2
Gloucester Dr	50	D2
Glover Pl	36	C1
Glyndon Ave	21	A3/B3
Glyndon Ct	21	B3
Goddard Ave	26	B3
Gold Pl	34	D1
Golden Ave	9	C1
Golden Gate Ave		
(1401-1600)	4	C3
(1601-1799)	5	C1
Golden St	29	C2
Goldenrod Pl	49	C1
W Goldenwood Dr	26	A3
Goldleaf Cir	10	D1
W Goldleaf Cir	10	D1
Goldmine Ln	42	A3
Goldsmith St	18	D2
Goldwyn Ter	24	B1
Goll Ave	44	A3
Gonzaga Ave	25	B3
Goode St	33	B2
Goodland Ave		
(3601-5450)	51	A1/B1/C1
(5201-5283)	50	A3
(5451-8199)	44	A1/B1/C1/D1
Goodland Dr	51	C1
Goodland Pl		
(3901-4099)	51	B1
(6201-6399)	44	C1
Goodman Ave	29	B2/C2/D2
Goodview Trl	52	C2
Goodwin Ave	47	C1
Gordon St	3	B2/C2
Gordon Ter	34	C2
Gorham Ave		
(11600-11849)	16	C3
(11850-12398)	19	A2
Gorham Pl	16	C3
Gosford Ave	44	A1
Goshen Ave	19	A2//B2
Goucher St	15	B2
Gould Ave		
(101-799)	29	B1
(8100-8298)	2	A2
Gould Ter	29	B1
N Gower St	3	A2/B2/C2/D2
Grace Ave		
(401-799)	13	B2
(1801-2099)	3	B2
Grace Dr	34	C2
Grace Ln	16	A2
Grace Ter	34	C2
Grace Walk	34	C2
Gracia St	5	A2/B2
Gracie Allen Dr	2	C1
Graciosa Dr	3	A3/A2
Gracita Pl	33	D1
Grafton St	5	C2/D2
Graham Ave	29	B3
E Graham Pl	46	C2
Graham Pl		
(901-999)	46	C2
(11200-11398)	19	C3
Gramercy Ave	32	A3/B3
Gramercy Dr	7	B3/C3
Gramercy Park	11	A2
N Gramercy Pl		
(101-250)	7	A3
(251-2099)	3	B3/D3
S Gramercy Pl		
(101-1199)	7	A3/B3/C3/D3
(2150-5798)	11	A2/B2/C2/D2
(5900-10798)	14	A2/B2/C2/D2
Granada Ave	35	D1
N Granada Ave	39	B3/A2/A3
S Granada Ave	39	B3/C3/D3
Granada Ct	21	C2
Granada Dr	41	B3
Granada St		
(500-798)	47	B2/C2
(2601-5113)	36	B3/C2/C1
(5114-5399)	33	D1
E Grand Ave		
(1-1199)	39	A3/B2
(101-2299)	27	A2/A3
Grand Ave	34	D1
N Grand Ave		
(1-799)	9	B2
(145-299)	34	B1
S Grand Ave		
(42-1248)	34	B2/C2/C1
(100-1786)	9	B2/C2/C1
(1788-5798)	12	A2/A1/B1/C1/D1
(10062-11098)	14	D3
W Grand Ave		
(2-2499)	39	B2/B1
(100-698)	27	A2/A1
(2500-2998)	38	B3
Grand Blvd	21	C2
Grand Canal		
(2201-3099)	21	C2/D2
(3100-3698)	25	A1
Grand Canal Ct	21	C2/D2
Grand Central Ave	46	D3
N Grand Oaks Ave	35	B2
S Grand Oaks Ave	35	B2/C2
Grand View Blvd		
(3000-3175)	19	D2
(3176-4598)	22	A1/B1/B2/C2
Grand View Dr		
(1600-2898)	38	C3
(8200-8598)	2	A2
S Grand View St		
(200-329)	9	A1
(330-1208)	8	B3/C3
S Grande Vista Ave	40	C3/C2/D2
Grandeza St	41	A3
Grandola Ave	33	B2
Grandview Ave		
(701-820)	46	D3
(821-1099)	47	A1
(2101-3699)	27	C2
(2300-2898)	21	B3/C3
Grandview Dr	38	C3
Grange St	47	A1
Granite Dr	34	C3
W Granito Dr	2	A2
Grant Ave		
(800-898)	47	A1
(1101-1199)	21	C3
(1700-2749)	29	C2/C3
(10100-10198)	24	B2
(21200-23398)	31	B3/C3
W Grant Ave		
(2750-2838)	29	C3
(2831-2999)	30	B1
Grant St	18	C2
Granville Ave		
(100-3249)	19	C2/A2/B2/C3/D3
(3250-3498)	22	A2
Grape Pl	3	A2
Gratian St	41	C2/C3
Gratiot St	38	C2
Grattan St	9	B1
Gravely Ct	29	C2
Graves Ave	42	C2/D2
Gravois Ave	38	C3
Gravois St	41	A2
Grayburn Ave	11	B1
Graynold Ave	47	A1
Grayridge Dr	24	D2
Grayson Ave	21	C2
Great Oak Cir	33	B3
Green Ave	9	B1
Green Ln	29	A2/B2/C2
Green Meadow Ct	48	B1
Green Meadow Dr	48	B1
Green Oak Dr	3	A3
Green Oak Pl	3	A3
E Green St		
(1-910)	34	B3/B2
(911-1411)	35	B1
Green St	47	C3
W Green St	34	B2
Green Valley Cir	26	A2
Green View Pl	51	D2
Green Vista Dr	48	C3
Greenacre Ave	2	B3
Greenbrier Ln	48	B1
Greenbush Ave		
(4101-8299)	44	A1/B1/C1/D1
(4151-5199)	50	A2/B2
N Greencraig Rd	16	B2
Greendale Dr	17	B3
Greene Ave	22	C2
Greenfield Ave		
(100-3798)	23	B1/C1/D1/D2
(150-2349)	20	C1/C2/D2
Greenlawn Ave	24	C1
Greenleaf St		
(12900-14544)	50	B1
(14545-16598)	49	B1/B2/B3
(17500-17598)	48	A2
Greenmeadows Ave	31	D3
Greenmeadows St	31	C2/D3
Greenock Ln	16	B2
Greensward Rd	5	A1
Greentree Ct	50	D1
Greentree Rd	15	B3
Greenvalley Rd	51	D2
Greenway Dr		
(801-827)	20	B3
(828-899)	1	C1
Greenwood Ave		
(1200-23198)	32	A2/B2
(3301-3798)	22	B1
N Greenwood Ave	35	B2
S Greenwood Ave	35	B2/C2
Greenwood Pl	4	B2
Greg Ave	45	A2
Gregory Ave	3	D2
Gregory Way		
(6600-9798)	1	D2/D3
(6650-9165)	6	A1/B1
Grenada Ct	27	C3
N Grenola Ave	15	B1/C1
S Gretna Green Way		
(100-749)	16	C2
(750-1198)	19	A2
Grevelia St	34	D2
Grevilia St	34	D2
Grevillea Ave		
(11400-15699)	28	A2/B2/C2/D2
(15700-20198)	30	A1/B1
N Grevillea Ave	13	B2
S Grevillea Ave	28	A2
(200-11398)	13	B2/C2/D2
Grey Dr	38	B1
Greydale Dr	47	A1
Grider Ave	28	C1
Griffin Ave		
(1701-1950)	40	A2
(1951-4699)	37	A3/B3/B2/C2/D2
Griffith Ave		
(1400-1637)	9	D2
(1638-3898)	12	A3/A2/B2/C2
Griffith Park Blvd		
(1500-2892)	4	A3/C3
(2073-2984)	5	A1/B1
Griffith Park Dr	5	A1
N Griffith Park Dr	46	B1/C1
S Griffith Park Dr	46	D1/D2
Griffith View Dr	5	A1
Grimes Pl	48	B1
Grimke Walk	33	C3
Grimsby Ave	26	B3
E Grinnell Dr	46	A2/B2
Grinnell Dr	46	B2
Grismer Ave	46	A1/B1
Griswold St	47	B3
Grosvenor Blvd		
(5300-5411)	22	D3
(5412-12499)	26	A1
Grosvenor St	13	B2
Groton Dr	46	A1
Grove Pl	47	B3
Groveland Dr	2	A1
Grover Ave	46	D3
Groverton Pl	17	C2
N Guadalupe Ave	31	A1/B2
S Guadalupe Ave	31	B2/B1
Guardia Ave	38	C2
Guerin St	51	B2
Guilford Pl	32	C3
Guirado St	40	C2/C3
Gulana Ave	25	B2/C2
Gull St	27	B1
N Gunston Dr	16	B3
S Gunston Dr	16	B3
Guthrie Ave	6	C1
Guthrie Cir	23	B3
Guthrie Ct	23	B3
Guthrie Dr	23	B3

H

Street	Page	Grid
Haas Ave	11	D2
(5800-10698)	14	C2/A2/B2/D2
(23599-23401)	32	C3
Haas St	32	C3
Hacienda Dr		
(12700-12742)	51	C1
(12793-12898)	50	C3
Hacienda Pl		
(1101-1199)	2	B1
(3700-3898)	50	C3
Hackett Pl	36	B3
Haddington Dr	23	B2/C2
Hadley Ct	16	C3
(2-98)	19	A3
Hadley Ln		
(2-398)	19	A3
(2401-2499)	29	C3
Hager Ave	22	C1
Hague Ct	47	C2
Hahn Ave	47	A1
Halbrent Ave		
(4601-7033)	43	B2/C2
(5401-5599)	49	A2
Haldeman Rd	15	C3
Halderman St	22	B1
Hale St	46	C3
Haley Way	27	D3
Halford St	35	D3
Halison Pl	31	A2
Halison St		
(4500-4910)	30	C1
(4911-5598)	31	A2/A3
Halkirk St		
(12700-12829)	51	B1
(12830-12898)	50	C3
Hall Ct	29	C3
Hall St	38	B2

Street Index

Street Index

Street	Page	Grid
Medford St		
(2401-2812)	40	A3
(2813-4098)	38	D1/D2
Media Dr	33	D2
Medill Pl	23	B2
S Medio Dr	16	C2
Medley Dr	48	B2/B1
Medley Pl	48	B2
Medlow Ave	33	B1
N Mednik Ave	41	B3/C3
S Mednik Ave	41	B3/C2/C3
Mei Ling Way	9	A3
Meier St	22	B1/C1
Meisner St	41	B1
Melbourne Ave	4	B3/B2
Melhill Way	16	B1
Melinda Dr	50	D2
Melita Ave	44	A1/B1
Mellon Ave	5	B2
Melrose Aly	33	B3
Melrose Ave		
(2-1008)	33	B3
(1009-5074)	4	D2/D1/D3
(5075-7049)	3	D3/D2/D1
(7050-9099)	2	C2/C3/C1
Melrose Hill St	4	D1
Melrose Pl	2	C2/C1
Melvil St	24	A3
Melville Dr	35	D3/D2
Mendips Ridge Rd	51	C2
Mendocino Ct	47	C3
Mendota Ave	33	C2
Menlo Ave		
(900-2098)	8	C2/D2
(2600-5834)	11	A3/B3/C3/D3
(5835-9198)	14	A3/B3/C3
(11400-12798)	28	A2/B2
Mentone Ave		
(1151-1393)	34	A2
(1394-3749)	23	C2
(3750-4498)	24	B1/B2
N Mentor Ave		
(1-305)	35	B1
(307-1439)	34	A3/B3
S Mentor Ave		
(2-357)	35	B1
(358-888)	34	C3
Mercantile Pl	34	B2
Merced St	36	C2/D2
Mercedes Ave	35	B3
Merchant St	9	D2
Mercury Ave		
(3701-4365)	37	B3
(4366-4599)	38	B1
Mercury Ct	9	C2
Meredith Pl	51	D2
Meridian Ave		
(300-1349)	34	D2
(1350-2098)	38	A3
S Meridian Ave	38	B3/C3
Meridian Pl	38	A3
Meridian St		
(4901-6399)	33	C2/C3
(6501-6599)	34	D1
Meridian Ter	33	C3
N Meridith Ave	35	B2
S Meridith Ave	35	B2/C2
Merit Pl	31	C3
Merlin Pl	48	A3
Merrick St	9	C3
Merrill Dr	32	C3
Merrill St	31	B3//C3
Merritt Dr	34	A3
Merrywood Dr	51	D3
Merrywood Ter	51	D3
Merrywood Trl	51	D3
Merton Ave	33	B1/B2
Merwin St	5	D1
Mesa Ave	33	C3
Mesa Rd		
(547-581)	15	C2
(1200-1298)	35	D1
Mesa St	31	D3
Mesa Verde Rd	34	C1
Mesa Way	41	A3
Mesita Way	15	C3
Mesmer Ave		
(5100-5398)	22	C3
(5400-5798)	26	A1/A2
Mesnagers St	37	D1
Mesquit St	9	C3/D3
Metcalf Aly	34	C3
Metropolitan Plz	2	D3/D2
Mettler Ave	12	D2/C2
Metz Pl	2	B1
Metzler Dr	37	C3
Meyer Ct	29	D2
Meyer Ln	29	C3
Miami Way	15	R1
Michael Ave	22	C1
Michaels St	43	A3
Michelle Dr		
(3500-4298)	30	D1/D2
(4700-5698)	31	A2/A3
Micheltorena St		
(301-399)	8	A3
(401-1550)	4	C3/D3
(1551-2599)	5	B1/C1
Michener Aly	34	A2
Michigan Ave		
(701-2199)	18	C3/C2
(1501-2999)	40	B1/B2/C2
(2301-2599)	19	C1
(3401-4699)	41	C2/C1
N Michigan Ave	35	A1/B1
S Michigan Ave	35	B1/C1
Michu Ln	28	B2
Middle Rd	38	D1
Middlebrook Rd	32	B3
Middlebury St	4	D2
Middlesex Ln	14	C1
Middleton Pl	11	B2
Midfield Ave	26	B3
Midland St	36	C3/D3
Midvale Ave	24	B1
(400-2349)	20	B1/C1/C2/D2
(2350-3798)	23	B1/C1/D2
Midvale Pl	38	C3
Midway Ave	24	B1
Midway Ln	9	C1
Midway Pl	9	C2/C1
Midwick Dr	38	C3
Mignonette St	9	B2
Milaca Pl	50	C1
Milan Ave		
(600-1306)	34	D2
(1307-2098)	39	A1
Milbank St		
(12300-12802)	51	B1
(12803-14498)	50	B2/B1
(15400-15798)	49	B2
Milburn Dr	41	A2/B2
Mildred Ave		
(101-699)	21	C2/C1/C3
(4100-4398)	22	C2
(20000-21498)	31	A2/B2
Miles St	34	C3
Milford St		
(100-898)	47	B2/B1
(698-600)	38	B2
Military Ave	23	B1/C1/D1/D2
Mill Canyon Rd	35	D1
Mill Creek Ln	39	A3
Mill Ln	35	D1
Mill Rd	34	C3
Mill St	9	C3
Millard Ave	34	B2
Millard Ct	34	B2
Millbrook Dr	50	B1
Milldale Ct	44	B2
Milldale Dr	49	D2
Miller Aly	34	B2
Miller Ave		
(801-1499)	41	A2/B2
(1501-1699)	38	D2
Miller Dr	2	B1
Miller Pl	2	B1
Miller Way	2	B1
Millicent Way	35	B3
Mills Pl	34	B2
Mills St	18	C1
Milne Dr	31	C2/C3
Milner Ave	3	B1
Milner Rd	3	B1
Milo Ter		
(601-662)	36	B3
(663-799)	33	C2
Milton Ave	38	C3
Milton Ct	36	B3
Milton Dr	35	D2
Milton St	22	D2
Milwaukee Ave	33	C3
Milwood Ave	21	B2/C2
Milwood Ct	21	B2
Mimosa Dr	36	A1
Mimosa St	38	B3
Mindanao Way		
(13000-13141)	22	C2/C1
(13142-13698)	25	A2
Minden Pl	33	B3
Mindora Dr	31	C2/C3
Minerva Ave	22	B2/B3
Mines Ave	40	D2
S Mines St	41	D2
Minneapolis St	5	A2
Minnesota St	37	C2/C3
Minorca Dr	15	B3
Minto Ct	38	B2/C2
Mioland Dr	10	D2
Mira Loma Ave	5	A2
Mira Monte Pl	34	B3
Mira St	29	C1
Mira Vista Ter	34	B1
Miradero Rd	1	A2
Miramar Dr	31	B2
Miramar St	9	A1/B1/B2
Miranda St		
(11200-12898)	44	D1/D2/D3
(14300-14498)	43	C3
(17400-18198)	42	D2/D1
Mirasol Dr	35	D3
Mirasol St	40	D3
Miriam St	33	C2
Mission Aly	34	D2
N Mission Dr		
(101-563)	39	A3
(564-699)	35	D2
S Mission Dr	39	A3/B3
Mission Dump Rd	49	D1
Mission Eastway St	40	B1
E Mission Rd	39	B3/C3
Mission Rd	47	C2
N Mission Rd		
(101-3522)	40	A2/B1
(3523-4198)	37	C3/D3
S Mission Rd	40	B1/C1
W Mission Rd		
(2-2298)	39	C2/C1
(2600-3298)	38	C3
Mission St	34	D3/D2/D1
Mississippi Ave		
(10300-11079)	20	C3/C2/D2
(11080-11998)	19	C3/C2
Missouri Ave		
(10200-11054)	20	C3/C2
(11055-11998)	19	B3/B2
Mitchell Ave	22	B2/C2
Mitchell Pl	40	B1
Mockingbird Ln	34	C2/D2
Mockingbird Pl	2	B1
Moco Ln	4	A1
Modesto Ave	32	B3
Modjeska Pl	22	B2
Modjeska St	5	B2
Moffatt St	38	A3
Mohawk St	35	B2
(1001-2511)	5	C2/C1/D1
Molino St	9	C3
Molony Rd	24	D2
Monaco Dr		
(1201-1474)	15	B3
(1475-1599)	16	C1
Monette Pl	8	C1
Monmouth Ave	11	A3
Mono St	40	B1
Monon St		
(1901-3999)	4	B3
(3601-3750)	5	B1
Monovale Dr	1	B1
Monroe St		
(4000-4798)	4	D2
(5300-5598)	3	D3
Mont Eagle Pl	36	A2
Montalvo St	36	C2
Montana Ave		
(101-2850)	18	A3/A2/A1
(2851-12798)	19	A2/A1
(11100-11398)	20	B1
(11400-11999)	16	B3/C3
Montana St	5	C1/D2
Montcalm Ave	52	C2
Montclair St	11	A1
Monte Bonito Dr	33	A3/B3
Monte Leon Dr	1	B3
Monte Leon Ln	1	B3
Monte Mar Dr		
(9000-9169)	6	C1
(9170-10398)	23	B3/B2
Monte Mar Pl	23	B2
Monte Mar Ter	23	B2
Monte Vista St		
(1411-2538)	35	B2/B1
(2539-5202)	36	B3
(5203-6199)	33	C3/C2/D1
Monte Vista Walk	33	C3
Montecito Cir	37	B3
Montecito Dr		
(401-2399)	35	C2
(451-1499)	37	B3
Montecito St	37	C2
Monteel Rd	2	B2
Montego Dr	17	C1
Monteith Dr	10	C2/C3
Monterey Ave	45	B2
W Monterey Ave		
(1400-1924)	46	B1
(1925-3098)	45	B3/B2
Monterey Blvd	29	B1/C1/D1
Monterey Ct		
(2-98)	27	C3
(25300-25398)	32	D3
Monterey Pass Rd	41	B3
Monterey Pl	35	D1
W Monterey Pl	45	B3
Monterey Rd		
(74-6535)	38	B1/A2/A1
(201-1299)	47	A2/A3
(300-2950)	34	D2/D3/D1
(2951-4299)	35	D2/D1
Monterey St		
(2500-3398)	32	A2/A1
(4101-4199)	36	C2
N Monterey St	39	A2/B2
S Monterey St	39	D3/B3/C3
Monterico St	36	C2
Montery Ct	32	D3
Montezuma Ave	41	A3
Montezuma St		
(5001-5072)	36	B3
(5073-5199)	33	C2
Montgomery Ave	43	C1
Montgomery Dr	29	C2
Montiflora Ave	33	B2
Montlake Dr	3	A2
Montline Ln	17	B3
Montreal St	25	C2
Montrobles Pl	34	D3
Montrose Ave	34	D3
Montrose Ln	34	D2
Montrose St	5	D1
Montuso Pl	48	C3
Monument St	15	B2
Moon Ave		
(701-835)	36	B3
(836-24698)	32	C2
Mooncrest Dr	48	B3
Mooncrest Pl	48	B3
Moonridge Dr	49	C2
Moonridge Terrace Pl	51	D2
Moonstone Ct	37	C3

Street Index

Street Index

Street	Page	Grid
Sinaloa Ave	35	A2/B2
Sinaloa Rd	25	B2
Sinclair Ave	47	B3
Sinova St		
(4001-4398)	37	B3
(4201-4499)	38	B1
Siskiyou St	41	D1
(3301-3799)	40	D2/D3
Sisson Aly	34	A3
Skelton Cir	24	B1
Sky Valley Rd	48	D2
Sky Way	26	C2/D2
N Skyewiay Rd	16	B2
Skyhill Dr	52	B1
Skylark Ln	2	B1
Skyline Dr		
(1-200)	46	B3
(201-8898)	51	D2
Skypark Dr		
(2509-3682)	32	C1/C2
(3683-3898)	31	D3
Skytop Rd	49	C1
Skywin Way	51	D2
E Slauson Ave	12	D3/D2/D1
S Slauson Ave	24	D2
(4400-5499)	22	C3
W Slauson Ave		
(100-537)	12	D1
(538-3598)	11	D3/D2/D1
(3599-5260)	10	D3/D2/D1
(5216-6398)	24	D3/D2
Slauson Ln	29	B3/C3
Slayton St	28	C3
Sloan Dr	49	D1
Sloat St	40	B3/C3
Smilax St	4	D2
Smiley Dr		
(5300-5933)	10	A1/A2
(5934-5998)	24	A3
Smith Aly	34	B2
Smith St	37	B2
Smithwood Dr	23	A3
Snow Dr	41	B1/B2
Solano Ave		
(400-610)	37	C1
(611-898)	5	D3
Solano Canyon Dr	5	C3
Solar Dr	52	D2
Solita Rd	34	A1
Solvang St	44	B2
Sombra Ave	30	A2
Sombrero Dr	41	A3
Somera Rd	17	B2
Somers Ave	47	C3
Somerset Dr	10	A3/B3/C3
Somerset Pl	35	D3
Somerset St	38	B3
Somma Way	17	B2
Sonata Ln	36	B3
Sonoma St	32	A2/A1
Sonora Ave	46	C3/D3
Soper Dr	52	C1
Sophia Ave		
(4701-5199)	49	A1/B1
(7001-7199)	43	B1
Sophia Ln	48	A1
Sophomore Dr	24	C2/C3
Sorrento Dr	16	C1
Sotello St		
(100-231)	9	A3
(232-298)	37	D1
N Soto St		
(101-1998)	40	B2/A3
(1801-2599)	37	C3/D3
S Soto St	40	D1/C2/C1
South Aly	34	D2
South Ln	38	A2
South Park Dr	11	C3
Southridge Ave	10	D2/D3
Southwest Dr	14	A1
Sovereign Ln	14	C1
Space Park Blvd		
(2-26)	27	C3
(27-98)	28	D1
Spad Pl	24	B1
S Spalding Dr		
(100-498)	20	C3
(200-298)	1	D2
N Sparks St	46	A1/B1/C1
S Sparks St	46	D1
N Spaulding Ave	2	B3/C3
S Spaulding Ave		
(500-598)	2	D3
(700-2299)	6	A2/B2/C2
(2300-2998)	10	A1
E Spazier Ave	46	B3/C3
W Spazier Ave	46	C2/D2
Speedway		
(109-295)	18	D1
(296-3249)	21	B1/C1/C2/D2
(3250-6699)	25	A1/B1/C1
Spence St	40	C3/D3/D2
Spencer St		
(801-4399)	30	D2/D1
(851-5398)	31	A2/A3/B2
W Spencer St	31	A3
Sperry St	47	B1
Speyer Ln	29	C2/C3
Spezia Pl	15	B3
Spinnaker Mall	25	B1
Spinnaker St	25	B1
Spinning Ave	14	D1
Spiros Pl	17	C1
Spokane St	10	A1
Spoleto Dr	15	C3
Spreading Oak Dr	3	A3
Spreckels Ct	30	C1
Spreckels Ln		
(1401-2750)	29	C3/C2
(2751-2899)	30	C1
Spring Oak Dr	3	A3
Spring Oak Ter	3	A3
N Spring St		
(101-1450)	9	A3/B3/B2
(1451-1799)	37	D1
S Spring St	9	B2/C2
Springdale Dr	10	D2
Springfield Ave	29	C1
Springhill Pl	10	D2
Springlet Trl	52	C2
Springpark Ave	26	A3
Springvale Dr	33	C3
Sproul Ave	23	C1
E Spruce Ave	13	B2/C2
W Spruce Ave		
(200-798)	13	C2/C1
(900-998)	26	C3
Spruce Ln	34	A2
Spruce St		
(600-798)	5	D3
(1200-1649)	38	A3
(1650-1998)	39	A1
W Spruce St	39	A2
Spurgeon Ave	29	A3
St Albans Rd	39	A3
St Albans St	33	C3
N St Andrews Pl		
(101-250)	7	A3
(251-1999)	3	B3/C3/D3
S St Andrews Pl		
(100-1898)	7	A3/B3/C3/D3
(2400-5798)	11	A2/B2/C2/D2
(5900-10898)	14	A2/B2/C2/D2
St Charles Pl	7	C1/D2
St Cloud Rd	17	C3
St Elmo Dr		
(4500-4924)	7	D1
(4925-4998)	6	C3
St Francis Ter	3	B1
St George St		
(2301-2750)	4	B3
(2751-3099)	5	B1
St Ives Dr	2	B1
St Ives Pl	2	B1
St James Park	12	A1
St James Pl	12	A1
N St John Ave	34	B2
N St Louis St	40	B2
S St Louis St	40	B2/C2/C1
St Paul Ave	9	B1
St Paul Pl	9	B1
St Pierre Rd	17	C3
St Susan Pl	22	A2
St Vincent Ct	9	C2
St Vincent Pl	9	C2
Staats Pl	34	D3
Stacy St	28	B1
Stadium	5	D3
Stadium Way	37	D1
(1282-2199)	5	C2/C3/D2/D3
(1495-1546)	9	A3
Stagg St		
(10100-10913)	45	A1/A2
(10914-13649)	44	B1/B2/B3
(13650-16398)	43	A3/A1/A2
(16700-17898)	42	A3/A2
Standard Ave	46	C3
Standard St	27	A2
Standish Dr	48	C3
Stanford Ave	21	C3
(300-1398)	9	C3/C2/D2
(1101-1899)	29	B2/C2
(1751-4498)	12	A2/B2/C2
Stanford Dr	47	C3
Stanford Rd	46	A1
Stanford St	19	A1/B1/B2/C2
Stanhurst Ave	32	C3
N Stanley Ave	2	A3/B3/C3
S Stanley Ave	6	A3/B2/C2
Stanley Ave	2	C3
(1101-1499)	47	B3
N Stanley Dr	2	D1
S Stanley Dr	6	A1
Stanley Hills Dr		
(2001-2143)	2	A1
(2144-2399)	51	D3
Stanley Hills Pl	2	A1
Stanmoor Dr	25	B3/C3
Stansbury Ave		
(3901-5138)	50	A1/B1/C1
(5501-8199)	43	A3/B3/D3
Stansbury Way	12	C3
Stanton Ave	46	D2
Stanton Dr	33	B1
Stanwood Dr		
(11300-12099)	19	D3
(12100-12998)	22	A1/B1
Stanwood Pl	22	A1
Star Cir	24	C1
Star Ridge Dr	41	B3
Starlight Cir	46	A1
Starling Way	36	C3
Stassi Ln	15	C3
State Dr	12	B1
State Hwy 110	33	C3
	38	A1
	36	B3/C3/D2
	37	B3/B2/C1/D1
	5	D3
	9	A2/B2/B1/C1
	12	A1
(2-1172)	34	B2/C2/D2/D1
State Hwy 134	47	A2
State Hwy 159	34	B1
State Hwy 170	44	A2
State Hwy 2		
	47	C3/D3
	33	B1/C1
	5	B2/C2
State Hwy 60	41	C3/C2/C1
	40	C3/C2/C1/D2
	9	D3
State Hwy 710	34	B2/C2
State Hwy 90	24	D2
	22	C3/D2
	26	A1
	25	A2
N State St	40	A2/B2/B1
S State St	40	B1/C1
State St	34	C2/D2
W State St	34	C2
State University Dr	38	D2
Staunton Ave	12	B3/C3/D3
Stearns Dr	6	B2/C2/C1
Stebbins Ter	2	B1
N Steele Ave	41	A2
Steele Ave	41	A2
Steele St	30	C1
Steiner Ave	18	D2
Steinhart Ave	29	B2/C2
Stellbar Pl	23	B2
Steller Dr	24	A3
Stephen Rd	46	A1
Stephen S Wise Dr	49	D2
Stephon Ter	24	D2
Stepney Pl	13	A2
Stepney St	13	B2
Sterling Pl	34	D2/D1
Sterling Walk	33	C3
Stern Ave	50	A2/B2
Stetson Aly	35	B1
Stetson Ave	26	B2
Steuben St	35	B1
Steveann St	31	B2
Stevely Ave	10	B2
Steven Dr	49	C1
Stevens Ave	24	D2
Stevens Cir	24	C2
Stevens Pl	9	B2
Stever Ct	24	D2
Stever St	24	D2
Stewart Aly	35	B3
Stewart Ave	19	D2
(3216-4498)	22	C2/A1/B1
(7400-8548)	26	B1
Stewart St	19	B1/C1/C2
Stillwater Dr	10	B2
Stillwell Ave	38	B3
Stockbridge Ave	38	B3/C3
Stocker Pl	11	C1
Stocker Plz	11	C1
Stocker St		
(3000-3559)	11	C1
(3560-4929)	10	C3/C2/C1/D2
(4930-5098)	24	C2/D3
Stoll Dr	33	C2
Stone Canyon Ave	49	B3/C3
S Stone Canyon Dr	17	C2
N Stone Canyon Rd	17	A2/B2
Stone Canyon Rd		
(101-233)	49	D3
(235-1635)	17	B2/C2
Stone Ct	41	B3
Stone Gate St	41	B3
Stone Oak Dr	48	D3
Stone Ridge Ln	49	C3
Stone St		
(901-1364)	40	B3
(1365-1399)	41	B1
Stonebridge Ln	14	C1
Stonehaven Way	16	C2
Stonehill Ln	16	B2
Stonehill Pl	50	C2
Stoneley Dr	35	C3
N Stoneman Ave	39	A2/B2
S Stoneman Ave	39	B2/C3/D2
Stoner Ave		
(1200-4698)	22	B2/A1/A2/C3
(1250-3174)	19	B2/C2/C3/D3
Stoneridge Dr	34	C2
Stoneridge Pl	50	C3
Stonesboro Pl	49	C3
Stoneview Dr		
(3900-5949)	24	B3
(5950-13699)	50	C2
Stonewell St	41	B3
Stonewood Dr		
(500-598)	1	A2
(3501-3599)	49	C2
Stonewood Ter	49	C2
Stoney Creek Rd	24	C2
Stoney Dr	34	D1
Stoneybrook Dr	49	C3
N Story Pl	39	A2
Story St	41	B1
Stowe Ter	33	C3
Strada Corta Rd	17	C3
Strada Vecchia Rd	17	B2
Stradella Ct	17	B2
Stradella Rd	17	B2/C2

Street Index

Street	Page	Grid
Thomas Ave	29	A3
Thomas St	37	C3/D3
Thompson Aly	35	B3
Thompson Ave	46	C3/D2
Thompson Dr	34	A3
Thoreau St		
(1800-2030)	14	D2
(2828-2898)	28	A3
Thornburgh Ave	30	A2
Thornburgh Pl	30	B2
Thornburn St	26	B3
Thorncroft Ln	13	C3
Thorndike Rd	35	C3
Thorne St	33	C3
Thornton Ave		
(1-99)	21	B1
(2300-3498)	45	B2/B3
Thornton Ct	21	B1
Thornton Pl	21	B1
Thornton St	41	B1
Thorpe Ave	36	C2/C1
Thrasher Ave	2	B1
Throop Aly	34	D2
Thrush Way	2	A1
Thurber Pl	46	B3
Thurman Aly	35	B1/B2
Thurman Ave		
(1800-2498)	6	C2/D2
(2500-2998)	10	A1
N Thurston Ave	17	C1
S Thurston Ave		
(100-148)	17	C1
(150-398)	20	B1
Thurston Cir	17	C1
Thurston Pl	17	C1
Tianna Rd	51	D3
Tiara St		
(10400-13498)	44	C2/D3/C1/D2
(14100-14698)	43	C3
(17100-18098)	42	D2
Tiburon Ct	27	C3
Tica Dr	4	A3
W Tichenor St	40	D1
Tierra Alta Dr	35	A2
Tiffany Cir	50	D1
Tiffany Ct	31	C3
Tiffany Ln	31	C3
N Tigertail Rd	16	B2/C2
S Tijera Blvd	13	A1
Tijera Blvd		
(6486-6572)	13	A1
(8300-8498)	26	B2
Tikita Pl	52	A2
Tilden Ave		
(200-398)	20	B1
(2500-3749)	23	C1/D1
(3750-3998)	24	B1
(4000-5299)	50	A1/B1
(5401-8299)	43	A3/C3/D3
Tillie St	36	C1
Tim Ave	38	D2
Timberlake Ter	24	C2
Timmons Trl	3	A2
Timothy Ave	29	B3
Tione Rd	17	C2
Tipton Ter	33	B3
Tipton Walk	33	B3
Tipton Way	33	B3
Titus St	43	A2/A3
Tiverton Ave	20	B1/C1
Tiverton Dr	20	B1
Tivoli Ave	22	C1
Toberman St		
(1300-1898)	8	D3
(1900-2598)	12	A1
Tobias Ave		
(4401-5696)	49	A3/B3
(5697-7699)	43	B3/B2/C2
Tobin Way	49	C1
Todd Ct	44	B2
Toland Ave	26	B3
Toland Pl	36	A2
Toland Way	36	A2/A1/A3
Toledo Ct	21	C2
Toledo St	33	C3

Street	Page	Grid
Toltec Way	38	A1
Toluca Ave	31	B2
Toluca Estates Dr	52	A1
Toluca Lake Ave	52	A2
W Toluca Lake Ave	52	A3
W Toluca Lake Ln	52	A2
N Toluca Park Dr	45	D2
Toluca Rd	52	A1
N Toluca St	9	B2
S Toluca St	9	B2
Tomlee Ave	31	A2/B2
Tompkins Way	24	B3
Tonawanda Ave	33	C1
Topacio Dr	41	B3
Topaz St		
(101-499)	31	B1
(4401-4799)	38	B1/C1
Topham St	42	C1/C2
Topock St	5	A2
Toppington Dr	50	D2
Topsail	25	B1
Topsail Mall	25	B1
Topsail St	25	B1
Topsfield St	35	C3
Toquet Dr	48	B2
Torrance Blvd		
(100-5598)	31	B2/B1/B3
(1678-3854)	32	A3/A1/A2
W Torrance Blvd	31	B1
Torrey Pines Ln	48	B1
Torreyson Dr	52	C1
Torreyson Pl	52	C1
Tortuoso Way	17	B2
Tottenham Ct	50	D2
Toucan St	30	C1
Toulon Dr	15	B3
Tourmaline St		
(4301-4451)	37	C3
(4498-4599)	38	C1
S Tower Dr	6	A2
Tower Rd	1	B1
Towers St	31	A3/A2
Towne Ave		
(300-5816)	12	D2/C2
(350-1198)	9	C2/D2
N Townsend Ave	41	B1/C1
S Townsend Ave	41	C1/D1
Townsend Ave	33	A2/B2
Townsend Pl	34	B2
Toyopa Dr	15	B2/C2
Traction Ave	9	C3
Tracy St		
(3600-3828)	5	B1
(3829-4298)	4	B3
Tracy Ter	5	B1
Traffic Circle Dr	16	C1
Trask Ave	25	C2
Travis St	16	B2
Treadwell St	47	D2
Treasure Trl	52	C2
S Tremaine Ave	7	B1/C1
Tremont St	40	A3/B3
Trent Ct	33	B1
Trent Way		
(4101-4199)	47	C3
(4201-4299)	33	B1
Trenton Dr		
(601-746)	1	C1
(747-799)	20	B3
Trenton St	9	C1
Trinity St		
(1600-1755)	9	D2
(1756-4198)	12	A2/B2/C1
Trino Way	15	C1
Trolley Pl	25	C1
Trolleyway	25	C1/C2
Troon Ave	23	B2
Troost Ave		
(4001-5450)	51	B2
(5451-8199)	44	A3/B3/C3/D3
Tropical Dr	51	C3
Tropico Way	36	B2
Troy Dr	52	B2
Trudi Ln	45	A3
Trudy Dr	50	D2

Street	Page	Grid
Truitt St	46	D3
S Truro Ave		
(900-11298)	13	C2/D2
(11300-11398)	28	A2
Truro Ave	28	A2/B2/C2
Truxton Ave	26	B2/C2
Tryon Rd	3	B3
Tuallitan Rd	16	B2
Tudor Dr	49	C1
Tufts Ave	46	A2/B1
E Tujunga Ave	46	B3/B2/C2
Tujunga Ave		
(4001-8323)	44	A3/B3/C3/D3
(4015-5423)	51	A3/B3
W Tujunga Ave	46	C2
Tulare Ave		
(501-1949)	46	A1
(1950-3499)	45	A2/A3
Tularosa Dr	4	D3
Tuller Ave		
(3500-3749)	23	D1
(3750-4398)	24	B1/C1
Tuller Rd	38	C2
Tura Ln	35	C3
Turner St	9	B3
Turquoise St		
(4101-4425)	37	C3
(4426-4599)	38	C1
Turrell St	32	C3
Tuscany Ave	25	B2/C2
Tustin St	49	B3
Tuxedo Ter	3	A3
Tweed Ln	16	C2
Twilight Ln	48	B2
Twin Palms Dr	35	D2
Twining St	38	B2/B1/C2
Tyburn St	47	D2
(2901-3630)	5	A2/B2
(3501-3629)	2	C1
Tyler Aly	35	B1
Tyler St	47	C3
Tyrone Ave		
(4301-5438)	50	A1/B1
(5439-8299)	43	A3/B3/C3/D3

U

Street	Page	Grid
Uclan Dr	46	A2
Udell Ct	4	C3
Udine Way	17	C2
Ulysses St	36	D2
Umbria St	33	C2
Umeo Rd	16	C1
N Union Ave	9	A1
S Union Ave		
(100-2398)	12	A1
(150-1049)	9	B1
(1050-1998)	8	C3/D3
Union Dr	9	B1
Union Jack St	25	B1
Union Pl	9	B1
E Union St		
(1-912)	34	B3/B2
(913-1199)	35	B1
W Union St	34	B2
Universal Center Dr	52	B2/C2
Universal City Plz	52	B1
Universal Terrace Pkwy	52	B1/B2
University Ave		
(101-999)	46	A2/B1
(2700-3441)	12	A1/B1
(3442-3585)	11	B3
University Dr	38	C2
Uplander Way	24	D3
(5899-5701)	26	A2
Upper Kress Rd	2	A1
Upper Kress St	2	A1
Upper Mesa Rd	15	C2
Upperton Ave	33	B2
Upperton Pl	33	B2
Upton Ct	33	A3
Upton Pl	33	A3
Urban Ave	19	C2
Urmston Pl	39	A2
Ursula Ave	10	B2
Utah Ave	27	B3

Street	Page	Grid
N Utah St	40	B1
S Utah St	40	B1
Utica Dr	2	A2
Utopia Ave	24	D1

V

Street	Page	Grid
Vaccaro Ave	31	B2
Vado Dr	51	D2
Vado Pl	51	D2
Vagabond Rd	41	B3
Vail Ave	29	A3/B3
Valdina Pl	10	D2
E Valencia Ave	46	B3/C3/C2
W Valencia Ave	46	C2
Valencia Ct	21	C2
N Valencia St	39	A3
S Valencia St	39	B3/C3/D3
Valencia St		
(600-1298)	9	B1/C1
(1300-1498)	8	D3
Valentine Pl	34	D3
Valentine St	5	C2
Valentino Pl	3	C2
Valerio St		
(10600-10914)	45	A1
(10915-13649)	44	B3/B2/B1
(13650-16614)	43	B1/B3/B2
(16615-18666)	42	B2/B3/B1
W Valerio St	45	A1
Valevista Trl	52	C2
W Valhalla Dr	45	B2
Valita St	21	B2
Valjean Ave		
(4801-5181)	49	A1
(6401-7599)	43	B1/C1
Valle Vista Dr	33	C1
Vallejo St	37	D2
Vallejo Villas	38	B1
E Valley Blvd	39	D3
Valley Blvd	39	D3
(3201-4187)	40	A2/A3
(4186-5699)	38	C3/C2/D2/D1
W Valley Blvd		
(1-2499)	39	D3/D2/D1
(2498-5698)	38	C3
N Valley Dr	27	C3/C2/D2
S Valley Dr	27	D2
Valley Dr		
(101-2813)	29	B1/C1/D1
(2814-3199)	27	D2
Valley Falls Rd	49	C1
Valley Glen Way	10	D3
Valley Home Rd	49	C1
Valley Meadow Pl	49	C1
Valley Meadow Rd	49	B2/B1/C1/C2
Valley Oak Dr	3	A3
Valley Park Ave	29	C1
Valley Ridge Ave	10	C3/D3
Valley Spring Ln		
(10000-10898)	52	A2/A1
(11100-12798)	51	B3/B1/B2
Valley Spring Pl	51	B3
N Valley St		
(101-299)	52	A2
(601-2399)	45	B2/C2/D2
S Valley St	52	A2
Valley St		
(2-198)	34	B2
(301-499)	27	A1
(2000-2398)	9	A1
Valley View Cres	46	A1
Valley View Dr	5	C2
Valley View Rd	38	A3
Valley Vista Blvd		
(13100-14571)	50	B1/B3/B2/C2/C3/C1
(14572-16098)	49	B1/B2/B3
(17700-18298)	48	A1/A2
Valley Vista Ct	49	B3
S Valley Vista Dr	41	B3
Valley Vista Dr	41	B3
Valley Wood Rd	49	A1
Valleybrink Rd	5	A1
Valleycrest Rd	51	C2
Valleydale Ave	10	C2

Street Index

Street	Page	Grid
Vig Center Dr	27	C3
N Vignes St	9	B3/C3
S Vignes St	9	C3
N Vignes Tunl	9	B3
Villa Grove Dr	15	B3
E Villa St		
(1-971)	34	B3/B2
(972-2999)	35	B3/B2/B1
Villa St	40	B1
W Villa St	34	B2
Villa View Dr	15	B3
Villa Woods Dr	15	B2/B3
Villa Woods Pl	15	B3
Village Cir	27	C3
Village Ct	31	B3
Village Grn	10	B1
Village Ln	31	B3
Village Pkwy	19	C2
Village Rd	25	C2
Villanova St	25	C3
Vincent Ave	33	A2/B2
Vincent Park	31	A2
Vincent St	31	A2/A1
Vincent Way	47	C3
Vine Aly	35	B3
Vine Ave	32	B2/C2
Vine St		
(300-698)	47	B2/B1
(701-2199)	3	A1/A2/B2/C2/D2
(1401-2198)	39	B1
Vine Way	3	A2
Vineburn Ave	38	D1
N Vinedo Ave	35	A3/B3
S Vinedo Ave	35	B3
Vineland Ave		
(3701-3713)	52	B1
(3715-5499)	51	A3/B3/C3/B1
(5498-8251)	44	A3/B3/C3/D3
Vineland Pl	51	A3/B3
Vineyard Ave		
(1600-2416)	7	C1/D1
(2418-3498)	10	A3
Vineyard Dr	35	D2
Vinton Ave		
(3300-3799)	23	C2
(3800-4498)	24	B2
Viola Pl	25	A1
Violet St	9	D3
Violeta Dr	39	D3
N Virgil Ave		
(101-265)	8	A3
(266-1499)	4	C2/D2
S Virgil Ave	8	A3/A2/B2
Virgil Pl	4	C2
N Virginia Ave	35	B3
S Virginia Ave	46	C1
Virginia Ave		
(2-498)	35	B3/C3
(2001-2234)	18	C3
(2235-3399)	19	C2/C1
(4200-5576)	4	C3/C1
(5577-5898)	3	C3
(10500-10898)	24	C2
Virginia Ct	21	C2
Virginia Pl		
(1000-1098)	47	C2
(1700-1798)	34	D2
(9500-9598)	20	C3
Virginia Rd		
(1000-1998)	35	C1/D1/D2
(1900-2322)	7	C2/D2/D1
(2324-3998)	10	A3/B3
Virginia St	27	A1/B1
Viscount St	38	C3
Viso Dr	52	C2
Vista Ave	35	B2
Vista Ct	47	C3
Vista De Oro Ave	10	D3
Vista Del Mar		
(101-355)	31	C1
(301-12798)	27	A1/B1
(6201-10399)	25	B1/C2/D2
Vista Del Mar Ave	25	D2
Vista Del Mar Ln	25	C2
Vista Del Mar Pl	3	A2
Vista Del Mar St	3	A2/B2
Vista Del Monte Ave		
(4401-5708)	50	A1/B1
(5709-7499)	43	B3
Vista Del Parque	31	C2
Vista Del Sol	31	D1
Vista Del Valle Dr	4	A2
Vista Del Vegas	31	D2
N Vista Dr	27	D2
Vista Dr		
(2201-3699)	27	C2/D2
(20500-20698)	30	D1
Vista Gloriosa Dr	36	C2
Vista Gordo Dr	5	C2
Vista Grande St		
(1001-1099)	46	A2
(8900-9098)	2	C1
Vista Haven Pl	49	C2
Vista Haven Rd	49	C2
Vista Largo	31	D3
Vista Linda Dr	48	C1
Vista Montana	31	D3
Vista Moraga	17	B1
Vista Pl		
(101-199)	21	B1
(301-399)	33	C3
(7400-7498)	2	B3
Vista Rdg	46	A1
N Vista St	2	A3/B3/C3
S Vista St	2	D3
Vista Superba St	47	C3
Vista Ter	15	C1
Vistacrest Dr	52	C2
Vlge Park Dr	19	C2
Vlge Park Way	19	C1
Voletta Pl	44	D1
Volney Dr	41	A2/B2
Voorhees Ave		
(1301-1999)	27	D3
(2001-2799)	29	B3
Vose St		
(11700-13698)	44	B2/B1
(14340-16098)	43	B2/B3/B1
(16900-17298)	42	B3
Voyage Mall	25	B1
Voyage St	25	B1
Voyager St	30	C2
Vulcan Dr	51	D3

W

Street	Page	Grid
Wabash Ave		
(2301-3199)	40	B2/B3
(3201-3299)	41	B1
Wabash St	34	A1
Waddell St	44	D1
Wade Ave	32	B2
Wade St	22	C2/B1
Wadena St	38	B2
Wadshan Aly	28	D3
Wadsworth Ave		
(101-199)	18	C1
(3200-5298)	12	B2/C2/D2
Wadsworth Pl	19	A3
Wagner St		
(1615-2499)	35	B2
(10800-11198)	24	C1
(11800-12598)	22	C3/C2
Wakefield Ave	43	A3
Walavista Rd	23	C2
Walcott Way	5	C2
Walden Dr		
(501-673)	1	C2
(675-899)	20	B3
Waldo Ave	34	C2
Waldo Ct	38	B1
Waldo Pl	33	A3
Waldran Ave	33	B2
Walgrove Ave		
(1300-1334)	19	D1
(1335-3998)	22	B1/C1
Wall St		
(300-1612)	9	C2/D2/D1
(1614-5198)	12	A2/B2/C1/D1
Wallace Ave	5	D2
Wallingford Dr	50	D2
Wallingford Rd	35	C3
Wallis St	34	C2
E Walnut Ave		
(101-1999)	27	A3/A2
(401-1499)	46	A2/B2
W Walnut Ave	27	A2/A1
Walnut Ave		
(1101-3699)	27	C2/B2
(2000-2522)	21	B3/C3
Walnut Ct	21	B3
Walnut Dr	2	A1
Walnut Ln	19	B2
E Walnut St		
(1-909)	34	B3/B2
(910-2999)	35	B1/B2/B3
W Walnut St	34	B2
Walnut St		
(600-1298)	13	C2/D2
(1301-1499)	12	B3
(22999-25998)	32	B3/C3/D3
Walsh Ave	22	C2
Walt Disney Dr	49	D2
Walter Ave	32	C2
Walther Way	16	B2
Walton Ave		
(1700-1898)	8	D2
(2800-4398)	11	A3/B3/C3
Wameda Ave	33	A2
Wanda Dr	4	B3
Warbler Pl	2	B1
Warbler Way	2	B1
Ward St	33	B2
(22300-24498)	32	B1/C1
Warehouse St	9	C3//D2/D3
Warfield Ave		
(1901-1999)	27	C3
(2001-2299)	29	A3
Waring Ave		
(5700-7074)	3	D2/D1
(7075-8498)	2	C2/C3/C1
Warmside Ave	31	C2
Warnall Ave	20	B2/C3
Warner Ave	20	B2/C2
W Warner Blvd	52	A3
Warner Blvd	52	A3/A2
Warner Dr		
(6100-6498)	6	A2
(8400-8598)	24	B3
Warren Ave	22	B1
Warren Ln	13	B2
Warren St	40	B1
Warwick Ave		
(101-3599)	38	A2/B2/C2
(1801-1999)	19	C2
Warwick Pl	38	A2
Warwick Rd		
(1700-1998)	35	D2
(2319-3398)	38	D3
Wasatch Ave	22	B1/B2/C2
Washburn Rd	33	B3
Washington Ave		
(101-2454)	18	B3/B2/B1
(2000-2168)	32	B3
(2455-2999)	19	A1/B1
(12800-14298)	28	B2/C2
E Washington Blvd		
(1-987)	34	A3/A2
(101-1899)	12	A2/B3
(1027-2884)	35	A3/A2/A1
(2701-2998)	40	D1
W Washington Blvd		
(2-424)	34	A2
(100-994)	12	A1/A2
(996-2256)	8	D2/D3/D1
(2257-4927)	7	D1/D3/D2
(4926-5703)	6	C3/C2/D2
(5704-5748)	10	A1
(11300-13398)	22	B3//C2/C1
(13399-13347)	21	B3/C2
Washington Blvd		
(1-13598)	21	C3//C2/D2
(5712-5996)	10	A1
(6016-11240)	24	A3/A2/B2/B1/C1
(11242-11298)	22	B3
Washington Cir	45	B3
Washington Pl		
(200-298)	34	A2
(2431-2477)	18	B3
(2478-11248)	24	C1
(11250-12774)	22	B3/B2/C2
W Washington St	39	B2
Washington St		
(301-899)	27	A2
(1900-1998)	8	D3
Washington Way	21	C2
Water And Power Pole Rd	48	D2
Waterford St	16	C3
Waterloo St	5	C2/C1/D1
Waterman Dr	43	A1
Waterview St	25	C2
N Watland Ave	41	B2
Watseka Ave		
(3600-3898)	24	B2/A2
(3625-3749)	23	C3
Watson Ave	32	A3
Watson St	46	B3
Watsonia Ct	3	A1
Watsonia Ter	3	A1
N Wattles Dr	52	D1
Wattles Dr	2	A3
Watts Way	11	B3
Wave Crest Ave	21	C1
Wave Crest Ct	21	C1
Wavecrest Ave	21	C1
Waverly Dr		
(2-430)	34	C2
(2-198)	38	B3
(2600-3498)	5	A1/B1/B2
Waverly Rd	35	D2
Wawona Pl	33	B1
Wawona St		
(3801-4099)	47	C3
(4138-4999)	33	B1
Wayland St	33	C3
Wayne Ave		
(1400-1898)	39	A1
(2201-2399)	4	A3
(20000-20598)	31	A2
Wearlham St	15	C2
Weatherford Dr	10	B2
Weaver Ln	33	C3
Weaver St	33	C3
Webb Ave	44	A2/A3
Weber Way	28	B3
Webster Ave	5	C1
Weddington St		
(10312-10949)	45	D1/D2
(10950-12798)	51	A3/A2/A1
(13000-14898)	50	A3/A2/A1
(14526-15398)	49	A3/A2
(16800-18298)	48	A1/A3/A2
Wedgewood Pl	3	B2
Weepah Way	2	A2
Weid Pl	3	A2
Weidlake Dr	3	A2
Weidlake Pl	3	A2
Weight Aly	34	C2
Weir Aly	35	B3
Weir St	22	C3
Welby Way		
(11100-13198)	44	C3/C1/C2
(17200-18298)	42	C2/C1
Welch Pl	4	B2
Welcome St	9	A1
Weldon Ave	47	D3
Welland Ave	11	B1/C1
Weller Rd	33	C1/C2
Wellesley Ave	19	A1/B2/C2
Wellesley Dr		
(1400-1598)	47	C3
(1601-1799)	18	D3
Wellesley Rd	35	D3

Street Index